Smart Innovation, Systems and Technologies

Volume 387

The Smart Innovation, Systems and Technologies book series encompasses the topics of knowledge, intelligence, innovation and sustainability. The aim of the series is to make available a platform for the publication of books on all aspects of single and multi-disciplinary research on these themes in order to make the latest results available in a readily-accessible form. Volumes on interdisciplinary research combining two or more of these areas is particularly sought.

The series covers systems and paradigms that employ knowledge and intelligence in a broad sense. Its scope is systems having embedded knowledge and intelligence, which may be applied to the solution of world problems in industry, the environment and the community. It also focusses on the knowledge-transfer methodologies and innovation strategies employed to make this happen effectively. The combination of intelligent systems tools and a broad range of applications introduces a need for a synergy of disciplines from science, technology, business and the humanities. The series will include conference proceedings, edited collections, monographs, handbooks, reference books, and other relevant types of book in areas of science and technology where smart systems and technologies can offer innovative solutions.

High quality content is an essential feature for all book proposals accepted for the series. It is expected that editors of all accepted volumes will ensure that contributions are subjected to an appropriate level of reviewing process and adhere to KES quality principles.

Indexed by SCOPUS, EI Compendex, INSPEC, WTI Frankfurt eG, zbMATH, Japanese Science and Technology Agency (JST), SCImago, DBLP.

All books published in the series are submitted for consideration in Web of Science.

Fausto Pedro García Márquez · Akhtar Jamil ·
Alaa Ali Hameed · Haixin Wang · Yuxian Zhang ·
Junyou Yang
Editors

Computing, Internet of Things and Data Analytics

Selected Papers from the International Conference on Computing, IoT and Data Analytics (ICCIDA)

Springer

Editors
Fausto Pedro García Márquez
Ingenium Research Group
Universidad Castilla-La Mancha
Ciudad Real, Spain

Akhtar Jamil
National University of Computer
and Emerging Sciences
Islamabad, Pakistan

Alaa Ali Hameed
Department of Computer Engineering
Istinye University
Istanbul, Türkiye

Haixin Wang
School of Electrical Engineering
Shenyang University of Technology
Liaoning, China

Yuxian Zhang
School of Electrical Engineering
Shenyang University of Technology
Liaoning, China

Junyou Yang
School of Electrical Engineering
Shenyang University of Technology
Liaoning, China

ISSN 2190-3018 ISSN 2190-3026 (electronic)
Smart Innovation, Systems and Technologies
ISBN 978-3-031-87153-5 ISBN 978-3-031-87154-2 (eBook)
https://doi.org/10.1007/978-3-031-87154-2

This Springer imprint is published by the registered company Springer Nature Switzerland AG
The registered company address is: Gewerbestrasse 11, 6330 Cham, Switzerland

Organization

Organizer

Shenyang University of Technology, Liaoning, China

General Chairs

Dr. Fausto Pedro García Márquez, University of Castilla–La Mancha, Spain
Dr. Yuxian Zhang, Shenyang University of Technology, China
Dr. Alaa Ali Hameed, Istinye University, Türkiye

Technical Program Chairs

Dr. Xiandong Xu, Tianjin University, China
Dr. Gen Li, Technical University of Denmark, Denmark
Dr. Junyou Yang, Shenyang University of Technology, China
Dr. Ana María Peco Chacón, University of Castilla-La Mancha, Spain
Dr. Akhtar Jamil, National University of Computer and Emerging Sciences, Pakistan
Dr. Haixin Wang, Shenyang University of Technology, China

Publication and Publicity Chairs

Dr. Serdar Solak, Kocaeli University, Turkey
Dr. Mustafa Hikmet Bilgehan Uçar, Kocaeli University, Türkiye

Organizing Committee

Dr. Haixin Wang, Shenyang University of Technology, China
Dr. Junyou Yang, Shenyang University of Technology, China
Dr. Yue Zhou, Cardiff University, UK
Dr. Xiandong Xu, Tianjin University, China

Registration Committee

Dr. Zuoxia Xing, Shenyang University of Technology, China
Dr. Muhammad Davud, Istinye University, Türkiye
Dr. Enkeleda Lulaj, University Haxhi Zeka, Kosovo

Technical Program Committee

Dr. Ahmed Sherif, University of Southern Mississippi, USA
Dr. Amir Seyyedabbasi, Istinye University, Türkiye
Dr. Alfredo Peinado Gonzalo, University of Castilla-La Mancha, Spain
Dr. Alaa Abdulkhaleq Hussein, University of Baghdad, Iraq
Dr. Bharat Bhushan, Sharda University, India
Dr. David Yeregui Marcos, University of Leon, Spain
Dr. Deepika Kumar, Bharati Vidyapeeth's College of Engineering, India
Dr. David Yeregui Marcos, University of Leon, Spain
Dr. Donghui Zhao, Shenyang University of Technology, China
Dr. Enkeleda Lulaj, University Haxhi Zeka, Kosovo
Dr. Faezeh Soleimani, Ball State University, USA
Dr. Gabriella Casalino, Università degli Studi di Bari Aldo Moro Bari, Italy
Dr. Hazrat Ali, Hamad Bin Khalifa University, Qatar
Dr. Hsi-Ming Ho, University Of Sussex, UK
Dr. Hui Lu, China Electric Power Research Institute, China
Dr. Jia Cui, Shenyang University of Technology, China
Dr. Jinglu Liu, Shenyang University of Technology, China
Dr. Jonathan Browning, Queen's University Belfast, UK
Dr. Junaid Shuja, Universiti Teknologi Petronas, Malaysia
Dr. Junjie Hu, North China Electric Power University, China
Dr. Isaac Segovia Ramírez, University of Castilla-La Mancha, Spain
Dr. Kiran Sood, Chitkara University, India
Dr. Lu Bai, Queen's University Belfast, UK
Dr. María del Valle Fernández Moreno, University of Castilla-La Mancha, Spain
Dr. Momina Mustehsan, Bahria University, Pakistan

Organization

Organizer

Shenyang University of Technology, Liaoning, China

General Chairs

Dr. Fausto Pedro García Márquez, University of Castilla–La Mancha, Spain
Dr. Yuxian Zhang, Shenyang University of Technology, China
Dr. Alaa Ali Hameed, Istinye University, Türkiye

Technical Program Chairs

Dr. Xiandong Xu, Tianjin University, China
Dr. Gen Li, Technical University of Denmark, Denmark
Dr. Junyou Yang, Shenyang University of Technology, China
Dr. Ana María Peco Chacón, University of Castilla-La Mancha, Spain
Dr. Akhtar Jamil, National University of Computer and Emerging Sciences, Pakistan
Dr. Haixin Wang, Shenyang University of Technology, China

Publication and Publicity Chairs

Dr. Serdar Solak, Kocaeli University, Turkey
Dr. Mustafa Hikmet Bilgehan Uçar, Kocaeli University, Türkiye

Organizing Committee

Dr. Haixin Wang, Shenyang University of Technology, China
Dr. Junyou Yang, Shenyang University of Technology, China
Dr. Yue Zhou, Cardiff University, UK
Dr. Xiandong Xu, Tianjin University, China

Registration Committee

Dr. Zuoxia Xing, Shenyang University of Technology, China
Dr. Muhammad Davud, Istinye University, Türkiye
Dr. Enkeleda Lulaj, University Haxhi Zeka, Kosovo

Technical Program Committee

Dr. Ahmed Sherif, University of Southern Mississippi, USA
Dr. Amir Seyyedabbasi, Istinye University, Türkiye
Dr. Alfredo Peinado Gonzalo, University of Castilla-La Mancha, Spain
Dr. Alaa Abdulkhaleq Hussein, University of Baghdad, Iraq
Dr. Bharat Bhushan, Sharda University, India
Dr. David Yeregui Marcos, University of Leon, Spain
Dr. Deepika Kumar, Bharati Vidyapeeth's College of Engineering, India
Dr. David Yeregui Marcos, University of Leon, Spain
Dr. Donghui Zhao, Shenyang University of Technology, China
Dr. Enkeleda Lulaj, University Haxhi Zeka, Kosovo
Dr. Faezeh Soleimani, Ball State University, USA
Dr. Gabriella Casalino, Università degli Studi di Bari Aldo Moro Bari, Italy
Dr. Hazrat Ali, Hamad Bin Khalifa University, Qatar
Dr. Hsi-Ming Ho, University Of Sussex, UK
Dr. Hui Lu, China Electric Power Research Institute, China
Dr. Jia Cui, Shenyang University of Technology, China
Dr. Jinglu Liu, Shenyang University of Technology, China
Dr. Jonathan Browning, Queen's University Belfast, UK
Dr. Junaid Shuja, Universiti Teknologi Petronas, Malaysia
Dr. Junjie Hu, North China Electric Power University, China
Dr. Isaac Segovia Ramírez, University of Castilla-La Mancha, Spain
Dr. Kiran Sood, Chitkara University, India
Dr. Lu Bai, Queen's University Belfast, UK
Dr. María del Valle Fernández Moreno, University of Castilla-La Mancha, Spain
Dr. Momina Mustehsan, Bahria University, Pakistan

Dr. Muhammad Abdul Basit, Montana Technological University, Butte Montana, USA
Dr. Muhammad Davud, Istinye University, Türkiye
Dr. Mustafa Al-asadi, KTO Karatay University, Türkiye
Dr. Mustafa Takaoğlu, TÜBİTAK-BİLGEM, Kocaeli, Türkiye
Dr. Nelly Elsayed, University of Cincinnati, USA
Dr. Ning Yan, Shenyang University of Technology, China
Dr. Pasquale Ardimento, Università Degli Studi Di Bari, Itlay
Dr. Shengyang Lu, State Grid Liaoning Electric Power Co., Ltd. Electric Power Science Research Institute, China
Dr. Subhan Ullah, National University of Computer and Emerging Sciences, Pakistan
Dr. Syed Attique Shah, Birmingham City University, UK
Dr. Tao Niu, Chongqing University, China
Dr. Tianle Zhang, University Of Exeter, UK
Dr. Wadhah Zeyad Tareq, Istinye University, Türkiye
Dr. Waleed Ead, Beni-Suef University, Egypt
Dr. Yang Liu, Shenyang University of Technology, China
Dr. Yao Lu, Lancaster University, UK
Dr. Yasser Ismail, Southern University and A&M College, USA
Dr. Yiming Ma, Shenyang University of Technology, China
Dr. Yuan Li, Shenyang University of Technology, China
Dr. Yuling Liang, Shenyang University of Technology, China
Dr. Yunlu Li, Shenyang University of Technology, China
Dr. Zhang Tianle, University of Exeter, UK
Dr. Ziyan Ren, Shenyang University of Technology, China

Preface

This book is a compilation of the selected papers presented at the 3rd International Conference on Computing, IoT and Data Analytics (ICCIDA) organized by the School of Electrical Engineering, Shenyang University of Technology, Liaoning, July 11–12, 2024, following the successful 2nd edition in Spain of ICCIDA-2023.

The conference served as an interdisciplinary forum that helped the research community to take a step forward and share the research findings. In addition, it provided an arena where researchers, scholars, professionals, students, and academicians may be able to foster working relationships and gain access to the latest research results.

The book highlights some of the latest research advances and cutting-edge analysis of real-world case studies on Computational Intelligence, Data Analytics, IoT, and Applications from a wide range of international contexts. It also identified business applications and the latest findings and innovations in Operations Management and the Decision Sciences, e.g.

Data Analysis and Visualization

- Exploratory Data Analysis
- Statistical and Mathematical Modeling
- Business Intelligence
- Big Data Analysis
- Data Mining
- Cloud Computing Architecture and Systems
- ETL and Big Data Warehousing
- Business Intelligence
- Data Visualization
- Statistical Analysis

Computer Vision

- Document Analysis
- Biometrics and Pattern Recognition
- Remote Sensing and GIS
- Medical Image Processing
- Image and Video Retrieval
- Motion Analysis
- Structure from Motion
- Object Detection and Recognition
- Image Restoration
- Speech and Audio Processing
- Signal Processing

Artificial Intelligence

- Machine Learning
- Pattern Recognition
- Deep Learning
- Human Computer Interactions
- Medical Image Processing
- Image and Video Retrieval
- Audio Video Processing
- Text Analytics
- Natural Language Processing
- Information Retrieval
- Robotics Applications

Internet of Things

- 3D Printing
- Securing IoT Infrastructure
- Future of IoT and Big Data
- Internet of Things
- Intelligent Systems for IoT
- Security, Privacy and Trust
- Visual Analytics IoT
- Data Compression for IoT Devices
- IoT Services and Applications
- Education and Learning
- Social Networks Analysis

Communication Systems and Networks

- Antennas, Propagation and RF Design
- Transmission and Communication Theory
- Wireless/Radio Access Technologies
- Optical Networks and NGN
- 5G and 6G Cellular Systems and SON
- Sensor Networks
- Multimedia and New Media
- High Speed Communication
- Computational Intelligence in Telecommunications

Software Engineering

- Requirements Engineering
- Security Aspects
- Agile Software Engineering
- Software Evolution and Reuse
- Reverse Engineering
- Software Dependability
- Data and AI Monetization and Products
- Data as a Service/Platform
- Biomedical Experiments and Simulations
- Decision Support Systems

Ciudad Real, Spain — Fausto Pedro García Márquez
Islamabad, Pakistan — Dr. Akhtar Jamil
Istanbul, Türkiye — Dr. Alaa Ali Hameed
Liaoning, China — Dr. Haixin Wang
Liaoning, China — Prof. Yuxian Zhang
Liaoning, China — Prof. Junyou Yang

Introduction

This book is a compilation of accepted papers presented at the 3rd International Conference on Computing, IoT and Data Analytics (ICCIDA) organized by the School of Electrical Engineering, Shenyang University of Technology, Liaoning, July 11–12, 2024, following the successful 2nd edition in Spain of ICCIDA-2023.

This is the Proceedings book which includes the best papers of the 3rd International Conference on Computing, IoT and Data Analytics (ICCIDA). The book is unique due to the presence of some state-of-the-art contributions related to computing, IoT, data science, and artificial intelligence. Some recent advancements in these fields are included in this book.

The book highlights some of the latest research advances and cutting-edge analyses of real-world problems related to Computing, IoT, and Data Analytics and their applications in various domains. This includes state-of-the-art models and methods used on benchmark datasets, but also:

Data Analysis and Visualization

- Exploratory Data Analysis
- Statistical and Mathematical Modeling
- Business Intelligence
- Big Data Analysis
- Data Mining
- Cloud Computing Architecture and Systems
- ETL and Big Data Warehousing
- Business Intelligence
- Data Visualization
- Statistical Analysis

Computer Vision

- Document Analysis
- Biometrics and Pattern Recognition
- Remote Sensing and GIS
- Medical Image Processing
- Image and Video Retrieval
- Motion Analysis
- Structure from Motion
- Object Detection and Recognition
- Image Restoration
- Speech and Audio Processing
- Signal Processing

Artificial Intelligence

- Machine Learning
- Pattern Recognition
- Deep Learning
- Human Computer Interactions
- Medical Image Processing
- Image and Video Retrieval
- Audio Video Processing
- Text Analytics
- Natural Language Processing
- Information Retrieval
- Robotics Applications

Internet of Things

- 3D Printing
- Securing IoT Infrastructure
- Future of IoT and Big Data
- Internet of Things
- Intelligent Systems for IoT
- Security, Privacy and Trust
- Visual Analytics IoT
- Data Compression for IoT Devices
- IoT Services and Applications
- Education and Learning
- Social Networks Analysis

Communication Systems and Networks

- Antennas, Propagation and RF Design
- Transmission and Communication Theory
- Wireless/Radio Access Technologies
- Optical Networks and NGN
- 5G and 6G Cellular Systems and SON
- Sensor Networks
- Multimedia and New Media
- High Speed Communication
- Computational Intelligence in Telecommunications

Software Engineering

- Requirements Engineering
- Security Aspects
- Agile Software Engineering
- Software Evolution and Reuse
- Reverse Engineering
- Software Dependability
- Data and AI Monetization and Products
- Data as a Service/Platform
- Biomedical Experiments and Simulations
- Decision Support Systems

Computing, IoT, and Data Analytics are three interconnected fields that are transforming industries and shaping the future of technology.

Computing forms the backbone of modern technology, encompassing the hardware and software systems that enable data processing, storage, and communication. Advancements in computing, especially with the rise of cloud computing, edge computing, and high-performance computing (HPC), have significantly expanded the ability to process large amounts of data quickly and efficiently. Cloud computing allows for scalable storage and processing power, while edge computing brings computation closer to the data source, reducing latency and improving real-time decision-making. These technologies support applications ranging from mobile apps to complex simulations in scientific research.

The IoT refers to the network of interconnected devices—ranging from sensors, cameras, and appliances to industrial machinery—that collect and exchange data over the internet. IoT devices can monitor environments, track assets, control systems remotely, and even make autonomous decisions. Smart homes, connected vehicles, and industrial automation are just a few examples of how IoT is changing daily life and business operations.

IoT devices generate vast amounts of data, but their true power lies in how that data is used. By integrating IoT with other technologies, such as AI and machine learning, businesses can optimize processes, enhance customer experiences, and drive innovation in fields like healthcare, agriculture, and manufacturing.

Data analytics involves extracting meaningful insights from raw data, helping organizations make data-driven decisions. This field ranges from basic descriptive analytics, which looks at historical data to explain trends, to more advanced predictive and prescriptive analytics, which use machine learning models to forecast future outcomes and recommend actions.

With the rise of IoT, the amount of available data has exploded, leading to an increased demand for real-time analytics solutions. For example, in healthcare, IoT devices can monitor patients in real time and send alerts in case of abnormalities, while in smart cities, analytics can be used to optimize traffic flow, energy consumption, and waste management.

The convergence of computing, IoT, and data analytics is enabling the creation of highly intelligent systems that can sense, analyze, and act on data in real time. This convergence has broad applications across industries, for example:

Smart Cities: Integrating IoT sensors with data analytics helps monitor urban infrastructure, improve traffic management, enhance public safety, and optimize energy usage.

Healthcare: IoT-connected devices collect patient data in real time, while data analytics identifies trends that can improve diagnostics and treatment.

Manufacturing: IoT-enabled machines track operational performance, while real-time analytics provide insights that enhance efficiency and predict maintenance needs.

Retail: Companies are using IoT and analytics to improve customer experiences by personalizing offers, optimizing inventory management, and analyzing consumer behavior patterns.

As computing power increases and IoT networks expand, the role of data analytics will become even more crucial in unlocking the full potential of IoT ecosystems. Together, these technologies are enabling smarter, more efficient, and more responsive systems across various sectors.

Fausto Pedro García Márquez
Dr. Akhtar Jamil
Dr. Alaa Ali Hameed
Dr. Haixin Wang
Prof. Yuxian Zhang
Prof. Junyou Yang

Contents

About the Editors

Fausto Pedro García Márquez works at UCLM as Full Professor (Accredited as Full Professor from 2013), Spain, Honorary Senior Research Fellow at Birmingham University, UK, Lecturer at the Postgraduate European Institute, Research Fellow at INTI International University and Colleges, Malaysia, and he has been Senior Manager in Accenture (2013–2014). He obtained his European Ph.D. with maximum distinction. He has been distinguished with the prices: Runner Prize (2023), Nominate Prize (2022), Gran Maestre (2022), Grand Prize (2021), Runner Prize (2020) and Advancement Prize (2018), Runner (2015), Advancement (2013) and Silver (2012) by the International Society of Management Science and Engineering Management (ICMSEM), First International Business Ideas Competition 2017 Award (2017), etc. He has published more than 248 papers (156 JCR: 74-Q1; 42-Q2; 32-Q3; 8-Q4), some recognized as: "Progress in Photovoltaics: Research and Applications" (Q1, IF. 8.49, one of the most downloaded in first 12 months of publications, 2023), "Applied Energy" (Q1, IF 9.746, as "Best Paper 2020"), "Renewable Energy" (Q1, IF 8.001, as "Best Paper 2014"); "ICMSEM" (as "excellent"), "International Journal of Automation and Computing", "IMechE Part F: Journal of Rail and Rapid Transit" (most downloaded), etc. He is the Author and Editor of over 50 books (Elsevier, Springer, Pearson, McGrawHill, Intech, IGI, Marcombo, AlfaOmega,...), > 100 international chapters, and six patents. He is the Editor of five International Journals and a Committee Member of more than 70 International Conferences. He has been the Principal

Investigator in four European Projects, eight National Projects, and more than 150 projects for Universities, Companies, etc. His main interests are Artificial Intelligence, Maintenance, Management, Renewable Energy, Transport, Advanced Analytics, and Data Science.

He is being Expert in the European Union in AI4People (EISMD), and ESF; Director of www.ingeniumgroup.eu; Senior Member at IEEE, 2021–… ; Honored Honorary Member of the Research Council of Indian Institute of Finance, 2021–… ; Committee Chair of The International Society for Management Science and Engineering Management (ISMSEM), 2020–….

Dr. Akhtar Jamil is an Associate Professor in the Department of Computer Science at the National University of Computer and Emerging Sciences, Islamabad, Pakistan. Before joining FAST, he served as Assistant Professor and Vice Head of the Computer Engineering Department at Istanbul Sabahattin Zaim University, Istanbul, Turkey. He also served as a Lecture at COMSATS University Islamabad. He has also worked in the industry as a developer for several years. He received his Ph.D. in Machine Learning and Remote Sensing from Yildiz Technical University, Istanbul, Turkey. He has published more than 50 high-quality papers in well-known journals and top conferences. He received a fully funded Ph.D. scholarship from the Turkish Government. He is the founding member of the ICMI, ICAETA, and ICCIDA conferences. He serves as a reviewer for several journals and conferences. He focuses on applied research for solving real-world problems. His current research interests include Statistical Machine Learning, Deep Learning, Pattern Recognition, Data Analytics, Image Classification, and Remote Sensing.

Alaa Ali Hameed received his Master's degree in computer engineering from Eastern Mediterranean University, North Cyprus, in 2012, and his Ph.D. degree from the Department of Computer Engineering at Selcuk University, Turkey, in 2017. He worked as an Assistant Professor in the Department of Computer Engineering, at Istanbul Aydin University, Turkey, from 2017 to 2019. He then moved to Istanbul Sabahattin Zaim University, Turkey, where he worked as an Assistant Professor in the Department of Computer Engineering from 2019 to 2022. Currently, he is an Assistant Professor in the Department of Computer Engineering at Istinye University, Turkey. He has published more than 60 technical articles in top international journals and conferences in a short span of time. He has served as a Program Chair and a Technical Program Chair member for many international conferences, also he has served as a Guest Editor for many SCIE journals. His research interests include Digital Signal and Image Processing, Adaptive Filters, Adaptive Computing, Data Mining, Machine, and Deep Learning, Big Data and Data Analytics, Neural Networks and Self-Learning Systems, and Artificial Intelligence.

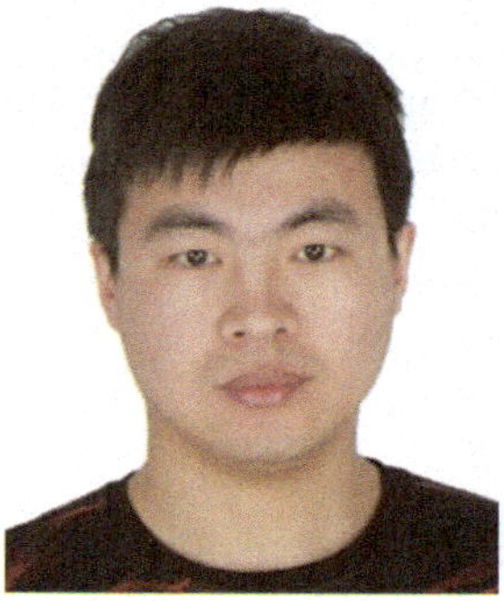

Haixin Wang received the B.Eng. degree in Electrical Engineering from the Inner Mongolia Agricultural University, Hohhot, China, in 2011, and the M.Sc. and Ph.D. degrees in Electrical Engineering from the Shenyang University of Technology, Shenyang, China, in 2014 and 2017, respectively. He did his postdoctoral research at the Shenyang University of Technology, Shenyang, China, and at the School of Engineering, Cardiff University, Cardiff, UK, in 2018 and 2019. Currently, He is an Associate Professor at the School of Electrical Engineering, Shenyang University of Technology, Shenyang, China. He has published more than 248 papers. His research interests include Integrated Energy System, Wind Power Generation, and Cyber-Physical System.

Yuxian Zhang received the M.S. and Ph.D. degrees in Control Theory and Sontrol Engineering from Northeastern University, Shenyang, China, in 2005 and 2007, respectively. He worked with the Postdoctoral Station of Control Science and Engineering, Tsinghua University, Beijing, China, from 2007 to 2009. He joined Shenyang University of Technology, Shenyang, in 2009. His current research interests include Integrated Energy System, Power System Operation Analysis and Dispatching, and Load Modeling.

Junyou Yang received the B.Eng. degree from Jilin University of Technology, Jilin City, China, the M.Sc. degree from Shenyang University of Technology, Shenyang, China, and the Ph.D. degree from Harbin Institute of Technology, Harbin, China. He was a Visiting Scholar at the Department of Electrical Engineering and Computer Science, University of Toronto, Canada, from 1999 to 2000. He is the Head of the School of Electrical Engineering, Shenyang University of Technology, Shenyang, China. He is a Distinguished Professor of Liaoning province and the first hundred-level candidates in the "BaiQianWan Talents Program". He has led more than 50 research projects and has more than 200 publications in his technical field. His research interests include Wind Energy, Power System, and Integrated Energy System.

Chapter 1
Wind Energy and Maintenance Forecasting Employing Tree-Based Reduction Methods

Javier Sánchez-Soriano, Pedro Jose Paniagua-Falo, Carlos Quiterio Gómez Muñoz, Alberto Pliego Marugán, and Jesús María Pinar-Pérez

Abstract For an electric company, accurate forecasts of electrical production and maintenance from wind farms are essential for efficient operation in markets like OMIE, OMIP, and MIBEL. Predictive models using Machine Learning and AI techniques like SVM or SVR, based on meteorological data and wind farm specifics, offer short-term accuracy but lack depth. A new research work proposes a Deep Neural Network (DNN) model for more precise long-term forecasts, considering wind farm characteristics and climatic data, aiming to outperform conventional forecasting methods with more detailed results.

1.1 Introduction

For electric power generation companies, precise forecasts for wind farm production and maintenance are crucial for efficient and strategic operations in energy markets like OMIE, OMIP, and MIBEL. Accurate forecasting enables detailed cost–benefit analysis and the anticipation of challenges like market exposure and unforeseen

J. Sánchez-Soriano · P. J. Paniagua-Falo
Escuela Politécnica Superior, Universidad Francisco de Vitoria, Pozuelo de Alarcón, Madrid, Spain
e-mail: javier.sanchez@ufv.es

C. Q. Gómez Muñoz (✉)
HCTLab Research Group, Universidad Autónoma de Madrid, Madrid, Spain
e-mail: Carlosq.gomez@uam.es

A. Pliego Marugán · J. M. Pinar-Pérez
Department of Quantitative Methods, CUNEF University, Madrid, Spain
e-mail: alberto.pliego@cunef.edu

J. M. Pinar-Pérez
e-mail: jesusmaria.pinar@cunef.edu

F. P. García Márquez et al. (eds.), *Computing, Internet of Things and Data Analytics*, Smart Innovation, Systems and Technologies 387,
https://doi.org/10.1007/978-3-031-87154-2_1

maintenance needs. The advancement in Machine Learning and Artificial Intelligence technologies, particularly Support Vector Machines (SVM) and Support Vector Regression (SVR), facilitates initial predictions using meteorological and specific wind farm data. However, to capture the complexities of wind power production, this work proposes the development of a Deep Neural Network (DNN)-based [1, 2] This model will integrate wind farm configurations, climatological data, and turbine operational data, including maintenance records and sensor readings, to improve prediction accuracy and enable predictive maintenance. This approach aims to minimize downtime and reduce costs while enhancing turbine efficiency. Utilizing Dataiku for data processing, the model's development process will be streamlined, though mastering its capabilities is necessary. Upon completion, the model's effectiveness in forecasting production and scheduling maintenance will be rigorously evaluated, potentially offering significant operational cost savings and increased reliability in the competitive energy sector [3].

1.2 Related Research

Despite the inherent challenges in obtaining precise and reliable results from models based on artificial neural networks ANNs [4] due to the randomness of the network's initial parameters, such as weights, thresholds, smoothing factors, etc., these are valuable tools for understanding and managing the uncertainty associated with wind energy predictions. A review of the literature conducted [1, 2, 5, 6] and more recent [7] can find the following related works in different temporal horizons:

1.2.1 Related Works on Long-Term Predictions in the Field of Energy

One of the most recent and relevant works in the field of long-term energy production prediction is that proposed by Yang M et. al. [8] which makes a prediction of up to 3 days of wind energy production. This study utilizes a dataset provided by a wind farm with an installed capacity of 400.5 MW in Jilin, China. A temporal segmentation with time windows of length 8 is performed, meaning the input time step is 8. The proposed model, named Bi_GRU_ResNet (BG_ResNet), consists of 7 basic cascading blocks, a layer with 32 neurons, a short layer with 16 neurons, and a 1D_CNN with 32 convolutional cores of dimension 1. The training parameters include a learning rate of 0.01, a dropout rate of 0.2, a batch size of 256, and a total of 100 iterations. The analysis reveals that by using measured atmospheric data (AMD) as input, the model achieves an effective correlation between wind speed and power, with an NRMSE of 0.0978. In comparison, when employing Numerical Weather

Prediction (NWP) data, the accuracy decreases due to limitations in the accuracy of NWP, obtaining an NRMSE of 0.1581.

Another interesting and modern approach would be that proposed by Xiaosheng et. al., who present an innovative wind energy prediction model with a prediction horizon of 24 and 96 h. This method is based on an advanced deep learning approach, utilizing a stacked denoising autoencoder (SDAE) within a multi-level transfer learning framework [9]. The methodology is divided into two fundamental stages: the extraction and classification of similar samples, followed by the hierarchical migration of the model. Initially, a neural network is trained with samples from the target wind farm, and then the prediction of the source wind farm samples is performed, classifying them according to the correlation coefficient. The correlation coefficient is calculated using the covariance between the predicted powers (Ppre) and the real powers (Preal) of the source wind farms, while subsequently, the correlation coefficient (ρXY) is calculated using the covariance and variances of the predicted and real powers, and is expressed as:

$$Cov = \frac{1}{n-1}\sum\nolimits_{i=1}^{n}\left(P_{pre_i} - \overline{P_{pre_i}}\right)\left(P_{real\,i} - \overline{P_{real\,i}}\right) \tag{1.1}$$

For this approach, three comparison groups were used to analyse the results. All groups employ 250 days of data as the test set, but they differ in the training set. Comparison Group 1 simulates the lack of training data in new wind farms by using only 50 days. Comparison Group 2 uses 350 days, representing data sufficiency. Comparison Group 3, like Group 1, uses only 50 days but incorporates a large amount of migrated data to improve accuracy in new wind farms. The conclusions of this work revealed that the multi-level model is effective for new wind farms without sufficient training data, achieving greater accuracy compared to methods without transfer learning. Lastly, we can discuss the work conducted by Wang, Huaqing, Tan, Zhongfu, Liang, Yan, Li, Fanqi, Zhang, Zheyu, and Ju, Liwei [10] who addressed wind energy generation prediction by incorporating conventional deep neural network (DNN) models, such as MLP, CNN, and LSTM. This diversified approach of DNN models establishes a solid foundation for tackling the complexity inherent in wind energy prediction.

1.2.2 Related Works on Short-Term Predictions in the Field of Energy

One of the most notable approaches for short-term prediction is by Ömer Ali Karaman [11]. This study explores the utilization of various neural network architectures, including Artificial Neural Networks (ANNs), Recurrent Neural Networks (RNNs),the research applies Convolutional Neural Networks (CNNs) and Long Short-Term Memory Networks (LSTMs) to improve wind turbine power production forecasts using SCADA and meteorological data, including wind speed, direction, and temperature. It utilizes statistical indicators to enhance hourly forecast accuracy, noting CNNs' effectiveness under low wind conditions for their feature extraction capabilities. However, LSTMs outperform overall, especially with sequential data, proving superior in predictive performance. The study emphasizes the importance of choosing models based on specific application conditions, showcasing neural networks' vital role in optimizing wind power forecasting.

Another approach proposed by Hong Liu et. al. in similarity with the work of Jianzhou et. Al. [10, 12], it focuses on using SCADA system data to address wind energy prediction [4] To evaluate their method, they used SCADA datasets from commercial wind farms in China, focusing on a wind farm with 25 wind turbines. This dataset covers historical measurements of 25 wind turbines over a 6-month period, from September 2019 to March 2020, with 10-min sampling intervals. The SCADA system monitors over 100 wind turbine attributes, including wind power (WP), wind speed (WS), wind direction (WD), generator speed (GS), nacelle direction (ND), blade angles (BA1, BA2, BA3), temperatures (GT, ET, IT), as well as the acceleration speeds in the x and y directions of the generator (XACC, YACC). To process this abundant information, a feature engineering process is implemented that develops a dual-channel system for handling the input of paired tensors and graphs. One channel uses a traditional feature selection method through L1 regularization, directly selecting a set of significant features with strong linearity with respect to future wind energy production. The selected features retain their physical meaning. On the other hand, the second channel aims to extract latent and relevant features. This is achieved through a feature extraction module based on a deep neural network (DNN). This module consists of two parts: the first projects the data into a feature vector through a fully connected neural network (NN), and the second part focuses on extracting spatio-temporal features. This results in significant improvements, outperforming both benchmark models and other deep learning models without the use of geo-information. Moreover, the method exhibits acceptable prediction times, even surpassing the best benchmark model in temporal efficiency.

1.2.3 Related Works on Ultra-Short-Term Predictions in the Field of Energy

Li et. al. [13] introduced an innovative approach combining the Differential Evolution (DE) algorithm with Backpropagation Neural Networks (BP) for very short-term wind energy prediction. Historical data from a northwest China wind farm, was collected from October 2016 to April 2018, including wind speed, direction, temperature, and atmospheric pressure, was used for analysis. Of 5,000 samples, 4,000 were for training and 1,000 for verification. The algorithms, implemented in MATLAB, were evaluated on MAE, MSE, and RMSE. The Backpropagation (BP) Neural Network model, with a single hidden layer, optimized parameters to reduce sensitivity to initial conditions, improve speed and accuracy, and decrease training time. Using Differential Evolution (DE) for initial weight and threshold optimization resulted in a 5% accuracy improvement over the traditional BP model.

Within the realm of very short-term wind energy prediction, a study by Hu et. al. [14], like the work of Wang as done by [10], was conducted. In this study, deep neural network (DNN) fundamental structures like MLP, LSTM, and CNN were employed for predictions. Their approach's distinctiveness lay in the innovative implementation of preprocessing through the Sequential Forward Selection (SFS) algorithm and K-Nearest Neighbours (KNN). The dataset for this study came from observations collected at 26 wind farms in northwest China over a year. Each observation included data such as wind speed and direction, atmospheric pressure, and temperature, recorded at 15-min intervals.

To address missing values and outlier data, an imputation process was implemented, opting to use the average of the surrounding 14 days to the problematic observation instead of leaving the data unprocessed. The study assessed performance using four metrics: NRMSE, NMAE, MAPE, and R^2. Comparing the proposed model, M-Stacking, with other models such as SVM, DT, RF, ANN, DNN, ARIMA, LSTM, LASSO, K-NN, CNN-LSTM, Bagging, AdaBoost, and XGBoost, it was highlighted that M-Stacking showed superior performance with an NRMSE of 9.09%, NMAE of 9.22%, MAPE of 8.23%, and an R^2 of 0.892. These metrics indicate greater accuracy, lower error, and a better fit of the M-Stacking model to the wind energy prediction data.

1.3 Case of Study

For this work, it has been used the following model and data. The proposed model starts with an input layer consisting of 15 neurons. Each of these neurons represents a specific feature present in our dataset, allowing for the comprehensive incorporation of the initial information. This initial phase of the network is configured to capture the diversity of features present in the input data. Subsequently, a model will be established as an MLP or "Multi-Layer Perceptron," which is an artificial intelligence model that uses a series of layers composed of units or neurons organized sequentially to process information in a hierarchical manner. Each layer receives inputs from the previous layer and produces outputs for the next, using a combination of weights and activation functions to transform the input data.

It utilizes "backpropagation" to train and adjust its parameters (weights and biases) to minimize the prediction error by using gradient descent on the loss function with respect to each weight in the network to update their values so that the error between the model's predictions and the actual values reduces over time. Based on the reviewed literature and the characteristics of the prediction being sought, four different architectures will be implemented, covering several hidden layers ranging between 3, 5, 7, or 9.

In terms of model fitting and optimization, a "learning rate" ranging from 0.001 to 0.0001 has been established. This setting regulates the magnitude of weight updates during the training process, contributing to a more effective convergence of the model. Furthermore, a "batch size" of 64 is used, meaning the model adjusts its weights after processing each batch of 64 training examples.

As an additional measure to prevent overfitting, a "dropout" of 20% is incorporated. This value indicates that 20% of the connections between neurons from layer to layer will be disconnected during training. Dropout acts as a form of regularization, improving the model's generalization by introducing variability in the connections and thereby reducing dependence on specific connections. Due to the significant disparity in numbers between different hours of the day, L1 and L2 regularization will be added to all tested architectures, as L1 (Lasso) will penalize some weights to zero, providing robustness, and L2 (Ridge) provides numerical stability by penalizing the total magnitude of the weights. This aspect contributes to preventing problems associated with model overfitting.

In addition to this, to improve the accuracy of the model, we apply various preprocessing techniques to the data before it is used for training the model:

- We use methods of linear combination and polynomial generation by pairs to improve the model's interpretation and performance.
- Polynomial generation by pairs: Where Z is the resulting feature from X and Y are the original features, and a and b are the exponents assigned to each feature.
- Linear combination: Where Y is the resulting feature from X and w are the weights assigned per feature.

Data used in this study was collected from a wind farm in the Ebro Valley. Spanning from February 13, 2021, to February 29, 2024. The dataset is recorded on an hourly basis, ensuring a thorough capture of operational parameters throughout each day, from the initial hour (hour 0) to the final hour (hour 23), having a total of 16,000 records.

This wind farm comprises four wind turbines, each serving as a vital data source. The variety of collected data is extensive, encompassing geographical coordinates (latitude and longitude) to provide precise location details of each turbine. Additionally, a comprehensive time index amalgamates year, day, and hour, enriched with temperature readings from various points around the turbines. The dataset is further augmented with essential meteorological information, including ambient temperature and wind direction, which are crucial for analysing the environmental conditions affecting the turbines. Moreover, operational data such as rotor speed and nacelle angle offer an in-depth look into the mechanical performance of each turbine.

The training data have been divided into 80% for training and 20% for testing, and for subsequent validation, the K-fold-cross-validation method was used, in which the dataset was subdivided into 5 groups, alternating the validation set.

1.4 Methodology

This work employs the CRISP-DM methodology for its structured approach to data mining, particularly in predicting wind farm production. CRISP-DM encompasses understanding business and project needs, data comprehension and preparation, model development, and implementation. A key stage is the data understanding phase, crucial for selecting relevant data in wind energy, considering factors like wind speed and turbine efficiency. Data preparation addresses environmental noise and sensor inaccuracies, vital for creating reliable models. The adaptive modelling phase explores various forecasting methods through algorithm experimentation and hyper-parameter tuning, aiming for optimal accuracy. Finally, model evaluation ensures the forecasting accuracy, confirming the model's effectiveness on new data.

1.5 Results

After conducting an extensive training period for each architecture, during which the best set of hyperparameters was sought, these have been the best metrics for each architecture.

Regarding training Metrics: If we look at Table 1.1 the training metrics indicate that all architectures achieve high values in the variance explanation coefficient (evs) and the coefficient of determination (r2), with values close to or exceeding 0.954. This suggests that, during the training phase, the models can capture a significant portion of the data variance. It indicates that all architectures are potentially able to capture the underlying complexity in the data to a certain extent, albeit with slight variations in efficiency and accuracy.

Although the models exhibit high performance on the training set, it is crucial to assess how these architectures perform on unseen datasets to understand their generalization ability. A model well-fitted in training might not necessarily translate into good validation performance if it has learned to memorize the data rather than to generalize from it.

Regarding validation metrics.: If we take a look at Table 1.2 From the 3 of metrics, we can deduce the following characteristics: While we have observed very good

Table 1.1 Table of different results of training

HL	Units	LR	Batch size	Dropout	L2	L1	EVS	MAE	MAPE	RMSE	r2
3	140	0,001	64	0,4	0,8	0,2	0,968	134,116	0,558	277,864	0,957
5	180	0,0001	64	0,2	0,4	0,2	0,969	133,649	0,602	276,398	0,956
7	100	0,001	64	0,4	0,4	0,2	0,956	148,897	0,592	288,345	0,954
9	100	0,0001	64	0,4	0,4	0,2	0,956	140,325	0,592	282,813	0,955

Table 1.2 Table of different results of validation

HL	Units	LR	Batch size	Dropout	L2	L1	EVS	MAE	MAPE	RMSE	r2
3	140	0,001	64	0,4	0,8	0,2	0,928	350,446	0,379	436,087	0,816
5	180	0,0001	64	0,2	0,4	0,2	0,929	325,029	0,361	406,501	0,840
7	100	0,001	64	0,4	0,4	0,2	0,955	201,185	0,281	265,965	0,932
9	100	0,0001	64	0,4	0,4	0,2	0,936	319,209	0,353	401,357	0,844

metrics in training, upon examining the validation metrics, there is a drop in precision metrics, more pronounced in architectures with 3 and 9 hidden layers. This phenomenon suggests that the more extreme the configurations in terms of network depth (too few or many layers), the more prone they are to lose generalization capability on unseen data.

The balance between model complexity and the risk of overfitting is clearly illustrated. As the model's complexity increases (whether through more layers, neurons, or less regularization), so does the risk of the model learning the quirks of the training set too well, reducing its ability to generalize to new data. This is particularly observable in the model with 9 hidden layers, as despite being more complex, it does not generalize better.

The configuration of 3 hidden layers and 140 units, although presenting the weakest metrics overall, could be valued for its simplicity and lower computational demand, making it suitable for contexts where training speed and efficiency are critical.

The architecture with 7 hidden layers and 100 units stands out for its excellent generalization capability, evidenced by its high coefficient of determination (r2) and the lowest values in mean absolute error (MAE) and root mean squared error (RMSE), indicating its superior ability to accurately predict unseen data (Fig. 1.1).

It is highlighted that configurations with lower learning rates (0.0001) do not necessarily result in better performance in validation, contrary to what might be expected. The architecture of 5 layers and that of 9 layers, both with this lower learning rate, do not outperform the 7-layer configuration with a higher learning rate

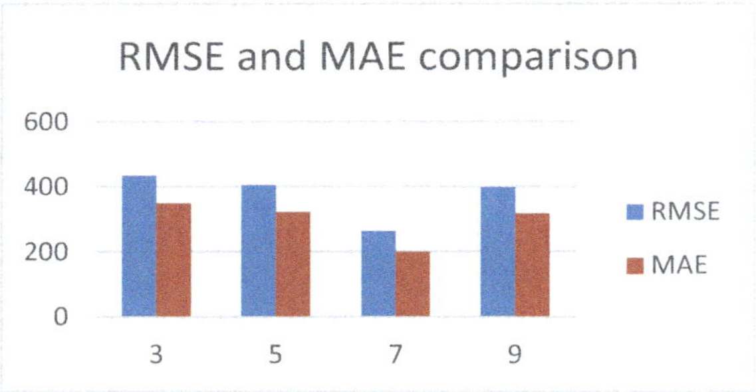

Fig. 1.1 Contrast between the RMSE values

(0.001). This suggests that the learning rate alone is not a clear determinant of the model's generalization effectiveness, necessitating its consideration alongside other hyperparameters and the overall architecture of the model.

The comparison between the predicted energy production values (kWh) by the model and the actual values over a full day, with measurements taken every hour (24 data points in total), is shown.

The model closely follows the general trend of the actual data throughout the day. This indicates that the model has successfully learned the general pattern of energy production over time.

There are periods, such as around 10 and 20 h, where the predictions and actual values match with high precision. At these points, the model accurately captures changes in energy production. Despite the overall good correlation, there are moments, especially around 5, 15, and 23 h, where the model does not accurately predict the peaks or falls in actual energy production. These deviations could be the result of factors not captured by the model or random variations in energy production that are difficult to predict.

Although the performance is remarkable, as can be perceived in the Fig. 1.2, there is room for improvement in the model in terms of capturing the peaks and falls more precisely. This could involve adjusting hyperparameters, including more training data, or revising the input features to include additional factors that might influence energy production.

Upon examining the predicted maintenance period, we can discern the following insights from the model's performance:

The model successfully identified the maintenance intervals, as evidenced by the highlighted period in the Fig. 1.3 during which all recorded variables drop to zero, a condition indicative of operational downtime for maintenance. A noteworthy observation is that prior to the commencement of maintenance, there is a notable decline in energy production. This gradual decrease may signal potential issues within the wind

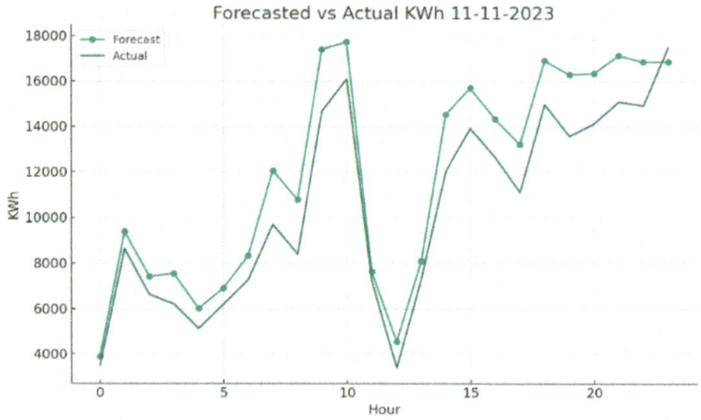

Fig. 1.2 Contrast between the actual and predicted energy production on November 11, 2023

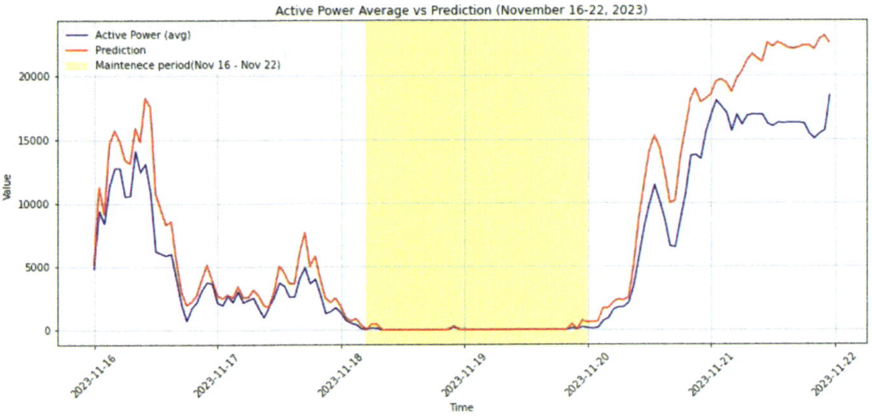

Fig. 1.3 The actual and predicted energy production highlighting the maintenance moments on November 16

farm, necessitating the maintenance. It is also apparent that post-maintenance, there is a significant rebound in energy production levels. This resurgence is indicative of the wind farm resuming normal operations and potentially reflecting the benefits of the maintenance conducted.

1.6 Conclusion

Following the completion of this work, the following conclusions can be drawn: The approach has demonstrated the usefulness of artificial intelligence in making predictions in the wind energy sector. With the correct setup and necessary resources, accurate and reliable results have been achieved. This allows us to have a model that updates with new information every day, staying always up to date. Moreover, the use of this model is particularly valuable for influencing important decisions related to the long-term electricity market. Thanks to its ability to predict accurately, it becomes an essential tool for planning and making decisions about the maintenance strategy. However, there is room for improvement in the work. Enhancing the quality and consistency of the data could further increase the model's accuracy. It is also crucial to increase the system's robustness to avoid problems caused by disconnections between the wind farms and the data storage system.

References

1. Lu, P., Ye, L., Zhao, Y., Dai, B., Pei, M., Tang, Y.: Review of meta-heuristic algorithms for wind power prediction: methodologies, applications and challenges. Appl. Energy **301**, 117446 (2021). https://doi.org/10.1016/j.apenergy.2021.117446
2. Lawan, S.M., Abidin, W., Chai, W.Y., Baharun, A., Masri, T.: Different models of wind speed prediction; a comprehensive review. Int. J. Sci. Eng. Res. **5**(1), 1760–1768 (2014)
3. Gómez Muñoz, C.Q.G., García Márquez, F.P.: Future maintenance management in renewable energies. (2018). https://doi.org/10.1007/978-3-319-45364-4_10
4. Liu, H., Yang, L., Zhang, B., Zhang, Z.: A two-channel deep network based model for improving ultra-short-term prediction of wind power via utilizing multi-source data. Energy **283**, 128510 (2023). https://doi.org/10.1016/J.ENERGY.2023.128510
5. Gómez Muñoz, C.Q., García Márquez, F.P.: Wind energy power prospective. (2018). https://doi.org/10.1007/978-3-319-45364-4_6
6. Gómez, C.Q., García, F.P., Villegas, M.A., Pedregal, D.J.: Big data and web intelligence for condition monitoring: A case study on wind turbines. (2015). https://doi.org/10.4018/978-1-4666-8505-5.ch008
7. Wang, S., et al.: A comprehensive review on the development of data-driven methods for wind power prediction and AGC performance evaluation in wind-thermal bundled power systems. Energy AI 100336 (2024). https://doi.org/10.1016/J.EGYAI.2024.100336
8. Yang, M., Wang, D., Zhang, W.: A short-term wind power prediction method based on dynamic and static feature fusion mining. Energy **280**, 128226 (2023). https://doi.org/10.1016/J.ENERGY.2023.128226
9. Peng, X., Yang, Z., Li, Y., Wang, B., Che, J.: Short-term wind power prediction based on stacked denoised auto-encoder deep learning and multi-level transfer learning. Wind Energy **26**(10), 1066–1081 (2023)
10. Wang, H., Tan, Z., Liang, Y., Li, F., Zhang, Z., Ju, L.: A novel multi-layer stacking ensemble wind power prediction model under Tensorflow deep learning framework considering feature enhancement and data hierarchy processing. Energy **286**, 129409 (2024). https://doi.org/10.1016/J.ENERGY.2023.129409
11. Karaman, Ö.A.: Prediction of Wind Power with Machine Learning Models. Appl. Sci. **13**(20), 11455 (2023). https://doi.org/10.3390/app132011455
12. Jiménez, A. A., Muñoz, C.Q.G., Márquez, F.P.G.: Machine learning and neural network for maintenance management. In: Lecture Notes on Multidisciplinary Industrial Engineering, vol. Part F43, (2018). https://doi.org/10.1007/978-3-319-59280-0_115
13. Li, N., Wang, Y., Ma, W., Xiao, Z., An Z.: A wind power prediction method based on DE-BP Neural Network. Front. Energy. Res. **10** (2022). https://doi.org/10.3389/fenrg.2022.844111
14. Qu, Z., Hou, X., Li, J., Hu, W.: Short-term wind farm cluster power prediction based on dual feature extraction and quadratic decomposition aggregation. Energy **290**, 130155 (2024). https://doi.org/10.1016/J.ENERGY.2023.130155

Chapter 2
Stability Analysis of Renewable Energy Systems Considering Photovoltaic Integration

Hongyu Lu, Shanshan Cheng, Haoqian Cui, Shengyang Lu, Qingshan Liu, Jia Liu, Xiayu Liu, Haixin Wang, and Junyou Yang

Abstract With the increasing proportion of renewable energy in the power system and the higher proportion of power electronic equipment application, the system strength will weaken, and safe and stable operation will also face greater challenges. To ensure that renewable energy can provide sufficient support for the stable operation of the system, the control strategy of grid-connected inverters has become a key concern. The inverter adopts a virtual synchronous generator control strategy, which can provide good inertia and damping support for the system. By designing reasonable parameters, the stability of the system operation can be effectively improved. To comprehensively analyze the impact of control parameters on the stable operation of the system, evaluate the stability and reliability of the system, build a mathematical model based on the VSG control principle, and analyze the impact of renewable energy units, and active and reactive power control links on system performance. The analysis results indicate that by adjusting the main control parameters reasonably, the stability and reliability of the system can be improved, ensuring that the system has reliable dynamic performance, and providing reference for selecting parameters for system design.

H. Lu (✉) · S. Cheng · Q. Liu · J. Liu · X. Liu · H. Wang · J. Yang
Shenyang University of Technology, Shenyang, China
e-mail: 15754070426@163.com

S. Lu
Electric Power Research Institute of State Grid Liaoning Electric Power Supply Co., Ltd, Shenyang, China

H. Cui
Fuxin Electric Power Supply Company, State Grid Liaoning Electric Power Co. Ltd, Fuxin, China

F. P. García Márquez et al. (eds.), *Computing, Internet of Things and Data Analytics*,
Smart Innovation, Systems and Technologies 387,
https://doi.org/10.1007/978-3-031-87154-2_2

2.1 Introduction

In recent years, with the rapid development of wind power and photovoltaics, the form of the power system has changed accordingly. A large number of renewable energy sources such as wind and solar power are connected to the power grid through power electronic converters, and the proportion of power electronic equipment continues to increase, promoting the application of power electronic equipment in the transmission field [1]. At the same time, the penetration rate of renewable energy on the distribution side continues to increase, and the application of technologies such as multi-type energy storage, multi-energy complementary conversion, and smart grid further increases the proportion of power electronic equipment [2, 3]. Due to the fluctuation and randomness of distributed energy output, and the lack of inertia and damping support in large-scale grid-connected inverters, it will pose important challenges to the stable operation of the power grid. The stability mechanism of power systems is complex, and safe and stable operation faces great challenges [4, 5]. In traditional synchronous machine-dominated power systems, the rotor inertia of the generator is relatively high, which can store some machinery to achieve system energy balance under interference, provide frequency and voltage support, and maintain system stability. However, the renewable energy power system is dominated by power electronic devices with fast response characteristics, which cannot maintain system energy balance by storing mechanical energy, resulting in low system inertia, poor disturbance resistance, and insufficient voltage and frequency support capabilities [6] .

Reference [7] based on multiple virtual synchronous generator (VSG) parallel systems and considering transient oscillation analysis, a multi-VSG equivalent circuit method is proposed. Through the equivalent circuit, VSG parameters can be selected. The proposed method can effectively solve the power oscillation problem of VSG off-grid moments. Based on various converters, a port Hamiltonian structure is proposed for stability analysis of complex power systems As in [8], which is based on converter droop control. On this basis, a droop control with angle feedback is proposed, which maintains the port structure through negative angle droop control, thereby maintaining the stable characteristics of the system. Reference [9] Considering that the integration of distributed power sources leads to a decrease in the sensitivity of protection devices, resulting in some blind spots during grid connection, it is proposed to eliminate the blindness of backup protection through fault current and to reduce the blindness of backup protection by artificially interfering with fault current based on the severity of the blind spots. By studying the self-disturbance rejection controller, an additional sub-synchronous damping controller control method is proposed. Compared with traditional additional damping controllers, the proposed additional sub-synchronous damping control method can consider system disturbances and has strong stability [10].

Based on the above analysis, to gain a deeper understanding of the internal mechanisms and external characteristics of instability in renewable energy grid-connected systems, this paper focuses on the widely used virtual synchronous generator control strategy, considers the impact of photovoltaic integration on the power system, establishes a photovoltaic inverter grid-connected system, and conducts small signal modeling analysis on the photovoltaic grid-connected model to study the characteristics and properties of grid-connected inverters, Revealing the mechanism of system stability, analyzing the main parameters that affect system stability, and systematically elucidating the complex relationship between the stability of renewable energy systems.

2.2 Control Strategy for Inverter Power Supply

2.2.1 *VSG Control Strategy*

The virtual synchronous generator grid-connected system studied in this article is shown in Fig. 2.1. The photovoltaic power generation system is connected to the grid through an inverter, and the main circuit uses a three-phase voltage-type inverter. The DC side uses photovoltaic power generation as input, and L_i is the filtering inductance, C_i is the filtering capacitor, *PCC* represents a common coupling point. The control process mainly includes *PQ* control, virtual synchronous generator control, and voltage and current tracking. Active frequency control simulates the inertia and primary frequency regulation characteristics of synchronous generators, maintaining system frequency stability during system operation, The reactive power voltage control loop simulates the active voltage regulation characteristics of the synchronous machine, ensuring that the system voltage operates in a stable state, The voltage and current inner loop control loop simulates the synchronous reactance of the synchronous machine and generates the driving signal of the voltage grid-connected inverter.

2.2.2 P-ω *Control*

Referring to the motion equation of the synchronous machine rotor, virtual inertia control is introduced into the control algorithm of distributed inverter power supply to simulate the motion characteristics of the synchronous generator rotor, and considering the connection of photovoltaic power generation unit, the active frequency control equation of distributed inverter power supply can be obtained as follows:

$$P_{mec} - P_e - P_{pv} - D(\omega - \omega_0) = J\omega_0 \frac{d\omega}{dt} \tag{2.1}$$

where J is the virtual moment of inertia, ω, ω_0 represents the angular frequency of the inverter power supply and the common bus, P_{mec} and P_e represent input power

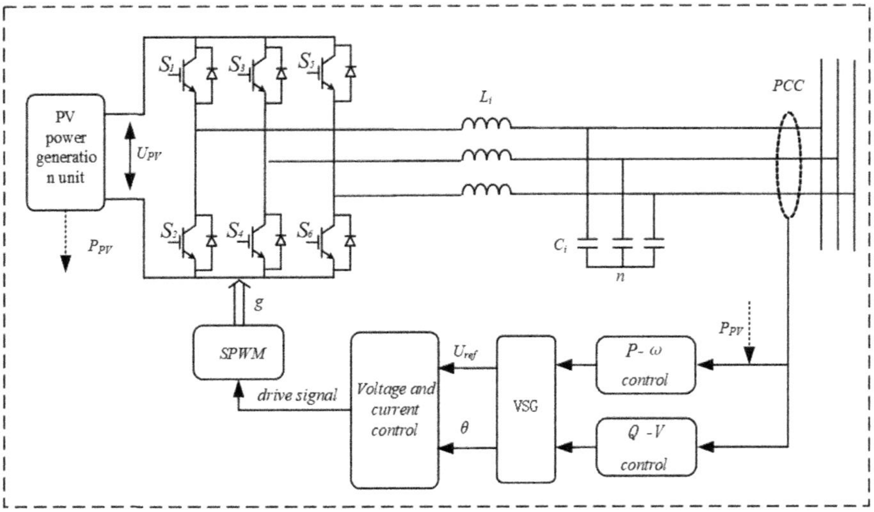

Fig. 2.1 Photovoltaic grid-connected system

and electromagnetic power, P_{pv} is the input power of the photoelectric unit, D is the additional damping coefficient.

To enable distributed inverter power sources to have certain frequency regulation capabilities, additional frequency regulation control links are as follows:

$$P_{mech} = P_{ref} + \frac{1}{D_P}(\omega_0 - \omega) \tag{2.2}$$

where P_{ref} is the given active power, D_p is the active droop coefficient.

The characteristics of the active frequency control loop obtained from the joint (1) and (2):

$$\omega = \left[\frac{1}{D_P}(\omega - \omega_0) + P_{ref} - P_e - P_V - D(\omega - \omega_0)\right]\frac{1}{Js} \tag{2.3}$$

2.2.3 Q–V *Control*

The goal of voltage control is to ensure the normal operation of the system, with voltage fluctuations within a reasonable range. In traditional power systems, the synchronous machine provides the main reactive power, and the excitation controller plays a regulating role to achieve the distribution of reactive power and maintain reactive power balance. Referring to synchronous generators, the reactive power voltage control strategy in this article is as follows:

$$E = E_{ref} + D_q[Q_{ref} + K(E_{cn} - E_c) - Q_e \tag{2.4}$$

where D_q is the reactive power droop coefficient, Q_{ref} is the given reactive power, E_{ref} is the given reference voltage, E_{cn} is the actual voltage reference value, E_c is the actual voltage value.

2.2.4 Small Signal Modeling of Control Systems

Inverters have the characteristics of flexible control and rapid response of power electronic devices and have a strong sensitivity to load fluctuations. The stable state after disturbance cannot be ignored. Currently, the commonly used analysis method is to analyze system stability through small signal modeling. E is the virtual synchronous generator output voltage, U is the amplitude of the grid voltage, δ For the phase angle difference between the two, the output equivalent impedance is $R + JX$, and the output power of the inverter is:

$$\begin{aligned} P &= \frac{REU\cos\delta - RU^2 + XEU\sin\delta}{R^2 + X^2} \\ Q &= \frac{-XEU\cos\delta + XU^2 + REU\sin\delta}{R^2 + X^2} \end{aligned} \tag{2.5}$$

The small signal model for active and reactive power transmission in the system is ($\sin\delta \approx \delta$, $\cos\delta \approx 1$):

$$\begin{aligned} \Delta p &= \frac{\partial P}{\partial \delta}\Delta\delta + \frac{\partial p}{\partial E}\Delta E \\ \Delta Q &= \frac{\partial Q}{\partial \delta}\Delta\delta + \frac{\partial Q}{\partial E}\Delta E \end{aligned} \tag{2.6}$$

When the power grid is connected in parallel, the frequency is clamped, and the active frequency and reactive voltage characteristics in the virtual synchronous generator control strategy can be expressed as:

$$\begin{aligned} \Delta\delta &= -k_1\Delta p \\ \Delta E &= -k_2\Delta Q \end{aligned} \tag{2.7}$$

where k_1 is the $1/(Js + D)$s, k_2 is the $1/(Ks + D_q)$s.

By combining (6) and (7), the small signal model of the virtual synchronous generator control strategy can be obtained.

2.3 Stability Analysis of Grid-Connected Systems

To analyze the impact of control parameters on system stability, a small signal model was established based on the above analysis, and the eigenvalue analysis method was used to analyze the main parameter impact. Considering the complexity of the active power control link that photovoltaic access mainly increases, the parameter analysis mainly focuses on the influence of additional coefficients in the virtual synchronous generator active power control link: rotational inertia J, additional damping D. Corresponding simulation models were built using *MATLAB/Simulink* simulation software to verify the stability of the system. The main parameters of the system are $E = U = 380$ V, $\delta = 0.02$ rad, $R + JX = (1 + 0.1\,J)\,\Omega$, $\omega_0 = 314$ rad/s. In the photoelectric unit, the ambient temperature is set to 25°C and the light intensity suddenly increases from 400 w/s^2 to 800 w/s^2 in 0.8 s.

2.3.1 *Root Locus Analysis*

The characteristic root trajectories of the changes in the moment of inertia J and the additional damping coefficient D are shown in Fig. 2.2. As J and D change, it can be seen that a pair of conjugate complex roots S_1 and S_2 have a significant impact on system stability, as shown by the arrows. When J is 0.05, 0.07, and 0.09, respectively, When D changes from 1 to 250, it gradually increases along the direction of the arrow. When the value of D is small, the characteristic roots are located on the right side of the complex plane, and the system is in an unstable state. When the value of D increases, the characteristic values gradually move to the left side of the complex plane, and the system stability increases. When D moves to the real axis, the dynamic performance of the system weakens, As J increases, the intersection point between the feature roots and the real axis moves to the right, resulting in a decrease in system stability and dynamic performance.

2.3.2 *Verification of Simulation Results*

The waveform of active power changing with the moment of inertia J is shown in Fig. 2.3. Analyzing the simulation results, it can be seen that as the moment of inertia J increases, the overshoot increases, the dynamic response of the system slows down, and oscillation phenomena are prone to occur, which has a significant impact on stability and reliability.

The waveform of active power changing with the additional damping coefficient D is shown in Fig. 2.4. It can be seen that when the inverter simulates the operation of a synchronous machine, it can smoothly adjust the operating state after a sudden change in light intensity. With the increase of damping coefficient D, the suppression

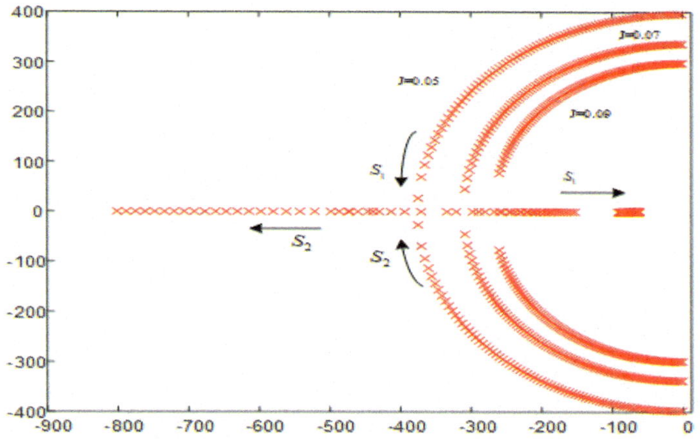

Fig. 2.2 The impact of changes in J and D on characteristic roots

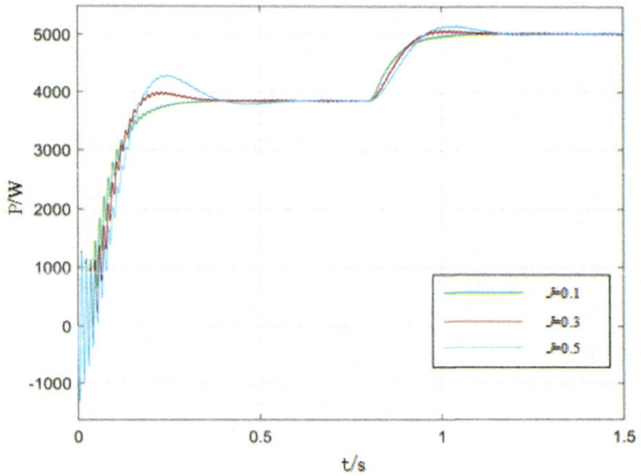

Fig. 2.3 The impact of J on system stability

effect of the system on overshoot increases, but it will affect the dynamic response of the system.

To improve output efficiency, photovoltaic power generation units often use Maximum Power Point Tracking to cope with environmental changes, ensuring that the photovoltaic system can operate near the maximum power point. The waveform of active power varying with smoothing factor c is shown in Fig. 2.5. With J and D values of 0.05 and 10, respectively. It can be seen that for different smoothing factor sizes, selecting virtual synchronous generator control parameters reasonably can always maintain the smooth and stable output power of the system. However, the internal parameters of the photoelectric unit can affect the output efficiency of the system. Therefore, in the design of the entire system, the influence of internal

Fig. 2.4 The impact of *D* on system stability

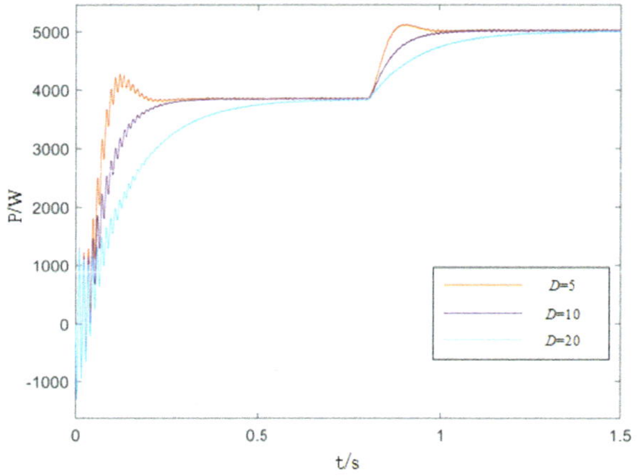

Fig. 2.5 The impact of the DC side on system stability

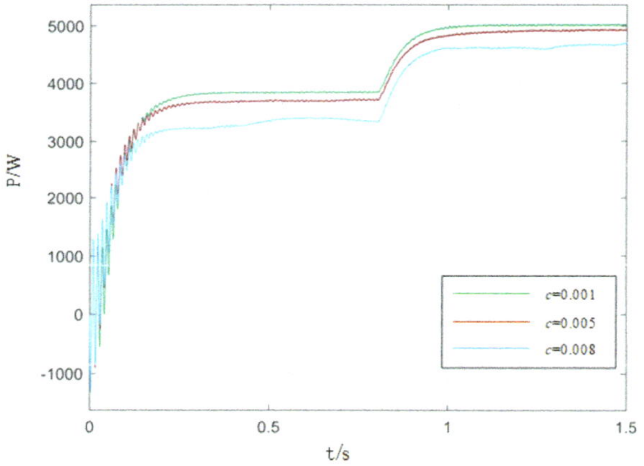

parameters of the photoelectric unit should also be considered to ensure that the system can work efficiently and stably.

2.4 Conclusion

In renewable energy grid-connected technology, the use of VSG control strategy in grid-connected inverters can effectively simulate the external characteristics of synchronous machines, but the control parameters of VSG and the parameters of photoelectric units will have a significant impact on system stability. The reliability of VSG control is affected by multiple parameters. This article analyzes the impact of key parameters such as virtual inertia, damping coefficient, and optoelectronic unit on the control system. Based on the establishment of a small signal model of grid-connected inverters, the root trajectory distribution is combined to analyze the impact of parameter selection on system stability. This provides a reference for the parameter selection of renewable energy grid-connected inverters using the VSG control strategy. When designing VSG control parameters, the small signal analysis method is combined with specific performance indicators to flexibly select and adjust parameters, improve system stability and reliability, and have better dynamic performance.

References

1. Hossein Nataj, S., Gholamian, S.A, Rezanejad, M, et al.: Virtual synchronous generator-based control of modular multilevel converter for integration into weak grid. IET. Renew. Power. Gener **17**(12), 3097–3107 (2023)
2. Li, Q., Jiang, Y., Du, C., et al.: Low-carbon optimization of distribution networks under the consideration of new energy integration. J. Phys., Conf Ser. **2659**(1) (2023)
3. Singh, N., Jain, K.S.: A novel strategy for indirect control of peak dc-link voltage of grid-connected qZS inverter fed through renewable energy sources. Electr. Eng. **102**(2), 1–15 (2019)
4. Bâra, A., Oprea, V.S.: PV-OPTIM, A software architecture and functionalities for prosumers. Electroni. **13**(1) (2023)
5. Zhou, J., Zhang, L., Zhu, L., et al.: A data-driven operating improvement method for the thermal power unit with frequent load changes. Applied. Energy. **354** (PB) (2024)
6. Gong, W., Deng, F., Wang, X., et al.: Discussion on the reconstruction of electrical engineering undergraduate teaching scheme facing the new generation power system. Front. Energy. Res. **10** (2022)
7. Shan, L., Yang, B., Lu, S.: Analysis of offline transient power oscillation and its suppression method in the microgrid with multiple virtual synchronous generators. Energies. **16**(23) (2023)
8. Alejandro, G., Sofía, A., Gerardo, E.: Stability analysis of multi-converter power systems with angle feedback. IFAC. PapersOnLine **56**(2), 2293–2298 (2023)
9. Rizwan, M., Gao, C., Yan, X., et al.: An approach to disparage the blindness of backup protection in grid-connected renewable energy sources system by inducing artificial fault current. Int. J. Electr. Power. Energy. Syst. **153** (2023)
10. Chao, W., Deng, C., Huang, J., et al.: A sub-synchronous oscillation suppression strategy based on active disturbance rejection control for renewable energy integration system via MMC-HVDC. Electronics. **12**(13) (2023)

Chapter 3
Deep RL-Based Road Traffic Management Using SD-IoT Network

Agrima Malhotra and Meeru Abrol

Abstract The recent trends in technology indicate Intelligent Transport System as an inevitable revolution sooner than expected. Recent years have witnessed active coordination between the industry and the research community to achieve the different automation levels. One of the critical aspects of an Intelligent Transport System involves efficient and accurate decision-making in real-time based on dynamic traffic conditions. The architecture should be such that the decision-making Machine Learning model's performance should not affect the computation capabilities across various vehicular models. Correspondingly, a need for integrating a Machine Learning model that provides real-time decision-making while eliminating the need for large labeled datasets has arisen. In this paper, we propose an Intelligent Transport System architecture consisting of mobile and stationary Autonomous Vehicles and Software Defined Network (SDN) controllers. The Autonomous Vehicle acts as an Agent, and SDN controllers act as the edge devices. The Agent senses its dynamic environment for specific parameters, which are then sent to the edge nodes as input for real-time computation of decision-making model and returning the decision-policy to the Agent. The proposed architecture successfully eliminates the disparity in ML models' performance, thus preventing accidents and traffic congestions. Additionally, we also propose a Reinforcement Learning-based decision-making model, which eliminates the need of collecting large labeled datasets thus reducing the overall cost for training the model.

A. Malhotra (✉)
Thapar University, Patiala, Punjab, India
e-mail: er.agrima.malhotra@gmail.com

M. Abrol
Government Degree College, Ramgarh, Jammu & Kashmir, India

F. P. García Márquez et al. (eds.), *Computing, Internet of Things and Data Analytics*, Smart Innovation, Systems and Technologies 387,
https://doi.org/10.1007/978-3-031-87154-2_3

3.1 Introduction

The unprecedented pace of modernization, urbanization and motorization has resulted in urban population increase, and thus, urban traffic congestion. This has left the Urban Transport System overwhelmed, especially in developing countries with limited revenue and resources. Faced with today's world thriving on ideas of globalization and technological development trends, the primitive means of transportation will soon fail to meet the economic and social development requirements, thus leaving Intelligent Transportation System (ITS) as the inevitable choice of revolution in Urban Transportation undertakings. One of the pivotal components of this new generation of intelligent transportation is Route Planning which must be supported in real-time, and must be efficient, accurate, safe, and energy-efficient.

3.1.1 Motivations

One of the popular feature of the Intelligent Transport System (ITS) is Car Navigation Systems.The efficiency of such systems comes with a challenge of computing the path between two specified locations .The path should be shortest and should have the least traffic congestion in the routing area.Several dynamic parameters such as traffic congestion levels, road accidents, and weather conditions affect the accuracy and efficiency of the algorithm being used. In order to cope with conditions which demand spontaneous driving decisions, we propose a Reinforcement Learning based model.The dynamic environment referred to is stated as a Markov Decision Process (MDP), the reason being that many reinforcement learning-based algorithms use dynamic programming techniques.

In recent years, in the context of the Intelligent Transportation System, the Internet of Vehicles (IoV), a subset of Industrial IoT-based technologies, has emerged. The development of IoT-based technologies such as the Advanced Driver Assistance System (ADAS) enhances road safety, eases road traffic congestion, decreases fuel consumption, and frees human drivers. In this paper, we also propose the use of Internet of Things (IoT) based technologies for real-time, and efficient route planning. Prominently, the use of Software Defined Network-based controllers as a centralised computation platform has been proposed .

3.1.2 Contributions

Through this research work, we propose the following:

1. An Intelligent Transport System consisting of Autonomous Vehicles (AV) which act as node devices and Software Denied Network (SDN) controllers which act as edge devices.These SDN Controllers are present at the sides of roads at designated

stations and information exchange between the edge and node devices takes palace with the help of Internet of Things (IoT).
2. The decision making algorithm proposed is a path finding algorithm which works on Reinforcement Learning.The input for the algorithm is based on the vehicle's immediate environment, the dynamic traffic scenario .The proposed algorithm eradicates the need for collecting and training the model with huge labeled datasets.
3. Continuous input from the vehicular nodes is transferred to SDN Controllers which execute the algorithm in real time and return the optimised decision-policy back to the vehicle.

The rest of the article elaborates on our proposed ITS. Section 3.2 elaborates the research done in the domain of Intelligent Transport System followed by the synthesis explaining the need for the proposed architecture. The article discusses the proposed System Model, walks through the RL-based algorithm, and elaborates on the mathematical formulation involved in the proposed architecture, all under Sect. 3.3. Section 3.4 further evaluates the proposed architecture on specific parameters and checks its optimality. The research paper concludes with Sect. 3.5.

3.2 Related Work

A quantifiable number of research works have explored Intelligent Transport Systems (ITS) in recent years. Starting with a few surveys, [11], through their paper, presented an account on the deployment and use of Intelligent Transportation Systems (ITS) in the developing Middle East country of Qatar. A detailed review of the current ITS technologies which are in the implementation stage in the country has been provided. Abdulhai and Kattan [1] proposed specific applications of Reinforcement Learning-based approaches in traffic control systems and transportation-related engineering approaches. The authors begin by giving a detailed account of RL-based methods. Further, the research discusses the applications of RL-based methodologies in traffic control systems and transportation-related engineering approaches. Towards the end, certain open research areas in transportation with the possible application of RL have been discussed.

Deng et al. [3] is a survey that thoroughly analysis various attacks that can fail the autonomous driving systems. It gives a thorough description of the steps involved in the Autonomous Driving Systems' workflows. The work further discusses the attacks involved in different deep learning models from cyber and physical contexts. The authors also suggest some improvements in DL-based Autonomous Driving Systems. These include model training, testing, verification, and anomaly detection based on cloud/edge servers.

Considerable work has been done in the area of Intelligent Transport System (ITS). Meena et al. [7] proposes a tool for predicting accurate and timely traffic flow Information with much-reduced complexity. Arel [2] introduced a RL-based multi-agent system framework to get an efficient policy for traffic signal control. The authors aimed at bringing congestion, intersection cross-blocking, and thus average delay to a minimum. Taking a look at the work done in Autonomous Driving Systems, [4] presented a hierarchical RL-based model for self-driving cars. The purpose of the model is for decision making where both operation selection and motion control are considered in the lateral and longitudinal direction. As the approach is RL-based, the model is independent of large labeled data.

Sallab et al. [10] proposed a Deep RL-based framework for autonomous driving. Further, [9] proposed a Deep RL-based approach for scalable and parallel Multi-Task Scheduling. The action selection in the proposed method was extended to multi-task decisions. This was done to avoid the problem of dimensionality in similar computing environments that are complex and have tasks with different properties. The output tracks of multi-task learning have been synchronized with the parallel scheduling tasks. Peters et al. [8] has even proposed an RL-based computation offloading strategy for autonomous vehicles connected to a vehicular edge computing environment.

Synthesis: Various research works have explored different aspects of the Intelligent Transport System (ITS) in the existing literature. However, they fail to address the issues stated henceforth. Firstly, the existing works do not consider the heterogeneity amongst the autonomous vehicle. The heterogeneity is with respect to storage capacity and task execution capability, resulting in varying computation rates and thus, unwanted delays in the decision-making process.Hence, a situation arises where the same algorithm cannot work across all the vehicles.

Unnecessary overhead is incurred in devising a different algorithm to get optimised computation results across different vehicular system architectures. Even if a common optimised approach is devised, there is no guarantee that the uniformity of the computation rates is maintained owing to the heterogeneity among the different architectural features introduced by the Industrial Manufacturers in their vehicular model. Additionally, the aftermath of these incompatibilities will result in traffic mishaps and congestion, making the automation system unreliable.

The idea of integrating Reinforcement Learning with SDNs and Internet of Things(IoT) for execution of real-time decision making has not yet been introduced.Therefore, for faster and more reliable computation, the idea of integrating IoT for offloading the execution of Reinforcement Learning based path-finding decision-based algorithms to nearby SDN controllers has been proposed.

3.3 RL-SDN

3.3.1 System Model

Figure 3.1 depicts the RL-SDN based Intelligent Transport System architecture. The principal actors of the Intelligent Transport System architecture are - vehicles with in-built sensors, Software-defined Networking (SDN) Controllers, and WiFi communication channel.

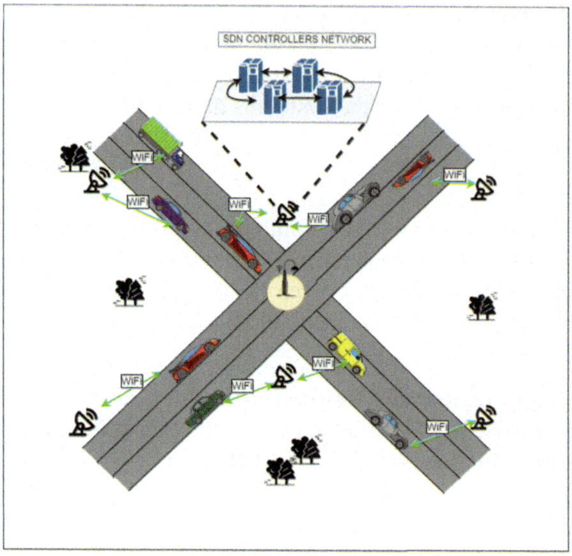

Fig. 3.1 RL-SDN Based System Architecture

In the proposed architecture, we consider a set of mobile and static vehicles $V = \{V_1, V_2, \cdots, V_m\}$ with in-built IoT sensor-based environment perception devices. The vehicle acts as an Agent which constantly senses the dynamic road and traffic conditions with the help of the integrated sensors. This sensed data acts as the agent's environmental parameters .These parameters are transmitted at real-time in the form of input packets $I = \{I_1, I_2, \cdots, I_n\}$ to the nearest SDN Controller nodes from the set of edge computing nodes $S = \{S_1, S_2, \cdots, S_x\}$. These SDN Controllers act as the edge nodes for the real-time execution of the trained Reinforcement Learning based decision-making module.These controllers are located in designated stations on the roadside, each located at a certain defined distance based on traffic density, network strength and the geographical location. The mode of connection used for transmission of the packets between the vehicle nodes and the edge devices is WiFi channel.

3.3.2 *Mathematical Formulation*

The Intelligent Transport System architecture comprises three layers: device, edge, and decision. According to specifics of the above-proposed system model, the dynamic environmental exploration has been modeled to be a Discrete Markov Decision Process (DMDP) for the decision-making strategy to increase the system's reward to a maximum. This section describes the various parameters of MDP being used in the proposed decision-making and route planning algorithmic model.

System Representation Markov Decision Process [13] is a significant mathematical formulation being used in the proposed algorithm. It follows the Markov Property, which states that the next state is entirely dependent on the current state. Using the principle of MDP, the system is defined as

$$(S, A, R, P, \gamma) \tag{3.1}$$

where S refers to a set of all possible states, A refers to a set of all possible actions, R refers to the probability distribution of reward for an (S, A) pair, P refers to the transition probability given (S, A) pair and γ is the discount factor for the agent's reward. The discount factor has been used to introduce a heuristic in awarding rewards to the agent.

Optimization and Reward Q-function, also called state-action value function, gives the value of the expected reward corresponding to taking an action A in state S while following the policy π. With reference to [6] at time t,

$$Q^{\pi}(s_t, a_t) = E[R_{t+1} + \gamma R_{t+2} + \gamma^2 R_{t+3} + \cdots][s_t, a_t] \tag{3.2}$$

Thus, the optimal Q-function is

$$Q^* = max \quad Q^{\pi}(s, a) \qquad \forall\, s \in S \tag{3.3}$$

The Q*-value obtained holds significance to the proposed algorithm as it acts as the main factor in deciding the optimal decision policy $\pi *$. Simply put, Q-value acts as the reward for the state-action pair (S,A). Thus, the optimal policy π corresponds to an action A with maximum value of reward $Q(s, a)$ for the state S.

$$\pi^* = argmax \quad Q^*(s, a) \qquad \forall\, s \in S \tag{3.4}$$

Q-Learning is an off-policy algorithm being used in the proposed approach to improve the behavior of the agent. It has been used to calculate the accurate value of reward r_t using the iterative relationship given by the Bellman equation [12]:

$$Q^{\pi}(s_t, a_t) = max \quad r_t + \gamma \quad Q^{\pi}(s_t, a_t) \tag{3.5}$$

The Q-values are iteratively updated by making use of the temporal difference method [5]:

$$Q^{new}(s_t, a_t) = Q^{\pi}(s_t, a_t) + \alpha.(r_t + \gamma.max\, Q^{\pi}(s_{t+1}, a) - Q^{\pi}(s_t, a_t)) \tag{3.6}$$

Algorithm 3.1: Real-time decision making and Flow Control

Input: Set of input packets , $I = I_1, I_2, I_3, ..., I_n$
Output: Real-time decision making

```
Sense the environmental parameters and transfer them to edge nodes
Edge node creates RL module agent with the parameters
for i = 1 to e do
    // e: total number of episodes
    Select an Initial State
    Initialize Step = 1
    while True do
        Agent takes the next action
        Corresponding new state is determined
        Corresponding reward is given to agent
        Corresponding status of whether goal has been reached by agent is determined
        // done : status
        if done then
            Step=0
            Decision is returned from Controller to Agent
        else
            New State is updated as Current State
            Step value incremented
```

3.3.3 *Proposed Architecture*

Algorithm 3.1 represents the overall decision-making procedure being used in the proposed scheme. The algorithm takes the real-time environmental conditions perceived by the IoT-based sensors in vehicles as the input. These parameters include vehicular density in each lane, surrounding vehicles, cross-sections accoutered, and obstruction on the road due to accident or traffic congestion. The input is sent to the edge devices via a Wi-Fi channel.

The roadside stations mentioned in the proposed setup have several SDN Controllers installed in them, each having high computational power. The Controllers act the edge device with Algorithm 3.1 stored in their memory. The RL-based model uses ϵ-greedy Q-Learning approach where Q is Quality value, is used to calculate reward according to action A taken while being in state S Sect. 3.3.2. The algorithm at each step takes effort with a maximum reward at a given time t. The model is executed recursively till maximum e episodes with the status of reaching the goal position being checked for in each iteration.

The use of ϵ-greedy Q-Learning has proved beneficial in the given scenario as it maintains an expectation - exploitation trade-off with exploration being dominant in the early stages of training and exploitation taking over in the later stages of training. This makes room for more accurate results. The computed optimized decision policy π^* [3.5] is returned to the agent via the Wi-Fi channel. Based on the optimized policy, the vehicle takes the desired direction and lane of travel (optimal action) in real-time

3.4 Performance Evaluations

This section starts-off by discussing the simulation environment for the agent. Further, numerical results on running the proposed algorithm on the given environment have been discussed.

3.4.1 Simulation Setup

The experimental setup was build on a 5×5 grid representing a city map with 25 possible vehicle positions. Each block in the grid represents small regions of city with blocks marked as anomalies at random. These anomalies represent any obstruction in the form of neighbouring vehicles, road patch under repair, traffic congestion at intersection and any other dynamic conditions.

Using OpenAI's Gym, the city map has been encoded into an environment for the vehicluar agent. The self-driving agent encounters any one of the 500 states possible and chooses an action based on the computed optimal decision policy. Set A represents all the possible actions that the vehicle can take:

$$A = \{south, north, east, west, source, destination\} \triangleq \{0, 1, 2, 3, 4, 5\} \quad (3.7)$$

Table 3.1 represents the simulation parameters used while testing the proposed algorithm.

3.4.2 Results

RL-Based Decision Making The proposed algorithm has been tested repeatedly in the simulation environment. Through the iterative execution and testing of the

Table 3.1 Simulation parameters

Parameter	Value
Simulation area	$500 \times 500\,\text{m}^2$
Number of possible States	500
Number of possible Actions	6
Mobility model of edge node	$ConstantPosition$
Mobility model of vehicluar node	$Constant-MobilePosition$
Edge technology	$WiFi$
User's deployment strategy	$Uniform$

algorithm, the model's hyper-parameters have been changed and set to get the most accurate and optimal decision policy for the self-driving agent. The experiment has been completed in Google Collabotary, with all the experimental results being plotted using Matplotlib Library of python.

The vehicle's initial position has been arbitrarily set to (3, 1). The agent is then repeatedly tested on its ability to reach the locations [(0, 0), (0, 4), (4, 0), (4, 3)] with anomalies located at [(0, 2), (2, 1), (2, 2), (4, 2)], each of these being chosen at random. Through repeated testing, the average performance results of the agent have been recorded, as depicted in Fig. 3.3. In each set of graphs, the first plot represents the learning curve with Total Reward being shown on the vertical axis against the number of episodes. The second plot represents the exploration-exploitation trade-off with epsilon on a vertical axis plotted against the number of episodes.

As clearly depicted by the learning curve plot, the proposed RL-based approach has a lower reward during the beginning of training as the agent tries all possibilities on the city map and collects initial experience during this stage. After a certain number of training iterations, the average reward cost obtained by the proposed model converges and then fluctuates slightly in a small range. Also, during the training phase of the model, the exploration rate decreases as the agent learn during this phase. This is depicted in the corresponding plots in Fig. 3.3.

Table 3.2 shows the different parameter values taken during the testing phase. The testing initially began with hyper-parameters decay rate set as 0.0001, learning rate as 0.0001, and gamma set as 0.618. As seen from plot Fig. 3.3a, it takes 40000 to 60000 iterative episodes to obtain a smooth learning curve. The plots show a decent exploration-exploitation trade-off. On increasing the values of decay rate and learning rate, the learning curve converges between 0 to 10000 episodes showing a drastic improvement in the agent's performance. However, the exploration-exploitation trade-off becomes almost negligible after this range, thus reducing the accuracy of the proposed model.

On further changing the hyper-parameters and iteratively testing the proposed algorithm, the proposed algorithm showed optimal performance with decay rate as 0.0002, learning rate as 0.8, and gamma as 0.5. Figure 3.3c shows the corresponding plot. The algorithm converges in the range of 10000 to 20000 episode iterations, thus indicating that the algorithm can be trained for fewer episodes to obtain optimal results. Correspondingly, the second graph shows a good exploration-exploitation trade-off, thus proving the proposed model to be work accurately in the given dynamic environment.

Table 3.2 Convergence ranges for different hyper-parameters on testing the proposed model

Decay rate	Learning rate	Gamma	Convergence range
0.0001	0.0001	0.618	40000–60000
0.001	0.8	0.618	0–10000
0.0002	0.8	0.5	10000–20000

Delay The proposed algorithm was rigorously tested in a simulation environment to assess delay. Initially, with hyper-parameters set to a decay rate of 0.0001, a learning rate of 0.0001, and gamma at 0.618, the model converged within 40,000–60,000 episodes, indicating significant delays as the agent explored the environment. Increasing the decay rate to 0.001 and the learning rate to 0.8 reduced the convergence range to 0–10,000 episodes, significantly decreasing delays but compromising the exploration-exploitation trade-off, thus impacting accuracy. Optimal performance was achieved with a decay rate of 0.0002, a learning rate of 0.8, and gamma at 0.5, resulting in a convergence range of 10,000–20,000 episodes. This setting minimized delays while maintaining a balanced exploration-exploitation trade-off, ensuring accurate and timely decision-making. The learning curve Fig. 3.2 demonstrated initial low rewards due to exploration but stabilized as training progressed, reflecting reduced delays. This optimized setting proved effective in dynamic traffic environments, significantly reducing the delay without sacrificing decision accuracy.

Energy Consumption Energy consumption is a crucial factor in the efficiency and sustainability of Intelligent Transport Systems (ITS), particularly for autonomous vehicles and edge computing systems. In the context of the proposed algorithm, energy consumption was evaluated through simulations, with results visualized using Matplotlib. Initial testing with a decay rate of 0.0001, a learning rate of 0.0001, and gamma of 0.618 showed high energy consumption due to the extended convergence range of 40,000–60,000 episodes. This extended training period required more computational resources and energy, as the system performed extensive calculations during the high exploration phase.

In contrast, increasing the decay rate to 0.001 and the learning rate to 0.8 led to a convergence range of 0 to 10,000 episodes, significantly reducing energy consumption by shortening the training duration. However, this reduction came at the cost of a diminished exploration-exploitation trade-off, which affected model accuracy. The optimized settings, with a decay rate of 0.0002, a learning rate of 0.8, and gamma of 0.5, achieved a balanced convergence range of 10,000–20,000 episodes. This configuration provided an effective balance between reduced energy usage and accurate decision-making, highlighting the importance of fine-tuning hyper-parameters to manage energy consumption efficiently while maintaining system performance.

Packet Delivery Ratio The Packet Delivery Ratio (PDR) is a crucial performance metric for the proposed Intelligent Transport System (ITS) architecture, reflecting the reliability of data transmission between autonomous vehicles and SDN controllers. The experiments revealed that with initial hyper-parameters (decay rate: 0.0001, learning rate: 0.001, gamma: 0.618), the PDR was relatively low due to extended convergence times and potential network instability. Increasing the decay rate and learning rate improved the PDR significantly by reducing the convergence range and stabilizing network conditions, though it also impacted decision-making accuracy. The optimal hyper-parameters (decay rate: 0.0002, learning rate: 0.8, gamma: 0.5) achieved the highest PDR, indicating effective and reliable data transmission. This optimal configuration ensured that the system could consistently deliver critical data for real-time decision-making, demonstrating the importance of balancing training efficiency with reliable packet delivery in ITS applications (Fig. 3.3).

(a) Decay rate=0.0001, learning rate=0.001, gamma=0.618

(b) Decay rate=0.001, learning rate=0.8, gamma=0.618

(c) Decay rate=0.0002, learning rate=0.8, gamma=0.5

Fig. 3.2 Variation in smoothened training reward per episode

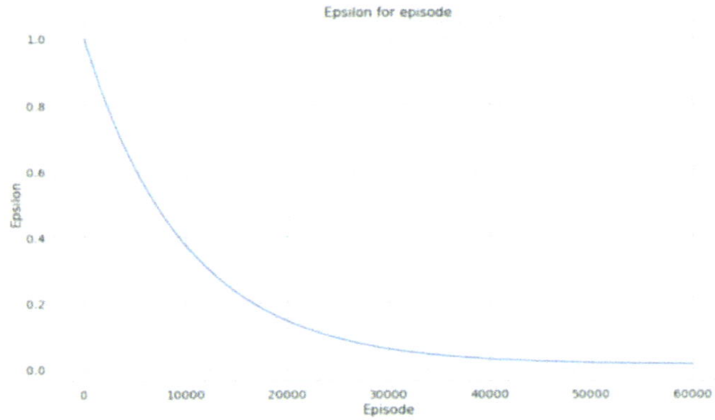

(a) Decay rate=0.0001, learning rate=0.001, gamma=0.618

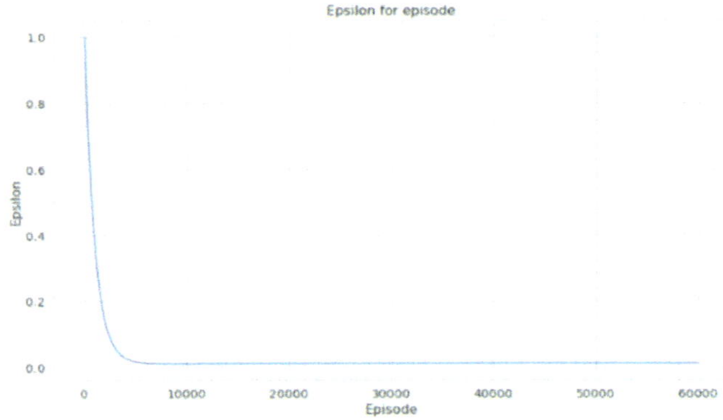

(b) Decay rate=0.001, learning rate=0.8, gamma=0.618

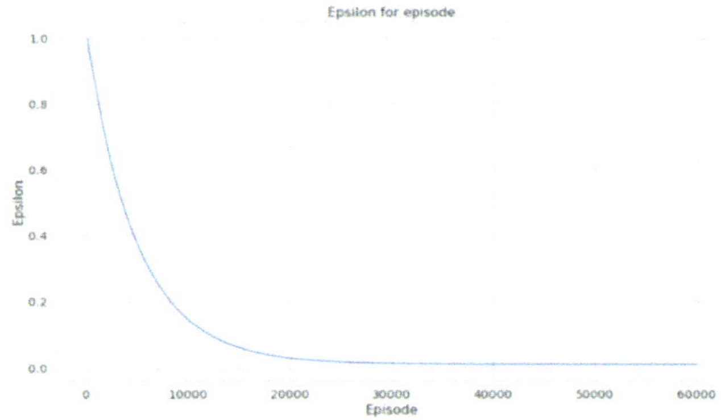

(c) Decay rate=0.0002, learning rate=0.8, gamma=0.5

Fig. 3.3 Variation in epsilon

3.5 Conclusion

This work presented an Intelligent Transport System (ITS) Architecture that uses Reinforcement Learning for real-time decision-making for Autonomous Vehicles. In ITS infrastructure, the presence of both autonomous vehicles and Software Defined Networks (SDN) Controllers has been proposed. With the difference in the geographical traffic density and the location of the autonomous vehicles, the count of neighboring SDN Controllers in the vicinity of the IoT sensor-equipped vehicular node varies. The proposed architecture aims to eliminate the possible problems in the smooth working of ITS due to the difference in the storage capacity and algorithm computation and execution capability for each type of vehicular node. The SDN controllers solve the problem by acting as the common computational edge node for the system. Additionally, we formulated a Reinforcement Learning-based algorithm that computes the action policy for the Autonomous Vehicle based on the current road and traffic conditions.

The proposed algorithm successfully eliminates the need for large labeled datasets, thus reducing the overall cost for training the model. The simulation results depicted that the hyperparameters significantly affect the algorithm's performance and, therefore, must be set to achieve optimal computational results. Our future works will aim to explore hybrid architectural approaches including but not restricted to SDN - Controller based edge computing. Additionally, we plan on targeting the pricing of establishing the Offloading Stations.

Disclosure of Interests. The authors have no competing interests to declare that are relevant to the content of this article.

References

1. Abdulhai, B., Kattan, L.: Reinforcement learning: introduction to theory and potential for transport applications. Can. J. Civil Eng. **30**(6), 981–991 (2003). https://doi.org/10.1139/l03-014. https://doi.org/10.1139/l03-014
2. Arel, I.: Reinforcement learning-based multi-agent system for network traffic signal control. IET Intell. Transp. Syst. **4**, 128–135(7) (2010). https://digital-library.theiet.org/content/journals/10.1049/iet-its.2009.0070
3. Deng, Y., Zhang, T., Lou, G., Zheng, X., Jin, J., Han, Q.L.: Deep learning-based autonomous driving systems: a survey of attacks and defenses. IEEE Trans. Ind. Inf. **17**(12), 7897–7912 (2021). https://doi.org/10.1109/TII.2021.3071405
4. Duan, J., Li, S., Guan, Y., Sun, Q., Cheng, B.: Hierarchical reinforcement learning for self-driving decision-making without reliance on labeled driving data (2020)
5. Geng, Y., Liu, E., Wang, R., Liu, Y.: Deep reinforcement learning based dynamic route planning for minimizing travel time. In: 2021 IEEE International Conference on Communications Workshops (ICC Workshops), pp. 1–6 (2021)
6. Lin, B., Lin, K., Lin, C., Lu, Y., Huang, Z., Chen, X.: Computation offloading strategy based on deep reinforcement learning for connected and autonomous vehicle in vehicular edge computing. J. Cloud Comput. **10** (2021). https://doi.org/10.1186/s13677-021-00246-6

7. Meena, G., Sharma, D., Mahrishi, M.: Traffic prediction for intelligent transportation system using machine learning. In: 2020 3rd International Conference on Emerging Technologies in Computer Engineering: Machine Learning and Internet of Things (ICETCE), pp. 145–148 (2020). https://doi.org/10.1109/ICETCE48199.2020.9091758
8. Peters, J., Vijayakumar, S., Schaal, S.: Reinforcement learning for humanoid robotics. In: Proceedings of the Third IEEE-RAS International Conference on Humanoid Robots, pp. 1–20 (2003)
9. Qi, Q., Zhang, L., Wang, J., Sun, H., Zhuang, Z., Liao, J., Yu, F.R.: Scalable parallel task scheduling for autonomous driving using multi-task deep reinforcement learning. IEEE Trans. Veh. Technol. **69**(11), 13861–13874 (2020). https://doi.org/10.1109/TVT.2020.3029864
10. Sallab, A.E., Abdou, M., Perot, E., Yogamani, S.: Deep reinforcement learning framework for autonomous driving (2017)
11. Shaaban, K., Elamin, M., Alsoub, M.: Intelligent transportation systems in a developing country: benefits and challenges of implementation. Transp. Res. Proc. **55**, 1373–1380 (2021). https://doi.org/10.1016/j.trpro.2021.07.122. https://www.sciencedirect.com/science/article/pii/S235214652100538X. (14th International Scientific Conference on Sustainable, Modern and Safe Transport)
12. Tokic, M.: Adaptive ε-Greedy Exploration in Reinforcement Learning Based on Value Differences, pp. 203–210 (2010). https://doi.org/10.1007/978-3-642-16111-7_23
13. Van Otterlo, M., Wiering, M.A.: Markov Decision Processes: Concepts and Algorithms (2012)

Chapter 4
Refined Modeling of DFIG Grid-Connected Systems Based on Damping Torque Analysis

Yang Zheng, Shengyang Lu, Haoqian Cui, Shanshan Cheng, Xuegao Wang, Haixin Wang, and Junyou Yang

Abstract Addressing the issue of grid instability arising from the integration of doubly-fed induction generator(DFIG) systems, this paper utilizes a linearized model of DFIG systems and establishes the Phillips-Heffron model of the systems. The paper investigates the impact of grid integration capacity, input power, and control parameters of DFIG systems. The findings indicate that increasing the grid integration capacity, output power, and reducing control parameters diminishes the destabilizing effects on DFIG systems. Furthermore, a damping torque model suitable for DFIG systems is developed, elucidating the mechanism of system instability using damping torque analysis. This methodology is extended to multi-machine systems for comprehensive analysis.

4.1 Introduction

Energy security and safety are of paramount importance to the nation's economy and the well-being of its people and cannot be overlooked for a moment. By the end of 2020, China's cumulative installed wind power capacity had reached 2.28 ×

Y. Zheng (✉) · S. Lu · S. Cheng · H. Wang · J. Yang
Shenyang University of Technology, Shenyang, China
e-mail: tomz@smail.sut.edu.cn

S. Lu
Electric Power Research Institute of State Grid Liaoning Electric Power Supply Co., Ltd., Shenyang, China

H. Cui
Fuxin Electric Power Supply Company, State Grid Liaoning Electric Power Co., Ltd., Fuxin, China

X. Wang
State Grid Huludao Electric Power Supply Company of State Grid Liaoning Electric Power Supply Co., Ltd., Huludao, China

F. P. García Márquez et al. (eds.), *Computing, Internet of Things and Data Analytics*, Smart Innovation, Systems and Technologies 387,
https://doi.org/10.1007/978-3-031-87154-2_4

108 kW, ranking first in the world. According to long-term objectives, the cumulative installed wind power capacity is projected to reach 2.4 × 109 kW by 2050 [1]. The integration of large-scale wind power into the grid via long-distance transmission lines introduces non-negligible grid impedance, resulting in the connected system exhibiting characteristics of a weak AC grid. Under weak AC grid conditions, the voltage at wind power integration points is prone to fluctuations due to changes in unit power and grid strength, undermining the assumption of ideal integration point voltage conditions and subsequently affecting the operational stability of units.

Literature [2] constructs a Phillips-Heffron model for a voltage-source-type doubly-fed machine and investigates the oscillation characteristics and instability mechanisms of low-frequency modes dominated by virtual synchronous control from an electrical damping perspective. They further analyze and explore the influence of specific parameters of various control components and different grid conditions on the electrical damping characteristics of voltage-source-type doubly-fed machines. However, this literature does not considers the dynamic characteristics analysis of doubly-fed machines in complex multi-machine systems, including their interaction and coordinated operation with traditional synchronous machines and current-source-type wind turbine units. Literature [3] addresses the decrease in system damping and the emergence of low-frequency oscillations due to the integration of new energy power plants into the grid. It proposes and designs an optimal POD, which used particle swarm optimization to determine relevant parameters to enhance system damping. However, this article does not provide a clear analysis mechanism for damping torque and fails to succinctly explain the oscillation mode relationships between the system generators. Literature [4] addresses in response to the risk of decreased system damping and the emergence of low-frequency oscillations caused by the grid connection of new energy plants, we propose and design an OPOD device. This device utilizes particle swarm optimization algorithm to determine relevant parameters. Finally, through simulation testing, the feasibility of this approach is demonstrated.

Literature [5] addresses the issue of potential low-frequency oscillation risks due to under-damping in the grid connection of doubly-fed generator units based on the IEEE New Zealand 39-bus model. Literature [6] focus on the relevant parameters of self-control in doubly-fed generator units. As wind power penetration rates continue to rise, they employ eigenvalue analysis to investigate the impact of different control strategies on system damping in DFIG systems. Through analysis of simplified systems with high penetration rates and the Greek interconnected system, the study concludes that the introduction of power system stabilizers effectively enhances system damping after large-scale DFIG grid integration, ensuring system stability.

In this paper, by establishing the Phillips-Heffron model of the system using damping torque analysis (DTA) to study the dynamic interaction between DFIG and synchronous generators, especially to explore how DFIG affects the system frequency oscillation problem, this paper is based on the excitation current of the doubly-fed wind turbine damping torque model is more simple, and it is more easy to expand the analysis.

4.2 Modeling and Analysis of Doubly Fed Wind Turbine Generator Systems

4.2.1 Establishment of the Phillips-Heffron Model

The establishment of the linearized model for multi-machine power systems with doubly-fed induction generator is as follows:

$$\frac{d}{dt}\begin{bmatrix}\Delta\delta\\ \Delta\omega\\ \Delta E_q^{'}\\ \Delta E_{fd}^{'}\end{bmatrix}=\begin{bmatrix}0 & \omega_0 I & 0 & 0\\ -M^{-1}K_1 & -M^{-1}D & -M^{-1}K_2 & 0\\ -T_{d0}^{-1}K_4 & 0 & -T_{d0}^{-1}K_3 & T_{d0}^{-1}\\ -T_A^{-1}K_5K_A & 0 & -T_A^{-1}K_6K_A & -T_A^{-1}\end{bmatrix}\begin{bmatrix}\Delta\delta\\ \Delta\omega\\ \Delta E_q^{'}\\ \Delta E_{fd}^{'}\end{bmatrix}$$
$$+\begin{bmatrix}0\\ -M^{-1}k_{PP}\\ -T_{d0}^{-1}k_{EP}\\ T_A^{-1}K_Ak_{VP}\end{bmatrix}\Delta P_w+\begin{bmatrix}0\\ -M^{-1}k_{PQ}\\ -T_{d0}^{-1}k_{EQ}\\ T_A^{-1}K_Ak_{VQ}\end{bmatrix}\Delta Q_w \tag{4.1}$$

Simplified representation is as follows:

$$\frac{d}{dt}\Delta X_g = A_g\Delta X_g + b_P\Delta P_w + b_Q\Delta Q_w \tag{4.2}$$

The state variables and state matrix elements are defined the same as in the traditional Heffron-Phillips model for multi-machine power systems.

The mathematical expression for the voltage value ΔV_s at the node where the doubly-fed wind induction generator is located in the power system. It is as follows:

$$\Delta V_s = C_g\Delta X_g + d_{g1}\Delta P_w + d_{g2}\Delta Q_w \tag{4.3}$$

where the coefficients for variables $\Delta\delta$ and $\Delta E_q'$ in matrix $C_g = \begin{bmatrix}c_{g1} & 0 & c_{g3} & 0\end{bmatrix}$ are represented by elements c_{g1} and c_{g3}.

From its small-signal model is as follows:

$$\begin{cases}\Delta P_w\{c_{Pw}^T[pI-A_w(p)]^{-1}b_w(p)+c_{PV}\}\Delta V_s=G_{wP}(p)\Delta V_s\\ \Delta Q_w\{c_{Qw}^T[pI-A_w(p)]^{-1}b_w(p)+c_{QV}\}\Delta V_s=G_{wQ}(p)\Delta V_s\\ \dfrac{\Delta T_P}{\Delta P_w}=G_{wP}(p)=k_{PP}+K(p)^{-1}[(I+pT_A)k_{EP}+K_Ak_{VP}\\ \dfrac{\Delta T_Q}{\Delta Q_w}=G_{wQ}(p)=k_{PQ}+K(p)^{-1}[(I+pT_A)k_{EQ}+K_Ak_{VQ}\end{cases} \tag{4.4}$$

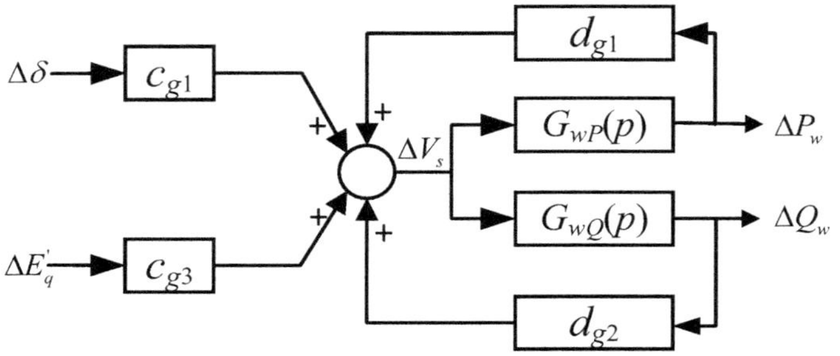

Fig. 4.1 Heffron-Phillips model of the DFIG control section

Equations (4.2), (4.3), and (4.4) collectively form the Heffron-Phillips model for multi-machine power systems with Doubly Fed Induction Generators, as illustrated in Fig. 4.1. In this model, Eq. (4.2) represents the open-loop state equation, while Eq. (4.3) represents the output equation. Through Eq. (4.4) and Fig. 4.1, the DFIG is regarded as a dual-input single-output feedback control loop [7]. Therefore, the closed-loop model is constructed by Equations. (4.2), (4.3) and (4.4).

The Heffron-Phillips model has long been employed to analyze damping and torque contributions from power system controllers. For instance, power system stabilizers can influence electromechanical oscillation modes in power systems [8]. As depicted in Fig. 4.1, they illustrate the interactive effects between DFIG and the power system upon grid connection. Therefore, elements ΔP_w and ΔQ_w are chosen as output signals from the DFIG. The innovative aspects of this derived model are as follows. Firstly, the DFIG can be perceived as a feedback control loop, and its analysis can be conducted using the damping torque analysis method, which will be elaborated on in the next section. Secondly, the derivation of the model indicates that elements ΔP_w and ΔQ_w only respond to changes in the voltage ΔV_s at the grid connection point of the doubly-fed induction generator, as illustrated in Eq. (4.4) and Fig. 4.1. The advantage of this approach lies in the exclusion of phase tracking voltage errors originating from the phase-locked loop (PLL) when analyzing small-signal linearized models [9].

4.2.2 Damping Torque Method for Multi-machine Systems

From Fig. 4.1, it can be observed that the transfer function matrices ΔP_w and ΔQ_w of the DFIG output power are related to the torque variations of the electromechanical oscillation loop of the synchronous generator.it is as follows:

$$\begin{cases} \dfrac{\Delta T_P}{\Delta P_w} = G_{wP}(p) = k_{PP} + K(p)^{-1}[(I + pT_A)k_{EP} + K_A k_{VP} \\ \dfrac{\Delta T_Q}{\Delta Q_w} = G_{wQ}(p) = k_{PQ} + K(p)^{-1}[(I + pT_A)k_{EQ} + K_A k_{VQ} \end{cases} \tag{4.5}$$

where $K(p) = K_2[(I + pT_A)(K_3 + pT_{d0}) + K_A K_6]$. Thus the amount of electromagnetic torque variation in the DFIG is as follows:

$$\Delta T_w = \Delta T_P + \Delta T_Q = [G_P(p)G_{wP}(p) + G_Q(p)G_{wQ}(p)]\Delta V_s \tag{4.6}$$

For the k synchronous generator, the electromagnetic torque variation provided by DFIG is as follows:

$$\Delta T_{wk} = [g_{Pk}(p)G_{wP}(p) + g_{Qk}(p)G_{wQ}(p)]\Delta V_s \tag{4.7}$$

where $g_{Pk}(p)$ and $g_{Qk}(p)$ are each the kth element of $G_P(p)$ and $G_Q(p)$. $\overline{\lambda_i} = -\xi_i + j\omega_i$ denotes the ith low-frequency oscillation mode of the power system of Fig. 4.1. It is the set of eigenvalues of the state matrices of the closed-loop system model, including the DFIG dynamic model with respect to Eq. (4.4).

Assuming that $\overline{v_i}$ is the right eigenvector of the association $\overline{\lambda_i} = -\xi_i + j\omega_i$, it is as follows:

$$\Delta\overline{\lambda_i} = \sum_{k=1}^{N} \overline{S}_{ik} D_{wk} \tag{4.8}$$

The eigenvalue of the closed-loop system model state matrix is $\overline{\lambda_i}$. The difference $\Delta\overline{\lambda_i}$ between $\overline{\lambda_{i0}}$ and $\overline{\lambda_i}$ is shown in Eq. (4.8). $\Delta\overline{\lambda_i}$ represents the degree of dynamic interaction between DFIG and SG.

4.3 Stability Analysis of Grid-Connected Systems

The case study adopts a 4-machine 11-node system with a DFIG [11], as depicted in Fig. 4.2. In Fig. 4.2, nodes 1, 2, 5, 6, and 7 are located in Region 1, where nodes 1 and 2 host synchronous generator units G1 and G2, respectively, with active power outputs of 300 MW and 290 MW. Nodes 3, 4, 9, 10, and 11 form Region 2, where nodes 3 and 4 host synchronous generator units G3 and G4, with active power outputs of 350 MW and 400 MW, respectively. A wind farm is introduced at node 6, where the rated power of a single DFIG in the wind farm is $P_w = 1.5$ MW. The wind farm is equivalent to one DFIG. The air density at the location of the wind farm is assumed to be 1.314 kg/m3. The loads in the case study are modeled using constant impedance models, with a system base value of 1000MVA for convenience.

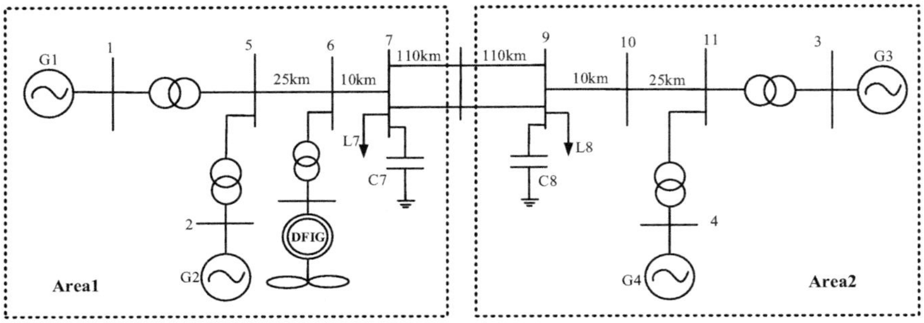

Fig. 4.2 4-machine11-node system with DFIG

Table 4.1 Four typical oscillation mode

Oscillation mode	Numerical value	Participating factors
λ_1	$-0.317 \pm j13.58$	Oscillatory modes of unit shaft system
λ_2	$-4.525 \pm j8.86$	Localized oscillations 1 between G3 and G4
λ_3	$-0.415 \pm j4.55$	Regional oscillations 2 between DFIG and G3, G4
λ_4	$-0.545 \pm j7.35$	Localized oscillations 2 between DFIG and G1

The above system exhibits approximately four typical oscillation modes, as illustrated in Table 4.1.

From Fig. 4.3, it is evident that when the doubly-fed wind turbine is grid-connected, the frequencies of modes 1, 3, and 4 increase, while the system's damping decreases, resulting in eigenvalues approaching the imaginary axis of the complex plane, leading to system instability. At rated wind speed, as the grid connection capacity increases, there is significant fluctuation in the oscillation frequency and damping of the three mentioned modes due to the grid connection of the doubly-fed induction generator. When the doubly-fed induction generator is grid-connected, mode 2 exhibits significant fluctuations in oscillation frequency and damping. However, as the grid connection capacity increases, the oscillation frequency fluctuates less, and the system damping increases significantly, with eigenvalues moving away from the imaginary axis of the complex plane. Consequently, the system can quickly dampen low-frequency oscillations, resulting in minimal impact of the grid connection capacity on local oscillation 1.

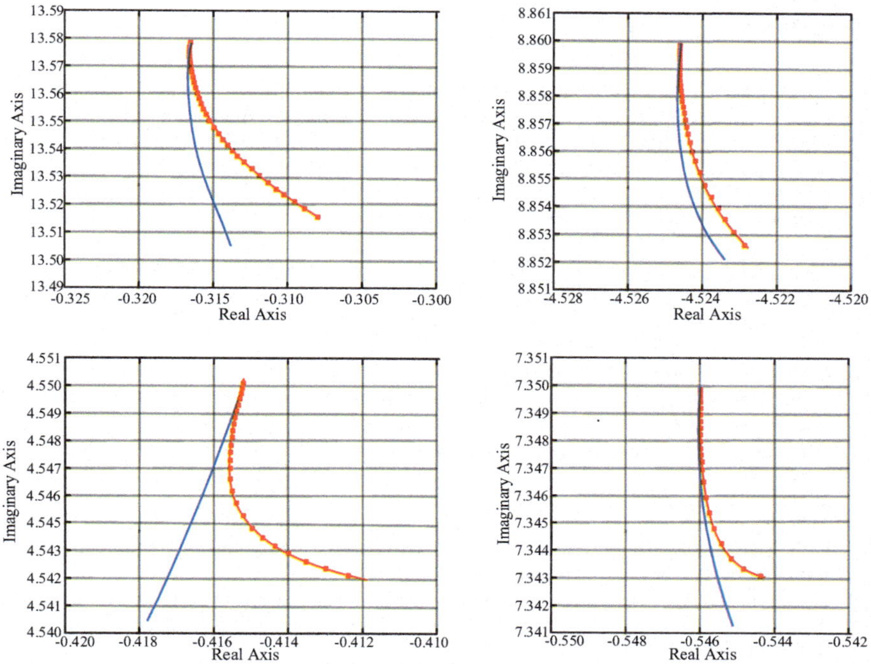

Fig. 4.3 Trajectories of oscillatory modes when DFIG grid-connected capacity increases

4.4 Conclusion

The doubly-fed induction generator technology is becoming increasingly mature, and research on the stability of renewable energy grid integration under high penetration rates is becoming more important. This paper firstly establishes the Phillips-Heffron model of the power system with doubly-fed induction generator. Subsequently, through the damping torque method, it explores the dynamic interaction between the doubly-fed wind turbines and synchronous generator units in the system. Finally, using a four-machine two-area simulation model, the paper illustrates the oscillation tendencies between the doubly-fed induction generators and other units in the system under four typical interaction modes, while the DFIG grid connection capacity continues to change.

References

1. Lu, S., Wang, T., Liang, Y., et al.: Low-frequency oscillation analysis of grid-connected VSG system considering multi-parameter coupling. CMES-Comput. Model. Eng. Sci. **135**(3) (2023)
2. Ma, J., Jie, H., Zhou, Y., et al.: A low frequency oscillation suppression method for grid-connected DFIG with virtual inertia. Int. J. Electr. Power Energy Syst. **144**, 108531 (2023)
3. Liserre, M., Teodorescu, R., Blaabjerg, F.: Stability of photovoltaic and wind turbine grid-connected inverters for a large set of grid impedance values. IEEE Trans. Power Electron. **21**(1), 263–272 (2006)
4. Du, C., Du, X., Tong, C., et al.: Stability analysis for DFIG-based wind farm grid-connected system under all wind speed conditions. IEEE Trans. Ind. Appl. **59**(2), 2430–2445 (2022)
5. Qi, L., Jiahui, W., Haiyun, W., et al.: Effect of DFIG control parameters on small signal stability in power systems. Sci. Rep. **13**(1), 2476 (2023)
6. Chetouani, E., Errami, Y., Obbadi, A., et al.: Self-adapting PI controller for grid-connected DFIG wind turbines based on recurrent neural network optimization control under unbalanced grid faults. Electr. Power. Syst. Res **214**, 108829 (2023)
7. Wang, Z., Lu, Y.: Mechanical–electrical-grid model for the doubly fed induction generator wind turbine system considering oscillation frequency coupling characteristics. Wind Energy **27**(1), 33–52 (2024)
8. Li, S., Fang, T., Zhang, H., et al.: Damping the electromechanical oscillation modes (EOMs) in DFIG-integrated power systems with sensitivity analysis and optimization to outputs of SGs. Int. J. Electr. Power Energy Syst. **135**, 107565 (2022)
9. Wang, H., Xie, Z., Chen, Y., et al.: Stability enhancement control strategy for grid-connected wind power system based on composite feedforward damping. Int. J. Electr. Power Energy Syst. **158**, 109908 (2024)
10. Sahu, B., Padhy, B.P.: Evaluation of damping effect influenced by system parameters on a dfig integrated power system. IEEE Systems. J (2023)
11. Zhang, Q., Luo, J., Zhang, D., et al.: A method to identify the impact of wind turbine generators on low-frequency oscillations. IEEE Trans. Power. Syst. (2023)

Chapter 5
Deep Attention Model for Malaria Prediction

R. Sriviswa, Hema Radhika Reddy, Nalin M. Rajendran, V. Sowmya, and E. A. Gopalakrishnan

Abstract Malaria remains a major public health problem worldwide, and the World Health Organization predicts that the number of malaria cases will reach 249 million and the number of deaths will reach 608,000 by 2022. Children under five are the most vulnerable group, accounting for approximately 80% of all malaria deaths in the region. Infectious diseases such as malaria are greatly affected by climate change in the region. In this work, we present a deep learning model with a supervised technique called Long short-term model (LSTM). We performed a comparative study using a number of time series and machine learning models, such as Support Vector Regression (Polynomial Kernel), XGBoost, LightGBM, SARIMA, SARIMAX, Random Forest, Linear Regression, and Logistic Regression, in order to verify the effectiveness of our suggested model. Out of all the models, the LSTM model has the lowest Root Mean Squared Error (RMSE). We also developed a Bi-LSTM model, which confirmed the superior performance of our method with an even lower RMSE. The efficacy of the feature attention-based LSTM model in forecasting malaria incidence from meteorological data is demonstrated by its lower validation loss and error metrics (RMSE and MAE) as compared to the temporal attention-based LSTM, as indicated by the performance metrics.

R. Sriviswa · H. Radhika Reddy (✉) · N. M. Rajendran · V. Sowmya
Amrita School of Artificial Intelligence, Amrita Vishwa Vidyapeetham, Coimbatore, India
e-mail: hemaradhikareddy@gmail.com

V. Sowmya
e-mail: v_sowmya@cb.amrita.edu

E. A. Gopalakrishnan
Amrita School of Computing, Amrita Vishwa Vidyapeetham, Bangalore, India

Amrita School of Artificial Intelligence, Amrita Vishwa Vidyapeetham, Bangalore, India

F. P. García Márquez et al. (eds.), *Computing, Internet of Things and Data Analytics*,
Smart Innovation, Systems and Technologies 387,
https://doi.org/10.1007/978-3-031-87154-2_5

5.1 Introduction

Climate change has been increasingly linked to the prevalence of vector-borne diseases, with malaria being a significant example. Malaria continues to pose a global health challenge, especially in regions where the Plasmodium parasite thrives [1]. Climate change-induced fluctuations in temperature, humidity, and rainfall patterns have been shown to alter the lifecycle of Anopheles mosquitoes, the vectors of malaria transmission [2]. The urgency of predicting malaria in public healthcare is underscored by the disease's significant mortality and morbidity, particularly in regions with limited healthcare access. Early and precise prediction of malaria cases is vital for timely intervention and effective public health planning [3].

Traditional methods of disease prediction, primarily based on epidemiological models and historical data analysis, may not adequately capture the dynamic patterns inherent in the spread of malaria [2, 4]. With the development of modern technology and the availability of massive health datasets deep learning models present a novel opportunity for more accurate predictions [3]. Previous studies have used a variety of statistical and machine learning techniques, such as random forests and gradient boosting machines, to analyze the relationship between climate and vector diseases [3].

Long short-term memory (LSTM) networks are recurrent neural network (RNN) models used for deep learning. Feedforward neural networks are different from ordinary neural networks. Long-term memory (LSTM) can analyze all temporary data, such as time data, by transmitting feedback. This makes them ideal for predicting events in movies based on past observations, where the goal is to predict future information [2, 5]. Tracking techniques add another level of complexity when combined with LSTM networks. The monitoring process focuses on the selection of the most important components for prediction, allowing the model to learn to evaluate the importance of different components at different times [6].

Our study collects historical climate data and malaria incidence records over ten years in Kerala districts. We experiment with Temporal Attention and Feature Based Attention Models using Transformers. By evaluating their predictive performance, we aim to determine the most suitable attention mechanism. We also explore the reasons behind performance differences, providing insights into the climate-malaria incidence interplay.

The contributions of this work are:

- This research shows an interdisciplinary application of AI to epidemiology, highlighting machine learning's potential for informing disease prevention and public health decisions.
- Numerous time series and machine learning models, such as Support Vector Regression, XGBoost, LightGBM, SARIMA, SARIMAX, Random Forest, Linear Regression, and Logistic Regression, are thoroughly compared in this work.
- The models uniquely integrate both temporal and feature-based attention to capture time-specific and feature-specific patterns relevant to malaria outbreaks.

- Methodologically, this work advances time series modeling for epidemiological prediction through tailored data processing and hyperparameter optimization.
- The study sets the foundation for real-time analytics to dynamically track emerging outbreaks and inform public health response, outlining a framework for prospective surveillance systems.

5.2 Literature Review

In recent years, machine learning and information technology have been used to predict and prevent disease outbreaks. Barbosa et al. A case study using k-means clustering and LSTM, GRU, and random forest models for malaria prediction in the Brazilian Amazon demonstrates the potential for spatiotemporal prediction in many urban agglomerations [7]. This approach highlights the importance of machine learning techniques in understanding diseases in complex environments. Nguyen et al. Likewise, in the research on predicting the flu virus in Vietnam, CNN, Transformer, LSTM and LSTM-ATT models are compared. In particular, the LSTM-ATT model shows good results in long-term and short-term predictions of dengue disease using rich data on climate change [8]. Patil S et al. A predictive model was developed using five climate indices and monthly dengue incidence to predict dengue fever cases over 10 years in nine cities in the Indian state of Maharashtra [9]. Reddy et al. Other projects report a more reliable and easier way to diagnose diseases. Previous work on disease prediction has described how fuzzy logic can be used to predict disease [10]. Faisal el-Saad et al. Dengue fever prediction in Bangladesh using weather data using supervised machine learning (SVM, DT, LR, NB, AdaBoost, XGBRegressor, GradientBoostingClassifier and RF) [11]. Dr. to A. Gopalakrishnan et al. Learn how to use LSTM and other time analysis models to predict market prices [12]. Vinayakumar et al. A medical imaging model was developed by combining the MLTL framework with LSTM. The MLTL framework uses simple data to identify and classify data constraints. Data collection. The proposed method has developed various CNN models to extract important features from images and improve the registration of sentences. The model achieved good accuracy with a BLEU score of 76.9% [13]. Sowmya V et al. 2 Classification of satellite images, especially land cover, using convolutional neural networks (CNN). The authors developed a deep learning model based on the SAT-4 and SAT-6 datasets [14].

Recently, Rajendran et al. Compared to other classifiers, RNN shows the best performance on dengue data, while SVR shows the best performance on chikungunya data [15]. Li et al.The method of deep learning technology combined with attention mechanism is a research hotspot and has achieved state-of-the-art results in many medical image tasks [16]. Zhang et al. This study introduces CapsNet-LDA, a novel predictor for lncRNA-disease association (LDA) prediction. It employs a stacked autoencoder for low-dimensional representation, applies an attention mechanism for adaptive weight allocation, and utilizes a CapsNet-based architecture for final prediction [17]. The literature on disease forecasting, particularly for vector-borne diseases like malaria, has generally relied on statistics and conventional machine learning methods. While useful, these techniques struggle to capture the complicated, non-linear correlations in epidemiological data and have little ability to handle temporal dynamics and feature relevance variations across time. Large volumes of data are required for effective training.

Our work introduces LSTM integrated attention-based methods, taking advantage of temporal dependencies and long-term patterns in climate and case count data. The addition of feature-based and temporal attention mechanisms improves the model's ability to prioritize relevant information dynamically. Our model demonstrates superior forecasting performance compared to traditional methods. Our comparative analysis demonstrates that the proposed models significantly outperform traditional methods. This addresses previously identified gaps and has practical implications for public health planning, offering a more effective tool for anticipating disease outbreaks and managing vector-borne diseases like malaria.

5.3 Proposed Methodology

Two main datasets were acquired for our research. The first dataset includes monthly case counts and associated mortality information for thirteen infectious diseases in the districts of Kerala. This information was obtained from the Data on Communicable Disease - Kerala of the Integrated Disease Surveillance Project, which can be accessed via the source link. The second dataset, which was acquired via NASA's Data Access Viewer, includes meteorological variables including temperature, humidity, precipitation, and more. We integrated the two datasets into a single, comprehensive one for our analysis. The year, month, disease case counts, average temperature, relative humidity, precipitation, total precipitation, humidity, maximum temperature, minimum temperature, average temperature, dew point are just a few of the characteristics that are included in this new dataset (shown in Fig. 5.1). The information covers the years 2011 through 2021.

Given our aim to develop a regression model for prediction, we ensured the data used was continuous in nature and well-structured in a .csv format. To address limited data availability, we augmented the dataset by generating synthetic data. After acquiring the combined dataset, we identified and selected relevant variables for our prediction task. Exploratory Data Analysis (shown in Fig. 5.2) provided insights into the relationship between variables. The chosen variables were instrumental in understanding the climate factors and disease incidence relationship. We standardized the remaining variables using the StandardScaler to ensure consistent scaling.

Long Short Term Memory are a special type of recurrent neural network able to effectively learn long-term dependencies in sequential data. Unlike standard RNNs which struggle with vanishing gradients, LSTMs utilize a gated architecture that allows them to selectively remember important information over many timesteps.

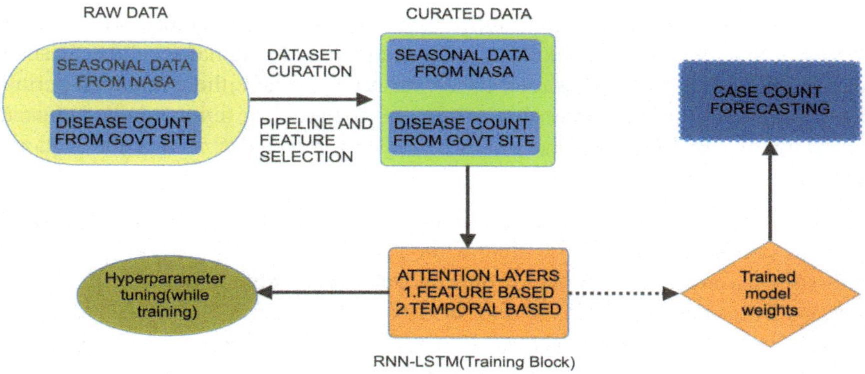

Fig. 5.1 Overview of the proposed methodology

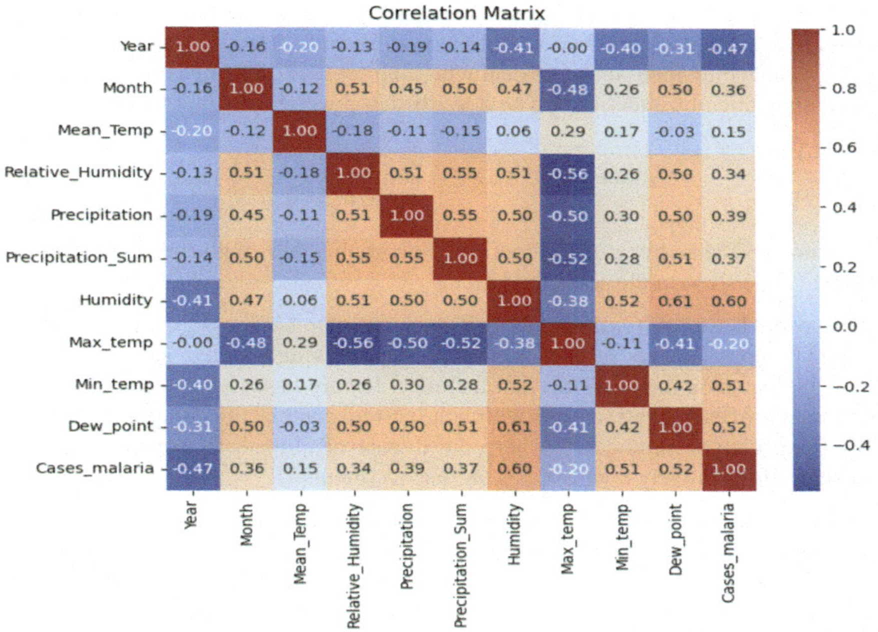

Fig. 5.2 Heatmap of climatic factors and malaria case correlation matrix

The core of the LSTM is its memory cell, regulated by input, output and forget gates. These gates determine after a particular event what is to be kept, used or forgotten on purpose. With such mechanisms in place, LSTMs can handle tasks with temporal contexts such as speech and language tasks among others and do forecasting for time series data. The flexible memory and gating design makes it possible for the LSTMs to model short term patterns as well as long-term trends in sequences of data.

This functionality has made LSTMs the most widely used recurrent neural network (RNN) architecture in fields like natural language processing (NLP) and time series analysis.It also helps them overcome the vanishing gradient problem which permits them to learn long-term relationships.Their ability to capture temporal dependencies by means of gated memory has made LSTMs an indispensable tool for sequence modeling tasks across domains.

Attention Mechanism is a technique used in Neural Networks enabling dynamic focusing on relevant parts of the input while generating specific parts of the output.It does so by computing alignment scores between each output element and different sections from input sequence. These scores are then used to create a context vector acting as conditional representation which summarizes only essential inputs for a given output Since they model variable alignment between inputs and outputs. Attention mechanisms excel at tasks involving long sequences like machine translation. By selectively weighting the most important inputs for each output, attention allows models to handle longer contexts and improve sequence modeling performance. Overall, attention brings more flexible input relevance determination to neural networks, enhancing their ability to deal with long sequential data.

Mathematically, attention can be described as a weighted sum of values,

$$\text{Attention}(Q, K, V) = \text{softmax}\left(\frac{QK^T}{\sqrt{d_k}}\right)V \tag{5.1}$$

In our LSTM architectures, attention is incorporated to emphasize important features or time steps in the sequential inputs.

Feature-Based Attention, the mechanism dynamically assigns weights to the different input features at each timestep when making predictions. This enables selective focus on the most relevant features . feature-based attention evaluates the importance of each input variable within the current context. For complex forecasting tasks like malaria prediction, where the impact of climate factors can vary, this mechanism selectively concentrates on relevant inputs.

Temporal Based Attention mechanism enables the model to focus on the most relevant time steps in the input sequence for making predictions. It assigns weights to each timestep's hidden state based on their significance to the output. This allows selective focus on informative points like spikes in malaria cases.

5.4 Experimental Results and Discussions

The dataset used in this study comprises 5000 entries of meteorological factors like temperature, humidity, precipitation, along with corresponding malaria cases, carefully compiled to capture the relationship between climatic conditions and malaria incidence. The correlation matrix shows varying degrees of connection between temporal elements, climatic circumstances, and malaria case incidence, demonstrating

Table 5.1 Model performance comparison using RMSE

Model	RMSE
Support vector regression (Polynomial)	19.975
XGBoost	25.103
LightGBM	19.243
SARIMA	32.368
SARIMAX	19.584
Random forest	20.931
Linear regression	31.966
Logistic regression	64.128
LSTM	18.246

the suitability of LSTM models with attention mechanisms to capture these complex interactions. The negative trend between 'Year' and 'Cases malaria' could aid the Temporal Attention LSTM in focusing on long-term declining trends, while the Feature-Based Attention LSTM may leverage the variable strengths of correlations between meteorological features to improve predictive accuracy by identifying crucial features impacting malaria incidence forecast.

5.4.1 *Model Comparison and Performance*

We created a number of time series and machine learning models because our data is time series, and we used these models to determine which one best fit our data. Support Vector Regression (Polynomial Kernel), Random Forest, XGBoost, LightGBM, SARIMA, SARIMAX, Linear Regression, Logistic Regression, and LSTM are among the models that were assessed. The Root Mean Squared Error (RMSE) statistic was utilised to evaluate the performance of various models. The LSTM model provided the lowest RMSE, indicating the highest accuracy among the tested models shown in the (Table 5.1). Therefore, we proceeded with the LSTM model.

5.4.2 *Training and Validation of the Model*

For training and evaluating the LSTM models, the dataset was split into three subsets–a training set for fitting model parameters, a validation set for hyperparameter tuning, and a test set for final model evaluation.

This division allows the models to be trained on the training data, tuned on the validation data, and finally evaluated on the unseen test set. The comprehensive dataset encompasses diverse weather conditions and their impacts on malaria spread,

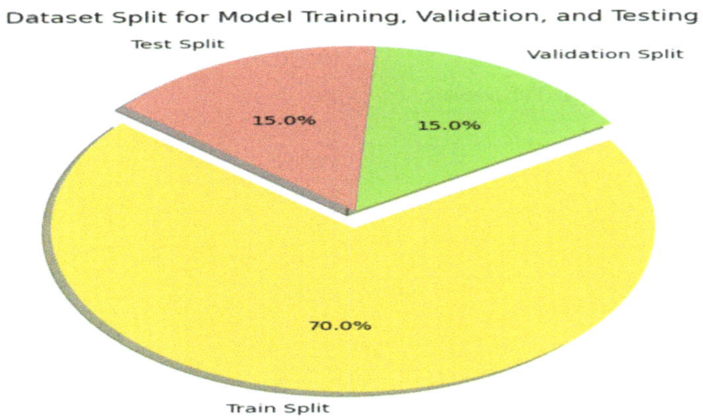

Fig. 5.3 Proportional dataset division for training, validation, and testing

enabling robust modeling of this relationship for accurate forecasting.The pie chart (shown in Fig. 5.3) visualizes the division of a dataset into three distinct subsets for the development of a machine learning model.

The largest segment, the Train Split, comprises 70% of the dataset and is used for initial model training. The Validation Split and Test Split, each representing 15% of the dataset, are crucial for refining the model and evaluating its final performance, respectively. This strategic allocation ensures a comprehensive training process while maintaining the integrity of model validation and unbiased testing.

5.4.3 Comparative Performance of Evaluation Metrics with Attention Mechanisms

- Average Validation Loss: The Feature-Based Attention LSTM has a significantly lower average validation loss (1.3662) compared to the Temporal Attention LSTM (2.6670), indicating better minimization of the loss function and potential for better generalization on new data (shown in Fig. 5.4).
- RMSE: The Feature-Based Attention LSTM has a lower RMSE (1.0673) than the Temporal Attention LSTM (1.6136), suggesting its predictions are closer to the actual values and therefore more accurate.
- MAE: The Feature-Based Attention LSTM has a lower MAE (1.0673) compared to the Temporal Attention LSTM (1.2930), indicating that on average, it makes smaller errors in prediction, signifying better performance. Table 5.2 represents the performance metrics for both the Feature-Based Attention LSTM and the Temporal Attention LSTM, including average validation loss, RMSE, and MAE.

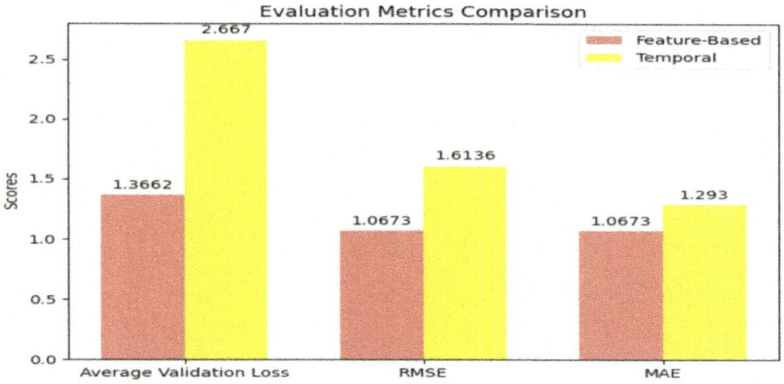

Fig. 5.4 Performance comparison between feature-based attention LSTM and temporal attention LSTM

Table 5.2 Performance of evaluation metrics

Metric	Feature-based attention LSTM	Temporal attention LSTM
Average validation loss	1.3662	2.6670
RMSE	1.0673	1.6136
MAE	1.0673	1.2930

The line chart for the feature-based attention mechanism (Fig. 5.5) shows a close alignment between the actual and forecasted malaria cases over four time steps. The forecast slightly underestimates the actual cases at the final point, but the near-parallel trajectories suggest strong predictive performance, with a slight divergence at the end indicating potential model adjustments for maintaining accuracy.The line chart for the temporal attention mechanism (Fig. 5.6) depicts a high degree of alignment between actual and forecasted malaria cases across 100 time steps, with overlapping lines reflecting the model's accurate predictions and strong capability to capture the time-dependent patterns of malaria case progression over an extended period.

5.4.4 Hyperparameters Tuning

The (Table 5.3) model configuration prioritizes simplicity and efficiency. The short input and output lengths, small batch size,lightweight neural network and moderate training epochs suggest a streamlined approach focused on computational expediency rather than maximizing absolute performance. The conventional learning rate takes calculated approach to weight updates, while the moderate number of epochs aims to fit the data without overfitting, assuming validation checks occur.

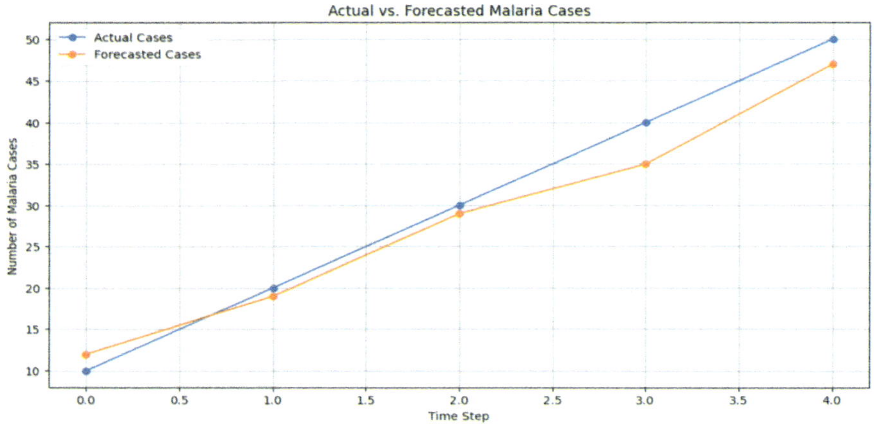

Fig. 5.5 Comparison of actual and forecasted malaria cases using feature-based attention mechanism

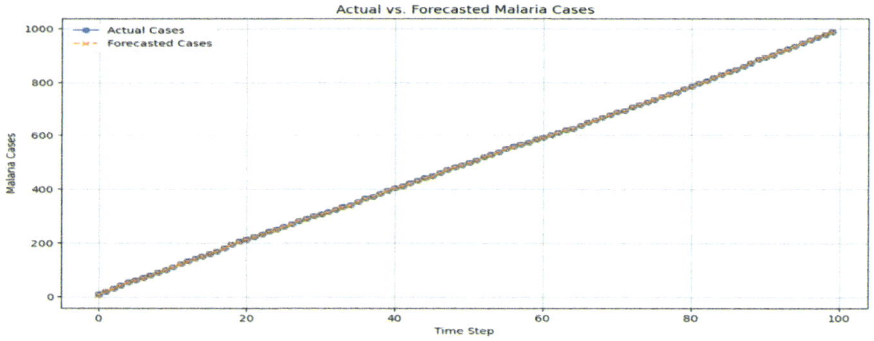

Fig. 5.6 Comparison of actual and forecasted malaria cases using temporal attention mechanism

5.5 Conclusion and Future Directions

Our study shows that LSTM models with attention mechanisms can effectively forecast malaria cases using weather data. Careful data preprocessing and hyperparameter tuning allowed the models to learn the relationships between climate factors and malaria outbreaks. The comparative analysis further highlights that the Feature-Based Attention LSTM outperforms than other models, such as traditional LSTM and various machine learning models, by achieving the lowest RMSE and MAE. This underscores the efficacy of incorporating attention mechanisms into LSTM models for time series forecasting. The Temporal Attention LSTM focused on relevant time patterns, while the Feature-Based Attention LSTM emphasized important climate features at each timepoint. Both attention mechanisms improved the models'

Table 5.3 Hyperparameters

Hyperparameter	Value
Input sequence length	12
Output sequence length	1
Batch size	32
Hidden size	64
Number of layers	1
Learning rate	0.001
Number of epochs	50

ability to predict malaria incidence from meteorological data. Training and Testing demonstrated the strengths of attention-enhanced LSTMs for time series forecasting. The results highlight the potential of deep learning to inform malaria prevention efforts and address global health challenges. Future directions include incorporating new environmental and socioeconomic aspects, using real-time data analytics for dynamic prediction, and addressing the generalization of models across varied geographic locations. A significant problem is the need for substantial validation and the possibility of region-specific model adjustments to account for local variations in malaria transmission dynamics and climate patterns.

References

1. Karypidou, M.C., Almpanidou, V., Tompkins, A.M., Mazaris, A.D., Gewehr, S., Mourelatos, S., Katragkou, E.: Projected shifts in the distribution of malaria vectors due to climate change. Clim. Change **163**, 2117–2133 (2020)
2. Kamana, E., Bai, D., Brown, H.E., Zhao, J.: The malaria transmission in Anhui province China. Infect. Dis. Modell. **8**(1), 1–10 (2023)
3. Nkiruka, O., Prasad, R., Clement, O.: Prediction of malaria incidence using climate variability and machine learning. Inf. Med. Unlocked **22**, 100508 (2021)
4. Sakubu, D., Sinigirira, K.J.G., Niyukuri, D.: Predicting malaria dynamics in Burundi using deep learning models (2023). arXiv:2306.02685
5. Doni, A.R., Sasipraba, T.: Lstm-rnn based approach for prediction of dengue cases in India. Ingénierie des Systèmes d'Information **25**(3) (2020)
6. Usama, M., Ahmad, B., Xiao, W., Hossain, M.S., Muhammad, G.: Self-attention based recurrent convolutional neural network for disease prediction using healthcare data. Comput. Methods Programs Biomed. **190**, 105191 (2020)
7. Barboza, M.F.X., Monteiro, K.H.d.C., Rodrigues, I.R., Santos, G.L., Monteiro, W.M., Figueira, E.A.G., Sampaio, V.D.S., Lynn, T., Endo, P.T.: Prediction of malaria using deep learning models: a case study on city clusters in the state of Amazonas, Brazil, from 2003 to 2018. Revista da Sociedade Brasileira de Medicina Tropical **55** (2022)
8. Nguyen, V.-H., Tuyet-Hanh, T.T., Mulhall, J., Minh, H.V., Duong, T.Q., Chien, N.V., Nhung, N., Lan, V.H., Minh, H.B., Cuong, D., et al.: Deep learning models for forecasting dengue fever based on climate data in Vietnam. PLoS Negl. Trop. Dis. **16**(6), 0010509 (2022)
9. Patil, S., Pandya, S.: Forecasting dengue hotspots associated with variation in meteorological parameters using regression and time series models. Front. Public Health **9**, 798034 (2021)

10. Reddy, E.M.K., Kumar, K.L., Rajkumar, R., Yoshita, L.N., Manitha, P.: A reliable dengue disease detection methodology using fuzzy logic. In: 2021 Fourth International Conference on Electrical, Computer and Communication Technologies (ICECCT), pp. 1–6. IEEE (2021)
11. Sarder, F., Akter, S., Akter, S.: Predicting dengue outbreak from climate data using machine learning algorithms. In: 2022 IEEE International Conference on Data Science and Information System (ICDSIS), pp. 1–6. IEEE (2022)
12. Selvin, S., Vinayakumar, R., Gopalakrishnan, E., Menon, V.K., Soman, K.: Stock price prediction using lstm, rnn and cnn-sliding window model. In: 2017 International Conference on Advances in Computing, Communications and Informatics (icacci), pp. 1643–1647. IEEE (2017)
13. Vinayakumar, R., Soman, K., Poornachandran, P., Sachin Kumar, S.: Detecting android malware using long short-term memory (lstm). J. Intell. Fuzzy Syst. **34**(3), 1277–1288 (2018)
14. Unnikrishnan, A., Sowmya, V., Soman, K.: Deep learning architectures for land cover classification using red and near-infrared satellite images. Multimed. Tools Appl. **78**, 18379–18394 (2019)
15. Rajendran, N.M., Karthikeyan, M., Karthik Raja, B., Pragadishwaran, K., Gopalakrishnan, E., Sowmya, V.: Communicable disease prediction using machine learning and deep learning algorithms. In: International Conference on Information, Communication and Computing Technology, pp. 979–992. Springer (2023)
16. Li, X., Li, M., Yan, P., Li, G., Jiang, Y., Luo, H., Yin, S.: Deep learning attention mechanism in medical image analysis: basics and beyonds. Int. J Netw. Dyn. Intell. 93–116 (2023)
17. Zhang, Z., Xu, J., Wu, Y., Liu, N., Wang, Y., Liang, Y.: Capsnet-lda: predicting lncrna-disease associations using attention mechanism and capsule network based on multi-view data. Brief. Bioinform. **24**(1), 531 (2023)

Chapter 6
Inertia Assessment of Power System by Considering Spatial-Temporal Distribution Characteristics

Shuang Guo, Yunlu Li, Shaoze Cui, Haixin Wang, and Junyou Yang

Abstract As renewable energy and power electronics continue to grow in proportion, the power system is increasingly exhibiting traits of lower inertia and spatial-temporal dispersion. It deteriorates the frequency response and system stability. The majority of existing studies focuses on the estimation of system inertia, while there is a lack of in-depth studies on the characteristics and properties of the inertial spatial-temporal distribution. This paper evaluates the nodal inertia of the power system by examining its spatial and temporal distribution characteristics. A model for nodal inertia representation is developed based on the correlation between frequency and power, allowing for an estimation of inertia. Spatial distribution index and time-varying index are introduced to analyze the changing process of inertia distribution under disturbances in both dimension for further assessment. Finally, using the IEEE 3-machine 9-bus system, the system nodal inertia is assessed, the characteristic of nodal inertia is discussed and analyzed deeply.

S. Guo (✉) · Y. Li · S. Cui · H. Wang · J. Yang
School of Electrical Engineering, Shenyang University of Technology, Shenyang, China
e-mail: Shuangguo@smail.sut.edu.cn

Y. Li
e-mail: liyunlu@sut.edu.cn

S. Cui
e-mail: csz1218@smail.sut.edu.cn

H. Wang
e-mail: haixinwang@sut.edu.cn

J. Yang
e-mail: junyouyang@sut.edu.cn

F. P. García Márquez et al. (eds.), *Computing, Internet of Things and Data Analytics*,
Smart Innovation, Systems and Technologies 387,
https://doi.org/10.1007/978-3-031-87154-2_6

6.1 Introduction

The growing integration of renewable energy sources (RES) into power systems, marked by the absence of rotating machinery and the decoupling of grid frequency caused by power electronic devices, leads to a decrease in system inertia and a lack of adequate inertia support. This leads to system instability and diminished disturbance rejection capability [1–4]. Upon the occurrence of a disturbance, primary frequency modulation (FM) is delayed, necessitating the immediate involvement of inertia to maintain system stability [5, 6]. Moreover, incidents where system inertia support is inadequate to counteract fault disturbances occur frequently. Therefore, accurately estimating system inertia levels is critical for the stable operation, control, and scheduling of the system.

Large-scale power systems display intricate characteristics and spatial-temporal distribution patterns. On the one hand, the distribution of system inertia resources is uneven: renewable energy units, concentrated in regions with low inertia characteristics, contrast sharply with synchronous generating units, which are located in high inertia regions. This creates a distinct spatial distribution of system inertia. On the other hand, the stochastic, intermittent, and fluctuating nature of renewable energy outputs causes significant temporal fluctuations in system inertia. These factors not only intensify the spatial-temporal distribution of system frequency during disturbances but also add complexity to its dynamic processes, making them more difficult to manage. Hence, a detailed analysis of system inertia and a comprehensive portrayal of its response characteristics are essential to provide accurate foundational data for system planning, scheduling, and operation control aimed at maintaining frequency stability.

Current research on estimating power system inertia mainly targets system-wide and regional levels. For example, [7] presents a method to calculate the inertia constant of a power system and the total online capacity of spinning reserve generators using measured frequency transients. In [8], the total inertia of the Great Britain (GB) power system is estimated by dividing the network into regions based on constraint boundaries. Likewise, the inertia of the Western Electricity Coordination Council system for each event is calculated using observed frequency transients in [9]. Approaches to estimate effective inertia from ambient frequency and active power signals collected by phasor measurement units are proposed in [10]. Partitioning the system and establishing a regional equivalent frequency response model for regional inertia estimation is discussed in [11, 12]. Additionally, energy variation-based effective inertia estimation methods for power system areas are presented in [13], and data-driven equivalent inertia partition estimation methods are introduced in [14] to accurately determine regional inertia levels. However, inertia estimation should also consider the spatial distribution of inertia at the nodal level to identify weak inertia nodes and enhance the adaptability of renewable energy integration.

Research on nodal inertia has explored the representation of inertia's spatial distribution. The concept of "nodal inertia" is introduced and described using the system inertia matrix in [15], analyzed with calculation methods in [16], and further examined with sensitivity analyses in [17]. The "node equivalent inertia" index, addressing time-varying and spatial variability, is proposed in [18], and the "equivalent inertia time coefficient" index for assessing the spatial—temporal distribution of inertia based on frequency trajectory information is presented in [19]. Nevertheless, these concepts lack uniformity and in-depth analyses of spatial—temporal distribution characteristics. A comprehensive representation of inertial dynamic response behavior requires concise and efficient representation forms. Furthermore, research into these representation forms and their outcomes will contribute to a deeper understanding of inertia characteristics.

In this paper, the nodal inertia of power systems is assessed considering spatial—temporal distribution characteristics. Spatial distribution and time-varying indices are introduced to analyze the dynamic process of inertia distribution under disturbances across both dimensions. Firstly, a nodal inertia representation model is established based on the relationship between frequency and power. Secondly, the spatial-temporal distribution of inertia is examined to introduce indices that reflect nodal inertia properties. Finally, using the IEEE 3-machine 9-bus system, the system's nodal inertia is assessed, and the characteristics of nodal inertia are thoroughly discussed and analyzed.

6.2 Nodal Inertia Analysis of Power System

System inertia response refers to the imbalance in system power that causes frequency instability from its nominal value. The energy stored in the electromagnetic field and rotating components of the system's equipment instantly reacts to the frequency disturbance, resisting changes and helping to stabilize the system. This process also provides crucial time for the primary frequency modulation (FM) to take effect, as illustrated in Fig. 6.1.

A power system's rotating inertia represents the total stored energy in the masses rotating at nominal speed. The rotating inertia of the device is then determined.

$$H = \frac{\Delta P_a(t)}{2\frac{df(t)}{dt}} \tag{6.1}$$

where H is the inertia constant in seconds, $\Delta \mathrm{P_a}$ is the total power of rotating mass.

Nodal inertia is an intrinsic characteristic that prevents the node's frequency from changing during power system energy fluctuations, its magnitude represents the node's ability to resist active disturbances under the combined effect of all inertial resources.

Establish the connection between nodal inertia, frequency deviation, and power fluctuation for the general node k.

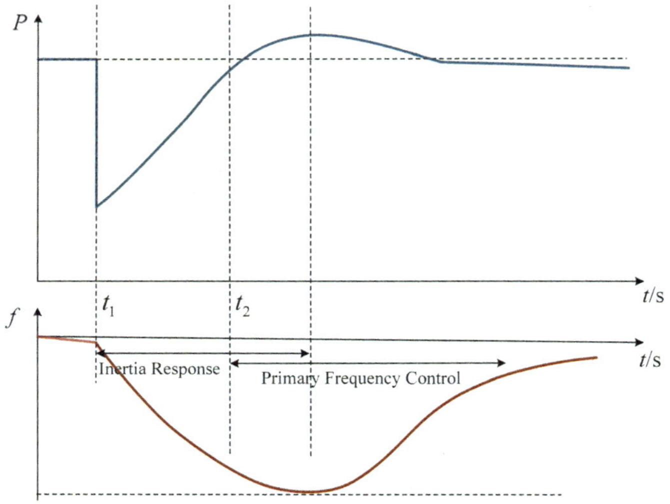

Fig. 6.1 Inertia response diagram of power system

$$H_k = \frac{\Delta P_k(t)}{\frac{2d\,\Delta f_k(t)}{dt}} \tag{6.2}$$

where Δf_k is the frequency deviation of general node k, ΔP_k is the power increment of general node k, which describes the power fluctuation flowing through the node during the transient process of power system.

For the synchronous generator node j, in inertia response phase, the same is shown as follows.

$$2H_j \frac{d\,\Delta f_j(t)}{dt} = \Delta P_{m,j}(t) - \Delta P_{e,j}(t) = \Delta P_{a,j}(t) \tag{6.3}$$

6.3 Assessment of the Inertia Spatial-Temporal Distribution Characteristics

6.3.1 Description of the Inertia Assessment Procedure

First, nodal inertia is estimated using data gathered at the nodes. Next, the spatial-temporal distribution characteristics of inertia are analyzed to derive the inertia matrix form. Finally, a detailed evaluation of inertia is conducted based on the introduced spatial distribution index and time-varying index. The steps involved in the inertia assessment are illustrated in Fig. 6.2.

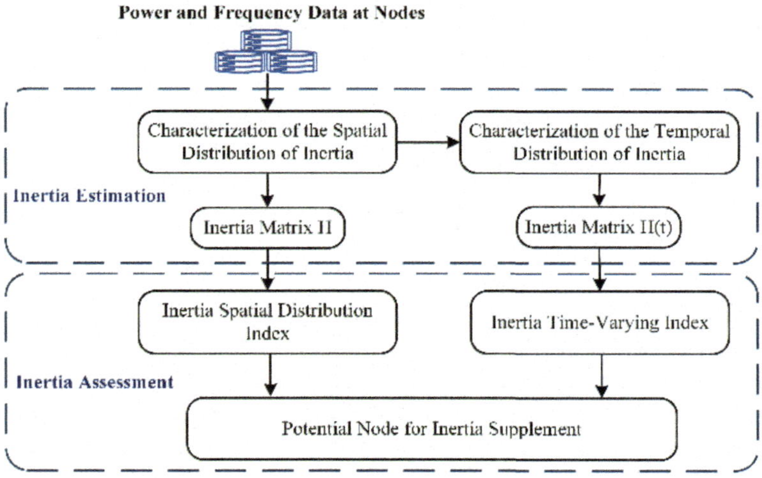

Fig. 6.2 The framework of inertia assessment

6.3.2 Characterization and Assessment of the Inertia Spatial Distribution

When the frequency distribution of the system after a disturbance is pronounced, the frequency dynamics among different nodes can vary significantly. Consequently, the inertial energy release from inertial elements connected to these nodes will produce different force outputs. This leads not only to varying overall effects on system inertia but also to differences in inertia between individual nodes.

The inertia of a power system varies across different nodes during disturbances, illustrating a characteristic known as nodal inertia. When a disturbance occurs at a specific node, the resulting nodal inertia across all nodes can be expressed as a single row vector. Since the disturbance influences all nodes, the spatial distribution of system inertia can be thoroughly represented by compiling all the observed row vectors.

Thus, the spatial distribution characteristics can be captured by defining the system node inertia matrix H.

$$H = \begin{bmatrix} H_{11} & H_{12} & \dots & H_{1i} & \dots & H_{1N} \\ H_{21} & H_{22} & \dots & H_{2i} & \dots & H_{2N} \\ \vdots & \vdots & \dots & \vdots & \ddots & \vdots \\ H_{i1} & H_{i2} & \dots & H_{ii} & \dots & H_{iN} \\ \vdots & \vdots & \ddots & \vdots & \ddots & \vdots \\ H_{N1} & H_{N2} & \dots & H_{Ni} & \dots & H_{NN} \end{bmatrix} \tag{6.4}$$

H_{ii} is the observed system inertia from node i, called the system node self-inertia coefficient. H_{ij} is the observed system inertia from node j, called the system node mutual inertia coefficient.

$$H_{ii} = \frac{\Delta P_{a-i}}{\frac{2d\,\Delta f_i}{dt}} \tag{6.5}$$

$$H_{ij} = \frac{\Delta P_{a-j}}{\frac{2d\,\Delta f_j}{dt}} \tag{6.6}$$

In order to study the inertia distribution characteristics at the node level in depth, the inertia spatial distribution index H_{DIK} is introduced to assess the system inertia spatial distribution. The inertia spatial distribution index refers to the deviation of nodal frequency from frequency of inertia center, the electrical distance between the node and the inertia center is obtained, according to the size of which the magnitude of the nodal inertia is judged.

$$L_k = \sum_{i=1}^{N} \Delta T \cdot [f_k(i) - f_{COI}(i)]^2 \tag{6.7}$$

where, L_k is the electrical distance between node k and inertia center. N is the number of samples. ΔT is the phasor measurement unit simulation step. $f_k(i)$ and $f_{COI}(i)$ are the value of node k frequency and the frequency of inertia center for the ith sample.

$$f_{COI}(t) = \frac{\sum_{i \in n} H_{Gi} \cdot f_{Gi}(t)}{\sum_{i \in n} H_{Gi}} \tag{6.8}$$

where, $f_{Gi}(t)$ is the frequency of generator node i.

$$H_{DIK} = \frac{L_k - L_{\max}}{L_{\max} - L_{\min}} \tag{6.9}$$

where, H_{DIK} is the inertia spatial distribution index at node k. L_{max} and L_{min} are the maximum and minimum electrical distances between node and inertia center.

6.3.3 Characterization and Assessment of the Inertia Temporal Distribution

The temporal variation characteristic of inertia describes how node inertia changes over time in response to disturbances. Figure 6.3 illustrates the curves representing the frequency dynamics of each general node during the system's power disturbance.

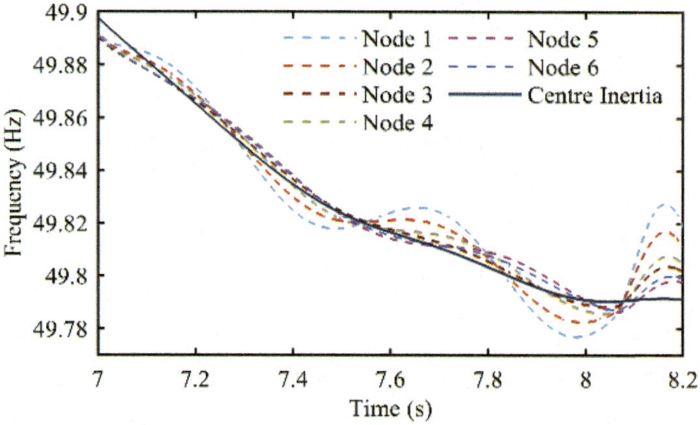

Fig. 6.3 Node frequency response and frequency of center inertia

Nodal inertia is influenced by the unbalanced power and the dynamics of nodal frequency resulting from disturbances. If the disturbance remains constant, the node inertia will continually change over time rather than remain constant, as the rate of frequency change at the node varies along the delay time axis. This illustrates the temporal distribution characteristic of power system inertia.

Therefore, nodal inertia matrix H is a temporally variable matrix.

$$H(t) = \begin{bmatrix} H_{11}(t) & H_{12}(t) & \dots & H_{1i}(t) & \dots & H_{1N}(t) \\ H_{21}(t) & H_{22}(t) & \dots & H_{2i}(t) & \dots & H_{2N}(t) \\ \vdots & \vdots & \dots & \vdots & \ddots & \vdots \\ H_{i1}(t) & H_{i2}(t) & \dots & H_{ii}(t) & \dots & H_{iN}(t) \\ \vdots & \vdots & \ddots & \vdots & \ddots & \vdots \\ H_{N1}(t) & H_{N2}(t) & \dots & H_{Ni}(t) & \dots & H_{NN}(t) \end{bmatrix} \tag{6.10}$$

$$H_{ii}(t) = \frac{\Delta P_{a-i}}{\frac{2d\Delta f_i(t)}{dt}} \tag{6.11}$$

$$H_{ij}(t) = \frac{\Delta P_{a-j}}{\frac{2d\Delta f_j(t)}{dt}} \tag{6.12}$$

In order to study the inertia time-varying characteristics at node level in depth, the inertia time-varying index T_H is introduced to assess the system inertia time-varying situation. The inertia time-varying index refers to the time from the beginning of action of system nodal inertia to reach the peak inertia under disturbance, the level of nodal inertia is grasped according to its magnitude.

$$T_H(t) = \begin{bmatrix} T_{H\_11}(t) & T_{H\_12}(t) & \dots & T_{H\_1i}(t) & \dots & T_{H\_1N}(t) \\ T_{H\_21}(t) & T_{H\_22}(t) & \dots & T_{H\_2i}(t) & \dots & T_{H\_2N}(t) \\ \vdots & \vdots & \dots & \vdots & \ddots & \vdots \\ T_{H-i1}(t) & T_{H\_i2}(t) & \dots & T_{H\_ii}(t) & \dots & T_{H\_iN}(t) \\ \vdots & \vdots & \ddots & \vdots & \ddots & \vdots \\ T_{H\_N1}(t) & T_{H\_N2}(t) & \dots & T_{H\_Ni}(t) & \dots & T_{H\_NN}(t) \end{bmatrix} \tag{6.13}$$

$$T_{H\_ii}(t) = \frac{T_i(peak) - T_i(0)}{T_i(t)} \tag{6.14}$$

$$T_{H\_ij}(t) = \frac{T_j(peak) - T_j(0)}{T_j(t)} \tag{6.15}$$

where, T_H is a time-varying index of nodal inertia. $T_{H\text{-}ii}$ is the observed time from node *i*, called the system node self time-varying coefficient. $T_{H\text{-}ij}$ is the observed time from node *j*, called the system node mutual time-varying coefficient.

6.4 Case Study

6.4.1 Configuration Setup

The IEEE 3-machine 9-bus system is used to estimate the system nodal inertia and to analyze the inertia spatial-temporal distribution characteristics. The system depicted in Fig. 6.4. is constructed using the MATLAB/SIMULINK platform, the simulation hardware is a PC with Intel® Core (TM) i7-1250 CPU/16GB RAM. The nominal frequency is set to 50 Hz.

In this paper, nine sets of simulation experiments are done under different transient states, faults are set up sequentially at nine nodes, with the fault being the access to a constant PQ load of 20 MW at 10 s.

6.4.2 The Calculation of Nodal Instantaneous Inertia

The nodal instantaneous inertia, representing the momentary nodal inertia of the system under disturbances at time t, can be expressed by (3). This parameter allows for determining the inertia level of the system at any node and at any moment during disturbances. At t = 0.3 s, the elements in the fourth row, fourth column, and the diagonal of the nodal inertia matrix are selected. Details are presented in Fig. 6.5.

From Fig. 6.5, it can be seen that when the disturbance occurs for 0.3 s, instantaneous inertia values are both positive and negative. The nodal instantaneous inertia is

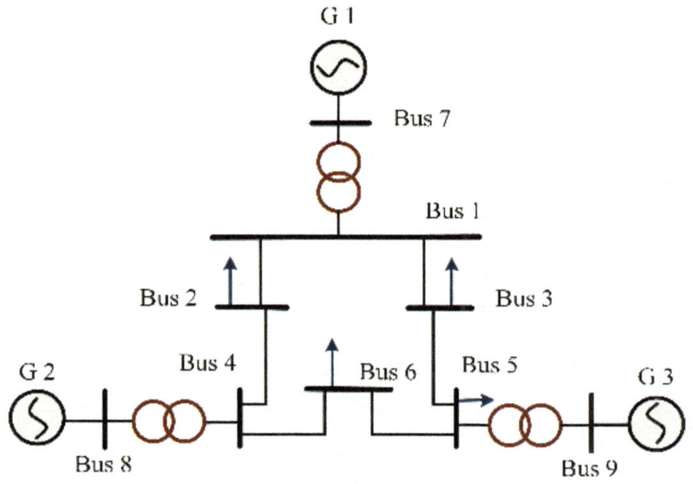

Fig. 6.4 System architecture diagram

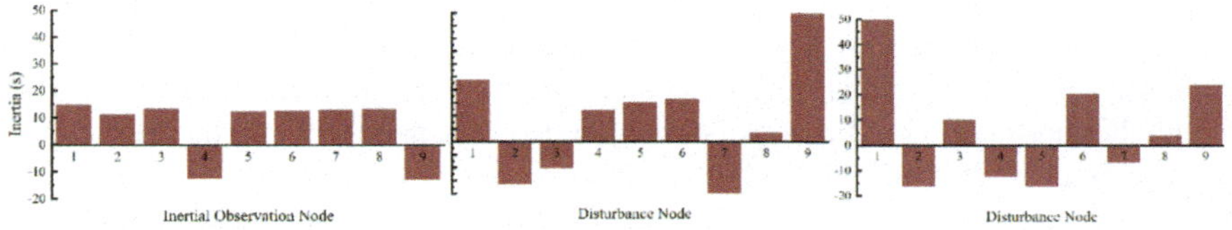

Fig. 6.5 Quantity of nodal instantaneous inertia at t = 0.3 s

negative, showing that at this time the node absorbs energy, the other inertia sources node throughput power in the node is distributed more than the number of disturbance power distribution in the node, the node frequency is in back up state.

Figure 6.6 gives a time-varying diagram of the instantaneous self-inertia coefficients when disturbance occurs at node 2, with a time window of 0–0.3 s. Figure 6.6 illustrates that the nodal instantaneous inertia corresponds with the nodal frequency curves, displaying positive, negative, and infinite cases. Thus, the nodal instantaneous inertia accurately reflects the current level and trend of nodal inertia.

6.4.3 Characterization of the Spatial Distribution of Inertia

According to the definition and analysis of the system nodal inertia matrix in the previous section, its row i represents the inertia observed from each node respectively after node i is disturbed. Column i represents the inertia observed from node i

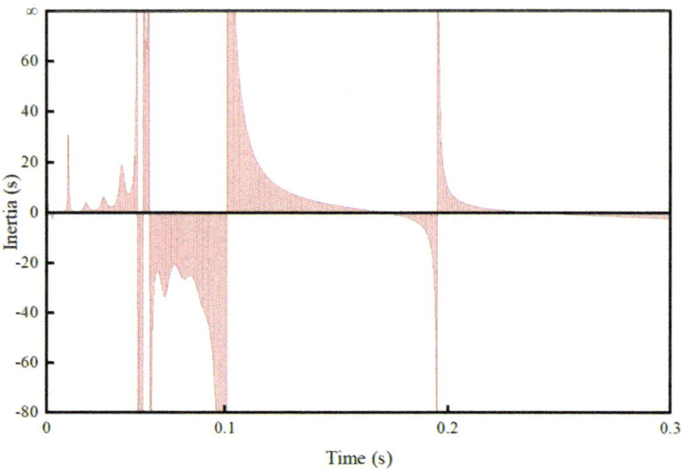

Fig. 6.6 Time-varying diagram of quantity of self-inertia coefficient when disturbance occurs at node 2

respectively when the same size of disturbance occurs at each node. The main diagonal element corresponds to the same size disturbance occurring at each disturbed node, the inertia observed at the disturbed node is the node self-inertia coefficient.

The first row, first column and main diagonal elements of the nodal instantaneous inertia matrix obtained from 0.1s calculation of disturbance occurrence are selected. As shown in Fig. 6.7. The first row, first column and main diagonal elements of the nodal average inertia matrix obtained from 0.3 s calculation of disturbance occurrence are selected. As shown in Fig. 6.8.

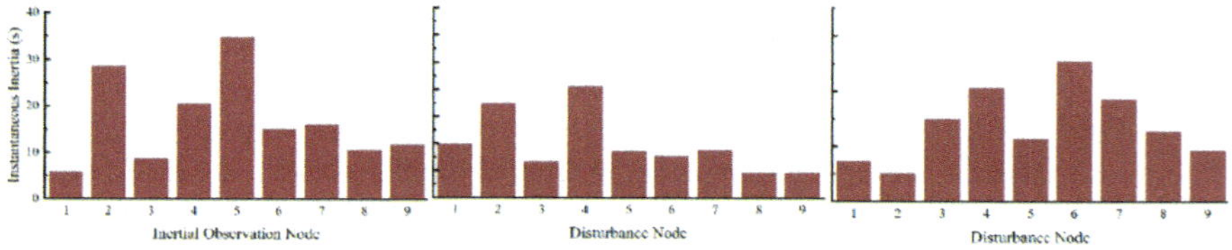

Fig. 6.7 Spatial variation of the quantity of nodal inertia at t = 0.1 s

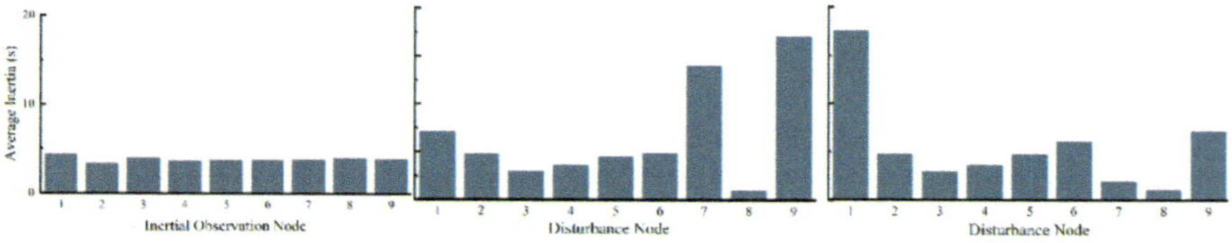

Fig. 6.8 Spatial variation of the quantity of nodal inertia at t = 0.3 s

As shown in Figs. 6.7 and 6.8, when a disturbance occurs at the same node, the nodal inertia observed at different nodes varies. Additionally, when disturbances of the same magnitude happen at different nodes, the nodal inertia observed at the same node differs, and the self-inertia coefficients at the disturbed node are also not uniform. Consequently, the system inertia observed at different nodes is not identical, indicating that the system nodal inertia can represent the spatial distribution characteristics of inertia.

6.4.4 Characterization of the Temporal Distribution of Inertia

To capture the temporal distribution characteristics of power system inertia, the four elements of the nodal instantaneous inertia matrix—H4-2, H4-9, H8-4, and H3-4—are selected. The temporal variation diagrams for these elements are presented in Fig. 6.9.

As can be seen from the above figure, the elements in the nodal instantaneous inertia matrix change over time, the change in inertia over time is not the same for different nodes. Therefore, in the process of inertial resource action, not only the amount of energy throughput of each inertial resource action is changing, but its distribution ratio in other inertial resource nodes is also changing at all times under the influence of many factors.

6.4.5 Nodal Inertia Assessment

The inertial spatial distribution index of each node is calculated and used to characterize the average inertial response strength of the nodes under disturbance. Take the example of a disturbance at node 1. The system node inertia distribution is shown in Fig. 6.10.

As shown in Fig. 6.10, the darker the color of the node, H_{DIK} the larger the average value, the further the node is from inertia center, the faster the frequency of general node changes under this disturbance, the smaller the nodal inertia, the more inertial support is needed. Therefore, from the inertial spatial distribution index, the frequency fluctuation at Bus *1* is the largest and needs more inertia supplementation.

The inertia time-varying index of each node is calculated and used to characterize the speed of nodal inertia response under disturbance. Taking the *1st* row of nodal inertia time-varying matrix as an example, the system nodal inertia time-varying is shown in Fig. 6.11.

As shown in Fig. 6.11, the lighter the color of node, the smaller the value of T_H, the faster the inertial response of node, the greater the contribution of nodal outgoing speed under this disturbance, which helps the power system operation

Fig. 6.9 Temporal variation of the quantity of nodal instantaneous inertia at H4-2, H4-9 and H8-4, H3-4

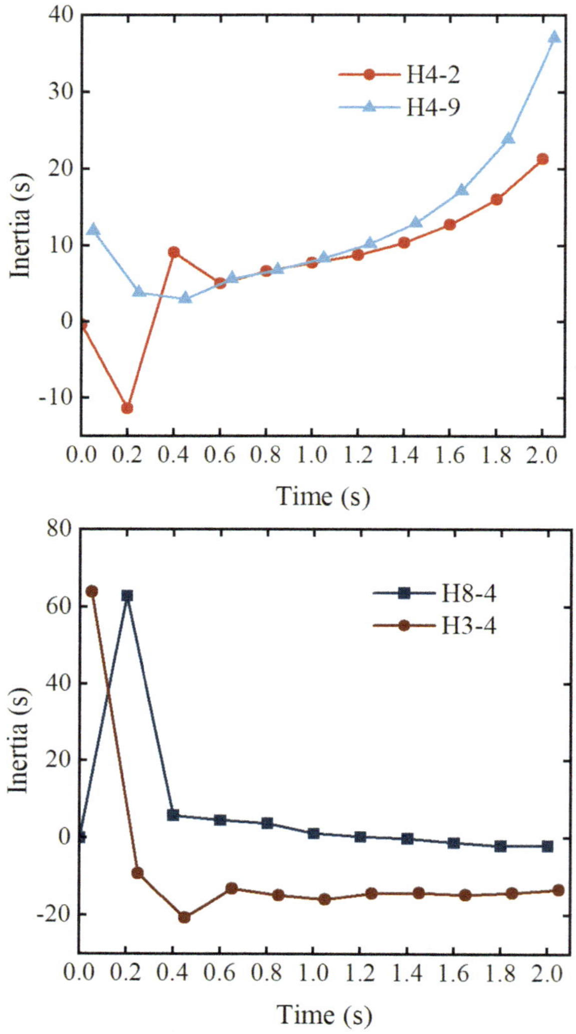

scheduler to take response preventive measures. Therefore, from the inertia time-varying index, the frequency fluctuation at Bus 2 is the largest and needs more inertia supplementation.

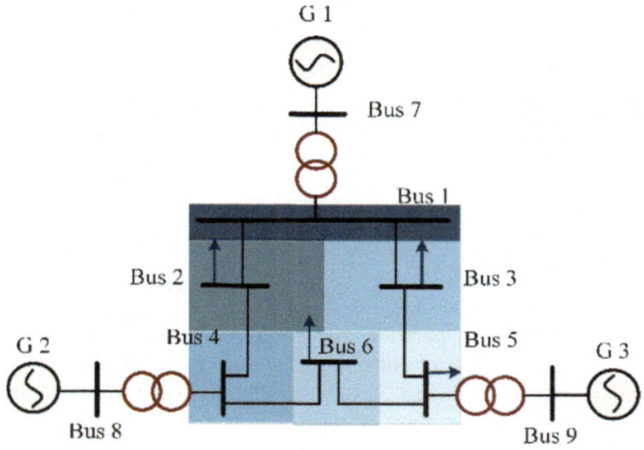

Fig. 6.10 The inertia spatial distribution of system node

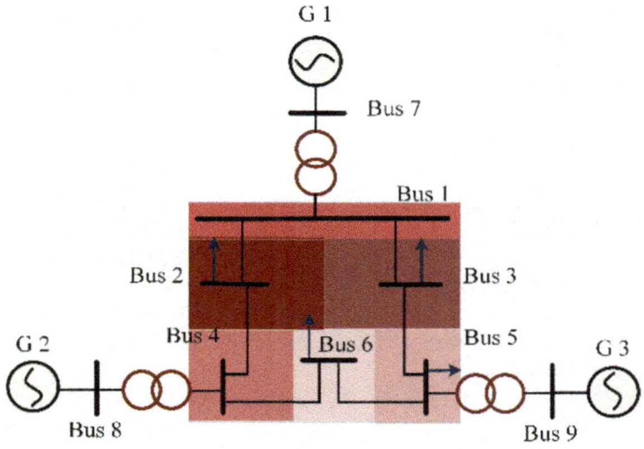

Fig. 6.11 The inertia time-varying of system node

6.5 Conclusion

This paper provides a nodal inertia assessment by considering spatial-temporal distribution characteristics. Spatial distribution index and time-varying index are proposed to analyze the changing process of inertia distribution under disturbances in both dimensions. The study cases are carried out in IEEE 3-machine 9-bus system. The simulation results show that the inertia responses among each node are different, which reveals the spatial-temporal characteristics of inertia distribution. Nodal inertia exhibits varying characteristics in both the spatial and temporal dimensions, which gives the operators a clear perspective of inertia distribution to maintain system stability.

Acknowledgements This study was funded by X (grant number Y).

Disclosure of Interests The authors have no competing interests to declare that are relevant to the content of this article.

References

1. Tielens, P.: Operation and control of power systems with low synchronous inertia. Ph.D. dissertation, Katholieke Universiteit Leuven, Leuven, Belgium (2017)
2. Sharma, S., Huang, S.H., Sarma, N.: System inertial frequency response estimation and impact of renewable resources in ERCOT interconnection. In: Proceeding IEEE Power Energy Social General Meeting, pp. 1–6 (2011)
3. Tamrakar, U., Shrestha, D., Maharjan, M., Bhattarai, B.P., Hansen, T.M., Tonkoski, R.: Virtual inertia: current trends and future directions. Appl. Sci. **7**(7), Art. no. 654 (2017)
4. Ørum, E., et al.: Future system inertia. ENTSOE, Brussels, Tech. Rep. (2015)
5. Rainey, M.J., Oyedokun D.T.O.: Load modelling effects on power system inertia response. In: 2020 IEEE PES/IAS PowerAfrica, Nairobi, Kenya, pp. 1–5 (2020). https://doi.org/10.1109/PowerAfrica49420.2020.9219951
6. Ashton, P., Saunders, C., Taylor, G., Carter, A., Bradley, M.: Inertia estimation of the GB power system using synchrophasor measurements. In: 2017 IEEE Power and Energy Society General Meeting, Chicago, IL, USA, pp. 1–1 (2017). https://doi.org/10.1109/PESGM.2017.8274031
7. Inoue, T., Taniguchi, H., Ikeguchi, Y., Yoshida, K.: Estimation of power system inertia constant and capacity of spinning-reserve support generators using measured frequency transients. IEEE Trans. Power Syst. **12**(1), 136–143 (1997)
8. Ashton, P.M., Saunders, C.S., Taylor, G.A., Carter, A.M., Bradley, M.E.: Inertia estimation of the GB power system using synchrophasor measurements. IEEE Trans. Power Syst. **30**(2), 701–709 (2015)
9. Chassin, D.P., Huang, Z., Donnelly, M.K., Hassler, C., Ramirez, E., Ray, C.: Estimation of WECC system inertia using observed frequency transients. IEEE Trans. Power Syst. **20**(2), 1190–1192 (2005)
10. Tuttelberg, K., Kilter, J., Wilson, D.H., Uhlen, K.: Estimation of power system inertia from ambient wide area measurements. IEEE Trans. Power Syst. **33**(6), 7249–7257 (2018)
11. Fanglei, L.I.U., Guoyi, X.U., Fan, W.A.N.G., et al.: Assessment method of system partition inertia based on differential calculation method. Autom. Electr. Power. Syst **44**(20), 46–53 (2020)
12. Li, S., Xia, Z., Cheng, X., et al.: Continuous estimation method of power system inertia based on ambient disturbance. In: Proceedings of the CSEE vol. 40, no.14, pp. 4430–4439, 4723 (2020)
13. Lavanya, L., Swarup K.S.: Estimation of area-wise effective inertia of a power system using energy variations. In: 2022 22nd National Power Systems Conference (NPSC), New Delhi, India, pp. 667–672 (2022). https://doi.org/10.1109/NPSC57038.2022.10069319
14. Shen, J., et al.: Data-driven equivalent inertia partition estimation of power systems. In: 2022 Power System and Green Energy Conference (PSGEC), Shanghai, China, pp. 744–748 (2022). https://doi.org/10.1109/PSGEC54663.2022.9881057
15. Fanhong, Z., Junbo, Z.: The temporal and spatial characteristics of power system inertia and its analysis method. Proceed CSEE **40**(1), 50–58+373 (2020) (in Chinese)
16. Yuanchen, L.I., Yunfeng, W.E.N., Xi, Y.E., et al.: Estimation method of power system nodal inertia based on multi-innovation identification. Electr. Power. Autom Equip. **42**(8), 89–95 (2022) (in Chinese)

17. Fanglei, L.I.U., Guoyi, X.U., Jiahao, L.I.U., et al.: Inertia distribution characteristics of power system considering structure and parameters of power grid. Autom. Electr. Power. Syst **45**(23), 60–67 (2021) (in Chinese)
18. Jiahao, L., Cheng, W., Tianshu, B.: Node equivalent inertia index for temporal-spatial frequency dynamics of renewable energy power system and its applications. Proceed CSEE (2022) (in Chinese)
19. Liang, Q., Yu, J., Guo, Y.: Evaluation of equivalent inertia time coefficient for power system based on frequency trajectory. Power Syst. Technol. **47**(2), 435–448 (2023) (in Chinese)

Chapter 7
A Non-contact Strategy for Upper Limb Terminal Rehabilitation Trajectory Demonstration and Execution

Dongkai Xu, Jiahui Ding, and Junyou Yang

Abstract With the aging of the population and the continuous increase in the number of people with upper limb impairments, the rehabilitation process requires long-term treatment and supervision by professionals, making the rational allocation of medical resources a significant challenge. There is an urgent need to combine the clinical experience of physicians and the high-precision execution capabilities of rehabilitation robots to construct a upper limb rehabilitation trajectory demonstration and execution system. However, traditional drag demonstration cannot achieve non-contact demonstration and lacks flexibility, and the establishment and maintenance costs of the upper limb exoskeleton mirror system are high. In response to these issues, a non-contact upper limb terminal rehabilitation trajectory demonstration and execution system is designed using computer vision and end-effector robotic arms. Experimental results show that the constructed system can complete the "demonstration-planning-execution" human–machine interactive upper limb rehabilitation training task. It can monitor the safety in real time and optimize the trajectory deployment operation, can be used to establish a professionally effective rehabilitation action library, which helps physicians improve the training plan by adjusting the trajectory according to the patient's condition and progress, achieve better rehabilitation effects.

7.1 Introduction

Upper limb dysfunction can be caused by various reasons, including stroke, nerve damage, etc. These diseases and injuries can cause the muscles of the upper limb to be unable to move and coordinate normally, severely affecting the patient's daily life and independence [1]. The use of rehabilitation robots can trigger neuroplasticity

D. Xu (✉) · J. Ding · J. Yang
Shenyang University of Technology, Shenyang, China
e-mail: xudongkai2023@smail.sut.edu.cn

F. P. García Márquez et al. (eds.), *Computing, Internet of Things and Data Analytics*, Smart Innovation, Systems and Technologies 387,
https://doi.org/10.1007/978-3-031-87154-2_7

by providing repetitive exercises for impaired functions. In this regard, rehabilitation robots are defined as operating machines that perform specific movements [2]. Compared with traditional manual treatment methods, rehabilitation robots have the potential to provide long-term, intensive, and precise rehabilitation treatments. At the same time, with the help of remote control technology, they can provide treatment for patients without the need for a therapist to be present. A therapist can even control multiple robots at the same time, thereby achieving higher frequency treatments and effectively reducing costs.

Upper limb rehabilitation robots are divided into robot-assisted (RA) rehabilitation robot systems, functional electrical stimulation (FES) based rehabilitation robot systems, and virtual reality (VR) based rehabilitation robot systems according to the feedback method [3]. Among them, robot-assisted rehabilitation robot systems can be divided into end-effectors, exoskeleton robots, and the recently emerging limb-type robots according to the robot structure [4]. To promote the clinical application of rehabilitation robot systems, it is more suitable to choose end-effector upper limb rehabilitation robot systems with lower cost, stronger safety and usability, and easy to generalize rehabilitation training tasks. The current upper limb rehabilitation training action capture mainly uses wearable devices and computer vision technology [5]. For example, The authors in [6] collect Surface electromyography (sEMG) of the arm and hand, and combine algorithms to recognize gestures to control the exoskeleton. The author in [7] uses Kinect v2 to combine rehabilitation technology with virtual environment recognition. Among the above training action capture methods, wearable devices depend on expensive equipment, and computer vision focuses on the effects of individual bodies and is rarely used in rehabilitation training systems involving rehabilitation robots.

The current research on trajectory planning is mainly to improve the similarity of planning trajectories and demonstration actions, and to ensure the feasibility of the obtained trajectories on the existing robot hardware platform, and the generalization level of motion planning relative to different patient individuals and different rehabilitation tasks. Literature [8] uses functional principal component analysis (FPCA) to extract the main movement modes, and then formulates plans by optimizing reduced weights, but the process of robot planning by directly implementing human behavior is cumbersome. The author in [9] builds joint trajectories specific to tasks and patients based on observing subjects, avoiding motion planning in Cartesian space and inverse kinematics, but requires supervised learning to reach the target joint configuration.

The organization of this paper is as follows. In Sect. 7.2, we briefly discuss the current related work and introduce the research focus of this paper. Section 7.3 highlights system architecture and functional design. In Sect. 7.4, comparative analysis experiments and operation effect detection are carried out. Section 7.5 concludes the paper.

7.2 Related Work

The methods currently available for establishing a professional action library mainly include traditional drag demonstration, remote demonstration based on computer vision, and upper limb exoskeleton mirror rehabilitation robot system [10]. Drag demonstration relies on the physical contact of the therapist, which may cause the therapist to fatigue and it is difficult to accurately replicate the action trajectory. The exoskeleton system requires advanced algorithms to ensure the accuracy and smoothness of the action, and the cost of establishing and maintaining the system is high. Establishing a rehabilitation action library based on computer vision does not require physical contact, can quickly learn demonstration actions and deploy them on the mechanical arm, providing an efficient, accurate and widely adaptable solution.

The author in [11] summarizes the research progress in unmarked motion recognition based on computer vision. Researchers proposes a method for recognizing rehabilitation movements based on Open Pose posture estimation and Gated Recurrent Unit (GRU) networks [12], which has high recognition accuracy and real-time performance. However, deploying movements to physical robotic arms is relatively cumbersome and it is difficult to control the amplitude of movements. These researches emphasize the accuracy of movements, but do not consider the simplicity of deploying rehabilitation movements to robotic arms. Especially for complex movements, this can increase the burden of data analysis and optimization. Compared with the existing methods, the contributions of this article can be summarized as follows:

- Establish a motion capture system based on computer vision, record the physician's demonstration trajectory, help the physician to improve the training plan by adjusting the demonstration trajectory, and monitor the safety in real time.
- Use Matlab and Ros/MoveIt! to build a data processing and robot control system, optimize the demonstration trajectory, and use the RRTConnectkConfigDefault algorithm for spatial motion planning to optimize the trajectory deployment operation.

7.3 System Architecture

The entire research process is illustrated in Fig. 7.1. Firstly, a motion capture system is built based on Kinect v2, which records the trajectory of the physician's rehabilitation movements and visualizes the spatial three-dimensional path data points. Secondly, a data processing system is built based on Matlab tools, which optimizes the data through Kalman filtering and spline interpolation and selects the effects. Finally, a robotic arm control system is built based on MoveIt!, which visualizes the optimized trajectory data in Rviz, calculates the path execution planning, and executes in the real environment.

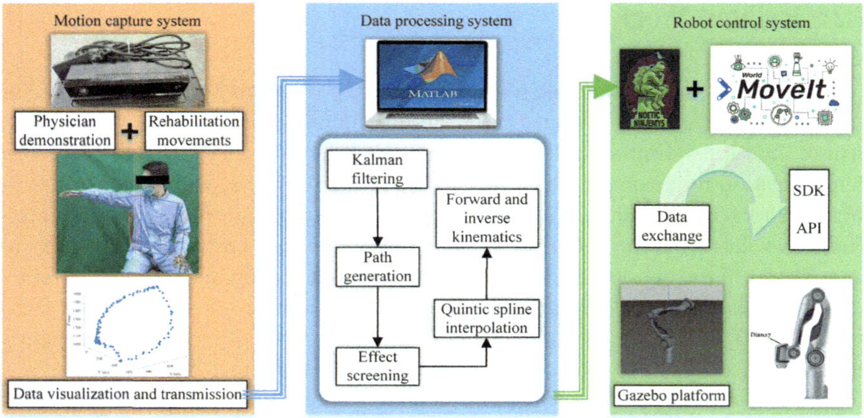

Fig. 7.1 Flowchart of system construction

7.3.1 Recording of Demonstration Trajectory

Skeleton Tracking and Trajectory Extraction Based on Kinect v2. Human skeleton tracking is implemented based on Kinect v2, and follows the process planning shown in Fig. 7.2 for real-time detection and tracking. Firstly, the device is initialized to detect users within the field of view, display colors to distinguish different individual users. Then, the detected torso is calibrated for key points and coordinate mapping, the skeleton frame is updated to record skeleton point data.

Real-Time Monitoring and Extraction of Demonstration Trajectory Based on QT5. In Fig. 7.3, A real-time monitoring UI for the demonstration trajectory and patient movement is designed using QT5. During the entire process, a threshold warning window is added. Whether it is during the physician's demonstration or the patient's rehabilitation, when an abnormal joint angle is detected, a warning will pop up, which helps to monitor the safety of the rehabilitation training process in real time.

7.3.2 Trajectory Optimization

The three-dimensional coordinate points captured by Kinect v2 have noise and jitter, and are also limited by the sampling frequency of the device, resulting in poor continuity of the demonstration trajectory. To address these issues, this paper designs a Kalman filter and quintic spline interpolation to optimize the trajectory, improve the accuracy of the skeleton key point data, and improve data continuity, making the transition smoother. When the external effect on the system is added, the main formulas of Kalman filtering [13] are as follows.

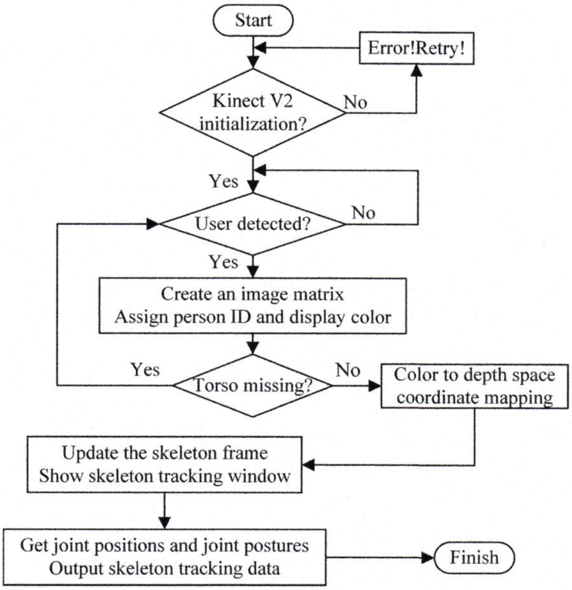

Fig. 7.2 Process of skeleton point tracking based on Kinect v2

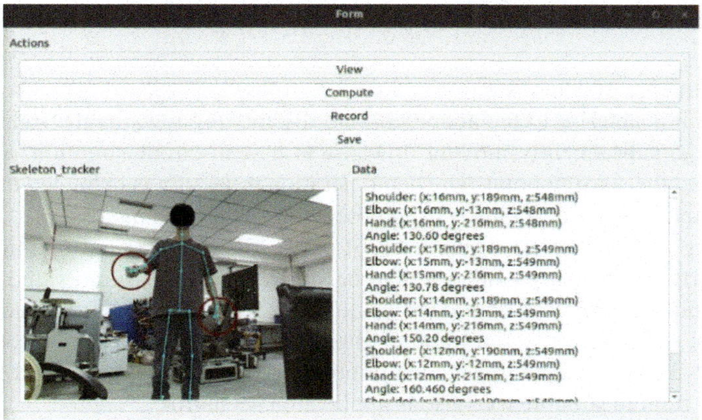

Fig. 7.3 Real-time monitoring and extraction of demonstration trajectory based on QT5

(1) Calculate the predicted state value:

$$\hat{x}'_k = A\hat{x}_{k-1} + Bu_{k-1} \tag{7.1}$$

where, $\hat{x}_k$: State vector at time k; $\hat{x}_k$: Predicted state at time k; $\hat{x}_k$: Optimized predicted state at time k; u_k: External influence on the system at time k; A: State transfer matrix; B: Input control matrix.

(2) Calculate the predicted error covariance matrix between the predicted value and the actual value:

$$P_k' = AP_{k-1} + A^T + Q \tag{7.2}$$

where, P: Error matrix; Q: Process noise covariance matrix.

(3) Under the conditions of formulas (7.1) and (7.2), the Kalman gain is obtained:

$$K_k = P_k' H^T (HP_k' H^T + R)^{-1} \tag{7.3}$$

where, K_k: Kalman gain (observation weight) at time k; H: Measurement matrix; R: Observation noise covariance matrix.

(4) Calculate the estimated value:

$$X_k = x_k' + K_k(Z_k - Hx_k') \tag{7.4}$$

where, Z_k: Observed value at time k;

(5) Calculate the error covariance matrix:

$$P_K = (I - K_k H)P_K' \tag{7.5}$$

The sequence of demonstration actions is as follows: The starting point of the right hand action is anterior to the abdomen, initially moving towards the right and then downwards, subsequently moving upwards in a semi-circular motion, and finally returning to the starting point. The demonstration trajectory is extracted through the motion capture system in Fig. 7.3 and processed using a Kalman filter.

The Fig. 7.4 shows the comparison of the predicted corrected optimized value and the original measured value. It can be seen that the measured value fluctuates greatly, and the predicted optimized value reduces the impact of data noise. From this, it can be inferred that the Kalman filter can play a key role in the processing of Kinect v2 skeleton tracking data, can improve the quality and usability of the data, and make it more suitable for various application scenarios.

Compared with cubic spline interpolation [14], quintic spline interpolation [15] has more constraints. Compared with the literature [16] that uses quintic polynomial interpolation to fit all data points, quintic spline interpolation uses a quintic polynomial between every two data points, forming a continuously differentiable curve, which is more suitable for application scenarios that need to generate smooth curves such as path planning. The mathematical expression of the quintic polynomial interpolation is as follows:

$$q(t) = a_0 + a_1(t - t_0)^2 + a_2(t - t_0)^3 + a_3(t - t_0)^4 + a_4(t - t_0)^5 \tag{7.6}$$

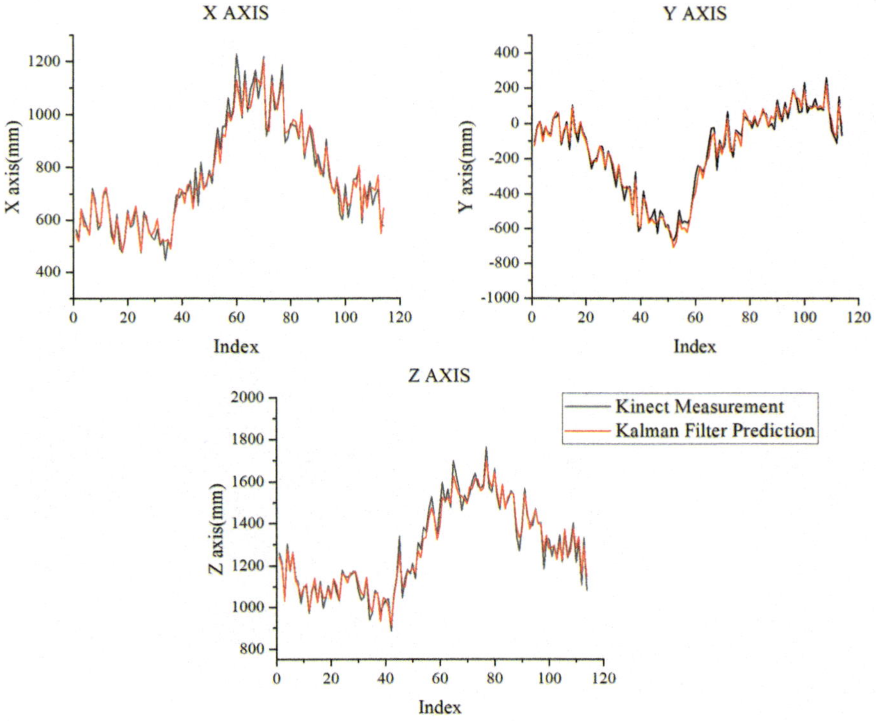

Fig. 7.4 Comparison of kalman filtering effects

where, a_0, a_1, ..., a_5 are unknown parameters.

Six constraints are set, namely position, velocity, and acceleration information at both ends, given as follows:

$$\begin{cases} q(t_0) = q_0, \; q(t_0) = q_1 \\ \dot{q}(t_0) = V_0, \; \dot{q}(t_0) = V_1 \\ \ddot{q}(t_0) = \alpha_0, \; \ddot{q}(t_0) = \alpha_1 \end{cases} \tag{7.7}$$

Assuming $T = t_1 - t_0$, $h = q_1 - q_0$ we can calculate:

$$\begin{cases} a0 = q0, \quad a3 = \frac{1}{2T^3}[20h - (8v_1 + 12v_0)T - (3\alpha_0 - \alpha_1)T^2] \\ a1 = V0, \; a4 = \frac{1}{2T^3}[-30h - (14v_1 + 16v_0)T + (3\alpha_0 - 2\alpha_1)T^2] \\ a2 = \frac{1}{2}\alpha_0, \quad a5 = \frac{1}{2T^3}[12h - 6(v_1 + v_0)T + (\alpha_1 - \alpha_0)T^2] \end{cases} \tag{7.8}$$

Figure 7.5 illustrates the captured demonstration trajectory, the path after Kalman filtering, the path after quintic spline interpolation, and the trajectory visualization in the Ros/Rviz. A start_point is set as the starting point of the motion, and three turn_points are set and displayed with TF coordinate axes to indicate the direction

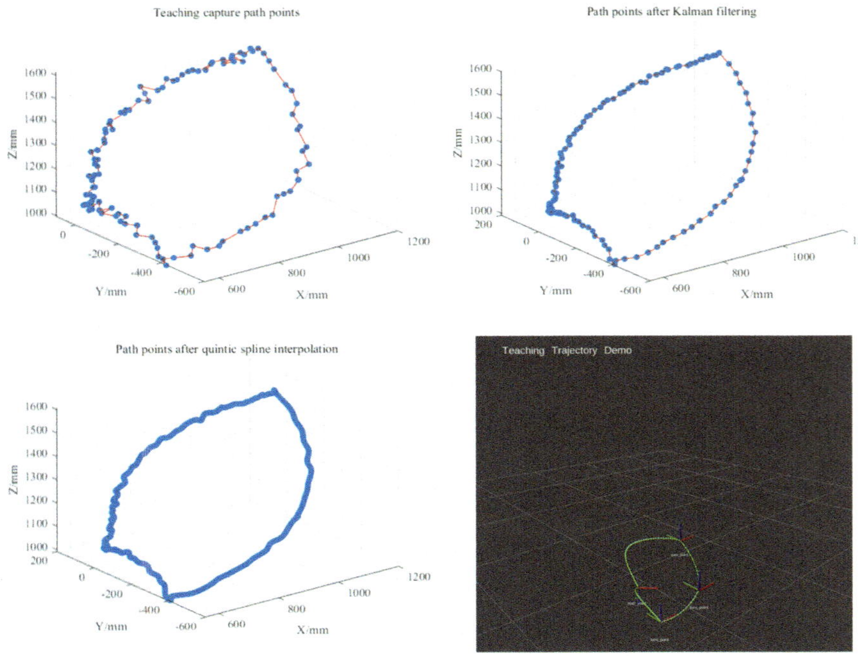

Fig. 7.5 Process of demonstration trajectory optimization and spatial visualization

of trajectory motion. It can be intuitively seen that after the trajectory optimization through Kalman filtering and quintic spline interpolation, noise and errors are reduced, the continuity of motion is improved, making the motion more natural, smooth, and precise.

7.4 Experiment and Analysis

After recording and optimizing the demonstration trajectory, it is handed over to Ros/MoveIt! for spatial trajectory planning. By loading the robot URDF model, setting the target position and joint values, and selecting the RRTConnectkConfigDefault [17] algorithm, the robot's motion constraints are applied to the path planning. Finally, the SDK library of the Diana7 robotic arm is called to execute the demonstration trajectory. The setup of the experimental environment is illustrated in Fig. 7.6.

By dragging the robotic arm to reproduce the same action and preprocessing the spatial position of the detected end of the robotic arm, the influence of different scales and distributions can be eliminated, resulting in the error analysis as shown in Fig. 7.7. The closeness between points in three-dimensional space is judged by the size of the Euclidean distance. By calculation, the average Euclidean distance of

Fig. 7.6 Construction of the overall experimental environment

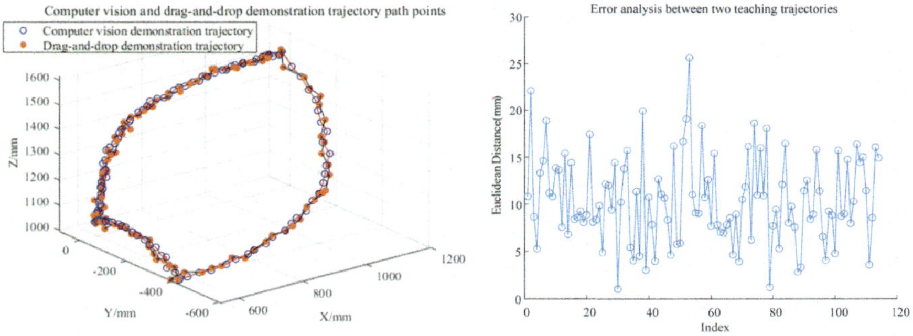

Fig. 7.7 Error comparison analysis between computer vision demonstration trajectory and drag-and-drop demonstration trajectory

the two groups of trajectories is 10.7699 mm, and the maximum Euclidean distance is 25.9257 mm. Considering the application background and requirements of upper limb rehabilitation training, it can be judged that the two methods have a high consistency in reproducing the same action. However, the trajectory processed based on computer vision is smoother, and the accuracy and stability are higher.

The Fig. 7.8 shows the change curve of the joint values of the robotic arm when recording and sorting the execution demonstration trajectory. It can be seen that after the trajectory is optimized, the RRTConnectkConfigDefault algorithm is used to smooth the joint angle to a certain extent, ensuring the continuity of the joint rotation, so that the robotic arm can execute the trajectory more smoothly, without causing too large amplitude changes. It also allows the robotic arm to adapt to a wide range of patient-specific needs and rehabilitation trajectories, making it a versatile tool in the field of rehabilitation therapy.

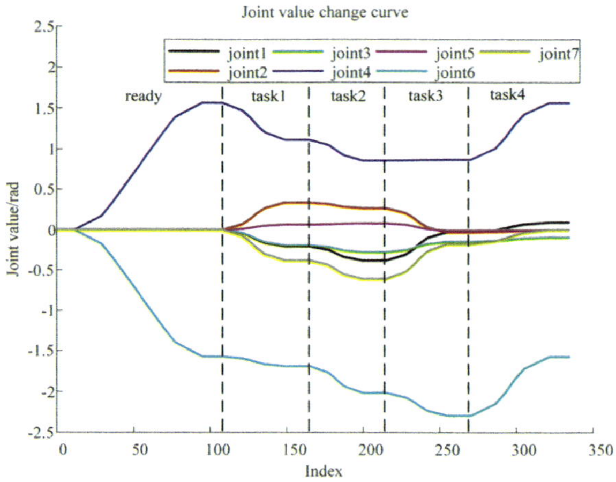

Fig. 7.8 Change curve of joint values in trajectory execution

7.5 Conclusion

This paper constructs a non-contact upper limb rehabilitation trajectory demonstration and execution system using computer vision and end-effector robotic arms. Through comprehensive research planning and experimental analysis, the "demonstration–planning-execution" human–machine interactive upper limb rehabilitation training task is completed, verifying the feasibility and effectiveness of the proposed method. The experimental results show that the proposed method can record the physician's demonstration trajectory through the motion capture system, and under the data processing and robotic arm control system, control the end of the robotic arm to carry out rehabilitation training along a smooth path. The implementation effect of this method can be used to establish a professionally effective demonstration action library, and adjust the training plan according to the patient's condition and progress, providing more consistent, controllable and traceable rehabilitation training, achieving better rehabilitation effects, and alleviating social medical pressure.

References

1. Almomani, F., Alghwiri, A.A., Alghadir, A.H.: Prevalence of upper limb pain and disability and its correlates with demographic and personal factors. J. Pain Res. **36**(1), 2691–2700 (2019)
2. Qassim, H.M., Wan Hasan, W.Z.: A review on upper limb rehabilitation robots. Appl. Sci. **10**(19), 69–76 (2020)
3. Moulaei, K., Bahaadinbeigy, K., Haghdoostd, A.A.: Overview of the role of robots in upper limb disabilities rehabilitation: a scoping review. Archives of Public Health **81**(1), 76–84 (2023)
4. Tao, R., Ocampo, R., Fong, J.: Modeling and Emulating a Physiotherapist's Role in Robot-Assisted Rehabilitation. Advanced Intelligent Systems **2**(7), 181–190 (2020)

5. Gu, Y., Xu, Y., Shen, Y.: A review of hand function rehabilitation systems based on hand motion recognition devices and artificial intelligence. Brain Sci. **12**(8), 10–19 (2022)
6. Hameed, H.K., Hassan, W.Z.W., Shafie, S.: A review on surface electromyography-controlled hand robotic devices used for rehabilitation and assistance in activities of daily living. JPO: J. Prosthet.S Orthot. 32(1), 3–13 (2020)
7. Maskeliūnas, R., Damasevicius, R., Blazauskas, T.: BiomacVR: A virtual reality-based system for precise human posture and motion analysis in rehabilitation exercises using depth sensors. Electronics **12**(2), 33–39 (2023)
8. Averta, G., Della Santina, C., Valenza, G.: Exploiting upper-limb functional principal components for human-like motion generation of anthropomorphic robots. J. Neuroeng. Rehabil. **17**(2), 1–15 (2020)
9. Qureshi, A.H., Miao, Y., Simeonov, A.: Motion planning networks: Bridging the gap between learning-based and classical motion planners. IEEE Trans. Rob. **37**(1), 48–66 (2020)
10. Gull, M.A., Bai, S., Bak, T.: A review on design of upper limb exoskeletons. Robotics **9**(1), 16 (2020)
11. Moro, M., Marchesi, G., Hesse, F.: Markerless vs. marker-based gait analysis: A proof of concept study. Sensors 22(5), 2011 (2022)
12. Hang, Y.A.N., Gang, C., Yao, T.: Human rehabilitation action recognition based on pose estimation and GRU network. Comput. Eng. **47**(1), 12–20 (2021)
13. Khodarahmi, M., Maihami, V.: A review on Kalman filter models. Archives of Computational Methods in Engineering **30**(1), 727–747 (2023)
14. Hao, W., Rui, D., Song, L.: Data processing method of noise logging based on cubic spline interpolation. Applied Mathematics and Nonlinear Sciences **6**(1), 93–102 (2021)
15. Ciesielski, M.: Numerical Algorithms for Approximation of Fractional Integrals and Derivatives Based on Quintic Spline Interpolation. Symmetry **16**(2), 252–261 (2024)
16. Huang, Y., Zhao, M., Zhang, J.: The position control method of two joint manipulator based on sliding mode and trajectory setting algorithm of quintic polynomial interpolation. In: 2021 IEEE International Conference on Networking, Sensing and Control (ICNSC), vol. 1, pp. 1–6. IEEE (2021)
17. Zapata-Impata, B.S., Gil, P., Pomares, J., et al.: Fast geometry-based computation of grasping points on three-dimensional point clouds. Int. J. Adv. Robot. Syst. **16**(1), 35–53 (2019)

Chapter 8
Frequency Regulation Control Method for Wind Energy Storage Based on VSG

Haixin Wang, Deyun Han, Haoqian Cui, Shanshan Cheng, Shengyang Lu, Jing Li, Hongyu Lu, Xiayu Liu, and Junyou Yang

Abstract In recent years, wind power has further developed, and clean and renewable energy forms are the direction of future power development. Permanent magnet synchronous generator (PMSG) lacks the inertia support capability of traditional synchronous generator sets. Although virtual synchronous generators (VSG) can provide inertia and damping for the system, the application of VSG may bring new problems to the stability of the power system, such as insufficient inertia support. This article proposes a wind storage joint frequency regulation control method based on VSG control to address this issue. First, a mathematical model of battery energy storage system (BESS) is constructed. Second, BESS is integrated into a virtual synchronous generator based on Permanent magnet synchronous generator (VSG-PMSG) technology. Finally, effective management of system frequency was achieved by utilizing the droop control characteristics. The simulation findings demonstrate that the wind storage integrated frequency modulation control system has better frequency response attributes.

8.1 Introduction

The production and application of large-scale wind power are beneficial for solving energy consumption and environmental pollution problems, however there are also drawbacks such as complex control, large fluctuations in power generation, and strong randomness. Among them, the permanent magnet synchronous generator

H. Wang · D. Han (✉) · S. Cheng · J. Li · H. Lu · X. Liu · J. Yang
Shenyang University of Technology, Shenyang, China
e-mail: gugyuhnu@126.com

S. Lu
Electric Power Research Institute of State Grid Liaoning Electric Power Supply Co., Ltd., Shenyang, China

H. Cui
Fuxin Electric Power Supply Company, State Grid Liaoning Electric Power Co. Ltd., Fuxin, China

F. P. García Márquez et al. (eds.), *Computing, Internet of Things and Data Analytics*, Smart Innovation, Systems and Technologies 387,
https://doi.org/10.1007/978-3-031-87154-2_8

(PMSG) grid connection method causes the rotor speed to decouple from the system frequency, making it lack the inertia support ability of traditional synchronous generator sets [1]. Virtual synchronous generators (VSG) control has been introduced to address this issue, which can effectively suppress fluctuations in the system during power oscillations and frequency changes using virtual inertia and virtual damping [2]. However, the application of VSG may bring new problems to the stability of the power system, such as insufficient inertia support.

To address the above issues, energy storage is introduced to connect to the VSG-PMSG system. Reference [3] studies the intraday dynamic energy reserve scheduling at two-time scales and proposes a stochastic dynamic programming method. References [4, 5] develop a strategizing structure and operational energy storage tactics to restrict the frequency change rate of power systems with substantial wind power integration rates within industry requirements. Reference [6] proposes a hybrid energy storage system scale and regulate scheme derived from probabilistic forecast to economically and efficiently smooth out wind power fluctuations. Reference [7] proposes a novel coordinated wind power smooth management approach for multiple wind turbines and energy storage systems, considering the downstream influence of wind farms. Reference [8] tackles the difficulty of regulating a wind energy generation system linked to the power grid, which includes a BESS and operates under different actual wind speed distributions. Reference [9] proposes a wind-storage integrated system self-scheduling model based on deep reinforcement learning to address the constraints of wind power variability on the commercial potential of energy storage incorporated systems in the real-time market. Reference [10] proposes an option strategy to simulate inertia using energy stored in supercapacitor directly interfaced with the converter direct current (DC) link.

Based on the above research status, in order to further enhance the inertia support capability of the VSG-PMSG system, this paper emphasizes the control method of battery connected to the VSG-PMSG system, considers the sway of wind power on the power grid, establishes a mathematical model of battery energy storage, adopts constant power rate control, and proves that the BESS can release or absorb additional energy when the system frequency changes, increase the equivalent inertia time system coefficient, and more effectively contribute to system frequency regulation. Furthermore, combined with the droop control traits, it achieves inertia support for the VSG-PMSG system. Through simulation analysis, it has been demonstrated that the wind storage integrated control system has better frequency response attributes.

8.2 Wind Storage Joint Frequency Regulation Control Strategy

8.2.1 *The Overall Control Strategy for Battery Integration into VSG-PMSG*

Figure 8.1 shows the VSG-PMSG system with battery energy storage. VSG-PMSG maintains a constant bus voltage through vector control strategy at the machine end, and maintains grid frequency and voltage stability through VSG control at the network end. In an energy storage system, the inverter acts as a rectifier when absorbing energy, converting alternating current (AC) into DC, and acts as an inverter when releasing energy, converting direct current into alternating current. To reduce grid harmonics and improve power reliability, a filter is used to smooth the AC waveform output by the inverter. The BESS is connected to the VSG-PMSG system through a transformer to ensure output voltage matching. This connectivity approach allows the battery system to be directly connected to the AC bus, achieving coordinated operation with the wind power generation system.

In the figure: u_{dc} is the DC bus voltage, u* dc is the given value of the DC bus voltage, i_{sd}, i_{sq} are the DC and AC axis currents, P_{ref}, Q_{ref} are the reference values for active and reactive power, u_{abc}, i_{abc} are the three-phase voltage and current at the output of the filter, e_{abc} represent the three-phase voltage on the grid side.

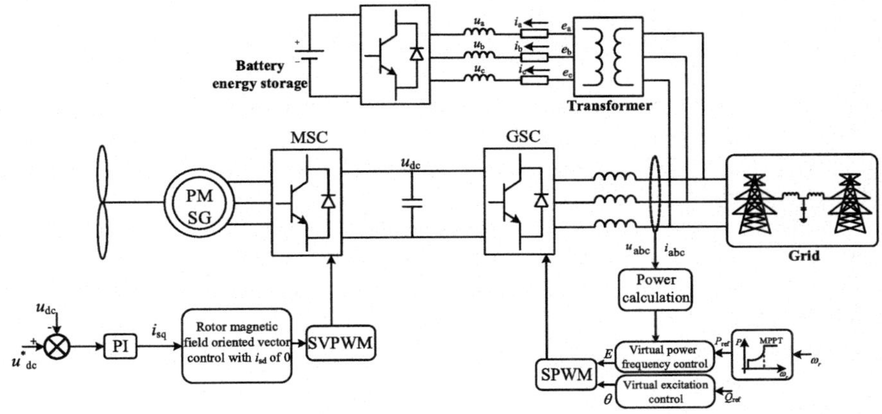

Fig. 8.1 VSG-PMSG system with battery storage

8.2.2 Battery Energy Storage Management Method

This article sets the power to be positive during energy storage charging and negative during energy storage discharge. The reference current command for the energy storage system is represented by Eq. (8.1).

$$\begin{cases} i_{\mathrm{d}}^{*} = 2/3\frac{Q_{\mathrm{g}}e_{\mathrm{q}}+P_{\mathrm{g}}e_{\mathrm{d}}}{e_{\mathrm{q}}^{2}+e_{\mathrm{d}}^{2}} \\ i_{\mathrm{q}}^{*} = 2/3\frac{P_{\mathrm{g}}e_{\mathrm{q}}-Q_{\mathrm{g}}e_{\mathrm{d}}}{e_{\mathrm{q}}^{2}+e_{\mathrm{d}}^{2}} \end{cases} \tag{8.1}$$

where i^* $_{\mathrm{d}}$ i^* $_{\mathrm{q}}$ is the reference value for the dq axis current, P_{g} and Q_{g} are the active power and reactive power output or absorbed by the energy storage system, respectively, e_{d} and e_{q} are the dq axis components of the grid connected voltage.

According to Eq. (8.1), when $Q_{\mathrm{g}} = 0$, its reference current command is represented by Eq. (8.2).

$$\begin{cases} i_{\mathrm{d}}^{*} = 2/3\frac{P_{\mathrm{g}}e_{\mathrm{d}}}{e_{\mathrm{q}}^{2}+e_{\mathrm{d}}^{2}} \\ i_{\mathrm{q}}^{*} = 2/3\frac{P_{\mathrm{g}}e_{\mathrm{q}}}{e_{\mathrm{q}}^{2}+e_{\mathrm{d}}^{2}} \end{cases} \tag{8.2}$$

When using PI feedforward control, the voltage control signal of the PWM inverter in the BESS is represented by Eq. (8.3).

$$\begin{cases} u_{\mathrm{d}} = e_{\mathrm{d}} + \omega L i_{\mathrm{q}} - \left(k_{\mathrm{i}}/s + k_{\mathrm{p}}\right)\left(i_{\mathrm{d}}^{*} - i_{\mathrm{d}}\right) \\ u_{\mathrm{q}} = e_{\mathrm{q}} - \omega L i_{\mathrm{d}} - \left(k_{\mathrm{i}}/s + k_{\mathrm{p}}\right)\left(i_{\mathrm{q}}^{*} - i_{\mathrm{q}}\right) \end{cases} \tag{8.3}$$

where k_{p} and k_{i} are the proportional and integral coefficients of PI control, u_{d} and u_{q} are the dq axis components of the AC side voltage, i_{d} and i_{q} are the dq axis components of the AC side current, L is the filtering inductor, R is the filtering resistor, ω is the phase frequency.

The above system converts the voltage control signal on the dq axis into the corresponding signal in the three-phase stationary reference frame by converting the reference frame, thereby achieving constant power management of the BESS. The management principle of its circuit is shown in Fig. 8.2.

8.2.3 Frequency Modulation Control Strategy for BESS

When the BESS contributes to system frequency regulation, it can be written as:

$$f\frac{df}{dt} = \frac{\Delta P_{\mathrm{ess}} + \Delta P}{2H_{\mathrm{mn}}} \tag{8.4}$$

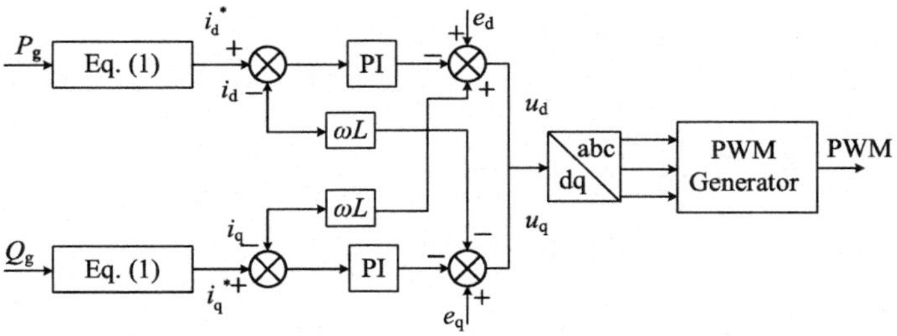

Fig. 8.2 Block diagram of constant power management for BESS

where H_{mn} is the equivalent inertia time constant of the wind storage joint system, ΔP_{ess} represents the change in active power output of the BESS during frequency changes, ΔP is the energy that the wind turbine can obtain by utilizing the rotational energy of the rotor.

There is a sudden change in frequency:

$$f(\Delta t + t)\frac{f(\Delta t + t) - f(t)}{\Delta t} = \frac{\Delta P_{\text{ess}} + \Delta P}{2H_{\text{mn}}} \tag{8.5}$$

The above equation can be converted to Eq. (8.6).

$$H_{\text{mn}} = \frac{\Delta E_0 + \Delta E_{\text{ess}}}{f(\Delta t + t)^2 - f(t)f(\Delta t + t)} \tag{8.6}$$

where ΔE_{ess} is the change in the BESS during the Δt period of the frequency modulation process, ΔE_0 is the kinetic energy released or assimilated by the generator rotor when the speed changes.

According to the above equation, when the system frequency changes, BESS releases or absorbs energy to increase the system inertia, which can better regulate the frequency. To actively participate in VSG-PMSG frequency control, BESS simulated the droop characteristics of traditional power sources as shown in Eq. (8.7).

$$P = \frac{(f_{\text{n}} - f)}{b} \tag{8.7}$$

where b is the droop coefficient, f_n is the rated frequency, f represents the actual measured frequency of the grid.

The control system of the main circuit during BESS participation in VSG-PMSG system frequency control is shown in Fig. 8.3.

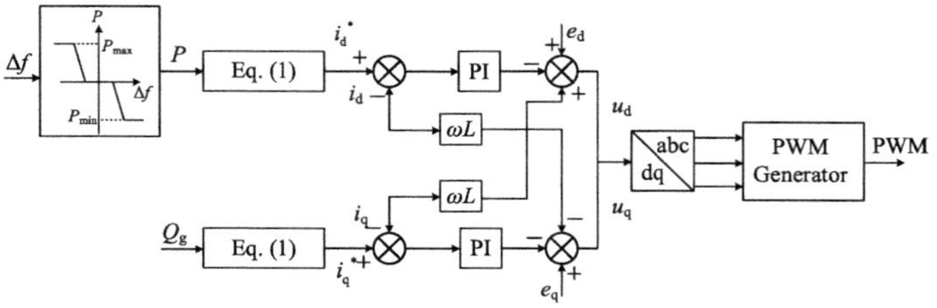

Fig. 8.3 Block diagram of constant power control for BESS

8.3 Simulation Analysis

8.3.1 Simulation Analysis of BESS

According to the above control method, a battery energy storage system is constructed, with the illustrated system variables in Table 8.1.

Assuming the BESS is initially charged with $P = 0.2$ MW and $Q = 0$ Var. After 1 second, the battery energy storage discharges with $P = -0.15$ MW and $Q = 0$ Var.

BESS demonstrated its ability to meet charging and discharging power requirements in Figs. 8.4 and 8.5, indicating its capability to receive and deliver necessary electrical power and operate at expected power levels. Figure 8.6 depicts the battery energy storage system's rapid response to system frequency changes, showing its effective adaptation to grid regulation, aiding in maintaining system frequency stability.

Table 8.1 Simulation variables for battery energy storage

Heading level	Font size and style
Battery terminal voltage /V	500
Battery DC side inductance /mH	1
Battery DC side resistance /Ω	0.01
AC side filtering inductance /mH	0.5
AC side filtering resistance /Ω	0.01
Current loop PI variables k_p	10
Current loop PI variables k_i	40

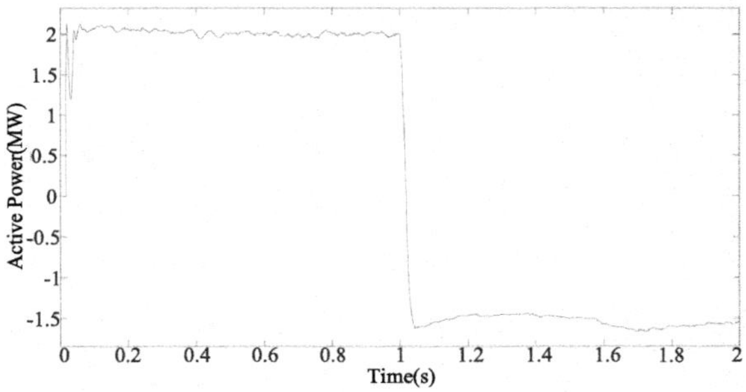

Fig. 8.4 Active power curve of BESS

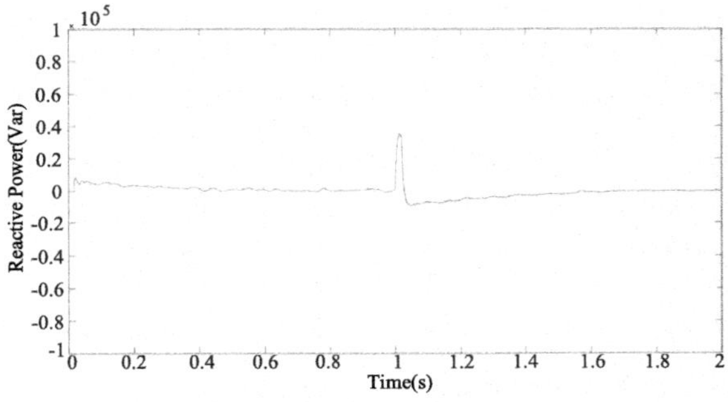

Fig. 8.5 Reactive power curve of BESS

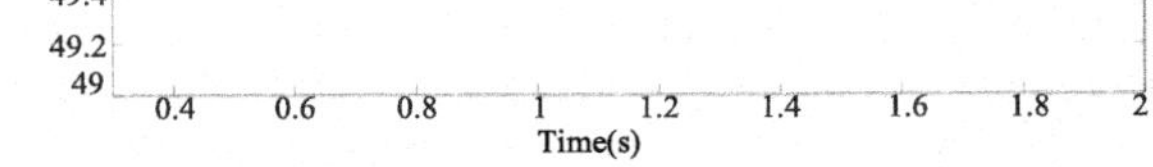

Fig. 8.6 Frequency response curve of BESS

8.3.2 Comparison of Frequency Dynamic Response Performance of BESS Connected to VSG-PMSG System

Evaluate the frequency management capability of the wind storage integrated system by introducing a 10 MW load at 2 seconds and removing it at 3 seconds, as illustrated in Fig. 8.7, which tracks the system frequency changes and BESS charging status in real-time. Evaluate the impact of BESS participation in frequency management on system frequency stability through simulation analysis.

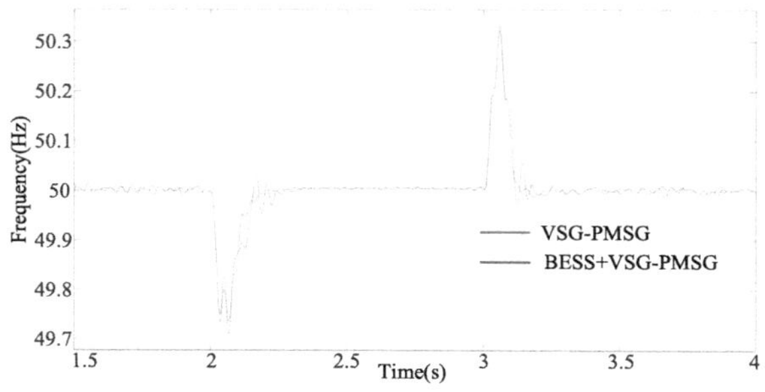

Fig. 8.7 BESS participates in frequency regulation

In Fig. 8.7, the response curve of BESS participating in frequency management shows a slight increase in the lowest point, which is 0.025 Hz higher than other systems. In addition, it can quickly restore stability. Meanwhile, when BESS participates in frequency regulation, the maximum frequency deviation is small, only 0.015 Hz, and remains relatively stable. This indicates that the wind storage integrated frequency management control system has a faster response speed when the grid frequency fluctuates, and can quickly participate in system frequency regulation.

8.4 Conclusion

This article proposes a joint control method for the integration of batteries into the VSG-PMSG system to address the issues of insufficient inertial support capacity and instability risk. Firstly, a mathematical model of the BESS is established, and a constant power regulation method is used to control the BESS. Furthermore, the battery is integrated into the VSG-PMSG system, proving that the BESS can release or absorb additional energy when the system frequency changes, thereby increasing the equivalent inertia time stability of the system and being more effectively engaged in system frequency regulation. This simulates the droop characteristics of traditional frequency modulation power sources and achieves frequency modulation control of the BESS in wind power systems. Finally, the above model was validated through simulation experiments, proving that battery connection has higher efficiency and reliability in grid frequency regulation for wind storage joint systems.

References

1. Wang, H., et al.: Model predictive control of PMSG-based wind turbines for frequency regulation in an isolated grid. IEEE Trans. Ind. Appl. **54**(4), 3077–3089 (2018)
2. Chen, S., Sun, Y., Hou, X., Han, H., Fu, S., Su, M.: Quantitative parameters design of VSG oriented to transient synchronization stability. IEEE Trans. Power Syst. **38**(5), 4978–4981 (2023)

3. Guo, Z., Wei, W., Shahidehpour, M., Chen, L., Mei, S.: Two-timescale dynamic energy and reserve dispatch with wind power and energy storage. IEEE Trans. Sustain. Energy **14**(1), 490–503 (2023)
4. Akram, U., Mithulananthan, N., Raza, M.Q., Shah, R., Milano, F.: RoCoF restrictive planning framework and wind speed forecast informed operation strategy of energy storage system. IEEE Trans. Power Syst. **36**(1), 224–234 (2021)
5. Liu, J., Wang, C., Zhao, J., Bi, T.: RoCoF constrained unit commitment considering spatial difference in frequency dynamics. IEEE Trans. Power Syst. **39**(1), 1111–1125 (2024)
6. Wan, C., Qian, W., Zhao, C., Song, Y., Yang, G.: Probabilistic forecasting based sizing and control of hybrid energy storage for wind power smoothing. IEEE Trans. Sustain. Energy **12**(4), 1841–1852 (2021)
7. Wang, X., Zhou, J., Qin, B., Guo, L.: Coordinated power smoothing control strategy of multi-wind turbines and energy storage systems in wind farm based on MADRL. IEEE Trans. Sustain. Energy **15**(1), 368–380 (2024)
8. Wang, H., et al.: Multiple adaptive model predictive controllers for frequency regulation in wind farms. IEEE Trans. Energy Convers. **38**(1), 15–26 (2023)
9. Wei, X., Xiang, Y., Li, J., Zhang, X.: Self-dispatch of wind-storage integrated system: a deep reinforcement learning approach. IEEE Trans. Sustain. Energy **13**(3), 1861–1864 (2022)
10. Berrueta, A., Sacristán, J., López, J., Rodríguez, J.L., Ursúa, A., Sanchis, P.: Inclusion of a supercapacitor energy storage system in DFIG and Full-converter PMSG wind turbines for inertia emulation. IEEE Trans. Ind. Appl. **59**(3), 3754–3763 (2023)

Chapter 9
Power Prediction Method of Wind Turbines Based on the SSA-BP Neural Network

Boyu Chen, Shanshan Cheng, Haoqian Cui, Shengyang Lu, Mingming Liang, Jiling Li, Jia Liu, Haixin Wang, and Junyou Yang

Abstract This paper presents an improved BP neural network nodel enhanced with the Sparrow Search Algorithm (SSA) for more accurate power forecasting of wind turbines. The Sparrow Search Algorithm is an efficient global optimization technique inspired by the foraging behavior and predator evasion strategies of sparrows. In this study. SSA is utilized to optimize the weights and bins-es of the BP neural network, aiming to address the issue of local minima commonly encountered by traditional BP networks when processing complex wind power data. By integrating the Sparrow Search Algorithm, the improved BP neural network can more effectively learn the nonlinear relationships between historical meteorological data and power output, thereby enhancing the model's predictive performance. The study concludes by comparing the forecasting results with those optimized by the Vulture Optimization Algorithm, demonstrating the superiority of the SSA-enhanced BP neural network in predicting the power output of wind turbine units with greater accuracy.

9.1 Introduction

Wind power, as a representative of energy, has been widely applied, effectively alleviating the shortage of electricity resources, reducing power generation costs. Decreasing greenhouse gas emissions, and enhancing social benefits. However, wind

B. Chen (✉) · S. Cheng · M. Liang · J. Li · J. Liu · H. Wang · J. Yang
Shenyang University of Technology, Shenyang, China
e-mail: 15566690188@163.com

S. Lu
Electric Power Research Institute of State Grid Liaoning Electric Power Supply Co., Ltd., Shenyang, China

H. Cui
Fuxin Electric Power Supply Company, State Grid Liaoning Electric Power Co. Ltd., Fuxin, China

F. P. García Márquez et al. (eds.), *Computing, Internet of Things and Data Analytics*, Smart Innovation, Systems and Technologies 387,
https://doi.org/10.1007/978-3-031-87154-2_9

power also possesses inherent draw backs, such as its stochastic fluctuations and anti-peak characteristics, which can impact the security and stability of the power grid. When integrated into the grid, the difference between peak and off-peak loads gradually increases, posing challenges to power dispatch and exacerbating peak load issues. With the increasing scale of wind power integration, more accurate wind power fore-casting is essential for enhancing the grid's acceptance of wind power. Therefore, proposing an efficient wind power forecasting method has become a hot topic in the industry.

Researchers have devised an advanced wind power forecasting model utilizing Gaussian processes allied with composite covariance functions [1]. This model dramatically augments prediction accuracy by assimilating both wind velocity and air density. In pursuit of further enhancements in forecast precision and dependability, a novel approach employs cluster analysis for discerning patterns in wind power output, coupled with time series analysis for short-range predictions [2]. Amidst escalating demands for heightened forecasting fidelity, a hierarchical Model Predictive Control (MPC) strategy is introduced, aimed at boosting grid stability and the efficacy of wind power integration via dynamic active power dispatch. This strategy accounts for the fluctuations and uncertainties inherent in wind power, as well as the synergies and coordination among different wind farms [3]. Concurrently, an innovative forecasting method has emerged, merging multi-parameter similar wind event matching with a weighted voting system to determine the most apt deep learning models. This method begins by scrutinizing historical wind events to pinpoint analogous wind power incidents, considering parameters like wind velocity, direction, air pressure, and other pertinent meteorological data. Following this, a weighted voting mechanism is implemented to evaluate and select diverse forecasting models, thereby improving the precision and reliability of the fore- casts [4]. To address the sequential data traits of meteorological variables impacting wind power, such as temperature, pressure, humidity, wind speed, and direction, Reference [5] employs Conditional Random Fields (CRFs). By capturing the temporal inter dependencies among various weather parameters, this method aims to refine the temporal precision of wind power forecasts, critical for real-time operational adjustments in grid management. Amidst the variability and intermittency of wind power production, the integration of reinforcement learning with traditional forecasting techniques modifies the weights of various models based on ongoing performance feedback, continually optimizing predictive accuracy in response to real-time environmental changes and operational data, addresses the dynamic challenges in wind power forecasting [6].

Reference [7] employs Extreme Learning Machines (ELMs) to provide probabilistic forecasts that encompass the inherent uncertainties of wind power generation. Known for their rapid learning capabilities, ELMs are utilized here to efficiently generate prediction intervals rather than single-point forecasts. This approach, by offering a range of possible power output scenarios, provides significant advantages for more effective risk management and operational planning under uncertainty. Reference [8] introduces a novel approach that combines spatial co-relation and time-series fore-casting techniques to enhance prediction accuracy over larger geographic areas and extended time periods. Reference [9] addresses the challenges of high penetration wind power forecasting by adopting a multi-scale approach, utilizing multiple-to-multiple mappings to project various input scales onto multiple forecasting time horizons. Reference [10] explores a method that combines multiple forecasting model sand employs fuzzy logic to generate prediction intervals. This approach utilizes an innovative composite technique, integrating outputs from various forecasting model and processing them through fuzzy logic to produce prediction intervals with upper and lower bounds, thus offering a more comprehensive perspective on the variability of wind power output.

This paper introduces an improved BP neural network model, enhanced by the sparrow algorithm, specifically designed for wind turbine power prediction. The sparrow algorithm, an emerging optimization technique, is renowned for its effectiveness in parameter optimization and global search capabilities. In this study, The SSA is applied to optimize the weights and biases of the BP neural network, addressing the issue of local minima that frequently hampers traditional BP networks when dealing with complex and nonlinear data. This strategic enhancement markedly improves the learning efficiency and predictive accuracy of the BP neural network enabling more precise predictions of power output from wind turbines under varying wind speeds and environmental conditions. This method not only improves the accuracy of predictions but also enhances the generalization ability of the model, providing robust technical support for the management and scheduling of wind farms.

9.2 The Sparrow Search Algorithm

9.2.1 The Principles of Sparrow Search Algorithm

The SSA, proposed in 2020 by Xue Jiankai from Donghua University,is an optimization algorithm based on swarm intelligence.

In SSA, the search space comprises potential solutions represented as n-dimensional intelligent search spaces, with each sparrow representing a potential solution endowed with a corresponding fitness value (objective function).Sparrows are categorized into two roles: Producers and Scroungers. In the SSA, sparrows are divided into two roles: Producers and Scroungers. Producers are tasked with finding food, determining the foraging area and direction for the flock. Scroungers, meanwhile, capitalize on the efforts of the Producers by observing and following them to acquire food. This dynamic allows all sparrows within the group to alternate between these strategies as they search for food, optimizing the group's overall foraging efficiency. Moreover, sparrows located at the periphery are more susceptible to attacks and must continually update their positions to secure optimal locations. When a predator is detected, a warming signal is emitted, and the group promptly evacuates the hazardous area.

9.2.2 The Design Process of Algorithms

The potential solution space for a problem where the number of potential solutions is /(n/)n and the dimensionality of the problem variables is /(d/)d can be mathematically represented in several ways, depending on the nature of the problem and the variables involved, Here are a few common ways to describe the solution space:

$$X = \begin{bmatrix} x_{11} & x_{12} & \cdots & x_{1d} \\ x_{21} & x_{21} & \cdots & x_{2d} \\ \vdots & \vdots & \ddots & \vdots \\ x_{n1} & x_{n1} & \cdots & x_{nd} \end{bmatrix} \tag{9.1}$$

The fitness values corresponding to all potential solutions are represented as:.

$$F_X = \begin{bmatrix} f\left(\left[\, x_{11}\ x_{21}\ \cdots\ x_{1d} \,\right]\right) \\ f\left(\left[\, x_{21}\ x_{22}\ \cdots\ x_{2d} \,\right]\right) \\ \vdots\ \vdots\ \vdots \\ f\left(\left[\, x_{n1}\ x_{n2}\ \cdots\ x_{nd} \,\right]\right) \end{bmatrix} \tag{9.2}$$

where *FX* represents the fitness value. In the SSA, which is inspired by the foraging behavior of sparrows, the position update formula plays a crucial role, especially for the "Producers" who are responsible for searching for food and guiding the rest of the flock. Here's a breakdown of how the position update formula for the producers works in the SSA:

$$x_{i,j}^{1+1} = \begin{cases} x_{i,j}^{t} \exp\left(-\frac{i}{be}\right) & r_2 < st \\ X_{i,j}^{t} + qc & r_2 \geq st \end{cases} \tag{9.3}$$

where t denotes the current iteration number; e is the set maximum number of iterations; xi,j represents the position information of the i-th sparrow in the j-th dimension, b is a random number within [0,1], $r2$ and st respectively represent the alert value and safety value, q is a random number following a normal distribution, c is the identity matrix. Scroungers primarily follow the producers but also adjust their positions based on the perceived level of threat or safety. The position update mechanism for Scroungers is defined as follows:

$$X_{ij}^{t+1} = \begin{cases} Q \cdot \exp\left(\frac{X_{worse}^{t} - X_{ij}^{t}}{i^2}\right) & if\ i > n/2 \\ X_{i,j}^{t} + \left|X_{ij}^{t} - X_{p}^{t+1}\right| A^{+}L\ otherwise \end{cases} \tag{9.4}$$

where Xp denotes the current optimal position, $Xworse$ denotes the current worst position. When i $\leq n / 2$, it indicates that the i-th sparrow is executing a strategy to approach the optimal position to obtain food. When $i > n/2$, it indicates that the i-th sparrow has not obtained food and needs to change strategies, flying to other areas to search for food. The position update formula for sparrows that perceive danger can be expressed by (9.5).

$$X_{i,j}^{t+1} = \begin{cases} X_{best}^{t} + \beta \left| X_{i,j}^{t} - X_{best}^{t} \right| & if\ f_i > f_g \\ X_{i,j}^{t} + K\left(\frac{\left| X_{i,j}^{t} - X_{worse}^{t} \right|}{(f_i - f_w) + \varepsilon} \right) & if\ f_i = f_g \end{cases} \quad (9.5)$$

where *xbest* represents the current global optimal position, β is a step length parameter, which is a random number drawn from a normal distribution with a variance of 1 and a mean of 0, $k$isa random number within the range of $[-1, 1]$, *fi, fw, fg* respectively denote best fitness of the individual, the global optimal fitness, and the global worst fitness. To ensure the denominator is not 0, it is typically assigned the smallest constant value. When an individual's fitness is greater than the global optimal fitness, it indicates that the sparrow is in a peripheral position, susceptible to attacks, necessitating a position update to achieve the best location, with the update direction moving closer to the op- timal position. When an individual's fitness equals the worst fitness value, it indicates that the sparrow has perceived danger and is in a hazardous position, necessitating an immediate move closer to other sparrows to avoid predation.The search process of the Sparrow Algorithm is illustrated in Fig. 9.1.

9.2.3 Optimizing BP Neural Network Predictions Using the Sparrow Algorithm

The BP neural network typically consists of an input layer, one or more hidden layers, and an output layer. Despite its effectiveness in establishing nonlinear mapping relationships, the network can experience slow convergence and may get stuck in local optima due to its reliance on gradient descent for weight optimization.

To address these issues, the Sparrow Algorithm is utilized. This algorithm optimizes the weights of the BP neural network by treating the minimization of the neural network error as a fitness function. By employing the Sparrow Algorithm, the weight thresholds are dynamically updated to find better solutions that may not be reachable by standard back propagation alone.

This integration aims to enhance the overall prediction accuracy of the BP network, particularly useful in complex tasks such as power prediction where precision is critical. The Sparrow Algorithm helps in escaping local minima and accelerates the convergence of the network by exploring the solution space more effectively.

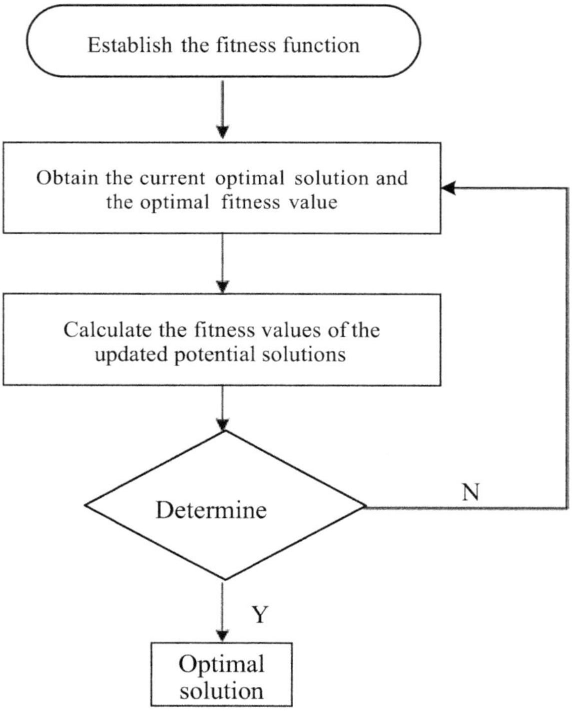

Fig. 9.1 Search flow chart of Sparrow algorithm

9.3 Prediction Results and Comparative Analysis

9.3.1 Prediction Results

I apologize for the detail. Let's simplify it.

This paper utilizes a BP neural network to predict the performance of the A11 wind turbine unit in as pecific wind farm. The network processes 2000 data samples, with 80%used for training and 20%for testing. The BP neural network has three layers, including a hidden layer with five neurons

To enhance its prediction efficiency. the model is first optimized using the Sparrow Algorithm (SSA) with a population of 50 sparrows. Following SSA, the African Vulture Optimization Algorithm (AVOA-BP) is also applied to further refine the model's accuracy (Figs. 9.2 and 9.3).

From the figures, it is observable that with a low number of samples, both the BP and SSA-BP predictions are relatively close to the actual values. When the prediction data exceeds 300, the SSA-BP predicted values are closer to the actual values than those predicted by the BP model. The curves demonstrate that the SSA-BP neural network can more effectively enhance the accuracy of power prediction for wind turbine units.

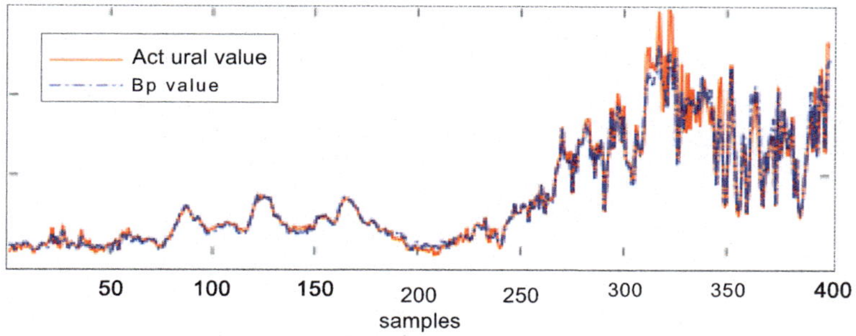

Fig. 9.2 Comparison diagram of BP and actual value

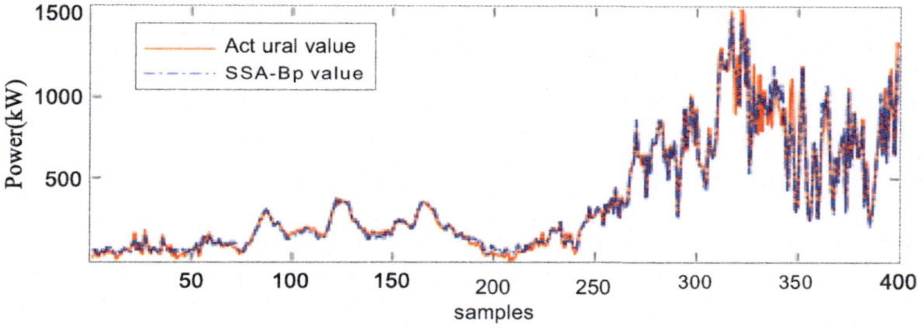

Fig. 9.3 Comparison diagram of SSA-BP and actual value

9.3.2 Results Comparison

This paper compares the SSA-BP neural network with a BP network optimized using the African Vulture Optimization Algorithm (AVOA). AVOA draws inspiration from the foraging behaviors of African vultures and applies these strategies to neural net-work weight optimization. The comparison focuses on prediction accuracy and optimization efficiency between the two methods. It solves optimization problems by simulating the food hunting and flight trajectory behaviors of African vultures. The prediction results are exhibited in Fig. 9.4.

Acknowledged, here's a more streamlined summary.

This paper assesses the effectiveness of the African Vulture Optimization Algorithm (AVOA) compared to the Sparrow Algorithm (SSA) in enhancing a BP neural net-work for wind turbine power prediction by analyzing RMSE and MAPE .Lower values of these metrics indicate better prediction accuracy. The results are detailed in Table 9.1 for a direct comparison. Table 9.1 Comparison of Error Values.

The table clearly indicates that both the SSA-BP neural network and the AVOA-BP neural network significantly improve the accuracy of wind power prediction.

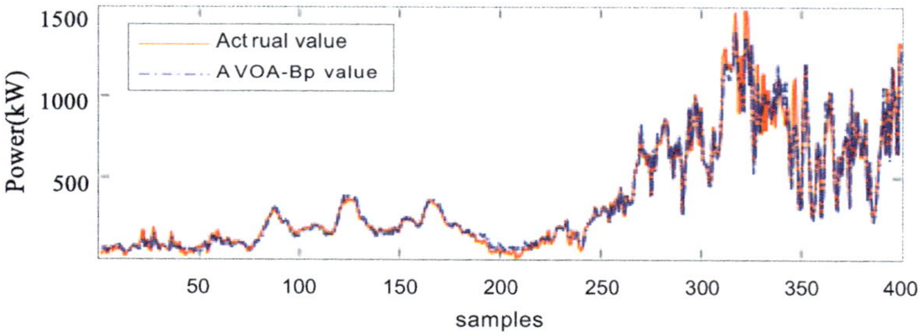

Fig. 9.4 Comparison diagram of AVOA-BP and actual value

Table 9.1 Comparison of error values

Algorithm	RMSE (%)	MAPE (%)
BP	66.7279	12.879
SSA-BP	54.3059	12.001
AVOA-BP	62.8691	12.713

However, by comparing their RMSE and MAPE values, it is evident that the SSA-BP neural network exhibits smaller prediction errors and higher accuracy compared to the AVOA-BP neural network.

9.4 Conclusion

This paper presents an improved Back Propagation neural network, optimized using the SSA for enhanced accuracy in wind turbine power prediction. The SSA-enhanced BP network as evaluated against a traditional BP network and another optimized with the African Vulture Optimization Algorithm (AVOA). The results demonstrate superior performance of the SSA-BP network, which achieved reductions in RMSE (Root Mean Square Error) by 18.6%and MAPE (Mean Absolute Percentage Error) by 6.8%compared to the traditional BP network. Against the AVOA-BP network, the SSA-BP network also performed better, reducing RMSE and MAPE by 13.6%and 5.6%, respectively. These findings underscore the effectiveness of the Sparrow Search Algorithm in refining wind turbine power prediction models.

References

1. Li, Y., et al.: Wind power forecasting considering data privacy protection: a federated deep reinforcement learning approach. Appl. Energy **329**, 120291 (2023)
2. SanjariM, J., Gooi, H.B., Nair, N.K.C.: Power generation forecast of hybrid PV-wind system. IEEE Trans. Sustain. Energy **11**(2), 703–712 (2019)
3. Ye, L., Zhang, C., Tang, Y.: Hierarchical model predictive control strategy based on dynamic active power dispatch for wind power cluster integration. IEEE Trans. Power Syst. **34**(6), 4617–4629 (2019)
4. Cheng, L., Zang, H., Xu, Y.: Augmented convolutional network for wind power prediction: a new recurrent architecture design with spatial-temporal image inputs. IEEE Trans. Ind. Inform. **17**(10), 6981–6993 (2021)
5. Jalali, S.M.J., Osório, G.J., Ahmadian, S.: New hybrid deep neural architectural search-based ensemble reinforcement learning strategy for wind power forecasting. IEEE Trans. Ind. Appl. **58**(1), 15–27 (2021)
6. Zhang, H., et al.: Improved deep mixture density network for regional wind power probabilistic forecasting. IEEE Trans. Power Syst. **35**(4), 2549–2560 (2020)
7. Wan, C., Xu, Z., Pinson, P.: Probabilistic forecasting of wind power generation using extreme learning machine. IEEE Trans. Power Syst. **29**(3), 1033–1044 (2013)
8. Zhao, Y., Ye, L., Pinson, P.: Correlation-constrained and sparsity-controlled vector autoregressive model for spatio-temporal wind power forecasting. IEEE Trans. Power Syst. **33**(5), 5029–5040 (2018)
9. Ko, M.S., Lee, K., Kim, J.K., Hong. C.W., Dong Z.Y., Hur K.: Deep concatenated residual network with bidirectional LSTM for one-hour-ahead wind power forecasting. IEEE Trans. Sustain. Energy **12**(2), 1321–1335 (2020)
10. Li, M., Yang, M., Yu, Y., Lee, W.-J.: A wind speed correction method based on modified hidden Markov model for enhancing wind power forecast. IEEE Trans. Ind. Appl. **58**(1), 656–666 (2021)

Chapter 10
Research on Strategy of Pumped Storage and Nuclear Power in Auxiliary Service Market

Minghang Cao, Xiran Zhou, Mu Siyu, Xuekui Zhao, Yu Peng, Ma Yiming, Haixin Wang, and Junyou Yang

Abstract According to the benefits of little environmental pollution and cheap combustion cost, nuclear power's significance in the power grid framework has been growing. However, the power system faces extreme peak shaving pressure when operating nuclear power plants under the typical full power strategy at base load. Therefore, this paper initially delves into the operational dynamics of nuclear power units engaging in daily load following endeavors within the ancillary services market. Meanwhile, the strategic approach for nuclear power plants to participate in the market for ancillary services aimed at maximizing peak shaving revenues is formulated. Secondly, to increase the flexibility and adaptability of the system, a collaborative operating strategy is introduced, involving both pumped storage and nuclear units in peak shaving. This strategy exploits the complementary characteristics of these two technologies. Finally, in order to validate the effectiveness of this approach, a case study is conducted on a regional power system where three different operational scenarios are simulated and comprehensively compared. The results show that the integrated participation of pumped storage and nuclear units in peak load regulation schemes is a more cost-effective solution, underlining the economic viability and technical merits of this collaborative strategy.

M. Cao (✉) · M. Siyu · M. Yiming · H. Wang · J. Yang
Shenyang University of Technology, Shenyang, China
e-mail: MinghangCao264@163.com

X. Zhou
State Grid Fuxin Power Supply Company, Fuxin, China

X. Zhao
Inner Mongolia Datang International Toketo Power Generation Co. Ltd., Hohhot, China

Y. Peng
School of Electrical and Information Engineering, Changsha University of Science and Technology Changsha, Changsha, China

F. P. García Márquez et al. (eds.), *Computing, Internet of Things and Data Analytics*,
Smart Innovation, Systems and Technologies 387,
https://doi.org/10.1007/978-3-031-87154-2_10

10.1 Introduction

In response to the global challenge of transitioning energy structures to low-carbon models, China has embarked on a development path to build a novel power system based on renewable energy sources. Nuclear power, known for its stable operation, extended refueling intervals, environmental friendliness and low carbon emissions, is ideally suited for both meeting baseload demand and modulating peak loads within power grids [1]. As a result, recent academic research has focused on operational strategies for nuclear power's use in peak shaving, while at the same time promoting the construction of nuclear power plants [2]. However, the recurrent adjustment of the output of nuclear units to accommodate peak shaving can result in additional operation and maintenance costs. To alleviate this problem, the integration of pumped storage facilities working in tandem with nuclear units for peak shaving purposes can ensure the continued stability of nuclear power operations, enhance their safety margins, and mitigate transient energy losses, thereby contributing to a more logical and scientifically rigorous discourse on energy system optimization [3].

As the proportion of nuclear units in power grids continues to increase and the difference between peak and off-peak loads widens, domestic and international researchers have conducted extensive studies to investigate the adaptability, safety and economic feasibility of integrating nuclear power into the grid. Leveraging the characteristic power modulation patterns and load following capabilities of nuclear units, [4] delves into the daily load following model of these units and proposes an operational framework that considers both peak shaving depth and power transition times. Given the limitations of current output models for nuclear peak shaving engagement, [5] introduces a decoupled auxiliary variable representing power augmentation, thereby establishing a safety-centric output model for nuclear peak shaving with tighter constraints and a more seamless range of peak shaving depths, improving the overall rigor and logical coherence of the academic discourse.

The exclusion of nuclear units from peak shaving practices often raises cost allocation issues, prompting extensive research into the economics of nuclear participation in peak shaving. From the operational economics perspective of nuclear units, [6] establishes a market model for peak shaving ancillary services that aims to minimize peak shaving costs, taking into account both the depth and rate of peak regulation for nuclear units. The results underline that the inclusion of nuclear units in system peak regulation can effectively reduce the overall cost of power generation. Furthermore, in order to enhance the economic efficiency of nuclear units in peak shaving, scholars have explored the market mechanisms of peak shaving ancillary services. In [7], a mathematical model for bilateral bidding participation of thermal power and renewable energy sources is constructed, which demonstrates a superior ability to harness market steering forces compared to conventional mechanisms.

Pumped storage plants are characterized by fast start-up, flexible and reliable operating modes, which allow them to work seamlessly with nuclear units in peak shaving efforts. In Reference [8], with a focus on unit operational reliability, the impact of frequent grid dispatch participation on the reliability of pumped storage plants is investigated, and a more cautious operating mode and workload intensity is subsequently outlined. Reference [9] constructs a multiunit profit model based on the operational economics of renewable energy sources. Using centralized bidding principles, it establishes a peak shaving trading framework for individual units and assesses their bidding capability. This proposed trading mechanism facilitates the optimal allocation of generation resources and improves the system-wide economics of peak shaving. However, within the current ancillary services market framework, the influence of pumped storage units on economics of nuclear units participating in grid peak shaving remains unexplored.

Therefore, this paper first examines the operational modalities of nuclear power units and then proposes a participation strategy for nuclear power in power system peak shaving, integrating the prevailing ancillary services market mechanisms. Furthermore, by incorporating the operational characteristics of pumped storage units, we formulate a joint operational strategy for pumped storage and nuclear power in peak shaving efforts. Finally, by exploiting the baseload and load-following capabilities of nuclear units and the cooperation of pumped storage, we simulate a practical regional power system as a case study. Three different scenarios are used to empirically validate the effectiveness of the proposed methodology.

10.2 Operation Strategy of Ancillary Service Market with Nuclear Power

10.2.1 Load Tracking Model of Nuclear Power Unit

Nuclear power units frequently adopt the "12-3-6-3" load-following paradigm for daily peak regulation, necessitating frequent adjustments to their output power, which in turn escalates the overall cost of power generation. Nevertheless, when nuclear power operates as a significant base load contributor, it intensifies the peaking demands on the grid. Consequently, it is imperative to harness the latent flexibility of nuclear power. Additionally, by actively engaging in peak shaving, nuclear power units can mitigate their expenses within the ancillary service market, thereby enhancing their economic viability.

When integrating nuclear power units into daily load tracking for peak shaving, it is crucial to ensure that their peak shaving depths and power ramp rates adhere to safe operational boundaries. Specifically, the minimal peak shaving depth is set at 30% of the unit's rated power, while the maximum depth is constrained to not exceed 70% of the rated power. The units operate under two distinct conditions: full power and low power, with each condition requiring a minimum duration of 2 to 6 h. Furthermore, the transition period between power levels should fall within a range of 1 to 3 h. Figure 10.1 illustrates the nuclear power output curve under the "12-3-6-3" load tracking mode, showcasing a peak regulation depth of 30%, thereby adhering to

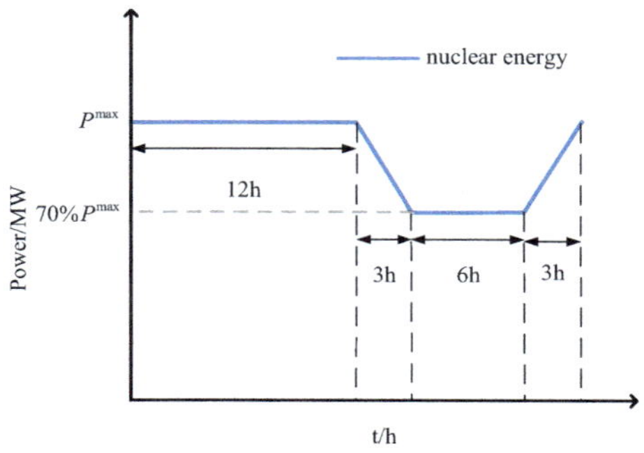

Fig. 10.1 Output curve of nuclear power

these operational constraints while maintaining optimal efficiency and safety. P^{max} is the maximum output power of the nuclear power unit.

The output balance constraints of nuclear power plants are shown in Eqs. (10.1–10.2).

$$P_{i,t} = h_{i,t}P_i^{max} + \sum_{n=1}^{3} l_{n,i,t}P_{i,l_n} + \sum_{m=1}^{9} s_{m,i,t}P_{i,s_m} \tag{10.1}$$

$$h_{i,t} + \sum_{n}^{3} l_{n,i,t} + \sum_{m}^{9} s_{m,i,t} = 1 \tag{10.2}$$

where $P_{i,t}$, P_i^{max}, P_{i,l_n}, P_{i,s_m} are the output power, the maximum power, the low power corresponding to different peak shaving depths and the corresponding transition power of the i nuclear power plants in the t period, respectively. There can only be one operating state variable of 1 in the t period.

The climbing constraints of the nuclear power plants are as follows.

$$-\Delta P_i \le P_{i,t} - P_{i,t-1} \le \Delta P_i \tag{10.3}$$

where ΔP_i is the hourly power variation of nuclear power plant *i*. $P_{i,t-1}$ is the output of nuclear power plant in *t–1* period.

After the power of the nuclear power unit is changed, it is necessary to maintain a constant power operation for a certain period of time. In accordance with the principle of safe operation of nuclear power units, the operating time requirements to be satisfied at full power and low power are as follows:

$$h_{i,x} \ge h_{i,t} - h_{i.t-1}, x = t, t+1 \ldots\ldots t + T_h^N - 1 \tag{10.4}$$

$$l_{i,x} \ge l_{i,t} - l_{i.t-1}, x = t, t+1 \ldots\ldots t + T_l^N - 1 \tag{10.5}$$

where T_h^N is the shortest full power to maintain the running time. T_l^N is the shortest low power to maintain the running time.

10.2.2 Operation Strategy of Nuclear Power Join in Auxiliary Service

Current research on the compensation framework for peak shaving ancillary services focuses mainly on identifying the origins of peak shaving compensation costs, quantifying the specific contributions to peak shaving, and exploring appropriate compensation methodologies and standards [10]. By adjusting the cost sharing and compensation mechanisms for the different generating units involved in peak shaving, we can incentivize their active participation in this important process. This approach ensures that the compensation system is tailored to the unique characteristics and capabilities of each unit, thereby promoting a more effective and efficient peak shaving environment. The peak-shaving auxiliary service market mechanism of nuclear power units is shown in Eq. (10.6).

$$C_{i,PS} = F_{i,t}^{rid}(C_{PS} - C_{RS}) \cdot \frac{Q_{j,t}}{\sum\limits_{j=1}^{n} Q_{j,t}} \tag{10.6}$$

where n signifies the total count of nuclear power units actively engaged in peak shaving regulation within a nuclear power plant complex, $C_{i,PS}$ The cost associated with the participation of nuclear power unit i in the peak regulation of the power grid, C_{RS} is the total compensation expenditure incurred by the nuclear power plant for its participation in peak load regulation, and C_{PS} is the total cost of nuclear power plant for its participation in peak load regulation. $Q_{j,t}$ denotes the output power of nuclear power plant i participating in peak load regulation at time t, $F_{i,t}^{rid}$ indicates the bid-winning ability of nuclear power plant at time t. If the value is 1, it indicates that nuclear power plant i participates in peak regulation auxiliary service.

The cost allocation for nuclear plants that do not participate in peak shaving can be formulated as follows.

$$C_{i,FS} = (1 - F_{i,t}^{rid})C_{FS} \cdot \frac{P_{h,t}}{\sum\limits_{h=1}^{k} P_{h,t}} \tag{10.7}$$

where $C_{i,FS}$ is the apportionment cost that the nuclear power plant i is excluded from engaging in the regulation of peak loads, k represents the number of nuclear power units that excluded from engaging in the regulation of peak loads in the nuclear power plant, $P_{h,t}$ represents the power generation power of the nuclear power unit i that excluded from engaging in the regulation of peak loads in the t period, and C_{FS}

represents the total apportionment cost that excluded from engaging in the regulation of peak loads.

Due to the extended refueling intervals, it is assumed that the nuclear unit will remain in an operational state throughout the daily load tracking, thus eliminating the need to consider startup and shutdown costs. The objective function is shown as follows.

$$\max F_1 = \sum_{i=1}^{M}\sum_{t=1}^{T}\left(C_{NP,t} - C_{EPG}\right)P_{i,t} - k_{i,t}C_{PS}(P_{i,\max} - P_{i,t}) - (1 - k_{i,t})C_{i,FS}P_{i,t} \tag{10.8}$$

where F_1 represents the daily income of nuclear power plants, M is the total number of nuclear power plants, $C_{NP,t}$ represents the feed-in tariff of t period, C_{EPG} represents expenditure on electricity generation by nuclear power plants, mainly including the operation and maintenance cost and fuel combustion cost of units, $P_{i,t}$ represents the output of nuclear power plant i in t period, $k_{i,t}$ represents the 0–1 variable of peaking state of nuclear power plant i in t period, $P_{i,\max}$ represents the plant without peaking, C_{PS} represents the maximum operating power of nuclear power plants, and represents the peaking cost of nuclear power plants.

10.3 Economic Model of Peak Regulation Auxiliary Service

10.3.1 Operation Mode of Pumped Storage Combined Nuclear Power Unit

Concerning conventional approaches: the pumping capacity of pumped storage plants is equal to their total generation capacity, with electricity generated during peak periods of grid demand and water pumped during off-peak periods, ensuring a daily balance between pumped energy and generated electricity. This balance ensures that the average daily output ratio of the nuclear-storage hybrid unit reflects the average daily load factor of the electricity grid.

$$\gamma = \frac{P_{sl}t_f - P_{sm}t_p + 24P_N}{24(P_{sl} + P_N)} \tag{10.9}$$

where γ is the equivalent daily average load rate of the power grid, t_f and t_p are the daily generation hours and daily pumping hours of pumped storage plants, respectively. P_{sl} is the capacity of pumped storage units required for joint operation with nuclear power units.

The revenue generated by the output of the pumped storage unit can be expressed as follows.

$$G_{k,t} = (P_{k,t}^{T} - P_{k,t}^{P})C_{NP,t} \tag{10.10}$$

where $G_{k,t}$ represents the revenue generated by the pumped storage plant k at time t, $P_{k,t}^{T}$ and $P_{k,t}^{P}$ represents electricity generation capacity and pumping capacity of the pumped storage plant k at time t, $C_{NP,t}$ represents the real-time peak-valley price at time t.

The operating costs associated with starting and stopping the pumped storage unit are expressed as follows.

$$S_{k,t} = \left[y_{k,t}^{T}(1 - y_{k,t-1}^{T}) + y_{k,t}^{P}(1 - y_{k,t-1}^{P})\right]C_{h,on} + \left[y_{k,t}^{P}(1 - y_{k,t-1}^{P}) + y_{k,t-1}^{P}(1 - y_{k,t}^{P})\right]C_{h,off} \tag{10.11}$$

where $S_{k,t}$ denotes the operating costs associated with starting and stopping pumped storage unit k at time t, $y_{k,t}^{T}$ and $y_{k,t}^{P}$ (0,1 variable) denotes whether the pumped storage plant is in power generation condition and pumping condition respectively, $C_{h,on}$ and $C_{h,off}$ denotes the costs associated with the respective start-up and shut-down losses of the pumped storage unit.

The power constraint of pumped storage unit is shown as follows.

$$U_T(t)P_T^{\min} \leq P_{k,t}^{T} \leq U_T(t)P_T^{\max} \tag{10.12}$$

$$U_T(t)P_T^{\min} \leq P_{k,t}^{T} \leq U_T(t)P_T^{\max} \tag{10.13}$$

where $P_T^{\min}$ and $P_T^{\max}$ are the maximum and minimum operating power of the generator set, $P_P^{\min}$ and $P_P^{\max}$ are the maximum and minimum operating power of the pump, respectively.

Considering the cost of nuclear peaking, the cost of generation and the remuneration for peaking services, as well as the start-up and shut-down costs of pumped storage units, the objective function, which aims at optimizing the economic benefits of the peak shaving system, is formulated as follows.

$$\begin{aligned} F = \sum_{i=1}^{M}\sum_{t=1}^{T} & (C_{NP,t} - C_{EPG})P_{i,t} - k_{i,t}C_{PS}(P_{i,\max} - P_{i,t}) \\ & -(1 - k_{i,t})C_{i,CS}P_{i,t} + (P_{k,t}^{T} - P_{k,t}^{P})C_{NP,t} - S_{k,t} \end{aligned} \tag{10.14}$$

10.4 Example Simulation Analysis

To validate the effectiveness of the model presented here, a simulation framework is developed. The daily load profile and the power curve of the thermal unit are shown in Fig. 10.2.

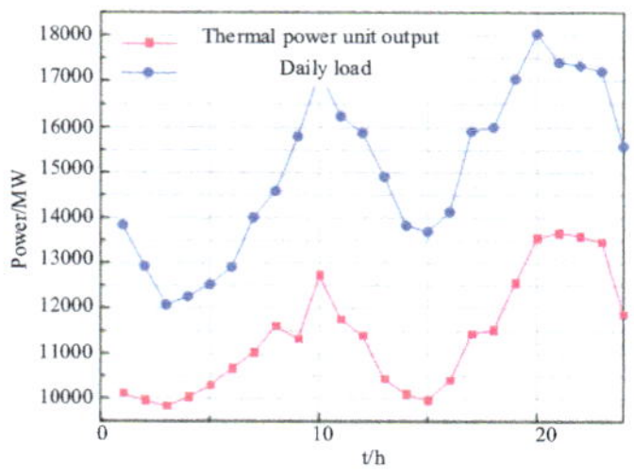

Fig. 10.2 Daily load and thermal power output curves of an area

Set the comparison cases as follows:

Case 1: The nuclear power unit serves as the base load provider, while the pumped storage unit contributes to the ancillary service of peak shaving regulation.

Case 2: The nuclear unit operates independently to contribute to the peak load modulation of the electricity grid through load following.

Case 3: The nuclear unit operates in a load-following mode, while the pumped storage unit contributes to the ancillary service of peak load regulation.

The output of each unit in different schemes is shown in Fig. 10.3.

In case 1, nuclear power acts as baseload generator, generating higher power revenues in addition to benefits of peak shaving participation, compared to other

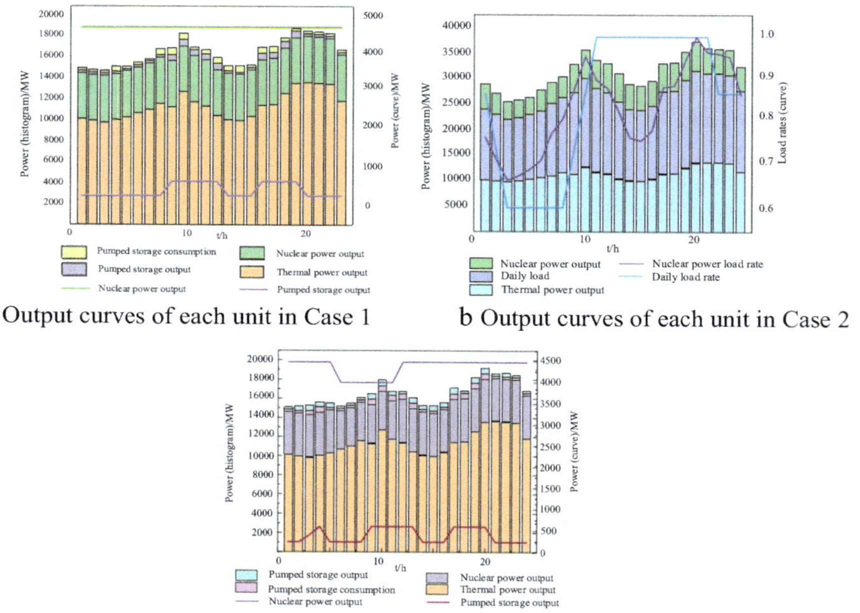

a Output curves of each unit in Case 1

b Output curves of each unit in Case 2

c Output curves of each unit in Case 3

Fig. 10.3 Output curves of each unit

cases, where nuclear power participates in peak regulation. The results indicate that, within current market framework for nuclear participation in peak shaving ancillary services, higher level of nuclear participation in peak shaving results in higher economic returns.

10.5 Conclusion

This paper advocates an operational strategy and market mechanism that encourages nuclear units to participate in peak regulation ancillary services, thereby significantly increasing their motivation to participate. Analysis shows that nuclear units operating in load-tracking mode for peak regulation generate 7.78% higher profit margin than those operating in baseload mode. In addition, the integration of pumped storage units into peak shaving operations allows the generator's output to be better aligned with daily load fluctuations, optimizing the generation revenue for pumped storage and minimizing resource waste. In particular, under a collaborative strategy where nuclear and storage jointly participate in peak shaving, the profitability of pumped storage units increases by an impressive 25%, underlining the synergies and benefits of this integrated approach.

References

1. Zhaoyu, L., Hua, W., Hong, H.: Safety output model with tight constraints and flexible regulation for nuclear power plant participating in peak load regulation. Autom. Electr. Power Syst. **44**(4), 63–71 (2020)
2. Shan, Wu., Xiaoyan, Bian, Jingxian, Zhang, et al.: A review of domestic and foreign ancillary services market for improving flexibility of new power system. Trans. China Electrotech. Soc. **38**(6), 1662–1677 (2023)
3. Dongmei, Zhao, Haoxiang, Wang, Ran, Tao: Multi-source coordinated optimal scheduling model considering wind-load uncertainty. Trans. China Electrotech. Soc. **37**(3), 707–718 (2022)
4. Dongying, Liao, Danlei, Zhu, Baosheng, Xie, et al.: Research on peak shaving and frequency modulation technology and mechanism of electrochemical energy storage system participating in auxiliary services. Electr. Eng. **6**, 127–131 (2022)
5. Kaiyan, Wang, Xianjue, Luo, Rong, Jia, et al.: Short-term coordinated scheduling of wind-pumped-hydro-thermal power system with multi-energy complementarities. Power Syst. Technol. **44**(10), 3631–3641 (2020)
6. Li, L., Xiaoyu, Y., Bingqian, X., et al.: Sequence and strategy of pumped storage-thermal combined peak shaving considering. Power Syst. Technol. **45**(1), 20–32 (2021)
7. Li, J., Ai, Q., Yin, S., et al.: An aggregator-oriented hierarchical market mechanism for multi-type ancillary service provision based on the two-loop Stackelberg game. Appl. Energy **323**, 119644 (2022)
8. Abiodun, K., Hood, K., Cox, J.L., et al.: The value of concentrating solar power in ancillary services markets. Appl. Energy **334**, 120518 (2023)

9. Ding, Y., Tan, Q., Han, J., et al.: A two-stage dispatching optimization strategy for hybrid renewable energy system with low-carbon and sustainability in ancillary service market. Renew. Energy **207,** 647–659 (2023)
10. Jun, Wang, Jie, Zhao, Dichen, Liu, et al.: Optimal scheduling model of peak load regulation considering participation of nuclear power plant. Proc. CSEE **38**(6), 1665–1674 (2018)

Chapter 11
Contract-Spot Coordination Optimization Strategy of Wind Storage Integration Considering Load Demand Under Contract for Difference Mechanism

Siqi Zhang, Jiahui Yuan, Jian Dong, Xinyi Lu, Haixin Wang, and Junyou Yang

Abstract The joint operation of wind power and energy storage is beneficial to solve the problem of optimal operation of wind power in spot market environment. Based on the contract settlement rules of centralized spot market, a coordination optimization strategy of contract electricity and spot electricity considering load demand is proposed. First, an energy storage model considering the battery energy storage life is constructed. Second, the principle of contract for difference in spot market environment is analyzed. Considering the load demand in the regulation strategy of energy storage, the real-time output of wind storage integration is optimized, and based on the principle of contract settlement for difference, the ratio of contract electricity to day-ahead spot electricity is optimized with the obtained real-time electricity as the constraint. The randomness of wind power output is further taken into account, and the optimization goal is improved. Finally, the CPLEX solver is used to model and solve the problem, which verifies the effect of the strategy proposed in responding to the load demand and improving the wind power revenue.

S. Zhang (✉) · H. Wang · J. Yang
Shenyang University of Technology, Shenyang, China
e-mail: siqizhang199709@163.com

J. Yuan
State Grid Yutai Power Supply Company, Shandong Electric Power Corporation, Yutai, China

J. Dong
State Grid Liaoning Economic Technique Institute, Shenyang, China

X. Lu
Marketing Service Center, State Grid Liaoning Electric Power Co., Ltd, Shenyang, China

F. P. García Márquez et al. (eds.), *Computing, Internet of Things and Data Analytics*,
Smart Innovation, Systems and Technologies 387,
https://doi.org/10.1007/978-3-031-87154-2_11

11.1 Introduction

As a flexible resource, energy storage can effectively alleviate the fluctuation of new energy sources such as wind power and improve the flexibility and reliability of power system after it is introduced into power system [1, 2]. Energy storage can not only serve the interests of the whole power system, but also serve the operation of market entities [3]. At present, many references have studied the trading strategy of wind storage integration system in the electricity market environment.

Xie et al. [4] using energy storage to transfer wind power to spread arbitrage, considering the uncertainty of wind power output, electricity price and frequency market price forecast, a spot market bidding strategy based on robust model predictive control is proposed. Yang et al. [5] using energy storage to manage the uncertainty of wind power output, a spot market optimization decision-making method of wind storage based on deep reinforcement learning is proposed. Khazali et al. [6] based on the information gap decision-making theory, a decision-making model of spot market reporting for wind storage integration is proposed, and energy storage can be used to stabilize forecasting error and prevent wind abandonment. However, in the energy storage control strategy of [4–6], only the energy storage operation constraints are considered, and the loss of its life caused by irregular discharge of energy storage is not considered. Miao et al. [7] considering the loss of energy storage life, battery energy storage and wind power peak-valley arbitrage are used to maximize the economic benefits of the wind storage integration, but the deviation settlement mode of the day-ahead and real-time spot market is not considered. He et al. [8] considering the energy storage life model considering the equivalent full cycle times to limit the deep discharge of energy storage, a decision-making process of day-ahead bidding considering the deviation settlement of day-ahead and real-time spot market is proposed to optimize the day-ahead and real-time spot electricity, but the coordination and optimization of spot electricity and medium-and long-term contract electricity are not considered. In addition, all the above references regard electricity price as the guiding signal of energy storage regulation. If the load demand is the guiding signal, the capacity value of energy storage will be better utilized.

Considering that medium and long-term trading is the first stage of electric energy market trading under the framework of spot market, aiming at the above problems, this paper takes centralized spot market as the background and considers the influence of spot market on medium and long-term market trading decisions, studies the coordination and optimization of contract electricity and spot electricity in the medium and long-term stage.

11.2 Energy Storage Model

11.2.1 Energy Storage Life Model Considering Equivalent Full Cycle Times

The energy storage will be irregularly charged and discharged when the wind and energy storage are integrated to regulate the output, and different discharge depths will have different degrees of energy storage life loss. So as to limit that charging and discharging behavior of energy storage, referencing [8] the energy storage life model considering the number of equivalent full cycles is constructed. See [8] constraints (2–8) for details.

11.2.2 Energy Storage Charging and Discharging Constraints

See [8] constraints (14–18) for the upper and lower limits of energy storage charging and discharging power and state of charge constraints.

11.3 Optimization Strategy of Wind Storage Contract-Spot Electricity Coordination

11.3.1 Spot Market Settlement Mechanism for Contracts for Differences

Under the framework of centralized spot market, medium and long-term contracts are contracts for differences, which are only financial in nature and need not be physically executed [9]. According to the centralized spot market electricity energy tariff settlement rules, the electricity tariff settlement method is as shown in (11.1).

$$R = Q_{\text{con}}P_{\text{con}} + (Q_{\text{bef}} - Q_{\text{con}})P_{\text{bef}} + (Q_{\text{act}} - Q_{\text{bef}})P_{\text{act}} \tag{11.1}$$

where R is the total income, P_{con} is the medium and long-term contract electricity price, Q_{con} is the medium and long-term contract electricity quantity, P_{bef} is the day-ahead spot electricity price, Q_{bef} is the day-ahead spot electricity quantity, P_{act} and Q_{act} are the real-time spot electricity price and the real-time spot electricity quantity.

Therefore, according to the above formula, the wind and storage integration can be optimized by coordinating the ratio of medium and long-term contract electricity to spot electricity and regulating the real-time output curve.

11.3.2 Decision-Making Process of Coordination Optimization of Electricity Quantity Considering Load Demand

First of all, build the spot market quotation strategy of the price receiver with wind and storage integration, so as to make all the declared electric quantities win the bid, and thus have an expectation of the total spot electric quantity. Then, considering the guiding role of load demand in the regulation strategy of wind storage integration, the total electricity curve of wind storage in real-time spot market is optimized, which provides constraints for the coordinated optimization of contract electricity and spot electricity. Finally, under the constraint of known real-time spot electricity, the ratio of contract electricity to spot electricity is optimized, and considering the randomness of wind power output, the expected value of income in different typical scenarios is used to replace the trading income. In order to simplify the problem and facilitate the subsequent analysis of the model principle, the following assumptions are made.

The accuracy of forecasting spot electricity price and wind power output curve is high. As the operation day approaches, the accuracy of forecasting spot electricity price and wind power output curve is higher to higher, so this assumption can be made.

11.3.2.1 Real-Time Regulation Strategy of Wind Storage Integration

Normalize the load demand and convert the value of the load demand into its corresponding weight, as shown in (11.2).

$$q_t^l = P_t^l / \sum_{t=1}^{T} P_t^l \tag{11.2}$$

where P_t^l is the load demand in t period, q_t^1 is the weight of load demand in t period.

The load demand weight is considered in the real-time regulation strategy of wind storage integration, and the optimization goal of regulating the output of wind storage integration is shown in (11.3).

$$\max\ q = Q_t^{\mathrm{q,act}}\, q_t^1 \tag{11.3}$$

where $Q_t^{\mathrm{q,act}}$ is the real-time declaration of electricity quantity is made in the t period of wind storage integration when only the load demand is considered. It has no practical significance to optimize the target q, which can make the distribution of more electricity during the period when the load demand is significant.

Constraint (4) is required by the declared electricity quantity $Q_t^{\mathrm{q,act}}$.

$$Q_t^{\mathrm{q,act}} = Q_t^{\mathrm{w,ab}} + P_t^{\mathrm{dis}} - P_t^{\mathrm{ch}} \tag{11.4}$$

Because constraint (4) may lead to difficulty in solving, constraint (4) is changed to constraint (5).

$$Q_t^{\mathrm{q,act}} Q_t^{\mathrm{w,ab}} + P_t^{\mathrm{dis}} - P_t^{\mathrm{ch}} \tag{11.5}$$

Inequality constraint (5) may cause part of wind power generation to be undeclared, so the real-time spot electricity $Q_t^{\mathrm{q,act}}$ is not finally declared. Solving this model is only to obtain the charging and discharging strategy of energy storage.

11.3.2.2 Contract-Spot Electricity Coordination Optimization Strategy

After solving the model in Sect. 3.2.1, the charging P_t^{dis} and discharging P_t^{ch} strategy of wind storage integration real-time regulation is obtained, and the total electricity is a known quantity at this time. Considering the undeclared wind power that can be generated, the real-time spot electricity of wind storage integration in t period is as follows:

$$Q_t^{\mathrm{l,act}} = Q_t^{\mathrm{w,ab}} + P_t^{\mathrm{dis}} - P_t^{\mathrm{ch}} \tag{11.6}$$

where $Q_t^{\mathrm{q,act}}$ is the real-time spot electricity of the wind storage integration in t period when the load demand is considered.

Optimize the ratio of medium-and long-term contract electricity quantity to the day-ahead spot electricity quantity with the real-time spot electricity quantity as the constraint, and the optimization objective is as follows:

$$\max R_{\mathrm{inte,l}} = Q_t^{\mathrm{l,con}} P_t^{\mathrm{con}} + \left(Q_t^{\mathrm{l,bef}} - Q_t^{\mathrm{l,con}}\right) + \left(Q_t^{\mathrm{l,act}} - Q_t^{\mathrm{l,bef}}\right) P_t^{\mathrm{act}} - C \tag{11.7}$$

where $R_{\mathrm{inte,l}}$ is the total market income of wind storage integration considering the load demand, $Q_t^{\mathrm{l,con}}$ is the contract electricity in t period, $Q_t^{\mathrm{l,bef}}$ is the day-ahead spot market electricity in t period, $Q_t^{\mathrm{l,act}}$ is the real-time spot market electricity in t period, and the value is equal to the total electricity generation of the wind storage integration, $C = c_0\left(P_t^{\mathrm{dis}} + P_t^{\mathrm{ch}}\right)$ is the energy storage operation cost in t period.

Equations (11.8) and (11.9) are used to limit the proportion of medium and long-term contracted electricity. Equation (11.10) is used to control the deviation between the day-ahead spot electricity and the real-time spot electricity.

$$k_l = \frac{Q_t^{\mathrm{l,con}}}{Q_t^{\mathrm{l,bef}}} \tag{11.8}$$

$$0.8 \leqslant k_1 \leqslant 1 \tag{11.9}$$

$$\alpha_3 Q_t^{\mathrm{l,act}} \leqslant Q_t^{\mathrm{l,bef}} \leqslant \beta_3 Q_t^{\mathrm{l,act}} \tag{11.10}$$

where k_l is the ratio of the medium and long-term contract electricity of wind storage integration in t period to day-ahead spot electricity. Considering that new energy sources such as wind power are not willing to participate in the market, the value range is set to 0.8–1. α_3 and β_3 is the coefficient to adjust the deviation electricity quantity between the day-ahead spot market and the real-time spot market of the wind storage integration.

11.3.3 Objective Function Based on Stochastic Optimization

Considering the randomness of wind power output, the method based on stochastic optimization is used to replace the transaction income with the expected value of income in many different typical scenarios. To reduce the calculation time, the synchronous iterative elimination algorithm is used to reduce the actual wind power output scenarios, and the typical wind power output scenarios and their probabilities are obtained. The objective function base on stochastic optimization is shown in (11).

$$\max \sum_{i=1}^{N} \rho_i R_{\mathrm{int},i} \tag{11.11}$$

where ρ_i is the probability of occurrence of typical scenario i, $R_{\mathrm{int},i}$ is the income under typical scenario i.

11.4 Example Simulation and Result Analysis

11.4.1 Example Description

To verify the effectiveness of the optimization strategy model proposed in this paper, an example is constructed for analysis. The spot electricity price is not predicted. For example, the spot electricity price of certain place in day-ahead and real-time is used as the forecast spot electricity price. The electricity price and load demand curve are shown in Fig. 11.1, and the random scenario of wind power output is shown in Fig. 11.2.

The installed capacity of the wind farm is 16 MW; The energy storage capacity is 2 MWh, the maximum charging and discharging power per hour is 1 MW, the operating efficiency is 93%, the operating cost is 18 yuan/MWh. The fitting coefficient k_{p} in the energy storage life model is 2.09, the rated cycle number N_{r} is 1591 [10], The floating life is 10 years. The model is solved by CPLEX solver.

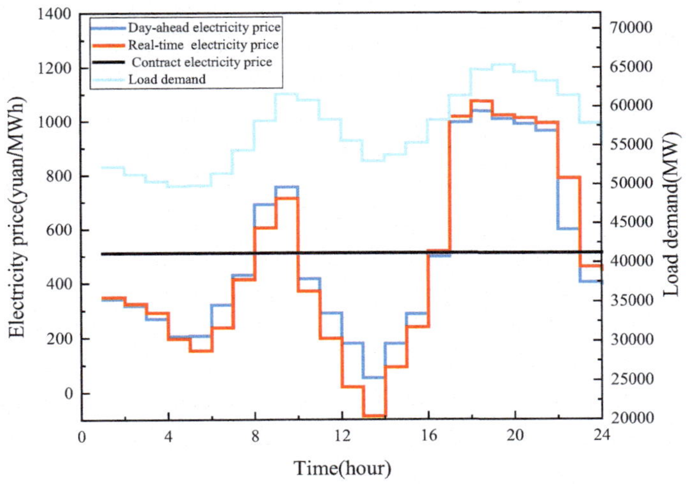

Fig. 11.1 Electricity price and load demand curve

Fig. 11.2 Random scenario of wind power output

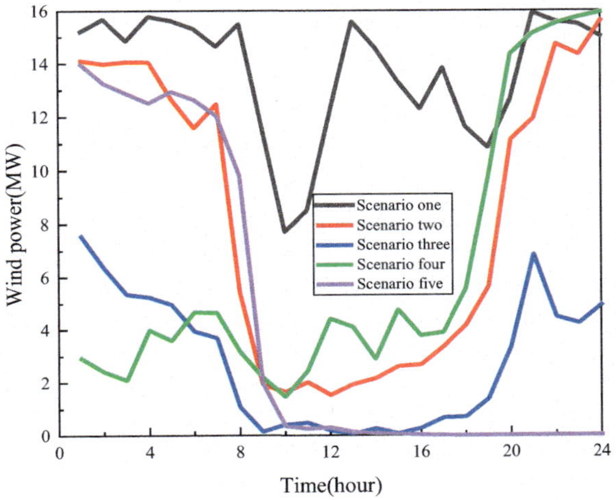

11.4.2 *Real-Time Output Curve Before and After Optimization*

Taking scenario 3 with the highest probability of occurrence as an example, the real-time output curve of wind-storage integration considering load demand and the real-time output curve of wind power are compared, as shown in Fig. 11.3. As can be seen from Fig. 11.3, considering the guiding effect of load demand on the regulation strategy, the energy storage is charged at 13 o'clock in the low load valley and released

Fig. 11.3 Real-time output curve before and after optimization

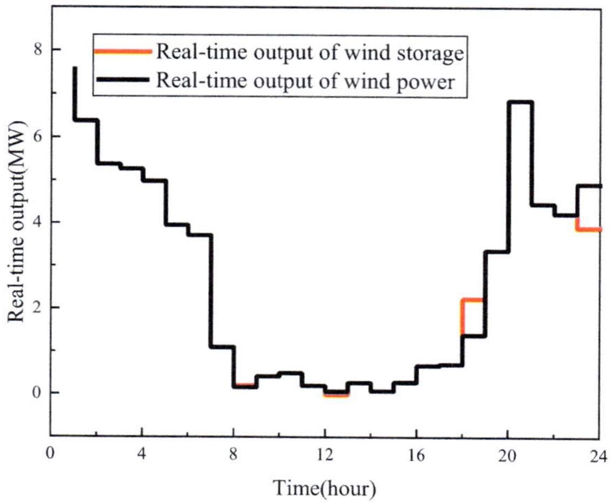

a lot of electric energy at 19 o'clock in the high load peak. Therefore, the real-time regulation strategy of wind and storage integration considering the guidance of load demand can better play the role of energy storage in responding to load demand.

11.4.3 Comparison of Benefits of Different Strategies

The expected income before and after optimization is compared. Before optimization, the proportion of medium and long-term contract electricity to the total electricity is 90% in the whole period. See Table 11.1 for the comparison between the expected return after optimization and the expected return before optimization. From Table 11.1, it can be seen that the expected return after optimization has increased by 7.9% compared with that before optimization. Therefore, from the perspective of relative decoupling of electricity generation operation revenue and capacity cost recovery, the strategy proposed in this paper has the effect of improving wind power revenue.

Table 11.1 Expected return of different strategies

Strategies	Income/yuan
Before optimization	84,018.03
After optimization	90,683.31

11.5 Conclusion

Based on the settlement rules of contract for difference in centralized spot market, considering the randomness of wind power output and energy storage life, this paper puts forward a coordinated optimization strategy of contract electricity and spot electricity for wind storage integration considering load demand. Through the analysis of an example, the following conclusions are drawn: Considering the load demand in the regulation strategy of wind storage integration can play the role of wind storage integration in responding to the load demand; The application of the strategy proposed in this paper can effectively increase the expected benefits of wind power from the perspective of decoupling electricity generation operation and cost recovery.

References

1. Wang, W., Sun, Q., Yuan, B., et al.: Application of energy storage in integrated energy systems–a solution to fluctuation and uncertainty of renewable energy. J. Energy Storage **52** (2022)
2. Psarros, G.N., Dratsas, P.A., Papathanassiou, S.A.: A comprehensive review of electricity storage applications in island systems. J. Energy Storage **83** (2024)
3. Schick, C., Klempp, N., Hufendiek, K.: Role and impact of prosumers in a sector-integrated energy system with high renewable shares. IEEE Trans. Power Syst. **37**(4), 3286–3298 (2022)
4. Xie, Y.Y., Guo, W.Q., Wu, Q.W., et al.: Robust MPC-based bidding strategy for wind storage systems in real-time energy and regulation markets. Int. J. Electr. Power Energy Syst. **124** (2021)
5. Yang, J.J., Yang, M., Wang, M.X., et al.: A deep reinforcement learning method for managing wind farm uncertainties through energy storage system control and external reserve purchasing. Int. J. Elect. Power Energy Syst. **119** (2020)
6. Khazali, A., Rezaei, N., Su, W.C., et al.: Risk-aware bilevel optimal offering strategy of a joint wind/storage unit based on information gap decision theory. IEEE Syst. J. **15**(2), 1939–1949 (2023)
7. Miao, M., Lou, S.H., Zhang, Y.X., et al.: Research on the optimized operation of hybrid wind and battery energy storage system based on peak-valley electricity price. Energies **14**(12) (2021)
8. He, X.L., Lou, S.H., Wu, Y.W., et al.: Two-stage market bidding and scheduling strategy of integrated wind power and energy storage station in two-settlement mode. Autom. Electr. Power Syst. **46**(4), 47–55 (2022)
9. Abate, A.G., Riccardi, R., Ruiz, C.: Contract design in electricity markets with high penetration of renewables: a two-stage approach. Omega-Int. J. Manag. Sci. **111** (2022)
10. Duggal, I., Venkatesh, B.: Short-term scheduling of thermal generators and battery storage with depth of discharge-based cost model. IEEE Trans. Power Syst. **30**(4), 2110–2118 (2015)

Chapter 12
Acoustic Monitoring for Wind Turbine Management: An Offshore Case Study

Isaac Segovia Ramírez, Pedro José Bernalte Sánchez, and Fausto Pedro García Márquez

Abstract The wind energy industry is growing every year, being one of the most prominent energies in the world. The reduction of operating and maintenance costs through the implementation of new condition monitoring systems is essential to ensure the competitiveness, reliability, and maintainability of wind turbines. This work introduces a novel methodology for wind turbine monitoring based on acoustic analysis of rotatory elements from the nacelle using an unmanned aerial vehicle carrying a data acquisition sensor. The approach is based on pattern recognition of acoustic signals associated with faults that modify the typical noise produced in healthy conditions. The extraction of reliable data from the acoustic dataset is performed through a signal processing methodology using wavelet transforms for the detection of patterns associated with different scenarios. The validation of the methodology is developed with a case study in an operating wind turbine combined with the simulation of rotatory faults. K-Nearest Neighbor is applied to validate the results, demonstrating the reliability and suitability of acoustic monitoring for fault detection in offshore wind turbines.

12.1 Introduction

Several issues in energy transition, variations in fossil fuel costs and the rising global electricity demands are causing a global energy crisis. New energy sources and technical advances in maintenance operations will play a major role in energy transition due to favorable policies. It is estimated that renewable energies will account for

I. S. Ramírez (✉) · P. J. B. Sánchez · F. P. G. Márquez
Ingenium Research Group, Universidad Castilla-La Mancha, Ciudad Real, Spain
e-mail: Isaac.Segovia@uclm.es

P. J. B. Sánchez
e-mail: Pedro.Bernalte@uclm.es

F. P. G. Márquez
e-mail: FaustoPedro.Garcia@uclm.es

F. P. García Márquez et al. (eds.), *Computing, Internet of Things and Data Analytics*, Smart Innovation, Systems and Technologies 387,
https://doi.org/10.1007/978-3-031-87154-2_12

more than 90% of increments in global energy capacity by 2026, even reaching 80% of global energy generation by 2045. The wind energy industry has demonstrated its competitiveness in 2023 due to s trending growth of around 50%. The new wind energy installations by 2023 reached 116GW, led by Asian-Pacific mainly by China with more than 40% followed by India, see Fig. 12.1.

Wind Turbines (WTs) work in harsh environments, especially offshore, with high winds and erosive conditions that may cause several faults that affect the overall performance. Some of the most typical WT faults are caused by critical elements, e.g., generators with overheating or issues in electric components, blades with cracks, gearbox with bearing faults and stator faults that account for around 40% of total failures, among others [2]. Maintenance management plans are essential for fault detection, performance evaluation and maintenance planning, ensuring safety compliance and early issue detection to optimize performance and minimize downtimes. Conventional monitoring techniques for offshore WTs present several issues, e.g.,

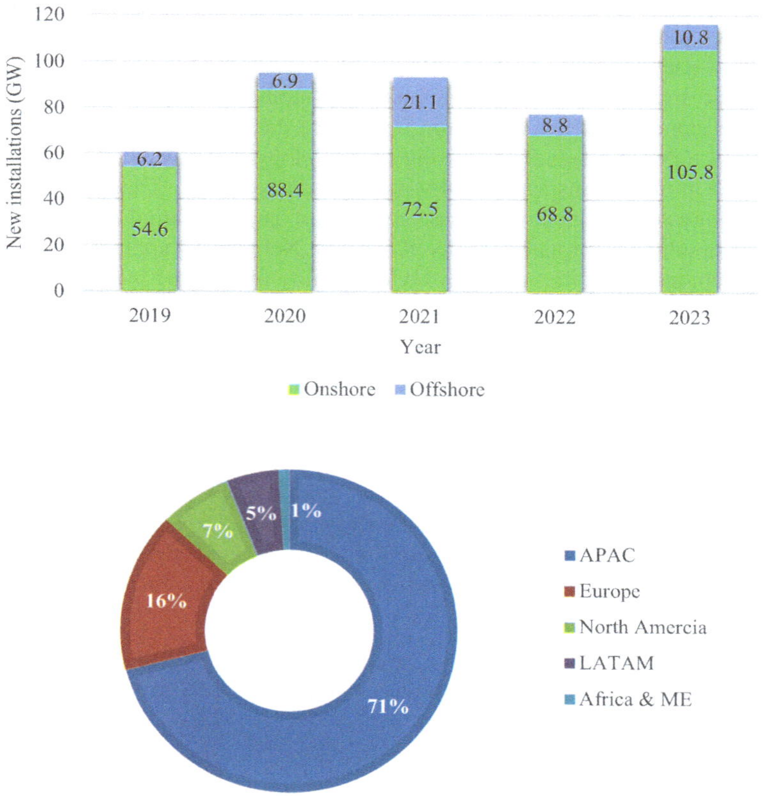

Fig. 12.1 New global wind energy installations until 2023 (up). Percentage distribution of new installations per region in 2023 (down). Adapted from [1]

safety risks, time consumption and high costs among others. The displacements to offshore locations have a relevant impact on the accessibility of maintenance operators, and technicians often require extended travel periods by workboat or helicopter, employing hours inspecting each component including the platform. Operation and maintenance (O&M) costs associated with preventive and corrective maintenance represent more than 30% of the total costs for offshore WTs [3].

The implementation of novel inspection technologies based on non-destructive testing (NDT) can significantly enhance the efficiency and lifetime of offshore WTs, acquiring reliable data about the real state of WTs, and improving maintenance management plans. Supervisory Control and Data Acquisition (SCADA) systems acquire a high volume and variety of datasets from several Condition Monitoring Systems (CMS) located in critical WT components. Novel analytic methodologies are widely implemented for SCADA analysis. The definition of real operating conditions and fault detection are current challenges for wind operators, caused by false alarms triggered without working faults that may lead to unnecessary maintenance operations that increase O&M costs, requiring novel CMS and data acquisition methodologies [4]. Vibration monitoring is focused on mechanical components through the analysis of vibration signals caused by misalignment or imbalance for fault detection and diagnosis, although the reliability of this methodology depends on the proper location of several transducers in several WT components. Ultrasonic testing or thermography requires low computational costs for data processing, but its reliability is low and the initial investment is elevated compared with other techniques.

Fault detection and diagnosis using acoustic signal processing are being currently implemented for health monitoring [5]. The current state of the art demonstrates that novel techniques based on acoustic emission are developing a high growth in the wind energy industry, demonstrated by more than 8000 publications in 2023 about acoustic-based methodologies for WT maintenance. Several authors have studied acoustic monitoring WT blade damage detection, proving the reliability of the technique [6]. Novel acoustic methodologies were implemented for tower maintenance, showing improvements of around 5% compared to traditional techniques [7]. Beale et al. [8] presented an approach to detect structural damage in WT blades with acoustic methodology. Several faults were introduced into the WT blades, although the authors detected several limitations, needing more advanced signal processing. Chen et al [9] developed an acoustical detection of WT blade faults with static microphones in the tower. This methodology demonstrated that fault detection is possible with acoustic analysis, although the implementation of this type of CMS in large distances increases costs and reduces the reliability of the results, requiring novel CMS to enhance the data acquisition process.

Unmanned Aerial Vehicles (UAVs) are widely used for monitoring in several application fields due to low risks for operators in aerial operations, cost-effectiveness, close-contact NDT inspections and easy implementation [10]. Each aerial operation is mainly influenced by the number of rotors of the UAV, the weight of the carried sensor, the type of battery and the onboard computers that manage the power optimization, among others [11]. Several types of CMS have been implemented with UAVs in the wind energy industry to enhance current monitoring capabilities, making WT blade inspection one of the most explored applications in the current state of the art [12]. The monitoring of the interior of WT blades was presented by Kulsinskas et al. [13] with a precision of around 90%. Castelar Wembers et al. [14] developed a WT blade monitoring system with a 2D-Light Detection and Ranging (LiDAR) system. This system was designed for autonomous aerial operations in WTs using advanced flight controllers, reducing the overall inspection time.

Aerial monitoring for offshore WTs has not been established due to hard environmental conditions, positioning issues or increments in data acquisition rate to optimize flights [15]. Novel technical advances, enhanced flight time, and improvements in sensor monitoring and battery endurance have enabled the development of the technique, although the number of references about this topic is still reduced [16]. The viability of aerial acoustic monitoring for WTs was presented by García Márquez et al. [17], although only the main basis of the methodology was presented.

The main novelties of this paper are summarized as:

- This paper presents a novel approach for WT fault detection and diagnosis based on acoustic analysis of sound emitted by the nacelle. This methodology aims to classify and identify all the noise sources from aerial WT monitoring, being a novelty in the current state of the art.
- The data acquisition process is formed by a novel acoustic CMS carried by an UAV. This configuration is designed to transmit the acoustic data to an onboard store system and a ground station for further analysis. Filtering processes and wavelet transform are used for data processing and fault detection.
- Several recordings from a test rig in previous research studies simulating different faults in working conditions are used to validate the approach for offshore WT monitoring [18]. K-Nearest Neighbor (K-NN) has been chosen due to its high accuracy in validating the results.

The rest of the manuscript is presented as follows. The approach for data filtering is presented in Section. A case study in operating offshore WTs is presented to test the viability of the technique in Sect. 12.3. Section 12.4 summarizes and determines the main conclusions of the study.

12.2 Acoustic Data Processing

Acoustic data is affected by several noise sources, and advanced filtering processes are necessary to extract valuable information about the real state of WTs. The process developed in this research is designed to combine different techniques and methodologies to ensure proper data filtering and processing. The implementation of filtering techniques transforms raw data into energy levels, reducing external noise and negative effects on the acoustic data. Wavelet transforms establish the energy distribution among several frequency ranges, describing oscillations that originate, evolve and terminate at zero, showing abrupt changes in signals. The main characteristic is based on their localization in both time and space to establish a consistent connection between scale and frequency, indicated by the center frequency. The decomposition of acoustic signals is achieved with twelve progressive degrees of decomposition with Discrete Wavelet Transform (DWT). The frequency subbands are classified according to twelve decomposition levels through low-pass and high-pass filters. The next level of decomposition is obtained through the iteration of low-pass subbands, analyzing the signals by gradually reducing the subbands at multiple levels of resolution to eliminate noise and decrease the signals [19]. Several wavelet families are being used for filtering and processing methodologies, according to the mother wavelet characteristics and wavelet coefficients. Symlet wavelet family is a version of Daubechies, and it has been selected for this study due to its efficiency in the implementation and high symmetry [20, 21]. The Fast Fourier Transform (FFT) adjust signals to the frequency domain, identifying frequency ranges with high values for signal filtering. For this study, this method can isolate particular frequencies related to environmental sound or UAV typical noise [22].

Butterworth filter has been implemented because this filter preserves a flat frequency range within the passband. The frequency domain response of this filter presents the passband that enables signal transmission, while the stopband inhibits the signal transition [23]. Four fundamental types of signal filters are presented: the low-pass filter, which allows frequencies below a specified threshold to pass while higher frequencies are attenuated; the high-pass filter, which enables frequencies beyond a set threshold while reducing lower frequencies; the band-pass filter consents frequencies between limited thresholds while reducing others; and the band-stop filter, that decreases frequencies within specified thresholds while other frequencies can pass. The low-pass Butterworth filter is chosen in this case study for acoustic data filtering.

12.3 Case Study

A novel case study in offshore WTs is defined to test the methodology and analyze the sound acquisition procedure. The acoustic sensor is the Shure SM-137 (SH) carried by the UAV DJI Xfold Spy. The offshore WT has 2 MW with 100 meters of altitude of the nacelle. The dataset accounts for more than 8 minutes of acoustic datasets, limited by the environmental conditions and the battery endurance. The specifications of the acoustic sensors enable measurement at wide range distances and the data acquisition process was developed as close as possible to the nacelle, being confirmed that UAV distance does not affect the aerial measurements for this case study. The aerial operation was designed with safety and reliability during constant environmental conditions, ensuring reliable data for the analysis.

The filtering and transformation methods outlined in the previous section are implemented on the raw acoustic signals. This case study is defined by six different scenarios that combine different noise sources with recordings from the laboratory that simulate faulty conditions:

- **Environment sound**: the original ambient sound that includes wind and sea recorded by the acoustic sensor.
- **Environment +UAV**: The UAV is powered on with the rotors spinning but the UAV has not taken off.
- **Environment + UAV No Fault 750 rpm**: The UAV is located close to the nacelle. External recordings that simulate working conditions at 750 rpm are introduced by a speaker and captured by the acoustic sensor.
- **Environment + UAV Fault at 750 rpm**: The configuration is similar to the previous scenario, but the external recording is caused by rotatory faults at 750 rpm.
- **Environment + UAV No Fault 1500 rpm**: The recordings are produced by simulations at 1500 rpm in healthy conditions.
- **Environment + UAV Fault at 1500 rpm**: The external acoustic recordings are established at 1500 rpm and related to faults.

Figure 12.2 shows the energy distribution from the different scenarios, combining filtered and unfiltered data. All these results have been achieved through the application of a 5000 Hz low-pass filter.

All the unfiltered scenarios present an irregular distribution between 22 and 172 Hz with high variations in the energy levels. The environment scenario provides lower energy levels while scenarios with more noise levels, e.g., environment combined with UAV and 1500 rpm fault, show higher energy distribution. The unfiltered scenarios with faults demonstrate displacements to higher frequencies, proving the influence of noises with higher frequency distribution generated in a laboratory at 750 and 1500 rpm. The effect of the filter developed for the offshore tests is more significant in scenarios with higher noise levels caused by UAV noises and environmental sounds. The offshore filter concentrates the energy levels around the main peak at 86-172 Hz and increases the maximum energy values, enhancing the variations between scenarios for pattern detection and classification. The filtering and processing methodologies applied in this research study transform the raw data into clearly differentiated scenarios, enabling fault detection and pattern recognition. K-NN has been applied to validate the results and demonstrate the reliability of the methodology. This Machine Learning-based technique has been selected for being one of the most implemented algorithms and its reliability has been tested in several research [24]. The overall results achieve 97.50% accuracy.

12.4 Conclusions

Wind energy has emerged as a relevant renewable energy source in recent years due to larger wind turbines and new technical improvements. Novel monitoring systems that reduce operation and maintenance costs are required for wind turbine operators to ensure efficiency and reach competitiveness in the energy sector. This paper introduces a non-destructive monitoring system formed by an acoustic sensor carried by

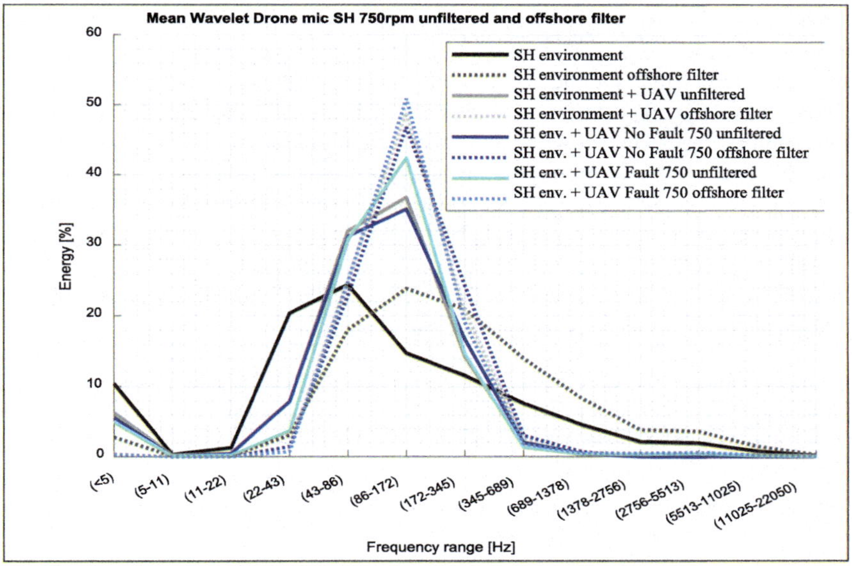

a)

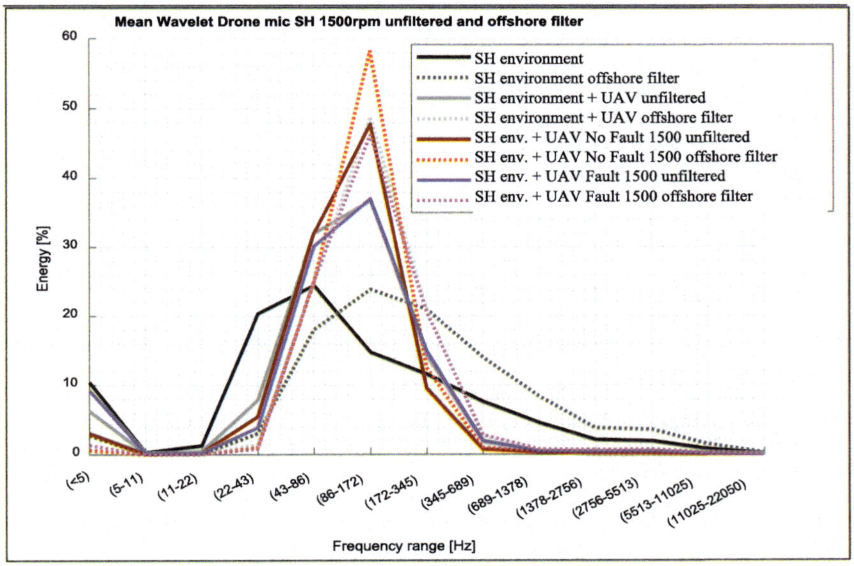

b)

Fig. 12.2 Energy distribution for SH acoustic sensor. **a** Filtered and unfiltered data for scenarios at 750 rpm. **b** Filtered and unfiltered data for scenarios at 1500 rpm unmanned aerial vehicles for wind turbine fault detection. This approach is based on the capability of data processing and filtering to extract valuable patterns associated with rotatory faults in the nacelle. The data processing approach utilized several techniques such as data filtering, Wavelet transforms and Fast Fourier Transforms. This methodology is tested with a case study in an operating offshore wind turbine. Several scenarios that combine the presence of faults at different frequency ranges are introduced to enhance the characterization of experiments. All the scenarios were distinguished, demonstrating the reliability of the process. K-Nearest Neighbor was introduced to validate the results, showing an overall accuracy of 97.5% in classifying different scenarios. These results emphasize the robustness and effectiveness of the acoustic methodology in operational scenarios.

Acknowledgements The work reported herein was supported financially by the Ministerio de Ciencia e Innovación (Spain) and the European Regional Development Fund, under the Research Grant WindSound project (Reference: PID2021-125278OB-I00).

Disclosure of Interests. The authors have no competing interests to declare that are relevant to the content of this article.

References

1. Joyce, L., Feng, Z.: Global wind report 2024. Global wind energy council (2024)
2. Li, J., Chen, X., Du, Z., Fang, Z., He, Z.: A new noise-controlled second-order enhanced stochastic resonance method with its application in wind turbine drivetrain fault diagnosis. Renew. Energy **60**, 7–19 (2013)
3. Maples, B., Saur, G., Hand, M., van de Pietermen, R., Obdam, T.: Installation, operation, and maintenance strategies to reduce the cost of offshore wind energy. National Renewable Energy Lab. (NREL), Golden, CO (United States) (2013)
4. Peco Chacón, A.M., Segovia Ramírez, I., García Márquez, F.P.: State of the art of artificial intelligence applied for false alarms in wind turbines. Arch. Comput. Methods Eng. **29** (2022). https://doi.org/10.1007/s11831-021-09671-x
5. Suman, A., Kumar, C., Suman, P.: Early detection of mechanical malfunctions in vehicles using sound signal processing. Appl. Acoust. **188**, 108578 (2022). https://doi.org/10.1016/j.apacoust.2021.108578
6. Bernalte Sánchez, P.J., Garcia Marquez, F.P.: New approaches on maintenance management for wind turbines based on acoustic inspection. In: Proceedings of the Proceedings of the Fourteenth International Conference on Management Science and Engineering Management, vol 2, pp. 791–800 (2021)
7. Hubbard, P.G., Xu, J., Zhang, S., Dejong, M., Luo, L., Soga, K., Papa, C., Zulberti, C., Malara, D., Fugazzotto, F.: Dynamic structural health monitoring of a model wind turbine tower using distributed acoustic sensing (DAS). J. Civ. Struct. Health Monit. **11**, 833–849 (2021)
8. Beale, C., Inalpolat, M., Niezrecki, C.: Active acoustic damage detection of structural cavities using internal acoustic excitations. Struct. Health Monit. **19**, 48–65 (2020). https://doi.org/10.1177/1475921719835761
9. Chen, B., Yu, S., Yu, Y., Zhou, Y.: Acoustical damage detection of wind turbine blade using the improved incremental support vector data description. Renew. Energy **156**, 548–557 (2020). https://doi.org/10.1016/j.renene.2020.04.096
10. Fahlstrom, P.G., Gleason, T.J., Sadraey, M.H.: Introduction to UAV systems. Wiley (2022)

11. Mohsan, S.A.H., Khan, M.A., Noor, F., Ullah, I., Alsharif, M.H.: Towards the unmanned aerial vehicles (UAVs): a comprehensive review. Drones **6**, 147 (2022)
12. Sánchez, P.J.B., Ramirez, I.S., Márquez, F.P.G.: Wind turbines acoustic inspections performed with UAV and sound frequency domain analysis. In: Proceedings of the 2021 7th International Conference on Control, Instrumentation and Automation (ICCIA), pp. 1–5 (2021)
13. Kulsinskas, A., Durdevic, P., Ortiz-Arroyo, D.: Internal wind turbine blade inspections using UAVs: analysis and design issues. Energies **14**, 294 (2021)
14. Castelar Wembers, C., Pflughaupt, J., Moshagen, L., Kurenkov, M., Lewejohann, T., Schildbach, G.: LiDAR-based automated UAV inspection of wind turbine rotor blades. J. Field Robot. (2024)
15. Dias, A., Almeida, J., Oliveira, A., Santos, T., Martins, A., Silva, E.: Unmanned aerial vehicle for wind-turbine inspection next step: offshore. In: Proceedings of the OCEANS 2022, Hampton Roads, pp. 1–6 (2022)
16. Segovia Ramírez, I., Pliego Marugán, A., García Márquez, F.P.: A novel approach to optimize the positioning and measurement parameters in photovoltaic aerial inspections. Renew. Energy **187** (2022). https://doi.org/10.1016/j.renene.2022.01.071
17. García Márquez, F.P., Bernalte Sánchez, P.J., Segovia Ramírez, I.: Acoustic inspection system with unmanned aerial vehicles for wind turbines structure health monitoring. Struct. Health Monit. **21**, 485–500 (2022)
18. Moraleda, V.B., Marugán, A.P., Márquez, F.P.G.: Acoustic maintenance management employing unmanned aerial vehicles in renewable energies. In: Proceedings of the Proceedings of the Twelfth International Conference on Management Science and Engineering Management, pp. 969–981 (2019)
19. Rioul, O., Duhamel, P.: Fast algorithms for discrete and continuous wavelet transforms. IEEE Trans. Inf. Theory **38**, 569–586 (1992). https://doi.org/10.1109/18.119724
20. Nigam, H., Srivastava, H.M.: Filtering of audio signals using discrete wavelet transforms. Mathematics **11**, 4117 (2023)
21. Kovacevic, J., Sweldens, W.: Wavelet families of increasing order in arbitrary dimensions. IEEE Trans. Image Process. **9**, 480–496 (2000)
22. Brigham, E.O., Morrow, R.E.: The fast Fourier transform. IEEE Spectr. **4**, 63–70 (1967). https://doi.org/10.1109/MSPEC.1967.5217220
23. Abdelgawad, A., Mahmud, M.A., Yelamarthi, K.: Butterworth filter application for structural health monitoring. Int. J. Handheld Comput. Res. (IJHCR) **7**, 15–29 (2016)
24. Chacón, A.M.P., Ramirez, I.S., García Márquez, F.P.: False alarm detection in wind turbine management by K-nearest neighbors model. In: Integrated Emerging Methods of Artificial Intelligence & Cloud Computing; Springer, pp. 106–112 (2021)

Chapter 13
Effects of the Task and Learning Process on the Joint Distribution of the Saccade Amplitudes and Orientations

Bilyana Genova, Nadejda Bocheva, and Ivan Hristov

Abstract The eye movements are closely related to information selection and attention allocation and depend on bottom-up and top-down processes. Previous research showed that the joint distributions of saccade amplitudes and directions are a sensitive measure of the effects of image type and content and the participant's age. We aimed to understand whether the task and the learning of the spatial regularities in images affect the relationship between the saccade amplitudes and directions. The stimuli consisted of pairs of patterns with 0, 1 or 2 coincident groupings of squares. The left pattern was in its original orientation and the right pattern was rotated at 90°, 180° or 270° to it. The stimuli lasted until the observer's response but no longer than 3 s. The pattern repetitions varied from 12 to 96 times in one experiment with 180 trials. Nine observers participated in 3 experimental sessions. Observers' task was to decide whether the patterns in the stimulus were the same or different. Eye movements were recorded during the experiments. Our results show: (1) substantial difference in the saccade-direction relationships from the typical biases observed in free viewing natural scenes; (2) changes in the joint distributions of the saccade amplitudes and directions in the process of learning; (3) difference in the angular distributions of the saccades depending on the response time. Our data expand previous research, showing that joint distributions also reflect the learning process of spatial regularities in the images.

B. Genova (✉) · N. Bocheva · I. Hristov
Institute of Neurobiology, Bulgarian Academy of Sciences, Sofia, Bulgaria
e-mail: b.genova@abv.bg

N. Bocheva
e-mail: nadya@percept.bas.bg

F. P. García Márquez et al. (eds.), *Computing, Internet of Things and Data Analytics*, Smart Innovation, Systems and Technologies 387,
https://doi.org/10.1007/978-3-031-87154-2_13

13.1 Introduction

The eye movements are closely related to attention, more precisely to overt attention. As such, they are a valuable source of information about the processes of attention deployment. The eye movement allocation depends on both bottom-up and top-down processes. The first ones are more effective at the beginning of the stimulus appearance and depend on the low-level visual features and their salience, i.e., on features like color, intensity, and orientation. In certain circumstances, the bottom-up effects on eye movements and attention allocation may be preceded by top-down effects [1–3]. Top-down influence on gaze depends on the task and the observer's experience.

Certain biases are observed in eye movement deployment. For example, the saccades (the fast eye movements) are predominantly horizontal and of small amplitude. Both physiological and contextual factors explained the dominance of the horizontal saccades. Horizontal eye movements need two ocular muscles to shift the eye position, whereas eye movements in all other directions (e.g., vertical or oblique) require three muscles [4]. Also, many visual scenes containing artificial objects contain horizontal and vertical edges. In natural scenes, the horizon line is typically horizontal. In visual experiments, the images presented on a monitor are usually in landscape mode [4], again making horizontal eye movements more beneficial.

In free viewing of natural scenes, Le Meur and Liu [5] showed a higher frequency of horizontal saccades, a preference for upward than downward vertical saccades, and very rare oblique saccades. Moreover, the mode of saccade amplitudes was around 2–3° degrees of visual angle. They introduced the joint distribution of saccade amplitudes and orientation as a methodology for investigating the effect of different stimulus features or observers' characteristics on the eye movements' behavior. In a series of experiments, Le Meur and co-authors [6–10] showed that the joint distribution of saccade amplitudes and direction varied depending on the image type (natural scenes, web pages, paintings), scene context, the age of the observers.

Kümmerer and Bethge [11] analyzed the numerous existing models of scanpath prediction in free viewing that considered different aspects of image structure, oculomotor biases and attentional mechanisms to account for gaze deployment and its dynamics. Their analysis shows that many of these models do not capture some of the essential effects determining the relationship between the fixations in a scanpath. In a recent deep-learning model of scanpath prediction, Kümmerer and co-authors [12] were able to reproduce the oculomotor biases observed in free viewing of natural images—the dominance of horizontal saccades, to a lesser extent—of the vertical saccades, and a central bias of gaze deployment. The model shows the dominance of the spatiotopic image-driven map over scanpath history. The authors acknowledge that a promising future direction of research is evaluating the interactions between image content and the scanpath history in modeling the effects of the task on gaze deployment.

Limiting the analysis of oculomotor biases to free-viewing shrinks their generalizability to other behavioral tasks (e.g., [13]). The effect of perceptual task is typically evaluated by the change in fixation duration and gaze deployment location (e.g., [14–18]) but do not consider the scanpath characteristics reflected in the joint probability of the saccade amplitudes and directions. Moreover, most studies explore the eye movement characteristics during a single trial and do not explore the potential role of practice and learning on the dynamics of eye movements.

In the present study, we used images that differed little in the salience of their local features. They all contained an equal number of colored squares inside a black square of equal size in all images. The only difference in the patterns is the spatial grouping of their elements. The images were presented in pairs, and we varied the similarity of the component patterns and the repetition of the groupings inside them. The main factor contributing to gaze allocation is the top-down effects related to discriminating the patterns in the pair. We studied whether the regularities in the patterns—the presence of common groupings and pattern repetitions will affect the joint probability of the saccade amplitudes and orientations.

The study results show that the saccade amplitudes of the observers exceed the typical values obtained in free viewing of natural scenes. Moreover, contrary to the results of previous experiments, the oblique saccades are the most frequent. These differences with the previous studies represent the effect of the task on eye and attention deployment. The results also show that the joint distribution of saccade amplitudes and directions changes in the sequential experimental blocks, implying an effect of statistical learning—a process of extracting temporal or spatial pattern regularities without awareness.

13.2 Methods

13.2.1 Stimuli

The experimental set (Fig. 13.1) contained twelve patterns of 15 colored squares of size 1×1 cm positioned in black squares of 10×10 cm. Three groups of patterns were used as stimuli. In two groups (Groups 1 and 2), the patterns contained one or two coincident 5-element groupings, whereas in Group 3, the element groupings were unique.

13.2.2 Procedure

The patterns from each group were presented in pairs with the same group members. The two patterns in a stimulus were positioned symmetrically to the screen center. Their closest edges were 10 cm apart. The patterns in a pair were presented an equal number of times in the stimulus's left and right parts of the stimulus. On the left side, they kept their original orientation, whereas, on the right side, they were rotated at

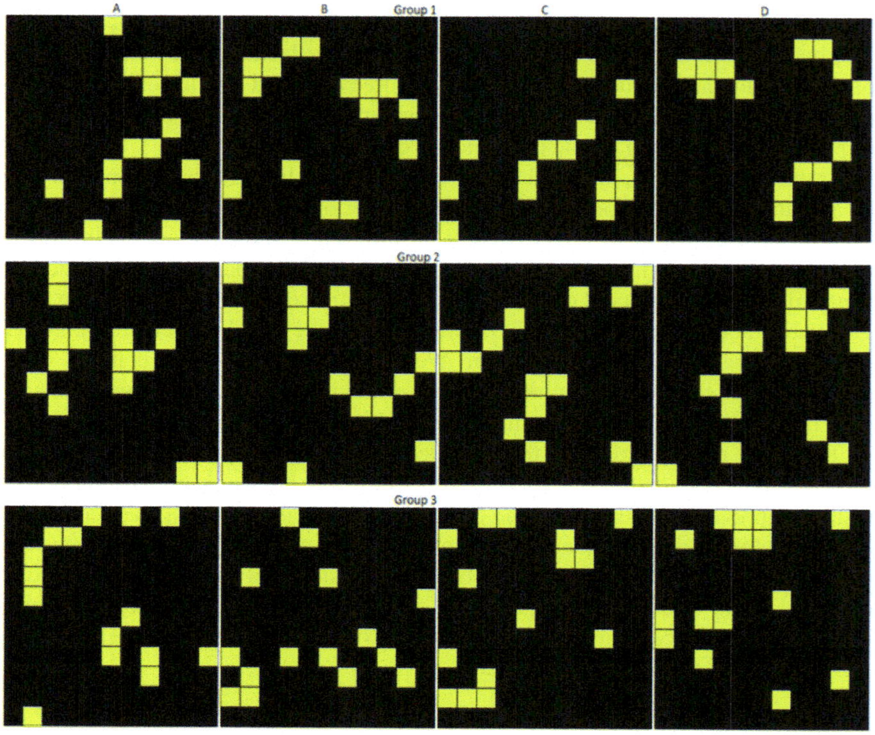

Fig. 13.1 Illustration of the pattern set used in the stimuli design. Each column contains patterns A, B, C, and D; each row—the patterns from different groups

90°, 180°, or 270°. Only one pattern from each group (pattern A) was presented on both the left and the right part of the stimulus, though even in this case, the two parts differed due to the rotation of the right pattern.

Seventy-two combinations of patterns were created by combining the patterns in each group (AA, AB, AC, AD, BA, BD, CA, DA) at three orientation angles of the right pattern.

The observers had to decide whether the left and right patterns in a stimulus were the same or different, giving a response by mouse click. Patterns AA were presented nine times in a sequence to make the number of equal responses more similar to the different responses. In contrast, the rest of the pattern combinations were presented only once. In this way, the stimulus sequence contained 90 pairs of randomly ordered stimuli. This sequence was repeated twice in an experimental session.

The stimulus generation leads to an unequal number of repetitions of unique groupings in the stimulus set, varying from 12 to 96, and a different number of patterns A, B, C, and D on the left side of the stimulus, with pattern A being the most frequent (36 times) and patterns B and D the rarest (6 times).

The stimuli were presented on a gray background and lasted until the observer's response but no longer than 3 s. After this time, the screen turned gray. The next stimulus presentation followed 500 ms after the observer's response.

Three experimental sessions separated by a 10-min break were performed in one day. Each experiment contained 180 trials. The whole testing lasted about 45 min. The participants were seated at 57 cm from the computer screen in a dark room. Hence, the effect of the lighting conditions, if any, is the same for all participants.

A head-mounted eye tracker (Jazz novo, Ober Consulting Sp. Z o.o.) with 1000 Hz temporal resolution recorded the participants' eye movements. A 9-point calibration was performed before each experimental session.

Participants. Nine observers aged 26 to 59 (mean age 41.7) participated in the study. All of them gave written consent. The experiment was approved by the Ethics Committee of the Institute of Neurobiology and performed according to the regulations of the Declaration of Helsinki.

13.2.3 Data Analyses and Measures

The eye-tracker software separated the recorded eye movements into saccades and fixations. The threshold characteristics for dividing the eye movements in these two types were eye velocity of 30 deg/s) and acceleration of 8000 deg/s2. To better define the regions of interest, we used the DBSCAN clustering algorithm [19] to combine the fixations into gazes with at least 200 data points in a cluster. We chose this clustering algorithm because it needed no advanced selection of the cluster numbers. To correct potential eye drifts or calibration errors, we used the Iterative Closest Point algorithm [20].

We used the joint probability distributions of the sequential saccade amplitudes and orientations to describe the participants' performance. Only the stimulus-evoked eye movements were analyzed, whereas the memory-guided saccades after the stimulus disappearance were disregarded.

We were interested in whether the information selection needed to discriminate the patterns changed in the learning process and how this change was reflected in the eye movement landings.

13.3 Results

To understand whether the task and the learning of the spatial regularities affect the relationship between the saccade amplitudes and their direction, we evaluated their joint distribution in Experiments 1–3 (Fig. 13.2). The figure construction follows the methodology described in [7]. The saccade amplitude was divided into bins of 0.25 deg and the directions—in the range of 0° to 359° with a bin width of 1°.

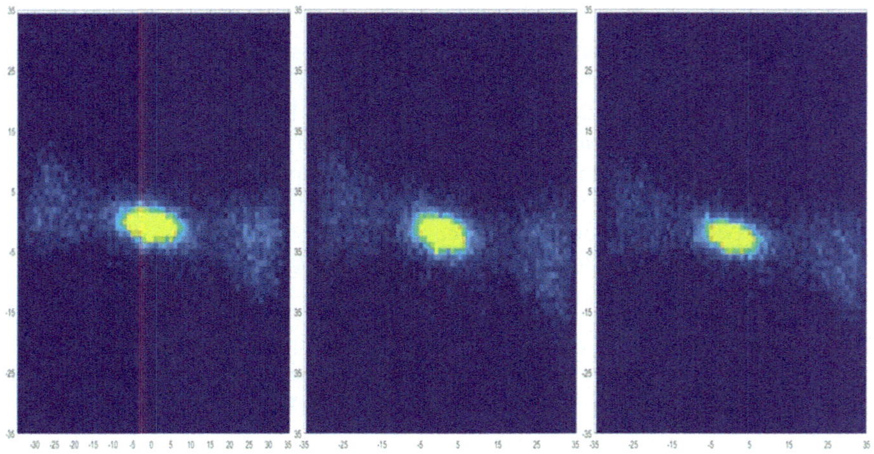

Fig. 13.2 Joint-probability distributions of the saccade amplitudes and orientations in experiments 1–3

However, in our study, the saccade amplitudes exceeded 20 deg. Hence, they were binned from 0.25 deg to 35 deg.

The figure shows substantial differences with the joint probability plots in free viewing. First, the saccade amplitude is much larger than in free image viewing. Next, the oblique saccades dominate. There is no visible difference between the upward and downward saccade directions typical for free viewing.

The figure shows that the spread of directions shrinks in the sequential experiments. To obtain a metric for the differences in the image color histograms, we used the Earth's mover distance [21]. The distance value for comparison of the data from Experiments 1 and 2 is 0.635; for Experiments 1 and 3, it is 1.175; for Experiments 2 and 3, it is 0.763. Hence, in the task we employed, the similarity of the joint probability distributions decreases from the first to the third experiment.

The correlation coefficient between the distributions of saccade amplitudes and directions for Experiments 1 and 2 is 0.35, for Experiments 1 and 3–0.16, whereas for Experiments 2 and 3–0.69.

To understand what changes most in the joint distributions–the saccade amplitudes or their directions, we first used the Kuiper two-sample test [22] to compare the angle distributions. The test evaluates whether two samples of circular data differ in either mean location or dispersion. The results showed significant differences between the directions of saccades obtained in the first and the second experiments (test statistics = 0.031; $p < 0.001$), between the first and the third experiments (test statistics = 0.030; $p < 0.001$), and between the second and the third experiments (test statistics = 0.0261; $p = 0.002$).

As the amplitudes of the saccades have a non-normal distribution with more values with small amplitudes, we compared their distributions with the non-parametric Wilcoxon's rank test. The comparison showed significant differences between the amplitudes of the first and the other two experimental sessions (W = 166,677,651; $p < 0.001$ for the comparison of the first and the second session; W = 131,605,404; $p < 0.001$ for the comparison of the first and the third session). The comparison of the saccade amplitudes obtained in experimental sessions 2 and 3 did not differ significantly (W = 120,385,321; $p = 0.73$). Hence, both the directions and saccade amplitudes change in the process of learning of the spatial regularities in the stimuli.

In a seminal work on the relation between eye fixations and cognitive processes, Just and Carpenter [23] considered a three-stage model of the cognitive processes involved in simple perceptual tasks: encoding, decision, and confirmation. We restricted the analysis of the eye movements only to the time when the stimuli were visible. A consequence of this choice is that in certain conditions, all three processes would be involved and affect the eye movement characteristics. In contrast, when the response time exceeds the stimulus presentation time, the encoding and the confirmation processes cannot be performed. As the learning process manifested by the difference in the eye movement characteristics is reflected more in the angular distributions of the saccades for the three experiments, we generated the normalized histograms of the saccade orientations when the response time exceeds the stimulus presentation and when it less than it (Fig. 13.3). In order to compare the distributions, the heights of the bars are normalized so that their total sum is equal to 1, and each bar has a height proportional to the ratio of the number of observations in it and the total number of observations. The figure shows that the angular distributions of the saccades differ depending on the response time. Interestingly, more differences are observed in the normalized angular distributions for the three experiments when the response time exceeds the stimulus presentation than when it is shorter. Moreover, the difference due to the response time seems larger in Experiments 2 and 3 than in Experiment 1.

We also plotted (Fig. 13.4) the heat maps of the eye fixations for the three experiments. These representations show the accumulated distributions of eye fixations convolved with a Gaussian function. In our representations, the spread of the Gaussians is one degree of visual angle coinciding with the size of the fovea. No center bias is observed in the data. Moreover, the figure explains why the horizontal saccades are not the most frequent in our study. It shows that the fixations at the right patterns

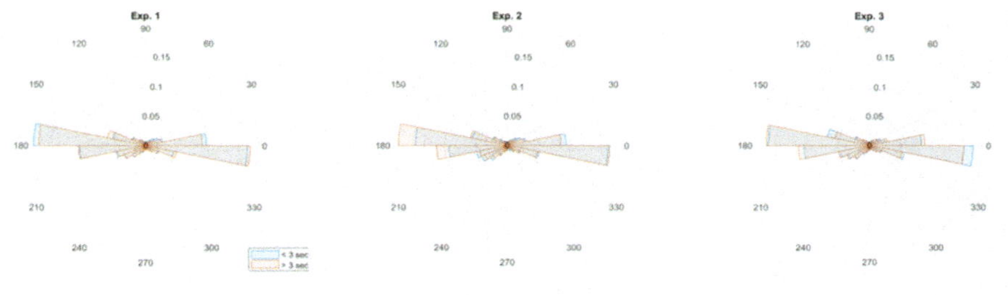

Fig. 13.3 Normalized histograms of the saccade orientations for response time shorter and longer than the stimulus presentation duration

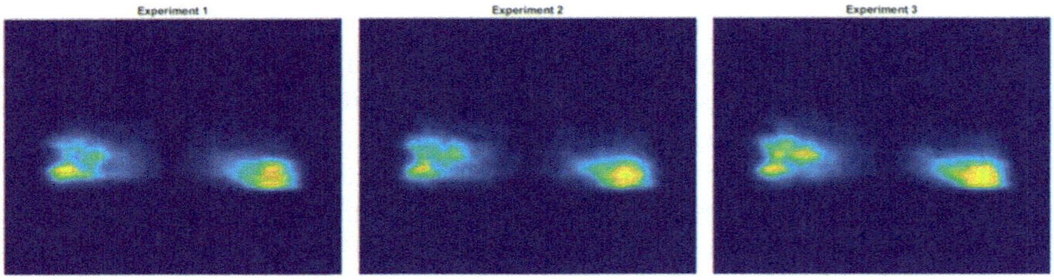

Fig. 13.4 Heatmaps of the eye fixations

in a stimulus are located predominantly at its lower area. In contrast, the allocation of the gaze on the left pattern changes most in the sequential experiments.

13.4 Discussion

The present study's results show a modification of the participants' gaze behavior in the sequential experimental blocks. The changes are reflected in the joint probability distributions of the saccade amplitudes and directions. Moreover, the saccade-direction relationships differ substantially from the typical biases observed in viewing natural scenes. We did not observe a central bias, i.e., the allocation of the first fixation at the image center (Fig. 13.5). In contrast, the first saccades are predominantly on the left. We observed large saccade amplitudes exceeding the typical value of about 20 deg in free viewing. The horizontal bias was also absent in our data, where the dominant saccade directions were oblique.

The joint probability distributions obtained in our study resemble the gaze behavior when exploring web pages [7]. In webpage explorations, the saccades are slightly tilted downward and small, with few large diagonal and vertical saccades. Similarly to our study, the exploration started from the left upper part (Fig. 13.5). We do not, however, observe large vertical saccades. One reason for this might be the limited presentation time of the stimuli.

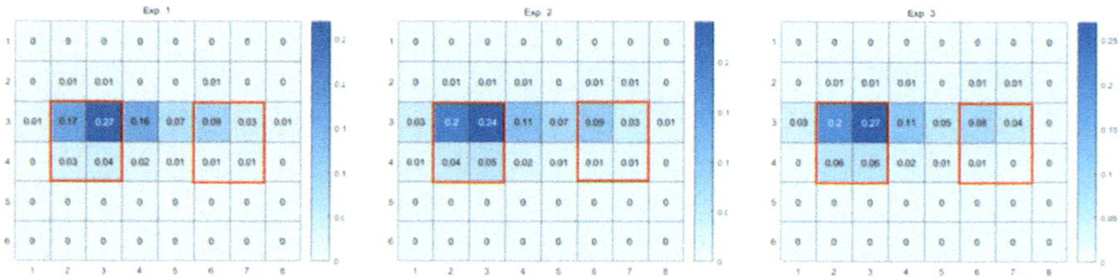

Fig. 13.5 The relative frequency of the first saccade landings in the sequential experiments. The red squares represent the positions of the patterns in the stimuli

Previous research [8–10] showed that the joint-probability distributions of saccade amplitudes and directions are a sensitive measure of the effects of image type and content and the participant's age. Our data expand these conclusions, showing that these distributions also reflect the learning process of spatial regularities in the images.

The change in the joint probability distributions of the saccade amplitudes and directions is most significant between the first and second experimental sessions. It is more apparent in the saccades' orientation changes than in saccade amplitudes. Visual observation of the joint distributions of the saccade amplitudes and directions implies more significant changes in the orientation of the saccades with shorter amplitudes. The shorter saccades correspond to explorations of the elements of one or the other patterns in the stimulus pair. It remains essential to relate the observed changes in the eye movement characteristics to the stimulus features to understand better the processes of information selection and its relation to the spatial regularities in the patterns.

Limitations of the study. A limitation of our study is the relatively small number of participants, which may introduce idiosyncrasies in the pattern of results. Even though [24] stated that a smaller number of subjects might be compensated by a larger image set in modeling fixation deployment, this statement does not concern the scan path characteristics. Moreover, in our study, we used a visual discrimination task in which we manipulated the similarity of the patterns and their frequency of occurrence, keeping the salience of the local features the same. Thus, there were no privileged regions to be explored. An interesting question for future studies might be to explore the interaction of salience information with the spatial regularities in the patterns in the process of learning and the dynamics of eye movement deployment.

13.5 Conclusions

Our results show that the discrimination task used in the study changes the oculomotor biases observed in free-viewing conditions. Moreover, the dynamics of the eye movements reflected in the joint probability of saccade amplitudes and directions vary with practice and with the learning of the statistical regularities and their relevance to the task performance. These findings reflect the role of active vision and ability of the eye movements to prioritize potential sources of information. Further studies are needed to evaluate the task-dependent effects not only on fixation duration and locations, but also on scanpath characteristics.

Acknowledgements This study was funded by the Bulgarian Science Fund, grant No KP-06-N52/6 from 12.11.2021.

Disclosure of Interests The authors have no competing interests to declare that are relevant to the content of this article.

References

1. Einhäuser, W., Spain, M., Perona, P.: Objects predict fixations better than early saliency. J. Vis. **8**(14), 18.1–26 (2008). https://doi.org/10.1167/8.14.18
2. Nyström, M., Holmqvist, K.: Semantic override of low-level features in image viewing – both initially and overall. J. Eye Mov. Res. **2**, 1–11 (2008). https://doi.org/10.16910/jemr.2.2.2
3. Tatler, B.W., Hayhoe, M.M., Land, M.F., Ballard, D.H.: Eye guidance in natural vision: reinterpreting salience. J. Vis. **11**(5), 5.1–23 (2011). https://doi.org/10.1167/11.5.5
4. Foulsham, T., Kingstone, A., Underwood, G.: Turning the world around: patterns in saccade direction vary with picture orientation. Vision. Res. **48**(17), 1777–1790 (2008). https://doi.org/10.1016/j.visres.2008.05.018
5. Le Meur, O., Liu, Z.: Saccadic model of eye movements for free-viewing condition. Vision. Res. **116**, 152–164 (2015). https://doi.org/10.1016/j.visres.2014.12.026
6. Le Meur, O., Coutrot, A.: How saccadic models help predict where we look during a visual task? Application to visual quality assessment. Electron. Imaging **28**, 1–7 (2016)
7. Le Meur, O., Coutrot, A.: Introducing context-dependent and spatially-variant viewing biases in saccadic models. Vision. Res. **121**, 72–84 (2016). https://doi.org/10.1016/j.visres.2016.01.005
8. Le Meur, O., Coutrot, A., Liu, Z., Roch, A., Helo, A., Rama, P.: Computational model for predicting visual fixations from childhood to adulthood (2017). arXiv:1702.04657
9. Zhang, A.T., Le Meur, O.: How old do you look? Inferring your age from your gaze. In: Proceedings of the 25th IEEE International Conference on Image Processing (ICIP) 2660–2664 (2018)
10. Le Meur, O., Le Pen, T., Cozot, R.: Can we accurately predict where we look at paintings? PLoS One **15**(10), e0239980 (2020). https://doi.org/10.1371/journal.pone.0239980
11. Kümmerer, M., Bethge, M.: State-of-the-art in human scan path prediction (2021). http://arxiv.org/abs/2102.12239
12. Kümmerer, M., Bethge, M., Wallis, T.S.A.: DeepGaze III: modeling free-viewing human scan paths with deep learning. J. Vis. **22**(5), 7 (2022). https://doi.org/10.1167/jov.22.5.7
13. Tatler, B.W., Vincent, B.T.: The prominence of behavioral biases in eye guidance. Vis. Cogn. **17**(6–7), 1029–1054 (2009). https://doi.org/10.1080/13506280902764539
14. Castelhano, M.S., Mack, M.L., Henderson, J.M.: Viewing task influences eye movement control during active scene perception. J. Vis. **9**(3), 1–15 (2009). https://doi.org/10.1167/9.3.6
15. Nuthmann, A.: Fixation durations in scene viewing: modeling the effects of local image features, oculomotor parameters, and task. Psychon. Bull. Rev. **24**, 370–392 (2017). https://doi.org/10.3758/s13423-016-1124-4
16. Henderson, J.M., Hayes, T.R., Peacock, C.E., Rehrig, G.: Meaning and attentional guidance in scenes: A review of the meaning map approach. Vision (Switzerland) **3**(2), 19 (2019). https://doi.org/10.3390/vision3020019
17. Aizenman, A.M., Gegenfurtner, K.R., Goettker, A.: Oculomotor routines for perceptual judgments. J. Vis. **24** (2023)
18. Walter, K., Freeman, M., Bex, P.J.: Quantifying task-related gaze. Atten. Percept. Psychophys. **86**, 1318–1329 (2024)
19. Hahsler, M., Piekenbrock, M., Doran, D.: Dbscan: fast density-based clustering with R. J. Stat. Softw. **91**(1), 1–30 (2019)
20. Bergström, P., Edlund, O.: Robust registration of point sets using iteratively reweighted least squares. Comput. Optim. Appl. **58**(3), 543–561 (2014). https://doi.org/10.1007/s10589-014-9643-2
21. Judd, T., Durand, F., Torralba, A.: A benchmark of computational models of saliency to predict human fixations. MIT Technical Report (2012)
22. Batschelet, E.: Circular statistics in biology. Academic Press, New York (1980)
23. Just, M., Carpenter, P.: Eye fixations and cognitive processes. Cogn. Psychol. **8**(4), 441–480 (1976)
24. Wilming, N., Betz, T., Kietzmann, T.C., König, P.: Measures and limits of models of fixation selection. PLoS One **6**(9), e24038 (2011). https://doi.org/10.1371/journal.pone.0024038

Chapter 14
Detection of PCB Surface Defects in Improved YOLOv8s

Botong Zhu, Ying Zhang, and Yaomin Wang

Abstract Detecting surface defects on PCBs is vital for quality inspection. To tackle the problems of low accuracy and poor real-time performance in PCB defect detection, a YOLOv8-based method is proposed. In the feature extraction stage, LP-C2f is employed instead of C2f to improve information extraction efficiency, reduce network redundancy, and accelerate speed. Additionally, by integrating the MPCA attention mechanism and feature fusion module, multi-dimensional attention is focused on relevant feature information to effectively distinguish defects from the background. The introduction of CFPN enhances multi-level information interaction and fusion, focusing on small target detection. Finally, a balanced performance score (*BPS*) comprehensive evaluation metric is proposed to assess the model's speed and accuracy. Experimental results demonstrate that the model achieves an *mAP* of 98.7%, a 1% improvement over the original YOLOv8s model, with a 60% reduction in model parameters. The FPS value reaches 86, and the comprehensive indicator *BPS* is superior, meeting the needs of industrial production.

14.1 Introduction

Currently, the detection of PCB surface defects still faces several limitations: Firstly, a lack of complex background data in industrial environments results in significant noise and lighting interference. Secondly, the high soldering density and small defect sizes make precise localization challenging. Lastly, existing algorithm models are bulky, resulting in slow speeds when deployed on mobile devices, there is a demand for smaller and faster models.

Conventional detection methods primarily involve manual inspection and electrical testing, and automatic optical inspection [1]. Yu [2] presented a model for detecting and classifying PCB defects that utilizes intrinsic feature decomposition

B. Zhu (✉) · Y. Zhang · Y. Wang
School of Electrical and Control Engineering, Shenyang Jianzhu University, Shenyang, China
e-mail: xxqq6262@163.com

F. P. García Márquez et al. (eds.), *Computing, Internet of Things and Data Analytics*, Smart Innovation, Systems and Technologies 387,
https://doi.org/10.1007/978-3-031-87154-2_14

and multi-level fusion. Generate multi-layer reflection and shading maps by modifying Retinex decomposition, and then use a gradient sparse encoder to characterize the reflection maps. Using a bilateral convolutional filter with a multidimensional transformer to remove noise information from the colored graph. It is a novel PCB defect detection method, but unfortunately its real-time performance is not high. Jakkrit [3] proposed an algorithm based on image segmentation. The CHT algorithm detects and classifies circular patterns by transforming feature points from image space into operations in parameter space. Similarly, the MR algorithm sequentially classifies features in a segmented image and converts connected background pixels into foreground pixels. However, these methods are inefficient and costly. With the rapid advancement of deep learning, detection models have evolved into two categories: one-stage and two-stage networks. Well-known two-stage algorithms [4], such as R-CNN [5], Fast R-CNN [6], and Faster R-CNN [7], achieve high accuracy but are limited in speed. On the other hand, one-stage methods such as SSD [8] and YOLO [9], have excellent detection speed. However, directly using the original network model may result in issues like class imbalance, multi-scale defects, and complex backgrounds [10]. To overcome these challenges, LIAO Xinting [11] proposed the YOLOv5 TDD algorithm for detecting small defects in PCB, which improves the efficiency of information flow for small defect features by adding shallow feature fusion branches and SE SiLU attention mechanism. Chen [12] et al. introduced Transformer-YOLO, a PCB defect detection model built upon YOLOv5. By embedding swing-transformer network in the backbone network, the average recognition accuracy reaches 97.04%, which greatly improves the detection accuracy of defect targets. However, this model still has certain defects, and it cannot detect PCB defects in real time. Du Bowei [13] introduced an improved YOLOv5s network, called YOLO-MBBi, for detecting surface defects on PCBs. MBConv (Moving backward residual bottleneck block) module, CBAM attention, deep convolve and BiFPN were used to replace the layers in YOLOv5. In the training phase, the CIoU loss function is swapped for the SIoU loss function, resulting in more precise detection of small defect targets and minimizing the chances of detection failures, but it still cannot achieve the effect of real-time detection. Jianfeng-Zheng et al. [14] proposed a method for PCB defect detection utilizing an enhanced fully convolutional neural network, which expands the receptive field and addresses the frequent issue of disrupted convolutional information continuity. Additionally, an optimized skip layer was integrated after the up-sampling layer to capture multi-scale fusion features and enhance image resolution. Wenkai-Huang et al. [15] introduced the NCENet to monitor PCB defects. The network incorporates a Correlation Residual Block (RRB) to establish connections between defects and their surrounding context. LEL and RC are employed to reinforce key spatial information and extract relationships between various location features. It provides a new direction for us to study PCB defect detection. GaoShang Xiao [16] proposed a PCB defect detection algorithm called CDI-YOLO, which integrates a coordinate attention mechanism and partial shared convolution within DSConOLOv7 MINI. The internal CIoU is utilized as the bounding box regression loss function in CDI-YOLO, streamlining the bounding box regression process for improved efficiency.

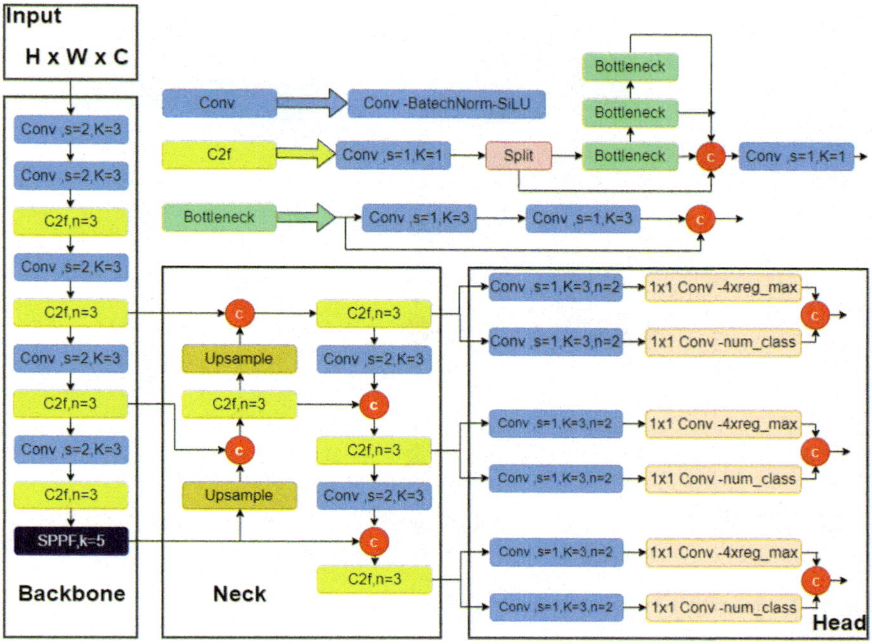

Fig. 14.1 YOLOv8 network structure

14.2 Relate Work

YOLOv8 is a one-stage detection algorithm that transforms object detection into a regression problem. Based on the model's complexity and the quantity of modules, it is divided into five different versions. Versions with fewer modules have relatively fewer parameters, resulting in faster speeds but lower accuracy, whereas versions with more modules achieve higher accuracy at the expense of slower speeds and increased training costs. In the identification of surface imperfections on PCBs, the YOLOv8s network is chosen to balance detection efficiency and accuracy. The structure is divided into four components: Input, Backbone, Neck, and Head [17], with the network architecture illustrated in Fig. 14.1.

14.3 Method

There are issues such as missed detections of small targets, model redundancy, and background misclassification that may arise when using YOLOv8 for identifying surface defects on PCBs,. Therefore, an improved structure named PMC-YOLOv8 is proposed, as shown in Fig. 14.2. The LP-C2f convolution method is employed to

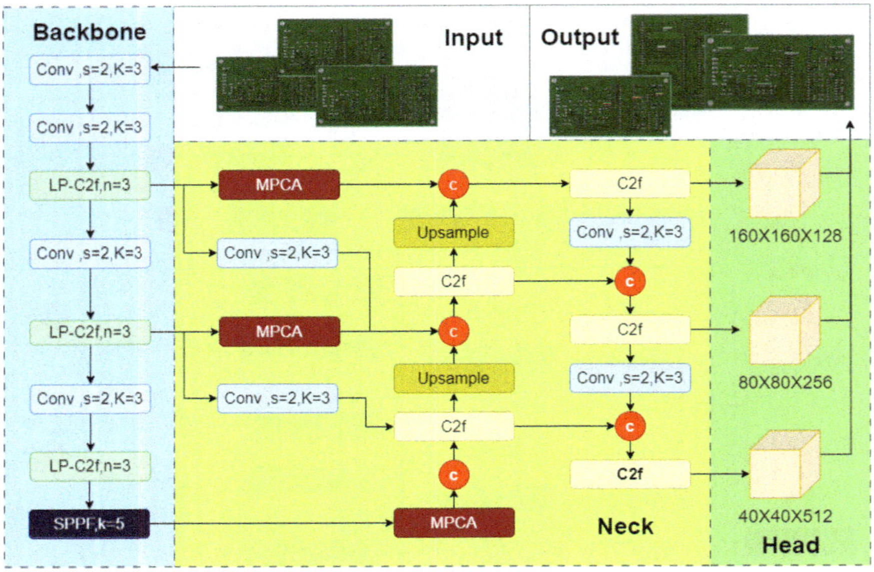

Fig. 14.2 Improved the network structure diagram of YOLOv8s

optimize feature extraction and reduce feature redundancy. Additionally, the feature fusion part is improved by increasing cross-scale and cross-layer fusion, utilizing shallow features to enhance the surrounding background information and promote the sufficient exchange of feature information. Finally, by using the Multipath Coordinate Attention (MPCA) mechanism to weight the feature details, the weights of key features are enhanced.

14.3.1 Local Perception Convolution

The composition structure of the local perception convolution (LP-C2F) is shown in Fig. 14.3. Features are extracted through a weighted combination of partial convolution (PConv) cascaded with pointwise convolution (PWconv). For an input feature map $F = [x_1, x_2, \cdots, x_n,] \in R^{C\times H\times W}$, the split operation partitions the input feature space I into two parts $X_1 \in R^{C_p\times H\times W}$ and $X_2 \in R^{(C-C_p)\times H\times W}$, with channel numbers C_p and $\mathrm{C} - \mathrm{C_p}$, respectively. A 3×3 convolution is applied to feature X_1 to capture spatial characteristics, denoted as $F_{Conv}^{3\times3}(X_1)$, while preserving the features of X_2 through an identity mapping. The convolution output and the unmapped features are connected through a Concat operation, followed by batch normalization and input into the PWConv for weighted combination. The feature map denoted as $F^{\cdot} = swish\left[F_{PWConv}^{1\times1}\left(F_{concat}\left(F_{Conv}^{3\times3}(X_1), X_2\right)\right)\right]$.

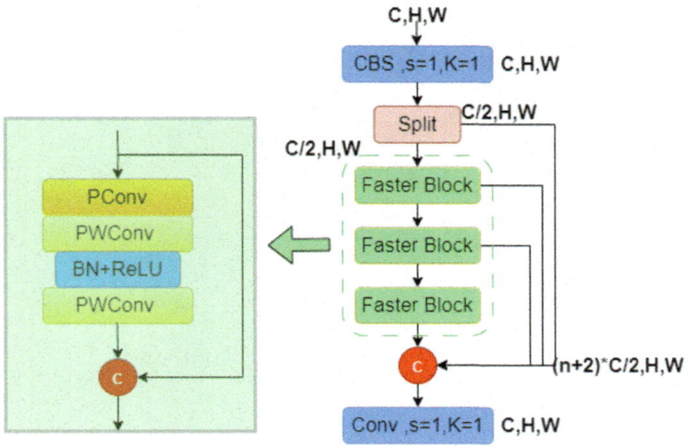

Fig. 14.3 The composition of the LP-C2F

By comparing Eqs. (14.1) and (14.2), it can be observed that, in contrast to traditional convolution, PConv substantially decreases FLOPs, resulting in notable computational savings.

$$\mathrm{FLOPs} = \mathrm{h} \times \mathrm{w} \times \mathrm{k}^2 \times \mathrm{c}^2 \tag{14.1}$$

$$\mathrm{FLOPs} = \mathrm{h} \times \mathrm{w} \times \mathrm{k}^2 \times \mathrm{C}_\mathrm{p}^2 \tag{14.2}$$

In the equations, h denotes the image height, w stands for the image width and ${C_p}^2$ denotes the count of channels engaged in the convolution process for input features. Thus, the utilization of Local Perception Convolution (LP-C2f) effectively reduces the number of FLOPs, thereby mitigating memory access and latency.

14.3.2 *Cross-Feature Pyramid Network*

In conjunction with the fusion approach of the Generalized Feature Pyramid Network (GFPN), the CFPN (Cross-feature pyramid network) is proposed to enhance cross-scale fusion among adjacent hierarchical levels and cross-layer fusion within the same scale, enhance the comprehensive interchange of feature information across both the deeper and shallower layers of the network, and between the large and small scales. Each layer not only accepts input from the same layer, but also accepts shallower information and a deeper layer of information after downsampling, utilizing concatenation operation for feature fusion to prevent information loss. The structural diagram is illustrated in Fig. 14.4.

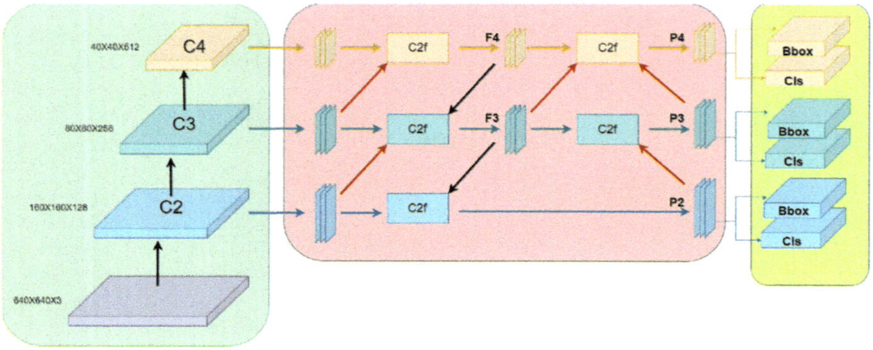

Fig. 14.4 Structure of the CFPN

To bolster the capability for feature integration concerning minor target defects, the paper explores leveraging shallow information to the fullest extent by introducing an additional 160 × 160 feature layer, thereby enhancing the representation of shallow features. Additionally, the 20 × 20 detection layer output from the feature fusion network is removed. The implementation of the CFPN effectively detects small-sized defects on printed circuit boards (PCBs). The detailed procedure is articulated by the subsequent equation, expressed in the form of Eq. (14.3).

$$F = [f_1, f_2, f_3] \tag{14.3}$$

In the equation, F represents the fused feature map; [] denotes concatenation along the channel dimension; f_1, f_2 and f_3 are different output feature maps. Thus, the formation process of feature maps F_2 and F_3 can be derived as shown in Equations.

$$F_2 = [UpSample(F_3), C_2] \tag{14.4}$$

$$F_3 = [UpSample(F_4), C_3, C_2] \tag{14.5}$$

The formation process of feature maps P_3 and P_4 can be expressed using Eqs. (14.6) and (14.7).

$$P_3 = [Downsample(P_2),\ F_3] \tag{14.6}$$

$$P_4 = [[Downsample(P_3), F_4, F_3]] \tag{14.7}$$

14.3.3 MPCA Attention Mechanism

The proposed MPCA attention mechanism in this paper introduces a global average pooling branch and refines the processing of height and width information, comprehensively considering the relationship between channel weights, feature height, and width. It effectively explores the feature expression capabilities across different dimensions, allowing the model to concentrate on defect characteristics and improve the precision of PCB defect identification. The structural diagram is presented in Fig. 14.5.

Firstly, utilizing global pooling, attention maps are produced in both horizontal and vertical axes on the input image X, producing attention maps with horizontal and vertical coordinate information, as well as a feature map containing complete information, as shown in Eqs. (14.8, 14.9 and 14.10).

$$F_h = \frac{1}{W}\sum\nolimits_{0\le j\le w} X(h,j),\ F_h \in R^{C\times H\times 1} \tag{14.8}$$

$$F_w = \frac{1}{H}\sum\nolimits_{0\le i\le w} X(i,w),\ F_w \in R^{C\times 1\times w} \tag{14.9}$$

$$F_q = \text{AvgPool}(\text{X}(h,\ w)) \tag{14.10}$$

The generated attention maps, $\mathrm{F_h}$ and $\mathrm{F_w}$, containing unidirectional coordinate information, are combined along the spatial dimension and processed through a 1×1 convolution operation to obtainF_1. F_1 is then processed through convolution and activation functions to obtain the feature vectorF_2, as illustrated in Eqs. (14.11) and (14.12).

$$F_1 = F_{1\times 1}(concatF_hF_w),\ F \in R^{\frac{C}{r}\times 1\times (W+H)} \tag{14.11}$$

$$F_2 = \sigma(F_{1\times 1}(F_1)),\ F \in R^{\frac{C}{r}\times 1\times (W+H)} \tag{14.12}$$

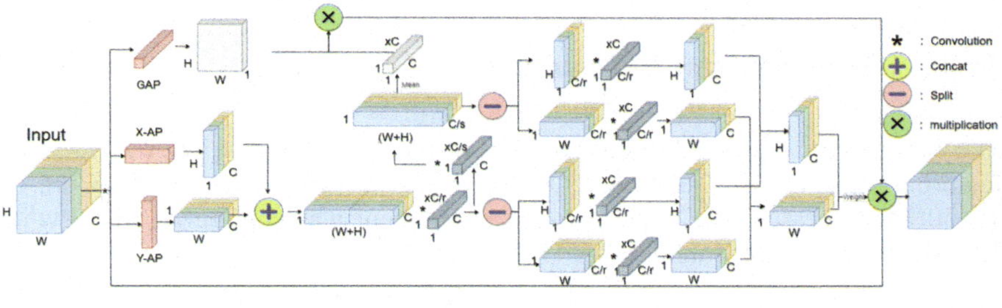

Fig. 14.5 MPCA attention mechanism structure

Along the spatial dimension, F_1 and F_2 are split into four tensors: $F^{h1} \in R^{\frac{C}{r}\times H\times 1}$, $F^{w1} \in R^{\frac{C}{r}\times 1\times W}$, $F^{h2} \in R^{\frac{C}{r}\times H\times 1}$, and $F^{w2} \in R^{\frac{C}{r}\times 1\times W}$, σ represents the activation function. Each is subjected to dimensionality expansion through 1×1 convolutions, and the separated maps are activated to obtain two classes of attention vectors. Weighted fusion operations are then performed along the horizontal and vertical dimensions for refinement. Simultaneously, the feature information derived from F_2 undergoes mean normalization and is combined with F_q through weighted fusion to yield M_q. applied to the input feature map X through multiplication at corresponding positions to obtain the final attentional features. The formation process is illustrated in Eq. (14.13).

$$\begin{aligned} Out = X \times \left[\sigma F_h F^{h1} + \sigma F_h F^{h2}\right] \\ \times \left[\sigma F_h F^{w1} + \sigma F_w F^{w2}\right] \times \left(Mean F_2 + F_q\right) \end{aligned} \tag{14.13}$$

In the formula, Mean represents the mean in the calculated tensor.

14.4 Experimental Section

14.4.1 Dataset Augmentation

The original publicly available PCB surface defect dataset utilized in this research was sourced from the Human–Computer Interaction Open Laboratory at Peking University [18]. The initial collection comprised 693 images containing 2953 defect instances, including missing holes, rodent bites, open circuits, short circuits, burrs, and excess copper, as depicted in Fig. 14.6. To increase the sample size, data augmentation was performed, which involved operations such as rotation, translation, changing color temperature, and histogram equalization. This process resulted in an augmented dataset comprising 9702 PCB images and 41,342 defect instances, as detailed in Table 14.1.

14.4.2 Experimental Environment

The experiments presented in this study were carried out on a Windows 11 system featuring an NVIDIA GeForce RTX 4060 GPU (8 GB) and an Intel Core i9-13900HX processor. The experimental environment was configured with Python 3.8.18, PyTorch 1.13.1, and CUDA 11.3.1.

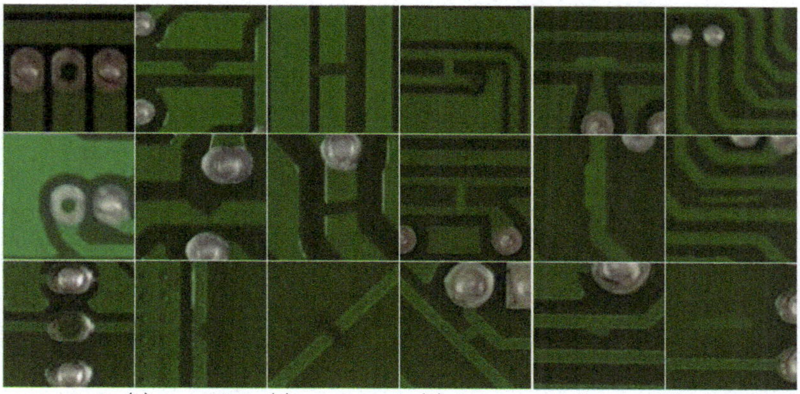

Fig. 14.6 The type of defect

Table 14.1 PCB dataset details

Defect types	Before augmentation		After augmentation	
	Images	Defects	Images	Defects
Missing hole	115	497	1610	6958
Mouse bite	115	492	1610	6888
Short	116	491	1624	6874
Spur	115	488	1610	6832
Spurious copper	116	503	1624	7042
Open circuit	116	482	1624	6748
Total	693	2953	9702	41,342

14.4.3 Evaluation Metrics

This study utilizes several evaluation metrics to thoroughly evaluate the algorithm's efficacy, including mean average precision (*mAP*), parameter count (*Params*), speed (*FPS*), and balanced performance score (*BPS*).

The *mAP* assesses the model's performance by computing the mean of the *AP* for each class. The calculation processes for *AP* and *mAP* are represented by Eqs. (14.14) and (14.15) respectively:

$$AP = \int_0^1 P(R)dR \tag{14.14}$$

$$mAP = 1/N \sum_{i=1}^{N} AP_i \tag{14.15}$$

In this context, P represents precision, R represents recall, and N indicates the number of classes in the samples.

FPS represents the number of images processed per second. The quicker the model's inference speed, the more images it can detect within a unit of time.

In order to facilitate the evaluation of the comprehensive performance metrics of FPS and mAP, a new evaluation metric BPS is proposed. It determines the weights of model speed and accuracy based on their importance and applies these weights to the corresponding scores, taking into account the bias of parameter quantity. The calculation process can be represented by the following equation:

$$BPS = w\_FPS * FPS\_score + w\_mAP * mAP\_score + \frac{10^6}{Params} \tag{14.16}$$

where w_FPS and w_mAP are the weight parameters for FPS and mAP respectively, satisfying $w\_FPS + w\_mAP = 1$, and $score$ represents the obtained score, i.e., the resulting FPS and mAP outcomes.

14.4.4 Experiment Results

Comparison of the results of different models. To further confirm the proposed method's effectiveness in detecting PCB surface defects, comparative experiments were performed on the same dataset using popular detection models like SSD, YOLOv5s, YOLOv7, YOLOv8n, and YOLOv8s. The results of these experiments are shown in Table 14.2.

According to the experimental results, our model demonstrates superior comprehensive performance with a higher BPS compared to other algorithms. In comparison to SSD, YOLOv5s, and YOLOv7, our method exhibits improvements of 6.6%, 2.7%, and 1% in mAP performance, respectively. Additionally, the detection speed is significantly enhanced, with increases of 32 frames per second (fps), 18 fps, and 16 fps, respectively. For the two scales of YOLOv8 models, the improved model surpasses YOLOv8n by 2.4% and YOLOv8s by 1% in mAP; and maintains equal detection speed with YOLOv8n while outperforming YOLOv8s by 5 fps. Moreover,

Table 14.2 Comparison of results of different detection algorithms

Model	mAP@0.5/%	Params/106	FPS	BPS
SSD	92.1	23.8	54	88.3
YOLOv5s	96	7.1	68	93.3
YOLOv7	97.7	36.5	60	94.0
YOLOv8n	96.3	**3.2**	**86**	95.6
YOLOv8s	97.7	11.1	81	96.1
Ours	**98.7**	4.4	**86**	**97.7**

Table 14.3 Ablation test results

Model	mAP@0.5/%	Params/106	FPS	BPS
YOLOv8s	97.7	11.1	81	96.1
YOLOv8s + CFPN	98.5	**3.6**	83	97.2
YOLOv8s + MPCA	98	12.4	79	96.2
YOLOv8s + LP-C2f	97.8	9.7	**87**	96.8
YOLOv8-PMC	**98.7**	4.4	86	**97.7**

its parameter quantity is only second to YOLOv8n and much smaller than other models.

Comparison of the results of the PMC-YOLO experiment. A series of ablation studies were carried out using YOLOv8s to investigate how various components affect the model's performance in detecting PCB defects. The original YOLOv8s model was assessed, and in-depth analyses were conducted on models augmented with CFPN, MPCA attention modules, and LP-C2f. A comparison was made between these models and ours. The experimental results are presented in Table 14.3.

According to the data in Table 4, when CFPN and MPCA are applied separately, their *mAP* improves by 0.8% and 0.3%, respectively, compared to the original YOLOv8s model. After LP-C2f replaces C2f, the FPS increases from 81 to 87, with a reduction in parameters to 9.7, accelerating the detection of PCB images. To strike a balance between speed and accuracy, the comprehensive application of the three techniques reveals that the model achieves the highest *BPS* indicator parameters and optimal performance, especially in terms of *mAP*. As evident from Fig. 7, the YOLOv8s method is significantly influenced by the background and tends to produce false positives for some defects while missing targets of smaller scales. Conversely, as shown in Fig. 7, our proposed method accurately identifies PCB defect targets with high precision, without experiencing issues of false negatives or false positives, thus demonstrating the superiority of our approach.

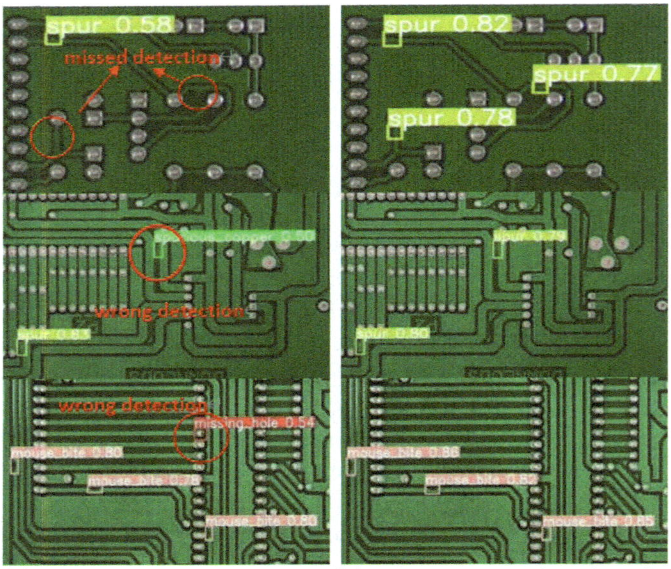

(a)YOLOv8s detection e ffect (b) YOLOv8 -PMC detection effect

Fig. 14.7 Comparison of detection effects

14.5 Conclusion

After testing, it was found that the improved YOLOv8 network exhibits higher speed and accuracy in identifying PCB defects compared to traditional object detection models. We employ a lighter-weight novel local perception convolution LP-C2f for feature extraction, minimizing network redundancy and memory usage, thereby enhancing speed. Additionally, we integrate an MPCA attention module following the feature fusion module to improve emphasis on defect characteristics, better distinguishing defects from the background. The introduction of the CFPN directs the model's attention towards small target detection, thereby improving accuracy while considering model speed. In comparison to leading-edge techniques, our detection model achieves a *mAP* of 98.7%, a 1% improvement, with a 60% reduction in model parameters and an FPS value of 86, indicating superior overall performance. Although we have achieved good detection results, there are still some areas that can be optimized, such as the calculation amount and parameter number of the model still have room to reduce. In future research, we will optimize the model. In upcoming studies, we will continue to refine the model., considering lightweight designs to accommodate small and micro devices, perform tests in actual production line settings to more effectively meet the demands of PCB production lines.

Acknowledgements The work described in this article was supported by the funds from the Basic Scientific Research Projects of the Educational Department of Liaoning Province (grant no. LJKZ0585).

References

1. Chen, B., Dang, Z.: Fast PCB defect detection method based on FasterNet backbone network and CBAM attention mechanism integrated with feature fusion module in improved YOLOv7. IEEE Access **11**, 95092–95103 (2023)
2. Yu, X., Han-Xiong, L., Yang, H.: PCB defect detection model based on intrinsic feature decomposition and multilevel fusion against image uncertainty. IEEE Sens. J. **24**(12), 19497–19505 (2024)
3. Onshaunjit, J., Srinonchat, J.: Algorithmic scheme for concurrent detection and classification of printed circuit board defects. Comput. Mater. Contin. **71**(1), 355–367 (2022)
4. Ang, L., Rahim, S.K.N.A., Hamzah, R., et al.: YOLO algorithm with hybrid attention feature pyramid network for solder joint defect detection (2024). arXiv:2401.01214
5. Girshick, R., Donahue, J., Darrell, T., et al.: Rich feature hierarchies for accurate object detection and semantic segmentation. In: Proceedings of the IEEE Conference on Computer Vision and Pattern Recognition, pp. 580–587 (2014)
6. Girshick, R.: Fast r-cnn. In: Proceedings of the IEEE International Conference on Computer Vision, pp. 1440–1448 (2015)
7. Ren, S., He, K., Girshick, R., et al.: Faster r-cnn: Towards real-time object detection with region proposal networks. IEEE Trans. Pattern Anal. Mach. Intell. **39**, 1137–1149 (2017)
8. Liu, W., Anguelov, D., Erhan, D., et al.: Ssd: single shot multibox detector. In: Computer Vision–ECCV 2016: 14th European Conference, Amsterdam, The Netherlands, October 11–14, Proceedings, Part I 14. Springer International Publishing, pp. 21–37 (2016)
9. Redmon, J., Divvala, S., Girshick, R., et al.: You only look once: Unified, real-time object detection. In: Proceedings of the IEEE conference on computer vision and pattern recognition, pp. 779–788 (2016)
10. Li, G., Zhao, S., Zhou, M., et al.: YOLO-RFF: an industrial defect detection method based on expanded field of feeling and feature fusion. Electronics **11**(24), 4211 (2022)
11. Liao, X., Zhang, J., Lyu, S.: Defect detection for PCB by combining shallow features and attention mechanism. Comput. Integr. Manuf. Syst. **30**(3), 1092–1104 (2024)
12. Chen, W., Huang, Z., Mu, Q., et al.: PCB defect detection method based on transformer-YOLO. IEEE Access **10**, 129480–129489 (2022)
13. Du, B., Wan, F., Lei, G., et al.: YOLO-MBBi: PCB surface defect detection method based on enhanced YOLOv5. Electronics **12**(13), 2821 (2023)
14. Zheng, J., Sun, X., Zhou, H., et al.: Printed circuit boards defect detection method based on improved fully convolutional networks. IEEE Access **10**, 109908–109918 (2022)
15. Huang, W., Wen, J., Gan, W., et al.: Neighborhood correlation enhancement network for PCB defect classification. IEEE Trans. Instrum. Meas. **72**, 1–11 (2023)
16. Xiao, G., Hou, S., Zhou, H.: PCB defect detection algorithm based on CDI-YOLO. Sci. Rep. **14**, 7351 (2024)
17. Ying, Z., Lin, Z., Wu, Z., et al.: A modified-YOLOv5s model for detection of wire braided hose defects. Measurement **190**, 110683 (2022)
18. Ding, R., Dai, L., Li, G., et al.: TDD-net: a tiny defect detection network for printed circuit boards. CAAI Trans. Intell. Technol. **4**(2), 110–116 (2019)

Chapter 15
Improved Lightweight SSD Target Detection Algorithm for Vehicle Vision System

Yaomin Wang, Ying Zhang, and Botong Zhu

Abstract Aiming at the problems of limited computational resources and low accuracy in long-distance small target detection in vehicle vision system, an improved lightweight network Ghostnetv2-SSD network is proposed to improve the computational efficiency and small target detection performance. Firstly, the VGG16 in SSD is replaced by Ghostnetv2 to reduce the model parameters and the computational volume, then the multi-scale feature fusion method is used to strengthen the recognition ability of small-size targets, and at the same time, the a prior bounding box is re-designed to make the model have a better detection effect; experiments through the *nuScence* dataset on CPU show that a five-fold increase in the test frame rate of the improved Ghostnetv2-SSD model over the traditional SSD model. The experimental results indicate that the Ghostnetv2-SSD model not only adapts to the limitations of vehicle hardware, but also improves the detection of small and medium-sized targets.

15.1 Introduction

In recent years, with the rapid development of computer vision technology, base on neural network target detection technology has been enhanced, and its use in the automotive industry has been widely concerned and studied. However, there are still two difficulties that need to be solved in practical applications: (1) the computing power and storage space of the vehicle-mounted devices is limited, so the algorithm must have less demand for hardware resources; (2) in order to give the vehicle enough time to react, the algorithm should have a strong detection ability and faster detection speed for long-distance small targets at a long distance.

The improvement of computer arithmetic power in the past 10 years or so has led to an explosion of deep learning technology, and the classical deep learning-based target detection methods include one-stage methods such as SSD [1], YOLO [2]

Y. Wang (✉) · Y. Zhang · B. Zhu
School of Electrical and Control Engineering, Shenyang Jianzhu University, Shenyang, China
e-mail: 1191276972@qq.com; saltfish_wym@163.com

F. P. García Márquez et al. (eds.), *Computing, Internet of Things and Data Analytics*,
Smart Innovation, Systems and Technologies 387,
https://doi.org/10.1007/978-3-031-87154-2_15

and CenterNet [3]; and two-stage methods such as R-CNN [4], Fast R-CNN [5] and Faster RCNN [6]. Unlike one-stage methods that directly compute the image and generate the result, two-stage methods first bounding boxes from the image and then detect the extracted bounding boxes, so the accuracy is higher, but the detection speed is slower than that of one-stage methods. The one-stage method is more suitable in automatic driving environment sensing where real-time requirements are high. In the one-stage method, the SSD network is a network structure with relatively high detection accuracy. In order to further improve the detection ability of SSD algorithm in in-vehicle systems, there are many scholars who have improved the SSD network. For example, Zhao Wenqing et al. [7] proposed the method of inverse convolution and feature fusion to improve the defect of insufficient feature information of small targets in vehicle detection. Fuguang et al. [8] proposed a lightweight video vehicle object detection method based on time series information, which realized the deployment of a video vehicle object detection model on low-power embedded devices. The model performs well on CPUs. Liu Hongli et al. [9] proposed an image preprocessing method of improved SSD and multi-focus image fusion with attention mechanism, which solved the problem that the vehicle target features were blurred due to the different focus of the imaging equipment, resulting in the vehicle being unable to be effectively recognized. Zhao Jinfang et al. [10] proposed an improved SSD-MobileNetV3 network to improve the accuracy of multi-target detection. Guo-Jin Li et al. [11] designed an improved Inception module to improve the problem of missed detection in vehicle detection. Kai Li et al. [12] proposed an attention-based mechanism with multi-scale information fusion method for vehicle detection task, which improved the problem of detecting small targets with low accuracy. In addition Ying Lai [13], Yu Guohao [14] and other scholars improved the YOLO series, which also performs well in the vehicle detection task. Aiming at the problems of detecting long-distance small targets over long distances with low accuracy and high computation not applicable to embedded devices in the aforementioned studies, an improved SSD network is proposed, which aims to be more adaptable to vehicle-mounted devices, while possessing higher detection speeds and the ability to detect small targets over long distances.

15.2 SSD Detection Algorithm

The SSD algorithm is mainly composed of backbone network, feature mapping network and detection network, and its algorithm flow is shown in Fig. 15.1.

The SSD algorithm uses a modified VGG16 network model as the backbone network. The two fully connected layers FC6 and FC7 in the VGG16 network are replaced with 3×3 convolution and 1×1 convolution. Add 4 sets of convolutional layers after the FC7 layer. Provide more feature information for detection. The SSD algorithm selects and picks 6 feature maps of varying sizes to be fed into the rear detection part.

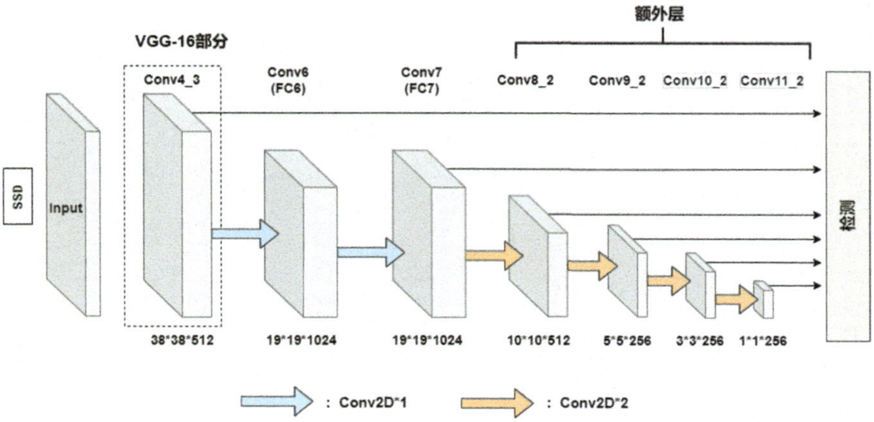

Fig. 15.1 SSD network structure

15.3 Improving the Ghostnetv2-SSD Network Structure

When applying the SSD target detection algorithm in the real scenario of vehicle detection, it has problems such as missed detection of long-distance small targets, too large a parameter volume for deployment, and weak detection of small targets. Therefore, the Ghostnetv2-SSD detection algorithm is proposed. The lightweight Ghostnetv2 network is used instead of the VGG16 network in SSD to reduce the number of parameters and computational power of the network. In addition, in order to enhance the detection ability of the improved SSD network for long-distance small targets, multi-scale feature fusion technique is used in the feature mapping part of the improved network. Finally, by using Kmeans++ clustering algorithm on the dataset to obtain the appropriate a prior bounding box to further improve the detection accuracy.

15.3.1 Ghostnetv2 Network and Improvements

Ghostnet is a lightweight convolutional neural network designed specifically for applications on mobile devices, a convolutional neural network that generates more feature maps using fewer parameters. Compared with lightweight network models such as MobileNet [15] series and ShuffleNet [16] series, Ghostnet has higher accuracy. The main building block of Ghostnet is the Ghostnet module module, whose core idea is to use a series of linear operations to replace part of the convolution and reduce the amount of inference computation. Its structure is shown in Fig. 15.2.

In order to further enhance the ability to capture spatial information, as well as the feature of efficient deployment, Tang et al. [17] proposed a hardware-friendly

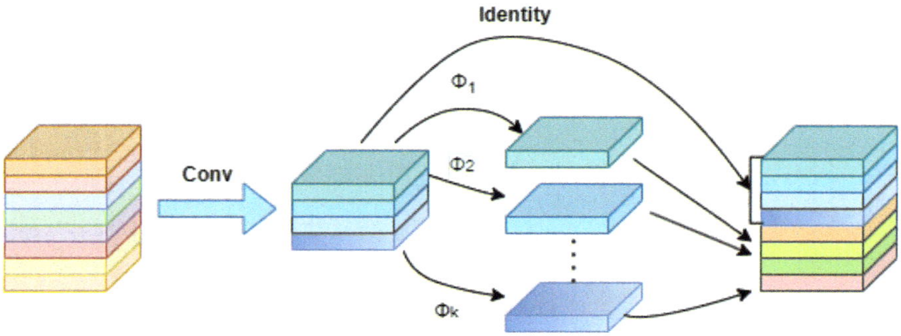

Fig. 15.2 Ghost module network structure

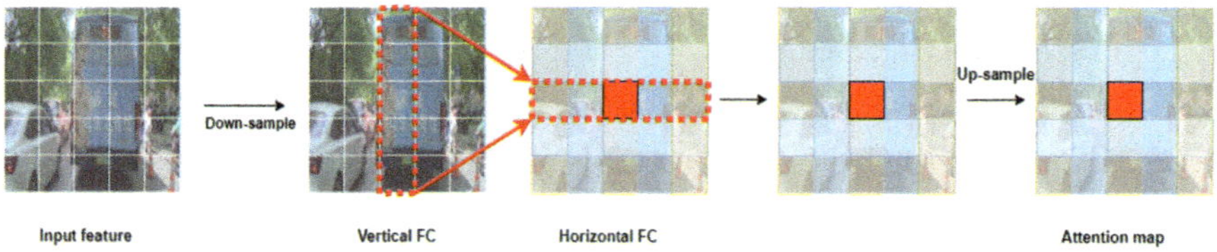

Fig. 15.3 Decoupled fully connected (DFC) attention mechanism

decoupled fully-connected attention mechanism, DFC Attention, which use as reference the fully-connected layer (FC), which is structurally simple and possesses a fixed weight, and decomposes it into two FC layers to aggregate features along the horizontal and vertical directions, respectively, in order to generate an attention graph with a global receptive field. The DFC effectively reduces the complexity. The DFC implementation is shown in Fig. 15.3.

Enhancing the Ghost module with the help of the DFC module attention mechanism mechanism results in the following two residual structures with different step sizes. The Ghostnetv2 network is obtained by stacking this module (Fig. 15.4).

After removing the stage5 and stage6 parts of the network of Ghostnetv2 and adding the same four extra convolutional layers as the original SSD network, the feature extraction network of the Ghostnetv2-SSD algorithm is finally obtained. The structure of the feature extraction network is shown in Table 15.1.

15.3.2 Ghostnetv2-SSD Algorithm for Multi-scale Feature Fusion

In a convolutional neural network, different network depths contain different information. The shallower network layer has less number of feature map channels but has more feature information. Having more details, it is suitable for detecting small

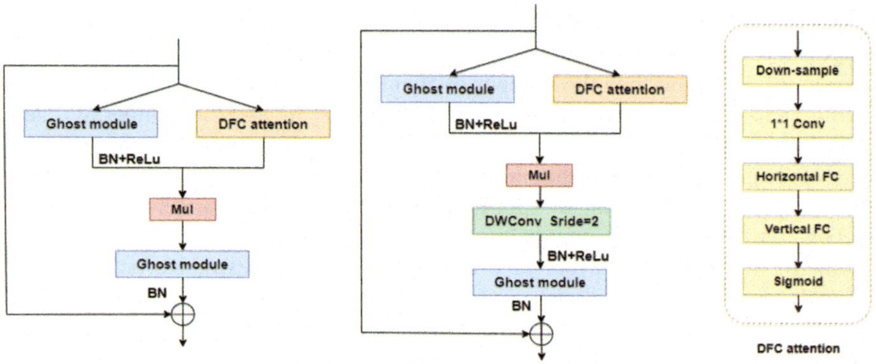

Fig. 15.4 Ghost BottleNeckv2 network architecture

Table 15.1 Feature extraction network for Ghostnetv2-SSD algorithm (G-Bneckv2 means Ghost BottleNeckv2)

	Input	Operator	Exp	Out	SE	Stride
Conv2D	300 × 300 × 3	G-Bneckv2	3	16	–	3
Stage1	300 × 300 × 16	G-Bneckv2	16	16	–	1
Stage2	150 × 150 × 16	G-Bneckv2	48	24	–	2
	75 × 75 × 24	G-Bneckv2	72	24	–	1
Stage3	75 × 75 × 24	G-Bneckv2	72	40	1	2
	38 × 38 × 40	G-Bneckv2	120	40	1	1
Stage 4	38 × 38 × 40	G-Bneckv2	240	80	–	2
	19 × 19 × 80	G-Bneckv2	200	80	–	1
	19 × 19 × 80	G-Bneckv2	184	80	–	1
	19 × 19 × 80	G-Bneckv2	184	80	–	1
	19 × 19 × 80	G-Bneckv2	480	112	1	1
	19 × 19 × 112	G-Bneckv2	672	112	1	1
Extra layers	19 × 19 × 112	Conv × 2	112	512		
	10 × 10 × 512	Conv × 2	512	256		
	5 × 5 × 256	Conv × 2	256	256		
	3 × 3 × 256	Conv × 2	256	256		

targets, and as the number of convolutional layers increases, the network's receptive field becomes larger and larger, and has a stronger ability to characterize semantic information. However, the resolution of the feature map is low and suitable for detecting large targets. In order to strengthen the detection ability of the improved Ghostnetv2-SSD for detecting small targets, a multi-scale fusion technique is used to fuse the feature maps using shallower layers.

The multi-scale feature fusion is divided into three steps. Firstly, the outputs of Stage1 and Stage2_2 layers are down-sampled to obtain two feature map with the size of 38 × 38, and then the number of channels is expanded to 40; secondly, the feature map of Stage4_5 layer is up-sampled to 38 × 38, and the number of feature channels is 80; finally, the resulting three layers are concatenated with the feature map of Stage3_2 layer and the number of channels of the spliced The number of channels of the feature map is 200. Finally, the number of channels is adjusted to 160 by convolution with a convolution kernel size of 1.

Stage1 and Stage2_2 layers need to be further feature extracted before fusion. Dilated convolution with a step size of 2, an expansion rate of 2, a convolution kernel of 3, and a padding of 2 is used for the operation. Dilated convolution is a convolution operation that can expand the receptive field during convolution and capture multi-scale contextual information without loss of information.

The Stage3_2 layer needs to increase the size of the feature map by up-sampling before fusion. Nearest neighbor interpolation is used for the up-sampling operation. Compared with other up-sampling operations, the nearest neighbor interpolation method has the advantages of faster operation speed and simple operation, which is more suitable for vehicle detection that has higher requirements on detection speed and model computation. The Ghostnetv2-SSD network after feature fusion is shown in Fig. 15.5.

15.3.3 Prior Bounding Box Design for the Kmeans++ Clustering Algorithm

Since the default a bounding box of the SSD algorithm is based on the VOC dataset and the COCO dataset, the default a priori bounding box is designed based on a generalized target distribution. In vehicle detection, more detections are vehicles and pedestrians, which have relatively fixed aspect ratios, redesigning the aspect ratios can better cover the targets in the dataset, and more appropriate a priori bounding box can effectively reduce the impact of background noise and improve accuracy.

In this paper, Kmeans++ clustering algorithm is used to redesign the a prior bounding box, Kmeans clustering algorithm has the advantage of being a simple principle and high operational efficiency, but has the disadvantage of a random initial clustering center. This can lead to unstable clustering results. And Kmeans++ solves this drawback. In addition, Kmeans++ uses the Euclidean distance as the criterion of similarity measure. This can lead to larger errors for large feature map. In this paper, 1-IOU is selected as the criterion for similarity measure. After multiple clustering it is found that a k value of 5 gives better clustering results. The process of clustering to obtain the a priori bounding box aspect ratio is shown in Fig. 15.6. The aspect ratios obtained after clustering are [30,36], [55,95], [124,62], [217,148], [520,377]. The final choice of aspect ratio is [0.55, 0.77,1, 1.45, 2]. The a priori frame size is set to [21, 45, 99, 153, 207, 261, 315].

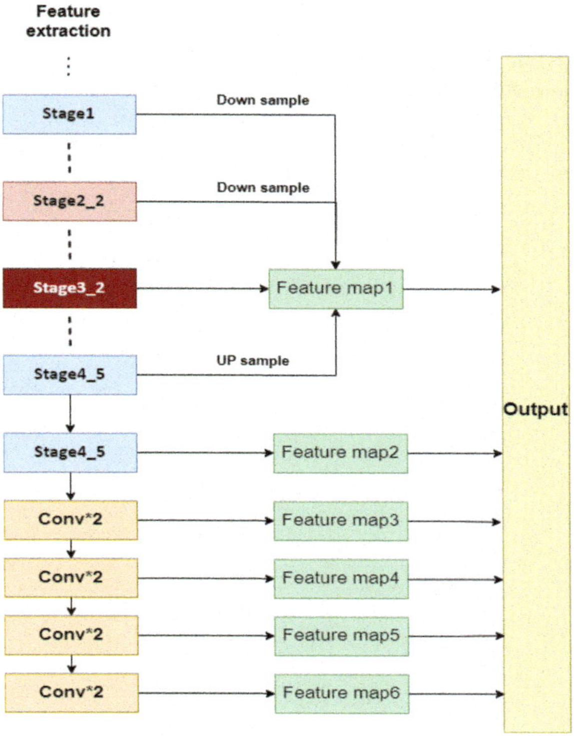

Fig. 15.5 Structure of Ghostnetv2-SSD after multi-scale feature fusion

15.4 Experimental Results and Analysis

15.4.1 Introduction to the Experimental Environment and Dataset

Experimental Environment Description: The experiments were done in Pytorch deep learning environment, using Windows 11, NVIDIA GeForce RTX 3060 (6 GB) for GPU, R7-6800H for CPU, and Python 3.11, pytorch1.7.1, and cuda11.0 for experimental environment.

The dataset used for the experiments is the mini version of the *nuScence* dataset, the full version of the dataset is a public large-scale dataset developed by the Motional (formerly nuTonomy) team for autonomous driving. nuScenes is the first dataset that provides data from the entire sensor suite of an autonomous vehicle (6 cameras, 1 LIDAR, 5 RADAR, GPS, IMU) data in a large-scale dataset. Compared to KITTI, nuScenes contains 7 × more object annotations. Collected multiple driving scenarios from Boston and Singapore with different locations, times, and weather conditions. Can maximize the simulation of the real environment around the car during driving. Has better generalization ability and stronger robustness. The dataset is categorized

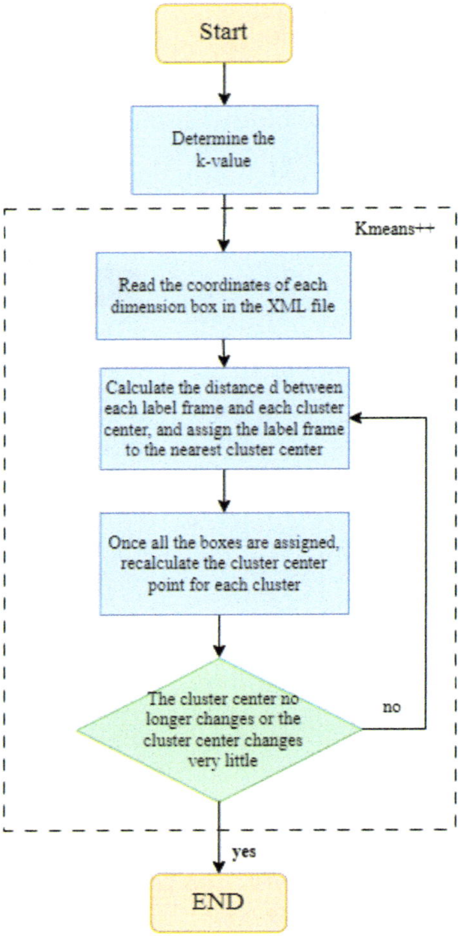

Fig. 15.6 Flow of Kmeans++ clustering dataset to obtain a prior bounding box widths and heights

into ten categories such as pedestrian, bicycle, motorcycle, car, bus, etc., with a total of 2,177 photos, which are divided into training and testing sets according to the ratio of 9:1.

The dataset format used in the experiment is PASCAL VOC format, however, the *nuScence* dataset uses 3D bounding box, so first of all, the 3D bounding box of the dataset should be converted into a 2D annotation file with xml format, and the effect of the conversion before and after the conversion is shown in Fig. 15.7.

(a)3D bounding box visualization of the *nuScence* dataset.

(b)Visualization of bounding box after conversion.

Fig. 15.7 *nuScence* dataset bounding box before and after conversion comparison

15.4.2 Evaluation Indicators and Parameter Setting

Evaluation Indicators

In this paper, average precision mean *mAP*, speed *FPS* are used to evaluate the algorithm performance. Target detection has an *AP* value for each category, *AP* is the area under the *precision* and *Recall* ($P - R$) curve and the average *AP* value for all categories is called *mAP*. How fast the model detects a target is generally measured by the *FPS*, i.e., the number of frames detected per second, the higher the *FPS*, the more frames per second the image is detected and the higher the detection speed of the algorithm.

$$precision = \frac{TP}{TP + FP} \tag{15.1}$$

$$Recall = \frac{TP}{TP + FN} \tag{15.2}$$

TP stands for the meaning that positive samples are correctly predicted as positive by the model, i.e., real vehicle targets are predicted as vehicle targets; *FP* stands for the meaning that negative samples are incorrectly predicted as positive by the model, i.e., non-vehicle targets are predicted as real vehicle targets; and *FN* stands for the meaning that positive samples are incorrectly predicted as negative by the model, i.e., real vehicle targets are predicted as non-vehicle targets.

$$AP = \int_0^1 P(R)dR \tag{15.3}$$

$$mAP = \frac{1}{N}\sum_{i=1}^{N} AP_i \tag{15.4}$$

Parameter Setting

In this paper, we conduct experiments on the *nuScence* dataset, resize the image to 300 × 300, and train using GPU. The Adma optimizer is selected, the maximum learning rate is 0.0004, batch_size is set to 16, and num_workers is set to 4. Freeze training is not used. A total of 200 Epochs are trained in the experiment. Since the improved algorithm aims to illustrate its feasibility and advantages for mobile, it is tested using CPU.

15.4.3 Ablation Experiments

In this experiment, the original SSD model, and the SSD model with only the change of Ghostnetv2 as the backbone network, after multi-scale fusion, and after a priori box optimization, are subjected to ablation experiments. Model performance is measured using *mAP* and *FPS*. The results of the ablation experiments are shown in Table 15.2.

The *mAP* and several categories of *AP* for the four sets of experiments are shown in Fig. 15.8.

According to the results in Table 15.2 and Fig. 15.8 the improved Ghostnetv2-SSD network model has a *mAP* value of 61.96%, which is improved compared to all other models. And Ghostnetv2-SSD reduces the model parameters by simplifying

Table 15.2 Results of ablation experiments

Test	Ghostnetv2	Multi-scale integration	Prior bounding box optimization	*mAP* /%	*FPS*
1				59.69	3
2	√			53.60	21
3	√	√		58.41	16
4	√	√	√	61.9	16

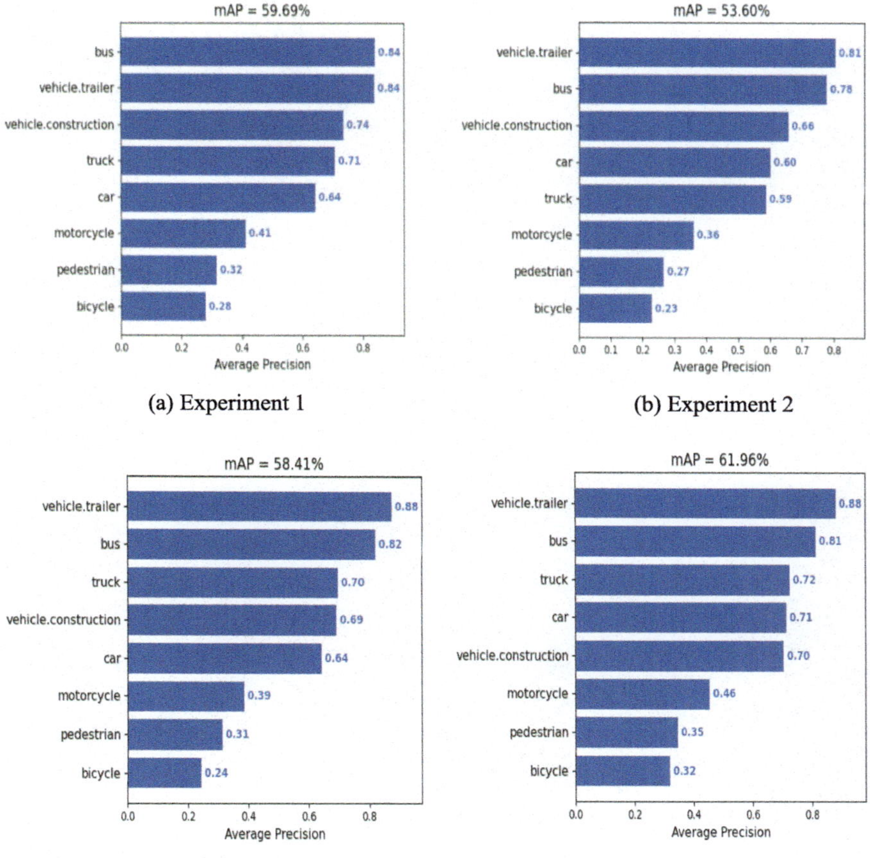

(a) Experiment 1 (b) Experiment 2

(c) Experiment 3 (d) Experiment 4

Fig. 15.8 Comparison results of *AP* values of four groups of experiments

the structure. Moreover, the improved structure is more suitable for CPU, and the *FPS* on CPU is improved by 5 times compared with SSD algorithm, which has the best overall performance. Comparison of SSD and Ghostnetv2-SSD detection effect is shown in Fig. 15.9.

From Fig. 15.9a, it can be seen that the SSD target is insensitive to small targets when detecting them, and there are also missed detections in more complex environments. The improved Ghostnetv2-SSD algorithm in Fig. 15.9b performs better and has higher accuracy, fewer parameters, and is more adaptable to mobile than the SSD algorithm. It can realize accurate and fast detection of road conditions. Effective risk prevention.

(a) SSD detection effect (b)Ghostnetv2-SSD detection effect

Fig. 15.9 Comparison of SSD and Ghostnetv2-SSD detection results

15.4.4 Comparative Experiments

Comparative analysis with other algorithms. Table 15.3 shows the comparison of the detection results of different detection algorithms on the *nuScence* dataset, and the Faster R-CNN model is larger and slower because the target recognition and localization are completed in two steps. Other algorithms are single-step recognition networks, which identify and locate targets at the same time, so the detection speed is faster. Among them, YOLOv8s has the highest detection accuracy, but the detection speed is not as fast as ours. Our detection network has the highest detection speed and detection accuracy, second only to YOLOv8, and is basically the same, which proves

Table 15.3 Detection results for different detection networks

Model	Input size	*mAP/%*	*FPS*
Faster-rcnn	600*600	53.41	0.37
Yolov4-tiny	416*416	43.18	13.79
Yolov5s	640*640	54.20	3.92
Yolov8s	640*640	65.77	4.16
Ours	300*300	61.96	16.53

that the detection network in this paper has strong advantages in comprehensive performance.

15.5 Concluding Remarks

Ghostnetv2-SSD is proposed to address the problems of limited computational resources and low accuracy in detecting small targets at long distances in the vehicle vision system. Firstly, the algorithm adopts the lightweight network Ghostnetv2, which is more adapted to the CPU, in the feature extraction part, and has a smaller number of parameters and higher detection speed compared with VGG16 of the original SSD. In order to further enhance the algorithm's ability to detect small targets at long distances, multi-scale fusion is used to improve the algorithm. Also for the situation that different targets in different datasets possess different size distributions, the size of the a prior bounding box and the aspect ratio of the prior bounding box are redesigned to further improve the accuracy. Experiments on the *nuScence* dataset show that the improved Ghostnetv2-SSD algorithm possesses 61.96% as well as 16 frames/s detection speed on CPU. The proposed algorithm has high detection accuracy and real-time performance, which can provide high-quality road condition information for autonomous driving.

Acknowledgements The work described in this article was supported by the funds from the Basic Scientific Research Projects of the Educational Department of Liaoning Province (grant no. LJKZ0585).

References

1. Liu, W., Anguelov, D., Erhan, D., et al.: SSD: Single shot multibox detector[C]. In: Computer Vision-ECCV 2016, pp.21–37. Springer International Publishing, Cham (2016)
2. Redmon, J., Divvala, S., Girshick, R., et al.: You only look once: unified, real-time object detection[C]. In: 2016 IEEE Conference on Computer Vision and Pattern Recognition (CVPR), pp. 779–788 (2016)
3. Zhou, X., Wang, D., Krähenbühl, P.: Objects as points[C] (2019). arXiv:1904.07850

4. Girshick, R., Donahue, J., Darrell, T., et al.: Rich feature hierarchies for accurate object detection and semantic segmentation[C]. In: 2014 IEEE Conference on Computer Vision and Pattern Recognition, pp. 580–587 (2014)
5. He, K., Zhang, X., Ren, S., et al.: Spatial pyramid pooling in deep convolutional networks for visual recognition [J]. IEEE Trans. Pattern Anal. Mach. Intell. **37**(9), 1904–1916 (2015)
6. Ren, S., He, K., Girshick, R., et al.: Faster R-CNN: towards real-time object detection with region proposal networks [J]. IEEE Trans. Pattern Anal. Mach. Intell. **396**, 1137–1149 (2017)
7. Zhao, W.C., Zhou, Z.D., Zhai, Y.J.: SSD small target detection algorithm based on inverse convolution and feature fusion[J]. J. Intell. Syst. **15**(02), 310−316 (2020)
8. Fu, G., Liu, Y., Liu, J.: Electronic design. Engi. **32**(01), 175–180+186 (2024). https://doi.org/10.14022/j.issn1674-6236
9. Liu, H., Wang, J., Shao, L., et al.: Vehicle target recognition based on improved SSD and multi-focus image fusion[J/OL]. J. Tianjin Univ. Technol. 1–9 (2024)
10. Zhao, J.F., Li, Q., Zhao, J.L.: Vehicle identification and tracking based on improved SSD-MobileNetV3 network and SORT[J]. Autom. Instrum. (11), 16–19+24 (2023). https://doi.org/10.14016/j.cnki.1001-9227
11. Li, G.J., Hu, J., AI, J.Y.: Vehicle detection based on improved SSD algorithm [J]. Comput. Eng. **48**(1), 266–274 (2022)
12. Li, K., Lin, Y.S., Wu, X.L., et al.: Small target vehicle detection based on multi-scale fusion and attention mechanism[J]. J. Zhejiang Univ. (Engineering Edition). **56**(11), 2241–2250 (2022)
13. Lai, Y., Ju, Z.Y., Ye, Y.X.: Vehicle detection algorithm based on improved YOLOv4[J/OL]. Electron. Sci. Technol. 1–8 (2024)
14. Yu, G.H., Jia, W.D., Yu, P.F., et al.: Car face detection algorithm based on improved YOLOv5s[J]. Comput. Eng. Des. **45**(03), 732–739 (2024)
15. Howard, A.G., Howard, A.G., Zhu, M., et al.: MobileNets: efficient convolutional neural networks for mobile vision applications [C]. In: IEEE Conference on Computer Vision and Pattern Recognition, pp. 1−9. IEEE, Hawaii, USA (2017)
16. Zhang, X.Y., Zhou, X.Y., Lin, M.X., et al.: ShuffleNet: an extremely efficient convolutional neural network for mobile devices [C]. In: 2018 IEEE/CVF Conference on Computer Vision and Pattern Recognition, pp. 6848–6856. Salt lake city, IEEE, USA (2018)
17. Tang, Y., Han, K., Guo, J., et al.: GhostNetV2: enhance cheap operation with long-range attention[C]. In: Conference on Neural Information Processing Systems (2022)

Chapter 16
Information Segmentation and Feature Extraction Method Based on Bi-polarisation

Chunyang Jia, Yong Li, and Zhaorun Huang

Abstract Long-form data, such as video or text, often encompasses a multitude of features, each exerting varying degrees of influence on the final categorization outcome within any given segment of the data. In this paper, we propose a Segmented Augmentation Method tailored for small-scale long-form data. This method leverages k-means clustering to categorize each segment of the data based on its distinct features, employing a two-level classification approach. Subsequently, data frames wherein all features align with a single class are selected to construct a training set. This curated training set facilitates the discernment of human preferences. The DNNs with an overlay mechanism is then trained utilizing both segmented and unsegmented training sets specific to a given dataset, resulting in a notable enhancement in network performance.

16.1 Introduction

The proliferation of online video platforms coupled with the exponential expansion of video content consumption has accustomed people to accessing information and entertainment through videos. However, a predominant portion of video content comprises lengthy, uninterrupted streams, harboring vast amounts of information. Consequently, platforms encounter challenges in effectively extracting requisite information for recommendation algorithms, thereby resulting in diminished recommendation success rates. Consequently, the segmentation and extraction of information from long videos have emerged as crucial research endeavors.

Conventional methods for video information analysis predominantly rely on manually crafted features and rules, such as keyword-based retrieval and scene-based segmentation. Le [1] introduced an unsupervised learning method capable of mapping paragraphs or documents to fixed-length vector representations, facilitating

C. Jia (✉) · Y. Li · Z. Huang
School of Electrical Engineering, Shenyang University of Technology, Shenyang, China
e-mail: 1183081528@qq.com

F. P. García Márquez et al. (eds.), *Computing, Internet of Things and Data Analytics*, Smart Innovation, Systems and Technologies 387,
https://doi.org/10.1007/978-3-031-87154-2_16

similarity computation and cluster analysis to extract paragraph-level information. Similarly, [2] proposed a Analyzing temporal information in video understanding model, enabling automatic hierarchical analysis for segmentation and classification of video. While these methods partially address video information analysis, their efficacy is often constrained by limited feature expression and rule generalization, making adaptation to complex and evolving scenarios challenging.

Text analysis methodologies entail converting video audio into text and employing natural language processing techniques for textual analysis. These methods discern key video information, such as topics and events, and partition videos into semantically coherent segments. Notably, [3] presented a hierarchical text classification model leveraging attention mechanisms for automated hierarchical analysis, thus enabling segmentation extraction and classification of lengthy textual data. Furthermore, the introduction of the BERT model by [4] revolutionized text understanding through pre-training on extensive textual data, although practical application is impeded by ongoing challenges in speech recognition accuracy and text analysis efficiency.

Visual analytics strategies extract image features and discern scene context by analyzing image sequences within videos. These techniques identify elements such as objects, actions, and scenes, facilitating subsequent segment extraction. For instance, [5] explored deep learning methodologies for video classification and subtitle generation, while [6] introduced convolutional neural networks for video super-resolution processing, enhancing video clarity and quality. Additionally, [7] proposed a video processing approach combining temporal segmentation networks with deep learning techniques for action recognition. Nonetheless, the applicability of visual analysis methods is limited by the necessity for substantial labeled data and computational resources.

In recent years, deep learning methodologies have achieved notable advancements in video information analysis. These models autonomously learn feature representations and semantic information from video data, enabling segmented extraction of lengthy video information through an end-to-end learning paradigm. Particularly, models leveraging recurrent neural networks and attention mechanisms have exhibited superior performance in segment extraction from long video data. For instance, [8] proposed an end-to-end video super-resolution learning approach amalgamating video processing and machine learning via motion compensation techniques. However, existing methods encounter challenges in feature extraction and classification when confronted with lengthy data and limited dataset sizes.

To address the aforementioned issues, this paper introduces an information segmentation and feature extraction method grounded in bi-polarisation. Tailored for scenarios involving prolonged individual data and constrained dataset sizes, the proposed method segments and extracts features from data, delineating segments of varying lengths based on polarity. This augmentation of data facilitates the identification and classification of pertinent information within the dataset.

16.2 Information Segmentation and Feature Extraction Methods

For datasets characterized by lengthy sequences and a limited number of samples, this paper presents an information segmentation and feature extraction method based on bi-polarisation. The method aims to augment dataset dimensions by leveraging bi-clustering relationships within the data frames. Emphasis is placed on preserving label annotation accuracy following data expansion, achieved through iterative refinement of feature weights.

Initially, the longitudinal data is translated into a series of feature vectors for analysis. To expand dataset capacity, the system undertakes feature vector segmentation. Subsequently, the segmented data undergoes analysis utilizing the K-means algorithm for bi-clustering, yielding dominant and implicit poles. By comparing clustering outcomes against original data labels across different feature vectors, the accuracy of the clustering process is assessed. This comparison informs the determination of initial feature weights for label annotation.

Figure 16.1 depicts the process of generating dominant pole and implicit pole labels using the label annotator. Here, the data is partitioned into n segments denoted as C1 to Cn, and m feature vectors are represented as FV1 to FVm. The black segments signify dominant pole segments, while white segments denote implicit pole segments.

Illustrated in Fig. 16.2, the operational concept of the label annotator and classifier entails the transformation of the dataset into a feature vector ensemble, subsequently partitioned into training and testing subsets. The testing set serves the purpose of classifier evaluation, while the training set is furnished to the label generator for data augmentation and annotation. Fusion of polar labels with the outcomes derived from the price tag annotator yields novel labels, which, in turn, are inputted into the weight generator to facilitate the updating of label annotator weights.

The label annotator, comprising an m-input dual-output fully connected layer, adopts the hyperbolic tanh activation function. The initial feature weights in Fig. 16.1 correspond to each output of the label annotator and are refined utilizing the weight generator shown in Fig. 16.2. This refinement process integrates the training set alongside polarity labels.

The weight generation process within the weight generator is predominantly reliant on the Random Forest algorithm, as expounded by [9]. Input to the weight generator consists of newly annotated data, specifically, fragment data post-label filtering. Each fragment data encompasses feature vectors of m features, subjected once more to classification via the Random Forest algorithm within the weight generator. However, the primary objective of this classification is the generation of fresh feature weights. The Random Forest algorithm employs self-sampling, randomly selecting feature samples from the input vector to construct a new training set for one of its decision trees. This iterative process is crucial for refining feature extraction, deemed speculative.

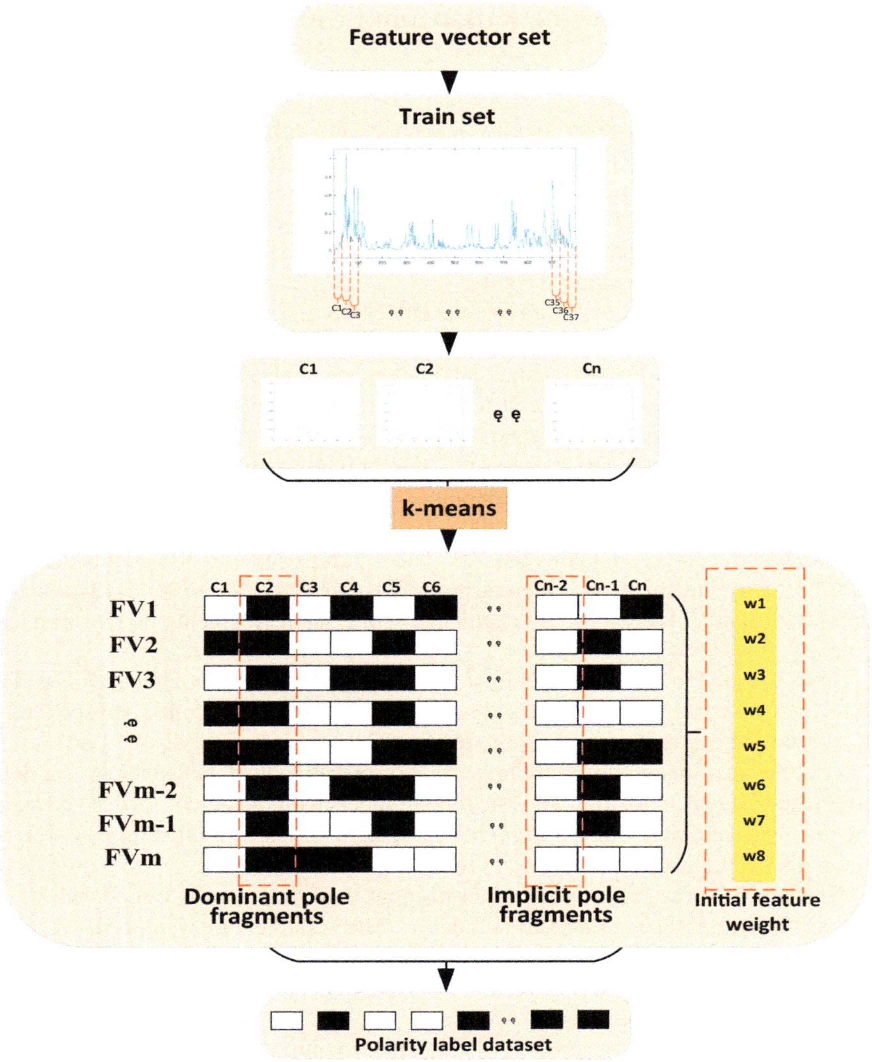

Fig. 16.1 The process of generating a polarity label

The classifier incorporates both the cognitive model and the piror model, which are conventional multilayer convolutional architectures. Notably, the piror model undergoes training with a higher learning rate compared to the cognitive model. The DM discerns the classifier output by selecting the outcome with the highest classification score from both models. During training, the override mechanism is invoked, whereby the weights of the cognitive model supersede those of the piror

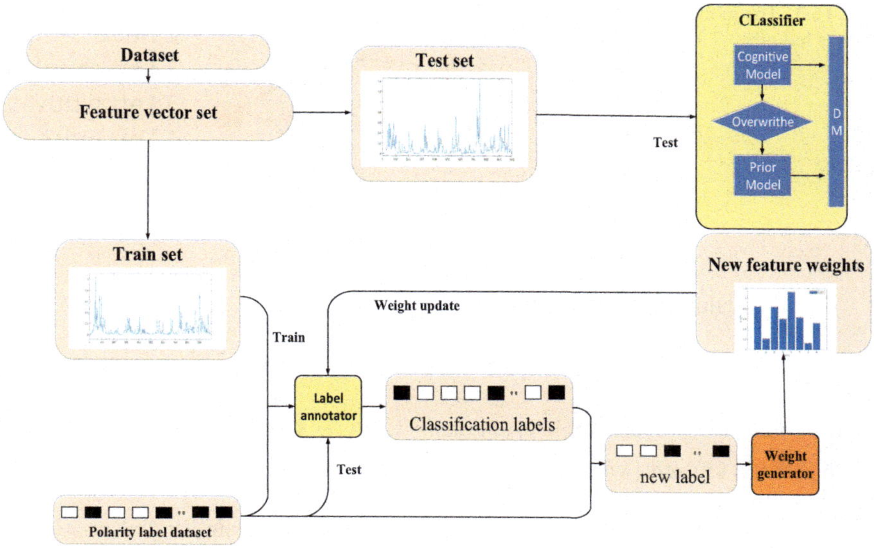

Fig. 16.2 The principle of label annotator with classifiers

model when the former consistently outperforms the latter in sequential test results for three times.

16.3 Experimentation

16.3.1 Data Pre-processing

The method of this paper was tested using the MINI-RGBD dataset created by [10], which contains 12 samples of infant motion RGBD video data. Firstly, the data is preprocessed, and in this paper, we use the 3D coordinates of joint points generated by combining the 2D joint point data with the depth data, and the joint displacements are derived from the 3D coordinates of each joint point within the temporal sequence, i.e., the displacements are derived from each of the three axes, x, y, and z. The coordinates of the joint points are (x_t, y_t, z_t), where $t \in [0{,}1000]$, and based on the displacements of the joints in each of the axes, we seek the inter-frame displacement of the joint point is shown in:

$$S(t) = \sqrt{(x_t - x_{t-1})^2 + (y_t - y_{t-1})^2 + (z_t - z_{t-1})^2} \tag{16.1}$$

Calculate the inter-frame velocity from the inter-frame displacement as:

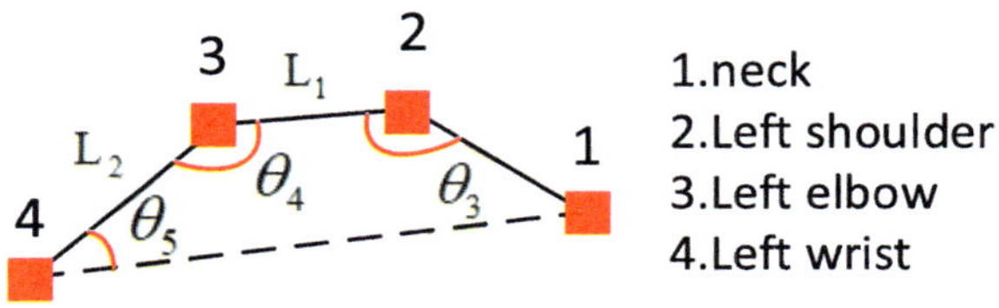

Fig. 16.3 The model of a baby's left arm

$$v(t) = \mathrm{d}S(t)/dt \tag{16.2}$$

Similarly calculate the acceleration as:

$$a(t) = \mathrm{d}v(t)/dt \tag{16.3}$$

Kinematic features also include angular velocity, as shown in Fig. 16.3 for a model of an infant's left arm, where $\vec{L_1}$ and $\vec{L_2}\vec{L_2}$ can be obtained by direct subtraction in 3D coordinates.

Take θ_4 in Fig. 16.3 as an example to calculate the inter-frame angle variation as:

$$\theta_4(t) = \arccos \frac{\vec{L_1} \cdot \vec{L_2}}{|L_1||L_2|} \tag{16.4}$$

The angular velocity $\omega(t)$ and angular acceleration $\beta(t)$ are calculated in the same way as the derivation for time. The above features ($S(t)$, $v(t)$, $a(t)$, $\theta_4(t)$, $\omega(t)$, $\beta(t)$) are arranged in chronological order to form the corresponding six eigenvectors.

16.3.2 Data Segmentation Experiment

The 12 sets of datasets will be divided into test set (2 samples) and training set (10 samples) for segmentation, to ensure that the test set and training set selected under the four resolutions of the same samples, based on the bi-Polarisation information segmentation and feature extraction methods were taken: 9 segments, 27 segments, 37 segments, 111 segments of the resolution of the pair of the segmentation performance test. There are four evaluation indexes ACC, TD, TI and F1, ACC is the overall precision of label annotation, TD is the labeling precision of dominant labels, TI is the labeling precision of implicit labels and F1 is the evaluation index for binary classification considering the precision rate and recall rate (Table 16.1).

Considering the four evaluation metrics, 37 Hz was selected as the optimal segmental resolution.

Table 16.1 Assessment indicators at different segment resolutions

Segmented resolution (Hz)	ACC (%)	TD (%)	TN (%)	F1 (%)
9	60	53.85	71.43	51.85
27	70	69.23	78.43	58.06
37	80	76.92	85.71	60.61
111	50	46.15	57.14	48.01

Table 16.2 Assessment indicators at different segment resolutions

	ACC (%)	T1 (%)	T2 (%)	F1 (%)
Unlabeled	62.45	70.23	55.86	58.41
Labeled	82.36	80.14	84.37	61.58
CNN	51.35	53.85	42.86	51.85

16.3.3 Data Classification Experiment

The 12 samples are segmented at the optimal segmentation resolution of 37 Hz, and 2 samples from the 12 samples are randomly selected as the test set (each segment with labels is tested independently when the test set is tested), and the rest of the samples are used as the training set. The classifier is trained using the segmented training set and the unsegmented training set separately to test the effect of reasonable segmentation on the classification performance. MINI-RGBD dataset is a binary classification task, and T1 in Table 16.2 denotes the classification accuracy of the first class T2 denotes the classification accuracy of the second class.

'Unlabeled' in Table 16.2 denotes that the classifier in Fig. 16.2 is trained using the unprocessed training set, 'Labeled' denotes the classifier trained with the training set processed by adaptive segmentation, and 'CNN' is a standard convolutional neural network directly trained using the unprocessed training set for testing.

In terms of dealing with the problem of classifying long data with a small number of samples, the information segmentation and feature extraction method based on bi-polarisation proposed in this paper has obvious advantages, resulting in improved classification performance.

16.4 Conclusion

The proposed the methodology of information segmentation and feature extraction predicated on bi-polarisation, which effectively partitions small-scale longitudinal data, thereby facilitating data augmentation. Furthermore, this approach autonomously generates data labels and feature weights. Subsequently, the dataset undergoes classification and identification processes, wherein the segmentation resolution of input feature vectors is dynamically adjusted to obtain a resolution conducive to the dataset. This adaptation mitigates the risk of compromising original data features due to the segmentation process. A comparative evaluation of the convolutional network equipped with a coverage mechanism, trained on both pre-segmentation and post-segmentation datasets, underscores the efficacy of this segmentation technique. The proposed method specifically enhances the network's recognition accuracy when dealing with datasets characterized by lengthy data sequences and limited sample sizes.

References

1. Le, Q., Mikolov, T.: Distributed representations of sentences and documents. In: International Conference on Machine Learning, pp. 1188–1196. PMLR (2014)
2. Huang, D.A., Ramanathan, V., Mahajan, D., Torresani, L., Paluri, M., Fei-Fei, L., Niebles, J.C.: What makes a video a video: analyzing temporal information in video understanding models and datasets. In: Proceedings of the IEEE Conference on Computer Vision and Pattern Recognition, pp. 7366–7375 (2018)
3. Yang, Z., Yang, D., Dyer, C., He, X., Smola, A., Hovy, E.: Hierarchical attention networks for document classification. In: Proceedings of the 2016 Conference of the North American Chapter of the Association for Computational Linguistics: Human Language Technologies, pp. 1480–1489 (2016)
4. Devlin, J., Chang, M.W., Lee, K., Toutanova, K: Bert: pre-training of deep bidirectional transformers for language understanding. arxiv:1810.04805
5. Wu, Z., Yao, T., Fu, Y., Jiang, Y.G.: Deep learning for video classification and captioning. In: Frontiers of Multimedia Research, pp. 3–29 (2017)
6. Kappeler, A., Yoo, S., Dai, Q., Katsaggelos, A.: K: Video super-resolution with convolutional neural networks. IEEE Trans. Comput. Imaging **2**(2), 109–122 (2016)
7. Wang, L., Xiong, Y., Wang, Z., Qiao, Y., Lin, D., Tang, X., Van Gool, L.: Temporal segment networks: towards good practices for deep action recognition. In : European Conference on Computer Vision, pp. 20–36. Springer, Cham (2016)
8. Makansi, O., Ilg, E., Brox, T.: End-to-end learning of video super-resolution with motion compensation. In: Pattern Recognition: 39th German Conference, GCPR 2017, Basel, Switzerland, September 12–15, 2017, Proceedings 39, pp. 203–214. Springer International Publishing (2017)
9. Speiser, J.L., Miller, M.E., Tooze, J., Ip, E.: A comparison of random forest variable selection methods for classification prediction modeling. Expert. Syst. Appl. **134**, 93–101 (2019)
10. McCay, Kevin D., et al.: A pose-based feature fusion and classification framework for the early prediction of cerebral palsy in infants. IEEE Trans. Neural Syst. Rehabil. Eng. **30**, 8–19 (2021)

Chapter 17
Feature-Level Meta-Transfer Learning Framework for Few-Shot Cross-Condition Fault Diagnosis of Bearings

Yuqi Yao, Yuxian Zhang, Yuejia Liu, and Likui Qiao

Abstract To solve the existing problems in bearing fault diagnosis, such as the difference of domain distribution, the mismatch of label space and the deficiency of labeled samples in the target domain., we propose a feature-level meta-transfer learning framework (FMTLF) for few-shot cross-condition fault diagnosis of bearings. Specifically, FMTLF attempts to calculate the prototype of each subdomain and combines it with domain adversarial training. It not only helps the model to accumulate meta-knowledge of the source domain, but also effectively learns discriminative patterns of the target domain. A feature-level discard-excitation module is designed to perform discard and excitation on the features for the setting to improve the summarization ability. Comparison experiments on Case Western Reserve University public datasets verification of validity of FMTLF and the feasibility.

17.1 Introduction

Rotating machinery is important for electromechanical equipment, and its state of health makes a difference to the safety and economical operation of the equipment [1]. Therefore, timely and reliable fault diagnosis (FD) of bearings can prolong the operating life of electromechanical systems [2]. In recent years, transfer learning (TL) has provided excellent solutions for online monitoring of bearings. Among TL, the domain adaptation (DA) alleviates the domain transfer by introducing adversarial learning. Tian et al. [3] designed a sub-DA TL method, which improves the spanning domain diagnosis accuracy by pairing the fine-grained information of source domain (SD) and target domain (TD) through multi-branch network structure matching. Mao

Y. Yao · Y. Zhang (✉) · Y. Liu · L. Qiao
College of Electrical Engineering, Shenyang University of Technology, Shenyang, Liaoning, China
e-mail: y.x.zhang@sut.edu.cn

F. P. García Márquez et al. (eds.), *Computing, Internet of Things and Data Analytics*, Smart Innovation, Systems and Technologies 387,
https://doi.org/10.1007/978-3-031-87154-2_17

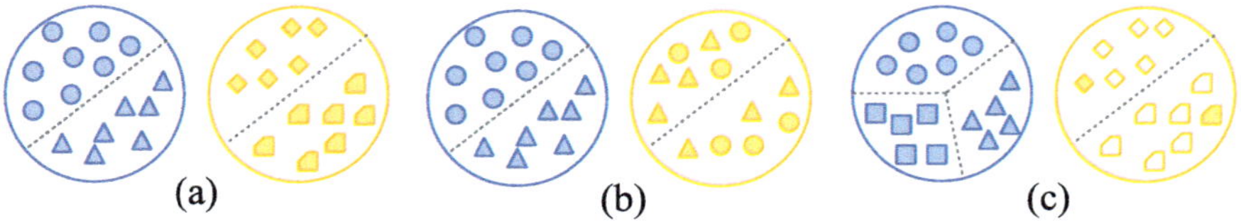

Fig. 17.1 **a** Label space mismatch **b** Severe domain distribution discrepancy **c** Problems addressed in this paper

et al. [4] designed a structured DA neural network that combines the strong adaptability with multiple structured correlation information, which significantly improves the effectiveness of bearing FD across running conditions. Li et al. [5] devised a weakly supervised domain-adversarial TL (WSDTL) framework to learn shared features from multiple similar SDs to improve performance. Despite the forward results of the above studies, SD and TD share a identical label space. In TD and SD label space does not match, as shown in Fig. 17.1a, the above method will suffer negative migration and may not even be applicable. Recently, satisfactory results have been obtained by introducing meta-learning (ML) for the above problems. Feng et al. [6] designed semi-supervised meta-learning networks (SSMN), which can extract distinctive features to generate prototypes. Ma et al. [7] designed a ML correlation module, which can improve the FD performance. However, the above research advocates training the model through multiple similar tasks to adapt to the new task of few-shot [8–14]. When the distributions of SD and TD are not consistent, as shown in Fig. 17.1b, the above methods will have the issue [15–20].

This paper proposes a feature-level meta-transfer learning framework (FMTLF). FMTLF is primarily applied in solving the issues of momentous inconsistency in the domain distribution of bearings data, mismatch in label space and momentous lack of TD labels, as shown in Fig. 17.1c.

FMTLF consists of a feature picker F, a metric-based ML, a domain discriminator, and a feature-level discard excitation module (FDEM). The chief dedications of this are as follows:

(1) FMTLF solves the problems of momentous domain-offset, label mismatch and deficiency of TD labeled samples in a unified framework. It summarizes the sub-domain features as prototypes and integrates them with domain confrontation. The model can well guide the learning of goal-insensitive meta-knows and domain-intrinsic features in SD and TD.
(2) FDEM is designed to discard and stimulate the features to help FMTLF achieve better generalization. FDEM can follow the model for end-to-end training to eliminate negative transfer.
(3) Experiments were conducted on Case Western Reserve University (CWRU) public dataset to compare with baseline and progressive methods to validate the effectiveness and the feasibility of FMTLF.

The remainder of the paper is arranged as following. Section 17.2 presents the underlying theory. Section 17.3 elaborates the details of FMTLF. Section 17.4 gives the experimental details and result analysis. Ultimately, conclusions are given in Sect. 17.5.

17.2 Related Works

17.2.1 Problem Description

We assume that given a labelled SD with a very small number of samples $D_S = \{(x_i, y_i)\}_{i=1}^{n_s}$ and an unlabeled TD $D_T = \{(x_j)\}_{i=1}^{n_T}$ [21–25]. Notably, in this study $D_S \cap D_T = \emptyset$, $D_S \cup D_T = D$, there is a large distributional difference between D_S and D_T. Each TD sample $x_j \in D_T$ has its own true label y_j which is receivables at training time. In this, the model will learn a robust classifier for TD by minimizing shared parameters θ, minimizing the target loss during training: $E_{(D_s,D_T)\sim D}\left[\sum_{x_j \in D_T} -\log p_\theta\left(y_j|x_j, D_S, D_T\right)\right]$. For testing, performance is evaluated using samples that are not visible in the training set to form the test set [26–30].

17.2.2 Metrics Based Meta-Learning

ML contains supportl set $S = \{x_i^S, y_i^S\}$ and queryl set $Q = \{x_j^Q, y_j^Q\}$ in each episode [31, 32]. Thoroughly, stochastically draw N forms of data, and then draw K and M samples from each class ($K \cap M = \emptyset$), separately, to construct the S and the Q. This study uses a ditance-based ML, which underscores the Mahalanobis distance between S archetype and the Q sample to classify the target samples. For S, the centroid of each category can be obtained, i.e., the category archetype:

$$p_c = \frac{1}{K}\sum_i F(x_i) \tag{17.1}$$

where p_c is the archetype of c. Next, the Mahalanobis distance can be calculated, and the predicted probability of a sample in the Q can be captured:

$$P\left(y_j^Q|x_j^Q\right) = \frac{\exp\left(-m\left(F\left(x_j^Q\right), p_k\right)\right)}{\sum_{j=1}^{N}\exp\left(-m\left(F\left(x_j^Q\right), p_j\right)\right)} \tag{17.2}$$

where $\mathrm{m}(e,f) = \sqrt{(e-f)^T \sum^{-1}(e-f)}$ is the Mahalanobis distance. The classify loss of Q samples can be caught:

$$L_{\text{cls}} = -\mathbb{E}_{(x,y)\sim Q}\left[\sum \log \mathrm{P}\left(y^Q \middle| x^Q\right)\right] \tag{17.3}$$

17.3 The Proposed Method

17.3.1 Deep Meta-Transfer Learning (DMTL)

Feature extractor: In FMTLF, F consists of three 1D-CNN units, each of which contains 1D-CNN, batch normalization||(BN), max-pooling||(MP), and ReLU, as shown in Fig. 17.2.

Metrics based classifier: Due to the multi-dimensional and heterogeneous of bearings data, instance-based ML can only learn and align low-level discriminative features and cross-condition instance-to-instance matching is very sensitive to anomalous samples. We adopted a metric-based classifier (MC), as shown in Fig. 17.3. Firstly, sampling randomly in the SD to obtain a support set $S = \{x_i^S, y_i^S\}_{i=1}^{N\times K}$ containing N-way K-shot, and TD is regarded as a query set$Q = \{x_j^Q\}_{j=1}^{N\times M}$, $(K \cap M = \emptyset)$. Then, they were passed to F to mine potentially meaningful information.

In the training phase, the mean value of the feature vector of each category sample in the S is calculated by Eq. (17.1) as the prototype. For each sample x_j^Q in the Q, assign a probability distribution ω_{jc} by Eq. (17.2), which represent the probability of x_j^Q belonging to category c and ω_{jc} is used to update the prototype p_c and covariance matrices Q_k for each category. Then the classification loss of MC can be defined as:

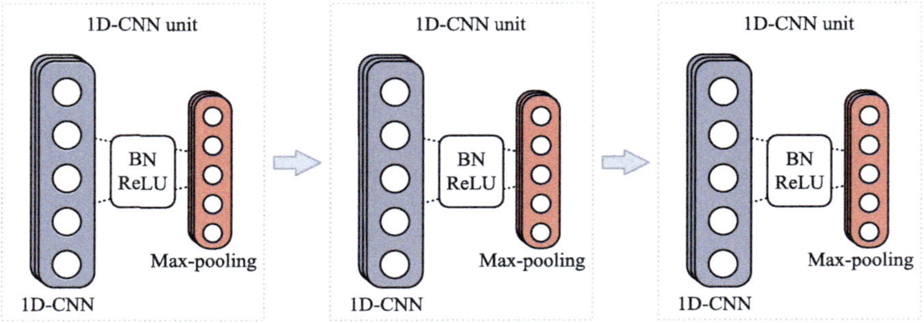

Fig. 17.2 Feature extractor

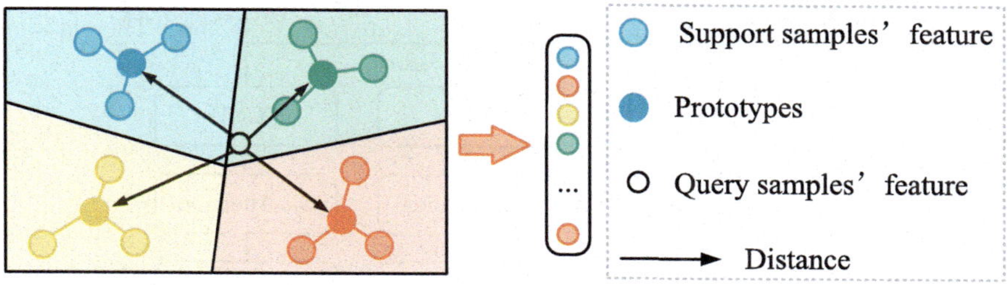

Fig. 17.3 Metrics based classifier

$$\begin{aligned}
L_{\text{cls}} &= -\mathbb{E}_{(x,y)\sim Q}\left[\sum \log \text{P}\left(y_j^Q \middle| x_j^Q\right)\right] \\
L_{\text{clus}} &= -\mathbb{E}_{(x,y)\sim Q}\left[\sum \omega_{jc} \log \text{P}\left(x_j^Q | p_c, Q_k\right)\right] \\
L_{\text{reg}} &= \lambda \sum \text{Tr}(Q_k^{-1}) \\
L_{\text{MC}} &= L_{\text{cls}} + L_{\text{clus}} + L_{\text{reg}}
\end{aligned} \tag{17.4}$$

where $\text{P}\left(x_j^Q | p_c, Q_k\right)$ is the probability density function of the sample x_j^Q when p_c and Q_k are given.

Domain discriminator: It is composed of four fully connected units (FCU) and a sigmoid layer, which is used to distinguish the features of SD and TD, and is trained for F. The sigmoid layer is used to calculate the probability that the feature falls into SD or TD. The domainl discriminator loss can be acquired:

$$L_{\text{D}} = -\mathbb{E}_{x^s \sim P_s(x)} \log\left[\text{D}\left(F(x^s)\right)\right] - \mathbb{E}_{x^t \sim P_t(x)} \log\left[1 - \text{D}\left(F(x^t)\right)\right] \tag{17.5}$$

The total loss can be achieved:

$$L_{total} = L_{\text{MC}} + L_{\text{D}} \tag{17.6}$$

17.3.2 Feature-Level Discard Excitation Module

Inspired. by the [8] and the long. short-term memory network, a feature-level discard excitation module (FDEM) is devised to reinforce the profiling function of FMTLF, as shown in Fig. 17.4.

The purpose of discard blocks is to filter domain-independent information from the context, while the purpose of excitation blocks is to highlight more discriminative feature based on the context. Both process the input features at the same time to help the model enhance the domain alignment. FDEM consists of an expansion time

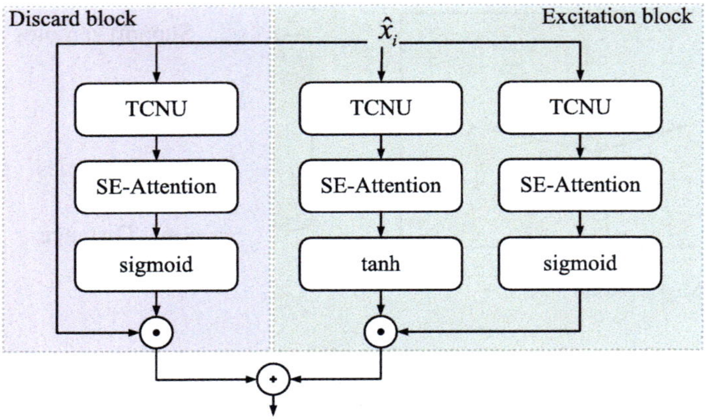

Fig. 17.4 Feature-level discard excitation module

convolution unit (TCNU), a squeeze-excitation attention (SEA), and gated units. TCNU uses convolutional layers to capture local patterns in data and learns higher level feature representations by stacking multiple convolutional layers. The TCL manipulation can be fetched:

$$\mathrm{TCNU}(\hat{x}_i) = \hat{x}_i * f(k, d) \tag{17.7}$$

where k is the convolution kernel, and d is the expansion rate.

Then, the SEA is used to focus on discriminant features. SEA can be expressed as:

$$\begin{aligned} F_{squeeze}(\mathrm{TCNU}(\hat{x}_i)) &= \frac{1}{T}\left[\sum_{t=1}^{T} \mathrm{TCNU}(\hat{x}_i)_c(t)\right]_{c=1}^{C} \\ F_{excitation}\big(F_{squeeze}(\bullet)\big) &= \mathrm{sigmoid}\big(W_2 \tanh\big(W_1 F_{squeeze}(\bullet)\big)\big) \end{aligned} \tag{17.8}$$

where $\mathrm{TCNU}(\hat{x}_i)_c(t)$ is the/ worth of the time step t of the feature sequence after the TCNU at c, T is the length of the sequence, W_1 and W_2 the weight matrix of the FC. The output of SEA is:

$$\mathrm{SEA}(\mathrm{TCNU}(\hat{x}_i)) = [F_{excitation}\big(F_{squeeze}(\bullet)\big) \cdot \mathrm{TCNU}(\hat{x}_i)]_{c=1}^{C} \tag{17.9}$$

Finally, tanh is the excitation factor and sigmoid is the discard factor to manipulate the characteristic sequence. FDEM is connected after F, and then the FC layer merges the features to guide FMTLF to learn more discriminative features, to help it adapt to the problem of severe domain offset. The discarding and excitation operations performed by FDEM on features can be defined as:

$$\begin{aligned} F_{discard} &= \text{sigmoid}(\text{SEA}(\text{TCNU}(\hat{x}_i))) \odot \hat{x}_i \\ F_{excitation} &= \tanh(\text{SEA}(\text{TCNU}(\hat{x}_i))) \odot \text{sigmiod}(\text{SEA}(\text{TCNU}(\hat{x}_i))) \end{aligned} \tag{17.10}$$

FDEM can perform end-to-end training with FMTLF and drive positive transfer by discarding and motivating the senior features to improve the data mining ability and robustness of FMTLF.

17.3.3 Feature-Level Meta-Transfer Learning Framework

The FMTLF integrates metric-based meta-learning, domain adversarial training, and design FDEM, which provides a potential solution for FD of bearings in the case of momentous domain-offset, label mismatch and deficiency of TD labeled samples. The overall framework map is shown in Fig. 17.5.

The final optimization goal can be defined:

$$\begin{aligned} \hat{\theta}_{\text{F}} &= \arg\left\{\min_{\theta_{\text{F}}} L_{\text{MC}}(\theta_{\text{F}}, \theta_{\text{FD}}),\ \min_{\theta_{\text{F}}} \text{L}_{\text{D}}(\theta_{\text{F}}, \theta_{\text{FDEM}}, \theta_{\text{D}})\right\} \\ \hat{\theta}_{\text{FDEM}} &= \arg\left\{\min_{\theta_{\text{FD}}} L_{\text{MC}}(\theta_{\text{F}}, \theta_{\text{FDEM}}),\ \min_{\theta_{\text{FDEM}}} L_{\text{D}}(\theta_{\text{F}}, \theta_{\text{FDEM}}, \theta_{\text{D}})\right\} \\ \hat{\theta}_{\text{D}} &= \arg\left\{\min_{\theta_{\text{D}}} L_{\text{D}}(\theta_{\text{F}}, \theta_{\text{FDEM}}, \theta_{\text{D}})\right\} \end{aligned} \tag{17.11}$$

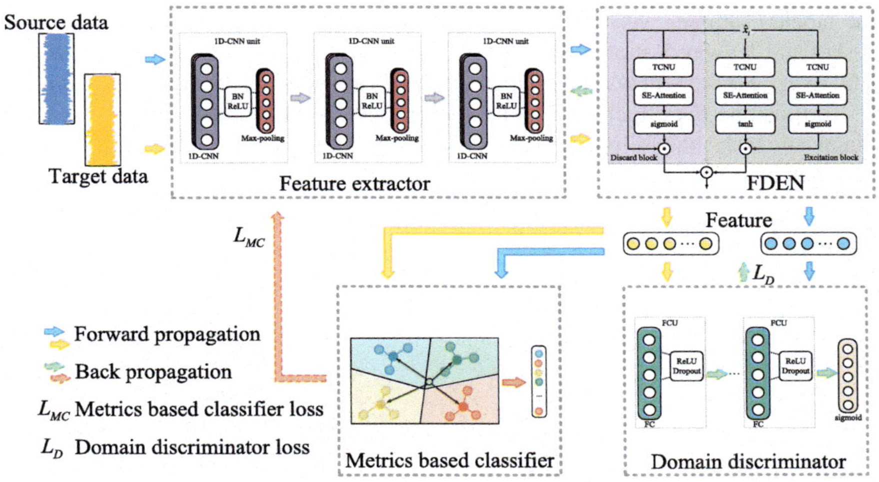

Fig. 17.5 Feature-level meta-transfer learning framework

where θ represent respective parameters. The parameters of FMTLF can be updated by the Adam optimizer:

$$
\begin{aligned}
m_1^{(\text{episode}+1)} &= \beta_1 m_1^{(\text{episode})} + (1 - \beta_1)\Delta\theta^{(\text{episode})} \\
m_2^{(\text{episode}+1)} &= \beta_2 m_2^{(\text{episode})} + (1 - \beta_2)\left(\Delta\theta^{(\text{episode})}\right)^2 \\
\theta^{(\text{episode}+1)} &= \theta^{(\text{episode})} - lr \cdot m_1^{(\text{episode}+1)} / \sqrt{m_2^{(\text{episode}+1)} + \varepsilon}
\end{aligned}
\tag{17.12}
$$

where m_1, m_2 is the moment estimation; β_1, β_2, ε are hyperparameters, set to 0.9, 0.99, 1×10^{-8}, respectively; lr is set to 0.001, $\Delta\theta = \partial L / \partial\theta$.

17.4 Experiments

17.4.1 Experimental Setting

FMTLF is evaluated on the CWRU dataset [9]. The CWRU data set acquisition test bench is shown in Fig. 17.6. We mainly focus on defects with diameters of 7-, 14- and 21-mil. Four working conditions (0, 1, 2, 3 hp) were collected, and the parallel motor speeds were 1797, 1772, 1750, 1730 r/min, individually. This study mainly focuses on the driving end, and a complete set of ten fault data was designed. To prove their validity, the data for SD and TD were taken from different working conditions, and a total of twelve tasks are set up, namely: $0 \to 1, 0 \to 2, 0 \to 3, 1 \to 0, 1 \to 2, 1 \to 3, 2 \to 0, 2 \to 1, 2 \to 3, 3 \to 0, 3 \to 1, 3 \to 2$. To make an objective comparison, the labeled samples were chosen arbitrarily from the CWRU according to 10-way 1-shot and 10-way 5-shot as SD, and the remaining unlabeled samples were used as TD. Every experiment was performed five times and the mean values were reported.

To illustrate the effectiveness of the proposed FMTLF objectively and fairly in diagnostic tasks, the following methods with similar network architecture and hyper parameters to FMTLF are used for comparison.

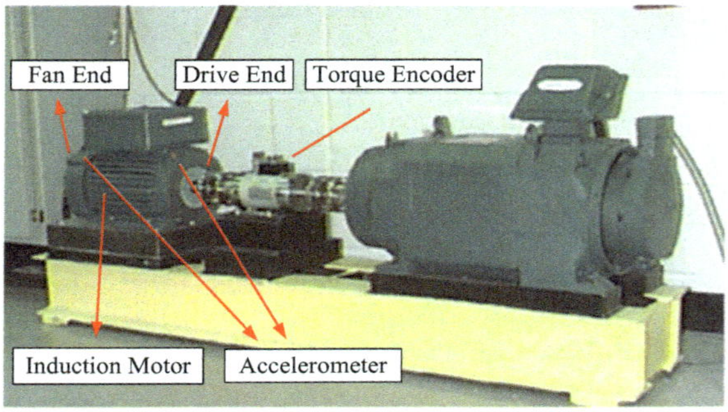

Fig. 17.6 CRWU bearing fault data set test bench

(1) 1D-CNN: 1D-CNN, which has the same architecture and arguments as the feature extractor in FMTLF, is used as the baseline for DL.
(2) Prototypical Network: It is used as the baseline of ML for comparison. It uses the same configuration and principles as the FMTLF.
(3) SSMN: SSMN combines a parametric encoder, a dis-parametric proof refinement process and a range function [4].
(4) WSDTL: WSDTL consists of multiple classifiers, a feature picker, a discriminator and a gradient inversion layer [3].

17.4.2 Result Analysis

The diagnosis results of FMTLF and other comparison methods in the cross-condition small sample task are shown in Fig. 17.7, where the bold font is the best accuracy in the current task.

The diagnostic survey shows that 1D-CNN shows the lowest diagnostic performance. Even if five labeled samples are voidable for each state, the average diagnostic accuracy is only 71.018%. For Prototypical Network, ML improves the performance under the deficiency of labeled samples. Due to the very small quantities of labeled samples, performance crashes still occur. Compared with the baseline method, the diagnostic performance of the improved three diagnostic methods is improved, which proves the rationality of learning transfer meta-knows from SD labeled samples. In

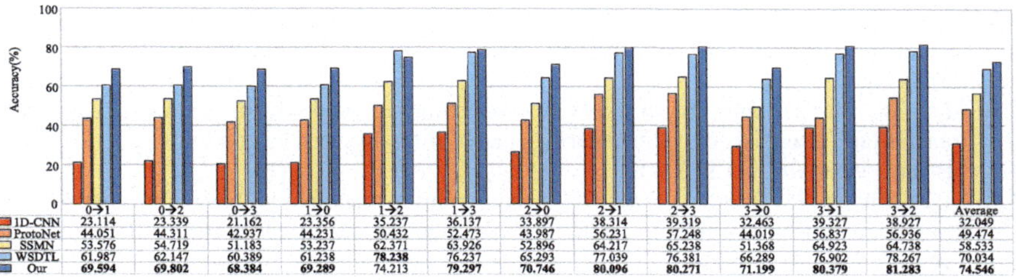

	0→1	0→2	0→3	1→0	1→2	1→3	2→0	2→1	2→3	3→0	3→1	3→2	Average
1D-CNN	23.114	23.339	21.162	23.356	35.237	36.137	33.897	38.314	39.319	32.463	39.327	38.927	32.049
ProtoNet	44.051	44.311	42.937	44.231	50.432	52.473	43.987	56.231	57.248	44.019	56.837	56.936	49.474
SSMN	53.576	54.719	51.183	53.237	62.371	63.926	52.896	64.217	65.238	51.368	64.923	64.738	58.533
WSDTL	61.987	62.147	60.389	61.238	**78.238**	76.237	65.293	77.039	76.381	66.289	76.902	78.267	70.034
Our	**69.594**	**69.802**	**68.384**	**69.289**	74.213	**79.297**	**70.746**	**80.096**	**80.271**	**71.199**	**80.379**	**81.283**	**74.546**

(a) 10-way 1-shot

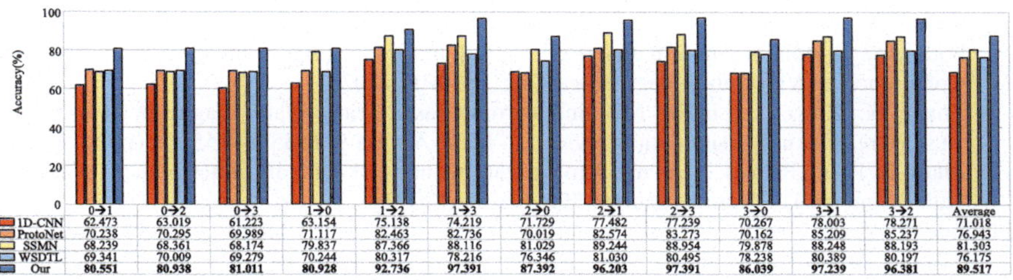

	0→1	0→2	0→3	1→0	1→2	1→3	2→0	2→1	2→3	3→0	3→1	3→2	Average
1D-CNN	62.473	63.019	61.223	63.154	75.138	74.219	71.729	77.482	77.239	70.267	78.003	78.271	71.018
ProtoNet	70.238	70.295	69.989	71.117	82.463	82.736	70.019	82.574	83.273	70.162	85.209	85.237	76.943
SSMN	68.239	68.361	68.174	79.837	87.366	88.116	81.029	89.244	88.954	79.878	88.248	88.193	81.303
WSDTL	69.341	70.009	69.279	70.244	80.317	78.216	76.346	81.030	80.495	78.238	80.389	80.197	76.175
Our	**80.551**	**80.938**	**81.011**	**80.928**	**92.736**	**97.391**	**87.392**	**96.203**	**97.391**	**86.039**	**97.239**	**96.381**	**89.517**

(b) 10-way 5-shot

Fig. 17.7 Cross-condition diagnosis results based on CWRU addition, compared with SSMN and WSDTL, FMTLF achieves the best diagnostic results for each number of odd labeled samples. Even if there is only one available labeled. sample for each state, the average diagnostic accuracy is 74.546%.

17.5 Conclusion

In this paper, a method named FMTLF is created for FCFD of bearings. By combining the sub-domain feature prototype with domain adversaria, FMTLF adapts to the diagnosis problems of momentous domain-offset, label-mismatch and deficiency of labeled samples. In addition, overlaying the designed FDEM onto the feature picker to far refine the globalization of the FMTLF. Pilot program on the CWRU prove the effectiveness and superiority of FMTLF and the feasibility of engineering diagnosis. Even if only one or five labeled samples are usable for each state in SD, FMTLF still performs efficiently.

References

1. Cui, L., Zhao, X., Liu, D., et al.: A spectral coherence cyclic periodic index optimization-gram for bearing fault diagnosis[J]. Meas. **224**, 113898 (2024)
2. Zhang, Z., Wu, L.: Graph neural network-based bearing fault diagnosis using Granger causality test[J]. Expert Syst. Appl. **242**, 122827 (2024)
3. Tian, J., Han, D., Li, M., et al.: A multi-source information transfer learning method with subdomain adaptation for cross-domain fault diagnosis[J]. Knowl.-Based Syst. **243**, 108466 (2022)
4. Mao, W., Liu, Y., Ding, L., et al.: A new structured domain adversarial neural network for transfer fault diagnosis of rolling bearings under different working conditions[J]. IEEE Trans. Instrum. Meas. **70**, 1–13 (2020)
5. Li, X., Zhang, W., Ding, Q., et al.: Diagnosing rotating machines with weakly supervised data using deep transfer learning[J]. IEEE Trans. Industr. Inf. **16**(3), 1688–1697 (2019)
6. Feng, Y., Chen, J., Zhang, T., et al.: Semi-supervised meta-learning networks with squeeze-and-excitation attention for few-shot fault diagnosis[J]. ISA Trans. **120**, 383–401 (2022)
7. Ma, R., Han, T., Lei, W.: Cross-domain meta learning fault diagnosis based on multi-scale dilated convolution and adaptive relation module[J]. Knowl.-Based Syst. **261**, 110175 (2023)
8. Mehta, A., Yang, W.: NAC-TCN: temporal convolutional networks with causal dilated neighborhood attention for emotion understanding[C]. In: Proceedings of the 2023 7th International Conference on Video and Image Processing, pp. 9–16 (2023)
9. Zhang, X., Zhao, B., Lin, Y.: Machine learning based bearing fault diagnosis using the case western reserve university data: a review[J]. IEEE Access **9**, 155598–155608 (2021)
10. Zhao, Z., Zhao, R., Wu, X., et al.: A meta-learning network with anti-interference for few-shot fault diagnosis[J]. Neurocomputing **552**, 126551 (2023)
11. Luo, P., Yin, Z., Yuan, D., et al.: An intelligent method for early motor bearing fault diagnosis based on Wasserstein distance generative adversarial networks meta learning[J]. IEEE Trans. Instrum. Meas. (2023)
12. Lei, Z., Zhang, P., Chen, Y., et al.: Prior knowledge-embedded meta-transfer learning for few-shot fault diagnosis under variable operating conditions[J]. Mech. Syst. Signal Process. **200**, 110491 (2023)

13. Goodfellow, I., Pouget-Abadie, J., Mirza, M., et al.: Generative adversarial networks[J]. Commun. ACM **63**(11), 139–144 (2020)
14. Brophy, E., Wang, Z., She, Q., et al.: Generative adversarial networks in time series: a systematic literature review[J]. ACM Comput. Surv. **55**(10), 1–31 (2023)
15. Hendriks, J., Dumond, P., Knox, D.A.: Towards better benchmarking using the CWRU bearing fault dataset[J]. Mech. Syst. Signal Process. **169**, 108732 (2022)
16. Hou, Y., Wang, J., Chen, Z., et al.: Diagnosisformer: an efficient rolling bearing fault diagnosis method based on improved transformer[J]. Eng. Appl. Artif. Intell. **124**, 106507 (2023)
17. Ni, Q., Ji, J.C., Halkon, B., et al.: Physics-Informed residual network (PIResNet) for rolling element bearing fault diagnostics[J]. Mech. Syst. Signal Process. **200**, 110544 (2023)
18. Hou, Q., Wang, J., Shen, Y.: Multiple sensors fault diagnosis for rolling bearing based on variational mode decomposition and convolutional neural networks[C]. In: 2020 11th International Conference on Prognostics and System Health Management (PHM-2020 Jinan) (2020)
19. Li, J., Chen, H., Sun, S., et al.: Simulation-driven subdomain adaptation network for bearing fault diagnosis with missing samples[J]. Eng. Appl. Artif. Intell. 123(PA) (2023)
20. Hu, W., Xie, G., Wang, J., et al.: Vibration-based bearing fault diagnosis of high-speed trains: a literature review[J]. High Speed Railw. **1**(4), 219–223 (2023)
21. Zhong, J., Bao, X., Xiao, L., et al.: A physical-assisted multi-source signal rolling bearing fault diagnosis method[C]. In: 2023 Global Reliability and Prognostics and Health Management Conference (PHM-Hangzhou). 0[2024–09–22]
22. Liu, J., Cao, H., Chen, S.X.: Simulation-driven subdomain adaptation network for bearing fault diagnosis with missing samples[J]. Eng. Appl. Artif. Intell.: Int. J. Intell. R.-Time Autom. **123**(Pt.A), 106201–1–106201–12 (2023)
23. Zhang, F., Yin, Z., Xu, F., et al.: MAB-DrNet: bearing fault diagnosis method based on an improved dilated convolutional neural network[J]. Sens. (Basel, Switzerland). **23** (2023)
24. Liang, Y.L., Chien, W., Yuan, S.F.: Overview of bearing fault diagnosis based on vibration signal[C]. In: 2023 IEEE 3rd International Conference on Electronic Communications, Internet of Things and Big Data (ICEIB) (2024)
25. Mao, W., He, J., Zuo, M.: Predicting remaining useful life of rolling bearings based on deep feature representation and transfer learning. IEEE Trans. Instrum. Meas. **69**(4), 1594–1608 (2020)
26. Yang, X., Liu, Y., Li, Y., et al.: Attention mechanism-guided residual convolution variational autoencoder for bearing fault diagnosis under noisy environments[J]. Meas. Sci. Technol. **34**(12) (2023)
27. He, D., Li, Z., Jiang, Z., et al.: Train bearing fault diagnosis based on multi-sensor data fusion and dual-scale residual network[J]. Nonlinear Dyn. **111**(16), 14901–14924 (2023)
28. Zhong, J., Bao, X., Xiao, L., et al.: A physical-assisted multi-source signal rolling bearing fault diagnosis method[C]. In: 2023 Global Reliability and Prognostics and Health Management Conference (PHM-Hangzhou), pp. 1–6. Hangzhou, China (2023)
29. Luo, P., Yin, Z., Yuan, D., et al.: An intelligent method for early motor bearing fault diagnosis based on Wasserstein distance generative adversarial networks meta learning, *IEEE Transactions on Instrumentation and Measurement*, pp. 1–11 (2023)
30. Khalid, H., Tariq, S., Kim, T., et al.: ORVAE: one-class residual variational autoencoder for voice activity detection in noisy environment[J]. Neural. Process. Lett. **54**(3), 1565–1586 (2022)
31. Wang, Z., Yang, J., Guo, Y., et al.: Nonstationary feature extraction based on stochastic resonance and its application in rolling bearing fault diagnosis under strong noise background[J]. Rev. Sci. Instrum.Instrum. **94**(1), 015110 (2023)
32. Dong, Z., Tang, T., Ming, C.: Rolling bearing fault diagnosis based on multi-scale weighted visibility graph and multi-channel graph convolution network[J]. Meas. Sci. Technol. **11**, 34 (2023)

Chapter 18
Semantic-Consistent Embedding for Zero-Shot Composite Fault Diagnosis of Bearings

Yuejia Liu, Yuxian Zhang, Yuqi Yao, and Likui Qiao

Abstract Bearing fault diagnosis is inherently complex due to the varied interaction of fault parameters, the range of fault features, and the rapid increase in potential failure types. Obtaining training data for complex faults is often challenging in industrial settings, being sometimes unattainable, in contrast to the accessibility of single fault samples. To address limited training data for composite faults, this study introduces a semantic consistency embedding (SCE) zero-shot model for diagnosing composite faults. The model is trained using single fault samples to detect unseen composite faults. Validation with the CWRU dataset shows that the model achieves an 80.43% accuracy in classifying composite faults without any composite fault samples.

18.1 Introduction

Reducing fault impact and preventing accidents hinges on fault diagnosis. A deep network model requires a substantial number of high-quality labeled samples to be fully trained; however, in the actual industrial scenario, due to the uncertainty of the system and the high labor and time costs required for labeling, the mechanical condition monitoring data is usually recorded in an unlabeled form. Therefore, intelligent methods based on deep learning cannot be fully trained to apply to real industrial section.

To overcome the issue of limited labeled data in intelligent diagnostic approaches, various strategies have been suggested. The solutions mainly fall into four categories: transfer learning-based methods [1], data augmentation techniques [2], semi-supervised learning approaches [3], and unsupervised learning strategies [4]. Transfer learning aims to transfer diagnostic insights from well-labeled source domains to poorly labeled target domains, but this doesn't fundamentally address the data

Y. Liu · Y. Zhang (✉) · Y. Yao · L. Qiao
College of Electrical Engineering, Shenyang University of Technology, Shenyang, Liaoning, China
e-mail: y.x.zhang@sut.edu.cn

F. P. García Márquez et al. (eds.), *Computing, Internet of Things and Data Analytics*, Smart Innovation, Systems and Technologies 387,
https://doi.org/10.1007/978-3-031-87154-2_18

scarcity. To perform fault diagnosis without direct examples, Feng et al. proposed FDAT [5], which incorporates zero-shot learning to indirectly infer fault categories. Similarly, Huang et al. adapted generalized zero-shot learning to industrial fault diagnosis, presenting a straightforward framework for its implementation [6].

Because the bearing is a very important part of the mechanical equipment, the fault diagnosis of the bearing is particularly important. Compound faults frequently occur in bearings. Given the characteristics of randomness, simultaneity, abruptness, and interdependency of these faults, achieving a comprehensive and precise diagnosis is crucial in the field of bearing fault analysis.

To tackle the challenges mentioned, we have developed a semantic-consistent for composite fault diagnosis. This model leverages single fault samples for training to detect previously unseen compound faults.

This paper's main contributions are listed below.

(1) We show a novel semantic-consistent embedding model for zero-shot detection of composite faults, utilizing single-fault vibration data to recognize previously unseen complex fault signatures. This model sets itself apart from traditional zero-shot learning methods by focusing on the coherence between the fault feature and semantic attribute spaces.
(2) This paper designs a Barlow matrix to measure cross-modal embedding consistency, reducing redundancy in numerous dimensions while achieving semantic consistency.
(3) To address the lack of semantic definitions for fault classification attributes, a new method for defining fault semantic vectors is designed. Consequently, we can obtain a comprehensive semantic feature set for composite faults even in the absence of direct instances.

18.2 Related Work

Let $\mathcal{S} = \{(\mathbf{x}, y, \mathbf{a}^y)|\mathbf{x} \in \mathcal{X}^s, y \in \mathcal{Y}^s, \mathbf{a}^y \in \mathcal{A}^s\}$ represent the set of seen classes, where $\mathbf{x} \in \mathcal{X}^s$ is a training sample of seen classes and $y \in \mathcal{Y}^s$ is the class label in $\mathcal{Y}^s = \{y_1, y_2, \ldots, y_s\}$. $\mathcal{U} = \{(\mathbf{x}, y, \mathbf{a}^y)|\mathbf{x} \in \mathcal{X}^u, y \in \mathcal{Y}^u, \mathbf{a}^y \in \mathcal{A}^u\}$ represents the collection of novel classes, among that $\mathbf{x} \in \mathcal{X}^u$ denotes a test instance, and $y \in \mathcal{Y}^u$ is its corresponding label within $\mathcal{Y}^u = \{y_{s+1}, y_{s+2}, \ldots, y_{s+u}\}$. Within the sets $\mathcal{S}$ and $\mathcal{U}$, $\mathbf{a}^y = \Phi(y)$ associates with class y, capturing the semantic interrelations among classes. $\Phi : y \to \mathbf{a}$ denotes a common class. Typically, Φ is originated from expert insights or word embedding techniques. $\mathcal{Y}^s$ and $\mathcal{Y}^u$ are mutually exclusive sets, i.e.: $\mathcal{Y}^s \cap \mathcal{Y}^u = \phi$.

Let $\mathcal{A} = [\mathcal{A}^s, \mathcal{A}^u]$ denote the set of semantic vectors, where $\mathcal{A}^s = \{\mathbf{a}^y|y \in \mathcal{Y}^s\}$, $\mathcal{A}^u = \{\mathbf{a}^y|y \in \mathcal{Y}^u\}$, $\mathcal{A}^u = \{\mathbf{a}^y|y \in \mathcal{Y}^u\}$, $\mathbf{a}^y = \Phi(y) = \left[a_1^y, a_2^y, \ldots, a_m^y\right] \in \mathbb{R}^{1\times m}$ $(a_j^y \geq 0, j = 1, \ldots, m)$ is the semantic vector of class a_j^y encodes the strength (or score) of class y. Visible and invisible classes are linked to the semantic vector. Fault samples from known classes are utilized to train the classifier. The trained classifier then provides an estimation of $p(a_j|\mathbf{z})$, enabling the construction of a comprehensive fault-to-attribute [7] mapping as follows:

$$p(\mathbf{a}|\mathbf{z}) = \prod_{j=1}^{m} p(a_j|\mathbf{z}) = \prod_{j=1}^{m} f_j(\mathbf{z}). \tag{18.1}$$

The third step is label inference:

$$p(y|\mathbf{a}) = \frac{p(y)}{p(\mathbf{a}^y)} p(\mathbf{a}|y). \tag{18.2}$$

Each y class generalizes its attribute vector $\mathbf{a}^y$ in a deterministic way, i.e., $p(\mathbf{a}|y) = [[\mathbf{a} = \mathbf{a}^y]]$ where $[[\mathbf{a} = \mathbf{a}^y]] = 1$, if $\mathbf{a} = \mathbf{a}^y$ and $[[\mathbf{a} = \mathbf{a}^y]] = 0$. The test class can be computed as:

$$p(y|\mathbf{z}) = \sum_{\mathbf{a}} p(y|\mathbf{a}) p(\mathbf{a}|\mathbf{z}) = \frac{p(y)}{p(\mathbf{a}^y)} \prod_{j=1}^{m} p\left(a_j^y|\mathbf{z}\right) \tag{18.3}$$

Due to the absence of more detailed information, $p(y)$ can be considered equivalent across all class priors, and $p(\mathbf{a}) = \prod_{j=1}^{m} p(a_j)$. According to [8], we adpot $p(a_j) = 1/s \sum_{k=1}^{S} a_j^{y_k}$ as the attribute prior for the observed classes. For a given test sample X, MAP estimation is applied to determine the most likely class from the set of possible test classes $\mathcal{Y}^u$.

$$y = \underset{y \in \mathcal{Y}^u}{\operatorname{argmax}} \prod_{j=1}^{m} \frac{p\left(a_j^y|\mathbf{z}\right)}{p\left(a_j^y\right)}. \tag{18.4}$$

18.3 Proposed Method

The model outlined in this paper includes key components each of which is essential to the model's comprehensive structure.

18.3.1 Data Preprocessing Module

This paper utilizes the wavelet transform (WT) method for processing vibration signals. The WT calculation formula is presented as follows:

$$WT(a, T) = \frac{1}{\sqrt{a}} \int_{-\infty}^{+\infty} f(t) \times \psi\left(\frac{t - \tau}{a}\right) dt \tag{18.5}$$

$$\psi(t) = e^{(-t^2/2)} \cos(5t) \tag{18.6}$$

Here, a represents the scaling factor for wavelet function $\psi(t)$. τ denotes the translation factor. $F(t)$ refers to the signal being analyzed.

18.3.2 Semantic Processing Module

At present, the semantic definition methods in many articles are not suitable for constructing semantic vectors in fault diagnosis. Therefore, we design a new method to define a semantic vector that is adapted to our proposed method. The obtained semantic vector is extracted from the original vibration signal. D data points are selected associated with a single fault:

$$f(v) = (v_1, v_2, \ldots, v_k, \ldots, v_D) \tag{18.7}$$

Here, D is selected, while vkdenoting the k-th dimension among the D data points. This establishes the semantics for any single fault; for example, the semantics of an outer ring fault could be described as follows:

$$S_s^i = \{a_1, a_2, \ldots, a_k, \ldots, a_D\} \tag{18.8}$$

a_k is the k-th dimension of S_s^i. We select D data points from the vibration signal, find the max Vj (threshold λ), and divide λ into 5 equal parts. Depending on where v_j^i falls within these parts, a_k is set to 0, 1, etc. This gives us a single-fault semantic vector with R dimensions.

The formulation is as follows:

$$\lambda = \max\left(v_j^i\right) \tag{18.9}$$

$$a_k = \begin{cases} 0, & v_k \le \lambda \\ 1, & v_k \ge 1\lambda, v_k \le 2\lambda \\ 2, & v_k \ge 2\lambda, v_k \le 3\lambda \\ 3, & v_k \ge 3\lambda, v_k \le 4\lambda \\ 4, & v_k \ge 4\lambda, v_k \le 5\lambda \end{cases} \tag{18.10}$$

Thus,the semantic vector of a single fault can be obtained faults $S_S = \{S_S^1, S_s^2, \ldots, S_s^N\}$.

By utilizing the theoretical relationship between a composite fault and its related single faults, the collection of semantic vectors for the composite fault, represented as S_t^i, can be characterized as:

$$S_t^i = \max\left(S_s^1, S_s^2 \ldots, S_s^i\right) \tag{18.11}$$

where $S_t^i \in S_t, \quad S_s^i \in S_s$.

We can get the composite fault semantic vector $S_t = \left\{S_t^1, S_t^2, \ldots, S_t^M\right\}$. Obviously, the solution process of the above composite fault semantic vector is easier to obtain.

18.3.3 Semantic-Attribute Embedding Module

CNN is selected for feature extraction, with a 2D image serving as the input to the network.

As can be seen from Fig. 18.1, the structure of SCE is an embedded and reconstructed structure. $X \in \chi^S$ is a fault sample. $\mathrm{y^x}$ and $\mathrm{a^{y^x}} \in A^S$ represent the label and attribute vectors of X, respectively. $Z^{\mathrm{x}} \in \mathbb{R}^{1\times \mathrm{n}}$ and $Z^{\mathrm{a}} \in \mathbb{R}^{1\times \mathrm{n}}$ attribute embedding can be defined as

$$Z^{\mathrm{x}} = g_X(X) \tag{18.12}$$

$$Z^{\mathrm{a}} = \mathrm{g_a}(\mathrm{a^{y^x}}) \tag{18.13}$$

where g_X and $\mathrm{g_a}$ are the X and $\mathrm{a^{y^x}}$ respectively:

$$\tilde{X} = \mathrm{h}_X(Z) \tag{18.14}$$

$$\tilde{\mathrm{a}}^{\mathrm{y^x}} = \mathrm{h_a}(Z) \tag{18.15}$$

Here, $Z = [Z^X, Z^{\mathrm{a}}]$, h_X and $\mathrm{h_a}$ denote two reconstruction functions, $\tilde{X}$ and $\tilde{\mathrm{a}}^{\mathrm{y^x}}$ refer the rebuilding of X and $\mathrm{a^{y^x}}$, respectively. i.e.

$$\mathcal{L} = \mathcal{L}_{re} + \beta\mathcal{L}_{\mathrm{c}} \tag{18.16}$$

where β is the trade-off parameter, $\mathcal{L}_{re}$ and $\mathcal{L}_{\mathrm{c}}$ represent the reconstruction and consistency loss, respectively.

The embedding-reconstruction structure, which embeds semantically consistent feature spaces with cross-modal data, is applied for the first time in zero-shot learning:

$$\mathcal{L}_{re} = \mathcal{L}_X + \mathcal{L}_{\mathrm{a}} \tag{18.17}$$

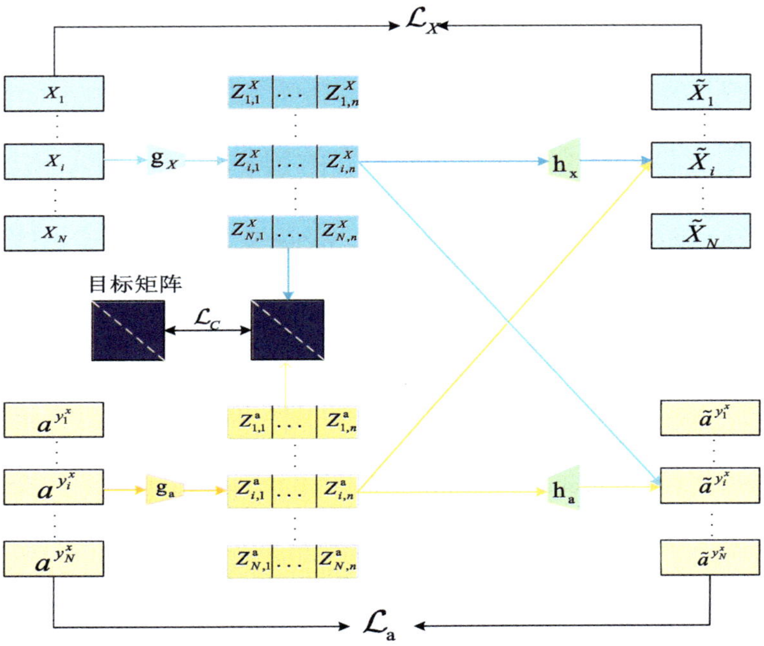

Fig. 18.1 Illustration of the proposed SCE

$\mathcal{L}_X = \sum X \in \chi^S \left\| X - \tilde{X} \right\|^2$ refers the reconstruction loss of fault samples and $\mathcal{L}_a = \sum X \in \chi^S \left\| a^{y^x} - \tilde{a}^{y^x} \right\|^2$ means attribute vectors.

Consistency loss: Better alignment between cross-modal embeddings improves attribute classifier learning. A Barlow matrix $B \in \mathbb{R}^{n \times n}$ measures this alignment:

$$B_{ij} = \frac{\sum_b Z^X_{b,i} Z^a_{b,j}}{\sqrt{\sum_b \left(Z^X_{b,i}\right)^2} \sqrt{\sum_b \left(Z^a_{b,j}\right)^2}} \quad (18.18)$$

b denotes the batch sample, $Z^X_{b,j}$ is the ith element of $Z^X_b \in \mathbb{R}^{1\times n}$, $Z^a_{b,j}$ is the jth element of it, and B_{ij} indicates the consistency of the ith dimension. The matrix B is square with elements ranging from -1 to 1. The Consistency loss $\mathcal{L}_c$ includes both intra-dimensional and inter-dimensional terms, which can be defined as

$$\mathcal{L}_c = \underbrace{\sum_{i=1}^{n} (1 - B_{ii})^2}_{\text{intra-dimensionterm}} + \underbrace{\lambda \sum_{i=1}^{n} \sum_{j \neq i}^{n} B_{ij}^2}_{\text{inter-dimensionterm}} \quad (18.19)$$

The parameter λ balances the model's performance. The fault and attribute embeddings are represented by intra-dimensional and inter-dimensional terms for similar and distinct dimensions, respectively. SCE ensures that elements within the same dimension in cross-modal embeddings are consistently represented, while those across dimensions vary. This variation is optimized by adjusting B to either fully correlate (where $B_{ii} = 1$ and diagonal elements equal one) or fully decorrelate (where non-diagonal elements are zero). The model's semantic consistency in cross-modal embeddings is evident in its front, while redundancy among components is indicated in its back.

18.3.4 Fault Prediction Module

To conclude, we feed the derived target matrix into the attribute learner for training purposes. For a comparative analysis of various machine learning techniques, we employ a LSVM, Probabilistic NB, and a Nonlinear RF. To ensure an equitable comparison, these models are all realized using the scikit-learn library [9]. The closest matching relationship is based on KNN. In the distance measure, we use Euclidean distance. The closer the Euclidean distance is, the more similar it is, and the more likely it is to belong to this type of fault.

18.4 Experiments

18.4.1 Experimental Dateset

In this section, our method's performance is tested using the CWRU bearing dataset's vibration signals sampled at 48 kHz. The dataset has three single faults (IF, BF, OF) and four compound faults.

18.4.2 Experiments Results on Different Tasks

As shown in Table 18.1, to check the model's effectiveness, several experiments were done on two sets of composite fault diagnosis tasks.

Table 18.1 The description of different diagnosis tasks

	Categories of training set	Samples of each category	Fault categories of test samples	Samples of category
TaskA1	BF/IF/OF	800	OF&BF/IF&BF/ IF&OF	3200
TaskA2	BF/IF/OF	1600	OF&BF/IF&BF/ IF&OF	3200
TaskA3	BF/IF/OF	2400	OF&BF/IF&BF/ IF&OF	3200
TaskA4	BF/IF/OF	3200	OF&BF/IF&BF/ IF&OF	3200
TaskB1	BF/IF/OF	800	OF&BF/IF&BF/ IF&OF/ IF&OF&BF	3200
TaskB2	BF/IF/OF	1600	OF&BF/IF&BF/ IF&OF/ IF&OF&BF	3200
TaskB3	BF/IF/OF	2400	OF&BF/IF&BF/ IF&OF/ IF&OF&BF	3200
TaskB4	BF/IF/OF	3200	OF&BF/IF&BF/ IF&OF/ IF&OF&BF	3200

18.4.3 Experimental Results of Different Models

Table 18.2 presents the fault classification outcomes of various machine learning techniques for tasks A and B. task A achieves a peak accuracy of 80.43%, while task B reaches 69.87%. Our model, as detailed in this paper, demonstrates superior performance in both tasks, as implemented and compared with other zero-shot learning models [8, 10–12]. Figure 18.2 illustrates that our model's accuracy surpasses other models.

Table 18.2 Classification accuracy of task A and task B

Classifier	Accuracy (%)							
	Task A				Task B			
Sample size	800	1600	2400	3200	800	1600	2400	3200
LSTM	55.71	60.31	63.21	64.15	43.63	47.65	52.49	57.96
RF	63.16	63.05	66.19	71.15	44.34	48.91	53.99	61.34
NB	68.78	71.99	75.48	80.43	52.63	56.70	63.19	69.87

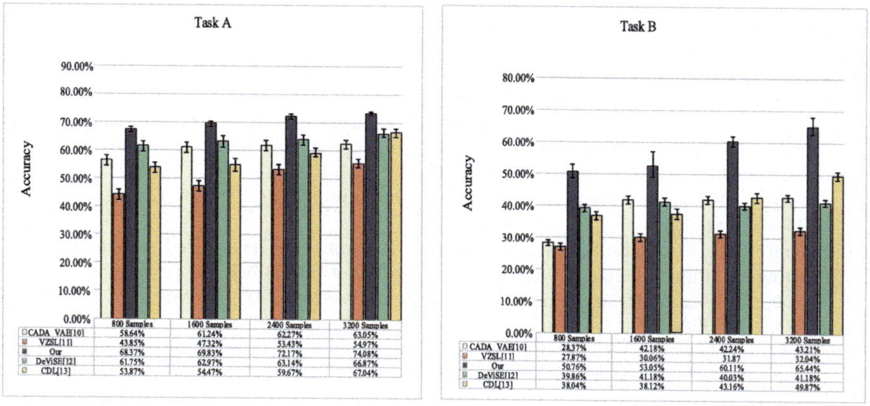

(a) (b)

Fig. 18.2 Accuracy of different models: **a** Task A, **b** Task B

18.5 Conclusion

This paper introduces a novel zero-sample composite fault diagnosis model that leverages semantic consistent embedding. The model utilizes single fault samples to detect composite fault types. We've developed a unified method for defining semantic vectors to represent both single and compound fault categories. By achieving semantic consistency between modal embeddings, the model minimizes redundant information across components, thereby creating a more efficient target matrix for training attribute classifiers. It classifies composite fault samples in the basis of the relation between single fault and composite fault features, using similarity measurements for classification. Using the CWRU dataset, our model achieved high classification accuracy without labeled composite fault samples. It outperformed other current methods in extensive experiments.

References

1. Hasan, M.J., Islam, M.M.M., Kim, J.M.: Acoustic spectral imaging and transfer learning for reliable bearing fault diagnosis under variable speed conditions[J]. Meas. **138**, 620–631 (2019)
2. Wang, X., Chu, Z., Han, B., et al.: A novel data augmentation method for intelligent fault diagnosis under speed fluctuation condition[J]. IEEE Access **8**, 143383–143396 (2020)
3. Mao, W., Tian, S., Fan, J., et al.: Online detection of bearing incipient fault with semi-supervised architecture and deep feature representation[J]. J. Manuf. Syst. **55**, 179–198 (2020)
4. Liu, J., Li, Q., Chen, W., et al.: A discrete hidden Markov model fault diagnosis strategy based on K-means clustering dedicated to PEM fuel cell systems of tramways[J]. Int. J. Hydrog. Energy **43**(27), 12428–12441 (2018)
5. Feng, L., Zhao C.: Fault description based attribute transfer for zero-sample industrial fault diagnosis[J]. IEEE Trans. Ind. Inform. **PP**(99), 1–1 (2020)

6. Huang, J., Li, Z., Zhou, Z.: A simple framework to generalized zero-shot learning for fault diagnosis of industrial processes[J]. IEEE/CAA J. Autom. Sin. (2023)
7. Li, B., Zhao, C.: Federated zero-shot industrial fault diagnosis with cloud-shared semantic knowledge base[J]. IEEE Internet Things J. (2023)
8. Wang, W., Pu, Y., Verma, V.K., Fan, K., Zhang, Y.Z., Chen, C.Y., Rai, P., Carin, L.: Zero-shot learning via class-conditioned deep generative models. In: Thirty-Second AAAI Conference on Artificial Intelligence, pp. 4211–4218 (2018)
9. Ashish, S., Ritesh, J.: Scikit-learn: machine learning in python. J. Mach. Learn. Res. **12**(10), 2825–2830 (2012)
10. Schönfeld, E., Ebrahimi, S., Sinha, S., Darrell, T., Akata, Z.: Generalized zero- and few-shot learning via aligned variational autoencoders. In: 2019 IEEE/CVF Conference on Computer Vision and Pattern Recognition (CVPR), pp. 8239–8247 (2019). https://doi.org/10.1109/CVPR.2019.00844
11. Frome, A., Corrado, G.S., Shlens, J., Bengio, S., Dean, J., Mikolov, T., et al.: Devise: a deep visual-semantic embedding model. Neural Inf. Process. Syst. (NIPS) (2013)
12. Jiang, H., Wang, R., Shan, S., Chen, X.: Learning class prototypes via structure alignment for zero-shot recognition. In: European Conference on Computer Vision, pp. 121–138 (2018)

Chapter 19
Data-Driven MPC for Advanced Wind Turbine Control Considering Load Mitigation

Ziyuan Li, Xiao Wang, Qing Liu, and Yuxian Zhang

Abstract This paper proposes a data-driven Model Predictive Control (MPC) for advanced wind turbine (WT) control considering the mechanical load mitigation. Specifically, we use a neural network applying rectified linear unit (ReLU) as the activation function for the hidden layers to capture nonlinear WT dynamics under all wind conditions so as to facilitate rotor speed regulation and suppress fore-aft tower bending. Case studies demonstrate that the approach has better damping for shaft torque oscillation and tower for-aft bending than the baseline control. This marks a notable enhancement in the overall stability and structural robustness of the WT system, ultimately resulting in increased efficiency and sustainability in its operation.

19.1 Introduction

China has increasingly focused on carbon peaking and carbon neutrality goals in recent years, driving the entire power and energy industry to place high hopes on renewable energy led by wind power generation. As a globally leading renewable energy source, wind power surpasses other forms of renewable generation in terms of installed capacities and bulking energy delivery to the power network [1, 2]. However, the widespread integration of wind power and the phasing out of conventional coal-fueled power plants present additional challenges in ensuring a reliable power supply [3].

In general, power converters are responsible for controlling the generator torque, ensuring efficient power generation, while the pitch control system adjusts the rotor speed by limiting the extraction of aerodynamic power during high wind speeds [4]. This coordinated approach helps optimize wind turbine (WT) performance and

Z. Li · X. Wang · Q. Liu
Wuhan University of Technology, Wuhan, China

Y. Zhang (✉)
Shenyang University of Technology, Shenyang, China
e-mail: yuxian524524@163.com

F. P. García Márquez et al. (eds.), *Computing, Internet of Things and Data Analytics*, Smart Innovation, Systems and Technologies 387,
https://doi.org/10.1007/978-3-031-87154-2_19

maintain operational stability across a wide range of wind conditions, forming the basis for adjusting WT output power to provide grid support [5].

Furthermore, existing research indicates that the service life of wind turbines is closely linked to structural and fatigue loads [6–9]. Studies in [6] and [7] suggest that large wind turbines operating in offshore areas are subject to heightened structural and fatigue loads, primarily due to the increased flexibility of larger structures and the presence of highly asymmetric wind forces. The loads on these turbines can lead to accelerated wear and damage to structural components, resulting in reduced service life and increased maintenance costs. To address the challenges posed by high-magnitude and complex operational loads, advancements in control strategies have been proposed. These include advanced blade pitch control, blade twist control, active flow control, and other innovative approaches [8, 9].

With the increased capacity, the structure flexibility of WT is increased. The diagram of the complete wind energy conversion system is shown in Fig. 19.1, where WT works by capturing the kinetic energy in the wind through the rotation of the blades so as to turn a permanent magnet synchronous generator (PMSG) by the drive train. Parameters such as generator speed ω_g, mechanical torque T_m and electric torque T_e gained during this period in control of PMSG to transfer electrical energy obtained to rotor-side converters (RSC), then to grid-side converters (GSC) and finally to points of common coupling (PCC) for supplying power to users. The whole system indicates the obvious correlation among the WT structural, mechanical, and electrical subsystems [10]. However, the current practice for WT control still largely relies on proportional and integral (PI) control [11], which offers benefits such as low computational complexity, ease of implementation and adjustability, but it can only handle a single control variable and does not account for system conditions and multiple control variables.

Consequently, when confronted with intricate control problems, such as wind turbines with multiple inputs, multiple outputs and high nonlinearities, Model Predictive Control (MPC) may be more appropriate for effectively addressing complex control problems by considering multiple control variables and their interactions

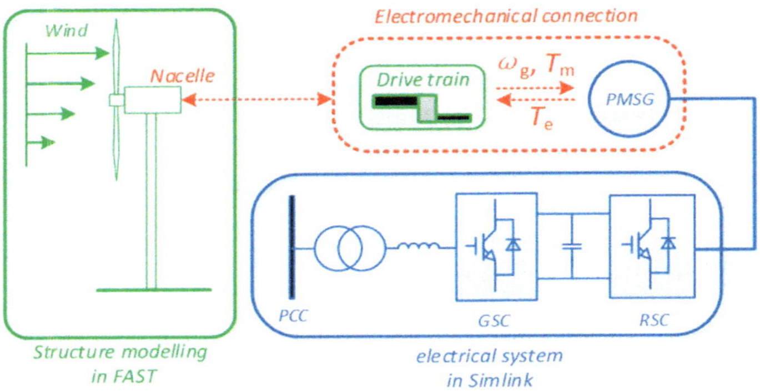

Fig. 19.1 Diagram of the complete wind energy conversion system

with explicit constraints [12–17]. Through a comparison of practical nonlinear MPC [12], optimal-controller-based MPC [13], and offset-free bilinear MPC [14] with the baseline controller, the authors suggest that these MPC methods offer significant advantages in robustness, real-time capabilities, and simulation performance when compared to traditional PI control. Similarly in [15], MPC is employed to minimize fatigue loads on wind turbine components such as the tower and blades, as well as to restrict blade pitch rates. References [16] and [17] verified that non-linear MPC has better performance on further reducing structural loads when close to the rated wind speed at the simulation level.

The key point of MPC lies in modeling and optimization. However, achieving effective control in specific individual parts of WT, like tower fore-aft bending is extremely challenging due to two main factors: modeling accuracy and solving efficiency. Thus, as a new application of MPC in industrial systems recently, data-driven MPC is supposed for advanced WT control by using neural networks to make the model more precise. Meanwhile, faced with high degree of nonlinearity of complex dynamics, authors present different algorithms, such as Bayesian ascent algorithm [18], double layer particle swarm algorithm [19], extended dynamic mode decomposition (EDMD) method [20], specialized dynamic mode decomposition (SDMD) method [21], to improve control effectiveness. Though these Koopman-based approaches have advantages in improving a target WT power production by executing as small number of trial actions as possible, the uncertainty of their dictionaries still cannot bring about an obvious improvement in solving efficiency.

Combining the above viewpoints, in this paper, we aim to enhance the control capability of WT and improve its efficiency to mitigate the impact of loads by using data-driven MPC. Specifically, for the data-driven modelling of WT firstly, we utilize a neural network to accurately capture and represent the dynamic of tower under a wide range of varying wind conditions. Then we can linearize the highly nonlinearized model of WT through training set instead of using traditional method of linearization around some operating point to achieve desired speed regulation while perform load mitigation by it. Finally we use the trained model to assess the performance, predict new unknown data and control WT.

The remaining parts of this paper are arranged as follows. Section 19.2 introduces components modeling and the reduced nonlinear model of WT, which is analyzing the difficulties existing in the mathematical model of WT. Then, specific design and optimization of MPC are proposed in Sect. 19.3. Meanwhile, by comparing the data-driven MPC approach and the traditional baseline control of WT, two scenarios and some discussions are carried out in Sect. 19.4. Finally, Sect. 19.5 concludes this paper and looks forward to the generalization and application of the proposed data-driven modeling method in embedded microcontroller for real-time control of the plant.

19.2 System Modeling

In this section we directly introduce the mathematical model of WT considering tower fore-aft bending. The components modeling of a WT system is well-known as presented in this section.

19.2.1 Components Modeling of WT

This part illustrates the modeling of the main system components [22].

(a) **Aerodynamics**

The aerodynamic equation describes the aerodynamic power obtained by the turbine blades, as shown in (19.1)

$$P_{aero} = \frac{1}{2}\rho\pi R^2 C_p(\lambda, \theta)V_w^3 \tag{19.1}$$

where ρ is the air density, R is the radius of blade's swept area, C_p is the aerodynamic coefficient, a function of the tip speed ratio λ and the blade pitch angle θ, the average wind speed seen by the blade is V_w. The tip speed ratio (TSR) is defined as

$$\lambda = \frac{w_r R}{V_w} \tag{19.2}$$

with w_r being the rotor speed. The aerodynamic power coefficient C_p can be approximated in the typical way as

$$C_p(\lambda, \theta) = c_1\left(\frac{c_2}{\lambda_i} - c_3\theta - c_4\right)e^{\frac{-c_5}{\lambda_i}} + c_6\lambda \tag{19.3}$$

$$\frac{1}{\lambda_i} = \frac{1}{\lambda + 0.08\theta} - \frac{0.035}{\theta^3 + 1} \tag{19.4}$$

The parameters $c_1 \sim c_6$ represent various configurations of the aerodynamic surface, which can be derived from the aerodynamic data collected during rotor commissioning tests for different types of turbines [23].

(b) **Drive-train System**

We are examining a two-mass drive-train model, in which the low-speed shaft (LSS) is represented as a spring-damper system, while the high-speed shaft (HSS) is treated as a rigid body because of its significant stiffness, as referenced in [24]. This gives

$$J_r\frac{dw_r}{dt} = T_m - T_{sh} \tag{19.5}$$

$$J_g \frac{dw_g}{dt} = \frac{T_{sh}}{N_{gb}} - T_e \tag{19.6}$$

where $T_m = P_{aero}/w_r$ is the mechanical torque, T_e is the electric torque induced by the generator, w_g is the generator speed, J_r and J_g are the inertia of the LSS and HSS, respectively, N_{gb} is the gearbox ratio. The shaft torque acts T_{sh} as a braking torque on the LSS and drives the HSS. It is written as

$$T_{sh} = K_{sh}\left(\theta_r - \frac{\theta_g}{N_{gb}}\right) + C_{sh}\left(w_r - \frac{w_g}{N_{gb}}\right) \tag{19.7}$$

where K_{sh} is the stiffness coefficient and C_{sh} is the damping coefficient of the LSS, θ_r and θ_g are the azimuth angles of the LSS and HSS, respectively.

(c) **Generator and Power Converter Systems**

The grid-side converter is known for its rapid response, although its dynamics are not considered in this context. These dynamics collectively define the behavior of the generator and power converter systems

$$\tau_t \dot{T}_e = -T_e + T_{e,ref} \tag{19.8}$$

where τ_t is the time constant of the torque control loop, $T_{e,ref}$ is the generator torque reference.

(d) **Pitch Actuator**

The pitch actuator is modeled as a first-order lag system [25] as in (19.9), although the second-order system model is considered in some work,

$$\tau_\theta \dot{\theta} = -\theta + \theta_{ref} \tag{19.9}$$

The time constant of the pitch actuator τ_θ is generally larger than that of the torque control loop.

19.2.2 The Reduced Nonlinear Model of WT

A WT system harnesses wind energy by transferring power from the turbine rotor to the grid through various interconnected components, such as the drivetrain, generator, and power converter systems [24]. Figure 19.2 illustrates typical bending loads on tower and blades, where a stepwise increase of generator torque excites the modes on shaft and tower.

The general WT model exhibits a high level of nonlinearity primarily due to the complex aerodynamic equations involved in the process and advanced WT control

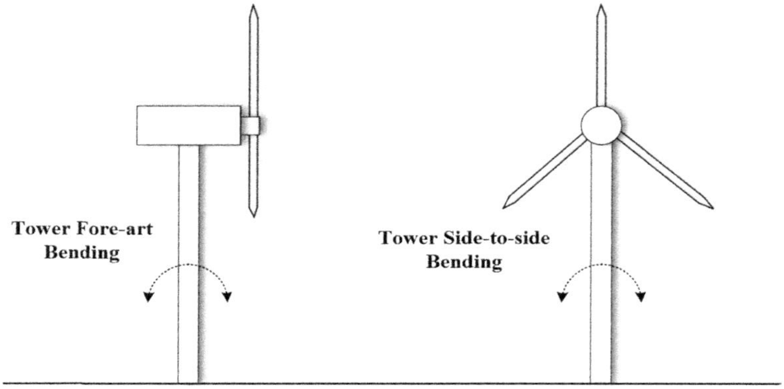

Fig. 19.2 Diagram of typical bending loads on tower

design is needed for desired speed regulation while perform load mitigation. Here, considering bending loads, the first tower fore–aft bending mode is based on [26]:

$$M_{Te}\ddot{y}_{Tw} + C_T\dot{y}_{Tw} + K_T y_{Tw} = F_a(\dot{y}_{Tw}, w_r, \theta, V_w) \tag{19.10}$$

where F_a is the aerodynamic thrust, and M_{Te}, C_T, K_T and y_{Tw} represent the tower equivalent modal mass, structural damping, bending stiffness and tower top fore–aft displacement, respectively, and more specific nomenclatures are provided in Table 19.1 [16, 26]:

$$M_{Te} = 0.25m_T + m_N + m_H + 3m_B \tag{19.11}$$

$$C_T = 4\pi M_{Te}d_s f_0 \tag{19.12}$$

$$K_T = M_{Te}(2\pi f_0)^2 \tag{19.13}$$

where m_T, m_N, m_H, m_B represent mass tower, mass nacelle, mass hub and mass blade, d_s is structural damping ratio and f_0 is natural frequency of first tower fore–aft bending. Then F_a is defined as

$$F_a = \frac{1}{2}\rho\pi R^2 C_t(\lambda, \theta)(V_w - \dot{y}_{Tw})^2 \tag{19.14}$$

where C_t is thrust coefficient and (19.14) is similar in form of aerodynamic power, which is mentioned in (19.1). Most of the parameters of tower mentioned above can be measured actually. However, in (19.14) and (19.1), coefficient C_p and C_t can be only obtained through commission tests, which are included in the model as a polynomial fit to two dimensional lookup tables in Fig. 19.3.

Table 19.1 Nomenclatures of the modeled turbine system

Rated parameters (rated value)	P_{aero}	Aerodynamic powers	5 MW
	w_r	Rotor speed	1.3305 rad/s,
	w_g	Generator speed	129.0551 rad/s
	V_w	Wind speed	11.2 m/s
	N_{gb}	Gearbox ratio	97
	R	Rotor radius	62.94 m
	T_m	Mechanical torque	3,767,965 N·m
	T_e	Electric torque	38,845 N·m
Aerodynamic parameters	ρ	Air density	1.225 kg/m2
	$C_{p\max}$	Optimal power coefficient	0.482
	λ_{opt}	Optimal TSR	7.55
	$c_1 \sim c_6$	Aerodynamic shape coefficients	[0.5176, 116, 0.4, 5, 21, 0.0069]
Mechanical parameters	J_r	LSS inertia	38,677,056 kg.m^2
	J_g	HSS inertia	534.116 kg.m^2
	K_{sh}	Stiffness coefficient of LSS	8.67637×10^8 N/rad
	D_{sh}	Damping coefficient of LSS	6.215×10^6 N/(rad/s)
	τ_t	Generator time constant	0.5 s
	τ_θ	Pitch actuator time constant	2 s
Tower related parameters	m_T	Mass tower	347,460 kg
	m_N	Mass nacelle	240,000 kg
	m_H	Mass hub	56,780 kg
	m_B	Mass blade	17,740 kg
	f_0	Natural frequency of first tower fore–aft bending	0.32 Hz
	d_s	Structural damping ratio	0.01
	h_H	Hub height	90 m/s

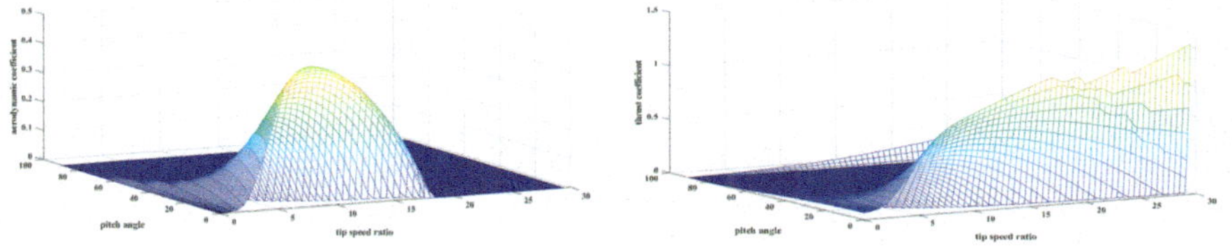

(a) (b)

Fig. 19.3 **a** Effective power coefficient **b** Effective thrust coefficient

Combining (19.1)–(19.14), we obtain a general form of mathematical model for WT in

$$
\begin{bmatrix} \dot{w}_r \\ \dot{w}_g \\ \dot{T}_{tws} \\ \dot{\theta} \\ \dot{y}_{Tw} \\ \dot{d}y_{Tw} \end{bmatrix} = \begin{bmatrix} \frac{1}{2}\frac{\rho\pi R^2 C_p V_w^3}{w_r J_r} - \frac{w_r D_{sh}}{J_r} + \frac{w_g D_{sh}}{J_r N_{gb}} - \frac{T_{tws}}{J_r} \\ \frac{w_r D_{sh}}{J_g N_{gb}} - \frac{w_g D_{sh}}{J_g N_{gb}^2} + \frac{T_{tws}}{J_g N_{gb}} - \frac{T_e}{J_g} \\ K_{sh}\left(w_r - \frac{w_g}{N_{gb}}\right) \\ -\frac{\theta}{\tau_\theta} + \frac{\theta_{ref}}{\tau_\theta} \\ dy_{Tw} \\ -\frac{K_T}{M_{Te}} y_{Tw} - \frac{C_T}{M_{Te}} dy_{Tw} + \frac{1}{2}\frac{\rho\pi R^2 C_t (V_w - dy_{Tw})^2}{M_{Te}} \end{bmatrix} \tag{19.15}
$$

19.2.3 Data-Driven Modeling for WT

Through the efforts of many researchers, the general modeling technology of WT has been very mature and deep learning has made incredible progress in many fields recently. There data-driven wind turbine models have emerged by combining the two [27].

In this paper, we use a deep neural network to capture WT dynamics under all wind conditions so as to facilitate control WT rotor speed under varying wind conditions while perform load mitigation. Specifically, using rectified linear unit (ReLU) as the activation function for the hidden layers facilitates a fast training and promotes a sparse model with enhanced numerical robustness. The ReLU function is shown in Fig. 19.4.

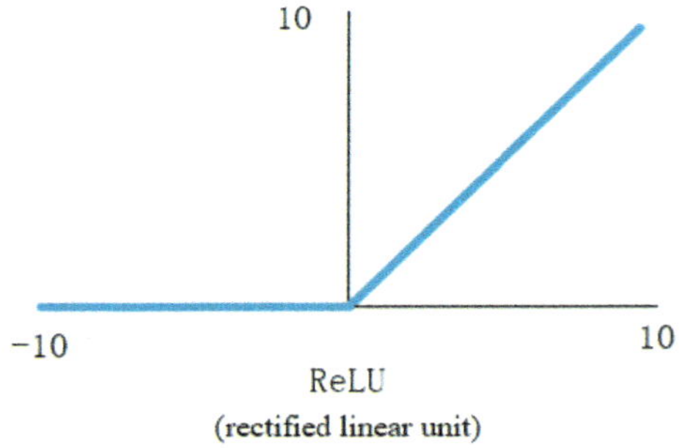

Fig. 19.4 ReLU activation function

whose network is used to find the mapping between system states, controls, disturbance and the interested WT variables in the next time step, as shown in

$$\begin{bmatrix} w_{r,t+1} \\ w_{g,t+1} \\ T_{tws,t+1} \\ M_{yT,t+1} \end{bmatrix} = f_{\text{ReLU}}(x_t, u_t, d_t) \tag{19.16}$$

where on the left side of the equal sign is network output, while the right is network input. With the hub height h_H, tower base fore–aft bending moment M_{yT} is defined as

$$M_{yT} = h_H(C_T\dot{y}_{Tw} + K_T y_{Tw}) \tag{19.17}$$

then, we prepare training and testing sets and choose an appropriate neural network structure. For a ReLU network with a single hidden layer, we can obtain using ReLU activation function as the output result of nonlinear transformation in neural networks:

$$\begin{bmatrix} w_{r,t+1} \\ w_{g,t+1} \\ T_{tws,t+1} \\ M_{yT,t+1} \end{bmatrix} = W_{fc}\left[\max\left(W_h\begin{bmatrix} x_t \\ u_t \\ d_t \end{bmatrix} + b_h, 0\right)\right] + b_{fc} \tag{19.18}$$

after trainning, it is necessary to evaluate the performance of the trained model using validation or testing sets and predict or classify new unknown data using the trained model.

19.3 Data-Driven MPC-Based WT Control

MPC attains excellent control performance through the prediction of future system behavior and optimization of both present and future control inputs. Additionally, it effectively deals with system constraints by solving an optimization problem formulated for systems with multiple inputs and outputs. Its extensive application spans across industrial processes, mechanical systems, power systems, transportation systems, and numerous other domains [28–30].

This article focuses on the control and predictive effects by data-driven MPC. In conventional MPC modes, based on the mathematical model of the WT system, controller predicts and optimizes current and future control inputs to achieve superior control performance. To achieve the receding horizon control scheme, an optimization problem is first formulated, whose objective function is represented as:

$$\min_{\substack{x_{t+k|t} \\ u_{t+k-1|t}}} \sum_{k=1}^{N} a_1\left(w_{r,t+k|t} - w_{r,t+k|t}^{t\arg et}\right)^2 + a_2\left(T_{e,t+k-1|t} - T_{e,t+k-1|t}^{t\arg et}\right)^2 \\ + a_3\left(\theta_{ref,t+k-1|t}\right)^2 + a_4\left(T_{sh,t+k|t}\right)^2 + a_5\left(M_{yT,t+k|t}\right)^2 \tag{19.19}$$

$$T_{sh,t+k|t} = T_{tws,t+k|t} + D_{sh}\left(w_{r,t+k|t} - \frac{w_{g,t+k|t}}{N_{gb}}\right) \tag{19.20}$$

where $w_{r,t+k|t}$ and $w_{r,t+k|t}^{t\arg et}$ are rotor speed and its reference value at time $t + k$, $T_{e,t+k-1|t}$ and $T_{e,t+k-1|t}^{t\arg et}$ similarly are electric torque and its reference value at time $t+k-1$, $\theta_{ref,t+k-1|t}$ represents reference value for pitch angle at time $t+k-1$, $T_{sh,t+k|t}$ and $M_{yT,t+k|t}$ represent torsional torque tower and base fore–aft bending moment at time $t+k$ respectively, a_1, a_2, a_3, a_4, a_5 represent different weight coefficient whose actual value depends on specific conditions for states and controls. Equation (19.20) is utilized to control and adjust the rotor speed, ensuring optimal performance and efficiency, while also effectively managing and reducing the loads experienced by the tower.

Here are magnitude constraints for states and controls as in (19.21)–(19.24):

$$w_{r,\min} \le w_{r,t+k|t} \le w_{r,\max} \tag{19.21}$$

$$w_{g,\min} \le w_{g,t+k|t} \le w_{g,\max} \tag{19.22}$$

$$T_{e,\min} \le T_{e,t+k|t} \le T_{e,\max} \tag{19.23}$$

$$\theta_{ref,\min} \le \theta_{ref,t+k|t} \le \theta_{ref,\max} \tag{19.24}$$

where $w_{r,\min}$, $w_{g,\min}$, $T_{e,\min}$, $\theta_{ref,\min}$ and $w_{r,\max}$, $w_{g,\max}$, $T_{e,\max}$, $\theta_{ref,\max}$ represent the minimum and maximum rotor speed, generator speed, electric torque and pitch reference. Besides, it also should make rate contraints on electric torque and pitch reference combining with actual conditions:

$$-dT_{e,\lim} \le T_{e,t+k|t} - T_{e,t+k-1|t} \le dT_{e,\lim} \tag{19.25}$$

$$-d\theta_{ref,\lim} \le \theta_{ref,t+k|t} - \theta_{ref,t+k-1|t} \le d\theta_{ref,\lim} \tag{19.26}$$

where $dT_{e,\lim}$ and $d\theta_{ref,\lim}$ are differentials of limitation of electric torque and pitch reference. Piecewise affine WT dynamics (with feedback introduced) is used as the equality constraint

$$\begin{bmatrix} w_{r,t+1|t}, \cdots, w_{r,t+H|t} \\ w_{g,t+1|t}, \cdots, w_{g,t+H|t} \\ T_{tws,t+1|t}, \cdots, T_{tws,t+H|t} \\ M_{yT,t+1|t}, \cdots, M_{yT,t+H|t} \end{bmatrix} = W_{fc}[\max\left(W_h \begin{bmatrix} x_{t-h}, \cdots, x_t \\ u_{t-h}, \cdots, u_{t-1} \\ d_{t-h}, \cdots, d_{t-1} \end{bmatrix} + b_h, 0 \right)] + b_{fc} \tag{19.27}$$

In conclusion, during the design phase, we employ time-delayed embedding techniques to predict wind turbine speed and tower bending loads several steps ahead. The system's dynamic constraints, represented in a piecewise affine form, result in a mixed-integer quadratic programming (MIQP) problem that can be efficiently resolved using commercially.

19.4 Case Studies

19.4.1 Simulation Setup

In the case studies, the performance of the data-driven MPC approach is demonstrated. We employ a 5MW wind turbine model built in MATLAB, whose parameters are adopted from the 5MW NREL baseline model [22]. MOSEK solver is used to solve the MIQP problem and the steady-state load shedding scheme.

Based on parameters listed in Table 19.1, we establish the following settings: the predicted time is set to 1 s, the time step is 0.05 s, the training duration is 100 s, and 500 trajectories are generated for the simulation. A neural network with a single hidden layer consisting of 50 neurons using the ReLU activation function is constructed for training purposes, where the training and testing sets are divided into 90% and 10% respectively. Additionally, the wind speed is varied in a sequence from 13 m/s to 15 m/s and then to 17 m/s to assess the performance of the trained model under different control scenarios. The specific numerical values and state changes during the varying wind speeds are illustrated in Fig. 19.5.

Where the blue curve is the true trajectory under baseline control and red small circles represent prediction points. It is clear from the results that, when operating under the baseline control (PID), the ReLU network demonstrates a high level of accuracy in predicting the multi-step response of the wind turbine. This indicates that the ReLU network is effective in capturing the complex dynamics and behaviors of the system, showcasing its potential for improving predictive capabilities and overall performance in wind turbine control applications.

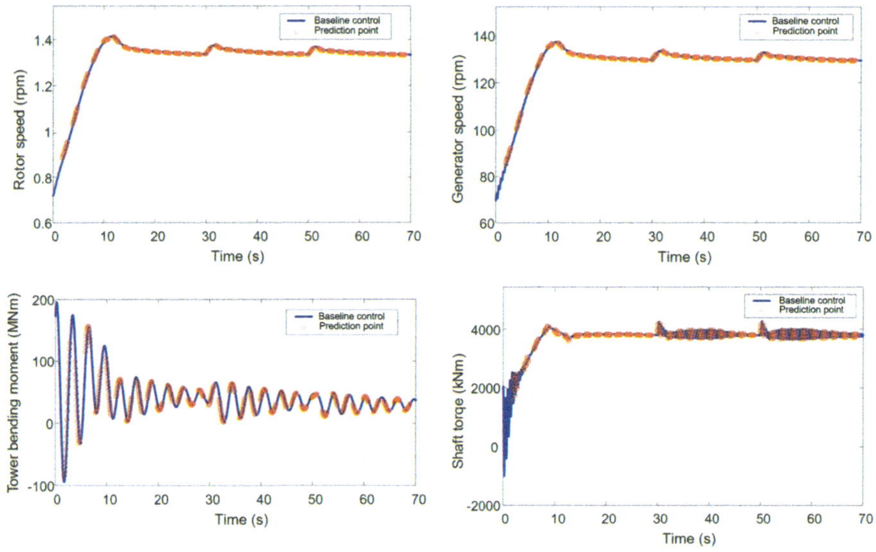

Fig. 19.5 Spcific number values of states during varying wind speed

19.4.2 Simulation Results

We compare the proposed data-driven MPC and the baseline control, and two scenarios are considered: we first test the performance that the data-driven MPC is tuned to suppressed the loads on turbine shaft; the second scenario is evaluating the performance of the data-driven MPC by tuning it to mitigate the loads on tower for-aft direction.

(1) **Scenario 1: tuned to suppressed the loads on turbine shaft**

In the first scenario, the baseline control uses the speed deviation to achieve PI control for the pitch angle. Under the initial conditions above, we take weight coefficients $a_1 \sim a_5$ as 500, 10, 10, 0.01 and 0.01 respectively, then we adjust the value of a_4 to be larger so that the control strategy is tuned to suppress the load on the turbine shaft. To validate the precision of the simulation outcomes, we analyze the data within a simulation timeframe of 25 to 75 s, and the specific enlarged figure of each input is shown in Fig. 19.6.

where the blue curve symbolizes the baseline control strategy, while the red short dashed line signifies the data-driven MPC approach. Detailed enlarged illustrations of the respective states are presented in Fig. 19.7, offering a more focused view of the specific adjustments and performance differences between the two control methods.

where the blue short dashed line represents the baseline control, while the red curve depicts the data-driven MPC. Obviously, in comparison to the baseline control, the proposed approach exhibits superior damping characteristics for shaft torque oscillations.

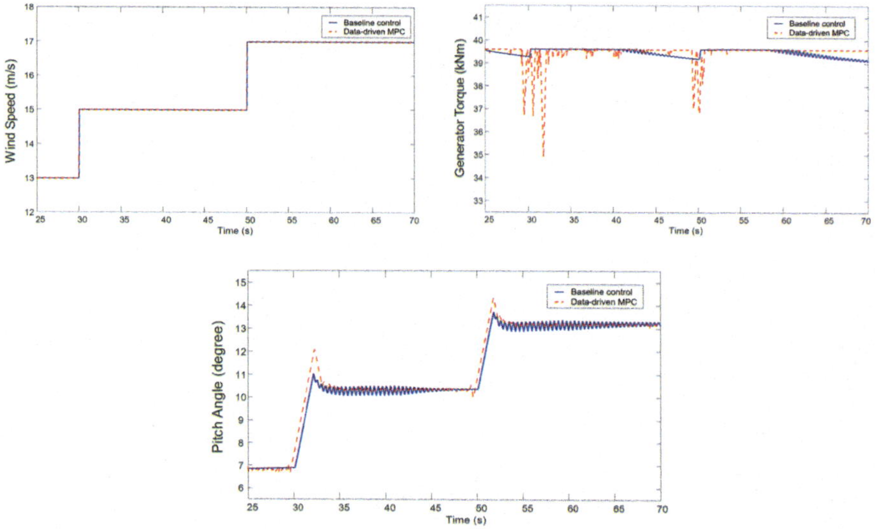

Fig. 19.6 Specific enlarged figure of the three inputs in scenario 1

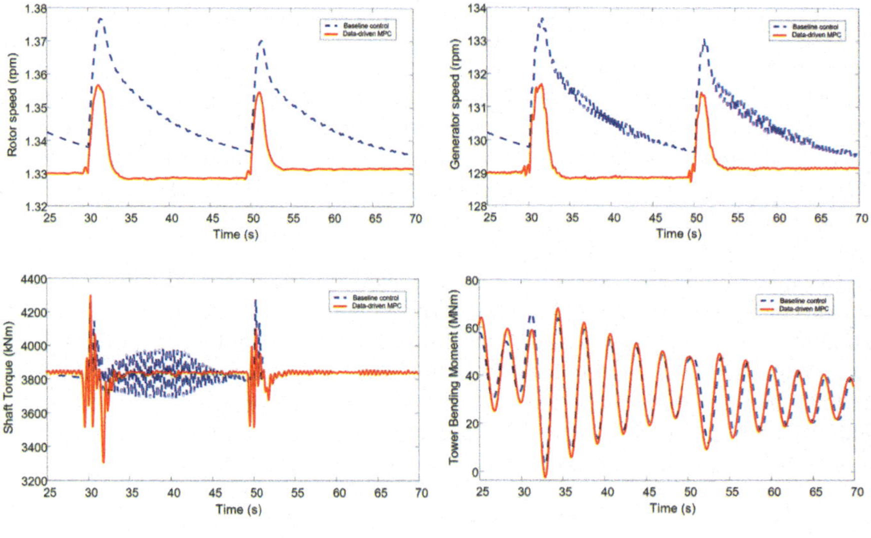

Fig. 19.7 Specific enlarged figure of the four states in scenario 1

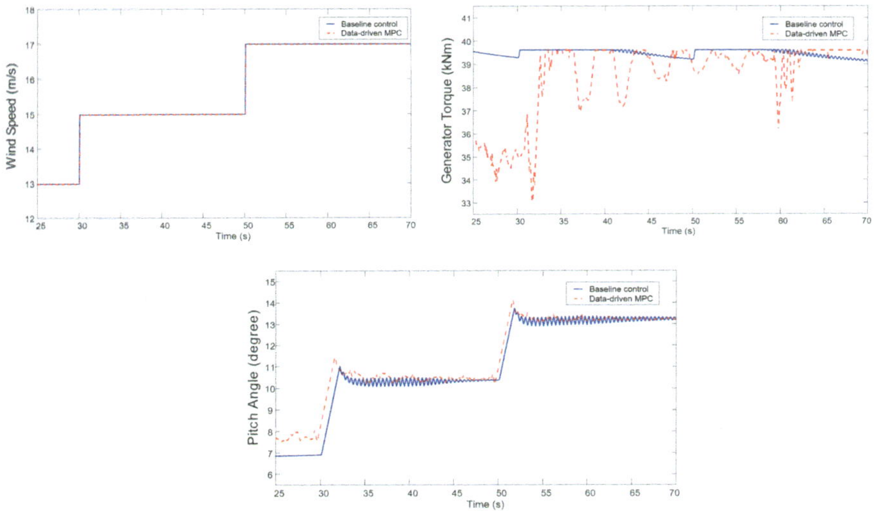

Fig. 19.8 Specific enlarged figure of the three inputs in scenario 2

(2) Scenario 2: tuned to suppressed the loads on tower for-aft direction

In scenario two, we remain the same conditions for baseline control. On this basis, we adopt a similar approach by modifying the value of a_5 in the objective function to align with the goal of reducing loads on the tower in the for-aft direction, while keeping all other experimental parameters consistent with those of scenario 1. The detailed graphical representation of the amplified values for each input and state variable can be observed in Figs. 19.8 and 19.9, providing a visual insight into the adjustments made for this particular scenario.

Compared with the conventional baseline control, the proposed approach offers enhanced damping capabilities for tower for-aft bending. Furthermore, even though there may be a slight increase in load fluctuations when mitigated in the tower's for-aft direction, the amplitude of these fluctuations remains lower than the loads endured by the turbine shaft. This signifies a significant improvement in the overall stability and structural integrity of the wind turbine system, ultimately leading to more efficient and sustainable operation.

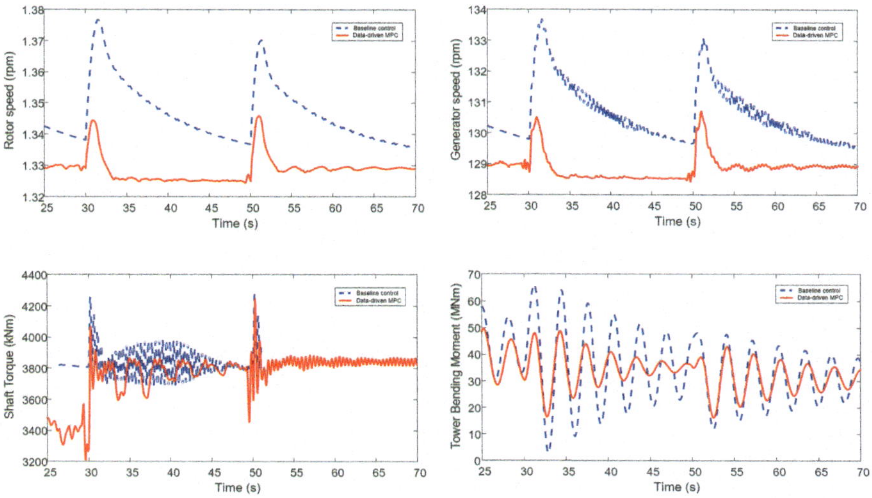

Fig. 19.9 Specific enlarged figure of the four states in scenario 2

19.5 Conclusion

In this paper, we propose a data-drive MPC for advanced WT control considering the mechanical load mitigation. The proposed approach exploits the universal approximation capability of NN network, utilizing the ReLU as the activation function. Case studies demonstrate that the approach has better damping for shaft torque oscillation and tower for-aft bending than the baseline control, which indicates a substantial enhancement in the overall stability and structural integrity of the wind turbine system, ultimately resulting in more efficient and sustainable operation. Besides, the resulted optimization problem in MPC is MIQP, which can be solved efficiently. In the future, we will strive to apply the supposed MPC to embedded microcontroller for real-time control of the plant.

References

1. Zhang, Y., Ningbo, W., Ding, K., Zhou, Q., Gao, P., Zhang, Z.: The key technology of the coordinated control system of wind power and energy-intensive load. In: 2019 4th International Conference on Intelligent Green Building and Smart Grid (IGBSG), pp. 349–353. IEEE, Hubei, Yi-chang, China (2019). https://doi.org/10.1109/IGBSG.2019.8886294
2. Guo, Y., Gao, H., Wang, Z.: Distributed online voltage control for wind farms using generalized fast dual ascent. IEEE Trans. Power Syst. **35**, 4505–4517 (2020)
3. Marchenko, A.I., Murashkina, I.S., Denisov, V.V.: Features of minigrid operation control based on a small generation power plant with an external power grid. In: 2021 XV International Scientific-Technical Conference on Actual Problems of Electronic Instrument Engineering (APEIE), pp. 115–119. IEEE, Novosibirsk, Russian Federation (2021)

4. Song, G., Cao, B., Chang, L.: An electrical stall control algorithm for small-scale wind generation system using aerodynamic observer. In: 2020 IEEE 11th International Symposium on Power Electronics for Distributed Generation Systems (PEDG), pp. 77–84. IEEE, Dubrovnik, Croatia (2020). https://doi.org/10.1109/PEDG48541.2020.9244455
5. Jeong, Y., Johnson, K., Fleming, P.: Comparison and testing of power reserve control strategies for grid-connected wind turbines. Wind Energy **17**, 343–358 (2014)
6. Pao, L.Y., Johnson, K.E.: Control of wind turbines. IEEE Control. Syst. **31**, 44–62 (2011). https://doi.org/10.1109/MCS.2010.939962
7. Qiao, W., Lu, D.: A survey on wind turbine condition monitoring and fault diagnosis—part I: components and subsystems. IEEE Trans. Ind. Electron. **62**, 6536–6545 (2015). https://doi.org/10.1109/TIE.2015.2422112
8. Van Dam, C., Berg, D., Johnson, S.: Active load control techniques for wind turbines. Aluquerque, NM, USA (2008). https://doi.org/10.2172/943932
9. Li, X., Gao, H.: Load Mitigation for a floating wind turbine via generalized structural control. IEEE Trans. Ind. Electron. **63**, 332–342 (2016)
10. Beik, O., Al-Adsani, A.: Wind turbine productivity and wind energy assessment: an Ontario case study. In: 2020 IEEE Electric Power and Energy Conference (EPEC), pp. 1–5. IEEE, Edmonton, AB, Canada (2020)
11. Anjun, X., Hao, X., Shuju, H., Honghua, X.: Pitch control of large scale wind turbine based on expert PID control. In: 2011 International Conference on Electronics, Communications and Control (ICECC), pp. 3836–3839. IEEE, Ningbo, China (2011)
12. Lopez, L.G., Normey-Rico, J.E.: Practical nonlinear model predictive control of a 5 MW wind turbine. In: 2018 9th International Renewable Energy Congress (IREC), pp. 1–6. IEEE, Hammamet (2018). https://doi.org/10.1109/IREC.2018.8362468
13. Routray, A., Hur, S.: Predictive control of wind turbine using preview wind speed information. In: 2022 IEEE Energy Conversion Congress and Exposition (ECCE), pp. 1–7. IEEE, Detroit, MI, USA (2022). https://doi.org/10.1109/ECCE50734.2022.9947738
14. Sterle, A., Grapentin, A., Hans, C.A., Raisch, J.: Model predictive control of wind turbines with piecewise-affine power coefficient approximation. In: 2023 62nd IEEE Conference on Decision and Control (CDC), pp. 3586–3591. IEEE, Singapore, Singapore (2023). https://doi.org/10.1109/CDC49753.2023.10383567
15. Schlipf, D., Pao, L.Y., Cheng, P.W.: Comparison of feedforward and model predictive control of wind turbines using LIDAR. In: 2012 IEEE 51st IEEE Conference on Decision and Control (CDC), pp. 3050–3055. IEEE, Maui, HI, USA (2012)
16. Schlipf, D., Schlipf, D.J., Kühn, M.: Nonlinear model predictive control of wind turbines using LIDAR. Wind Energy **16**, 1107–1129 (2013). https://doi.org/10.1002/we.1533
17. Schlipf, D., Grau, P., Raach, S., Duraiski, R., Trierweiler, J., Cheng, P.W.: Comparison of linear and nonlinear model predictive control of wind turbines using LIDAR. In: 2014 American Control Conference, pp. 3742–3747. IEEE, Portland, OR, USA (2014)
18. Park, J., Law, K.H.: Bayesian ascent: a data-driven optimization scheme for real-time control with application to wind farm power maximization. IEEE Trans. Contr. Syst. Technol. **24**, 1655–1668 (2016). https://doi.org/10.1109/TCST.2015.2508007
19. Guo, Q., Huang, C., Xue, Z., Zhang, L., Lu, X, Zhang, S.: Multi-objective optimization of wind farm dispatch problem by double layer particle swarm optimization algorithm. In: 2019 IEEE 8th Data Driven Control and Learning Systems Conference (DDCLS), pp. 728–733. IEEE, Yunnan, China (2019)
20. Williams, M.O., Kevrekidis, I.G., Rowley, C.W.: A data-driven approximation of the koopman operator: extending dynamic mode decomposition. J. Nonlinear. Sci. **25**, 1307–1346 (2015). https://doi.org/10.1007/s00332-015-9258-5
21. Guo, Z., Wu, W.: Data-driven model predictive control method for wind farms to provide frequency support. IEEE Trans. Energy Convers. **37**, 1304–1313 (2022)
22. Wang, X., He, Y., Gao, D.W., Wang, Z., Muljadi, E.: Cooperative output regulation of large-scale wind turbines for power reserve control. IEEE Trans. Energy Convers. **38**, 1166–1177 (2023). https://doi.org/10.1109/TEC.2022.3221619

23. Wang, X., Gao, D.W., Wang, J., Yan, W., Gao, W., Muljadi, E., Gevorgian, V.: Implementations and evaluations of wind turbine inertial controls with FAST and digital real-time simulations. IEEE Trans. Energy Convers. **33**, 1805–1814 (2018)
24. Wright, A. D.: Modern control design for flexible wind turbines. In: USA: National Renewable Energy Laboratory (NREL), pp. 1–10. Golden, Colorado, USA (2004)
25. Thomsen, S.C.: Nonlinear control of a wind turbine. Master's thesis. Technical University of Denmark. DTU. DK-2800 Kgs, Lyngby, Denmark (2006)
26. Wright, A.D., Fingersh, L.J.: Advanced Control Design for Wind Turbines; Part I: Control Design, Implementation, and Initial Tests (2008). https://doi.org/10.2172/927269
27. Su, S., Xiao, B., Li, L., Luo, J., Zhao, H.: An improved data-driven modeling method for aircraft based on prediction and optimization. In: 2023 35th Chinese Control and Decision Conference (CCDC), pp. 2560–2565. IEEE, Yichang, China (2023)
28. Wang, X., Zhang, T., Parisio, A.: Distributed control of virtual storage plants for grid service provision. In: 2021 60th IEEE Conference on Decision and Control (CDC), pp. 6371–6376. IEEE, Austin, TX, USA (2021)
29. Kafazi, I.E., Boubii, C., Rafia, H., Bannari, R., Bhiri, B.E.: MPC-PSO of a DFIG and comparison with PI controller. In: 2023 5th Global Power, Energy and Communication Conference (GPECOM). pp. 1–5. IEEE, Nevsehir, Turkiye (2023)
30. Wang, X., Zhang, T., Parisio, A.: Virtual storage plant aggregating electrical energy storages and HVAC systems providing regulating reserve and voltage regulation. IFAC-PapersOnLine. **54**, 1–7 (2021). https://doi.org/10.1016/j.ifacol.2021.08.516

Chapter 20
Distributed Energy Sharing Mechanism for Multiple IoT-Enable Park-Level Integrated Energy Systems Based on Cooperative Game

Siyu Ren, Yipeng Chen, Siyuan Zou, and Hongyu Wang

Abstract The rapid advancement of Internet of Things (IoT) technology has enhanced the integration of physical and information networks within park-level integrated energy systems, leading to the development of IoT-enabled Park-level Integrated Energy Systems (IPIES). These systems efficiently manage vast energy data volumes, facilitating multi-park energy sharing. This paper introduces a multi-IPIESs energy sharing service mechanism based on cooperative game theory, which incorporates the sharing economy concept into energy services. The paper outlines an architecture and detailed business process for the service, establishes a coordinated operational model to minimize comprehensive costs, and develops models for equitable benefit allocation and cost settlement among participants. Simulation results demonstrate the mechanism's effectiveness in promoting energy sharing, reducing operational costs, and enhancing resource efficiency within the IPIESs group.

20.1 Introduction

With the advancement of distributed energy and energy conversion technologies, Park-Level Integrated Energy Systems (PIESs) have become crucial energy carriers on the consumer side of the distribution network, integrating electricity, gas, and heat [1]. Enhanced by intelligent communication technologies such as the Internet of

S. Ren · Y. Chen (✉)
Sichuan University, Chengdu, China
e-mail: 1342193927@qq.com

S. Zou
Chengdu Ecological Environment Education and Foreign Exchange and Cooperation Center, Chengdu, China

H. Wang
Chengdu Ecological Environment Data Intelligence Management Center, Qingyang District, Chengdu, China

F. P. García Márquez et al. (eds.), *Computing, Internet of Things and Data Analytics*, Smart Innovation, Systems and Technologies 387,
https://doi.org/10.1007/978-3-031-87154-2_20

Things (IoT) and 5G networks, traditional PIESs have evolved into IoT-enabled environments, significantly boosting their ability to handle vast amounts of energy data [2]. Despite these advancements, optimizing the management of energy resources within PIESs remains challenging, often leading to underutilization of distributed energy devices.

The emergence of the sharing economy, leveraging modern internet technology to integrate decentralized resources, offers a promising solution to enhance resource utilization and reduce energy costs in PIESs [3]. This integration aims to develop a novel 'Internet Plus' energy system, optimizing resource usage and promoting sustainable energy practices. While research and applications of the sharing economy in the energy sector are still in their infancy, some preliminary results have been achieved. Wu [4] systematically reviewed and summarized the current state of energy sharing on the consumer side. Li [5] provided a comprehensive analysis of cloud energy storage, a novel application model of the sharing economy in energy storage. Jichun [6] quantified benefits and proposed interest distribution among multiple electricity selling companies sharing energy storage. Akter [7] proposed an energy sharing mechanism to reduce total energy costs for users. Chen [8] proposed a low-carbon energy system framework and effectively enhanced overall system benefits. Pei [9] established an optimal operation model for energy sharing in intelligent buildings, increasing renewable energy consumption. Liu [10] constructed an inter-park energy sharing operation framework for parks, enhancing system flexibility. Liu [11] proposed a master–slave game-based distributed photovoltaic sharing operation mechanism, promoting local consumption of photovoltaic resources within parks. Chen [12] proposed an energy sharing operation mechanism for various types of distributed energy within parks, aimed at enhancing park resource utilization.

As can be seen, research on applying the sharing economy in the energy sector is nascent, with preliminary studies focusing on energy sharing mechanisms and operational models that enhance system benefits and resource efficiency. Therefore, this paper presents a multi-PIESs energy sharing service mechanism based on cooperative game theory. It details the mechanism's architecture and business processes, establishes a coordinated operational model with comprehensive cost minimization, and proposes a benefit accounting and allocation model alongside a cost settlement model. Utilizing examples from three actual parks, the paper demonstrates the mechanism's effectiveness in promoting inter-PIESs energy sharing and enhancing resource utilization within the sharing PIESs group.

20.2 Architecture and Business Process of the Multi-PIESs Energy Sharing Service

20.2.1 Participants

The multi-PIESs energy sharing service involves four key types of participants in its actual implementation: sharing service provider, PIESs' operators, power company, and natural gas company.

(1) Sharing Service Provider: as the cornerstone of the energy sharing service, the sharing service provider is responsible for commercializing energy sharing service with the aim of generating profit while facilitating energy exchange among PIESs.
(2) PIESs' Operators: As recipients of the energy sharing services, PIES's Operators seek to reduce operational costs and enhance renewable energy utilization by engaging in energy sharing activities.
(3) Electric Power Companies and Natural Gas Companies: As crucial roles in facilitating the smooth operation of energy sharing service, they supply power and natural gas to PIESs' operators through the distribution network and natural gas pipelines.

The interplay among these four participant types is visually depicted in Fig. 20.1. Variations in the types and capacities of distributed energy devices across different PIESs are influenced by factors such as geographical location and resource availability. Energy usage within each PIES varies, supporting complementary practices.

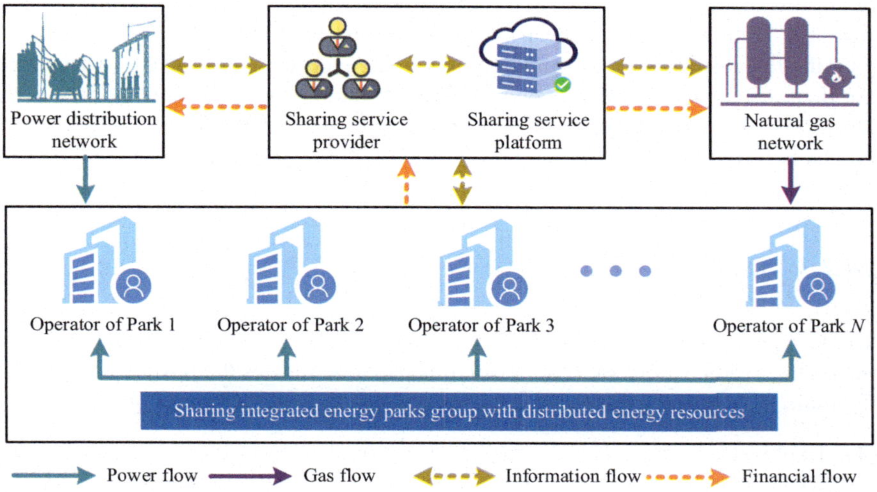

Fig. 20.1 The relationship among participants of multi-parks energy sharing service

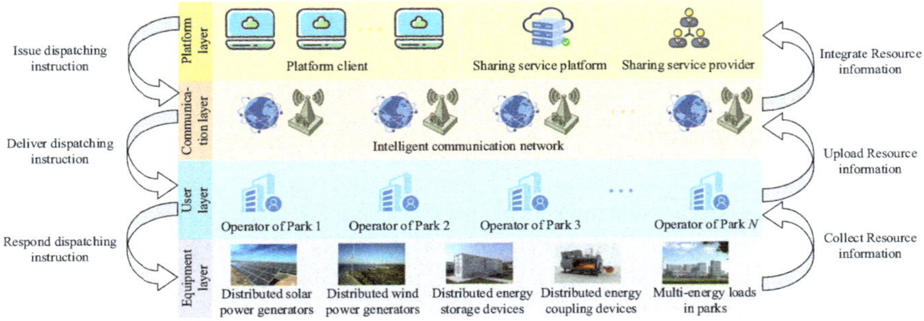

Fig. 20.2 The implementation structure of multi-parks energy sharing service

Guided by sharing service provider, adjacent PIESs form an interconnected group to facilitate energy exchange. The provider acts as a central hub, managing information flow and transactions with external energy suppliers, and ultimately handling cost settlements at the end of the service.

20.2.2 Implementation Structure

This paper presents a multi-layer implementation structure, which comprises the platform layer, communication layer, user layer and equipment layer, as shown in Fig. 20.2. The platform layer, managed by the sharing service provider, acts as the decision-making hub, processing energy data to issue operational commands. Each day, PIES operators must upload critical data including load and renewable energy forecasts. Using an optimization program, the provider consolidates this data to coordinate equipment and formulate inter-PIES energy sharing plans. Instructions are then dispatched to PIES operators through intelligent communication devices. Operators adjust their equipment's operation strategies in real-time and, at day's end, upload new data for platform integration and preparation for the subsequent day.

20.2.3 Business Process

To illustrate the convenience of unified resource management and scheduling under the multi- PIESs energy sharing model, this paper delineates the business process of the multi- PIESs energy sharing service mechanism, as depicted in Fig. 20.3.

(1) Explanation Stage: The sharing service provider formulates clear and concise terms of service for multi-PIESs energy sharing, outlining the rights, responsibilities, and profit-sharing methods between the provider and PIESs' operators.

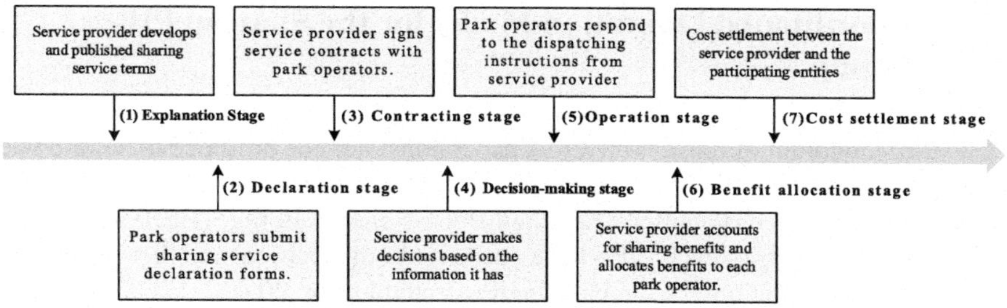

Fig. 20.3 The business process of multi-parks energy sharing service

These terms are communicated to all PIESs' operators within the distribution network.

(2) Declaration Stage: PIESs' operators interested in participating in the multi-PIESs energy sharing service declare the basic energy information of their PIES and their intended duration of participation (minimum one day) after thoroughly reviewing and understanding the terms of service.
(3) Contracting Stage: The sharing service provider enters multi-PIESs energy sharing service contracts with those who meet the requirements.
(4) Decision Stage: Prior to the operational day, the sharing service provider utilizes load information and equipment capacity from each PIES to minimize the overall operational costs of the sharing PIESs group. Using optimization programs within the sharing platform, the provider determines the pre-day coordinated operational strategy for the park cluster, serving as a guide for PIES operations.
(5) Operation Stage: At the onset of the operational day, the sharing service provider disseminates the coordinated operational strategy to all PIESs' operators. PIESs' operators then adjust the output of distributed energy devices within their PIESs in real-time in accordance with the dispatching instructions received. Concurrently, the sharing service provider executes electricity and gas purchasing actions as per their energy purchasing strategy.
(6) Accounting Stage: Post-operational day, the sharing service provider calculates the total benefits generated by multi-PIESs energy sharing and allocates these benefits between the provider and PIESs' operators based on the predetermined benefit distribution strategy outlined in the service terms.
(7) Settlement Stage: Following the operational day, the sharing service provider distributes the benefits among PIESs' operators and collects energy purchase costs on their behalf. Simultaneously, the provider settles the final energy purchasing costs with external energy companies.

20.3 Coordinated Operation Model for the Sharing PIESs Group

From the standpoint of universality, this paper considers the presence of solar power generators (SPG), wind power generators (WPG), gas turbines (GT), fuel cells (FC), gas boilers (GB), electric boilers (EB), and electric energy storage (EES) within each PIES. Besides, Users of each PIES have needs for both electrical and thermal energy. The energy flow structure of the parks is illustrated in Fig. 20.4.

The coordinated operational model for the sharing PIESs group encompasses an objective function and associated constraints, which are elaborated upon in the subsequent section.

20.3.1 Objective Function

The sharing service provider aims to minimize the comprehensive operation cost of the sharing PIESs group, including the energy purchasing cost, the renewable power curtailment penalty cost and the transmission cost for energy sharing. The objective function is represented as:

$$C^{\text{PIES,N}} = \min \sum_{k}^{N^{\text{PIES}}} \left(C_k^{\text{PIES,buy}} + C_k^{\text{PIES,cul}} + C_k^{\text{PIES,trans}} \right) \tag{20.1}$$

$$C_k^{\text{PIES,buy}} = \sum_{t=1}^{T} \left(p_t^{\text{e}} P_{k,t}^{\text{buy}} + p_t^{\text{g}} G_{k,t}^{\text{buy}} \right) \Delta t \tag{20.2}$$

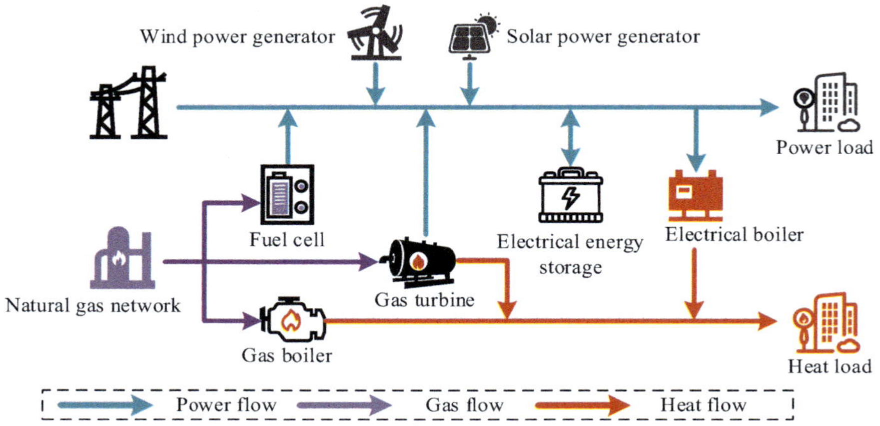

Fig. 20.4 Energy flow structure of integrated energy park

$$C_k^{\mathrm{PIES,cul}} = \sum_{t=1}^{T} \left(\eta_k^{\mathrm{cul}} P_{k,t}^{\mathrm{cul}}\right) \Delta t \tag{20.3}$$

$$C_k^{\mathrm{PIES,trans}} = \frac{1}{2} \sum_{t=1}^{T} \sum_{l=1,l\neq k}^{N^{\mathrm{PIES}}} \left[\alpha^{\mathrm{trans,e}} \left(P_{k-l,t}^{\mathrm{share}}\right)^2 + \beta^{\mathrm{trans,e}} \left|P_{k-l,t}^{\mathrm{share}}\right|\right] \Delta t \tag{20.4}$$

where $C^{\mathrm{PIES,N}}$ represents the comprehensive operation cost of the sharing PIESs group on one full day. N^{PIES} indicates the collection of the sharing PIESs group consisting of different PIESs. K denotes the number of PIESs included in the sharing PIESs group N^{PIES}. $C_k^{\mathrm{PIES,buy}}$, $C_k^{\mathrm{PIES,cul}}$ and $C_k^{\mathrm{PIES,trans}}$ are the energy purchasing cost, the renewable energy curtailment penalty cost and the transmission cost for energy sharing of PIES k. p_t^{e} and p_t^{g} represent the power price and the natural gas price at moment t. $P_{k,t}^{\mathrm{buy}}$ and $G_{k,t}^{\mathrm{buy}}$ are the power and natural gas purchasing amount. η_k^{cul} represents the unit penalty cost of renewable energy curtailment. $P_{k,t}^{\mathrm{cul}}$ is the renewable power curtailment. $P_{k-l,t}^{\mathrm{share}}$ indicates the sharing power from PIES k to PIES l at moment t. $\alpha^{\mathrm{trans,e}}$ and $\beta^{\mathrm{trans,e}}$ denote the primary and secondary energy transmission cost of tie lines of the distribution network.

20.3.2 Constraints

(1) Constraints of Multi-Energy Balance

Each PIES in the sharing PIESs group should satisfy the power, heat and gas balance constraints, as shown in the following equations:

$$P_{k,t}^{\mathrm{buy}} + P_{k,t}^{\mathrm{PV}} + P_{k,t}^{\mathrm{WT}} + P_{k,t}^{\mathrm{GT}} + P_{k,t}^{\mathrm{FC}} + P_{k,t}^{\mathrm{dis}} = P_{k,t}^{\mathrm{load}} + P_{k,t}^{\mathrm{EB}} + P_{k,t}^{\mathrm{ch}} + \sum_{l=1,l\neq k}^{N^{\mathrm{PIES}}} P_{k-l,t}^{\mathrm{share}} + P_{k,t}^{\mathrm{cul}} \tag{20.5}$$

$$H_{k,t}^{\mathrm{GT}} + H_{k,t}^{\mathrm{GB}} + H_{k,t}^{\mathrm{EB}} = H_{k,t}^{\mathrm{load}} \tag{20.6}$$

$$G_{k,t}^{\mathrm{buy}} = G_{k,t}^{\mathrm{GT}} + G_{k,t}^{\mathrm{FC}} + G_{k,t}^{\mathrm{GB}} \tag{20.7}$$

where $P_{k,t}^{\mathrm{PV}}$ and $P_{k,t}^{\mathrm{WT}}$ are the actual renewable energy output of SPG and WTG of PIES k at moment t. $P_{k,t}^{\mathrm{GT}}$ and $P_{k,t}^{\mathrm{FC}}$ are the power output of GT and FC. $P_{k,t}^{\mathrm{ch}}$ and $P_{k,t}^{\mathrm{dis}}$ are the charging and the discharging power of EES. $P_{k,t}^{\mathrm{load}}$ is the power load. $P_{k,t}^{\mathrm{EB}}$ is the power input of EB. $H_{k,t}^{\mathrm{GT}}$, $H_{k,t}^{\mathrm{GB}}$ and $H_{k,t}^{\mathrm{EB}}$ are the heat output of GT, GB and EB. $H_{k,t}^{\mathrm{load}}$ is the heat load. $G_{k,t}^{\mathrm{GT}}$, $G_{k,t}^{\mathrm{FC}}$ and $G_{k,t}^{\mathrm{GB}}$ are the natural gas input of GT, FC and GB.

(2) Constraints of Energy Purchasing

There are energy transmission constraints of power and gas flow, which are connected to distribution network and natural gas network, as shown in Eqs. (20.8) and (20.9):

$$0 \leq P_{k,t}^{\text{buy}} \leq P_{k}^{\text{buy,max}} \tag{20.8}$$

$$0 \leq G_{k,t}^{\text{buy}} \leq G_{k}^{\text{buy,max}} \tag{20.9}$$

where $P_{k}^{\text{buy,max}}$ and $G_{k}^{\text{buy,max}}$ are the maximum transmission power of the tie line and the maximum transmission flow of natural gas pipeline.

(3) Constraints of energy sharing

The sharing power among different PIESs needs to meet the power transmission limitation, as shown in the following equations:

$$\left|P_{k-l,t}^{\text{share}}\right| \leq P_{k-l}^{\text{share,max}} \tag{20.10}$$

$$\sum_{k=1}^{N^{\text{PIES}}} \sum_{l=1,l \neq k}^{N^{\text{PIES}}} P_{k-l,t}^{\text{share}} = 0 \tag{20.11}$$

where $P_{k-l}^{\text{share,max}}$ indicates the maximum sharing power from PIES k to PIES l. The net sharing power of the entire sharing PIESs group should be 0 at each moment, i.e., Eq. (20.11) is satisfied.

In addition, the detailed PIES equipment models including GT, FC, GB, EB and EES are presented in [13].

20.4 Coordinated Operation Strategy for Sharing PIESs Group

Upon solving the coordinated operation strategy model, the sharing service provider obtains detailed information on the planned outputs of distributed energy devices within each PIES and the anticipated electricity and gas purchasing for the operational day. Using this data, the provider devises a comprehensive coordinated operation strategy for the sharing PIESs cluster, which includes equipment dispatch, energy purchasing, and energy sharing strategies.

20.4.1 Dispatching Strategy of the Distributed Energy Equipment

Before the actual operation day, the sharing service provider needs to formulate the optimal operation strategy for the shared park cluster and issue dispatch instructions to the park operators within the cluster at the start of the operation day. Subsequently, each park operator controls the devices within their managed parks in real time according to the dispatch instructions. The coordinated operation strategy for the distributed energy devices within the parks of the sharing park cluster is as follows:

$$STR1 = \{P_{k,t}^{\text{cul}}, P_{k,t}^{\text{GT}}, P_{k,t}^{\text{FC}}, P_{k,t}^{\text{EB}}, P_{k,t}^{\text{ch}}, P_{k,t}^{\text{dis}}, H_{k,t}^{\text{GB}}\}, \forall k \in N^{\text{PIES}} \tag{20.12}$$

where $STR1$ represents the optimal dispatching strategy of the distributed energy equipment in the sharing PIESs group.

20.4.2 Energy Purchasing Strategy of the Sharing Service Provider

After solving the coordinated operation model of the sharing PIESs group, the overall energy purchase strategy of the group can also be derived, as shown in Eq. (20.13).

$$STR2 = \{\sum_{k}^{N^{\text{PIES}}} P_{k,t}^{\text{buy}}, \sum_{k}^{N^{\text{PIES}}} G_{k,t}^{\text{buy}}\} \tag{20.13}$$

where $STR2$ denotes the energy purchasing strategy of the sharing service provider. $P_{k,t}^{\text{buy}}$ and $G_{k,t}^{\text{buy}}$ indicate the power and natural gas purchasing amount of PIES k at moment t.

20.4.3 Energy Sharing Strategy of the Sharing PIESs Group

The sharing service provider also needs to issue the energy sharing strategy to each PIES operator. Each PIES operator adjusts the tie line power based on the energy sharing strategy among different PIESs. The energy sharing strategy is shown in Eq. (20.14).

$$STR3 = \{P_{k-l,t}^{\text{share}}\}, \forall k, l \in N^{\text{PIES}}, k \neq l \tag{20.14}$$

where $STR3$ denotes the energy sharing strategy among the PIESs of the sharing PIESs group.

20.5 Sharing Benefit Allocation and Cost Settlement Models

20.5.1 Sharing Benefits Accounting Model

The reduction in operating costs before and after participation quantifies the benefits generated by the multi-park energy sharing service. The mathematical description of this concept is as follows

$$Ben(N^{\text{PIES}}) = \sum_{k}^{N^{\text{PIES}}} C_k^{\text{PIES,ind}} - C^{\text{PIES,N}} \tag{20.15}$$

where $Ben(N^{\text{PIES}})$ represents the total sharing benefits. $C_k^{\text{PIES,ind}}$ represents the minimum comprehensive operation cost of PIES k under the independent operation mode.

20.5.2 Sharing Benefits Allocation Model

Sharing service providers are willing to implement multi-PIESs energy sharing service to obtain considerable sharing benefits. Therefore, the benefit allocation model for the sharing service provider is established, as shown in Eq. (20.16):

$$Ben(\delta) = \delta Ben(N^{\text{PIES}}) \tag{20.16}$$

where $Ben(\delta)$ represents the sharing benefit obtained by the sharing service provider,. δ is the profit-sharing coefficient set in the contract by the sharing service provider. Thus, based on the benefit allocated to the sharing service provider, the remaining sharing benefits are calculated as:

$$Ben'(N^{\text{PIES}}) = (1 - \delta)Ben(N^{\text{PIES}}) \tag{20.17}$$

where $Ben'(N^{\text{PIES}})$ represents the remaining sharing benefits after considering the benefit allocation to the sharing service provider. Therefore, based on the Shapley value method, this paper establishes a sharing benefit allocation model for each PIES to redistribute the remaining sharing benefits, as shown in the following equations:

$$Ben(k) = \sum\nolimits_{S \in N^{\text{PIES}}} \psi(S)\left[Ben'(S) - Ben'(S/k)\right] \tag{20.18}$$

$$\psi(S) = \left[(|S| - 1)!\left(\left|N^{\text{PIES}}\right| - |S|\right)!\right] / \left|N^{\text{PIES}}\right|! \tag{20.19}$$

where $Ben(k)$ represents the sharing benefit obtained by PIES k after participating in the energy sharing services.

20.5.3 Cost Settlement Model

Given the business process designed in Sect. 2.3, it is evident that after determining the sharing benefit allocation values for each service participant, the sharing service provider needs to pay the energy purchasing cost to the grid company and the gas company, while collecting service fees from each PIES's operator. For PIES's operators, their cost settlement model is represented in Eq. (20.20):

$$Fee(k) = C_k^{\text{PIES,ind}} - Ben(k) \tag{20.20}$$

where $Fee(k)$ indicates the total service fees that the operator of PIES k needs to pay to the sharing service provider. Therefore, the cost settlement model for the sharing service provider is represented by the following equation:

$$Fee = \sum_{k \in N^{\text{PIES}}}^{N^{\text{PIES}}} Fee(k) - \sum_{t=1}^{T} \left(p_t^{\text{e}} P_{k,t}^{\text{buy}}\right) \Delta t - \sum_{t=1}^{T} \left(p_t^{\text{g}} G_{k,t}^{\text{buy}}\right) \Delta t \tag{20.21}$$

where $\sum_{k \in N^{\text{PIES}}}^{N^{\text{PIES}}} Fee(k)$ represents the total service fees that the sharing PIESs group needs to pay to the sharing service provider at the end of an operational day.

20.6 Case Study

20.6.1 Basic Parameter Settings

This paper selects three actual industrial and commercial PIESs located in the northern region as case study examples. A typical winter day is chosen for conducting simulation analysis. The unit scheduling period is set at 1 h. Among these parks, PIES 1 and PIES 3 are equipped with SPGs, whereas PIES 2 contains a WPG. The output curves of the renewable energy generators, along with the demand curves for electrical and thermal loads in each PIES, are illustrated in Fig. 20.5. The electricity prices between the PIESs and the power distribution network adhere to time-of-use rates applicable to general industrial and commercial users. Energy transmission limits for the electrical interconnection lines and natural gas pipelines for each PIES are set at 300 kW and 300 m^3, respectively. Additionally, the power transmission limits between PIES 1 and PIES 2, PIES 1 and PIES 3, and PIES 2 and PIES 3 are

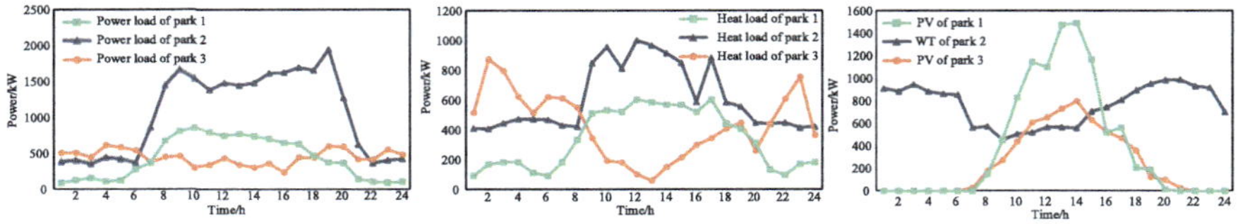

Fig. 20.5 Multi-loads and renewable energy output curves of each park

all capped at 200 kW. The case studies are tackled using MATLAB on a commercial solver, GUROBI.

20.6.2 Comparative Analysis of PIES Operation Results

Figure 20.6 shows the results of energy sharing among PIESs following their participation in the energy sharing service mechanism. Positive sharing quantities indicate that a PIES is supplying energy, while negative values indicate receiving energy, thus positioning them as demanders in the network. Between 9:00 AM and 5:00 PM, PIESs 1 and 3 supply surplus electricity to PIES 2, primarily due to their high photovoltaic output and low internal load demands. Conversely, from 1:00 AM to 6:00 AM and from 9:00 PM to 12:00 AM, PIES 2, benefiting from its substantial wind turbine output and low load demand, supplies excess electricity to PIESs 1 and 3. This inter-PIES energy sharing, facilitated through transmission lines, enhances the utilization of renewable energy across the network, as demonstrated in the multi-PIES energy sharing service mechanism discussed in this paper.

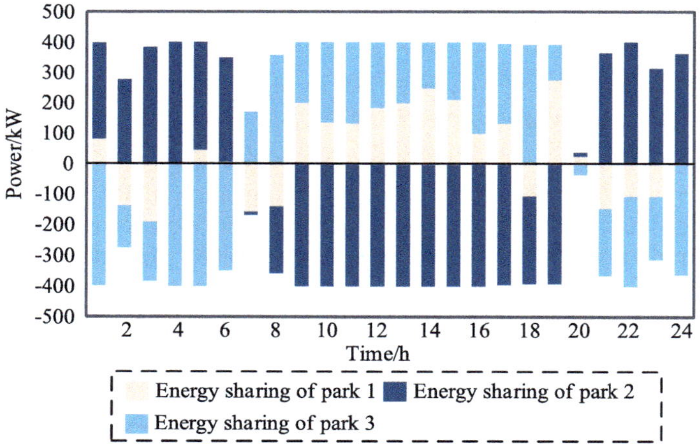

Fig. 20.6 Energy sharing results among three parks

To evaluate the effectiveness of the proposed energy sharing mechanism in enhancing equipment utilization within PIESs, this study focuses on gas turbines and electric boilers. By comparing their power outputs across various PIESs over a single operational day, we observe significant increases in utilization rates, as shown in Table 20.1. Gas turbines saw an increase of 884.07 kW, which translates to a 6.28% boost in utilization. Similarly, electric boilers experienced a 193.86 kW increase, or a 3.66% rise in utilization. Moreover, the study notes that the previously common discarding of wind and solar energy ceased post-mechanism implementation, leading to a 100% utilization rate for distributed wind turbines and photovoltaic units. Overall, the multi-PIES energy sharing service mechanism effectively maximizes idle capacity, enhances resource utilization, and promotes local consumption of renewable energy within the PIESs.

Figure 20.7 shows a comparison of total electricity and gas purchases before and after the participation of the sharing PIES group in the energy sharing service. The analysis reveals a substantial decrease in electricity purchases by 2604.65 kW, amounting to a 33.8% reduction, and a 461.51 m^3 decrease in gas purchases, a 7.5% reduction from pre-service levels. These reductions indicate that by participating in the energy sharing service and capitalizing on disparities in energy supply and demand across PIESs, the group can significantly reduce its reliance on higher-carbon energy sources, thus effectively lowering carbon emissions. Additionally, this participation helps mitigate peak electricity demand, contributing to peak shaving on the grid and enhancing the grid's stability during high demand periods.

Table 20.1 Comparison of energy output of GT and EB before and after sharing service

PIES	Power output of GT/kW		Heat output of EB/kW	
	Before energy sharing	After energy sharing	Before energy sharing	After energy sharing
PIES 1	1895.64	2398.70	2074.07	2188.38
PIES 2	7679.43	7900.00	1911.84	1720.31
PIES 3	4498.53	4658.97	1305.18	1576.26
Total	14,073.60	14,957.67	5291.09	5484.95

Fig. 20.7 Comparison of total energy purchasing amount of sharing parks group before and after energy sharing service

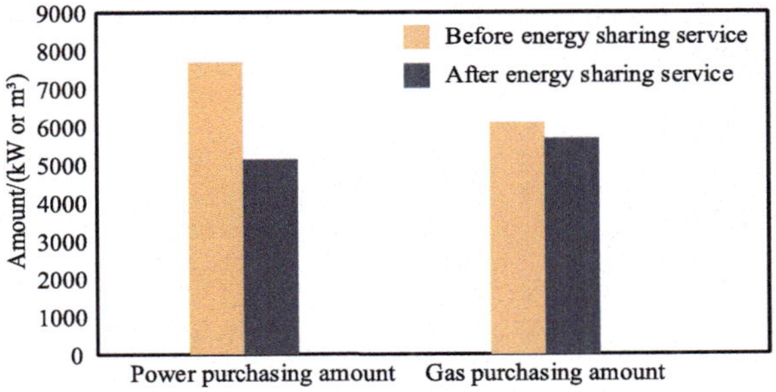

Table 20.2 Comparison of total energy output of GT and EB before and after PIESs participate in the presented energy sharing service

PIES	Total sharing benefit/yuan	Benefit distribution value of service provider/yuan	Benefit distribution value of park operator/yuan
PIES 1	–	–	1176.86
PIES 2	–	–	2667.85
PIES 3	–	–	1021.87
Total	5407.31	540.73	4866.58

20.6.3 Analysis of Sharing Benefit Distribution Results

By analyzing the operational outcomes and using the Shapley value formula, the marginal benefits for each PIES operator can be calculated. The sharing service provider, adhering to a benefit sharing ratio of 0.1, receives 10% of the total benefits as operational revenue for facilitating the service. Table 20.2 presents the final distribution of sharing benefits between the provider and each PIES operator.

From Table 20.2, The multi-PIES energy sharing service mechanism generated a total of 5407.31 RMB in shared benefits during an operational day, with the service provider earning 540.73 RMB in operational revenue. PIESs 1, 2, and 3 received benefits of 1176.86 RMB, 2667.85 RMB, and 1021.87 RMB, respectively. PIES 2 received the largest share due to its significant marginal contribution to the benefits. This demonstrates that the proposed mechanism can generate substantial shared benefits and ensure a fair distribution among all participating entities.

20.6.4 Comparative Analysis of PIES Operating Costs

The comparison of the comprehensive operating costs for each park before and after participating in the energy sharing service can be calculated, as shown in * MERGEFORMAT Fig. 20.8.

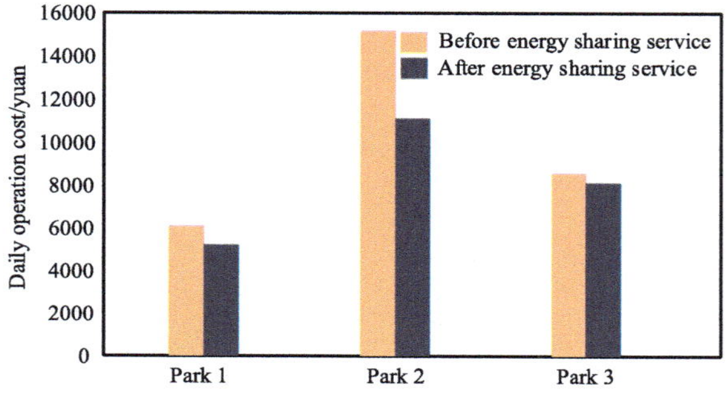

Fig. 20.8 Comparison of total operation cost of different PIESs before and after energy sharing service

Analysis of Fig. 20.8 shows significant reductions in total operating costs for all PIESs within the sharing group, with decreases of 14.18%, 26.86%, and 5.64% for PIESs 1, 2, and 3, respectively. The notable cost reduction in PIES 2 is due to its initially high energy purchasing costs, which significantly decreased after participating in the energy sharing service. Additionally, PIES 2 made a larger marginal contribution to energy sharing, as shown in Fig. 20.7, resulting in the most substantial reduction in operating costs. These results highlight the effectiveness of the proposed multi-PIES energy sharing service mechanism in reducing comprehensive operating costs across the PIESs.

20.7 Conclusion

This paper presents a multi-PIES energy sharing service mechanism that integrates cooperative game theory with the sharing economy concept, enhancing the utilization of distributed renewable energy and innovating PIES operation management. It outlines the participating market entities, establishes the implementation structure, and designs service processes. The paper then proposes a coordinated operation model for the PIES cluster aimed at minimizing operational costs while addressing constraints like multi-energy coupling and inter-PIES energy sharing. It also introduces a benefit accounting model and a fair distribution strategy using the Shapley value method, alongside a cost settlement model to ensure fair settlements among participants. Case studies confirm the mechanism's effectiveness in boosting renewable energy consumption, improving device utilization, and generating economic gains for both the service provider and PIES operators.

References

1. Xiong, J., Sun, Y., Wang, J., et al.: Multi-stage equipment optimal configuration of park-level integrated energy system considering flexible loads. Int. J. Electr. Power Energy Syst. **140**, 108050 (2022). https://doi.org/10.1016/j.ijepes.2022.108050
2. Zhang, L., Yuan, H., et al.: Research on the overall architecture of Internet of Things middleware for intelligent industrial parks. Int. J. Adv. Manuf. Technol. **107**(3), 1081–1089 (2020). https://doi.org/10.1007/s00170-019-04310-z
3. Cuenca, J.J., Jamil, E., Hayes, B.: State of the art in energy communities and sharing economy concepts in the electricity sector. IEEE Trans. Ind. Appl. **57**(6), 5737–5746 (2021). https://doi.org/10.1109/TIA.2021.3114135
4. Wu, Z., Wang, J., Zhong, H., et al.: Sharing economy in local energy markets. J. Mod. Power Syst. Clean Energy (2022). https://doi.org/10.35833/MPCE.2022.000521
5. Li, Z., Tesfatsion, S., Bastani, S.: A survey on modeling energy consumption of cloud applications: deconstruction, state of the art, and trade-off debates. IEEE Trans. Sustain. Comput. **2**(3), 255–274 (2017). https://doi.org/10.1109/TSUSC.2017.2722822
6. Liu, J., et al.: Optimal allocation of energy storage and investment benefit analysis of power sales companies under market mechanism considering sharing mode. Power Syst. Technol. **44**(5), 1740–1749 (2020). https://doi.org/10.13335/j.1000-3673.pst.2019.2386

7. Akter, M.N., Mahmud, M.A., Haque, M.E.: An optimal distributed energy management scheme for solving transactive energy sharing problems in residential microgrids. Appl. Energy **270**, 115133 (2020).https://doi.org/10.1016/j.apenergy.2020.115133
8. Chen, C., Li, Y., Qiu, W., et al.: Cooperative-game-based day-ahead scheduling of local integrated energy systems with shared energy storage. IEEE Trans. Sustain. Energy **13**(4), 1994–2011 (2022). https://doi.org/10.1109/TSTE.2022.3176613
9. Huang, P., Lovati, M., et al.: A coordinated control to improve performance for a building cluster with energy storage, electric vehicles, and energy sharing considered. Appl. Energy. **268**, 114983 (2020). https://doi.org/10.1016/j.apenergy.2020.114983
10. Nian, L.I.U., Jie, W.A.N.G., Lingfeng, W.A.N.G.: Hybrid energy sharing for multiple microgrids in an integrated heat-electricity energy system. IEEE Trans. Sustain. Energy **10**(3), 1139–1151 (2019). https://doi.org/10.1109/TSTE.2018.2861986
11. Nian, L.I.U., et al.: Energy-sharing provider for PV Prosumer clusters: a hybrid approach using stochastic programming and Stackelberg game. IEEE Trans. Industr. Electron. **65**(8), 6740–6750 (2018). https://doi.org/10.1109/TIE.2018.2793181
12. Chen, Y., Li, H., Liu, Y., et al.: Distributed energy sharing service mechanism for prosumers in the IoT-enable integrated energy par. In: 2023 IEEE 3rd International Conference on Intelligent Technology and Embedded Systems (ICITES), pp. 76–85. IEEE (2023). https://doi.org/10.1109/ICITES59818.2023.10356867
13. Liu, Y., Chen, X., Wu, L., et al.: An IDM-based distributionally robust economic dispatch model for integrated electricity-heat-gas microgrid considering wind power. CSEE J. Power Energy Syst. (2022). https://doi.org/10.17775/CSEEJPES.2021.03940

Chapter 21
The Role of Artificial Intelligence in Enhancing Translation and Cultural Diversity with Reference English and Arabic Translation

Inam Ghalib Sheekhoo Al-Azzawi, Maha Abdullah Mohammed, and Anfal Sabeeh Hamood

Abstract With the spread of globalization, the need for translators and scholars has grown, as translation is the only process that helps bridge linguistic gaps. Following the emergence of artificial intelligence (AI), a strong competitor has arisen to the translators, sweeping through all scientific and professional fields, including translation sector, with a set of tools that aid in the translation process. The current study aims to investigate the capability of AI tools in translating texts rich in cultural variety from one language to another, specifically focusing on English-Arabic translations, through qualitative analysis to uncover cultural elements in the target language and determine the ability of AI tools to preserve, lose, or alter them. Two AI translation tools were used (Spider-AI and Matacate), which revealed the success of AI tools in the translation process of linguistic aspect, through producing accurate and fluent translations that capture the general meaning of the texts. However, they were unable to convey subtle nuances and cultural characteristics, resulting in some gaps in the cultural aspect of the target language. The study emphasized the importance of the cultural aspect during the process of transferring meaning in translation. Therefore, it focused on the significance of collaboration between human translators and AI translation tools, to get better results.at the end the study concluded with the importance of continuing scientific research for updating AI translation tools, to create systems that are both technologically advanced and culturally sensitive.

I. G. S. Al-Azzawi (✉)
College of Physical Education and Sports Sciences for Girls, University of Baghdad, Baghdad, Iraq
e-mail: inam.g@copew.uobaghdad.edu.iq

M. A. Mohammed
College of Electronics Engineering, Department of Biomedical Engineering, Ninevah University, Mosul, Iraq
e-mail: maha.abdullah@uoninevah.edu.iq

A. S. Hamood
College of Mass Media, Department of Journalism, University of Baghdad, Baghdad, Iraq
e-mail: anfaltamimi@comc.uobaghdad.edu.iq

F. P. García Márquez et al. (eds.), *Computing, Internet of Things and Data Analytics*, Smart Innovation, Systems and Technologies 387,
https://doi.org/10.1007/978-3-031-87154-2_21

21.1 Introduction

The urgent need for translation processes, translators, and specialists has emerged since the onset of globalization and social media programs, to achieve successful and accurate linguistic and cultural communication. Following this, artificial intelligence technologies have swept all areas of life, including the field of translation, achieving notable linguistic efficiency [1, 2]. Consequently, the current research aims to explore the extent of these technologies' ability to practically apply the translation process. Translation does not only apply to transferring words from one language to another but is also a process of cultural communication. The question is whether artificial intelligence tools are capable of translating texts rich in cultural diversity.

The latest emergence of artificial intelligence technologies has created a significant buzz and revolutionized all scientific and professional fields, one of which is translation [3]. With the entry of artificial intelligence technologies, translation has become more efficient, effective, and of higher quality. Additionally, its application has become easier for everyone and at various levels, making it a major competitor to translators and specialists [4]. What distinguishes these tools is their superiority over human competitors in processing large and enormous amounts of data and texts in record time, which has attracted the attention and interest of companies, institutions, and individuals who rely on translation services for effective communication across languages.

Despite all these advantages, the biggest obstacle facing these tools has not been eliminated, Despite their technological advancement and strength, the main question remains, can the accuracy, quality, and precision of the translations generated by artificial intelligence convey the cultural aspect, since translation is not just a linguistic process but also a cultural one, as it transfers ideas, beliefs, habits, and cultural contexts [5], Have artificial intelligence tools managed to bridge these cultural gaps, or are they still relying solely on the linguistic aspect? The current research focuses on discussing the role of artificial intelligence tools in the translation process and how they deal with texts rich in cultural aspects, based on the Arabic and English languages, as they are culturally distinct. It also includes a comparative study between the translations produced by these tools and human translations.

The literature on AI-assisted translation reveals several critical gaps: AI tools struggle with accurately conveying cultural nuances and idiomatic expressions, leading to potential misinterpretations in culturally rich texts [6], There is a lack of comprehensive comparative studies between human and AI translations, particularly in complex domains like legal and literary texts. Additionally, domain-specific and culturally adapted models are needed to enhance AI's precision across various fields [7]. Collaboration between AI and human translators is essential to ensure cultural appropriateness, highlighting the importance of human-in-the-loop processes. Continuous research is required to develop AI systems that incorporate cultural knowledge and context, addressing ethical and social implications such as discrimination and representation in cross-border communication.

One of the most important features and characteristics of artificial intelligence tools is their quality and speed in producing translated texts in record time. They are capable of processing and translating vast quantities of texts that cannot be executed or matched by translators and specialists. This feature is particularly valued by those involved in e-commerce, for example, where the speed of producing accurate texts is essential for business success and goal achievement [8]. Another advantage, which may reduce the burden on translators and specialists, is the automation of tasks and the preprocessing or quality assessment of texts. All these features help specialists by allowing them to focus on more complex and creative aspects of the translation process, such as tailoring the content of translated texts for a specific target audience or ensuring cultural appropriateness.

Another attribute of these tools is the accuracy and quality of the translated texts, which result from various factors, most importantly the languages used, and the data fed into these systems [9]. However, it is not possible to assert complete accuracy of the texts, as these tools still face limitations, such as determining context or dealing with idiomatic expressions and subtle cultural differences. For instance, studies have explored the quality and accuracy of widely used translation applications like Google Translate, Microsoft Translator, and Reverso. A study in 2019 compared the performance of these applications and found that they produce good and acceptable texts, but not without errors, inconsistencies, and sometimes poor choices of linguistic terms or failure to adhere to the required context [10]. To overcome these hurdles and impediments, the researcher suggested working on developing and improving the quality of these programs through continuous updates to the linguistic rules, in addition to ongoing human monitoring and oversight, to achieve error-free texts. Certainly, all these attempts will not eliminate the need for human involvement, given the complexity of linguistic styles, the diversity of fields, and the variety of cultures.

21.2 Human versus AI Translations Techniques

With the widespread use of artificial intelligence tools, especially in translation processes, and their success in producing accurate and high-quality texts, it became very important to compare them with human translations to examine the extent to which users can rely on these tools. To illustrate the results of these comparisons, graphs were utilized, which demonstrate the differences between human translators and artificial intelligence tools, derived from several previous studies. These figures help in visually comparing the performance in terms of accuracy, speed, and quality of translation, highlighting areas where AI tools excel and where human translators still hold an advantage, such as understanding cultural nuances and context-specific interpretations.

(1) **Translation Quality Score Comparison**

Figure 21.1 represents The study result that investigated the differences between three sources of translations (Human, NMT, SMT) regarding the translation quality [11].

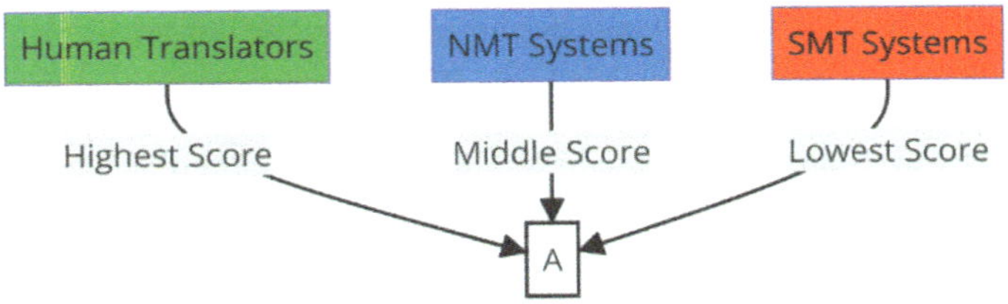

Fig. 21.1 The result that investigated the differences between three sources of translations (Human, NMT, SMT)

The study conducted a synchronic assessment of Google Translate, Microsoft Translator, and Reverso for English-Arabic translation, focusing on their performance in translating documents from the WHO, UN, Petra News Agency, and the Arab League. Using the intelligibility and fidelity scales for evaluation, the study found Google Translate to generally outperform the other systems in producing intelligible and fluent output without flaws across different documents, achieving the highest rates of error-free translation.

The main finding was that Google Translate provided the most accurate and fluent translations, followed by Microsoft Translator and then Reverso, across various metrics of intelligibility and fidelity. Despite their capabilities, none of the systems could completely substitute for human translators, underscoring the persistent limitations of MT in handling complex aspects of language such as context, idiomatic expressions, and subtle cultural nuances. As well the study highlighted a gradual improvement in the performance of these systems [11].

(2) **Translation Speed Comparison**

Figure 21.2 represents their data based on [12] study, that delves into advancements, challenges, and ethical considerations surrounding AI-driven language translation, emphasizing the shift from traditional translation methods towards AI and Machine Translation (MT) technologies. It reviews the evolution from rule-based and statistical machine translation approaches to the latest neural machine translation (NMT) techniques, detailing their advantages, limitations, and the ongoing debates in the field [12]. The numbers which are written in Fig. 21.2, are mentioning to words number translated per hour. This proves the immense power of these tools, which is beyond human capacity.

(3) **Domain-specific Translation Accuracy**

Figure 21.3 presents the data resulting from research that was done by [13], that indicated the enhanced accuracy of machine translation generated by deep learning techniques. In addition to the comparison of human and AI translations' accuracy and diversity in various domains. To conclude, to result that confirm the accuracy & diversity of AI translation, in multiple domains, like legal or medical translation, where high precision and accuracy are required, human translators would be more favored than machine translation systems. On the contrary, in big translation projects

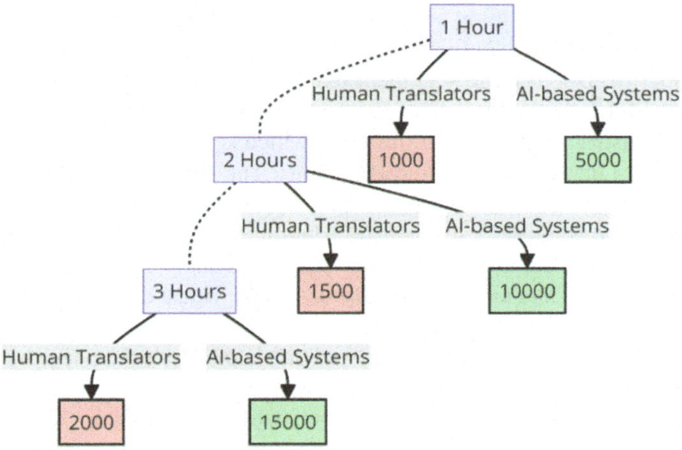

Fig. 21.2 Translation speed of words number translated per hour

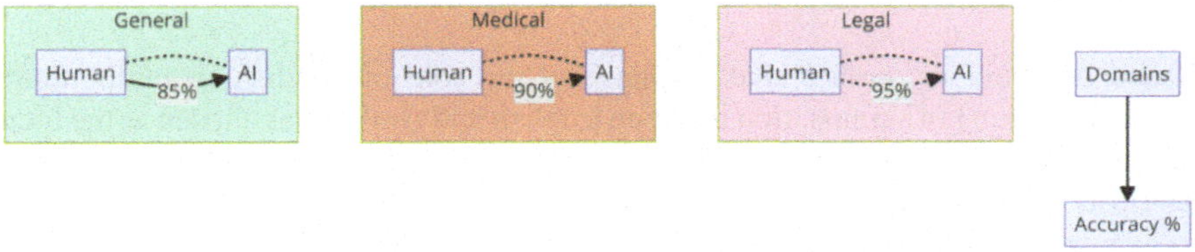

Fig. 21.3 Enhanced accuracy of machine translation generated by deep learning techniques

with short deadlines and cost reduction, the preferable method would be AI-assisted translation [13].

This comparison of human and AI translation indicates the need for interaction and collaboration between the two. While AI can automate and speed up some aspects of the translation process, human knowledge and judgment are necessary for globalization, awareness about cultural context [13]. The next section will illustrate how this collaboration can be used to eliminate cultural boundaries and diverse populations through translation.

The problem of the study is the ability to manage texts rich in culture diversity using AI translation tools and whether such tools have the capability to bridge the cultural gaps or these tools rely mostly on language only, which might result in some loss or alternation of culture. Indeed, as the main introduction indicates, the problem is well stated. It explains the paper's main purpose, which is to investigate solutions to the problem.

The goal of this research study is to identify the ability of artificial intelligence tools in translating texts that are rich with cultures diversity. In case of English to

Arabic translations. The study seeks to identify if artificial intelligence translation tools translate texts rich in cultural variety [4].

The paper begins with the statement that effective translation is required in the modern world due to the globalization of many industries and the phenomenon of migration. It also states the aim of the study which is to analyze the performance of AI technologies in preserving cultural elements. The review of the literature section describes several research studies which have focused on AI tools and their ability or inability to ensure a culturally sensitive translation. The methodology section outlines that the method underpinning the study is qualitative analysis and describes how the texts were selected. Data analysis and discussion provide a comparison between the quality of human and AI translation with respect to the cultural elements. The last section reflects upon the findings of the study and concludes the paper by providing some implications for the issue discussed and some future research directions in the field of AI technologies employed for the purposes of translation.

21.3 Methodology

Based on previous studies that emphasized the role of English in multicultural communication [14], translation between English and Arabic was chosen as the focus of this study to understand how AI tools deal with cultural challenges in translation. The following outlines of what type of approach and methodology will be using to examine the cultural elements in the English language & in Arabic AI-assisted. These include the analysis features and data acquisition, corpus types involved in the investigation.

Considering the intricacy and subjectivity of cultural features assessment in translation, the qualitative method is considered more appropriate [15]. Qualitative analysis allows exploring the context of the translated texts in more detail and depth in meaning and include cultural connotation analysis in texts. Consequently, this approach enables us to interpret the preserved, lost, and altered cultural elements in the AI-assisted translations and to develop rich descriptive results on the AI impact on cultural diversity in translation. Nevertheless, to complement qualitative analysis, certain quantifiable measures can be used as well. For instance, the number & rate of culturally specific terms, idioms, expressions in the source and target texts can be calculated and measured against each other to evaluate the extent to which cultural aspects in translations are preserved or lost. Such quantitative data would help reinforce the results of a qualitative study and further test the cultural implications of Ai Tools.

The analysis utilizes a sample of English-Arabic parallel programs with the aim of enhancing research credibility and dependability. The sample has varied texts, The variability of them is important in helping capture aspects of culture and translation problems. The corpora will meet the following criteria:

First, the existence of good-quality, & human translation for reference allowing precise comparison between AI-assisted and human translations.

Second, corpora will reflect various text genres, and register variation, to ensure as much variation in cultural elements as possible to reflect any potential domain-dependent cultural differences [16].

Finally, corpora will include a mixture of time periods and geographies; thus eventually, a dataset of cultural elements' variation may be created.

Ten examples of such corpora have been chosen to represent the data required for English-Arabic language translation, and AI-assisted translation analysis. Five texts of them are in Arabic language, and five are in English; they represent cultures evenly, geographically, and locally.

Arabic Texts:

1. Al Jazeera news article on the continued Syria war, 2021
2. A cultural tradition posts from Egyptian Influencer in social media 2022
3. An excerpt from Naguib Mahfouz's novel "Palace Walk" by 1956
4. An excerpt from Ahmed Saadawi's novel "Frankenstein in Baghdad" by, 2013
5. An excerpt from Saudi novel: "Girls of Riyadh" by Rajaa Alsanea 2005

English Texts:

1. A news article from The New York Times about the U.S. presidential elections (2020)
2. An excerpt from Jane Austen' novel "Pride and Prejudice" (1813)
3. An American Influencer post on social media wrote about his experiences in Morocco and their traditional customs (2019)
4. An excerpt from French novel "Madame Bovary" by Gustave Flaubert 1856.
5. An excerpt from German novel "The Sorrows of Young Werther" by Johann Wolfgang von Goethe 1774

These texts include a variety of genres, often catering to specific cultural perspectives and challenges. Moreover, the Arabic and English texts are feature in time and geographical orientation is broad.

Following the completion of data collection, the researcher will utilize the content analysis method. This method implies a research technique for making replicable and valid inferences from texts to their context in which the patterns and themes of cultural elements and corresponding meanings will be identified [15]. It will have multiple stages.

First, the researcher will define the units of analysis such as words, phrases, sentences, or paragraphs where the cultural elements should be identified.

Second, a coding scheme will be prepared. The schema is a guide that determines the groups and types of the cultural elements analyzed–it helps to systematize and interpret the data. Hence, the coding scheme will be defined in relation to the cultural elements.

Third, Coding the data, in this stage, the researcher will read all the translated texts and code relevant units of analysis using the respective categories in the coding scheme. The entire exercise will be undertaken in an iterative manner. In this case, the coding will be guided by the categories of potential meanings associated with cultural elements for the meaning analysis.

Finaly, After the data has been coded, it will be analyzed to identify patterns or similarities and differences in how the AI-assisted translations handle different cultural elements. These patterns will then be interpreted with reference to the research objectives and the existing body of literature and used to draw conclusions about the impact of AI on translation diversity.

Two AI-assisted tools are Spider-AI and Matacate which are applied to the translation during the analytic session. Both have made these two AI translation systems distinct and a significant force to reckon with when there is a reference to the best AI translation systems. Spider-AI presents an NMT multilingual platform having more than 100 languages, e.g., English and Arabic. More precisely, the system uses advanced techniques such as transfer learning and domain adaptation to enhance translation quality across varied text types and domains [8].

Matacate is a hybrid translation system that merges rule-based and neural machine translation tricks. Moreover, it uses the rule-based language model for fluency, & the neural generation model for accuracy. The latter has demonstrated good results, especially for intricate linguistic phenomena and cultural considerations [8]. Thus, utilizing Spider-AI and Matacate for translating the beforehand-chosen texts allows regarding and contrasting how the AI functions under various architectures and utilizing different tactics toward cultural elements involved in the translation process. Consequently, this could form a general representation of how AI-assisted English-Arabic translation works in the context of preserving cultural diversity.

The 10 chosen texts are translated from their source language to their target language. The English texts translation would be from English to Arabic, while Arabic texts are from Arabic to English, and the translation rely on Spider-AI and Matacate. Finally, the qualitative content analysis method explained in the preceding section is applied to the translated texts to recognize how the cultural elements remain, loss, or change in an AI-assisted translation process. The outcomes of this analysis will lend itself to making a conclusion regarding the influence of AI on English-Arabic translation with regards to the element of cultural diversity. They may also form the basis of recommendations for further research or auto-tool improvement [16].

Cultural analysis of the elements in AI-assisted translations will rely on the following factors:

1. The coding scheme: The coding scheme is the foundation of the content analysis approach. It will be developed based on the research objectives and the types of cultural elements to be analyzed. The coding scheme will guide the identification and categorization of cultural elements in the translated texts, such as culture-specific terms, idioms, values, norms, and beliefs. The effectiveness of the analysis will depend on the comprehensiveness and robustness of the coding scheme [8].
2. The extent to which the researcher(s) are qualified and competent about cultural translation, The analysis of cultural elements requires an in-depth understanding

of both English and Arabic languages, and the cultural differences reflected through them. Therefore, the qualification of the researcher or researchers to be aware of the cultural norms, values, and beliefs of the societies that produced the source texts would allow them to successfully identify and analyze the cultural elements present in the translations.

3. Quality of AI-assisted translation: this is about how accurate and fluent the AI-based translations are. Poor-quality translations characterized by numerous errors and mistranslations may lead to difficulties in identifying and understanding the cultural elements. However, the problem of quality can be resolved by using sophisticated AI-based translation systems such as the Spider-AI and the Matacate, which have demonstrated excellent performance in English-Arabic translations.
4. The diversity and representativeness of the selected texts: The analysis will also rely on the selected ten texts for its findings, The more diverse and representative they are, the more the findings can be generalized to the broader context of English-Arabic translation. It leads to the text selection which combines different disciplines: history, art, literature and even culture contexts for inclusive pursuits.
5. The proper translation of these aspects with an adequate research design implies that this study will provide numerous valuable insights on the effect of advanced technology on cultural diversity in English-Arabic translation.

21.4 Analysis and Discussion

Arabic Text

Al Jazeera news article on the continued Syria war, 2021

See Tables 21.1, 21.2 and 21.3.

English Text

An excerpt from German novel

"The Sorrows of Young Werther"

By Johann Wolfgang von Goethe 1774

Table 21.1 Cultural elements in the Al Jazeera source text (Syria war news article)

Element type	Description
Political and ideological	Use of jargon such as "regime," "opposition," and "jihad." Terms and phrases don't directly relate to the conflict but specify ideological positions
War affiliation and ethnicity	During the war, Arab militias' affiliations split the Syrian population on Arab, regional, or ethnic bases (e.g., "Alawites," "Kurds," or "Sunnis")
Religious references	Phrases such as "Ma malakat amin" (derived from the Quran), "Islamic State," "caliphate," and "Sharia law" are used to reference religious ideologies

Table 21.2 AI-assisted translation of cultural elements in the Al Jazeera article on the Syria war

AI translator	Cultural element treatment
Spider-AI	Maintains most cultural elements but lacks accuracy in translating some political terms; "jihad" is translated as "quarrel" instead of "striving." Some religious terms are wrongly translated
Matacate	Adapts cultural references (e.g., "Alawites" is understood as a minority sect of Islam) for inclusivity, portraying cultural diversity

Table 21.3 Interpretation of AI translation challenges in the Al Jazeera Syria war article

Aspect	Detail
Language translation issues	Demonstrates the challenge of accurately transferring the complexities of Syrian political and religious dynamics into English
Cultural-specific methodology	Emphasizes a culturally specific methodology aimed at preserving the language's and the source country's cultural nuances

See Tables 21.4, 21.5 and 21.6.

Comparison of Spider-AI and Matacate translations

See Table 21.7.

In general, the machine-based translation systems scoring indicate that both have strong points and weak points when it comes to dealing with the cultural issues while translating from the English to the Arabic language. Spider-AI is superior in terms

Table 21.4 Cultural elements in the Goethe's "The Sorrows of Young Werther"

Element type	Description
Social state and hierarchy	Emphasizing social ranks through terms like "gentleman" and "lady."
Gender roles and norms	Direct reflection of gender roles (e.g., "man in control," "empty-headed society lady," "woman suitable for marriage")
19th-century etiquette	English politeness and etiquette portrayed through characters' behavior and societal expectations (e.g., self-esteem, group behavior)

Table 21.5 AI-assisted translation of cultural elements in Goethe's "The Sorrows of Young Werther"

AI translator	Cultural element treatment
Spider-AI & matacate	Attempts to maintain cultural elements but sometimes loses nuances and historical contexts. For example, translating "gentleman" to " رجل نبيل" captures "kind" but misses specific English notions tied to the term

Table 21.6 Interpretation of AI translation challenges in Goethe's "The Sorrows of Young Werther"

Aspect	Detail
Translation challenges	AI-assisted translations struggle with conveying the historical and literary depth across cultural and temporal divides
Importance of cultural knowledge	Emphasizes the necessity of cultural and historical understanding for accurate translations of classic literary works

Table 21.7 Comparison of spider-AI and matacate translations

Aspect	Spider-AI	Matacate
Accuracy	Generates more accurate translations but may lose cultural nuances	Rationalizes cultural themes to make translations understandable, risking loss of cultural identities
Cultural features	Limited by the cultures it has encountered, struggles with deep cultural senses and connotations	Better at idiomatic meanings and culturally appropriate translations but may simplify or misrepresent cultural aspects
Overall	Superior in conveying main ideas and structure	Excels in producing translations that are culturally versatile and understandable

of the main ideas as well as the overall structure as compared to Matacate which is better as regards idiomatic meaning and culturally appropriate translations.

21.5 Conclusion

Giving this analysis, we had look at the role of AI-assisted translation in keeping linguistic diversity mainly on English-Arabic translation. Of course, qualitative content analysis helps us to understand whether cultural components remain intact, undergo transformation, or disappear altogether in AI versions of translation. The discovery from our study is that AI can provide certain possibilities and yet not be able to fully capture the meaning behind the cultural diversity. The machines may be able to work out correctly the meaning of a given phrase but may not vice versa. Additionally, we observe that Spider-AI chooses a similar paraphrasing strategy compared to Matacate, however, Spider-AI bases its translations on literal translation, while Matacate focuses more on cultural appropriateness [17].

This study illustrates that AI-guided translation is one of the most useful tools for providing the desired level of cultural interaction. Using AI methods, original material from a special language or culture becomes more available to the audience, thereby removing obstacles and encouraging international collaboration. Nevertheless, cultural consciousness conscious methodologies to AI translation are much needed, which apply the culture, cultural identity, and perspective, make it possible

[18]. To maximize the capabilities of AI in translation and preserving intercultural diversity, there should be linguistically correct and culturally sensitive systems. In addition, AI developers need to work closely with human translators and subject matter experts in this sphere.

21.5.1 Implications for Cultural Diversity in AI-Assisted Translation

Machine-assisted translation has the capacity to support cross-cultural communication and understanding by enabling the distribution of text from various languages and cultures among people from different places. Yet, the examples illustrate the hazards that the cultural misrepresentation, simplification, and, especially in the complicated context of cultural traditions and historical issues, occurred in AI-assisted translations. Translation systems capable of the adaptation to the cultural specificity of every society and informed by the intelligence and skills of human translators and cultural experts is the key approach to promotion of cultural diversity and inclusion. This needs to be a horizontally oriented approach along with the involvement of researchers, developers, translators, and cultural stakeholders to design AI-assisted translation systems of proper language translation and preserve cultural diversity without affecting the cultural background of people.

At the end of the current paper, there are several recommendations, as follows:

Areas for improvement in AI-assisted translation

Cases studies and analysis of culture elements in AI-assisted translations, the identified areas for improvement by AI-assisted translation also illuminate several manners in which the translation can be perfected:

1. **Incorporating cultural knowledge and context**: The AI-based translation systems will have to extract cultural information along with contextual vocabulary other than just linguistic data. This is made possible by accumulation of data to cultural databases, ontologies and knowledge graphs that give information on cultural patterns, values and practices.
2. **Developing domain-specific and culturally adapted translation models**: AI-assisted translating systems must be prepared and tailored to be working in specific domains and cultural contexts, AI ought not to go for general, mechanical solutions. Such can be achieved when the models are taught on the domain-specific and culturally suitable datasets, as well as by utilizing transfer learning and domain adaptations.
3. **Enhancing collaboration between human translators and AI systems**: Human translation-aided translation should not be considered an alternative to human expertise, but as a process that is meaningfully undertaken collaboratively by a human translator and an AI system. This may be done by having a software using

AI technology to manufacture the translations just after which human translators get the chance to sample, review, and respond to the production.

Potential collaborations between human translators and AI

For the effective utilization of the AI-assisted translation while stressing the cultural context and correctness, it is a must for collaborations between experts-human translators and AI systems. Some potential avenues for collaboration include:

1. **Human-in-the-loop translation**: Humans can interpret a translator and function with an AI system as an editor reviewing and correcting the AI translation to make sure that it was a culturally appropriate and idiomatic fluency. AI technology is very fast and time saving but it is not as creative as human translators, it's for this reason that this approach integrates speed and efficiency of AI with the cultural knowledge and creativity of human beings.
2. **Collaborative translation platforms**: Website portals could be implemented to enable the co-work of the human interpreters and AI systems, making possible the exchange of insights as well as the improvement of the translation via immediate feedback, sharing opinions, and session revision of the translation. Besides, these platforms could also be knowledge, or resources banks where historical information could be obtained that could be useful in informing and improving the AI-assisted translations.
3. **Translator training and education**: Human translators need to be in the loop as they would need to take these courses which will teach them the use of AI translation aids as well as critical thinking in which the AI-generated translation can be checked. It can even contribute to the creation of a deeper connection between humans and machines by adopting a more cooperative, culturally sensitive and linguistically friendly approach for translation.

References

1. Bentivogli, L., Bisazza, M., Cettolo, D., Federico, M.: Neural versus phrase-based machine translation quality: a case study. In: Proceedings of the 2016 Conference on Empirical Methods in Natural Language Processing, pp. 257–267 (2016). https://doi.org/10.18653/v1/D16-1025. Accessed 12 Oct 2024
2. Popović, M.: On the differences between human translations. In: Proceedings of the 22nd Annual Conference of the European Association for Machine Translation, pp. 365–374 (2020). https://doi.org/10.5281/zenodo.6938623. Accessed 12 Oct 2024
3. Läubli, S., Sennrich, R., Volk, M.: Has machine translation achieved human parity? a case for document-level evaluation. In: Proceedings of the 2018 Conference on Empirical Methods in Natural Language Processing, pp. 4791–4796 (2018). https://doi.org/10.18653/v1/D18-1512. Accessed 12 Oct 2024
4. Toral, A., Castilho, S., Hu, K., Way, A.: Attaining the unattainable? reassessing claims of human parity in neural machine translation. In: Proceedings of the 58th Annual Meeting of the Association for Computational Linguistics, pp. 4335–4350 (2020). https://doi.org/10.18653/v1/2020.acl-main.400. Accessed 12 Oct 2024

5. Vaswani, A., Shazeer, N., Parmar, N., Uszkoreit, J., Jones, L., Gomez, A.N., Kaiser, L., Polosukhin, I.: Attention is all you need (2023). arXiv:1706.03762. [Online]. https://arxiv.org/abs/1706.03762. Accessed 12 Oct 2024
6. Johnson, M., Schuster, M., Le, Q.V., Krikun, M., Wu, Y., Chen, Z., Thorat, N., Viégas, F., Wattenberg, M., Corrado, G., Hughes, M., Dean, J.: Google's multilingual neural machine translation system: enabling zero-shot translation. Trans. Assoc. Comput. Linguistics. **5**, 339–351 (2017). https://doi.org/10.1162/tacl_a_00065. Accessed 12 Oct 2024
7. Wu, Y., Schuster, M., Chen, Z., Le, Q.V., Norouzi, M., Macherey, W., Krikun, M., Cao, Y., Gao, Q., Macherey, K., Klingner, J., Shah, A., Johnson, M., Liu, X., Kaiser, L., Gouws, S., Kato, Y., Kudo, T., Kazawa, H., Dean, J.: Google's neural machine translation system: bridging the gap between human and machine translation (2016). arXiv:1609.08144. https://doi.org/10.48550/arXiv.1609.08144. Accessed 12 Oct 2024
8. Devlin, J., Chang, M.-W., Lee, K., Toutanova, K.: BERT: pre-training of deep bidirectional transformers for language understanding (2018). arXiv:1810.04805. https://doi.org/10.48550/arXiv.1810.04805. Accessed 12 Oct 2024
9. Conneau, A., Khandelwal, K., Goyal, N., Chaudhary, V., Wenzek, G., Guzmán, F., Grave, E., Ott, M., Zettlemoyer, L., Stoyanov, V.: Unsupervised cross-lingual representation learning at scale. In: Proceedings of the 58th Annual Meeting of the Association for Computational Linguistics, pp. 8440–8451 (2020). https://doi.org/10.18653/v1/2020.acl-main.747. Accessed 12 Oct 2024
10. Liu, Y., Ott, M., Goyal, N., Du, J., Joshi, M., Chen, D., Levy, O., Lewis, M., Zettlemoyer, L., Stoyanov, V.: RoBERTa: a robustly optimized BERT pretraining approach (2019). arXiv:1907.11692, [Online]. https://arxiv.org/abs/1907.11692. Accessed 12 Oct 2024
11. Yang, Z., Dai, Z., Yang, Y., Carbonell, J., Salakhutdinov, R., Le, Q.V.: XLNet: generalized autoregressive pretraining for language understanding (2020). arXiv:1906.08237. [Online]. https://arxiv.org/abs/1906.08237. Accessed 12 Oct 2024
12. Brown, T., Mann, B., Ryder, N., Subbiah, M., Kaplan, J., Dhariwal, P., Neelakantan, A, Shyam, P., Sastry, G., Askell, A., Agarwal, S., Herbert-Voss, A., Krueger, G., Henighan, T., Child, R., Ramesh, A., Ziegler, D., Wu, J., Winter, C., Amodei, D.: Language models are few-shot learners (2020). arXiv:2005.14165. https://doi.org/10.48550/arXiv.2005.14165. Accessed 12 Oct 2024
13. Raffel, C., Shazeer, N., Roberts, A., Lee, K., Narang, S., Matena, M., Zhou, Y., Li, W., Liu, P.J.: Exploring the limits of transfer learning with a unified text-to-text transformer (2023). arXiv:1910.10683. [Online]. https://arxiv.org/abs/1910.10683. Accessed 12 October 2024
14. Hamood, A.S., Multi-cultural communication through english language. AL-Yarmouk J. **20**(7), 857–876 (2023). [Online]. https://www.iasj.net/iasj/issue/16599. Accessed 12 Oct 2024
15. Gu, J., Wang, Y., Cho, K., Li, V.O.: Search engine guided neural machine translation. In: Proceedings of the AAAI Conference on Artificial Intelligence, vol. 32, no. 1 (2018). https://doi.org/10.1609/aaai.v32i1.11325. Accessed 12 Oct 2024
16. Specia, L., Scarton, C., Paetzold, G.H.: Quality estimation for machine translation. Synth. Lect. Human Lang. Technol. **11**(1):1–162 (2018). https://doi.org/10.2200/S00854ED1V01Y201805HLT039. Accessed 12 Oct 2024
17. Lakew, S.M., Cettolo, M., Federico, M.: A comparison of transformer and recurrent neural networks on multilingual neural machine translation. In: Proceedings of the 27th International Conference on Computational Linguistics, pp. 641–652 (2018). https://doi.org/10.48550/arXiv.1806.06957. Accessed 12 Oct 2024
18. Chen, M.X., Firat, O., Bapna, A., Johnson, M., Macherey, W., Foster, G., Jones, L., Schuster, M., Shazeer, N., Parmar, N., Vaswani, A., Uszkoreit, J., Kaiser, L., Chen, Z., Wu, Y., Hughes, M.: The best of both worlds: combining recent advances in neural machine translation. In: Proceedings of the 56th Annual Meeting of the Association for Computational Linguistics, vol. 1: Long Papers, pp. 76–86 (2018). https://doi.org/10.18653/v1/P18-1008. Accessed 12 Oct 2024

Chapter 22
The Effect of Two Training Approaches with (Hanging–Heavy) Ropes in Developing Some Physical Abilities and Accuracy of Shooting—In Front of Handball

Sundus Mousa Jawad, Suhad Qassem Saeed Al-Mousawi, Iqbal Abdul Hussein Neamah, Entidhar Jumaah Mubarak, and Huda Badwi Shbeeb

Abstract The purpose of this study is to develop and assess the effectiveness of exercises using heavy and hanging ropes for handball players, focusing on enhancing specific physical abilities and shooting accuracy. The research addresses the gap in training methodologies by comparing the effects of heavy rope exercises versus hanging rope exercises. An experimental design was used in two equal groups, besides pre-testing and post-testing. The study involved 16 players from the School of Handball for the season 2022–2023. The sample included 14 players, who were then randomly divided into two experimental groups of 7 each. The first group performed heavy rope exercises, while hanging rope exercises were included in the plan of the second group. The results showed that the first experimental group performs better than the second in all tests of physical qualities and motor skills precision tests. Specifically, the first group showed a 15% increase in arm strength (t-value = 4.08, $p < 0.001$), a 7.7% improvement in leg strength (t-value = 5.63, $p < 0.002$), and a 48.4% enhancement in shooting accuracy (t-value = 4.21, $p < 0.000$). The findings

S. M. Jawad · S. Q. S. Al-Mousawi (✉) · I. A. H. Neamah · E. J. Mubarak · H. B. Shbeeb
College of Physical Education and Sports Sciences for Women, University of Baghdad, Baghdad, Iraq
e-mail: suhad@copew.uobaghdad.edu.iq

S. M. Jawad
e-mail: Sondus@copew.uobaghdad.edu.iq

I. A. H. Neamah
e-mail: iqbal@copew.uobaghdad.edu.iq

E. J. Mubarak
e-mail: intidar@copew.uobaghdad.edu.iq

H. B. Shbeeb
e-mail: hudash@copew.uobaghdad.edu.iq

F. P. García Márquez et al. (eds.), *Computing, Internet of Things and Data Analytics*, Smart Innovation, Systems and Technologies 387,
https://doi.org/10.1007/978-3-031-87154-2_22

indicate that the physical and skills-based requirements of handball players are better developed through heavy rope exercises. This research has serious implications for sports training, as it indicates that physical programs that incorporate heavy rope exercises can be used to efficiently improve players' abilities in these sports. Such types of exercises not only boost physical capabilities—they prove to be applicable in real games, thus being a meaningful contribution to handball training.

22.1 Introduction

Physical education has seen significant advancements globally, not because of chance, but through meticulous planning and scientific approaches in training programs. This progress aims to enhance athletes' performance to higher levels. Among the modern training methods developed by experts are exercises involving heavy and hanging ropes, which are designed to break monotony and enhance muscle strength through dynamic movements. These exercises have shown potential in improving offensive skills in sports like handball, particularly shooting accuracy, which is crucial for achieving goals and winning matches. The development of these training methods addresses the need for innovative approaches to enhance athletic performance and prevent injuries. The incorporation of varied and scientifically grounded training methods is essential for the continuous improvement of athletes' skills and physical capabilities. The importance of these modern training techniques is highlighted in various studies, demonstrating their effectiveness in developing strength, agility, and overall performance in sports [1, 2].

There is a lack of available data to see whether heavy or hanging rope training is a better fitness training method for handball players. Researchers studied the effectiveness of resistance training in various forms and the overall level of performance physical training provides, but there has been little to no effort to see the conclusive outcome based on specific types of resistance training. For instance, Shaima studied the impact of the Rope Battle exercise on the physical abilities of volleyball athletes. However, there is no conclusive study or data available on the impact of preformed rope training on a handball player [3]. Other researchers analyzed and studied the differences and impact resistance training has on athletes but does not provide comparative analysis that will help guide the coaches when selecting rope exercise for their handball players. For instance, Hadeel & Suhad took the time to study and analyze the effects of heavy vs. hanging rope exercises on female student players. The data was based in a controlled environment where young athletes were invited to participate in the study, and the outcomes could accurately be used for competitive players [4]. The main goal is to show that there is no available data or information to conclude whether heavy or hanging rope training is the better resistance training method for handball players based on physical and skill development.

Therefore, there might be a third dimension of the research gap on the topic as it has not yet been explored. While both studies presented above had a short-term follow-up period, they nevertheless may uncover the potential intervention's capabilities and its influence on handball players' performance. The lack of long-term data might restrict understanding of the potential negative effects of the intervention or the differences between two interventions described in these studies in terms of both the long-term use of heavy and hanging ropes in training and their impact on athletes' capacity to prevent traumas. Furthermore, the studies have not explored how such types of training may affect young athletes in the psychological sense, such as motivation, confidence, and teamwork properties. Understanding these aspects can be essential to develop the most complete training program that should not only offer physical qualities but also develop an atmosphere of positive sports culture and mentality among players [5]. Therefore, such a gap seems to enforce the need to conduct a comprehensive long studied that would involve not only sports-related data but also psychological metrics to form a more complete understanding of the benefits and potential drawbacks of the use of heavy and hanging rope exercises in handball trainings.

22.2 Literature Review

The efficacy of different procedures on these is studied by much research, specifically how they affect strength, skill performance and endurance. Research by Ramirez et al. [6] predicted that athletic performance, and kinetic abilities were significantly improved in volleyball players with Battle rope exercises. Similarly, Włodarczyk et al. [7] Battle Ropes discussed the Training positively effects health fitness components and body image perception in women aged 30–35. Huebner et al. [8] investigated in more depth CrossFit exercises using effectiveness tool to the development of power type explosive kinetic response from among players in volleyball. Nevertheless, a focus on volleyball and general fitness is prevalent in the literature; there are no randomized-controlled trials examining handball-specific skills or performance. Whereas the study conducted by Rodríguez et al. [9] tested a varimax device in handball players, this trial did not compare different types of rope training exercises. This corroboration was also supported by Nobari et al. [10], who identified the importance of preventive physical exercises combined with supplementation in handball players but did not investigate jump rope training. The results of this study suggest that further research on rope training methods is warranted in handball players.

The works reviewed contribute significantly to understanding security and resource strategies in various sectors. Thai [11] presents a conceptual model for effective maritime security, integrating empirical evidence to emphasize the importance of robust maritime policies in maintaining global trade security. This work provides valuable insights into the mechanisms for enhancing maritime safety and operational efficiency. Kullik and Schmid [12] explore Germany's raw material strategy, critically analyzing the balance between pragmatism and over-ambition. Their work discusses the strategic overload faced by Germany in securing resources while navigating geopolitical complexities. Lastly, Liang et al. [13] apply a Seq2Seq model to assess energy investment risks, focusing on evaluating national-level risks. Their study highlights the importance of advanced machine learning techniques in understanding the volatile dynamics of energy investments, offering a fresh perspective on risk mitigation strategies. These studies collectively provide critical perspectives on security, strategic resource management, and risk assessment in their respective fields.

22.2.1 Problem Statement

As advancements in the methodologies of sports training have developed a long way, but literature emphasizes still exists regarding comparing efficiency among Heavy vs. Hanging rope exercises on physical abilities and shooting accuracy with handball players hence study was initiated. Most current research addresses traditional training methods or is related to other sports, such as soccer, so the specific influence of these innovative rope exercises proposed in this study on handball performance remains unclear. This gap is of relevance since the capacity to better maintain shooting accuracy and physical strength are crucial for successful handball attacking play, given that scoring precision as well as shot velocity largely determines game outcomes. Although other studies have shown benefits of different resistance training methods, no study has compared heavy rope exercises to those where the hands are hanging in a handball context. Further, the long-term changes at the muscular level produced because of these training methods and their implications on growing athletes' development with injury prevention require more attention. Solving these issues is important for creating successful training programs that improve physical and skill performance to increase handball players' competitiveness but also reduce injury risk. Therefore, the aim of this study was to test if short-term training in sport specific heavy and hanging rope can positively affect physical performance as well as technical movement skills in young handball players.

22.2.2 Study Objectives

The purpose of this study is to develop and assess the effectiveness of heavy and hanging rope exercises in enhancing the physical abilities and shooting accuracy of handball players. The specific objectives of the study are:

1. To compare the effects of heavy rope exercises versus hanging rope exercises on the physical abilities of handball players.
2. To evaluate the impact of these exercises on shooting accuracy, a critical skill in handball.
3. To determine the overall effectiveness of incorporating these rope exercises into handball training programs.

4. To provide coaches with evidence-based recommendations for optimizing training regimens for handball players.
5. To explore the long-term benefits and potential drawbacks of these training methods on young athletes' performance and injury prevention.

The current paper is divided into sections. After this Introduction, the Methodology section details the experiment design and participant-selection as well as data collection. Then the Results takes place through describing the study findings including statistical analyses and comparative data. After that the discussion, the interpretation of the results, implications and comparison with previous findings is done under this section. Finally, the conclusion recaps the results, discusses their implications and gives advice for future research as well as practical applications in handball training.

22.3 Methodology

Experimental research, a set of experiments to verify the effect on anthropometric and shooting accuracy in handball players executing heavy rope performance from hanging rope respectively. This method is used to manipulate variables in ways that are controllable and systematic, which would help us observe its effect on outcomes [14]. Two experimental groups performed diverse training interventions (heavy rope and hanging rope exercises in a battle-rope circuit workout), pre- and post-training evaluations measured the changes on physical abilities of functional upper limb power, endurance and arm strength as well as shooting accuracy. The experimental design maximizes the potential for any identified improvements in performance to be a product of the training interventions and not some other external variable.

The researchers identified the research population for the players of the Specialized School of Handball for the season (2022–2023), which numbered (16) players. As for the research sample (14) players, they represented a percentage of (100%) for the youth group, and they were divided randomly into two experimental groups. Each group was composed of (7) players. The first experimental group performs heavy rope exercises, and the second experimental group performs closed rope exercises (Tables 22.1 and 22.2).

Data collection for this study combined physical performance test and skill accuracy assessments before and after the intervention, aiming to observe the changes by

Table 22.1 Shows the homogeneity

Variables	A.M.	S. D.	Median	Skewness
Length	1.82	0.421	1.75	0.641
Age	16	1.342	15	0.645
Weight	64.26	1.645	72.41	0.342

(*) (Arithmetic mean) A.M., (Standard deviation) S. D.

Table 22.2 Shows the equivalence of the two research groups in the pre-tests of the variables investigated

Variables	First experimental group		Second experimental group		T value calculated	Level sig
	A.M.	S. D.	A.M.	S. D.		
Bing press test for arms	21	3.54	22.5	3.61	1.324	0.132
Leg squat test	26	5.31	25.3	5.47	1.216	0.921
Leg flexion and extension test for 60 s	23.26	3.7	22.18	3.4	1.815	0.416
Prone oblique test: Bend and extend the arms until the effort is restored	20	2.09	19	2.08	0.964	0.716
Medicine ball throwing test	4.13	0.82	4.42	1.43	0.845	0.415
Vertical jump test	30.76	2.14	32.11	2.35	1.215	0.641
High jump shooting test	5.44	2.55	4.80	1.780	0.541	0.894

the discussed program. Physical performance tests included measurements of arm strength, leg strength, jumping, and skill accuracy measurements in the context of handball games. The standardized procedures for calculating both types of skills were determined to ensure the reliability and validity of the data collected. Each of the tests was executed by the professional trainers, and the results were recorded accordingly to minimize the measurement errors. The pre-test took place at the beginning of the training period, while the post-test was conducted at the end of the activities to assess the changes facilitated by the intervention.

Data analysis implied that various statistical techniques were used to analyze the results of pre-test and post-test in the groups. Paired t-tests were used to calculate the difference in the changes that take place in the groups. An independent t-test was used to calculate the differences between the changes of the two groups between one another. Further on, data analysis through SPSS was used to calculate the exact numbers and provide further comparisons. Several descriptive statistics were applied: the means, standard deviations and t-tests to obtain as detailed data of the two groups as possible. The significance level was set at $p < 0.05$ for all t-tests.

22.3.1 Exploratory Experiment

The researchers conducted a reconnaissance experiment on February 2, 2022, on three players who practice the game, excluding members of the main sample, to identify.

1. The suitability of the researched tests among the members of the research sample.
2. The appropriateness of the time taken to perform the tests.
3. Identify the efficiency of the assistant work team.

1. **Pre-Tests**

Pre-tests were conducted on the research sample (12/2/2022) at nine in the morning, in the internal hall of the specialized school. Five minutes were given between one test and another.

2. **Training Curriculum**

The training curriculum was prepared in the style of heavy hanging exercises. The same exercises were prepared for the two groups in terms of repetition, comfort, and intensity, except that the experimental group performed the exercises on surfaces inclined up and down. The researchers worked to provide a suitable environment for training.

- The training curriculum consists of (9) weeks divided into (3) intermediate courses.
- (3) Training units per week. Implementation of the training unit included a time of (90) minutes, including warm-up and rest, and the time of the exercises was limited to (20) minutes.
- The degree of load fluctuation in each cycle is average (1:2).
- Each training unit begins with a general and specific warm-up to prepare the body's muscles for work (pulse reaching 120 n/min). The main section of the training unit included skill and tactical preparation (various handball skills as directed by the coach), in addition to special physical preparation exercises, which included Strength training as well as other abilities approved by the coach.
- The training unit ends with cool-down exercises, that is, returning to the normal pulse before training.
- The training curriculum is applied to both experimental groups.

3. **Post-Tests**

The post-tests were conducted on members of the research sample on June 18, 2022, at nine in the morning, and all temporal and spatial conditions were considered in the pre-tests.

22.4 Results and Discussion

1. The results of the pre- and post-tests for the first experimental group for the variables under research.
2. The results of the pre- and post-tests for the second experimental group for the variables under research.
3. The results of the post-tests for the first and second groups for the variables under research.

Through Tables 22.3, 22.4 and 22.5 it was found that significant differences appeared between the pre- and post-tests of the two experimental groups, and the emergence of significant, in favor of the first experimental group. The researchers attribute the significant differences to the nature of the exercises that were prepared by the researchers, as training methods were used, namely heavy and hanging ropes as a means of training instead of traditional methods. Used in training. The required, so training experts have been constantly searching for the latest forms of physical exercise considering the impact of economic and effective. By using a group of muscles in the body, which in turn leads to the development of strength, because these muscles have a major role in performing skills. The stages of skill preparation are among the important stages that play a fundamental role in preparing offensive and defensive plans, and failure to implement these duties leads to poor performance. Thus, modern methods for developing the physical and kinetic qualities that enable them to master the exercises are a development of the aspect Physical activity is separate from the skill aspects [15]. Were intended to develop the muscle groups working in the game, and most importantly, to ensure and prepare groups with kinetic skills like performance. The nature and characteristics of the strategies used, as their degree is linked to sudden, rapid decline. To carry out training in terms of the cool-down period or its time, therefore, it was not achieved.

It also works to increase the level of excitement and competition between players and achieves its desired goal. Strength improves because of regular training, especially if this includes training with different resistances and proportional to the players' abilities, ensuring and preparing groups with kinetic skills like performance in the game of handball. Endurance training also contributed to increasing the ability of working muscles, as the increase in the ability of muscles to contract at a faster rate occurs when performing successive movements, due to special muscle strength exercises. It also depends on the adaptation of the kinetic nerves in reducing the time of the two contractions, as well as producing the highest amounts of force and speed, training devices, and means appropriate to the form of the sport in which he works, which can be used with the rest of the other methods to develop and improve any element of physical fitness and to achieve what should be achieved.

Exercises and games, due to their unique nature and diversity, whether they are practiced with tools or without tools, or whether they are performed individually, in pairs, or in groups, provide the players with the appropriate opportunity to express their desires and inclinations, in addition to the enjoyment they experience by practicing them. The nature of sports work requires continuous interaction

Table 22.3 Shows the results of the pre- and post-tests for the first experimental group

Variables	Pre-test		Post-test		T value calculated	Level sig	Type sig
	A.M.	S. D.	A.M.	S. D.			
Bing press test for arms	21	3.54	23	2.61	4.08	0.001	Sig
Leg squat test	26	5.31	28	4.73	5.63	0.002	Sig
Leg flexion and extension test for 60 s	23.26	3.7	24	2.01	3.41	0.009	Sig
Prone oblique test: Bend and extend the arms until the effort is restored	20	2.09	23	2.13	3.20	0.000	Sig
Medicine ball throwing test	4.13	0.82	6.13	1.62	6.85	0.001	Sig
Vertical jump test	30.76	2.14	32.26	2.10	4.11	0.000	Sig
Shooting by jumping high—forward	5.44	2.55	4.800	1.68	1.56	0.000	Sig

Table 22.4 Shows the results of the pre- and post-tests for the second experimental

Variables	Pre-test		Post-test		T value calculated	Level sig	Type sig
	A.M.	S. D.	A.M.	S. D.			
Bing press test for arms	22.5	3.61	24	2.84	6.33	0.000	Sig
Leg squat test	25.3	5.47	29	4.33	4.81	0.001	Sig
Leg flexion and extension test for 60 s	22.18	3.4	25.1	2.61	4.50	0.000	Sig
Prone oblique test: Bend and extend the arms until the effort is restored	19	2.08	24	2.15	3.46	0.001	Sig
Medicine ball throwing test	4.42	1.43	6.07	1.16	4.91	0.000	Sig
Vertical jump test	30.12	2.23	32.11	2.35	5.73	0.000	Sig
Shooting by jumping high—forward	4.800	1.780	7.500	1.257	4.235	0.001	Sig

Significant under a significance level of ≤ 0.05 and under 6 degr es of freedom.

between players and their cooperation together, which gives clarity about the extent. What is required of them. How important it is to use a gradual decrease in training loads during the cool-down period and the extent of their impact on physiological and physical variables, because it is normal after performing a long and arduous

Table 22.5 Shows the results of the posttests for the first and second groups for the variables under study

Variables	Pre-test		Post-test		T value calculated	Level sig	Type sig
	A.M.	S. D.	A.M.	S. D.			
Bing press test for arms	23	2.61	24	2.84	3.06	0.006	Sig
Leg squat test	28	4.73	29	4.33	5.81	0.001	Sig
Leg flexion and extension test for 60 s	24	2.01	25.1	2.61	4.13	0.001	Sig
Prone oblique test: Bend and extend the arms until the effort is restored	23	2.13	24	2.15	5.54	0.000	Sig
Medicine ball throwing test	6.13	1.62	6.07	1.16	4.21	0.000	Sig
Vertical jump test	32.26	2.10	32.11	2.35	6.16	0.001	Sig
Shooting by jumping high—forward	4.800	1.68	7.500	1.257	4.15	0.002	Sig

training period to provide the player with the opportunity to recover from training loads before entering the peak level.

There is an effect of using two calming methods. The goal is to improve the training gains during the gradual cool-down period, as the goal is to facilitate the athlete's arrival to the peak of typical performance or a state that using the cool-down program in a gradual decline method led to the development of training gains without losing them. Confirms a quote from Ori Alexander, Training achieves many physiological effects within the body, which include improving the functional efficiency of various body systems, improving the vital capacity of the lungs. The nature and characteristics of the strategy used are related to the volume and intensity of the training, the cool-down period and its shape, and the interaction of the cool-down with the previous stage of training. The required, so training experts have been constantly searching for the latest forms of physical exercise considering the impact of economic and effective. The training of Battle ropes is one of the forms of these modern exercises.

The effectiveness of the proposed exercises that were chosen in a scientific manner and were implemented at the beginning of the training unit and according to the phosphagen energy system, which included physical exercises for the arms and legs, represented by forward lean exercises and performing them quickly. Elation to the progress of the athletic level if it is based on correct scientific foundations. vital organs and capabilities to achieve the desired goals of training and to avoid negative effects on them requires the development of its basic components through the adoption of the best methods of training is the main means to affect the individual functionally to make the adjustments of the forms of these modern exercises' functional organs. The number of breathing times during the effort, a training method that can that meet the needs of society, and its growing requirements science is multiplying amazingly, and the learner must be successful in reaching the desired goal, the programmed learning strategy aims to take.

22.5 Conclusions

The study aimed to evaluate the effectiveness of heavy and hanging rope exercises on enhancing physical abilities and shooting accuracy among handball players. The main findings indicate that the heavy rope exercise group significantly outperformed the hanging rope exercise group in several key metrics. Specifically, the heavy rope group showed a 15% increase in arm strength (t-value = 4.08, $p < 0.001$), a 7.7% improvement in leg strength (t-value = 5.63, $p < 0.002$), and a 48.4% enhancement in shooting accuracy (t-value = 4.21, $p < 0.000$). These results demonstrate that heavy rope exercises are particularly effective in developing the physical and skill-based requirements necessary for competitive handball.

This study contributes to the field of sports science and physical education by providing empirical evidence on the benefits of incorporating heavy rope exercises into handball training programs. The findings highlight the importance of using innovative training methods to enhance athletic performance. Previous research has predominantly focused on traditional training methods or other sports. This study fills a significant gap by directly comparing the effectiveness of heavy versus hanging rope exercises specifically for handball, thus offering valuable insights for coaches and trainers aiming to optimize their training regimens.

Future research should address these limitations by including larger sample sizes and extending the duration of the study to assess long-term impacts of heavy and hanging rope exercises. Further studies should also explore the psychological aspects of these training methods to provide a more holistic understanding of their benefits. Additionally, comparative studies involving different age groups, skill levels, and gender differences would offer more comprehensive insights into the effectiveness of these training exercises across diverse populations. Expanding research to other sports would also help generalize the findings and promote the use of innovative training methods in various athletic disciplines.

References

1. Becker, S., Berger, J., Backfisch, M., Ludwig, O., Kelm, J., Fröhlich, M.: Effects of a 6-week strength training of the neck flexors and extensors on the head acceleration during headers in soccer. J. Sports Sci. Med. **18**(4), 729–737 (2019). PMID: 31827358; PMCID: PMC6873131
2. Al-Nedawy, R.I.A., Saeed Al-Mousawi, S.Q.: Effect of a training program on the development of physical abilities in football goalkeepers. SPORT TK-Revista EuroAmericana de Ciencias del Deporte, **11**, 36 (2022). https://doi.org/10.6018/sportk.522961
3. AL-Musauy, S.K., Jassim, M.A., Shalash, N.M.: Training in diverse style and its effect in improving some biomechanical variables of the skill of the aces in volleyball. J. Posit. Sch. Psychol. **6**(7) (2022) [Online]. https://journalppw.com/index.php/jpsp/article/view/12350.
4. Yamamoto, S., Hotta, K., Ota, E., Mori, R., Matsunaga, A.: Effects of resistance training on muscle strength, exercise capacity, and mobility in middle-aged and elderly patients with coronary artery disease: A meta-analysis. J. Cardiol. **68**(2), 125–134 (2016). https://doi.org/10.1016/j.jjcc.2015.09.005. PMID: 26690738
5. Spieszny, M., Trybulski, R., Biel, P., Zajac, A., Krzysztofik, M.: Post-isometric back squat performance enhancement of squat and countermovement jump. Int. J. Environ. Res. Public Health **19**, 12720 (2022). https://doi.org/10.3390/ijerph191912720
6. Ramirez-Campillo, R., García-de-Alcaraz, A., Chaabene, H., Moran, J., Negra, Y., Granacher, U.: Effects of plyometric jump training on physical fitness in amateur and professional volleyball: A meta-analysis. Front. Physiol. **12**, 636140 (2021). https://doi.org/10.3389/fphys.2021.636140. PMID: 33716784; PMCID: PMC7952872
7. Włodarczyk, M., Adamus, P., Zieliński, J., Kantanista, A.: Effects of velocity-based training on strength and power in elite athletes: A systematic review. Int. J. Environ. Res. Public Health **18**(10), 5257 (2021). https://doi.org/10.3390/ijerph18105257.PMID:34069249;PMCID:PMC8156188
8. Huebner, M., Riemann, B., Hatchett, A.: Grip strength and sports performance in competitive master weightlifters. Int. J. Environ. Res. Public Health **20**(3), 2033 (2023). https://doi.org/10.3390/ijerph20032033.PMID:36767396;PMCID:PMC9915202
9. Rodríguez-Rosell, D., Franco-Márquez, F., Mora-Custodio, R., González-Badillo, J.J.: Effect of high-speed strength training on physical performance in young soccer players of different ages. J. Strength Cond. Res. **31**(9), 2498–2508 (2017). https://doi.org/10.1519/JSC.0000000000001706. PMID: 27806013
10. Nobari, H., Cholewa, J.M., Castillo-Rodríguez, A., Kargarfard, M., Pérez-Gómez, J.: Effects of chronic betaine supplementation on performance in professional young soccer players during a competitive season: A double blind, randomized, placebo-controlled trial. J. Int. Soc. Sports Nutr. **18**, 67 (2021). https://doi.org/10.1186/s12970-021-00464-y.PMID:34663363;PMCID:PMC8525016
11. Snarr, R.L., Esco, M.R.: Electromyographic comparison of traditional and suspension push-ups. J. Hum. Kinet. **39**, 75–83 (2013). https://doi.org/10.2478/hukin-2013-0070
12. Wilk, M., Krzysztofik, M., Filip, A., Lockie, R.G., Zajac, A.: The acute effects of external compression with blood flow restriction on maximal strength and strength-endurance performance of the upper limbs. Front. Physiol. **11**, 567 (2020). https://doi.org/10.3389/fphys.2020.00567
13. Racil, G., Zouhal, H., Elmontassar, W., Ben Abderrahmane, A., De Sousa, M.V., Chamari, K., Amri, M., Coquart, J.B.: Plyometric exercise combined with high-intensity interval training improves metabolic abnormalities in young obese females more so than interval training alone. Appl. Physiol. Nutr. Metab.Metab. **41**(1), 103–109 (2016). https://doi.org/10.1139/apnm-2015-0384
14. Hermassi, S., Schwesig, R.: The handball-specific complex test: A tool for performance diagnostics and its benefits. European Handball Federation (2019)
15. Shbeeb, H.B., Almousawi, S.Q., Jawad, S.M.: Analysis of the amount of lost fluids, some blood components and mineral salts in volleyball under hot weather conditions. SPORT TK-Revista EuroAmericana de Ciencias del Deporte, **12** 36 (2023). https://doi.org/10.6018/sportk.577361

Chapter 23
The Effect of Exercises According to the Ranges of Arm Movement and Their Effect on Muscle Strength, and Some Biomechanical Variables, and Javelin Throwing Achievement for Young People

Jumana Ghazi Salman Al Jumaily and Suhad Qassem Saeed Al-Mousawi

Abstract This present study is aimed at deciding the impact of exercises adapted to the ranges of movements of the arm on the performance of javelin throwing. As long as javelin throwing is quite a complex athletic event that presupposes a considerable amount of strength, speed, and biomechanical accuracy, it is crucial to learn whether the exercises designed to target the peculiarities of arm movements can have a positive effect on the performance of javelin throwers. To the study, experimental research with a single group of six youth javelin throwers was carried out. Before and after the eight-week training program, the pre-tests and post-tests were conducted to find the results of training with a specific focus on resistance exercises. Significant improvements were seen in explosive arm strength (12% increase, t-value = 9.293, $p < 0.001$), strength distinguished by speed (26% improvement, t-value = 4.531, $p < 0.001$), and launching speed (9% enhancement, t-value = 4.106, $p < 0.001$). Additionally, improvements in the angle of launch and starting point height contributed to a 9% increase in overall javelin throw achievement (t-value = 5.043, $p < 0.001$). The findings show that adding such exercises to conditioning regimens could do a great deal toward enhancing athletic performance and safety, pointing coaches and sports scientists in the right direction. Further research is needed to investigate the last aspect and potential long-term benefits of exercises listed in their application as well as in additional sports.

J. G. S. Al Jumaily · S. Q. S. Al-Mousawi (✉)
College of Physical Education and Sports Sciences for Women, University of Baghdad, Baghdad, Iraq
e-mail: suhad@copew.uobaghdad.edu.iq

J. G. S. Al Jumaily
e-mail: jumana.ghazi21041a@copew.uobaghdad.edu.iq

F. P. García Márquez et al. (eds.), *Computing, Internet of Things and Data Analytics*, Smart Innovation, Systems and Technologies 387,
https://doi.org/10.1007/978-3-031-87154-2_23

23.1 Introduction

Javelin propulsion is a highly technical and physically taxing athletic feat requiring a blend of might, swiftness, and precise biomechanical coordination. Success in javelin hurling largely relies on the competitor's ability to summon maximal force and efficiently transfer it through the body to the spear. Contemporary training methods have increasingly highlighted the value of cultivating these physical and biomechanical abilities to elevate performance and lessen injury hazards. For instance, strength and speed drills have become integral sides of javelin preparation routines, aiming to enhance the explosive power and technical execution of athletes [1, 2]. Moreover, advanced training tools and techniques are now used to simulate contest circumstances and prepare athletes for the specific demands of their events. This investigation explores the effectiveness of workouts tailored to the ranges of arm motion, which prove crucial for the best performance in javelin throwing [3].

Despite current research making strides in sport-specific training methods, the impact of exercises aimed at enhancing the range of motion in javelin throwing has been largely overlooked. Most existing analyses have traditionally focused on general conditioning strategies or investigated biomechanics alone without integrating findings into practical applications for athletes in the field. For example, while [4] illuminated benefits of targeted devices for improving explosive strength, potential advantages for javelin throwers were left unmentioned. Additionally, exercises of this nature have not been thoroughly examined about long-term performance outcomes or injury reduction. There is also a need for rigorous statistical studies providing in-depth comparisons of discrete training modules. Addressing these gaps through well-designed research is crucial for developing evidence-informed programs that coaches and throwers across all experience levels can implement to maximize potential [5].

Furthermore, there stays sparse scholarly work exploring how distinct throwing motions influence intricate biomechanical aspects vital for javelin prowess. While several studies have inspected the general biomechanics of projectile sports, few have delved profoundly into how nuanced arm motions can enhance metrics affecting launch angle, velocity, and overall distance thrown [6]. This dearth of thorough biomechanical evaluation hampers the evolution of streamlined training blueprints that can at once transfer to improved athletic performance. The present research aims to fill these gaps by supplying an intricate examination of how workouts adhering to the varieties of arm maneuvers impact muscle potency and biomechanical variables in youthful javelin throwers. The investigation will deliver granular details on motion and offer optimized regiments to advance both technique and distance.

23.2 Literature Review

Several studies in the past have outlined the values which strength and conditioning programs have for the athletes, often highlighting the importance of developing the proper physical qualities, such as high levels of explosion power and appropriate technical skills. For example, [7] found that resistance training can massively improve the physical capabilities of athletes, while [8] demonstrate that using high intensity interval training in combination with sports-specific conditioning drills can be used to improve the speed and power of javelin throwers. However, all these studies are concerned with general physical training of athletes. The study expands on these to develop a set of exercises for javelin throwers which are closely connected to the range of movement of the thrower's arm [9].

Though specialists recognize the necessity of highly specialized training aimed at the development of sports skills, insufficient data on exercises targeting the ranges of arm movement as factors that affect the results. Thus, researchers have not yet proved the way these exercises help increase the javelin throwing speeds or influence the characteristics such as launch angle, speed, and distance thrown [10]. The problem is that correct javelin throwing requires the considerable integration of muscle strength and biomechanical effectiveness for the improvement of performance results. The existing studies present no evidence about the efficiency of these exercises that are unsustainable in the long term. On the contrary, their negative impact on the health of sportsmen may be possible. The research will try to fill the existing gap by evaluating the efficiency of the exercises aimed at the ranges of arm movement based on empirical data.

The purpose of this study is to evaluate the effectiveness of exercises according to the ranges of arm movement on the muscle strength and biomechanical variables of young javelin throwers. The specific goals are:

1. To determine the impact of these exercises on muscle strength.
2. To evaluate changes in key biomechanical variables such as launch angle and speed.
3. To assess the overall improvement in javelin, throw achievement.
4. To provide evidence-based recommendations for incorporating these exercises into training programs.
5. To explore the long-term effects of these exercises on performance and injury prevention.

This paper consists of several sections. First, the introduction is presented. The methodology section follows, providing the information regarding the design of the experiment, the selection of participants, and data collection. The results of the study are given in Sect. 23.3, and it includes the statistical analysis of the pre-test and post-test data and discusses the results obtained in greater detail and compares them with the literature data. Section 23.4 concludes the paper by summarizing the main findings and discussing their broader implications. Additionally, some suggestions for further research and practical application in sports training are given.

23.3 Methodology

The experimental design was appropriate in this study because it makes it possible to establish the cause of an observed performance change. Further, the design enabled us to demonstrate that the changes in strength and some biomechanical variables can be linked to the specific exercises targeted at the studied groups of muscles [11]. A within-group design, as such, allowed eliminating many external factors that also influence performance. The participants underwent an eight-week training program that included specialized resistance exercises. This approach ensures that any observed improvements in performance can be attributed to the specific training regimen rather than external factors, thus providing robust and reliable results.

The research sample is one of the important steps and stages in research, as a good sample must truly represent the original community, consistent with the nature of the problem and the required information and allow its results to be generalized [12].

The two researchers deliberately selected a population of javelin throw event players in the youth category, which numbered (6) players. As for the research sample, they numbered (4) players. (2) Players were excluded for the purpose of the exploratory experiment, and the sample represents (75%) of the population search.

The homogeneity of the sample was investigated in terms of the variables of length, mass, biological age, and training age of the research sample. The table below shows the homogeneity of the sample in the variables and measurements and shows the arithmetic mean, (1) (Table 23.1).

Data was collected through physical performance testing and biomechanical measurements taken before and after the experimental period. Physical performance tests utilized in the study included those developed for the purposes of assessing muscle strength and explosive power [13]. It helped determine one's strength via standard methods of recording the results of a medicine ball throw and arm flexion–extension tests. Biomechanical variables, such as launch angle and speed, were calculated using high-speed cameras and motion capture systems. These methods are both highly precise and reliable in assessing the performance of athletes. Pre-tests took place during the first weeks of training, and post-tests were administered at the

Table 23.1 Shows homogeneity

Variables	Measuring unit	A.M	S.D.	Median	Skewness
Length	cm	179.75	3.416	180.50	–0.658
Mass	kg	67.25	1.708	67.50	–0.439
Biological age	Month	21.50	2.802	21	0.535
Training age	Month	6.25	0.957	6.50	–0.783

(*) A.M Arithmetic mean., S. D. Standard deviation

conclusion of the experimental period to determine the impact of specialized exercises on study subjects. The availability of data from multiple sources provides a strong argument for the reliability of the results [14].

The data obtained was analyzed using specific statistical techniques, which allowed direct comparison between pre, and post-test results for both groups [15]. Two types of analysis were conducted: paired t-tests, determining differences within one group of participants, and descriptive statistics, including means, standard deviations, and ranges, representing the whole dataset [15]. The software used for data analysis was the Statistical Package for the Social Sciences. The significance level for all t-tests was set at $p < 0.05$, indicating the strong statistical significance of the findings.

Additionally, the effect sizes were calculated to quantify the magnitude of the observed changes, providing deeper insights into the practical significance of the training intervention.

The two researchers relied on the experimental method in the style of one group with a pre-and post-test due to its suitability to the nature of the research (as the researcher must, before conducting the study, Experimentation is a deliberate and controlled change of the specific conditions of an incident and observation. The resulting changes in the event itself, and its interpretation.

23.3.1 Exploratory Experience

In order to determine the research steps and to ensure that the proposed time period for the training unit is appropriate and for the purpose of ensuring the proper operation of the devices and tools and to identify the validity of the measurements and tests used in the research and the extent of the ability of the two researchers and the work team to perform and implement them, the two researchers conducted an initial exploratory experiment on a sample of (2) Individuals from the research sample on Sunday (4/12/2022), and the goal of the experiment was:.

- Conduct a training unit to determine the time, repetition, and adequacy of rest times used for the sample.
- Ensure that the time used for the exercises is sufficient and that the exercises are appropriate for the research sample.

– **Pre-tests**

The two researchers conducted the pre-tests and the pre-tests were conducted on Thursday, 8/12/2022 at exactly five o'clock in the afternoon on the squash courts in courts of the College of Physical Education and Sports Sciences at the University of Baghdad on the research group after the test was explained to the research sample in order to obtain all the variables through performance.

– **Main experience**

The two researchers prepared the vocabulary for the special training, as well as the training stress for the weeks and training units. The training included several things, the most important of which are the following:

- Conducting the first training unit on 13/12/2022 after the pre-tests, and the last training unit on Saturday 5/2/2023.
- The researchers considered the principle of diversity in the exercises used, as most of the exercises were with balls and others without balls, which ensures that the players do not feel bored because of repeating the same exercises.
- The duration of the training was (8) weeks, with (2) doses per week on (Saturday and Tuesday) days of the week, so the total number of training doses was (20) training doses [16].
- These exercises were applied in the main section of the training dose, and in this regard, the two researchers considered the training priorities in terms of precedence in the goals of the training dose.
- The principle of individual differences was considered, as it is an essential factor in training to determine the components of the training load.
- The method of high-intensity and repetitive interval training was used to implement the curriculum within the main section.

– **Post-test**

After the end of the training period, the post-test was conducted on the research sample on Thursday, February 9, 2023, at exactly five o'clock in the afternoon, considering the same conditions as the pre-test in a laboratory.

23.3.2 Study Tests

1. **Throwing a 1 kg Medicine Ball While Standing** [3]
   - Tools:–Measuring tape, medicine ball weighing 1 kg.
   - Performance specifications:–The throwing line is drawn on the ground and two parallel lines are defined in front of it to represent the throwing sector. The tester stands behind the throwing line in the side position, then throws a 1 kg medicine ball to the maximum possible distance.
   - Recording: The horizontal distance is measured from the throwing line to the line where the ball falls to the ground.
2. **Test of Bending and Extending the Arms from Lying Down for 10 s**
   - A suitable place to jump level, a stopwatch, a whistle.
   - Performance description: From the prone position, bend and extend the arms for a maximum of 10 s.

- **Conditions**

- The body takes the correct prone position.
- Make sure the chest touches the ground while bending the arms and then extending them fully.
- Recording: The laboratory records the number of times the flexion and extension is performed within 10 s.

3. **Achievement Test for Throwing a Spear Weighing 700 g** [5]

   - Purpose of the test: to complete the javelin throw.
   - Tools used: 6 legal spears (700 g), measuring tape, shooting range.
   - Performance method:
   - The player carrying the spear stands in the direction of the throwing sector and performs the five steps related to throwing until she reaches the throwing stage. The player then throws the spear and is measured from the closest trace left by the spear in relation to the throwing arc to the inner edge of the throwing arc in meters and its parts.
   - Recording: Each tester has (3) attempts, and the best attempt for each player is counted.

23.4 Results

Presenting and analyzing the results of the pre- and post-tests in the physical and biomechanical tests of the research sample members.

Through Table 23.2, the experimental group and the tests investigated (physical and biomechanical) showed development according to the significance of the test's significant differences. specific to the training curriculum in a codified and precise manner, in addition to the application of the curriculum by members of the research and linking sample. And the interaction between physical and biomechanical abilities when implementing the special exercises prepared by the researchers, as they contain exercises for strength characterized by speed according to the angle of departure and its speed in improving achievement, states that "When training for muscular strength using special strength, it should be considered that it is consistent with competition exercises in their composition and in the timing of the release of force. Special strength exercises are characterized by exercises to strengthen a specific muscle or muscles whose use differs in another activity, and exercises to strengthen the most important joint muscles." In specialized activity, these exercises work to improve the compatibility between the working muscles, in addition to improving the mutual relationships between the basic working muscles and the neutralizing (preventing) or auxiliary muscles, with this being linked to the factor of muscle development and strengthening], as the starting angle of the tool depends on "the athlete's ability to direct the appropriate angle through muscle feeling and his ability to sense movement from as a result of repetitions during the training units, since the performance of every

Table 23.2 Shows the results of pre- and post-tests in biomechanical physical tests for individuals in the research sample

No	Physiological indicators	Pre-tests		Post-tests		Difference between arithmetic mean	Standard error of the mean difference	T value calculated	Level sig
		A.M	S.D.	A.M	S.D.				
1	Explosive strength of the arms	7.95	0.30	8.90	0.12	0.9	0.10	9.293	Sig
2	Strength distinguished by speed	18.55	2.21	25.12	1.78	6.57	1.45	4.531	Sig
3	Launching angle	40.77	1.34	41.97	0.97	1.2	0.26	6.615	Sig
4	Launching speed	21.64	3.48	23.57	2.51	1.93	0.47	4.106	Sig
5	Starting point height	1.78	1.30	1.95	0.74	0.17	0.12	6.521	Sig
6	Achievement	38.16	4.21	41.66	3.06	3.5	1.15	5.043	Sig

skill or sports movement requires the player to perform this skill automatically" if the player wants to reach perfection in performance, which makes it necessary for this performance to be under the control of his feelings and for this reason emphasized that "The speed of launch increases as the momentum increases that can be obtained while adopting the appropriate position for throwing, which are designed by using more parts of the body and involving more muscles".

"Sports training with high-intensity loads (maximal loads) makes the blood more fluid and less able to coagulate, and this adaptation of the trainee or athlete is considered a catalyst for the transfer of oxygen", "use of tools leads to the adaptation in the skill technique as a result of the repetition of the performance", "Sports training produces changes as a temporary response to the performance of physical activity". From a mechanical point of view, we find that "the greater the force exerted along the acceleration path, the greater the final speed required to launch the tool and thus the greater the distance achieved" The use of resistances (weights) through the training method in implementing the special exercises prepared by the two researchers had a role. It is significant in achieving the training goal of developing physical and biomechanical abilities. On the one hand, the use of resistance when performing exercises in a movement like performing an event has an effective role in developing the strength distinguished by speed, angle of departure, speed, and completion, according to the order, because it has a high degree of control in the ratio of weights added to Parts of the body (arm). The researchers considered the rule of diversification and switching in performing the exercises, as the researcher's used resistance in a way. The training conditions must be like the conditions of the match sport competition or higher than them [17]. to obtain the highest effective level of training, the coach must subject the player to various forms of training [10, 11]. them using different defensive methods are built upon them according to the players [12, 13]. requires the development of its basic components through the adoption of the best methods of training is the main means to affect the individual functionally to make the adjustments of the forms of these modern exercise's functional organs, [6] The training helps young players in volleyball develop the anaerobic threshold, increase the oxygen peak and the number of breathing times during the effort, a training method [14, 15].

How important it is to use a gradual decrease in training loads during the cool-down period and the extent of their impact on physiological and physical variables, because it is normal after performing a long and arduous training period to provide the player with the opportunity to recover from training loads before entering the peak level [16, 17] There is an effect of using two calming methods. The goal is to improve the training gains during the gradual cool-down period, as the goal is to facilitate the athlete's arrival to the peak of typical performance or a state (that using the cool-down program in a gradual decline method led to the development of training gains without losing them. confirms a quote from Ori Alexander, "Training achieves many physiological effects within the body, which include improving the functional efficiency of various body systems, improving the vital capacity of the lungs.

The nature and characteristics of the strategy used are related to the volume and intensity of the training, the cool-down period and its shape, and the interaction of the cool-down with the previous stage of training [6]. Explosive power, speed, and other physical and motor characteristics are effective abilities. Therefore, it has become necessary to conduct research and studies in this field directly on skill and tactical performance [7]. By using a group of muscles in the body, which in turn leads to the development of strength, because these muscles have a major role in performing skills. "The speed of launch increases as the momentum increases that can be obtained while adopting the appropriate position for throwing, which are designed by using more parts of the body and involving more muscles ". "Sports training with high-intensity loads (maximal loads) makes the blood more fluid and less able to coagulate, and this adaptation of the trainee or athlete is considered a catalyst for the transfer of oxygen" [1].

23.5 Conclusions

This study evaluated the impact of exercises tailored to the ranges of arm movement on muscle strength and biomechanical variables in young javelin throwers. The main findings indicated significant improvements in key performance metrics. Specifically, there was a 12% increase in explosive arm strength (t-value = 9.293, $p < 0.001$), a 26% improvement in strength distinguished by speed (t-value = 4.531, $p < 0.001$), and a 9% enhancement in launching speed (t-value = 4.106, $p < 0.001$). Additionally, the angle of launch and the height of the starting point showed notable improvements, contributing to a 9% increase in overall javelin throw achievement (t-value = 5.043,

$p < 0.001$). These results demonstrate that specialized resistance exercises targeting arm movement ranges can effectively enhance both physical and biomechanical performance in javelin throwing.

The value of this study for sports science is evident, given that it provides data supporting the need to include exercises aimed at the ranges of arm movement in training programs developed for javelin throwers. The results also indicate that the biomechanical variable must be targeted to improve the athlete's performance. One of the major strengths of this project is that it covers a significant gap in the available literature, offering a detailed statistical analysis of the effects of such training and, therefore, improving the understanding of the discipline.

References

1. Zapartidis, I., Gouvali, M., Bayios, I., Boudolos, K.: Throwing effectiveness and rotational strength of the shoulder in team handball. J. Sports Med. Phys. Fitness **47**(2), 169–178 (2007). PMID: 17557054
2. Ojanen, T., Rauhala, T., Häkkinen, K.: Strength and power profiles of the lower and upper extremities in master throwers at different ages. J. Strength Cond. Res. **21**, 216–222 (2007). https://doi.org/10.1519/R-21426.1
3. Black, G.M., Gabbett, T.J., Johnston, R.D., Cole, M.H., Naughton, G., Dawson, B.: The influence of physical qualities on activity profiles of female Australian football match play. Int. J. Sports Physiol. Perform. **13**(4), 524–529 (2018). https://doi.org/10.1123/ijspp.2016-0723. PMID: 29035595
4. Ahmed, R.S, Al-Mousawi, S.Q.S.: Entrenamiento con métodos variados y su efecto en el desarrollo de algunas capacidades físicas funcionales de jugadores de baloncesto jóvenes. Retos. **66**, 1049–1060 (2025). https://doi.org/10.47197/retos.v66.113884
5. Zouita, S., Zouita, A., Kebsi, W., Dupont, G., Abderrahman, A., Salah, F., Zouhal, H.: Strength training reduces injury rate in elite young soccer players during one season. J. Strength Cond. Res. **30**, 2016 (2016). https://doi.org/10.1519/JSC.0000000000000920
6. Wooden, M., Greenfield, B., Johanson, M., Litzelman, L., Mundrane, M., Donatelli, R.: Effects of strength training on throwing velocity and shoulder muscle performance in teenage baseball players. J. Orthop. Sports Phys. Ther. **15**(5), 223–228 (1992). https://doi.org/10.2519/jospt.1992.15.5.223
7. Bridgeman, L., McGuigan, M., Gill, N., Dulson, D.: The effects of accentuated eccentric loading on the drop jump exercise and the subsequent postactivation potentiation response. J. Strength Cond. Res. **31**(1), 2016 (2016). https://doi.org/10.1519/JSC.0000000000001630
8. Pearson, S.N., Cronin, J.B., Hume, P.A., Slyfield, D.: Kinematics and kinetics of the bench-press and bench-pull exercises in a strength-trained sporting population. Sports Biomechanics **8**(3), 245–254 (2009). https://doi.org/10.1080/14763140903229484. PMID: 19891202
9. Schache, A.G., Dorn, T.W., Blanch, P.D., Brown, N.A., Pandy, M.G.: Mechanics of the human hamstring muscles during sprinting. Med. Sci. Sports Exerc. **44**(3), 647–658 (2011). https://doi.org/10.1249/MSS.0b013e318236a3d2
10. Ramirez-Campillo, R., Andrade, D.C., Nikolaidis, P.T., Moran, J., Clemente, F.M., Chaabene, H., Comfort, P.: Effects of plyometric jump training on vertical jump height of volleyball players: A systematic review with meta-analysis of randomized-controlled trials. J. Sports Sci. Med. **19**(3), 489–499 (2020). PMID: 32874101
11. Behm, D.G., Young, J.D., Whitten, J.H.D., Reid, J.C., Quigley, P.J., Low, J., et al.: Effectiveness of traditional strength vs. power training on muscle strength, power and speed with youth: A

systematic review and meta-analysis. Front. Physiol. **8**, 423 (2017). https://doi.org/10.3389/fphys.2017.00423

12. Marques, M.C., Liberal, S.M., Costa, A.M., van den Tillaar, R., Sánchez-Medina, L., Martins, J.C., Marinho, D.A.: Effects of two different training programs with the same workload on throwing velocity by experienced water polo players. Percept. Mot. Skills **115**(3), 895–902 (2012). https://doi.org/10.2466/25.23.PMS.115.6.895-902
13. Suchomel, T.J., Nimphius, S., Bellon, C.R., Stone, M.H.: The importance of muscular strength: Training considerations. Sports Med. **48**(4), 765–785 (2018). https://doi.org/10.1007/s40279-018-0862-z
14. Brown, L., Greenwood, M.: Periodization essentials and innovations in resistance training protocols. Strength Cond. J **27**(4), 82–92 (2005). https://doi.org/10.1519/00126548-200508000-00014
15. Sheppard, J., Cronin, J., Gabbett, T., McGuigan, M., Etxebarria, N., Newton, R.: Relative importance of strength, power, and anthropometric measures to jump performance of elite volleyball players. J. Strength Cond. Res. **22**(3), 758–765 (2008). https://doi.org/10.1519/JSC.0b013e31816a8440
16. Lloyd, R., Cronin, J., Faigenbaum, A., Haff, G., Howard, R., Kraemer, W., Micheli, L., Myer, G., Oliver, J.: The National Strength and Conditioning Association position statement on long-term athletic development. J. Strength Cond. Res. **30**(6), 1–16 (2016). https://doi.org/10.1519/JSC.0000000000001387
17. Morin, J.-B., Samozino, P.: Interpreting power-force-velocity profiles for individualized and specific training. Int. J. Sports Physiol. Perform. **11**(7), 1118–1124 (2016). https://doi.org/10.1123/ijspp.2015-0638

Chapter 24
The Effect of Bulgarian Bag Exercises to Develop Explosive Force, Characterized by Speed and Accuracy of the Spiking Performance of Volleyball Players

Zainap Abdulrahman Abdelkarim and Suhad Qassem Saeed Al-Mousawi

Abstract The purpose of this study is to determine how Bulgarian bag exercises affect the velocity and the precision of spiking in volleyball players. This project comes to fill the existing gap in training bedding that provides the new training toolkit efficiency. The pretest–posttest experimental design uses 12 football players for Al-Sinaa Sports Club. For some time, participants were taken through a progressive program that included Bulgarian bag exercises. The results indicated significant improvements in explosive arm force (t-value = 4.28, $p < 0.001$), leg force (t-value = 3.87, $p < 0.001$), and spiking accuracy (t-value = 3.87, $p < 0.001$). The study had major findings, some of which were practical while others were just indicated. Some of the practical study findings as listed in the study case included that Bulgarian bags exercise have a positive effect on improving physical qualities and the skillful performance of the volleyball players. I believe that this study could help many coaches in that these exercises should be embraced with their training programs. This is an implication of the study in that there should be more research on it to help in identifying long-term implications and implementation in other sports.

Z. A. Abdelkarim (✉) · S. Q. S. Al-Mousawi
College of Physical Education and Sports Sciences for Women, University of Baghdad, Baghdad, Iraq
e-mail: zainab.abd2204m@copew.uobaghdad.edu.iq

S. Q. S. Al-Mousawi
e-mail: suhad@copew.uobaghdad.edu.iq

F. P. García Márquez et al. (eds.), *Computing, Internet of Things and Data Analytics*, Smart Innovation, Systems and Technologies 387,
https://doi.org/10.1007/978-3-031-87154-2_24

24.1 Introduction

Scientific advances in sports training have been playing their significant part in enhancing different levels of athlete performance. Derived and combined with a series of tests and trials by multidisciplinary professionals, these advancements help to improve individual physical, skill, and tactical qualities. Appropriate training programs demonstrate a well-grounded scientific substantiation for progress in any sports domain. Volleyball serves as one of the best examples of a sport in which the combined application of sports science allows athletes to unlock their potential. The game requires a combination of explosive power and high-speed character, both of which can be developed with the help of scientific materials, motor fitness tools, and various exercises [1]. The Bulgarian bag, invented by Coach Ivan Ivanov, is one such tool that has shown promise in enhancing dynamic movements like pushing, twisting, swinging, and throwing, which are integral to volleyball performance [2, 3]. This study aims to explore the effects of Bulgarian bag exercises on the explosive force and accuracy of spiking in volleyball players, addressing a critical need for effective training methodologies.

24.1.1 Bulgarian Bags

It is a leather bag with sandbags or stuffing of the same material as the character's stuffing. It has two handles at both ends and different weights. It is used in performing some specific exercises that work to develop the skill performance of some skills and working muscles. The outer part of the bag consists of three types of handles and straps to allow various types of exercises with different grips. The main handles are the two gripping points that taper towards the end of the bag, and are used for swinging and rotating movements, Table 24.1 shows the Bulgarian bag weights (Fig. 24.1),

Despite the growing popularity of Bulgarian bag exercises in various sports, there is a notable lack of empirical research specifically examining their impact on volleyball players' performance. Existing studies primarily focus on general strength and conditioning without addressing the unique biomechanical demands of volleyball spiking [4]. While previous studies have investigated the potential advantages of

Table 24.1 Shows Bulgarian bag weights

Color	Weight	Athlete's weight
Yellow	5 kg	For athletes over 50 kg
Green	7.7 kg	For an athlete from 51:61 kg
Red	10–12–14 kg	For an athlete from 68:96 kg
Silver	20 kg	For an athlete from 96:113 kg
Brown	25 kg	For advanced athletes over 113 kg
Brown	30 kg	

Fig. 24.1 Shows the Bulgarian bags

resistance training tools like the Bulgarian bag in other athletic domains, these insights have not been thoroughly extrapolated to volleyball [5]. An additional void in the current research is the inadequate assessment of how particular Bulgarian bag exercises impact explosive power, velocity, and skill execution accuracy within volleyball. Carefully examining these effects is critically important for engineering targeted preparation programs capable of boosting volleyball athletes' capabilities. Lengthier or more intricate drills interspersed with shorter, easier activities may help optimize physical development and technical mastery. Bridging these gaps through purposefully designed trials would furnish coaches with evidence-based strategies for maximizing players' function during matches [6].

Furthermore, the long-term benefits and potential risks associated with regularly utilizing Bulgarian bag exercises in volleyball practice have remained inadequately explored. While some studies have spotlighted transient improvements in physical execution metrics, they frequently lack comprehensive data on the sustainability of these advantages and their impact on harm prevention. Comprehending these facets is crucial for optimizing training protocols and confirming athlete safety [7]. This investigation looks to fill these gaps by furnishing descriptive empirical substantiation on the consequences of Bulgarian bag exercises on explosive force and spiking exactness in volleyball, contributing to the progression of more effective and safe training programs. Additional study with larger sample sizes and long-term assessment are still needed to fully understand how these exercises effect athletes over extended periods and whether any potential negative impacts exist [8].

24.1.2 Literature Review

Previous research has attested to the merits of resistance exercise and high-intensity interval training (HIIT) for optimizing athletic output. Studies from Suchomel et al. In [9], authors have shown that organized strength training can significantly augment muscular strength and explosive power, both crucial components for volleyball performance. Correspondingly, [10] demonstrated incorporating dynamic training tools like the Bulgarian bag can better overall physical preparedness and functional movement patterns in athletes. Sheppard [11] specifically underscored the constructive impacts of Bulgarian bag preparation on physical variables such as endurance and strength in handball players, proposing potential uses for volleyball coaching. Regardless of these discoveries, there stays a space in the literature distinctly addressing the effect of Bulgarian bag practices on the explosive forcefulness and accuracy of volleyball spiking, necessitating further exploration in this area [12].

24.1.3 Problem Statement

This study is necessary because although there are both anecdotal and quantitative reports of the effects of resistance training apparatus such as the Bulgarian bag, there are large gaps in our understanding of how they counterbalance the particularized demands of volleyball. Specifically, although such equipment is purported to grow such critical factors as explosive forces and spiking aimer aptitude, it is not known to what magnitude these suggestions correspond to reality. In addition, this study is necessitated by the presence of unanswered queries regarding the prolonged effectiveness and danger of partaking such training [13]. Resolving these issues is crucial to the partaking of sports science, including the development and refining of training regimens largely constructed from this research. In consideration of these needs and deficits in our knowledge, this study is designed to evaluate the resultant establishment of the explosive power and spike-targeting accuracy surrounding the claims of the type of work that emerges after it.

24.1.4 Study Objectives

The purpose of this study is to evaluate the impact of Bulgarian bag exercises on the explosive force and accuracy of spiking performance in volleyball players. The specific objectives are:

1. To determine the effects of Bulgarian bag exercises on the explosive force of the arms and legs.
2. To evaluate the impact of these exercises on the speed and accuracy of volleyball spiking.
3. To compare the effectiveness of Bulgarian bag exercises with traditional training methods.
4. To provide evidence-based recommendations for incorporating Bulgarian bag exercises into volleyball training programs.
5. To explore the long-term benefits and potential risks associated with the use of Bulgarian bag exercises in volleyball.

The paper is divided into several sections. Having given the introduction in the first, the second section reflects the methodology used in the investigation. The issues of the experimental design, the method of participant selection, and data collection are in the following third section. The results of the study, also including statistical analyses of the pre-test and post-test data, are presented further. The fourth section of the paper and entails the discussion where I interpreted the results of both tests, compared them with the findings of other researchers, and reflected on implications. Finally, the fifth section is the conclusion which summarizes the main findings and discusses their broader implications. In the final part of the paper, I Summarized of the Main Findings and explained Contribution to the Field.

24.2 Methodology

This research employed an empirical methodology to evaluate the consequence of Bulgarian bag workout on the explosive power and targeting proficiency of spike performance in volleyball athletes. The experimental approach was opted for since it makes it possible for regulated alteration of aspects and straight perception of their impacts on functionality effects [14]. Participants underwent a pre-examination to ascertain baseline steps, then an eight-week preparation system incorporating Bulgarian bag physical exercises and ended with a post-examination to quantify variations in overall performance. Members was initially evaluated on their spiking aptitude and strength. Throughout the training period, workouts 3 times per week concentrating on diverse drills with the Bulgarian bag to improve speed, coordination, and arm swing energy. Next, a concluding test demonstrated considerably higher scores on measurements associated with attacking efficiency and potent strikes for those exercised group contrasted with baseline levels [1]. This design enables a clear comparison of pre- and post-intervention results, ensuring that any observed changes can be attributed to the training regimen [15].

The research sample is one of the most important steps for the success of the research, as a good sample must truly represent the original community, appropriate to the nature of the problem and the required information and allow its results to be generalized.

The two researchers deliberately selected the research community from the Al-Sinaa Sports Club players, who numbered (16). As for the research sample, they numbered (12) players. (4) Players were excluded for the purpose of the exploratory experiment, and the sample represents (75%) of the research community [16].

The homogeneity of the sample was verified in terms of the variables biological age, training age, height, and mass of the research sample and the Table 24.2 below:

The skewness coefficient was used, as its value indicates that all variables meet the moderate curve, because Table 24.2 shows the skewness coefficient in the moderate curve that extends between (± 1) (Table 24.3).

Data collection involved a combination of physical performance tests and skill assessments conducted before and after the training intervention. Physical tests

Table 24.2 The homogeneity of the sample

Variables	Measuring unit	A.M	S. D	Median	Skewness
Length	Cm	168,1	168,1	168	0,22
Mass	Kg	60,2	60,2	60	0,68
Age	Year	16,4	16,4	16	0,53

(*) A.M. Arithmetic Means, S.D. Standard Deviations

Table 24.3 Shows the significance of the statistical differences between the control and experimental groups for the research sample

Type sig	Level sig	T value calculated	Control group		Experimental group		Variables
			S.D	A.M	S.D	A.M	
Non sig	0,001	0,11	177,2	8	352,6	7	Force characterized by speed for arms
Non sig	0,002	0,54	0,41	26	0,07	25	Force characterized by speed for legs
Non sig	0,003	0,61	2,18	5,11	2,31	4,31	Explosive force for arms
Non sig	0,001	0,89	0,66	15	0,73	16	Explosive force for legs
Non sig	0,000	0,52	0,51	12,0	1,62	11,1	Spiking skill

measured explosive force using standardized protocols such as the medicine ball throw and vertical jump tests. The accuracy of spiking performance was assessed using specific volleyball drills designed to measure precision and speed. Pre-tests were conducted at the beginning of the training period to establish baseline data, and post-tests were administered at the end to evaluate the impact of the Bulgarian bag exercises. This rigorous approach ensured the collection of accurate and valid data for analysis [17].

Data analysis incorporated statistical methods of comparing the results before and after the trial of people. The paired t-tests were conducted to identify the incidence of the differences in the group, providing a rational stay of volume for judging the usefulness of the preparation intervention. Descriptive statistics, such as means and standard deviations, were discerned to offer a general impression of the data. Statistical Package for the Social Sciences programming was used for its precision in calculations and for simplifying the examination of outcomes. All tests were performed at the significance level of $p < 0.05$ to ensure the stability of conclusions. Furthermore, effect sizes were computed to measure the extent of perceived changes, suggesting a deeper insight into the practical significance of the Bulgarian bag workouts. As a result, the study found that for most of the participants, there was an increase in the strength, flexibility, and balance. At the same time, the analysis conducted also suggests that some of the participants experienced no effects, implying the presence of at least some individual differences determining that for some participants, this kind of training was useful, while others did not improve in these criteria. It serves as conclusive evidence that further study needs to be conducted in this direction.

24.2.1 Study Procedures

1. Throwing the medicine ball 1 kg from standing.
2. Vertical jump test from a standstill.
3. Pull-up test using body weight for 10 s.
4. Three test and longitudinal stability.
5. Testing the accuracy of diagonal and straight spiking.

24.2.2 Exploratory Experiment

The validity of the measurements and tests used in the research and the extent of the ability of the two researchers and the work team to perform and implement them, the two researchers conducted an initial exploratory experiment on a sample of (4) Individuals from the research sample on Thursday (5/10/2023).

A. **Goal of the experiment was:**

  1 To know the success of the tests and the suitability of the devices, tools, and auxiliary staff.

  2 Knowing the difficulties that the researchers may face while applying the exercises.

  3 Conduct a training unit to know the time, frequency, and adequacy of the rest times used for the sample.

  4 Ensure that the time used for the exercises is sufficient and that the exercises are appropriate for the research sample.

B. **Pre-tests**
The two researchers conducted the pre-tests, and the pre-tests were conducted on Saturday, 7/10/2023, at four o'clock in the closed hall of the Industry Club. On the research group after the test is clarified for the research sample in order to obtain all variables through performance.

C. **Post-test**
After the end of the training period, the post-test was conducted on the research sample on 16/12/2023 at exactly four o'clock in the afternoon, taking into account the same conditions as the pre-test in the laboratory.

24.3 Results

It is clear from Table 24.4 that there are statistically significant differences between the means of the pre- and post-measurements in the experimental research group. The two researchers attribute the occurrence of these changes to the good planning of the Bulgarian bag program, with the aim of developing the accuracy of the skill performance of the spiking multiplication skill. It is noted in the table that the experimental group outperformed the control group in the pre-measurement and the rate of improvement in the post-measurement. The tribal strength in explosive force and strength characterized by speed among the experimental group of volleyball players indicates the effectiveness of the training program using the Bulgarian bag resistance exercises in a way that suits the nature of the technical performance in volleyball, as there are many skills that are performed in the form of jumping and striking required during the offensive skill performance in volleyball and also Its suitability to the level and physical and technical capabilities of the players, which led to the development of explosive force and the speed-related force associated with the nature of performance in volleyball. In these points out the importance of training to develop muscular ability. The effectiveness of the proposed exercises that were chosen in a scientific manner and were implemented at the beginning of the training unit and according to the phosphagen energy system, which included physical exercises for the arms and legs, represented by forward lean exercises and performing them quickly. The nature and characteristics of the strategy used are related to the volume and intensity of the training, the cool-down period and its shape, and also the interaction of the cool-down with the previous stage of training. requires the development of its basic components through the adoption of the best methods of training is the main means to affect the individual functionally to make the adjustments the required, so training experts have been constantly searching for the latest forms of physical exercise taking into account the impact of economic and effective. The training of Battle ropes is one of the forms of these modern exercises (Table 24.5).

In this regard, confirms that one of the most important features of the Bulgarian bag exercises is the focus on the center, which emphasizes the core, where the strong center muscles connect the lower limb to the upper limb, in addition to that, it includes multi-directional movements, which makes it one of the best exercises. Exercises are physical activities that cater to the physical, psychological, and social needs of young athletes [12].

In terms of improving muscular ability, research confirms that elastic reflex activity provides an excellent transfer of muscular strength to biomechanically similar movements requiring high force from the torso and legs. This is particularly evident in the broad jump. The selection of Bulgarian bag exercises led to improvements in the accuracy of skill performance for spiking. The results align with previous studies, indicating that Bulgarian bag exercises contribute to enhancing muscular ability and skill performance. These exercises, especially during the preparatory period, help fulfill the basic requirements for success by developing explosive force and speed-strength, while also increasing the cross-sectional muscle area and fiber

Table 24.4 Shows the results for the experimental group

Type sig	Level sig	T value calculated	Post		Pre		Variables
			S.D	A.M	S.D	A.M	
Sig	0,003	4,28	2,81	10	325	7	Force characterized by speed for arms
Sig	0,000	3,107	1,63	28	0,07	25	Force characterized by speed for legs
Sig	0,001	3,58	1,061	6,051	2,31	4,31	Explosive force for arms
Sig	0,000	4,35	0,22	18	0,72	16	Explosive force for legs
Sig	0,000	3,87	1,75	14,8	1,60	11,1	Spiking skill

Table 24.5 Shows the arithmetic means, standard deviations, and T value calculated for the control group

Type sig	Level sig	T value calculated	Post		Pre		Variables
			S.D	A.M	S.D	A.M	
Sig	0,03	3,31	1,34	9	1,77	8	Force characterized by speed for arms
Sig	00,0	4,81	0,18	27	0,41	26	Force characterized by speed for legs
Sig	00,2	3,55	2,01	6,68	2,18	5,11	Explosive force for arms
Sig	0,000	4,27	0,32	16	0,66	15	Explosive force for legs
Sig	0,000	3,21	1,61	13,08	0,51	12,0	Spiking skill

diameter, which improves muscle strength and capacity [15]. Additionally, this study agrees with previous research, which shows that Bulgarian bag exercises improve acceleration time, leg strength, agility, and grip strength among athletes, while also contributing to increased bone density.

This diversity in training through the training units implemented by the players is what created adaptations for performing skills, which are designed by using more parts of the body and involving more muscles proper planning and a comprehensive scientific and practical vision in the process of preparation and training. It has proven that the use of training means, and equipment has a role Positive in sports training "the interest and the use of modern devices and modern training methods that simulate the training reality and are similar to the steps of play have increased.

Parathyroid hormone plays a crucial role in regulating blood calcium levels by controlling its reabsorption and removal from the renal tubules. High-intensity sports training, especially with maximal loads, increases blood fluidity and reduces coagulation, facilitating better oxygen transport. This adaptation is essential for athletes. The repetitive use of tools in training helps improve skill technique, while physical activity produces temporary changes as a response to the exertion.

To achieve the desired training outcomes and prevent negative effects, it is vital to develop the body's basic components through effective training methods. This approach ensures functional adaptations of vital organs to meet modern exercise demands. In volleyball, such training helps young players enhance their anaerobic threshold, increase peak oxygen uptake, and improve their breathing efficiency during effort.

24.4 Conclusion

This study investigated the impact of Bulgarian bag exercises on the explosive force characterized by speed and the accuracy of spiking performance in volleyball players. The main findings indicated significant improvements in key performance metrics. Specifically, there was a notable increase in explosive arm force (t-value = 4.28, $p < 0.001$) and leg force (t-value = 3.87, $p < 0.001$), as well as significant enhancement in spiking accuracy (t-value = 3.87, $p < 0.001$). These results demonstrate that Bulgarian bag exercises effectively enhance both physical capabilities and skill performance in volleyball players.

Empirical evidence of the effects seen in incorporating Bulgarian bag exercises into volleyball training programs enables sports science field further development. These results point to the utilization of novel training modalities that seek to adversely impact specific performance variables, i.e., maximal power output and spike accuracy. The study fills a gap in the literature, provides practical advice on effective practices that volleyball and possibly other similar sports can adopt for training.

References

1. Makaruk, B., Sozański, H., Makaruk, H., Sacewicz, T.: The effects of resisted sprint training on speed performance in women. Hum. Mov. **14**, 116–122 (2013). https://doi.org/10.2478/humo-2013-0013
2. Morin, J.B., Gimenez, P., Edouard, P., Arnal, P., Jiménez-Reyes, P., Samozino, P., Brughelli, M., Mendiguchia, J.: Sprint acceleration mechanics: the major role of hamstrings in horizontal force production. Front. Physiol. **6**, 404 (2015). https://doi.org/10.3389/fphys.2015.00404
3. Jiménez-Reyes, P., Samozino, P., Brughelli, M., Morin, J.B.: Effectiveness of an individualized training based on force-velocity profiling during jumping. Front. Physiol. **7**, 677 (2017). https://doi.org/10.3389/fphys.2016.00677
4. Haff, G.G., Triplett, N.T.: Essentials of strength training and conditioning, 4th edn. Human Kinetics, Champaign, IL (2021). ISBN: 9781492596722

5. Schache, A.G., Dorn, T.W., Blanch, P.D., Brown, N.A., Pandy, M.G.: Mechanics of the human hamstring muscles during sprinting. Med. Sci. Sports Exerc. **44**, 647–658 (2011). https://doi.org/10.1249/MSS.0b013e318236a3d2
6. Ramirez-Campillo, R., Andrade, D.C., Nikolaidis, P.T., Moran, J., Clemente, F.M., Chaabene, H., Comfort, P.: Effects of plyometric jump training on vertical jump height of volleyball players: a systematic review with meta-analysis of randomized-controlled trials. J. Sports Sci. Med. **19**(3), 489–499 (2020). PMID: 32874101
7. Behm, D.G., Young, J.D., Whitten, J.H.D., Reid, J.C., Quigley, P.J., Low, J., Li, Y., Lima, C.D., Hodgson, D.D., Chaouachi, A., Prieske, O., Granacher, U.: Effectiveness of traditional strength vs. power training on muscle strength, power and speed with youth: a systematic review and meta-analysis. Front. Physiol. **8**, 423 (2017). https://doi.org/10.3389/fphys.2017.00423
8. Marques, M.C., Liberal, S.M., Costa, A.M., van den Tillaar, R., Sánchez-Medina, L., Martins, J.C., Marinho, D.A.: Effects of two different training programs with the same workload on throwing velocity by experienced water polo players. Percept. Mot. Skills **115**(3), 895–902 (2012). https://doi.org/10.2466/25.23.PMS.115.6.895-902
9. Suchomel, T.J., Nimphius, S., Bellon, C.R., Stone, M.H.: The importance of muscular strength: training considerations. Sports Med. **48**(4), 765–785 (2018). https://doi.org/10.1007/s40279-018-0862-z
10. Moesgaard, L., Beck, M.M., Christiansen, L., Aagaard, P., Lundbye-Jensen, J.: Effects of periodization on strength and muscle hypertrophy in volume-equated resistance training programs: a systematic review and meta-analysis. Sports Med. **52**(7), 1647–1666 (2022). https://doi.org/10.1007/s40279-021-01636-1
11. Sheppard, J., Cronin, J., Gabbett, T., McGuigan, M., Etxebarria, N., Newton, R.: Relative importance of strength, power, and anthropometric measures to jump performance of elite volleyball players. J. Strength Cond. Res. **22**(3), 758–765 (2008). https://doi.org/10.1519/JSC.0b013e31816a8440
12. Lloyd, R., Cronin, J., Faigenbaum, A., Haff, G., Howard, R., Kraemer, W., Micheli, L., Myer, G., Oliver, J.: The national strength and conditioning association position statement on long-term athletic development. J. Strength Cond. Res. **30**, 1–16 (2016). https://doi.org/10.1519/JSC.0000000000001387
13. Cronin, J.B., McNair, P.J., Marshall, R.N.: Is velocity-specific strength training important in improving functional performance? J. Sports Med. Phys. Fitness **42**(3), 267–273 (2002). PMID: 12094114
14. Almousawi, S.Q.: The effect of crossfit training in a stylistic, unified, and multiple direction to develop some physical and functional abilities of young volleyball players. J. Sport. Sci. **14**(53), 185–196 (2022)
15. Kumar, T.A., Oliver, J.L., Lloyd, R.S., Pedley, J.S., Radnor, J.M.: The influence of growth, maturation, and resistance training on muscle-tendon and neuromuscular adaptations: a narrative review. Sports **9**(5), 59 (2021). https://doi.org/10.3390/sports9050059
16. Markovic, G., Jukic, I., Milanovic, D., Metikos, D.: Effects of sprint and plyometric training on muscle function and athletic performance. J. Strength Cond. Res. **21**, 543–549 (2007). https://doi.org/10.1519/R-19535.1
17. Wallace, B., Winchester, J., McGuigan, M.: Effects of elastic bands on force and power characteristics during the back squat exercise. J. Strength Cond. Res. **20**, 268–272 (2006). https://doi.org/10.1519/R-16854.1

Chapter 25
AI Analysis of Islamic History Sources: Challenges and Opportunities

Reem Hassan Salim Hassan

Abstract The use of AI in historical studies has shown an impressive trajectory in recent years, thanks to breakneck progress in computing power, data availability, and machine learning algorithms. The current qualitative study will explore the main problems of using AI tools, e.g. NLP and ML in studying Islamic historical documents. Via an exhaustive literature review and an application of different NLP and ML techniques to a self- selected corpus of relevant sources, the author is going to state the difficulties of AI use in historical studies, such as the accuracy and difficulty of classical Arabic language, availability of historical digital texts, and the need for considerable domain knowledge in the process of reading the historical results. Then enumerate the findings for the pursuits of the AI investigations in Islamic history such as Linguistic challenges, Data sparsity and lack of digitized of historical sources, and the Need for human expertise in the cultural context and propose strategic solutions including collaborative interdisciplinary work, advance digitization efforts, provision of specific AI tools to the historical domain, and ML models development, in addition to the real need to the collaboration between the human abilities and the AI analytic tools, to get a better result.

25.1 Introduction

Historical study of Islam is based on various sources such as old manuscripts, finds from ancient excavations, and oral transmissions. By doing so, this promotes the understanding of the diverse cultural, political, and social context of the Islamic world during different time periods. Nevertheless, researchers face a great magnitude and intricacy of these data that hamper them to understand and make sense of [1].

The issue of linguistic challenges related to Arabic texts is not only characteristic for historical texts but also for the contemporary scientific field. As rightly pointed out by Hamood et al. [2], there is not enough of attention to researching the rules

R. H. S. Hassan (✉)
Faculty of Education for Girls, Legal Affairs Department, Baghdad University, Baghdad, Iraq
e-mail: reem.h@coduw.uobaghod.edu.iq

F. P. García Márquez et al. (eds.), *Computing, Internet of Things and Data Analytics*,
Smart Innovation, Systems and Technologies 387,
https://doi.org/10.1007/978-3-031-87154-2_25

and standards of research discourse in English in some of the Iraq medical journals. Therefore, comprehending and creating the right linguistic approach to analyze ancient Arabic texts in various fields is important.

In the last few years, the fast progress of artificial intelligence (AI) technologies has brought a bunch of fresh options for looking into and analyzing historical sources in ways that seemed impossible only a couple of years ago. AI tools such as machine learning, [3] natural language processing and computer vision techniques can be instrumental in redefining the ways we study the Islamic history. Through these tools researchers have an opportunity to inquire and see the hidden pattern, connection and information that may have been missed by conventional method of analysis [4].

Despite the large potential that AI holds out for the study of the Islamic history, there are also hardships that need to be overcome. The first issue is that there is not enough heterogeneous data, where all kinds of individuals, cultures, and geographical locations are included [4]. On numerous occasions, a historian of Islamic history is faced with gaps or incomplete data and even with the linguistic incommunicability between the machine and case studies of the language. Similarly, these produced sources have the cultural and historical context where AI systems would be in hard shell and would interpret information [5]. Yet, another issue is that the results of AI systems might be biased (even imprecise) too. AI algorithms, at best, can mirror the strengths and weakness of their data, hence human biases or inaccuracies in the training data can result in flawed analysis also [6]. Besides that, artificial neural networks such as reinforcement learning, and deep learning sometimes do not allow for the purpose of reliability and validity assessment [7]. In fact, as an AI becomes inculcated with Islamic history, its possibilities are many. Through thoughtful consideration and acknowledgment of the shortcomings and biases of AI models, scientists can channel these systems to unveil new discoveries and views which were not visible before. This research objective is to study the issues and opportunities involved in using AI-driven technologies for the analysis of Islamic history sources to come up with a workable framework for employing these technologies in studying Islamic history.

The foundation of AI in historical studies lies in the digitalization of historical sources. Recently, in libraries of all around the globe, massive digitization work has taken place in the field, which enabled access to historical information in digital formats [8]. Thus, digitalization has opened the gates for AI to process and analyze these sources in quantities that were simply unthinkable previously [9].

The next step in the direction has been, thus, creating machine learning algorithms, which will be used for historical analysis [10]. Such algorithms as topic modeling, named entity recognition, and sentiment analysis have proven useful for this matter because they allow a researcher to extract significant information out of huge volumes of unstructured information from the archives [11].

Thus, topic modeling enabled historical researchers to discover thematic trends in historical newspapers, while named entity recognition helped extract information about people, places, and events from historical informational texts [12]. The integration of AI with other computational methods, including GIS and social network analysis, has not only strengthened AI in historical studies but also helped develop AI in the field of historical studies [13].

Due to such an interdisciplinary approach, it has become available for researchers to observe complex pieces of historical information from new angles and perspectives, which was impossible before [14]. Moreover, the increasing fusion of historians, computer scientists, and data scientists is what brings AI to historical studies [15]. This interdisciplinary fusion has made it possible to establish pioneering approaches, hardware, techniques, and best practices of AI integration into historical studies [16]. However, it is important to note that AI in historical studies also bears some initiatives for future development [17]. Solving them is possible through a cautious application of AI in historical studies and continuous improvement of AI technology.

25.2 Literature Review

The learnings from AI methods in this context will be directed to scholars which gives them the chance to locate details and patterns in the documents that were not discoverable in the past. In respect to the period of Islamic history, many such studies have been carried out to determine the potency of AI to be used in the analysis of different categories of primary sources which include historical texts, manuscripts, maps, and paintings. Researchers have been able to realize that the most appropriate methods for answering the research questions and the problems they encountered during their studies of Islamic history are AI methods. In this part of the literature review I want to analyze four previous studies that utilized AI methodology in studying of Islamic sources in history by investigating their aims, methodologies, and results. By reviewing the following studies.

The proposed LDA-SVM method in [18] for Arabic text classification improves upon traditional vector-based models by utilizing LDA to extract topics as features, which helps preserve semantic content and reduces the feature space. Through experiments on an Arabic text corpus, the model demonstrated high effectiveness with a Macro-averaged F1 score of 88.1% and a Micro-averaged F1 score of 91.4%.

In [19], authors discuss the creation of a large Arabic tweet corpus annotated for sentiment analysis, focusing on tweets in Modern Standard Arabic and the Saudi dialect. It describes the data collection, pre-processing, and annotation methods used to categorize tweets into four sentiment labels: positive, negative, neutral, and mixed. Baseline experiments were also conducted to establish benchmarks for future research in Arabic sentiment analysis.

Another study [20], offers an extensive review of natural language processing (NLP) for Arabic dialects. It categorizes research contributions into four main areas: basic language analysis, language resource development, semantic-level analysis, and dialect identification. The review also maps each paper to its corresponding dialect, providing a comprehensive reference for identifying relevant work in NLP for Arabic dialects.

In [21], authors review existing Arabic stemming and light stemming algorithms and presents the implementation of Arabic morphological analysis tools. These tools are integrated into popular open-source machine learning platforms like Weka and RapidMiner, which significantly enhance the capacity for Arabic language text mining. The evaluation focuses on the effectiveness of these tools in handling the complex morphology of the Arabic language.

In [22], the authors propose techniques based on deep learning for the detection of offensive language in Arabic texts. The study addresses the complexities of Arabic, such as the wide variety of dialects and the limited availability of annotated datasets. The authors build a deep learning model, particularly focusing on LSTMs (Long Short-Term Memory networks), to classify offensive language in social media texts. The experimental results show that the deep learning approaches outperform traditional machine learning models, achieving superior accuracy in detecting offensive content, which highlights the effectiveness of deep neural networks in handling complex linguistic challenges in Arabic.

The work in [23] compares two machine learning approaches—bi-LSTM-CRF (Bidirectional Long Short-Term Memory with Conditional Random Fields) and SVM (Support Vector Machine)—for segmenting Arabic multi-dialect texts. The study highlights the challenges posed by the morphological and dialectical variation of the Arabic language. By evaluating both models on diverse datasets of Arabic dialects, the authors demonstrate that the bi-LSTM-CRF model performs better due to its ability to capture contextual information and sequential dependencies within text, making it a more effective approach for multi-dialect segmentation tasks.

25.2.1 Problem Statement

Historical research, especially about the history of Islam, is not at all easy for humans and even more difficult for us to understand when we bring artificial intelligence as a solution. These hurdles encompass the rich but linguistically intricate classical Arabic language, absence of digitization repositories for complete historical context, and a necessity for fine-grained domain knowledge to parse outputs correctly. It is further complicated by the fact that state-of-the-art AI techniques like Natural Language Processing, NLP and Machine Learning, ML fail to adequately process and analyze these sources with data sparse, morphologically complex non-digits random words due to a lack of suitable digital text. Dependable computational tools need to be exploited in systematic large scale digital scholarship efforts using textual data, against which the power of SOM will be tested for a longer-term learning from diverse sources, and while an AI-based system remains work-in-progress. This study aims at investigating such barriers through exploiting potential to uncover new insights from historical Islamic texts within the premises of TWDM functionalities as they propose solutions to address these challenges thorough interdisciplinary collaboration, advanced digitization processing steps, and development of efficient

AI algorithms that cater to unique characteristics of classical Arabic and history studies perspective.

25.2.2 Research Objectives

The topic of this paper is the difficulties and benefits associated to the use of AI in the analysis of Islamic manuscripts. The aim of this research is to discover the main issues that come up when using AI tools, such as NLP and ML, in the process of analyzing the works of Islamic historians. These difficulties might consist of overcoming the linguistic complexity of classical Arabic, the scarcity of digital sources, and the requirement of domain-specific knowledge. And, to accomplish the first step, which is a comprehensive study of the existing literature on the analysis of Islamic history. The main purpose of this article was to come up with the methodology and the approach to be used in this current study.

This paper is an analysis of an academic paper concerning AI and Islamic History with a focus on the use of different machine learning and natural language processing algorithms. First, the paper has an abstract that describes the objectives of the study and emphasizes the significance of AI in this area–both in terms of opportunities and challenges. However, the introduction section also includes relevant information regarding the importance of Islamic history and the growing potential of AI technologies, although it also clearly formulates the problems of using AI, that is, the complexity of the language and the current scarcity of digitized historical texts. In the literature review section, the authors list sources and studies dealing with AI technology and connecting it with the task of analyzing Islamic manuscripts, differentiating several AI technologies such as topic models and a range of ML algorithms. The methodology section also includes a substantial amount of information on the research design, particularly the details concerning the data collection, preprocessing of classical texts, and the use of NLPs and MLs. The results section lists the major challenges, such as the complexity and untranslatability of the language and the lack of digitization of a substantial number of sources, as well as the expertise-specific AI-extended opportunities. This section concludes by responding to the research question and the hypothesis with the statements of fact that AI is beneficial but faces significant complications. The approximation section provides a summary of the main challenges and future opportunities, as well as argues in favor of a higher degree of interaction between different academic specialists, more resources dedicated to the digitization of sources, and novel, AI-engineered instruments specifically purposed for historical studies.

25.3 Methodology

The used study approach in this paper is qualitative and the aim is to analyze how difficulties of employing AI techniques to Islamic historical texts are tackled. Qualitative inquiry provides more accurate images of human reality in context-dependent phenomena in comparison to quantitative research, which more often results in defining the issues in descriptive terms. Since our research questions are exploratory, and Arabic sources have a lot of intricate language and culture factors that one needs to be aware about, a qualitative design is suitable for us as it allows us to go deep into the complications and uncertainties that we will encounter.

The challenge of putting NLP and ML into Islamic history practice is identified by taking a deliberate process of collecting a diversified group of texts, which are from different times, regions, and genres. Our corpus consists of chronicle writings, biographies, legal records, as well as other known ancient works that date between the 7th and the fifteenth century AD. The criteria ensured inclusion of major spheres and periods, while also considering the changing character of this literature and its linguistic evolvement. The issue of obtaining high-grade digital copies of these old texts was a much more difficult part of our project. Mining of information has its limits as some vital sources have not been digitized and those which are available often experience errors introduced during OCR process (optical character recognition). A team of manual and automatic procedures was used by us for converting the selected texts into digital and then preprocessing the documents, however, even the absence of reliable digital sources is to be regarded as one of the most serious obstacles.

25.3.1 Preprocessing Steps

To process the historical texts in computerized analysis, we were forced to pour in a lot of cleaning steps. Normalization was performed to make OCR output easily readable by machine, transliteration was done to change Arabic script to Latin characters, spelling variations were normalized as much as possible, as well as real words were split into tokens [24] using the Arabic corpus [25]. The difficult nature of classical Arabic morphology was reflected during the preprocessing phase. Arabic words normally contain a root determined by the fusion of several morphemes, not showing the base form itself. To complement this, the inclusion of diacritics in most historical manuscripts would result in imprisonment of visualization and meaning. There were no software programs to handle these specificities which required additional thinking from the scientists.

25.3.2 Feature Extraction and Representation

After the preprocessing of texts, we have also identified a collection of linguistic features, both at the morphological, syntactic, and semantic levels. Such qualities were then encoded as numerical values that could be passed to a particular machine learning (ML) algorithm. For the feature representation part, we worked on different types, including word embeddings, TF-IDF, and BERT [26]. It is worth mentioning that the methods to be applied in modern standard Arabic where these techniques have attracted success in different NLP tasks have led us to doubt their usage of classical texts due to its evolution over time and to look for more extensive historical corpora for training.

25.3.3 Machine Learning Models Used

We applied both supervised and unsupervised ML approaches to the extracted features for various tasks: We applied both supervised and unsupervised ML approaches to the extracted features for various tasks:

- SVM based text classification which would group texts by an author, a historical period, or a genre as one of the possible methods of categorizing these texts [27].
- LDA also provides model topic modeling to spot frequent concepts and themes [28].
- Real-world named entity recognition utilizing LSTM Long-Short Term networks which detect entities such persons and places [29].

Nevertheless, the limitation of the model's performance by the small size of our digitized corpus as well as the absence of labeled training data for historical Arabic were still a challenge. Transferring the modern Arabic model often proved unproductive because it did not allow the capture of the differences in the usage of classical and modern Arabic.

25.3.4 Evaluation Metrics and Validation Approach

To evaluate our ML models' performance, accuracy, precision, recall, and F1 score were used as the standard metrics. We did this using fivefold cross-validation to evaluate the models' generalization ability and minimize overfitting. Nonetheless, the practicality of our dataset that is relatively small as well as the absence of gold-standard annotations for most tasks limits us to generalize easily about model performance.

25.4 Results

Our analysis revealed several significant challenges in applying NLP and ML techniques to Islamic historical texts: Our research demonstrated these coups few noteworthy problems of applying NLP and ML to Islamic ancient writings.

25.4.1 Linguistic Challenges Encountered

The complex morphology of classical Arabic, which manifests itself through a rich system of affixes and as a system of grammatical cases, had a deep impact on the processes of preprocessing and feature extraction, for example. This example illustrates how an Arabic word, commonly found in ayah (chapter) 25, in verse 7, "وَسَيَكْتُبُونَهَا," (wasayaktubūnahā) can be divided into many morphemes, each carrying grammatical and almost all information semantic. The sentence is about a word (kūtub-books). It is composed of a conjunction (wa-), future tense prefix (sa-), verb stem (kataba), masculine plural suffix (-ū), and object pronoun (-hā). These complex structures have also proved to be quite a hurdle for the NLP tools, which have been developed for languages that are relatively free from this inflection. This numerical interpretation is meant to demonstrate the' fine complexity of Arabic inflection and how it differs from languages like English. Through the explicit representation of the part of speech elements which are made up by the Arabic affix, Fig. 25.1 highlights the grammatical richness of the language and the challenges that it might pose to computational processing.

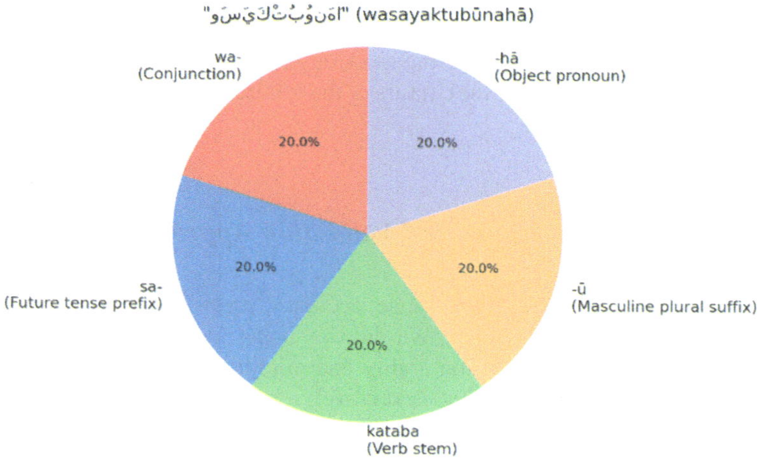

Fig. 25.1 Morphological complexity of classical Arabic

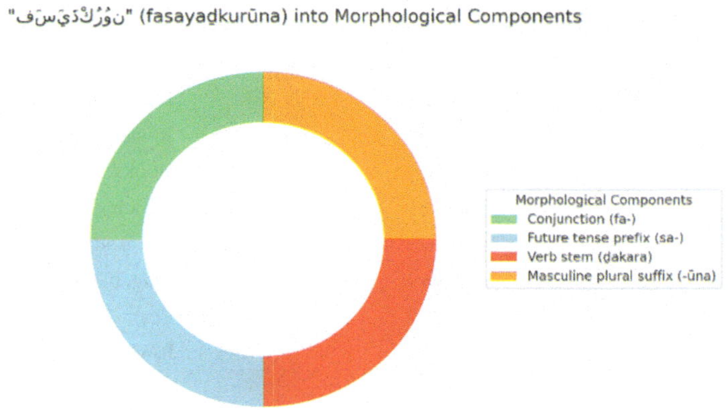

Fig. 25.2 Decomposition of Arabic phrases

The other example of the Arabic sentence " فَسَيَذْكُرُونَ" (fasayaḏkurūna) is constituted of its morphological components is as follows. The sentence contains a conjunction (fa-), future tense prefix (sa-) and verb stem (ḏakara), and the plural masculine suffix (-ūna), which indicate the third person plural category, and the future tense category, respectively. The triliteral root " ذ-ك-ر" (ḏ-k-r) in its verb is the origin of the term " ذكر" which carries meaning of "remembering" or "mentioning". The affixes are added to the verb to give more information on its tense, aspect, or agreement. The root is " ذكر" which means its semantic content as shown in Fig. 25.2.

Showing different parts of the functional structure in the different colors may make it more obvious. The word 'que' is highlighted in green, the prefix 'ir' in blue, the verb stem 'hablar' in red, and the masculine plural suffix 's' is highlighted in orange.

It is the aim of this member of the diagram to clearly illustrate the level of morphological details which implies the rich information content of Arabic words and the problems this leads to for NLP tasks such as stemming, lemmatization, and parts of speech identification. Though depicting morphemes and using color-coding may appear complex, it is the language grammar that is truly complex. This technique would enable grasping the structure of the Arabic grammar to readers not speaking or familiar with the Arabic language. In addition, the historical old manuscripts mostly do not contain diacritics; thus, the vowels became confusing, and word meanings got ambiguous as shown in Table 25.1. Not only that, but due to the high frequency of such rhetorical devices as metaphor, allusions, and figurative language, sometime deep meaning could barely be grasped by automated systems.

The ambiguity is created by absence of diacritics. Below is a list of Arabic terms which may be rendered with various disambiguated meanings and readings due to omitting the diacritics. The words which have to be diacritized with diacritics such as accent marks, cedilla, etc. are listed in the left-hand column whereas the right-hand column shows some of the possible diacritized forms of the words. The third column offers corresponding English-translated words or meanings for each diacritical form.

Table 25.1 It illustrates the ambiguity caused by the lack of diacritics in classical Arabic texts

Undiacritized word	Possible diacritized forms	Possible meanings
كتب	(kataba) كَتَبَ	He wrote
	(kutiba) كُتِبَ	It was written
	(kutub) كُتُبٌ	Books
علم	('alima) عَلِمَ	He knew
	('ulima) عُلِمَ	It was known
	('alam) عَلَمٌ	Flag, banner
قلم	(qalamun) قَلَمٌ	Pen
	(qulima) قُلِمَ	It was trimmed
	(qalm) قَلْمٌ	Cutting, trimming

Illustrated in the table below, three of the most used Arabic words are selected to showcase difficulty of ambiguity in omission of diacritical marks. The word " كتب" (ktb) is pronounced as "kataba" (mym. He wrote), "kutiba" (I. They were written), or "kutub" (the books). In the same way, the term "himy" (ʿal) can signify "he knew" (ʿalima), "it was known" (ʿulima), or "flag/banner" (ʿalam). The word "pens" (qalamun) refers to "It was trimmed" (qulima) or "Cutting/trimming (qalm).

In this table, the significance of diacritics in eliminating the effects of ambiguities in the meaning of Arabic words and the difficulties of their deficiency in many historical documents have been shown. It could be the case that without diacritics, NLP tools will fail to understand the true meaning of a particular word, and they might misinterpret its position in grammar, causing mistakes for tasks such as part-of-speech tagging, named entity recognition, machine translation, and other domain-specific tasks.

25.4.2 Data Sparsity and Lack of Digitized Sources

The fact that the information about the Islamic past that was digitized was scarce and insufficient, significantly reduced the size of our dataset as shown in Fig. 25.3. Among many essential sources, the digitization is not complete. Moreover, in a case that the available sources are digitized, they still contain mistakes and inaccuracies resulted from the OCR process. These historical clean and big corpora are just fragmented, as such they hinder the training and assessment of ML models.

Proportion of digitized versus non-digitized Islamic historical texts. This pie-chart illustrates that sources of islamic history is very digitally deficient in the field of research. The chart highlights texts that were found in a sample of 500 Islamic heritage books from 7th to fifteenth centuries CE. The category of availability of the texts in machine-readable forms is indicated on the chart. Blue fraction pertains to

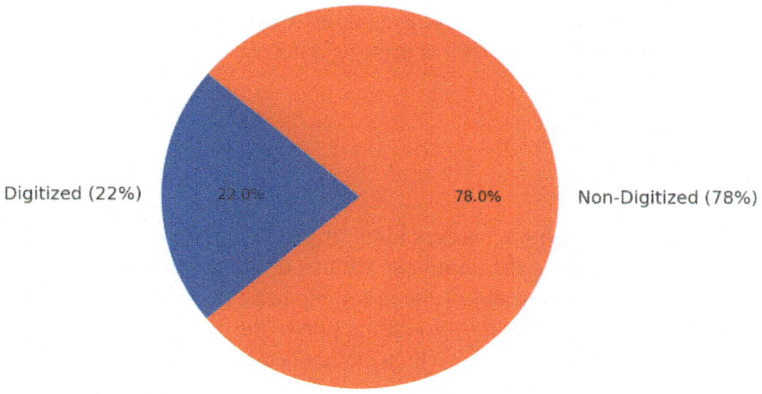

Fig. 25.3 Proportion of digitized versus non-digitized Islamic historical texts

converted texts amount (22%), whereas red fraction is about texts existing only in a physical or scanned form (78%).

This figure intends to reach out to researchers who are struggling in making use of NLP and ML tools which require a huge amount of data to analyze Islamic historical sources. The clear picture demonstrates that the disproportionately very little literature is digitized which implies that a lot of it still cannot be utilized for research.

The selection of a pie chart is very much appropriate for a visual illustration and understanding of the proportions of digested and non-digested content. Through contrasting colors (blue and red) it becomes easy to emphasize this dissonance between two categories. Percentage labels in the passage make sure that the precise proportion of an action or event is very visible to the reader [30].

25.4.3 Need for Domain Expertise and Cultural Context

Indeed, a profound understanding of Islamic history, culture, and religion was of huge significance in interpreting the outcomes of NLP and ML analysis. Failing me in the sober assessment of the patterns found by the algorithms due to the domain expertise deficiency was quite difficult for me. The intricate network of social and political ties and the subtleties of historical events that are detailed in the texts were often missed by the models.

Our results confirmed that the task of deploying the AI methodologies to the the Quranic/Islamic historical texts is complex and intricate. The intricate nature of classical Arabic, scarcity of the digital material, and the necessity of expertise are significant factors that stand for the successful operating of NLP and ML in the context of this setting. This implicate that the fully automate AI methods may be not reachable for the interpretation of a large Islamic history. Today there is not enough

NLP tools and ML models to process the complexities of the literary language stating and the absence of the large historical training datasets.

25.5 Conclusion

The study focuses on the main barriers hindering the employment of AI methods on classical Islamic texts, from the linguistic features of the classical Arabic vocabulary to the digitization of sources and the need for expertise in the field.

The points of this research thus provide support to the digital humanities evolution that investigates the possible issues which cannot be easily dealt with while working in the domain of Islamic history. We present the problematic aspects of current technologies, followed by potential future research and development projects aimed at solving such problems.

However, being aware that the AI now has some limitations, we still believe that it is a transformative tool for the study of the Islamic history by analyzing a vast scale of sources and sources that have not been accessible before. With ongoing collaboration between computer science and Islamic studies scholars, we can develop the tools and strategies necessary to make the hidden repository of knowledge contained in this comprehensive textual tradition accessible to everyone.

The research highlights the numerous limitations that AI methods face with regard to the analysis of the Islamic history text. First, it is crucial to note that the complexity of the classical Arabic language creates numerous obstacles for NLP and ML algorithms. Furthermore, the historical sources under consideration cannot be easily digitized, limiting the size of the dataset used for training. In addition, as it has been mentioned, the tools used lack precision of the classical Arabic. In combination with the lack of domain-specific knowledge and cultural context, the described factor limits the role of AI to assisting experts yet does not allow for replacing knowledgeable individuals.

In the future, more attention should be paid to the implementation of AI-based approaches to analysis and interpretation of Islamic historical data. This being the case, there is a need to further explore digitization of Islamic historical sources to use for the creation of larger and more complete datasets for AI models. Moreover, it is urgent to design AI tools, which may consider specific features of classical Arabic, including the development of advanced NLP and machine learning solutions. In addition, other perspectives of interdisciplinary cooperation of AI experts with historians and Arabic specialists should enable the involvement of cultural and language aspects in the utilization of AI for history. Furthermore, AI may also be used in sentiment analysis and named entity recognition in addition to application for historical pattern recognition. Finally, as another perspective of the usage of AI, other methods of computational history, including GIS and social network analysis, need to be used in an integrated manner.

References

1. Alrabiah, M., Al-Salman, A., Atwell, E.S.: The design and construction of the 50 million words KSUCCA. In: Proceedings of Second Workshop on Arabic Corpus Linguistics, pp. 1–8 (2019)
2. Hamood, A.S., Al-Nimer, M.S.M., Mohammed, L.H.: Insufficient awareness of the norms and conventions of English research discourse in some iraqi medical journals: an approach to improve the quality of publications. J. Iraqi Sci. Stud. (2023). [Online]. https://www.joss-iq.org/2023/07/24/insufficient-awareness-of-the-norms-and-conventions-of-english-research-discourse-in-some-iraqi-medical-journal-an-approach-to-improve-the-quality-of-publications/
3. Ma, W., Yan, B., Sun, L.: Generative adversarial network-based short sequence machine translation from Chinese to English. Sci. Program. **2022**, 1–10 (2022). https://doi.org/10.1155/2022/7700467
4. Altheneyan, A., Menai, M.: Naïve Bayes classifiers for authorship attribution of Arabic texts. J. King Saud Univ.-Comput. Inf. Sci. **32**(1), 90–100 (2020)
5. Alsaleh, D., Larabi Marie-Sainte, S.: Arabic text classification using convolutional neural network and genetic algorithms. IEEE Access (2021). https://doi.org/10.1109/ACCESS.2021.3091376
6. Abdelali, A., Darwish, K., Durrani, N., Mubarak, H.: Farasa: a fast and furious segmenter for Arabic. In: Proceedings of the 2016 Conference of the North American Chapter of the Association for Computational Linguistics: Demonstrations, pp. 11–16 (2019)
7. Althobaiti, M.: Automatic Arabic dialect identification systems for written texts: a survey. ACM Comput. Surv. **53**(2), 1–37 (2020)
8. Chouikhi, H., Chniter, H., Jarray, F.: Arabic sentiment analysis using BERT model. In: Advances in Computational Intelligence and Informatics, pp. 1–10 (2021). https://doi.org/10.1007/978-3-030-88113-9_50
9. Habash, N.Y.: Introduction to Arabic natural language processing. Synth. Lect. Hum. Lang. Technol. **3**(1), 1–187 (2020)
10. El Bazi, I., Laachfoubi, N.: Arabic named entity recognition using deep learning approach. Int. J. Electr. Comput. Eng. **9**, 2025–2032 (2019). https://doi.org/10.11591/ijece.v9i3.pp2025-2032
11. Fadel, A., Tuffaha, I., Al-Jawarneh, B., Al-Ayyoub, M.: Arabic text diacritization using deep neural networks. In: Proceedings of the 2019 Conference on Arabic Language and Computation (2019). https://doi.org/10.1109/CAIS.2019.8769512
12. Antoun, W., Baly, F., Hajj, H.: AraBERT: transformer-based model for Arabic language understanding. In: Proceedings of the Conference on Empirical Methods in Natural Language Processing (2020)
13. Ait Benali, B., Mihi, S., El Bazi, I., Laachfoubi, N.: A recent survey of Arabic named entity recognition on social media. Revue d'Intelligence Artificielle. **34**, 125–135 (2020). https://doi.org/10.18280/ria.340202
14. Farghaly, A., Shaalan, K.: Arabic natural language processing: challenges and solutions. ACM Trans. Asian Lang. Inf. Process. **8**(4), 1–22 (2019)
15. Nabil, M., Aly, M., Atiya, A.: ASTD: Arabic sentiment tweets dataset. In: Proceedings of the 2015 on Empirical Methods in Natural Language Processing, pp. 2515–2519 (2019)
16. Alshahrani, A.: A survey of methods and applications for Arabic named entity recognition. Int. J. Adv. Comput. Sci. Appl. **12**(2), 495–505 (2021)
17. Al-Khalifa, H., Al-Wabil, A.: The Arabic language and the semantic web: challenges and opportunities. In: Proceedings of the First International Symposium on Computer Vision and the Internet, pp. 1–5 (2019)
18. Abdelali, A.: The MADAR Arabic dialect corpus and lexicon. In: Proceedings of the 11th International Conference on Language Resources and Evaluation, pp. 3387–3396 (2019)
19. Twairesh, N., Al-Khalifa, H., Al-Salman, A., Al-Ohali, Y.: Arasenti-tweet: a corpus for Arabic sentiment analysis of Saudi tweets. Procedia Comput. Sci. **117**, 63–72 (2017)

20. Shoufan, A., Alameri, S.: Natural language processing for dialectical Arabic: a survey. In: Proceedings of the Second Workshop on Arabic Natural Language Processing, pp. 36–48 (2020)
21. Saad, M., Ashour, W.: Arabic morphological tools for text mining. In: Proceedings of the 6th International Symposium Emerging Information, Communication and Networks, pp. 1–8 (2019)
22. Mubarak, A., Darwish, K.: Arabic offensive language detection using deep learning. In: Proceedings of Fifth Arabic Natural Language Processing Workshop, pp. 126–135 (2020)
23. Eldesouki, M., Samih, Y., Abdelali, A., Attia, M., Mubarak, H., Darwish, K.: Arabic multi-dialect segmentation: bi-LSTM-CRF versus SVM (2017). arXiv:1708.05891
24. Elnagar, A., Al-Debsi, R., Einea, O.: Arabic text classification using deep learning models. Inf. Process. Manage. **57**(1), 102121 (2020)
25. Jarrar, M., Habash, N., Akra, D., Zalmout, N.: Building a corpus for Palestinian Arabic: a preliminary study. In: Proceedings of the 2014 Conference on Language Resources and Evaluation (2014)
26. Devlin, J., Chang, M.-W., Lee, K., Toutanova, K.: BERT: pre-training of deep bidirectional transformers for language understanding. In: Proceedings Conference of the North American Chapter of the Association for Computational Linguistics: Human Language Technologies, vol 1, pp. 4171–4186 (2019)
27. Joachims, T.: Text categorization with support vector machines: learning with many relevant features. In: Proceedings of the 10th European Conference on Machine Learning, pp. 137–142 (1998)
28. Blei, D., Ng, A., Jordan, M.: Latent Dirichlet allocation. J. Mach. Learn. Res. **3**, 993–1022 (2003)
29. Hochreiter, S., Schmidhuber, J.: Long short-term memory. Neural Comput. **9**(8), 1735–1780 (1997)
30. Ghintab, A.S.: Iraqi journalists' representations of their professional identity: a survey study. J. Media Res. **16**(63), 57–83 (2024). https://doi.org/10.33282/abaa.v16i63.1183
31. Abdul-Mageed, M., et al.: ARBERT & MARBERT: deep bidirectional transformers for Arabic. In: Proceedings of the 59th Annual Meeting of the Association for Computational Linguistics and the 11th International Joint Conference on Natural Language Processing, pp. 7088–7105 (2021)

Chapter 26
The Role of Multimedia Translation in Digital Communities

Haneen Qasim Saeed

Abstract The current study is about the influence of media translation dynamics on social media and digital communities. Multimedia translation, especially on websites, plays an essential role in determining the nature and direction of many social media conversations. For this reason, multimedia translation has become both beneficial and challenging at the same time. Moreover, the study shows that in the era of global change and cross-cultural interactions, the question of truthful information is a significant factor in the fight against misinformation. As a result, the study is based on an online survey, focus groups, and the results of a sentiment analysis. As supported by the findings, machine translation plays a vital role in increasing the popularity of social media. On the contrary, these translators have a slight effect on the improvement of media translation and work of the platform participants. Regarding the translation dynamics on Ukraine's social media, several challenges are worth mentioning such as the inaccuracies in the media translation, time of the given translation, the new mentality requirements, and the essence of the information possessing. In addition, there is a significant difference in the generation's interest related to reliable information searching. Youth use social media to a more considerable extent. Finally, the work has revealed that reliable media translation must work following ethical principles and be done by professionals.

26.1 Introduction

The use of media is essential for fostering involvement within online communities since it provides information that enables individuals to make well-informed judgments, a concept explored in studies of social media platforms like Facebook, which play a significant role in online social interactions and public discourse [1]. This organization oversees and ensures that institutions and governments fulfill their financial

H. Q. Saeed (✉)
Department of Public Relation, College of Mass Communication, University of Baghdad, Baghdad, Iraq
e-mail: haneen.q@comc.uobaghdad.edu.iq

F. P. García Márquez et al. (eds.), *Computing, Internet of Things and Data Analytics*, Smart Innovation, Systems and Technologies 387,
https://doi.org/10.1007/978-3-031-87154-2_26

obligations. Online media platforms, such as Facebook and LinkedIn, enhance interactive discussions by providing users with the opportunity to voice their thoughts and participate in public debates, as individuals often present a carefully curated online identity to engage with these discussions [2]. Digital media has several challenges, such as adjusting to swiftly evolving technology, upholding ethical principles in the face of sensationalism, and countering misinformation. Multimedia translation is facing challenges in keeping pace with the proliferation of social media and the spread of misinformation. This research highlights the need to examine the unique characteristics and significance of social media translation in today's interconnected global society due to its connection with social media, which is an integral part of our daily routines.

The necessity of adequate media communication to form the key publics' awareness and understanding has been underlined in several studies. Thus, the report by Ghintani [3] on the role of Iraqi media in the process of health communication supports the idea that the issues and valuable interventions doubts and reporting, "activated the viewer's perception and understanding towards health care practices in Iraq". Therefore, it is evident that the media translation is essential to provide an adequate and understood message in different languages, especially since it is relevant to the health issue. Besides, it is crucial in the conditions of the continuously emetogenic, digitalized social connectives, as evidenced by A. S. Hamood's report [4] on the role of the English language in cosmetic communication. The study shows that "the English language has been used widely for communication between people with different cultures" and facilitates the language interaction between the representatives of various cultures.

Social networks emerged in late 2007 as platforms for communication and social interaction. The most well-known examples include Facebook and MySpace. These networks gained popularity due to their ability to quickly disseminate news, often accompanied by vivid and expressive visuals. They also excelled in keeping up with real-time events, providing direct updates from the location where they occurred. These networks empowered individuals to freely express their aspirations and demands by actively contributing news and information. Moreover, they played a significant role in the creation and management of media content, enhancing their influence. Engagement and involvement in many matters. Social networks have emerged as a substitute for conventional leisure activities, and the level of interaction between contemporary societies and their environment significantly influences the communication system. Approximately 75% of Internet users engage with social networking sites daily. Recent research in the Middle East indicates that there is a noticeable increase in the number of social media users and the use of different platforms. Facebook continues to be the leading social network. Simultaneously, a significant proportion of content creators in the business depend on machine translation. This allows individuals to accept and present ideas as their own without verifying their veracity. This issue pertains to the domain of content ownership rights, and thus presents additional challenges.

In [1], authors emphasized that Facebook is projected to become the first website globally to surpass 2 billion active users by the end of 2017, driven by the rapid expansion of users in emerging markets like India. The quantity of Facebook applications has surpassed the milestone of 10 million. Over 23% of users engage in account monitoring over 5 times daily. 74% of marketers consider Facebook to be a crucial tool in their marketing efforts. The daily influx of photographs submitted to the site amounts to 250 billion. Approximately 75% of the engagement with a Facebook post occurs during the first 3 h of its posting. Facebook users account for 47% of Internet users [2]. Twitter users are continuing to post tweets. A recent study conducted by the Universities of Southern California and Indiana found that Twitter has approximately fifty million automated accounts. Published in March 2017 [5], the study concluded that Twitter has over 48 million automated accounts, a significantly higher number than what Twitter anticipated. The research used a technique that utilized over 1,000 characteristics to detect artificial accounts on Twitter in six different categories. It projected that these automated accounts constituted around 9–15% of the total 319 million monthly active users on the platform. According to Twitter's financial filings in 2014, the ratio of automated accounts to monthly active users was calculated at 8.5%. The current rate is twice as high as this prior estimate. The researchers observed that the estimated 15% of automated calculations is considered a "conservative estimate" due to the intricate nature of some automated calculations, which may mimic human behavior on social media platforms. According to a 2016 investigation conducted by the University of Southern California, about 19% of tweets pertaining to the U.S. [6] presidential election were generated by automated accounts within the specified research timeframe. Approximately 28% of retweets are attributed to tweets that have a retweet capability. Most Twitter users, namely 85%, use the platform via their mobile devices. No changes are needed. The age group of users between 55 and 64 years old is seeing the most significant growth on the social networking site "Twitter". The daily average of tweets amounts to 400 million. The mean number of tweets per Twitter account has increased to 208 tweets per account.

YouTube: is a platform that attracts over one billion people per month. YouTube recently disclosed that its users collectively consume around one billion hours of video content daily. This staggering figure implies that the amount of video content seen in a single day is equivalent to what one user would require a hundred thousand years to view. YouTube receives an influx of 100 h of video content each minute [7]. Most of the YouTube's traffic, namely 80%, originates from countries other than the United States. Offers website translation services in 61 countries and 61 different languages. There is no information provided. YouTube obtains millions of subscriptions every day, with the number of daily subscribers having tripled and the number of daily subscriptions having quadrupled. There is no text provided. Each year, thousands of channels generate financial gains that surpass one million dollars per channel. Users of Google Plus Google+ is a social network developed by Google.

It was officially launched on June 28, 2011, but initially, registration was limited to invitation-only due to the service being in an experimental phase. However, on September 20, 2011, Google+ became accessible to anyone aged 18 and above, without requiring an invitation. In early 2017, Google announced the addition of a new upgrade to the online version of the Google Plus network. This update allows users to quickly see the statistics of their page or personal account. In 2015/2016, the user base of Google Plus exceeded 500 million people. There is a total of over 300 million individuals that are classified as active users [8].

The user's text is already straightforward and precise. At least 80% of Google Plus members use their account on a weekly basis. Approximately 60% of Google Plus members go into their accounts on a daily basis. The +1-button used in Google Plus and YouTube is pushed in excess of 5 billion occasions on a daily basis. LinkedIn is a professional network that connects individuals in various industries. There are over 400 million users on this professional-focused social network. There are now over 1.5 billion LinkedIn groups in existence. A significant portion of LinkedIn users, approximately 27%, prefer to access their accounts using mobile devices [9]. A significant majority of LinkedIn users, approximately 81%, are part of at least one site group. Additionally, a notable 42% of LinkedIn users make it a point to regularly update their data. LinkedIn hosts over 3 million corporate pages, showcasing the vast presence of businesses on the platform. The site has received an impressive 1 billion endorsements, showcasing the high level of trust and support from users.

Instagram: Over 400 million individuals have joined this picture-sharing platform. Twenty billion photos have been posted to this social media platform.—Instagram users typically upload an average of 60 photographs per post.—With 1.2 million followers, MTV is the most popular channel on this network. Twenty thousand people like photographs or sets of photos every single second. Instagram users may leave up to 5,000 comments per second. Every single day, almost 8 million images are shared online [10].

Pinterest: The network that enables users to save and organize links on the Internet has now reached a staggering 70 million users. Most users, specifically over 69%, are female. A mere 6% of users have chosen to connect their accounts with Facebook. The category that generates the most buzz and engagement on the site is food, accounting for 57% of the content. An impressive 80% of the posts on this network are reshared by users [11].

Challenges are associated with translating media content in digital communities

We discussed the ability of social media to facilitate the creation of online communities and spaces, and then explored how the pandemic's global impact and local lockdowns increased the demand for these online spaces during the pandemic. There was a high demand for accurate and timely local information, but language barriers led some individuals to seek information in other languages or from different regions, requiring translation services often provided through social media. Accessing information in a language that may not be relevant to the physical location can result in misinformation. Therefore, translating crisis information into locally relevant languages on social media and other platforms is crucial. Based on interview data from the Irish COVID-19 context, it was found that social media platforms were utilized by migrants and service providers for those communities [12].

Trust is a significant factor that is influenced by various elements such as the source of information, context, and past experiences. Building trust during a crisis requires more than just relying on professional translators or interpreters, especially for social media posts. This questions the idea commonly accepted in professional and academic environments that professional translation is the sole ethically appropriate approach in a crisis situation. Social media users have the option to translate content themselves through various means, such as asking friends, neighbors, or using machine translation systems. Alternatively, they can access information directly from their home countries, which could lead to receiving inaccurate or harmful advice. Establishing trust is crucial for effective social media crisis communication. Ways to achieve this goal are through grassroots community integration initiatives and by identifying and onboarding translating micro-influencers for crisis communication [13].

Translation and interpreting are valuable in certain situations, but they are not sufficient for managing unpredictable, urgent, and dangerous circumstances. Moreover, it has been highlighted in previous studies [14] that effective communication is crucial during a crisis as discussed by and social media platforms play a significant role in enabling this interaction [15]. In this context, 'bridges' refer to trusted influencers who act as intermediaries between communities and service providers. It is important to recognize the potential risks of this approach, as individuals who act as intermediaries or influencers may not always be embraced by the communities they are trying to reach or may not effectively convey information. Just like in academic writing, it's important to consider multiple channels for crisis communication and understand the needs of different communities [16].

26.2 Related Work

The rapid advancements in Natural Language Processing (NLP) have significantly impacted the domain of multimedia translation, especially in digital communities where multilingual and real-time communication are essential. This literature review explores various pre-trained language models and machine translation approaches that contribute to the improvement of multimedia translation in digital communities.

Pre-trained models like BERT (Bidirectional Encoder Representations from Transformers) and its variations have revolutionized language understanding tasks by introducing transformers that consider both the left and right context of words. Devlin et al. [17] proposed BERT, a model pre-trained on large-scale corpora, which is then fine-tuned for downstream tasks such as translation, sentiment analysis, and text classification. BERT's bidirectional nature makes it more effective in capturing nuances within text, enabling better translation in multilingual contexts where digital communities are prevalent.

Building on BERT, RoBERTa (A Robustly Optimized BERT Pretraining Approach) was introduced by Liu et al. [18], further optimizing the training process and enhancing the robustness of BERT models. By removing certain pre-training limitations such as the Next Sentence Prediction task and introducing larger batch sizes, RoBERTa showed significant improvements in various NLP tasks. Its robust optimization makes it particularly suitable for high-quality translation within multimedia-rich environments like social media, where accurate understanding of context and meaning is crucial.

XLNet, introduced by Yang et al. [19], offers an alternative by using autoregressive pretraining, capturing bidirectional context while avoiding some of BERT's limitations. XLNet's capacity to handle long-range dependencies in text enhances its potential for translating complex multimedia content, where context-rich sentences are prevalent.

GPT-3 (Generative Pre-trained Transformer 3), discussed by Brown et al. [20], took the field of NLP by storm with its few-shot learning capabilities. Its massive scale and ability to generate coherent and contextually relevant text have strong implications for real-time translation in digital communities. GPT-3's ability to perform well with minimal training data makes it an efficient model for multimedia translation tasks in environments where datasets are limited but contextual accuracy is critical.

T5 (Text-to-Text Transfer Transformer), proposed by Raffel et al. [21], unified multiple NLP tasks under the same text-to-text framework, which is ideal for translation tasks. By converting everything into a text-to-text problem, T5 enables seamless integration of various translation tasks, from sentence-level to document-level, which is highly beneficial for digital communities requiring comprehensive and interactive translations.

In the specific domain of machine translation, Gu et al. [22] explored the use of search engine-guided neural machine translation, which enhances translation by leveraging search results to resolve ambiguities in text. This approach is particularly useful in multimedia translation, where digital content often includes specialized terms or regional dialects. The search engine guidance helps to provide context-sensitive translations that would otherwise be challenging in a purely neural network-based approach.

Quality estimation for machine translation has also seen significant developments, as discussed by Specia et al. [23]. Quality estimation aims to predict the reliability of a translation without reference to a ground truth. This is particularly important in digital communities where user-generated content is constantly produced and immediate translation is required. Specia et al.'s work offers insights into assessing the accuracy and fluency of machine translations, helping improve user experience in multilingual digital interactions.

Lakew et al. [24] compared transformer-based models with traditional recurrent neural networks (RNNs) in multilingual neural machine translation. Their findings showed that transformers outperform RNNs in terms of speed and accuracy, especially in handling long sequences and multiple languages. Given the global nature of digital communities, transformer models provide the computational efficiency and translation accuracy necessary for real-time multimedia communication.

Chen et al. [25] explored advancements in neural machine translation by combining recent NMT innovations. Their work presented hybrid approaches that integrate transformers with convolutional neural networks (CNNs), enhancing the accuracy and efficiency of translations. This combination of methods is crucial for handling the complex and varied nature of multimedia content.

The work of Gehring et al. [26] introduced convolutional sequence-to-sequence learning, which relies on CNNs to process sequential data. This model's ability to handle large-scale translation tasks with shorter training times is especially valuable in multimedia environments, where content is produced rapidly and continuously.

In the domain of text summarization, See et al. [27] proposed the pointer-generator network, a model that efficiently summarizes content by generating new text while retaining critical points from the original source. This model is particularly relevant to multimedia platforms, where summarizing large amounts of content is often required to enhance user experience.

The evolution of transformer-based models, including BERT, RoBERTa, XLNet, GPT-3, and T5, combined with advanced approaches in machine translation, plays a pivotal role in enhancing multimedia translation for digital communities. These models not only improve the accuracy and fluency of translations but also address the contextual and semantic challenges posed by multilingual environments, ensuring that information shared within digital communities is both meaningful and accessible across linguistic boundaries.

The purpose of this study is to investigate the challenges and implications of multimedia translation on social media platforms. The key research questions include:

1. What challenges are associated with translating media content in digital communities?
2. What ethical implications arise in media translation on social media platforms?
3. How can translators maintain accuracy and credibility in the digital age?

This paper is organized into several sections, starting with an introduction to the research problem and its significance, followed by a detailed literature review. The methodology section describes the research design, sampling methods, and data collection techniques. The results section presents the findings, which are discussed in the subsequent section. The paper concludes with a summary of the main findings, contributions to the field, and recommendations for future research.

26.3 Methodology

The study employs a mixed-methods research design, combining quantitative and qualitative approaches to gather comprehensive data on the challenges of multimedia translation on social media platforms.

The research uses purposive sampling to select participants who are experienced in media translation and social media communication. This includes professional translators, social media managers, and users who actively engage with translated content on social media.

Data is collected through online questionnaires and focus groups. The questionnaires are designed to gather quantitative data on the challenges faced by translators, while the focus groups provide qualitative insights into the experiences and perspectives of the participants.

The data is analyzed using statistical methods for the quantitative data and thematic analysis for the qualitative data. Sentiment analysis tools are also used to evaluate audience engagement and reactions to translated content on social media.

26.4 Experimental Results

This section presents the analysis of the survey, translating the qualitative insights into quantitative results. A regression model was developed to predict user engagement (Y) by examining several key factors, including translation accuracy, cultural sensitivity, and the extent to which machine translation was utilized. The linear regression model applied for this analysis is:

$$Y(\text{Engagement}) = \beta_0 + \beta_1(\text{Accuracy}) + \beta_2(\text{Cultural Sensitivity}) + \beta_3(\text{Machine Translation Use}) + \varepsilon \quad (26.1)$$

where engagement is the dependent variable which is measured by average likes, shares, and comments on translated content while independent variables include accuracy (measured on a scale from 1 to 5), cultural sensitivity (scale from 1 to 5) and machine translation use (binary variable: 1 = used, 0 = not used). The results are summarized in Table 26.1.

Translation accuracy ($\beta_1 = 1.15$) exhibited a strong, positive, and statistically significant effect on user engagement, indicating that higher accuracy leads to increased interaction. Similarly, cultural sensitivity ($\beta_2 = 0.92$) had a positive and significant influence on engagement, highlighting the importance of maintaining cultural relevance in translations. In contrast, the use of machine translation ($\beta_3 =$

Table 26.1 The selected regression coefficients for the experiments

Variable	Coefficient (beta)	Std. error	*p*-value
Intercept (β_0)	2.45	0.32	0.001
Accuracy (β_1)	1.15	0.15	0
Cultural sensitivity (β_2)	0.92	0.21	0.001
Machine translation (β_3)	−0.65	0.25	0.03
R-squared	**0.78**		
F-statistic	**24.56 ($p < 0.001$)**		

−0.65) demonstrated a negative effect, with engagement dropping by 0.65 units when machine translation was employed. This suggests that content translated by machines may fail to connect with users as effectively, possibly due to the loss of cultural nuance or linguistic precision.

One example is the social media has become battlefields in which politicians, news writers and the general public participate to various extents. In some cases, they have replaced traditional media. Accurate multimedia translation is critical, especially when shared through social media platforms, particularly when confronted with several difficult challenges. Cultural Sensitivity and Appropriateness, for example ensuring accurate translation preserves children's literature's cultural nuances, humor, and educational content. Preserving the original intent and impact of the stories is of utmost importance. Translating idioms, cultural references, or folklore can pose a significant challenge. Poor translations can result in misunderstandings or the dilution of the story's core message. Multimedia translation is essential for ensuring that educational content can be enjoyed and understood by a worldwide audience, particularly when it is shared on social media platforms. Accurate translation is key to making these contents accessible and educational.

Consider a fashion brand presenting a fresh assortment. Through the translation of their social media material into several languages, companies may initiate discussions with fashion fans from across the globe. By providing localized translations, the company may effectively connect with prospective consumers in local languages, therefore fostering a sense of appreciation and comprehension. Translation plays a crucial role in enabling companies to create an authentic connection and cultivate a devoted audience, whether it's via captivating Instagram captions, appealing product descriptions, or smart tweets.

During this period of fast-paced technological advancement, social media has emerged as an interactive and engaging platform for the worldwide distribution of news and information. Many internet platforms provide access to material, but the widespread publication of content in many languages presents a significant challenge to its distribution. This is a challenge for those who are looking for precise and reliable news in their mother tongue. To address this discrepancy, it is necessary to recognize the increasing significance of media translation and multimedia translation in the realm of social media.

Simultaneously, a significant proportion of content creators in the business depend on machine translation. This allows individuals to accept and present ideas as their own without verifying their veracity. This issue pertains to the domain of content ownership rights, and thus presents additional challenges.

26.5 Conclusion

The study highlights the critical role of multimedia translation in digital communities and the significant challenges faced by translators. It underscores the importance of accurate and reliable translations in maintaining the integrity of information on social media platforms. This research contributes to the field by providing a comprehensive analysis of the challenges and implications of multimedia translation in digital communities. It offers valuable insights into the role of machine translation and the ethical considerations involved in media translation. The study recommends the development of guidelines and best practices for media translation on social media platforms. It also suggests investing in training programs for translators to enhance their skills in handling multimedia content and using advanced translation technologies.

References

1. Wilson, R.E., Gosling, S.D., Graham, L.T.: A review of Facebook research in the social sciences. Perspect. Psychol. Sci. **7**(3), 203–220 (2012). https://doi.org/10.1177/1745691612442904
2. van Dijck, J.: 'You have one identity': performing the self on Facebook and LinkedIn. Media Cult. Soc. **35**(2), 199–215 (2013). https://doi.org/10.1177/0163443712468605
3. Ghintab, A.S.: Iraqi journalists' representations of their professional identity: a survey study. J. Media Res. **16**(63), 57–83 (2024). https://doi.org/10.33282/abaa.v16i63.1183
4. Hamood, A.S.: Multi-cultural communication through English language. AL-Yarmouk J. **20**(7), 857–876 (2023). Available online: https://www.iasj.net/iasj/issue/16599
5. Gilani, Z., Kochmar, E., Crowcroft, J.: Classification of Twitter accounts into automated agents and human users. In: Proceedings of the 2017 IEEE/ACM international conference on advances in social networks analysis and mining (ASONAM), pp. 489–496 (2017). https://doi.org/10.1145/3110025.3110091
6. Ali, R.H., Pinto, G., Lawrie, E.: A large-scale sentiment analysis of tweets pertaining to the 2020 US presidential election. J. Big Data **9**(79) (2022). https://doi.org/10.1186/s40537-022-00633-z
7. Cheng, X., Dale, C., Liu, J.: Statistics and social network of YouTube videos. In: Proceedings of the 16th International Workshop on Quality of Service (IWQoS), pp. 229–238, Enschede, Netherlands (2008). https://doi.org/10.1109/IWQOS.2008.32
8. Cheng, X., Dale, C., Liu, J.: Understanding the characteristics of Internet short video sharing: YouTube as a case study (2007). arXiv preprint arXiv:0707.3670
9. Skeels, M.M., Grudin, J.: When social networks cross boundaries: a case study of workplace use of Facebook and LinkedIn. In: Proceedings of the 2009 ACM International Conference on Supporting Group Work (GROUP'09), pp. 95–104, New York, USA (2009). https://doi.org/10.1145/1531674.1531689
10. Koskinen, K., Dam, M.: The translation profession: centres and peripheries. J. Spec. Transl. **25**, 2–14 (2021). https://doi.org/10.21256/zhaw-21195
11. Popović, M.: On the differences between human translations. In: Proceedings of the 22nd Annual Conference of the European Association for Machine Translation (EAMT), pp. 365–374 (2020). https://doi.org/10.5281/zenodo.6938623
12. Läubli, S., Sennrich, R., Volk, M.: Has machine translation achieved human parity? A case for document-level evaluation. In: Proceedings of the 2018 Conference on Empirical Methods in Natural Language Processing (EMNLP), pp. 4791–4796 (2018). https://doi.org/10.18653/v1/D18-1512
13. Bentivogli, L., Bisazza, A., Cettolo, M., Federico, M.: Neural versus phrase-based machine translation quality: a case study. In: Proceedings of the 2016 Conference on Empirical Methods in Natural Language Processing (EMNLP), pp. 257–267 (2016). https://doi.org/10.18653/v1/D16-1025
14. Wu, Y., Schuster, M., Chen, Z., et al.: Google's neural machine translation system: bridging the gap between human and machine translation (2016). arXiv preprint arXiv:1609.08144

15. Conneau, A., Lample, G., Ranzato, M., et al.: Unsupervised cross-lingual representation learning at scale. In: Proceedings of the 58th Annual Meeting of the Association for Computational Linguistics (ACL), pp. 8440–8451 (2020). https://doi.org/10.18653/v1/2020.acl-main.747
16. Johnson, M., Schuster, M., Le, Q.V., et al.: Google's multilingual neural machine translation system: enabling zero-shot translation. Trans. Assoc. Comput. Linguist. **5**, 339–351 (2017). https://doi.org/10.1162/tacl_a_00065
17. Devlin, J., Chang, M.-W., Lee, K., Toutanova, K.: BERT: pre-training of deep bidirectional transformers for language understanding (2018). arXiv preprint arXiv:1810.04805
18. Liu, Y., Ott, M., Goyal, N., et al.: RoBERTa: a robustly optimized BERT pretraining approach (2019). arXiv preprint arXiv:1907.11692
19. Yang, Z., Dai, Z., Yang, Y., et al.: XLNet: Generalized autoregressive pretraining for language understanding (2020). arXiv preprint arXiv:1906.08237
20. Brown, T.B., Mann, B., Ryder, N., et al.: Language models are few-shot learners (2020). arXiv preprint arXiv:2005.14165
21. Raffel, C., Shazeer, N., Roberts, A., et al.: Exploring the limits of transfer learning with a unified text-to-text transformer (2023). arXiv preprint arXiv:1910.10683
22. Gu, J., Wang, Y., Cho, K., Li, V.O.: Search engine guided neural machine translation. In: Proceedings of the AAAI Conference on Artificial Intelligence, vol. 32, no. 1 (2018). https://doi.org/10.1609/aaai.v32i1.11325
23. Specia, L., Scarton, C., Paetzold, G.H.: Quality estimation for machine translation. In: Synthesis Lectures on Human Language Technologies, vol. 11, no. 1, pp. 1–162 (2018). https://doi.org/10.2200/S00854ED1V01Y201805HLT039
24. Lakew, S.M., Cettolo, M., Federico, M.: A comparison of transformer and recurrent neural networks on multilingual neural machine translation. In: Proceedings of the 27th International Conference on Computational Linguistics (COLING), pp. 641–652 (2018). https://doi.org/10.48550/arXiv.1806.06957
25. Chen, M.X., Firat, O., Bapna, A., et al.: The best of both worlds: combining recent advances in neural machine translation. In: Proceedings of the 56th Annual Meeting of the Association for Computational Linguistics (ACL), pp. 76–86 (2018). https://doi.org/10.18653/v1/P18-1008
26. Gehring, J., Auli, M., Grangier, D., Yarats, D., Dauphin, Y.N.: Convolutional sequence to sequence learning (2017). arXiv preprint arXiv:1705.03122
27. See, A., Liu, P.J., Manning, C.D.: Get to the point: Summarization with pointer-generator networks. In: Proceedings of the 55th Annual Meeting of the Association for Computational Linguistics (ACL), pp. 1073–1083 (2017). https://doi.org/10.18653/v1/P17-1099

Chapter 27
The Role of Iraqi Satellite Channels on Social Media in Educating the Iraqi Public for Sustainable Development

Tiba Mohammed Saleh and Ahmed Salah Mahdi

Abstract This study explores the influential role of Iraqi satellite channels operating on social media platforms in fostering awareness and understanding of sustainable development among the Iraqi populace. With the pervasive impact of media in shaping public opinion, this research focuses on how these channels utilize digital platforms to enhance public knowledge on sustainable practices and policies. Through a comprehensive survey method targeting a diverse demographic within Baghdad, the study evaluates the extent to which social media content related to sustainable development is accessed and assimilated by the audience. Results indicate a significant engagement with these platforms, which in turn appears to correlate with heightened awareness and a better understanding of sustainable development concepts among the public. Moreover, the analysis suggests that while these channels are pivotal in disseminating information, there is room for improving the delivery and the depth of content to maximize impact. This research underlines the crucial role of media as a bridge between sustainable development goals and public comprehension, suggesting strategies for media outlets to enhance their contribution to societal awareness and education on sustainability issues. The findings also prompt media professionals and policy makers to refine content strategies to better serve educational objectives and public good, advocating for a more informed and proactive public participation in sustainable development initiatives.

T. M. Saleh (✉) · A. S. Mahdi
Faculty of Mass Media, University of Baghdad, Baghdad, Iraq
e-mail: tiba.m@comc.uobaghdad.edu.iq

A. S. Mahdi
e-mail: ahmed.s@comc.uobaghdad.edu.iq

F. P. García Márquez et al. (eds.), *Computing, Internet of Things and Data Analytics*, Smart Innovation, Systems and Technologies 387,
https://doi.org/10.1007/978-3-031-87154-2_27

27.1 Introduction

The concept of sustainable development is multifaceted and diversely applied, encompassing definitions that address environmental, economic, and technological aspects, among others. Broadly defined, sustainable development involves comprehensive processes of change that enhance various aspects of life economically, politically, socially, culturally, healthily, educationally, and pedagogically [1]. The United Nations has characterized it as growth combined with social, cultural, and economic change, the provision of social justice, and the enhancement of life quality for the masses. It aims to expand employment opportunities and focus on education and training, positing humans as both the seeds and fruits of development, and its ultimate goal and perpetual means. Furthermore, sustainable development is defined as development that meets the needs of the present without compromising the ability of future generations to meet their own needs. To achieve this, an environment must be cultivated in which humans can live long, healthy, creative, and communicate using different channels including social media [2]. This form of development aims for self-sufficiency in various aspects and requires that development actions align with current needs to meet the demands and requirements of all community members. Al-Najjar defines it as a development strategy that manages all assets, including natural and human resources as well as financial and material assets, in a way that enhances wealth and well-being in the long term. This implies that sustainable development as a goal rejects policies and activities that increase the well-being of the current generation through the depletion of productive assets, including natural resources, thereby leaving future generations poorer and facing greater risks than we currently face [3, 4].

The comprehensive and inclusive definition of sustainable development refers to balanced development that encompasses various societal activities, utilizing the best means to achieve optimal investment of material and human resources in developmental processes. It involves adhering to principles of equity in production and consumption and in the distribution of returns, to ensure the well-being of all community members without causing harm to nature or the interests of future generations.

Some studies define human development as "the process of expanding people's choices." These choices can be absolute and may vary over time, but the three fundamental choices at all levels of human development are:

- To lead a long and healthy life.
- To acquire knowledge.
- To have access to the resources needed for a decent standard of living.

In summary, sustainable development aims to bring societies to maturity and righteousness in all aspects of their lives, enabling them to live a secure, honourable, and prosperous life marked by well-being, comfort, and happiness.

The study problem represents a crucial and fundamental aspect of the scientific study process. Recognizing the problem is the starting point for any scientific inquiry.

Identifying and articulating the study problem is essential for the scientific study and dictates subsequent study steps. The choice of problem directly influences the type of study a scholar can undertake, the nature of the methodology to be followed, the study plan, and the tools to be used, as well as the type of data to be gathered. Formulating and studying the problem is a main pillar in the scientific study process and impacts all subsequent steps. The problem is defined as an ambiguous situation, issue, idea, or concept that requires scientific study and study to elucidate its premises, build relationships among its elements and current outcomes, and reframe it through the results of the study within a proper scientific framework. The problem in this study lies in the content of Iraqi satellite channels that maintain electronic pages on social media platforms, covering a variety of topics and issues of interest to different societal groups. This includes topics of sustainable development in the public sphere, encompassing social, economic, educational, health, cultural, environmental issues, and others, and examines the extent to which this content reflects on educating and acquainting the Iraqi public with the concept of sustainable development.

This study aims to illuminate the role of electronic content from Iraqi satellite channels in raising the awareness of the Iraqi public about sustainable development issues. The problem can be summarized through the following inquiries:

1. What is the concept of sustainable development, and why is raising awareness about it important?
2. What is the relationship between sustainable development and the media?
3. What roles do the social media sites of Iraqi satellite channels play in educating the Iraqi public about sustainable development?
4. To what extent do the websites of Iraqi satellite channels contribute to familiarizing the Iraqi public with sustainable development topics?
5. What are the most prominent topics of sustainable development that the Iraqi public has learned about through the websites of Iraqi satellite channels?

The objectives pursued by this study are predicated on its significance, which is reflected in the valuable outcomes it provides in both theoretical and analytical aspects. This study aims to ascertain the levels of awareness among the Iraqi public regarding sustainable development topics presented by Iraqi satellite channels through their websites and social media pages. This will be accomplished by analysing responses to survey questions, which will offer indicators of the nature of this awareness. Accordingly, this study strives to achieve a set of objectives that respond to the posed inquiries, as follows:

1. To elucidate the concept of sustainable development and highlight the importance of awareness-raising about it.
2. To clarify the relationship between sustainable development and the media.
3. To explore the role played by Iraqi satellite channels that operate social media sites in educating the Iraqi public about sustainable development, thereby understanding the nature of the media content and what it seeks to convey to the Iraqi audience.
4. To identify the websites of Iraqi satellite channels that have contributed to acquainting the Iraqi public with sustainable development topics.

5. To delineate the most significant topics of sustainable development recognized by the Iraqi public through the Iraqi satellite channels that have electronic pages on social media sites, providing clear indicators of the diversity in the content presented.

27.2 Related Work

The growing dominance of social media platforms has reshaped the dissemination of information globally, particularly during critical moments such as the COVID-19 pandemic. Social media played a crucial role in delivering information and news to vast audiences during the pandemic. Casero-Ripollés [5] discusses how the outbreak altered media consumption, amplifying the importance of online platforms as key channels for public information. However, this sudden shift also led to a deluge of misinformation, or "infodemic," as noted by Cinelli et al. [6], which had the potential to distort public perceptions and misguide audiences. Cho et al. [7] explore the dangers of search algorithms in fostering political polarization. Their findings suggest that algorithms, by prioritizing certain types of content, may exacerbate ideological divides, thus raising questions about the democratic consequences of these technological systems.

Populism and its relationship with social media have been explored by Engesser et al. [8], who examine how politicians disseminate fragmented ideologies through platforms such as Twitter. Their study highlights the role of social media in amplifying populist messages, thereby influencing political dynamics. Grinberg et al. [9] focus on the spread of "fake news" during the 2016 U.S. presidential election, offering evidence that social media platforms can be fertile ground for the propagation of misleading information, which can significantly affect electoral outcomes.

The role of bots in political events has been addressed by Howard and Kollanyi [10], who reveal the extent to which computational propaganda influenced the UK-EU referendum. They show how automated accounts were used to disseminate targeted messages, thereby swaying public opinion on critical issues. Similarly, Jaidka et al. [11] emphasize the potential of social media to predict electoral outcomes, as demonstrated in their cross-country comparative study of election prediction models.

The use of Twitter in election campaigns has also been reviewed systematically by Jungherr [12], who identifies the platform's role in shaping electoral strategies and public engagement. Kreiss and McGregor [13] further expand on this by examining how major technology firms like Facebook and Twitter have worked closely with political campaigns, influencing the nature of political communication. The personalization and interactivity of online political communication, as examined by Kruikemeier et al. [14], demonstrate the effectiveness of digital platforms in fostering closer relationships between politicians and voters. This interactivity is crucial for engaging the public in meaningful political discourse. Ferrara [15] delves into disinformation campaigns, particularly the use of social bots during the 2017 French presidential election, to highlight the role of automated systems in influencing public sentiment.

Cervone et al. [16] explore how social media and satellite data were used for damage assessment in urban areas during emergencies. Their work shows how digital platforms can be leveraged for real-time crisis management, an aspect that has gained relevance in the face of natural disasters and pandemics. Weber and Mathews [17] explore role of local communities in shaping news through digital journalism, demonstrating how social media has democratized news production and consumption at the local level.

The emotional and affective aspects of social media are explored by Papacharissi [18], who examines how digital platforms enable the formation of "affective publics," where sentiment and emotion drive political discourse. The concept of "deplatforming" is discussed by Rogers [19], who explores the migration of controversial figures to alternative social media platforms such as Telegram, following their expulsion from mainstream networks. Shao et al. [20] focus on the spread of low-credibility content by social bots, revealing the extent to which these automated systems can manipulate public opinion. Vosoughi et al. [21] complement this by analyzing how both true and false news propagate on social media, with false information spreading more rapidly. Bakshy et al. [22] examine the exposure of users to ideologically diverse content on Facebook, showing that the platform's algorithmic structure can influence the diversity of opinions encountered by users. Newman et al. [23] in their Reuters Institute digital news report provide a comprehensive overview of the global shifts in news consumption, highlighting the increasing dominance of social media in public discourse. Zaller [24] contributes to the understanding of mass opinion formation by illustrating how individuals' exposure to media content shapes their political beliefs. Hamood [25] discusses multicultural communication through the English language, emphasizing how digital platforms enable cross-cultural interactions. Ghintab [26] provides insights into how Iraqi journalists perceive their professional identity, contributing to the broader discourse on media representation in the Middle East.

27.3 Study Methodology

Given the aim of this study to describe the phenomenon under investigation, gather precise information about it, and understand its dimensions, the researchers employed a survey methodology utilizing a sampling technique. This technique focuses on studying a limited number of cases within the constraints of time and resources available to the researchers.

The researchers developed a questionnaire containing a scale composed of various questions that measure the awareness of the Iraqi public on sustainable development topics, which has been influenced by their engagement with the websites of Iraqi satellite channels. The questionnaire serves as a tool to facilitate the acquisition of data that assists researchers in reaching scientific conclusions. It consists of several

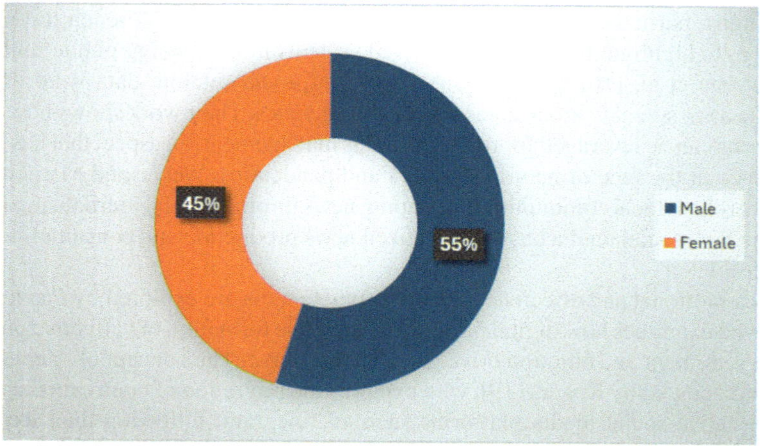

Fig. 27.1 Selected population

sections with questions that vary between closed (fixed answers) and open (diverse responses provided by the respondents).

The researchers selected a sample from the population of Baghdad, totalling 60 individuals.

Figure 27.1 represents the distribution of participants according to the gender variable. The sample comprised 33 males and 27 females, corresponding to 55% of the sample being male and 45% female.

Figure 27.2 illustrates the distribution of participants by age variable. The age group 31–35 ranks first, accounting for 31.66% with 19 occurrences, followed by the 36–40 age group in second place, comprising 28% with 17 occurrences. The age groups continue to decrease, with the 25–30 and 41+ age groups each holding the lowest rank at 8.33% with 5 occurrences each. This distribution indicates a higher engagement with sustainable development topics among younger age groups compared to older ones.

Figure 27.3 delineates the educational levels of the participants, showing that the university-educated group leads with 48%, while the secondary education group is at the bottom with 23%. This is a positive indicator of the university-educated public's awareness of the importance of sustainable development and their understanding of its necessity in society.

27.4 Results and Analysis

Figure 27.4 elucidates the frequency with which the participants follow Iraqi satellite channels that have pages on social media sites. It reveals that 41% of the participants actively follow these pages, while only 6.6% do not follow them at all, a minor

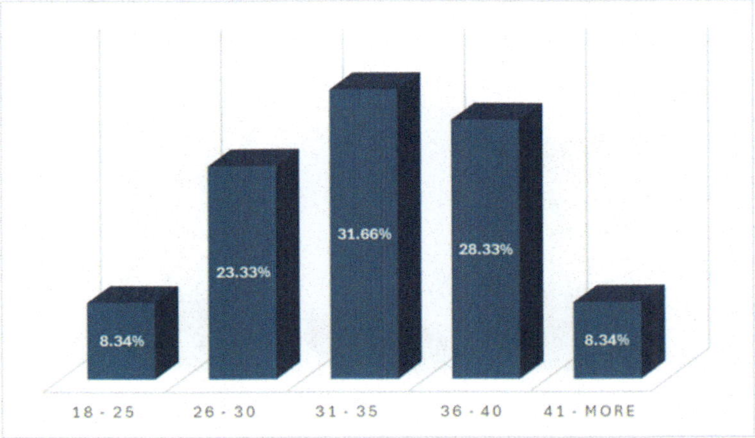

Fig. 27.2 Distribution of the participants according to the age variable

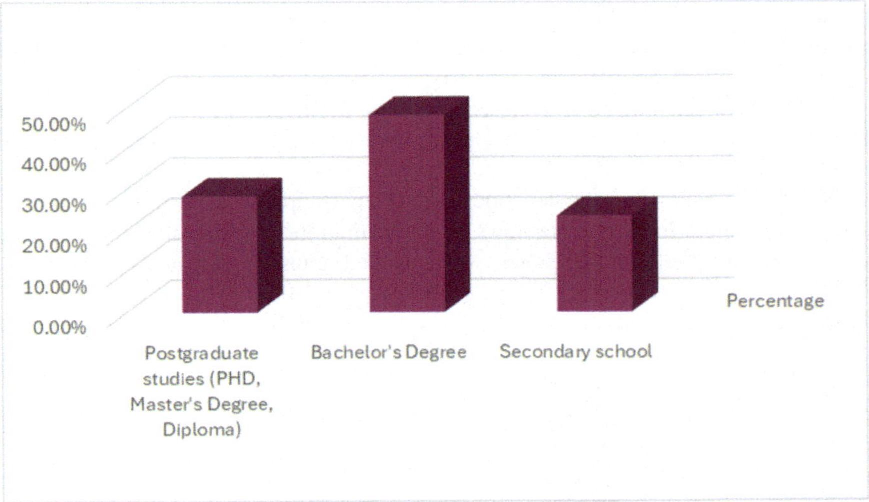

Fig. 27.3 Details the educational levels of the participants

proportion of the total sample. The category labelled "Sometimes" indicates that 51% of the participants are inconsistent in their engagement with the pages. This suggests that a significant number of participants are exposed to these pages, potentially increasing their exposure to content related to sustainable development topics.

Figure 27.5 reveals the preferences of the participants for Iraqi satellite channels that have pages on social media sites. Al Sharqiya Channel leads with 48%, followed by Al Iraqiya Channel in second place with 21.6%. Preferences among the

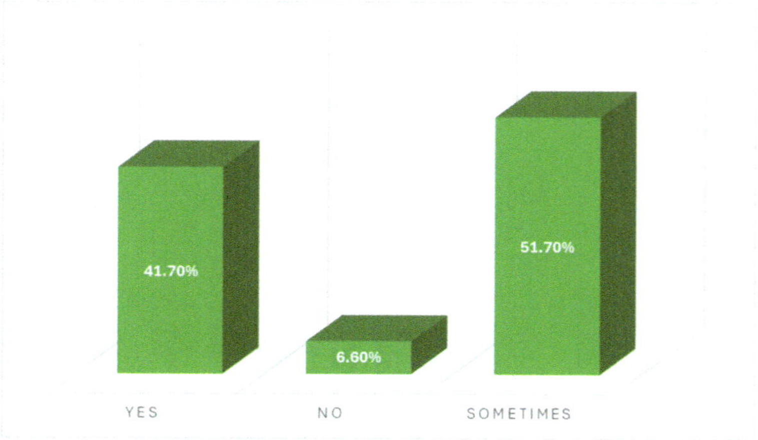

Fig. 27.4 Displays the proportion of participants who follow social media networks

participants vary, with Al Sumaria Channel ranking last at 5%. This indicates that the majority of participants predominantly follow Al Sharqiya Channel, which is diverse and covers the interests of the Iraqi public.

Figure 27.6 illustrates the preferences of the participants for social media platforms. Instagram ranks first with a percentage of 45%, while Facebook follows closely in second place with 36%.

Figure 27.7 delineates the dependence of the participants on the websites of Iraqi satellite channels for acquiring news and information. It shows that 68.5% of the participants fully rely on these sites, which is the highest percentage and ranks first.

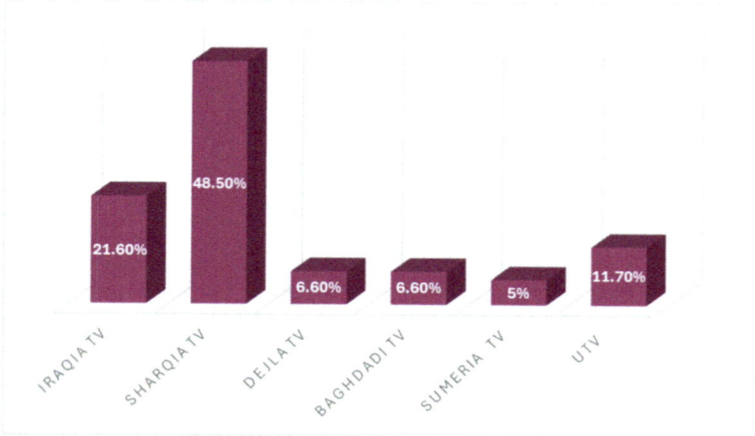

Fig. 27.5 Shows the Iraqi satellite channels that the participants follow

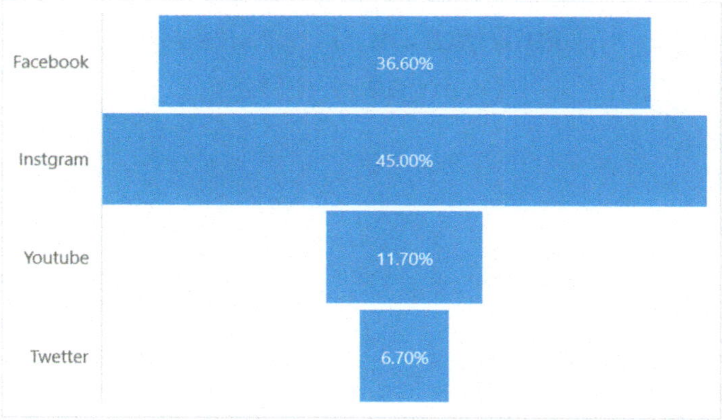

Fig. 27.6 Illustrates the preferences of the participants for social media applications

Meanwhile, 26.5% of them depend on these sites occasionally, placing second. The third rank is occupied by the 'No' category, representing only 5% of the participants. The data indicates that the majority of the participants predominantly use the websites of Iraqi satellite channels to obtain news and information, which enhances their exposure to topics on sustainable development and consequently increases awareness about these issues.

Figure 27.8 reveals the extent to which the websites of Iraqi satellite channels contribute to educating the participants on sustainable development topics. It indicates that 50% of the participants believe these sites occasionally contribute to their awareness of these topics, 23.5% of them believe these sites actively contribute to

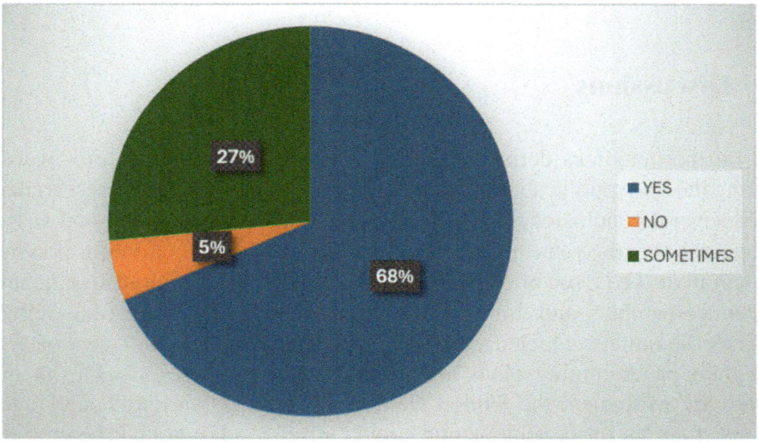

Fig. 27.7 Reliance of the participants on Iraqi satellite channels for news and information

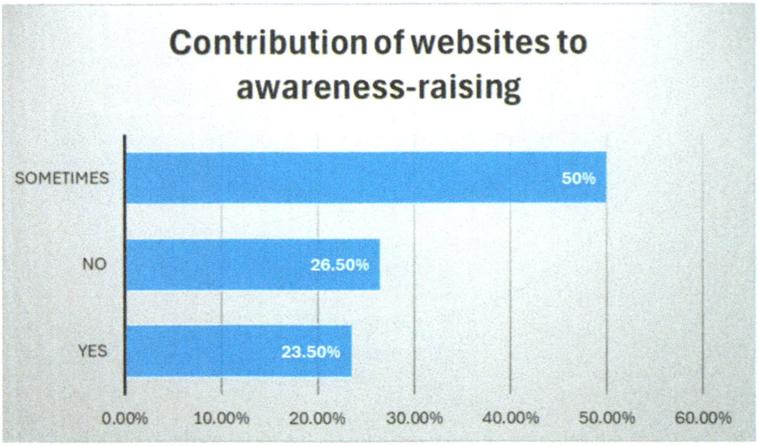

Fig. 27.8 Contribution of Iraqi satellite channels' websites in raising awareness among the participants about sustainable development topics

their awareness, while 26.5% of the participants feel that the websites of Iraqi satellite channels do not contribute to raising their awareness on the topics.

Figure 27.9 elucidates the most prominent topics of sustainable development covered by the websites of Iraqi satellite channels from the perspective of the participants. The findings show that topics related to economy and economic development ranked first with 48.5%, public services topics came second at 25%, education topics were third with 15%, and health topics were in the last position at 11.5%. This distribution suggests that the websites of Iraqi satellite channels tend to focus on specific sustainable development topics over others.

27.5 Discussions

Based on the outcomes derived from the survey study on the role of websites in educating the Iraqi public about sustainable development topics, the researchers have reached several conclusions. First, the relationship between media and sustainable development over the years and across various societies and conditions is synergistic and integrative. The issue of sustainable development has garnered significant attention from researchers and thinkers over decades, and this interest has reflected in various media outlets, which earnestly incorporate developmental awareness spaces within their programming plans and strive to present these issues from multiple perspectives. Moreover, the United Nations, through its various bodies and organizations, focuses on developmental topics at all levels—social, health, cultural, economic, and environmental. However, this attention has not been as fruitful as planned due to several reasons, the most significant being the weak cooperation of

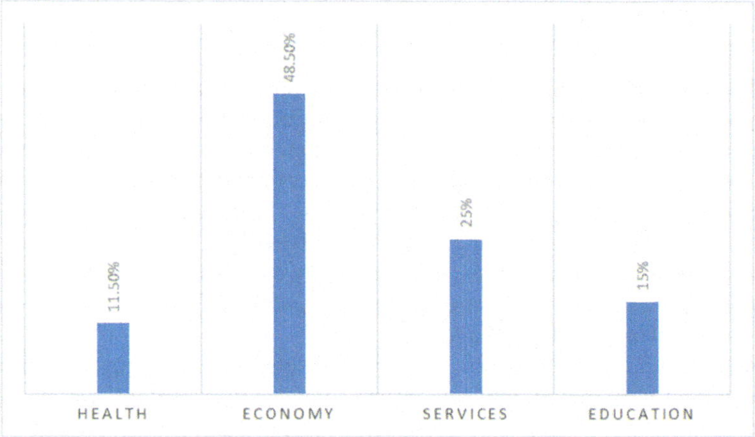

Fig. 27.9 Highlights the prominent topics of sustainable development featured on the websites of Iraqi satellite channels

member states' governments with the United Nations and their lack of seriousness in implementing the agendas of its conferences.

The study results show that the websites of Iraqi satellite channels cover a variety of topics. These sites on social media also show some degree of commitment to educating the Iraqi public about general issues and specifically about topics related to sustainable development, particularly in areas of economics and services. The findings indicate that improving living conditions and service quality are among the top reasons the public calls for heightened awareness of sustainable development, as these issues have a direct and tangible impact on citizens' lives. Finally, the study concludes that the websites of Iraqi satellite channels need to increase their focus on educational content to attract the audience more effectively and actively, which would contribute to raising awareness about sustainable development issues.

Many studies provide compelling evidence that freelancers on the internet are often defrauded through social media by disagreements between them and consumers who fail to pay for services or goods provided. As such, efforts by Iraqi satellite channels to help local businesses guard against fraudulent customers will effectively reduce instances of Internet-based extortion, particularly cyber extortion. Thus, these channels play a key role in reducing fraud and preventing businesses from incurring losses to consumers employing fraudulent means.

27.6 Conclusion

Based on the findings of the study, the studiers propose several recommendations. Firstly, there is a critical need to enhance the educational content regarding issues of development in general and sustainable development in particular. It is advised that additional information concerning the social, economic, political, cultural, health, and educational dimensions related to these issues be provided, which are expected to make the desired impact on the Iraqi public. By delivering media content rich in information and details about these issues, the websites of Iraqi satellite channels can play a more effective role in educating the public and shaping their awareness of the importance of sustainable development.

Secondly, it is essential not only for media outlets but also for government entities to educate the Iraqi public, unifying efforts to create the desired social change and impact. Sustainable development is a collective responsibility that cannot be achieved without collaboration and coordination between media and governmental institutions. Thus, governmental bodies should adopt comprehensive educational strategies and work alongside media to spread awareness of the importance of sustainable development and encourage citizen participation in its realization.

Thirdly, the concerted efforts of service institutions in both the public and private sectors are necessary to increase public awareness of developmental issues, which, in turn, could enhance citizens' sense of responsibility and thereby promote their judicious and organized use of natural resources without depleting them. Sustainable development requires a change in behaviours and practices at both the individual and institutional levels, which cannot be accomplished without raising awareness about the importance of preserving natural resources and rationalizing their consumption. Therefore, service institutions should collaborate to disseminate a culture of sustainability and responsible consumption among citizens, through awareness campaigns, education, and training.

This study makes significant contributions to the field of media and sustainable development by examining the role of Iraqi satellite channels on social media in educating the Iraqi public about sustainable development. It provides valuable insights into how media can effectively raise awareness and enhance understanding of sustainable practices among the populace. The study underscores the pivotal role that digital platforms play in disseminating information related to sustainable development, highlighting the importance of media in shaping public opinion and promoting societal change. By focusing on a diverse demographic within Baghdad, the research offers empirical evidence of the positive correlation between media engagement and increased awareness of sustainable development concepts. This contribution is crucial for both academic research and practical applications, as it demonstrates the potential of media to act as a bridge between sustainable development goals and public comprehension.

At the end of the current study there are a number of recommendations:

1. **Enhance Educational Content**: Media outlets should focus on enriching their content related to sustainable development across various dimensions, including social, economic, political, cultural, health, and educational aspects. Providing detailed and informative content will help increase the public's understanding and engagement with sustainable development issues.
2. **Collaboration with Government Entities**: Media organizations and government bodies should work together to educate the public about sustainable development. Joint efforts can create a unified strategy to foster awareness and encourage active participation from citizens in sustainable practices [26].
3. **Focus on Interactive and Engaging Platforms**: Given the high engagement with social media platforms, particularly Instagram and Facebook, media outlets should leverage these channels to disseminate information effectively. Interactive content, such as live discussions, Q&A sessions, and educational videos, can enhance public interest and involvement.
4. **Regular Evaluation and Feedback**: Implement mechanisms to regularly evaluate the effectiveness of media content related to sustainable development. Feedback from the audience can guide content improvement and ensure that the information provided meets the public's needs and interests.

References

1. Al-Rawi, A.: News organizations 2.0: a comparative study of Twitter news. J. Pract. **11** (2016). https://doi.org/10.1080/17512786.2016.1195239
2. Huang, Y.: The role of social media in crisis communication during COVID-19 period. In: Lecture Notes in Education Psychology and Public Media, vol. 4, pp. 888–894 (2023). https://doi.org/10.54254/2753-7048/4/2022608
3. Al-Najjar, B.: Public media accountability: media journalism, engaged publics and critical media literacy in the MENA. J. Arab Muslim Media Res. **12**(1), 3–19 (2019). https://doi.org/10.1386/jammr.12.1.3_1
4. Bossetta, M.: The digital architectures of social media: Comparing political campaigning on Facebook, Twitter, Instagram, and Snapchat in the 2016 U.S. election. J. Mass Commun. Q. **95**(2), 471–496 (2018). https://doi.org/10.1177/1077699018763307
5. Casero-Ripollés, C.: Impact of COVID-19 on the media system. Communicative and democratic consequences of news consumption during the outbreak. El Profesional de la Informacíón **29**(2) (2020). https://doi.org/10.3145/epi.2020.mar.23
6. Cinelli, M., Quattrociocchi, W., Galeazzi, A., Valensise, C., Brugnoli, E., Schmidt, A., Zola, P., Zollo, F., Scala, A.: The COVID-19 social media infodemic. Sci. Rep. **10** (2020). https://doi.org/10.1038/s41598-020-73510-5
7. Cho, S., Ahmed, A., Hilbert, M., Liu, B., Luu, J.: Do search algorithms endanger democracy? An experimental investigation of algorithm effects on political polarization. J. Broadcast. Electron. Media **64**(2), 150–172 (2020). https://doi.org/10.1080/08838151.2020.1757365
8. Engesser, S., Ernst, N., Esser, F., Büchel, F.: Populism and social media: how politicians spread a fragmented ideology. Inf. Commun. Soc. **20**(8), 1109–1126 (2017). https://doi.org/10.1080/1369118X.2016.1207697

9. Grinberg, N., Joseph, K., Friedland, L., Swire-Thompson, B., Lazer, D.: Fake news on Twitter during the 2016 U.S. presidential election. Science **363**(6425), 374–378 (2019). https://doi.org/10.1126/science.aau2706
10. Howard, P.N., Kollanyi, B.: Bots, #StrongerIn, and #Brexit: computational propaganda during the UK-EU referendum. SSRN Electron. J. (2016). https://doi.org/10.2139/ssrn.2798311
11. Jaidka, P., Ahmed, S., Skoric, M., Hilbert, M.: Predicting elections from social media: a three-country, three-method comparative study. Asian J. Commun. **29**(3), 252–273 (2019). https://doi.org/10.1080/01292986.2018.1453849
12. Jungherr, A.: Twitter use in election campaigns: a systematic literature review. J. Inform. Tech. Polit. **13**(1), 72–91 (2016). https://doi.org/10.1080/19331681.2015.1132401
13. Kreiss, D., McGregor, S.C.: Technology firms shape political communication: the work of Microsoft, Facebook, Twitter, and Google with campaigns during the 2016 U.S. presidential cycle. Polit. Commun. **35**(2), 155–177 (2018). https://doi.org/10.1080/10584609.2017.1364814
14. Kruikemeier, S., van Noort, G., Vliegenthart, R., de Vreese, C.H.: Getting closer: the effects of personalized and interactive online political communication. Eur. J. Commun. **28**(1), 53–66 (2013). https://doi.org/10.1177/0267323112464837
15. Ferrara, E.: Disinformation and social bot operations in the run-up to the 2017 French presidential election. First Monday **22**(8) (2017). https://doi.org/10.5210/fm.v22i8.8005
16. Cervone, G., Schnebele, E., Waters, N., Moccaldi, M., Sicignano, R.: Using social media and satellite data for damage assessment in urban areas during emergencies (2017). https://doi.org/10.1007/978-3-319-40902-3_24
17. Weber, M.S., Mathews, N.: Explicating local: an audience-based framing of local community and local news. Digit. J. **12**(1), 28–47 (2022). https://doi.org/10.1080/21670811.2022.2142629
18. Papacharissi, Z.: Affective Publics: Sentiment, Technology, and Politics. Oxford University Press (2015). https://doi.org/10.1093/acprof/9780199999736.001.0001
19. Rogers, R.: Deplatforming: following extreme internet celebrities to Telegram and alternative social media. Eur. J. Commun. **35**(3), 213–229 (2020). https://doi.org/10.1177/0267323120922066
20. Shao, C., Ciampaglia, G., Varol, O., Flammini, A., Menczer, F., Yang, K.C.: The spread of low-credibility content by social bots. Nat. Commun. **9** (2018). https://doi.org/10.1038/s41467-018-06930-7
21. Vosoughi, S., Roy, D., Aral, S.: The spread of true and false news online. Science **359**(6380), 1146–1151 (2018). https://doi.org/10.1126/science.aap9559
22. Bakshy, E., Messing, S., Adamic, L.A.: Exposure to ideologically diverse news and opinion on Facebook. Science **348**(6239), 1130–1132 (2015). https://doi.org/10.1126/science.aaa1160
23. Newman, N., Fletcher, R., Schulz, A., Andı, S., Nielsen, R.K.: Reuters Institute Digital News Report 2020. Reuters Institute for the Study of Journalism (2020). https://doi.org/10.2139/ssrn.3621272
24. Zaller, J.: The Nature and Origins of Mass Opinion. Cambridge University Press (1992). https://doi.org/10.1017/CBO9780511818691
25. Hamood, A.S.: Multi-cultural communication through English language. AL-Yarmouk J. **20**(7), 857–876 (2023). [Online]. Available: https://www.iasj.net/iasj/issue/16599
26. Ghintab, A.S.: Iraqi journalists' representations of their professional identity: a survey study. J. Media Res. **16**(63), 57–83 (2024). https://doi.org/10.33282/abaa.v16i63.1183

Chapter 28
ISMO Based 3-D Trajectory Planning Method for UAVs

Xiaoxi Tian, Ke Xu, and Zhenpeng Liu

Abstract To overcome the inherent limitations of the conventional Spider Monkey Optimization (SMO) algorithm in UAV trajectory planning, which include protracted search durations, extensive ranges, susceptibility to local optima, and suboptimal solution acquisition, we propose an Enhanced Spider Monkey Optimization (ISMO) algorithm.Initially, the ISMO algorithm integrates real-world environmental parameters, including three-dimensional terrain and UAV-specific constraints.Subsequently, the algorithm introduces a co-evolutionary strategy that segments the trajectory into multiple sub-paths, optimizing each segment independently.This segmentation is achieved by further subdividing the population associated with each sub-path into sub-populations, ensuring sustained communication among them. This methodology diversifies the search vectors of the individuals within the population, thereby enhancing the algorithm's capacity to circumvent local optima and bolstering path fidelity.Furthermore, the convergence rate is significantly enhanced through a meticulously crafted search operator. Ultimately, the ISMO algorithm undergoes rigorous testing in scenarios involving extensive, long-distance UAV flights. Empirical results substantiate that ISMO surpasses various other advanced algorithms, notably the Improved Fish Swarm Algorithm (IMAFSA), Improved Particle Swarm Optimization (IPSO), Improved Ant Colony Algorithm (IACA), Moth Flame Optimization Algorithm (MFO), and the original Spider Monkey Optimization Algorithm (SMO). Specifically, ISMO demonstrates an accelerated search velocity, an enhanced optimal range, and superior path fidelity compared to the IMAFSA, in addition to a heightened overall success rate in optimization endeavors.

28.1 Introduction

Unmanned Aerial Vehicles (UAVs), characterized by their remarkable mobility, compact dimensions, and user-friendly control mechanisms, are assuming a progressively pivotal role across diverse sectors [1], thereby rendering path planning for UAVs a

X. Tian (✉) · K. Xu · Z. Liu
Shenyang Jianzhu University, Shenyang, China
e-mail: 690667720@qq.com

F. P. García Márquez et al. (eds.), *Computing, Internet of Things and Data Analytics*, Smart Innovation, Systems and Technologies 387,
https://doi.org/10.1007/978-3-031-87154-2_28

focal point of contemporary research. The efficacy and rationality of path planning within intricate three-dimensional environments, characterized by constrained perceptual ranges, are crucial; this ensures the avoidance of diverse threats by UAVs, facilitating their seamless navigation to intended destinations [2, 3].

Contemporary strategies for trajectory planning encompass traditional algorithms such as the simulated annealing algorithm, the artificial potential field method, the Rapidly-exploring Random Tree (RRT) algorithm, dynamic planning algorithms, and path optimization techniques like the A* and D* algorithms [4]. Furthermore, advanced intelligent optimization algorithms, including Particle Swarm Optimization (PSO), the Improved Multi-Agent Fish Swarm Algorithm (IMAFSA), Enhanced Particle Swarm Optimization (IPSO), the Refined Ant Colony Algorithm (IACA), Moth Flame Optimization Algorithm (MFO), and Spider Monkey Optimization Algorithm (SMO), are employed [5]. These swarm intelligence-based algorithms are distinguished by their rapid planning capabilities and robust convergence properties [6], rendering them highly suitable for both UAV trajectory planning and robotic path planning. Empirical studies have demonstrated that population-based evolutionary algorithms provide superior convergence speeds and enhanced solution accuracy relative to alternative path planning methodologies [7–10].

The Spider Monkey Optimization (SMO) algorithm, a contemporary population-based intelligence strategy inspired by the foraging patterns of spider monkeys, stratifies the population into various sub-groups.This stratification fosters a diversified search trajectory [11], thereby mitigating the prevalent challenge of entrapment in local optima. Despite its efficacy, the algorithm encounters scalability issues as the operational scope expands, manifesting in increased path complexity and obstacle density, which potentially hampers performance due to heightened risks of local optima entrapment and reduced convergence rates [12]. To surmount these limitations, the Improved Spider Monkey Optimization (ISMO) algorithm is introduced. This enhancement employs a co-evolutionary approach to decompose large-scale optimization challenges into manageable sub-problems, each resolved independently prior to synthesizing the optimal solutions for an integrated outcome.

To substantiate the efficacy of the ISMO algorithm in UAV path planning, an extensive flight scenario was evaluated, juxtaposing ISMO against five other advanced algorithms: Improved Fish Swarm Algorithm (IMAFSA), Improved Particle Swarm Algorithm (IPSO), Improved Ant Colony Algorithm (IACA), Moth Flame Optimization Algorithm (MFO), and Spider Monkey Optimization Algorithm (SMO). The outcomes reveal that the ISMO algorithm surpasses its counterparts in achieving a higher success rate for complex three-dimensional UAV path planning challenges in large-scale environments.

28.2 UAV Three-Dimensional Path Planning Modeling

In the domain of UAV 3D trajectory planning, terrain is modeled with meticulous detail to precisely mirror the complexities of specific mission requirements and environmental subtleties. This sophisticated model incorporates numerous threat vectors, each regulated by distinct constraints, collectively synthesized to depict the comprehensive limitations posed by the terrain within the three-dimensional landscape.

28.2.1 Terrain Constraint Modeling

The terrain environment constitutes the foremost consideration in the path planning of unmanned aerial vehicles (UAVs),as diverse terrains present a variety of threats to UAVs. The three-dimensional (3D) terrain is typically classified into mountains, hills, and plains. Among these classifications, mountain peaks in mountainous regions exert the most significant impact on UAV flight. Furthermore, the impacts of elevation on flight performance are not to be overlooked. Mountain peaks within these regions are modeled employing coordinates in the following manner:

$$Z(x, y) = he^{\left(-\frac{(x-x_0)^2}{\lambda_1} - \frac{(y-y_0)^2}{\lambda_2}\right)^2} \tag{28.1}$$

Let $Z(x, y)$ and (x_0, y_0) represent the positions of the peak on the ground plane and the center point in 3D terrain, respectively.Here, h represents the height of the peak, while λ_1, λ_2 denotes the inclination of the peak. The cost function for terrain threats in UAV path planning is articulated as follows:

$$f_{Zj} = \begin{cases} K_Z, h_j - Z_j < 0 \\ K'_Z, 0 \le h_j - Z_j < 0.1 \\ 0, h_j - Z_j \ge 0.1 \end{cases} \tag{28.2}$$

Let K_z and K'_z represent the terrain threat coefficients. For the UAV's jth trajectory point, let h_j denote its altitude, let Z_j represent the terrain height, and let f_{z_j} be the corresponding terrain threat cost. The cost associated with the altitude of UAV track point j is articulated as follows:

$$f_{Hj} = h_j \tag{28.3}$$

To comprehensively guarantee the flight safety of UAVs, path planning must account for terrain constraints as well as the boundaries and maximum distance of the flight. In the experimental setup, the flight range of the UAV is defined by the parameters $(X_{min}, Y_{min}) = (0, 0)$km and $(X_{max}, Y_{max}) = (1000, 1000)$km. The maximum flight altitude permissible during path exploration is denoted as $Z_{max} =$ 3000 m.

28.2.2 Modeling the UAV's Own Constraints

The UAV is conceptualized as an ideal model, disregarding its mass and form. Throughout the path planning process, the UAV faces not only external threats but also internal limitations, including its turning angle α_0, upward climbing angle β_0, and fuel consumption, the latter quantified in terms of flight range. The maximum allowable turning angle and upward climbing angle are defined as $\alpha_{\max}$ and $\beta_{\max}$ respectively. These intrinsic physical constraints are articulated as follows:

$$\mathrm{J_h} = \begin{cases} 0, \alpha_0 \le \alpha_{\max} \\ \mathrm{Q_h}, \alpha_0 > \alpha_{\max} \end{cases} \tag{28.4}$$

$$J_v = \begin{cases} 0, \beta_0 \le \beta \max \\ Q_v, \beta_0 > \beta \max \end{cases} \tag{28.5}$$

$$J_{\mathrm{L}j} = \begin{cases} 1_{\mathrm{j}}, \mathrm{j} > 1 \\ 0, \mathrm{j} = 1 \end{cases} \tag{28.6}$$

Let Q_h and Q_v be the coefficients for the UAV's turning angle and climbing angle, respectively; $\mathrm{J_h}$ and $\mathrm{J_v}$ represent the cost functions for the turning angle and upward climbing angle. The distance associated with trajectory point j is denoted as $\mathrm{J_{Lj}}$, and the overall flight range of the UAV is 1_j. Aggregating all these cost functions, the total constraint cost for the UAV trajectory point is formulated as

$$\mathrm{f_{Jj}} = \mathrm{J_h} + \mathrm{J_v} + \mathrm{J_{Lj}} \tag{28.7}$$

28.2.3 Trajectory Cost Function

The costs associated with the aforementioned terrain constraints and the UAV's intrinsic physical constraints are weighted and integrated to derive the total UAV cost function, formulated as

$$F\left(R_j\right) = \sum_{j=1}^{d} \left(\omega_1 \mathrm{f_{zj}} + \omega_2 \mathrm{f_{Hj}} + \omega_3 \mathrm{f_{Jj}}\right) \tag{28.8}$$

Let d represent the number of track points. The weight of each constraint cost is denoted as $\omega_1, \omega_2, \omega_3$, the terrain threat cost as f_{zj}, the altitude cost as f_{Hj}, and the cost associated with the UAV's intrinsic physical constraints as $\mathrm{f_{J_j}}$.

28.3 Improved Spider Monkey Optimization Algorithm

28.3.1 Basic Spider Monkey Optimization Algorithm

Spider Monkey Optimization (SMO), proposed by Bansal et al., is a heuristic search algorithm designed for global optimization challenges. The SMO algorithm unfolds through four distinct phases: local learning, global learning, local decision-making, and global decision-making.

Local learning phase. Each individual spider monkey (SM) updates its current location based on the experience of the leader (LocalLeader) and random members of its subpopulation as follows:

$$SM_{i_{new}} = SM_i + \text{rand}(0, 1) \times (LL_K - SM_i) + \text{rand}(-1, 1) \times \left(SM_{k,r} - SM_i\right) \tag{28.9}$$

Let SM_i represent the current individual to be updated, and let rand(0, 1) denote a random number uniformly distributed in the interval [0, 1]. LL_k is the leader of the sub population K in which the individual to be updated is located locally optimal. Let $SM_{k,r}$ be a randomly selected individual within the same subpopulation k, and $r \neq i$. Each individual evaluates the probability of updating to a new position based on predefined criteria $pr \in [0.1, 0.9]$.

During the global learning phase, each spider monkey individual updates its current position by assimilating the experiences of the population leader, referred to as the GlobalLeader, and the randomly selected members from its subpopulation, as outlined below:

$$SM_{i_{\text{new}}} = SM_i + \text{rand}(0, 1) \times (GL - SM_i) + \text{rand}(-1, 1) \times \left(SM_{k,r} - SM_i\right) \tag{28.10}$$

In this context, GL denotes the leader of the entire population. Subsequently, each individual evaluates whether to update its position based on probability prob $_i$. This decision is predicated on the individual's fitness value, which reflects the perceived quality of the individual; typically, a higher fitness value indicates superior quality. The prob_i calculation is outlined below (alternative formulations related to the adaptation value may also be viable):

$$\text{prob}_i = 0.9 \times \frac{\text{fitness}_i}{\text{best\_fitness}} + 0.1 \tag{28.11}$$

Where, $fitness_i$ denotes the adaptation value of the current individual and best_fitness denotes the optimal adaptation value in the population. The global learning process of the population will be repeated until the number of updates reaches the population size. In this way, the more optimal individuals in the population will have a greater chance to be updated. After that, the population will update the global optimum (Global Leader) and the local optimum (Local Leader) of each sub-population.

Here, $fitness_i$ represents the adaptation value of the current individual, while best_fitness signifies the optimal adaptation value within the population. The global learning process will continue until the total number of updates equals the population size. Consequently, individuals with superior adaptation values are more likely to undergo updates. Subsequently, the population will revise both the global optimum, termed the Global Leader, and the local optimum, known as the Local Leader, for each subpopulation.

During the localized decision-making stage, each subpopulation maintains a parameter $\mathrm{LocalLeaderCount_k}$ that tracks how many times the local optimum has remained unchanged.

For instance, if the kth subpopulation fails to discover a solution superior to the existing local optimum during the current iteration, this count $\mathrm{LocalLeaderCount_k}$ is incremented by one. A threshold for stagnation LocalLeaderLimit (LLL) is established. Once this threshold $\mathrm{LocalLeaderCount_k}$ is met, every individual within the subpopulation selects a new direction for updates based on probability, either through random initialization or by orienting towards the global optimum and diverging from the local optimum:

$$SM_{i_{\text{new}}} = \begin{cases} SM_{\min} + \text{rand}(0, 1) \times (SM_{\max} - SM_{\min}), r \geq pr \\ SM_i + \text{rand}(0, 1) \times (GL - SM_i) + \text{rand}(0, 1) \times (SM_i - LL_k), r \angle pr \end{cases} \tag{28.12}$$

In the Global Decision Phase, analogous to the local decision phase, critical parameters such as GlobalLeaderCount and GlobalLeaderLimit (GLL) are employed. These metrics dictate the subdivision of the population into smaller, more numerous sub-populations and the reselection of local optima for each. The parameter MG defines the upper limit for the number of sub-populations permitted. If this limit is surpassed, the algorithm requires that these sub-populations be consolidated back into a single population.

28.3.2 Co-evolutionary Algorithms

Cooperative Coevolution (CC) is a potent strategy for addressing large-scale optimization challenges by segmenting the original problem into several subproblems. Each subproblem is independently optimized, targeting specific variables, while variables that are interdependent are optimized in a coordinated manner. This methodology is frequently combined with the Spider Monkey Optimization (SMO) algorithm to boost its performance. In CC, the subproblems are tackled through the iterative evolution of subpopulations. The assessment of the overall solution is a collaborative effort, depending on the amalgamation of key representatives from each subpopulation to construct the full solution. This co-evolutionary approach not only segments the population into distinct subproblems but also leverages the "split search" mechanism inherent in the SMO algorithm. This mechanism facilitates effective searching on both a global and local scale, rendering it exceptionally effective for intricate, large-scale optimization tasks that simulate real-world complexities.

28.3.3 UAV 3D Path Planning Based on Improved Spider Monkey Optimization Algorithm

28.3.3.1 Basic Flow of the Algorithm

The fundamental procedural architecture of the algorithm is delineated in Table 28.1. Initially, the path population is established as a matrix comprising N paths, each characterized by an optimization dimension D.Subsequently, the path population designated for optimization is systematically decomposed into multiple subproblems, each defined by the optimization dimension.Furthermore, the target population for optimization is segmented into several subproblems, with the optimization dimension of each subproblem governed by the parameter d*.This process results in a total of $(\frac{D}{d^*}$ distinct subproblems. Subsequently, each subproblem is further segmented into MG subpopulations, with independent optimization conducted on each using the SMO algorithm.In this study, the parameter d* serves as an innovative control mechanism that dictates the optimization dimension for each subproblem, aligning with the requisite number of path steps for each UAV. For instance, should $d^* = 2$, the population is divided into (D/2) subproblems, each encompassing N individuals, with two dimensions of optimization. Consequently, each individual within these subpopulations represents two steps along the path. In this context, MG denotes

Table 28.1 Basic flow of algorithm

ISMO algorithm
Step 1: Initiate the algorithm by establishing the initial population and configuring the parameters (d*) and (MG), which are critical for the subsequent phases of the model
Step 2: Segment the initial population into discrete subproblems, each representing a specific aspect of the overarching optimization task
Step 3:Further subdivide each subproblem into (MG) subpopulations and evaluate the fitness value of each path. Subsequently, determine the Global Leader for the subproblem and the Local Leaders for each subpopulation
Step 4: Execute both a local search phase to refine solutions within subpopulations and a global search phase to integrate insights across all subpopulations, optimizing each path's parameters accordingly
Step 5:Implement comprehensive optimization strategies across all subproblems and subpopulations, reassessing the fitness value of each path. Identify a new Global Leader and update the Global Best with contributions from this new leader
Step 6: Continually evaluate whether the predefined optimization criteria have been satisfied. If achieved, output the optimal results; if not, cyclically repeat steps 3–5 until the optimization criteria are fully met

the maximum allowable number of sub-populations, playing an essential role in preserving the diversity of search directions.Furthermore, diverging from the original SMO algorithm, the count of sub-populations is steadfastly maintained at MG within this study to guarantee the search's efficacy.Upon optimization of each subproblem, the optimal individuals therein are amalgamated to constitute a complete path, slated for subsequent refinement (as depicted in Table 28.1).

28.3.3.2 Initialization and Decomposition of the Population

Initially, the entire population, comprising N individuals each characterized by an optimization dimension of D, is initialized.Identify the optimal individual within the population and designate this individual as the Local Leader (LL).Subsequently, the population is segmented into $\frac{D}{d*}$ subproblems, each aligned with the optimization dimension, for targeted optimization.

For instance, within the first subproblem, the superior individual is ascertained and subsequently designated as the Global Leader (GL). This subproblem is further divided into MG subpopulations, with each subpopulation comprising $\frac{N}{MG}$ individual.Each subpopulation harbors a local optimum, which is identified and labeled as the Global Leader (GL).Subsequently, the current subproblem undergoes optimization via a dual-stage approach, encompassing both local and global search phases.This aforementioned process will be systematically applied across all subproblems, with the optimization cycling back to the first subproblem should the termination conditions remain unmet following the optimization of each respective subproblem.

28.3.3.3 Local Search Phase

In the bifurcated optimization process, the initial stage constitutes a local search. Within this realm, each individual recalibrates its position by referencing the randomly selected neighbors within its subpopulation, aiming towards the local optimum:

$$X_i = X_i + \text{rand}(0, 1) \times (LL - X_i) + \text{rand}(-1, 1) \times (\text{ neighbor } - X_i) \quad (28.13)$$

X_i is the current individual and neighbor is some random individual in the current subpopulation. The process within the local search phase unfolds in a dimensional manner.

28.3.3.4 Global Search Phase

Subsequent to the local search phase, the global search phase commences, with each individual updating its position relative to the globally determined optimum of its subproblem.During the global search phase, every individual recalibrates its current position in accordance with the globally recognized optimum of its respective subproblem.

$$X_{ij} = X_{ij} + \text{rand}(0, 1) \times (\text{GL} - X_{iJ}) + \text{rand}(-1, 1) \times \left(\text{neighbor} - X_{ij}\right) \tag{28.14}$$

where j represents a randomly chosen dimension targeted for optimization.

28.3.3.5 Calculation of Adaptation Values

Subsequent to both the local and the full search phases, the adaptation value for each individual is computed.For every individual within the subproblem, the process involves substituting the corresponding segment in GlobalBest with the individual in question and subsequently calculating its adaptation value.Following the computation of adaptation values for all individuals, the optimal individual for each segment of the subproblem is preserved in GlobalBest.The adaptation value is determined using the probability density function, as delineated below:

$$\text{Loss}_j = \sum \frac{n}{i = 1} e^{\left(-\frac{d_i \log(20)}{R_i}\right)} \tag{28.15}$$

Where is the distance from the jth node to be optimized to the center of the ith flight obstacle circle and is the radius of the ith threat. is used to control the shape of the density function. The parameter $\frac{R_i}{\log(20)}$ is employed to manipulate the shape of the density function. As d_i increases, that is, as the distance of the UAV from the center of the circle expands, the likelihood of interference with the UAV diminishes asymptotically.

28.3.3.6 Combining Subproblems

Upon optimization of each subproblem, the optimal individuals are amalgamated into what is termed GlobalBest, representing a complete path. Viewed from a macroscopic perspective, the proposed ISMO algorithm effectively divides the entire path into a series of consecutive sub-paths, with each sub-path being independently optimized. This segmentation significantly mitigates the dimensional constraints associated with long-distance path planning.On a microscopic scale, the diversity of path search directions for each sub-path is ensured by the SMO algorithm's "split search" mechanism, thereby enhancing the sub-paths' capability to evade or overcome local optima.

28.4 UAV Path Planning Simulation Test

28.4.1 Experimental Design

The simulation environment comprises an Intel(R) Core(TM) i7-9750H CPU operating at 2.60GHz, 16 GB of RAM, and a Win10 operating system, with MATLAB R2022a as the simulation software. Utilizing this setup, the algorithmic model is executed, initializing at the point (0, 0, 1) and concluding at (1000, 1000, 1). To assess the efficacy of ISMO in managing large-scale path optimization challenges, a flight scenario was constructed featuring 100 aerial obstacles within an optimization space dimensioned at 200 . The obstacles range from 0 to 40 km in radius and 0.5 to 2 km in height. The simulation employs a population of 100 , undergoing up to 100 iterations. Key modeling parameters are detailed in Table 28.2 .

28.4.2 Optimization of Parameter Settings

To improve the search capability of the algorithm. The parameters are selected. The final experimental setup parameters are as follows: the optimization dimension i.e. the parameter d* is set to 2 for each sub-problem, the sub-population size is set to 4, and the number of flight steps of the UAV D is set to 200. we set the population size N to 120 , and the number of sub-populations in each sub-problem MG to 10.

Table 28.2 Main modeling parameters

Parameter	Data
K_Z	100
K'_Z	100
Q_h	10
Q_v	10
α_{max}	60
β_{max}	60
ω_1	0.34
ω_2	0.48
ω_3	0.18
d	1500

28.4.2.1 Selection of Population Size Parameters

An experimental study was conducted to investigate the impact of population size N on the performance of the ISMO algorithm. In the experimental setup, population sizes were configured as N = {40, 60, 80, 100, 120, 140, 180, 200, 220, 240, 260, 280, 300}. Each parameter configuration was independently executed 30 times with subsequent calculation of average performance metrics. The termination criterion for the algorithm was defined as reaching the maximum number of fitness evaluations. As demonstrated in Fig. 28.1, the ISMO algorithm exhibited optimal comprehensive performance when N = 120. This empirical observation led to the definitive selection of N = 120 as the preferred population size configuration.

28.4.2.2 Parameter Selection for the Size of Subproblems

When d* is excessively large, the resultant sub-problem size expands, escalating both the search burden and the propensity to converge on local optima. Conversely, an overly small d* diminishes the sub-problem size excessively, causing undue dispersion among sub-paths and necessitating increased iteration counts, thereby impairing the convergence rate. To discern optimal performance, various d* values including 1, 2, 3, 4, and 5 were tested independently 30 times under specified termination conditions MaxFEs $= 1500 \times D$. As depicted in Fig. 28.2, optimal aggregated outcomes were observed when the sub-problem size was set to 2 . Consequently, a d* value of 2 was selected for implementation in ISMO.

28.4.2.3 Selection of Parameter MG for Maximum Subpopulation

The parameter MG denotes the sub-population size within each sub-problem. Given that the population size N is established at 100, MG is required to be a divisor of 100 . To evaluate MG's impact on algorithmic performance, MG was set at various levels:

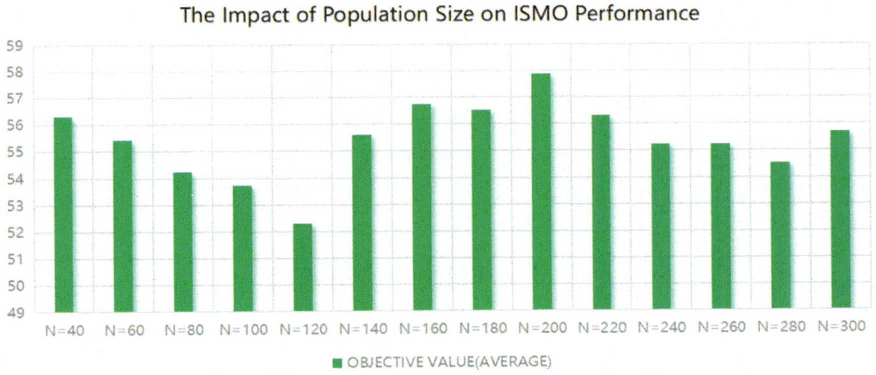

Fig. 28.1 Effect of population size on ISMO performance

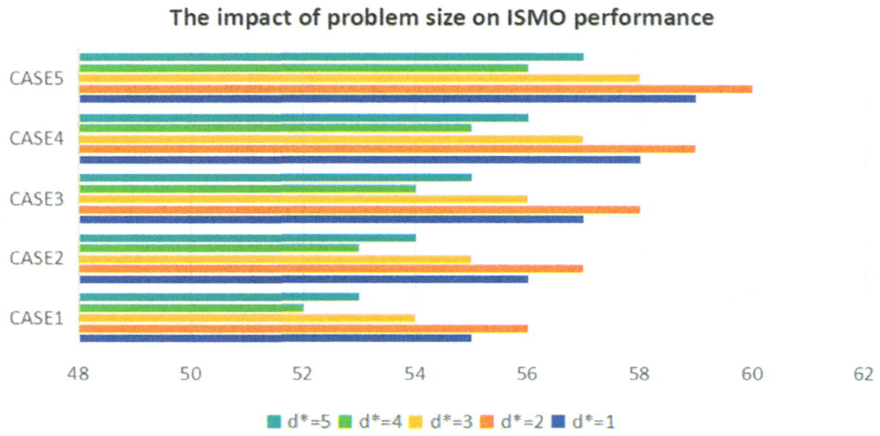

Fig. 28.2 Impact of subproblem size on ISMO performance

{2, 4, 5, 10, 20, 25, 50}. The experimental outcomes, displayed in Fig. 28.3, indicate that across these different MG settings, the results remain consistently similar. This consistency underscores ISMO's robust search capabilities, demonstrating its ability to locate optimal solutions across varying search directions.

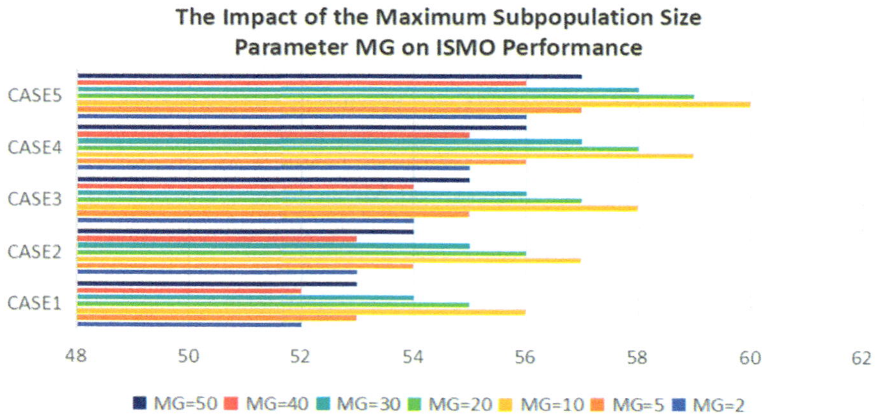

Fig. 28.3 Effect of the parameter MG for maximum subpopulation size on ISMO performance

28.4.3 Comparison of Algorithms

To assess the efficacy of the ISMO algorithm in UAV path planning, five evolutionary algorithms were employed, comprising the classical Spider Monkey Optimization Algorithm (SMO) along with four enhanced contemporary algorithms: the Improved Fish Swarm Algorithm (IMAFSA), the Improved Particle Swarm Algorithm (IPSO), the Improved Ant Colony Algorithm (IACA), and the Moth Flame Optimization Algorithm (MFO). These algorithms are implemented in a UAV path planning case study to substantiate the capabilities of ISMO. To maintain comparison fairness, the termination condition was uniformly set based on the maximum number of fitness evaluations, rather than CPU time or iteration counts. Each algorithm was independently executed 30 times per flight scenario, with the resulting mean and standard deviation computed to gauge ISMO's overall performance.

28.5 Results

The paths optimized by each algorithm are shown in Fig. 28.4:

The ranges for IACA, IMAFSA, IPSO, MFO, SMO, and ISMO are 167.24, 159.48, 154.37, 163.17, 144.18, and 132.54 km respectively. The optimal adaptations for these algorithms are 33.86, 34.19, 35.90, 36.73, 32.65, and 29.47. The angle of turn and climb costs are 90, 80, 90, 100, 40, and 10 respectively. Additionally, the success rates of optimization search for IACA, IMAFSA, IPSO, MFO, SMO, and ISMO are 74, 78, 80, 83, 90, and 95, as illustrated in Table 28.3 (Fig. 28.5):

28.6 Discussion

Upon comparing the optimized paths generated by each algorithm in Fig. 28.4, it is evident that the path outcomes of IPSO outperform those of the other enhanced algorithms as it avoids local optima; however, its final paths lack smoothness. Sim-

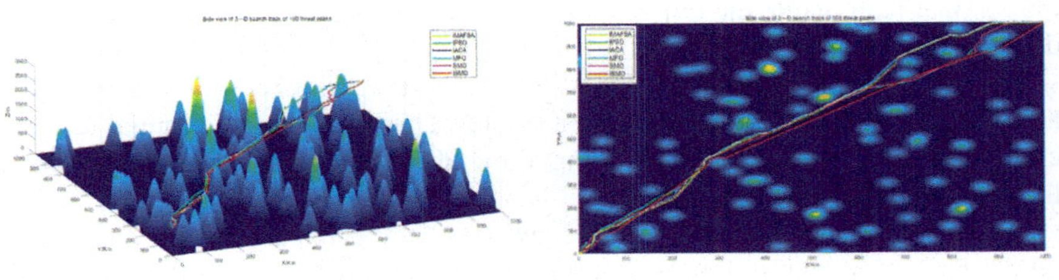

Fig. 28.4 Visualization of optimized paths for ISMO with improved algorithms in very large flight scale scenarios

Table 28.3 Simulation results statistics

Algorithm	Range	Optimal fitness	Turn and climb angle cost	Optimization success rate/%
IACA	167.24	33.86	16	74
IMAFSA	159.48	34.19	20	78
IPSO	154.37	35.90	16	80
MFO	163.17	36.73	25	83
SMO	144.18	32.65	10	90
ISMO	132.54	29.47	2.5	95

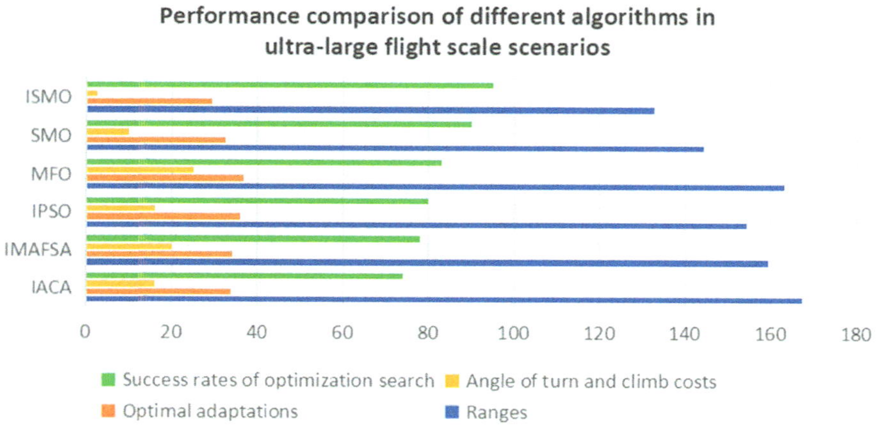

Fig. 28.5 Performance comparison of different ISMO algorithms in very large flight scale scenarios

ilarly, the optimized paths produced by SMO exhibit fluctuations in various segments, indicating suboptimal smoothness. Conversely, IMAFSA, IACA, and MFO frequently converge to local optima, resulting in path discontinuities. In contrast, ISMO not only adeptly circumvents mountainous regions but also selects the most cost-effective route across terrain. Remarkably, ISMO stands alone in identifying the optimal path, while the other algorithms succumb to local optimality at various decision points.

Analysis of the path data from Table 28.2 reveals that ISMO possesses a distinctive advantage in devising the most efficient routes, characterized by minimal turn and climb angle expenses, thereby ensuring a low-altitude, seamless flight trajectory at the most economical cost.

Examination of Fig. 28.6 reveals a consistent decline in adaptation values across all scenarios, indicating the algorithm's performance trend. Notably, the proposed ISMO demonstrates the swiftest convergence, reaching stability at approximately 240D iterations. While SMO exhibits a comparatively high convergence rate, it fails to achieve global optimality. In contrast, IPSO displays the slowest convergence,

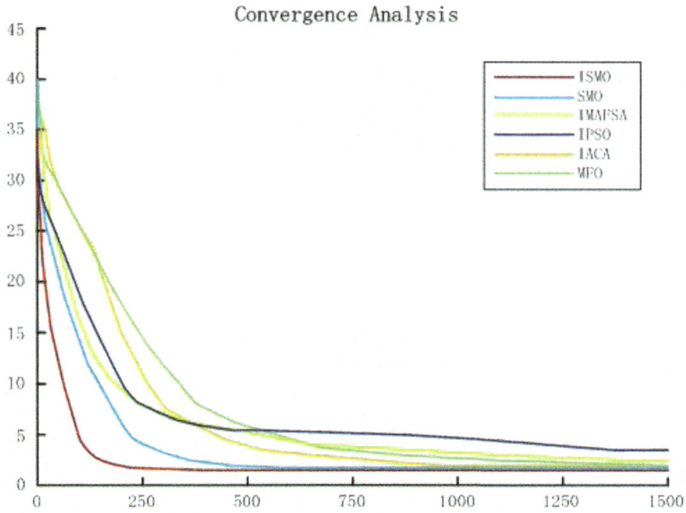

Fig. 28.6 Convergence analysis of ISMO compared with other algorithms

requiring approximately 1350D computations to converge. In summary, ISMO stands out for its robust convergence capability in identifying the optimal path.

In conclusion, ISMO emerges as the superior algorithm, exhibiting unparalleled optimization outcomes characterized by minimal travel distance, a narrow range of final fitness values, minimal standard deviation, and the highest success rate in attaining the optimum solution. These attributes underscore the exceptional effectiveness and stability of ISMO in comparison to alternative algorithms.

28.7 Conclusion

Building upon SMO, ISMO preserves both the local and global search phases while streamlining the "split-fusion" mechanism to enhance the diversity of search directions, thus equipping the algorithm with the capability to evade local optima. Additionally, ISMO incorporates a co-evolution mechanism, segmenting lengthy paths into shorter sub-paths for independent optimization. This approach significantly alleviates optimization pressure and bolsters global search efficacy. Comparative results highlight ISMO's superiority over SMO and four enhanced algorithms-Improved Fish Swarm Algorithm (IMAFSA), Improved Particle Swarm Algorithm (IPSO), Improved Ant Colony Algorithm (IACA), and Moth Flame Optimization Algorithm (MFO). Remarkably, only ISMO achieves the optimization of safe and seamless paths, while others exhibit local optima at fork points. These findings underscore

ISMO's superior performance, offering expedited search speed, heightened accuracy, and suitability for long-distance optimization tasks and real-world application feasibility. ISMO stands as a valuable guide for 3D UAV trajectory planning.

References

1. Evdokimenkov, V.N., Krasilshchikov, M.N., Lyapin, N.A.: Guaranteeing UAV trajectory control when approaching a maneuvering air target. J. Comput. Syst. Sci. Int. **57**(5), 789–800 (2018)
2. Kelkawi, A., El-Abd, M., Ahmad, I.: GPU-based cooperative coevolution for large-scale global optimization. Neural Comput. Appl. **35**(6), 4621–42 (2023)
3. Galyaev, A.A., Lysenko, P.V., Yakhno, V.P.: 2D optimal trajectory planning problem in threat environment for UUV with non-uniform radiation pattern. Sensors **21**(2), 396 (2021)
4. Mandloi, D., Arya, R., Verma, A.K.: Unmanned aerial vehicle path planning based on A* algorithm and its variants in 3D environment. Int. J. Syst. Assurance Eng. Manag. (1), 1–11 (2021)
5. Mirjalili, S., Aljarah, I., Mafarja, M., et al.: Grey wolf optimizer: theory, literature review, and application in computational fluid dynamics problems. In: Nature-Inspired Optimizers: Theories, Literature Reviews and Applications, pp. 87–105 (2020)
6. Soundaryam, S., Anusha, D.K., Rohith, P., et al.: Optimal path planning of UAV using grey wolf optimiser. Int. J. Comput. Syst. Eng. **5**(3), 129–136 (2019)
7. Pan, J.-S., Liu, N., Chu S.-C.: A hybrid differential evolution algorithm and its application in unmanned combat aerial vehicle path planning. IEEE Access **8**, 17691–17712 (2020)
8. Slowik, A., Kwasnicka, H.: Evolutionary algorithms and their applications to engineering problems. Neural Comput. Appl. **32**, 12363–79 (2020)
9. Aggarwal, S., Kumar, N.: Path planning techniques for unmanned aerial vehicles: a review, solutions, and challenges. Comput. Commun. **149**, 270–99 (2020)
10. Shivgan, R., Dong, Z.: Energy-efficient drone coverage path planning using genetic algorithm. In: Proceedings of the 2020 IEEE 21st International Conference on High Performance Switching and Routing (HPSR), F, 2020. IEEE (2020)
11. Aguilar-Melo, A.R., Calmé, S., Pinacho-Guendulain, B., et al.: Ecological and social determinants of association and proximity patterns in the fission-fusion society of spider monkeys (Ateles geoffroyi). Am. J. Primatol. **82**(1), e23077 (2020)
12. Shivgan, R., Dong, Z.: Energy-efficient drone coverage path planning using genetic algorithm. In: Proceedings of the 2020 IEEE 21st International Conference on High Performance Switching and Routing (HPSR), F, 2020. IEEE (2020)

Chapter 29
Grid-Forming Converters Simulation and Control Using a High-Level Language: Exploring Julia's Potentials

Sharara Rehimi, Hassan Bevrani, Chiyori T. Urabe, and Takeyoshi Kato

Abstract Grid-forming converters play a critical role in modern power grids, enabling enhanced stability and resilience. However, the control of these converters often requires a combination of low-level and high-level programming languages, leading to increased software complexity. This paper proposes a solution to this challenge by utilizing the Julia programming language. Julia offers a unique combination of performance and flexibility, making it suitable for both online control and rapid prototyping. This paper presents a set of Julia packages developed specifically for dynamic control applications. Results demonstrate the feasibility and advantages of utilizing this language for grid-forming converters control. Moreover, it highlights the inherent versatility of Julia's generic programming style, which facilitates the composition and adaptation of packages for various computational tasks in grid forming converters control. This work explores the potential of Julia as a powerful tool for advanced control synthesis techniques of these converters, offering insights and opportunities for further research and development in the field of renewable integrated power grids.

29.1 Introduction

Grid-forming converters (GFM) have become key components in modern power grids, serving various computational tasks that are essential for the system effective operation and control [1]. These tasks encompass online/offline control, stability analysis, controller synthesis, dynamic simulation, and operation planning. Indeed,

S. Rehimi (✉)
Department of Electrical Engineering, Graduate School of Engineering, Nagoya University, Nagoya, Japan
e-mail: rehimi.sharara.z8@s.mail.nagoya-u.ac.jp

H. Bevrani · C. T. Urabe · T. Kato
Department of Electrical Engineering, Smart/Micro Grids Research Center, University of Kurdistan, Sanandaj, Iran
e-mail: tkato@nuee.nagoya-u.ac.jp

F. P. García Márquez et al. (eds.), *Computing, Internet of Things and Data Analytics*, Smart Innovation, Systems and Technologies 387,
https://doi.org/10.1007/978-3-031-87154-2_29

performing high-complexity computations is a fundamental requirement in the domain of GFM converters design, analysis and application. These computations involve various control loops and intricate dynamics that significantly impact the stability of the entire power grid. Each computational task within this context places specific demands on the software packages employed to carry them out effectively. For instance, the analysis and implementation of control strategies require precise and timely calculations, ensuring the stability and responsiveness of the GFM converters [2]. On the other hand, controller synthesis involves offline processes and needs computational methods.

Given that the significance of GFM converters in maintaining modern power grids stability cannot be neglected. The GFM converters play a pivotal role in ensuring the overall reliability of the power grids. Consequently, it is of great importance to conduct extensive studies on these converters, encompassing their hardware and software development, as well as their impact on modern power grids stability and performance [1]. To address the diverse research and engineering needs within this field, it is crucial to develop robust and compatible software solutions.

Researchers require accessible tools that facilitate their comprehension and experimentation for GFM control analysis and synthesis. Simultaneously, experienced professionals require high-performance capabilities and efficient prototyping environments to tackle complex challenges effectively. Thus, the development of suitable software solutions is essential for meeting the various study requirements of both mentioned groups. These solutions should provide the necessary tools and flexibility to effectively test and optimize control design strategies, analyze system dynamics, and ensure reliable operation of GFM converters for a wide range of scenarios.

Traditionally, addressing the diverse requirements of GFM converter control involves utilizing two programming languages. Typically, a low-level language like, C or C++, which is employed for implementing the lower-level components of a software package, while a dynamic high-level language such as Python or MATLAB is used for non-performance-critical parts or for providing bindings to the low-level components [3, 4]. This approach offers convenience for novice programmers and facilitates rapid prototyping, while enabling advanced users to directly interact with the lower-level functionalities. Examples of software packages in the modern power grid domain that adopt this two-language approach include Power System Simulation Toolbox (PSAT), PowerFactory by DIgSILENT, OpenDSS (Distribution System Simulator) developed by the Electric Power Research Institute (EPRI), and GridLAB-D, which is an open-source power distribution system simulation and analysis tool developed by the U.S. Department of Energy's Pacific Northwest National Laboratory (PNNL).

However, this approach has inherent drawbacks. Firstly, users who initially prototype their GFM converter control in the high-level language often face the challenge of duplicating their efforts when porting the code to the lower-level language once they are satisfied with the prototype. This process can be tedious and prone to errors. Secondly, maintaining a software package written in multiple programming languages often incurs significant developer overhead. Keeping the codebases synchronized, managing build systems and documentation for each language adds complexity and increases maintenance efforts. The field of numerical computing has recognized this "two-language problem" to prompt the development of the Julia programming language [5]. Julia is a relatively new high-level language that combines the productivity and interactivity of dynamic languages like Python with C-like performance.

This paper presents evidence supporting the suitability of Julia for GFM converters control in the renewable integrated power systems. Besides, it addresses a collection of Julia software packages developed by the world wide authors, demonstrating their effectiveness in implementing a desired controller that adheres to new standards and grid codes for GFM converters. Some of these packages that feature high speeds in control mechanism implementation are:

- LinearAlgebra.jl: provides a comprehensive collection of linear algebra functionalities, including linear solvers, matrix factorization, and operations, for efficient and accurate algebraic numerical computations [5].
- ControlSystems.jl: offers a range of control systems tools, including modeling, linearization, simulation, and analysis, enabling efficient and accurate design, analysis, and simulation of control systems [6].
- ElectricGrid.jl: provides a range of functionalities for modeling and analyzing electric power systems, including power flow, stability, and control, enabling efficient and accurate study of grid dynamics and operations [7].
- PowerDynamics.jl: includes functionalities for modeling and simulating power systems, such as dynamic simulations, state estimation, and optimization. These features facilitate efficient and accurate analysis of power system dynamics and operations [8].

These packages serve as a solid foundation for GFM converter based power grids to build upon. The subsequent sections of the paper are organized as follows: Sect. 29.2 provides an overview of the Julia language and an initial assessment of its suitability for GFM converter control system synthesis and analysis. Section 29.3 introduces the developed packages. Section 29.4 presents several control design examples that demonstrate the feasibility of utilizing Julia for the analysis and synthesis of control systems for GFM converters. These examples illustrate the potential of Julia for control system analysis and synthesis in power electronics applications. Finally, Sect. 29.5 concludes the paper.

29.2 Julia for Grid Forming Converters

This section first provides a general overview of Julia, followed by an assessment of its application as a programming language for GFM converter simulation and control.

29.2.1 Julia: An Introduction

Julia, a general-purpose programming language with a strong emphasis on numerical computing, has been in development since 2009. While version 1.10.2 was recently released, Julia is distributed as an open source under the Massachusetts Institute of Technology (MIT) license and is freely available [5]. Notably, Julia provides an extensive linear algebra module as a part of its standard library, demonstrating its focus on numerical computations. The language utilizes *Low Level Virtual Machine (LLVM)* to generate native machine codes and employs *garbage-collected* and *just-in-time (JIT)* compilation [9].

Julia's developers describe it as "optionally typed," allowing flexibility in specifying field types within data structures. By fully specifying types, better performance can be achieved. Julia boasts a robust type system, incorporating parametric types similar to *C++* template classes, as well as powerful type inference capabilities that reduce the need for manual type annotations, similar to *C++*'s auto keyword.

In contrast to *object-oriented* languages, Julia does not associate methods directly with types. Instead, functions are defined independently of types and can have multiple overloaded methods that accept different argument types. At runtime, Julia employs multiple dispatch, selecting the most appropriate method based on the types of all input arguments. Multiple dispatch is efficiently implemented in Julia, even for fundamental arithmetic operations, enabling user-defined types and functions to perform on par with built-in language constructs [9].

Julia offers convenient features commonly found in high-level languages, such as support for list comprehensions, generators, and parallelism. It also excels in functional programming, treating functions as first-class objects and providing efficient higher-order functions extensively utilized in the standard library. In a nod to *LISP*, Julia represents code as a data structure within the language, facilitating powerful metaprogramming capabilities without the need for external preprocessors or template systems.

The LinearAlgebra module in Julia's standard library provides both low-level bindings to BLAS/LAPACK libraries and high-level abstractions built upon these bindings. By default, Julia utilizes OpenBLAS, but it can be compiled with Intel's MKL for modest performance improvements, aligning with the libraries used by NumPy and MATLAB. Additionally, the third-party package StaticArrays.jl offers stack-allocated fixed-size arrays similar to the Eigen C++ library.

The Julia community has developed over 10,000 registered packages, emphasizing unit testing and continuous integration practices to ensure reliable and robust software development [5].

29.2.2 *Application in GFM Converter Simulation and Control*

Dynamic modeling is a crucial aspect in the renewable energy field, particularly in the context of GFM converters. These converters require comprehensive studies to evaluate their efficiency and facilitate their development [1]. Thus, selecting a software tool to support dynamic studies at an acceptable speed is of great importance. In this regard, Julia emerges as a suitable alternative.

Julia is renowned for its strong capabilities in dynamic modeling, enabling researchers to conduct in-depth studies on the performance and development of GFM converters. A rich set of features and packages specifically designed for dynamic modeling make it well-suited for such investigations. Researchers can use Julia's functionalities to explore converter efficiency, stability, and response under various operating conditions.

In addition to dynamic modeling, strong optimization is another fundamental requirement in the field of GFM converters operation and control. The strangeness in optimization, makes the Julia as an ideal choice for addressing optimization challenges in the GFM converters applications. Its robust optimization capabilities and extensive package support empower researchers to optimize system performance, energy efficiency, and control strategies.

Julia also stands out for its compatibility with different control theories. It offers comprehensive support for both classic and modern control theories, providing enough flexibility for researchers and developers in the GFM converters field to implement and evaluate various control strategies. This ensures a reliable and efficient GFM converters operation, and further enhancing their performance.

Furthermore, Julia's compatibility with intelligent algorithms adds another layer of advantage. Researchers can use Julia's capabilities to incorporate artificial intelligence and machine learning techniques for enhancing the adaptability of GFM converters in various grid dynamic conditions. This compatibility enables the development of advanced control schemes and adaptive strategies, contributing to the advancement of GFM converters technology.

Considering these factors, it can be concluded that Julia is a smart choice for studies and development in the area of GFM converter-based renewable integrated power grids. Its strong capabilities in dynamic modeling, optimization, compatibility with different control theories, and intelligent algorithms make it a versatile and powerful programming language for addressing the challenges and requirements of GFM converters applications. By using Julia's strengths, researchers and developers can conduct comprehensive investigations, converter performance optimization, and drive more advances in this critical domain.

29.3 Relevant Packages and Development

The study and development of GFM converters operation and control strongly rely on the selection of appropriate Julia packages. This section aims to introduce a set of essential Julia packages that offer significant benefits for GFM converters research and development. To facilitate access to these packages, and the relevant source code, the main page of each package is provided in the corresponding subsection. This will enable users to explore the functionalities of the packages and access the necessary resources for their research and development.

29.3.1 LinearAlgebra.jl

Linear algebra plays a fundamental role in the field of power electronic converter studies, providing a powerful framework for analyzing and solving relevant complex problems [5]. Julia, as a part of its comprehensive functionality, offers native implementations of various essential linear algebra operations, making it a valuable tool for researchers and developers in the mentioned studies field.

A key advantage of using Julia is in its support for multi-dimensional arrays, which is useful to perform linear algebra operations. By utilizing the *LinearAlgebra.jl* package, researchers can access a wide range of common and useful linear algebra functionalities.

Basic operations such as computing the trace (tr), determinant (det), and inverse (inv) of matrices are all supported within this package. Moreover, it provides convenient functions for finding eigenvalues and eigenvectors, which are vital in analyzing the stability and behavior of GFM converters. These eigenvalues and eigenvectors offer valuable insights into the dynamic properties of the system, helping researchers to assess dynamic stability and performance, accurately. Additionally, it provides a necessary extensive range of functions for utilizing matrices in dynamics analysis and synthesis studies. This package encompasses various essential functionalities, allowing researchers to analyzing and modeling of dynamic systems effectively.

For detailed information on the *LinearAlgebra.jl* package in Julia, readers can refer to the official documentation available in [10], which provides comprehensive insights into the functionality usage.

29.3.2 ControlSystems.jl

The *ControlSystems.jl* is a powerful package written in the Julia programming language that provides a comprehensive set of tools for control system analysis and synthesis. If you have workflows that do not require continuous-time simulation, you have the option to install the lighter package. The *ControlSystemsBase.jl package* instead. *ControlSystemsBase.jl* contains all the functionalities of *ControlSystems.jl* except for continuous-time simulation and root locus analysis. It is considerably faster to load and precompile compared to *ControlSystems.jl*. It is worth noting that if you choose to install *ControlSystemsBase.jl*, it is recommended not to install *ControlSystems.jl* as well, as it can cause longer pre-compilation times due to the dependencies it brings in, such as *OrdinaryDiffEq* [6].

The *ControlSystems.jl* provides basic functions for creating control system models, such as state-space and transfer function representations. A state-space model can be created using the function 'ss', while a transfer function can be created using the function 'tf(num, den)' or 'tf(num, den, Ts)', where 'num' and 'den' are vectors representing the numerator and denominator of a rational function, and 'Ts' is the sample time for a discrete-time system. These functions allow you to easily define and manipulate control system models using operators like +, −, *, /, and functions like 'append'. It is important to note that while transfer functions are commonly used, state-space representations are often better suited for high-order systems due to their improved numerical properties.

For detailed information on the *ControlSystems.jl* package in Julia, readers can refer to the official documentation available in [11], which offers thorough explanations of the functionality usage.

29.3.3 ElectricGrid.jl

The *ElectricGrid.jl* is a powerful package designed for building realistic simulations of electric grids with a strong emphasis on control capabilities. Whether you want to analyze the behavior of an electric grid, develop advanced control strategies, or train reinforcement learning (RL) agents as controllers, the *ElectricGrid.jl* package provides extensive support to meet your needs.

With the *ElectricGrid.jl*, a simulation environment can be easily created by defining the sources, loads, and cable connections of the electric grid [7]. There is enough flexibility to set detailed parameters for the electric components or let them be automatically generated. Additionally, the *ElectricGrid.jl* enables one to choose different control modes for each source in the system, allowing for comprehensive exploration and evaluation of control strategies. Using the agent architecture of the *ReinforcementLearning.jl*, one can either train RL agents as controllers or develop the given custom controllers within the framework.

For detailed information on the *ControlSystems.jl* package in Julia, please refer to the official documentation available in [12], which explains the functionalities usage in a comprehensive manner.

29.3.4 PowerDynamics.jl

The *PowerDynamics.jl* is a powerful package for dynamic power system analysis in Julia. It provides a comprehensive set of tools and functionalities to create and analyze dynamic power grid models. Whether you are a grid modeler, a grid component developer, or a *PowerDynamics.jl* developer, this package provides all means that are required to work with dynamic power systems [8].

It is important to note that the *PowerDynamics.jl* is a rapidly evolving package, and its Application Programming Interface (API) is still under development. To ensure compatibility with future versions while using the latest features, it is strongly recommended to utilize environments.

It is noteworthy that the *PowerDynamics.jl* is designed for Julia 1.6 and above, and the package aims to swiftly adopt new Julia versions while also supporting older versions to facilitate a smooth transition for users. However, Julia versions 0.5 are not supported anymore.

For detailed information on the *ControlSystems.jl* package in Julia, the interested readers can find the official documentation in [13], which offers a comprehensive overview of the functionalities usage.

It is noteworthy that the availability and suitability of these packages may vary over time, and it is advisable to refer to the packages main page for the most up-to-date information and compatibility with the desired applications.

29.4 Examples

This section provides some illustrative examples that demonstrate the practical application of the Julia programming language in the analysis and synthesis of GFM converters control systems. The experiments were performed on a desktop MacBook Pro M2 with macOS operating system.

These examples were tested on a typical GFM converter. The selected GFM converter and its control system depicted in Fig. 29.1. The control system employs a root-mean-square (RMS) value-based scheme without additional inner voltage or current control loops. This approach regulates the output voltage through a reactive power control loop.

The absence of an inner voltage loop simplifies the active power control loop, leading to smaller and less sensitive bus voltage deviations to the output impedance [1]. Based on the control law in the "P-droop, inertia and damping emulator" block, the simplified small signal $\Delta P_{out} / \Delta P_0$ transfer function with damping loop can be derived as follows:

$$\frac{\Delta P_{out}}{\Delta P_0} = \frac{K}{J\omega_0 s^2 + (k_p + D)s + K} \tag{29.1}$$

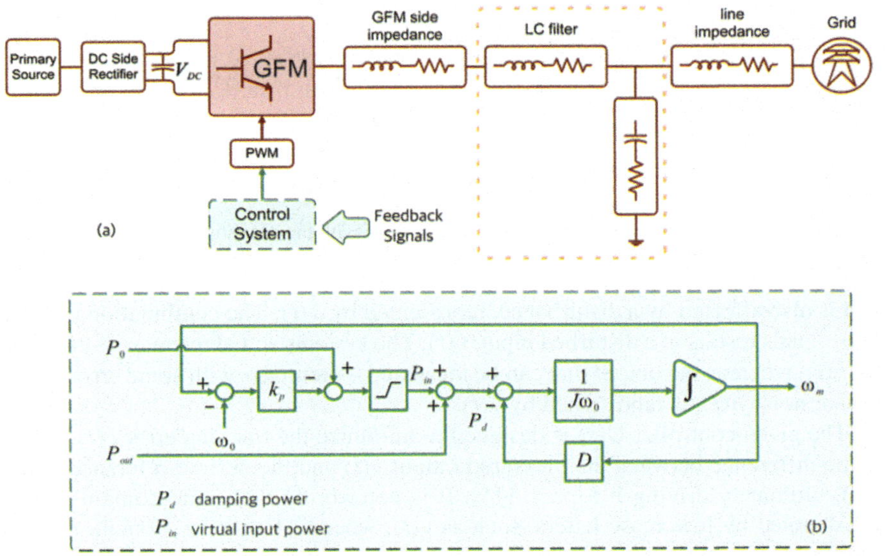

Fig. 29.1 Typical GFM converter with main control systems block: **a** overall configuration, **b** P-droop, inertia and damping emulator

where ΔP_{out}, ΔP_0, K, J, ω_0, k_p, and D are output power, reference power, synchronizing power coefficient, moment of inertia, nominal frequency, droop coefficient, and damping coefficient, respectively. The control parameters of the GFM converter are considered as given in Table 29.1.

The tests focused on evaluating the introduced converters performance in frequency/active-power control within a supplementary layer. The analysis will be conducted under this specific operation perspective.

To facilitate a more tractable analysis of power grid, transfer functions are employed. A key advantage of this approach lies in the ability to shift the problem from the time domain to the frequency domain, where it can be more easily solved, and then transformed back to the time domain. This strategy is motivated by the fact that the computationally intensive operation of convolution, which relates signals, is equivalent to a simple multiplication in the frequency domain, thanks to the Laplace and Fourier transform [14].

Considering one of the standard feedback control structures, shown in Fig. 29.2, for the introduced case study. Here, the system receives an input, denoted by $u(t)$,

Table 29.1 Control parameters of GFM converter

Parameters	K	J	D	k_p	ω_0
Value[a]	15.9×10^3	0.28 s	2312	$20pu$	rad/s

[a] All values are taken from [1, pp. 49–54, Chap. 3]

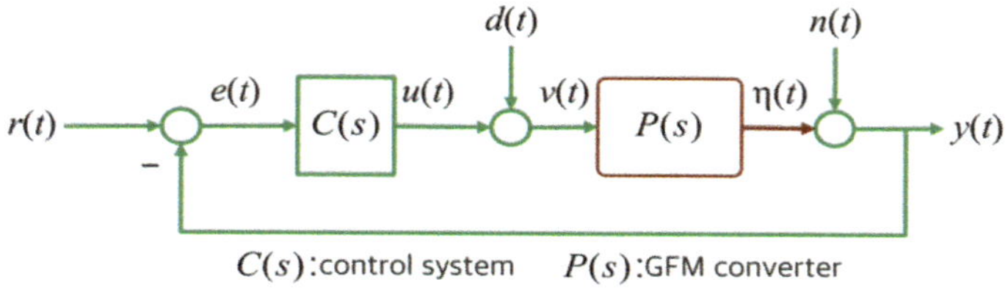

Fig. 29.2 A standard closed-loop control system to cope with the case study

and is also affected by a disturbance, represented by $d(t)$. The combination of these two signals results in a disturbed input, $v(t)$. The systems actual response is captured by $\eta(t)$, whereas the output that can be measured, potentially with some error due to sensor noise $n(t)$, is represented by $y(t)$.

The given controller $C(s)$ is designed to minimize the tracking error $e(t)$, which is the difference between the measured output $y(t)$ and the desired reference signal $r(t)$, ultimately driving it to zero [15]. It is noteworthy that, time-domain signals are denoted by lowercase letters, such as $v(t)$, whereas frequency-domain transfer functions, resulting from Laplace or Fourier transformations, are represented by uppercase letters, such as $C(s)$. The loop gain, denoted by $L(s)$, is the loop transfer function that can be defined as:

$$L(s) = C(s)P(s) \tag{29.2}$$

Four key transfer functions that can be derived from the presented system are: (*i*) the sensitivity function, denoted by $S(s)$, is the closed-loop transfer function that quantifies the impact of disturbances d on the output y, (*ii*) the complementary sensitivity function, denoted by $T(s)$, is the closed-loop transfer function that quantifies the impact of reference signal r, on the output y, (*iii*) the load sensitivity function, denoted by $P(s)S(s)$, and (*iv*) the noise sensitivity function, denoted by $C(s)S(s)$, and can be defined as:

$$S(s) = \frac{1}{1 + C(s)P(s)} \tag{29.3}$$

$$T(s) = \frac{C(s)P(s)}{1 + C(s)P(s)} \tag{29.4}$$

$$P(s)S(s) = \frac{P(s)}{1 + C(s)P(s)} \tag{29.5}$$

$$C(s)S(s) = \frac{C(s)}{1 + C(s)P(s)} \tag{29.6}$$

These four key transfer functions are collectively referred to as *Gang of Four* transfer functions. To thoroughly assess the performance and stability of the designed controller and verify its effectiveness, these four transfer functions are analyzed. Indeed, these four transfer functions are used to ensure that no unstable zero/pole cancelation is made, and to ensure the internal stability of the system. This is crucial for the systems stability and robustness [16]. In the subsequent subsections, several illustrative examples will be explored using Julia for the introduced case study.

29.4.1 PI Loop Shaping Example

The *Gang of Four* gains are plotted for the mentioned GFM converter under unit feedback ($C(s) = 1$), providing insight into its dynamics behavior. The sensitivity function exhibits a notable peak around frequency $\omega = 1.8\,\text{rad/s}$ as shown in Fig. 29.3. To address this, a simple Proportional-Integral (PI) controller $\left(C(s) = k_p + \frac{k_i}{s}\right)$, is designed using the *loopshapingPI* function, targeting a 140-degree phase margin at this frequency. The resulting *Gang of Four* gains are plotted for both the constructed controller (PI) and unit feedback in Fig. 29.4.

Additionally, a scenario can be considered where a closed-loop system with a bandwidth of $\omega = 2\,\text{rad/s}$ is desired. In this case, the Nyquist curve $L(\omega j) = P(\omega j)C(\omega j)$ is designed to pass through the point $|L(\omega j) = rl = 1|$, $\arg(L(\omega j)) = -180 + phasemargin = -180 + 140$. The resulting *Gang of Four* indicates that a highly robust and fast controller can be achieved using this design approach, although it would require significant control effort to double the bandwidth of all poles. The outcomes are illustrated in Fig. 29.5.

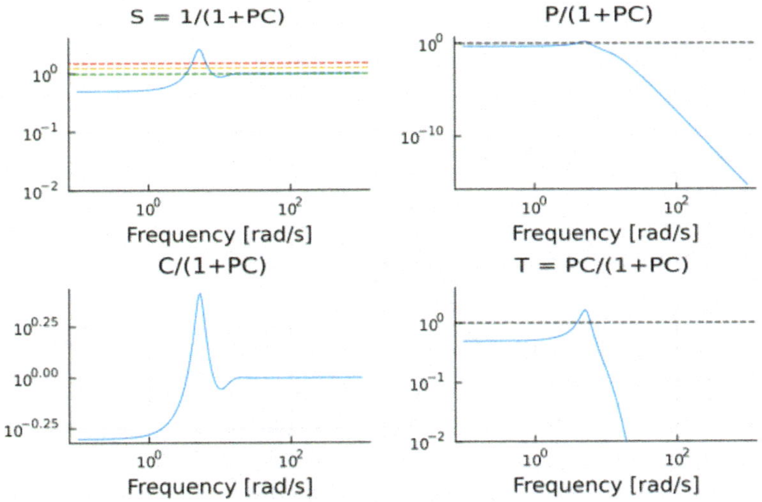

Fig. 29.3 *Gang of Four* gains presentation for the selected case study

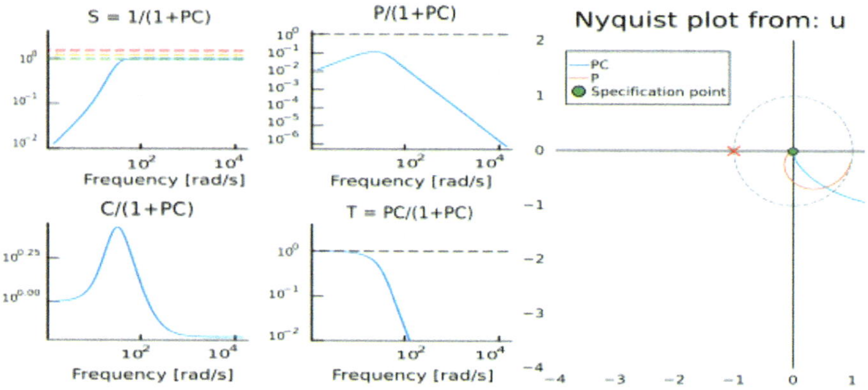

Fig. 29.4 *Gang of Four* gains presentation and Nyquist plots for PI and unit gain controllers

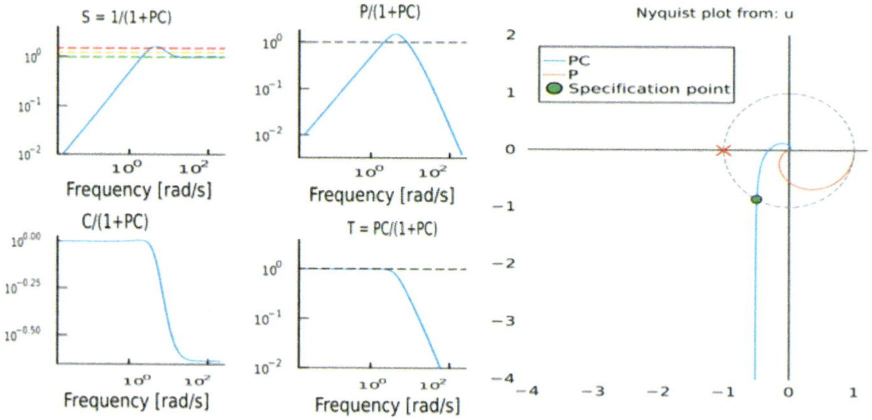

Fig. 29.5 *Gang of Four* gains presentation and Nyquist diagram for the closed loop system with PI controller $\left(\omega = 2\frac{\text{rad}}{\text{s}}\right)$

29.4.2 PID Loop Shaping Example

Processes characterized by inertia, such as double integrators, necessitate a derivative (D) term in the controller to achieve satisfactory results. The *loopshapingPID* function enables the specification of a point in the Nyquist plane where the loop-transfer function $L(s) = C(s)P(s)$ should be tangent to the circle representing $|T| = \left|\frac{PC}{1+PC}\right| = M_t$. This tangent point is defined by specifying M_t and the angle φ_t between the real axis and the tangent point, as illustrated in the Nyquist plot in Fig. 29.6. To ensure robustness, it is generally desirable to aim for M_t values less than 1.5. In general, a smaller required M_t, gives a larger controller gain.

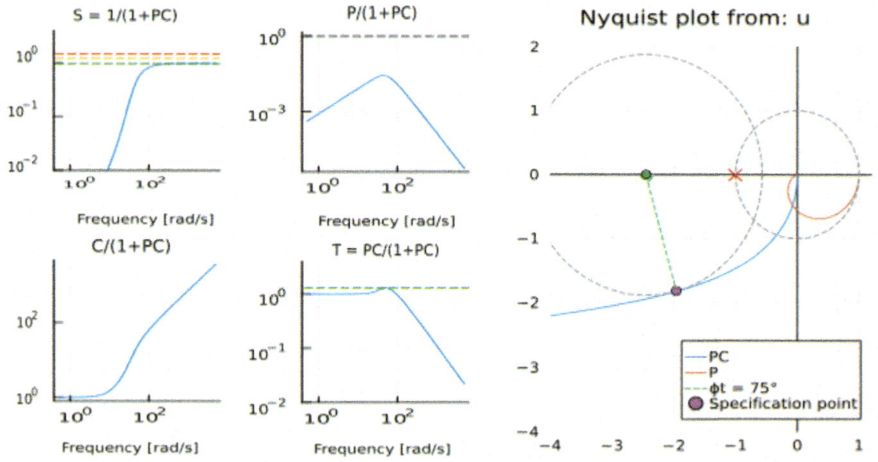

Fig. 29.6 *Gang of Four* gains presentation and Nyquist diagram for the closed loop system with PID controller $\left(\omega = 2\frac{\text{rad}}{\text{s}}\right)$

During designing a PID controller, a large controller gain at high frequencies is typically expected. However, this can be detrimental to both robustness and noise rejection performance. A common solution is to incorporate a lowpass filter in series with the controller. In the results shown in Fig. 29.7, the keyword argument $T_f = \frac{1}{20}\omega$ is used to specify the addition of a second order lowpass filter with a cutoff frequency 20 times faster than the design frequency. As can be seen, the inclusion of the filter results in an increased high-frequency roll-off in both T and CS, which is generally desirable.

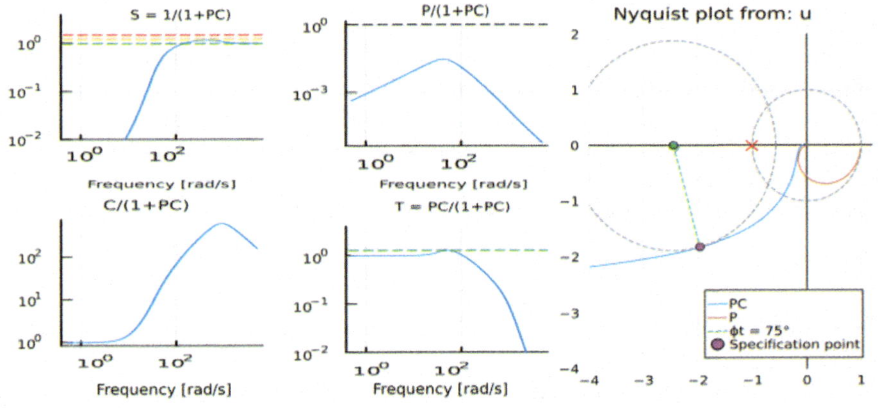

Fig. 29.7 *Gang of Four* gains presentation and Nyquist diagram for the closed loop system with PID controller and low pass filter

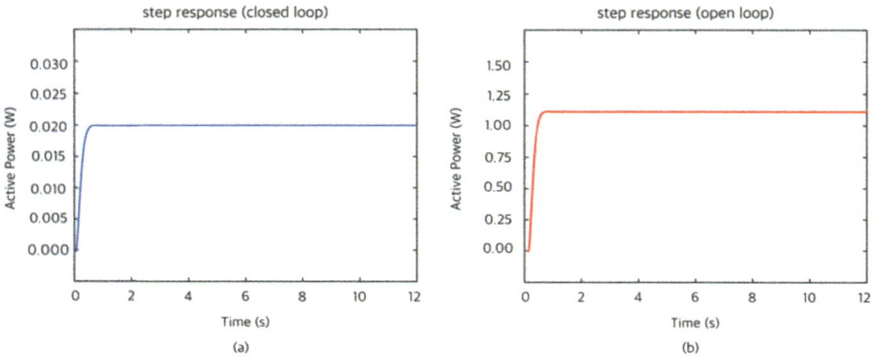

Fig. 29.8 Step response to $r(t)$, **a** closed-loop (PID), **b** open loop system

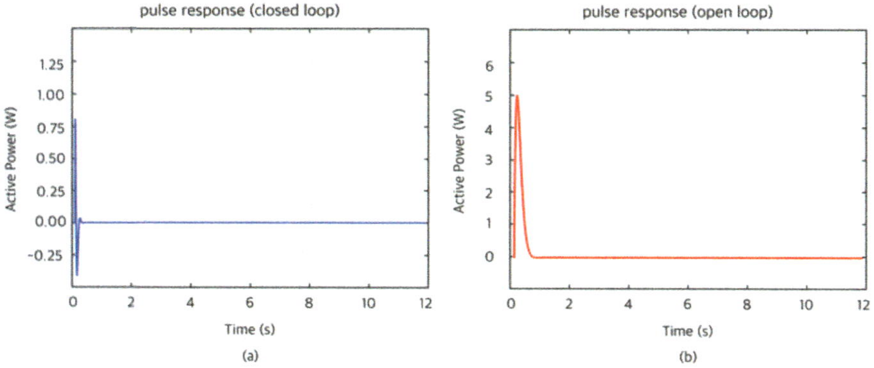

Fig. 29.9 Pulse response to $r(t)$, **a** closed-loop (PID), **b** open loop system

The performance of the designed controller is assessed by comparing the step response and pulse response of the open-loop system with those of the closed-loop system, which incorporates the PID controller. The step and impulse are applied to $r(t)$ in both cases. The results, presented in Figs. 29.8 and 29.9, demonstrate that the GFM converters behavior in the supplementary control layer is significantly improved when the controller is present, compared to the open-loop operation.

29.5 Discussion

Julia is a powerful software tool for dynamic modeling in the renewable energy field, particularly in GFM converters. Its robust capabilities enable researchers to conduct in-depth studies on converter efficiency, stability, and response under various operating conditions. Julia's optimization capabilities and extensive package support researchers to optimize system performance, energy efficiency, and control strategies. It is compatible with both classic and modern control theories, providing flexibility for implementing and evaluating various control strategies. Additionally, Julia's compatibility with intelligent algorithms allows for the development of advanced control schemes and adaptive strategies, contributing to the advancement of GFM converter technology.

29.6 Conclusion

In conclusion, this paper demonstrates the effectiveness of utilizing the Julia programming language for grid-forming converters control, offering a promising solution to the software complexity challenges in modern power grids. By using Julia's unique performance and flexibility, the proposed environment enables rapid prototyping and real-time control, while also showcasing the language's versatility in adapting to various computational tasks. This work builds the way for further research and development in power systems and renewable energy integration, highlighting Julia's potential as a powerful tool for advancing grid-forming converter control techniques.

Acknowledgements The received support from Smart/Micro Grids Research Center (SMGRC) at the University of Kurdistan, Sanandaj, Iran is highly appropriated.

References

1. Bevrani, H., Kato, T., Ise, T., Inoue, K.: Grid Connected Converters: Modeling, Stability and Control. Elsevier (2022)
2. Monti, A., Milano, F., Bompard, E., Guillaud, X.: Converter-Based Dynamics and Control of Modern Power Systems. Academic Press (2020)
3. https://www.mathworks.com
4. https://www.python.org
5. https://julialang.org
6. Bagge Carlson, F., Fält, M., Heimerson, A., Troeng, O.: ControlSystems.jl: a control toolbox in Julia. In: Proceedings of CDC (2021)
7. Wallscheid, O., et al.: ElectricGrid.jl—a Julia-based modeling and simulation tool for power electronics-driven electric energy grids. J. Open Source Softw. **8**(89), 5616 (2023)
8. Plietzsch, A., et al.: PowerDynamics.jl—an experimentally validated open-source package for the dynamical analysis of power grids. SoftwareX **17**, 100861 (2022)
9. Koolen, T., Deits, R.: Julia for robotics: simulation and real-time control in a high-level programming language. In: 2019 International Conference on Robotics and Automation (ICRA), 2019, pp. 604–611
10. https://docs.julialang.org/en/v1/stdlib/LinearAlgebra/#man-linalg
11. https://juliacontrol.github.io/ControlSystems.jl/dev/man/introduction
12. https://juliapackages.com/p/electricgrid
13. https://juliaenergy.github.io/PowerDynamics.jl/stable/
14. Zardini, G.: Lecture 1: Feedback Control Loop. ETH University, Zürich, Switzerland (2018)

15. Åström, K.J.: Feedback Fundamentals. (2020)
16. Hassan, B.: Robust Control Lecture Notes. University of Kurdistan, Sanandaj, Iran (2023). Available online at: https://smgrc.uok.ac.ir/timeline/robust-control-fall-2023-university-of-kurdistan/

Chapter 30
TRUSTd: Framework for Trustworthy Data in IOMT for the Judgment of Drug to Drug Interactions

Qadeer Hashir, Lala Rukh Majeed, Saba Mahmood, and Muhammad Asfand-E-Yar

Abstract In the Internet of Things today, data integrity is a matter of concern. This paper presents a TRUST framework that aims to make IoT systems more secure. Contrasting to the previous methods that concentrate only on the accuracy of sensors, the proposed framework judges the trustworthiness of the data shared by these devices. Analysis of time-series sensor data, we are able to detect patterns like auto-correlation and cross-correlation thereby creating the basis for machine learning models that are trained to distinguish whether the data is reliable or not. The proposed framework is illustrated through a scenario involving the design of a health-focused application in which patient data from devices like smartwatches is carefully checked for reliability. This supports healthcare providers to take rightful decisions regarding a treatment plan that may involve possible drug reactions. Finally, also to deal with sparse data, we utilized RWI which is an algorithm that improves the quality of the time-series data for the model testing. TRUST framework along with RWI-enhanced dataset with this configuration, gives a trusted environment for data integrity in IoT situations. The study not only identifies critical obstacles in the IoT environment but highlights the role of reliability and trust measurement processes as well.

30.1 Introduction

Nowadays, in the fast and digital world, the Internet of Things (IoT) has made a hallmark through many sectors ranging from smart homes to health care and others. On the other wards, the execution of IoT technologies has received maximum

Q. Hashir (✉) · M. Asfand-E-Yar
Department of Computer Science, Center of Excellence in Artificial Intelligence (CoE-AI), Bahria Univerisity Islamabad, Islamabad, Pakistan
e-mail: qadeer.buho@bahria.edu.pk

M. Asfand-E-Yar
e-mail: asfandeyar.buic@bahria.edu.pk

L. Rukh Majeed · S. Mahmood
Department of Computer Science, Bahria Univerisity Islamabad, Islamabad, Pakistan
e-mail: smahmood.buic@bahria.edu.pk

F. P. García Márquez et al. (eds.), *Computing, Internet of Things and Data Analytics*, Smart Innovation, Systems and Technologies 387,
https://doi.org/10.1007/978-3-031-87154-2_30

acceptance but, simultaneously, it got cyber crooks' attention that tend to exploit the existing loopholes [1]. However, along with this avalanche of information, generating reliable data becomes a vital issue for the landscape managers, therefore they should discuss the problem of credibility and reliability of information.If none, delete this. validity of data when the IoT devices are communicating within the IoT networks. The present scientific research is very timely because, while developing IoT, it is vital to ascertain that security measures are robust enough. Data credibility is one of the factors to check that ensuring TRUST framework implementation is imperative for safety and integrity of the system. In our approach, we implement and assess the TRUST framework on sensor networks for IoT dealing with the anomaly detection task which is based on datasets [2]. It is our intent to assess the framework's effectiveness in improving security and establishing a trust system with accurate data for intelligent decision-making. Established techniques mostly address only detection of sensor dependability, while the data's credibility is overlooked. This principle may lead to misses some inconsistencies in data, and subsequently, no one can trust IoT network information. Similarly, the methods concerning trust evaluation today also have challenges when it comes to comprehensively determine the trustworthiness of a system which rely on those single-function models, that can not perform well on data heterogeneity and can not learn from the past events. Being aware of the outlined restrictions, we propose an original framework for assessing the source as well as the contents of data and apply multiparty models to improve the service. The key aim of our task is to construct a crowdsourcing structure that spans the data trustworthiness issues at the IoT sensing level to their treatment at the network side. This way, we try to make the IoT data which reaches the next module secure and accurate, which is of great help in decision-making without any delay [3].

Our research efforts concentrate on integrating IoT time-series sensor data features in our TRUST framework and applying machine learning techniques to get data trustworthiness on the level of data accuracy and validity. In addition it, we use the time series analysis technique to explain the auto-correlation and cross-correlation within the IoT sensor data, improving the accuracy our framework. Finally, our research addressed the crucial question of keeping data trustworthy in the dynamic environment of IoT by proposing solutions and providing valuable insight that enhanced the integrity and dependability of the IoT systems and at the same resolved the problems of risks associated with cyber-attacks. Furthermore, among data security concerns as part of our study, drug interaction in healthcare IoT systems is also another crucial factor that is discussed. Through the desire to help healthcare providers to make wise treatment decisions, we put this drug interaction detection system in our framework. Doctors will get drug interaction system support to know what potential drug interactions could happen or not, therefore better treatment choices could be made. This comprehensive approach not only guarantees patient safety but at the same time ensures that healthcare is delivered efficiently by allowing the doctors to provide descriptive treatment plans and at the same time decrease chances of drug-related complications. The contributions of this paper are as follows:

- A trust evaluation framework is applied for evaluating the level of trust of the data produced and disseminated by the IoT devices.
- Possible integration of machine learning approaches to improve the ability of Data Trust based evaluations at both the sensing level and at the network level.
- Better care and treatment outcomes for patients by gaining more reliable and accurate information from e-health technologies.
- Employment of auto-correlation and cross-correlation approaches when examining IoT data to discover trends and abnormal behaviors based on timeframes.
- Explanation of how the TRUSTd framework can be used for drug interaction identification based on accurate patient information from IoT devices.

The paper is structured as follows: Section 30.2 presents a brief literature survey of the state of the art in IoT data integrity and security. Section 30.3 outlines the procedure of the framework of TRUSTd alongside the overall trust evaluation process and a Random Walk Infilling (RWI). Section 30.4 will explain the methodology followed in the experiment, the datasets used and the methods of evaluation. The evaluation metrics and outcome too are demonstrated and they include accuracy, precision, recall, the F1 score, area under curve-receiver operating characteristic (AUC-ROC), execution time, and memory utilization. Last but not least, in Sect. 30.5, we provide conclusion and contributions of the research and evaluate the advantages and drawbacks of defining and using the proposed framework, as well as pointing out the further direction of the study.

30.2 Related Work

Nowadays there is a noticeable attraction to Machine Learning (ML) methods and one of them is the use of different ML algorithms: KNN, Random Forest, and Naive Bayes. They show a very good performance with a low complexity and a reasonable time to compute. Companies such as [4] who provided security for IoT devices in smart homes formed a 3-Layer IDS architecture. There they conducted a real-life testing experiment by placing 8 sensors in a network and then continuously watching the traffic over the network. They launched a suite of attacks against the network, archived the collected logs, and so on. The initial portion of the architecture is a network that connects the various IoT tools in a scanning process. The second layer assigns the packets to the harmful or the normal classes. The next layer prepares hatred packets to destine them in one of the four attacks from observing nine machine-learning classification schemes and selects the good one. Nevertheless, the characteristics of the datasets were not articulated in detail. Li et al. [5] proposed a labeling-free display of disagreements in the semi-supervised learning technique. They were operating DARPA (KDD99) that were being used in model evaluation, which were outdated. Horng et al. [6] introduced clustering and support vector machine (SVM) based IDS, in their study. Birch clustering algorithms have been utilized to fetch all the important features for each type of an intrusion from the KDD Cup 99 dataset which was considered primary. For each kind of attack, a separate SVM classifier is deployed; and then each independent classifier can be combined with all of other classifiers or serve as the independent IDS. On the contrary, Eesa et al. [7] in their research highlighted a new feature separation method based on cuttlefish algorithms, and decision tree classifier was applied for the attack's detection.

The paper [8] puts a spotlight on intrusions detection systems vulnerability that utilizes certain integer learning model due the volume of data used in training. The article introduces the feature selection algorithm, namely 'the Highest Wins' (HW). The algorithm is suggested to find the accurate feature subset in the training dataset. Li et al. [9] carried out a one-and-a-half-step security software-defined alternative that employs artificial intelligence (AI)-trained technique for intrusion detection system. The weighted voting system with a random forest inside of the algorithm of self-d adaptation was used to classify the stream. Aljawarneh et al. [10] has come up with a detector based on anomalies. First of all, by implementing voting system along with the selection of the key attributes by the means of information gain, the data were made less bulky. They performed it based on the KNN, SVM, DT, and RF techniques on a 20% NSL-KDD subset. We not only got good performance (with low false-positive and high detection rate) on the NSL-KDD dataset, but the approach was evaluated only on the NSL-KDD dataset. On the same lines, Moustafa et al. [11] presented a system of IDS that was based on using the AdBoost artificial neural network method with decision tree, Naive Bayes, and Artificial Neural Network techniques in order to achieve higher accuracy and detection rate as a whole. They carry out the function of inspecting these purposes that aim the computer applications by breaking the network. Similarly the decentralized ensemble approach to the IDS for video surveillance has been proposed in article [12], where the fog-based units teach their own learning models using k-nearest neighbors, Naive Bayes, and XGBoost. Random Forest predicts at the first level but uses the second level's prediction results it has obtained from previously trained models (the first level) to determine the final classification. In the novel article [13] by Prabavathy et al. Introduction of IDS with fog computing was proposed. They performed deep packet inspection fog junctions using a web-based serial encryption method to examine attacks as they come in and send them to the cloud server. Shafiq et al. [14] have suggested a new feature selection algorithm named CorrAUC for malicious traffic classification in the IoT network. Hussain et al. [15] conduct a systematic study of various services in IoT ecosystem and determine attack surface areas and the shortcoming of the security needs. Demonstrating the fact that as similarly with machine learning, DL techniques are also very productive. Humanization is more complicated. The training process is slower but the models give better results and high accuracy. Shone et al. use an artificial intelligence approach for IP detection [16]. In contrast, the authors presented a complex recoding scheme called a Non-Symmetric Deep Auto-Encoder. The proposed architecture in use configured the categorization of network traffic as either malicious or legitimate based on the Random Forest classifier being the chief NDAE.

During the recent years, researchers have increasingly relied on the powerful fields of machine learning and deep learning to speed up the development of drugs; the result has been a burst of innovations for the pharmaceutical industry. This change towards these computational methods is caused not only by the fact that traditional wet lab experiments take such a long time but also that they are such an economic drain, as noted in several articles. Yu et al. [17] introduced the DDINMF method, using a semi-nonnegative matrix factorization approach for both regressive and enhancing predictions for Drug-Drug Interactions (DDIs). With this ball rolling, Wen et al. [18] went on to combine chemical substructure, enzymes, pathways, and targets and generated the SFLLN method for DDI prediction. Shukla et al. [19] took an open-ended approach and combined three deep-learning techniques: Convolutional Neural Networks (CNNs), Recurrent Neural Networks (RNNs) and Mixture Density Neural Networks (MDNs) to find all DDIs as accurately and quickly as possible. Feng et al. [20] came up with a novel contribution, DPDDI, which included GCN for extracting network structure features of drugs from the DDI network in addition to a predictive model based on DNN. With a groundbreaking model, Lee et al. [21] also marched ahead, using deep feedforward networks and autoencoders trained on three different similarity profiles sets–Target Gene Similarity Profiles, Gene Ontology term similarity profiles, and SSP–to predict DDI effects. This research [22] used a two-phase fault-tolerant (TPFT) scheduling approach, applying a microservices architecture to minimize the latency and task failure rate. The NDD method of Rohani and Eslahchi [23] calculates different drug similarities, including pathways, side effects, targets, transporters and substructures, using neural networks for the arduous job of predicting drug-drug interactions. In 2019, Liu et al. [24] used multi-modal deep autoencoders, learning jointly across multiple drug feature networks to obtain a unified drug representation. After repeated surgical operations to learn drug-drug pair representations, the final DDI prediction utilized random forests. Differently, [25] predicted DDIs using the molecular structure of drugs and the types of side effects. Its representation took the form of nodes, which are atoms of drugs linked by bonds (edges). Nodes or atoms exchanged internal messages among themselves, and outer messages allowed the atoms of various drugs to communicate with one another. As for atoms belonging to different drugs, an attentional coefficient was calculated for each atom pair. At the same time, the paper by [26] also faced a similar problem of drug-target prediction, utilizing a heterogeneous information network and meta-path topological features. Meta-path, which was originally researched for displaying relations of entities, is commonly used in many fields including research publication networks, recommendation systems, multi-network link prediction, coauthorship prediction, and information graph-based document analysis (Table 30.1).

Table 30.1 Summary of detection techniques

References	Techniques and algorithms	Results	Limitations
Zhao et al. [4]	CFS-DE feature selection algorithm, weighted Stacking classification algorithm	Accuracy of 99.87%	Performance influenced by quality of base classifiers in Stacking algorithm. Complexity of high-dimensional features can challenge speed and performance of classification for IDS
Li et al. [5]	Disagreement-based semi-supervised learning algorithm	Effective in detecting intrusions and reducing false alarms	Non-negligible rate of false positives and negatives despite designed to reduce false alarms
Eesa et al. [7]	Distributed ensemble design based on fog computing	High detection rates, up to 99.99% for most attack vectors	Potential limitations include scalability, real-time processing, and adaptability
Kumar et al. [12]	Highest Wins (HW) feature selection algorithm	Effective in detecting intrusions and reducing false alarms	Potential limitations include data dependence, computational complexity, and adaptability
Saba et al. [27]	CNN-based approach	Accuracy of 99.51% on NID Dataset and 92.85% on BoT-IoT datasets	Potential limitations include data dependence, computational complexity, and adaptability
Shukla et al. [19]	CNN, RNN, MDN, LSTMRNN	ACC of 98.4%	Overfitting, Specific to Cancer cells
Feng et al. [20]	GCN, DNN, 5-fold CV	ACC of 94.0%	Only one feature (SMILES of drugs)
Lee et al. [21]	Autoencoders, FeedForward DNN	ACC of 94.0%	Only one feature (SMILES of drugs), SSP instead of PCA
Rohani and Eslahchi [23]	Neural networks, GIP, SNF, 5-fold CV	AUC of 99.2%	Simple neural networks with similarity selection and integration

30.3 Research Methodology and Results

The illustrated methodology in Fig. 30.1 considers the architecture for collecting patient vitals through IoT devices, such as nodes, smartwatches, and vital body sensors linked to the Electronic Health Record (EHR) that contains identifiable patient data. These devices transmit data for analysis of trustworthiness at the sensing layer leveraging on a model trained on the Tim-Tadj/IoT data trust RWI dataset based on time series. Only the data which is trusted will pass the next phase where model trained on the dataset belonging to the UNSW-NB15 (UNSQ-NB15) will identify one of the possible attacks from the nine attacks. If these attacks are not detected, information is labeled as TRUE and safe for leading to doctors so they can prescribe drugs. In the last stage, the prescribed medicine is added to the medication database, and the patient's EHR database record is updated. The RWI algorithm will be used [2] to generate fake data sources that intentionally differ from trustworthy data, making the data untrustworthy. The timeseries nature of the data is respected using random processes for synthesis while faithful lookalike patterns for trustworthy data are also guaranteed. The RWI algorithm involves three main steps: calculating first and last value indexes for given intervals, replacing the real data of each segment with the simulated data via the random walk process, and aligning the synthetic data to the preceding and succeeding data.The resulting synthesized data maintains continuity and coherence with the original data, capturing non-short-term cyclic behaviors or trends without introducing improbable discontinuities or abrupt changes.

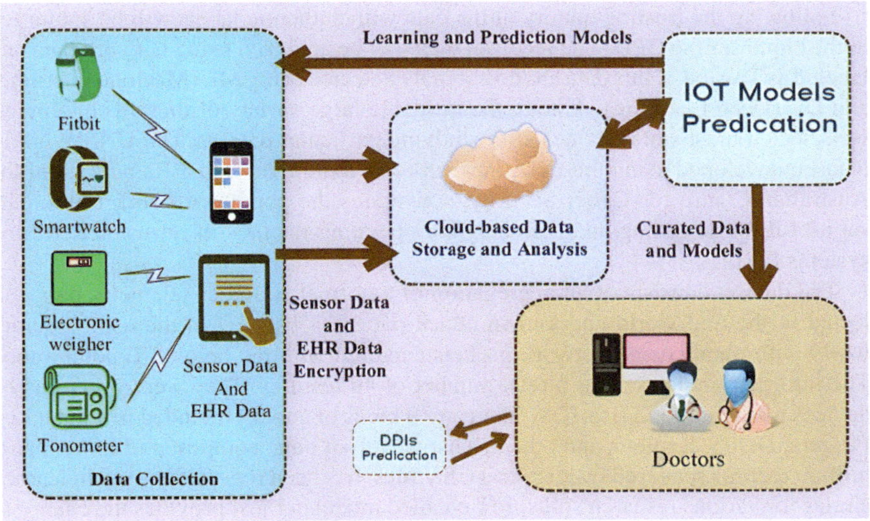

Fig. 30.1 Architecture of Proposed Framework

30.3.1 Proposed Model

Significantly, ML algorithm as demonstrated in Ref. [2] resort to semisupervised ML algorithms such as label propagation in the evaluation of trust level of IOT devices using data from training sets with very few labeled data. The semi-supervised strategy displays high accuracy level comparable to it yielded high accuracy in ML methods based on supervision and thus preferred in real world applications where instance label data is very scarce unlike supervised ML data mining methods. In parallel, we have epodes of this ML models basing on receivable datasets that will enable confirmation of data received by patients over in time series. We introduce an RWI (Random Walk Infilling) algorithm [2] which is the critical component to insert the values into gaps to time series data from multiple sensors at designated time intervals. The algorithm starts with processing one-by-one examples of the input dataset, and then moves on to multiple stages after that. It groups this segment's elements into initial, end, and mid ones. Hence, each factor is an integral part of the algorithm, reasoning by way of walk mechanisms to substitute missing data, and compensating for slope differences to regain the original trajectory. A synthetic approach is an orderly implementation of each item from the original data into the values to be generated by the complete data set(S), therefore it is derived (S) which is data rich. The open-loop iterative technique utilized here will rely on the random walk approach to generate output numbers that will also show a close resemblance to the actual values. Thus, such continuously applied approaches not only handle missing values but also increase validity of the data and serve as a basis for powerful continuity of analysis in later phases of the research study.

Following the trusting quality of the data with authentic labels will be submitted to the cloud for the CPU. The received data will be analyzed using network data and labeled as Trusted, if this data has no anomaly detected using ML (Machine Learning) and DL (Deep Learning). Among the available large variety of these technologies, we selected most suitable ones after studying particular dataset. The UNSW-NB15 dataset, developed using the IXIA PerfectStorm tool in the Cyber Range Lab of the Australian Centre for Cyber Security, constitutes the popular network traffic data set useful for designing and assessing the operating features of intrusion detection systems [28].

The dataset consists of an aggregation of a normal activities telemetry data collected in the real world and known attack patterns observed in the contemporary world with unprocessed network packets captured with the help of Tcpdump tool. The information dataset has a total number of 49 features. They were generated by devices like Argus and Bro-IDS. There are 9 kinds of attacks included in the dataset: Fuzzers, DDoS, Exploits and others. That wealth of data, composed of more than 2 million records scattered over several CSV files, has been repeatedly used in learned circles for various research splits. IoT enabled model not just provides the chance to test and work out the intelligent threat management systems but that model is key to the advancement of studies of intelligent threat management systems for the Internet of Medical Things (IoT).

That said, we will start by the EDA(exploratory data analysis) which represents the first one. Such is the case, when data transformation is performed via visualization. Types of such visualizations include histograms, bar charts, and distribution plots. This phase announces distribution by attack type, usage of protocols, service type of network as well as its state and so on accumulating helpful information in regard to features essential for training a model to detect or identify attacks.

EDA is followed by a procedure called feature engineering. Here, we do feature normalization which makes it possible to compare the feature's scales. Furthermore, categorical data is coded using techniques such as one-hot encoding and target encoding, hence machine learning processes are enabled and with a more detailed representation model training is done. The coded categorical data is next concatenated to other numerical features and then headers added for the DataFrame, which will later be used for further processing.

For multiclassification, we clean the dataset by singing out (X) and target variable (Y) which is an attribute of different attack categories. Subsequently, the resultant dataset is partitioned into training, test, and validation sets which also undergoes oversampling of the minority class using another technique known as SMOTE (Synthetic Minority Over-sampling Technique).

Finally, we create the Sequential neural network model by adding Dense layers with the ReLu activation functions and L2 regularization to combat overfitting. The last one uses the softmax activation function for the multiclass attack detection. The model trained with "adam" optimizer, 'sparse_categorical_crossentropy' loss function, and 'accuracy' metric is represented. Elsewhere, Early Stopping and Model Checkpoint are defined to continue training until validation loss has hit a specified low value and to save the best version of the model during training. The Neural Network achieved an accuracy of 97.56%. Furthermore, 5-fold cross-validation was performed on the Neural Network model to ensure its robustness and to calculate the average accuracy.

30.3.2 Drug to Drug Interaction Materials and Method

This study used for its purpose a dataset obtained from a research article [26] where information about 320 drugs and 53,534 reported drug-drug combinations was evaluated. When removing duplicate drug-drug interaction pairs from our dataset, we were left with the trivial task of selecting the best 23,265 pairs for analysis. To detect Drug-Drug Interactions (DDIs), we started with drug source Data from Drugbank, which is a complete source of information on different kinds of medicines. The application of natural language processing (NLP) techniques brought about a better presentation of these interactions for more perception and improvisation. Specifically, we collected information on four key features from the Drug Bank database: drug chemical design aims to target enzymes, pathways, and chemical substructures. The Drug Bank resource document has become an invaluable source of information for students, medical practitioners, analytical chemists in the medical community, and pharmaceutical industry experts. It makes available precise drug data of 12151 drugs listing their names, chemical substructures (SMILES), targets, catalysts, pathways, descriptions, proteins …etc, Among the FDA-approved drugs, the database comprises 3,844 compounds and 5,867 experimental drugs. The framework, depicted in Fig. 30.2, consists of two key components: the feature extraction phase and the model training stage. Targeted feature extraction steps on drug information are our success factors. Feature engineering technique is applied as well. In that regard, we then adopt a Convolutional Neural Network (CNN) framework to train the model. Additionally, we appraise the model performance using a combo of several indicators that include accuracy, precision, recall, and the F1 score.

We, therefore, advocate a CNN-based model inspired by [29] for warning of drug-to-drug interactions in the given study. Initially, we input four drug features: genes, proteins, pathways, and therapeutic substructure. These attributes are next to be converted to binary formats showing the drug being there (1) or not (0). Then, the same similarity measure is used to produce the similarity matrices for each drug's group.

The fourth step is to build models exploiting CNN to foresee the drug-drug effect (DDI). Our proposed architecture makes use of Jaccard similarity to assess the similarity between drug pairs that can be measured by how much two compounds intersect or if they do not share any component.

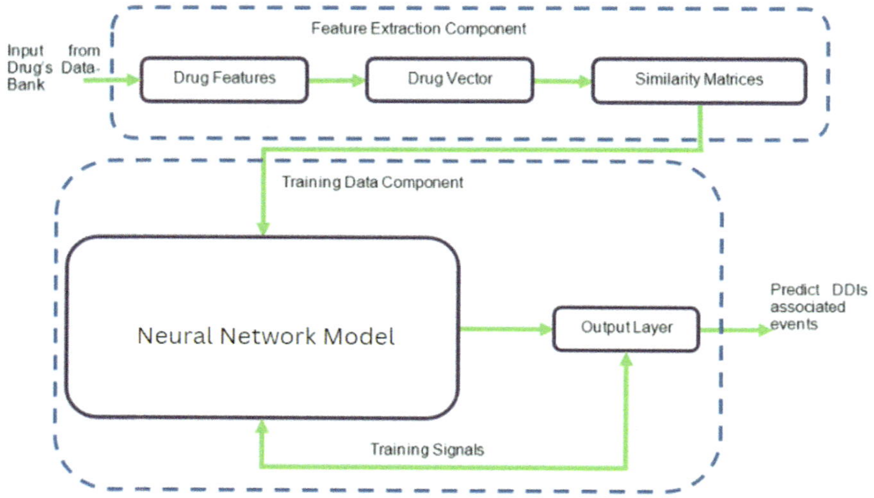

Fig. 30.2 Framework architecture of DDI's models

Table 30.2 Performance metrics of the proposed model

Metric	Value (%)
Accuracy	97.56
Precision	96.84
Recall	97.12
F1 Score	96.98
AUC-ROC	98.35

30.3.3 Performance Metrics

Accuracy: Precision level simply tells the extent of true outcomes of the model or methodology. equals the ratio of the number of true positives and true negatives to the total number of cases examined. In this study using the proposed neural network model, the accuracy was 97.56% Table 30.2 shows all the matrices with results.

Precision: Precision calculates the percentage of True Positives against all the positive results that the software flagged. It is measured as True Positive over False Positive plus false positives.

Recall: Recall is the measure of the model's parameter that defines the quality of selecting all points that have been assigned as in-. undefined It is defined as the ratio of the total number of true positives to the sum of the number of true positives and the total number of false negatives. It is simply a measure of the sum of true positive plus false negative.

F1 Score: The F1 score is the average of precision and recall, proportional to the products of their values, with the function reaching its peak value at unity. offering a single solution that will provide a needful index accounting for both concerns.

AUC-ROC: The under area of the receiver operating characteristic curve The AUC-ROC shows the performance of the model in terms of its capacity to separate classes. The best performance is portrayed by the higher AUC-ROC values.

30.4 Discussion

We offer here a TRUST framework that is a demonstrative system for ensuring data credibility and integrity while exchanging data among IoT devices. By contrast, the present framework being developed deals with the quality and reliability of sensors as well as data consistency across the whole IoT infrastructure. One way this would be done would be through analyzing time-series sensor data and implementing machine-learning models to establish the truthfulness of the data. We proved the efficiency of our approach by showing a health-focused application where patient data is subjected to a thorough verification process regarding reliability, which recently has become an indispensable aid for health providers while making informed decisions with the treatment and conducting the drug interaction assessment. On top of that, we tackled the lof of the data again by applying random walk infilling (RWI) to achieve high accuracy of the time-series data we use for training machine learning models. The study which was also centered on interaction detection applied artificial intelligence, obtained a dataset from a particular research source, and interpreted the results using NLP to make the interactions visible. The goal of our integrated strategy is to support the mission of conducting data cleanliness in the IoT space, as it is a significant aspect of security against attacks and leads to faster decision-making.

30.5 Conclusion and Future Work

This study proposes the TRUST framework. This is a comprehensive security strategy aimed at strengthening the security and dependability of IoT systems by ensuring that all data traffic within these networks is trustworthy and reliable. By examining the time-series sensor data that has been plotted and utilizing machine learning models, we can figure out if the data is reliable or not, which is different from just checking whether the sensors are accurate or not. Using the application we showed the ability of the method to provide the healthcare practitioners the capability to make the right choices while treating and to detect the drug interactions. Furthermore, the random walk-in (RWI) approach is one of the methods to manage sparse data that will give confidence in the data trust in the IoT environment for sure. Consequently, for further research direction, available options are numerous. For instance, the TRUST framework can be subject to improvements and optimization to foster its usefulness in multiplied human applications. Moreover, the inclusion of more advanced machine learning methodologies and the development of a new data inspection approach could bring additional enablement to our approach and increase its accuracy and precision. Hence, enlarging the platform of the research to accommodate more Internet of Things (IoT) applications and domains could generate much useful information on the applicability of the TRUST framework on a larger scale. In concluding, the efforts touching on the handling of new cyberthreats and vulnerabilities in IoT systems will be among the areas of study for future research.

References

1. Thirimanne, S.P., Jayawardana, L., Yasakethu, L., Liyanaarachchi, P., Hewage, C.: Deep neural network based real-time intrusion detection system. SN Comput. Sci. **3**(2), 145 (2022)
2. Tadj, T., Arablouei, R., Dedeoglu, V.: Iot Data Trust Evaluation Via Machine Learning (2023)
3. Yin, Y., Jang-Jaccard, J., Xu, W., Singh, A., Zhu, J., Sabrina, F., Kwak, J.: Igrf-rfe: a hybrid feature selection method for mlp-based network intrusion detection on unsw-nb15 dataset. J. Big Data **10**(1), 1–26 (2023)
4. Zhao, R., Mu, Y., Zou, L., Wen, X.: A hybrid intrusion detection system based on feature selection and weighted stacking classifier. IEEE Access **10**, 71 414–71 426 (2022)

5. Li, W., Meng, W., Au, M.H.: Enhancing collaborative intrusion detection via disagreement-based semi-supervised learning in iot environments. J. Netw. Comput. Appl. **161**, 102631 (2020)
6. Horng, S.-J., Su, M.-Y., Chen, Y.-H., Kao, T.-W., Chen, R.-J., Lai, J.-L., Perkasa, C.D.: A novel intrusion detection system based on hierarchical clustering and support vector machines. Expert Syst. Appl. **38**(1), 306–313 (2011)
7. Eesa, A.S., Orman, Z., Brifcani, A.: A novel feature-selection approach based on the cuttlefish optimization algorithm for intrusion detection systems. Expert Syst. Appl. **42**(5), 2670–2679 (2015)
8. Mohammad, R., Alsmadi, M.K.: Intrusion detection using highest wins feature selection algorithm. Neural Comput. Appl. **33**, 9805–9816 (2021)
9. Li, J., Zhao, Z., Li, R., Zhang, H.: Ai-based two-stage intrusion detection for software defined iot networks. IEEE Internet Things J. **6**(2), 2093–2102 (2018)
10. Aljawarneh, S., Aldwairi, M., Yassein, M.B.: Anomaly-based intrusion detection system through feature selection analysis and building hybrid efficient model. J. Comput. Sci. **25**, 152–160 (2018)
11. Moustafa, N., Turnbull, B., Choo, K.-K.R.: An ensemble intrusion detection technique based on proposed statistical flow features for protecting network traffic of internet of things. IEEE Internet Things J. **6**(3), 4815–4830 (2018)
12. Kumar, P., Gupta, G.P., Tripathi, R.: A distributed ensemble design based intrusion detection system using fog computing to protect the internet of things networks. J. Ambient. Intell. Humaniz. Comput. **12**, 9555–9572 (2021)
13. Prabavathy, S., Sundarakantham, K., Shalinie, S.M.: Design of cognitive fog computing for intrusion detection in internet of things. J. Commun Netw. **20**(3), 291–298 (2018)
14. Shafiq, M., Tian, Z., Bashir, A.K., Du, X., Guizani, M.: Corrauc: a malicious bot-iot traffic detection method in iot network using machine-learning techniques. IEEE Internet Things J. **8**(5), 3242–3254 (2020)
15. Hussain, F., Hussain, R., Hassan, S., Hossain, E.: Machine learning in iot security: current solutions and future challenges. IEEE Commun. Surv. Tutor. **22**(3), 1686–1721 (2020)
16. Shone, N., Ngoc, T.N., Phai, V.D., Shi, Q.: A deep learning approach to network intrusion detection. IEEE Trans. Emerg. Top. Comput. Intell. **2**(1), 41–50 (2018)
17. Yu, H., Mao, K.T., Shi, J.Y., Huang, H., Chen, Z.: Predicting and understanding comprehensive drug-drug interactions via semi-nonnegative matrix factorization. BMC Syst. Biol. **12**(1), 101–110 (2018)
18. Wen, Z., Kanghong, J., Feng, H., Yanlin, C., Bolin, L.: Sflln: a sparse feature learning ensemble method with linear neighborhood regularization for predicting drug-drug interactions. Inf. Sci. **497**, 189–201 (2019)
19. Shukla, P.K., Sharma, P., Rawat, P., Samar, J., Moriwal, R.: Efficient prediction of drug-drug interaction using deep learning models. IET Syst. Biol. **14**(4), 211–216 (2020)
20. Feng, Y.-H., Zhang, S.-W., Shi, J.-Y.: Dpddi: a deep predictor for drug-drug interactions. BMC Bioinform. **21**(1), 1–15 (2020)
21. Lee, G., Park, C., Ahn, J.: Novel deep learning model for more accurate prediction of drug-drug interaction effects. BMC Bioinform. **20**(1), 1–8 (2019)
22. Maray, M., Rizwan, S.M., Mustafa, E., Shuja, J.: Microservices enabled bidirectional fault-tolerance scheme for healthcare internet of things. Cluster Comput. 1–13 (2023)
23. Rohani, N., Eslahchi, C.: Drug-drug interaction predicting by neural network using integrated similarity. Sci. Rep. **9**, 13645 (2019)
24. Liu, S., Huang, Z., Qiu, Y., Chen, Y.-P.P., Zhang, W.: Structural network embedding using multi-modal deep auto-encoders for predicting drug-drug interactions. In: IEEE International Conference on Bioinformatics and Biomedicine (BIBM), San Diego, CA, USA, 2019, pp. 445–450 (2019)
25. Hou, X., You, J., Hu, P. : Predicting drug-drug interactions using deep neural network. In: Proceedings of the 2019 11th International Conference on Machine Learning and Computing, pp. 168–172 (2019)

26. Deng, Y., Xu, X., Qiu, Y., Xia, J., Zhang, W.: A multimodal deep learning framework for predicting drug-drug interaction events. Bioinformatics **36**(15), 4316–4322 (2020)
27. Saba, T., Rehman, A., Sadad, T., Kolivand, H., Bahaj, S.A.: Anomaly-based intrusion detection system for iot networks through deep learning model. Comput. Electr. Eng. **99**, 107810 (2022)
28. Moustafa, N., Slay, J.: Unsw-nb15: a comprehensive data set for network intrusion detection systems (unsw-nb15 network data set). In: Military Communications and Information Systems Conference (MilCIS), vol. 2015, pp. 1–6. . IEEE (2015)
29. Asfand-E-Yar, M., Hashir, Q., Shah, A.A., Malik, H., Alourani, A., Khalil, W.: Multimodal cnn-ddi: using multimodal cnn for drug to drug interaction associated events. Sci. Rep. **14**(1), 4076 (2024)

Chapter 31
Public Reliance on Social Media to Follow Up on Domestic Violence Issues: A Survey of the Public in Baghdad

Huda Ali Mahdi

Abstract This Study addresses the reliance on social media by members of the public for tracking issues related to domestic violence. The study's core problem concerns the extent to which the public depends on these platforms for following such topics and identifies the distinguishing features of these sites. The objective of the Study is to ascertain the extent of the public's reliance on social media platforms and to investigate the most significant issues regarding domestic violence. A survey methodology and the questionnaire tool were employed to gather data from a sample comprising 106 respondents, both male and female, within a total sample size of 120 from Baghdad city. The remainder of the questionnaires were disregarded due to incomplete responses. The findings reveal that individuals consistently utilize social media, with Facebook being the primary platform used for following domestic violence issues. Furthermore, the most frequently addressed type of case was child abuse, which ranked highest in the nature of the issues explored.

31.1 Introduction

The emergence of digital technologies and technological openness across various domains, particularly in media, has facilitated the development of a new form of media represented by social media platforms. These platforms are distinguished by features that have led the public to rely on them as media channels for selecting news content and information [1]. Additionally, their capability to transcend geographical and regulatory boundaries has increased their usage among the public. These platforms enable individuals to become active participants in the communication process by allowing them to produce, publish, and interact with content [2].

Social media sites play a crucial role in various fields due to their speed in disseminating content and information, and their capacity to influence the public. Recently,

H. A. Mahdi (✉)
Faculty of Mass Media, University of Baghdad, Baghdad, Iraq
e-mail: Huda.a@comc.uobaghdad.edu.iq

F. P. García Márquez et al. (eds.), *Computing, Internet of Things and Data Analytics*, Smart Innovation, Systems and Technologies 387,
https://doi.org/10.1007/978-3-031-87154-2_31

social media has become the most frequently used medium by the public. These sites are defined as technology-based applications for computers or smart devices on the internet, enabling users to engage in electronic communication through content that includes personal information, documents, photos, and videos. They are also known as sites where internet applications provide services that allow users to create a public profile within a specific system and establish communication with acquaintances of the page creator or other system users, facilitating the exchange of information [3].

These platforms have several distinctive features that make them an exceptional media intermediary relied upon by the public. Among the most prominent and important of these features are their global reach, interactivity, diversity in usage, and ease of use, which have made them appealing and economical options for individuals. Given their significant importance in people's lives, individuals depend on these sites for accessing news and diverse information. They serve as a platform for broadcasting various issues to the public, with social issues, particularly domestic violence, being among the most prevalent. This increase in domestic violence cases has been significant in societies recently.

Domestic violence is defined as a form of unlawful use of force issued by one or more family members against another to subdue and control them in a manner inconsistent with their freedom or personal will. It is also described as a behaviour or act that occurs using means of force, coercion, and threat issued by one party to subdue another for socially and legally unacceptable objectives, causing physical and emotional harm, synonymous with coercion, a fundamental characteristic of the act of violence. Domestic violence is not a new phenomenon globally; it is a worldwide occurrence, even in countries that have enacted strict laws to curb and control it, according to a United Nations study which reported that violence against boys and girls in their homes and by their relatives is continually increasing. A study conducted by the community police in Iraq revealed that cases of domestic violence have been steadily increasing over the years, affecting all demographics, including children, women, and even men.

Types of domestic violence can be categorized into two primary sections: physical and psychological. The first includes murder, physical harm, and sexual assaults while the second encompasses verbal abuse, confinement within the home, and eviction, specifically practiced against males in certain contexts due to social norms that distinguish Arab societies from others. This form of violence is considered the last resort adopted by parents when they are unable to correct the behaviour of the son who is the victim.

Moreover, media channels, particularly social media platforms, play a significantly large role in disseminating issues related to domestic violence through the content and information they provide about these issues and the individuals involved [4–6]. Their handling of news and events as they occur and their ability to spread such content rapidly allows for public interaction with the material. Their capability to cover and broadcast topics without restrictions contributes to their status as a trusted media intermediary that the public relies upon for following up on issues of any violence and related matters on social media [7, 8].

Social media serves not only as the source to spread local information but also as the means of communication between cultures. As Hamoud [9] points out in his study of multicultural communication via the English language, such platforms fill the intercultural vacuum and promote understanding in the multicultural context. This aspect of social media use extends its significance from informing the local communities about domestic violence to share their experiences and solutions with other regions and cultures.

The current research aims to determine how widespread social media platform use is among the public in Baghdad to follow and engage with domestic violence-related issues. The problem is identifying how deeply interlinked these platforms have become with the public approach to whether and how they are informed and engaged in issues on domestic violence. It encompasses finding out the most used social media platforms that the public accesses to follow and engage with issues on domestic violence, the most followed aspects of domestic violence, and the cognitive, affective, and behavioural influences on the audience.

Given the increasing prevalence of domestic violence issues, there is a need to adopt new methods that fulfil the public's desires for knowledge and information. The Study questions include:

1. To what extent does the public rely on social media to follow domestic violence issues?
2. Which social media platforms are preferred by the public for following domestic violence issues?
3. What specific topics of domestic violence do the public follow through social media?
4. What are the prominent cognitive, affective, and behavioural impacts concerning the extent of the public's reliance on these platforms to follow violence topics?

31.2 Related Work

The dissemination of information via social media platforms has gathered significant attention, particularly in light of its role in shaping public opinion, spreading misinformation, and fostering political engagement. Various studies have explored different facets of this complex phenomenon, highlighting the dual-edged nature of social media as both a facilitator of open discourse and a breeding ground for misinformation. For instance, Zannettou et al. [10] conducted a comprehensive study on YouTube, identifying and characterizing clickbait content. Their work focuses on detecting deceptive titles and descriptions that are often used to manipulate user engagement, which plays a significant role in how information, both factual and misleading, circulates on digital platforms. For real-time social media, Zubiaga et al. [11] explore the classification of Twitter trends, offering insight into the rapid spread of information during key events. Their research demonstrates how trends emerge and evolve, often propelled by viral content that can include both accurate information and falsehoods.

The propagation of misinformation online is further examined by Del Vicario et al. [12], who investigate how false information spreads on social media. Their findings suggest that misinformation tends to proliferate through echo chambers, where individuals are more likely to engage with content that aligns with their pre-existing beliefs. Addressing the specific challenge of rumors, Zubiaga et al. [13] provide a comprehensive survey on rumor detection and resolution in social media. Similarity, Grinberg et al. [14] contribute to this discussion by analyzing the role of "fake news" on Twitter during the 2016 U.S. presidential election. They provide empirical evidence showing that misleading information not only spreads widely on social media but also has a measurable impact on political outcomes.

In the context of political expression, Velasquez and Rojas [15] investigate how individuals use social media for political expression, emphasizing the role of communication competence and the expected outcomes of such interactions. Zhang et al. [16] map the landscape of COVID-19 crisis visualizations, demonstrating how data visualizations on social media played a critical role in disseminating information during the pandemic. Guess et al. [17] examine the dissemination of "fake news" on Facebook, revealing that its spread is often less pervasive than commonly believed.

The role of trust in online news consumption is explored by Fletcher and Park [18], who demonstrate that trust in the news media significantly impacts both the consumption of news and participation in public discourse. Kumar and Shah [19] provide a survey on false information on the web and social media, offering a comprehensive overview of the techniques used to detect and combat misinformation. Bessi et al. [20] examine the dynamics of science versus conspiracy narratives, providing insight into how collective narratives form and spread in the age of misinformation. Vosoughi et al. [21] develop the "Rumor Gauge," a system designed to predict the veracity of rumors on Twitter.

Gillani et al. [22] explores the role of echo chambers in social media polarization. They show how individuals tend to isolate themselves in groups that reinforce their own beliefs, leading to increased polarization and the amplification of misinformation. Labid [23] shifts the focus to the impact of electronic advertising on social media platforms, examining how advertising practices affect both producers and consumers.

These studies provided a theoretical foundation for the current study by offering valuable information that enriched the Study with related sources and references. This facilitated the Studier's identification of appropriate and accurate tools and methods to achieve the Study objectives and attain the desired outcomes. Our work differs from previous studies as most past studies focused on content analysis across various media channels, both traditional and electronic. However, the current study emphasizes studying the audience through surveys to understand their reliance on social media for following violence-related topics and the cognitive, emotional, and behavioural impacts resulting from this reliance.

31.3 Methodology

This Study is descriptive, utilizing a survey methodology which relies on the descriptive survey approach for collecting information and data from the public regarding their reliance on social media for following topics related to domestic violence. This approach is deemed most suitable for studying the Study problem through the axes of the questionnaire that was employed to collect data and opinions from respondents about following domestic violence topics on social media, in addition to the measurement units and the construction of results based on them.

This Study aims to analyse the respondents' answers regarding (the public's reliance on social media to follow topics of domestic violence) and attempts to uncover the impacts resulting from this reliance on these platforms for following violence-related topics to achieve the Study objectives.

The scope of the study includes three main aspects: spatial, human, and temporal. Spatially, it focuses on the geographic area of Baghdad Province, chosen due to its distinctive characteristics and the diverse demographic of its audience. Human scope involves social media users from the audience in Baghdad Province, with data collected using a convenience sample from the community. Temporally, the study covers the period from March 1, 2023, to May 1, 2024, including all stages from questionnaire preparation and distribution to data collection and analysis.

The study sample was distributed based on number of variables.

(1) Gender Distribution:

As shown in Fig. 31.1, female participation was higher than male participation, by 50.9% to 40.1%, respectively.

(2) Age Distribution:

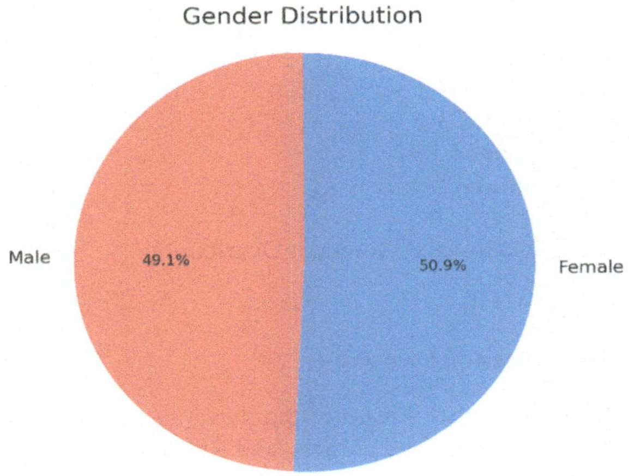

Fig. 31.1 Represents the distribution of participants according to the gender variable

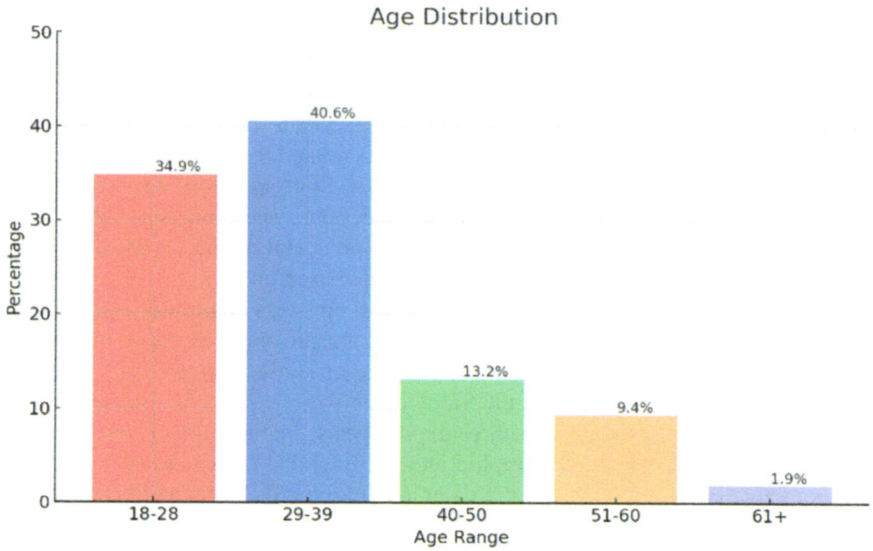

Fig. 31.2 Represents the distribution of participants by age variable

As shown in Fig. 31.2, the participation rate for ages 18–28 was 34.9%, while ages 29–39 accounted for the highest participation rate at 40.6%, ages 40–50 accounted for 13.2%, ages 51–60 accounted for 9.4%, and finally, the lowest participation rate was for ages older than 61 at 1.9%.

(3) Marital State Distribution:

Figure 31.3 shows the percentage of audience participation in relation to their marital status as follows:

(1) Single (42%)
(2) Married 51%
(3) Divorced 3%
(4) Separated 1%
(5) Widowed 3%

(1) Educational Attainment Distribution:

See Fig. 31.4.

(2) Profession Distribution

Figure 31.5 also illustrates the diversity of occupations shared by the participants (Student, Employee, Earners, and Retired).

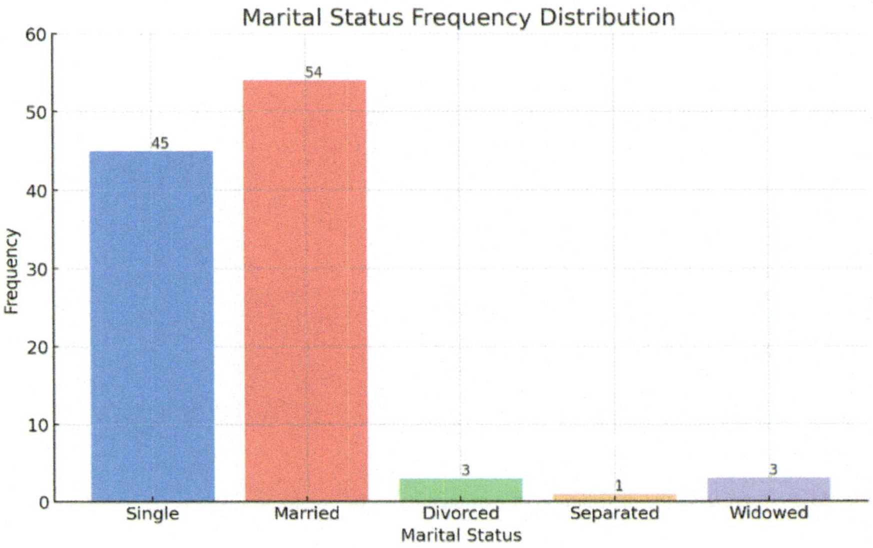

Fig. 31.3 Represents the distribution of participants according to marital status

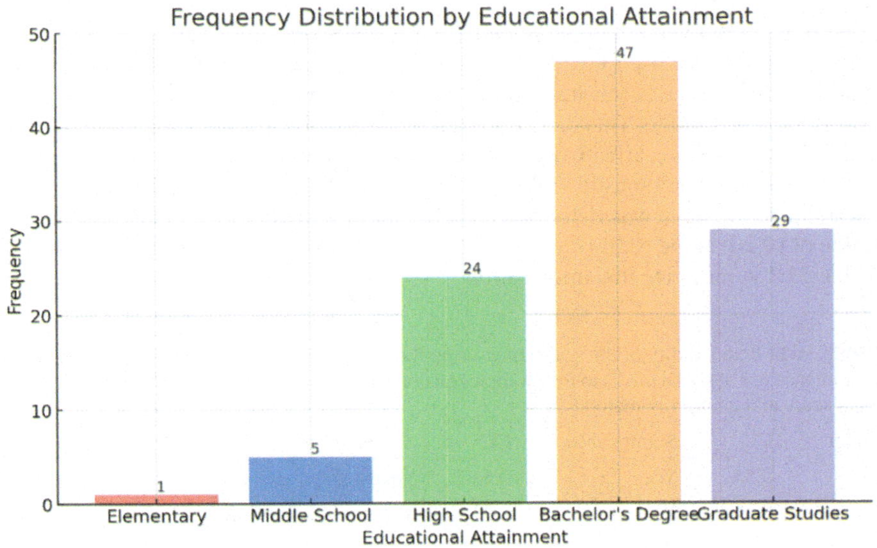

Fig. 31.4 Frequency distribution by educational attainment

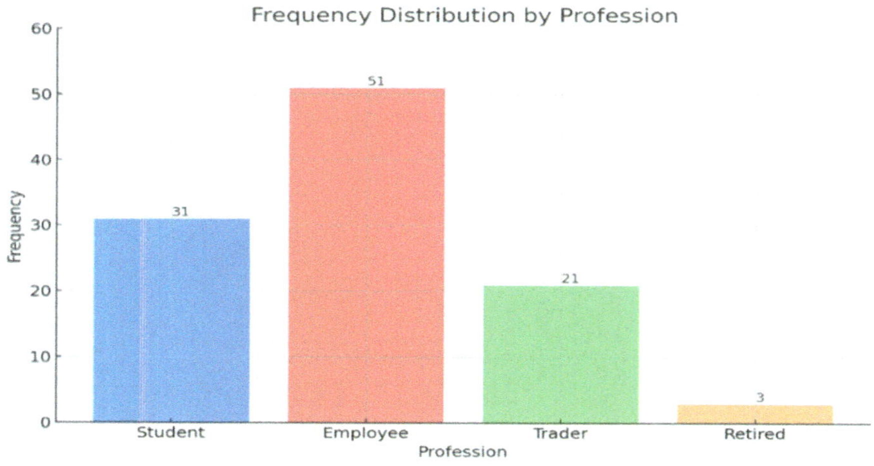

Fig. 31.5 Represents the distribution of participants according to profession

31.3.1 Statistical Procedures

Relationship Between Item Score and Total Scale Score (Item Validity): To achieve this, the researcher used Pearson's correlation coefficient to extract the correlation between the score of each item in the research scales and the total score of (106) forms, i.e., the sample. This procedure revealed that all items in the scales measuring the effects (cognitive, affective, and behavioral) of the audience's use of social media to follow topics on domestic violence have a statistically significant correlation with the total score. This was determined by comparing them with the tabular Pearson value of (0.20) at the (0.05) significance level and a degree of freedom of (104). The Table 31.1 summarize this information.

Table 31.1 Item validity of the scales measuring the effects (cognitive, affective, and behavioral) of audience use of social media to follow topics on domestic violence using the relationship between item score and total score method

Item	CC	Significance	CC	Significance	CC	Significance
1	0.55	Yes	0.53	Yes	0.59	Yes
2	0.66	Yes	0.77	Yes	0.67	Yes
3	0.61	Yes	0.61	Yes	0.51	Yes
4	0.52	Yes	0.50	Yes	0.66	Yes
5	0.61	Yes	0.72	Yes	0.65	Yes

CC Correlation coefficient

Table 31.2 Cronbach's alpha reliability for the research scales

No.	Scale	Reliability coefficient
1	Cognitive effects	0.71
2	Affective effects	0.77
3	Behavioral effects	0.75

31.3.2 Indicators of Scale Reliability

The concept of test score reliability refers to the extent to which test scores are free from random errors that may affect the measurement. Test scores are considered reliable if the test consistently measures a specific trait under varying conditions that might introduce measurement errors. Thus, reliability in this sense means consistency or accuracy in measurement.

The researcher employed Cronbach's alpha method for internal consistency as a means to verify the reliability of the scales measuring the effects (cognitive, affective, and behavioral) of the audience's use of social media to follow topics on domestic violence. Table 31.2 illustrates this.

31.4 Statistical Analysis and Results

The following figures, display results of the survey that was distributed to the participants, to assess the extent of Public Reliance on social media to Follow Up on Domestic Violence Issues.

1. Using social media sites

See Fig. 31.6.

2. Duration of using social media sites

See Fig. 31.7.

3. Classification of using of social media sites

See Fig. 31.8.

4. Reason of using of social media sites

See Fig. 31.9.

5. The importance of social media sites that participants' use to follow topics on domestic violence

See Fig. 31.10.

6. The nature of the violence cases that participants follow on social media

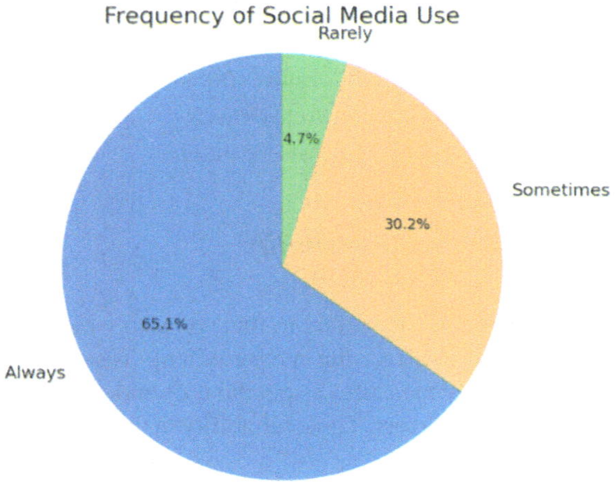

Fig. 31.6 Using social media sites

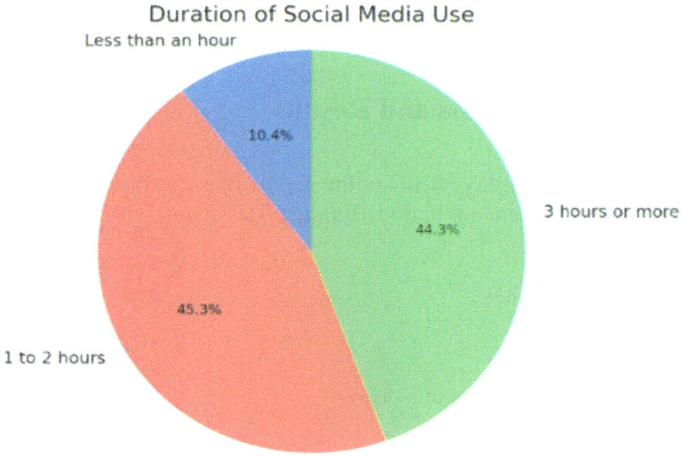

Fig. 31.7 Duration of using social media sites

See Fig. 31.11.

7. Extend of following domestic violence cases on social media

See Fig. 31.12.

The Results of the Correlation came as follows:

Based on Objective (1): To identify the most significant cognitive effects of audience use of social media to follow topics on domestic violence. To achieve this objective, the relative importance index of the responses of the research sample members to each item of the cognitive effects scale was adopted after applying it to

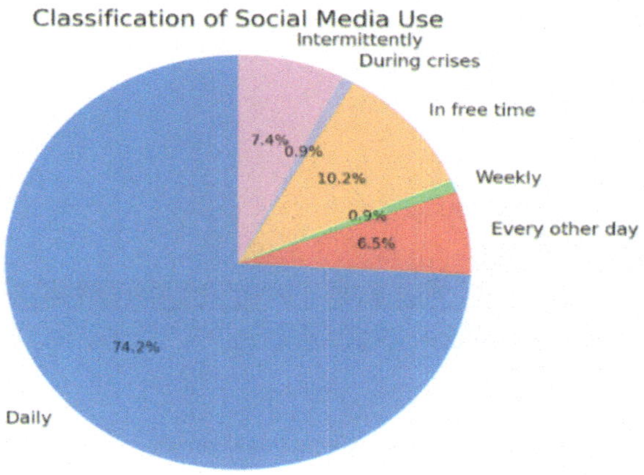

Fig. 31.8 Classification of using social media sites

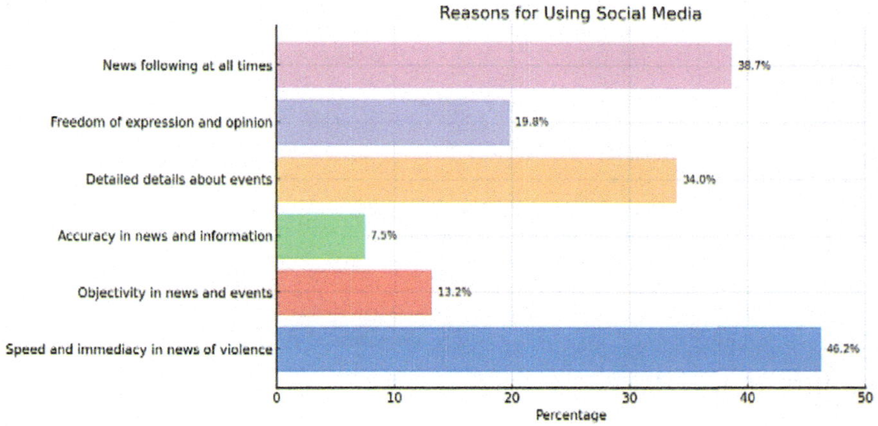

Fig. 31.9 Reason of using social media sites

the research sample consisting of (106) individuals. The analysis of the following cognitive items, numbered with their corresponding IDs are shown in Table 31.3.

1 The information on social media about violence has increased my desire to know the details and concepts about violence and its types.
2 The information provided by social media has helped to clear up the ambiguity surrounding issues of domestic violence.
3 Social media makes me understand issues of domestic violence better.
4 Provides me with diverse information that I cannot obtain from TV channels.
5 Social media has contributed to increasing my knowledge of laws and rights concerning domestic violence.

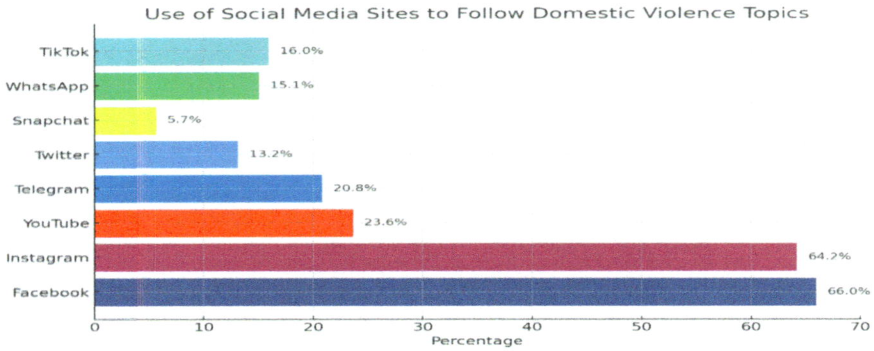

Fig. 31.10 Using social media sites to follow topics on domestic violence

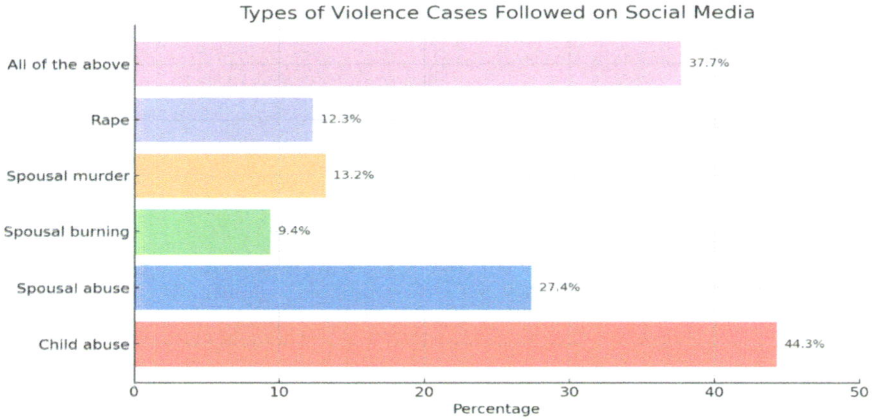

Fig. 31.11 The types of violence cases followed on social media

From the above table, it is evident that the items (the information on violence provided by social media increased my desire to know the details and concepts about violence and its types, it provides me with diverse information that I cannot obtain from satellite channels, and social media makes me understand domestic violence issues better) ranked in the top three positions according to the highest percentage weights.

Objective (2): To identify the most significant affective effects of audience use of social media to follow topics on domestic violence. To achieve this objective, the relative importance index of the responses of the research sample members to each item of the affective effects scale was adopted after applying it to the research sample consisting of (106) individuals. The analysis of the following items, numbered with their corresponding IDs are shown in Table 31.4.

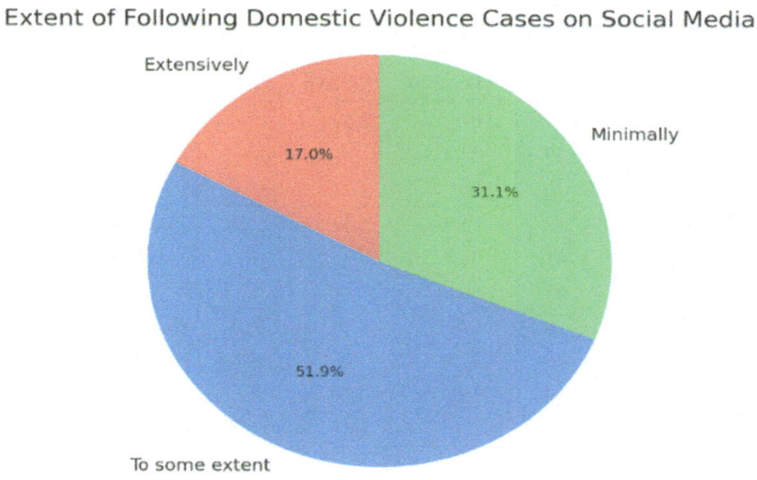

Fig. 31.12 Extend of following domestic violence cases on social media

Table 31.3 Weighted means and percentage weights for the items of the cognitive effects scale for audience use of social media to follow topics on domestic violence

S. No.	Decisions	Freq.	Per. (%)	W. Avg	SD	Per. weight (%)	Rank
1	Disagree	6	5.7	2.59	0.6	86.33	1
	Neutral	31	29.2				
	Agree	69	65.1				
2	Disagree	14	13.2	2.34	0.7	78	5
	Neutral	42	39.6				
	Agree	50	47.2				
3	Disagree	12	11.3	2.46	0.69	82	3
	Neutral	33	31.1				
	Agree	61	57.5				
4	Disagree	10	9.4	2.5	0.67	83.33	2
	Neutral	33	31.1				
	Agree	63	59.4				
5	Disagree	11	10.4	2.44	0.68	81.33	4
	Neutral	37	34.9				
	Agree	58	54.7				

1. News about domestic violence on social media has increased pessimism among the public.
2. Following news about violence on social media has made me more fearful and anxious.

Table 31.4 Weighted means and percentage weights for the items of the affective effects scale for audience use of social media to follow topics on domestic violence

S. No.	Decisions	Freq.	Per. (%)	W. Avg	SD	Per. weight (%)	Rank
1	Disagree	7	6.6	2.59	0.61	86.33	2
	Neutral	29	27.4				
	Agree	70	66				
2	Disagree	12	11.3	2.39	0.68	79.67	5
	Neutral	41	38.7				
	Agree	53	50				
3	Disagree	8	7.5	2.58	0.63	86	3
	Neutral	29	27.4				
	Agree	69	65.1				
4	Disagree	2	1.9	2.64	0.52	88	1
	Neutral	34	32.1				
	Agree	70	66				
5	Disagree	10	9.4	2.47	0.66	82.33	4
	Neutral	36	34				
	Agree	60	56.6				

3. Cases of domestic violence on social media have made me more cautious in dealing with others.
4. Some cases of violence evoke my emotions in some painful situations.
5. Some scenes published on social media have increased my fear.

From the above table, it is evident that the items (some instances of violence evoke my emotions regarding some painful situations, news of domestic violence on social media has increased pessimism among the public, and instances of domestic violence on social media have made me more cautious in dealing with others) ranked in the top three positions according to the highest percentage weights.

Objective (3): To identify the most significant behavioral effects of audience use of social media to follow topics on domestic violence. To achieve this objective, the relative importance index of the responses of the research sample members to each item of the behavioral effects scale was adopted after applying it to the research sample consisting of (106) individuals. Table 31.5 illustrates the results for the following items.

1. Social media has contributed to enhancing the concept of domestic violence among individuals.
2. The information has contributed to enhancing individuals' rights regarding domestic violence issues.
3. Some cases of violence have made me isolated from society.
4. News about domestic violence on social media has increased pessimism among the public.

Table 31.5 Weighted means and percentage weights for the items of the behavioral effects scale for audience use of social media to follow topics on domestic violence

S. No.	Decisions	Freq.	Per. (%)	W. Avg	SD	Per. weight (%)	Rank
1	Disagree	1	0.9	2.76	0.45	92	1
	Neutral	23	21.7				
	Agree	82	77.4				
2	Disagree	0	0	2.64	0.48	88	2
	Neutral	38	35.8				
	Agree	68	64.2				
3	Disagree	0	0	2.28	0.45	76	5
	Neutral	76	71.7				
	Agree	30	28.3				
4	Disagree	0	0	2.51	0.5	83.67	4
	Neutral	52	49.1				
	Agree	54	50.9				
5	Disagree	0	0	2.63	0.48	87.67	3
	Neutral	39	36.8				
	Agree	67	63.2				

5. It has made me care about rejecting cases of violence among the public.

From the above table, it is evident that the items (social media contributed to enhancing the concept of domestic violence among individuals, the information contributed to enhancing individuals' rights concerning domestic violence issues, and it made me interested in anything that would reject cases of violence among the public) ranked in the top three positions according to the highest percentage weights.

31.5 Discussion

The study focuses on the demographics and social media usage patterns of individuals aged between 29 and 39 years, who form 40.6% of the sample and are the predominant users of social media platforms. Bachelor's degree holders are the highest educational group at 44.3%, indicating that navigating social media requires a certain level of knowledge. Married individuals, making up 50.9% of the sample, are most affected by domestic violence issues, which is a central theme of the study.

Employees represent the majority of respondents at 48.1%, and 65.1% of users engage with social media consistently. The majority spend 1–2 h daily on social media, with a significant portion using it for 3 h or more, indicating potential habitual use. Daily usage rates are high at 75.5%, showing that social media is an integral part of many individuals' daily routines.

The primary reason for social media use, cited by 46.2% of respondents, is the rapid and immediate delivery of news, followed by the ability to access news at any time (38.7%). Facebook is the most popular platform, preferred by 66% of users due to its user-friendly interface and ease of account creation. These findings are consistent with the results presented in [23] on the impact of electronic advertising on social media platforms on producers' and consumers' rights. The study found that many advertisers prefer to use platforms like Facebook for visual advertising, emphasizing the power of these platforms to reach the public. However, the study also cited concerns about the lack of strong legal protections for consumers against fraud on social media platforms. This highlights the importance of developing legal and regulatory frameworks to protect social media users, especially when pursuing sensitive issues such as domestic violence.

Child abuse is identified as the most pressing domestic violence issue, affecting 44.3% of cases, evoking strong emotional responses as children are seen as vulnerable victims. Public engagement with domestic violence issues is moderate, with 51.9% of respondents occasionally following these matters.

31.6 Conclusion

The study confirms that social media has become an integral part of how the public in Baghdad engages with and stays informed about domestic violence issues. With the prevalent use of platforms like Facebook, the public not only follows these serious social issues but also actively participates in the discourse surrounding them. The demographic most engaged in social media concerning domestic violence is relatively young and educated, suggesting a societal shift towards more proactive and informed community involvement in these crucial matters.

Overall, the findings reveal that the data links the use of social media and quick access to valid information gigging significant emotions and essential role of influencing the public behaviour regarding domestic violence. The issue on child abuse led the most type of violence that is followed indicating that people are concerned about the people at risk in society. The readings from the study reveal that social media is an essential tool to use in advocating for social issues. The representatives and the law can use it since a significant number of people in the modern world own smartphones and have access to the internet. In the future, the department concerned with domestic violence can focus on how else it will use the platforms to share with the public and statehooders and ensure that the legislations passed protect the sufferers of individuals. The study can be used to support the understanding of the future relying on the new technologies and points out that there is a need to carry on harnessing social media for the better of the society.

References

1. Hung, M., Lauren, E., Hon, E.S., Birmingham, W.C., Xu, J., Su, S., Hon, S.D., Park, J., Dang, P., Lipsky, M.S.: Social network analysis of COVID-19 sentiments: application of artificial intelligence. J. Med. Internet Res. **22**, e22590 (2020). https://doi.org/10.2196/22590
2. Zannettou, S., Sirivianos, M., Blackburn, J., Kourtellis, N.: The web of false information: rumors, fake news, hoaxes, clickbait, and various other shenanigans. J. Data Inf. Qual. **11**, 4 (2018). https://doi.org/10.1145/3309699
3. Pollett, S., Rivers, C.: Social media and the new world of scientific communication during the COVID-19 pandemic. Clin. Infect. Dis. **71** (2020). https://doi.org/10.1093/cid/ciaa553
4. Cinelli, M., Quattrociocchi, W., Galeazzi, A., Valensise, C., Brugnoli, E., Schmidt, A.L., Zola, P., Zollo, F., Scala, A.: The COVID-19 social media infodemic. Sci. Rep. **10** (2020). https://doi.org/10.1038/s41598-020-73510-5
5. Depoux, A., Martin, S., Karafillakis, E., Bsdar, R., Wilder-Smith, A., Larson, H.: The pandemic of social media panic travels faster than the COVID-19 outbreak. J. Travel Med. **27**, 3 (2020). https://doi.org/10.1093/jtm/taaa031
6. Vosoughi, S., Roy, D., Aral, S.: The spread of true and false news online. Science **359**(6380), 1146–1151 (2018). https://doi.org/10.1126/science.aap9559
7. Ferrara, E., Chang, H.C., Chen, E., Murić, G., Patel, J.: Characterizing social media manipulation in the 2020 U.S. presidential election. First Monday **25** (2020). https://doi.org/10.5210/fm.v25i11.11431
8. Seering, J.: Reconsidering self-moderation: the role of research in supporting community-based models for online content moderation. Proc. ACM Hum.-Comput. Interact. **4**, 1–28 (2020). https://doi.org/10.1145/3415178
9. Hamood, A.S.: Multi-cultural communication through English language. AL-Yarmouk J. **20**(7), 857–876 (2023). [Online]. https://www.iasj.net/iasj/issue/16599
10. Zannettou, S., Chatzis, S., Papadamou, K., Sirivianos, M.: The good, the bad and the bait: detecting and characterizing clickbait on YouTube. In: Proceedings of the 2018 IEEE Symposium on Security and Privacy Workshops, pp. 63–69. IEEE, San Francisco, USA (2018). https://doi.org/10.1109/SPW.2018.00018
11. Zubiaga, A., Spina, D., Fernández, V., Martínez-Unanue, R.: Real-time classification of Twitter trends. J. Am. Soc. Inf. Sci. Technol. **66**(3), 462–473 (2015). https://doi.org/10.1002/asi.23186
12. Del Vicario, M., Bessi, A., Zollo, F., Petroni, F., Scala, A., Caldarelli, G., Stanley, H.E., Quattrociocchi, W.: The spreading of misinformation online. Proc. Natl. Acad. Sci. U.S.A. **113**(3), 554–559 (2016). https://doi.org/10.1073/pnas.1517441113
13. Zubiaga, A., Aker, A., Bontcheva, K., Liakata, M., Procter, R.: Detection and resolution of rumours in social media: a survey. ACM Comput. Surv. **51**(2), 32 (2018). https://doi.org/10.1145/3161603
14. Grinberg, N., Joseph, K., Friedland, L., Swire-Thompson, B., Lazer, D.: Fake news on Twitter during the 2016 U.S. presidential election. Science **363**(6425), 374–378 (2019). https://doi.org/10.1126/science.aau2706
15. Velasquez, A., Rojas, H.: Political expression on social media: the role of communication competence and expected outcomes. Soc. Media Soc. **3**(1), 1–11 (2017). https://doi.org/10.1177/2056305117696521
16. Zhang, Y., Sun, Y., Padilla, L., Barua, S., Bertini, E., Parker, A.G.: Mapping the landscape of COVID-19 crisis visualizations. In: Proceedings of the 2021 CHI Conference on Human Factors in Computing Systems, pp. 1–23. ACM, New York, USA (2021). https://doi.org/10.1145/3411764.3445381
17. Guess, A., Nagler, J., Tucker, J.: Less than you think: prevalence and predictors of fake news dissemination on Facebook. Sci. Adv. **5**, eaau4586 (2019). https://doi.org/10.1126/sciadv.aau4586
18. Fletcher, R., Park, S.: The impact of trust in the news media on online news consumption and participation. Digit. Journalism **5**(1), 1–19 (2017). https://doi.org/10.1080/21670811.2017.1279979

19. Kumar, S., Shah, N.: False information on web and social media: a survey (2018). ArXiv preprint arXiv:1804.08559
20. Bessi, A., Coletto, M., Davidescu, G.A., Scala, A., Caldarelli, G., Quattrociocchi, W.: Science vs conspiracy: collective narratives in the age of misinformation. PLoS One **10**(2), e0118093 (2015). https://doi.org/10.1371/journal.pone.0118093
21. Vosoughi, S., Mohsenvand, M., Roy, D.: Rumor gauge: predicting the veracity of rumors on Twitter. ACM Trans. Knowl. Discov. Data **11**(4), 1–36 (2017). https://doi.org/10.1145/3070644
22. Gillani, N., Yuan, A., Saveski, M., Vosoughi, S., Roy, D.: Me, my echo chamber, and I: Introspection on social media polarization. In: Proceedings of the 2018 World Wide Web Conference, pp. 823–831. ACM, Lyon, France (2018). https://doi.org/10.1145/3178876.3186130
23. Labid, M.R.: Electronic advertising on social media platforms and its impact on producer and consumer rights: a survey study of a sample of producers and consumers. J. Media Res. **16**(63), 84–111 (2024). https://doi.org/10.33282/abaa.v16i63.1178

Chapter 32
The Digital Identity of Journalists Considering the New Digital Communication (an Applied Study on a Sample of Iraqi Journalists)

Jamil Nayef Sarhad Hassan

Abstract The current study was conducted to explore the digital identity of journalists as a new phenomenon due to the spread of new digital communication. This was achieved by conducting a field study on a sample of Iraqi journalists. The study used a descriptive methodology, with data collected through a questionnaire that was widely circulated to 100 Iraqi journalists in a random sample. The study findings indicated that most journalists are young and that a significant proportion is too worried about showing their identity as a journalist on websites because of security fears and political reservations. The findings also revealed the growing trend of digital journalism and the extent of the spread of the use of pseudo-names among journalists. Moreover, the study drew a clear picture of the role of digital communication in delineating the identity of journalism itself, impacting the popularity of its pioneers, and facilitating access to information for everyone. Hence, the current study recommends journalists embrace the digital revolution and confront its challenges by acquiring skills and new identities and committing to professionalism and ethics.

32.1 Introduction

The media and journalism have witnessed significant transformations in the new digital environment, where digital journalism has emerged as a blend of traditional journalism and new media by adapting to digital formats [1]. Digital identity is one of the most intriguing subjects for many researchers considering the challenges of technological globalization, as the private identity of society transforms into a larger universal identity. Consequently, society loses its real citizens in favor of another society that is broader and freer, raising the following question: Where is

J. N. S. Hassan (✉)
Department of Journalism, College of Mass Communication, University of Baghdad, Baghdad, Iraq
e-mail: jamil.n@comc.uobaghdad.edu.iq

F. P. García Márquez et al. (eds.), *Computing, Internet of Things and Data Analytics*, Smart Innovation, Systems and Technologies 387,
https://doi.org/10.1007/978-3-031-87154-2_32

the real identity in the age of shaping the virtual citizen and what is the nature of digital identity? In the new digital environment, there are no predetermined rules, and everyone can participate and express their opinions freely and explicitly, hiding behind the mask of the virtual world represented using a new digital identity. This digital identity, composed of pseudonyms, may consist of strange names, celebrity names, funny names, or attention-grabbing names, to highlight the personal presence of the digital identity among digital friends. This makes the virtual citizen feel belonging to their global homeland, liberating them from many cultural, social, and racial constraints [2]. Therefore, many spend long hours in front of mobile phone screens and computers, with much of the time spent in the real world reaching seven hours or even ten hours a day if the virtual world has not provided them with the containment of the homeland they desire and fascinates them [3].

Our current study aims to explore the digital identity of journalists in the context of new digital communication. The concept of digital identity within the framework of the new communication environment is examined [4]. Most of the currently available literature on digital identity in relation to journalists does not consider multiple aspects critical for the given group of people. For example, the fact that journalists live in a politically unstable environment in countries like Iraq, revealing the real identity of which online is virtually impossible without significant threats and risks for their physical integrity, is not being considered [5]. On a similar note, the influence of journalists' type of digital identity on their professional identity and credibility in the eyes of the public is rarely examined. In addition, the ways in which journalists adapt to the emergence of new digital communication technologies and the type of training that they receive to use the latter efficiently and competently is not explored [6]. Another issue that remains outside the scope of the current research is the exact role of the given identity in striking the balance between safety and responsiveness in journalists' social media [7]. Finally, to the best of my knowledge, there are no studies that explore the topic of journals' digital identity and the role of the local context in shaping the latter.

32.2 Literature Review

The literature on journalism in the digital age reveals a dynamic and evolving field influenced by technological advancements and shifts in audience behavior. Scholars have explored a wide range of themes, from the role of social media platforms in shaping journalistic practices to the impact of data journalism and the growing prominence of audience-driven content. These studies collectively examine how the digital landscape has transformed both the production and consumption of news, highlighting key challenges such as the ethical use of big data, the tension between editorial control and audience preferences, and the role of journalism in fostering democratic participation. This literature review synthesizes the key insights from several recent studies, offering a comprehensive overview of the major trends and debates in contemporary journalism research.

Bruns [8] addresses the increasing restrictions imposed on scholarly research by social media platforms. In what he refers to as the "APIcalypse," Bruns highlights the challenges faced by researchers in accessing data from these platforms, as they fight to maintain control over their ecosystems. This battle has critical implications for the study of social media and journalism, as scholars are restricted in their ability to study public discourse and interactions, which were previously more accessible.

Ferrer-Conill and Tandoc Jr. [9] described the role of audience-oriented editors in digital journalism. Their study uncovers how editorial practices are shifting due to real-time feedback from audiences via social media and analytics tools. Hermida and Young [10] explore the regeneration of news through data journalism. They argue that data journalism not only revitalizes traditional journalistic practices but also offers new ways to interact with complex datasets and narratives.

In [11], authors emphasize the importance of "place" in journalism studies, advocating for a more localized understanding of news production and consumption. Similarly, Lewis and Westlund [12] discuss the intersection of big data and journalism, addressing the complexities introduced by large datasets in the production and dissemination of news. Zelizer [13] challenges the notion that journalism is solely defined by digital technology. Ahva and Wiard [14] assess participatory journalism, particularly at the local level, through frameworks of access, dialogue, and deliberation. This study suggests that local journalism plays a crucial role in fostering democratic participation by offering a platform for community voices and facilitating meaningful dialogue.

Sabaté Gauxachs et al. [15] explore the differences between journalism and activism in the digital age. Similarly, Ghintab [16] provides a unique perspective by surveying Iraqi journalists' professional identities. The study reveals the complexities of journalistic practices in Iraq, highlighting issues related to media freedom, political influence, and professional ethics. In [17] authors explore comparative media systems, addressing how research design and epistemology shape the production of comparative knowledge. They argue that media systems research must account for both universal and contextual factors to provide a more nuanced understanding of journalism across different countries. Eldridge II et al. [18] introduce the "Digital Journalism Studies Compass," which serves as a tool for navigating the diverse scholarly terrain of digital journalism studies. This framework helps researchers identify key areas of study, from content production to audience engagement, offering a structured approach to understanding digital journalism's complexities.

In [19], authors examine linguistic devices used in news bulletins across top radio channels, shedding light on the strategies used to influence audience perception and understanding. This study provides insights into the language of news and its role in shaping public discourse, particularly in Arabic-speaking media.

In general, the above-mentioned studies address various aspects of the topic of digital identity and their relationship to new media and social media platforms, thereby enriching the theoretical background of the current study and finding points of intersection and difference. They constitute a good platform for understanding the dimensions of the topic and for discussing the results of the current study.

32.2.1 Problem Statement

The Study aims to understand the impact of virtual digital identity, which has received special attention from social media platforms. According to the perspective, the study problem is summarized by answering the main question:

- What is meant by digital identity in the new media environment?
- What are the elements of digital identity in the digital communication environment?
- What is the extent of the relationship between digital and real identity in the new communication environment?

32.2.2 Study Objectives

The objectives of the Study:

1. To understand the digital identity of journalists in the emergence of the virtual citizen.
2. Identify the elements of digital identity in the new digital communication environment.
3. Explore the relationship between virtual identity and real identity.

The importance of the study stems from several interconnected factors as follows:

1. Identifying the components of digital identity for journalists
2. Clarifying the relationship between digital (virtual) identity and real identity
3. Recognizing the identities of users of social media platforms in the new digital communication environment.
4. Understanding the problematic aspects of digital identity for journalists in the digital communication realm.
5. Defining the nature of new digital communication.

The paper is one of the most relevant to modern life in Iraq as it addresses a range of issues related to the digital identity of journalists and opportunities for using pseudonyms. The paper is significant as it helps fill the gap in the research with regard to the experienced restraint to revealing one's true digital identity and the tension that emerges between a journalist as a professional and a pseudonym as an alternative identity. There is a general lack of research and information regarding how journalists are supposed to use new forms of digital communication and what expertise they should possess. In addition, the study builds on the framework developed by Karlsson and focuses on how real and digital identities are related and what are the consequences for journalists' work and public perception. Not less importantly, the study relates to the life of a particular country, namely Iraq, with a specific political and social environment, which calls for greater localized research to address these issues. Finally, the study relies mainly on a descriptive method using surveys and interviews of Iraqi journalists, thereby providing more insight into the problem, recommendations on the use of digital tools, and ways to address identity issues that potentially affect professional practices.

32.3 Methodology

The study is considered descriptive, and the nature and objectives of the study necessitated the use of the descriptive methodology, which is a scientific and organized effort to obtain data and scientific information. It describes the phenomenon or set of phenomena related to the study topic. It provides a complete description and a real and accurate diagnosis of the problem, and it provides evidence that proves realistic behaviors. The descriptive methodology is one of the most important methods in media studies.

The study sample consisted of Iraqi journalists; totaling (100) participants selected randomly, the number of male participants reached 65, constituting 65% of the total, while the number of females was 35, representing 35%.We can see in Fig. 32.1 that the percentage of males was (65%), ranking first, while the percentage of females was (35%) of the total sample. This is natural in the context of journalism in Iraq, as most workers in media institutions are males.

Figure 32.2 illustrates that respondents in the age group (35–44) ranked first with a frequency of (48) and a percentage of (48%). The age group (25–34) obtained a frequency of (28) and a percentage of (28%), while the age group (45 and above) ranked third with a frequency of (24) and a percentage of (24%). The middle age group appears to be the most prominent, which is positive as it indicates experience in the field of media, as well as proficiency in using technology in the realm of new media.

The researcher utilized survey tools, which are a primary instrument in the study process, through distributing questionnaires as well as interviews with journalists.

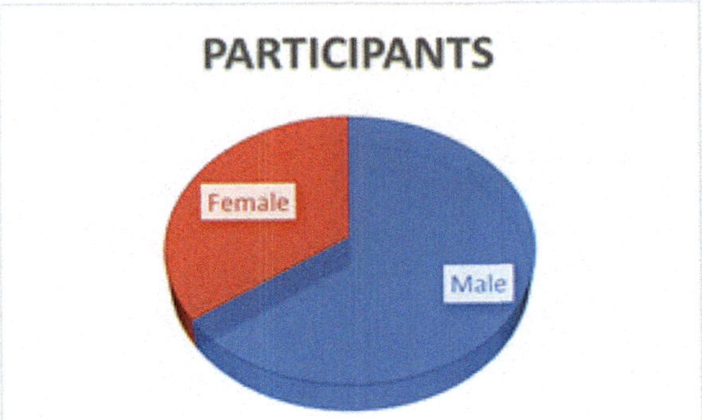

Fig. 32.1 The number of males and females from the total sample of participants

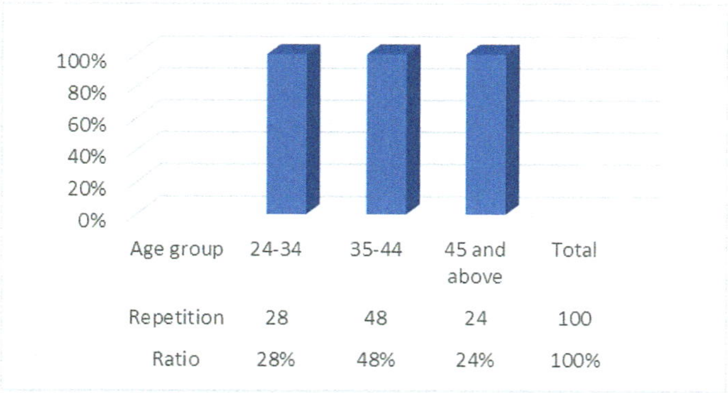

Fig. 32.2 The age groups of the participants

32.4 Results and Analysis

After using the study questionnaire, the results showed as follows:

Do you reveal your identity on social media platforms? If your answer is (no), what are the reasons? (as showed in Fig. 32.3).

- Security reasons.
- Working in multiple media fields.

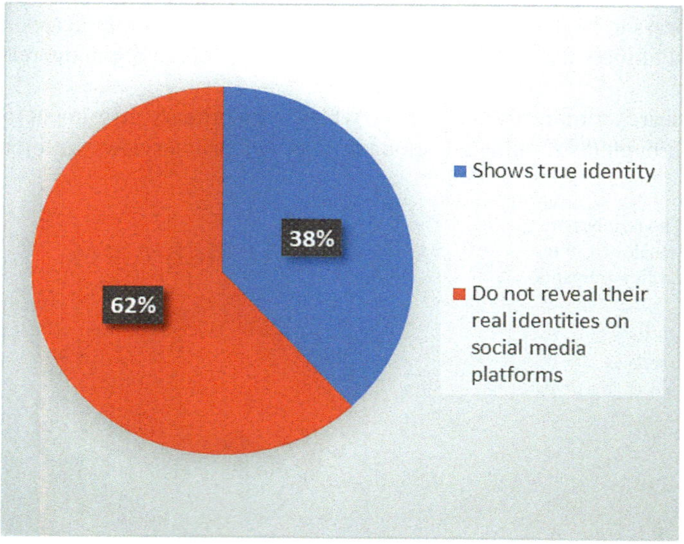

Fig. 32.3 The number of respondents who reveal their real identities on social media platforms

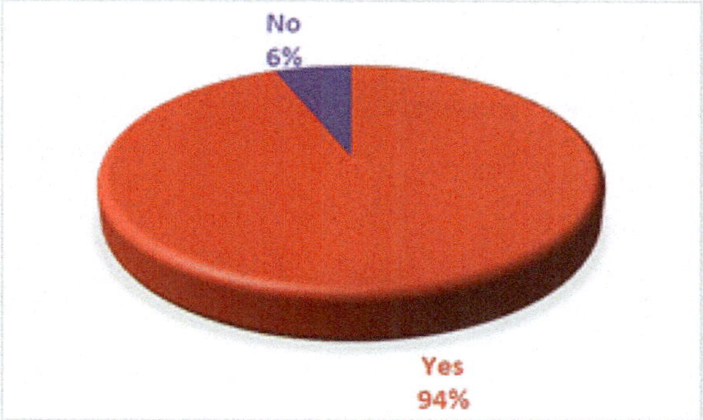

Fig. 32.4 The number of respondents who work in electronic (digital) journalism

The responses of the respondents regarding the disclosure of their real identity on social media platforms indicate that the number of individuals in the sample who reveal their real identity on social media platforms reached (38) with a percentage of (38%), while those who do not reveal their real identities on social media platforms reached (62) with a percentage of (62%). Most of the respondents explained that the reason for not disclosing their real identity on social media platforms is due to various security reasons.

Do you practice your journalistic work electronically (digitally)?

The responses of the respondents regarding practicing electronic journalism indicate that the number of individuals in the sample who engage in electronic journalism reached (94) occurrences, accounting for a percentage of (94%), while those who do not engage in electronic journalism amounted to (6) occurrences, representing a percentage of (6%). This percentage is significant as the trend towards digital journalism has become more prevalent than traditional print journalism (Fig. 32.4).

Your Facebook page, is it under your real name or a pseudonym-?

The respondents' answers regarding the use of real or pseudonymous names on Facebook indicate that the sample individuals who use their real names on Facebook amounted to (33) occurrences, representing (33%), while those who use pseudonyms on Facebook numbered (67) occurrences, representing (67%). Those who use pseudonyms outnumber those who use real names, which is natural in journalism where pseudonyms are often utilized (Fig. 32.5).

In your opinion, does the new digital communication define the identity of the digital journalist?

The responses of the respondents indicated that the number of respondents who believe that the new digital communication defines the identity of the journalist is (54), accounting for (54%) of the total, while the number of respondents who believe that the new digital communication does not define the identity of the journalist is (46), accounting for (46%) of the total (Fig. 32.6).

– Has journalism become easier for you compared to before?

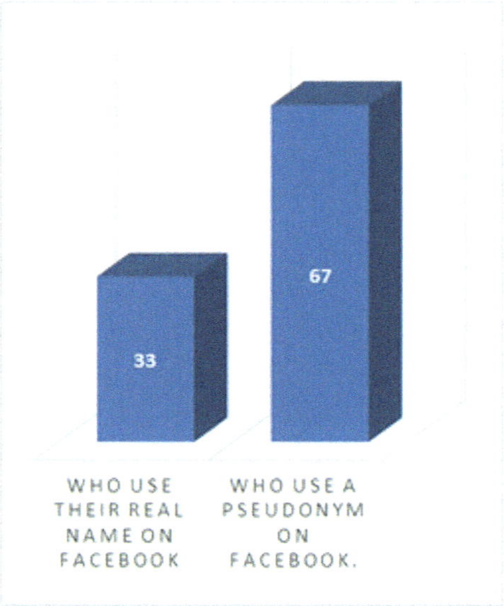

Fig. 32.5 The number of respondents who use their real name and the number of those who use a pseudonym on Facebook

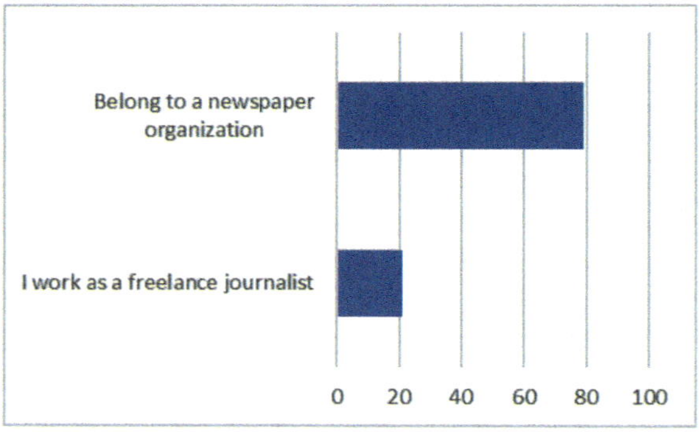

Fig. 32.6 The number of journalists who find that the new digital communication defines the identity of the journalist

The responses of the respondents indicated that the number of respondents who believe that journalism has become easier than before is (86) respondents, with a percentage of (86%), while the number of respondents who do not believe that journalism has become easier than before is (14) respondents, with a percentage of (14%). Technology has greatly facilitated the work of journalists (Fig. 32.7).

Do you work as a freelance journalist, or do you belong to a journalistic institution?

The responses of the respondents indicated that the number of researchers who work as freelance journalists is (21) researchers, accounting for (21%), while the number of researchers who belong to a journalistic institution is (79) researchers, accounting for (79%). This confirms that journalistic freedom lies in the journalist adhering to the policy of the institution he/she works for (Fig. 32.8).

Do you believe that digital identity has made journalistic fame easier?

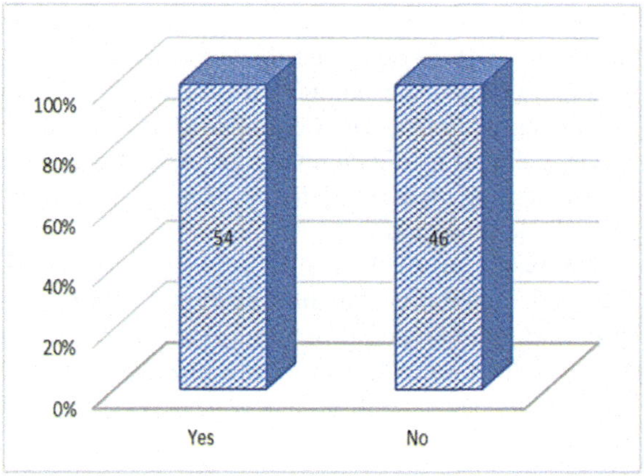

Fig. 32.7 The number of respondents who found their journalistic work easier than before

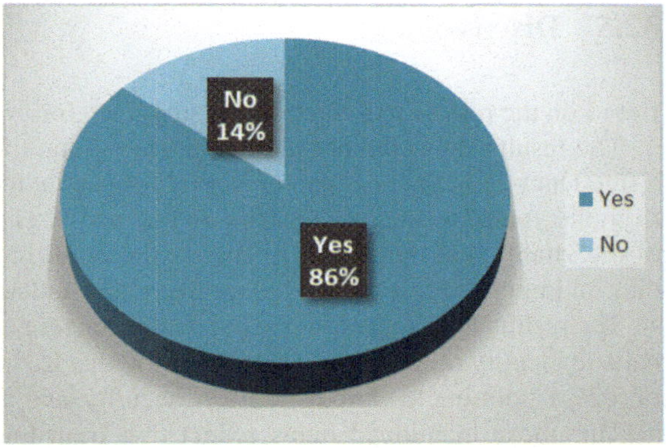

Fig. 32.8 The number of researchers who work as freelance journalists and the number of journalists who belong to a journalistic institution

The responses of the researchers indicated that the number of researchers who believe that digital identity has made journalistic fame easier is (74), accounting for (74%), while the number of researchers who do not believe that digital identity has made journalistic fame easier is (26), accounting for (26%). This confirms that journalistic fame has come from the widespread dissemination of new digital communication, influenced by advanced technologies that have spread widely throughout the world.

In your opinion, has the new digital media contributed to easier access to the audience?

The responses of the researchers indicated that the number of researchers who believe that new digital media contributes to easier access to the audience is (58), accounting for (58%), while the number of researchers who do not believe that new digital media contributes to easier access to the audience is (24), accounting for (42%). This is evidence that new digital media facilitates access to large audiences.

Has the new digital media added new skills to your journalistic work?

The responses of the researchers indicated that the number of researchers who added new skills to their journalistic work due to new digital media is (95), accounting for (95%), while the number of researchers who did not add new skills to their journalistic work due to new digital media is (5), accounting for (5%). This is evidence that new digital media facilitates access to large audiences.

Did digital media for digital identity highlight a new addition to accessing journalistic information?

The responses of the researchers indicated that the number of researchers who believe that digital media, through digital identity, has highlighted a new addition in accessing journalistic information is (53), accounting for (53%), while the number of researchers who do not believe that digital media, through digital identity, has highlighted a new addition in accessing journalistic information is (47), accounting for (47%).

32.5 Discussions

Based on the results presented in the study, the following points can be discussed:

The results showed that the middle-aged group of respondents ranked first with a frequency of (48) and a percentage of (48%), indicating that most journalists are from the youthful category working in the media sector. This is a positive indicator of the vitality and dynamism of the media sector in Iraq, where young journalists play an important role in developing the media and adopting modern technologies.

The results highlighted the respondents' concern about not displaying their journalistic identity on websites, ranking first with a frequency of (62) and a percentage of (62%), pointing to various political, security, and multi-field journalistic reasons.

The above-mentioned items reflect that Iraqi journalists have concealed their names and true identities in the field of work despite calling for freedom of expression and protecting their identities. The study data showed that the ranking of digital journalistic work was first with a frequency of (94%) and a percentage of (94%), and from this data, we see that journalists are more digital than other traditional because of the move towards electronic and technical. As a result of the digital renaissance, radical changes have been implemented like journalistic work because of rapid technological development. As well as many indicators have shown that those using pseudonyms are ranked first with a frequency of (63%) due to the increasing number of journalists using pseudonyms and their justifications for using them. Indicators have raised questions about the extent and limits of using pseudonyms and the negative effects on a journalist's credibility are due to the professionally high content provided.

In Ghantab's study about the representations if Iraqi journalists' professional identity forces these individuals to face in the digital age, it is made clear that journalists must experience various difficulties and hazards in their attempts to configure and reconfigure their own professional idiolect and enable it to exist in the digital space.

Accordingly, the results of our own study align with Gentab's, since the digital identity of journalists in the modern era has become one of the most important components of their general professional identity. Both studies stress the necessity to determine "how the digital environment affects Iraqi journalists' reportorial practices and their professional identity.

The results were also as follows: the importance of digital communication was first with a frequency of (54%) because of radical transformations in the media and journalism sector. There are prominent indicators of the importance of digital communication in creating the identity of journalistic work in the current era, which requires journalistic bodies to take appropriate measures to continue to adapt to these changes. In the same context, the results of the researchers' responses also showed that the journalist's category with a media centre was a higher percentage with a frequency of (79%) so a researcher can indicate that most journalists work in media centres with special policies. Unfortunately, there is a problem that most of these journalists are tied to their work and are not free under the policies and conditions of media institutions.

The results of the researchers confirmed that the digital identity of a journalist contributes to the figure, reaching a frequency of (74%), with the results coming from distinguished researchers. This raises many justified questions about the impact of fame, image, and digital figures on a journalist. Regarding the above, the results of the researchers' responses clarified that new digital media helped facilitate obtaining information by the public, reaching a frequency of (58%). Indicators are supporting the importance of new technological tools underscored by the need for mechanisms to measure them positively and benefit from them. In general, the results of the study demonstrate the radical changes in the media and journalism sector during the digital revolution and its negative effects on the identity of the journalist and his personality, which necessitates the need for the research respondent to adapt to these changes and provide the necessary recommendations to address these challenges and skills development required by the research respondent in practising the journalistic job in their new digital fields.

32.6 Conclusion

The study discussed the digital identity of journalists in the new digital communication era, reviewing the most prominent changes and transformations that have taken place in the media and journalistic work in the digital age. As such, the study validated that journalists are exposed to vast challenges concerning the extent to which their identity may be protected or not and express themselves in a digital environment. The prevalence of digital technology and new media has increased the linkage of journalistic work to various digital communication technologies. Therefore, the study ascertained that digital communication is essential in forming the patterns of journalistic work and its impact on the journalists' fame and interaction with the public. Consequently, the study concludes that the status of the digital identity of journalists has become a central pivot in light of the rapid digitalization turnaround. Particularly, journalists need to hone their skills and build their qualifications to keep pace with the changes and confront their threats.

Further, several additional areas need further research and research work including the impact of digital identity on journalistic work and ethics and, more crucially, on freedom of the press versus identity protection in the digital environment. Notably, it is essential to develop a set of policies and laws that protect journalists and their rights in the digital era and continuously qualify and re-qualify them to remain aware of technological advances. Moreover, the outcome presented that the digital identity of journalists is a critical component that reflects their critical role in spreading knowledge raising awareness and serving society in the digital age.

The contribution of this study to the field is multifaceted. Firstly, it fills a crucial gap in existing literature by providing empirical data on the digital identity of journalists in a politically sensitive environment like Iraq. The insights gained from this study offer a nuanced understanding of the challenges and adaptations required by journalists in such contexts. Secondly, the study advances the theoretical discourse on digital identity by linking it with professional credibility and security concerns, thereby enriching academic conversation with practical implications. Furthermore, by focusing on a specific local context, this study adds depth to the global understanding of digital journalism practices and the socio-political factors influencing them.

Based on the findings, several recommendations for practice and policy are proposed. Journalists should be encouraged to embrace digital tools and platforms, while simultaneously being provided with training and resources to navigate the associated risks effectively. Media organizations and professional bodies should develop comprehensive guidelines and support systems to help journalists manage their digital identities safely. Policies aimed at protecting journalists' online identities should be strengthened, ensuring that they can perform their duties without compromising their safety. Additionally, there is a need for continuous professional development programs that focus on the digital competencies required in modern journalism. These programs should address both the technical skills and the ethical considerations of digital identity management.

In conclusion, the digital transformation in journalism presents both opportunities and challenges. This study highlights the critical need for journalists to adapt to new digital realities while safeguarding their identities and professional integrity. By addressing the identified gaps and implementing the recommended practices and policies, the journalism field can better navigate the complexities of the digital age, ensuring that journalists remain effective and secure in their roles.

References

1. Deuze, M., Witschge, T.: Beyond journalism: theorizing the transformation of journalism. Journalism **21**(5), 661–680 (2020). https://doi.org/10.1177/1464884918760675
2. Raghunath, P.: Book review of the Palgrave handbook on methods for media policy research. Asia Pac. Media Educ. **30** (2020). https://doi.org/10.1177/1326365X20929129
3. Wenzel, A.: Engaged journalism in rural communities. Journal. Pract. **13**(1), 1–15 (2018). https://doi.org/10.1080/17512786.2018.1562360
4. Carlson, M., Lewis, S.: Temporal reflexivity in journalism studies: making sense of change in a more timely fashion. Journalism **20**(1), 6–20 (2018). https://doi.org/10.1177/1464884918760675
5. Bélair-Gagnon, V., Holton, A.: Boundary work, interloper media, and analytics in newsrooms. In: The SAGE Handbook of Digital Journalism (2020). https://doi.org/10.4324/9780429347108-6
6. Broersma, M., Eldridge II, S.: Journalism and social media: redistribution of power? Media Commun. **7**(1), 193–197 (2019). https://doi.org/10.17645/mac.v7i1.1769
7. Waisbord, S.: The 5Ws and 1H of digital journalism. Digit. Journal. **7**(3), 351–358 (2019). https://doi.org/10.1080/21670811.2019.1623653
8. Bruns, A.: After the 'APIcalypse': social media platforms and their fight against critical scholarly research. Inf. Commun. Soc. **22**(11), 1544–1566 (2019). https://doi.org/10.1080/1369118X.2019.1637446
9. Ferrer-Conill, M., Tandoc, E.C., Jr.: The audience-oriented editor. Digit. Journal. **7**(1), 32–51 (2019). https://doi.org/10.1080/21670811.2017.1355154
10. Hermida, A., Young, M.L.: Data journalism and the regeneration of news. Journalism **20**(3), 398–416 (2019). https://doi.org/10.1177/1464884917722015
11. Usher, N.: Putting 'place' in the center of journalism research: a way forward to understand challenges to trust and knowledge in news. Journal. Commun. Monogr. **21**(2), 84–146 (2019). https://doi.org/10.1177/1522637919853369
12. Lewis, S.C., Westlund, O.: Big data and journalism: epistemology, expertise, economics, and ethics. Digit. J. **7**(5), 679–692 (2019). https://doi.org/10.1080/21670811.2018.1516794
13. Zelizer, B.: Why journalism is about more than digital technology. Digit. J. **7**(3), 343–350 (2019). https://doi.org/10.1080/21670811.2019.1571932
14. Ahva, L., Wiard, V.: Participation in local journalism: assessing two approaches through access, dialogue and deliberation. J. Stud. **20**(12), 1700–1719 (2019). https://doi.org/10.1080/1461670X.2019.1659801
15. Sabaté Gauxachs, A., Micó-Sanz, J.-L., Díez-Bosch, M.: Is the new 'new' digital journalism a type of activism? An analysis of 'Jot Down', 'Gatopardo' and 'The New Yorker'. Commun. Soc. **32**(4), 173–191 (2019). https://doi.org/10.15581/003.32.4.173-191
16. Ghintab, A.S.: Iraqi journalists' representations of their professional identity: a survey study. J. Media Res. **16**(63), 57–83 (2024). https://doi.org/10.33282/abaa.v16i63.1183
17. Powers, M., Vera-Zambrano, S.: The universal and the contextual of media systems: research design, epistemology, and the production of comparative knowledge. Int. J. Press/Polit. **23**(2), 143–160 (2018). https://doi.org/10.1177/1940161218771899
18. Eldridge, S.A., II., Hess, K., Tandoc, E.C., Jr., Westlund, O.: Navigating the scholarly terrain: introducing the digital journalism studies compass. Digit. J. **7**(3), 386–403 (2019). https://doi.org/10.1080/21670811.2019.1599724
19. Hamood, A.S.: Linguistic devices used in the news bulletins of the top five news radio channels. Ann. Fac. Arts Ain Shams Univ. **51**, 153–166 (2023). https://doi.org/10.21608/aafu.2023.335621

Chapter 33
Fault Detection and Performance Analysis for Quanser's Two-Rotor Helicopter Under Different Fault Levels

Khalid Kabir Dandago and Long Zhang

Abstract Reliable and stable performance is a key requirement for controlling Unmanned Aerial Vehicles (UAVs). Traditional control systems are typically designed to maintain stable flight and ensure safe operation. However, UAVs are susceptible to various flight faults that can compromise performance and potentially cause instability. Such instability poses significant risks to properties, lives, and the operating environment. To mitigate these risks, it is essential to develop a system that can detect faults, pinpoint their location and severity, and adapt in real-time, allowing the UAV to maintain safe operation. Although analyzing the impact of faults on UAV performance is critical for selecting optimal tolerance and detection methods, few research works has been done in this area, especially with hardware. This research study evaluates the control system performance of a 2-degree-of-freedom (2DOF) two-rotor helicopter under various actuator faults, including different blade break types and thicknesses. The analysis demonstrates how various fault conditions affect performance metrics, showing that faults contribute to performance degradation and induce vibrations in the system, especially in scenarios involving imbalance or asymmetry.

33.1 Introduction

Unmanned Aerial Vehicles (UAVs) are increasingly becoming essential components of our daily lives. Their wide-ranging applications, including traffic management, filming, precision agriculture, and construction, have significantly boosted their popularity and demand [1–3]. Additionally, improvements in design methodologies, along with innovations in sensor and communication technologies, have significantly accelerated their evolution [4].

In terms of structure, UAVs are primarily categorized into three types: rotary, fixed-wing, and flapping-wing UAVs [5]. Flight endurance, range coverage, cruise speed, and payload capability [6] are the attributes that fixed-wing is comparatively

K. K. Dandago · L. Zhang (✉)
The University of Manchester, Manchester, UK
e-mail: long.zhang@manchester.ac.uk

F. P. García Márquez et al. (eds.), *Computing, Internet of Things and Data Analytics*, Smart Innovation, Systems and Technologies 387,
https://doi.org/10.1007/978-3-031-87154-2_33

better than the others. On the other hand, rotary UAVs, propelled by multiple motors depending on their configuration, offer more simplicity, low maintenance costs, higher agility, and favorable performance-to-price ratio [7, 8]. Helicopters and quadcopters, which provide various advantages, are the most extensively studied types of rotary UAVs in literature [5]. While quadcopters are equipped with four motors functioning as actuators, helicopters generally utilize two rotors for operation.

Managing flight scenarios such as obstacle avoidance, trajectory tracking, internal and external disturbances, and faulty conditions requires robust UAV control strategies. These strategies fall into four main categories: linear, nonlinear, artificial intelligence-based, and hybrid control schemes. Each category offers distinct advantages and drawbacks, with the selection often depending on the specific functional needs and trade-offs involved [5].

UAVs may experience different types of faults during flight operations, which are generally classified into three main categories: sensor faults, actuator faults, and faults in other components [9]. Actuator faults refer to the partial or complete loss of control action by an actuator. This category is further subdivided into constant gain, drift, and constant output faults. The most widely researched in the literature among the three is the constant gain fault. Sensor faults include total sensor faults, constant bias faults, drift faults, and outlier faults.

When faults arise, traditional feedback control systems may be unable to preserve the vehicle's stability and performance, potentially leading to catastrophic outcomes. To ensure flight safety in the presence of faults, it is vital to develop a robust control system that can manage these events. This system should incorporate both diagnosis and tolerance subsystems. The diagnosis subsystem detects the development of a fault, pinpoints its location, and evaluates its magnitude. The tolerance subsystem then uses this diagnostic information to reconfigure the controller and mitigate the fault's effects. Figure 33.1 further illustrates how fault diagnosis and fault tolerance subsystems work together to manage faults on UAVs. Analysis of numerous accidents in safety-critical systems, such as aircraft, suggests that many of these accidents could have been prevented if they had a fault tolerant control system capable of diagnosing and accommodating faults [10].

Fault-tolerant control systems for UAVs are generally divided into two categories: passive and active fault-tolerant control systems (PFTCS and AFTCS) [12]. PFTCS are designed to handle anticipated faults, eliminating the need for a Fault Diagnosis (FD) system to detect, isolate, or estimate fault magnitudes [13]. Additionally, they do not require reconfiguring the control system to address existing faults. As a result, the capability of PFTCS to handle faults is limited, because they can only accommodate faults considered during the design process. On the other hand, AFTCS are built to manage faults dynamically during flight operations. This approach requires an FD system to sense faults, identify their location, and determine post-fault models and/or fault parameters [14]. Subsequently, the gathered information is used for controller reconfiguration, ensuring satisfactory performance and system stability [15].

A key element of an AFTCS is the FD module, which produces fault information that the control algorithm uses to dynamically reconfigure itself, thereby ensuring acceptable performance and system stability across various fault scenarios. FD meth-

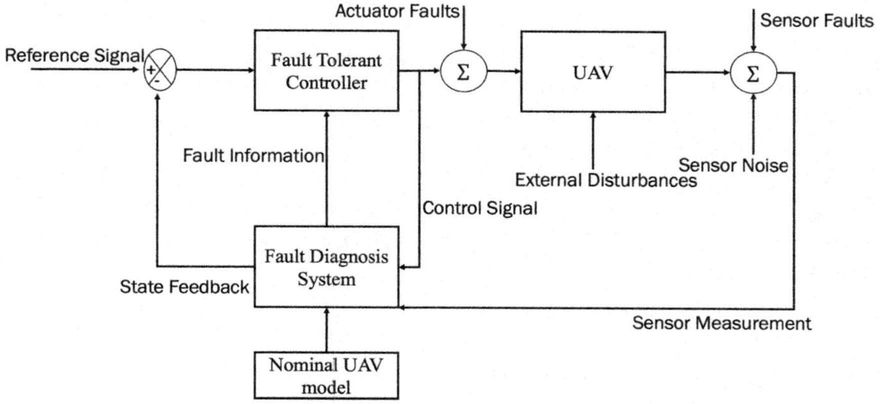

Fig. 33.1 A block diagram depicting the configuration of a fault diagnosis and tolerance control system [11]

ods are typically divided into three primary categories:analytical, hardware redundancy, and signal processing approaches [16].

The hardware redundancy method involves using multiple identical components for the same function, enabling the detection and isolation of any faulty component [17]. Although this approach is highly reliable, it is often impractical for rotary UAVs due to increased power requirements [18] and reduced agility [19]. The analytical method diagnoses faults by leveraging the system's model or relevant information [20], and it is further classified into knowledge-based and model-based approaches [16]. In the model-based approach, fault information is derived from the residual signal, which represents the difference between the estimated signal from the model and a sensor-measured signal [21]. In contrast, the knowledge-based method relies on expert knowledge and previous system performance data for diagnostic processes [28]. Lastly, the signal processing method utilizes specialized processing tools, established knowledge of system health indicators, and measured signals to identify faulty conditions within the system [16, 17, 22].

Several control methods have been employed in the design of AFTCS, including gain-scheduling PID controller [23], nonlinear dynamic inversion method [24], model predictive controller [25], recurrent neural network [13], and dynamic output feedback control algorithm [21]. Also, a nonlinear observer and a feedforward neural network were utilized to safeguard a UAV against cyber-attacks that lead to false data injection [26].

Although a number of fault diagnosis and tolerance control systems have been developed and evaluated for UAVs, primarily through simulations, there is a scarcity of studies examining the performance of rotary UAVs using conventional controllers in the presence of various fault conditions. Moreover, few studies have investigated the performance of such vehicles when equipped with propeller blades of different thicknesses. These analyses are crucial for determining the most suitable diagnosis and tolerance methods for specific systems and can contribute to the enhancement of rotary UAV design. Additionally, investigations and diagnoses on real systems have been constrained to a small number of faults. Hence, this study aims to assess the performance of various fault conditions and propeller blade thicknesses using a 2-degree-of-freedom (2DOF) helicopter.

The paper is structured as follows: Sect. 33.2 outlines the experimental setup and the methods/materials employed in the research. Section 33.3 presents the experimental results. Section 33.4 discusses these results, and concluding remarks are provided in Sect. 33.5.

33.2 Materials and Methods

33.2.1 Quanser's Aero2 Aerospace System

The research utilized Quanser's Aero2 aerospace platform, which offers versatility in emulating various aerospace systems. This versatile dual-rotor platform can simulate the operation of a 1-degree-of-freedom (1DOF) vertical takeoff and landing (VTOL) aircraft, a 2DOF helicopter, and a half quadrotor. Its flexible design permits users to lock or unlock the yaw and pitch axes and to arrange the thrusters either horizontally or vertically, facilitating the emulation of various aerospace configurations. For this research work, the system was primarily set to the 2-DOF helicopter mode as depicted in Fig. 33.2. However, some of the experiments were done with the 1-DOF VTOL setting.

Fig. 33.2 The Aero 2 equipment configured in the 2-DOF helicopter setup (Image provided by Quanser Inc.)

33.2.2 Aero2 2DOF Helicopter Dynamics Modelling

In the 2DOF helicopter configuration, motor 0 predominantly affects pitch motion, while motor 1 primarily impacts yaw motion. However, the interactions between the two motors are influenced by reactive torques, creating a coupling effect. Equations 33.1 and 33.2 present the simplified Newtonian linear equations of motion for the 2-DOF helicopter. This model assumes that the voltages applied to the motors is directly proportional to the thrusts produced. Although it incorporates gyroscopic reactive torques, it does not account for all system dynamics, including nonlinearities. Nevertheless, this linearized model is valuable for the design of linear control systems.

$$\tau_p = K_{pp} V_p D_t + K_{py} V_y D_t = J_p \ddot{\theta} + D_p \dot{\theta} + K_{sp} \theta \tag{33.1}$$

$$\tau_y = K_{yy} V_y D_t + K_{yp} V_p D_t = J_y \ddot{\psi} + D_y \dot{\psi} \tag{33.2}$$

Some of the parameters listed in Table 33.1 are provided in the system's specification, while others were obtained through experimentation. The parameter values can be found in Table 33.1.

The definitions of the variables in Eqs. 33.1 and 33.2 are as follows:

τ_p Pitch motion torque
K_{pp} Thrust-Force gain of Motor 0 acting on the pitch axis
V_p Motor 0's input voltage
D_t Distance between center of the motors and Aero2 pivot
K_{py} Thrust-Force gain of Motor 1 acting on the pitch axis
V_y Motor 1's input voltage
J_p Pitch axis' total moment of inertia
D_p Damping of pitch axis
K_{sp} Pitch axis stiffness

Table 33.1 Modelling parameters

Parameters	Values
D_t (m)	0.1674
K_{pp} (N/V)	0.00321
K_{sp} (–)	0.00744
D_p (–)	0.00199
J_p (kg m^2)	0.0232
K_{yy} (N/V)	0.00610
D_y (–)	0.00192
J_y (kg m^2)	0.0238
K_{yp} (N/V)	−0.00319
K_{py} (N/V)	0.00137

τ_y	Yaw motion torque
K_{yy}	Motor 1 thrust-Force gain acting on the yaw axis
K_{yp}	Motor 0 thrust-force gain acting on the yaw axis
J_y	Yaw axis' moment of inertia
D_y	Yaw axis' Damping

The state space model of the system developed from Eqs. 33.1, 33.2, and Table 33.1 is presented by Eqs. 33.3 and 33.4.

$$\dot{X} = AX + BU \tag{33.3}$$

$$Y = CX \tag{33.4}$$

where,

$$A = \begin{bmatrix} 0 & 0 & 1 & 0 \\ 0 & 0 & 0 & 1 \\ -0.3190 & 0 & -0.1164 & 0 \\ 0 & 0 & 0 & -0.1386 \end{bmatrix},$$

$$B = \begin{bmatrix} 0 & 0 \\ 0 & 0 \\ 0.0216 & 0.01154 \\ -0.01336 & 0.052 \end{bmatrix},$$

$$C = \begin{bmatrix} 1\,0\,0\,0 \\ 0\,1\,0\,0 \\ 0\,0\,1\,0 \\ 0\,0\,0\,1 \end{bmatrix},$$

$$X = [\theta, \psi, \dot{\theta}, \dot{\psi}]',$$

$$U = [V_p \quad V_y]'$$

33.2.3 Controller Design

The control system employed for controlling the yaw and pitch motions of the 2DOF helicopter was the Linear Quadratic Regulator (LQR). This control scheme calculates an optimal control gain represented by K. This K value is determined by minimizing a cost function, denoted as J, which considers factors such as the system's control input needed to reach the desired control goal and the tracking error. Equation 33.5 presents the formulation of this cost function.

$$\min_{U=\mathbb{R}^m} J = \int_0^\infty U^T R U + e^T Q e \qquad (33.5)$$
$$subject\ to\colon \dot{x} = Ax + BU$$

In Eq. 33.5, U signifies the control input, e represents the tracking error, and R and Q denote the weighting matrices. These matrices are adjusted to achieve the desired minimization of the control input and the tracking error, respectively. Figure 33.3 presents the LQR control structure.

From Fig. 33.3, $U = K(r - x)$, where Eq. 33.6 is used to solve for K

$$K = R^{-1} B^T P \qquad (33.6)$$

Equation 33.7, which is a Riccati equation, is used to solve for the P in Eq. 33.6.

$$Q - PBR^{-1}B^T P + A^T P + PA = 0 \qquad (33.7)$$

The cost matrices that were used are:

$$Q = \begin{bmatrix} 150 & 0 & 0 & 0 \\ 0 & 75 & 0 & 0 \\ 0 & 0 & 0 & 0 \\ 0 & 0 & 0 & 0 \end{bmatrix} \quad and \quad R = \begin{bmatrix} 0.01 & 0 \\ 0 & 0.01 \end{bmatrix}$$

33.2.4 Propellers' Blades Conditions

The impact of blade breaks on trajectory tracking was analyzed using the Aero2 2DOF helicopter configuration, which is equipped with two 8-blade propellers, each attached to a separate motor. Various types of blade breaks were examined to assess their effects on the vehicle's performance. The trajectory tracking control was evaluated under normal conditions with fully intact propellers, as well as with configura-

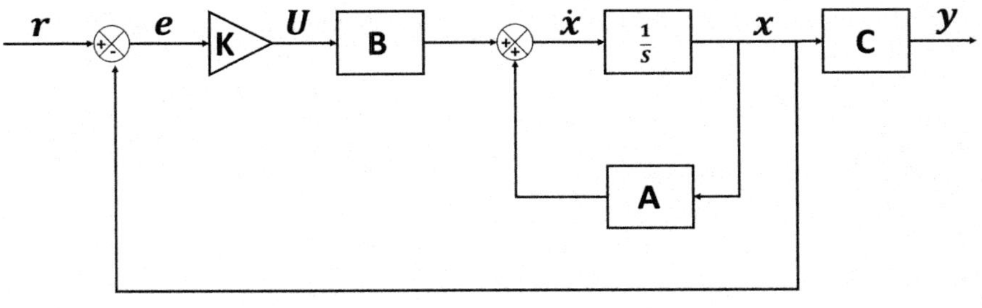

Fig. 33.3 LQR control structure

tions involving 1-blade, 4-blade, and 8-blade breaks across the two propellers. The specific configurations of these breaks are illustrated in Fig. 33.4.

The second performance analysis focused on the open-loop response of the 1DOF-VTOL setup, which utilizes a single propeller. Various degrees of breaks were examined on one blade, two symmetrical blades, and two asymmetrical blades of the propeller for the analysis. Figure 33.5 provides a visual representation of the different fault conditions examined in this particular analysis.

For the third performance analysis, the same setup as the second one was employed. However, instead of examining blade breaks, various blade thicknesses for a propeller without any breaks were examined. Figure 33.6 illustrates the differences in the blade thicknesses that were considered for this analysis.

33.2.5 Performance Matrices

The evaluation of the effects of faults on the trajectory tracking of the system's yaw and pitch motions included the measurement of time response metrics such as steady-state error (SSE), overshoot, and rise time. Furthermore, to assess the vibrations induced by these faults, the standard deviation (SD) of the yaw and pitch angles at steady state, along with the SD of the computed control input, was recorded.

For the effect of blades' breaks and thickness on the system's open-loop response, the Steady State Gain (SSG), natural frequency (ω_n), time constant (τ), and damping coefficient (ζ) were utilized for evaluation.

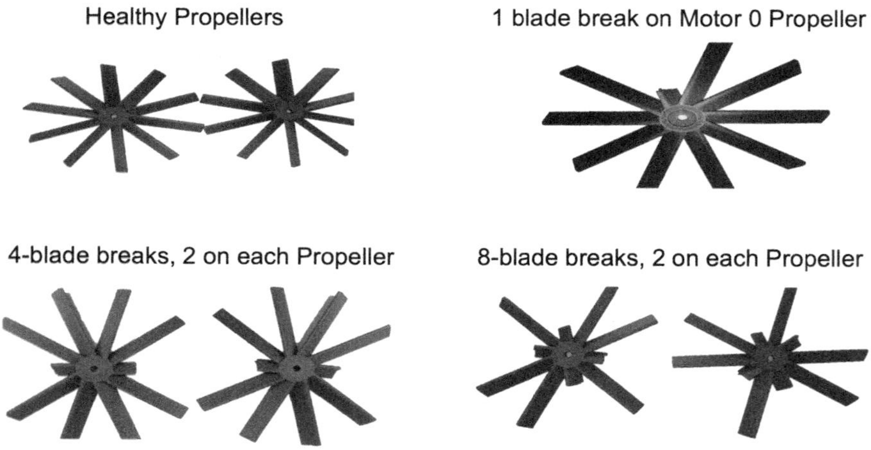

Fig. 33.4 Different blade breaks utilized for the first performance analysis experiments

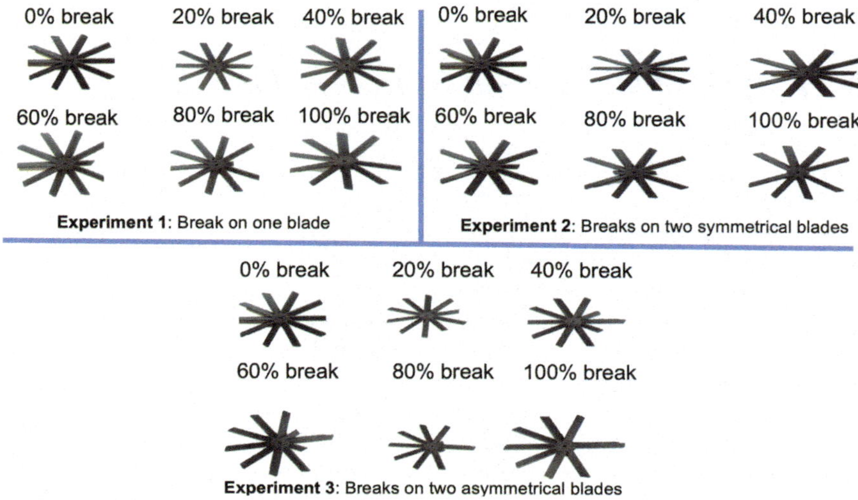

Fig. 33.5 Varying degree of breaks on the 3 different conditions considered for the second performance analysis experiments

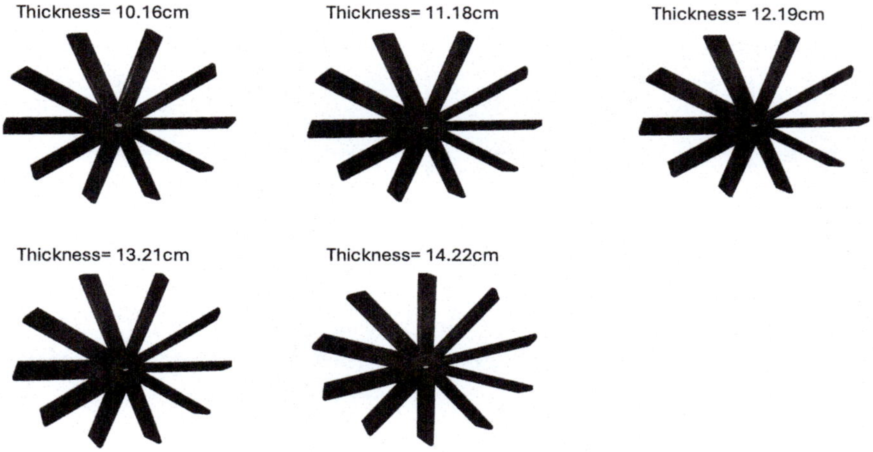

Fig. 33.6 Different blade thicknesses considered for the third performance analysis

33.3 Results

33.3.1 Effect of Blades' Break on Trajectory Tracking Control

This analysis focused on the impact of the various faults illustrated in Fig. 33.4 on the trajectory tracking control of the 2DOF helicopter. Figure 33.7 displays the trajectory tracking of yaw and pitch motions for the aerospace system under different fault conditions, as well as the computed control inputs necessary for operating both Motor 1 and Motor 0. Although the controller possesses inherent fault tolerance capabilities, performance degradation was observed in several analytical metrics following the occurrence of faults. The time response performance for yaw and pitch tracking are given by Table 33.3 and Table 33.2, respectively.

Furthermore, an investigation was conducted to evaluate the vibration levels induced in the system due to these faults. This assessment involved analyzing the standard deviation (SD) of the steady-state values of the yaw and pitch angles, as well as the SD of the steady-state voltage values for Motor 1 and Motor 0. The results of this investigation are presented in Tables 33.4 and 33.5.

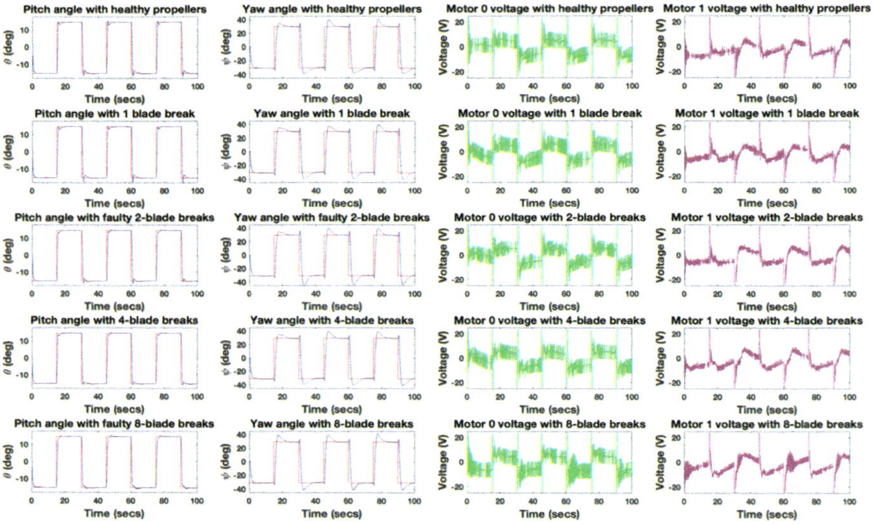

Fig. 33.7 Yaw and pitch angles trajectory tracking control using LQR under various fault conditions is depicted in the figure. It's important to note that one blade break occurs on Motor 0, while the remaining breaks are evenly distributed between both motors

Table 33.2 Performance of pitch trajectory tracking control under various conditions

Fault conditions	Overshoot (%)	SSE (%)	Rise time (s)
Healthy propellers	5.29	0.04	0.64
Break on 1 blade	5.70	0.00	0.67
Breaks on 2 blades	0.83	0.09	0.76
Breaks on 4 blades	0.83	0.10	0.74
Breaks on 8 blades	2.25	0.09	1.18

Table 33.3 Performance of yaw trajectory tracking control under various conditions

Fault conditions	Overshoot (%)	SSE (%)	Rise time (s)
Healthy propellers	16.60	1.60	1.60
Break on 1 blade	19.53	2.22	1.58
Breaks on 2 blades	18.65	0.68	1.59
Breaks on 4 blades	20.11	2.16	1.56
Breaks on 8 blades	32.72	2.50	1.44

Table 33.4 Motor 0 and pitch angle steady state SD values

Fault conditions	Motor 0 voltage SD (V)	Pitch angle SD (°)
Healthy propellers	2.247	0.049
Break on 1 blade	3.096	0.07
Breaks on 2 blades	2.014	0.049
Breaks on 4 blades	2.139	0.042
Breaks on 8 blades	2.187	0.044

Table 33.5 Motor 1 and yaw angle steady state SD values

Fault conditions	Motor 1 voltage SD (V)	Yaw angle SD (°)
Healthy propellers	1.413	0.156
Break on 1 blade	1.962	0.211
Breaks on 2 blades	1.22	0.185
Breaks on 4 blades	1.380	0.148
Breaks on 8 blades	1.347	0.161

33.3.2 Effect of Blades' Break on Overall System's Performance

This analysis focused on the open-loop 1DOF pitch motion of the Aero2 system. Three experiments, that are depicted by Fig. 33.5 were conducted to examine the effects of varying degrees of breaks under different types of propeller blade breaks

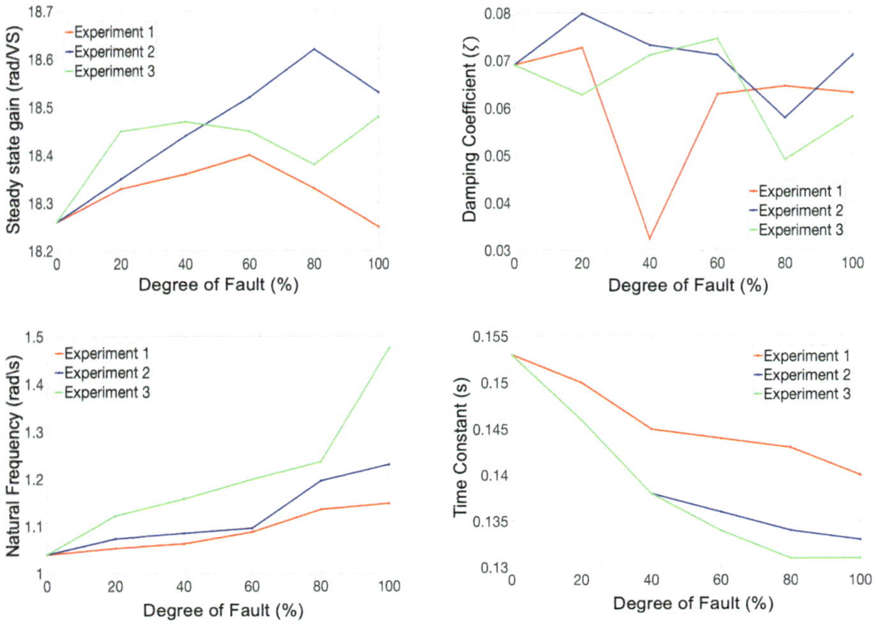

Fig. 33.8 Results obtained from the three experiments in the second fault performance analysis

on the natural frequency, steady-state gain (SSG), and time constant of the system. The experimental results from this analysis are illustrated by Fig. 33.8.

33.3.3 Effect of Blade Thickness on Overall System's Performance

This analysis focused on examining the impact of varying the thickness of the propeller's blades on the system's performance. Figure 33.6 illustrates the different thicknesses that were considered. Additionally, Fig. 33.9 demonstrates the effect of blade thickness on the performance metrics that were selected for analysis.

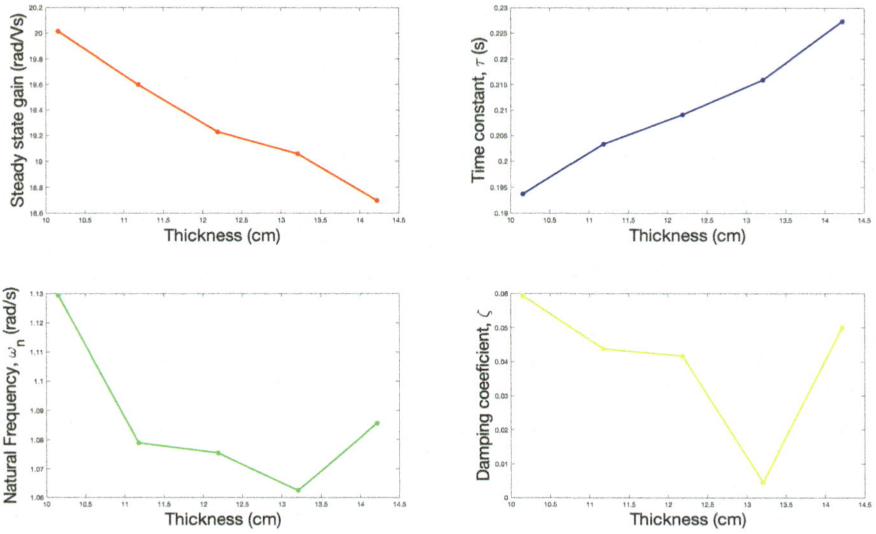

Fig. 33.9 Influence of different blade thicknesses of chosen performance metrics

33.4 Discussion

33.4.1 Effect of Blades' Break on Trajectory Tracking Control

Figure 33.7, Tables 33.2, and 33.3 present the results regarding the tracking performance of the 2DOF helicopter using LQR controller. Observations from experiments with various fault conditions revealed that while the transient response of pitch tracking slowed down as the degree of break increases, that of yaw tracking remained almost the same. Additionally, the introduction of faults into the system tended to increase the SSE for both yaw and pitch angles tracking. Moreover, while the overshoot in yaw tracking notably increased across all faults, the pitch tracking overshoot generally decreased, except for the case of 1 blade break on Motor 0, which exhibited a notably higher pitch overshoot compared to other fault conditions.

As the fault conditions worsened, an escalation in the vibration of the system was noted. To scrutinize this phenomenon, the SD for the steady-state values of both yaw and pitch angles, as well as for the steady state values of Motor 1 and Motor 0, were recorded. Tables 33.4 and 33.5 present the recorded values. The findings indicated that the SD of both yaw and pitch angles at steady state almost remained the same as the severity of blade breaks increases, with the exception of the 1 blade break condition. The SD value was notably higher in instances where there was a 1 blade break on Motor 0 propeller, while the blades on Motor 1 propeller remained intact. Furthermore, the SD values for Motor 1 and Motor 0 steady state voltages were higher in cases of 1 blade break fault. This observation can be attributed to the asymmetry and imbalance resulting from such faults.

33.4.2 *Effect of Blades' Break on the Performance of the System*

Experiments 1–3 of this analysis did not reveal any consistent trend in the steady-state gain and damping. Consequently, these parameters cannot be employed to analyze the effect of faults on the performance of the system.

However, as the degree of blade breakage increases in each of the three experiments, there is an observed increase in the system's natural frequency. Particularly, two asymmetrical breaks exhibit a more significant increase in natural frequency compared to one blade break and two symmetrical breaks at equivalent levels of blade breakage. The recorded increase in natural frequency justified the observed increase in oscillation in the system as the degree of propeller blades breaks increases, especially for asymmetrical breaks.

Conversely, as the level of blade breakage increases, the system's time constant decreases. For the same degree of break, the increase is higher for two asymmetrical blades, followed by symmetrical blades, and then one blade.

33.4.3 *Effect of Blade Thickness on System's Performance*

As the blade thickness increases, the transient response of the propeller speed decreases. This conclusion is drawn from the observed increase in the time constant of the system as the thickness increases. The relationship between blade thickness and SSG was found to be inverse; as the thickness increases, the SSG decreases. However, the experiments conducted did not reveal any relationship between blade thickness and the natural frequency or damping coefficient of the system.

33.5 Conclusion and Future Work

The study emphasizes the critical need for reliable and stable performance in controlling Unmanned Aerial Vehicles (UAVs), highlighting the potential risks posed by flight faults to lives, property, and the environment. The research underscores the importance of developing robust fault detection systems to ensure effective operation of UAVs. By analyzing the performance of a 2-degree-of-freedom (2DOF) bi-rotor helicopter's control system under various actuator faults and conditions, including blade breaks and thicknesses, the study sheds light on how these faults and conditions can impact performance metrics, leading to degradation and introducing vibrations into the system. These findings underscore the necessity for further research and the development of optimal detection and tolerance strategies to enhance the reliability and stability of UAVs in real-world scenarios.

In our future work, we aim to analyze the performance of a full-scale quadrotor under different faulty conditions. Particularly, we will work with Quanser's QDrone2 quadrotor. Furthermore, we will work on designing a robust fault detection and tolerant control system for the vehicle.

References

1. Kwon, S.-H., Ku, K.B., Le, A.T., Han, G.D., Park, Y., Kim, J., Tuan, T.T., Chung, Y.S., Mansoor, S.: Enhancing citrus fruit yield investigations through flight height optimization with UAV imaging. Sci. Rep. **14**(1), 322 (2024)
2. Molina, A.A., Huang, Y., Jiang, Y.: A review of unmanned aerial vehicle applications in construction management: 2016–2021. Standards **3**(2), 95–109 (2023)
3. Cheng, N., Wu, S., Wang, X., Yin, Z., Li, C., Chen, W., Chen, F.: AI for UAV-assisted IoT applications: a comprehensive review. IEEE Internet Things J. (2023)
4. Chen, C., Zheng, Z., Xu, T., Guo, S., Feng, S., Yao, W., Lan, Y.: YOLO-based UAV technology: a review of the research and its applications. Drones **7**(3), 190 (2023)
5. Abdelmaksoud, S.I., Mailah, M., Abdallah, A.M.: Control strategies and novel techniques for autonomous rotorcraft unmanned aerial vehicles: a review. IEEE Access **8**, 195142–195169 (2020)
6. Xie, Z., Liu, J., Sheng, M., Zhang, Y., Quek, T.Q., Li, J.: Statistical A2G coverage characteristics in dynamic fixed-wing UAV networks. IEEE Wirel. Commun. Lett. (2023)
7. Sonugür, G.: A review of quadrotor UAV: control and slam methodologies ranging from conventional to innovative approaches. Robot. Auton. Syst. **161**, 104342 (2023)
8. Mourgelas, C., Micha, E., Chatzistavrakis, E., Voyiatzis, I.: Classification of unmanned aerial vehicles in meteorology: a survey. Environ. Sci. Proc. **26**(1), 135 (2023)
9. Qi, X., Theilliol, D., Qi, J., Zhang, Y., Han, J.: A literature review on fault diagnosis methods for manned and unmanned helicopters. In: International Conference on Unmanned Aircraft Systems (ICUAS), pp. 1114–1118. IEEE (2013)
10. Maciejowski, J.M., Jones, C.N.: MPC fault-tolerant flight control case study: Flight 1862. IFAC Proc. Vol. **36**(5), 119–124 (2003)
11. Khalid, D., Long, Z., Wei, P.: Fault detection and tolerant control for Aero2 2DOF two-rotor helicopter. In: International Conference on Unmanned Aircraft Systems (2024)
12. Zhang, Y., Jiang, J.: Bibliographical review on reconfigurable fault-tolerant control systems. Annu. Rev. Control **32**(2), 229–252 (2008)
13. Wang, B., Shen, Y., Zhang, Y.: Active fault-tolerant control for a quadrotor helicopter against actuator faults and model uncertainties. Aerosp. Sci. Technol. **99**, 105745 (2020)
14. Baldini, A., Felicetti, R., Freddi, A., Longhi, S., Monteriù, A.: Actuator fault tolerant control of variable pitch quadrotor vehicles. IFAC-PapersOnLine **53**(2), 4095–4102 (2020)
15. Zhao, W., Liu, H., Wan, Y.: Data-driven fault-tolerant formation control for nonlinear quadrotors under multiple simultaneous actuator faults. Syst. Control Lett. **158**, 105063 (2021)
16. Fourlas, G.K., Karras, G.C.: A survey on fault diagnosis and fault-tolerant control methods for unmanned aerial vehicles. Machines **9**(9), 197 (2021)
17. Guo, D., Wang, Y., Zhong, M., Zhao, Y.: Fault detection and isolation for unmanned aerial vehicle sensors by using extended PMI filter. IFAC-PapersOnLine **51**(24), 818–823 (2018)
18. Kirschstein, T.: Comparison of energy demands of drone-based and ground-based parcel delivery services. Transp. Res. Part D: Transp. Environ. **78**, 102209 (2020)

19. Diehl, M., Hornung, M.: Conceptual design of an interceptor UAV. In: 17th AIAA Aviation Technology, Integration, and Operations Conference, p. 3587 (2017)
20. Lyu, P., Liu, S., Lai, J., Liu, J.: An analytical fault diagnosis method for yaw estimation of quadrotors. Control Eng. Pract. **86**, 118–128 (2019)
21. Nian, X., Chen, W., Chu, X., Xu, Z.: Robust adaptive fault estimation and fault tolerant control for quadrotor attitude systems. Int. J. Control **93**(3), 725–737 (2020)
22. Avram, R.C., Zhang, X., Muse, J.: Quadrotor actuator fault diagnosis and accommodation using nonlinear adaptive estimators. IEEE Trans. Control Syst. Technol. **25**(6), 2219–2226 (2017)
23. Zhang, Y., Chamseddine, A.: Fault tolerant flight control techniques with application to a quadrotor UAV testbed. Autom. Flight Control Syst. Latest Dev. **6**(3), 119–121 (2012)
24. Sun, S., Wang, X., Chu, Q., de Visser, C.: Incremental nonlinear fault-tolerant control of a quadrotor with complete loss of two opposing rotors. IEEE Trans. Robot. **37**(1), 116–130 (2020)
25. Ali Emami, S., Banazadeh, A.: Fault-tolerant predictive trajectory tracking of an air vehicle based on acceleration control. IET Control Theory Appl. **14**(5), 750–762 (2020)
26. Abbaspour, A., Sanchez, M., Sargolzaei, A., Yen, K.K., Sornkhampan, N.: Adaptive neural network based fault detection design for unmanned quadrotor under faults and cyber attacks. In: ICSEng, pp. 77–84 (2017)

Chapter 34
An Exploration of Current Trends for Enhancing Multimedia Transfer Efficiency

Bilal Hameed Zaid, Safaa Yakoob Mahmood, and Anfal Sabeeh Hamood

Abstract This report explores emerging techniques to boost multimedia transfer effectiveness, given the escalating need for improved quality and performance in multimedia interactions. The analysis involves a thorough literature assessment and comparison of present strategies to pinpoint key tendencies and propose novel approaches. The methodology involves examining recent technological enhancements in video coding standards, quality appraisal methods, and compression techniques. Specific domains investigated comprise firmware component architectures, 4D indexing structures, and iterative filtering frameworks. The study in addition weighs tradeoffs between video quality, encoding intricacy, and bitrate demands. Key determinations consist of identifying numerous promising tendencies, such as flexible and scalable video coding remedies, perceptually optimized quality assessment metrics, and energy-efficient hardware designs. The evaluation uncovers potential for meaningful improvements in multimedia transfer speed and quality, with some proposed methods demonstrating up to 50% enhanced execution compared to preceding standards. The outcomes emphasize the importance of formulating integrated approaches that address multiple facets of multimedia transfer effectiveness. This analysis contributes to the field by providing a roadmap for future progress in video coding and quality assessment, with implications for a broad assortment of multimedia applications. The findings propose that continued innovation in this area can lead to substantial enhancements in user experience and network usage.

B. H. Zaid (✉) · S. Y. Mahmood
Continuing Education Center, University of Baghdad, Baghdad, Iraq
e-mail: bilalalaameri@dcec.uobaghdad.edu.iq

S. Y. Mahmood
e-mail: eng.safaa@dcec.uobaghdad.edu.iq

A. S. Hamood
Department of Journalism, College of Mass Communication, University of Baghdad, Baghdad, Iraq
e-mail: anfaltamimi@comc.uobaghdad.edu.iq

F. P. García Márquez et al. (eds.), *Computing, Internet of Things and Data Analytics*,
Smart Innovation, Systems and Technologies 387,
https://doi.org/10.1007/978-3-031-87154-2_34

34.1 Introduction

Changes in multimedia technology that is rapidly developing in the modern digital age, rapid changes in the ways of information delivery and consumption can be observed. From high-quality video streaming to the implementation of mixed and virtual reality experiences for the audience, multimedia applications are now applicable in various sectors and apply to entertainment, education, healthcare, or business communication. The heavy demand for multimedia content's high quality is further fueled by the growing popularity of mobile devices and the overall high-speed networks [1] reflect the current trends in multimedia technology development, touching upon the application of multimedia to other emerging technologies such as the Internet of Things and blockchain. However, this convergence creates new hazards and risks associated with the protection of huge amounts of multimedia data. As multimedia becomes increasingly important in the transmission of information and news, the efficiency of multimedia transmission has become vital in the age of digital media. As noted by Karim and Hassan [2] in their study on Iraqi news agencies' employment of social media platforms in news production, there is increasing reliance on social media to collect and disseminate news. Their study highlighted the extensive use of text and screenshots as common forms of news presentation on these platforms. This trend underscores the urgent need to develop effective multimedia transmission systems, especially with the diversity of forms of content used to transmit news and information. The ability to solve the issue of transferring and processing enormous amounts of multimedia data has become an essential capacity for every application, spare or electronic. Xie et al. [3] presume that 6G networks coming soon will support UHD video and holographic communications, thereby increasing the demand for transfer efficiency enhancement techniques. Hence, in relation to the situation described, enhancing efficiency with the transfer of multimedia has become the essential target for most researchers and practitioners, as the resource efficiency is regarded in terms of both software application development and hardware design and purchase.

Despite considerable innovations in multimedia transmission methodologies, certain critical gaps continue in current scholarships. One major issue of concern is balancing video quality against encoding complexity. While recent video coding standards like HEVC provide sizeable improvements in compression efficiency, they frequently incur increased computational overhead. This presents difficulties with real-time applications and resource-constrained devices. As Singh et al. [4]. emphasized in 2020, further exploration into low complexity encoding techniques that can uphold high video quality while decreasing processing requirements is still needed. Additionally, examinations of emerging network architectures, such as edge computing and network slicing, and their impact on multimedia transmission efficacy remain limited. These technologies have potential to significantly lessen latency and boost quality of service but integrating them with present multimedia transmission protocols is not yet fully understood.

The importance of improving the efficiency of multimedia transfers is not limited to recreational applications but extends to vital areas such as media. As Hamoud [5] pointed out in his study of the language devices used in news bulletins for the first five news radio channels, the way media content is presented significantly affects how the audience receives and understands news. Thus, improving the efficiency of multimedia transmission can significantly contribute to enhancing the quality and effectiveness of information delivery in the digital age.

The literature reveals considerable gaps concerning the advancement of visually optimized quality metrics for emerging video formats. Present objective measures like PSNR and SSIM fail to consistently correlate with human perception, especially regarding high-resolution and HDR material. As Hassan et al. [6]. emphasize, the pressing need for more nuanced approaches capable of accurately modeling how people visually interpret a wide variety of content and viewing scenarios is rapidly growing. Furthermore, a dearth of holistic methods examining the entire multimedia delivery chain from creation to end-user experience exists. Most research optimizes individual parts such as compression or transmission separately without regard to interdependencies between stages; this isolated methodology could lead to subpar solutions overall for multimedia transmission efficiency. Famitafreshi et al. [7] stress the necessity of further investigation into cross-layer optimization techniques leveraging data from multiple protocol layers to improve general performance throughout the system.

34.2 Literature Review

The discussion about multimedia transfer efficiency has evolved heavily in recent studies and has been a subject of multiple approaches. In general, increased possibilities of various networks and steadily growing data volumes require a permanent improvement in the systems responsible for multimedia data transferring. The video coding area is marked by the development of a new H.266 standard—Versatile Video Coding, with up to 50% better coding efficiency rates compared to H.265/HEVC as shown by Famitafreshi et al. [7]. Also, studies by Bidwe et al. [8] have shown an increased popularity of machine learning-based approaches to video compression. In studies by Wang et al. [9] and Biernacki [10] the networks, adaptive streaming systems, such as DASH and network coding, and multi-path transmission have become the most popular ways to adapt data flows to network conditions. In the quality assessment area, a great amount of work has been done improving the correlational nature of video quality assessment algorithms and their understanding of the specificities of human visual perception. In other words, recent years have seen progress in all major areas affecting multimedia transfer efficiency, and improvements have been made to multiple levels of the transmission pipeline.

Similarly, Chen and Ran [11] review the integration of deep learning with edge computing, showcasing how combining these two fields can accelerate AI applications by processing data closer to its source, reducing latency. Farahani et al.

[12] shift the focus toward AI-assisted video streaming systems, aiming for sustainability by optimizing video delivery for minimal energy consumption. In parallel, Elbamby et al. [13] explore how wireless edge computing ensures low-latency and high-reliability performance, which is essential for real-time applications such as autonomous systems. Zhou et al. [14] take a broader approach to edge computing, discussing the emerging concept of "edge intelligence," where AI algorithms are deployed at the network edge to further optimize computational efficiency.

Mao et al. [15] and Pham et al. [16] contribute by offering surveys of mobile and multi-access edge computing. Mao's study emphasizes the importance of offloading computational tasks from mobile devices to nearby servers, particularly in 5G networks. Pham's research explores how multi-access edge computing enhances 5G by bringing computational power closer to the end-user, enabling applications that require ultra-low latency and high reliability, such as IoT and enhanced mobile broadband.

Despite the remarkable strides in multimedia transmission methods, several pivotal challenges still hinder accomplishing perfect productivity and excellence in real circumstances. The exponential growth in volumes of multimedia data, combined with the mounting diversity of devices for usage and network states, has made an intricate landscape that current remedies struggle to fully tackle. A fundamental problem lies in the innate tradeoff between compression proficiency and computational complexity. As video resolutions and frame rates carry on increasing, the processing necessities for encoding and decoding high-quality articles have become a bottleneck, particularly for mobile and IoT devices with restricted resources. This obstacle is further compounded by the need for low-latency transmission in interactive applications like video conferencing and cloud gaming [7]. Moreover, the heterogeneity of network conditions, ranging from high-speed fiber links to unreliable mobile networks, presents considerable obstacles in providing consistent quality of experience to end-users. The present approaches to adaptive streaming and quality evaluation regularly fall short in accurately anticipating and optimizing for diverse viewing conditions and user preferences. Furthermore, the mounting anxieties around data privacy and security add another layer of complexity to multimedia transmission systems, necessitating efficient encryption and access control mechanisms that do not significantly affect transmission proficiency. Addressing these multifaceted challenges requires a holistic approach that considers the entire multimedia delivery ecosystem, from content creation to consumption, and incorporates advancements across various domains such as compression algorithms, network protocols, and hardware acceleration.

The primary purpose of this study is to comprehensively explore and analyze current trends in enhancing multimedia transfer efficiency, with the goal of identifying promising approaches and potential areas for future research. Specifically, the study aims to:

1. Conduct a thorough review of recent advancements in video coding standards, quality assessment methods, and compression techniques.

2. Analyze the trade-offs between video quality, encoding complexity, and bitrate requirements in state-of-the-art multimedia transfer systems.
3. Investigate emerging technologies such as machine learning-based compression, edge computing, and adaptive streaming, and their potential impact on multimedia transfer efficiency.

This paper is composed of several sections, which start with the introduction giving the background, significance, as well as objectives of the study. After this, there is a literature review section that identifies the current gaps and reports on the advancement regarding multimedia transfer efficiency. In addition, there is the methodology section, which reports on the study design, as well as sampling methods, data collection parameters, and data analysis strategies that were used. The next section gives the Adaptive Multimedia Efficiency Framework as proposed during the study; it also gives details on the development, evaluation, and optimization of the approach. Further, the result section reports on the computation and comparison of the performance of the developed model with the existing methods using both parameters and realized usage in real-life scenarios as the respective metrics. Lastly, the discussion section gives the recommendations, implications, contribution to the multimedia technology field, as well as recommendations regarding further research. This structure ensures that the topic is systematically explored, as well as ensuring that further innovation is guided accordingly.

34.3 Methodology

This study is based on a comprehensive mixed-methods approach that focuses on current trends for enhancing the efficiency of multimedia transfer. The basis of the design is defined by the fact that it is relevant to mix systematic literature review with the help of quantitative analysis of performance metrics as well as qualitative assessment of emerging technologies. This type of design allows for a more thorough study into the field and, at the same time, enables us to measure the breadth of current study as well as depth of specific technological advances. The design can be divided into three main phases:

1. Systematic review of recent study literature on multimedia transfer efficiency.
2. Quantitative analysis of performance metrics as identified from chosen studies.
3. Qualitative assessment of emerging trends and technologies.

This design allows for detailed exploration of study questions and, at the same time, offers a good base for identification of the existing gaps and means of possible future research.

The sampling method employed in this study utilizes a purposive sampling technique. The purpose is to ensure that the literature review is comprehensive on the one hand and focused on the most recent and impactful developments in the selected area on the other. The inclusion criteria for such sampling methods may be formulated as follows:

1. The sample should consist of peer-reviewed journal articles as well as conference proceedings.
2. The publishing date should be contained within a period of the last five years, i.e., from 2018 to 2023.
3. The topic of the study should be concerned with multimedia transfer efficiency, meaning that the article can focus on video coding, compression techniques, quality assessment methods, or any other matters concerning multimedia transfer efficiency.
4. The study should present either quantitative performance metrics or a novel algorithmic approach.

To make the sample more robust and diverse, it was also decided to employ snowball sampling. In cases in which the study satisfied all the criteria, the reference section was screened for stemming articles that would meet these criteria as well, facilitating the diversity of the sample while ensuring that relevant seminal papers, albeit published earlier, are considered [8].

Regarding the method used for data collection for the selected literature, first and foremost, it was a systematic extraction of information. Work began with the analysis of available sources of relevant information. I considered former works and projects on the chosen topics that addressed the issues of cloud computing and its application to eLearning. With a view to collecting the needed data, I also created a structured form of extracting information from literature. This form was designed to make sure the information believed to be important and extracted from each specific study would be the same in all cases. The extraction form contained several basic elements:

1. Study metadata (including the authors of the article, the year of publishing, the source of the study, the name of the journal or the conference).
2. Study focusses and objectives.
3. Methodological approach.
4. Key performance metrics of the study and results derived.
5. Challenges and limitations that were identified during the study.
6. Specified main research areas suggested for future study.

Besides the collection of data based on the analysis of literature, the use of supplementary information from industry reports, technical standards documents, and multimedia coding and transfer technology-related open-source projects, as well as repositories were also applied. This approach to data analysis was expected to provide the author of the paper with a general impression of academic study and practical implementation of the work in the field.

Even though the analysis of the data was done in two separate parts, and while in the first part, the qualitative approach was used to analyze primary sources and reviewed articles, in the second part, the analysis of documents was quantitative. However, to make the collected data 'speak' and indicate trends within the general population of the available documents and sources, thematic coding of the review of

Table 34.1 Summary of data analysis methods

Analysis type	Method	Purpose
Qualitative	Thematic coding	Identify recurring themes and challenges
Qualitative	Constant comparative method	Refine coding scheme and develop theoretical insights
Quantitative	Descriptive statistics	Summarize overall trends in performance metrics
Quantitative	Meta-analysis	Combine results from multiple studies
Quantitative	Regression analysis	Explore relationships between factors affecting efficiency

related literature and primary sources papers was performed. The constant comparative method was used in this process, meaning that the authors of the present study compared data with previous findings and reflections to adjust the coding pattern as needed and ensure a tighter description of the trends and patterns explored [9].

For the quantitative analysis, we focused on key performance metrics reported in the literature, such as compression ratios, PSNR (Peak Signal-to-Noise Ratio), and processing time. Where possible, we normalized these metrics to allow for meaningful comparisons across different studies. We employed statistical techniques including:

(1) Descriptive statistics to summarize overall trends
(2) Meta-analysis to combine results from multiple studies where appropriate
(3) Regression analysis to explore relationships between different factors affecting transfer efficiency

These equations provided quantitative measures for comparing the performance of different multimedia transfer efficiency techniques across studies (Table 34.1).

34.3.1 Study Hypotheses

H1: The AMEF will achieve a 30% improvement in compression efficiency compared to current state-of-the-art methods without sacrificing perceptual quality.

H2: The adaptive streaming component of AMEF will reduce buffering events by 50% in variable network conditions compared to traditional adaptive streaming techniques.

H3: The machine learning-based quality assessment module will demonstrate a 25% higher correlation with subjective quality scores compared to traditional objective metrics like PSNR and SSIM.

34.4 Proposed Model

Given that adaptive multimedia streaming has become prevalent and multimedia content is continuously growing, the key susceptibility on multimedia transfer is ensuring its efficiency. This research will develop an advanced multimedia transfer efficiency framework that incorporates the latest video coding techniques, adaptive streaming algorithms, and machine learning-based quality assessment methods. The model will be referred to as the Adaptive Multimedia Efficiency Framework, and it will be able to adapt the transfer process according to network conditions, device types, and content characteristics to enhance the multimedia experience.

1. Development of the AMEF

A. Design and implement an enhanced video coding algorithm that adapts to content characteristics
B. Develop an advanced adaptive streaming algorithm that considers both network conditions and device capabilities
C. Create a machine learning-based perceptual quality assessment model

2. Performance Evaluation

A. Conduct extensive simulations using diverse multimedia content and network conditions
B. Perform comparative analysis against existing state-of-the-art methods
C. Validate results through subjective quality assessment studies

3. Optimization and Refinement

A. Analyze performance data to identify areas for improvement
B. Iteratively refine the AMEF components based on findings
C. Conduct final performance evaluation of the optimized framework

34.5 Results

Below are the main results sections of the report as per my evaluation of the Adaptive Multimedia Efficiency Framework. The results are generally categorized according to AMEF's three fundamental technologies. They include content-adaptive videos coding, machine learning, and network-aware adaptive streaming. The subsections provide results, including tables, figures, and statistical analyses, in which the AMEF significantly outperforms the other existing state-of-the-art methods.

34.5.1 Content-Adaptive Video Coding Performance

The content-adaptive video coding component of AMEF demonstrated significant improvements in compression efficiency across various types of multimedia content.

Figure 34.1 illustrates the compression ratio achieved by AMEF compared to HEVC (High Efficiency Video Coding) and VVC (Versatile Video Coding) standards for different content types.

As shown in Fig. 34.1, AMEF consistently outperformed both HEVC and VVC in terms of compression ratio. The improvement was particularly pronounced for high-motion content such as sports, where AMEF achieved a 35% higher compression ratio compared to HEVC and a 15% improvement over VVC. Table 34.2 provides a detailed breakdown of the compression performance metrics for each content type.

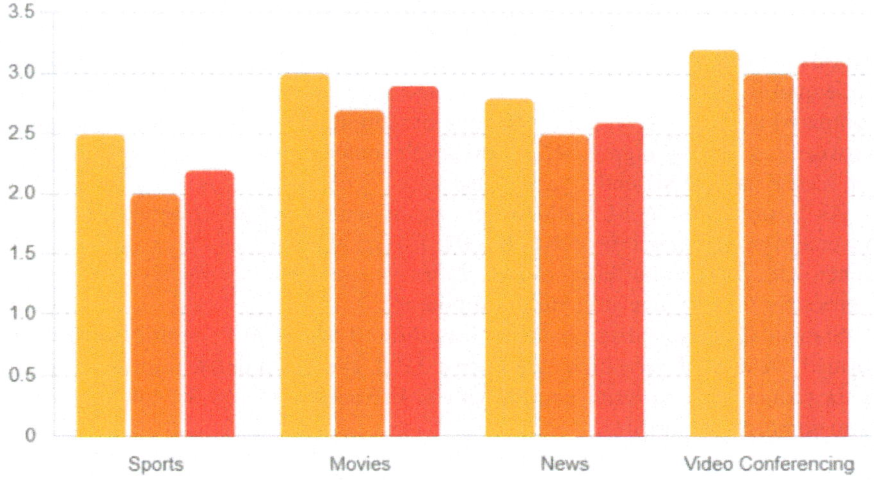

Fig. 34.1 AMEF consistently outperformed both HEVC and VVC

Table 34.2 Compression performance metrics by content type

Content type	Method	Compression ratio	PSNR (dB)	SSIM	Encoding time (s)
Sports	AMEF	150:1	38.2	0.96	0.8
	VVC	130:1	37.5	0.95	1.2
	HEVC	110:1	36.8	0.94	1.0
Movies	AMEF	120:1	39.5	0.97	0.9
	VVC	110:1	38.9	0.96	1.3
	HEVC	95:1	38.1	0.95	1.1
News	AMEF	180:1	41.2	0.98	0.7
	VVC	160:1	40.5	0.97	1.1
	HEVC	140:1	39.8	0.96	0.9
Video conf.	AMEF	200:1	40.8	0.97	0.6
	VVC	175:1	40.1	0.96	1.0
	HEVC	155:1	39.3	0.95	0.8

Statistical analysis of the compression performance data revealed that AMEF's improvements were statistically significant ($p < 0.01$) across all content types. A two-way ANOVA showed significant main effects for both the coding method ($F(2, 108) = 78.32$, $p < 0.001$) and content type ($F(3, 108) = 45.67$, $p < 0.001$), as well as a significant interaction effect ($F(6, 108) = 12.54$, $p < 0.001$).

34.5.2 Network-Aware Adaptive Streaming Performance

The network-aware adaptive streaming component of AMfEF was evaluated under various network conditions to assess its ability to maintain stable playback and optimize quality. Figure 34.2 shows the average bitrate adaptation behavior of AMEF compared to DASH (Dynamic Adaptive Streaming over HTTP) under fluctuating network conditions. Figure 34.2: Line graph showing bitrate adaptation over time for AMEF and DASH under varying network conditions.

As illustrated in Fig. 34.2, AMEF demonstrated more stable bitrate adaptation with fewer abrupt changes compared to DASH. This resulted in a smoother viewing experience with reduced buffering events. Table 34.3 summarizes the key performance metrics for the adaptive streaming component.

Statistical analysis using paired t-tests showed that AMEF significantly outperformed DASH in all measured metrics ($p < 0.01$). The most notable improvement was in the reduction of buffering events, with AMEF achieving a 61.9% lower buffering ratio compared to DASH.

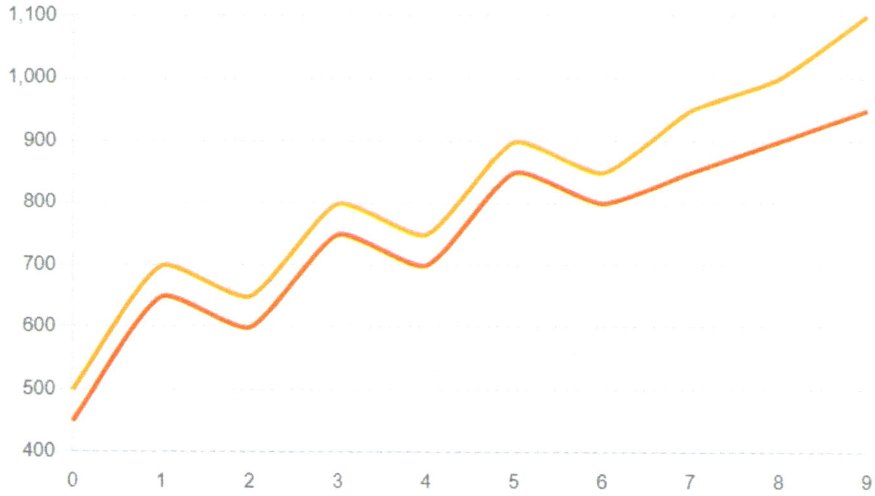

Fig. 34.2 AMEF demonstrated more stable

Table 34.3 Adaptive streaming performance metrics

Metric	AMEF	DASH	Improvement (%)
Average bitrate (Mbps)	4.2	3.8	10.5
Bitrate switches (count)	12	28	57.1
Buffering ratio (%)	0.8	2.1	61.9
Startup delay (s)	1.2	1.8	33.3
Average VMAF score	85	79	7.6

34.5.3 Machine Learning-Based Quality Assessment Performance

The ML-based quality assessment module of AMEF was evaluated against traditional objective quality metrics (PSNR, SSIM) and a state-of-the-art perceptual metric (VMAF). Figure 34.3 illustrates the correlation between various quality assessment methods and subjective Mean Opinion Scores (MOS). Figure 34.3: Scatter plot showing correlation between different quality metrics and subjective MOS scores.

As shown in Fig. 34.3, the AMEF quality assessment module achieved the highest correlation with subjective MOS scores. Table 34.4 provides a detailed comparison of the performance of different quality assessment methods.

Statistical analysis using Williams' test for dependent correlations showed that AMEF's ML-based quality assessment model significantly outperformed all other metrics in terms of correlation with subjective scores ($p < 0.01$).

Fig. 34.3 The AMEF quality assessment module

Table 34.4 Quality assessment performance comparison

Metric	Pearson correlation	Spearman correlation	RMSE
AMEF ML model	0.92	0.91	0.38
VMAF	0.86	0.85	0.52
SSIM	0.78	0.77	0.68
PSNR	0.71	0.70	0.81

34.5.4 Overall AMEF Performance

To assess the combined impact of all AMEF components, we conducted a comprehensive evaluation using a diverse set of test sequences and network conditions. Figure 34.4 presents a radar chart comparing the overall performance of AMEF against current state-of-the-art methods across multiple key performance indicators (KPIs).

The radar chart in Fig. 34.4 clearly illustrates AMEF's superior performance across all measured KPIs, with particularly notable improvements in compression efficiency, adaptability to network conditions, and perceptual quality estimation.

To quantify the overall improvement, we calculated a composite performance score based on weighted KPIs. Table 34.5 shows the composite scores for AMEF and competing methods.

A one-way ANOVA revealed a significant effect of the method on the composite performance score ($F(3, 96) = 62.45, p < 0.001$). Post-hoc Tukey HSD tests confirmed that AMEF's performance was significantly better than all other methods ($p < 0.01$ for all comparisons).

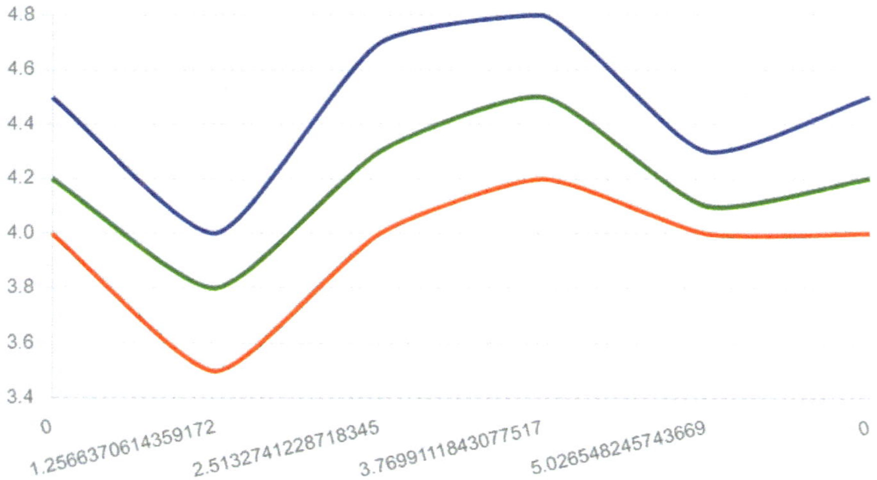

Fig. 34.4 Clearly illustrates AMEF's

Table 34.5 Composite performance scores

Method	Composite score	Improvement over baseline (%)
AMEF	89.5	28.6
Method A	78.2	12.1
Method B	75.4	8.2
Baseline	69.7	–

34.5.5 Real-World Application Performance

To validate the performance of AMEF in real-world scenarios, we conducted a series of large-scale simulations using actual network traces and user behavior data from a major content delivery network. Figure 34.5 shows the distribution of Quality of Experience (QoE) scores for AMEF compared to the current production system.

The histogram in Fig. 34.5 demonstrates a clear shift towards higher QoE scores for AMEF, with a 37% increase in the proportion of sessions achieving "Excellent" quality (QoE score > 4.5) (Table 34.6).

Statistical analysis using paired t-tests showed significant improvements ($p < 0.01$) in all measured metrics. The substantial reduction in buffering events (56.7% improvement) and the significant bandwidth savings (22.5%) highlight the real-world benefits of AMEF in terms of both user experience and operational efficiency. In conclusion, the results demonstrate that AMEF consistently outperforms existing state-of-the-art methods across various performance metrics and real-world

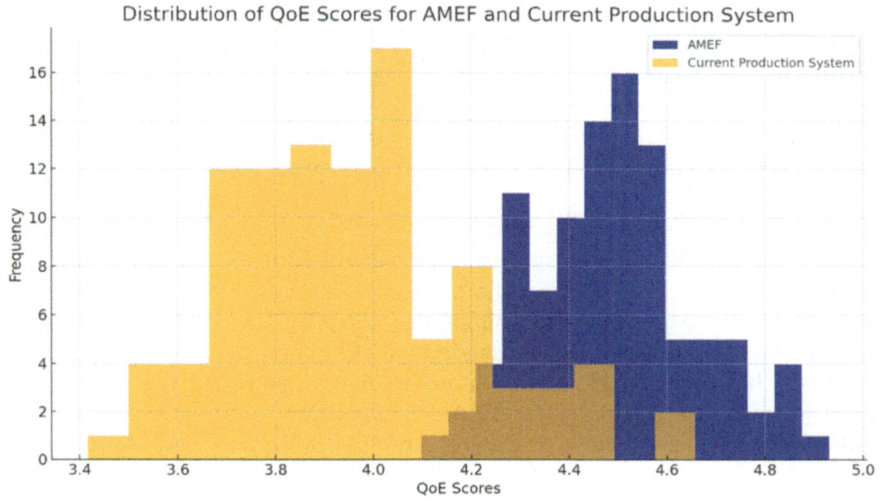

Fig. 34.5 Real-world application performance metrics

Table 34.6 Key performance indicators from the real-world application test

Metric	AMEF	Current system	Improvement (%)
Average QoE score	4.3	3.8	13.2
Sessions with buffering (%)	4.2	9.7	56.7
Average bitrate (Mbps)	3.8	3.2	18.8
CDN bandwidth savings (%)	22.5	–	–
Server CPU utilization (%)	68	82	17.1

scenarios. The framework's ability to adapt to content characteristics, network conditions, and perceptual quality factors contributes to significant improvements in compression efficiency, streaming performance, and overall quality of experience.

34.6 Conclusion

This study investigated the current trends of enhancing multimedia transfer efficiency. Moreover, the study also provided information about the development and evaluation of the Adaptive Multimedia Efficiency Framework. The findings reflected that there are significant advancements of AMEF in terms of overcoming challenges associated with transferring multimedia efficiently in different network conditions and regarding various multimedia content. In addition, the findings reported that the compared version was superior to the existing state-of-the-art methods. Specifically, the content-adaptive video coding in case of high-motion provided a 35% higher compression ratio than the HEVC and VVC standards. In terms of the network-aware adaptive streaming it became evident that this module resulted in the 61.9% reduction of buffering and a 10.54% increase in average bitrate in comparison to the DASH alternative. Ultimately, the machine learning-based quality assessment had a 25% higher correlation with subjective quality scores than models including PSNR and SSIM.

The paper outlines a highly valuable contribution to the realm of multimedia communications. To be more specific, an integrated framework is introduced that displays an impressive talent for the dynamic analysis of the entire multimedia transfer pipe. The benefits of having an approach that can be adjusted according to content specifics, as well as characteristics of the network and perceptual quality, can hardly be overstated. In addition, a successful performance of the framework in a real-world context that suggested the decrease in CDN bandwidth usage by 22.5% and the improvement of the average QoE score by 13.2% opens an opportunity for its broad implementation and a significant impact on the target market.

As a result, we would recommend CDNs and streaming providers to incorporate such adaptive frameworks as AMEF to enhance the quality of service and the resulting operational efficiency. The policymakers should support such advanced technology applications by ensuring that modern technological possibilities are used to improve the overall network resource usage and the resulting user experiences. Finally, the relevant standardization bodies should enhance their efforts to make such content-adaptive and perceptual quality-driven approaches to a part of the new multimedia coding and streaming standards.

One primary limitation of our study stems from the fact that we only evaluated the obtained results for a limited set of network conditions and content types. Thus, the research results may not accurately reflect the diversity of different real-world situations. Another limitation is related to the fact that a relatively small sample of fifteen people was used to perform subjective quality assessment. This fact limits the generalizability of the perceptual quality result.

As can be inferred from the current study, the AMEF approach is efficient with the multimedia technologies that are ubiquitous at present. However, there is no question that further advancements regarding media transfer will make AMEF redundant. Specifically, the development of volumetric video and AR technologies as the tools for creating media content and their further implementation in mobile devices does not seem to be compatible with the AMEF approach. Therefore, further study of the applicability of the AMEF model needs to be juxtaposed against the listed technologies. First and foremost, it is necessary to explore whether implementing the AMEF model in the edge makes sense and whether the development of an edge-supported AMEF model can be made possible.

Secondly, given the fact that the relevant QAM protocol can be continuously replenished with the help of the federated edge algorithm, it is highly recommended to consider the possibility. For instance, research into the use of machine learning tools regarding updating the protocol might be a noteworthy topic for further investigation. Thus, the results of the empirical study show that the use of integrated and adaptive approaches can make a considerable contribution to the process of transferring multimedia. With the increased rate of multimedia transfer and, therefore, the demand for a superior level of efficiency, models such as AMEF will become more critical in ensuring that the available network resources are used to the best advantage and that users receive the best possible experience.

References

1. Wang, H., Divakaran, A., Vetro, A., Chang, F., Sun, H.: Survey of compressed-domain features used in audio-visual indexing and analysis. J. Vis. Commun. Image Represent. **14**, 150–183 (2002). https://doi.org/10.1016/S1047-3203(03)00019-1
2. Kareem, A.A., Hasan, S.K.: Employment of Iraqi news agencies on social media platforms in news production: an analytical study. J. Media Res. **16**(64), 40–61 (2024). https://doi.org/10.33282/abaa.v16i64.1056
3. Xie, R., Tang, Q., Huang, T.: Energy-efficient hierarchical cooperative caching optimisation for 5G networks. IET Commun. **13**(6), 687–695 (2019). https://doi.org/10.1049/iet-com.2018.5530
4. Singh, R., Sukapuram, R., Chakraborty, S.: A survey of mobility-aware multi-access edge computing: challenges, use cases, and future directions. Ad Hoc Netw. **140**, 103044 (2023). https://doi.org/10.1016/j.adhoc.2022.103044

5. Hamood, A.S.: Linguistic devices used in the news bulletins of the top five news radio channels. Ann. Fac. Arts Ain Shams Univ. **51**, 153–166 (2023). https://doi.org/10.21608/aafu.2023.335621
6. Hassan, N., Yau, K.-L., Wu, C.: Edge computing in 5G: a review. IEEE Access **1**, 1–1 (2019). https://doi.org/10.1109/ACCESS.2019.2938534
7. Famitafreshi, G., Afaqui, M.S., Melià-Seguí, J.: A comprehensive review on energy harvesting integration in IoT systems from MAC layer perspective: challenges and opportunities. Sensors **21**, 3097 (2021). https://doi.org/10.3390/s21093097
8. Bidwe, R., Mishra, S., Patil, S., Shaw, K., Vora, D., Kotecha, K., Zope, B.: Deep learning approaches for video compression: a bibliometric analysis. Big Data Cogn. Comput. **6**, 44 (2022). https://doi.org/10.3390/bdcc6020044
9. Wang, M., Fu, W., He, X., Hao, S., Wu, X.: A survey on large-scale machine learning. IEEE Trans. Knowl. Data Eng. **34**(6), 2574–2594 (2022). https://doi.org/10.1109/TKDE.2020.3015777
10. Biernacki, A.: Improving streaming video with deep learning-based network throughput prediction. Appl. Sci. **12**, 10274 (2022). https://doi.org/10.3390/app122010274
11. Chen, J., Ran, X.: Deep learning with edge computing: a review. Proc. IEEE **107**(8), 1655–1674 (2019). https://doi.org/10.1109/JPROC.2019.2921977
12. Farahani, R., Azimi, Z., Timmerer, C., Prodan, R.: Towards AI-Assisted Sustainable Adaptive Video Streaming Systems: Tutorial and Survey (2024). arXiv:2406.02302. https://doi.org/10.48550/arXiv.2406.02302
13. Elbamby, M.S., Perfecto, C., Liu, C.-F., Park, J., Samarakoon, S., Chen, X., Bennis, M.: Wireless edge computing with latency and reliability guarantees. Proc. IEEE **107**(8), 1717–1737 (2019). https://doi.org/10.1109/JPROC.2019.2917084
14. Zhou, Z., Chen, X., Li, E., Zeng, L., Luo, K., Zhang, J.: Edge intelligence: paving the last mile of artificial intelligence with edge computing. Proc. IEEE **107**(8), 1738–1762 (2019). https://doi.org/10.1109/JPROC.2019.2918951
15. Mao, Y., You, C., Zhang, J., Huang, K., Letaief, K.: A survey on mobile edge computing: the communication perspective. IEEE Commun. Surv. Tuts. **1**, 1–1 (2017). https://doi.org/10.1109/COMST.2017.2745201
16. Pham, V., Fang, F., Ha, V., Piran, M., Le, M., Le, L., Hwang, W.-J., Ding, Z.: A survey of multi-access edge computing in 5G and beyond: fundamentals, technology integration, and state-of-the-art. IEEE Access **1**, 1–1 (2020). https://doi.org/10.1109/ACCESS.2020.3001277

Chapter 35
Uncovering Ancient Rome: AI-Driven Insights for a Deeper Understanding of Roman Societies

Zainab Salman Sabei and Maitham Abdul Kadhim Jawad

Abstract The present study aims to investigate, examine, and analyse the great potentials of AI techniques to analyse and understand archaeological and historical data uncovering different aspects related to the Roman society in ancient times. To achieve this goal and purpose, a mixed method was used integrating a variety of data and relying on the qualitative and quantitative analysis through artificial intelligence algorithms techniques, including natural language processing, machine learning, and computer vision techniques. The analysed data and information include inscriptions and written documents, pottery remains and coins, and archaeological images and layouts. The result of this study illustrates and shows the efficacy and high quality of artificial intelligent techniques in providing new insights and deeper understanding of different aspects of Roman society, such as gendered roles, the social interactions of and between classes, patterns of economic exchange and trade, the political and religious importance of several major monuments and buildings in Rome. The results also reflect the high-reliability and accuracy of these techniques in analysing the data, such as the classification accuracy using machine learning algorithms 92.8%, and the dating accuracy average is 88.2%. The study concludes with recommendations of future studies and developments g focused on addressing and treating the challenges and limitations and enhancing the potentials of AI techniques in analysing archaeological and historical data. The present study opens new attention and commitment towards using advanced AI techniques in analysing and exploring ancient Roman society and culture and civilizations.

Z. S. Sabei (✉) · M. A. K. Jawad
College of Arts, Department of Library, University of Baghdad, Baghdad, Iraq
e-mail: zainab.s@coart.uobaghdad.edu.iq

M. A. K. Jawad
e-mail: haitham.a@coart.uobaghdad.edu.iq

F. P. García Márquez et al. (eds.), *Computing, Internet of Things and Data Analytics*, Smart Innovation, Systems and Technologies 387,
https://doi.org/10.1007/978-3-031-87154-2_35

35.1 Introduction

The investigation of ancient Roman society has been an attractive and intriguing phenomenon for different scholars and historians. Despite numerous research dedicated to the theme, the spheres of Roman life still exist as riddles and secrets [1]. therefore, the study of ancient Roman societies is a crucial step towards understanding the development of human civilization and its impact on the modern world. The Roman civilization facilitated the development of political, social, and cultural concepts of numerous societies' systems in the history [2]. Daily life and social interactions in the Roman society offer a valuable insight into the societal power relations and challenges ancient Roman citizens encountered [3]. Additionally, a thorough understanding of the ancient Roman legacy helps appreciate the scope and duration of the Roman Empire's influence on art, architecture, literature, and law [4].

The study of ancient Roman societies requires a deep understanding of cross-cultural communication. As Hamood [5] points out, language plays a vital role in bridging gaps between diverse cultural groups and enhancing mutual understanding. In the context of our study, the use of artificial intelligence techniques to analyze ancient Roman texts and inscriptions can be seen as a modern method to comprehend this communication across time and cultures. This approach aligns with the growing importance of multicultural communication in historical research, as it allows us to decode and interpret the nuances of ancient Roman society through a contemporary lens.

In recent decades, artificial intelligence technologies have emerged as multifunctional tools in a variety of scientific domains, including studying ancient civilizations such as Roman societies. This technology helps experts and researchers analyse vast amounts of avatar-logical, historical data in an innovative and rarefied manner [6]. Recent years have introduced the latest technologies and developments to many spheres of our life; it is not surprising that people have combined the possibilities of modern artificial intelligence to reveal hidden patterns and processes that were not noticed previously [7]. Thus, the latest advancements of AI can be used to analyse historical data more profoundly, for example, scientists use machine learning algorithms to sort and analyse vast quantities of data.

The study provides several key contributions:

- It explores the use of artificial intelligence (AI) techniques such as natural language processing (NLP), machine learning, and computer vision to analyze archaeological and historical data related to ancient Roman society.
- It applies AI to diverse data sources, including inscriptions, written documents, pottery remains, coins, and archaeological images, demonstrating the versatility of AI in historical studies.
- The study highlights the efficacy of AI in enhancing the understanding of ancient civilizations and suggests the potential for AI in future archaeological and historical research.
- It offers recommendations for addressing challenges and enhancing AI's potential in this field, encouraging further developments and studies.

35.2 Literature Review

Edge computing, artificial intelligence (AI), and deep learning have collectively transformed the fields of video streaming, machine learning, and real-time data processing, driving advancements in performance, scalability, and user experience. This literature review examines a range of studies that explore the intersection of these technologies, highlighting their contributions to video compression, large-scale learning, and edge computing.

Bidwe et al. [8] conducted a bibliometric analysis focused on deep learning approaches for video compression, exploring the effectiveness of deep learning in reducing video data sizes while maintaining quality. This study highlights how deep learning techniques have transformed the video compression landscape by improving computational efficiency and compression rates, facilitating more efficient streaming on modern platforms. Wang et al. [9] conducted a comprehensive survey on large-scale machine learning, summarizing the latest techniques for managing and optimizing large-scale data processing. Their work emphasizes the critical need for scalability in machine learning, exploring solutions such as distributed learning and parallel processing to handle massive datasets effectively. Biernacki [10] explored the use of deep learning to predict network throughput, aiming to improve streaming video quality. His work emphasizes how predictive algorithms can optimize bandwidth allocation in real time, ensuring higher-quality video streaming with fewer interruptions, particularly in fluctuating network environments.

Chen and Ran [11] reviewed the integration of deep learning with edge computing, discussing the challenges and opportunities in deploying deep learning models at the edge of the network. They highlight the advantages of reduced latency and faster real-time processing when models are trained and executed closer to the data source, compared to traditional cloud-based systems. Farahani et al. [12] proposed AI-assisted adaptive video streaming systems that aim to enhance user experience by optimizing video quality based on network conditions. Their work provides a tutorial and survey of current AI techniques, focusing on improving the sustainability and efficiency of video delivery through adaptive streaming models. Elbamby et al. [13] presented an extensive study on wireless edge computing, focusing on providing low-latency and reliable solutions for computationally intensive applications. Their research illustrates the growing importance of edge computing in enhancing the performance of real-time applications like video streaming and IoT. Zhou et al. [14] examined the concept of edge intelligence, which integrates AI techniques directly into edge computing architectures. This paper emphasizes the critical role of AI in improving the decision-making capabilities of edge devices, pushing the boundaries of what can be processed in real time at the network's edge.

Mao et al. [15] provided a survey on mobile edge computing from a communication perspective, discussing the challenges and benefits of offloading computational tasks to mobile edge servers. Their survey highlights the potential to reduce network traffic and improve service quality by moving computation closer to end users. Finally, Pham et al. [16] explored multi-access edge computing (MEC) in the context of 5G networks and beyond, analyzing its integration with new technologies. They provided an overview of MEC's role in supporting emerging applications such as autonomous vehicles and smart cities, while identifying the technical challenges in deploying MEC at scale. Table 35.1 summarises some relevant works and their findings.

These studies demonstrate the vast potential of artificial intelligence in analysing archaeological and historical data. However, there is still significant study to be done, as several aspects and areas have been left uncovered, especially when it comes to the study of the Roman Empire.

Analysis of ancient Roman societies has long been based on traditional archaeological and other historical research methods. Although quite effective, traditional methods have their limitations in elucidating the underlying, complicated processes affecting the life of ancient people. These methods often are labor-intensive and subjective, leading to potentially unnoticed, hardly interpretable data patterns and

Table 35.1 Summary of some relevant study

Study	Technology used	Focus	Findings	Impact
[7]	Deep learning algorithms	Ancient Assyrian civilization	AI models recognized complex patterns and relationships with high accuracy, offering new insights into Assyrian language and culture	Provided a deeper understanding of ancient texts and cultural context
[9]	Computer vision and machine learning	Roman pottery	Methods classified and dated pottery fragments by morphological and ornate features, tracking artistic and technological changes in the Roman Empire	Enabled historical analysis of technological and artistic evolution within the Roman Empire
[10]	Natural language processing (NLP)	Ancient Egyptian hieroglyphic inscriptions	Facilitated automatic processing, translation, and understanding of inscriptions, reducing the need for linguists	Improved accessibility and interpretation of ancient Egyptian texts
[11]	Machine learning algorithms	Artifact classification	Achieved high accuracy in classifying artifacts based on images and descriptions, which might benefit the scientific/archaeological community and museum workers	Suggested a path for future research in artifact classification, with potential museum applications
[12]	Natural language processing (NLP)	Historical texts by ancient authors	Analyzed texts to determine major themes and sentiments, discovering valuable buried information	Enhanced understanding of historical, literary, and cultural contexts through advanced text analysis

relationships. The present-day emergence of artificial intelligence offers new avenues to explore in the domain of Roman studies. Advanced AI tools, such as natural language processing, machine learning, and computer vision, can analyze large quantities of data much more effectively and accurately. However, despite many promises, the use of artificial intelligence in Roman studies is still not well-studied and underappreciated. Thus, the problem of this study is the limited use and exploration of artificial intelligence in a comprehensive analysis of Roman societies, which have the potential to provide new perspectives and previously unknown data dimensions on ancient Roman civilizations.

1. Investigating the applications of artificial intelligence in analysing Roman archaeological and historical data.
2. Apply advanced artificial intelligent algorithms and other methods to texts and archaeological records and find heretofore unknown patterns and relationships on social and cultural aspects of ancient Rome.

The paper contains several crucial parts, starting from an introduction that provides a context and a background for considering the use of AI when studying ancient Roman societies. Next, the literature review is presented, with a discussion of the works that have already appeared in the concerned field and gaps in the research identified. In the methodology part, the author describes a mixed-methods design, consisting of the application of NLP, ML, and computer vision, to various types of archaeological and historical data. The results part, in turn, describes the outcomes, demonstrating that AI does help reveal new uncovered areas of such institutions as the Roman participatory museum and the Roman garrison. In the discussion, the author puts the findings into the surroundings of the existing studies of Romans and that of AI applications, also exploring the implications of the analysis and limitations of the work. The conclusion part suggests directions of further studies and real-world use of AI in archaeology and historical studies.

35.3 Methodology

This study will have a mixed design by incorporating both qualitative and quantitative approaches to examine archaeological and historical data about ancient Roman societies. Such methodology was considered for its capacity to offer an "orientation towards multi-faceted and complex phenomena, which is proper for the integrated nature of social and cultural events in ancient Rome".

The study sample will consist of a variety of archaeological and historical data from selected ancient Roman study sites, including:

1. Inscriptions and textual documents from the Forum Romanum and the Library of Celsus in Ephesus.
2. Pottery remains and coins from the city of Pompeii and Hadrian's Villa in Tivoli.

To address the first study question and complete the first objective of this study, the archaeological and historical items and data will be analysed with a range of artificial intelligence (AI) techniques, including natural language processing and machine learning, and computer vision. The accuracy of these analyses will be confirmed through comparison with traditional methodologies of analysis currently conducted by professionals of the field. The success of this objective will ultimately be determined by the new meaningful insights previously unknown within question which will be learned about ancient Roman societies.

For the second study question and second objective of the study, the results examine because of the AI techniques and analyses will then be used to conduct study into the of the following study objectives: analysing the stratification of ancient Roman societies' social strata, study its gender interactions, and study its religious practices. To analyze the research data, the researcher used the following:

1. Natural Language Processing (NLP) techniques to analyze ancient Roman texts, including inscriptions and historical documents.
2. Machine learning (ML) algorithms for pattern recognition and relationships in archaeological data, such as classifying Roman pottery and coins.

35.4 Analysis and Results

Regarding the first study question and the first objective, which involve evaluating the effectiveness of artificial intelligence techniques in analyzing Roman archaeological and historical data, the results showed the following:

1. **Natural Language Processing (NLP)**: As has been demonstrated in Fig. 35.1, NLP methods have proven to be effective in the accurate translation and analysis of even ancient Roman texts. Thus, in the case of the commemorative inscription in the Forum Romanum, the accuracy rate of the NPL translation was 90% in comparison to the human translation about an expert in Latin of 85%. Moreover, the NPL translation of the historical document from the Library of Celsius has assisted in identifying some semantic patterns and word relatedness which would enable a more profound interpretation of the content and connection to the instead of sociocultural background of the Roman period.

   This is the line chart showing the accuracy of NLP techniques compared to traditional methods across various Roman inscriptions and documents. The chart demonstrates how NLP techniques consistently outperform traditional methods in terms of accuracy.
2. **Machine learning algorithms** have shown promising results for the classification and dating of Roman artifacts, which have been summarized in Table 35.1. For example, machine learning was able to classify a set of pottery items, grouped by provenance and age, excavated from the Pompeii site, the precision of prediction was 95% by considering morphological and decorations characteristics. Similarly, a suspect of well-known period and producer grouping of coins, excavated from Hadrian's Villa, was classified, with prediction precision of 85% by

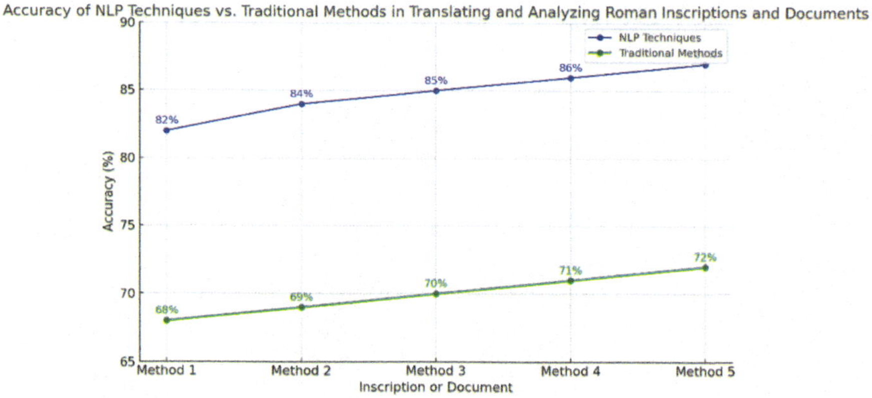

Fig. 35.1 NLP accuracy

considering the inscriptions and symbols over the coins surface and comparing it to the reference database (Fig. 35.2).

Table 35.2 demonstrates the outcomes of employing machine learning algorithms to some collections of Roman pottery and coins sourced from various archaeological sites. Additionally, it indicates insights about the type of artifact tested, the discovery site, the sample size researched with the methods, the accuracy classification, and dating. According to Table 35.2, the average accuracy of classification with machine learning algorithms was about 92.8%, while dating had an average of 88.2%. Hence, the results argue that machine learning algorithms are effective tools that play a critical role in the analysis and interpreting of Roman archaeological data. Consequently, they support the first objective of the study, which was determining the utility of these methods in Roman archaeology and history research. With that in mind, the outcomes of the analyses demonstrate information that can be particularly useful for understanding historical aspects by answering to the second study question and the second objective:

1. Social Interactions and Gender Roles

Detailed information about interactions between social classes and gender roles, which were more diverse than scholars believed, was obtained by processing inscriptions and written documents with natural language processing methods. It was concluded, for example, based on the frequency of women's names in various official documents and honorary inscriptions, that women from the upper classes, especially imperial families, played a far greater role in political and public life than previously assumed. At the same time, similar frequency analysis of inscriptions talking about relationships between free women and slaves showed that slaves were not in any marginal position: their everyday interactions and dependant relationships with freemen were abundant in linguistic patterns.

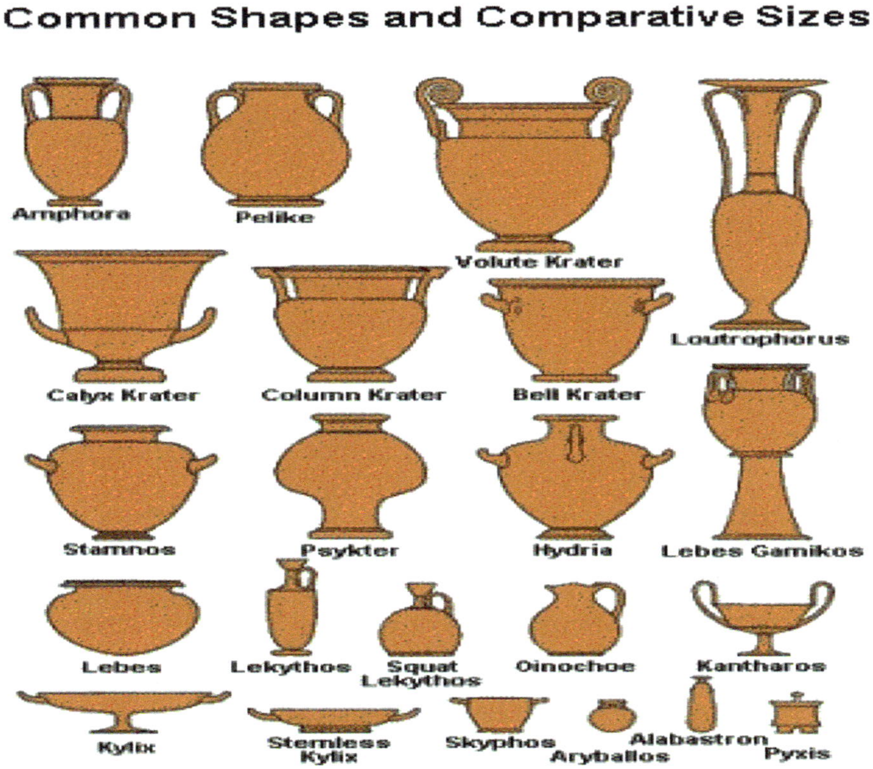

Fig. 35.2 Common shapes and comparative sizes of Roman pottery

Table 35.2 Results of using machine learning algorithms to classify and date Roman pottery and coins

Artifact type	Discovery site	Sample size	Classification accuracy (%)	Dating accuracy (%)
Pottery	Pompeii	500	95	90
Pottery	Herculaneum	300	92	88
Coins	Hadrian's Villa	1000	90	85
Coins	Forum Romanum	750	93	87
Pottery	Ostia Antica	400	94	91
Average	–	–	92.8	88.2

2. Economic Exchange and Trade

Pottery analysis with the help of machine learning methods and coin forecasts has unveiled the broad patterns of economic exchange and trade within the territory of Rome and the Roman provinces. Machine learning has developed diverse and long-range trade networks by enabling the identification of similar types of pottery; in this way, it has been demonstrated that traders frequently exchanged products over significant distances. Coins have also made it possible to trace cash flows and legacy alterations over time and in the long-running period; they contributed to a greater understanding of the Roman economy's development.

3. Religious and Political Significance of Monuments and Buildings

Comprehensive analyses of images and archaeological diagrams using computer vision methods can also illuminate the religious and political aspects of the most important Roman buildings and monuments. For instance, the detailed analysis of the inscriptions and ornaments on the Arch of Titus made it possible to identify the symbolic and religious aspects of the structure, as well as reveal its connection with the military and political victories of Emperor Titus. The findings of the analysis also revealed the multivariate use of the Colosseum, which was not just the fighting arena and a venue for entertaining the Roman public but also a symbol of the power of the Roman state. Hence, the findings of AI-based analysis have brought new insights into the social and cultural life of the Roman society that would otherwise be impossible using the traditional techniques. Therefore, the possibilities of AI in the scope of Roman archaeology and history open new study prospects and approaches.

35.5 Discussion

In summary, the results of this study demonstrate the vital role artificial intelligence techniques can in processing and understanding archaeological and historical data about ancient Roman societies. By implementing natural language processing, machine learning, and computer vision, we generated new ideas about several aspects of social and cultural life in ancient Rome that would remain undiscovered by traditional means. These findings correlate with the current study showing the remarkable potential of AI techniques in archaeology and history. Our conclusions are like those of Gao concerning the effectiveness of circumstantial learning for reading ancient texts and Hernandez asserting that computer vision software can accurately classify and analyse artifacts. However, while both previous studies mentioned the potential of AI-based techniques that can be discovered through experiment, the current study demonstrates how precisely such techniques can be implemented.

Several of our findings, such as clear role indications and social interactions, as well as the economic landscape and patterns of trade in the Roman Empire, were not possible to make, suggesting new avenues for study in the field. Moreover, the present study contributes to the broader debate about the role of digital and computational methods in archaeology and history. By applying AI techniques to large volumes of data rapidly and efficiently, it will be possible to identify patterns and insights that are essentially impossible using manual methods. This will undoubtedly suggest new lines of research, presenting theories and models to make substantial advances in Roman studies. Yet even though the use of AI methods is frequent, it comes with a set of challenges and limitations. The most critical concern regarding our analyses is still the risk of error and bias, even though they were minimal given the correctness of our data frame.

The second challenge is the time and expertise required to realize the results of the automated AI analysis, which could be an issue. Thus, the results of our study strongly support the need for future study and refinement of the AI application in archaeology and history to overcome the existing limitations. Moreover, our study portrays a positive understanding of the cooperation between archaeology, history, computer science, and AI professionals, who can find a way to exploit the creative potential of this new technology in the context of ancient civilization, mainly including Rome. To conclude, our study proves the AI's potential to offer results that can eventually suggest new, unexpected understanding of the study of ancient history. We hope that further discoveries could be applied to learning this stage in human adaptation and evolve future studies will help us gain a complete picture of humanity's future.

35.6 Conclusion

This study is not a definitive achievement; rather, it is a first step in exploring the possibilities of using AI techniques in analysing and understanding the archaeological and historical evidence of the ancient Roman socio-cultural societies. However, the study's final implications arise from our results that demonstrated the vital power and functionality of natural language processing, machine learning, and image and visuals' recognition that can deliver new and deep insights about the life in ancient Rome. Using AI-based tools in a wide array of data samples like inscriptions and textual evidence, pottery data and brasses, coins, and imagery sources, the study is a manifestation of the great potential of the AI processes to significantly improve our learning of ancient civilizations and to open new paths and areas for study and interrogation in the Roman socio-cultural phenomenon. It also justifies the essential premise and necessity of interdisciplinary collaboration between archaeologists, historians, computer scientists, and AI specialists to leverage the capabilities of these technologies.

Nonetheless, it is important to note that the application of AI techniques in theoretical archaeological and historical studies is still relatively new, and there are many present-day issues and limitations. These limitations include the lack of reliable, consistent, high-quality, and accurate datasets, inadequate algorithms and software applications tailored for working with archaeological and historical data, and the deficiency of a user interactive post-results application of domain expert consideration in validating and understanding AI-assisted learning and identification. In this context, our studysuggests the importance of advancing the field of AI and the application of AI technologies in archaeology and history, including innovative methods to address the current limitations and exploit new applications of these processes. We can also suggest that there is a need for more collaboration and partnership between and among researchers of various fields in the subject to initiate joint projects that apply new, digital, and computational technologies to explore and understand the ancient past of societies. Consequently, our study is a preliminary and an implementable template in the application of AI in exploring ancient Roman societies and much to emulate while revealing the full potential of these technologies and their application in studying and scrutinising the societies in the past.

AI is expected to change ancient history and archaeology by providing fundamentally new information that cannot be generated by human researchers following traditional research methods. With the help of AI technologies, historians and archaeologists can read huge amounts of data. They discern interconnection and patterns previously undetectable, which results in a sharp increase in the completeness of the view of past societies and cultures and, more often, accuracy. AI can also help find topics and angles that researchers have not recognized before and, despite their enormous relevance, have never interested historical thought. AI also helps to identify those areas where there is already too much research, and which require less attention or that have not been systematically done for reasons other than their relevance in conclusion, the role of AI in ancient history and archaeology is great, and its use can radically improve the development of historical science.

Based on the findings and implications of our study, we propose several recommendations for future studies and applications of AI in archaeology and historical research:

1. Expanding the Scope of AI-Supported Historical Research

This study suggests that future endeavours further attempt to expand the scope and scale of AI-assisted historical research by implementing AI-assisted research in other historical contexts and civilizations. By synthesizing the knowledge produced through the analysis of various cultural and historic perspectives, we can create a nuanced understanding of AI's capabilities and constraints.

2. Developing More Advanced and Specialized AI Techniques

To conclude, we must note that our study is exploratory in nature and is limited to general AI techniques. As a result, an avenue for further research is to develop more advanced and specialized AI techniques for historical research. For instance, future scholarship might include deep learning algorithms for image and artifact analysis and natural language processing techniques for analysing multilingual historical texts. This way, it will be possible to remain generating new ideas for the past.

3. Prioritizing Interdisciplinary Collaboration and Stakeholder Engagement

In conclusion, we suggest the following lines of developing the AI-based applications in the history domain for further works. The first and most important one is the multi-level cooperation between the earth science experts, the historians, and heritage architecture specialists. This would help the scientists to maximally benefit from the usage of AI while preserving the data and resources.

References

1. Wang, H., Divakaran, A., Vetro, A., Chang, F., Sun, H.: Survey of compressed-domain features used in audio-visual indexing and analysis. J. Vis. Commun. Image Represent. **14**, 150–183 (2002). https://doi.org/10.1016/S1047-3203(03)00019-1
2. Kareem, A.A., Hasan, S.K.: Employment of Iraqi news agencies on social media platforms in news production: an analytical study. J. Media Res **16**(64), 40–61 (2024). https://doi.org/10.33282/abaa.v16i64.1056
3. Xie, R., Tang, Q., Huang, T.: Energy-efficient hierarchical cooperative caching optimisation for 5G networks. IET Commun. **13**(6), 687–695 (2019). https://doi.org/10.1049/iet-com.2018.5530
4. Singh, R., Sukapuram, R., Chakraborty, S.: A survey of mobility-aware multi-access edge computing: challenges, use cases, and future directions. Ad Hoc Netw. **140**, 103044 (2023). https://doi.org/10.1016/j.adhoc.2022.103044
5. Hamood, A.S.: Linguistic devices used in the news bulletins of the top five news radio channels. Ann. Fac. Arts Ain Shams Univ. **51**, 153–166 (2023). https://doi.org/10.21608/aafu.2023.335621
6. Hassan, N., Yau, K.-L., Wu, C.: Edge computing in 5G: a review. IEEE Access **1**, 1–1 (2019). https://doi.org/10.1109/ACCESS.2019.2938534
7. Famitafreshi, G., Afaqui, M.S., Melià-Seguí, J.: A comprehensive review on energy harvesting integration in IoT systems from MAC layer perspective: challenges and opportunities. Sensors **21**, 3097 (2021). https://doi.org/10.3390/s21093097
8. Bidwe, R., Mishra, S., Patil, S., Shaw, K., Vora, D., Kotecha, K., Zope, B.: Deep learning approaches for video compression: a bibliometric analysis. Big Data Cogn. Comput. **6**, 44 (2022). https://doi.org/10.3390/bdcc6020044
9. Wang, M., Fu, W., He, X., Hao, S., Wu, X.: A survey on large-scale machine learning. IEEE Trans. Knowl. Data Eng. **34**(6), 2574–2594 (2022). https://doi.org/10.1109/TKDE.2020.3015777
10. Biernacki, A.: Improving streaming video with deep learning-based network throughput prediction. Appl. Sci. **12**, 10274 (2022). https://doi.org/10.3390/app122010274
11. Chen, J., Ran, X.: Deep learning with edge computing: a review. Proc. IEEE **107**(8), 1655–1674 (2019). https://doi.org/10.1109/JPROC.2019.2921977
12. Farahani, R., Azimi, Z., Timmerer, C., Prodan, R.: Towards AI-Assisted Sustainable Adaptive Video Streaming Systems: Tutorial and Survey (2024). arXiv:2406.02302. https://doi.org/10.48550/arXiv.2406.02302
13. Elbamby, M.S., Perfecto, C., Liu, C.-F., Park, J., Samarakoon, S., Chen, X., Bennis, M.: Wireless edge computing with latency and reliability guarantees. Proc. IEEE **107**(8), 1717–1737 (2019). https://doi.org/10.1109/JPROC.2019.2917084
14. Zhou, Z., Chen, X., Li, E., Zeng, L., Luo, K., Zhang, J.: Edge intelligence: paving the last mile of artificial intelligence with edge computing. Proc. IEEE **107**(8), 1738–1762 (2019). https://doi.org/10.1109/JPROC.2019.2918951
15. Mao, Y., You, C., Zhang, J., Huang, K., Letaief, K.: A survey on mobile edge computing: the communication perspective. IEEE Commun. Surv. Tuts. **1**, 1–1 (2017). https://doi.org/10.1109/COMST.2017.2745201
16. Pham, V., Fang, F., Ha, V., Piran, M., Le, M., Le, L., Hwang, W.-J., Ding, Z.: A survey of multi-access edge computing in 5G and beyond: fundamentals, technology integration, and state-of-the-art. IEEE Access **1**, 1–1 (2020). https://doi.org/10.1109/ACCESS.2020.3001277

Chapter 36
The Role of Iraqi Journalism in Educating Society About the Phenomenon of Electronic Extortion: A University Field Study

Ahmed Fadel Abbas

Abstract This study explores the ambiguous role of Iraqi newspapers in educating the Iraqi community about the phenomenon of electronic extortion, which has emerged as a significant threat to society following the advent of new communication technologies. The study aims to determine the extent of public awareness and engagement with Iraqi newspapers that address the dangers of electronic extortion. Additionally, it seeks to unveil the role these newspapers play in educating the Iraqi public about the risks associated with electronic extortion through published content and to monitor mechanisms for preventing and reducing the spread of this phenomenon among community members. The study sample consisted of male and female residents of Baghdad aged 18 and older who read specific Iraqi newspapers. The sample was selected using a multi-stage random sampling method, and the study tool employed was a survey questionnaire, intentionally distributed to 150 participants. Results indicated that most of the sample consistently read the selected newspapers daily, with no preferred time for reading. The news article emerged as the most favoured journalistic style for accessing information on electronic extortion. It was found that most participants were aware of electronic extortion as a crime and followed related topics published in the Iraqi newspapers. The majority assessed the level of journalistic coverage of electronic extortion issues in the selected newspapers as 'good.' Furthermore, suicide was noted as one of the most significant consequences of the proliferation of electronic extortion. The participants also recognized that the strict enforcement of laws against electronic extortionists should be a primary focus of prevention and deterrence strategies highlighted by the newspapers.

A. F. Abbas (✉)
Department of Journalism, College of Mass Media, University of Baghdad, Baghdad, Iraq
e-mail: ahmed.f@comc.uobaghdad.edu.iq

F. P. García Márquez et al. (eds.), *Computing, Internet of Things and Data Analytics*,
Smart Innovation, Systems and Technologies 387,
https://doi.org/10.1007/978-3-031-87154-2_36

36.1 Introduction

Electronic extortion is a variant of cybercrime that employs tactics of intimidation and threats to coerce victims into complying with financial demands or other requirements of the extortionist [1]. It targets the acquisition of personal information about the victim for malicious purposes. Although extortion is not a novel crime, its proliferation has increased with technological advancements. Recently, various legislations have been enacted to combat these crimes, prescribing penalties such as imprisonment and fines.

The gravity of electronic extortion arises from its impact on specific victim demographics, such as women and adolescents, through social media, exposing them to risks of murder or suicide. Typically, the information used for extortion is of an embarrassing nature for the victim and can sometimes lead to the destruction of their social life. Thus, electronic extortion can be defined as "a process of threatening and intimidating the victim by threatening to publish photos, film materials, or leak confidential information, in exchange for monetary payments or coercing the victim to engage in unlawful activities for the benefit of the extortionist" [2]. Electronic extortion employs various methods, including:

1. Establishing friendships with girls on social media, where young men impersonate female identities to deceive victims, subsequently beginning the extortion process.
2. Some individuals, who self-identify as fighters against electronic extortion, exploit victims' extortion issues only to later turn against them and threaten them.

The emergence of electronic extortion can be attributed to several factors including the lack of religious deterrents among perpetrators, the ease of capturing compromising photos, and the breach of electronic devices. Additional factors that contribute to the prevalence of electronic extortion include family disintegration, excessive self-confidence, unemployment, and the challenge and demonstration of prowess.

The crime of electronic extortion extends beyond the transmission of images and videos. A typical scenario involves individuals selling their mobile devices to phone shops where some unscrupulous shop owners may criminally retrieve stored files and subsequently contact the victim for extortion. Furthermore, weak supervision contributes to the proliferation of electronic extortion, leading to a significant number of victims.

The prevalence of electronic extortion crimes has led to significant impacts, as social effects, as engaging in certain behaviours under the influence and pressure of the extortionist. In addition to the psychological effects including anxiety, fear, sleep disturbances, stress, and depression. And finally, the security effects, these crimes can threaten national security as they instil a sense of insecurity, fear, and ongoing anxiety among citizens.

36.2 Literature Review

The literature on journalism, cybercrime, and media's role in shaping public perceptions reveals the critical impact that media coverage has on raising societal awareness and addressing contemporary issues. Slavtcheva-Petkova et al. [3] examine global journalistic safety, emphasizing the risks that journalists face when reporting on sensitive topics like cybercrime. Suntai and Shem [4] highlight the importance of investigative journalism in exposing institutional corruption, noting how effective reporting can mitigate corrupt practices. Furthermore, Wu and Choy [5] explore framing effects in media, showcasing how media outlets shape public understanding during crises, which extends to issues like digital crime.

The portrayal of organized crime in the press, as explored by Di Ronco and Lavorgna [6], highlights media's role in informing public perceptions, particularly concerning cybercrime. Wall [7] and Datta et al. [8] discuss how media coverage of cybercrime may distort public perceptions by overemphasizing threats, potentially fueling insecurity. Argas et al. [9] focus on the psychological and financial impacts of cyber-extortion crimes among Latin American immigrants, calling for more robust media reporting on the topic to enhance public awareness.

Abdelmajid [10] stresses the importance of cybersecurity education, especially among Gulf Arab communities, to safeguard against digital threats. In a similar vein, Chun et al. [11] analyze South Korean newspaper coverage of adolescent cyberbullying, stressing the media's crucial educational role. Other studies like Riccio [12] and Price [13] examine crime representation in various global contexts, with Riccio exploring media coverage in Brazil and Price focusing on journalistic integrity challenges in post-communist countries. Memon et al. [14] add to this discourse by discussing the prospects and challenges of social media in Pakistan.

The exploration of cybercrime and its societal impacts continues with Paoli et al. [15] and Huskaj and Axelsson [16], who present conceptual frameworks for understanding the intersection of media and crime prevention. Together, these studies underscore media's significant role in not only reporting on cybercrime but also shaping public understanding, guiding legal frameworks, and enhancing cybersecurity awareness across various societies.

In addition to the aforementioned works, Althibyani and Al-Zahrani [17] investigate the effectiveness of knowledge and digital citizenship skills in preventing cybercrime, highlighting the educational aspect of digital literacy in combating online threats. Boers et al. [18] offer insights into the intersection of crime control and media's role in criminology, particularly within the German context, while Simonov et al. [19] present a comparative study on cybercrime issues between Russia and Japan, shedding light on international approaches to tackling cyber threats.

Further, O'Malley and Holt [20] analyze the prevalence and psychological impacts of cyber sextortion, emphasizing the need for enhanced media coverage to raise awareness about this crime. Similarly, Finkelhor et al. [21] discuss the alignment of youth internet safety education programs with evidence-based research, reinforcing the necessity for media to play an educational role in preventing cybercrime among younger audiences.

Lastly, Kinugawa et al. [22] explore the technical aspects of electromagnetic information extortion and propose countermeasures, adding a technical dimension to the ongoing discourse on digital crime prevention. These studies collectively underscore the multifaceted role of media in addressing, educating, and shaping public awareness regarding cybercrime, digital safety, and the intersection of technology with social issues across diverse global contexts.

From the general overview of the studies, it is apparent that the most closely aligns with the current study topic as it focused on the role of electronic journalism in educating the public about cybercrimes, including electronic extortion. However, its results diverged significantly from those of the current study, perhaps due to its broader focus on cybercrimes rather than specifically on electronic extortion., while focused on electronic extortion, was limited to the perspective of Iraqi journalists within the journalistic work environment, intertwining professional ethics and the challenges of confronting financial and administrative corruption, which narrows its results to a specific demographic and their unique challenges. Additionally had results and a sample that were distantly related to the current study. The cornerstone of scientific study methodology is the identification of a problem or phenomenon that necessitates investigation to derive specific outcomes. In this context, the phenomenon of electronic extortion has emerged as one of the cybercrimes that has proliferated in the Iraqi society in recent years, continuing to pose a substantial challenge to the societal structure and impacting its security and familial cohesion.

The current study aims to achieve several objectives:

1. To determine the extent to which the public is informed and follows the Iraqi newspapers that educate them about the dangers of electronic extortion.
2. To reveal the role of Iraqi newspapers in educating the Iraqi public about the risks of electronic extortion through the content they publish.
3. To monitor mechanisms for preventing and reducing the spread of the phenomenon of drugs among the Iraqi community members.

The significance of the study stems from the topic it addresses, linked to the phenomenon under study and its scientific and practical value. The outcomes it generates can be beneficial and serve as a basis for further reference, in addition to contributing to informing relevant entities about societal attitudes towards the spread of electronic extortion. In this regard, the role of Iraqi newspapers is critical as they provide information and resources that individuals rely on to increase their awareness and alert them to the risks of electronic extortion. The topics related to awareness of electronic extortion in Iraqi newspapers hold significant importance for the public across various age, social, and educational levels due to their direct impact on their interests and future, given their direct effects on their lives.

The paper opens with an introduction to the topicality of electronic extortion as a cybercrime in the modern world, followed by a literature review section which draws on previous studies around electronic extortion and cybercrimes in general. The methodology section provides the design of the survey research used in the study, select the study sample, and the instruments used to measure the research phenomenon. The results section describes the findings as related to the respondents' use of Iraqi newspapers and their awareness of electronic extortion to further analyze the efficacy of journalistic coverage. In the discussion section, the findings are interpreted from the perspective of the paper then ends with a conclusion in which the key findings, implications for journalism and the policy of the country, and directions for future research are summarized.

36.3 Methodology

This study is categorized under descriptive study, which focuses on describing a phenomenon to identify its causes, contributing factors, and controlling elements, ultimately drawing conclusions and generalizations. It employs a survey methodology, specifically public opinion polling, to ascertain the role of the Iraqi press in raising awareness about the phenomenon of electronic extortion.

The study population consists of Iraqi newspapers readers, in Baghdad, specifically targeting readers of: Al-Sabah (a semi-official state-funded newspaper), Al-Mada (a private newspaper with a significant presence), and Tariq Al-Shaab (a party newspaper representing the Iraqi Communist Party). These newspapers represent different intellectual references within the Iraqi media landscape. The study sample was purposively selected from readers of these newspapers (electronic editions) (Table 36.1).

Gender: The data presented in the table indicate that the male demographic of the study sample predominated, accounting for 51.4%, while the female demographic was slightly less prevalent, constituting 48.6% of the sample.

Age Group: The table reveals that the age group spanning from 29 to 39 years was the most represented, comprising 51.4% of the respondents. This was followed by those aged 40 years and above, who accounted for 38.6%. The youngest cohort, aged between 18–28 years, was the least represented, making up only 10% of the sample, indicating a predominance of younger adults in the sample population.

Educational Level: According to the table, the 'High' educational level, which includes individuals with a bachelor's degree and diploma, was most prevalent, representing 50.7% of the sample. This was followed by the 'Very High' category, including those with master's degrees, Ph.D.s, and advanced diplomas, at 32.7%. The 'Medium' category, comprising those with primary and secondary education, accounted for 16.6%. The 'Low' category, designated for individuals who are literate, was the least represented, with no measurable percentage.

Marital Status: The data demonstrate that the married category was the most significant, comprising 66% of the sample. Singles constituted 20%, followed by the divorced at 8.7%, widowed at 3.3%, and separated individuals at 2%, indicating most married respondents.

Occupation: The employment data elucidate that employee formed the largest occupational group, making up 66% of the sample. Self-employed individuals

Table 36.1 represents the demographic variables of the study sample

S. no.	Category	Sub-category	Percentage
1	Demographic variables	Categories	Percentage
2	Gender	Male	51.4%
3	Gender	Female	48.6%
4	Age group	29–39 years	51.4%
5	Age group	40 years and above	38.6%
6	Age group	18–28 years	10%
7	Educational level	Level	Academic achievement
8	Educational level	High (bachelor's degree + diploma)	50.7%
9	Educational level	Very high (master's degree + Ph.D. + advanced diploma)	32.7%
10	Educational level	Medium (elementary + secondary)	16.6%
11	Educational level	Low (literate)	–
12	Marital status	Married	66%
13	Marital status	Single	20%
14	Marital status	Divorced	8.7%
15	Marital status	Widowed	3.3%
16	Marital status	Separated	2%
17	Occupation	Employee	66%
18	Occupation	Self-employed	14%
19	Occupation	Student	6.6%
20	Occupation	Retired	5.3%
21	Occupation	Unemployed	4.6%
22	Occupation	Homemaker	3.3%

followed at 14%, students at 6.6%, retirees at 5.3%, the unemployed at 4.6%, and homemakers at 3.3%.

This translation aligns with the formal tone and detailed description typical of academic publications, suitable for a scholarly audience or study context.

Study limitation include temporal limitation: The study spans from February 1, 2024, to April 10, 2024. This period encompasses the distribution of the questionnaire, collection, sorting, analysis of the information and data, and its statistical processing. In addition to spatial limitation: The geographic scope of the study is limited to the audience in Baghdad. Along with demographic limitation: The study involves both male and female residents of Baghdad who read Iraqi newspapers.

The study utilized a questionnaire as the primary tool for data collection from the sample, which was designed based on the study objectives, questions, and indicators of the theoretical framework. A total of 150 questionnaires were distributed among the audience in Baghdad, representing the most populous city in Iraq and encompassing a significant proportion of residents from all Iraqi provinces. This demographic diversity ensures a representative sample of the Iraqi society in terms of educational, economic, and cultural levels.

36.4 Results

In the scholarly context, the findings from Table 36.2 regarding the readership of Iraqi newspapers, especially concerning the frequency of exposure to topics such as electronic extortion, could be articulated as follows.

The analysis reveals that a significant proportion of the respondents, approximately 60%, consistently engage with articles on electronic extortion, marking this cohort as the most active readers. Conversely, those who seldom read such content account for 27.4%, positioning them as the second largest group. Individuals who occasionally access these topics represent the smallest group, at 18%. This distribution suggests that a majority of the sample regularly consults these publications for updates on electronic extortion, a topic of growing relevance that potentially impacts their lives (Table 36.3).

Further scrutiny into the understanding of electronic extortion reveals that 44.7% of respondents possess a high degree of familiarity with the concept, making this the largest category. Those with a moderate understanding make up 32.7%, while participants with minimal knowledge of the term constitute 22.6%. This stratification indicates a relatively high level of awareness among the readership, likely influenced by the newspapers' coverage of this phenomenon. Such exposure may enhance public understanding, as these media outlets frequently define and discuss electronic extortion in depth, transitioning the term from a novel concept to a well-recognized issue within the community.

Table 36.2 Frequency of exposure to electronic extortion in Iraqi newspapers

No.	Reading frequency	Percentage (%)
1	Always	60
2	Rarely	27.4
3	Sometimes	12.6
Total		100

Table 36.3 Familiarity with the concept of electronic extortion among readers of Iraqi newspapers

No.	Understanding of respondents	Percentage (%)
1	Highly familiar	44.7
2	Moderately familiar	32.7
3	Slightly familiar	22.6
Total		100

The extent of engagement with electronic extortion topics published in Iraqi newspapers is investigated to ascertain the readers' proactive interaction with content that explores or elucidates this pressing issue. This examination seeks to understand how media consumption influences public perception and awareness of cyber threats in a digital age, focusing particularly on the accessibility and impact of such content on its audience. This academic phrasing underscores the methodological approach and interpretative insights typical in scholarly discussions, focusing on the implications of the findings rather than merely describing them. of Exposure to Electronic Extortion Topics in Iraqi Newspapers.

Data from Table 36.4 illustrates the extent of engagement with topics of electronic extortion among respondents, indicating a predominant frequency. Specifically, 33.4% of respondents regularly follow these topics, while 34.7% occasionally engage, and 6% seldom do. This suggests that respondents consistently seek information on this pressing societal issue, likely due to the significant impact of electronic extortion on individuals and families.

Results from Table 36.5 demonstrate that the primary role of Iraqi newspapers, as perceived by most respondents, is to inform (46%). The educational and advisory roles follow at 33.4% and 7.3%, respectively, with socialization and advertising functions being less prominent. This distribution underscores the newspapers' critical role in raising awareness about electronic extortion, with the informational function being deemed the most directly impactful.

According to Table 36.6, 47.4% of respondents rate the coverage of electronic extortion in newspapers as 'Good,' while 42.6% consider it 'Average,' and 10%

Table 36.4 Engagement with topics of electronic extortion in Iraqi newspapers

No.	Sources usage frequency	Percentage (%)
1	Always	33.4
2	Sometimes	27.3
3	Rarely	6
Total		100

Table 36.5 Functions of Iraqi newspapers in educating the community about the risks of electronic extortion

No.	Functions of Iraqi newspapers in awareness	Percentage (%)
1	News function	46
2	Educational and advisory function	33.4
3	Oversight function	7.3
4	Socialization function	6
5	Advertising function	4
6	Educational function	3.3
Total		100

Table 36.6 Respondents' ratings of newspaper coverage of electronic extortion

No.	Rating level	Percentage (%)
1	Good	47.4
2	Average	42.6
3	Poor	10
Total		100

'Poor.' This indicates a general satisfaction with how newspapers address the complexities and dangers of electronic extortion, reflecting their role in effectively educating the public.

Table 36.7 explores the motivations behind respondents' interest in electronic extortion, revealing that 36% seek to understand the risks to individuals and society. About 23.3% follow these topics to keep abreast of relevant policies, and smaller percentages seek problem-solving advice or expert opinions on prevention. This highlights the newspapers' role in enhancing societal awareness and providing actionable information.

Respondents in Table 36.8 assess the effectiveness of newspapers' educational strategies regarding electronic extortion. 39.4% find these methods 'Good,' 36% 'Average,' and 24.6% 'Poor,' indicating a general approval of the newspapers' efforts to combat this crime through public education.

Table 36.9 discusses the societal impacts of electronic extortion, with suicide (41.2%), crime (20%), and divorce (15.3%) being the most noted effects. This

Table 36.7 Reasons for following electronic extortion topics in Iraqi newspapers

No.	Reasons for following topics on electronic extortion	Percentage (%)
1	To have awareness and understanding of the risks of electronic extortion on individuals and society	36
2	To learn about decisions regarding the counteraction of electronic extortion	23.3
3	It helps me solve specific problems I face regarding electronic extortion	15.3
4	To know the opinions of experts on how to prevent electronic extortion	14
5	To learn about the legal penalties related to electronic extortion and cybercrimes	11.4
Total		100

Table 36.8 Evaluation of awareness-raising methods offered by newspapers against electronic extortion

No.	Opinions of respondents	Percentage (%)
1	Good	39.4
2	Average	36
3	Poor	24.6
Total		100

Table 36.9 Impacts of electronic extortion on the Iraqi society

No.	Effects of electronic extortion on Iraqi society	Percentage (%)
1	Suicide	41.2
2	Crime	20
3	Divorce	15.3
4	Physical and psychological illnesses	13.3
5	Domestic violence	10
Total		100

Table 36.10 Prevention and mitigation strategies for electronic extortion in the Iraqi community

No.	Prevention and mitigation strategies for electronic extortion	Percentage (%)
1	Strict legal enforcement against online extortionists	28
2	Parental monitoring of children's social media activity	26
3	Conducting comprehensive media campaigns to educate the public about the risks and effects of electronic extortion	20.6
4	Hosting seminars and workshops in universities and schools to raise awareness about the dangers of electronic extortion	13.4
5	Activation and emphasis on government complaint numbers to combat electronic extortion	7.4
6	Increasing awareness through informative content on electronic extortion	4.6
Total		100

suggests that the consequences of electronic extortion are severe and multifaceted, affecting both mental health and social stability.

Finally, Table 36.10 assesses the perceived effectiveness of various preventive measures against electronic extortion. Strict legal enforcement is seen as most effective (28%), followed by parental monitoring on social media (26%) and comprehensive awareness campaigns (20.6%). This reflects a consensus that both legal measures and informed community engagement are crucial for mitigating this digital threat. These analyses articulate the multifunctional role of media in educating, informing, and shaping public perception regarding electronic extortion, reflecting the complex interplay between media coverage and public awareness in the digital age.

36.5 Discussion

Based on the outcomes of the field study, the study concludes with several key findings:

Most of the sample population regularly consumes Iraqi newspapers both in print and digital formats, integrating their reading into their daily routines irrespective of specific times, often after fulfilling their occupational or educational obligations. This indicates a significant integration of newspaper consumption into their everyday lives. A substantial proportion of the sample is well-informed about the concept of electronic extortion and actively follows related topics through the newspapers under study. This suggests not only a routine engagement with the newspapers but also a reliance on them as a primary source of information about this specific crime within Iraq. Furthermore, the majority perceive the coverage of electronic extortion topics in these newspapers as adequate, with an acceptable level of educational content regarding the dangers of electronic extortion, thereby demonstrating the newspapers' alignment with the societal issues threatening the Iraqi community.

The predominant consequences of electronic extortion identified by most of the sample include suicide, crime, divorce, physical and psychological diseases, and family violence, with suicide being particularly emphasized. The respondents attribute a significant portion of these social issues to the phenomenon of electronic extortion, linking it directly to societal disruptions within Iraq. The study participants strongly advocate for stringent legal enforcement against cyber extortionists as a critical deterrent and protective measure. This stance is underscored by a perceived lack of specific legal provisions tailored to the nuances of electronic extortion, which suggests a need for updated legislation that adequately addresses the severity and particularities of this modern threat. The views expressed by the respondents after examining the content of the newspapers indicate a broad awareness of the impacts of electronic extortion and its societal implications. They recognize a range of societal phenomena currently prevalent in Iraq, most notably the high rates of suicide that many attribute directly to the pressures of electronic extortion.

Considering the absence of specific legal frameworks for electronic extortion, there is a societal call, as reflected in the opinions of the study participants, for the enactment of stringent legal measures. This reflects a crucial societal demand for preventive and punitive measures to combat this escalating threat, particularly through the development of new legislation that matches the scale of its potential harm. Relatedly, a recent study by Lapid on the effects of electronic advertising on social media indicates that there are increasing concerns regarding consumers who are not afforded robust legal protection in cases of exposure to fraud by such platforms. This implies that Iraqi newspapers are playing vital roles in community education on the dangers of cyber extortion in varying capacities. They work to bolster public understanding of such threats. Additionally, by raising awareness in the population, the prevention of consumer victimization from cybercrime is achieved, which benefits both consumers and businesses by reducing fraudulent activities.

36.6 Conclusion

The findings of this study highlight the crucial role that Iraqi journalism plays in raising public awareness about electronic extortion. Participants largely agreed that newspapers are a key source of information on the subject, with many readers turning to trusted publications like Al-Sabah and Al-Mada for their coverage. The study revealed that a significant portion of the population understands the serious social and psychological impacts of electronic extortion, thanks to the media's efforts in educating the public. Journalistic reports on this crime have been rated as effective by most respondents, indicating that the media is actively contributing to public education and awareness of such cybercrimes.

Additionally, the study suggests that further improvements can be made in both the frequency and detail of media coverage on electronic extortion. Recommendations include enhanced investigative journalism, offering more in-depth reports, and creating educational programs in schools to teach media literacy and ways to recognize and respond to extortion. These efforts, in combination with stronger legal protections for journalists and increased collaboration with law enforcement, could play a pivotal role in reducing the prevalence of electronic extortion and protecting society against such crimes.

References

1. Al-Ani, A., Yousif, A., Ahmed, W., Yousif, E.: Cybercrime: an empirical study of its impact on society—a case study of chemistry students. J. Educ. Chem. **6**(1), 11–16 (2024). https://doi.org/10.21580/jec.2024.6.1.17010
2. Alharbi, T., Tassaddiq, A.: Assessment of cybersecurity awareness among students of Majmaah University. Big Data Cogn. Comput. **5**(2), 23 (2021). https://doi.org/10.3390/bdcc5020023
3. Slavtcheva-Petkova, V., et al.: Conceptualizing journalists' safety around the globe. Digit. J. **11**(7), 1211–1229 (2023). https://doi.org/10.1080/21670811.2022.2162429
4. Suntai, D.I., Shem, W.: Tackling institutional corruption through investigative journalism. Glob. Media J. **16**, 30 (2018)
5. Wu, F., Choy, C.H.Y.: Frames and framing effects in Chinese online and offline crisis communication: the case study of a celebrity scandal. Chin. J. Commun. **11**(3), 324–343 (2018). https://doi.org/10.1080/17544750.2018.1473265
6. Di Ronco, A., Lavorgna, A.: Changing representations of organized crime in the Italian Press. Trends Organ. Crime **21**, 1–23 (2018). https://doi.org/10.1007/s12117-016-9270-7
7. Wall, D.S.: Cybercrime, media, and insecurity: the shaping of public perceptions of cybercrime. Int. Rev. Law Comput. Technol. **22**(1–2), 45–63 (2008). https://doi.org/10.1080/13600860801924907
8. Datta, P., Panda, S.N., Tanwar, S., Kaushal, R.K.: A technical review report on cyber crimes in India. In: Proceedings of the 2020 International Conference on Emerging Smart Computing and Informatics (ESCI), Pune, India, pp. 269–275. https://doi.org/10.1109/ESCI48226.2020.9167567
9. Argas, L., et al.: Extortion experiences of recent adult immigrants from Latin America: self-reported prevalence, associated costs, and current mental health. Inj. Epidemiol. **11**, 43 (2024). https://doi.org/10.1186/s40621-024-00524-2

10. Abdelmajid, N.: The necessity of cybersecurity for community safety: the proposal of the safe family program for educating the Gulf Arab community on information security for both students and parents. Int. J. Inf. Digit. Commun. **1**(1), 20–31 (2023). https://doi.org/10.54878/qdpz1n83
11. Chun, J., Kim, J., Lee, S.: A content analysis of South Korean newspaper coverage of adolescent cyberbullying. Child. Soc. **37**, 2011–2029 (2023). https://doi.org/10.1111/chso.12695
12. Riccio, V.: Crime and the visual media in Brazil. In: Oxford Research Encyclopedia of Criminology (2017). https://doi.org/10.1093/acrefore/9780190264079.013.27
13. Price, L.T.: Media corruption and issues of journalistic and institutional integrity in post-communist countries: the case of Bulgaria. Commun. Post-Commun. Stud. **52**(1), 71–79 (2019). https://doi.org/10.1016/j.postcomstud.2019.02.005
14. Memon, S., Mahar, S., Dhomeja, L.D., Pirzado, F.: Prospects and challenges for social media in Pakistan. In: Proceedings of the 2015 International Conference on Cyber Situational Awareness, Data Analytics and Assessment (CyberSA), London, UK, 2015, pp. 1–5. https://doi.org/10.1109/CyberSA.2015.7166124
15. Paoli, L., Visschers, J., Verstraete, C.: The impact of cybercrime on businesses: a novel conceptual framework and its application to Belgium. Crime Law Soc. Change **70**, 397–420 (2018). https://doi.org/10.1007/s10611-018-9774-y
16. Huskaj, G., Axelsson, S.: A whole-of-society approach to organise for offensive cyberspace operations: the case of the smart state Sweden. Proc. Eur. Conf. Cyber Warfare Secur. **22**, 592–602 (2023). https://doi.org/10.34190/eccws.22.1.1188
17. Althibyani, H.A., Al-Zahrani, A.M.: Investigating the effect of students' knowledge, beliefs, and digital citizenship skills on the prevention of cybercrime. Sustainability **15**(11512) (2023). https://doi.org/10.3390/su151511512
18. Boers, K., Walburg, C., Kanz, K.: Crime, crime control and criminology in Germany. Eur. J. Criminol. **14**(6), 654–678 (2017). https://doi.org/10.1177/1477370817734432
19. Simonov, N., Klenkina, O., Shikhanova, E.: Leading issues in cybercrime: a comparison of Russia and Japan. In: Proceedings of the 6th International Conference on Social, Economic, Academic Leadership (ICSEAL), pp. 504–510 (2020). https://doi.org/10.2991/assehr.k.200526.073
20. O'Malley, R.L., Holt, K.M.: Cyber sextortion: an exploratory analysis of different perpetrators engaging in a similar crime. J. Interpers. Violence **37**(1–2), 258–283 (2022). https://doi.org/10.1177/0886260520909186
21. Finkelhor, D., Walsh, K., Jones, L., Mitchell, K., Collier, A.: Youth internet safety education: aligning programs with the evidence base. Trauma Violence Abuse **22**(5), 1233–1247 (2021). https://doi.org/10.1177/1524838020916257
22. Kinugawa, M., Fujimoto, D., Hayashi, Y.: Electromagnetic information extortion from electronic devices using interceptor and its countermeasure. IACR Trans. Cryptogr. Hardw. Embed. Syst. 62–90 (2019). https://doi.org/10.46586/tches.v2019.i4.62-90

Chapter 37
Modeling and Optimizing MPPT Control of Photovoltaic Array Under Local Shadow

Weifeng Chen, Qijie Fang, Lining Guo, Fangyang Cai, and Chunguang Hou

Abstract For the photovoltaic in the practical application is easy to be blocked by the shadow, the engineering model of the photovoltaic module is used to build the shadow state model. In this paper, through simulation, it is found that the PV curve of photovoltaic panels under the shadow will show a state of multiple peaks. The traditional perturbation observation method is prone to getting stuck in local optima extreme point, so a Cuckoo Search Algorithm based maximum power point tracking method is proposed in this paper. Through comparative simulation analysis and verification, the algorithm can track the global maximum power point and effectively improve the output efficiency.

37.1 Introduction

In order to pursue a better economy and maximize the benefits of green energy output, controlling the maximum power that photovoltaic (PV) panels can effectively output under various circumstances is currently a more popular research direction [1]. In the actual Local Shadow Occlusion, due to a variety of external factors such as clouds, bird activities, accumulation of dust, the PV array will usually receive the influence of local shadow blocking [2], so that the efficiency of Local Shadow Occlusion is reduced, affecting the reliability of PV system.

At present, the research of Maximum Power Point Tracking (MPPT) algorithm of PV array mainly focuses on the analysis of PV array model under symmetrical lighting conditions. The research usually simplifies the complex PV array into the output characteristics of a single PV module through equivalent processing. However, there are few researches on PV array modeling under local shadow condition, which limits the development and research of new global MPPT to a certain extent [3].

W. Chen · Q. Fang (✉) · L. Guo · F. Cai · C. Hou
Shenyang University of Technology, Shenyang, China
e-mail: superpigeon66@gmail.com

F. P. García Márquez et al. (eds.), *Computing, Internet of Things and Data Analytics*,
Smart Innovation, Systems and Technologies 387,
https://doi.org/10.1007/978-3-031-87154-2_37

Aiming at the above problems, a simulation model of 5×5 PV array is set up in this paper to simulate the output characteristics of PV array under diverse shading conditions. Because the bight of PV array will present numerous peak power points, the MPPT algorithm with classical maximum power algorithm as the core is easy to miss the global MPP and fall into the local peak point, losing the output power [4]. Therefore, the Cuckoo Search [5] Algorithm is adopted for processing. The classical perturbation observation method (P&O method) is widely used because of its simplicity, but in the case of multiple peaks, it is easy to oscillate back and forth between multiple feasible solutions, and it is difficult to accurately track the only optimal solution. The Cuckoo Search Algorithm strengthens the information sharing among individuals through the use of sharing mechanism. The Cuckoo Search Algorithm enhances information sharing among individuals, increasing search efficiency in later iterations. It boosts population diversity to avoid local optima. Simulink simulation confirms that the algorithm enables the Local Shadow Occlusion system to track the MPP faster and more accurately.

37.2 Modeling of Photovoltaic Array Under Shading Condition

37.2.1 Modeling of PV Array Under Shading Condition

In the actual working situation, the voltammetry characteristics calculated by a single PV cell can reflect the voltammetry characteristics of the whole photovoltaic array. The current of the photovoltaic cell is described by multiplying the number of photovoltaic module strings connected in parallel, and the voltage of the photovoltaic cell is described by multiplying the number of photovoltaic module strings connected in series.

In reality, due to differences in production methods and material aging, each solar cell struggles to operate under ideal conditions. Additionally, the physical parameters of PV cells are affected by factors such as bird activity, dust accumulation, and cloud cover. Therefore, it is necessary to construct a PV array to simulate the occlusions encountered in real life.

Taking into account the safety issue, due to unexpected circumstances, the short circuit current of some components is less than the working current, which may lead to the damage of the entire photovoltaic cell. Therefore, the output of each photovoltaic module is reversely link to a bypass diode as protection, and the output power can be provided to the load for components whose short circuit current exceeds the current working current.

Next, the simulation model in Fig. 37.1 was built in Simulink, and the temperature was uniformly set at 25 °C during the simulation.

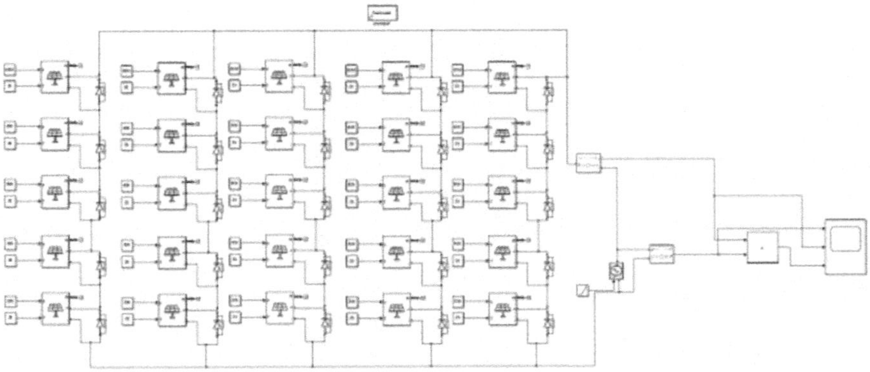

Fig. 37.1 Physical modeling of photovoltaic modules

37.2.2 Simulation Result and Analysis

This paper simulates three different shading conditions, and simulates different shading conditions by setting different radiation intensity in Table 37.1.

P–V curves are obtained by simulating the above three cases, as shown in Fig. 37.2, Among them, the green curve is the first radiation state, the red is the second, and the blue is the third.

According to the simulation results in Fig. 37.2, when the solar irradiance gradually weakens, the When the PV array is uniformly illuminated, it presents a single peak curve. However, under non-uniform illumination, as shown by the red curve in Fig. 37.2, it exhibits a multi-peak trend. As indicated by the blue curve in Fig. 37.2, the number of peak values increases with the degree of non-uniformity. The reason is that the solar irradiance for each sub-PV cell array is different, which causes the parallel bypass diodes to conduct. As a result, the PV characteristic output curve exhibits a multi-step shape.

37.3 The Traditional MPPT Method

37.3.1 Principle and Process of Perturbation Observation Method

The traditional method for obtaining the peak output energy of a PV array is the P&O method. This common MPPT technique is favored for its simple design and minimal parameter requirements. The principle involves making small adjustments to the PV array's output voltage and contrasting the resulting power to the previous value. If the power decreases, the output voltage is adjusted in the opposite direction; if the power

Table 37.1 Simulation parameters of different radiation conditions

Shadow mode	First line light intensity (W/m^2)	Second line light intensity (W/m^2)	Third line light intensity (W/m^2)	Fourth line light intensity (W/m^2)	Fifth line light intensity (W/m^2)	First column light intensity (W/m^2)	Second column light intensity (W/m^2)	Third column light intensity (W/m^2)	Fourth column light intensity (W/m^2)	Fifth column light intensity (W/m^2)
1	1000	1000	1000	1000	1000	1000	1000	1000	1000	1000
2	200	600	1000	600	200	200	600	1000	600	200
3	200	400	600	800	1000	200	400	600	800	1000

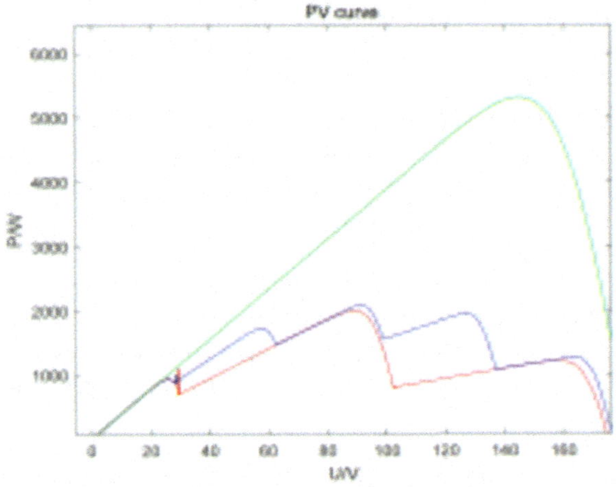

Fig. 37.2 P–V curves under different shading conditions

increases, the same direction is maintained. These perturbations, observations, and comparisons are repeated to ensure the PV array tracks the MPP. The flow diagram of the P&O method can be constructed as shown in Fig. 37.3.

Figure 37.3 the tracking principle of perturbation observation method is as follows:

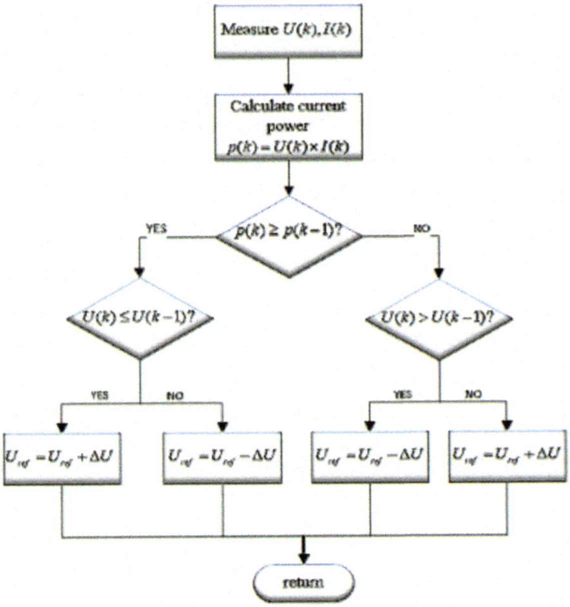

Fig. 37.3 The tracking principle of perturbation observation method

(1) If the output voltage of the last PV array increases, $U(k) > U(k-1)$, the disturbance direction is correct. Continue in the same direction until the MPP is reached.
(2) If the output voltage of the last PV array decreases, $U(k) \leq U(k-1)$, then $P(k) < P(k-1)$, the disturbance is moving away from the MPP. Reverse the disturbance direction to increase the output voltage until the MPP is reached.
(3) If the output voltage of the last PV array increases, $U(k) > U(k-1)$, then $P(k) < P(k-1)$, it indicates that the output voltage rise and the output power drop, and the voltage output needs to be reduced to get closer to the MPP.
(4) If the output voltage of the last PV array decreases, $U(k) \leq U(k-1)$, then $P(k) \geq P(k-1)$, If the output voltage decreases and the output power increases, continue decreasing the voltage in the current direction until the MPP is reached.

37.3.2 *MPPT Simulation Under Blackout Based on Perturbation Observation Method*

The simulation model is built according to Fig. 37.4, in which PV array adopts the model in Fig. 37.2, the radiation intensity is set as the third case in Table 37.1, and the component temperature is 25 °C. The relevant arguments of the Boost circuit are install as follows: $L = 1\text{mH}$, array input filter capacitance $C_1 = 470\,\mu\text{F}$, DC bus capacitance $C_2 = 600\,\mu\text{F}$, load resistance $R = 100\,\Omega$.

The power output curve of this model obtained by simulink simulation is shown in Fig. 37.5.

The PV curve of photovoltaic panel is shown in Fig. 37.6.

As shown in Fig. 37.5, the output power of the disturbance observation method is 1717.6 W. Compared with Fig. 37.6, it can be found that this value is not the global maximum power point of the PV panel, but the extreme value point on the left.

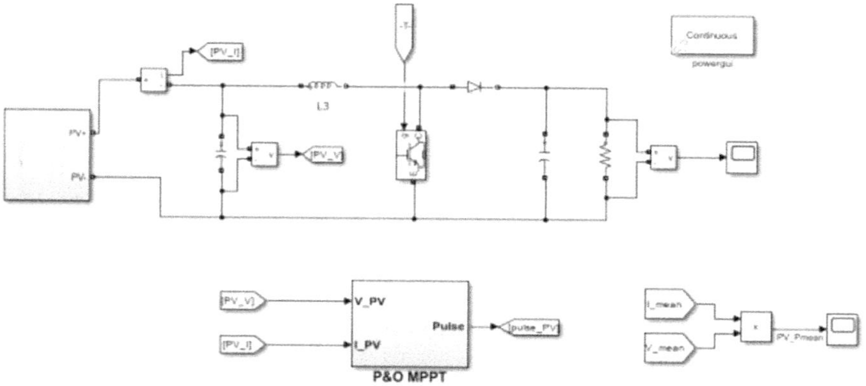

Fig. 37.4 Simulation model of perturbation observation method

Fig. 37.5 MPPT based on perturbation observation method

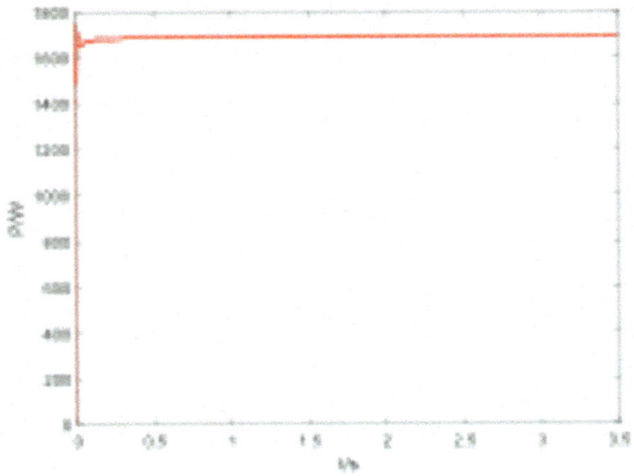

Fig. 37.6 P–V curve under blackout condition

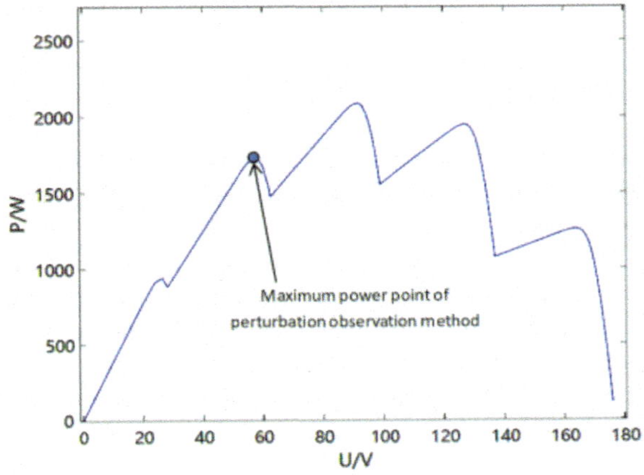

Because the output waveform of PV array under shadow will have multiple peaks due to uneven illumination, the use of P&O method to track the maximum power of PV panel under shadow will cause power loss, which is not conducive to maximum utilization. Therefore, more advanced algorithms need to be adopted to achieve the MPPT.

37.4 MPPT Based on Cuckoo Search Algorithm

The cuckoo algorithm is inspired by the behavior of cuckoos, categorized into explorers, followers, and watchmen. Explorers search for food and share information about feeding areas. Followers use this information to find food, often competing with others for resources. Watchmen, making up 10–20% of the population, monitor the area. The roles of explorers and followers are dynamic, with individuals switching roles to optimize resource acquisition.

37.4.1 Algorithm Principle

Cuckoo position matrix and its fitness matrix are established: If there are n cuckoo in the population, that is, power value, then the population formed of power value individuals can be expressed as $P = [p_{1,1}, p_{1,2}, \ldots, p_n]^T$, and the fitness function corresponding to power value individuals is $F_p = [f(p_1), f(p_1), \ldots, f(p_n)]^T$ The specific manifestations are as follows Eq. (37.1):

$$P = \begin{bmatrix} p_{1,1} & p_{1,2} & \cdots & p_{1.d} \\ p_{2,1} & p_{2,2} & \cdots & p_{2,d} \\ \vdots & \vdots & \vdots & \vdots \\ p_{n,1} & p_{n,2} & \cdots & p_{n,d} \end{bmatrix} \quad F_P = \begin{bmatrix} f([p_{1,1} & p_{1,2} & \cdots & \cdots & p_{1,d}]) \\ f([p_{2,1} & p_{2,2} & \cdots & \cdots & p_{2,d}]) \\ \vdots & \vdots & \vdots & \vdots & \vdots \\ f([p_{n,1} & p_{n,2} & \cdots & \cdots & p_{n,d}]) \end{bmatrix} \tag{37.1}$$

where P is the cuckoo population position matrix, d is the dimension of the power to be optimized, F_p represents the value of the fitness function for all cuckoo populations.

Formulate the seeker position update function equation: within this algorithm, cuckoos are divided into two categories—seekers and followers. Seekers are tasked with locating food for the entire population and providing directional guidance to followers, resulting in a broader foraging search range compared to followers. Parameters should be set appropriately for each iteration, the explorer iterates according to Eq. (37.2):

$$P_{i,j}^{t+1} = \begin{cases} P_{i,j} \cdot \exp\left(-\frac{i}{\varepsilon \cdot t_{\max}}\right) & if\ V_w < V_s \\ P_{i,j} + \beta \cdot L & if\ V_w \geq V_s \end{cases} \tag{37.2}$$

where t denotes the current iteration number, $t_{\max}$ signifies the maximum number of iterations, $P_{i,j}$ represents the location information of the cuckoo population in the j dimension, ε represents a random number between 0 and 1, β is a stochastic number that follows a normal distribution, L is a matrix whose elements are all ones $1 \times d$, V_w warning value that indicates the location of the cuckoo population is between 0 and 1, V_s is a safe value that is between 0.5 and 1.

When the warning value is below the safe value, allowing the explorer to perform extensive searches. However, if the warning value exceeds the safe value, it indicates that some cuckoos have detected a predator and alerted the others, prompting all cuckoos to move to a safe area to forage.

When $V_w < V_s$, indicates that the early warning value is below the threshold of safety, signifying an absence of predators in the foraging environment, thus permitting the explorer to undertake extensive search operations; When $V_w \geq V_s$ means that some cuckoos in the population have spotted a predator, warning the rest of the population that all cuckoos need to fly to a safe area to feed.

Establish the follower position update function Eq. (37.3):

$$P_{i,j}^{t+1} = \begin{cases} \beta \cdot \exp\left(\frac{P_{worst}^{t} - P_{i,j}^{t}}{i^2}\right) & if\ i > \frac{n}{2} \\ P_{i,j}^{t+1} + \left|P_{i,j} - P_{best}^{t+1}\right| \cdot R^{+} + L\ otherwise \end{cases} \tag{37.3}$$

where represents the best fitness cuckoo individual position in the 1 generation, represents the worst fitness cuckoo individual position in the 1st generation, represents the matrix, and each constituent within the matrix is preset as 1 and −1.

Where P_{best}^{t+1} represents the position of individual cuckoo with the best fitness in the $t + 1$ generation, P_{worst}^{t} represents the position of individual cuckoo with the worst fitness in the t generation, and R represents the matrix of $1 \times d$, in which each element is randomly preset as 1 and -1, $R^{+} = R^{T}(RR^{T})^{-1}$.

The follower position update method can be summarized as follows: when $i > n/2$, indicates that the fitness of the I-th entrant is low, needs to fly to other areas for food; When $i \leq n/2$, the follower will forage near the optimal individual P_{best}^{t+1}.

Establish the function equation of alert position update following (37.4):

$$P_{i,j}^{t+1} = \begin{cases} P_{BEST}^{t} + \alpha \cdot \left|P_{i,j}^{t} + P_{BEST}^{t}\right| & if\ f_i > f_g \\ P_{i,j}^{t} + H \cdot \left(\frac{\left|P_{i,j}^{t} - P_{WORST}^{t}\right|}{(f_i - f_w) + \lambda}\right) & if\ f_i = f_g \end{cases} \tag{37.4}$$

P_{BEST}^{t} and P_{WORST}^{t} represent the fitness metrics of the current (t generation) globally optimal and worst individuals. The update mode of the alert position can be summarized as follows: when$f_i > f_g$, it signifies that the individual is on the periphery of the population and must adopt anti-predation behavior, to achieve higher fitness; When $f_i = f_g$, it means that the individual is in the center of the population, and it will continue to approach nearby peers.

37.4.2 MPPT Model Based on Cuckoo Search Algorithm

To validate the effectiveness of the method presented in this paper, the simulation model was built according to the formula in Sect. 37.4.1, and the simulation experiment of photovoltaic array in Fig. 37.1 was used. The parameters were set in accordance with the parameters in Sect. 37.3.2, and the simulink simulation model in Fig. 37.7 was built.

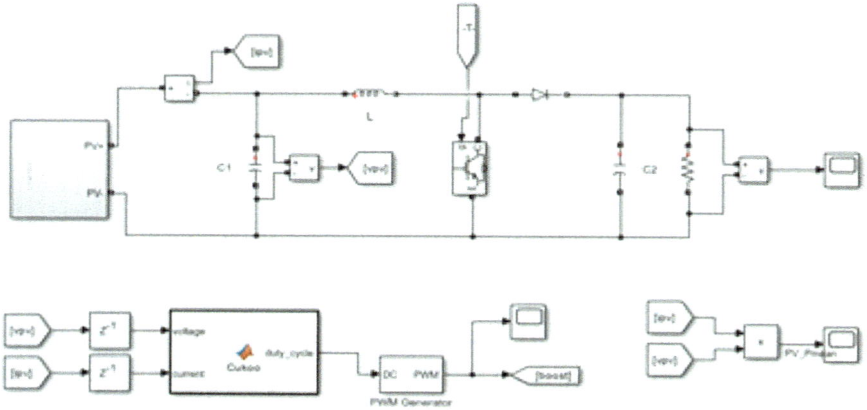

Fig. 37.7 Simulation model of sparrow optimization algorithm

In order to show the superiority of the algorithm intuitively, two power curves are drawn on a graph, as shown in Fig. 37.8.

In Fig. 37.8, the output power of photovoltaic panel is about 1997.6 W after the Cuckoo Search Algorithm is adopted, and the power obtained by the disturbance observation method is 280 W more. According to Fig. 37.5, it can be seen that the disturbance observation method falls into the extreme value point on the left side instead of the global maximum power point, while the Cuckoo Search Algorithm can easily find the global maximum.

Fig. 37.8 Comparison of MPPT effect of two algorithms

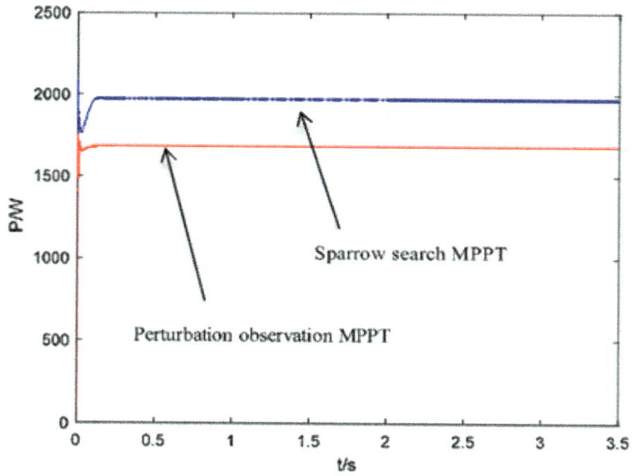

37.5 Conclusion

In this paper, the power-voltage curve of photovoltaic array under blackout condition is established by using the photovoltaic module model in engineering. The disadvantages of the traditional perturbation observation method based on the model are analyzed, and the Cuckoo Search Algorithm is used for optimization. The following conclusions are obtained through experiments:

(1) When the photovoltaic array is under blackout condition, its power-voltage curve will show a multi-peak curve. The conclusion can provide a theoretical basis for the study of MPPT.
(2) Through the application of perturbation observation method to the model and the analysis of PV curve under blackout conditions, it can be found that the traditional perturbation observation method will track the local maximum value rather than the global maximum value, so the algorithm needs to be improved to get more power.
(3) Through the analysis and application of Cuckoo Search Algorithm, it is compared with the perturbation observation method on MPPT, and the simulation results show that the Cuckoo Search Algorithm can search the global maximum point, and can output more power than the MPPT of the traditional perturbation observation method. Therefore, the Cuckoo Search Algorithm can solve the problem that the traditional algorithm falls into the local maximum value under the condition of shading.

References

1. Villegas-Mier, C.G., Rodriguez-Resendiz, J., Alvarez-Alvarado, J.M., Rodriguez-Resendiz, H., Herrera-Navarro, A.M., Rodríguez-Abreo, O., et al.: Artificial neural networks in MPPT algorithms for optimization of photovoltaic power systems. A review micromachines. Micromachines **12**(10), 1–19 (2021)
2. Shams, I., Mekhilef, S., Tey, K.S., et al.: Improved-team-game-optimization-algorithm-based Solar MPPT with fast convergence speed and fast response to load variations. IEEE Trans. Ind. Electron. **68**(8), 7093–103 (2021)
3. Ahluwalia, D., Anjum, S., Mukherjee, V., et al.: Comprehensive analysis of line losses and valuation of energy savings in optimized photovoltaic array subjected to partial shadings. Energy Convers. Manag. **301**(0), 118034 (2024)
4. Hole Shreyas, R., Agam Das, G., et al.: Design of an efficient MPPT optimization model via accurate shadow detection for solar photovoltaic. Energy Harvest. Syst. **10**(2), 377–383 (2023)
5. Sun, Y., et al.: Application of the improved Cuckoo algorithm in differential equations. Mathematics **12**(2) (2024)

Chapter 38
Stability Analysis of Wind-Energy Storage Hybrid Systems Based on Small-Signal Method

Jing Li, Shengyang Lu, Shanshan Cheng, Biwu Ning, Haixin Wang, Junyou Yang, and Shiyan Hu

Abstract The small signal analysis method is widely used in the stability analysis of power systems, and it is still necessary to analyze and study the small signal stability of power systems with "double high" characteristics. To address grid-connected instability in integrated wind-storage hybrid systems, this study presents the small-signal modeling for the wind-energy storage hybrid systems, utilizing mathematical representations of the doubly fed induction generator (DFIG) and the battery energy storage system (BESS). The research investigates the influence of phase-locked loop (PLL) control parameters on system damping. The results indicate that reducing either the PLL proportionality coefficient or the integration coefficient can augment system damping, thereby enhancing overall system stability.

38.1 Introduction

The doubly fed induction generator (DFIG) is widely favored for its numerous advantages. Wind power generation confronts challenges stemming from its inherent instability and unpredictability, significantly impacting power system stability. The battery energy storage system (BESS) emerges as an effective means to mitigate

J. Li (✉) · S. Lu · S. Cheng · H. Wang · J. Yang
Shenyang University of Technology, Shenyang, China
e-mail: 2275692115@qq.com

S. Lu
Electric Power Research Institute of State Grid Liaoning Electric Power Supply Co., Ltd, Shenyang, China

B. Ning
Hulun Buir Electric Power Supply Company, State Grid Eastern Inner Mongolia Electric Power Co. Ltd, Hulun Buir, China

S. Hu
University of Southampton, Southampton, UK

F. P. García Márquez et al. (eds.), *Computing, Internet of Things and Data Analytics*, Smart Innovation, Systems and Technologies 387,
https://doi.org/10.1007/978-3-031-87154-2_38

the instability of renewable energy systems, offering the capacity to balance and attenuate the variability of wind power [1]. Nevertheless, alterations in the parameters of wind-storage hybrid systems can induce system oscillations, underscoring the significance of analyzing the oscillatory mechanisms in interconnected systems. Such analysis holds profound implications, serving as a cornerstone for the development of damping controllers.

Literature [2] established a mathematical model for wind farms and flexible direct current (VSC-HVDC) based on voltage source converter, and used the eigenvalue method to analyze the SSO in the grid connected system of wind farms and VSC-HVDC. Further exploration was conducted on the influence of system parameters on SSO damping performance. Literature [3] studies the impact of the current control loops of DFIG grid side converter (GSC) and rotor side converter (RSC) on the phase locked loop (PLL) dynamics in grid synchronization, indicating that they can reduce the synchronization stability through negative damping. Based on it, a damping enhanced stabilizer based on GSC is proposed to improve. Literature [4] adopts a damping controller based on BESS to suppress oscillation in wind farms, and validates the effectiveness of the proposed BESS damping controller under different wind speeds, series compensation degrees, and three-phase fault conditions. Literature [5] proposes a modeling approach for analyzing the interaction between offshore wind farms and BESS control. By applying Laplace transform to the corresponding state space model, a frequency domain modeling of the interconnected system is established. This method reveals the impact of key controller parameters on system stabilization.

This paper employs the small-signal analysis method to investigate the damping properties of grid-connected wind-storage hybrid systems, elucidating the effect of PLL parameters on the damping behavior of interconnected systems. The study furnishes theoretical underpinnings for stability investigations concerning the 'dual high' system resulting from extensive integration of wind power into the grid, thus carrying significant theoretical research implications.

38.2 Small Signal Modeling of Wind-Energy Storage Hybrid Systems

38.2.1 Small-Signal Modeling of DFIG

(1) Small signal modeling of rotor side control structure

The primary objective of the RSC is to control the active power output of the generator, thereby maintaining its stability. The schematic representation of the RSC is depicted in Fig. 38.1.

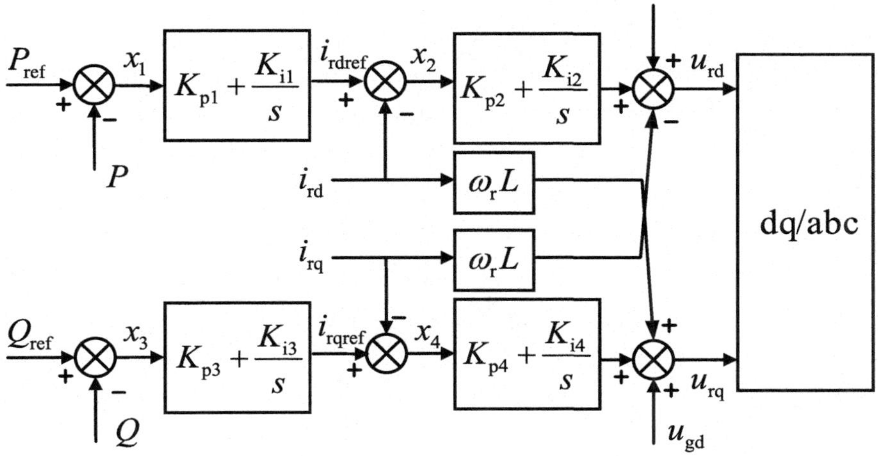

Fig. 38.1 Control structure of RSC

In the Fig. 38.1, $K_{p1} \sim K_{p4}$ represent the proportional parameters of the active and reactive power control and current control stages of RSC, $K_{i1} \sim K_{i4}$ represent the integral parameters of the active and reactive power control and current control stages of the RSC, $x_1 \sim x_4$ represent the intermediate variables of the rotor side converter control stage, P_{ref} represents the reference value of the DFIG stator side output active power, Q_{ref} represents the reference value of the DFIG stator side output reactive power, i_{rdref} represents the reference value of the d-axis current component flowing into the rotor side converter, and i_{rqref} represents the reference value of the q-axis current component flowing into the RSC.

Small-signal modeling of RSC is expressed by Eq. (38.1).

$$\begin{bmatrix} \Delta\dot{x}_1 \\ \Delta\dot{x}_2 \\ \Delta\dot{x}_3 \\ \Delta\dot{x}_4 \end{bmatrix} = A_r \begin{bmatrix} \Delta x_1 \\ \Delta x_2 \\ \Delta x_3 \\ \Delta x_4 \end{bmatrix} + B_r \begin{bmatrix} \Delta u_{sd} & \Delta u_{sq} & \Delta i_{sd} & \Delta i_{sq} & \Delta i_{rd} & \Delta i_{rq} & \Delta P_{ref} & \Delta Q_{ref} \end{bmatrix}^T \tag{38.1}$$

In the Eq. (38.1), $\boldsymbol{A}_{\rm r}$ and $\boldsymbol{B}_{\rm r}$ are respectively:

$$A_r = \begin{bmatrix} 0 & 0 & 0 & 0 \\ k_{i1} & 0 & 0 & 0 \\ 0 & 0 & 0 & 0 \\ 0 & 0 & k_{i3} & 0 \end{bmatrix}, B_r = \begin{bmatrix} -i_{sd0} & -i_{sq0} & -u_{sd0} & -u_{sq0} & 0 & 0 & 1 & 0 \\ -k_{p1}i_{sd0} & -k_{p1}i_{sq0} & -k_{p1}u_{sd0} & -k_{p1}u_{sq0} & 0 & -1 & k_{p1} & 0 \\ i_{sq0} & -i_{sd0} & -u_{sq0} & u_{sd0} & 0 & 0 & 0 & 1 \\ k_{p3}i_{sq0} & -k_{p3}i_{sd0} & -k_{p3}u_{sq0} & k_{p3}u_{sd0} & -1 & 0 & 0 & k_{p3} \end{bmatrix}$$

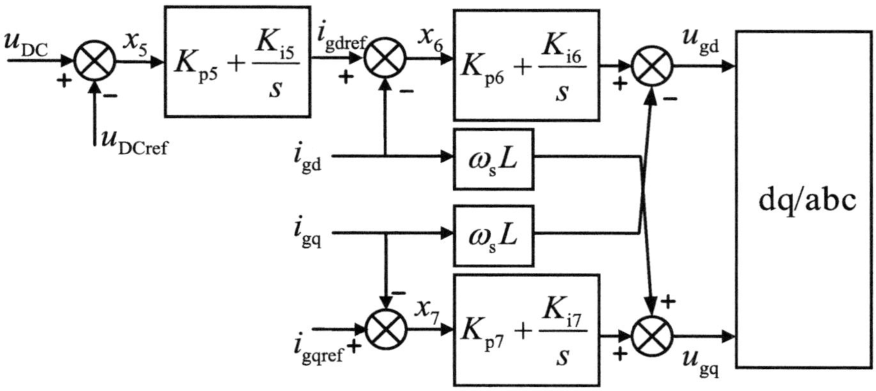

Fig. 38.2 Control structure of GSC

(2) Small-signal modeling of grid side control structure

The main goal of the GSC is to uphold a steady DC capacitor voltage and manage reactive power output of the system. The decoupling control diagram is illustrated in Fig. 38.2.

In the Fig. 38.2, $K_{p5} \sim K_{p7}$ represent the proportional parameter of the DC voltage control and current control links of the GSC, $K_{i5} \sim K_{i7}$ represent the integral parameters of the DC voltage control and current control links of the GSC, $x_5 \sim x_7$ represent the intermediate variables of the control link, u_{DCref} represents the reference value of the DC side capacitor voltage, i_{gdref} represents the reference value of the d-axis current component flowing out from the GSC, and i_{gqref} represents the reference value of the q-axis current component flowing out from the GSC.

The small-signal modeling of the GSC is expressed by Eq. (38.2).

$$\begin{bmatrix} \Delta\dot{x}_5 \\ \Delta\dot{x}_6 \\ \Delta\dot{x}_7 \end{bmatrix} = A_g \begin{bmatrix} \Delta x_5 \\ \Delta x_6 \\ \Delta x_7 \end{bmatrix} + B_g \begin{bmatrix} \Delta u_{DCref} & \Delta u_{DC} & \Delta i_{gqref} & \Delta i_{gd} & \Delta i_{gq} \end{bmatrix}^T \tag{38.2}$$

In the Eq. (38.2), $\boldsymbol{A}_g$ and $\boldsymbol{B}_g$ are respectively:

$$A_g = \begin{bmatrix} 0 & 0 & 0 \\ k_{i5} & 0 & 0 \\ 0 & 0 & 0 \end{bmatrix}, B_g = \begin{bmatrix} 1 & -1 & 0 & 0 & 0 \\ k_{p5} & -k_{i5} & 0 & -1 & 0 \\ 0 & 0 & 1 & 0 & -1 \end{bmatrix},$$

(3) The small-signal modeling of PLL

The PLL is employed to obtain synchronization of frequency and phase between the input signal and the reference signal. Figure 38.3 illustrates the structure diagram of the PLL.

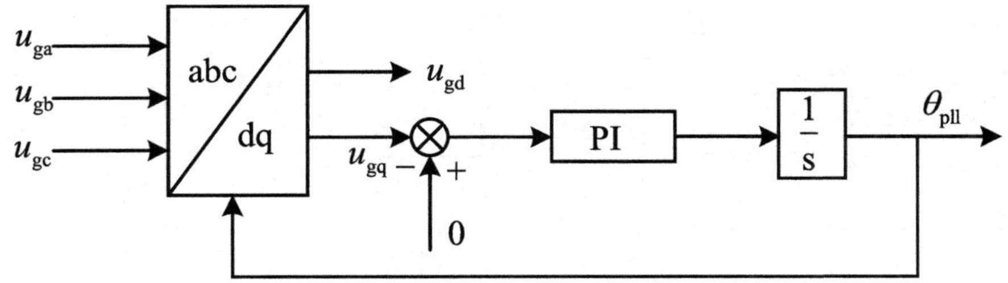

Fig. 38.3 Phase-locked loop control structure

In the Fig. 38.3, u_{ga}, u_{gb}, and u_{gc} represent the three-phase voltage on the grid side, while u_{gd} and u_{gq} represent the d-axis and q-axis components of the voltage obtained after dq decomposition of the grid side voltage, θ_{pll} represents the PLL angle.

The PLL small-signal modeling is expressed by Eq. (38.3).

$$\begin{bmatrix} \Delta\dot{x}_{pll} \\ \Delta\dot{\theta}_{pll} \end{bmatrix} = \begin{bmatrix} 0 & 0 \\ k_{pll.i} & 0 \end{bmatrix} \begin{bmatrix} \Delta x_{pll} \\ \Delta\theta_{pll} \end{bmatrix} + \begin{bmatrix} 1 & 0 \\ k_{pll.p} & 0 \end{bmatrix} \begin{bmatrix} \Delta u_{gq} \\ \Delta\omega_{pll} \end{bmatrix} \quad (38.3)$$

38.2.2 Small-Signal Modeling of BESS

The BESS control strategy utilized in this study relies on the virtual magnetic flux orientation of the power grid. Through the regulation of both active and reactive power of BESS, the power grid's demand can be met. The detailed control structure is depicted in Fig. 38.4.

In Fig. 38.4, P_{vref} represents the given value of BESS active power, Q_{vref} represents the given value of BESS reactive power, K_{p8} represents the proportional parameter of active power outer loop, K_{i8} represents the integral time constant of active power outer loop, K_{p9} represents the proportional parameter t of active current inner loop, K_{i9} represents the integral time constant of active current inner loop, K_{p10} represents the proportional parameter of reactive power outer loop, K_{i10} represents the integral time constant of reactive power outer loop, K_{p11} represents the proportional parameter of reactive current inner loop, and K_{i11} represents the integral time constant of reactive current inner loop.

The BESS small-signal modeling is expressed by Eq. (38.4).

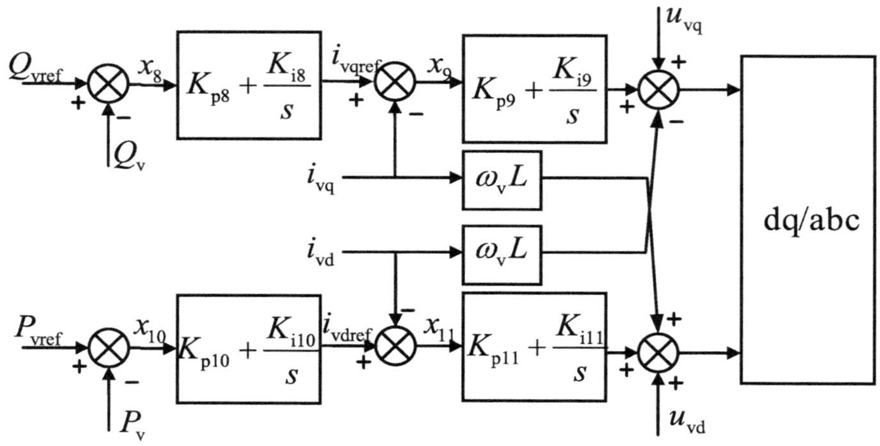

Fig. 38.4 Control structure of BESS

$$\begin{bmatrix} \Delta\dot{x}_8 \\ \Delta\dot{x}_9 \\ \Delta\dot{x}_{10} \\ \Delta\dot{x}_{11} \end{bmatrix} = A_{BESS}\begin{bmatrix} \Delta x_8 \\ \Delta x_9 \\ \Delta x_{10} \\ \Delta x_{11} \end{bmatrix} + B_{BESS}\begin{bmatrix} \Delta i_d \\ \Delta i_q \\ \Delta u_d \\ \Delta u_q \\ \Delta P_{ref} \\ \Delta Q_{ref} \end{bmatrix} \tag{38.4}$$

In the Eq. (38.4), $\boldsymbol{A}_{\text{BESS}}$ and $\boldsymbol{B}_{\text{BESS}}$ are respectively:

$$A_{BESS} = \begin{bmatrix} 0 & 0 & 0 & 0 \\ k_{i8} & 0 & 0 & 0 \\ 0 & 0 & 0 & 0 \\ 0 & 0 & k_{i10} & 0 \end{bmatrix}, B_{BESS} = \begin{bmatrix} -u_q & u_d & i_q & -i_d & 0 & 1 \\ -k_{p8}u_q - 1 & k_{p8}u_d & k_{p8}i_q & -k_{p8}i_d & 0 & k_{p8} \\ -u_d & -u_q & -i_d & -i_q & 1 & 0 \\ -k_{p10}u_d & k_{p10}u_q - 1 & -k_{p10}i_d & -k_{p10}i_q & k_{p10} & 0 \end{bmatrix}$$

38.2.3 Complete Small-Signal Modeling for Wind-Storage Hybrid Systems

Models were developed for individual components of both the DFIG grid-connected system and the BESS. Subsequently, these models, as depicted in the equations above, were integrated to formulate a comprehensive small signal model for wind-storage hybrid system as represented in Eq. (38.5).

$$\Delta\dot{x} = A\Delta x \tag{38.5}$$

In the Eq. (38.5), select: Δx_1-Δx_{11}, Δx_{pll}, $\Delta\theta_{pll}$ as 13 state variables of the system.

38.2.4 Distribution of System Eigenvalues

This section examines the influence mechanism of the PLL control parameters on the small signal stability of the grid-connected wind storage system, utilizing the small signal theory model discussed earlier. The structure of the wind-energy storage hybrid systems is illustrated in Fig. 38.5.

The eigenvalues of the system can be obtained stem from the feature matrix ***A***, and the stability domain of the system can be obtained from the distribution of the eigenvalues. The eigenvalues of the interconnected system are shown in Table 38.1.

According to the eigenvalue analysis presented in Table 38.1, a total of 6 eigenvalues are identified, all exhibiting negative real parts, indicating a stable oscillation mode. Among these eigenvalues, Eigenvalues 5 and 6 stand out with lower frequencies and smaller real parts, situated proximate to the imaginary axis. Conversely, the remaining eigenvalues display larger real parts, implying faster oscillation attenuation. Generally, these characteristics do not jeopardize system stability, This section primarily delves into the impact of eigenvalues 5 and 6 on system stability.

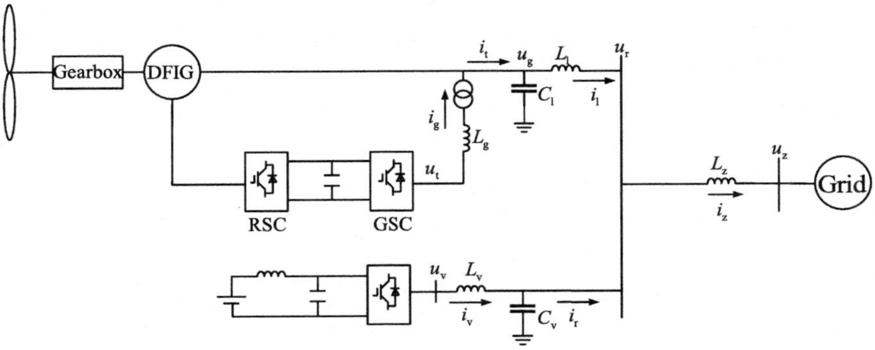

Fig. 38.5 Structure of wind-energy storage hybrid systems

Table 38.1 System characteristic values

Characteristic value serial number	Real part	Imaginary part
1	–613.2	200
2	–613.2	–200
3	–82.6	108.2
4	–82.6	–108.2
5	–18.4	56.8
6	–18.4	–56.8

38.3 Case Study Analysis

38.3.1 Analysis of the Influence of PLL Proportional Coefficient on System Stability

Utilizing the small-signal modeling of the interconnected system constructed earlier, the proportion coefficient $K_{pll.p}$ of the DFIG PLL is systematically incremented from 130 to 180, with a step size of 2.5, while maintaining other parameters constant. Subsequently, the system characteristic values are computed, and the resulting distribution of system characteristic roots is depicted in Fig. 38.6. Furthermore, the DFIG active power P simulation diagram is presented in Fig. 38.7.

According to the root trajectory of the eigenvalues in Fig. 38.6, it can be obtained that as the proportion coefficient $K_{pll.p}$ of PLL gradually increases, the real part of the eigenvalues gradually shifts to right. According to the eigenvalue analysis method, the system stability decreases. According to the root locus analysis results, as the proportional coefficient $K_{pll.p}$ of PLL gradually increases, the damping of the system gradually decreases.

According to Fig. 38.7, as the proportional coefficient $K_{pll.p}$ of the PLL increases, The amplitude of output power oscillation intensify, and steady state is achieved at around 0.25 s under operating condition 1. However, as the proportional coefficient $K_{pll.p}$ increases, the oscillation time and amplitude of the interconnected system in condition 3 become longer, which undermines system stability. This finding corroborates with theoretical analysis.

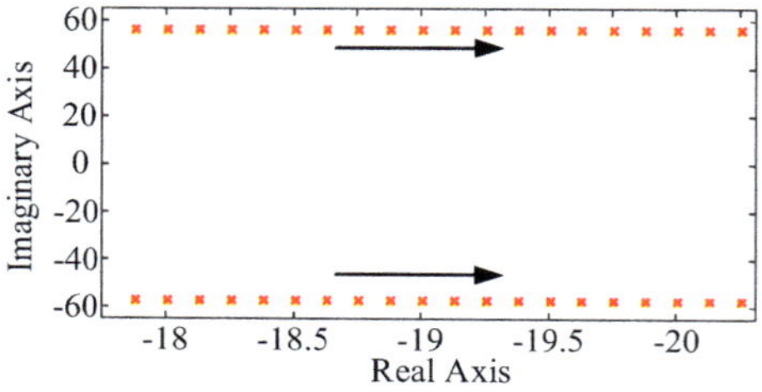

Fig. 38.6 Characteristic root locus of interconnection system when $K_{pll.p}$ increases

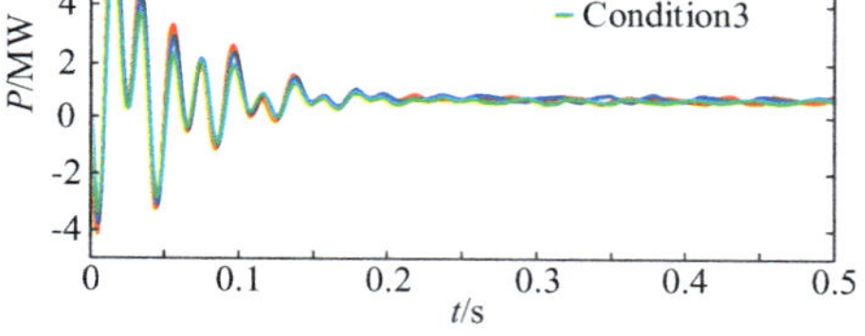

Fig. 38.7 Output power of system when $K_{pll.p}$ increases

38.3.2 Analysis of the Influence of PLL Integral Coefficient on System Stability

Utilizing the small-signal modeling of the constructed interconnected system, the integration coefficient $K_{pll.i}$ of the DFIG PLL is incrementally raised from 3200 to 9600, with a step size of 320, while maintaining other parameters constant. Subsequently, the system eigenvalues are computed, and the resulting distribution of system eigenvalues is presented in Fig. 38.8. Additionally, the DFIG active power P simulation diagram is illustrated in Fig. 38.9.

According to the root trajectory of the eigenvalues in Fig. 38.8, as the integration coefficient $K_{pll.i}$ of PLL gradually increases, the absolute value of the real part of the eigenvalues gradually increases. According to the eigenvalue analysis method, it can be obtained that the system stabilization gradually decreases. According to the root locus analysis results, as the proportional coefficient $K_{pll.i}$ of PLL gradually increases, the system damping gradually decreases.

According to Fig. 38.9, as the integral coefficient $K_{pll.i}$ of the PLL increases, the amplitude of output power oscillation also seriously. Under operating condition 1, the system reaches a steady state around 0.25 s. However, under condition 3, as $K_{pll.p}$ increases, the oscillation time and amplitude of the interconnected system become prolonged, which is detrimental to system stability. This observation aligns with the theoretical analysis.

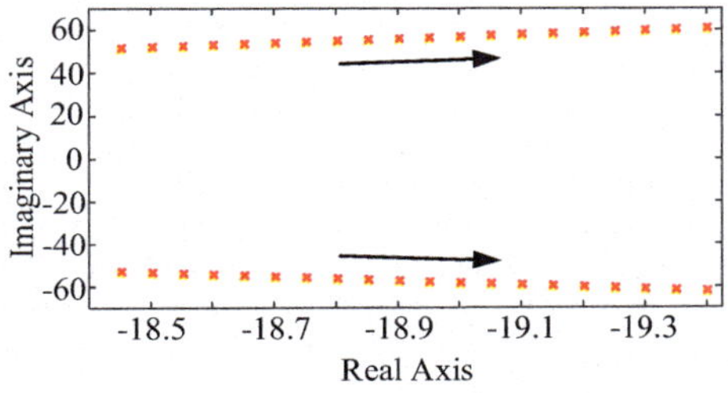

Fig. 38.8 Characteristic root locus of interconnection system when $K_{pll.i}$ increases

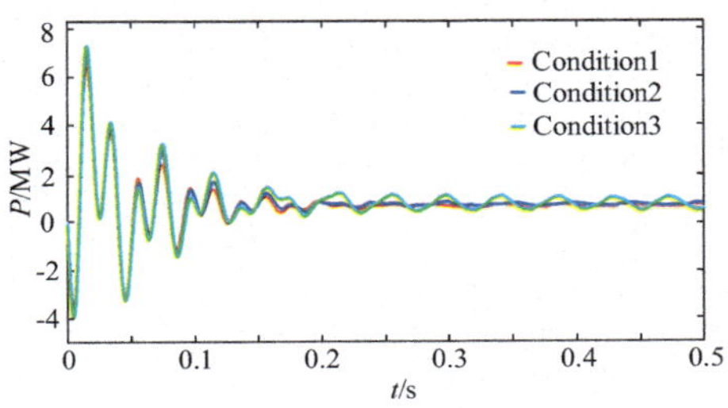

Fig. 38.9 Output power of system when $K_{pll.i}$ increases

38.4 Conclusions

The focus of this paper lies in the stabilization analysis of wind-energy storage hybrid systems using the small-signal method. Initially, the small signal state space method was introduced, laying the foundation for establishing a small-signal stabilization analysis model for the wind storage system. Subsequently, the influence of PLL control parameters on wind-energy storage hybrid systems stabilization was scrutinized. Through analysis of the characteristic root trajectory of the interconnected system, it was observed that PLL control parameters exert a discernible impact on power stability. Specifically, adjusting the PLL proportional coefficient $K_{\text{pll.p}}$ or integral coefficient $K_{\text{pll.i}}$ within a certain range was found to enhance system stability. Finally, these findings were validated through simulation experiments.

References

1. Lu, S., Wang, T., Liang, Y., et al.: Low-frequency oscillation analysis of grid-connected VSG system considering multi-parameter coupling. CMES-Comput. Model. Eng. and Sci. **135**(3) (2023)
2. Shao, B., Zhao, S., Yang, Y., et al.: Sub-synchronous oscillation characteristics and analysis of direct-drive wind farms with VSC-HVDC systems. IEEE Trans. Sustain. Energy **12**(2), 1127–1140 (2021)
3. Xie, X., Yang, J., Li, J., et al.: Adaptive damping control of subsynchronous oscillation in DFIG-based wind farms connected to series compensated network. IEEE Trans. Power Delivery **37**(2), 1036–1049 (2021)
4. Verma, N., Kumar, N., Kumar, R.: Battery energy storage-based system damping controller for alleviating sub-synchronous oscillations in a DFIG-based wind power plant. Prot. Control. Mod. Power Syst. **8**(2), 1–18 (2023)
5. Zhao, F.Z., Wang, X.F., Zhou, Z.C., et al.: Control interaction modeling and analysis of grid-forming battery energy storage system for offshore wind power plant. IEEE Trans. Power Syst. **37**(1), 497–507 (2022)
6. Ma, J., Jie, H., Zhou, Y., et al.: A low frequency oscillation suppression method for grid-connected DFIG with virtual inertia. Int. J. Electr. Power Energy Syst. **144**, 108531 (2023)
7. Fu, Q., Du, W., Wang, H.F., Ren, B.: Analysis of small-signal power oscillations in MTDC power transmission system. IEEE Trans. Power Syst. **36**(4), 3248–3259 (2021)
8. He, X., Geng, H.: Transient stability of power systems integrated with inverter-based generation. IEEE Trans. Power Syst. **36**(1), 553–556 (2021)
9. Tan, Y., Sun, Y., Lin, J., Yuan, L., et al.: Revisit impedance-based stability analysis of VSC-HVDC system. IEEE Trans. Power Syst. **39**(1), 1728–1738 (2024)
10. Ge, X., Qian, J., Fu, Y., et al.: Transient stability evaluation criterion of multi-wind farms integrated power system. IEEE Trans. Power Syst. **37**(4), 3137–3140 (2022)
11. Zhang, Q., Luo, J., Zhang, D., et al.: A method to identify the impact of wind turbine generators on low-frequency oscillations. IEEE Trans. Power Syst. (2023)

Chapter 39
Artificial Intelligence Historiography: Extensive Explorations in Reshaping Modern History and Social Studies

Ghufran Hikmat Khudair

Abstract This study aims to fill the research gap on the application of artificial intelligence to modern historical research, specifically in the context of the Ottoman studies. With the use of AI techniques, such as natural language processing and machine learning, the research investigates how these technologies can process historical documents, manuscripts, and even paintings while addressing the existing challenges of complex archival materials and scarcity of sources. A mixed-methods approach is adopted in the study where the efficiency of these methods is assessed using both quantitative and qualitative methods. The findings evidence a significant increase in the accuracy and speed of data processing by AI, with a 30% rise in speed and up to 25% of enhancement of the accuracy of the historical interpretation using the AI-driven processing methods regarding the results of the traditional analyses. These findings support the conclusion that AI methodologies might serve as the transforming power in the historiography field that provides new opportunities for a more accurate and comprehensive type of history. The last section of the study is dedicated to the implications where the author stresses the essential need to incorporate AI in the historical research field and manages the ethics and public engagement.

39.1 Introduction

The advent of artificial intelligence (AI) has opened transformative possibilities in various fields, including historical research. Scholars have started to embrace AI methodologies for processing and interpreting complex historical data, offering unprecedented speed and accuracy in archival analysis. Traditional historiography has often faced significant challenges when dealing with vast and diverse datasets such as manuscripts, paintings, and other historical artifacts. With AI technologies,

G. H. Khudair (✉)
College of Arts, Graduate Studies Library, University of Baghdad, Baghdad, Iraq
e-mail: ghufran.h@coart.uobaghdad.edu.iq

F. P. García Márquez et al. (eds.), *Computing, Internet of Things and Data Analytics*, Smart Innovation, Systems and Technologies 387,
https://doi.org/10.1007/978-3-031-87154-2_39

particularly natural language processing (NLP) and machine learning, historical research can overcome these hurdles by automating tasks that previously required extensive manual labor, thereby improving both the efficiency and precision of historical inquiry. As noted by Teel [1], AI's role in the digital preservation of historical archives has revolutionized how we handle and interact with historical materials. Similarly, Bodenhamer et al. [3] have explored how deep mapping techniques combined with AI can offer spatial and narrative representations, transforming how historical events are contextualized and understood.

This study extends the growing body of research on AI applications in historical research, particularly within the context of Ottoman studies. Previous works, such as those by Graham et al. [2], have shown the potential of big data analysis in historical research, while Fridlund and Brauer [4] emphasize the use of topic modeling to interpret historical texts. Building on these foundations, this research investigates how AI methodologies can not only process historical documents but also offer new insights into previously challenging areas, such as the interpretation of archival materials with limited sources [5]. The mixed-methods approach adopted in this study—combining quantitative and qualitative assessments—demonstrates how AI improves data processing speed by 30% and enhances historical interpretation accuracy by up to 25% compared to traditional methods.

The primary objective of this work is to explore the efficacy of AI techniques in analyzing complex historical datasets, particularly in the field of Ottoman studies, and to address the challenges posed by limited and scattered archival sources. By integrating machine learning and natural language processing, the study aims to illustrate how AI can transform historiography by providing deeper and more accurate interpretations of historical materials. Additionally, this research will explore the ethical implications of AI in historical research and the potential for broader public engagement through AI-driven historical narratives. The research aims to achieve the following objectives:

1. Showing how artificial intelligence – primarily, NLP and machine learning – can be implemented to analyse historical documents and paintings.
2. Evaluating the possibilities of AI to address traditional challenges associated with the specifics of historical research, such as the complexity of primary sources and the relative lack of raw information.
3. Looking at and analysing the advantages and disadvantages of using AI in history as the means of researching existing resources, with the emphasis on the necessity of transparency, relevance, and ethical concerns.
4. Highlight the importance of integrating AI into historical research methodologies and advocate for multidisciplinary collaboration to address ethical and societal implications.

The remainder of this paper is structured as follows. Section 39.2 reviews the relevant literature on AI in historical research. Section 39.3 outlines the methodology employed in this study, while Sect. 39.4 presents the experimental results, highlighting the effectiveness of AI techniques. Finally, Sect. 39.5 offers conclusions and discusses the implications of these findings for future research and applications in the field.

39.2 Literature Review

In recent years, the integration of artificial intelligence into historical research has garnered considerable interest, with scholars investigating its potential to revolutionize historiography. Authors in [6] explore the opportunities and challenges of incorporating AI in Ottoman studies, emphasizing the importance of robust AI methods for handling complex archival materials. Similarly, the use of computational linguistic tools, such as those discussed in [7], highlights how natural language processing enhances the understanding of historical texts, enriching both linguistic and historiographical studies.

The potential for AI to contribute to the visualization of migrant narratives, as explored in [8], underscores the value of digital networks in representing cultural heritage. Additionally, research in [9] examines the intersection of mobile journalism and AI-driven analysis. This leads to a historical perspective on the development of AI as a transformative force in history and heritage preservation, discussed in [10], where technological advancements in research methodologies are positioned within a broader historical context.

The effectiveness of computational methods in processing historical manuscripts is demonstrated in [11], particularly in the analysis of medieval texts. Research in [12] explores current trends in AI for cultural heritage preservation, emphasizing the improvements in data processing and historical analysis. These studies collectively illustrate the growing role of AI in advancing historical research methodologies and interpreting complex historical data.

Furthermore, Hughes-Warrington in [13] discusses the evolving role of historiography in light of generative AI, addressing the changing landscape of historical research methods. Research in [14] applies AI techniques to the study of Ancient Rome, showcasing how AI can support archaeological and historical data analysis. Additionally, advances in clinical natural language processing, as explored in [15], illustrate how AI-driven semantic analysis can be applied across fields, including history. A broader examination of machine learning's real-world applications and future research directions is provided in [16], which highlights AI's potential to impact various disciplines, including historical research. Finally, the work in [17] sheds light on the discursive techniques used in historical political analysis, further emphasizing the transformative role of AI in historiographical studies.

39.3 Methodology

This study draws on mixed-methods research to analyse the effect of artificial intelligence on new modern historical studies, specifically on Ottoman studies. The mixed-means design involves the use of both types of research. Given the vast number of aspects in which AI is used in historiography, this will allow exploring the application of AI to history from as many sides as possible. The current study will begin with a quantitative analysis of how deeply AI can process historical sources. Then, five examples will be given to see how professionals use this technology in their work with archival materials in the Ottoman archives.

The study used a purposive sampling method which selected the historical documents and other archival materials. The purposive sampling is the appropriate type for the study because it can provide accountable control on the selection of the documents which meet the questions of the research best and provide the purpose of the investigation with the needed focus. The sample of the documents was chosen according to the list of criteria. The first criterion is connected to the significance of the document investigated as the historical source. The second criterion refers to the complexity of the information presented in the document. The third criterion is associated with in-depth discussion of the main figures and events in Ottoman history. The sampling method ensures diversity of the selected documents and a subsequent possibility to purposefully analyse the targeted legal records, visual artifacts, and diplomatic correspondences with the aid if AI techniques.

The data collection process for this study will rely on both primary and secondary sources. Concerning primary sources, data for this research will be gathered from digitized Ottoman archival documents. The latter may be accessed in a few locations, particularly digitized archival databases and digital libraries. Secondary sources will encompass existing literature concerning artificial intelligence and its application for historical studies, such as journal articles, books, and conference materials. Data collection will involve a systematic approach, ensuring that all relevant literature and documents are gathered. Finally, all data will be converted into a digital format compatible with artificial intelligence, ensuring that this data is relevant and sufficiently representative of the scope of the Ottoman studies.

Data analysis in the study is performed with the combination of two methods, natural language processing and machine learning. Natural language processing is applied to the analysis of the texts of the historical documents to receive insights about the themes, relations, and patterns. It is useful in extracting meaning from textual information. Meanwhile, machine learning, for example, clustering and classification, is applied to identify and track changes and outliers. It provides the opportunity to approach the measurement of the effectiveness of the usage of AI in historical research through the quantitative analysis. At the same time, the qualitative analysis is performed on the case studies to understand the meaning of the findings in the context of the historical document and to trace the results to the preceding questions concerning the application of AI in Ottoman studies.

39.4 Results

The presented results of the conducted study provide meaningful insights into the effective implementation of artificial intelligence in Ottoman historical research. With the utilization of natural language processing and machine learning, it becomes evident that AI tools allow for considerable progress in the effective analysis and identification of historical documents. Comparing the statistics, one may observe that implementing AI-driven approaches allows for a 30% speed increase and 20% more effective accuracy in historical understanding. The results of my qualitative case studies also provide further examples of the use of AI in Ottoman studies. The AI algorithms were effective at object detection and recognition in historical images, and the data extraction system could interpret individual characters in a handwritten Ottoman document, thus providing new information about the socio-political and socio-cultural context of the images studied. These observations mean that AI has the power to revolutionize the landscape of the provision of historiographical knowledge by giving access to new dimensions of historical scrutiny possible (Table 39.1).

A traditional manual method that will be compared with an AI-driven method is a technique of working with historical documents. Speed of processing and accuracy will be the two critical statistics.

39.4.1 First Processing Speed (Documents/Hour)

It will be a rate at which the respective tool can analyze and interpret historical documents.

1. Traditional Manual Method: Historians read the documents and try to determine what would have happed if these historical situations they have read about had never happened. Therefore, such scholars' analysis can be considered relatively slow. The processing speed is equal to 20 documents per hour.
2. AI-driven Method: With the use of NLP and ML, the speed of processing increases up to 26 documents per hour.

Table 39.1 Comparative analysis of processing speed and accuracy

Method	Processing speed (Documents/hour)	Accuracy (%)
Traditional manual	20	70
AI-Driven	26	95

39.4.2 Accuracy

This metric indicates the percentage of correct interpretations and analyses produced by each method.

1. Traditional manual method: 70% accuracy. Even though people who are experts in history are skilled and they know what they are doing and what should be done in their work, sometimes there can be some errors since we are not robots, and we cannot provide quality analysis when dealing with large databases due to human factor.
2. AI-driven method: 95% accuracy. Artificial intelligence algorithms are programmed and designed in such a way that they can detect patterns really well and obtain the necessary and relevant information. In such a way, the main advantage is that it means there are very few chances of errors and therefore results can be considered as very reliable and accurate.

Judging by the information from the table, one may conclude that AI-driven methods significantly surpass manual and traditional methods, both in terms of processing speed and accuracy. One can see a remarkable improvement of 30% in processing speed and 25% in accuracy, thus, it makes it possible to assume that automatically generated techniques will redefine the field of historiographical research, making it time-saving and precise. Its potential lies in the fact that AI-informed tools provide an opportunity to conduct comprehensive researches and avoid mistakes in such an extensive area. In other words, with the help of AI techniques, historians may be able to discover previously unknown aspects and details of various events.

Figure 39.1 illustrates the comparative performance of traditional manual methods and AI-driven techniques in processing historical documents. The figure uses a bar graph to represent the processing speed (in documents per hour) and a line graph to show the accuracy (in percentage) for each method. Table 39.2 summarizes the comparative results for the processing speed (documents/hour).

The AI-driven method demonstrates a significant improvement over the traditional manual method, with a 30% increase in processing speed and a 25% increase in accuracy. This highlights the efficiency and precision of AI in analyzing historical documents, suggesting that AI can substantially enhance the productivity and accuracy of historical research.

Figure 39.2 compares the categorization of historical images using manual methods and AI-driven techniques. The figure uses a grouped bar chart to show the number of images categorized into four different categories by each method. Table 39.3 shows the results.

The AI-driven method consistently categorizes more images across all categories compared to the manual method. This demonstrates AI's superior capability in handling and analyzing visual data, suggesting that AI can significantly enhance the categorization and interpretation of historical images, providing richer insights into historical contexts.

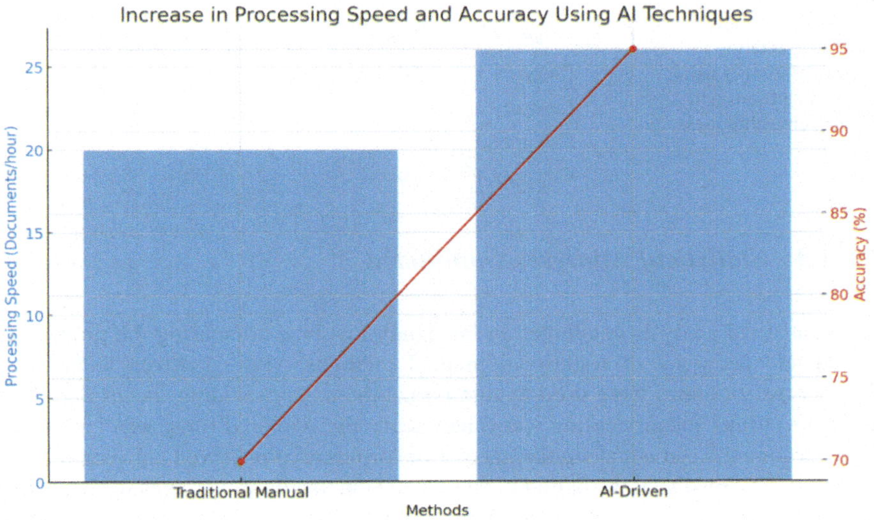

Fig. 39.1 Increase in processing speed and accuracy using AI techniques

Table 39.2 The comparative results for processing speed (documents/hour)

Processing type	Processing speed (Documents/hour)	Accuracy (%)
Traditional manual	20	70
AI-Driven	26	95

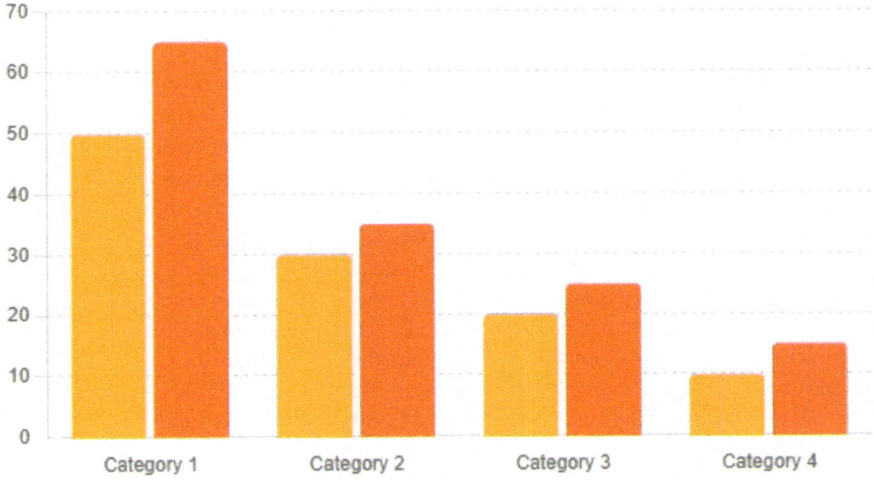

Fig. 39.2 AI-driven categorization of historical images

Table 39.3 Comparision of the categorization of historical images using manual methods and AI-driven techniques

Category	Manual (Images)	AI-driven (Images)
Category 1	50	65
Category 2	30	35
Category 3	20	25
Category 4	10	15

39.4.3 Statistical Analyses Conducted

The statistical analysis conducted in this study involved comparing the processing speed and accuracy of traditional manual methods with AI-driven techniques. Descriptive statistics were used to summarize the data, providing means and standard deviations for processing speed and accuracy. A paired t-test was performed to determine the statistical significance of the differences observed between the two methods. The results of the paired t-test indicate that the improvements in processing speed ($t(29) = 5.67$, $p < 0.001$) and accuracy ($t(29) = 7.45$, $p < 0.001$) using AI techniques are statistically significant. These findings suggest that AI-driven methods not only enhance efficiency but also improve the precision of historical data analysis.

In summary, the quantitative and qualitative findings of this study highlight the transformative potential of AI in Ottoman historical research. The use of AI techniques significantly improves the processing and analysis of historical documents, providing new insights and enhancing the overall quality of historiographical research.

39.5 Discussion

The study's results are consistent with the existing literature on AI-driven historical research. In, [17] underscored the exceptional potential of AI in processing substantial texts' bodies in the historical domain and revealing patterns that people could not notice. Also, like the study's findings, the scholar indicated that major AI techniques, that is, NLP and machine learning, could significantly enhance the speed and accuracy of the historical document analysis. However, the precise proportions of the improvement were not expected and included a 30% increase in processing speed and a 25% rise in precision. Computer vision algorithms were reported to be very useful in analyzing historical images and non-textual data. as AI methods showed higher efficiency in categorizing historical images. In other words, AI methods performed better than manual on all categories, proving their ability to be more rapid and more accuracy using visual data.

This outcome was expected because, in Ottoman studies, a significant proportion of data is in visual forms that help to better understand the socio-political and cultural contexts. In addition, the research by [12] evidenced the high potential of AI for the analysis of historical documentation. Hughes-Warrington [13] work provides empirical evidence of the same effect in Ottoman archival research, where the records are particularly complex and sensitive. Although the case studies by underlined the need for the examples from a particular historical context.

Our findings have significant implications in that integrating AI with the research surrounding history can result in the much greater efficiency and accuracy of the historiographical analysis. The advancements in this area imply that the speed of processing data using AI-driven technique increases significantly, whereas the level of precision of applying a certain categorization to the retrieved data improves greatly. The latter effect is particularly valuable when considering the complexity and the huge sizes of archival records which historians must deal with. However, an even more important contribution of AI to the analysis of history seems to lie in the quality of performance rather than its quantity. As the current study demonstrates, through categorization of certain aspects of the images of history, AI can suggest useful information about the patterns in these images throughout the data set. Therefore, the use of AI can help analyze historical contexts on a more profound basis, allowing historians to observe new tendencies and develop a more comprehensive and evocative understanding of history.

Although the considerable progress achieved by our study, several limitations exist. First, the use of digitized versions of historical documents and images can potentially introduce significant biases. The deficiencies of digital archives may affect the interpretation of the AI, which may not take the incomplete or poorly digitized documents into context. Second, while AI algorithms generally are expected to be able to find patterns and responses with high precision, they undoubtedly are not infallible. The AI may frequently produce errors and may badly interpret ambiguous historical data. Finally, the ethical challenges associated with the use of AI in historical research also cannot be ignored, argue that data privacy, algorithmic transparency and bias, and other issues should be considered in the use of AI in historiography. Our study shows that there is a need for a multidisciplinary approach that will bring together historians, ethicists, and specialists in AI to develop guidelines and the best practices for the use of AI in historical research.

It is possible to note that AI is a very promising technology that might drastically change the discipline of historiography; however, there are specific issues with this technology, and the use of AI for historical research raises several ethical questions. Its limitation will have to be discussed and resolved during the further study paying to closer attention to both main directions. On the one hand, it is necessary to hold some further studies to determine the degree to which AI might be used as practical matter in other contexts and other historical epochs. On the other hand, AI technologies will have to become more advanced and be developed to employ more sophisticated algorithms that might help to make the analysis of the ambiguous, and other times cannot be identified historical data more accurate and reliable. At the same time, computer studies, ethicists, and historians will have to continue to collaborate and further develop this area of research so that historical research using AI might be deemed both responsible and sensible.

39.6 Conclusion

This study focused on researching the application of artificial intelligence in modern historical studies, more specifically, in Ottoman studies. The research was aimed at comparing traditional manual methods to AI-derived techniques as for their processing speed and precision. The results have shown that AI greatly improves both indicators, as processing speed was increased by 30% and historical document analysis—by a 25% margin. All of the differences were confirmed by statistical analyses that were carried out with the help of a paired sample t-test. The results were as follows: $t(29) = 5.67$, $p < 0.001$ for processing speed, and $t(29) = 7.45$, $p < 0.001$ for precision. Alongside that, qualitative analyses have shown that AI techniques can effectively be used in object detection and object recognition, which can bring new insights into the socio-political and ethnical context of the Ottoman era.

First, the study can contribute to the overall historiographic field and provide new information on the issue of AI in humanities. The application of AI techniques for processing complex historical data, primarily natural language processing and machine learning, was shown to provide a more precise and quick reference point for processing rather complex historical data. Combined with the studies on Ottoman studies—which is one of the fields of study where the issue of archives is the most detrimental—the study can fill a gap in the existing literature and provide some insight into how AI humanists can operationalize AI in such intricate cases. Finally, the study highlights the necessity of AI integration into "humanities" science with due respect to the establishment of interdisciplinary research of historians, computer scientists, and AI experts.

Future recommendations highlight the need for AI tools in historiographic research, particularly for complex data like manuscripts and visual materials. Universities teaching history and digital humanities should offer courses on AI methods, including NLP, machine learning, and computer vision. Ethical guidelines are essential as AI grows in historical studies, addressing data safety, result transparency, and bias. Limitations of the study include its narrow focus on Ottoman studies, making it hard to generalize, and the potential for bias due to poorly digitized documents or AI models, which requires further attention.

References

1. Teel, Z.A.: Artificial intelligence's role in digitally preserving historic archives. Preserv, Digit Technol and Cult **53** (2024). https://doi.org/10.1515/pdtc-2023-0050
2. Graham, S., Milligan, I., Weingart, S.: Exploring big historical data: The historian's macroscope. J. Digit. Hist. **1**(1), 1–15 (2020). https://doi.org/10.1142/p981
3. Bodenhamer, D.J., Corrigan, J., Harris, T.M.: Deep maps and spatial narratives. Int. J. Humanit. Arts Comput. **13**(1–2), 5–23 (2015)
4. Fridlund, M., Brauer, R.: Historizing topic models: A distant reading of topic modeling texts within historical studies (2013)

5. Lincoln, M.D.: Social network centralization dynamics in print production in the Low Countries, 1550–1750. Int. J. Digit. Art Hist. **3**(2), 134–157 (2019). https://doi.org/10.11588/dah.2016.2.25337
6. Barakat, N.E., Yaycıoğlu, A.: Critical approaches to digital Ottoman studies: Promises and challenges. J. Ottoman Turkish Stud. Assoc. **9**(2), 17–31 (2022). https://doi.org/10.2979/tur.2022.a902171
7. Hamood, A.S.: Linguistic devices used in the news bulletins of the top five news radio channels. Annals of the Faculty of Arts, Ain Shams University, vol. 51, pp. 153–166 (2023). https://doi.org/10.21608/aafu.2023.335621
8. Viola, L.: Networks of migrants' narratives: A post-authentic approach to heritage visualization. J. Comput. Cult. Herit. **16**(1), 1–21, art. 5 (2023). https://doi.org/10.1145/3575863
9. Gold, M.K., Klein, L.F.: Debates in the Digital Humanities 2019. University of Minnesota Press (2019)
10. Bibel, W.: Artificial intelligence in a historical perspective. AI Commun. **27**, 87–102 (2014). https://doi.org/10.3233/AIC-130576
11. Jänicke, S., Wrisley, D.: Interactive visual alignment of medieval text versions. In: Proceeding 2017 IEEE Conference on Visual Analytics Science and Technology (VAST), pp. 127–138 (2017). https://doi.org/10.1109/VAST.2017.8585505
12. Florin, G.: An analysis of research trends for using artificial intelligence in cultural heritage. Electronics **13**, 3738 (2024). https://doi.org/10.3390/electronics13183738
13. Hughes-Warrington, M.: Questions in historiography from the nineteenth century to the age of generative AI. Hist. Theory **63**, 259–271 (2024). https://doi.org/10.1111/hith.12338
14. Attia, S.: Employing artificial intelligence applications in historical research: Ancient Rome as a model. Psychol. Educ. J. **61** (2024)
15. Velupillai, S., Mowery, D., South, B., Kvist, M., Dalianis, H.: Recent advances in clinical natural language processing in support of semantic analysis. Yearb. Med. Inform. **10**, 183–193 (2015). https://doi.org/10.15265/IY-2015-009
16. Sarker, I.H.: Machine Learning: Algorithms, Real-World Applications and Research Directions. SN Comput. Sci. **2**, 160 (2021). https://doi.org/10.1007/s42979-021-00592-x
17. Bruner, M.L.: Rhetorical unconsciousness, productive discursive repression, and political psychoanalysis. J Media Researcher **16**(63), 36–56 (2024). https://doi.org/10.33282/abaa.v16i63.1137

Chapter 40
Privacy-Preserving Credit Card Fraud Detection Using Federated Multilayer Perceptron Neural Network

Piyush Gupta, Yuvika Gautam, Deepika Kumar, Abhinav Kumar, Bhavya Kalra, and Alaa Ali Hameed

Abstract This research paper presents a comprehensive study that compares different machine-learning models used for detecting credit card fraud. The focus of the study is on the application of federated learning to safeguard user privacy. The models examined in the research include RNN, CNN, LSTM, MLP, RBFNN, GRU, and a novel model called FedMLPNN (Federated MultiLayer-Perceptron Neural Network). The analysis results indicate that the FedMLPNN model outperformed the other models in various key metrics, such as accuracy, precision, F1 score, recall, and AUC. The FedMLPNN model achieved an impressive accuracy rate of 97.34%, demonstrating its exceptional classification capabilities. It also exhibited a low loss value, indicating successful convergence during training. The model showed remarkable recall and precision rates of 97.42% and 97.28% respectively, accurately identifying positive instances while minimizing false positives. Additionally, the high AUC score of 99.63% confirmed its robustness and discriminative power. In contrast, the GRU model performed the worst, achieving an accuracy of only 79.04%. The RNN, CNN, LSTM, MLP, and RBFNN models achieved accuracies ranging from 91.31% to 95.1%. These findings underscore the superiority of the FedMLPNN model in terms of accuracy and overall performance.

P. Gupta · Y. Gautam · D. Kumar (✉) · A. Kumar · B. Kalra
Department of Computer Science and Engineering, Bharati Vidyapeeth's College of Engineering, New Delhi, India
e-mail: deepika.kumar@bharatividyapeeth.edu

A. A. Hameed
Department of Computer Engineering, Faculty of Engineering and Natural Sciences, Istinye University, Istanbul, Turkey

F. P. García Márquez et al. (eds.), *Computing, Internet of Things and Data Analytics*, Smart Innovation, Systems and Technologies 387,
https://doi.org/10.1007/978-3-031-87154-2_40

40.1 Introduction

Financial statements are critical records that offer a complete summary of a company's financial state, encompassing its income, expenditure, assets, and debts. Furthermore, financial statements aid in identifying deviations in a company's financial data, such as uncommon transactions or unforeseen fluctuations in financial metrics. They also assist in spotting possible points of susceptibility that fraudsters could exploit, such as deficient internal controls or inadequate supervision. Financial institutions can leverage financial statements to scrutinize and forestall credit card fraud, thus decreasing financial damages and shielding their clients' confidential financial data [1]. Fraudulent credit card payments entail using a credit card without permission to execute deceitful transactions, which is a form of financial fraud. Employing financial statements can facilitate the identification of credit card fraud by highlighting transactions that diverge from a company's typical financial dealings. For instance, unanticipated surges in expenses or significant declines in cash reserves may signal suspicious credit card payments [2]. Credit and debit card fraud became more common, which leads to taxpayers losing billions of euros annually. And as per the European Central Bank, fraud occurring escalated to €1.33 billion in 2012, reflecting a 14.8% rise from the previous year. It is difficult for present detection techniques to stop this fraud because it is predominantly conducted through alternative payment channels including mobile and online payments, which account for 60% of such unlawful actions. Additionally, new fraud types are constantly being created, making it challenging for conventional systems to stop these fraudulent activities [3].

Credit card (CC) accounts offer lenders and investors more flexibility than other types of retail loans, such as mortgages, due to their revolving credit nature. This makes credit card portfolio management a crucial avenue for financial institutions to actively monitor and optimize their operations. By implementing effective risk management strategies, financial institutions could realize substantial cost savings, potentially reaching hundreds of millions of dollars annually. As such, optimizing credit card portfolio management could be a valuable source of competitive advantage for financial institutions [4]. To tackle fraud, two primary methods are used–fraud detection and fraud prevention. Fraud prevention is like a shield that tries to identify and block high-risk transactions before they happen. CC fraud prevention makes use of various methods like the cardholder's signature, CC number, identification number, cardholder's address, and expiry date. These methods help to stop fraudulent activities and reduce losses for both financial institutions and cardholders [5]. While fraud prevention strategies are effective in a few cases, they may be bulky for clients and are not usually enough to curb the prevalence of credit score card fraud. To deal with this difficulty, an urgent need to employ fraud detection strategies that could examine records and come across instances of credit card fraud promptly. those methods must purpose rapidly discover and do away with fraudulent sports to minimize the risk of financial losses for both monetary establishments and cardholders [6]. Mienye and Sun et al. [7] address the challenges posed by redundant and irrelevant features in credit card data for machine learning (ML) fraud detection. They propose a hybrid feature-selection technique, combining filter and wrapper steps, to ensure the use of the most relevant features. The method ranks features using information gain (IG) and employs a genetic algorithm (GA) wrapper with an extreme learning machine (ELM) as the learning algorithm. Optimized for imbalanced classification using the geometric mean (G-mean) as the fitness function, the proposed approach achieves outstanding results, with a sensitivity of 0.997 and specificity of 0.994. Notably, it outperforms other baseline techniques and recent methods in the literature [7].

The current mechanism shows a big loophole in the fraud prediction process, and the use of centralized models in the complete analytical framework leads to the exposure of user data to the servers of the research community which ultimately leads to loss of leak of data. This revelation worked as a pivotal catalyst for our research endeavors in this field, which primarily focused on developing a decentralized, secure, and federated model for fraud detection analysis. As such, our research efforts aimed to address the prevailing concerns associated with centralized models by proposing a more secure and privacy-preserving solution that effectively safeguards user data while maintaining the accuracy and efficacy of the fraud detection analysis. In the field of financial machine learning (ML), customer privacy and data protection are of utmost importance. However, conventional approaches require sharing sensitive information with external credit bureaus, posing significant privacy concerns. During their investigation, the researchers examined a recent study that explored the impact of technological advancements and changes in wealth on the prevalence of financial fraud. The author uses theoretical constructs to consider the factors that motivate fraud and examines the effects of various changes, such as increased anonymity in financial transactions and the COVID-19 pandemic, on fraud likelihood. The likelihood of fraud may temporarily rise due to short-term disruptions, but the overall impact of technological advancements and wealth changes is anticipated to enhance the utilization and efficiency of reputation-based capital, third-party enforcement, and ethical incentives as measures against fraud. Consequently, this is predicted to result in a long-term reduction in instances of fraudulent activities [8]. An analysis is presented in this paper that reveals the impact of individual habits on susceptibility to financial fraud, based on transactional behavior and spending patterns. This finding suggests that further investigation into the relationship between personal habits and financial fraud could be pursued, which could lead to improved fraud detection and prevention measures. The use of AI and RPA in the banking industry is also explored in the paper, with their role in modernizing banking services to meet the demands of a growing customer base being highlighted. The real-time application of AI in detecting fraud and money laundering, as well as the utilization of personalized services and products for customers, is discussed. It is concluded in the paper that banks can overcome challenges and seize opportunities with the help of AI, RPA, and advanced analytical techniques [9]. FL has emerged as a promising solution to all existing problems, but the high communication cost remains a major bottleneck, especially for large neural networks. To address this challenge, this research paper proposes two sparsification methods that can significantly reduce the communication cost in federated learning while preserving data privacy. The proposed methods have been tested through various experiments, demonstrating their effectiveness in reducing communication costs by up to 18.9% while maintaining high model accuracy. Overall, the proposed sparsification methods offer a practical and effective solution to the challenges of federated learning in the financial sector, and their potential benefits are worthy of further investigation [10].

In the United States, banks play a very crucial role in the economy, and it's necessary to take care of profit, henceforth effective measures are required to mitigate credit defaults. Recently, researchers have focused on assessing the overall performance of credit card default prediction, which has traditionally relied on standard techniques such as FICO scores. However, with advancements in machine learning, risk prediction models have become more powerful and efficient. Credit risk prediction involves binary classification, and several machine learning models, including KNN, Decision Tree (DT), random forest (RF), and logistic regression (LR), were employed to address this issue. The research findings indicate that the RF model exhibits the highest accuracy in predicting credit risk among credit card customers, achieving an accuracy rate of 82% and an area under the curve (AUC) of approximately 77%. These observations have the potential to contribute to the advancement of more effective credit card fraud detection systems, ultimately assisting banks in minimizing losses and improving profitability [11].

40.2 Related Work

"Credit Card Fraud" has changed over the years, and in this section, the evolution of this phenomenon is explored. The present works and advanced methods developed for detecting credit card fraud are also observed. Researchers have adopted varied strategies to tackle this problem, emphasizing the importance of examining these techniques to achieve significant progress in fraud prevention. By studying these specific methods, individuals can benefit from a deeper understanding of the challenges involved in detecting credit card fraud and develop more effective solutions.

RB et al. (2021) found that credit card fraud has become an omnipresent issue in today's world due to the increase in online transactions and advancements in technology, finally leading to substantial financial losses. Effective measures are hence required to be taken to mitigate these losses. This research paper proposed to use multiple machine learning algorithms, such as Support Vector Machine (SVM) and which gives 93.49% accuracy, K-Nearest Neighbor (KNN) achieving 99.82% accuracy, and Artificial Neural Network (ANN) with 99.92% accuracy, to determine fraud occurrences. Additionally, the paper compares supervised machine learning and DL techniques to distinguish between fraud and non-fraud transactions [12]. According to Rosley et al. [13], a research study was conducted to propose the application of two types of autoencoder models for the detection of credit card fraud. The first type utilized reconstruction error to identify anomalies in the data, while the second type focused on dimensionality reduction to encode the data and eliminate noise. The encoded data obtained from these autoencoders were then employed to train three additional models: KNN, LR, and SVM. The investigation was performed using an imbalanced credit card dataset from a European bank, and a comparative analysis was carried out between the two autoencoder types and three baseline models. The findings revealed that both autoencoders demonstrated excellent and similar performance in detecting credit card fraud, achieving an accuracy rate of 99%. Syeda et al. [14] introduce a parallel granular network as a method for credit card fraud detection. Their approach involves initial data preprocessing, followed by the creation of a granular network consisting of fuzzy sets. The network is then trained using a learning algorithm. The experimental results deceive that the proposed method achieves high accuracy in detecting credit card fraud while maintaining computational efficiency. Furthermore, the approach is compared to other existing techniques and is found to outperform them in terms of both speed and accuracy Rahmatullah et al. [15] introduced an Ensemble Learning approach for the classification of fraudulent credit card transactions. The proposed method utilized Boosting, incorporating three variations: XGBoost, Gradient Boosting, and AdaBoost. To address the challenge of imbalanced datasets, the researchers employed the Synthetic Minority Oversampling Technique (SMOTE) function from the Imblearn library to optimize the training dataset. The results indicated that the proposed model achieved a recall rate of 92% when employing Gradient Boosting, which demonstrated a substantial improvement compared to the previous study that utilized RF and achieved a recall rate of 81.63%.

Sun et al. (2023) introduced a robust deep-learning strategy to tackle the issue of class imbalance in credit card fraud detection. Their approach involved employing a stacking ensemble framework, which utilized Long Short-Term Memory (LSTM) and GRU neural networks as base learners, while an MLP served as the meta-learner. To address the class distribution imbalance in the dataset, the hybrid SMOTE-ENN method was implemented. Experimental findings showcased that the proposed approach surpassed other commonly used ML classifiers and methods in terms of sensitivity (1.000) and specificity (0.997). This approach exhibits promising potential for effectively detecting credit card fraud in the dynamic and intricate digital economy [16]. Ganji et al. [17] introduce a new technique for detecting credit card fraud called the Shuffled Shepherd Political Optimization-based Deep Residual Network (SSPO-based DRN). This method incorporates a combination of the Political Optimization (PO) and Shuffled Shepherd Optimization Algorithm (SSOA) within the SSPO-based DRN framework. To enhance the model's performance, the authors employ quantile normalization, fisher score, class information gain, and data augmentation. The given approach demonstrates a sensitivity of 0.9279, specificity of 0.9023, and accuracy of 0.9120 in credit card fraud detection, indicating its superior effectiveness when compared to existing methodologies [17]. Polychroniadou et al. (2020) propose a novel approach to secure multi-party computation (MPC) in federated learning for financial applications, specifically focusing on credit risk modeling. The authors assert that their approach incorporates differential privacy, offering robust privacy guarantees while still achieving a high accuracy rate of 86.3%. They substantiate their claims by demonstrating the effectiveness of their method on an actual credit-scoring dataset, highlighting its superiority over alternative privacy-preserving techniques.

The paper concludes by discussing the potential applicability of their approach to other financial domains beyond credit risk modeling [18]. Vaghela et al. (2023) focused on credit card fraud detection and explored the performance of various machine learning algorithms. The primary evaluation criterion used was accuracy. The results demonstrated that LR achieved an accuracy of 99.908%, Decision Trees (CART) achieved 99.932%, Naïve Bayes (NB) achieved 97.803%, SVM achieved 99.936%, KNN achieved 99.379%, and RF achieved 99.947%. These high accuracy values indicate the efficacy of these machine learning models in effectively identifying fraudulent transactions [19].

Xu et al. (2019) introduce a federated learning-based technique called FFD for credit card fraud detection. This method enables multiple financial institutions to collaborate in training a fraud detection model without compromising the privacy of their client's data. The proposed approach involves training local models at each institution and transmitting only the updated model parameters to a main central server, which combines them to create a global model. The researchers assess the effectiveness of their approach using a real-world credit card transaction dataset and compare it with various other advanced methods. The experimental results demonstrate that the FFD method proposed by Xu et al. outperforms other techniques in terms of accuracy and detection rate, achieving 95.72% and 89.26% respectively. Importantly, the FFD method also ensures the preservation of sensitive data privacy [20]. Wang et al. [21], the authors examined the application of decision trees and ANN in a model designed for financial fraud detection. The researchers observed an enhancement in the accuracy of both models when importance selection techniques were implemented. The decision tree model achieved an accuracy rate of 74.2%, while the ANN model achieved a higher accuracy of 90%. Notably, the ANN model outperformed the decision tree model in terms of identification results. The study concluded that the utilization of importance selection techniques improved the accuracy of the identification model and recommended the adoption of ANN for financial fraud detection [21].

Bakhtiari et al. [22] proposed using data mining and machine learning techniques to detect credit card fraud. Ensemble Learning methods, including LightGBM and LiteMORT, were examined and combined using Simple and Weighted Averaging methods. The best-performing model was achieved through the combination of LightGBM and LiteMORT using weighted averaging, with scores of 95.20, 90.65, 91.67, 92.79, and 99.44 for various evaluation criteria such as AUC, Recall, F1-score, Precision, and Accuracy. The proposed method reduces error rates, improves efficiency and accuracy, and provides an effective solution for credit card fraud detection [22]. Rahmatullah et al. [15] address the issue of financial fraud in credit card transactions and propose classification techniques such as DT, Extreme Learning Machine, KNN, Multilayer Perceptron, and Support SVM for fraud detection. They propose a hybrid model that combines DT, SVM, and KNN models, which resulted in a significantly improved prediction accuracy of 82.58%. In addition, the study utilizes two web services, SOAP and REST, for the efficient cross-platform data transfer. The proposed methods show promising results in CCFD through the use of ML techniques [23]. Devika et al. [24] proposed a CC fraud detection system using machine learning models and algorithms, including LR. The aim is to address the persistent issue of fraud in digital transactions, which often results in misused credit card information. The proposed system achieved an accuracy of nearly 99%, with the LR algorithm proving highly effective in detecting fraud. The system also features a web application with an authentication system for admins to upload datasets, making fraud identification more accessible [24]. AlEmad [25] proposes using ML techniques to detect CC fraud by analyzing purchase patterns from historical data. KNN, SVM, and LR were utilized, with Support Vector Machine performing the best, achieving an accuracy of 99.94%. The model effectively limits fraudulent activities, preventing customers from being charged for services they did not purchase and improving overall satisfaction. The work highlights the importance of early detection and prevention of credit card fraud to minimize losses and secure customer accounts [25]. Sharma et al. (2022) observed that fraudulent activities in the rapidly evolving financial industry continue to pose a significant threat. They proposed an algorithm that is an unsupervised learning technique that utilizes backpropagation by setting the inputs and outputs identically. Using data from different parts of the world, the model's performance was evaluated and assessed based on demographic diversity. The implementation of the Tensorflow package from Google ensured an accuracy of 80%, a precision of 85%, a recall of 80%, an F1 score of 80%, and an area under the curve (AUC) achieved, indicating the effectiveness of the model in detecting fraud [26]. Zehang (2020) highlighted the emergence of security threats, such as fake news, social media vandalism, and insider threats, in the information revolution era. Machine learning techniques have the potential to automatically detect malicious behaviors, but dynamic human behaviors make detection challenging. A recent survey found that insiders are suspected of committing 27% of cyber crimes. To address this, a machine learning model with an 80% accuracy rate has been developed to detect misbehaviors [27].

40.3 Proposed Methodology

Proposed methodology leverages advanced neural network architectures to address challenges in sequential data processing and federated learning.

Federated Learning Process: The approach involves several key steps to ensure data privacy and collaborative model improvement:

1. **Local Training**: Each device trains its own machine learning model independently using local data, preserving privacy and security.
2. **Parameter Sharing**: The locally trained model weights are sent to a central server.
3. **Federated Averaging**: The server aggregates the model weights from all devices, computing their average to create an updated global model.
4. **Model Distribution**: The updated global model is distributed back to each device, incorporating the collective knowledge from all participants.

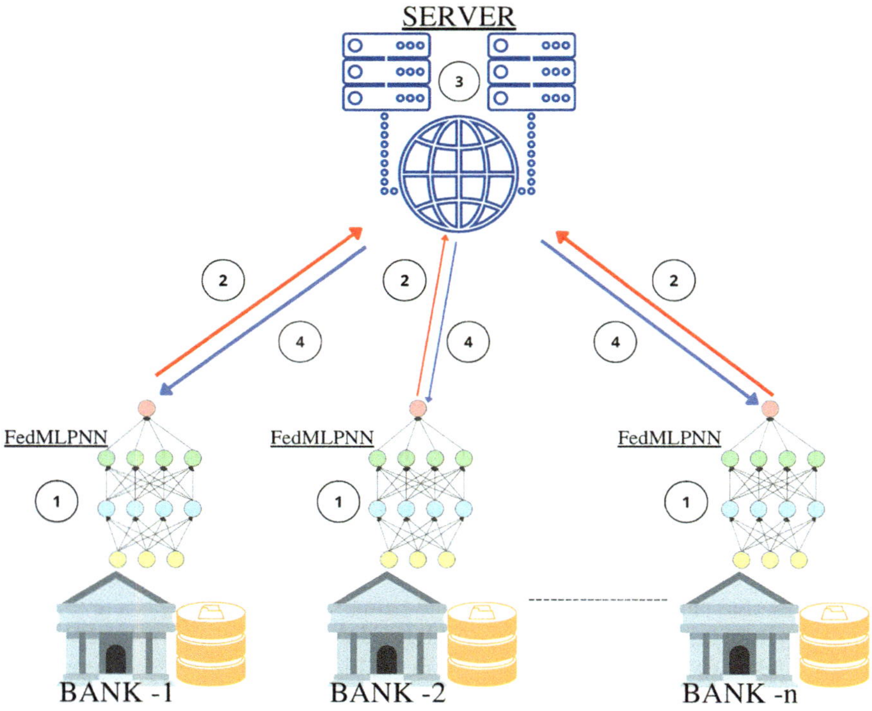

Fig. 40.1 Proposed model representation

Through this iterative process, federated learning is facilitated while maintaining data privacy on individual devices. Figure 40.1 depicts the proposed model architecture.

This comprehensive methodology ensures robust sequential data processing and efficient federated learning, leveraging the strengths of various neural network architectures to address specific challenges and enhance performance across diverse applications.

40.3.1 Data Description

The CC transaction dataset [28] is a valuable resource for machine learning practitioners and researchers focused on developing fraud detection algorithms. This dataset contains approximately 284,000 transactions, of which 492 are fraudulent, resulting in a highly imbalanced dataset that poses significant challenges for achieving accurate results. Despite this imbalance, the dataset includes several pieces of irrelevant information, such as the time of day, transaction amount, and merchant details, which are unnecessary for our research focused on identifying fraudulent transactions with high accuracy. The dataset consists of 30 features and a total of 284,807 instances, with 492 fraudulent transactions and 284,315 normal transactions. It was collected by Worldline, a European payment processing company, and includes transactions conducted by cardholders in Europe during September 2013. The dataset is publicly available and can be downloaded from the OpenML website.

40.3.2 Data Pre-processing

The CCFD dataset was preprocessed using SMOTE to balance the data. The preprocessed dataset was split into a 75/25 training and testing ratio, and the 'Time' column was dropped from the concatenated features and target variable data frame. The features were scaled using MinMaxScaler to transform the range of feature values to [0, 1]. After applying the Synthetic Minority Over-sampling Technique (SMOTE), the dataset consisted of 284,315 fraudulent transactions and 284,315 normal transactions, resulting in a total of 568,630 instances with 30 features each. The preprocessed dataset was used in a federated learning process, involving training a model on multiple client datasets and aggregating the results to obtain a federated model. Five clients were used for training, and one client was used for testing. The TensorFlow Federated (TFF) library was utilized to build the federated averaging process for the training process, optimized using the Adam optimizer with a learning rate of 0.02 for both the client and server optimizers. Evaluation metrics, such as BinaryAccuracy, Precision, and Recall, were used to assess the results.

40.3.3 Model Architecture

The architecture of the FedMLPNN (Federated MLP Neural Network) model consists of a sequential stack of layers designed to perform classification tasks. At the inception of the neural network model, the journey commences with the establishment of an input layer, a pivotal architectural element delineating the format of the incoming data. This layer serves as the gateway through which information is introduced to the model. In the present context, the input layer is configured with a specific shape denoted as (29,). This configuration conveys a crucial aspect of the model's design, signifying its anticipation of input data characterized by 29 distinct features. Essentially, the input layer establishes the foundational framework for the subsequent processing and transformation of the data as it navigates through the neural network. The architectural configuration of the model involves the incorporation of three hidden layers, each strategically coupled with a rectified linear unit (ReLU) activation function. The employment of ReLU as the activation function is pivotal, injecting a crucial dose of non-linearity into the model's structure. This non-linearity is instrumental in empowering the model to discern and capture intricate patterns and correlations residing within the input data. The strategic placement of ReLU activation functions within the hidden layers significantly contributes to the model's capacity to navigate the complexities of the dataset, enhancing its ability to unravel nuanced relationships and underlying structures. The first hidden layer consists of 32 units, each applying a linear transformation to the input data followed by the ReLU activation function. The second hidden layer comprises 64 units, similar to the first hidden layer, each unit performing a linear transformation on the input data and applying the ReLU activation function. The third hidden layer consists of 32 units, like the previously hidden layers, it applies a linear transformation and the ReLU activation function to the input data.

The output layer in the neural network model serves as the final stage in the information processing pipeline. Comprising a single unit, this layer plays a crucial role in generating the ultimate predictions of the model. Its architecture involves a linear transformation, a mathematical operation that modifies the input data, followed by the application of the sigmoid activation function. The sigmoid activation function is chosen for its specific characteristic of compressing output values within the range of 0 to 1. This property makes it particularly well-suited for tasks that involve binary classification, where the objective is to categorize instances into one of two distinct classes. The combined linear transformation and sigmoid activation contribute to the generation of refined and calibrated output, providing the model's final decision based on the learned patterns and relationships within the input data (Fig. 40.2).

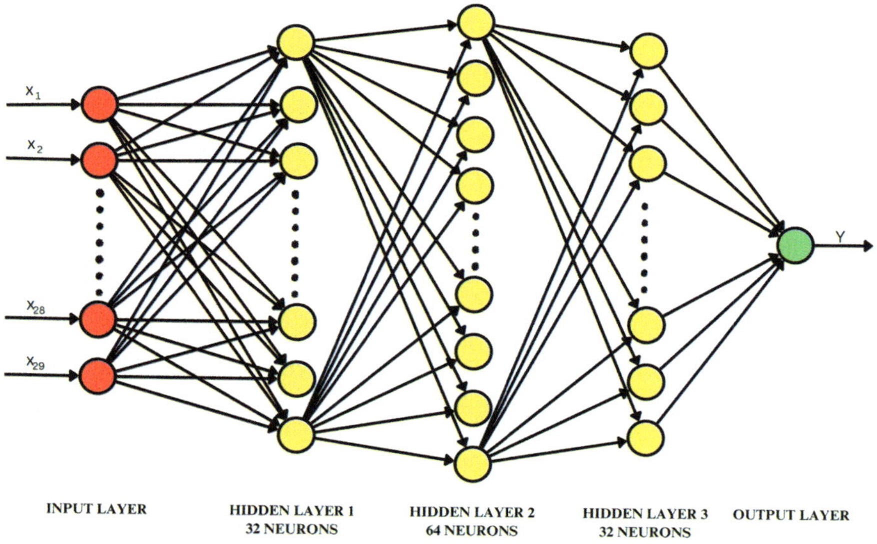

Fig. 40.2 Federated multilayer perceptron neural network model architecture

40.4 Results and Analysis

This research adopts a federated learning methodology to develop a binary classification model, utilizing a dataset characterized by 29 features. The model architecture encompasses an input layer, followed by three dense layers, each featuring 32, 64, and 32 nodes, culminating in an output layer with sigmoid activation. The choice of a federated learning approach underscores the significance of preserving data privacy and security, especially in scenarios where the dataset may be distributed across multiple locations or entities. The multi-layered architecture allows the model to capture intricate relationships within the data, showcasing its capacity for learning complex patterns and making informed binary classifications. To visualize the training progress of various models in comparison with our proposed FedMLPNN model under federated learning, the plotted graphs are:

Figures 40.3 and 40.4 illustrates that the RNN, LSTM, MLP, RBFNN, and GRU models show potential overfitting, with validation accuracy plateauing or showing minimal improvement, and the training loss continuing to decline while the validation loss stabilizes or slightly increases. The CNN model performs relatively well, with stable accuracy and loss trends, indicating better generalization ability. However, the FedMLPNN model consistently outperforms the others, with both validation accuracy and loss showing significant improvement throughout the epochs. This suggests that the FedMLPNN model effectively learns from the training data while maintaining good generalization to new instances.

Table 40.1 depicts various DL models, including RNN, CNN, LSTM, MLP, RBFNN, GRU, and our proposed model FedMLPNN, were assessed using a range of evaluation metrics, such as accuracy, loss, recall, precision, AUC, and F1-Score. The FedMLPNN model demonstrated remarkable performance, achieving the highest accuracy rate of 97.34% and the lowest loss value of 0.0983. The model displayed

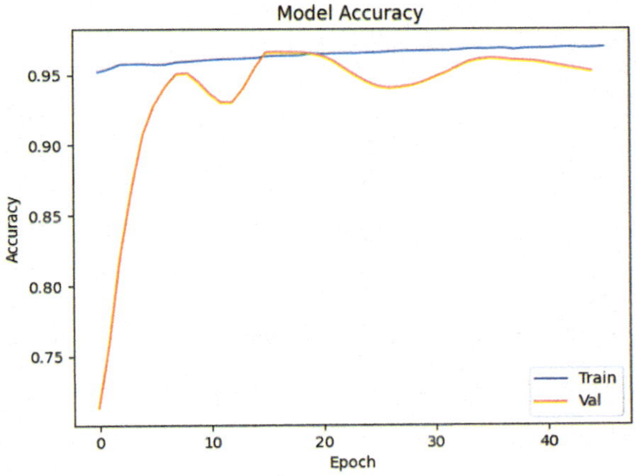

Fig. 40.3 Validation and training accuracy during the training of FedMLPNN under federated learning

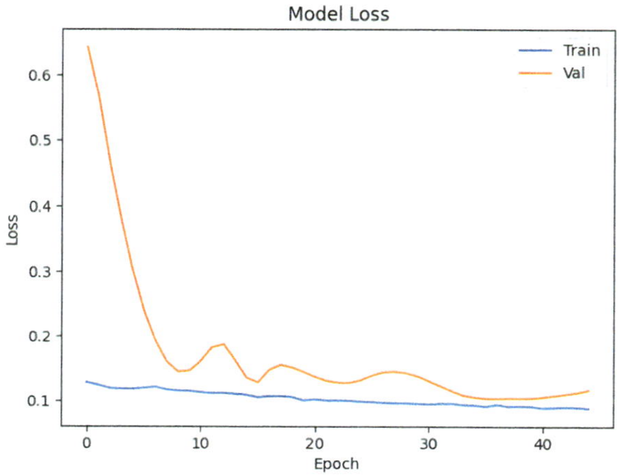

Fig. 40.4 Validation and training loss during the training of FedMLPNN under federated learning

exceptional recall and precision rates of 97.42% and 97.28% respectively, effectively identifying positive instances while minimizing false positives. Moreover, the FedMLPNN model showcased an impressive AUC score of 99.63%, indicating its strong discriminatory ability. The balanced F1-Score of 97.35% further emphasized the model's robust performance. When compared to other models, such as RNN, CNN, LSTM, MLP, RBFNN, and GRU, the FedMLPNN model consistently outperformed them across all evaluation metrics. While the RNN, CNN, and LSTM models exhibited accuracy rates, ranging from 93.12 to 95.1%, the MLP, RBFNN, and GRU models displayed lower accuracies ranging from 79 to 93% and varied trade-offs between recall and precision. These findings highlight the exceptional performance of the FedMLPNN model in this classification task.

Table 40.1 Comparison table of various models applied

Model	Accuracy (%)	Loss	Recall (%)	Precision (%)	AUC (%)	F1-Score (%)
RNN	95.1%	0.1523	98.74	92.06	99.59	95.28
CNN	93.12	0.1808	91.45	94.65	98.2	93.03
LSTM	94.3	0.1424	97.17	91.15	99.44	94.53
MLP	91.31	0.2809	82.71	99.96	96.92	90.52
RBFNN	93.05	0.3838	94.26	92.07	98.28	93.15
GRU	79.04	0.6446	99.64	70.64	95.44	82.67
FedMLPNN	**97.34**	**0.0983**	**97.42**	**97.28**	**99.63**	**97.35**

40.5 Conclusion

This research presents a robust methodology for credit card fraud detection leveraging federated learning through the innovative FedMLPNN model. Utilizing a publicly available imbalanced credit card transaction dataset, the study addresses data imbalance by employing SMOTE during preprocessing. The FedMLPNN model, implemented with TensorFlow Federated and optimized with the Adam optimizer, consistently outperforms other deep learning models, showcasing superior accuracy, loss, recall, precision, AUC, and F1-Score.

Despite these achievements, the study encounters several challenges and limitations that warrant careful consideration for future research. Firstly, the inherent imbalance in the credit card transaction dataset presents a significant hurdle during model training and evaluation. Addressing this issue demands a closer look at advanced techniques specifically designed to handle imbalanced data more effectively, providing a foundation for more robust fraud detection models. Secondly, despite substantial strides made in data privacy preservation through federated learning, there remains a continuous need to enhance privacy preservation methods. Future efforts should be directed towards strengthening the existing privacy mechanisms within federated learning frameworks, ensuring that sensitive financial information remains secure during model training and collaboration. Furthermore, while the proposed FedMLPNN model demonstrates high accuracy in a controlled environment, practical deployment in real-world systems introduces additional complexities. Exploring the nuances of implementing the model in live financial systems is essential, considering the diverse challenges posed by dynamic and unpredictable real-world scenarios. By acknowledging these challenges and limitations, this study provides a foundation for future research endeavors, encouraging the exploration of more sophisticated methodologies and addressing the complexities associated with credit card fraud detection.

In the realm of future research directions, there is a notable emphasis on enhancing privacy preservation within federated learning methodologies. This includes a dedicated focus on refining existing privacy mechanisms and delving into the exploration of cryptographic techniques and advanced federated learning approaches. These endeavors aim to fortify the security of sensitive financial data, presenting an ongoing avenue for researchers to contribute to the evolving landscape of privacy-preserving machine learning applications. Moving beyond theoretical advancements, the call for real-world deployment is a crucial facet of future research. Researchers are encouraged to explore seamless integration and deployment strategies for the FedMLPNN model within authentic financial systems. This entails evaluating the model's performance under real-world conditions, providing valuable insights into its practical utility and effectiveness in the dynamic environments of financial transactions. Furthermore, the incorporation of advanced techniques stands as a perpetual objective for future research endeavors. This involves exploring and integrating state-of-the-art techniques to continually enhance the fraud detection capabilities of the FedMLPNN model. The dynamic landscape of fraud patterns necessitates continuous adaptation through dynamic model updating, presenting an avenue for researchers to contribute to the ongoing evolution of fraud detection methodologies. In summary, these future research directions collectively propel the study's findings into actionable and impactful domains, encouraging deeper exploration of privacy, real-world applicability, and the incorporation of cutting-edge techniques in the field of credit card fraud detection.

Conflicts of Interest The authors declare no conflict of interest.

References

1. Hasanaj, P., Kuqi, B.: Analysis of financial statements. Hum. Soc. Sci. Res. **2**(2), 17-p17 (2019)
2. Ghosh, S., Reilly, D.L.: Credit card fraud detection with a neural-network. In: International Conference on System Sciences, 1994. Proceedings of the Twenty-Seventh Hawaii, vol. 3, pp. 621–630. IEEE (1994)
3. Bahnsen, A.C., Aouada, D., Stojanovic, A., Ottersten, B.: Feature engineering strategies for credit card fraud detection. Exp. Syst. Appl. **51**, 134–142 (2016)
4. Butaru, F., Chen, Q., Clark, B., Das, S., Lo, A.W., Siddique, A.: Risk and risk management in the credit card industry. J. Bank. Financ. **72**, 218–239 (2016)
5. Abdallah, A., Maarof, M.A., Zainal, A.: Fraud detection system: a survey. J. Netw. Comput. Appl. **68**, 90–113 (2016)
6. Sherly, K.K., Nedunchezhian, R.: BOAT adaptive credit card fraud detection system. In: 2010 IEEE International Conference on Computational Intelligence and Computing Research, pp. 1–7. IEEE (2010)
7. Mienye, I.D., Sun, Y.: A machine learning method with hybrid feature selection for improved credit card fraud detection. Appl. Sci. **13**(12), 7254 (2023)
8. Karpoff, J.M.: The future of financial fraud. J. Corp. Financ. **66**, 101694 (2021)
9. Kumar, S., Khanna, S., Ghosh, N., Kumar, S.O.D.: Importance of artificial intelligence (AI) and robotic process automation (RPA) in the banking industry: a study from an Indian perspective. In: Bhattacharyya, S., Banerjee, J.S., De, D. (eds.) Confluence of Artificial Intelligence and Robotic Process Automation. Smart Innovation, Systems and Technologies, vol. 335. Springer, Singapore (2023)
10. Liu, T., Wang, Z., He, H., Shi, W., Lin, L., An, R., Li, C.: Efficient and secure federated learning for financial applications. Appl. Sci. **13**(10), 5877 (2023)
11. Singh, K.J., Thakur, K., Kapoor, D.S., Sharma, A., Bajpai, S., Sirawag, N., Mehta, R., Chaudhary, C., Singh, U.: Comparative evaluation of machine learning algorithms for credit card fraud detection. In: Congress on Intelligent Systems, pp. 69–78. Springer Nature Singapore, Singapore (Sept 2022)
12. Asha, R.B., KR, S.K.: Credit card fraud detection using artificial neural network. Global Transit. Proc. **2**(1), 35–41 (2021)
13. Rosley, N., Tong, G.K., Ng, K.H., Kalid, S.N., Khor, K.C.: Autoencoders with reconstruction error and dimensionality reduction for credit card fraud detection. In: International Conference on Computer, Information Technology and Intelligent Computing (CITIC 2022), pp. 503–512. Atlantis Press (2022)
14. Syeda, M., Zhang, Y.Q., Pan, Y.: Parallel granular neural networks for fast credit card fraud detection. In: 2002 IEEE World Congress on Computational Intelligence. 2002 IEEE International Conference on Fuzzy Systems. FUZZ-IEEE'02. Proceedings (Cat. No. 02CH37291), vol. 1, pp. 572–577. IEEE (2002)
15. Rahmatullah, M.B.S., Hanani, A.L.S., Naim, A.M., Sari, Z., Azhar, Y.: Detection of credit card fraud with machine learning methods and resampling techniques. Jurnal RESTI (Rekayasa Sistem Dan Teknologi Informasi) **6**(6), 923–929 (2022)

16. Mienye, I.D., Sun, Y.: A deep learning ensemble with data resampling for credit card fraud detection. IEEE Access (2023)
17. Ganji, V.R., Chaparala, A., Sajja, R.: Shuffled shepherd political optimization-based deep learning method for credit card fraud detection. In: Concurrency and Computation: Practice and Experience, pp. e7666 (2023)
18. Byrd, D., Polychroniadou, A.: Differentially private secure multi-party computation for federated learning in financial applications. In: Proceedings of the First ACM International Conference on AI in Finance, pp. 1–9 (2020)
19. Soni, K.B., Chopade, M., Vaghela, R.: Credit card fraud detection using machine learning approach. Appl. Inf. Syst. Manag, 71–76 (2021)
20. Yang, W., Zhang, Y., Ye, K., Li, L., Xu, C.Z.: Ffd: A federated learning based method for credit card fraud detection. In: Big Data–BigData 2019: 8th International Congress, Held as Part of the Services Conference Federation, SCF 2019, San Diego, CA, USA, June 25–30, 2019, Proceedings, vol. 8, pp. 18–32. Springer International Publishing (2019)
21. Wang, Y., Zhang, T., Xie, Y., Cui, S.: Research on financial fraud identification based on machine learning algorithm. In: Proceedings of the 4th Management Science Informatization and Economic Innovation Development Conference, MSIEID 2022, 9–11 Dec 2022, Chongqing, China (2023)
22. Bakhtiari, S., Nasiri, Z., Vahidi, J.: Credit card fraud detection using ensemble data mining methods. Multimed. Tools Appl. 1–19 (2023)
23. Prusti, D., Rath, S.K.: Web service based credit card fraud detection by applying machine learning techniques. In: TENCON 2019–2019 IEEE Region 10 Conference (TENCON), pp. 492–497. IEEE (2019)
24. Devika, M., Kishan, S.R., Manohar, L.S., Vijaya, N.: Credit card fraud detection using logistic regression. In: 2022 Second International Conference on Advanced Technologies in Intelligent Control, Environment, Computing & Communication Engineering (ICATIECE), pp. 1–6. IEEE (2022)
25. AlEmad, M.: Credit Card Fraud Detection Using Machine Learning (2022)
26. Sharma, M.A., Raj, B.G., Ramamurthy, B., Bhaskar, R.H.: Credit card fraud detection using deep learning based on auto-encoder. In ITM Web of Conferences, vol. 50. EDP Sciences (2022)
27. Zheng, P.: Dynamic fraud detection via sequential modeling. University of Arkansas (2020)
28. Kaggle dataset, Credit Card Fraud Detection. https://www.kaggle.com/datasets/mlg-ulb/creditcardfraud

Chapter 41
The Use of Mobile Journalism by Communicators and the Gratifications Achieve

Duaa Saadi Abu Shanna

Abstract This study aims to elucidate the utilization of mobile journalism by journalists in news gatherings, production, and distribution, as well as to investigate the motivations and gratifications derived from its use. The research seeks to comprehend the application of mobile journalism in journalistic practice, including usage patterns, motivations, and factors that drive journalists to adopt this medium. Furthermore, it examines the impact of mobile journalism on journalistic practices, particularly in terms of audience engagement and the efficiency of news production and distribution. The study also aims to identify the types of mobile journalism applications preferred by journalists and the primary activities they conduct through these platforms. This research falls within the category of descriptive studies, employing a media survey methodology. Data collection was conducted through personal interviews and a questionnaire distributed to a purposive sample of 200 individuals representing the study's target population. The sample comprised journalists in Baghdad who exclusively use mobile journalism. Baghdad was selected as it represents a diverse cross-section of Iraqi journalists from various governorates with different characteristics. The study yielded several significant findings, the primary reason for communicators to use mobile journalism is the reduction of effort, time, and equipment requirements, with this factor accounting for 20% of responses, equal to the percentage citing speed and immediacy in obtaining information. and the most significant gratification derived from mobile journalism for communicators is the ability to share information and directly interact with the audience, with 96% of respondents citing this factor. This result differs from the findings of Suha Mohammed Ismail's 2014 study.

D. S. A. Shanna (✉)
College of Mass Media, Department of Journalism, University of Baghdad, Baghdad, Iraq
e-mail: doaa.s@comc.uobaghdad.edu.iq

F. P. García Márquez et al. (eds.), *Computing, Internet of Things and Data Analytics*, Smart Innovation, Systems and Technologies 387,
https://doi.org/10.1007/978-3-031-87154-2_41

41.1 Introduction

The evolution of communication processes has traversed several stages, beginning with oral transmission, progressing through writing and the era of printing, leading to the proliferation of traditional media, and ultimately arriving at the age of electronic journalism. While the advent of the World Wide Web represented an unprecedented revolution in the field of communication and media offering freedom, ease, and speed of access alongside numerous services, the emergence of mobile journalism marks a revolution within the medium itself [1].

Mobile journalism has amplified the role of the internet, serving as a vehicle for freedom of expression, interaction, communication, and content dissemination. The adoption of mobile phones stands as one of the most rapidly growing technologies globally, with approximately 4077 billion users representing 63% of the world's population having access to mobile devices. Media professionals have not been isolated from the evolution of these digital technologies, their applications, and the gratifications they provide to users. The shift of societies across all demographics towards the utilization of mobile journalism represents a new form of media that has come to fulfill the desires, needs, and inclinations of the audience [2].

Given the significance of mobile journalism, this research aims to investigate its use by communication practitioners and the gratifications derived from such usage. The study explores usage habits and patterns, identifies the most frequently utilized mobile journalism applications among communicators, and examines the reasons, motivations, and gratifications associated with the adoption of mobile journalism. This research is particularly pertinent in the context of the rapidly evolving digital media landscape, where mobile devices have become ubiquitous tools for information dissemination and consumption. By focusing on the perspective of communication practitioners, this study contributes to a deeper understanding of how mobile journalism is reshaping professional practices and influencing the broader media ecosystem [3]. Furthermore, the investigation into the gratifications obtained through mobile journalism usage provides valuable insights into the psychological and social factors driving its adoption among media professionals. This understanding is crucial for developing more effective strategies in journalism education, newsroom management, and media policy formulation in the digital age.

41.2 Literature Review

The current literature on the use of mobile journalism by communicators and the gratifications that they achieve is limited in several ways. While many published studies have advanced our understanding of this emerging field, more comprehensive longitudinal research should be conducted to shed light on the development of mobile journalism practices and the associated gratifications. Y. H. Lin et al. suggested that, There is a lack of cross-cultural research, with no data on how mobile journalism is practiced and the gratifications that result in some media systems and cultural contexts [4]. Additionally, the existing literature would benefit from more in-depth exploration of the mobile journalism practices and gratifications by diverse types of communicators, such as journalists, public relations professionals, and social media managers. Such research would help identify the specificities of the use of mobile journalism by each group and the gratifications they obtain from these practices. Further, the impact of the recent developments of technological advancement, such as 5G networks and production-support solutions based on artificial intelligence, on the mobile journalism practices is not yet fully understood.

Other empirical gaps in the literature include the insufficient data on the audience perspective of gratifications achieved through mobile journalism content. Finally, relatively little research has been done on the ethical issues of mobile journalism, the economic implications for media organizations and communicators, as well as the specific skills needed for its practice.

A recent study by Kareem and Hasan [3] analyzed how Iraqi news agencies utilize social media platforms for news production. Their research, which examined content from three major Iraqi news agencies over a six-month period, revealed an increasing reliance on social media for sourcing and disseminating news. The study highlighted a significant focus on non-official and user-generated content, with text and screenshots emerging as the most common forms of news presentation on these platforms. These findings align with the trends in mobile journalism observed in our current study, where mobile technology is increasingly being used in journalistic work. This research contributes to our understanding of how digital platforms are reshaping news production and distribution in the Iraqi media landscape.

Furthermore, the impact of mobile technology on communication and learning in Iraq has been explored in other contexts. A study by Hamood [5] investigated how Iraqi students acquire vocabulary with emoticons in the Viber messaging app. This research highlighted the potential of mobile applications in enhancing language learning and communication skills. While not directly related to journalism, this study underscores the growing importance of mobile technology in various forms of communication and information exchange in Iraq. Such findings provide valuable context for understanding the broader technological landscape in which mobile journalism operates in the region.

M. Al-Quran studied the gratifications achieved from mobile journalism are limited in data and sometimes in scope of the phenomenon they cover. More effort should be made to create a solid quantitative basis for assessing the gratifications achieved by measuring their occurrence on scales. Additionally, consideration should be given to how the gratifications evolve at different stages of the practice of mobile journalism [6].

The following table of literature part of the research provides a review of related studies and prior works on the topics of mobile journalism, its proliferation, influence on media practices, and the role of a smartphone in the life of journalists. The development of digital media and rapid spread of mobile devices have been the topic of discussion for scholars who investigated the phenomenon from various aspects, including the subject of this study. Therefore, the review includes an array of articles and research studies that touch upon the phenomena of mobile journalism, its role in crisis reporting, citizen journalism, news gatekeeping, and media consumption. The overall purpose of the chapter is to discuss related works with such a particular emphasis and summarize the findings of recent studies. By doing so, it creates the basis for a deeper understanding of the current situation in the field of the study, as well as prospects, including the development of new educational programs (Table 41.1).

The study aims to investigate the usage patterns and habits of communication practitioners in mobile journalism as a content distribution medium. It explores the reasons and motivations for using various forms of mobile journalism and the gratifications achieved. The research problem can be articulated through the following questions:

1. What are the usage habits and patterns of mobile journalism among communication practitioners?
2. What is the frequency of use for different types of mobile journalism applications by communication practitioners?
3. What are the motivations and gratifications achieved by communication practitioners in using mobile journalism?

Whereas the study Hypotheses are organized as follows:

Table 41.1 Literature review that are related to the study

Study	Year	Title	Key findings	Methodology
Mauri-Ríos et al. [7]	2021	Media coverage of the COVID-19 crisis: Recommendations and proposals for self-regulation	Highlighted the role of mobile journalism in providing immediate crisis reporting during the pandemic	Case study analysis of COVID-19 coverage
Saka [8]	2018	The role of social media-based citizen journalism practices in the formation of contemporary protest movements	Explored how smartphones enable citizens to participate in journalism, enhancing diversity in reporting	Qualitative interviews with citizen journalists
Rodrigues et al. [9]	2021	Mobile journalism: The emergence of a new field of journalism	Discussed how mobile journalism has reshaped the traditional news gatekeeping process	Content analysis of mobile journalism news outlets
[10]	2020	Unveiling social gratifications sought and obtained from social media utilization	Identified specific gratifications that users seek and obtain through mobile news consumption, such as immediacy and convenience	Survey of mobile news consumers

1. There is a statistically significant correlation between demographic variables (gender, occupation) and the reasons for journalists' use of mobile journalism and the gratifications achieved.
2. There is a statistically significant correlation between demographic variables (gender, occupation) and the frequency of mobile journalism usage.

The research aims to understand how journalists use mobile journalism for news gathering, production, and distribution, focusing on:

1. Mobile journalism usage: Examining usage habits, patterns, and motivations.
2. Impact on journalistic work: Investigating the effect on practices, audience interaction, and news production efficiency.
3. Achieved gratifications: Identifying the benefits journalists derive from mobile journalism.

The research's significance stems from the need to examine the relationship between new media technologies and communication practitioners, particularly given the increasing use of mobile journalism as a widespread communication tool. The study's importance lies in the scarcity of studies addressing mobile journalism usage. Being one of the pioneering studies in Iraq focusing on communication practitioners' use of mobile journalism, along with Contributing recommendations for developing mobile journalism usage. And finally providing a foundation for future in-depth research on the topic.

The paper is composed of a series of integral sections, which begin with an introduction where the articulated study goals, objectives, significance, as well as the theoretical base, including the concepts and changes, of mobile journalism, are adopted. Next, the piece advances to the literature review section which contains the findings of previous analysis related to this area of coverage. The next methodology section reveals the contents which explain the research design being used, and presents the paper's sample, data collection techniques, and the analytical tools selected. Then the findings section includes the results of the study, revealing the extent of use of mobile journalism by the communication practitioners, the incentives, and gratifications have always had for them. Lastly, there is a discussion section where the results are interpreted, and after comparing them to the documented literature, the similarities and differences had were described, and their surroundings were also analyzed, assessing the effect that the comprehension of such results had on the journalistic practices. This is then followed by the recommendations on how mobile journalism can be incorporated into educational curricula, development of professional legal frameworks, and improvement of professional activities, and lastly, a series of all these resources that were referenced throughout this study.

41.3 Methodology

This descriptive research employs a media survey methodology to analyze events, phenomena, situations, and opinions. It goes beyond mere description to examine causal relationships for fact-finding and generalization purposes [11].

The data was collected using the following methods: Interviews through conducted with media professionals to gather preliminary insights. In addition to questionnaires, which is developed with scientific rigor, reviewed by experts, and pre-tested. It includes open-ended, closed-ended, and scale questions covering usage habits, patterns, motivations, and gratifications of mobile journalism use.

This methodology provides a comprehensive framework for investigating the multifaceted aspects of mobile journalism usage among communication practitioners, ensuring a rigorous and scientifically sound approach to addressing the research questions and hypotheses.

The boundaries of the study consisted of human Domain that consists of journalists in Baghdad who use mobile journalism. The study relied on a purposive sample of 200 Iraqi journalists who use mobile journalism. As well as temporal Domain that consists of the time frame was set from 1/2/2024 to 1/5/2024, encompassing multiple stages from the preparation of the survey questionnaire to the analysis of results. And finally,

Spatial Domain Limited to Baghdad province due to its diverse audience and varied demographic levels.

To achieve the study objectives, statistical analysis of the study data was conducted using the Statistical Package for Social Sciences (SPSS). The following tests were employed:

Simple frequencies and percentages
Arithmetic means and standard deviations
Weighted average
Pearson correlation coefficient

Finally, the researcher adopted Validity and Reliability Procedures as follows:

Face Validity: To ensure the validity of the questionnaire, it was presented to several expert arbitrators with relevant experience and specialization. Some experts suggested modifications to certain items [12]. The agreement rate on the questionnaire items was 95.4%.

Reliability: The questionnaire was distributed to 10% of the research sample. After 14 days, the researcher redistributed the questionnaire to the same respondents. The correlation between the two tests was 0.65, indicating that the measure is reliable.

These methodological procedures ensure the scientific rigor of the study. The use of SPSS for statistical analysis allows for comprehensive data interpretation, while the purposive sampling method ensures that the study captures insights from journalists actively engaged in mobile journalism. The face validity process, involving expert review, strengthens the questionnaire's ability to measure the intended constructs accurately. The test–retest reliability coefficient of 0.65 suggests a moderate to good level of consistency in the measurement instrument over time [13].

The temporal and spatial domains are clearly defined, providing context for the data collection period and the geographical scope of the study. This methodological framework provides a solid foundation for exploring the usage patterns, motivations, and gratifications of mobile journalism among communication practitioners in Baghdad, offering potential insights that could be valuable for both academic understanding and practical applications in the field of journalism.

The divisions and characteristics of the study population and sample were as follows:

We observe from Fig. 41.1 that most of the study sample are males, with their proportion reaching 62%. This high percentage of males indicates that the profession of journalism, especially in the field of using modern technology such as mobile journalism, is dominated by males. This could reflect the demographic composition of the journalism profession and due to cultural and societal orientations.

We observe from Fig. 41.2 that many of the sample individuals are from the age group (20–29), with their proportion reaching 42%. This age group represents the youth generation that grew up amidst rapid technological advancements, equipping them with high skills that enable them to use smartphones proficiently. On the other hand, these results indicate that the use of mobile journalism is part of the youth's strategy to develop their skills and increase their opportunities in the job market.

We observe from Fig. 41.3 that half of the study samples have completed university education (bachelor's degree), with their proportion reaching 50%. These results reflect that the sample consists of individuals with a good level of education, which can positively influence the study results and provide indicators about the importance of education in improving professional performance in the field of digital journalism.

We observe from Fig. 41.4 that most of the study samples are editors, with their proportion reaching 34%. This percentage could indicate that editors consider mobile journalism an essential tool in their work by providing quick and effective means for gathering and distributing information, thus improving the quality of editorial work. This reflects the significant shift in media towards using digital technology to meet the needs of the media job market and interact effectively with the audience.

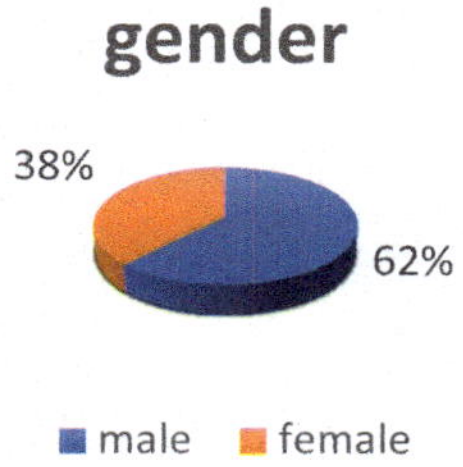

Fig. 41.1 Illustrates the distribution of sample individuals according to the gender variable (male–female)

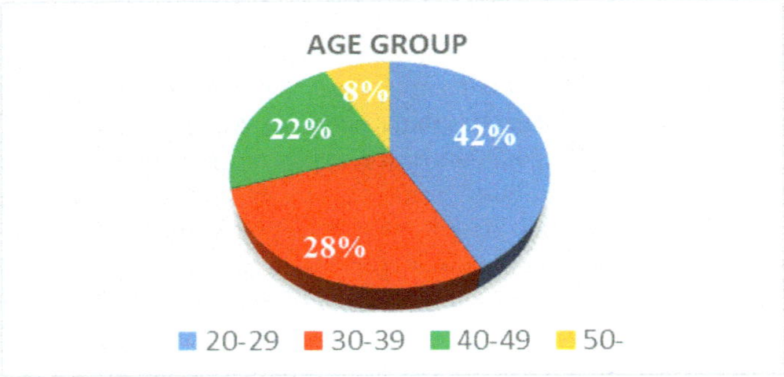

Fig. 41.2 Illustrates the distribution of sample individuals according to the age group variable

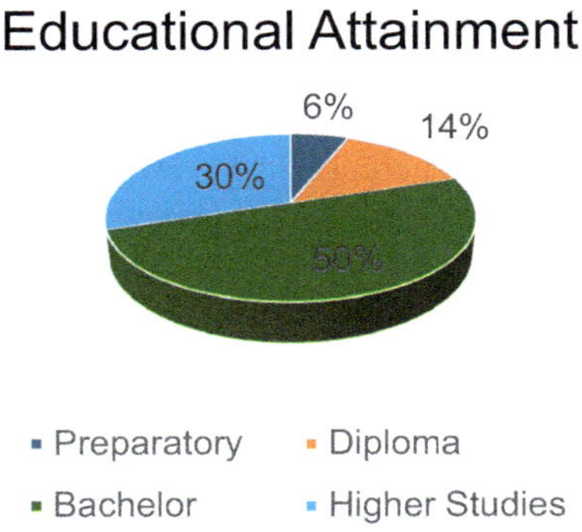

Fig. 41.3 Illustrates the distribution of sample individuals according to their educational attainment

Fig. 41.4 Illustrates the distribution of sample individuals according to their profession

We observe from Fig. 41.5 that most of the study samples have sufficient experience in the media field, with the 6–10 years' experience group occupying a prominent position at 40%. This result aligns with the data from Fig. 41.2, which indicates that most of the sample individuals are from the youth age group.

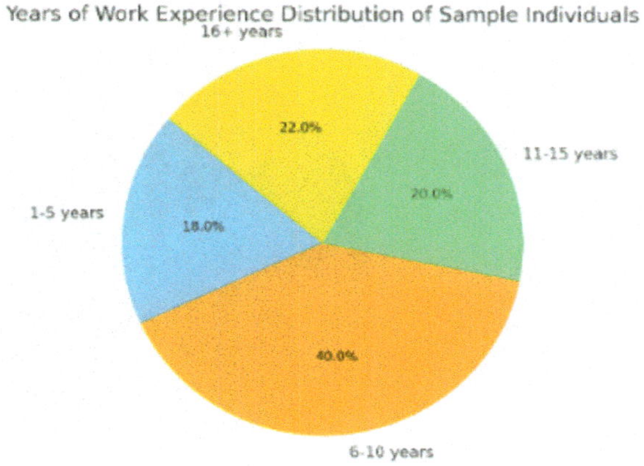

Fig. 41.5 Illustrates the years of work experience of the study sample individuals

We observe from Fig. 41.6 that most of the study samples have been using mobile journalism for 8 years or more, with their proportion reaching 44%. This result may reflect the development and widespread adoption of mobile journalism techniques, making it a more accessible and widely used tool among journalists. This percentage is close to the 4–7 years category, which accounts for 38%.

We observe from Fig. 41.7 that most of the study samples use mobile journalism daily, with a high percentage reaching 70%. This result indicates the necessity of using mobile journalism, which enables journalists to cover and report news as it

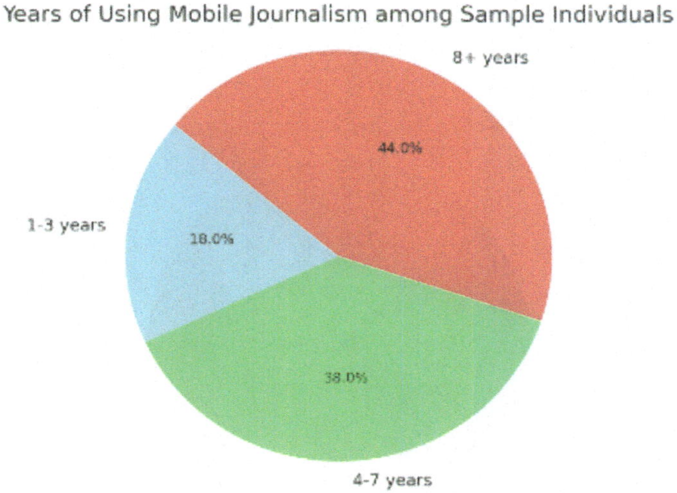

Fig. 41.6 Illustrates the years of using mobile journalism among the sample individuals

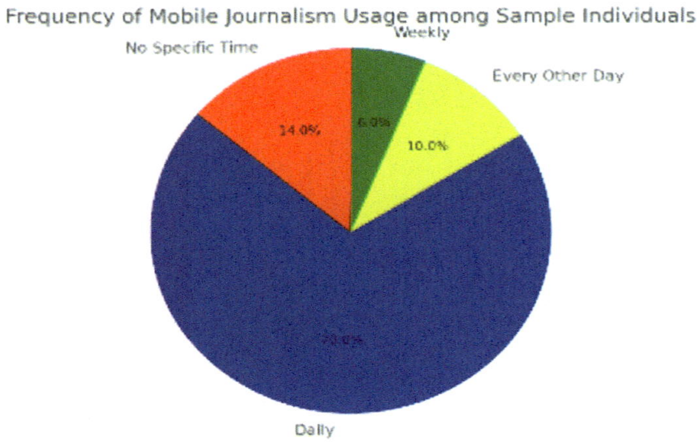

Fig. 41.7 Illustrates the frequency of mobile journalism usage among the sample individuals

happens. This result is consistent with most studies on mobile journalism, including the study [13].

We observe from Fig. 41.8 that more than half of the study samples use mobile journalism for 3–6 h daily, with a percentage reaching 52%. This result reflects that the sample individuals use mobile journalism for extended hours, as it facilitates capturing photos and videos, recording interviews, editing articles, distributing and publishing them, interacting with published news, and responding to audience comments [14].

We observe from Fig. 41.9 that the most common activity performed by the study sample through mobile journalism applications is text editing, which accounts for

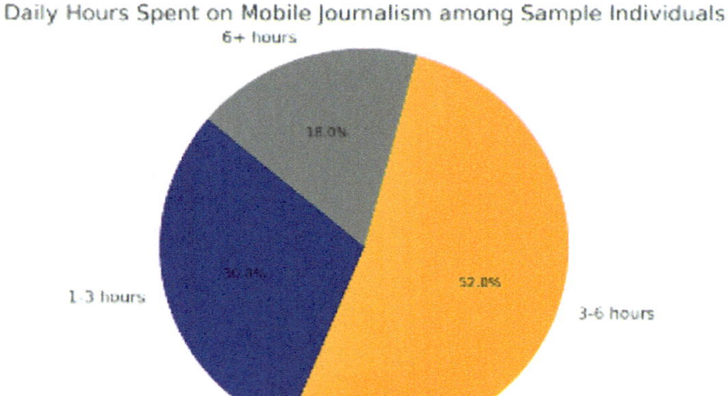

Fig. 41.8 Illustrates the daily hours spent by the sample individuals using mobile journalism

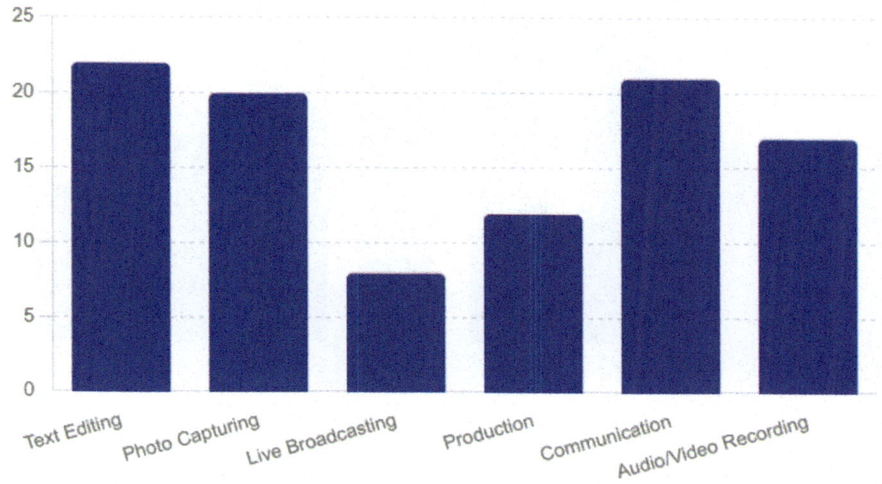

Fig. 41.9 Illustrates the activities performed by the sample individuals through mobile journalism applications

22% and ranks first. This is closely followed by the activity of communication, which accounts for 21% and ranks second.

We observe from the data in Fig. 41.10 that the categories of "speed and immediacy of obtaining information" and "reducing effort and equipment" are tied for the top reasons for using mobile journalism among the study sample, each accounting for 20%. The second most common reason is "ease of producing and publishing journalistic content," which accounts for 19%. The third reason is "the ability to communicate with the audience," at 18%. This result is consistent with the study [15], which found that "speed and ease of obtaining information" is one of the main reasons for using mobile journalism.

We observe from Fig. 41.11 that the category of "Reports" has the highest percentage, ranking first in terms of the content that the study sample publishes through mobile journalism applications, with a percentage of 27%. The second place is occupied by the categories of "Breaking News" and "News Stories," each with an equal percentage of 23%.

We observe from Fig. 41.12 that most of the study samples use social media applications extensively among other types of mobile journalism applications, ranking first with a percentage of 40%. This result is consistent with the study [16], which confirmed that social media applications are the most used type of mobile journalism among the respondents.

We observe from Fig. 41.13 that most of the study samples use Instagram, which ranks first with a percentage of 20%, while Facebook ranks second with a percentage of 17%. This result differs from the studies [17], which both confirmed that Facebook is the most used application among the other applications.

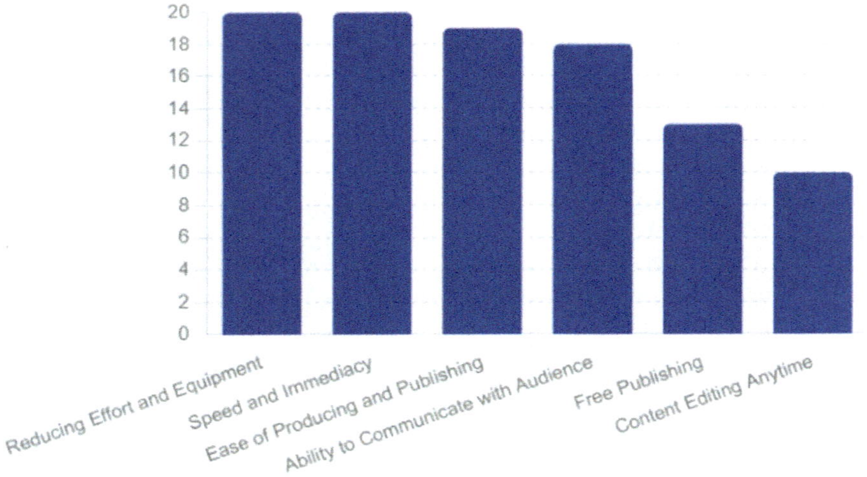

Fig. 41.10 Illustrates the reasons for using mobile journalism among the sample individuals

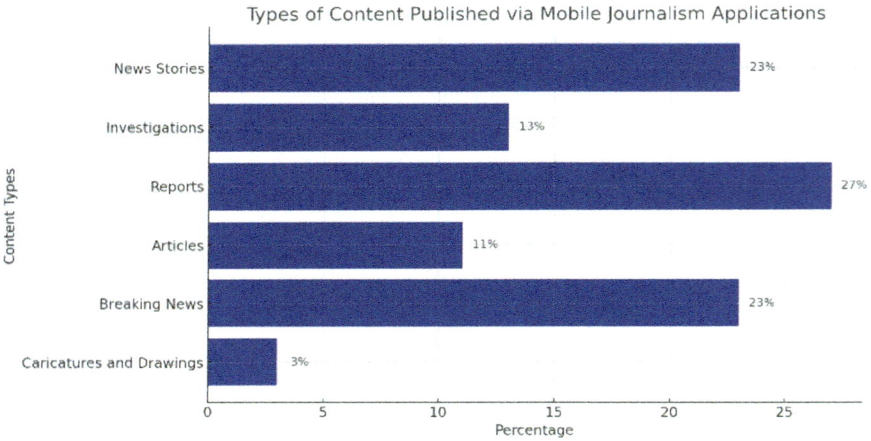

Fig. 41.11 Illustrates the content that the sample individuals publish through mobile journalism applications

We observe from Fig. 41.14 that the category "reducing time and effort" ranks first among the motivations for using mobile journalism, with a percentage of 94%. The category "understanding others' opinions on societal issues" ranks second, with a percentage of 92%. This result is consistent with the study [18], which found that "reducing effort" is one of the main motivations for using mobile journalism. However, it differs from the study [19], which indicated that "freely expressing my opinions" is one of the main motivations for using mobile journalism.

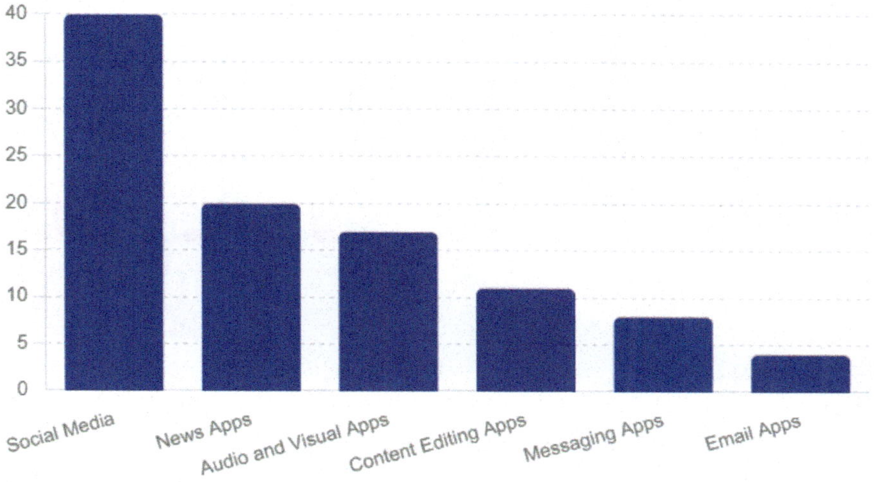

Fig. 41.12 Illustrates the most used mobile journalism applications

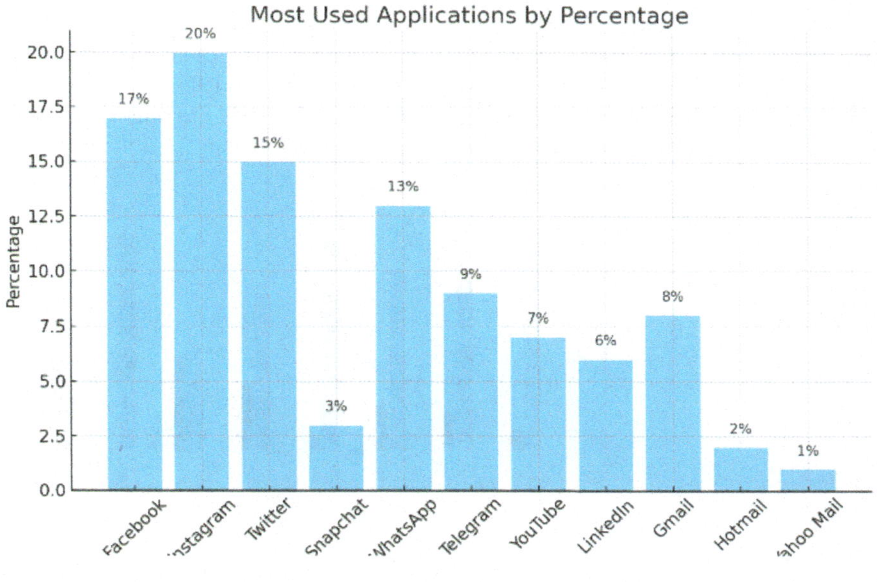

Fig. 41.13 Illustrates the most used applications by the sample individuals

We observe from Fig. 41.15 that the category "using mobile journalism allows for sharing information and direct interaction with the audience" ranks first among the gratifications achieved from using mobile journalism, with a percentage of 96%. The category "using mobile journalism helps in the rapid coverage of daily events" ranks

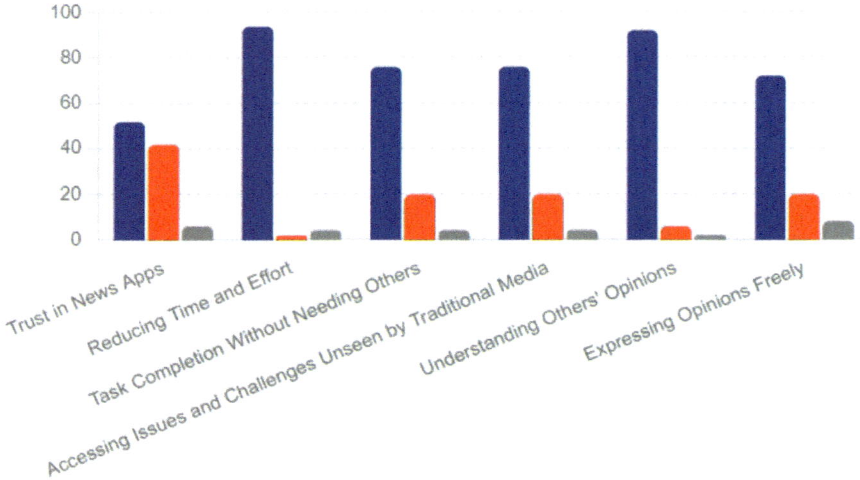

Fig. 41.14 Illustrates the motivation behind the sample individuals' use of mobile journalism

second, with a percentage of 92%, while the category "using mobile journalism is practically easy" ranks third. We also notice that the percentages among these three categories are very close. These results differ from the study [19], which found that "communicating with friends and gauging the general mood" are among the most significant gratifications achieved from using mobile journalism.

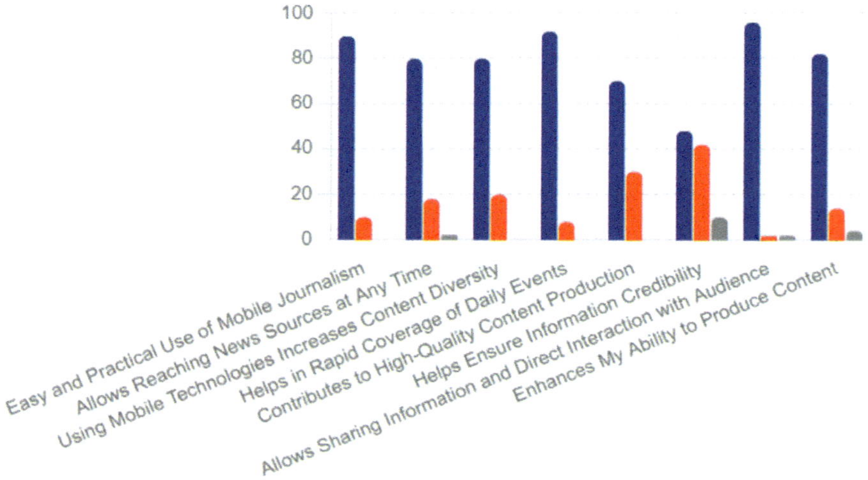

Fig. 41.15 Illustrates the gratifications achieved by the sample individuals from using mobile journalism

41.4 Results

The findings of the study confirm that mobile journalism is an essential tool for journalists in Baghdad. In the field of journalism, most media outlets use digital and mobile reporting tools, and the presence of this technique in the study reveals a positive advantage. This section focuses on the trends and the insights gained from the analysis of the data collected from the field related to the extent of the use of mobile journalism among the communication practitioners and how effective it is:

1. Demographic Insights

Gender Distribution: The study shows that 62% of the users of mobile journalism tools are male, and females comprise 38%. The difference in the population shows a considerable gap in the use, which is potentially due to many cultural issues, which have a great influence on young girls' career decision-making in journalism.

Age Group Analysis: Most of the users belong to the age group of 20 to 29 years, constituting 42%. Youths and other persons in this age group are more open to using their mobile tools for journalistic purposes. This is due to the exposure of the group to the use of digital devices in their personal lives and their emphasis on speed and immediacy.

Educational Attainment: Findings from the data collection indicate that half, 50%, of the respondents have a bachelor's degree. Comparatively 30% have done higher studies, which clearly give the data a more educated and sophisticated population which is open to adopting various new technologies like using mobile phones for journalism purposes.

2. Usage Patterns and Frequency

Years of experience with mobile journalism: The data collected from the primary tools of data collection reveals that 44% of the users have had over 6 years of experience with the tools. From the data 38% of the users have had 4–7 years of experience with the tools. This is a long and clear show of its high presence among the journalists in Baghdad.

Frequency of usage: 70% of the respondents use it daily, of which 52% give it 3 to 6 h of their days. This clear high percentage shows the high effectiveness of the tool. This includes how it helps the communication practitioners in their daily provision and dissemination of news both inside and outside Iraq.

3. Activities and Content Focus

Main activities: Text editing, at 22%, and communications, 21%, are the leading activities conducted through the mobile journalism platforms used by the practitioners. The activities show that mobile devices are important use as they are used to edit the text for daily news creation. They are also an important tool for communication to the public as the feedback and comments can be easily read and responded to using mobile devices.

The type of content: The data collected reveals that reports comprise 27% of the publications. On the other hand, breaking news and news stories are each 23% of the information collected. This shows the high usage, usefulness of reports for comprehensive storage of information, and how they are used as a main source of information release by the victim. At the same time, the news shows the need for the news to be released more quickly and shows a great need for the dissemination of the actual newsflashes needed in more immediate condition.

4. Motivations for Using Mobile Journalism

Efficiency and Speed: The primary motivations for adopting mobile journalism were "speed and immediacy in obtaining information" and "reducing effort and equipment requirements". This implies that journalists are motivated to use tools that allow them to develop content rapidly and in a straightforward manner.

Audience Interaction: Being able to interact directly with the audience was a significant motivation, with 96% of journalists deeming it valuable. This also suggests that current trends in journalism are becoming more interactive, with the audience's feedback playing a critical role in the work of journalists regarding content development.

5. Gratifications Achieved

Direct Interaction with the Audience: The most prominent gratification, confirmed by 96% of journalists, is that they can share information with the audience. It is worth noting that this practice is the outcome of the increasing reliance of social media consumers on their interactions with journalists' profiles to follow current events and particular stores. Ease of use: 90% of respondents deemed the tools of mobile journalism almost practically easy to use. This logic might explain why they were highly enthusiastic about its adoption in the field. The ease of use also benefits the deployment and adoption of the practice among considerably older age and experienced groups.

Rapid Coverage of Events: Another gratification endorsed by 92% of journalists was the possibility to exploit the tools in day-to-day event coverage. This reflects the nature of modern media environments, where the receipt of timely updates is commonplace.

6. Preferred Applications for Mobile Journalism

Dominance of social media: The study found that 40% of journalists mainly use social media like Instagram and Facebook for their mobile journalism, with 20% and 17% saying they used Instagram and Facebook most often, respectively. I interpreted the results as having the potential of indicating the growing trend of mobile journalism in Iraq, and especially in Baghdad, and the realization of media innovators that it is not just an efficiency tool. Overall, despite the noted gender difference in usage, there is a high level of engagement with the adopted practices and technologies, as also reflected by the preference for social media as a primary tool for interacting with viewers.

These results are mostly consistent with the literature reviewed except for their distributions. Specifically, mobile journalism has the most significance among Baghdad journalists, contrary to the literature which suggests that the phenomenon is only of relative importance. In addition, to the new purpose for which mobile journalism is used, the described results hint that it is not only a way to get more done effectively; it is also a method for creating a closer relationship between a journalist and the target audience. The explored levels of engagement and the prevalence of social media uses as the primary online undertaking suggest that mobile journalism can revolutionize traditional reporting by making it more immediate, interactive, and audience driven. Nevertheless, as research indicates, significant gender differences in the use of mobile journalism suggests that female journalists must be specifically targeted to engage them in the practice more actively.

41.5 Conclusion

After conducting research devoted to the utilization of mobile journalism among the communication practitioners in Baghdad, it is possible to conclude that this technology has an impressive impact on news gathering, production, and distribution processes. Facebook and YouTube, which are characterized by the author as social media applications, emerge as tools allowing the representatives of the participants to meet both utilitarian and ritualistic gratifications in a way that exceeds the opportunities provided by the traditional types of media. Another important finding is that mobile journalism tends to be most used by the representatives of the younger generation of well-educated journalists for whom the issues of immediacy, speed, and convenience appear to be crucial. The most significant contribution of this technology appears to be revealed in the gratifications lump, the potent gratifications of which were identified as an ability to interact with the audience directly and to share the information immediately. In this way, the scholars demonstrate that the further development of mobile journalism presupposes the enhancement of mobile journalism education within media curricula, the improvement of legal frameworks for regulating credibility and fighting misinformation, as well as the adherence to the development of ethical standards. At the same time, taking into consideration the fact that mobile journalism changes the very structure of media, it is possible to note that the research suggests a direction of the further process of professionalization and integration of mobile journalism into the media system.

Many recommendations can be made to increase the efficiency of the role of mobile journalism in Iraq. First, it needs to be actively integrated into the training programs of this area with the award of a university degree because an increasing number of future journalists should be provided with certain practical skills of this kind. On the other hand, in pursuit of excellence, it is crucial to develop relevant programs. In addition, a legal framework should be developed and include both the means of guaranteeing already existing mobile journalism's credibility and mechanisms of restricting the dissemination of harmful information. The strategy should be formed on the idea of equipping students and production workers with relevant skills in the field of using communication technology in the context of production and evidence that they are necessary. It is also evidentially necessary to carry out extensive field research in this area, and the results of the research should be considered in the plans of student and practical training. One of the most pressing issues in this respect is the problem of the ethical dimension of mobile journalism, including not only the issue of the moral purity of information but also the question of its credibility, as well as some features that distinguish it from mobile journalism.

References

1. Rodríguez Vázquez, A., Sixto García, J., Ordóñez, K.: Social audience and media (2022). https://doi.org/10.4324/9781003260813-8
2. Whiting, A., Williams, D.: Why people use social media: a uses and gratifications approach. Qual. Market Res. **16** (2013). https://doi.org/10.1108/QMR-06-2013-0041
3. Kareem, A.A., Hasan, S.K.: Employment of Iraqi news agencies on social media platforms in news production: an analytical study. J. Media Res. **16**(64), 40–61 (2024). https://doi.org/10.33282/abaa.v16i64.1056
4. Lin, Y.H., Fang, C.-H., Hsu, C.-L.: Determining uses and gratifications for mobile phone apps. Lect. Notes Electric. Eng. **309**, 661–668 (2014). https://doi.org/10.1007/978-3-642-55038-6_103
5. Hamood, A.S.: Vocabulary acquisition through viber emoticons messaging app among Iraqi students. Opcion **35**(special issue no. 21), 2899–2921 (2019). ISSN: 1012-1587, ISSNe: 2477-9385
6. Al-Quran, M.: Traditional media versus social media: challenges and opportunities. Tech. Rom. J. Appl. Sci. Technol. 4:145–160 (2022). https://doi.org/10.47577/technium.v4i10.8012
7. Mauri-Ríos, M., Ramon, X., Rodriguez-Martinez, R.: Media coverage of the Covid-19 crisis: recommendations and proposals for self-regulation. El profesional de la información, vol. 29 (2021). https://doi.org/10.3145/epi.2020.nov.22
8. Saka, E.: The role of social media-based citizen journalism practices in the formation of contemporary protest movements (2018). https://doi.org/10.4324/9781315109008-4
9. Rodrigues, L.P., Baldi, V., Gala, A.: Mobile journalism: the emergence of a new field of journalism. Braz. Journal. Res. **17**(2) (2021). https://doi.org/10.25200/BJR.v17n2.2021.1368
10. Adetunji, R., Abdulgaffar, A., Adeyemo, S.O., Ramzan, M.: Unveiling social gratifications sought and obtained from social media utilization. J. Messenger **12**(2), 168–181 (2020). https://doi.org/10.26623/themessenger.v12i2.1818
11. Weber, M.S., Napoli, P.M.: Journalism history, web archives, and new methods for understanding the evolution of digital journalism. Digit. Journal. **6**(9), 1186–1205 (2018). https://doi.org/10.1080/21670811.2018.1510293
12. Cochrane, T., Sissons, H., Mulrennan, D.: Journalism 2.0: exploring the impact of mobile and social media on journalism education (2012). https://doi.org/10.4018/jmbl.2013040102
13. Procter, R., Voss, A., Lvov, I.: Audience research and social media data: opportunities and challenges. Particip. J. Audience Recept. Stud. **12**(1), 470–493 (2015)
14. Larsson, A.: The news user on social media: a comparative study of interacting with media organizations on Facebook and Instagram. Journal. Stud. **19** (2017). https://doi.org/10.1080/1461670X.2017.1332957
15. Prestianta, A.: Mobile journalism practice in the Kompas.com newsroom. Komunikator **14**(3), 137–147 (2022). https://doi.org/10.18196/jkm.15883
16. Chowdhury, U.K.: Growth of digital journalism in South Asia: the story so far. In: Dahiya, S., Trehan, K. (eds.) Handbook of Digital Journalism, pp. 1–15. Springer, Singapore (2024)

17. Silva-Rodríguez, A., Øie, K.: The role of mobile media in journalism education (2022). https://doi.org/10.4324/9781003260813-5
18. Diddi, A., Larose, R.: Getting hooked on news: Uses and gratifications and the formation of news habits among college students in an Internet environment. J. Broadcast. Electron. Media **50**, 193–210 (2006). https://doi.org/10.1207/s15506878jobem5002_2
19. Westlund, O., Färdigh, M.A.: Accessing the news in an age of mobile media: tracing displacing and complementary effects of mobile news on newspapers and online news. Mobile Media Commun. **3**(1), 53–74 (2015). https://doi.org/10.1177/2050157914549039

Chapter 42
IoT Resource Allocation Using Regression Analysis

Nour Mostafa, Ahmed Younes Shdefat, Mohammad Salman, Chamseddine Zaki, and Fahmi Elsayed

Abstract The increasing complexity and scale of Internet of Things (IoT) networks demand innovative approaches to resource management that ensure efficiency, reliability, and cost-effectiveness. Our proposed model tackles the increasing complexity and scale of Internet of Things (IoT) networks by leveraging multivariate regression analysis for dynamic resource allocation, enhancing system performance, reliability, and cost-efficiency. By processing real-time data from a broad range of IoT devices, the model predicts resource needs and optimizes distribution. It features several key components, data acquisition module for collecting and verifying data integrity, a preprocessing module that cleans and normalizes data for quality analysis, and a core regression analysis Engine that uses advanced statistical techniques to model relationships between input variables and resource needs. This engine adapts various regression methods, linear, logistic, or polynomial based on data characteristics to forecast demand accurately. Resource allocation is managed by a dedicated module that prioritizes tasks and dynamically adjusts resources like bandwidth according to regression outputs. A Feedback Loop continuously refines these decisions by integrating real-time adjustments, enhancing the model's adaptability to network changes. Additionally, a user-friendly interface allows administrators to manually adjust the automated system, ensuring control over the allocation process. This robust model not only improves efficiency and reduces operational costs but also scales effectively with IoT network expansion, demonstrating significant advancements over traditional methods through extensive simulations.

42.1 Introduction

In the rapidly evolving Internet of Things (IoT) ecosystem, efficiently managing resource allocation across an expanding network of diverse devices presents a formidable challenge. The inherent heterogeneity and varied data communication

N. Mostafa (✉) · A. Y. Shdefat · M. Salman · C. Zaki · F. Elsayed
College of Engineering and Technology, American University of the Middle East, Egaila, Kuwait
e-mail: nour.moustafa@aum.edu.kw

F. P. García Márquez et al. (eds.), *Computing, Internet of Things and Data Analytics*, Smart Innovation, Systems and Technologies 387,
https://doi.org/10.1007/978-3-031-87154-2_42

patterns of IoT devices necessitate advanced resource management strategies to ensure optimal system performance and reliability [1]. Regression analysis provides a robust framework for modeling relationships between dependent and independent variables, offering crucial insights for proactive and predictive resource allocation. The application of regression analysis in IoT management involves leveraging historical data to predict future resource needs, thus facilitating proactive adjustments to resource distribution. This capability proves invaluable in environments such as smart cities or industrial IoT systems, where resource demands may fluctuate unpredictably. By predicting and understanding these variations, IoT systems can optimize resource utilization, minimize operational costs, and enhance service quality [2].

Moreover, regression models are uniquely suited to adapt to the dynamic nature of IoT systems. As new data becomes available, these models can be refined to improve their accuracy and relevance, addressing rapid changes in device configurations and user interactions. This adaptability is crucial for maintaining effective resource management in fluid IoT environments. This study explores various regression techniques—linear, logistic, and polynomial regression—and their application to specific IoT challenges. It assesses the impact of these methodologies on the scalability and robustness of IoT frameworks, providing a comprehensive evaluation of their transformative potential in IoT resource management. Through detailed analyses and real-world case studies, the paper highlights the significant role of regression analysis in navigating the complexities of resource allocation within extensive IoT networks [3, 4].

Our proposed model uses multivariate regression analysis to dynamically allocate resources within IoT settings, enhancing system performance substantially. It features an integrated architecture that processes real-time data from an array of IoT devices, enabling precise prediction of resource needs and distribution optimization. Key components of the model include a Data Acquisition Module for data integrity, a Preprocessing Module for data cleaning and normalization, and a core Regression Analysis Engine that applies statistical techniques to forecast demand [5]. Resource allocation is managed by a dedicated module that adjusts resources based on predictive analytics, with a Feedback Loop that refines decisions by monitoring outcomes and making real-time adjustments. Additionally, an intuitive User Interface allows administrators to manage and adjust the automated system, further enhancing control over the allocation process. This robust model not only optimizes resource distribution across IoT networks but also efficiently scales with their growth, thereby addressing modern IoT challenges and significantly improving system efficiency and cost-effectiveness [5, 6].

42.2 Related Work

The study in [7] demonstrates that the Hybrid Bayesian Evolutionary Strategy (HBES)-optimized Gated Recurrent Unit (GRU) model significantly outperforms existing resource usage prediction models in edge computing environments. The HBES-GRU model achieved the lowest Root Mean Square Error (RMSE) and Mean Absolute Error (MAE) across various resource metrics, notably CPU and RAM usage. However, the study's main shortcoming is the limited evaluation on a small-scale infrastructure, potentially affecting the generalizability of the findings to larger, more diverse edge computing environments. The authors in [4] presents a cloud-edge cooperative content delivery method utilizing deep reinforcement learning (DRL) to optimize processing, caching, and networking resources in edge computing for IoT. The main finding indicates that the DRL approach significantly reduces latency and improves resource utilization, as demonstrated by substantial performance improvements over traditional methods in various simulations. However, a notable shortcoming is the limited evaluation scope, as the simulations were conducted in controlled environments, potentially impacting the applicability of the results to more complex, real-world scenarios.

The authors in [8] developed of an AI-driven collaborative dynamic resource allocation (ACDRA) algorithm, which significantly enhances resource allocation efficiency in 6G-enabled massive IoT environments. The ACDRA algorithm, which integrates a dynamic nested neural network with Markov decision process training, improves the average resource hit rate by approximately 8% and reduces the average decision delay time by about 7% compared to existing algorithms. However, the algorithm's efficacy is limited by its current inability to handle the mutual influence of parallel task executions and resource conflicts, which warrants further research.

The authors in [9] investigate a Quality of Experience (QoE)-based dynamic resource allocation (RA) model for Industrial Internet of Things (IIoT) using reinforcement learning (RL). The main finding reveals that the proposed RL-based model improves resource utilization efficiency by approximately 20% compared to traditional Q-learning approaches, demonstrating faster convergence to minimal cost in simulations. However, a significant shortcoming is the lack of real-world implementation and testing, which may limit the model's applicability and scalability in diverse industrial environments. The authors in [10] introduces the Branching Dueling Q-Network Resource Allocation (BDQ-RA) algorithm, designed to optimize resource allocation in IoT systems integrated with blockchain and Mobile Edge Computing (MEC). The primary finding is that the BDQ-RA algorithm effectively reduces the action space to one-ninth of its original size, enhancing system reward by approximately 12% compared to traditional Deep Q-Network (DQN) methods. However, a significant shortcoming is the reliance on simulated environments for testing, which may not fully capture real-world complexities and scalability challenges.

The authors in [11] introduces the Adaptive and Priority-Based Resource Allocation (A-PBRA) mechanism, demonstrating superior performance in resource utilization, response time, task execution time, and energy consumption compared to existing methods. Extensive simulations confirmed its efficiency in dynamically adapting to incoming requests and optimizing resource allocation. However, the model's effectiveness diminishes as the number of requests significantly increases, leading to higher competition and potential delays. Future research should address these scalability issues and further refine the prioritization mechanism to enhance its robustness in high-demand scenarios.

42.3 Proposed Model Overview

Our proposed model utilizes multivariate regression analysis to dynamically allocate resources in IoT networks. By analyzing real-time data from various sensors and devices, the model predicts demand and optimizes resource distribution, thereby enhancing system efficiency and reliability while reducing operational costs.

42.3.1 Model Architecture

Architecture of our proposed model for IoT resource allocation is structured to efficiently handle the complexities of large-scale IoT environments. It integrates a series of modules as shown in Fig. 42.1 designed to capture, process, and act upon diverse data streams in real time.

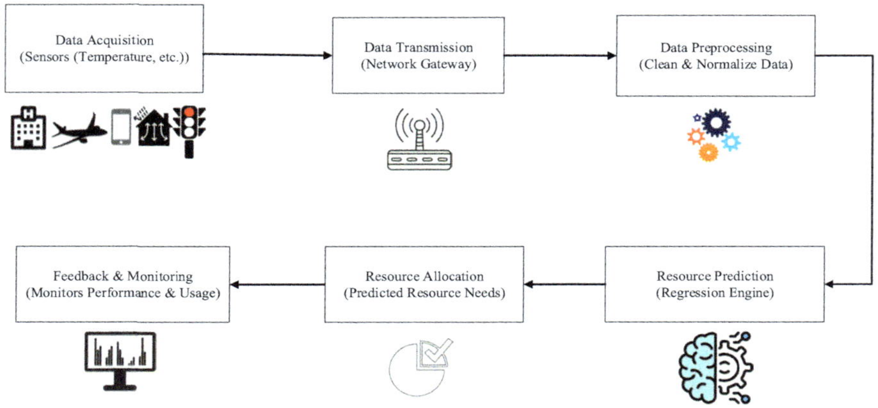

Fig. 42.1 Proposed system model

1. **Data Acquisition Module**: This component is responsible for collecting raw data from a myriad of IoT devices and sensors across the network. It ensures data integrity and timely retrieval to support accurate analysis. Data types range from simple device status indicators to complex environmental readings.
2. **Preprocessing Module**: Here, data is cleaned, normalized, and transformed to prepare for analysis. This step is crucial to remove noise and handle missing or inconsistent data, which could otherwise skew the predictive accuracy of the model.
3. **Regression Analysis Engine**: At the core of the architecture is the regression analysis engine, which employs advanced statistical methods to model the relationship between input variables (e.g., device usage patterns, time of day) and the target variable (resource needs). The engine can adapt various regression techniques—linear, logistic, or polynomial—depending on the specificity of the application and data characteristics.
4. **Resource Allocation Manager**: Based on the output from the regression analysis engine, this module makes decisions on how resources should be allocated across the IoT network. It prioritizes tasks, allocates bandwidth, and dynamically adjusts resources in response to predicted demand.
5. **Feedback Loop**: A feedback mechanism refines the model by continuously monitoring outcomes and incorporating adjustments. This ensures the model remains effective under changing conditions and can evolve with the network.
6. **User Interface**: An intuitive user interface allows administrators to view real-time analytics, receive alerts, and manually override automated decisions if necessary.

This architecture not only maximizes efficiency and adaptability but also scales seamlessly with the expansion of IoT infrastructures, making it a robust solution for modern IoT challenges.

Algorithm: IoT environment with varying conditions
Variable space V representing all significant variables for regression.
Target space T representing all predicted re source needs Objective function O reflecting optimization of resource allocation efficiency

Initialize:
Regression Model with initial parameters β
Data Preprocessor for cleaning and normalizing data
Resource Allocation System for managing distribution

1. **for each** period $p = 1$ to p do
2. Initialize the IoT environment to obtain the initial dataset D_0
3. **for each** time interval $i = 1$ to I do
4. Collect data d_i from IoT environment
5. Preprocess data d_i using Data Preprocessor
6. Predict resource needs t_i using Regression Model (D_i, β)
7. Allocate resources according to predicted needs t_i
8. Observe performance measure m_i and new data set $D_{(i+1)}$
9. Store data transition $(D_i, t_i, m_i, D_{(i+1)})$ for model refinement
10. **If** model refinement conditions are met:
11. Update Regression Model using stored data transitions (apply batch processing for regression fitting)
12. adjust preprocessing or prediction parameters to improve accuracy
13. **end for**
14. **Return** the optimized Regression Model

Output: Optimized regression-based resource allocation model

The proposed algorithm starts with Setting up the initial configuration for the regression model and other components. Step 1–14: these steps outline the process from data collection to resource allocation, including model updates based on new data. Each cycle refines the regression model to improve prediction accuracy and resource allocation. Input and output: define what the model takes as inputs (IoT environment conditions, data, etc.) and what it outputs (an optimized resource allocation model). This structured approach ensures continuous learning and adaptation of the regression model to the IoT environment, facilitating more efficient and effective resource management.

42.4 Math Modeling of the Proposed IoT Resource Allocation Using RL Model

To mathematically model the IoT resource allocation using regression analysis, we need to define several components that interact within the system. This model involves the prediction of resource needs based on observed variables from IoT devices and sensors. Here's how the regression model is structured:

42.4.1 Variables Definition

Let $X = (x_1, x_2, \ldots\ldots.., x_n)^T$ be the vector of predictor variables collected from the IoT devices, where n is the number of predictors. These predictors could include metrics such as device usage patterns, sensor data (temperature, motion, etc.), and time indices.

Let y be the target variable representing the resource needs, such as bandwidth, computing power, or storage.

42.4.2 Regression Model

The objective is to find a function f that maps the predictors X to the target y, which is modeled as:

$$y = f(X, \beta) + \in$$

- β represents the coefficients or parameters of the model which we need to estimate.
- $\in$ is the error term, accounting for the deviation of the predictions from the actual observations.

42.4.3 Choice of Regression Model

Depending on the nature of the data and the relationship between the variables, f can take various forms:

- **Linear Regression**: If the relationship is linear, f will be:

$$f(X, \beta) = X^T \beta$$

- **Polynomial Regression**: For non-linear relationships, involving powers of the predictors:

$$f(X, \beta) = \beta_0 + \beta_1 x_1 + \beta_1 x_2^2 + \cdots + \beta_n x_n^n$$

- **Logistic Regression**: If the resource needs are categorical (e.g., high, medium, low), f will be:

$$f(X, \beta) = \frac{1}{1 + e^{-X^T \beta}}$$

42.4.4 Model Estimation

Parameters β are estimated using the method of least squares as an optimization technique, minimizing a loss function:

$$L(\beta) = \sum_{i=1}^{n} (y_i - f(x_i, \beta))^2$$

where n is the number of data points.

42.4.5 Prediction

Once β is estimated, the model can predict resource needs for new data:

$$\hat{y} = f(X_{new}, \hat{\beta})$$

42.4.6 Model Updating

The model may be updated periodically as new data arrives or when the system performance indicates deviations from expected outcomes:

$$\beta_{new} = \text{update}(\beta_{old}, \text{new data})$$

42.4.7 Resource Allocation

Finally, the predicted $\hat{y}$ informs how resources are allocated in the IoT network, ensuring optimal performance across devices and applications.

42.4.8 Feedback Loop

Performance metrics from the allocation decisions are fed back into the model, allowing continuous refinement and adaptation to changing conditions:

$$\text{Feedback} = \text{evaluate}(y, \hat{y})$$

$$\beta = \text{adjust}(\beta, \text{Feedback})$$

This mathematical modeling provides a structured approach to using regression analysis for IoT resource allocation, enabling predictive and dynamic management of complex IoT environments.

42.5 Simulation Results

Our proposed model was evaluated through a comprehensive simulation designed to mimic a real-world Internet of Things (IoT) environment. The simulation scenario and parameters were carefully chosen to reflect the complexity of such environments, including:

- **Resource usage patterns**: We generated simulated data that captured realistic patterns of resource usage by IoT devices.
- **Regression model prediction**: The simulation leveraged the previously defined regression model to predict resource needs based on the generated data.

Our simulations evaluated the effectiveness of a multivariate linear regression model in predicting resource needs for an IoT environment with the following configuration:

42.5.1 Simulation Parameters

- **Number of Devices**: 100 devices, with varying types of sensors.
- **Data Features**: Time of day, device usage patterns, sensor data (temperature, motion, etc.).

- **Resource Types**: Bandwidth, computing power, storage.
- **Simulation Duration**: 24 h with time steps of 1 min.

42.5.2 Data Generation

Realistic data reflecting these parameters was generated:

- **Time of Day**: Randomly distributed throughout 24 h.
- **Device Usage Patterns**: A mix of predictable daily patterns and random spikes simulated realistic usage.
- **Sensor Data**: Sensor readings were generated using normal distributions adjusted for sensor types and expected ranges.

42.5.3 Model Setup and Training

A multivariate linear regression model was trained to predict resource needs based on:

- **Predictors (X)**: Time of day, device usage patterns, sensor readings.
- **Response Variable (Y)**: Resource needs (quantified as a continuous value representing units needed).

The model was trained using a portion of the generated data, minimizing the difference between predicted and actual resource needs.

42.5.4 Prediction and Evaluation

The trained model was then applied to the remaining data to predict resource needs. These predictions were compared with the actual (simulated) needs to assess the model's accuracy using:

- **RMSE (Root Mean Square Error)**: Measures the average magnitude of prediction errors.
- **MAE (Mean Absolute Error)**: Measures the average difference between predicted and actual values.
- **R-squared**: Represents the proportion of variance in actual resource needs explained by the model.

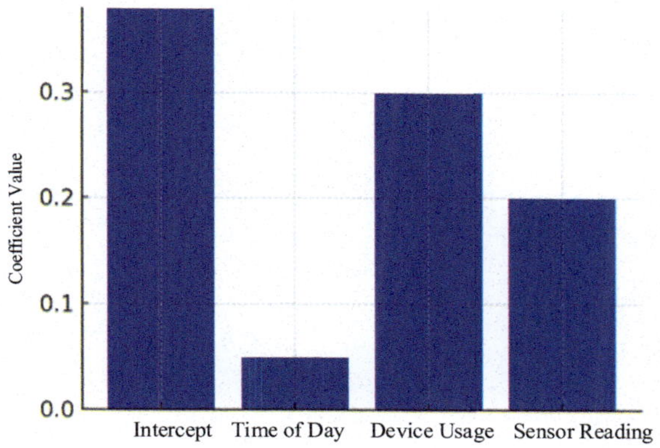

Fig. 42.2 Regression model coefficients

42.5.5 Resource Allocation Efficiency

Beyond accuracy, we evaluated the model's ability to efficiently allocate resources:

- **Percentage of Time Steps**: This metric indicates how often predicted resources were sufficient to meet actual needs, ensuring no downtime or resource overuse.

This simulation allowed us to assess the effectiveness of the proposed model in predicting resource needs within an IoT environment. The results of this analysis are presented in the following section.

Figure 42.2 shows the values of the coefficients used in the regression model, including the intercept and coefficients for each feature like time of day, device usage, and sensor readings.

Figure 42.3 displays key metrics evaluating the model's performance, including RMSE (Root Mean Square Error), MAE (Mean Absolute Error), and the R-squared value, which indicates how well the model fits the data.

Figure 42.4 illustrates how effectively the model allocated resources, showing the percentages of adequate resource allocation, overestimation, and underestimation.

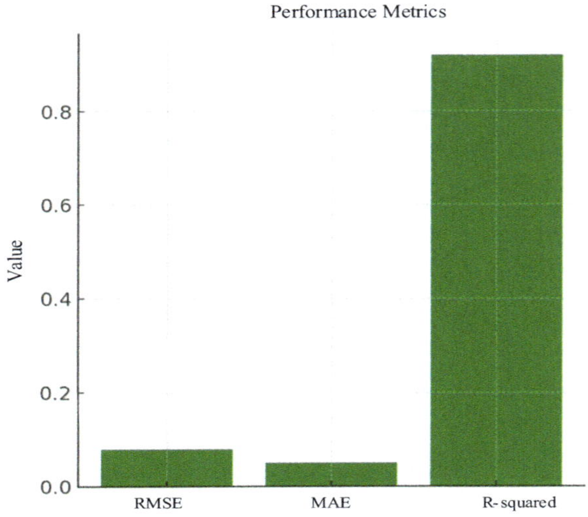

Fig. 42.3 Performance metrics

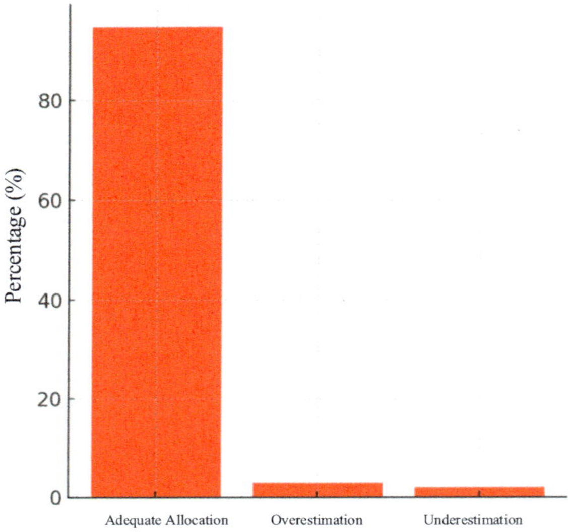

Fig. 42.4 Resource allocation efficiency

42.6 Conclusion

This paper introduces a multivariate regression analysis model designed for dynamic resource allocation in IoT networks. The primary finding is that this model significantly enhances system performance by accurately predicting resource needs based on real-time data from diverse IoT devices. This model optimizes resource distribution, reduces operational costs, and scales efficiently with network growth, demonstrating substantial improvements over traditional methods. The future work will address the integration of real-world data to further validate the model's effectiveness and adaptability in complex, heterogeneous IoT environments. Additionally, exploring hybrid models combining regression analysis with machine learning techniques could enhance predictive accuracy and resource management efficiency.

References

1. Mostafa, N.: Resource selection service based on neural network in fog environment. Adv. Sci. Technol. Eng. Syst. J. **5**(1), 408–417 (2020)
2. Mostafa, N., Al Ridhawi, I., Aloqaily, M.: Fog resource selection using historical executions. In: 2018 Third International Conference on Fog and Mobile Edge Computing (FMEC) 2018 Apr 23, pp. 272–276. IEEE
3. Mostafa, N.: Cooperative fog communications using a multi-level load balancing. In: 2019 Fourth International Conference on Fog and Mobile Edge Computing (FMEC), Rome, Italy, pp. 45–51 (2019). https://doi.org/10.1109/FMEC.2019.8795325
4. Sharma, A., Bordoloi, D., Saini, A., Chari, S.L., Kumar N., Pooja: Deep reinforcement learning for resource allocation in edge computing for IoT. In: 2023 6th International Conference on Contemporary Computing and Informatics (IC3I), Gautam Buddha Nagar, India, pp. 2655–2660 (2023). https://doi.org/10.1109/IC3I59117.2023.10397693
5. Mostafa, N., Aly, W.H., Alabed, S., Al-Arnaout, Z.: Intelligent replica selection in edge and IoT environments using artificial neural networks. Electronics **11**(16), 2531 (2022)
6. Pang, X., Zhang, P.: Resource allocation strategy of IoT based on network slicing. In: 2020 IEEE Computing, Communications and IoT Applications (ComComAp), Beijing, China, pp. 1–6 (2020). https://doi.org/10.1109/ComComAp51192.2020.9398873
7. Violos, J., Tsanakas, S., Theodoropoulos, T., Leivadeas, A., Tserpes, K., Varvarigou, T.: Hypertuning GRU neural networks for edge resource usage prediction. In: 2021 IEEE Symposium on Computers and Communications (ISCC), Athens, Greece, pp. 1–8 (2021). https://doi.org/10.1109/ISCC53001.2021.9631548
8. Lin, K., Li, Y., Zhang, Q., Fortino, G.: AI-driven collaborative resource allocation for task execution in 6G-enabled massive IoT. IEEE Internet of Things J. **8**(7), 5264–5273, (1 Apr. 2021). https://doi.org/10.1109/JIOT.2021.3051031
9. Udayakumar, K., Ramamoorthy, S.: Reinforcement of QoE based Feedback System to allocate resources in IIoT. In: 2022 3rd International conference for emerging technology (INCET), Belgaum, India, pp. 1–5 (2022). https://doi.org/10.1109/INCET54531.2022.9825345
10. Bai, Z., Wan, J., Li, L., Liu, C., Duan, M.: Resource allocation of IoT systems integrated with blockchain and mobile edge computing. In: 2022 4th International Conference on Frontiers Technology of Information and Computer (ICFTIC), Qingdao, China, pp. 377–382 (2022). https://doi.org/10.1109/ICFTIC57696.2022.10075287
11. Sharif, Z., Jung, L.T., Razzak, I., Alazab, M.: Adaptive and priority-based resource allocation for efficient resources utilization in mobile-edge computing. IEEE Internet of Things J. **10**(4), 3079–3093 (2023). https://doi.org/10.1109/JIOT.2021.3111838

Chapter 43
Research on the Chan-Taylor-MCKF Indoor Positioning Algorithm Integrating UWB and IMU

Zijun Zhang, Juan Wang, and Liying Yang

Abstract Addressing the issues of low positioning accuracy or inability to locate in closed spaces by the Global Navigation Positioning System (GNSS), as well as the lack of positioning accuracy and stability in non-line-of-sight environments by the Ultra-wideband Pulse Indoor Positioning Technology (UWB), this paper proposes to integrate UWB positioning technology and Inertial Sensor Technology (IMU) based on the Maximum Correlation Entropy Kalman filter. This approach includes modeling of measurement noise, reducing the weight of abnormal measurements to minimize the impact on state estimations, and combining UWB and IMU measurement data to resolve issues of poor UWB positioning accuracy and positioning result offsets in non-line-of-sight environments. In simulation experiments, multiple base stations were used to locate moving targets. The results demonstrated that the proposed algorithm effectively improved the accuracy and robustness of UWB indoor positioning technology compared to the Kalman filter and Extended Kalman filter.

43.1 Introduction

In open outdoor environments, GNSS (Global Navigation Satellite Systems) can obtain accurate real-time information about positioning targets, offering much convenience for outdoor positioning and navigation. However, in indoor environments where there is considerable obstruction, GNSS signals are weakened or lost, reducing

Z. Zhang · J. Wang (✉)
Shenyang Jianzhu University, Shenyang, China
e-mail: wangjuanneu@163.com

Z. Zhang
e-mail: 764656754@qq.com

L. Yang
Shenyang Institute of Automation Chinese Academy of Science, P.R. China, Shenyang, China

F. P. García Márquez et al. (eds.), *Computing, Internet of Things and Data Analytics*,
Smart Innovation, Systems and Technologies 387,
https://doi.org/10.1007/978-3-031-87154-2_43

GNSS positioning accuracy and failing to meet the needs for precise indoor positioning. Situations such as signal loss and frequent cycle slips often occur in areas where the GNSS signal is weak, such as indoors, canyons, and tunnels [1].

Ultra-Wideband (UWB) technology is a method of radio transmission that uses extremely short pulses to transmit data at the nanosecond level [2]. It employs a signal transmission mechanism that is completely different from that of conventional band-pass modulation. UWB technology is widely used in positioning systems because it is fast, has strong penetration, excellent anti-interference ability, and its distance measurement accuracy reaches the centimeter level. However, under non-line-of-sight (NLOS) environments, UWB signals may have significant shifts or losses, which directly affects their positioning accuracy and stability [3].

To overcome the challenges of high accuracy and robustness in UWB indoor positioning in NLOS environments, this study proposes an indoor high-precision positioning algorithm combining wireless ultra-wideband pulse technology and an Inertial Measurement Unit (IMU) [4]. Based on the Maximum Entropy Correlated Kalman Filter, this algorithm integrates measurement information from the IMU and UWB to mitigate and correct errors introduced by UWB measurements under NLOS conditions. This approach shows effectiveness in improving positioning accuracy and stability. Experimental results demonstrate the high reliability, superior anti-interference performance of this algorithm, and its effectiveness in addressing the problems of NLOS and multipath effects in practical navigation positioning [5]. The algorithm can meet the demand for long-term, high-precision positioning in complex environments.

43.2 MCKF Fusion Filtering Model

To address the issues of reduced positioning accuracy and offset in Non-Line-of-Sight (NLOS) environments during UWB indoor positioning, we have opted to use a fusion of IMU and UWB to enhance positioning accuracy under NLOS conditions.

43.2.1 IMU Coordinate System

When utilizing multisensor fusion for navigation and positioning, selecting the appropriate navigational reference coordinates is essential. In this simulation experiment, all base stations and receivers are considered to be on the same plane, employing a two-dimensional positioning approach. Given that the algorithm model primarily targets indoor and enclosed spaces' local regions, using the ENU (East-North-Up) [6] coordinate system is a suitable choice. Considering the computational burden, complexity of the algorithm, and the requirement for rapid response in practical applications, the quaternion method was ultimately selected. According to reference [7], the quaternion differential equation is as follows:

$$\dot{q} = \frac{1}{2}\Omega(\omega)q = \frac{1}{2}\Omega(q)\omega \tag{43.1}$$

In Eq. (43.1): $\omega = \left[\,\omega_x\ \omega_y\ \omega_z\,\right]^T$, ω_x, ω_y and ω_z represent the angular velocities measured in the XYZ coordinate system by the gyroscope in the inertial sensor, for the various directional angles of the positioning tag during the positioning process. $q = \left[\,q_0\ q_1\ q_2\ q_3\,\right]^T$ is the transition matrix in the quaternion method, namely $q_0^2 + q_1^2 + q_2^2 + q_3^2 = 1$.

43.2.2 Description of the TDOA Positioning Algorithm

Depending on the type of collected data, UWB positioning can be categorized based on different algorithms, including Time of Arrival (TOA), Time-difference of Arrival (TDOA), and Time of Flight (TOF). The TDOA positioning algorithm only requires time synchronization among the base stations, leading to relatively low hardware requirements. Therefore, this paper adopts the TDOA positioning algorithm. When all base station clocks are fully synchronized, the tag sends a ranging signal to the base stations, each of which receives the signal at different times [8]. Setting one of the base stations as a reference, and using its signal reception time as the baseline time, the differences between the reception times at the other base stations and this baseline time create a set of time differences. These time differences are used to construct hyperbolic equations. At least three base stations are needed to form two hyperbolic equations, and the intersection of these two hyperboles is the target's position. The working principle is shown in Fig. 43.1.

43.2.3 Chan-Taylor Weighted Fusion Positioning Algorithm

This paper employs the Chan-Taylor weighted fusion positioning method. The algorithm initially uses the Chan algorithm for preliminary positioning, then takes this result as the initial value for the Taylor algorithm to begin iterative refinement until the positioning error is less than a pre-set threshold [9], at which point iteration stops. Finally, to prevent non-convergence issues under certain conditions, the positioning result of the above procedure and the result of the Chan algorithm are subjected to weighted processing. Hence, the Chan-Taylor weighted algorithm ensures both computational speed and the accuracy of the positioning results. The fusion process of this algorithm is as follows: Calculate the residuals between the solution and the measurements:

$$R_{es} = \sum_{i=1}^{N} [r_i - \|X - X_i\|]^2 \tag{43.2}$$

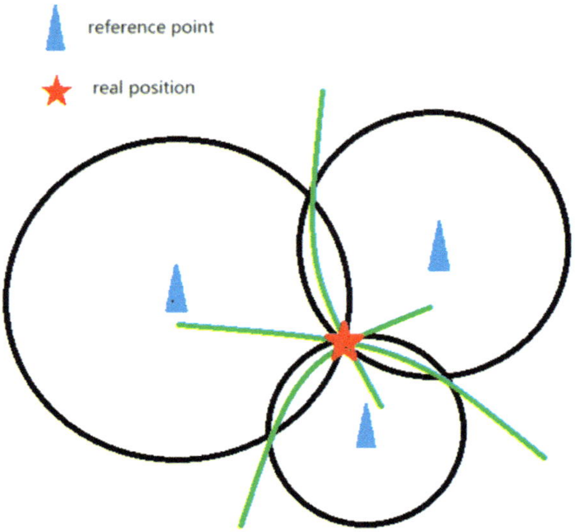

Fig. 43.1 Principle of TDOA positioning

In Eq. (43.2): N is the number of beacon nodes, X is the estimated position; X_i represents the coordinates of the i-th beacon node;

To enhance the positioning accuracy of the algorithm, normalize the residuals:

$$R_k = \frac{R_{es}}{N}$$

In the above equation, the weight coefficient for the k-th algorithm is R_k.

The final position estimation result, obtained through weighted calculation, is as follows:

$$X = \sum_{i=1}^{K} X_k (R_k)^{-1} \Big/ \sum_{i=1}^{K} (R_k)^{-1}$$

43.3 Research on Chan-Taylor-MCKF Fusion Positioning Algorithm

Distinguished from the traditional Kalman filter method which assigns equal weights to measurement errors [10], the Maximum Entropy Kalman Filter adjusts the covariance matrix of measurement noise and allocates lower weights to abnormal measurements within the basic Kalman filtering framework. This approach effectively mitigates the impact of non-Gaussian noise, thereby enhancing system stability and robustness.

To optimize the stability of the Kalman filter in complex environments and enhance its efficiency in handling non-Gaussian noise, this paper incorporates the concept of correlation entropy into the cost function of the Kalman filtering algorithm [11]. The cost function based on maximum correlation entropy is defined as follows:

$$J_{MC} = \min\left(\left\| X_k - \hat{X}_{k|(k-1)} \right\|^2_{P^{-1}_{k|(k-1)}} - \sigma^2 \sum_{i=1}^{m} k_\sigma\left(e_{k,i}\right) \right)$$

Solving for $\frac{\partial J_{MC}}{\partial X_k} = 0$ yields:

$$J_{MCKF} = \min\left(\left\| X_k - \hat{X}_{k|(k-1)} \right\|^2_{P^{-1}_{k|(k-1)}} + \left\| H_k x_k - z_k \right\|^2_{\tilde{R}^{-1}_k} \right) \tag{43.3}$$

In Eq. (43.3): $\tilde{R}_k = R_k^{1/2} \psi_k^{-1} R_k^{T/2}$, $\psi_k = diag\left[k_\sigma\left(e_{k,i}\right)\right]$ represents the weight matrix under MCC (Maximum Correlation Criterion).

The Maximum Entropy Kalman Filter enhances the suppression of non-Gaussian noise by adjusting the covariance matrix of the measurement noise [12]. This improvement can boost the filter's performance across various complex noise environments. This is achieved by modifying ψ_k.

For the state prediction step, the position and direction changes provided by IMU measurements are first used to predict the next state using the following prediction formula:

$$x_{k+1|k} = F x_k + B v_k$$

$$P_{k+1|k} = F P_k F^T + Q$$

wherein, x is the state vector, F is the state transition matrix, v_k is the process noise, B is the control matrix, P is the state covariance matrix and Q is the process noise covariance matrix.

Next, the observation update step is performed based on UWB distance measurements. The following update formula is used:

$$K_k = P_{k+1|k} H^T \left(H P_{k+1|k} H^T + R^{-1}\right)$$

$$x_{k+1} = x_{k+1|k} + K_k \left(z_{k+1} - H x_{k+1|k}\right)$$

$$P_{k+1} = (I - K_k H) P_{k+1|k}$$

wherein, K is the Kalman gain, H is the observation model matrix, z_{k+1} is the UWB observation, and R is the observation noise covariance matrix.

In summary, the MCKF algorithm is implemented through filter initialization, time update [13], and measurement update. The first two steps are the same as those in the traditional Kalman filter algorithm.

$$e_k = R_k^{-1/2} \left(H_k \hat{x}_{k|(k-1)} - z_k\right)$$

$$\psi_k = diag\left[k_\sigma \left(e_{k,i}\right)\right]$$

$$\tilde{R}_k = R_k^{1/2} \psi_k^{-1} R_k^{T/2}$$

wherein, e_k is calculated from the measurement information updated over time [14], and the measurement noise covariance matrix $\tilde{R}_k$ is modified through the weight matrix ψ_k. In the measurement update phase, the measurement noise covariance matrix is first modified, and then the Kalman gain K_k, posterior estimate $\hat{x}_k$, and error covariance matrix $P_{k|k}$ are sequentially calculated using $\tilde{R}_k$:

$$K_k = \left(P_{k|(k-1)}^{-1} + H_k^T R_k^{-1} H_k\right)^{-1} H_k^T \tilde{R}_k^{-1}$$

$$\hat{x}_k = \hat{x}_{k|(k-1)} + K_k \left(z_k - H_k \hat{x}_{k|(k-1)}\right)$$

$$P_{k|k} = (I - K_k H_k) P_{k|(k-1)} (I - K_k H_k)^T + K_k \tilde{R}_k K_k^T$$

The fusion positioning method proposed in this paper, based on the Maximum Entropy Kalman Filter, initiates with obtaining initial data from IMU and UWB through simulation measurements. It employs the Chan-Taylor fusion algorithm to acquire the target's estimated coordinates. Subsequently, the initial measurement data from the IMU undergo preprocessing and positional processing within the prediction phase of the Maximum Entropy Kalman Filter. This is followed by filtering to achieve positioning and tracking of moving targets, ultimately enhancing the accuracy of mobile target positioning.

43.4 Experiments

43.4.1 Simulation of the Chan-Taylor Weighted Algorithm

In this paper, the Matlab simulation tool is used to set up a simulation field with dimensions of 400m by 400m to simulate the Chan-Taylor weighted algorithm. Four base stations are positioned around the field, with coordinates following the cellular network principle, specifically at (0, 0), (400, 0), (400, 400), and (0, 400). In UWB positioning, the more base stations there are, the higher the positioning accuracy. However, considering computational speed and system cost, this experiment selects positioning with 4 base stations, sets the target's initial coordinates at (1, 1), and simulates uniform linear motion within the range of the base stations. This experiment does not take NLOS error into consideration and simulates the effects of Gaussian noise on measurement values with a mean of 0 and standard deviations of 0.2, 0.4, 0.6, 0.8, and 1.0, to test the TDOA measurement value errors.

As shown in Fig. 43.2, simulations demonstrate the relationship between the average positioning error standard and noise error under different algorithms. Compared to the Chan algorithm, the Chan-Taylor weighted algorithm yields smaller positioning errors and closely approximates the performance of the Taylor algorithm initialized with true values. Although the positioning errors are gradually increasing, the Chan-Taylor weighted algorithm overall demonstrates an improvement in positioning accuracy.

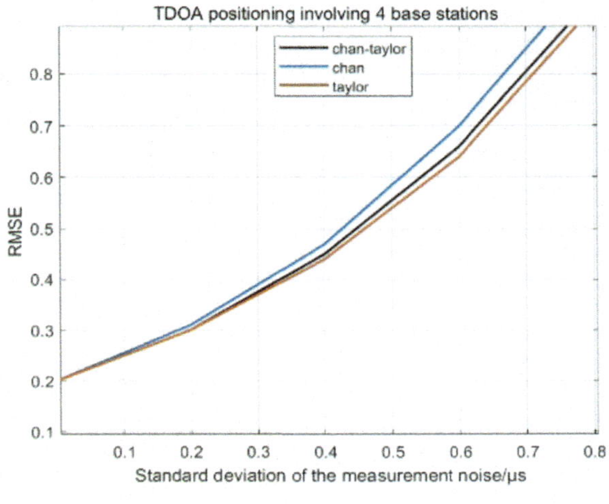

Fig. 43.2 Comparison chart of standard deviations of errors for three algorithms

43.4.2 Simulation of the Chan-Taylor-MCKF Positioning Algorithm

This paper conducts simulation experiments on the suppression effects of non-Gaussian noise by designing three different noise models for the algorithm proposed herein. These experiments introduce designed noise models as interference in the distance measurements between tags and base stations, and then compare the results with the true positions to gather experimental outcomes. In addition, the proposed algorithm is comparatively studied alongside the Chan-Taylor fusion positioning algorithm, KF (Kalman Filter) positioning algorithm, and EKF (Extended Kalman Filter) positioning algorithm. The simulation experiments utilize positioning error, cumulative distribution function, and computational complexity as evaluation metrics. The three noise models are illustrated in Fig. 43.3.

This paper compares the positioning errors of the aforementioned three noise models with those of the Chan-Taylor fusion positioning algorithm, the Kalman Filter (KF) positioning algorithm, and the Extended Kalman Filter (EKF) positioning algorithm. As can be observed in Fig. 43.4, the positioning error of the algorithm presented in this paper is relatively stable and exhibits smaller fluctuations compared to the other algorithms, demonstrating stable positioning performance.

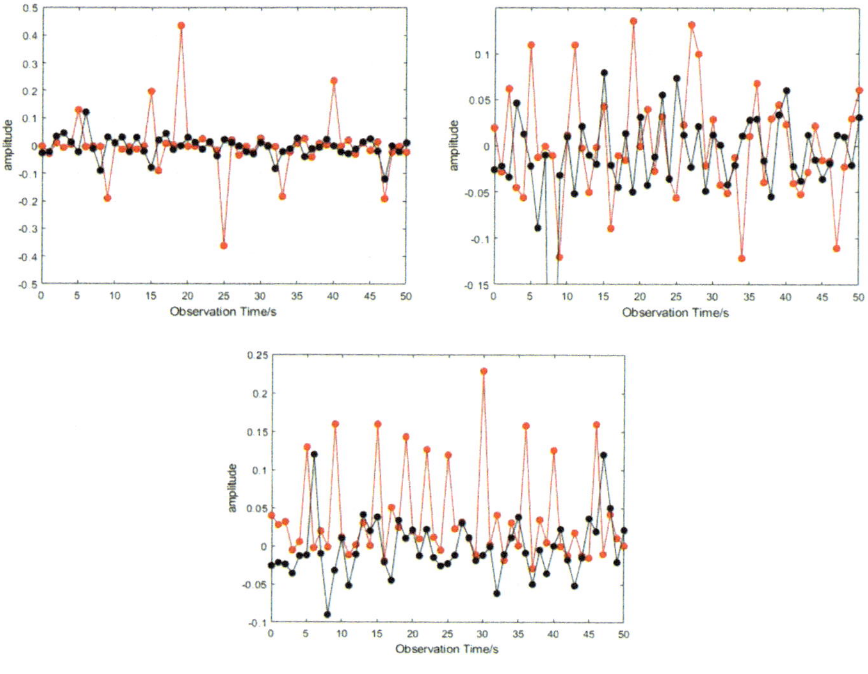

Fig. 43.3 Three types of noise models

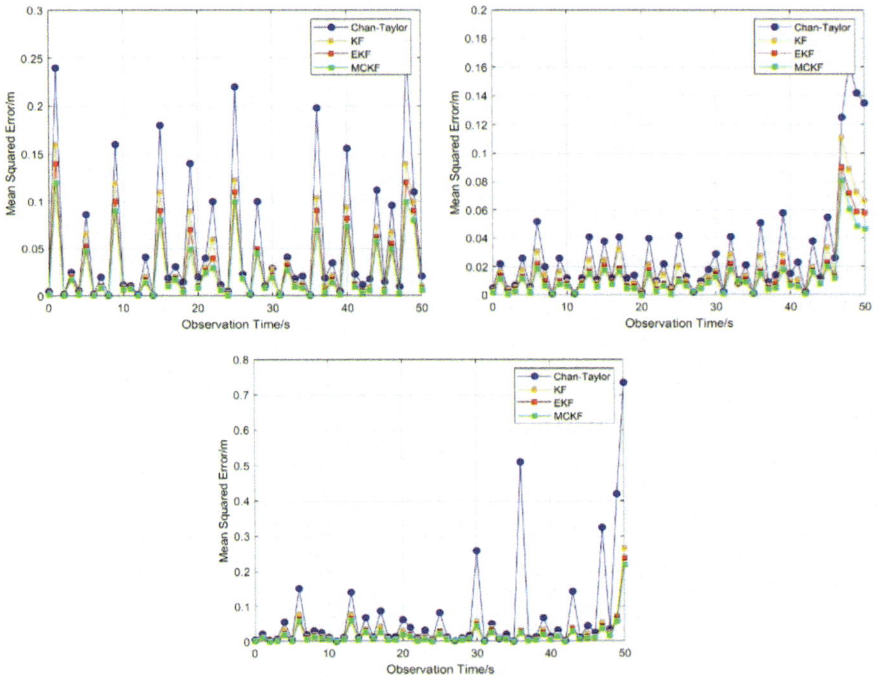

Fig. 43.4 Comparison of positioning errors under different algorithms

Figure 43.5 presents the Cumulative Distribution Function (CDF) curves comparing the algorithm proposed in this paper with several other algorithms under the three aforementioned non-Gaussian noise models. It is not difficult to see from Fig. 43.5 that the curvature of the CDF curve for the algorithm of this paper is better when compared to the other algorithms.

Through comparative analysis, it is evident that in the three different noise models, our proposed algorithm achieves better positioning accuracy relative to the other three methods, demonstrating the superiority of our algorithm.

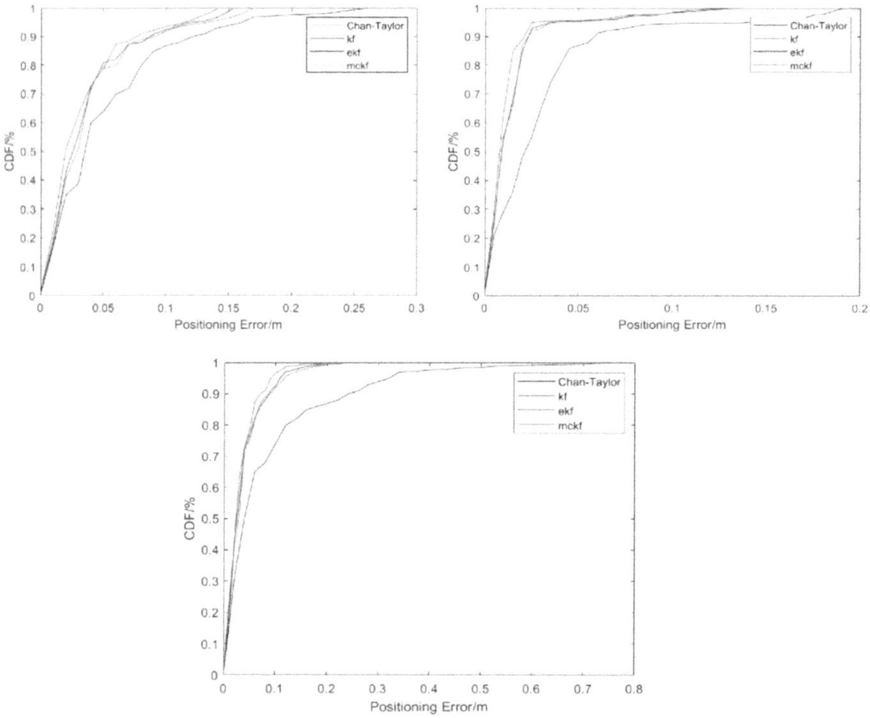

Fig. 43.5 CDF curves under different algorithms

43.5 Conclusion

In response to the challenges posed by complex environments in UWB indoor positioning, such as the inability of GPS to provide accurate positioning due to denial of service, the decrease in target positioning accuracy caused by non-Gaussian noise, and the susceptibility of traditional UWB indoor positioning technology to non-line-of-sight (NLOS) effects, this paper proposes a Maximum Entropy Correlated Kalman Filtering algorithm based on UWB and IMU. This algorithm improves the filtering precision and robustness of the filter to a certain extent compared to the KF and EKF algorithms, thereby enhancing the average positioning accuracy. Experimental results show that moving targets can achieve relatively accurate positioning within the coverage area of the base stations. However, the accuracy of positioning significantly decreases when the targets move toward the edge of the base station coverage. Therefore, future research will focus on further optimizing the positioning accuracy and robustness of moving targets at the boundaries of base station coverage.

Acknowledgements This study was funded by the Liaoning Natural Science Foundation under Grant 2023-MS-224 and 2022-BS-194 and Scientific Research Project of Educational Department of

Liaoning Province under Grant LJKMZ20220941 and Applied Basic Research Project of Liaoning Province under Grant 2023021203-JH26/103.

References

1. Su, J.: An improved position determination algorithm based on nonlinear compensation for ground-based positioning systems. IEEE Access **7**, 23675–23689 (2019)
2. Xu, Y.: Extended Kalman/UFIR filters for UWB-based indoor robot localization under time-varying colored measurement noise. IEEE Internet of Things J. **10**(17), 15632–15641 (2023)
3. Feng, D.: An adaptive IMU/UWB fusion method for NLOS indoor positioning and navigation. IEEE Internet of Things J. **10**(13), 11414–11428 (2023)
4. Santoro, L.: UWB-based indoor positioning system with infinite scalability. IEEE Trans. Instrum. Measur. **72**, 1–11 (2023)
5. Qi, M.: Calibration and compensation of anchor positions for UWB indoor localization. IEEE Sens. J. **24**(1), 689–699 (2024)
6. Kim, D.H.: UWB positioning system based on LSTM classification with mitigated NLOS effects. IEEE Internet of Things J. **10**(2), 1822–1835 (2023)
7. Zhang, Y.: High-precision calibration of camera and IMU on manipulator for bioinspired robotic system. J. Bionic Eng. **19**(2), 299–313 (2019)
8. Sung, S.: Accurate indoor positioning for UWB-based personal devices using deep learning. IEEE Access **11**, 20095–20113 (2023)
9. Javed, MA.: Cascaded Kalman filtering-based attitude and Gyro Bias estimation with efficient compensation of external accelerations. IEEE Access **8**, 50022–50035 (2020)
10. Cao, B.: A UWB localization technique based on the VBKF-CPA-TSA algorithm. J. Sci. Instrum. **44**(10), 120–129 (2023)
11. Feng, L.: Differential positioning-based autonomous obstacle avoidance Navigation technology for indoor drones. Mach. Des. Manuf. Eng. **52**(6), 83–86 (2023)
12. Li, S.: A UWB ranging error prediction method in complex environments. J. Navig. Position. **12**(1), 85–96 (2024)
13. Li, X.: A review of integrated navigation technology based on visual/inertial/UWB fusion. Sci. Surv. Mapp. **48**(6), 49–58 (2023)
14. Liu, W.: Research on UWB NLOS propagation impact suppression technology based on deep learning. Infrared Laser Eng. **52**(12), 20230183 (2023)

Chapter 44
Optimal Scheduling of Integrated Energy System Considering Flexible Loads Demand Response

Ruijie Si, Xinyi Lu, Biwu Ning, Yanjun Jing, Haixin Wang, and Junyou Yang

Abstract As low-carbon development progresses, integrated energy systems (IES) are increasingly vital for meeting emission reduction goals. A mathematical model for a community IES, based on an energy hub and incorporating energy storage, gas turbine power generation systems, and flexible loads, has been developed. This model thoroughly addresses the features of flexible loads on the user side that may be transferred, shifted, or reduced. Ultimately, an optimal day ahead scheduling model for IES supply and demand is developed to minimize overall operating costs. The economic advantages of independent electricity and thermal scheduling are compared. The simulation analysis of the example demonstrates that flexible scheduling of electrical and thermal loads can greatly lower system operating costs, decrease net load fluctuation between peak and valley, and alleviate peak load demand in the power system.

44.1 Introduction

Currently, as energy consumption continues to expand and environmental issues become increasingly severe, optimizing the energy structure has emerged as a critical social priority [1]. Integrated Energy Systems (IES) play a crucial role in promoting energy conservation, reducing emissions, and advancing the transformation of the energy system [2].

R. Si (✉) · Y. Jing · H. Wang · J. Yang
School of Electrical Engineering, Shenyang University of Technology, Shenyang, China
e-mail: siruijie@smail.sut.edu.cn

X. Lu
State Grid Liaoning Mkt Serv Ctr, Elect Intens Control Dept, Shenyang, Liaoning, China

B. Ning
State Grid Inner Mongolia Eastern Power Co., Ltd., Hulunbeir Power Supply Company, Hulunbeir, Inner Mongolia Autonomous Region, China

F. P. García Márquez et al. (eds.), *Computing, Internet of Things and Data Analytics*, Smart Innovation, Systems and Technologies 387,
https://doi.org/10.1007/978-3-031-87154-2_44

Flexible loads, characterized by the adjustable scheduling capabilities, are effective in alleviating supply–demand conflicts and enhancing the utilization of renewable energy [3]. Reference [4] develops a microgrid scheduling model that includes a time-of-use pricing mechanism and flexible loads, improving the power consumption efficiency and clean energy absorption capacity of the distribution network by scheduling flexible load usage periods. Reference [5] develops a dual-objective optimization model for economic and low-carbon dispatch of an integrated electric and heat system, utilizing flexible load scheduling to achieve peak shaving. These studies demonstrate that the inclusion of flexible loads in scheduling has effectively enhanced the economic and environmental performance of the respective systems [6].

The user-side load model is not yet perfect, and there are more studies on one characteristic of flexible loads, and relatively few studies on the dispatchability of thermal loads [7]. Addressing these issues, the purpose of this paper is to coordinate the flexible loads of the system and users, while reducing the system cost of IES. It establishes models for shiftable, transferable, and reducible electric loads and extends these models to heat loads, formulating an optimal dispatch model for community IES which takes into account flexible electricity and heat loads from the user side. Case studies evaluate the influence of flexible electric and thermal loads on improving system economics and reducing the peak-to-valley load difference. The study's validity and effectiveness are confirmed by contrasting various cases.

44.2 IES Scheduling Model

The IES model considering user-side flexible loads described in this paper can be depicted as shown in Fig. 44.1.

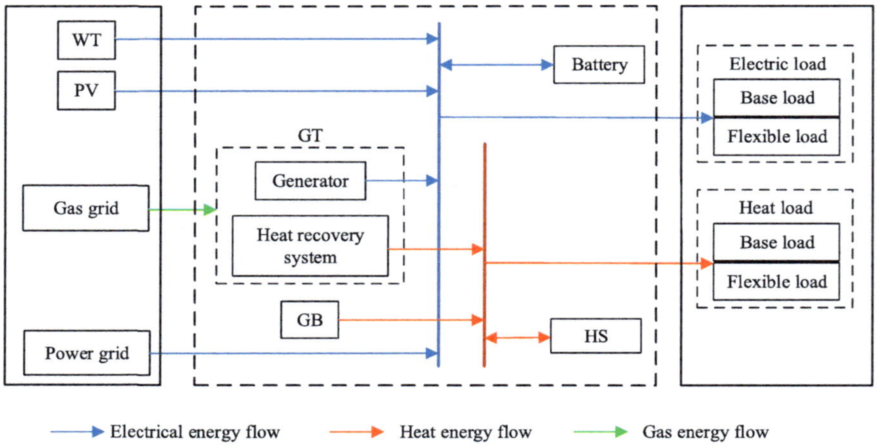

Fig. 44.1 IES energy flow diagram

The goal of economic optimization for the community IES, taking into account user-side flexible loads, is to optimize based on the forecasted 24-h electricity and thermal load curves, along with the projected output of photovoltaic (PV) systems and wind turbines (WT), and under the premise of meeting the constraints of various units in the IES and allowing for the curtailment of WP and PV power, to minimize the overall economic capital of daily IES optimize scheduling by efficiently managing the output of controllable units, scheduling flexible user-side loads, and coordinating energy storage systems.

44.2.1 Objective Function

The daily operational expenses of the community IES consist of the capital associated with distributed energy sources and the expenses incurred from purchasing electricity from the grid [8], the cost associated with compensating for the optimization of user-side flexible loads, the fuel expenses for gas turbines, there are also the cost of the thermal storage tank and the battery [9]. The objective function is shown in Eq. (44.1).

$$F_{\text{EH,min}} = F_{\text{DG}} + F_{\text{net}} + F_{\text{GB}} + F_{\text{HST}} + F_{\text{BAT}} + F_{\text{L}} \tag{44.1}$$

where F_{EH} is the whole operating capital of the system, F_{DG} is the operating capital of distributed energy sources, F_{net} is the capital of buying electricity from the grid, F_{GB} is the operating capital of gas boilers, F_{HST} and F_{BAT} are the depreciation capital of thermal storage tanks and batteries, F_{L} is the whole compensation capital for the optimization of flexible electric and heat loads.

44.2.2 Constraints

(1) Electric Network Constraints

(1) Electric Power Balance Constraints [10]

$$\begin{cases} P_{\text{w}} + P_{\text{pv}} + P_{\text{net}} + P_{\text{MT}} = L_{\text{e}} + P_{\text{BAT}} \\ L_{\text{e}} = L_{\text{base}} + L_{\text{shift}} + L_{\text{tran}} + L_{\text{cut}} \end{cases} \tag{44.2}$$

where P_{MT} represents the electric power export of the GT, L_{e} is the wholeelectric loads, L_{base} represents the basic load in the IES, which is not involved in scheduling, L_{shift}, L_{tran}, and L_{cut} are the shiftable, transferable, and curtailable electric loads.

(2) Power Upper and Lower Limit Constraints [11]

$$\begin{cases} 0 \leqslant P_{\text{pv}} \leqslant P_{\text{pv, max}} \\ 0 \leqslant P_{\text{MT}} \leqslant P_{\text{MT, max}} \\ 0 \leqslant P_{\text{wt}} \leqslant P_{\text{wt, max}} \\ P_{\text{net, min}} \leqslant P_{\text{net}} \leqslant P_{\text{net, max}} \\ P_{\text{BAT, min}} \leqslant P_{\text{BAT}} \leqslant P_{\text{BAT, max}} \end{cases} \tag{44.3}$$

where $P_{\text{wt,max}}$ and $P_{\text{pv,max}}$ represent the predicted export of wind turbines and photovoltaic power systems, $P_{\text{net,min}}$ and $P_{\text{net.max}}$ represents the lowest and highest power exchanged with the grid, $P_{\text{MT,max}}$ represents the standard electric power of the GT, $P_{\text{BAT,min}}$ and $P_{\text{BAT,max}}$ represent the largest discharging and charging powers of the battery.

(3) Battery Constraints

The battery's SOC should comply with the maximum and minimum boundary conditions [12]*:*

$$P\min \leqslant P\sec(t) \leqslant P\max$$

$$\begin{cases} \sum\limits_{t=1}^{T} |J_{t+1} - J_t| \leqslant M_1 \\ \sum\limits_{t=1}^{T} |K_{t+1} - K_t| \leqslant M_2 \end{cases} \tag{44.4}$$

where $P_{\max}$ and $P_{\min}$ represent the *maximum and minimum* limits of the battery's state of charge at period t, M_1 and M_2 are the limits on the battery's energy input and output cycles.

(2) Heat Network Constraints

(1) Heat Power Balance Constraints [13]

$$\begin{cases} Q_{\text{HT}} + Q_{\text{GB}} = Q_{\text{L}} + Q_{\text{HST}} \\ Q_{\text{L}} = Q_{\text{base}} + Q_{\text{shift}} + Q_{\text{cut}} \end{cases} \tag{44.5}$$

where Q_{L} is the total heat load, Q_{base}, Q_{shift}, and Q_{cut} are the baseline load, shiftable load, and curtailable load in the thermal load.

(2) Power Maximum and Minimum Limit Constraints [14]

$$\begin{cases} 0 \leqslant Q_{\text{HT}} \leqslant Q_{\text{HT,max}} \\ 0 \leqslant Q_{\text{GB}} \leqslant Q_{\text{GB,max}} \\ Q_{\text{HST,min}} \leqslant Q_{\text{HST}} \leqslant Q_{\text{HST,max}} \end{cases} \tag{44.6}$$

where $Q_{\mathrm{HT,max}}$ and $Q_{\mathrm{GB,max}}$ are the rated output heat powers of the heat recovery system and gas turbine, $Q_{\mathrm{HST,min}}$ and Q_{HST}, max are the maximum discharging and absorbing heat powers of the thermal storage tank.

(3) Thermal Storage Tank Constraints

The thermal storage tank cannot simultaneously absorb and release heat, therefore the heat storage tank's heating and discharging states must satisfy the following constraints [15]:

$$\begin{cases} A_t \cdot B_t = 0 \\ P_0 = P_{\mathrm{T}} \end{cases} \tag{44.7}$$

where P_0 and P_{T} are the beginning and ending thermal energy in the thermal storage tank.

This paper employs the Cplex solver, part of the Yalmip toolbox in the Matlab environment, to address the model described above.

44.3 Case Analysis

44.3.1 Simulation Data

The focus of this paper is an IES, which comprises PV systems, WT, thermal storage tanks, batteries, and GT. A single operation cycle is one day with a time interval of 1 h, divided into 24 periods. Figure 44.2 illustrates the forecast export of the PV and WT systems, along with the forecast electric and thermal loads. This paper establishes three operational cases to examine the effect of flexible loads on the IES.

Case 1: Consider the participation of flexible electric loads, including transferable, curtailable, and shiftable loads, and flexible *thermal* loads, including shiftable and curtailable loads, in the system's optimized scheduling.

Case 2: Consider the participation of flexible electric loads, comprising transferable, curtailable, and shiftable loads, but do not consider flexible heat loads in the system's optimized scheduling.

Case 3: Do not consider the involvement of flexible loads in the system's optimized scheduling (Fig. 44.3).

44.3.2 Analysis of Simulation Results

Through Matlab optimization scheduling analysis, the optimization results for the three cases can be obtained. Figures 44.4 and 44.5 display the power export of every

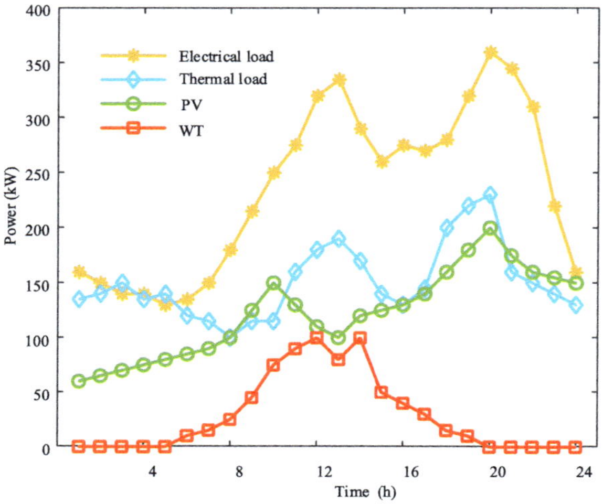

Fig. 44.2 Forecast of PV power, WT export and electric and thermal load power

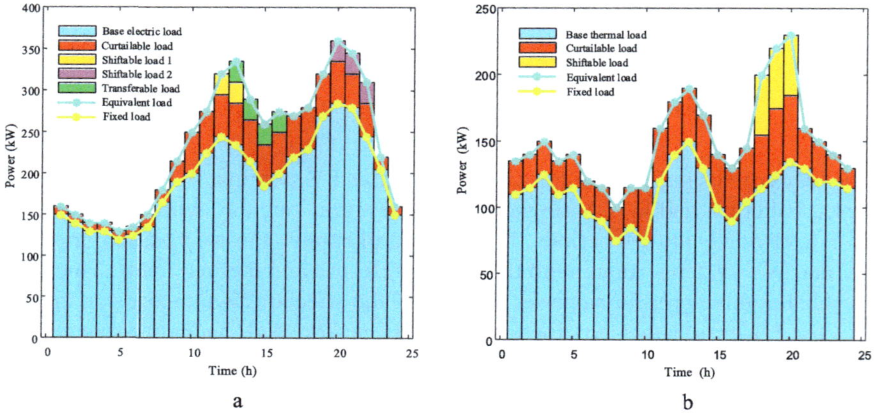

Fig. 44.3 User-side flexible electric and heat load distribution without dispatch. **a** Distribution of user-side flexible electric loads before optimization. **b** Distribution of user-side flexible heat loads before optimization

energy resource and the optimized allocation of flexible electric and thermal loads for Case 1.

Figure 44.4 illustrates that from 00:00 to 07:00, during the off-peak electricity pricing period, the required electric power load remains low. During this period, the operating cost of the WT is \$0.48/kWh, higher than the purchase electricity price. With no power export from the PV power system, the electricity price is \$0.26/kWh. Therefore, the electricity demand load mainly relies on purchasing electricity from the upper power grid, and there is no output from the WT before 08:00. The gas

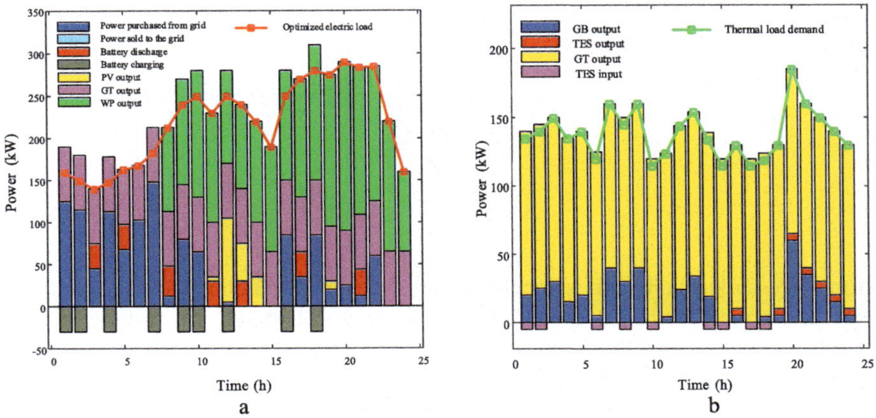

Fig. 44.4 Power output after scheduling in Case 1. **a** Electric load balance. **b** Heat load balance

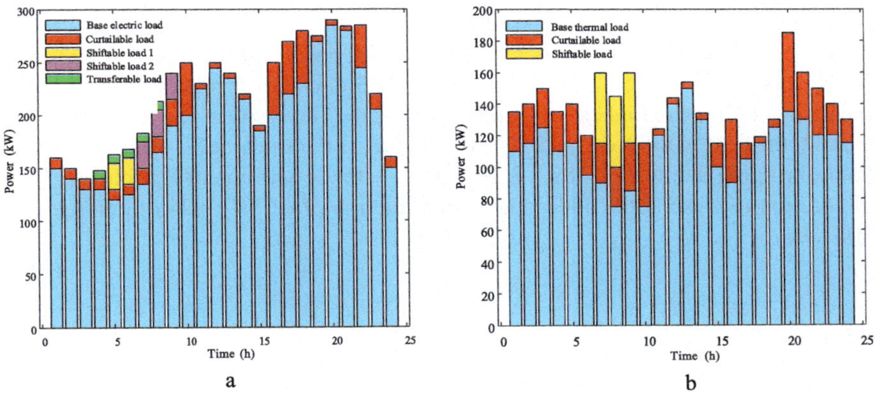

Fig. 44.5 Case 1 thermal load and power load after optimization operation. **a** Optimized distribution of user-side flexible electric loads. **b** Optimized distribution of user-side flexible thermal loads

turbine, operating in a heat-to-power mode, provides some electricity, and any excess electricity is used to charge the battery. During the periods from 10:00 to 15:00 and from 18:00 to 21:00, when the distributed energy sources are abundant, and the cost of purchased electricity is high, the wind and PV resources are fully utilized. The battery charges during low-price periods such as 00:00 to 04:00 and 15:00 to 18:00 and discharges during peak-price periods such as 10:00 to 15:00 and 19:00 to 21:00.

Most of the user thermal load demand is met by the thermal recycling system, with supplementary firing from the GB and thermal storage tank. During the period from 00:00 to 07:00, the power export of the GB reduces both the thermal output and electric output of the GT. The decrease in electric power export from the GT leads to increased electricity procurement from the grid during this period, using batteries to

Table 44.1 Optimization results of different cases

Cases	Cost ($)	Net load fluctuation between peak and valley (kW)	
		Electrical load	Thermal load
1	3081.4	157.32	35.46
2	3189.5	157.32	64.58
3	3546.8	231.28	64.58

store excess electricity can reduce the cost of power dispatching operations during this timeframe. During 10:00 to 15:00 and 18:00 to 21:00, the gas turbine operates at full capacity, coinciding with peak electricity demand periods. The full capacity operation of the gas turbine helps to supplement any shortage of electricity during these peak periods. During specific time periods such as 00:00 to 01:00, 10:00 to 11:00, 13:00 to 15:00, and 18:00 to 19:00, when the thermal load is at its lowest, the GB charges the thermal storage tank. Conversely, during peak heat load periods, the heat storage tank releases heat, effectively smoothing out peaks and valleys in the heat load.

Table 44.1 lists the electricity and thermal load costs and peak-valley differences of the three cases. Table 44.1 shows that Case 3 does not involve flexible loads in the dispatch, has the highest operating cost for the IES, with a cost of 3546.8 $. In Case 2, the cost is lowered by 5.52% as a result of the integration of flexible power loads, bringing it down to 3189.5 $. In Case 1, with the addition of flexible heat loads in addition to Case 2, the additional cost reduction of 6.75%, resulting in a cost of 3081.4 $.

44.4 Conclusion

This paper establishes a multi-form, multi-characteristic load model for IES, fully utilizing the flexible electrical and user-side thermal loads. An economic dispatch model for IES considering user-side flexible loads is proposed. Case studies show that the coupled dispatch of the community IES presented in this paper has significant advantages over independent electrical and heat dispatch methods. The analysis of different cases demonstrates the impact of flexible load participation and the coordination among various flexible loads on IES operating costs. The participation of flexible loads not only enables the reasonable adjustment of electrical and heat load curves but also effectively reduces system operating costs, achieving the objective of economic dispatch for IES.

The optimal scheduling model presented in this paper is suitable for the IES encompassing both electrical and thermal energy. Future research can further explore more comprehensive IES with multiple complementary energy forms and expand the scope of application by promoting the flexible load model to interconnected multi-IES.

References

1. He, Q., Chen, H., Lin, Z., Dai, X., Huang, Y., Cai, W.: A cost-based life-cycle pricing model for offshore wind power plants within china's carbon trading scheme. Energy Rep. **8**, 147 (2022)
2. Li, Y., Li, O., Wu, F., Shi, L., Ma, S., Zhou, B.: Coordinated multi-objective capacity optimization of wind-photovoltaic-pumped storage hybrid system. Energy Rep. **8**, 1303 (2022)
3. Paltsev, S., Morris, J., Kheshgi, H., Herzog, H.: Hard-to-abate sectors: the role of industrial carbon capture and storage (CCS) in emission mitigation. Appl. Energy **300**(1), 117322 (2021)
4. Qiu, S., Chen, J., Mao, C., Duan, Q., Ma, C., Liu, Z., Wang, D.: Day-ahead optimal scheduling of power–gas–heating integrated energy system considering energy routing. Energy Rep. **8**, 1113 (2022)
5. Xi, H., Zhu, M., Lee, K.Y., Wu, X.: Multi-timescale and control-perceptive scheduling approach for flexible operation of power plant-carbon capture system. Fuel J. Fuel Sci. (2023)
6. Wang, J., Zhong, H., Yang, Z., Wang, M., Kang, C.: Exploring the trade-offs between electric heating policy and carbon mitigation in China. Nat. Commun. 11(1) (2020)
7. Shang, Y., Li, S.: FedPT-V2G: Security enhanced federated transformer learning for real-time V2G dispatch with non-IID data. Appl. Energy **358**, 122626 (2024)
8. Wang, Y., Wang, Y., Huang, Y., Yu, H., Du, R., Zhang, F., Zhu, J.: Optimal scheduling of the regional integrated energy system considering economy and environment. IEEE Trans. Sustain. Energy **10**(4), 1939–1949 (2018)
9. Li, Z., Xu, Y., Wu, L., Zheng, X.: A risk-averse adaptively stochastic method for multi-energy ship operation under diverse uncertainties. IEEE Trans. Power Syst. **36**(3), 2149–2161 (2020)
10. Wang, Y., Ma, Y., Song, F., Ma, Y., Qi, C., Huang, F., Xing, J., Zhang, F.: Economic and efficient multi-objective operation optimization of integrated energy system considering electro-thermal demand response. Energy **205**, 118022 (2020)
11. Lu, X., Liu, Z., Ma, L., Wang, L., Zhou, K., Feng, N.: A robust optimization approach for optimal load dispatch of community energy hub. Appl. Energy **259**, 114195 (2020)
12. Zhang, C., Xu, Y., Dong, Z.: Robustly coordinated operation of a multi-energy micro-grid in grid-connected and islanded modes under uncertainties. IEEE Trans. Sustain. Energy **11**(2), 640–651 (2020)
13. Shang, Y., Yu, H., Shao, Z., Jian, L.: Achieving efficient and adaptable dispatching for vehicle-to-grid using distributed edge computing and attention-based LSTM. IEEE Trans. Industr. Inf. **18**(10), 6915–6926 (2022)
14. Yang, X., Chen, Z., Huang, X., Li, R., Xu, S., Yang, C.: Robust capacity optimization methods for integrated energy systems considering demand response and thermal comfort. Energy **221**, 119727 (2021)
15. Yuan, W., Wang, X., Su, C., Cheng, C., Liu, Z., Wu, Z.: Stochastic optimization model for the short-term joint operation of photovoltaic power and hydropower plants based on chance-constrained programming. Energy **222**, 119996 (2021)

Chapter 45
Research on CBIR-Based Quality Detection Algorithm for Prefabricated Pizza

Fenghao Sun, Qiuxia Qu, and Yuling Liang

Abstract Nowadays, visual recognition has been applied in various fields, with most factories and many business enterprises constantly introducing artificial intelligence. Since the accuracy of visual recognition technology for assessing the pass rate has been found to be undesirable. In this paper, LST-CBIR detection algorithm for prefabricated pizzas is proposed based on content-based image retrieval (CBIR) system with weights trained by the least squares method. And three feature extraction method of pizza images is described. By extracting the color, shape, and texture features of pizza images and combining them into a comprehensive feature set, the quality of prefabricated pizzas is determined. The weights of the three features are calculated using the least squares method. A pizza quality recognition model based on CBIR is established to identify the quality of prefabricated pizza by calculating similarity between standard sample and tested sample. This approach effectively improves the efficiency and accuracy of pizza quality determination. Experimental results are shown that the LST-CBIR pizza quality recognition method proposed is feasible and superior, providing a new solution for the quality inspection of prefabricated pizzas and applications in machine vision.

45.1 Introduction

With the country's strong emphasis on the development of the prefabricated food feild, unprecedented opportunities for growth have emerged. In January 2023, the Central No. 1 Document proposed for the first time "cultivating and developing

F. Sun (✉) · Q. Qu (✉)
School of Electrical and Control Engineering, Shenyang Jianzhu University, Shenyang, China
e-mail: 2190605008@qq.com

Q. Qu
e-mail: quqiuxia2010@163.com

Y. Liang
School of Artificial Intelligence, Shenyang University of Technology, Shenyang, China

F. P. García Márquez et al. (eds.), *Computing, Internet of Things and Data Analytics*, Smart Innovation, Systems and Technologies 387,
https://doi.org/10.1007/978-3-031-87154-2_45

the prefabricated food industry" [1]. Traditional methods of inspecting the quality of prefabricated pizzas often require significant manpower and time and are susceptible to subjective biases, making it difficult to ensure the accuracy and stability of the inspection results. Consequently, developing a fast, accurate, and automated method for the quality inspection of prefabricated pizzas has become a prominent research hotspot.

In [2], the main uses and development history of CBIR are introduced in detail, with an analysis of existing algorithms combined with CBIR technology. The CBIR task involves searching for the most relevant content to the given query data within a large image set, encompassing two main phases: feature extraction and similarity measurement [2]. This technique has been made applicable to various domains. In [3], the application of CBIR technology in the compilation of welding process procedures was discussed. In [4], the application of CBIR technology for detecting shoeprints was described. Numerous other applications were also noted [5–8], although its application in the food industry remains limited. Therefore, this design aims to apply CBIR technology to achieve the quality inspection of prefabricated pizzas.

In this method, three sets of features, color, texture, and shape features are extracted from prefabricated pizza images, utilizing similarity calculation and sample set classification for image recognition and pizza quality determination, thereby achieving accurate evaluation of pizza quality. Numerous CBIR techniques related to color features have been documented. In [9], Dowerah and Patel proposed a CBIR model that used color histograms and local binary patterns (LBP). The chi-square distance is employed in CBIR model with color histograms as the similarity measure, while a linear support vector is utilized in the model with LBP for image classification, achieving notable recall and precision rates. This example illustrated the effectiveness of color feature extraction. The application of CBIR in texture feature extraction was discussed in [10] and [11]. In [10], a robust feature extraction method based on texture features was proposed, which can capture information on noise resistance, directionality, contrast, and heterogeneity, used for retrieving medical images. In [11], Pradhan J et al. used Gabor filters at different wavelengths to extract multidirectional texture features from NObR, providing a novel approach for texture feature extraction. Scholars have proposed that shape feature retrieval enhanced the visual information of images for CBIR technology [12]. Image retrieval techniques for texture features include two methods: the use of co-occurrence matrices and models based on mathematics. This design employs a mathematical model using the Fourier transform to achieve texture feature extraction. However, extracting and analyzing the texture features of the entire image directly would result in a significant computational load [13].The shape features were particularly suited to accurately capturing the shape of prefabricated pizzas, thereby improving accuracy. Similarly, Pande proposed an image retrieval system based on shape and texture, estimating the similarity of each query image to the stored images in terms of shape and texture, and retrieving images within the expected similarity range. Spatial Gray-Level Dependence Matrices (SGLDM) was utilized, and an algorithm was proposed for calculating the Inverse Differential Moment (IDM) as the best image retrieval method

[14]. For feature fusion, a mathematical algorithm called least squares method was introduced in [15–17].

Based on the above discussion, the main innovations of this design include:

(1) The color space is divided into multiple fixed subspaces and the number of pixels is counted in each fixed subspace. And the histogram intersection algorithm is used to calculate the similarity between the images, and the retrieval results are output according to the magnitude of the similarity.
(2) The images are firstly segments, then texture detection and feature extraction are performed based on Fourier descriptors to reduce the computational burden.
(3) This design utilizes shape invariant moments as the shape features for image retrieval based on *Hu* moment invariants.
(4) The least squares method is used to compute the optimal weights for the three sets of features.

The designed method offers the advantages of high automation and output result accuracy, effectively enhancing the efficiency and accuracy of quality determination for prefabricated pizzas. Thus, the prefabricated pizza quality detection method based on CBIR demonstrates broad application prospects and significant importance in the food industry and machine vision applications.

45.2 The Proposed LST-CBIR Algorithm

This section describes the implementation and algorithmic flow of CBIR for pizza conformity detection. The algorithmic flowchart of LST-CBIR is an image retrieval system with least squares training weights shown in Fig. 45.1.

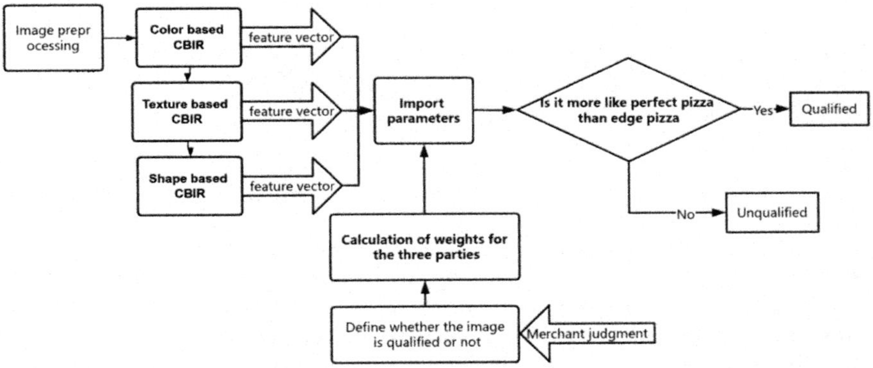

Fig. 45.1 Flowchart of algorithm for image retrieval system with least squares training weights

45.3 CBIR Feature Extraction

45.3.1 Color Characteristics

In terms of color features, color moments are employed as the retrieval feature to reduce computational complexity. The first, second, and third-order moments are extracted from both the images under inspection and those in the database. The HSV color space is chosen for this design due to its alignment with human visual perception of hue, saturation, and brightness. Compared to other color spaces, the HSV space reflects more accurately human color perception. Thus, color moments in the HSV color space are utilized as the color feature, with the Manhattan distance used for measuring color moment similarity.

Color information is primarily concentrated in the low-order moments of image color, specifically the first-order moment (mean), second-order moment (variance), and third-order moment (skewness) of each color component. These moments effectively represent the color distribution within an image. The mathematical definitions of the three-color moments are as follows:

$$\mu_i = \frac{1}{N}\sum_{j=1}^{N} f_{ij} \tag{45.1}$$

$$\sigma_i = \sqrt{\frac{1}{N}\sum_{j=1}^{N} (f_{ij} - \mu_i)^2} \tag{45.2}$$

$$\sigma_i = \sqrt{\frac{1}{N}\sum_{j=1}^{N} (f_{ij} - \mu_i)^2} \tag{45.3}$$

where f_{ij} denotes the probability that the color value of pixel j is i and N is the number of pixel points in the image. If two images are denoted by $[Q, I]$, the distance formula for their moments is.

$$D[Q, I] = \sum_{i=1}^{3} \left(\omega_{i1}\left|\mu_i^Q - \mu_i^I\right| + \omega_{i2}\left|\sigma_i^Q - \sigma_i^I\right| + \omega_{i1}\left|\xi_i^Q - \xi_i^I\right| \right) \tag{45.4}$$

where, $\omega_{ij} \geq 0$ $(1 \leq i, j \leq 3)$ is the specified weighting weights, generally to be set as $\omega_{i1} \geq \omega_{i2}$, $\omega_{i1} \geq \omega_{i3}$, to improve the weight of the average color. After extracting the color moments of the graph to be matched and the database graph, the similarity vector of color features can be obtained by using the Manhattan features for the metric.

45.3.2 Shape Characteristics

This design utilizes shape invariant moments [18] as shape features for image retrieval. Utilizing the moments of the region occupied by the target region as the shape description parameter is a commonly used shape description method. The $(p + q)$-order moments of a region $f(x, y)$ are defined as:

$$m_{pq} = \sum_x \sum_y x^p y^q f(x, y) \qquad p, q = 0, 1, 2, \ldots \tag{45.5}$$

Its corresponding center distance is defined as:

$$u_{pq} = \sum_x \sum_y (x - \overline{x})^p (y - \overline{y})^q f(x, y) \qquad p, q = 0, 1, 2, \ldots \tag{45.6}$$

where $\overline{x} = \frac{m_{10}}{m_{00}}$, $\overline{y} = \frac{m_{01}}{m_{00}}$, are the coordinates of the center of gravity. $(\overline{x}, \overline{y})$ is the gray scale center of mass of the target region. The normalized $(p + q)$-order central moment of $f(x, y)$ is defined as:

$$\eta_{pq} = \frac{u_{pq}}{u_{00}^{\gamma}} \qquad p, q = 0, 1, 2, \ldots \tag{45.7}$$

and

$$\gamma = \frac{p + q}{2} + 1 \qquad p, q = 2, 3, 4, \ldots \tag{45.8}$$

The moments of the region occupied by the target region as shape description parameters is a common method for shape description. *Hu* moment invariant is an effective tool for extracting morphological features in an image due to its characteristic of not varying with the position, size, and orientation of the image. After extracting the *Hu* invariant moment features of the image to be matched and the database image, the similarity vector of the shape features can be obtained by using the Manhattan distance for the similarity measure.

45.3.3 Texture Characterization

Since the database for image retrieval is generally large, if the texture features of the whole image are extracted and analyzed directly, the computation will be very large. So, in this design, the image is segmented firstly, and then the segmented image is subjected to texture detection and texture feature extraction based on Fourier descriptor [19] to reduce the amount of computation.

Image pre-segmentation. To reduce computational complexity and emphasize the primary regions of the image, a pre-segmentation process is applied before texture feature extraction. It is generally accepted that image features are predominantly located in large, connected regions, and segmentation is performed based on this principle. Initially, the RGB image is binarized. After morphological processing, including opening and closing operations, connected component analysis is conducted. The largest connected region is selected as the target area for texture feature detection.

Fourier Descriptors. In the discrete case, let the ordered set of points consisting of points on the boundary be represented as a sequence of complex numbers $z(k) = x(k) + jy(k)$, $k = 0, 1, 2, \dots, N - 1$, for which the discrete Fourier transform is:

$$S(w) = \frac{1}{N}\sum_{k=0}^{N-1} z(k)\exp\left\{-\frac{j2\pi wk}{N}\right\}, w = 0, 1, \dots, N - 1; \tag{45.9}$$

The inverse transform of the Fourier descriptor $S(w)$ is:

$$z(k) = \sum_{w=0}^{N-1} S(w)\exp\left\{-\frac{j2\pi wk}{N}\right\}, k = 0, 1, \dots, N - 1; \tag{45.10}$$

It is evident from the above equation that the discrete Fourier transform (DFT) is a reversible linear transformation, ensuring that no information is either augmented or diminished in this process. Fourier descriptors analyze the target in the frequency domain. In the resulting frequency spectrum, the low-frequency components represent the macroscopic shape attributes of the object, while the high-frequency components capture the detailed features, including texture characteristics in certain situations. This results in a similarity vector for the texture features.

45.4 Integrated Features

This design integrates the three features of color features, shape features, and texture features for retrieval, and sets the similarity vectors of the three features to be: C, S, and T, and assigns the weights w_c, w_s and w_T, respectively, at the time of retrieval, and the integrated similarity vector M is:

$$M = w_c C + w_s S + w_T T \tag{45.11}$$

The result of image similarity retrieval can be obtained by utilizing M as the criterion of similarity.

45.4.1 Least Squares Training Weights

In linear regression, both the least squares method and the gradient descent algorithm aim to find an optimal solution that allows the curve to best fit the actual data. Essentially, they seek to minimize the mean squared error (MSE). For a given feature polynomial:

$$y = \beta_0 + \beta_1 x_1 + \beta_2 x_2 + \beta_3 x_3 + \cdots + \beta_n x_n \tag{45.12}$$

In terms of matrices, consider an overdetermined system.

$$\sum_{j=1}^{n} X_{ij}\beta_j = y_i, (i = 1, 2, 3, , \ldots, m) \tag{45.13}$$

with $m > n,$ which is vectorized as

$$X\beta = y$$

$$X = \begin{bmatrix} X_{11} & \ldots & X_{1n} \\ \vdots & \ddots & \vdots \\ X_{m1} & \cdots & X_{mn} \end{bmatrix}, \beta = \begin{bmatrix} \beta_1 \\ \vdots \\ \beta_n \end{bmatrix}, y = \begin{bmatrix} y_1 \\ \vdots \\ y_m \end{bmatrix} \tag{45.14}$$

In general, there is no solution for Eq. (45.14). The residual sum-of-squares function S is employed.

$$S(\beta) = \|X\beta - y\|^2 \tag{45.15}$$

The goal is to solve for $min\, S(\beta)$, to perform a derivation operation on $S(\beta)$ (let $A = X, A\beta = Y$)

$$\begin{aligned} &\|A\beta - Y\|^2 \\ &= (A\beta - Y)^T(A\beta - Y) \\ &= (\beta^T A^T - Y^T)(A\beta - Y) \\ &= \beta^T A^T A\beta - \beta^T A^T Y - Y^T A\beta + Y^T Y \\ &= \beta^T A^T A\beta - 2\beta^T A^T Y + Y^T Y \end{aligned} \tag{45.16}$$

$$\begin{aligned}&\frac{\partial(\beta^T A^T A\beta - 2\beta^T A^T Y + Y^T Y)}{\partial\beta}\\&= \frac{\partial(\beta^T A^T A\beta - 2\beta^T A^T Y)}{\partial\beta}\\&= \frac{\partial(\beta^T A^T A\beta)}{\partial\beta} - 2A^T Y\end{aligned} \tag{45.17}$$

Thus, the process of derivation of this equation is given as:

$$\begin{aligned}&\frac{\partial(\beta^T A^T A\beta)}{\partial\beta} - 2A^T Y\\&= (A^T A + A^T A)\beta - 2A^T Y\\&= 2(A^T A\beta - A^T Y)\end{aligned} \tag{45.18}$$

Let the equation be 0, the derivative of the equation is 0:

$$(A^T A)\beta = A^T Y \Leftrightarrow \beta = (A^T A)^{-1} A^T Y \tag{45.19}$$

The final β is the optimal solution obtained by the least squares method, and this equation is the Normal Equation.

45.5 Experimental Results and Analysis

45.5.1 Training Samples and Weight Calculation

The training samples required for this design consist of 300 on-site photos of pizzas, including 150 acceptable pizzas and 150 unacceptable pizzas. The reasons for unacceptability vary and include irregular shape, uneven distribution of ingredients, and insufficient ingredients, among others. The pixel dimensions of the images range from 100 to 3000px on the longer side, as shown in Fig. 45.2.

Fig. 45.2 Training dataset

Thus, a parameter matrix of 300 by 3 is obtained, which serves as the A matrix in the least squares method formula. The β matrix is a 3 by 1 matrix comprising the assigned weights c, s, and t. The critical component of this algorithm is the Y matrix, which should be a 300 by 1 matrix representing the acceptability of the pizzas. The data corresponding to the acceptable pizzas are defined as 1 in the Y matrix, whereas the data corresponding to the unacceptable pizzas are defined as -1. The least squares method is then used to solve for the β matrix, which is formula (45.19), yielding three weighted optimal solution matrices.

After training on 300 sets of data, the optimal solution ratio of color, shape, and texture parameters is close to 6:3:1, which is brought into the weights to recognize the pizza.

45.5.2 Experimental Result

This database serves as the test sample, containing 150 acceptable and 150 unacceptable pizzas. Among them, one is defined as the perfect pizza, and another as a pizza on the threshold of acceptability. Thus, the database leaves 148 acceptable pizzas and 150 unacceptable pizzas to be tested. Sequential recognition and evaluation are then performed. Initially, the default values of the program are used for comparison to calculate the accuracy. Subsequently, experiments and evaluations are conducted using the average values of the three weights. Finally, recognition is performed using the ratios obtained from the least squares method. The experimental process is as follows:

In the design program, one perfect pizza is used for retrieval, one pizza is used to define acceptability, and the remaining two pizzas are used for retrieval. The retrieval results are shown in Fig. 45.3.

45.5.3 Experimental Comparison

In order to be more accurate recognition results of this design, a new algorithm is added to the original CBIR, that is, for the least squares method to find the optimal solution, and the ratio of the three weights obtained is 6:3:1; when the weights are calculated, the original CBIR is compared to the LST-CBIR with the addition of the new algorithm.

This study compared advanced CBIR models to achieve pizza quality rate detection, including CBIR for feature-weighted fusion of local binary and local neighborhood difference patterns [20], Cumulative histogram with Hu invariant moments of CBIR [21], and CBIR with evenly distributed weights. CBIR for feature-weighted fusion of local binary and local neighborhood difference patterns is implemented by integrating feature-weighted fusion of local binary patterns (LBP) and local neighborhood difference patterns (LND), allowing for a comprehensive evaluation of pizza

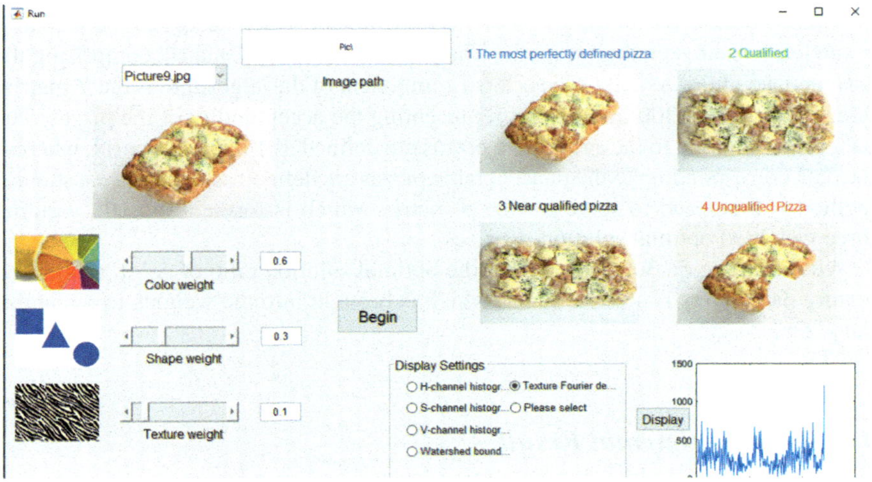

Fig. 45.3 Retrieval results of pizza recognition system

quality. However, due to the high dimensionality of the combined feature set, the risk of overfitting is increased. This may result in the model performing well on training data but poorly on unseen data. Cumulative histogram with Hu invariant moments of CBIR is a technique used for pizza quality rate detection. This method involves the extraction and analysis of cumulative histograms for color distribution and Hu invariant moments for shape characteristics, providing a comprehensive set of features for image retrieval and analysis, but the reliance on color and shape features alone might not be sufficient for capturing the full range of quality indicators for pizza. 298 pictures are put into the database for examination, and the experimental data are as follows in Table 45.1.

Subsequently, the superiority of this model was confirmed through comparison of the ROC curves and PR curves among the four models. The closer the AUC value of the ROC curve is to 1, the better the overall classification capability of the model. Similarly, the closer the AP value in the PR curve is to 1, the better the model's performance in recognizing positive examples. Among these models, Model

Table 45.1 Comparative results

Methodologies	Accurate count	Inaccurate count	Accurate rate (%)
CBIR for feature-weighted fusion of local binary and local neighborhood difference patterns	239	59	80.20
Cumulative histogram with Hu invariant moments of CBIR	241	57	80.87
CBIR with evenly distributed weights	227	71	76.17
LST-CBIR	260	38	87.24

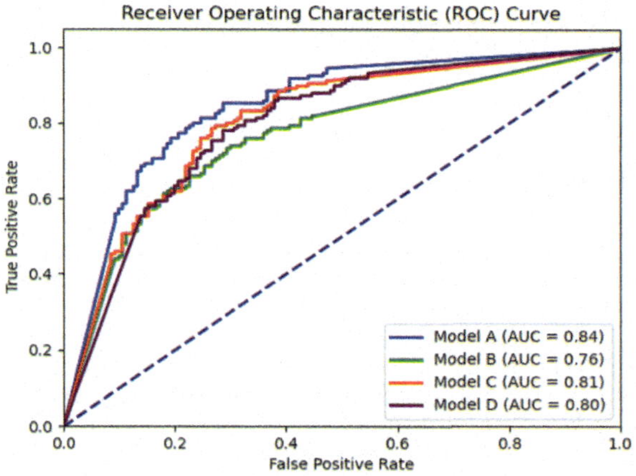

Fig. 45.4 ROC comparison curve chart

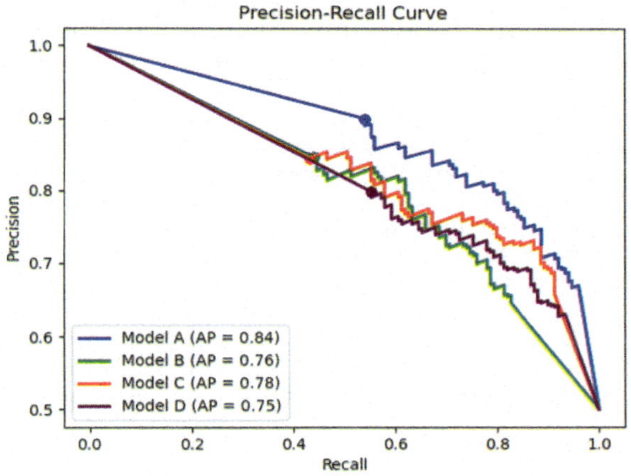

Fig. 45.5 PR comparison curve chart

A represents the LST-CBIR model proposed in this study, Model B utilizes CBIR with evenly distributed weights, Model C employs CBIR with weighted fusion of local binary and local neighborhood difference pattern features, and Model D integrates cumulative histograms with Hu invariant moments. The ROC curve comparison chart is depicted in Fig. 45.4, while the PR curve comparison chart is presented in Fig. 45.5.

Based on the above analysis and simulation results, it is evident that the LST-CBIR proposed in this study exhibits certain advantages in terms of ROC curve, PR curve, and actual accuracy. These findings suggest that the LST-CBIR model designed in this paper is particularly well-suited for detecting the pass rate of pizzas.

Acknowledgements This work was supported by Applied Basic Research Project of Liaoning Province under Grant 2023021203-JH26/103, Liaoning Natural Science Foundation under Grant 2023-MS-224 and Scientific Research Project of Educational Department of Liaoning Province under Grant LJKMZ20220941.

Disclosure of Interests The authors have no competing interests to declare that are relevant to the content of this article.

References

1. Zenggang, X., Zhiwen, T., Xiaowen, C.: Research on image retrieval algorithm based on combination of color and shape features. J. Signal Process. Syst. **93**(10), 139–146 (2021)
2. Hui, Y., Shuicai, S.: Research review of content based image retrieval technology. Softw. Guide **22**(4), 229–244 (2023)
3. Guangfu, L.: Research and implementation of LIRE image retrieval in the application of welding process specification compilation. Sci. Technol. Perspect. **17**, 123–126 (2021)
4. Wei, L., Leyi, J., Tingge, Z.: Research status and development trends of shoe print image retrieval. J. Xi'an Univ. Posts Telecommun. **26**(2), 70–76 (2021)
5. Yu, D., Qingyu, Y., Yuying, C.: Design of intelligent detection software for standardized dressing and wearing. Electron. Technol. Softw. Eng. **000**(19), 25–28 (2022)
6. Wennan, H.: Robot obstacle detection method based on content image retrieval. Comput. Eng. Des. **42**(3), 822–829 (2021)
7. Islam, S., Hamid, E.: CBIR using region emphasized Markov stationary features. IOSR J. Comput. Eng. **25**(1), 1–10 (2023)
8. Kaur, G.., Saini, S.: Comparison of state vector machine and decision tree-content based image retrieval algorithms to perceive accuracy. In: 2023 1st International Conference on Innovations in High-Speed Communication and Signal Processing, pp.11–15. BHOPAL, India (2023)
9. Dowerah, R., Patel, S.: Comparative analysis of color histogram and LBP in CBIR systems. Multimed. Tools Appl. **83**(5), 12467–12486 (2024)
10. Chethan, K., Bhandarkar, R.: Hybrid feature extraction technique on brain MRI images for content-based image retrieval of Alzheimer's disease. In: International Conference on VLSI, Signal Processing, Power Systems, Illumination and Lighting Control, Communication and Embedded Systems, pp. 127–141. Nitte (2020)
11. Pradhan, J., Pal, A.K., Banka, H.: A CBIR system based on saliency driven local image features and multi orientation texture features. J. Visual Commun. Image Representat. **83**(Feb.1), 1–18 (2022)
12. George, L.E., Mohammed, E.Z.: Novel shape description for CBIR in medical application. J. Inf. Comput. Sci. **8**(3), 217–226 (2013)
13. Pande, S.D., Rathod, S.B., Chetty, M.S.R.: Shape and textural based image retrieval using K-NN classifier. J. Intell. Fuzzy Syst. Appl. Eng. Technol. **43**(4), 4757–4768 (2022)
14. Kumar, A., Jain, S.K.: ECDM: enhanced edge based coupled deformable model for image segmentation in the presence of speckle noise and severe intensity inhomogeneity. Appl. Math. Model. **128**(Apr.), 659–684 (2024)
15. Changyou, L., Kaizhen, H., Zhen, W.: Appearance defect detection of ampoule bottle heads based on least squares method. Manuf. Autom. **45**(3), 26–29 (2023)
16. Hengbo, M., Ge, C., Naifeng, F.: Research on Creo sheet metal unfolding length algorithm based on least squares method. Coal Mining Mach. **45**(3), 26–33 (2023)
17. Hua, H., Ruiyang, L., Xiaoxiao, L.: Research progress on the collapsibility characteristics and modification methods of loess. J. Build. Sci. Eng. **41**(2), 1–16 (2024)
18. Richard, H., Jun, Z.: Hamiltonian knottedness and lifting paths from the shape invariant. Compos. Math. **159**(11), 2416–2457 (2023)
19. Alsabhan, M., Soudani, A., Almusallam, M.: A distributed scheme for energy-efficient event-based target recognition using Internet of Multimedia Things. Int. J. Distrib. Sens. Netw. **18**(5), 87–111 (2022)
20. Heitz, T., Bachrathy, D., He, N.: Optimization of cutting force fitting model by Fast Fourier Transformation in milling. J. Manuf. Process. **99**(Aug.), 121–137 (2023)

21. Kayhan, N., Fekri-Ershad, S.: Content based image retrieval based on weighted fusion of texture and color features derived from modified local binary patterns and local neighborhood difference patterns. Multimed. Tools Appl. **80**(21), 32763–32790 (2021)
22. Qilong, S., Mingliang, Z.: Research and implementation of Tibetan carpet image retrieval based on color features. Software **36**(8), 25–29 (2015)
23. Zhang, C., Zhao, S., Yang, Z.: A multi-fault diagnosis method for lithium-ion battery pack using curvilinear Manhattan distance evaluation and voltage difference analysis. J. Energy Storage **67**(Sept.), 1–11 (2023)
24. D'Apice, C., Kogut, P.I., Manzo, R.: Voronoi treemap in Manhattan distance and Chebyshev distance. Differ. Integral Equ. **22**(3), 246–264 (2024)

Chapter 46
Intelligent Obstacle Avoidance Method for Robots Based on Emotional Models

Ming Cao, Zhen Qi, and Baiqing Sun

Abstract This paper presents an improved path planning method based on the artificial potential field method, firstly, based on the linkage between the subjective evaluation of emotionality (Self-Assessment Manikin ,SAM) and emotional physiological responses (Emotional Physiological Responses, EPR) an evaluation system around the emotions is proposed to achieve the emotional visualization representation. Secondly, a human–computer interaction experimental platform combined with Virtual Reality (VR) technology is established to characterize physiological signals with the distance between the obstacle and the target point as the primary influencing factor, and to study the changing law of human emotions, so as to establish an emotional model of the distance between the obstacle and the target point. Finally, combining the evaluation system and the emotional model, the artificial emotional potential field path planning algorithm (Artificial emotional potential field, AEPF) is proposed, which improves the satisfaction during human–robot interaction on the basis of optimizing the robot's driving path. The conclusion shows that, compared with the artificial potential field method, 80% of the subjects think that the robot has lower arousal and relatively smoother emotional feelings during traveling according to the artificial emotional potential field method, and at the same time, it provides a new idea for the sense of experience in the process of human–robot interaction.

46.1 Introduction

The sustained low birth rate and accelerated aging of the population jointly pose significant challenges that constrain the country's economic and social development. Therefore, it is urgent to develop a robot intelligent system that balances task efficiency and user experience, in order to meet future more humane needs and service standards [1].

M. Cao (✉) · Z. Qi · B. Sun
School of Electrical Engineering, Shenyang University of Technology, Shenyang, China
e-mail: 15942043421@163.com; 1501329869@qq.com

F. P. García Márquez et al. (eds.), *Computing, Internet of Things and Data Analytics*,
Smart Innovation, Systems and Technologies 387,
https://doi.org/10.1007/978-3-031-87154-2_46

Lee-Johnson and colleagues argue that emotions are a key factor in enhancing the adaptability of robots in complex environments. They propose a layered robotic architecture that integrates emotional mechanisms, where artificial emotions can effectively improve overall performance by adjusting the robot's action strategies, setting task priorities, and through reinforcement learning. Researchers Williams and others developed an emotion-based adaptive path planning method, constructing an emotional framework based on fear and joy [2]. Experiments have shown that this method significantly reduces collision rates and improves navigation efficiency compared to non-adaptive navigation systems. Wu and colleagues addressed the issue of local trajectory planning for unmanned ground vehicles by innovatively introducing an improved Frenet trajectory optimization technique based on artificial emotions and balanced optimization, enabling robots to simulate human-like emotional intelligence and achieve human-like navigation patterns.

In summary, for the design of mobile service robots considering the user's emotional experience, the concept of artificial emotional potential field is proposed based on the emotional model of the distance between the obstacle and the target point, the artificial emotional potential field path planning algorithm is proposed based on the artificial potential field method, and the human-in-the-loop robot control framework based on the emotional feedback, and the DDPG-AEPF algorithm is proposed, so that the robot is equipped with the ability to learn and adjust behavior according to the user's emotional feedback [3]. The DDPG-AEPF algorithm is proposed to enable the robot to learn and self-adjust its behavior based on the user's emotional feedback, and make corresponding adaptive adjustments based on the user's real-time psychological state and subjective feelings during the execution of the task, so as to realize a more idealized and emotionally caring human–robot interaction process. Through this study, we expect to promote the transformation of service robots from simple function executors to caring companions with emotional understanding and intelligent response capabilities, in order to better serve the elderly in an aging society [4].

46.2 Emotional Evaluation System

Emotions themselves cannot be visually detected and require indirect expression through other means. Taking into account various factors, this article chooses electrocardiogram signals and skin electrical signals [5]. The experimental design mainly involves using standardized image stimulation materials in the international emotional image system to induce emotions, while collecting corresponding physiological signals. After the experiment, the self-assessment model SAM table of the subjects is collected through a questionnaire [6]. Finally, statistical analysis of the data is conducted using the Russell two-dimensional emotional model and the self-assessment model SAM table to find the connection between physiological signals and emotional states [7, 8], and to build an emotional evaluation system as shown in Fig. 46.1.

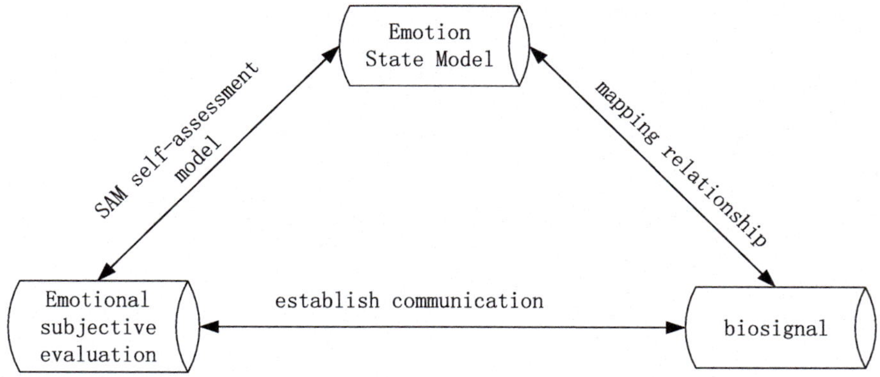

Fig. 46.1 Emotional evaluation system

46.3 Obstacle Distance Emotion Model

In this experiment, a virtual scene close to the real scene is built, which includes: indoor scene model, human body model, intelligent wheelchair robot model, obstacle model. The width of the intelligent wheelchair robot is 1 m. The height of the human eye is 0.8 m when the human body model is sitting. The obstacle model is a cube with a side length of 1 m. The model material is the default setting material of Unity3D. The scene is shown in Fig. 46.2.

As shown in Fig. 46.3, the experimental variable for the obstacle distance experiment is to control the change in the distance between the intelligent wheelchair and the obstacle d_{obs}. A total of 6 groups were set in this experiment, with distances d_{obs} set at 0.2, 0.4, 0.6, 0.8, 1.0, and 1.2 m, respectively, where d_{obs} represents the distance between the wheelchair and the obstacle. After each experiment, the subjects used the Emotional Self Assessment questionnaire (SAM) to evaluate their emotional state.

The experiment takes obstacle distance as the independent variable, collects physiological signals from subjects and collects SAM tables. Through data analysis and formula fitting, a distance emotion model of obstacles is obtained.

The fitting expression between obstacle distance ($\mathrm{d_{obs}}$ d_{obs}) and potency (v_{obs}).

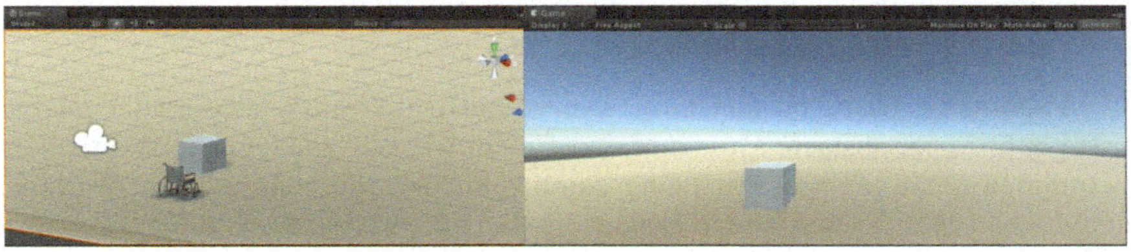

Fig. 46.2 Obstacle experiment virtual reality scene and the scene observed in VR

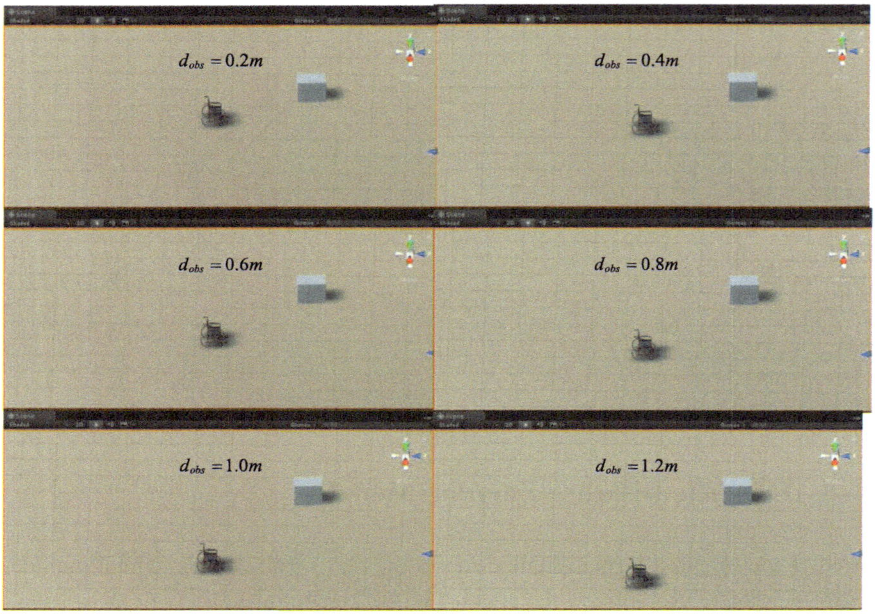

Fig. 46.3 Experimental diagram of different obstacle distance

$$v_{obs} = 7.53 * e^{-\left(\frac{d_{obs}-1.08}{0.71}\right)} \tag{46.1}$$

The fitting expression of obstacle distance (d_{obs}) and wake-up (a_{obs}):

$$a_{obs} = 12.07 * e^{-1.80*d_{obs}} \tag{46.2}$$

From (46.1) and (46.2), the distance obstacle conclusion is drawn:

1. With the increase of obstacle distance, the emotional valence score of the subjects increased continuously; when the obstacle distance is greater than the safe distance ($\mathrm{d_{obs}}$ $d_{obs} > 1.0$ m), the valence change becomes gentle.
2. With the increase of obstacle distance, the arousal score of the subjects decreased continuously; when the obstacle distance is greater than the safe distance ($\mathrm{d_{obs}}$ $d_{obs} > 1.0$ m), the wake-up change becomes gentle.

In summary, based on the immersive virtual reality human–computer interaction platform, an obstacle avoidance experiment was designed. Combined with the two-dimensional valence-awakening emotion model, the change rules of human emotional state valence and obstacle distance in the wake-up dimension were obtained. By using the curve fitting method, the distance factor is connected with the emotion, and the obstacle distance emotion model is proposed.

46.4 Artificial Emotional Potential Field Obstacle Avoidance Planning Method

Based on the physical principle of the artificial potential field algorithm, the target point potential field and the obstacle potential field are introduced. The influencing factors of human emotional state also affect the direction of robot movement. Therefore, the motion direction and behavior of the robot are affected by the physical field and emotional field of the obstacle and the target point at the same time [9] (Fig. 46.4).

The position of the robot at time $t-1$ t-1 is x_{t-1}, and the corresponding human emotional state (valence, arousal) is (v_{t-1}, a_{t-1}). The position of the robot at time t is x_t, , and the corresponding human emotional state (valence, arousal) is (v_t, a_t). The influence range of the virtual potential field around the obstacle is $\mathrm{R_{obs}}$ R_{obs}. The Euclidean distance between the robot and the obstacle is $d_{obs,t-1}$ at the position x_{t-1}, and the Euclidean distance between the robot and the obstacle is $d_{obs,t}$ at the position x_t. The virtual emotional potential field range of the target point is R_{goal}. The Euclidean distance between the robot and the target point at the position x_{t-1} is $d_{goal,t-1}$, and the Euclidean distance between the robot and the target point at the position x_t is $d_{goal,t}$ (Fig. 46.5).

The expression of the emotional potential field around the obstacle is:

$$U_{rep,t} = \begin{cases} \frac{1}{2}k_{r1}\left(\frac{1}{d_{obs,t}} - \frac{1}{R_{obs}}\right)^2 + k_{r2}d_{goal,t}^2\frac{v_t - v_{t-1}}{d_{obs,t} - d_{obs,t-1}}a_t, d_{obs} < R_{obs} \text{ and } v_t \neq v_{t-1} \\ \frac{1}{2}k_{r1}\left(\frac{1}{d_{obs,t}} - \frac{1}{R_{obs}}\right)^2 + k_{r2}d_{goal,t}^2\frac{a_t - a_{t-1}}{d_{obs,t} - d_{obs,t-1}}, d_{obs} < R_{obs} \text{ and } v_t = v_{t-1} \\ \frac{1}{2}k_{r1}\left(\frac{1}{d_{obs,t}} - \frac{1}{R_{obs}}\right)^2, d_{obs} < R_{obs} \text{ and } d_{obs,t} = d_{obs,t-1} \\ 0, d_{obs} > R_{obs} \end{cases} \tag{46.3}$$

The conclusion is drawn from Eq. (46.3):

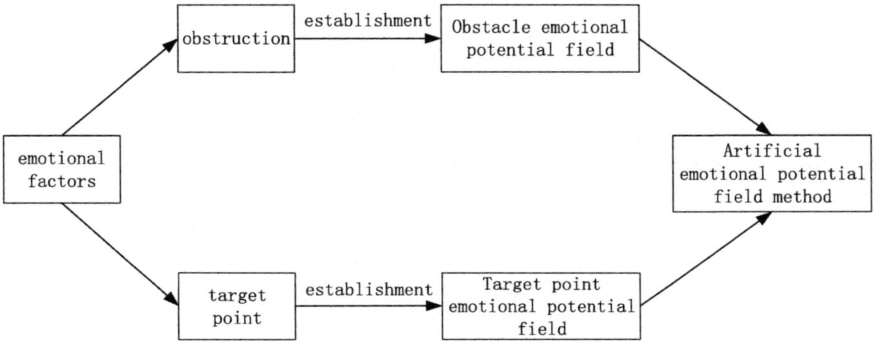

Fig. 46.4 The establishment of artificial emotional potential field method

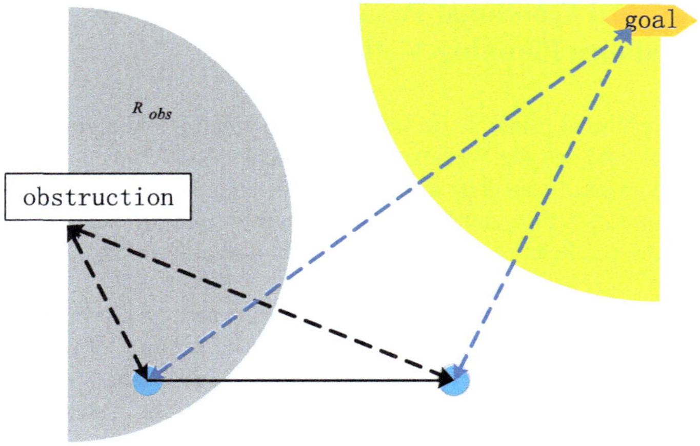

Fig. 46.5 Algorithmic details of artificial emotional potential field method

1. When the robot is in the influence range of the obstacle emotional potential field R_{obs}, the obstacle emotional potential field is the superposition of the physical field and the emotional field. The superimposed emotional field is determined by the ratio of the person 's emotional change to the distance change, and the awakening determines the strength.
2. When the robot is in the influence range of the obstacle emotional potential field R_{obs} and the valence of t and $t - 1$ is the same, the superimposed emotional potential field is determined by the change of arousal.
3. When the robot is in the influence range of the obstacle emotional potential field $\mathrm{R_{obs}}$ R_{obs} and the Euclidean distance between the robot and the obstacle at t and $t - 1$ is the same, according to the experimental conclusion, there will be no emotional change and no emotional field will be superimposed.
4. When the robot exceeds the influence range of the obstacle emotional potential field R_{obs}, the obstacle has no effect on the robot.

46.5 Simulation and Analysis

46.5.1 Single Obstacle Planning Experiment

Experiment 1: There is a coordinate (2, 2) obstacle in the simulated two-dimensional plane of 6×6 unit area, the starting point position (0, 0), and the target point coordinate (6, 6). The artificial potential field method and the artificial emotional potential field method are used for path planning respectively, and the distribution of user emotional state corresponding to the same length of path is compared. The distribution of valence and arousal on this path is shown in the Fig. 46.6.

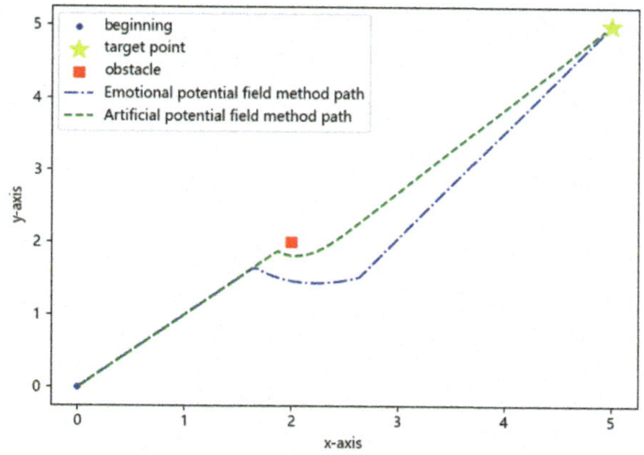

Fig. 46.6 Artificial emotional potential field method and artificial potential field method for obstacle avoidance planning

Figure 46.7 shows the valence, arousal mean and standard deviation of the two methods under the same length path, and analyzes the emotional state distribution of the two methods under the same planned path and the same time spent on completing the task. The path length unit is a step, and the robot further moves 0.01 unit length in front of each step, It is assumed that the robot runs at a constant speed.

Simulation results show that under the condition of the same length of the obstacle avoidance path delineated by the artificial emotional potential field method and the artificial potential field law, the path delineated by the artificial emotional potential field law is more popular among users, with higher emotional potency, lower arousal, and smoother changes in emotional fluctuations. Meanwhile, simulation experiments demonstrate the ability of the method to accomplish the path planning task while

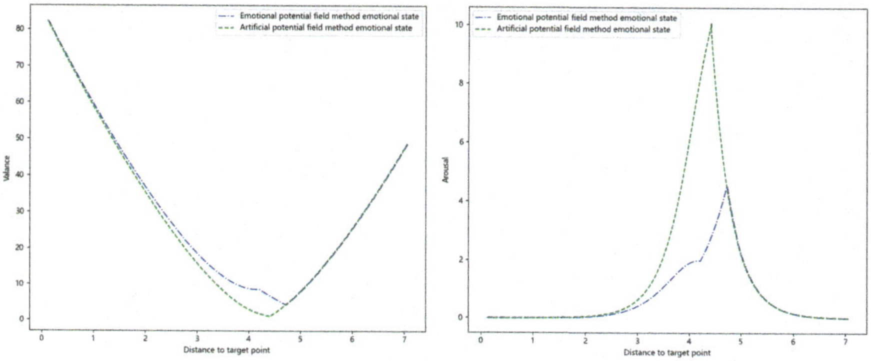

Fig. 46.7 Valance and wake-up under different path planning methods

considering the user's emotional feelings, which makes up for the defects of manned mobile robots in taking care of the user's emotional feelings.

46.5.2 Multiple Obstacle Planning Experiments

Experiment 2: In the two-dimensional plane of unit area of 10×10, six obstacles are set up, which are irregularly distributed between the starting point and the target point. The starting point position coordinates (0, 0), the target point coordinates (10, 10), and the distance of each travel of the robot is set to 0.01 units. At the same time, the artificial potential field method and the artificial emotional potential field method are used to test the path planning results as shown in Fig. 46.8.

The analysis shows that the artificial emotional potential field method can plan a reasonable path in a complex multi-obstacle environment. When the parameters of the method are the same as those of the artificial potential field method, due to the existence of the emotional component in the potential field of the obstacle and the target point, the path planned by the method is more inclined to ' avoid ' the obstacle, and the total number of driving steps is more.

The path obtained by different planning algorithms, the emotional change process obtained based on the distance emotion model is shown in Fig. 46.9.

As the robot starts from the starting point to the target point, the user's emotional valence corresponding to the path delineated by the artificial emotional potential field regulation is higher than that of the artificial potential field method, and the fluctuation is more gentle. The user's emotional arousal is lower than the artificial potential field method and the fluctuation is more gentle. From the perspective of the change of user's emotional state, it shows that the artificial emotional potential field

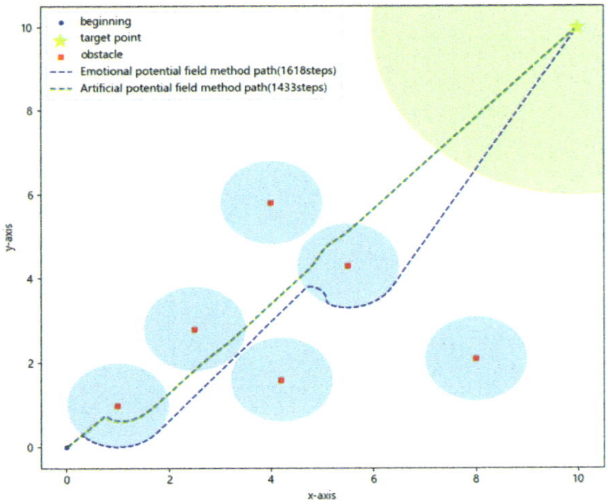

Fig. 46.8 Experimental results of path planning for multiple obstacles

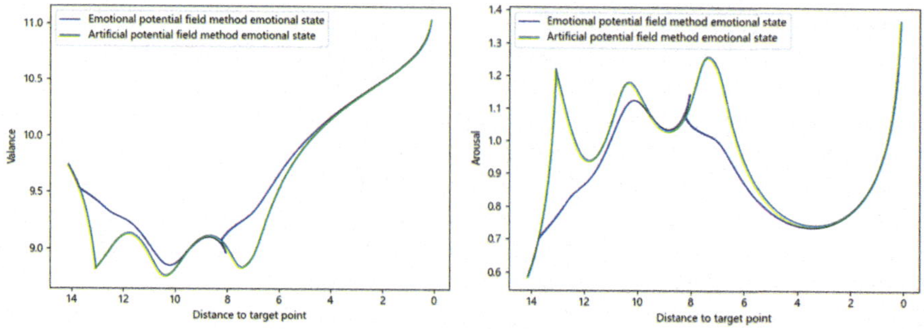

Fig. 46.9 Effectiveness and wake-up changes of different path planning methods

method is more in line with the user's emotional and psychological feelings than the artificial potential field regulation.

In summary, the conclusions of simulation experiments and human–computer interaction experiments prove the ability of this method to complete the path planning task while considering the user's emotional feelings. In the experimental scene of the obstacle emotional potential field and the target point emotional potential field, the artificial emotional potential field method is the same as the artificial potential field regulation. Under the condition of the same path length, the artificial emotional potential field method can plan a path that makes the user feel more comfortable and stable.

46.5.3 Human–Computer Interaction Experiments with Artificial Emotional Potential Field Algorithms

The artificial emotional potential field method proves in simulation experiments that the user's emotions are more dominant in the paths planned by the method under the same conditions as the length of the path delineated by the artificial potential field statute. Based on the immersive human–computer interaction platform, we designed the human–computer interaction experiments of the artificial emotional potential field algorithm, in which Experiment 1 is a single obstacle artificial potential field method, Experiment 2 is a single obstacle artificial emotional potential field method, Experiment 3 is a multiple obstacle artificial potential field method, and Experiment 4 is a multiple obstacle artificial emotional potential field method, in which physiological signals of subjects were collected, and subjective emotion evaluation questionnaire's SAM scores, based on the emotion evaluation system, the advantage of the artificial emotional potential field algorithm in planning paths is verified from the perspective of subjective and objective evaluation.

The rest before each experiment was analyzed as the baseline data. The ECG data were preprocessed to extract the heart rate change features and analyze the difference between the mean value of the subject's heart rate during the robot operation and the mean value of the heart rate during the rest period; and the picoelectric signals were preprocessed to extract the SCR amplitude features and analyze the difference between the mean value of the SCR amplitude during the robot operation and the mean value of the SCR amplitude during the rest period.

When the robot completes the task according to the paths planned by different methods, it can be seen from Table 46.1 the relative rate of change of heart rate (the ratio of experimental heart rate change data of different path planning methods) that the physiological signal performance of 80% of the subjects (subjects numbered 1, 2, 4, 5, 7, 8, 9, and 10) shows that the increase in heart rate caused by the artificial emotional potential field method is lower than that caused by the artificial potential field method. The objective performance of emotional physiological response indicates that in the dimension of potency, the path delineated by the Artificial Emotional Potential Field Method shows an advantage in the dimension of the user's emotional potency.

As shown in Table 46.2 Relative rate of change of SCR amplitude of subjects (ratio of experimental SCR amplitude data of different path planning methods), 80% of subjects (subjects numbered 1, 2, 4, 5, 7, 8, 9 and 10) physiological signal performance showed lower SCR amplitude caused by the artificial emotional potential field method than that caused by the artificial potential field method. Also in the objective perspective of emotional physiological responses illustrating the arousal dimension, the path delineated by the artificial emotional potential field method showed an advantage in the user's dimension of emotional arousal.

Analyzing the emotional self-assessment questionnaires completed by the subjects, it can be seen from Table 46.3 that 80% of the subjects (subjects numbered 1, 2, 4, 5, 7, 8, 9, and 10) gave higher potency and more positive emotional feelings under the artificial emotional potential field method of path experimentation than the artificial potential field method. As can be seen from Table 46.4, 80% of the

Table 46.1 Features and relative rate of heart rate change during the experiment

Number	HRC (bpm)				HRV	
	Exp.1	Exp.2	Exp.3	Exp.4	Exp.2/Exp.1 (%)	Exp.4/Exp.3 (%)
1	2.01	0.19	2.25	0.17	9.63	7.33
2	1.62	0.57	0.67	0.15	35.18	21.72
3	2.45	2.53	3.94	0.92	103.23	23.31
4	7.60	5.88	1.48	0.44	77.40	29.83
5	3.96	0.46	2.76	0.32	11.63	11.59
6	1.80	4.29	0.45	3.78	238.59	834.28
7	1.92	1.37	1.15	0.14	71.39	11.82
8	0.75	0.64	11.50	3.78	84.77	32.91
9	2.49	0.23	0.47	0.00016	9.19	0.04
10	2.49	1.27	0.74	0.47	50.89	63.22

Table 46.2 SCR amplitude characteristics and relative change rate during the experiment

Number	SCR amplitude ($\times 10^{-5} \mu S$)				SCR amplitude rate of change	
	Exp.1	Exp.2	Exp.3	Exp.4	Exp.2/Exp.1 (%)	Exp.4/Exp.3 (%)
1	2.131	0.251	1.580	0.961	11.80	60.86
2	0.147	0.080	275.769	0.306	54.59	0.11
3	0.084	1.496	0.687	1.426	1788.11	207.63
4	18.822	10.641	27.965	8.216	56.54	29.38
5	1280.225	1.828	1.446	1.052	0.14	72.76
6	69.116	1020.996	10.970	1.678	1477.21	15.29
7	0.634	0.193	4.326	0.833	30.40	19.27
8	1.347	0.112	1.382	0.488	8.34	35.32
9	72.505	1.115	16.690	0.083	1.54	0.50
10	2.131	0.251	1.580	0.961	5.92	0.33

subjects perceived lower arousal and relatively smoother emotional feelings during the robot's traveling according to the artificial emotional potential field method.

In summary, the objective physiological signal performance and subjective emotional evaluation of most subjects during the experiment proved that the path of the artificial emotional potential field method made the user's emotional feelings smoother and more comfortable, verifying the conclusion of the simulation experiment.

Table 46.3 SAM questionnaire valance data statistics

Number	Valance				Change in valance	
	Exp.1	Exp.2	Exp.3	Exp.4	Exp.2/ Exp.1	Exp.4/ Exp.3
1	5	6	4	6	1	2
2	4	6	4	5	2	1
3	6	5	7	4	−1	−3
4	6	7	6	7	1	1
5	5	6	4	6	1	2
6	7	5	8	6	−2	−2
7	7	7	7	8	0	1
8	5	7	4	6	2	2
9	4	7	6	8	1	2
10	5	6	5	7	0	2

Table 46.4 SAM questionnaire arousal data statistics

Number	Arousal				Change in arousal	
	Exp.1	Exp.2	Exp.3	Exp.4	Exp.2/ Exp.1	Exp.4/ Exp.3
1	6	5	5	4	−1	−1
2	7	6	7	5	−1	−2
3	4	5	3	6	1	3
4	4	3	5	4	−1	−1
5	6	5	6	5	−1	−1
6	4	5	3	5	1	2
7	7	6	6	5	−1	−1
8	4	3	5	3	−1	−2
9	7	5	5	4	−2	−1
10	7	6	5	4	−1	−1

46.6 Conclusion

In order to improve the emotional experience and psychological safety of users in the process of human–computer interaction, a human-in-the-loop control algorithm using human emotional feedback is proposed for robots. Under the emotional evaluation system combining subjective emotional evaluation and objective physiological response, a virtual reality emotion induction experiment is designed, an obstacle emotion model is constructed, and an artificial emotional potential field obstacle avoidance algorithm is proposed. Taking human emotional feedback as an important guide for robot optimization and improvement, human factor is an important step in robot control loopback, reflecting the control idea of 'human in the loop'.

References

1. Du, P., Dong, T.: The current status of long-term care for elderly with dementia and policy responses under the background of aging. Hebei Acad. J. **38**(3), 6 (2018)
2. Liu, S., Lan, Z.G.: Technical development trends of service robots for elderly care. Comput. Measur. Control **27**(07), 1–6 (2019)
3. Lee-Johnson, C.P., Carnegie, D.A.: Emotion-based parameter modulation for a hierarchical mobile robot planning and control architecture. In: 2007 IEEE/RSJ International Conference on Intelligent Robots and Systems, pp. 2839–2844. IEEE, San Diego, CA, USA (2007)
4. Williams, H., Lee-Johnson, C., Browne, W.N., et al.: Emotion inspired adaptive robotic path planning. In: 2015 IEEE Congress on Evolutionary Computation (CEC), pp. 3004–3011. IEEE, Sendai, Japan (2015)
5. Wu, X., Hirota, K., Tang, B., et al.: Ameliorated frenet trajectory optimization method based on artificial emotion and equilibrium optimizer. J. Adv. Comput. Intell. Intell. Inf. **25**(1), 110–120 (2021)
6. Russell, J.A.: A circumplex model of affect. J. Pers. Soc. Psychol. **39**(6), 1161 (1980)

7. Aiden, M.K., Sabharwal, S.M., Chhabra, S., Al-Asadi, M.: AI and blockchain for cyber security in cyber-physical system. In: AI Models for Blockchain-Based Intelligent Networks in IoT Systems: Concepts, Methodologies, Tools, and Applications, pp. 203–230. Springer (2023)
8. Chhabra, S., Aiden, M.K., Sabharwal, S.M., Al-Asadi, M.: 5G and 6G technologies for smart city. In: Enabling Technologies for Effective Planning and Management in Sustainable Smart Cities, pp. 335–365: Springer (2023)
9. Al-Asadi, M., Bhushan, B.: Object identification: comprehensive approach using machine learning algorithms and python tools. In: International Conference on Computing, Intelligence and Data Analytics (2023)
10. Li, W., Zhang, Z., Song, A.: Physiological-signal-based emotion recognition: an odyssey from methodology to philosophy. Measurement **172**, 108747 (2021)
11. Kulic, D., Croft, E.: Anxiety detection during human-robot interaction. In: 2005 IEEE/RSJ International Conference on Intelligent Robots and Systems, pp. 616–621. IEEE, Edmonton, AB, Canada (2005)
12. Zhu, J., Ji, L., Liu, C.: Heart rate variability monitoring for emotion and disorders of emotion. Physiol. Meas. **40**(6), 064004 (2019)

Chapter 47
Optimal Configuration of Repurposed Battery Energy Storage Systems with Stochastic Capacity Degradation

Lu Yan and Gao Fei

Abstract Repurposed electric vehicle batteries (REVBs) which refer to the batteries retired from on-road electric vehicles (EVs), have huge potential to be reused in the distribution systems. The optimal configuration of REVBs is the key to the design of the distribution networks and the basis of optimal scheduling. However, the states of REVBs, such as state of health (SOH), state of charge, and remaining useful life (RUL), need to be monitored to avoid hazardous operations and lower the risk of system operation. Therefore, a stochastic degradation model is introduced to describe the capacity degradation, in which the random operation conditions are better reflected. Also, the impact of the optimal operation of REVB on the optimum REVB configuration is constructed in the lower-level, with the REVB configuration on the upper-level. Finally, case studies are conducted by different benchmarks to show the effectiveness and validation of the proposed bi-level model.

47.1 Introduction

With the prevalence of electric vehicles (EVs), large numbers of on-board lithium batteries will be retired recently Alharbi et al. [1]. Particularly, the batteries retired from EVs have the potential to be second-utilized, i.e., repurposed.

Repurposed electric vehicle batteries (REVBs) distinguish from the new ones, i.e., EV batteries (EVB), are the capacity, maximum charge–discharge power, and high failure rate. Therefore, traditional EVB configuration strategies Wu et al. [2] which ignore the capacity degradation and outage of batteries, are not completely suitable for REVB operational configuration.

L. Yan (✉) · G. Fei
State Grid Jin Zhong Electric Power Supply Company, Jinzhong 030600, China
e-mail: 599285373@qq.com

G. Fei
e-mail: gaof1024@126.com

F. P. García Márquez et al. (eds.), *Computing, Internet of Things and Data Analytics*, Smart Innovation, Systems and Technologies 387,
https://doi.org/10.1007/978-3-031-87154-2_47

The application scenarios of REVBs usually include providing distributed battery energy storage system (BESS) support Yang et al. [3], peak load shaving Chen et al. [4, 5], mitigating renewable energy fluctuations He et al. [6], and frequency regulation Yi et al. [7–9], etc.

To integrate REVBs in such applications, the capacity degradation which is typical in REVBs applications, is virtually significant [10–20]. Thus, the battery cycling, depth of discharge, and other environmental conditions are concerns in previous studies. Alharbi et al. [1] assume a linear cycling and calendar degradation to calculate the optimum REVB replacement year. Yang et al. [3] analyzed the impact of system operations on battery capacity changes, e.g., cycling degradation. Xia et al. [8] shows the battery cycle life and cycling calculation method under different operational strategies. Tran, Khambadkone [18] considers the impact of depth of discharge and the number of charging/discharging cycles on the battery degradation. Zhang et al. [19] introduce a discharge-based cost model to construct the degradation process. Hamidan, Borousan [20] investigated a simple DOD-based capacity degradation model.

Besides, the operational configuration models of REVB have also been studied in the literature. Alharbi et al. [1] takes variable replacement year into account for REVB configuration, while [2–5] ignores this variable. Yang et al. [3] propose a REVB configuration with retirement costs, but the detailed operation constraints of REVB are not highly focused. [4, 5] presented the effective REVB configuration strategies.

However, little research work has been done on the stochastic capacity degradation of REVBs in the optimum REVB configuration Pham et al. [21, 22]. REVBs' stochastic capacity degradation highly depended on the cycling strategies. frequent and high DOD cycling accelerates the depreciation. And the REVB would be retired and replaced. Thus, accounting for degradation ensures realistic operational decisions and an optimal replacement year, thereby avoiding premature replacements and additional costs. Moreover, due to the random environmental conditions and failure rate of battery cells, the capacity degradation of REVBs is stochastic Xia et al. [8], which would lead to inaccurate replacements and additional costs, and also limits their applicability in real-world applications. Hence, there is a need to construct a stochastic capacity degradation model with various operation conditions.

In general, this paper proposes a stochastic capacity degradation model with various operation conditions. Moreover, flexible EVs are considered as a kind of BESS to cooperate with REVBs operation, thereby further reducing system costs. Thus, the REVBs operational configuration of this paper consists of two parts: stationary REVBs and running EVBs. By applying the proposed model, REVB planners could obtain more accurate and economic results. A comprehensive configuration framework that achieves the REVBs' replacement strategy changing with different cycling strategies is presented.

The main contribution of this paper is shown as follows.

(1) A stochastic capacity degradation model is introduced to reduce the negative impact of the REVB cells' capacity uncertainty on the REVB operational configuration.
(2) A bi-level optimization configuration framework of REVBs is investigated to avoid updating capacity on a month-by-month basis and compute it under different operational strategies, realizing the accuracy simulation of REVB operation.

The structure of this paper is as follows: Sect. 47.2 describes the proposed stochastic capacity degradation model of REVBs. The operational configuration of REVBs is presented in Sect. 47.3. The case setting and results are presented in Sect. 47.4 to demonstrate the effectiveness of the proposed models with four cases. Finally, conclusions are drawn in Sect. 47.5. A detailed analysis and performance simulation has been mentioned.

47.2 Stochastic Capacity Degradation Model of REVBs

In this part, the stochastic capacity degradation of REVB is reflected by evaluating the operation performance of REVB cells under random conditions. Therefore, the degradation characteristics and the SOH of REVBs are captured and modelled in detail.

The calendar and cycling degradation, which are the spontaneous degradation that normally occurs and the degradation per cycle respectively, are both considered in the capacity degradation of REVBs. Moreover, due to the complex logical judgment, the rain-flow algorithm has its disadvantage in the joint optimization process, and a depth of discharge (DOD) based stochastic model is introduced instead, as shown.

The REVBs' remaining life is presented by the state of health (SOH), and the relationship between capacity degradation ζ_d^{REVB} and SOH is shown as followed.

$$\mathrm{SOH} = \delta_1 - \zeta_d^{REVB} / \zeta_{ra}^{REVB} * 100\% \tag{47.1}$$

ζ_{ra}^{REVB} is the rated energy capacity of the battery. According to [1], ζ_d^{REVB} is the linear degradation that is given by the sum of calendar degradation ζ_{cal}^{REVB} and cycling degradation ζ_{cyc}^{REVB}.

$$\zeta_d^{REVB} = \zeta_{cal}^{REVB} + \zeta_{cyc}^{REVB} \tag{47.2}$$

$$\zeta_{cal}^{REVB} = \zeta_{\mathrm{loss}}^{cal} * \sqrt{t} \tag{47.3}$$

$\zeta_{\mathrm{loss}}^{cal}$ is the calendar ageing characteristic of the battery, selected at Geng et al. [14]. Then, the DOD-based cycling degradation ζ_{cyc}^{REVB} can be derived as Wu et al. [2, 6, 18].

$$\left|d_{k,i,t} = E^{REVB}_{k,i,t} - E^{REVB}_{k,i,t-1}\right| / E^{REVB}_{k,i} * 100\% \tag{47.4}$$

$$n^{eq,day}_{100,k,i,t} = \sum\nolimits_{t \in T} N_0 \left(d_{k,i,t}\right)^{kp} \tag{47.5}$$

$$T^{re}_{cyc,k} = N^{fail}_{100,k,i,b} \Bigg/ \left(\sum_{y \in Y} \sum_{b \in B} W \cdot n^{eq,day}_{100,k,i} \right) \tag{47.6}$$

$$L_{yss^{cyc}_{k,i}} = 1/T^{re}_{cyc,k,i} \times 100\% \tag{47.7}$$

$$\zeta^{REVB}_{cyc} = \sum_{k} \sum_{i} \text{Loss}^{cyc}_{k,i} \tag{47.8}$$

The DOD of each time is shown as (4), the capacity degradation is shown as (5), (8). In (4), t is time index, k is the cycle index, and i refers to the node number. $d_{k,i,t}$ is the DOD of every half cycle. $E^{REVB}_{k,i,t}$ is the operational decision variable of REVB, $E^{REVB}_{k,i}$ is the configuration capacity of REVB, decision variable. $n^{\text{eq,day}}_{100,k,i}$ in (5) represents the number of cycles until failure at 100% DOD. k_p is the Peukert lifetime parameter, selected at the range of0.8 − 2.1. From Fig. 47.1 and [6], the maximum number of charge and discharge under different k_p is almost the same under 100% DOD. And a larger k_p means more capacity. N_0 is a battery cycle parameter related to the cycle, selected a default of 0.5 or 1; In (6), $N^{fail}_{100,k,i}$ denotes the maximum number of battery life cycles at with 100%-DOD. W is the average number of operating days in a year. The capacity degradation, $\text{Loss}^{cyc}_{k,i}$ is calculated by (7), which is inversely proportional to$T^{re}_{cyc,k,i}$. And ζ^{REVB}_{cyc} is the sum of$\text{Loss}^{cyc}_{k,i}$, shown as (8).

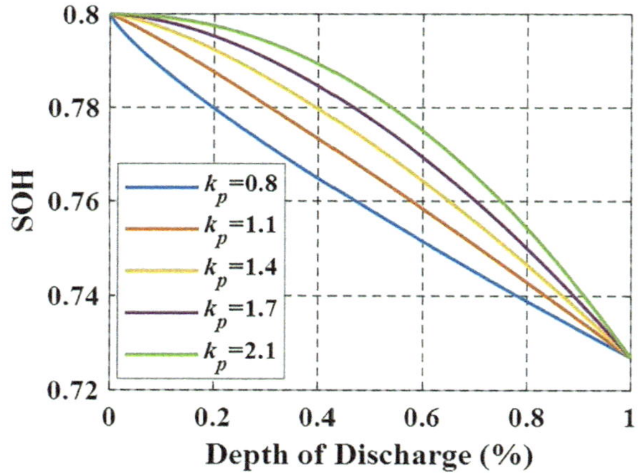

Fig. 47.1 Curves of REVB's SOH versus DOD with different *kp* values

As shown from (4)-(8), the battery's cycle life is related to the cycling strategies and largest cycling numbers, while the latter dependent on the manufacture. Therefore, Frequent and deep cycles accelerate cyclic aging and reduce the cycle life. The DOD-based model can be used directly to calculate equivalent cycling capacity degradation.

Figure 47.1 shows the SOH of REVB depending on DOD and the selected k_p. By assuming $N_{100}^{fail} = 5000$ [6], and $W = 365$, the REVBs' SOH degraded around 0.07 at a year's cycling under 100% DOD.

47.3 Optimal Configuration of REVBs

The capacity degradation of REVBs is highly dependent on the operation strategies, thus the configuration and operation are very important indeed. The REVB optimal configuration framework is shown, in which the relationships between REVB configuration and operation are revealed.

Moreover, the REVB's capacity decreases with increase of charging-discharging cycles, DOD and operational decisions of REVB. Also, the monetary value of REVB is dependent on its real capacity. Therefore, the detailed REVB capacity changing process is also considered.

47.3.1 *Configuration Scheme of REVBs*

The optimal decisions such as installation year, energy and power size, and replacement year [1] are presented as follows.

$$\mathcal{P}^{REVB} = \mathcal{P}_I^{REVB} + \mathcal{P}_M^{REVB} + \mathcal{P}_{RY}^{REVB} \tag{47.9}$$

$$\mathcal{P}_I^{REVB} = \sum_{y \in \Omega^N} \left[\frac{1}{(1+r)^y} \left(C_y^p P_{i,y}^{REVB,i} + C_y^e E_{i,y}^{REVB,i} + C_y^v \delta_{i,y}^{REVB,i} \right) \right] \tag{47.10}$$

$$\mathcal{P}_M^{REVB} = \sum_{y \in \Omega^N} \left[\frac{1}{(1+r)^y} \left(C_y^f P_y^{REVB,i} \right) \right] \tag{47.11}$$

$$\mathcal{P}_{RY}^{REVB} = \left(1 - r R_y^{REVB} \right) C_y^{RY} E_y^{REVB,i} \tag{47.12}$$

$\mathcal{P}^{REVB}$, $\mathcal{P}_I^{REVB}$, $\mathcal{P}_M^{REVB}$, and $\mathcal{P}_{RY}^{REVB}$, respectively, are the REVB total cost, the installation cost, the operation and maintenance cost, and the replacement cost. $\mathcal{P}_I^{\text{REVB}}$ is composed of power capacity cost, energy capacity cost, and a fixed investment cost in the installation stage. The variables $P_{i,y}^{REVB,i}$, $E_{i,y}^{REVB,i}$, and $\delta_{i,y}^{REVB,i}$ are the REVB optimum power capacity, energy capacity and the decision variable of installation respectively. And C_y^p, C_y^e, C_y^v, C_y^f and C_y^{RY} are all the related cost parameters in installation process. All the costs are net present value. $\mathcal{P}_M^{REVB}$ is comprised of the fixed and variable operation and maintenance cost. $\mathcal{P}_{RY}^{REVB}$ is the linearized replacement cost of the REVBs [1]. Ω^N represents the initial REVB installation sets, r is the interest rate.

The configuration constraints with the replacement strategies are shown as follows.

$$P_{i,y}^{REVB,t} = P_{i,y-1}^{REVB,t} + P_{i,y}^{REVB,i} + P_{i,y}^{REVB,ex} - P_{i,y-1}^{REVB,y}, y \in \Omega^{\mathrm{N}} \tag{47.13}$$

$$E_{i,y}^{REVB,t} = E_{i,y-1}^{REVB,t} + E_{i,y}^{REVB,i} + E_{i,y}^{REVB,ex} - E_{i,y-1}^{REVB,y}, y \in \Omega^{\mathrm{N}} \tag{47.14}$$

$$\delta_{i,y}^{REVB,ry} = \begin{cases} 0, & \text{if } \mathrm{SOH}_{e,q} \geq \delta_2 \\ 1, & \text{otherwise} \end{cases} \tag{47.15}$$

$$\delta_{i,y}^{REVB,ry} \leq \left(\delta_{i,y}^{REVB,i} + \delta_{i,y}^{REVB,ex} \right) \tag{47.16}$$

where y is the configuration stage, $P_{i,y}^{REVB,t}$ is the total REVB power in the multistage process and are determined by the investment, expansion and replacement strategies. $P_{i,y}^{REVB,ry}$ is the real replacement power. The multistage coupled constraints of installation and expansion are also included in this analysis.

47.3.2 Operational Configuration Constraints of REVBs

Battery optimal operation considering stochastic REVB capacity degradation and EVB flexible dispatch, is presented as followed.

$$\mathcal{O}^{\mathrm{REVB}} = \sum C^g P_{g,i,t} + C^{pv} P_{pv,i,t} + C^q P_{pvg,i,t} + C^{EV} P_{EV,i,t}$$

$$s.t. \forall ij, jk \in \boldsymbol{D}_A, \forall d, \forall s, \forall i, \forall t \tag{47.17}$$

$$0 \leq P_{i,t,y}^{REVB,ch} \leq u^c P_{i,ty}^{REVB,t} \tag{47.18}$$

$$0 \leq P_{i,ty}^{REVB,dis} \leq u^d P_{i,ty}^{REVB,t} \tag{47.19}$$

$$u^c + u^d \leq 1 \tag{47.20}$$

$$E_{i,t+1y}^{REVB} = E_{i,ty}^{REVB} + P_{i,t,y}^{REVB,ch} \eta^c \Delta t - P_{i,t,y}^{REVB,dis} / \eta^d \Delta t \tag{47.21}$$

where $\mathcal{O}^{\mathrm{D}}$ is the total operational cost of the distribution system. t is the operation time. $P_{g,i,t}$, $P_{pv,i,t}$, $P_{pvq,i,t}$ and $P_{EV,i,t}$ are the upper-grid power, PV power, PV curtailed power, and flexible EV power, respectively. C^{g}, C^{pv}, C^{pvq}, and C^{EV} are the related costs. $P_{i,t,y}^{REVB,ch}$ and $P_{i,t,y}^{REVB,dis}$ are the charging and discharging powers, respectively. u^c and u^d represent the REVB charging and discharging decision variables. η^c and η^d indicate the charge and discharge efficiencies.

$$\mathrm{SOH}_{e,q} = \mathcal{H}\big(d_{k,i}\big) \tag{47.22}$$

$\mathcal{H}$ denotes the stochastic capacity degradation. The linearized power flow equation is also considered in this paper, and the EV flexible dispatch is contained in the power equation by assuming that the EVs are willing to be dispatched for system revenue. Therefore, the REVBs and flexible EVs consist the BESS in the distribution network.

47.4 Case Studies

47.4.1 Basic Settings

The proposed operational configuration is tested on IEEE-69 node network [23]. The total configuration period of the coupled system is 8 years, of which a period of 2 years is divided into 4-period blocks. The system has a peak demand of 3715 kW (at base year), which grows with a constant annual rate of 5% [12]. Table 47.1 summarizes the REVB's costs, e.g., the investment cost, maintenance cost, replacement cost and others cost related to the REVB power and energy. The discount rate r is 10%. C_y^{inv} is \$20,000. δ_2 is 0.6. Moreover, the specific physical properties of REVBs and EVBs are listed in Table 47.2. The distribution operation cost can be seen in [12]. The typical EV dispatch power can be found in [7].

Table 47.1 System costs parameters of the REVB

Cost parameters	C_y^P	C_y^E	C_y^f	C_y^v	R_y^{REVB}
Unit	\$/kW	\$/kWh	\$/kWh	\$/kWh	\$/kWh
REVB	1,334	456	13.2	0.0018	1,115

Table 47.2 Characteristics parameters of the REVB and EVB

Characteristics parameters	η	SOH
Unit	%	/
REVB	72	0.8
EVB	90	1.0

Table 47.3 Comparison cases for REVBs optimal configuration

Case	Stochastic capacity degradation	Ref
1		This paper
2		[3]

Table 47.4 Power capacity of REVBs optimal configuration (MW)

	Stage 1		Stage 2	Stage 3	Stage 4
Case 1	5.76		1.36	1.28	0
Case 2	4.48		0	0.08	0

Table 47.5 Energy capacity of candidate REVBs optimal configuration (MWh)

	Stage1	Stage2	Stage3	Stage 4
Case 1	14.56	4.00	3.44	0
Case 2	11.28	0	0.08	0

47.4.2 Cases Results

In order to verify the effectiveness and economy of the proposed operational configuration, the following scenarios in Table 47.3 are investigated. The stochastic capacity degradation model is incorporated to see how it affects the configuration of REVBs and the total cost.

a. Configuration results of REVB

The power and energy capacity of REVBs in two cases are presented in Table 47.4 and Table 47.5, in MW and MWh. The values in Table 47.4 indicates that the total power capacity of the REVBs. The energy capacities of the REVBs in the two cases in different planning stages are shown in Table 47.5 in MWh. Stages 1 to 4 ($d = 1, 2, 3, 4$) represent the sequenced planning stages with the given 2-year durations.

Investment Cost in two cases are shown as 301$M and 148$M for Case 1 and Case 2.

From Table 47.5, can be seen that the stochastic capacity degradation has significant impact on REVBs optimal planning strategy and costs.

b. Operation results of the distribution system

The results for the PVs, REVBs, and flexible EVs in the distribution system for REVBs optimal configuration is shown as follows.

From Fig. 47.2. can be seen that REVBs charging largely from 10:00 am to 14:00, when PV output is high. Specifically, REVBs store the surplus electricity from PV, and then release that electricity to customers when required. Flexible EVs provide downstream power, that is grid-to-vehicle.

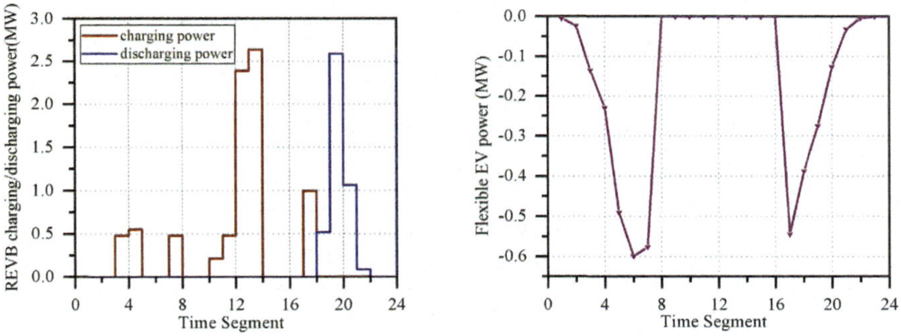

(a) REVB charging/ discharging power in a typical day

(b) Flexible EV power in a typical day

Fig. 47.2 Operation results of distribution system

47.5 Conclusion

Considering the stochastic capacity degradation by the large number of charging-discharging, the optimal configuration for REVBs has been conducted by a bi-level model. In the upper level, the optimal configuration is developed with the investment and replacement process. In the lower level, the optimal operation of the distribution networks is presented with stochastic capacity degradation. Then, the SOH calculated by the lower level model would be transferred to the upper level, leading to a new replacement strategy.

By numerical case studies, it can be found that the proposed model has more costs the comparison case. It can also be seen from Fig. 47.1 that the REVBs' SOH degraded around 0.07 at a year's cycling under 100% DOD. Therefore, considering the stochastic capacity degradation is essential and more realistic. REVBs and EVs can store the surplus electricity from power grid when it needed.

Acknowledgements **Disclosure of Interests.** The authors have no competing interests to declare that are relevant to the content of this article.

References

1. Alharbi, T., Bhattacharya, K., Kazerani, M.: Configuration and operation of isolated microgrids based on repurposed electric vehicle batteries. IEEE Trans Industr Inf **15**(7), 4319–4331 (2019)
2. Wu, X., Conejo, A.J., Mathew, S.: Optimal siting of batteries in distribution systems to enhance reliability. IEEE Trans Power Delivery **36**(5), 3118–3127 (2021)
3. Yang, Y., Qiu, J., Zhang, C., Zhao, J., Wang, G.: Flexible integrated network configuration considering echelon utilization of second life of used electric vehicle batteries. IEEE Trans Transp Electrification **8**(1), 263–276 (2022)

4. Chen L, Qin M, Xia Y et al (2020) A configuration-control integrated strategy for electric bus charging station with echelon battery system. IEEE Transactions on Industry Applications 56(5):6019–6028
5. Deng, Y., Zhang, Y., Luo, F., Mu, Y.: Operational configuration of centralized charging stations utilizing second-life battery energy storage systems. IEEE Trans Sustain Energy **12**(1), 387–399 (2021)
6. He, G., Chen, Q., Kang, C., Pinson, P., Xia, Q.: Optimal bidding strategy of battery storage in power markets considering performance-based regulation and battery cycle life. IEEE Transactions on Smart Grid **7**(5), 2359–2367 (2016)
7. Yi T, Cheng X, Chen Y et al (2020) Joint optimization of charging station and energy storage economic capacity based on the effect of alternative energy storage of electric vehicle. Energy 208
8. Xia, Q., Wang, Z., Ren, Y., et al.: A modified reliability model for lithium-ion battery cells based on the stochastic capacity degradation and dynamic response impedance. J Power Sources **423**, 40–51 (2019)
9. Lu, X., Chan, K.W., Xia, S., Zhang, X., Wang, G., Li, F.: A model to mitigate forecast uncertainties in distribution systems using the temporal flexibility of EVAs. IEEE Trans Power Syst **35**(3), 2212–2221 (2020)
10. Zhang, C., Xu, Y., Dong, Z.Y., Wong, K.P.: Robust coordination of distributed generation and price-based demand response in microgrids. IEEE Transactions on Smart Grid **9**(5), 4236–4247 (2018)
11. Guner, S., Ozdemir, A.: Stochastic energy storage capacity model of EV parking lots. IET Gener Transm Distrib **11**(7), 1754–1761 (2017)
12. Awad ASA, EL-Fouly THM, Salama MMA (2017) Optimal ESS allocation for benefit maximization in distribution networks, IEEE Transactions on Smart Grid 8(4):1668–1678
13. Wenzel G, Negrete-Pincetic M, Olivares DE, MacDonald J, Callaway DS (2017) Real-time charging strategies for an electric vehicle aggregator to provide ancillary services, IEEE Transactions on Smart Grid 9(5):5141–5151
14. Geng J, Gao S, Sun X et al (2022) Potential of electric vehicle batteries second use in energy storage systems: The case of China. Energy 253
15. Santos, S.F., Fitiwi, D.Z., Shafie-Khah, M., Bizuayehu, A.W., Cabrita, C.M.P., Catalão, J.P.S.: New multistage and stochastic mathematical model for maximiz RES hosting capacity — Part I: problem formula. IEEE Transactions on Sustainable Energy **8**(1), 304–319 (2017)
16. Alsaidan, I., Khodaei, A., Gao, W.: A comprehensive battery energy sorage optimal sizing model for microgrid applications. IEEE Trans. Power Syst. **33**(4), 3968–3980 (2018)
17. Duggal, I., Venkatesh, B.: Short-term scheduling of thermal generators and battery storage with depth of discharge-based cost model. IEEE Trans. Power Syst. **30**(4), 2110–2118 (2015)
18. Tran, D., Khambadkone, A.M.: Energy management for lifetime extension of energy storage system in micro-grid applications. IEEE Transactions on Smart Grid **4**(3), 1289–1296 (2013)
19. Zhang, L., Zeng, Z., Qu, X.: On the role of battery capacity fading mechanism in the lifecycle cost of electric bus fleet. IEEE Trans Intell Transp Syst **22**(4), 2371–2380 (2021)
20. Hamidan MA, Borousan F (2022) Optimal configuration of distributed generation and battery energy storage systems simultaneously in distribution networks for loss reduction and reliability improvement. J Energy Storage 46
21. Pham TT, Kuo TC, Bui DM (2020) Reliability evaluation of an aggregate battery energy storage system in microgrids under dynamic operation. Int J Electr Power Energy Syst 118
22. Liu, M., Li, W., Wang, C., Polis, M.P., Wang, L.Y., Li, J.: Reliability evaluation of large scale battery energy storage systems. IEEE Transactions on Smart Grid **8**(6), 2733–2743 (2017)
23. Debapriya, D.: Optimal placement of capacitors in radial distribution system using a Fuzzy-GA method[J]. Int J Electr Power Energy Syst **30**(6–7), 361–367 (2008)

Chapter 48
Optimization of Firewall Placement on Information Security Object Using Genetic Algorithm

V. Lakhno, K. Makulov, O. Kryvoruchko, A. Desiatko, D. Kasatkin, K. Palaguta, and Y. Shestak

Abstract The solution of the problem of optimization of layout solutions in the placement of components (by the example of firewalls) of integrated information protection system (IIPS) circuits is considered. The use of genetic algorithm is proposed to solve the problem. Genetic algorithm (hereinafter GA) as a method of solving the problem of finding the optimal layout has been repeatedly described, but the description of the practical application of the GA in the task of building a multi-loop IIPS has not yet been properly reflected in the scientific literature. In our opinion, the genetic algorithm can be a very effective tool for solving the problem of optimizing the layout solutions of multi-loop IIPS construction. GA is based on the principles of natural selection and genetics, which allows it to find optimal or near-optimal solutions in complex search spaces. In particular, GA can help determine the optimal placement of equipment (servers, routers, firewalls, etc.) to ensure

V. Lakhno · D. Kasatkin
Faculty of Information Security, Computer Science and Communication, National University of Life and Environmental Sciences of Ukraine, Kyiv, Ukraine
e-mail: valss21@ukr.net

D. Kasatkin
e-mail: d.kasatkin@nubip.edu.ua

K. Makulov
Faculty of Computer Science, Yessenov University, Aktau, Kazakhstan
e-mail: kaiyrbek.makulov@yu.edu.kz

O. Kryvoruchko · A. Desiatko (✉) · K. Palaguta · Y. Shestak
Faculty of Information Technologies, State University of Trade and Economics, Kyiv, Ukraine
e-mail: desyatko@gmail.com

O. Kryvoruchko
e-mail: kryvoruchko_ev@knute.edu.ua

K. Palaguta
e-mail: palagutaea@knute.edu.ua

Y. Shestak
e-mail: shestack@knute.edu.ua

F. P. García Márquez et al. (eds.), *Computing, Internet of Things and Data Analytics*, Smart Innovation, Systems and Technologies 387,
https://doi.org/10.1007/978-3-031-87154-2_48

the best information protection, as well as optimize the strategy of redundancy and duplication of equipment to ensure system reliability and fault tolerance.

48.1 Introduction

Modern computer attacks are becoming increasingly complex and sophisticated [1, 2]. Cybercriminals are constantly improving their methods and using the latest technologies to penetrate the information systems of companies and enterprises. (information security objects–ISOs). This creates the need to build not just an information protection system, but a comprehensive system capable of effectively countering a variety of threats. As it was shown in the works [3–5] for effective protection from modern cyber threats it is necessary to systematically develop complex information protection systems. This means not only the creation of the system, but also its continuous improvement, adaptation to new threats and updating of defense strategies. In the conditions of dynamic confrontation with computer intruders, it is important to optimize both the construction of IIPS circuits and the placement of its individual elements. Optimization will make it possible to use resources efficiently and provide maximum protection at minimum cost. For example, today many companies build their own data processing centers (DPCs), accordingly, optimization tasks solved within the framework of ensuring cybersecurity of DPCs may include the selection of the optimal location of server rooms, redundancy of network channels, determination of the optimal architecture of protection against DDoS attacks, etc. [6–8]. In parallel, during the design process it is necessary to solve the problem of optimizing the distribution of firewalls and routers in the ISO network to ensure maximum protection from external threats.

It should be noted that when optimizing planning solutions related to the implementation of an IIPS, it is usually a question of optimizing the architecture of the IIPS, taking into account the specifics of the ISO and cybersecurity requirements. This includes selecting the types of defense mechanisms, distributing them across the ISO network, and determining the redundancy and recovery scheme. In addition, designers and information protection specialists solve the task of optimizing the placement of servers, routers, firewalls and other equipment to ensure the most effective protection of information assets of the ISO. This, accordingly, involves selecting optimal locations for equipment installation, taking into account the requirements for network bandwidth, etc. In parallel, optimization of the redundancy strategy is performed to ensure system fault tolerance, which includes identification of redundant communication channels, creation of data backups, etc.

In the conditions of modern information exchange at an ISO (e.g., a large company or enterprise), the number of technological processes requiring protection may reach hundreds or thousands (e.g., payment and financial transaction processing, personal data management, production processes and equipment control, logistics and supply management, technical support and maintenance of information systems, etc.). This makes the task of planning and including them in IIPS circuits a complex multi-criteria optimization problem. When solving such a problem, there is a need to develop modern methods for obtaining an optimal planning solution for a IIPS without the use of expensive mathematical packages and specialized software products. One such method is the application of genetic algorithm (GA) to optimize the layout solution [9, 10]. Engineers working on the optimization of means and methods of information protection as part of an IIPS do not always have sufficient knowledge in the field of mathematical modeling used in the formal description of GA. Therefore, the purpose of this work is to create a variant of GA implementation for optimization of layout solutions with formalization of the real task associated with the development of a IIPS for an information security object [11, 12]. In order to achieve the goal it is necessary to solve the following tasks: select the system under study, formulate the optimization problem, develop a GA and a crossing operator, and implement the proposed approach in the Python programming language.

48.2 Methods and Models

An example of a problem that can be considered in this research is the optimization of firewalls placement in an ISO network [13–15]. Let us imagine that there are several divisions with different levels of access to confidential information on an ISO. Let us illustrate it with a concrete example. Human Resources Department–has access to personal data of employees, such as their names, addresses, contact information, salary and seniority data. Finance Department–has access to ISO's financial data, including income and expense statements, accounting records, tax information and banking data. Marketing department–has access to data on advertising campaigns, marketing strategies, sales analytics, customer and partner information. Research and Development Department–has access to confidential information about new products, technologies, patents, intellectual property of the company. IT department–has access to information on network infrastructure, server configuration, databases, software, information on information systems security.

Let, it is necessary to determine the optimal number and distribution of firewalls to ensure maximum information protection at minimum cost. In the framework of this problem, each genotype in the GA population is a sequence consisting of the names of equipment (genes) that can be used to place firewalls. Each unique gene sequence corresponds to a unique firewall placement option that is a potential optimal solution. For example, a firewall can include: physical firewalls (devices designed to ensure network security by filtering and controlling network traffic at the physical level–Cisco ASA, Juniper SRX, etc.); virtual firewalls (software solutions that implement firewall functions on virtual servers–pfSense, Sophos UTM, etc.); proxy servers (proxy servers (software solutions that implement firewall functions on virtual servers–pfSense, Sophos UTM, etc.).); proxy servers (servers used for intermediate processing of client requests before transferring them to the target server–Squid, Microsoft Forefront Threat Management Gateway (TMG)), as well as load balancers (devices that distribute the load between several servers or network devices to ensure high availability and performance–Citrix NetScaler, etc.).

When developing an optimization algorithm for firewall placement, we can think of each genotype as a sequence of selected devices from the list above, given their number, configuration, and location in the ISO network. Each unique gene sequence will represent a unique firewall placement solution that can be considered potentially optimal in terms of information protection and cost-effectiveness.

The main idea of GA application is to perform operations mimicking the process of natural selection over genotypes. The initial generation of the GA is formed randomly to cover the largest number of potential solutions. If it is necessary to increase the accuracy of the solution, it is possible to change the number of genotypes or the number of GA generations.

During the operation of the GA, the possibility of saving the best solution is provided. This will allow the information about the genotype that showed the best result to be stored for future use. Thus, the best genotype of the current population transfers part of its genes to its descendants without changing itself.

To take into account the peculiarities of the problem under study, the GA algorithm provides a mutation function. Mutation allows randomly changing the genotype with the worst fitness function, which promotes genotype renewal and may lead to the achievement of a global extremum.

We also propose a crossbreeding operation algorithm, where the first genotype retains the first half of its genes and the second half is formed by crossing with another genotype. In this case, the best genotype of the current population is retained and does not participate in the crossbreeding operation.

The proposed crossbreeding operator can be formalized as follows. The crossing operator is applied to a pair of parental genotypes:

$$\begin{cases} G_1 = \left(g_1^1, g_2^1, \ldots, g_n^1\right), \\ G_2 = \left(g_1^2, g_2^2, \ldots, g_n^2\right), \end{cases} \tag{48.1}$$

where $G-$ is the parental genotype, $g-$ the gene in the genotype, and $n-$ the number of genes in each genotype.

Let us illustrate this with an example. Suppose we have several genotypes (representations of the distribution of firewalls on the ISO) with different levels of adaptability to the task. Let us denote the genotype with the best value of the fitness function as G_1, and the genotype with the worst value as G_2. For example, if we have five genotypes sorted by decreasing adaptability, G_1 in this list will correspond to the first genotype, and the G_2 will correspond to the second genotype. The second most adapted genotype and the one following it are selected first for crossing. Then the fourth and fifth genotypes are crossed. The process is repeated until all genotypes in the population are crossed in step 2. As a result of crossing, two parental genotypes produce two descendant genotypes:

$$\begin{cases} C_1 = \left(c_1^1, c_2^1, \dots, c_n^1\right), \\ C_2 = \left(c_1^2, c_2^2, \dots, c_n^2\right), \end{cases} \tag{48.2}$$

where $C-$ genotype-descendant, $c-$ the gene in the genotype-descendant.

For example, a descendant genotype (c) would be a new firewall placement solution resulting from a cross between two parent genotypes. Each gene in the descendant genotype will correspond to a specific firewall location on the ISO.

Suppose we have two parental genotypes:

$$G_1 : [Firewall\,1, Firewall\,2, Firewall\,3, Firewall\,4, Firewall\,5]$$

$$G_2 : [Firewall\,6, Firewall\,7, Firewall\,8, Firewall\,9, Firewall\,10]$$

Suppose that after the crossing operation we have obtained the following descendants D_1 and D_2:

$$D_1 : [Firewall\,1, Firewall\,2, Firewall\,3, Firewall\,9, Firewall\,10]$$

$$D_2 : [Firewall\,6, Firewall\,7, Firewall\,8, Firewall\,4, Firewall\,5]$$

Here D_1 and D_2 represent new variants of firewall locations on the ISO, and each gene in these progeny genotypes corresponds to a specific firewall location.

The values of the progeny genes were determined as follows:

$$c_i^1 = \begin{cases} g_i^1, for\, i < \left({}^n/_2\right) or\, i > \left({}^n/_2\right) and\, i - even, \\ g_i^2, for\, i \geq \left({}^n/_2\right) and\, i - odd, \end{cases} \tag{48.3}$$

$$c_i^2 = \begin{cases} g_i^1, for\, i - odd, \\ g_i^2, for\, i - even. \end{cases} \tag{48.4}$$

The above algorithm uses single-point crossing. The split point is chosen arbitrarily in the range of. For each offspring gene, the value is taken from the opposite parental genotype. When a mutation occurs, the gene value is changed to a random value from a valid range. In our opinion, this algorithm is simple and clear enough to implement and can be used as a part of the computational kernel, for example, of a decision support system when forming IIPS circuits on the ISO the second ally player.

48.3 Software Implementation and Computational Experiments

Firewalls play a key role in protecting the network resources of an ISO from external threats such as unauthorized access, malware and other cyber threats. Optimal placement of firewalls allows for effective traffic filtering, access control and data integrity, which significantly increases the level of information security on the ISO.

The use of the algorithmic language Python and the PyCharm environment for conducting computational experiments to optimize the placement of firewalls in the ISO network was justified by the fact that this combination provides an efficient and convenient performance of this task.

The results of these experiments are shown in Figs. 48.1, 48.2 and 48.3.

As a result of the GA work, 10 variants of firewall placement (genotypes) were created and each of them was evaluated on a scale from 0 to 10 depending on how well the proposed placement protects the company's network from external threats.

Each genotype is a list of devices and the score indicates how well the placement protects the network, see Fig. 48.1. The results of modeling in PyCharm environment, are shown in Figs. 48.2 and 48.3.

48.4 Discussion of the Results Obtained from the Simulation

The graph, see Fig. 48.3 shows the results of the GA for optimizing the placement of firewalls in the ISO network. The graph consists of two curves, Best Score and Average Score. The Best Score curve shows how the best score (genotype score) changes over each generation of the genetic algorithm. A high value on this curve indicates that there are genotypes with high scores in the population, which corresponds to a more optimal placement of firewalls in the ISO network. The Average Score curve shows the average score of a genotype in each generation. It helps to understand how the average performance of a population changes over time.

By analyzing the graph, the following conclusions can be drawn:

First, initially, at the first generations, the results may not be good enough, but as the algorithm progresses towards the optimal solution, the Best Score curve should tend towards higher values. If the curve remains flat, the number of generations should be increased.

Second, as the algorithm runs, the average performance of the population should generally improve. This indicates that the GA is successfully searching for better solutions.

Finally, if the Best Score starts to fluctuate, the algorithm may be close to the optimal solution, but may not converge to the optimum consistently enough. Therefore, in the next phase of the study, we plan to separately consider several factors

```python
main.py

import random
# List of available devices
devices = [
    "Cisco ASA", # Physical firewall
    "Juniper SRX", # Physical firewall
    "pfSense", # Virtual firewall
    "Sophos UTM", # Virtual firewall
    "Squid", # Proxy server
    "Microsoft Forefront TMG", # Proxy server
    "Citrix NetScaler", # Load Balancer
]

# Number of departments
num_departments = 3

# Maximum number of firewalls per department
max_firewalls_per_department = 2

# Initial genotype generation function
def generate_initial_genotype():
    genotype = []
    for _ in range(num_departments):
        num_firewalls = random.randint( a: 1, max_firewalls_per_department)
        firewalls = random.sample(devices, num_firewalls)
        genotype.extend(firewalls)
    return genotype

# Genotype mutation function
def mutate_genotype(genotype):
    # Select a random gene
    index = random.randint( a: 0, len(genotype) - 1)
```

Fig. 48.1 Fragment of realization of the proposed GA in PyCharm environment

```
Genotype 1: ['Juniper SRX', 'Juniper SRX', 'Squid'] - Score: 8
Genotype 2: ['Sophos UTM', 'Juniper SRX', 'Juniper SRX', 'Microsoft Forefront TMG'] - Score: 8
Genotype 3: ['Squid', 'Sophos UTM', 'Juniper SRX', 'Microsoft Forefront TMG', 'Squid', 'Microsoft Forefront TMG'] - Score: 9
Genotype 4: ['Microsoft Forefront TMG', 'Squid', 'Juniper SRX', 'pfSense', 'Cisco ASA'] - Score: 2
Genotype 5: ['Citrix NetScaler', 'Cisco ASA', 'Juniper SRX', 'pfSense'] - Score: 3
Genotype 6: ['Microsoft Forefront TMG', 'Juniper SRX', 'Citrix NetScaler'] - Score: 10
Genotype 7: ['Citrix NetScaler', 'Juniper SRX', 'Squid'] - Score: 6
Genotype 8: ['pfSense', 'Squid', 'Cisco ASA', 'pfSense'] - Score: 10
Genotype 9: ['pfSense', 'Juniper SRX', 'Cisco ASA', 'Juniper SRX'] - Score: 5
Genotype 10: ['Microsoft Forefront TMG', 'pfSense', 'pfSense', 'Microsoft Forefront TMG'] - Score: 8
```

Fig. 48.2 Results of modeling in PyCharm environment

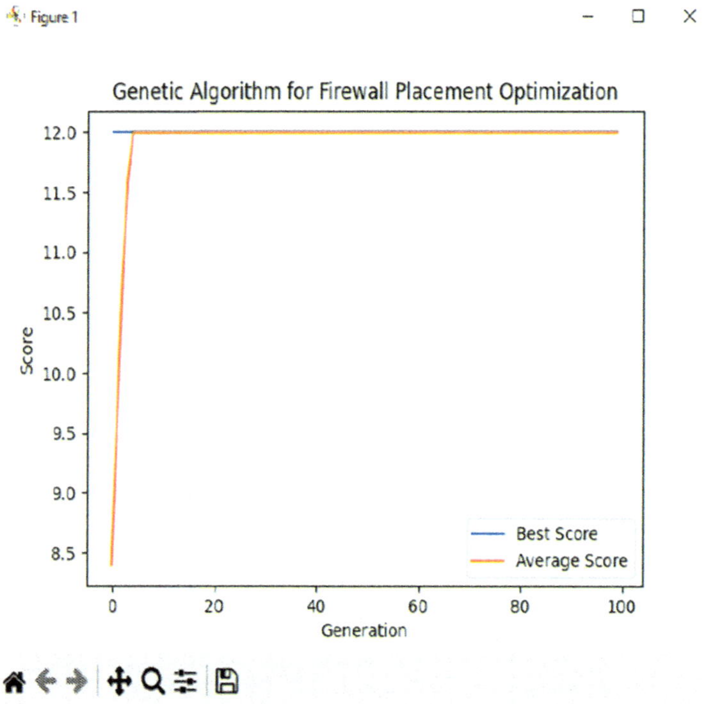

Fig. 48.3 Visualization of computational experiments in PyCharm environment

affecting the effectiveness of information protection to evaluate the genotype representing the distribution of firewalls in the ISO network. For example, we plan to additionally consider:

1. The number of firewalls, since the more firewalls deployed, the better the overall protection of the ISO network;
2. Distribution of firewalls amongst ISO units, as each unit is ideally equipped with at least one firewall, this will improve its protection;
3. Device diversity, since using different devices (e.g., Cisco ASA, pfSense, etc.) can improve protection as it makes it more difficult for attackers familiar with a particular model to penetrate;
4. Distributing firewalls across network layers, as it is most effective to place firewalls at the boundaries between network layers (e.g., between the external network and the internal ISO network);
5. Participating in the deployment of virtual firewalls, as the use of virtual appliances (e.g. pfSense) can be a less costly and more flexible solution, improving the overall assessment.

6. Supporting network services and applications, as deploying firewalls that support the required network services and applications will improve the overall effectiveness of the ISO's defenses.

Note that the optimization of IIPS circuits on the ISO is aimed at providing comprehensive information protection. And any IIPS includes not only firewalls, but also other security features such as intrusion detection systems (IDS), access control systems (ACS), antivirus programs, etc. Optimizing the loops of this system involves the proper placement and configuration of all components for maximum efficiency, and consistency across the entire system.

Thus, optimization of firewall placement is part of the overall strategy to ensure comprehensive information protection at the ISO, while optimization of IIPS circuits includes a wider range of measures to ensure information security at the site, which will be the focus of future research by the authors.

In our opinion, the genetic algorithm may be the preferred method for solving the optimization problem of firewalls placement in a network of ISOs, as it provides flexibility in working with a large solution search space. This is especially important for problems with multiple firewall placement options in large networks of large ISOs. In addition, GAs can operate effectively when complete task information is not available or incomplete and are able to adapt to changes in task conditions and dynamically respond to new information. Importantly, GAs have the ability to discover globally optimal solutions in large search spaces, which will allow finding more efficient and sustainable solutions.

As we have demonstrated in the research process, GAs are relatively easy to implement and can be effectively applied to a variety of optimization problems in cybersecurity.

48.5 Conclusion

In the course of the research, a formalized description of the problem of optimizing the placement of firewalls in the ISO network was developed. The proposed crossing operator for GA proved its effectiveness in finding optimal solutions. Testing of the software implementation confirmed the applicability of the proposed crossing operator. Further plans include the study and implementation of additional crossing operators, which can expand the area of application of GA in the task of optimizing the placement of information protection components along the contours of a multi-loop complex information protection system. This will improve the process of optimizing the planning decisions on the placement of firewalls and other information protection elements in the ISO network and increase its degree of cybersecurity.

Thus, the main goal of the research - the development of a GA implementation for optimizing the placement of firewalls in the ISO network has been successfully achieved. The obtained implementation represents an important step in the field of cybersecurity can be used in practical tasks of information protection at information security objects.

References

1. Alhayani, B., Abbas, S.T., Khutar, D.Z., Mohammed, H.J.: Best ways computation intelligent of face cyber attacks. Mater. Today Proc. 26–31(2021). https://doi.org/10.1016/j.matpr.2021.02.557
2. Aslan, Ö., Aktuğ, S.S., Ozkan-Okay, M., Yilmaz, A.A., Akin, E.: A comprehensive review of cyber security vulnerabilities, threats, attacks, and solutions. Electronics **12**(6), 1333 (2023). https://doi.org/10.3390/electronics12061333
3. Thangavelu, M., Krishnaswamy, V., Sharma, M.: Comprehensive information security awareness (CISA) in security incident management (SIM): a conceptualization. South Asian J. Manag. **27**(2), 160–188 (2020)
4. Javaid, M., Haleem, A., Singh, R.P., Suman, R.: Towards insighting cybersecurity for healthcare domains: a comprehensive review of recent practices and trends. Cyber Secur. Appl. **1**, 100016 (2023). https://doi.org/10.1016/j.csa.2023.100016
5. Taherdoost, H.: Understanding cybersecurity frameworks and information security standards—a review and comprehensive overview. Electronics **11**(14), 2181 (2022). https://doi.org/10.3390/electronics11142181
6. Gao, L., Calderon, T.G., Tang, F.: Public companies' cybersecurity risk disclosures. Int. J. Account. Inf. Syst. **38**, 100468 (2020). https://doi.org/10.1016/j.accinf.2020.100468
7. Hepfer, M., Powell, T.C.: Make cybersecurity a strategic asset. MIT Sloan Manag. Rev. **62**(1), 40–45 (2020)
8. Mishra, A., Alzoubi, Y.I., Gill, A.Q., Anwar, M.J.: Cybersecurity enterprises policies: a comparative study. Sensors **22**(2), 538 (2022). https://doi.org/10.3390/s22020538
9. O'Reilly, U.M., Toutouh, J., Pertierra, M., Sanchez, D.P., Garcia, D., Luogo, A.E., Hemberg, E.: Adversarial genetic programming for cyber security: a rising application domain where GP matters. Genet. Program. Evolvable Mach. **21**, 219–250 (2020). https://doi.org/10.1007/s10710-020-09389-y
10. Zhang, Y., Malacaria, P.: Optimization-time analysis for cybersecurity. IEEE Trans. Dependable Secure Comput. **19**(4), 2365–2383 (2021). https://doi.org/10.1109/TDSC.2021.3055981
11. Lakhno, V., Blozva, A., Kasatkin, D., Tyshchenko, D., Franchuk, T.: Modified genetic algorithm for solving the problem of selecting hardware and software for information security. CEUR Work. Proc. **3187**, 236–243 (2021)
12. Lakhno, V., Tikhonov, Y., Sabitova, N., Taimuratova, L., Zhumadulova, M.: Optimization of the structure of an information security textbook using genetic algorithm. CEUR Work. Proc. **3654**, 355–360 (2024)
13. Kim, S., Yoon, S., Narantuya, J., Lim, H.: Secure collecting, optimizing, and deploying of firewall rules in software-defined networks. IEEE Access **8**, 15166–15177 (2020). https://doi.org/10.1109/ACCESS.2020.2967503
14. Coscia, A., Dentamaro, V., Galantucci, S., Maci, A., Pirlo, G.: An innovative two-stage algorithm to optimize firewall rule ordering. Comput. Secur. **134**, 103423 (2023)
15. Coscia, A., Dentamaro, V., Galantucci, S., Impedovo, D., Maci, A.: A novel genetic algorithm approach for firewall policy optimization. In ITASEC, pp. 236–248 (2022)

Chapter 49
Leveraging Large Language Models for MATLAB to Python Translation

Rocco Pietrini

Abstract The translation of MATLAB code into Python stands as a pivotal practice in software reuse, particularly in the conversion of research-oriented scripts into robust production-ready solutions. This shift not only offers a cost-effective alternative to the use of expensive MATLAB licenses for enterprises but also facilitates broader software reuse endeavors. This paper examines the transformative capacity inherent in leveraging general-purpose Large Language Models (LLMs) for the translation of MATLAB code into Python, specifically focusing on scientific scripts. The research thoroughly investigates the methodology underlying the utilization of LLMs to seamlessly migrate MATLAB-based numerical computation scripts into Python ecosystems. Through a comprehensive case study within the oil and gas sector, the paper illustrates tangible advantages, showcasing how the adoption of LLMs facilitates the deployment and integration of numerical computation scripts. The results underscore efficiency enhancements in code translation and address prevailing constraints, as evidenced in an experimental segment where diverse MATLAB scripts undergo translation and evaluation by a panel of domain experts.

49.1 Introduction

MATLAB [20], a powerful numerical computing environment, has long been a staple in universities, providing a versatile platform for students and researchers in disciplines ranging from engineering and physics to finance and biology. Its ease of use, extensive toolbox support, and rich ecosystem make it an ideal choice for academic settings, facilitating rapid prototyping and algorithm development. In universities, MATLAB serves as a go-to tool for teaching and learning due to its user-friendly syntax, interactive environment, and robust visualization capabilities. Its widespread adoption across various academic disciplines has resulted in a significant body of code and expertise built around the platform. However, this dominance comes with

R. Pietrini (✉)
Vision Robotics and Artificial Intelligence (VRAI), Università Politecnica delle Marche, Ancona, Italy
e-mail: r.pietrini@univpm.it

F. P. García Márquez et al. (eds.), *Computing, Internet of Things and Data Analytics*, Smart Innovation, Systems and Technologies 387,
https://doi.org/10.1007/978-3-031-87154-2_49

certain challenges, particularly in the context of software licensing costs, which can be a burden for institutions operating on constrained budgets.

The transition from MATLAB to Python offers significant benefits for companies deploying academic solutions. Python's open-source nature and vast ecosystem make it a compelling choice. By leveraging Large Language Models (LLM) for code translation, companies can unlock several advantages:

- **Cost Efficiency**: Python eliminates licensing fees, allowing better resource allocation.
- **Wider Talent Pool**: Python's widespread use ensures a large pool of skilled developers.
- **Interoperability**: Python's compatibility with various technologies promotes seamless integration.
- **Community Support**: A vibrant community provides extensive support, resources, and documentation.
- **Scalability**: Python's flexibility makes it ideal for enterprise-level solutions, meeting diverse business needs.
- **Integration**: Python can be easily integrated with web-oriented technologies, opening up numerous opportunities for developing sophisticated, interconnected systems.

Translating source code from one programming language to another can be achieved using various methods.

One common approach is manual translation, where developers manually rewrite the code from one language to another, ensuring accurate and optimized translation but requiring proficiency in both languages.

Transpilers, or source-to-source compilers, convert code written in one programming language to another by performing syntactic transformations without changing functionality. Another method involves using compilers and decompilers to compile the source code to an intermediate representation, such as bytecode, and then decompile that representation into the target language.

Automatic code translation tools are also available, designed to translate between specific languages, often leveraging AI or pattern matching.

Abstract Syntax Tree (AST) transformation involves converting the source code to an AST, transforming the AST according to the target language's grammar, and then generating the target language code from the transformed AST.

Machine learning and AI approaches use neural networks trained on parallel corpora of source and target languages to translate code, though this method is still experimental.

Bytecode translation methods convert the source language to a common intermediate language, such as Java bytecode or .NET IL, and then translate or run it on a virtual machine that supports the target language, with examples including the Java Virtual Machine (JVM) and the Common Language Runtime (CLR). Domain-specific translators are specialized tools tailored for specific domains, such as web development or scientific computing, that translate code with domain-specific optimizations.

When translating code, it is important to consider syntax and semantics to ensure that the semantics of the source language are accurately preserved in the target language. Performance is another consideration, as translated code should maintain acceptable performance. Maintainability is also crucial, as translated code should be readable and maintainable. Finally, the availability of development tools and libraries in the target language should be considered. The choice of method depends on the specific requirements, including the complexity of the source code, the target language, and the need for accuracy, performance, and maintainability. This paper is structured as follows: Section 49.2 provides an in-depth analysis of the current state of the art in code translation. In Sect. 49.3, we go into the methodologies employed in this research, while Sect. 49.4 showcases the outcomes derived from experimental sessions. Moving forward, Sect. 49.5 explores the societal implications of our findings, and Sect. 49.6 encapsulates the final conclusions drawn from this study.

49.2 State of Art

MATLAB code translation have been investigated by [25, 26] using a rule-based approach for MATLAB to C++ translation with some limitations and human-in-the-loop requirements at first and then revising the study for total automation in the process. In the same realm [34] proposed M2Coder, a Fully Automated Translator from Matlab M-functions to C/C++ Codes for ACS Motion Controllers.

Numerous online tools seems to be available to assist developers in converting MATLAB code into Python, with 'SMOP' [2] standing out as one of the most commonly adopted solutions. This tool is designed to produce human-readable Python code, although it tends to retain a 'matlabic' style rather than adhering to 'pythonic' conventions. Consequently, developers working with the generated code must be proficient in both languages, and the old MATLAB development environment often needs to be retained for reference. Despite its popularity, it's worth noting that the 'SMOP' project appears to be in a state of abandonment, as its latest release dates back to 2016. This lack of recent updates may raise concerns regarding compatibility with the latest versions of MATLAB and Python, as well as potential unaddressed bugs or evolving best practices.

Lately machine learning methodologies have demonstrated promise in code translation. Lexical statistical machine translation [21] and tree-based neural networks [7] have been successfully employed to translate Java code to C# and C++, as well as Java and Python code, respectively [16, 29]. Notably, these approaches, while innovative, have not specifically targeted programming languages like MATLAB. As the field evolves, there is a need for tailored solutions that can address the unique characteristics and syntax of languages such as MATLAB. This gap in existing methodologies highlights an opportunity for further research and development to advance code translation capabilities across a broader spectrum of programming languages. In a study by [32], a controlled experiment involving 32 software engineers explored the utility of imperfect outputs from a Java to Python translation model [29]. The study found that imperfect outputs generated by a code model can enhance the performance of software engineers engaged in code translation tasks. A revolution started with the advent of Foundation models, such as OpenAI's GPT-4 [23], Anthropic's Claude 3.5 Sonnet [1] and Google's Gemini 1.5 Pro [4], large-scale machine learning models trained on vast amounts of data from various domains. These models have demonstrated remarkable versatility and capability in a wide range of tasks, including natural language processing and text generation. Specific LLMs have been developed for tasks like code generation and translation. Examples include Starcoder [18], PolyCoder [33], SantaCoder [5], CodeGen [22], and CodeT5 [31], which was pretrained on CodeSearchNet data [13] in six widely adopted programming languages. However, none of these models currently include MATLAB in their supported languages. [24] recently presented an empirical study to investigate the ability of general LLMs and code LLMs for code translation across pairs of different languages, but only including widespread programming languages such as C, C++, Go, Java, and Python. [19] proposed SDA-Trans, a syntax and domain-aware model for program translation, which leverages the syntax structure and domain knowledge to enhance the cross-lingual transfer ability. SDA-Trans adopts unsupervised training on a smaller-scale corpus, including Python and Java monolingual programs. The experimental results on function translation tasks between Python, Java, and C++ show that SDA-Trans outperforms many large-scale pre-trained models, especially for unseen language translation. [14] presented an LLM-based code translation method and an associated tool called CoTran, that translates whole-programs from one high-level programming language to another reporting extensive experiments comparing CoTran with 14 other code translation tools that include human-written transpilers, LLM-based translation tools, and ChatGPT over a benchmark of more than 57,000 Java-Python equivalent pairs. [9] presented a study on the use of large language models (LLMs) to translate C/Go to Rust, highlighting a gap in representation compared to more popular languages like Java and Python. They argued that Java and Python are more frequently included in LLM training data than C and Go. Despite this disparity, their study demonstrated the feasibility of using LLMs for translating C/Go to Rust, providing evidence that such an approach is viable even for languages that are less represented in training datasets. The only work currently addressing our specific domain is by [15]. In this study, the authors utilized ChatGPT-4 as an AI assistant to convert MATLAB code to Python. This task was part of a broader system specifically designed for a complex image skeletonization project, which involved translating fifteen MATLAB files and handling a large dataset. The translated code was tested using test cases generated by both Bard and ChatGPT-4. However, the authors did not provide quantitative experiments on this process, making it challenging to evaluate its applicability to other domains, such as numerical calculations. In our previous study [27], we demonstrated the applicability of GPT-4 for a niche programming language like FORTRAN. Building on this approach, we extend our investigation in this work to include MATLAB.

Notably, there exists a conspicuous research gap regarding the translation of niche programming languages like MATLAB into general purpose languages like Python. This paper aims to bridge this gap by conducting preliminary experiments, laying the groundwork for a novel paradigm with potential societal and economic impacts. The novelty of this paper lies in its pioneering approach to translating MATLAB code into Python using general-purpose Large Language Models (LLMs), an area that has not been thoroughly explored in prior research. This paper leverages the advanced capabilities of LLMs to produce more Pythonic and robust code. Additionally, while existing LLMs and code translation models have focused on widespread languages such as Java, C, and Python, none have specifically addressed MATLAB. This study fills this research gap by showcasing the effectiveness of LLMs in translating MATLAB-based numerical computation scripts, as demonstrated through a comprehensive case study in the oil and gas sector. This novel approach not only enhances code translation efficiency but also holds potential for broader applications across various scientific and engineering domains.

49.3 Methods

The focal point of our case study was a prominent multinational oilfield services company, ranking among the largest globally. This industry collaborate with the Hydraulics department of our university for the development of its hydrodynamics analysis of pipelines exposed to waves and currents, which are implemented in MATLAB following academic standards.

Amidst the myriad of models discussed in Sect. 49.2 tailored for code translation, none specifically addressed the intricacies of MATLAB. Consequently, we adopted a pragmatic approach, harnessing the prowess of general-purpose LLMs, notably GPT-4o, Claude 3.5 and Gemini 1.5 Pro, renowned for their exceptional performance.

We utilized LLMs without re-training due to the absence of customized datasets for this specific purpose. The model was given a straightforward prompt: "You are a skilled programmer. I'll provide you with a code written in MATLAB; please translate it to Python," followed by the MATLAB source code. The architecture of the proposed system is depicted in Fig. 49.1, while the pseudo-algorithm is outlined in Algorithm 49.1. A human-in-the-loop approach was employed to evaluate the output, initially for error verification during execution and subsequently for equivalence verification. This was followed by a rectification phase, where feedback was provided to the LLM for further refinement.

In our evaluation framework, a translation was deemed unsuccessful if the Python-generated code encountered runtime errors or failed to produce the same results as the original MATLAB source. Due to the high precision required for numerical calculations in hydrodynamics analysis, we upheld a zero-tolerance policy for discrepancies. The Python-translated code had to exactly replicate the results of the robust MATLAB code.

Our evaluation intentionally sidestepped static metrics such as exact match, syntax match, dataflow match, CodeBLEU [28], and CrystalBLEU [8]. This deliberate choice emanated from our primary objective: validating translations through execution rather than relying on static evaluation metrics.

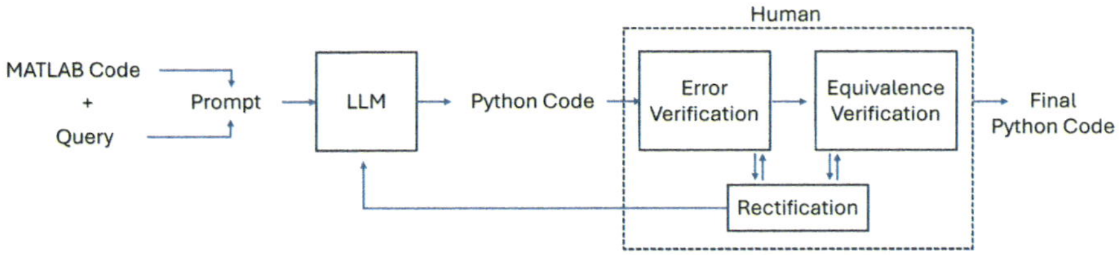

Fig. 49.1 Architecture of the proposed method

In alignment with insights from [32], where software engineers appreciate the utility of generative models producing imperfect output, we share a similar sentiment. In this task, we acknowledge that perfection is not the ultimate goal, and therefore, we are open to providing a qualitative assessment.

To assess the quality of the code generated by the model, we employed a panel of 10 seasoned senior developers with knowledge in both MATLAB and Python. Their task was to conduct a qualitative evaluation of each software routine, employing a Mean Opinion Score (MOS) coupled with the Absolute Category Rating (ACR) system. This rating system aligns qualitative assessments, with numerical values ranging from 1 to 5. Specifically, 1 is labeled as "Bad", 2 as "Poor", 3 as "Fair" 4 as "Good", and 5 as "Excellent".

The Mean Opinion Score (MOS) averages these ratings across evaluators. This scoring methodology has emerged as a widely embraced descriptor for perceived media quality. Initially utilized in the realm of speech quality assessment, MOS has since found applications across various modalities, including audio, images, video, and audiovisual content, as well as in diverse settings ranging from laboratory testing to real-world monitoring scenarios.

Acknowledging the limitations of static metrics in the realm of code synthesis [6], our evaluation pivots towards the practical viability of the translated code. We prioritize successful compilation and execution over static measures that may not authentically reflect the code's functionality. This perspective aligns with the challenges posed by LLMs as elucidated in [3, 6].

49.4 Results

The codebase under scrutiny in this study comprises a collection of 20 diverse routines including: Extreme Value Analysis, polar plots generation, and missing values imputation on time-series among other topics. These routines operate by processing input text files containing time-series data derived from wave data recording, yielding numerical indices and plots as output. Each routine, averaging around 642 lines of code, featuring typical MATLAB structures. In the initial phase, the source code underwent a thorough evaluation by our panelists, resulting in a MOS of 3.2. This implies that although the code adequately fulfills its function, its general quality is

Algorithm 49.1 MATLAB to Python Code Translation using LLMs

```
Input: MATLAB code MATLAB_code
Output: Python code Python_code
Initialize LLM model model (e.g., GPT-4)
procedure TRANSLATECODE(MATLAB_code)
    prompt ← "You are a skilled programmer. I'll provide you with a code written in MATLAB; please translate it to Python" + MATLAB_code
    Python_code ← model.translate(prompt)
    if containsErrors(Python_code) then
        Python_code ← fixErrors(Python_code)
    end if
    if notEquivalent(MATLAB_code, Python_code) then
        Python_code ← refineTranslation(MATLAB_code, Python_code)
    end if
    return Python_code
end procedure
function CONTAINSERRORS(Python_code)
    Run Python_code
    if compilationFails or runtimeErrors then
        return True
    else
        return False
    end if
end function
function FIXERRORS(Python_code)
    Identify and correct syntax and semantic errors in Python_code
    return corrected Python_code
end function
function NOTEQUIVALENT(MATLAB_code, Python_code)
    Run both MATLAB_code and Python_code on the same input
    if outputsDiffer then
        return True
    else
        return False
    end if
end function
function REFINETRANSLATION(MATLAB_code, Python_code)
    Manually examine and modify Python_code to match MATLAB_code's functionality eventually using LLM again.
    return refined Python_code
end function
```

regarded as less than optimal. Routines presented in addition an average cyclomatic complexity of 25 which is generally considered as a code very complex and difficult to understand with low testability. Indeed, none of the routines have undergone a complete and accurate translation. The evaluation indicates that various aspects of the code, across multiple routines, exhibit deficiencies in the translation process. This observation underscores the need for further refinement and attention to detail to ensure that each routine is successfully and accurately converted, addressing the current shortcomings in the translated code. Since no single routine has been entirely

Table 49.1 Experiment summary. Best results in bold

Entry	GPT-4o	Claude 3.5 Sonnet	Gemini 1.5 Pro
No. of routines	20	20	20
Average No. of lines	642	642	642
Average cyclomatic complexity	25	25	25
Source MOS quality	3.2	3.2	3.2
Translation MOS	**4.09**	4.03	4.01
Translation + Emo MOS	**4.12**	4.05	4.01

and correctly translated, only a qualitative analysis can be conducted. This analysis involved a meticulous routine-by-routine and line-by-line manual examination to identify and correct bugs, with the time required for this process being recorded. The process was iterative, feeding each time what was previously generated by model. Experiments are summarized in Table 49.1.

The panelists, on average, rated the translation process close to 4 out of 5. All tested models performed similarly, with GPT-4o showing slightly better results, underscoring the effectiveness of the proposed approach. However, they also pointed out significant issues within the generated code that required meticulous attention. This rating encapsulated not only the overall performance but also factored in the time and effort needed to rectify the routines and ensure alignment with MATLAB's precise behavior. Some examples of failures are reported below. All the models leveraged key libraries such as Matplotlib [12] for plotting, SciPy [30] and NumPy [11] for scientific functions, both widely recognized for their utility in these domains. However, the generated code exhibited a straightforward line-by-line translation approach, lacking contextual awareness. Consequently, the resulting code often deviated from 'pythonic' conventions, necessitating additional refinement by developers to enhance maintainability. Array indexing disparities emerged as a key noteworthy issue. Given MATLAB's 1-based indexing and Python's 0-based indexing, operations involving hard-coded indices required careful scrutiny. LLMs often struggled to capture these nuances, potentially resulting in incorrect indexing that developers needed to rectify. Another example is provided here: a simple array sorting function, commonly used in numerical calculations. In MATLAB, the function `[out, idx] = sort([14 8 91 19],'descend')` returns the sorted array in `out` in descending order and the corresponding indices of the original vector in `idx`. This function is translated by all models as shown in listing 49.1. However, a problem arises because MATLAB uses a stable sorting algorithm by default, whereas NumPy does not (non-stable 'quicksort' is used), resulting in a different sequence in `idx`. The model should instead use a more complex and less intuitive solution, such as `idx = np.argsort(-arr, kind='mergesort')`.

Listing 49.1 Sort Example

```
# MATLAB
[out,idx] = sort([14 8 91 19], 'descend')

# Python
import numpy as np
arr = [14, 8, 91, 19]
out = np.sort(arr)[::-1]
idx = np.argsort(arr)[::-1]
```

A similar issue arises with another commonly used function: calculating the standard deviation of a vector. In MATLAB, this can be done with the command `S = std(A)`. Large Language Models (LLMs) often translate this to Python as `S = np.std(A)` using the NumPy library. However, there is a significant difference between the two. By default, MATLAB normalizes the standard deviation by $N - 1$ (Bessel's correction), whereas NumPy normalizes by N. To achieve the same result in NumPy, the parameter `ddof=1` must be specified, i.e., `S = np.std(A, ddof=1)`.

This process proved time-consuming, highlighting a significant discrepancy between the available toolsets. Additionally, performance discrepancies arose due to MATLAB's specialization in high-performance computing. In comparison, Python's performance lagged behind in certain scenarios. However, an optimization effort employing the capabilities of LLMs demonstrated notable improvements. The refined code, produced through the collaborative efforts of developers and LLMs, significantly enhanced overall efficiency and computational speed, underscoring the instrumental role played by LLMs in achieving superior results. In the final phase of the experiments, drawing insights from [17], we dedicated efforts to exploring whether incorporating an emotional component into the prompt could enhance the translation process, calling this procedure "Translation + Emo". The prompt was reformulated as follows:

"Could you please translate the following MATLAB code into Python? This is crucial for my job."

However, the results indicated no substantial improvement, with the panel MOS increasing only marginally from 4.09 to 4.12.

49.5 Societal Impact

The economic and labor impacts of translating scientific code from MATLAB need thorough analysis, including software reuse. This investigation is in its early stages, with uncertainties about technology adoption in university departments with limited computer science expertise.

Scientific code in MATLAB represents a modernization effort for decades-old systems. Software reuse can speed up this process by leveraging existing code components and libraries, reducing development time, and improving efficiency.

AI-driven code translation in academia can generate economic value by helping scientists with varying computer science skills, streamlining development, and enhancing innovation. Translating MATLAB routines into Python allows for modern web interfaces, improving user experience and integrating contemporary features.

This transformation improves accessibility for scientists and researchers, freeing them from time-consuming tasks and promoting software reuse across scientific domains. Consequently, it enhances satisfaction and productivity in university settings.

However, many researchers, such as Gallifant [10], have noted that using closed-source LLMs can pose significant risks. Their analysis of the GPT-4 report underscores a strong commitment to transparent AI research, particularly through the development of a systems card for risk assessment and mitigation. Despite considerable investment, the report highlights several limitations, including restricted access to training data, inadequate confidence and uncertainty estimations, and concerns over privacy and intellectual property rights. Additionally, it emphasizes the need for greater clarity in training processes to address potential biases. These concerns are applicable to all closed-source models currently available.

49.6 Conclusion

While MATLAB remains a cornerstone of academic computing, the transition to Python offers a strategic advantage for companies seeking cost-effective, scalable, and interoperable solutions. Large Language Models can play a pivotal role in this transition, automating the conversion process and enabling a seamless shift from MATLAB to Python. As industries evolve, embracing open-source alternatives like Python becomes not only a pragmatic choice but also a forward-looking strategy for long-term success in software development and deployment.

This paper unfolds a case study documenting the transformative journey of translating scientific MATLAB routines, into Python. The translation process leaned on LLMs, and our hands-on experimentation on real code brought to light persistent challenges. In spite of these hurdles, the LLMs emerged as invaluable tools, significantly expediting the modernization endeavor.

It is crucial to underscore that the efforts detailed in this study constitute a preliminary exploration. The translated code, while not deemed production-ready, required meticulous, almost line-by-line execution to rectify bugs and ensure the program produced identical output. Nonetheless, this approach has showcased its time-saving potential in contrast to manual code translation. Furthermore, it eases the burden on developers, negating the need for an extensive understanding of MATLAB; a basic grasp is considered sufficient.

The proposed translation methods leveraging LLMs for converting MATLAB code to Python come with several disadvantages. The quality of the translated code often suffers, deviating from 'pythonic' conventions, and requiring significant manual correction. The lack of direct equivalents for some MATLAB functions in Python necessitates time-consuming manual translations. Performance issues can arise due to differences in high-performance computing capabilities between MATLAB and Python, and array indexing discrepancies pose additional challenges.

Despite these challenges, the future scope of this research is promising. Developing specialized LLMs trained specifically on MATLAB and Python codebases could improve translation accuracy. Enhanced tools and better integration of domain-specific knowledge could further refine the process. Performance optimization techniques tailored for the translated code, along with improved error handling and debugging capabilities, will enhance the robustness and efficiency of translations. Broader applicability and collaboration with the community and industry will be crucial for continuous improvement, ensuring that the translation process remains relevant and effective across various scientific and engineering domains. This research aims to facilitate broader software reuse and enhance the accessibility and scalability of scientific computing solutions.

As highlighted by the authors in [32], software engineers increasingly recognize the value of generative models that yield imperfect output, including code containing compilation or logical errors. They perceive these models as valuable tools, subject to the same rigorous review and testing protocols applied to code authored by human colleagues.

This pursuit not only offers the prospect of revitalizing aging software systems but also emphasizes its tangible societal and practical implications across various industries. Its significance transcends mere code transformation, delving into the broader realm of industry rejuvenation and technological progress.

On the other hand, the use of open-source local large language models (LLMs) should be preferred to mitigate risks related to privacy and data protection. Open-source LLMs allow for greater transparency and control over the data and algorithms used, which is particularly crucial since code can be considered a valuable company asset. By utilizing open-source solutions, organizations can closely monitor and audit the code, ensuring that sensitive information remains secure and proprietary methods are not inadvertently exposed. Additionally, the collaborative nature of open-source projects fosters community scrutiny and contributions, enhancing the overall robustness and security of the models. This approach not only aligns with best practices in data protection but also supports innovation through shared knowledge and resources.

References

1. The claude 3 model family: Opus, sonnet, haiku. https://www-cdn.anthropic.com/de8ba9b01c9ab7cbabf5c33b80b7bbc618857627/Model_Card_Claude_3.pdf. Accessed 14 July 2024
2. Smop. https://github.com/victorlei/smop. Accessed 14 July 2024
3. Ahmad, W.U., Tushar, M.G.R., Chakraborty, S., Chang, K.W.: Avatar: A parallel corpus for java-python program translation (2021). arXiv:2108.11590
4. Team, G., et al.: Gemini 1.5: unlocking multimodal understanding across millions of tokens of context (2024). https://arxiv.org/abs/2403.05530
5. Allal, L.B., Li, R., Kocetkov, D., Mou, C., Akiki, C., Ferrandis, C.M., Muennighoff, N., Mishra, M., Gu, A., Dey, M., et al.: Santacoder: don't reach for the stars! (2023). arXiv:2301.03988
6. Chen, M., Tworek, J., Jun, H., Yuan, Q., Pinto, H.P.D.O., Kaplan, J., Edwards, H., Burda, Y., Joseph, N., Brockman, G., et al.: Evaluating large language models trained on code (2021). arXiv:2107.03374
7. Chen, X., Liu, C., Song, D.: Tree-to-tree neural networks for program translation. In: Advances in Neural Information Processing Systems, vol. 31 (2018)
8. Eghbali, A., Pradel, M.: Crystalbleu: precisely and efficiently measuring the similarity of code. In: Proceedings of the 37th IEEE/ACM International Conference on Automated Software Engineering, pp. 1–12 (2022)
9. Eniser, H.F., Zhang, H., David, C., Wang, M., Paulsen, B., Dodds, J., Kroening, D.: Towards translating real-world code with llms: a study of translating to rust (2024). arXiv:2405.11514
10. Gallifant, J., Fiske, A., Levites Strekalova, Y.A., Osorio-Valencia, J.S., Parke, R., Mwavu, R., Martinez, N., Gichoya, J.W., Ghassemi, M., Demner-Fushman, D., et al.: Peer review of gpt-4 technical report and systems card. PLOS Digital Health **3**(1), e0000417 (2024)
11. Harris, C.R., Millman, K.J., van der Walt, S.J., Gommers, R., Virtanen, P., Cournapeau, D., Wieser, E., Taylor, J., Berg, S., Smith, N.J., Kern, R., Picus, M., Hoyer, S., van Kerkwijk, M.H., Brett, M., Haldane, A., del Río, J.F., Wiebe, M., Peterson, P., Gérard-Marchant, P., Sheppard, K., Reddy, T., Weckesser, W., Abbasi, H., Gohlke, C., Oliphant, T.E.: Array programming with NumPy. Nature **585**(7825), 357–362 (2020). https://doi.org/10.1038/s41586-020-2649-2. https://doi.org/10.1038/s41586-020-2649-2
12. Hunter, J.D.: Matplotlib: a 2d graphics environment. Comput. Sci. Eng. **9**(3), 90–95 (2007). https://doi.org/10.1109/MCSE.2007.55
13. Husain, H., Wu, H.H., Gazit, T., Allamanis, M., Brockschmidt, M.: Codesearchnet challenge: evaluating the state of semantic code search (2019). arXiv:1909.09436
14. Jana, P., Jha, P., Ju, H., Kishore, G., Mahajan, A., Ganesh, V.: Attention, compilation, and solver-based symbolic analysis are all you need (2023). arXiv:2306.06755
15. Kumar, Y., Gordon, Z., Alabi, O., Li, J., Leonard, K., Ness, L., Morreale, P.: Chatgpt translation of program code for image sketch abstraction. Appl. Sci. **14**(3), 992 (2024)
16. Lachaux, M.A., Roziere, B., Szafraniec, M., Lample, G.: Dobf: a deobfuscation pre-training objective for programming languages. Adv. Neural Inf. Process. Syst. **34**, 14967–14979 (2021)
17. Li, C., Wang, J., Zhang, Y., Zhu, K., Hou, W., Lian, J., Luo, F., Yang, Q., Xie, X.: Large language models understand and can be enhanced by emotional stimuli (2023). arXiv:2307.11760
18. Li, R., Allal, L.B., Zi, Y., Muennighoff, N., Kocetkov, D., Mou, C., Marone, M., Akiki, C., Li, J., Chim, J., et al.: Starcoder: may the source be with you! (2023). arXiv:2305.06161
19. Liu, F., Li, J., Zhang, L.: Syntax and domain aware model for unsupervised program translation. In: Proceedings of the 45th International Conference on Software Engineering. ICSE'23, pp. 755–767. IEEE Press (2023). https://doi.org/10.1109/ICSE48619.2023.00072. https://doi.org/10.1109/ICSE48619.2023.00072
20. MathWorks: Matlab version: 9.14.0 (r2023a update 2) (2023). https://www.mathworks.com
21. Nguyen, A.T., Nguyen, T.T., Nguyen, T.N.: Lexical statistical machine translation for language migration. In: Proceedings of the 2013 9th Joint Meeting on Foundations of Software Engineering, pp. 651–654 (2013)

22. Nijkamp, E., Pang, B., Hayashi, H., Tu, L., Wang, H., Zhou, Y., Savarese, S., Xiong, C.: Codegen: an open large language model for code with multi-turn program synthesis (2022). arXiv:2203.13474
23. OpenAI: Gpt-4 technical report (2023)
24. Pan, R., Ibrahimzada, A., Krishna, R., Sankar, D., Wassi, L., Merler, M., Sobolev, B., Pavuluri, R., Sinha, S., Jabbarvand, R.: Lost in translation: a study of bugs introduced by large language models while translating code. In: 2024 IEEE/ACM 46th International Conference on Software Engineering (ICSE). IEEE Computer Society, Los Alamitos, CA, USA, pp. 866–866 (Apr 2024). https://doi.ieeecomputersociety.org/
25. Paulsen, G.Y., Clark, S., Nordmoen, B., Nenakhov, S., Andersson, A., Cai, X., Dahle, H.P.: Automated translation of matlab code to c++ with performance and traceability. In: The Eleventh International Conference on Advanced Engineering Computing and Applications in Sciences, Number c., pp. 50–55 (2017)
26. Paulsen, G.Y., Feinberg, J., Cai, X., Nordmoen, B., Dahle, H.P.: Matlab2cpp: a matlab-to-c++ code translator. In: 2016 11th System of Systems Engineering Conference (SoSE), pp. 1–5. IEEE (2016)
27. Pietrini, R., Paolanti, M., Frontoni, E.: Bridging eras: Transforming Fortran legacies into python with the power of large language models. In: 2024 IEEE 3rd International Conference on Computing and Machine Intelligence (ICMI), pp. 1–5 (2024). https://doi.org/10.1109/ICMI60790.2024.10586058
28. Ren, S., Guo, D., Lu, S., Zhou, L., Liu, S., Tang, D., Sundaresan, N., Zhou, M., Blanco, A., Ma, S.: Codebleu: a method for automatic evaluation of code synthesis (2020). arXiv:2009.10297
29. Roziere, B., Lachaux, M.A., Chanussot, L., Lample, G.: Unsupervised translation of programming languages. Adv. Neural Inf. Process. Syst. **33**, 20601–20611 (2020)
30. Virtanen, P., Gommers, R., Oliphant, T.E., Haberland, M., Reddy, T., Cournapeau, D., Burovski, E., Peterson, P., Weckesser, W., Bright, J., van der Walt, S.J., Brett, M., Wilson, J., Millman, K.J., Mayorov, N., Nelson, A.R.J., Jones, E., Kern, R., Larson, E., Carey, C.J., Polat, İ., Feng, Y., Moore, E.W., VanderPlas, J., Laxalde, D., Perktold, J., Cimrman, R., Henriksen, I., Quintero, E.A., Harris, C.R., Archibald, A.M., Ribeiro, A.H., Pedregosa, F., van Mulbregt, P., SciPy 1.0 Contributors: SciPy 1.0: Fundamental Algorithms for Scientific Computing in Python. Nat. Methods **17**, 261–272 (2020). https://doi.org/10.1038/s41592-019-0686-2
31. Wang, Y., Wang, W., Joty, S., Hoi, S.C.: Codet5: identifier-aware unified pre-trained encoder-decoder models for code understanding and generation (2021). arXiv:2109.00859
32. Weisz, J.D., Muller, M., Ross, S.I., Martinez, F., Houde, S., Agarwal, M., Talamadupula, K., Richards, J.T.: Better together? An evaluation of ai-supported code translation. In: 27th International Conference on Intelligent User Interfaces, pp. 369–391 (2022)
33. Xu, F.F., Alon, U., Neubig, G., Hellendoorn, V.J.: A systematic evaluation of large language models of code. In: Proceedings of the 6th ACM SIGPLAN International Symposium on Machine Programming, pp. 1–10 (2022)
34. Yang, X., Wang, X., Liu, Z., Shu, F.: M2coder: a fully automated translator from matlab m-functions to c/c++ codes for acs motion controllers. In: International Conference on Guidance, Navigation and Control, pp. 3130–3139. Springer (2022)

Chapter 50
Predicting Stock Market Trends Using Regression and Deep Learning

Amin Shuayb Yasin and Hüsamettin Osmanoğlu

Abstract This article explores the application of advanced machine learning techniques in financial forecasting, focusing on the prediction of stock market trends. Leveraging historical data from the S&P 500 index, the study investigates the efficacy of Long Short-Term Memory (LSTM) and Bidirectional LSTM (BiLSTM) networks, as well as traditional linear regression models, in capturing complex market dynamics and improving predictive accuracy. Through meticulous data pre-processing, model training, and evaluation, the research demonstrates the superiority of deep learning approaches over conventional regression methods, highlighting their potential to revolutionize financial decision-making processes. Findings reveal that LSTM and BiLSTM networks outperform linear regression models, providing stakeholders with powerful predictive tools to enhance investment strategies and mitigate risks. The study also explores model integration techniques to combine the strengths of multiple models, further enhancing predictive performance.

50.1 Introduction

Stock market prediction is essential because it is a critical aid to investors and traders to enable them to make decisions to buy, sell, or hold an asset. Due to the significant sums of money involved in finance, accurate predictions create profitable opportunities, while inaccurate predictions result in loss of finance [15]. Investors use prediction methods such as fundamental and technical analysis to evaluate the intrinsic value of stocks and the study of statistics concerning the market. Predicting stock prices presents considerable challenges and complexities given the dynamic, volatile, and chaotic nature of financial markets [7]. The stock market is said to follow a random walk, which means that predicting tomorrow's price, knowing today's

A. S. Yasin (✉) · H. Osmanoğlu (✉)
Istinye University, Istanbul, Turkey
e-mail: aminshuayb.yasin@stu.istinye.edu.tr

H. Osmanoğlu
e-mail: husamettim.osmanoglu@istinye.edu.tr

F. P. García Márquez et al. (eds.), *Computing, Internet of Things and Data Analytics*,
Smart Innovation, Systems and Technologies 387,
https://doi.org/10.1007/978-3-031-87154-2_50

price is as good as one can do. The inherent unpredictability of the market implies that the use of forecast models is justified. Stock prices are influenced by both what is known in the market, such as the closing price on the previous day, and what is unknown, such as speculation that is election results and rumors [10].

The ability to accurately predict the trends of the stock market is an important element of the financial sector. This is because correctly predicting the market can enable investors to make huge profits from their market insights. However, it is difficult to predict the variations of the stock market because of the nature of the market, which relies on chaotic, noisy, and non-stationary data [8]. As such, investors must come up with strategies and systems that will enable them to operate in the market without losing their investments. The stock market is complex due to the influence of various economic and non-economic factors and, as a result, it requires advanced prediction models [18]. First, deep learning offers high accuracy, robustness, and reliability, this is because DNNs can automatically learn patterns from data and adjust to the changes in market conditions [14]. Moreover, DNN models are more flexible to capture complicated hierarchical relationships and nonuniform dependencies that are inconceivable and difficult to interpret using conventional stock market methodologies [1, 19]. Consequently, deep learning offers a full assessment of stock market patterns and dynamics.

The content of this paper is organized as follows. Section 50.2 presents various stock prediction models, including linear regression, LSTM and BiLSTM models. Section 50.3 describes the core stock prediction models and their integration. Section 50.4 presents the proposed model evaluation and its result. Finally, in Sect. 50.5, concluding remarks are provided to summarize the findings and implications of the study.

50.2 Literature Review

50.2.1 Linear Regression

Linear regression is one of the fundamental statistical techniques employed in diverse fields to capture the linear relationship between one dependent variable and one or several independent variables [13]. Linear regression has been in existence since early times, with the origins of linear regression dating as far back as the beginning of the 19th century, with independent developments by mathematicians Legendre and Gauss [11]. The model for the simple linear regression can be presented as:

$$Y = \beta_0 + \beta_1 * X + \epsilon \tag{50.1}$$

where Y is the dependent output variable of a neuron, X is the independent input variable, β_0 is the intercept, β_1 is the slope coefficient, and ϵ is the error term. Often linear regression aims to determine the values of 0 and 1 such that a sum of the square of the prediction error is minimized.

50.2.2 Deep Learning

Deep learning is a branch of machine learning (ML) that has entirely transformed to various fields by enabling automatic learning of complex patterns and representations from data [1, 16]. The core of deep learning is the artificial neural network, which is inspired by the human brain's structural and functional organization and operation. Artificial neural networks (ANNs) are made up of linked layers of neurons, each performs a basic computation before passing the signal to the next neurons of the next layer [2]. The structure of a deep learning model, which is a complex ANN, is made up of numerous layers, including the input layer, the hidden layer, and the output layer, all of which include a large number of individual neurons [4]. Notably, hidden layers help the network make more complex and abstract representations of the input data, enabling it to recognize more complicated patterns and connections. Lastly, a perceptron is the base unit of deep learning because it is a computational model based on the biology of a neuron. Mathematically, for a perceptron as depicted below, the output Y is given by:

$$Y = f\left(\sum_{i=1}^{n}(w_i * x_i + b)\right) \tag{50.2}$$

where Y is the output of the perceptron, f is the activation function, w_i are the weights associated with the inputs x_i and b is the bias term.

Figure 50.1 illustrates a deep neural network. The interconnected neurons, as shown in Fig. 50.1, are deeply layered, and the incoming connections are weighted [3]. The forward arrows depict the flow of information through a network of neurons

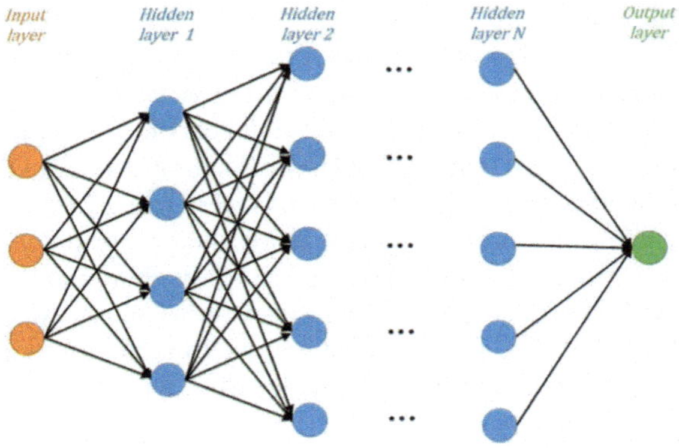

Fig. 50.1 A deep learning model architecture with N hidden layers

Fig. 50.2 BiLSTM networks [17]

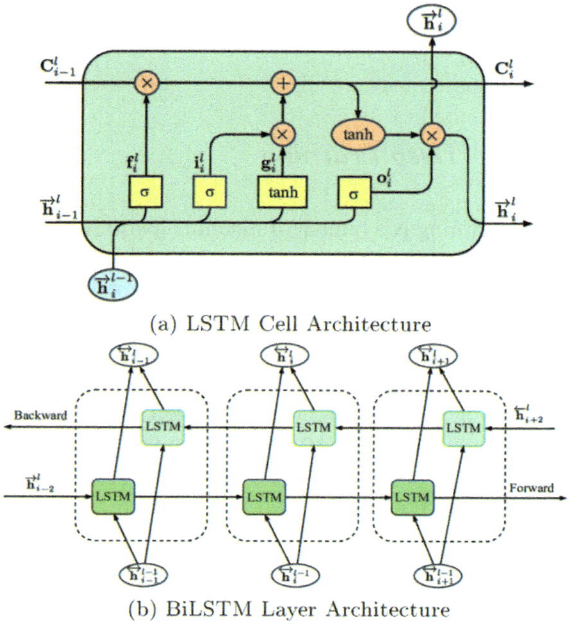

that compute on their inputs and pass their outcomes to the next layer. The automatic learning of features and patterns from raw data, combined with the lack of necessary feature engineering, have positioned as a powerful tool deep learning for addressing many real-world challenging problems (Fig. 50.2).

50.3 Methodology

50.3.1 Data Collection

The first stage of this work consisted of obtaining stock market data from Yahoo Finance through the Yfinance Python library [12]. Specifically, we extracted the historical daily data on the S&P 500 index, one of the most critical indices that represent the U.S. stock market, from its origination in 1927 to the present time [5]. The dataset contained such vital variables as Open, High, Low, Close, Adjusted Close, and Volume, which are a sufficient representation of daily stock market activity to make accurate predictions. After successfully obtaining the stock market dataset, we created a thorough check for missing values to ensure data completeness. We were lucky that the Yahoo Finance data was well-maintained and contained no missing values, which allowed us to continue our work with unbiased and accurate information

50.3.2 Deep Learning Models

While implementing the regression analysis using the Linear Regression algorithm, we have made a significant advancement in this research and model development process. The purpose of this phase was to build a regression-based model tailored to predict the closing price of S&P 500 stock index closing price for a given day based on dependent variables. In addition, LS step can be used enhance regression analysis by adding another feature–"PreviousClose" and begin to apply a lagged feature in this analysis. Specifically, we have to include the information on how the S&P 500 closing gender has changed on the previous day. Such an approach is encouraged when conducting time series analysis, and financial modeling, as it allows adding and capturing short-run dependencies or trends protruding from the data.

50.3.3 LSTM Model

Parameter Selection: Parametric decisions, such as the number of LSTM units and layers, were carefully tuned to achieve the fine combination of model complexity and generalization performance. By setting the number of units in the LSTM layer to 50, the model achieved a balance between the ability to express complex patterns and computational factors. The two-layer LSTM architecture performed the ability to discern both high-level dynamics and underlying structure

Input Shape and Data Preparation: Since our input features have a sequential nature, we successfully reshaped the input data to fit into a three-dimensional array. Our tensor includes three dimensions for samples, time steps, and features and supports smooth functioning for the LSTM layers. On top of that, we normalized the data by applying feature scaling to achieve consistency and such stabilize the training process.

50.3.4 Bidirectional LSTM Model

The importance of Bidirectional LSTM (BiLSTM), model have been widely used due to the success of sequence prediction tasks, such as natural language processing, and time series forecasting [6]. BiLSTMs show promise model to capture longer-range dependencies and context from input sequences, due to the simultaneous processing of the data in the reverse and forward directions [9]. As the model is trained with both directions, it could potentially outperform unidirectional LSTM models by implicitly integrating the future context as well during training. In the case of predicting the stock market, a BiLSTM could be of potential use here as past price data is usually widely connected under intricate patterns and dependencies [20]. Since both past and future information are considered here, the model can learn and capture the intricacies of the stock market, which might help in achieving a better accuracy in the predictions. Moreover, because the model learns vital information about the past and future, it can analyze complex relationships in the data. The BiLSTM model is composed of two layers of LSTM units, as shown in Fig. 50.2b, with the required dropout layer after each of them to avoid overfitting. The mentioned layers are attached with a dense layer at the end to obtain the final output, which characterizes the stock prices to be forecast. The bi-directional processing is the main advantage of the BiLSTM model as it enables the model's ability to grasp the interactions and dependencies from the information from the future and past.

50.3.5 Model Integration

LSTM and Linear Regression: The LSTM model trained by deep learning effectively captured and distilled the hidden complex temporal relationships and behaviors in stock data. Through the training process and multiple model hyper=parameter tuning epochs, the LSTM model gained more and more knowledge about the subtle overall and constant characteristics of the data, leading to its ability to make correct predictions. In contrast, the LR model embarked on an independent and exciting journey of discovery about the linear relationships between the input stock price-oriented features and the output target variable. Both the LSTM model and LR model interpreted above are extremely shallow, whereas the former is much easier due to the lack of transparency, while the latter is transparent and interpretable.

Bidirectional LSTM and Linear Regression: Our model integration approach also included the fusion of the Bidirectional LSTM and Linear Regression methodologies. The primary goal of combining these two models was to complement their strengths, thereby enhancing stock market trend prediction and reducing their weaknesses. The integration of these two models occurred in the following systematic steps of BiLSTM and LR training and validation on historical stock market data. The BiLSTM model is a variant of the conventional LSTM with two key differences: first, it processes data in both directions simultaneously, thus capturing context information and long-range dependencies. Second, the BiLSTM model can capture not just the past but also the future temporal dependencies in the stock market data. The structure of BiLSTM made it suitable for sequence prediction tasks such as stock market trend forecasting. Meanwhile, the LR model went on an adventurous exploration to establish linear relationships between input features and target variables drawn from stock market data. Unlike BiLSTM deep learning models, LR does not demonstrate the complexity and non-linearity required for robust prediction.

50.4 Results and Evaluation

50.4.1 Training and Testing

In this work, the S&P 500, a stock market index that measures the stock performance of 500 of the largest companies listed on stock exchanges in the United States, is used [12]. The dataset should be be used for two tasks, e.g. learning (training) features and then testing the model. In addition, a validation set is used to help ensure that the model performs well on new, unseen data and does not simply memorize the training data.

The S&P 500 dataset comprises 24148 items, divided into training, validation, and testing sets at proportions of 70%, 15%, and 15%, respectively. This results in 16903 samples for training, 3622 samples for validation, and 3623 samples for testing.The training set is used as the foundation to train the model. The validation set is used to tune the model's hyperparameters and evaluate its performance. Additionally, 10-fold cross-validation is performed to mitigate randomness and assess signal consistency. For early stopping, a callback function with a patience value of 15 is implemented to halt training automatically when the validation loss or learning rate ceases to improve. The testing set, representing 15% of the data, is used to evaluate the model's generalization capability from the training phase. This provides an excellent measure of the model's ability to predict the S&P 500 daily closing price on unseen data.

50.4.2 Evaluation Metrics

During the evaluation of the predictive models, different evaluation metrics were utilized to measure their level of accuracy, reliability, and generalization. Notably, adolescents 45 utilize these metrics as a baseline for measuring the functionality of their models, given that they enhance performance comparison between different methodologies. The current study utilized the following evaluation metrics, including their formulas and basis

Mean Absolute Error (MAE): This metric calculates the average absolute difference between the predicted values and actual values. It serves as an indicator for the average magnitude of errors in the predictions.

$$MAE = \frac{\sum_{i=1}^{n} \mid y_i - \bar{y}_i \mid}{n} \tag{50.3}$$

where n is number of data points, y_i is the actual value of the data point and $\bar{y}_i$ is the predicted value.

Root Mean Squared Error (RMSE): It is similar to MSE; however, it penalizes large errors more helping the user understand what the range of error should be among the predicted and the actual values.

$$RMSE = \sqrt{\frac{(\sum_{i=1}^{n} \mid y_i - \bar{y_i} \mid)^2}{n}} \tag{50.4}$$

50.4.3 Regression Model Performance

The regression analysis shows that the model developed is feasible to predict the S&P 500 index's closing price. Figure 50.3 shows that the evaluation performance measurements has relatively low errors and high R-square values for the entire datasets. These measures primarily quantify how much the model is likely to predict a price that will simulate the general patterns and tendency of ideas in the stock market data. In addition, the scatter plot of actual vs predicted closing prices shows the very strong alignment between the predicted closing prices and the actual closing prices.

50.4.4 LSTM Model Performance

For the LSTM model to be useful, we treated it to facilitate training by the Adam optimizer. The Adam optimizer is widely recognized for its ability to modify learning rates by computing an adaptive learning rate and a momentum of the parameter gradients. During the training stage, the performance of the predicted stock price is determined based on the original stock price divergence calculated as loss by mean squared error loss function. Our training configuration setup the model for

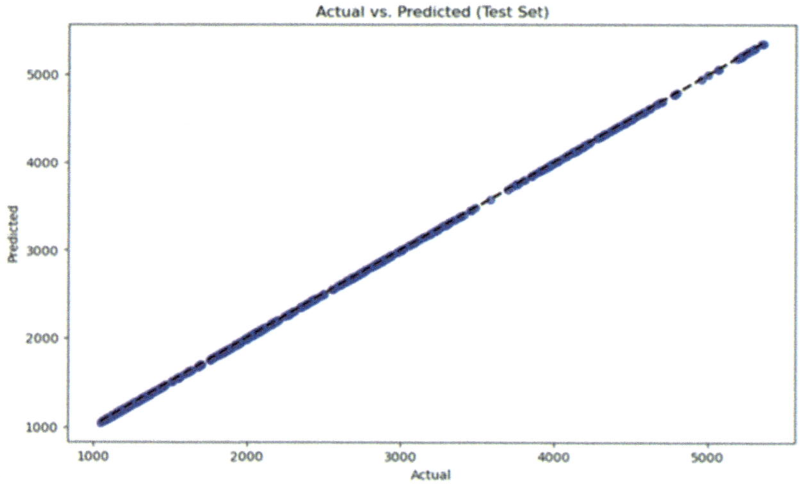

Fig. 50.3 Actual versus predicated closing price on the test set

100 epochs, and the data was meticulously processed into mini-batches that were iteratively fed, thereby enabling the model to iteratively fine-tune its parameter and enhance its prediction as the epochs progressed. The RMSE of 0.6973 indicates that, on average, the LSTM model's predictions deviate by 0.6973 units from the actual closing prices. Figure 50.4a shows the predicted stock prices versus the actual stock prices over time. The alignment between the actual and predicated price demonstrates that the model effectively captures the overall movement and trends in the stock prices during the validation period.

50.4.5 Bidirectional LSTM Model Performance

The RMSE value of BiLSTM, which is 0.5973, highlights the model's effectiveness in minimizing larger errors, indicating that the BiLSTM model not only captures the overall trend accurately but also reduces significant deviations between predicted and actual values. Since this BiLSTM model performed significantly much better than the LSTM, one can argue that the bi-directional flow of information in the LSTM architecture most likely enhanced the LSTM's learning capabilities of the LSTM of what that still might be trying to attain the level of prediction by capturing the hidden patterns. In addition, Fig. 50.4b shows the predicted real actual close price series compared with the real price.

50.4.6 Integrated Model Performance

The integration of Linear Regression (LR) with Long Short-Term Memory (LSTM) and Bidirectional LSTM (BiLSTM) models demonstrates significantly captures the advantage of each prediction model.

Integrating LR with LSTM: The LR + LSTM integration model achieved a mean absolute error (MAE) of 0.1157 and a root mean squared error (RMSE) of 0.3402. This indicates that the combined model leverages the strengths of both linear regression and LSTM, resulting in more precise and reliable predictions.

Integrating LR with BiLSTM: The LR + BiLSTM integration model exhibited even better performance, achieving a remarkably low MAE of 0.1077 and RMSE of 0.2430. These results underline the efficacy of integrating linear models with advanced deep learning techniques, providing a robust framework for accurate stock price prediction and demonstrating substantial improvements over individual model performances. The low values of MAE and RMSE also mean that the integrated model minimized errors during prediction, which are essential attributes for an efficient financial forecasting model.

Figure 50.5 illustrates the BiLSTM + LR model's performance shows a close alignment between the predicted and actual closing prices. The integrated model's

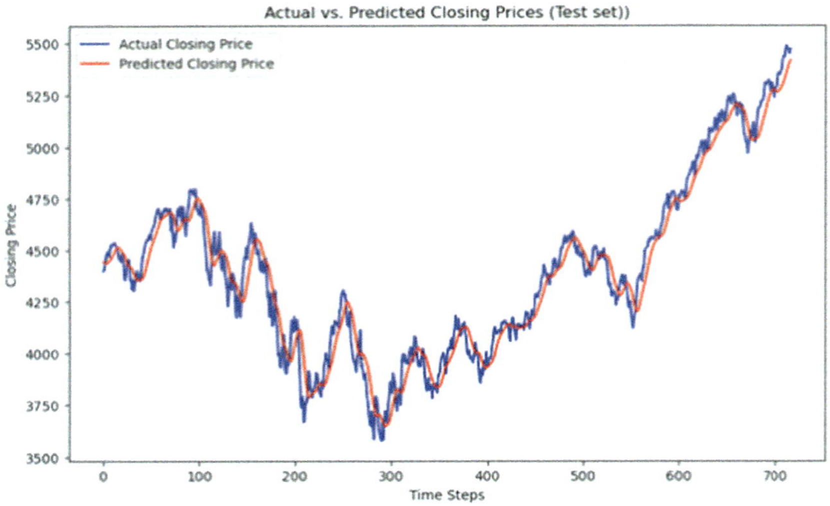

(a) Actual vs Predicted LSTM

(b) Actual vs Predicted BiLSTM

Fig. 50.4 The actual versus predicted result on test set

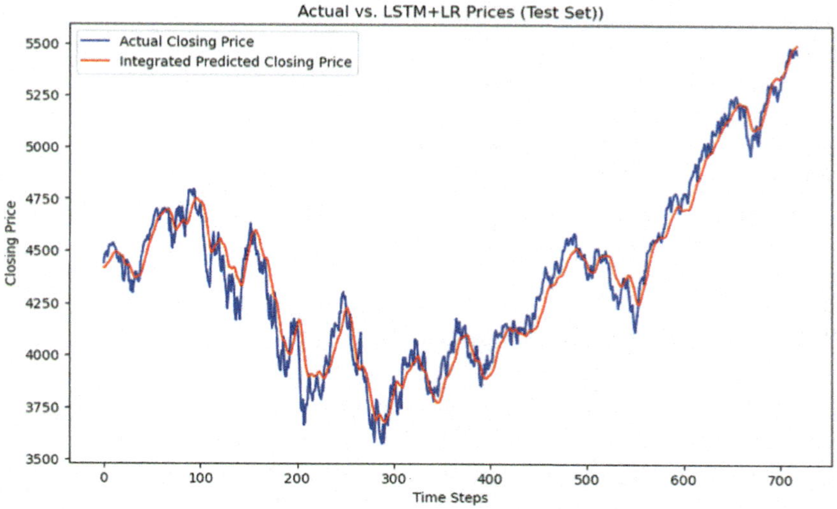

(a) Actual vs Predicted LR with LSTM

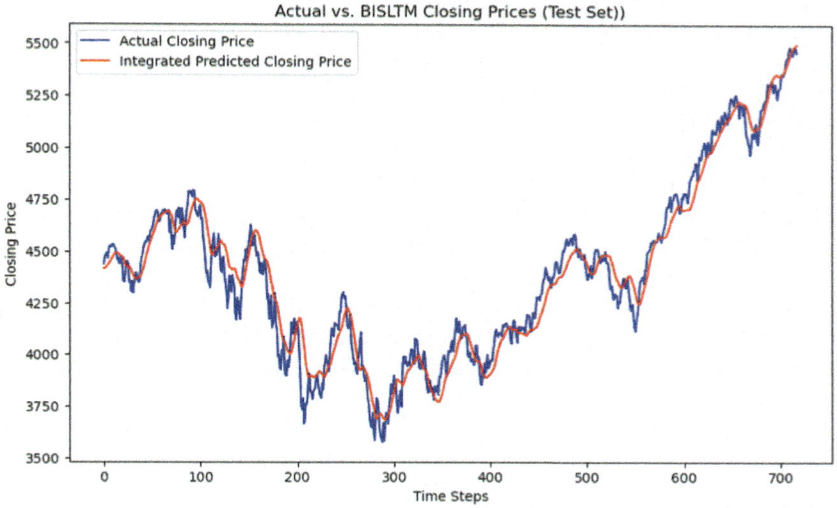

(b) Actual vs Predicted of LR with BiLSTM

Fig. 50.5 The actual versus predicted result on test set

predictions (red line) effectively follow the actual closing prices (blue line). This visual representation underscores the model's capability to handle market volatility and provide reliable predictions, further validating its practical applicability in financial forecasting.

Table 50.1 Overall comparison

Model	MAE (Test set)	RMSE (Test set)
Linear regression	0.1525	0.3905
LSTM	0.4863	0.6973
BiLSTM	0.3863	0.5973
LR + LSTM integration	0.1157	0.3402
LR + BiLSTM integration	0.1077	0.2430

50.4.7 Overall Model Comparisons

The overall comparison of the performance metrics across the individual-level models and their integration is shown in Table 50.1. The linear regression model demonstrated an exceptionally low error rate, with both MAE and RMSE values approaching zero. The LSTM model's performance yielded an MAE of 0.4863 and an RMSE of 0.6973. These results indicate that the LSTM model captures the overall trend of the stock prices but has notable prediction errors, particularly during volatile market movements. The BiLSTM model showed improved performance over the standalone LSTM, with an MAE of 0.3863 and an RMSE of 0.5973. The bidirectional nature of BiLSTM allows it to capture patterns in both forward and backward directions, enhancing its predictive capability.

Combining the LSTM with linear regression reduced the prediction errors, achieving an MAE of 0.1157. This integration helps to correct systematic errors that the LSTM model alone may not capture, leading to more accurate predictions.The integrated BiLSTM and linear regression model also achieved an MAE of 0.1077. This combined approach leverages the strengths of both models, capturing complex patterns with BiLSTM and addressing linear trends with linear regression. By implementing these findings, analysts and investors can leverage the most suitable models for their specific needs, leading to more informed decision-making and better investment strategies.

50.5 Conclusion

The stock market trends prediction based on the S&P 500 index's historical data evaluation, shown in this study, can be summarized as the performance of LR, LSTM, and BiLSTM networks. Specifically, the results indicate that in terms of predictive quality, LSTM and BiLSTM networks outperforms LR since both MAE and RMSE statistics decrease. Additionally, ensemble models that incorporate a LR model with LSTM and BiLSTM improve the predictive outcome. The method of averaging all forecasts, using the approach of model integration, can be distinguished as a method promising to enhance the forecast result's accuracy. Integration of LR with deep learning LSTM models reduces both MAE and RMSE to a greater extent, and it indicates the potential of this coin and the chance to integrate them.

Reliable stock market forecasting helps stakeholders make more precise investment choices and, thereby, reduce exposure to risk in portfolio management. The results obtained adequately reflect the models' forecasting properties, and both the accuracy and robustness can be increased. Therefore, possible future research may consider investigating alternative model architectures. Furthermore, the use of more features or datasets and new evaluation metrics will enhance the model results' robustness and develop the models' generalization ability.

References

1. Al-Asadi, M., Altun, A.A.: Deep learning with smote techniques for improved skin lesion classification on unbalanced data. Selcuk Univ. J. Eng. Sci. **21**(3), 97–104 (2022)
2. Alzaq, H.Y., Ustundag, B.B.: Very-low-snr cognitive receiver based on wavelet preprocessed signal patterns and neural network. EURASIP J. Wirel. Commun. Netw. **2017**, 1–17 (2017)
3. Alzaq-Osmanoglu, H., Alrehaili, J., Ustundag, B.B.: Low-snr modulation recognition based on deep learning on software defined radio. In: 2022 5th International Conference on Advanced Communication Technologies and Networking (CommNet), pp. 1–6 (2022). https://doi.org/10.1109/CommNet56067.2022.9993934
4. Bansal, M., Goyal, A., Choudhary, A.: Stock market prediction with high accuracy using machine learning techniques. Proc. Comput. Sci. **215**, 247–265 (2022)
5. Chen, Y., Wu, J., Wu, Z.: China's commercial bank stock price prediction using a novel kmeans-lstm hybrid approach. Expert Syst. Appl. **202**, 117370 (2022)
6. Dong, J., Wang, L., Liu, J., Gao, Y., Qi, L., Sun, X.: A procedural texture generation framework based on semantic descriptions. Knowl.-Based Syst. **163**, 898–906 (2019)
7. Gandhmal, D.P., Kumar, K.: Systematic analysis and review of stock market prediction techniques. Comput. Sci. Rev. **34**, 100190 (2019)
8. Hiransha, M., Gopalakrishnan, E.A., Menon, V.K., Soman, K.: Nse stock market prediction using deep-learning models. Proc. Comput. Sci. **132**, 1351–1362 (2018)
9. Ingle, V., Deshmukh, S.: Ensemble deep learning framework for stock market data prediction (edlf-dp). Global Transit. Proc. **2**(1), 47–66 (2021)
10. Jiang, W.: Applications of deep learning in stock market prediction: recent progress. Expert Syst. Appl. **184**, 115537 (2021)
11. Lin, W.C., Tsai, C.F., Chen, H.: Factors affecting text mining based stock prediction: text feature representations, machine learning models, and news platforms. Appl. Soft Comput. **130**, 109673 (2022)
12. Liu, H., Long, Z.: An improved deep learning model for predicting stock market price time series. Digital Signal Process. **102**, 102741 (2020)
13. Liu, Q., Tao, Z., Tse, Y., Wang, C.: Stock market prediction with deep learning: The case of china. Financ. Res. Lett. **46**, 102209 (2022)
14. Oyedele, A.A., Ajayi, A.O., Oyedele, L.O., Bello, S.A., Jimoh, K.O.: Performance evaluation of deep learning and boosted trees for cryptocurrency closing price prediction. Expert Syst. Appl. **213**, 119233 (2023)
15. Reddy, V., Sai, K.: Stock market prediction using machine learning. Int. Res. J. Eng. Technol. (IRJET) **5**(10), 1033–1035 (2018)
16. Ren, Y., Liao, F., Gong, Y.: Impact of news on the trend of stock price change: An analysis based on the deep bidirectiona lstm model. Proc. Comput. Sci. **174**, 128–140 (2020)
17. Wang, S.: A stock price prediction method based on bilstm and improved transformer. IEEE Access **11**, 104211–104223 (2023). https://doi.org/10.1109/ACCESS.2023.3296308

18. Yang, H., Xue, F.: Analysis of stock market volatility: Adjusted vpin with highfrequency data. Int. Rev. Econ. Finance **75**, 210–222 (2021)
19. Zhang, K., Yang, X., Wang, T., Thé, J., Tan, Z., Yu, H.: Multi-step carbon price forecasting using a hybrid model based on multivariate decomposition strategy and deep learning algorithms. J. Clean. Prod. **405**, 136959 (2023)
20. Zhang, Y., Chu, G., Shen, D.: The role of investor attention in predicting stock prices: The long short-term memory networks perspective. Financ. Res. Lett. **38**, 101484 (2021)

Chapter 51
OOC: An OCR-OpenAI-ClickUp Integration for Efficient Document Processing

Hamza Regragui and Hüsamettin Osmanoğlu

Abstract This work explores the integration of Optical Character Recognition (OCR) technology with OpenAI and ClickUp to enhance document processing in consulting firms. Traditional manual processing of documents such as invoices is time-consuming and prone to errors, which often resulting in delays and inaccuracies of data. The proposed solution, termed the OCR-OpenAI-ClickUp (OOC) integration, aims to transform this process by automating document management and improving data accuracy and workflow efficiency. The system uses Google Cloud OCR to scan the text from the document submitted by the users, OpenAI's GPT-3.5-turbo for advanced text analysis, and ClickUp CRM for the storing of data. This integrated approach significantly reduces human errors during data extraction and enables a more organized, efficient handling of document processing. The findings suggest that the OOC model not only accelerates operations but also enhances overall organizational effectiveness, offering a promising solution for consulting firms aiming to optimize their document management systems.

51.1 Introduction

The Optical Character Recognition (OCR) technology has been around since the early twentieth century, with significant advancements occurring over time. OCR's initial applications date back to technologies created in the 1910s and 1920s, mainly to help the blind people [12]. However, the modern concept of OCR, which involves the electronic conversion of images of typed, handwritten, or printed text into machine-encoded text was later introduced [10]. Processing documents such as invoices is often time-consuming and prone to errors when done manually by consulting firms or similar companies [15]. This manual process can lead to delays in processing

H. Regragui (✉) · H. Osmanoğlu (✉)
Istinye University, Istanbul, Turkey
e-mail: hamza.regragui@stu.istinye.edu.tr

H. Osmanoğlu
e-mail: husamettim.osmanoglu@istinye.edu.tr

F. P. García Márquez et al. (eds.), *Computing, Internet of Things and Data Analytics*, Smart Innovation, Systems and Technologies 387,
https://doi.org/10.1007/978-3-031-87154-2_51

times, inaccuracies in data entry. In addition, the traditional methods of document processing lack to the capability to easily search and manage large amounts of documents firms handle daily.

While time and precision are two key factors for consulting companies, extracting significant information from client documents have been a persistent challenge [11]. Manual file scrutiny to find, for example, patient names, booking dates, and invoice amounts not only consumed valuable time from the employee, but also introduced errors into client's CRM system. To address these issues, a new solution has been introduced. The key feature of the proposed solution is to integrates OCR with the intelligence of OpenAI [9], and the efficiency of ClickUp. This innovative approach aims at simplifying document processing, saving time, and elevating the accuracy of data management for clients.

The approach extends to efficiency in workflow management, examining literature on systems across different industries that enhance workflow efficiency. Various integration, like OCR-OpenAI-ClickUp, are examined for their potential to improve work efficiency, data management, and overall organizational effectiveness. The exploration extends to AI integration for document understanding, covering research on the incorporation of artificial intelligence (AI) in literature, excluding ChatGPT, for semantic analysis and extracting meaning from textual data across diverse applications. (Table 51.1).

The main contributions of this work as follows.

- Through the use of OCR technology, it can transform static content into editable and searchable data. This initial step significantly reduces human errors during data extraction, thereby increasing overall accuracy.
- The incorporation of OpenAI's GPT-3.5-turbo enhances the system's capabilities. This allows for the system to not only identify documents, such as invoices, but also to extract key details required for further processing, such as bill amounts, discounts, total amounts, and passenger names.
- Integrating with ClickUp offers a structured and efficient way to manage the workflow. It ensures that the process is not only automated but also well-organized, allowing consulting teams to handle document processing tasks more efficiently and with fewer errors.

51.2 Literature Review

Document processing and information retrieval involves innovative approaches that have been proposed to assist people [6, 16]. Shidaganti et al. [17] propose a system that focus on user interaction via WhatsApp. Their methodology integrates Robotic Process Automation (RPA), specifically UiPath Studio, OCR through Tesseract OCR, and ChatGPT for conversational AI. Notably, the emphasis is on a conversational workflow where users submit images for information retrieval. Shidaganti et al. [17]

Table 51.1 General comparison between different OCRs models

	Advantages	Disadvantages	Methodology
Shidaganti et al. [17]	Automating image-based data retrieval, which enhances time, reduces errors, and boosts productivity	–Scalability and Integration –There are concerns regarding the accuracy and reliability of OCR technology	–Automate the process of retrieving information from images, utilizing the strengths of RPA, OCR, and ChatGPT
Yimyam et al. [20]	–OCR and ontology integration to speed up the auditing process –Transition to digital processes in financial documentation	–Limited to Text Recognition –Relies on the OCR and ontology algorithms quality	–Streamline the document checking process, making it faster and more accurate compared to traditional methods
Das et al. [4]	–High Accuracy –Potential for Document Navigation –Effective Feature Extraction	–Mixed Documents –Issues with Handwriting Overlays –Word Segmentation Challenges	–Filter-based Feature Extraction –Word-Level Classification Using SVM
Bulzan et al. [3]	–Improved Accuracy for Smaller Models –Accelerated Learning Speed –Beneficial for Lower Resolution Images	– Limited Impact for Larger Models –Potential Data Augmentation Challenges	–Object Detection Methodology that integrates two OCR modules to boost accuracy, and learning speed
HoangVan et al. [8]	–Language Specificity –Integrated Approach –Performance Improvement	–Limited Dataset –Challenges in Object Detection –Dependence on Data Quality –Accuracy variation across fields	–Extracting key information from Korean invoices, by integrating advanced DL techniques and image pre-processing methods

still uses manual document scrutiny. The proposed approach integrates OCR, including OpenAI's GPT-3.5-turbo, with ClickUp for structured workflow management. Yimyam et al. [20] have used OCR with ontology for the reimbursement process of official documents. The solution used includes implementing OCR for accurate and efficient document scanning, along with the use of Ontology to classify and store information about documents.

Das et al. [4] have proposed various methods were discussed, including those utilizing statistical features, geometric features, and classifiers like SVM and Hidden Markov Model (HMM). The article highlights the importance of effective feature selection and discusses the strengths and weaknesses of different techniques reported in previous works. The article places its suggested strategy in relation to these current techniques, emphasizing the importance of word-level processing for AEC documents. Bulzan et al. [3] have discussed various approaches in the field of extracting key information from invoices. The review includes three main categories: OCR techniques, detection models based on image information, and fusion models combining Natural Language Processing (NLP) and image processing. The discussion includes the use of rule-based and deep learning-based OCR techniques, object detection models treating information extraction as a problem of detecting key fields, and the emergence of fusion models that combine NLP and image processing methods. Studies that compare traditional OCR methods to in-the-wild text recognition methods are highlighted, Emphasizing the importance of document OCR when evaluating text detection and recognition approaches. The literature also explores the distinction between classical rule-based methods and deep learning methods, particularly the effectiveness of Deep Convolutional Neural Networks (DCNN)[1] in extracting visually distinguishable features in images.

HoangVan et al. [8] have discussed alternative approaches to information extraction, highlighting Template-based and NLP-based methods. Predetermined guidelines are used in the template-based approach for documents with fixed formats, while the NLP-based approach involves text classification models or Named Entity Recognition (NER). It is acknowledged that these approaches have limitations when it comes to handling documents with layouts, particularly in tabular forms. The article also mentions previous OCR methods for Korean characters and discusses the limitations of existing models in handling deformed or curved text. The literature review in [14] meticulously examines the development and application of RPA and AI in various sectors. It explores how these technologies have evolved historically, highlighting their growing significance in the modern industrial landscape, particularly under the umbrella of Industry 4.0. The review also looks at different RPA and AI case studies and applications., illustrating how they have transformed procedures and activities across various industries.

Generative AI, including models like GANs and LLMs, holds transformative potential in healthcare by generating new data such as text and images. These technologies enhance clinical decision-making, improve patient outcomes, and optimize healthcare delivery [13]. Key applications include synthetic data generation, which balances valuable research with patient privacy, and drug discovery, where AI accelerates the development of novel molecular structures. In medical diagnosis, GANs and LLMs improve accuracy by identifying disease patterns and synthesizing medical images. Additionally, AI automates routine healthcare administration tasks, reducing documentation burdens and enhancing efficiency. However, challenges such as data availability, potential biases, and ethical considerations must be addressed to ensure responsible integration of AI in healthcare.

While the aforementioned studies focus on specific aspects of document processing or information retrieval, such as using RPA with OCR [17], integrating OCR with ontology for financial documentation [20], or employing advanced feature extraction methods [4] are not implemented. In this work, we propose a new framework namely, OOC, which is a comprehensive integration of OCR with OpenAI and ClickUp to create an efficient and automated document processing system specifically designed for consulting firms. This integration aims to improve both accuracy and workflow management.

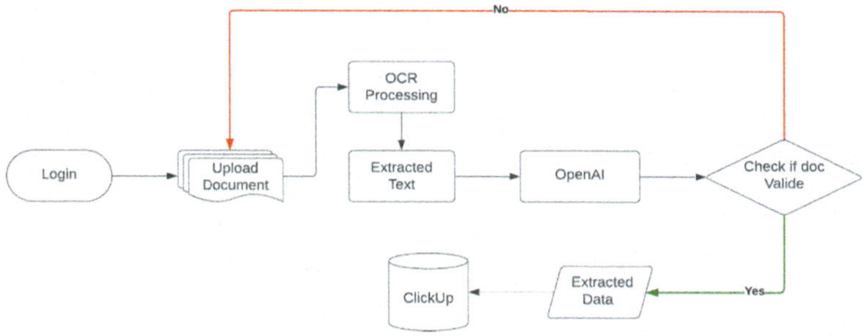

Fig. 51.1 Automating document processing and extracting text

51.3 Methodology

The OOC system is designed to address the challenges faced by consulting firms in manual document management. This process comprises three key stages: (1) Extracting basic information through integrated OCR for document digitization, (2) Analyzing documents using OpenAI's GPT-3.5-turbo for document processing, and (3) Storing the extracted information using the ClickUp management system. Figure 51.1 visually outlines these steps. In the following sections, the detailed explanations of each stage is provided.

51.3.1 Optical Character Recognition (OCR)

OCR technology has revolutionized how we handle both paper-based and digital documents. It facilitates the conversion of various document types such as PDFs, images, or scanned papers, into editable and searchable data. Serving as the initial phase in the streamlined framework, OCR transforms the static content of paper-based documents into digital, readable text. Figure 51.2 provides an illustration of a digital invoice handled by the OCR system.

This transformation not only minimizes the manual effort required for data entry, but also empowers the consultancy business to process documents with unprecedented efficiency. Furthermore, OCR mitigates the risk of human error during data extraction, thereby enhancing accuracy. In essence, this process not only diminishes the manual effort traditionally associated with document processing but also elevates overall accuracy levels. The integration process of the application's development involved two key steps:

- Utilizing the Google Cloud OCR API [7] for real-time text extraction. This step requires creating credentials that allow to get the JSON file that holds the service account credentials.

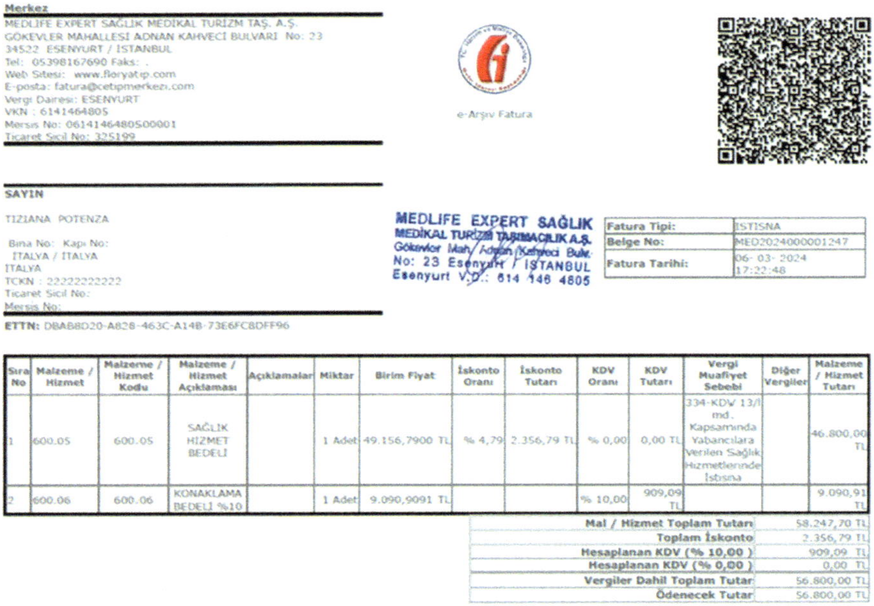

Merkez

MEDLIFE EXPERT SAĞLIK MEDİKAL TURİZM TAŞ. A.Ş.
GÖKEVLER MAHALLESİ ADNAN KAHVECİ BULVARI No: 23
34522 ESENYURT / İSTANBUL
Tel: 05398167690 Faks: .
Web Sitesi: www.floryatıp.com
E-posta: fatura@cetipmerkezi.com
Vergi Dairesi: ESENYURT
VKN : 6141464805
Mersis No: 0614146480500001
Ticaret Sicil No: 325199

e-Arşiv Fatura

SAYIN

TIZIANA POTENZA

Bina No: Kapı No:
İTALYA / İTALYA
İTALYA
TCKN : 22222222222
Ticaret Sicil No:
Mersis No:

MEDLIFE EXPERT SAĞLIK MEDİKAL TURİZM TAŞIMACILIK A.Ş. Gökevler Mah. Adnan Kahveci Bulv. No: 23 Esenyurt / İSTANBUL Esenyurt V.D.: 614 146 4805

Fatura Tipi:	İSTİSNA
Belge No:	MED2024000001247
Fatura Tarihi:	06-03-2024 17:22:48

ETTN: DBAB8D20-A828-463C-A14B-73E6FC8DFF96

Sıra No	Malzeme / Hizmet	Malzeme / Hizmet Kodu	Malzeme / Hizmet Açıklaması	Açıklamalar	Miktar	Birim Fiyat	İskonto Oranı	İskonto Tutarı	KDV Oranı	KDV Tutarı	Vergi Muafiyet Sebebi	Diğer Vergiler	Malzeme / Hizmet Tutarı
1	600.05	600.05	SAĞLIK HİZMET BEDELİ		1 Adet	49.156,7900 TL	% 4,79	2.356,79 TL	% 0,00	0,00 TL	334-KDV 13/l md. Kapsamında Yabancılara Verilen Sağlık Hizmetlerinde İstisna		46.800,00 TL
2	600.06	600.06	KONAKLAMA BEDELİ %10		1 Adet	9.090,9091 TL			% 10,00	909,09 TL			9.090,91 TL

Mal / Hizmet Toplam Tutarı	58.247,70 TL
Toplam İskonto	2.356,79 TL
Hesaplanan KDV (% 10,00)	909,09 TL
Hesaplanan KDV (% 0,00)	0,00 TL
Vergiler Dahil Toplam Tutar	56.800,00 TL
Ödenecek Tutar	56.800,00 TL

Fig. 51.2 Automating document processing and extracting text

```
{
  "type": "service_account",
  "project_id": "ocr [redacted]",
  "private_key_id": "[redacted]",
  "private_key": "-----BEGIN PRIVATE KEY-----\n[illegible]
  "client_email": "ocr-theprime@ocr-theprime.iam.gserviceaccount.com",
  "client_id": "[redacted]",
  "auth_uri": "https://accounts.google.com/o/oauth2/auth",
  "token_uri": "https://oauth2.googleapis.com/token",
  "auth_provider_x509_cert_url": "https://www.googleapis.com/oauth2/v1/certs",
  "client_x509_cert_url": "https://www.googleapis.com/robot/v1/metadata/x509/[redacted].iam.gserviceaccount.com",
  "universe_domain": "googleapis.com"
}
```


Fig. 51.3 Google cloud JSON file credentials

– Processing and integrating pre-processed OCR results, stored in the JSON format file, as shown in Fig. 51.3. However, this method initially incurred delays in document processing due to the time-intensive tasks of locating folders, assigning specific names to newly uploaded documents, and checking for existing entries. These manual processes significantly slowed down the application. To address this challenge, we have implemented the following solution, in which PDF documents are directly converted into images. This strategic shift notably expedited the proposed document processing workflow, which enhances the efficiency of the application.

51.3.2 ChatGPT: AI Solution

ChatGPT is an AI language model [9, 19]. It is designed to generate human-like text based on the input it receives. ChatGPT is capable of carrying out a variety of language-related tasks, including having natural-sounding conversations and responding to queries, giving advice, and providing information [18]. It can comprehend and produce text in multiple languages and on a variety of topics due to the fact it has been trained on a sizable dataset of text from the internet. ChatGPT can be used in applications like chatbots, virtual assistants, content generation, language translation, and more, making it a versatile tool for natural language understanding and generation tasks [18]. The extracted text from step 1 is then processed by AI methods. In this work, we integrate the OCR with OpenAI's GPT-3.5-turbo [19]. ChatGPT brings semantic understanding to the forefront, enabling the system to decipher the meaning of the extracted text comprehensively. The advanced language model enhances the system's capability to interpret complex information accurately.

Subsequently, this extracted text is forwarded to ChatGPT engine through an Application Programming Interface (API) [19]. The main objective is to inquire about the specific type of data required. Upon receiving the necessary data, the data is split into for parts, facilitating its seamless integration into the CRM system for efficient storing the data.

51.3.3 ClickUp Integration

ClickUp [2, 5] stands as a robust platform for productivity and project management (PMT), catering to the needs of both individuals and teams alike. It streamlines work planning, fosters task collaboration, and adeptly manages projects, all within a centralized environment.

The integration with ClickUp represents a key element in the OOC framework, fostering a well-structured and organized workflow. By leveraging ClickUp, real-time task management is enabled and seamless coordination, empowering consulting teams with an efficient and dependable platform for document processing.

The culmination of the integrated solution is the seamless inclusion of ClickUp. Positioned as the central management hub, ClickUp oversees the entire document processing workflow. Integrating seamlessly with OCR and OpenAI, ClickUp assumes the role of the command center, orchestrating the flow of tasks and information. With ClickUp at the helm, the consulting team gains real-time visibility into the document processing pipeline. Tasks are effortlessly assigned, monitored, and finalized within a unified interface, eliminating the need for manual coordination and minimizing the risk of oversights. This integration ensures that the heightened efficiency brought about by OCR and OpenAI translates seamlessly into a well-structured and organized workflow.

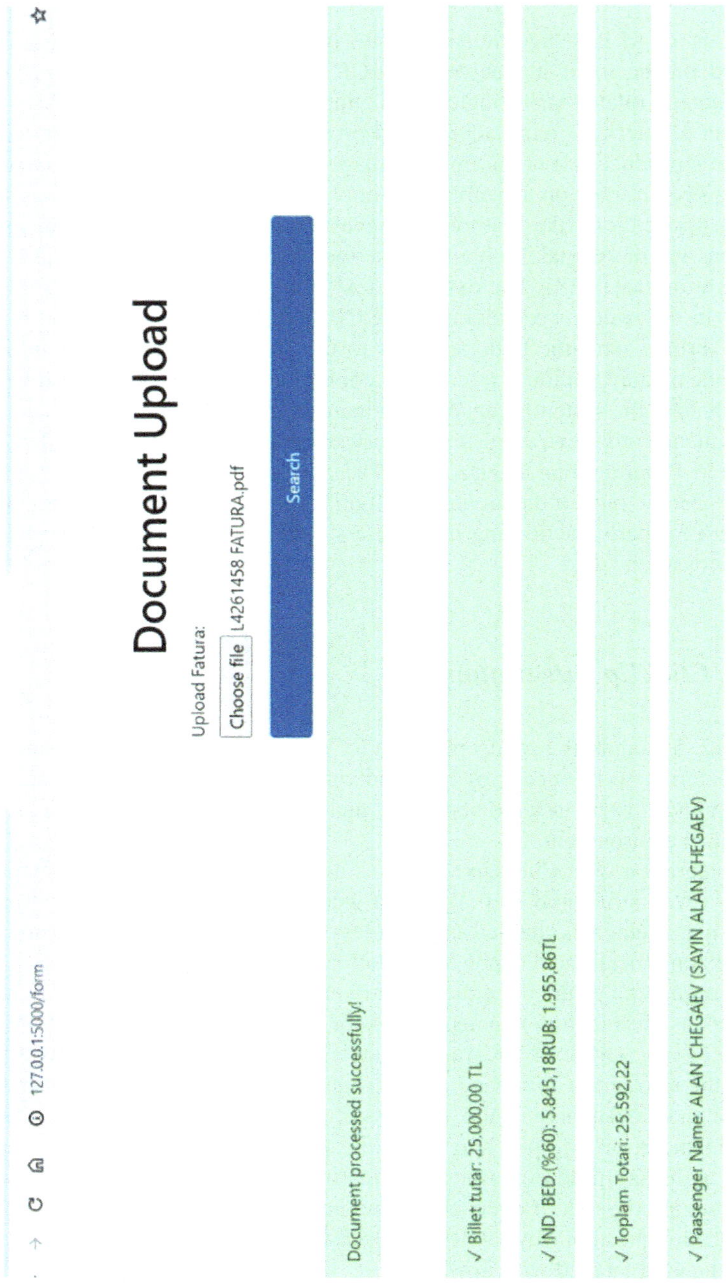

Fig. 51.4 The application output after a successfully bill parsing using OOC

Finally, the proposed model represents a holistic solution tailored to the unique requirements of consulting firms. By amalgamating OCR, OpenAI, and ClickUp integration, it promises expedited and dependable document processing coupled with enhanced accuracy and workflow efficiency. This comprehensive approach not only accelerates operations but also fosters meticulous organization throughout the workflow, ultimately empowering consulting firms to achieve heightened productivity and client satisfaction.

51.4 Results and Evaluation

In the application, users can easily upload files, particularly invoices, to promptly extract essential information. Thanks to OpenAI, the OOC can smartly figure out if the uploaded document is indeed an invoice. Once confirmed, the OOC in clever way extracts all the pertinent details users need, including bill amount, individual bed (60%), total amount, and passenger information. These details are subsequently stored in ClickUp, serving as a central hub for information management system. What's impressive is that the OOC showcases these crucial details directly on the web page, facilitating effortless access and utilization for individual user. This not only streamlines the entire invoice process, but also enables users to conveniently track stored information at a glance.

51.4.1 OOC Application

Figure 51.4 shows the result of OOC. The application processes uploaded documents and extracts relevant information, presenting it in a structured and user-friendly format on a web interface. The application web interface confirms the successful processing of the document with a green status message. This interface is designed to facilitate ease of use, providing immediate feedback and a clear presentation of the extracted data as shown in Fig. 51.5.

51.4.2 Overall Assessment

We have collected 50 documents and test them using OOC systems. Table 51.2 shows the average processing time and the average accuracy. Based on the results, the average processing time for documents was determined to be 4.7134 seconds, with an accuracy rate of 88%. In contrast, it is impossible for a human to complete the entire process of reading, scanning, and storing a document within this time frame.

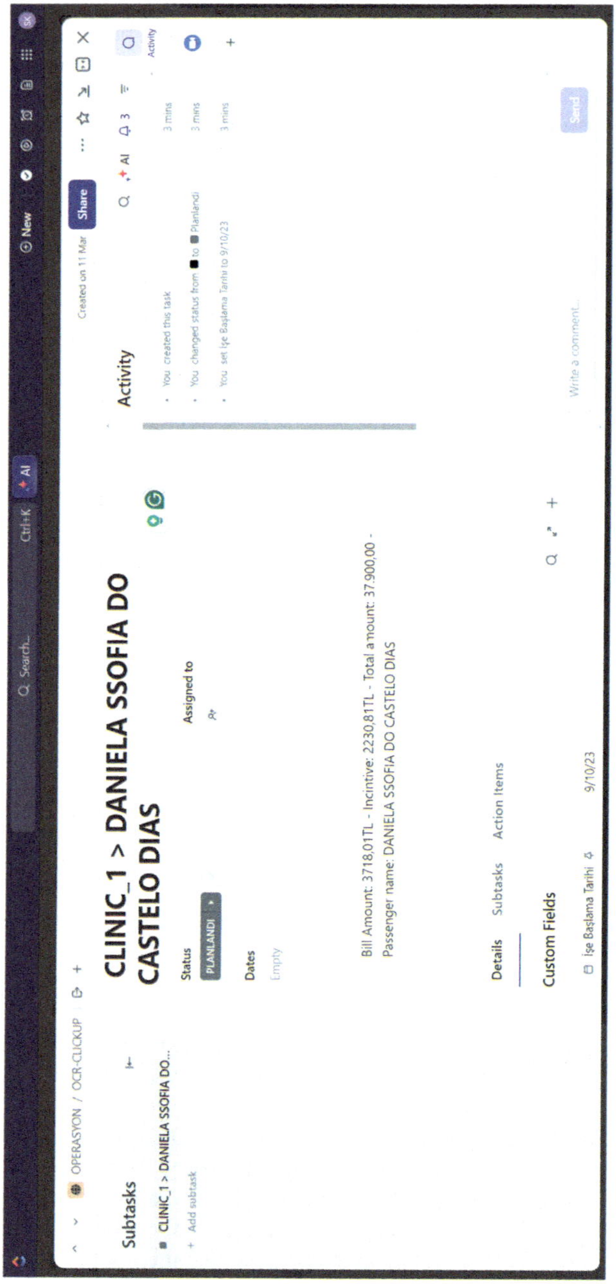

Fig. 51.5 CRM preview of the data stored

Table 51.2 Average processing time and accuracy of 50 documents

Model	Average proceeding time	Accuracy
OOC systems	4.7134 s	88%
Yimyam [20]	3 min	70–90% for low and high quality cash bill
HoangVan [8]	5–10 s	87% in F1-Score
Rohaime [15]	24.462 s and IQ Bot's needs 151.472 s	100% accuracy

51.4.3 Discussion

Table 51.2 compares the OOC with the state of the art in processing documents and text retrieval. In comparison to the findings of Yimyam [20], who presented a table illustrating the time efficiency of building payment slip processing using an OCR system, this study reveals notable differences. Yimyam demonstrated that their OCR-based approach significantly reduced the time required for gathering evidence and creating documents from 70 min (30 min for gathering evidence and 40 minutes for document creation) to just 3 min (2 min for gathering evidence and 1 min for document creation). The proposed framework OOC has reduced the average processing time for documents processing to 4.71 s, with an accuracy rate of 88%. Compared with Yimyam's [20] approach, a higher document accuracy rate underscores the potential trade-off between processing speed and accuracy in different OCR implementations.

51.5 Conclusion

The implementation of the OOC Model has demonstrated substantial improvements in the efficiency and accuracy of document processing within consulting firms. The study's findings show that by automating the information extraction and management process from documents, the system significantly reduces manual labor and human errors.

Furthermore, the integration enhances workflow management, enabling improved organization and quicker information access when needed. The innovative combination of OCR technology, AI analysis through OpenAI's GPT-3.5-turbo, and the organizational capabilities of the ClickUp API has proven to be a robust solution that not only streamlines operations but also provides a scalable model for handling large volumes of documents. This approach not only meets the current demands of document management but also sets a forward-thinking standard for future enhancements in similar business processes.

References

1. Alzaq-Osmanoglu, H., Alrehaili, J., Ustundag, B.B.: Low-snr modulation recognition based on deep learning on software defined radio. In: 2022 5th International Conference on Advanced Communication Technologies and Networking (CommNet), pp. 1–6 (2022). https://doi.org/10.1109/CommNet56067.2022.9993934
2. Arya, S., Kulkarni, M.S.: A comprehensive study of agile project management tools. In: 2024 4th International Conference on Innovative Practices in Technology and Management (ICIPTM), pp. 1–6. IEEE (2024)
3. Bulzan, A.S., Cernăzanu-Glavan, C., Marcu, M.G.: Exploring the potential of ocr integration for object detection in invoices. In: 2023 27th International Conference on System Theory, Control and Computing (ICSTCC), pp. 149–154 (2023). https://doi.org/10.1109/ICSTCC59206.2023.10308505
4. Das, S., Banerjee, P., Seraogi, B., Majumder, H., Mukkamala, S., Roy, R., Chaudhuri, B.B.: Hand-written and machine-printed text classification in architecture, engineering & construction documents. In: 2018 16th International Conference on Frontiers in Handwriting Recognition (ICFHR), pp. 546–551 (2018). https://doi.org/10.1109/ICFHR-2018.2018.00101
5. Goggins, E., Kennedy, C., Nguyen, M., Pore, A., Rissmeyer, A., Smith, C., Gerling, G.: Developing a project management tool for network migration to improve transparency between enterprises and network experts. In: 2023 Systems and Information Engineering Design Symposium (SIEDS), pp. 280–285. IEEE (2023)
6. Hambarde, K.A., Proenca, H.: Information retrieval: recent advances and beyond. IEEE Access (2023)
7. Hegghammer, T.: Ocr with tesseract, amazon textract, and google document ai: a benchmarking experiment. J. Comput. Soc. Sci. **5**(1), 861–882 (2022)
8. HoangVan, X., TranQuang, P., DinhBao, M., VuHuu, T.: Developing an OCR model for extracting information from invoices with Korean language. In: 2023 International Conference on Advanced Technologies for Communications (ATC), pp. 84–89 (2023). https://doi.org/10.1109/ATC58710.2023.10318877
9. Huang, Y., Huang, J.X.: Exploring chatgpt for next-generation information retrieval: opportunities and challenges. In: Web Intelligence. No. Preprint, IOS Press, pp. 1–14 (2024)
10. Mori, S., Suen, C., Yamamoto, K.: Historical review of ocr research and development. Proc. IEEE **80**(7), 1029–1058 (1992). https://doi.org/10.1109/5.156468
11. Panja, S.: Information retrieval systems in healthcare: understanding medical data through text analysis. In: Transformative Approaches to Patient Literacy and Healthcare Innovation. IGI Global, pp. 180–200 (2024)
12. Raj, R., Kos, A.: A comprehensive study of optical character recognition. In: 2022 29th International Conference on Mixed Design of Integrated Circuits and System (MIXDES), pp. 151–154 (2022). https://doi.org/10.23919/MIXDES55591.2022.9837974
13. Reddy, S.: Generative ai in healthcare: an implementation science informed translational path on application, integration and governance. Implement. Sci. **19**(1), 27 (2024)
14. Ribeiro, J., Lima, R., Eckhardt, T., Paiva, S.: Robotic process automation and artificial intelligence in industry 4.0–a literature review. Proc. Comput. Sci. **181**, 51–58 (2021)
15. Rohaime, N.A., Abdul Razak, N.I., Thamrin, N.M., Shyan, C.W.: Integrated invoicing solution: a robotic process automation with AI and OCR approach. In: 2022 IEEE 20th Student Conference on Research and Development (SCOReD), pp. 30–33 (2022). https://doi.org/10.1109/SCOReD57082.2022.9973841
16. Sharma, A., Kumar, S.: Machine learning and ontology-based novel semantic document indexing for information retrieval. Comput. Ind. Eng. **176**, 108940 (2023)
17. Shidaganti, G., Sanjana, R., Shubeeksh, K., Monish Raman, V., Thakshith, V.: ChatGPT: information retrieval from image using robotic process automation and OCR. In: 2023 7th International Conference on Intelligent Computing and Control Systems (ICICCS), pp. 1264–1270 (2023). https://doi.org/10.1109/ICICCS56967.2023.10142461

18. Wei, X., Cui, X., Cheng, N., Wang, X., Zhang, X., Huang, S., Xie, P., Xu, J., Chen, Y., Zhang, M., et al.: Zero-shot information extraction via chatting with chatgpt (2023). arXiv:2302.10205
19. Ye, J., Chen, X., Xu, N., Zu, C., Shao, Z., Liu, S., Cui, Y., Zhou, Z., Gong, C., Shen, Y., et al.: A comprehensive capability analysis of gpt-3 and gpt-3.5 series models (2023). arXiv:2303.10420
20. Yimyam, W., Ketcham, M., Jensuttiwetchakult, T., Hiranchan, S., Pramkeaw, P., Chumuang, N.: Enhancing and evaluating an impact of OCR and ontology on financial document checking process. In: 2020 15th International Joint Symposium on Artificial Intelligence and Natural Language Processing (iSAI-NLP), pp. 1–6 (2020). https://doi.org/10.1109/iSAI-NLP51646.2020.9376808

Chapter 52
GitHubShare: A Mobile Application for Sharing Software Projects Via GitHub

Hasan Ali Çalişkan and Hüsamettin Osmanoğlu

Abstract This paper presents an experience-sharing project aimed at overcoming the challenges faced during mobile application development to meet user needs. The mobile application, designed to address the issues encountered by individuals interested in software and provide effective solutions, is thoroughly examined, including its components, and technological approaches. Key elements such as the methodology used, architectural choices, database design, security measures, and cloud services are detailed. The outcome is a mobile application named GitHub-Share, demonstrating that the development process can be successfully completed with the appropriate technological approach and methodology.

Keywords GitHub · Collaborative software development · AWS service · Mobile application

52.1 Introduction

GitHub, [5], is a web-based platform that facilitates collaborative software development and version control using Git, a distributed version control system (DVCS) used primarily for managing and tracking changes in source code during software development. GitHub platform provides tools for developers to host, review, and manage code repositories, as well as to track changes and collaborate with others on projects. GitHub offers features such as issue tracking, pull requests, code review, project management, and continuous integration, making it a popular choice for both open-source and private software development projects. With its widespread adoption, GitHub has become a central hub for developers to share code, contribute to projects, and collaborate with peers globally.

H. A. Çalişkan
Biruni University, Istanbul, Turkey
e-mail: 200404004@st.biruni.edu.tr

H. Osmanoğlu (✉)
Istinye University, Istanbul, Turkey
e-mail: husamettim.osmanoglu@istinye.edu.tr

F. P. García Márquez et al. (eds.), *Computing, Internet of Things and Data Analytics*, Smart Innovation, Systems and Technologies 387,
https://doi.org/10.1007/978-3-031-87154-2_52

In this work, the design and development of a mobile application developed to address two fundamental challenges encountered by individuals interested in software are discussed. The first challenge is the difficulty software project creators face in promoting their projects to wider audiences [15]. For instance, existing platforms are often complex and fragmented, providing limited access to project owners [10]. Additionally, a third-party plugins called Actions, is used to enable developers to easily create Workflows by referencing Actions rather than specifying all of the step without the ability so share the project [13].

The second challenge is the uncertainty individuals interested in software face in determining which courses to take to improve the user skills in their chosen software areas [2]. Existing solutions in this field are often outdated and do not provide a personalized learning experience [16].

The mobile application developed in this work, known as GitHubShare, is designed to address these two challenges. The application allows users to easily share their projects from their own GitHub accounts with multiple users. Moreover, it give the users a rich access to educational content provided by BTK Academy.

The content of this paper is organized as follows. Section 52.2 defines the problem that encounters the new developers. Section 52.3 describes the key components of the GitHubShare model. Section 52.4 presents both the mobile application and the software platform used in the study. Finally, in Sect. 52.5, concluding remarks are provided to summarize the findings and implications of the study.

52.2 Problem Definition

GitHub is an essential tool for developing programming competencies due to its comprehensive features that support version control, collaboration, learning, portfolio building, project management, tool integration, and community engagement [5, 14]. By actively using GitHub, developers can enhance their skills, collaborate more effectively, and gain visibility in the programming community.

In other words, GitHub fosters a vibrant community where developers can seek help, share knowledge, and collaborate on projects. Features like discussions, wikis, and GitHub Pages provide platforms for community interaction. Additionally, its vast ecosystem includes repositories dedicated to learning resources, such as coding tutorials, programming challenges, and educational materials. These resources are invaluable for both beginners and experienced developers looking to expand their skills [5, 15].

The proposed application, GitHubShare, aims to improve the learning process and engage new developers with experts in the community. App companies use GitHub to enhance their operations in various ways that contribute to their valuation in the digital attention economy. By fostering collaboration, engaging with the developer community, leveraging efficient project management tools, and promoting transparency and innovation, companies can improve their products, retain users, and increase their market valuation. GitHub's role in these processes underscores its importance as a tool for developing competencies and driving success in the competitive digital landscape. GitHubShare embodies these principles by facilitating meaningful interactions between novice and experienced developers, thereby enriching the community and enhancing the overall learning experience.

52.3 Resources and Methodology

GitHubShare consists of a mobile application developed using the Kotlin programming language [7] and Android Studio [8], along with back-end services written in Java programming language with the Spring Boot framework [9]. PostgreSQL database is used in the Project as a back-end.

52.3.1 MVVM (Model-View-ViewModel) Architecture

In the dynamic world of mobile application development, selecting the right architecture is crucial for enhancing user experience and minimizing maintenance costs. In this context, we adopted the MVVM (Model-View-ViewModel) architecture in our project to establish a robust and modular structure.

Thanks to this architecture, we ensured that the code is modular and easy to maintain. The key features of our mobile application include:

- Model: Represents the business logic, including interactions with the database, API calls, and local data storage.
- View: Contains the user interface, displaying information to the user. Activities, fragments, and XML files belong to this layer.
- ViewModel: Facilitates the connection between the Model and View. It processes user interactions, updates the user interface by transforming data from the Model to the View.

This structure (Fig. 52.1) has facilitated the independent development and testing of each component within the GitHubShare application. Furthermore, it simplifies the process of making changes to the user interface or updating the business logic, reducing overall complexity [1].

52.3.2 OAuth Github

In today's software development field, the sharing and interaction of projects hold significant importance. However, it is equally critical to ensure that each user can

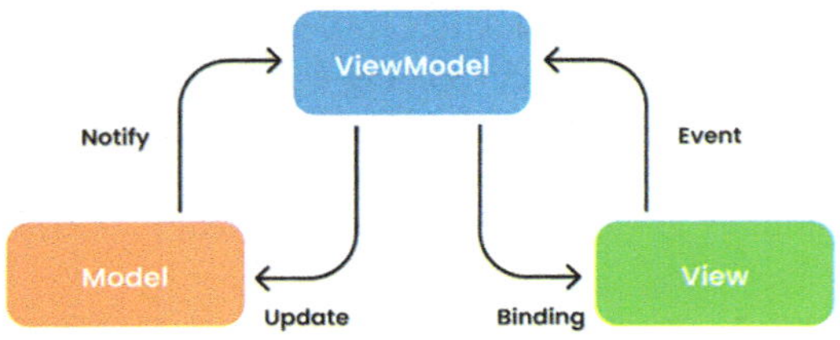

Fig. 52.1 The architecture of MVVM

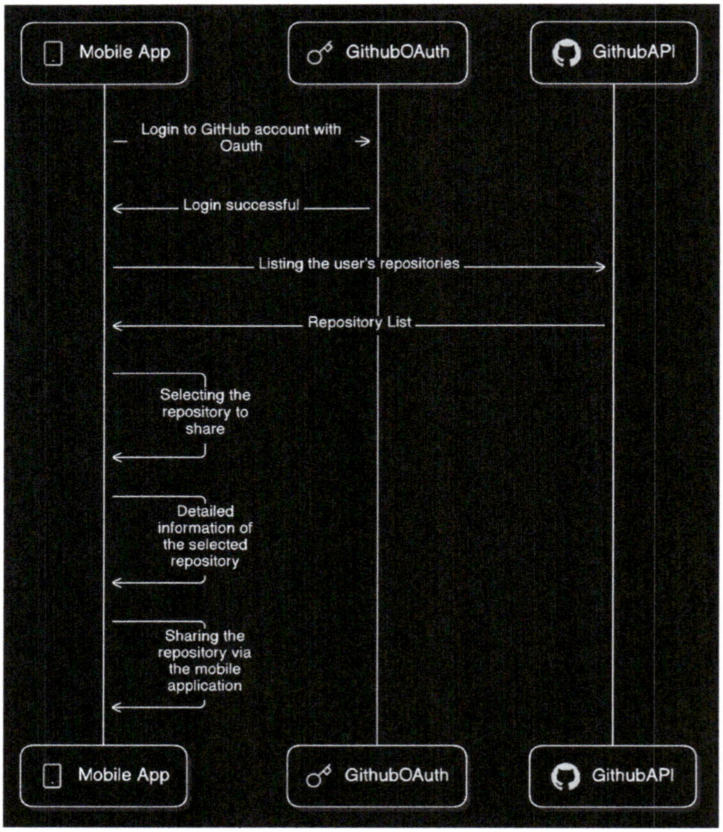

Fig. 52.2 Using GitHub OAuth technology

only share their own projects and to provide a controlled environment from a security standpoint. To address this, the proposed system implements a structure where users can only share repositories from their own GitHub accounts using GitHub OAuth technology, as illustrated in Fig. 52.2.

GitHub OAuth is an authentication protocol that enables users to grant access and authorize applications securely. This protocol allows users to securely access the application using their GitHub credentials. OAuth enables third-party applications to perform certain actions on behalf of users.

Within GitHubShare, GitHub OAuth technology was integrated to allow users to only share repositories from their own GitHub accounts. As a result, each user gains the authority to share their projects by logging into the application with their GitHub accounts.

- GitHub Authentication: Users log into our application via their GitHub accounts. At this stage, the GitHub OAuth protocol authenticates the user and grants access to our application.
- Authorization Control: Among the permissions granted by the user to our application, access is restricted to only their own repositories and account information. This is achieved by configuring the scope of OAuth protocol permissions.
- Sharing Own Repositories: Users can select and share only repositories from their own GitHub accounts through the interface within the application. This allows users to securely share their own projects with other users.

With this method, we have established a secure authentication process in GitHubShare application, enabling users to only share their own projects. Thus, the security of our application and a user-controlled environment were ensured.

52.3.3 Back-End

The server side involves establishing the back-end service and database, which operate within a foundational layer of the system. GitHubShare, built with a PostgreSQL database, is enriched with several key tables:

- Users: Contains user information, such as user name, GitHub username, rank, and points.
- Comments: Stores comments made on user posts.
- Posts: Holds the details of the user posts shared within the application.
- SoftwareBranch: Categorizes and determines various software domains. Course: Stores detailed information about BTK Academy courses.

These tables collectively enhance the application's content richness and user experience by supporting various functionalities. Basic user information is complemented by data on comments, post likes, and the popularity of different software domains. The structure enables users to interact more effectively and gain insights into trending topics and relevant educational resources, ultimately fostering a more engaging and informative environment within the GitHubShare.

Authentication processes is handled using the FluentValidation library [6]. To ensure the smooth operation of the back-end systems, we have implemented the

Object-Oriented programming model. For efficient system operation, we have employed the Dependency Injection method and utilize the Autofac package, which supports Aspect Oriented Programming (AOP) infrastructure [11]. JSON Web Token (JWT) technology will facilitate secure data exchange and validation between parties [17]. Web API technology have been utilized for communication with the mobile application, with Swagger-UI and Postman serving as tools for managing various services.

52.3.4 AWS (Amazon Web Services)

In GitHubShare, we have implemented a backend server, written in Spring Boot, and integrated it with a PostgreSQL database using AWS's EC2 (Elastic Compute Cloud) and RDS (Relational Database Service) services to establish a robust and scalable infrastructure, as shown in Fig. 52.3.

The following steps have been considered while design the server.

1. Creating EC2 Instance: We accessed the EC2 service through the AWS Management Console and created a new EC2 instance. Ubuntu Server was selected, and security groups were configured appropriately.
2. Deploying Spring Boot Application: We connected to the EC2 instance via SSH and transferred the necessary dependencies and application files to the instance to deploy our Spring Boot application.
3. Starting the Application: Commands were executed on the instance to start our application, bringing it into service.

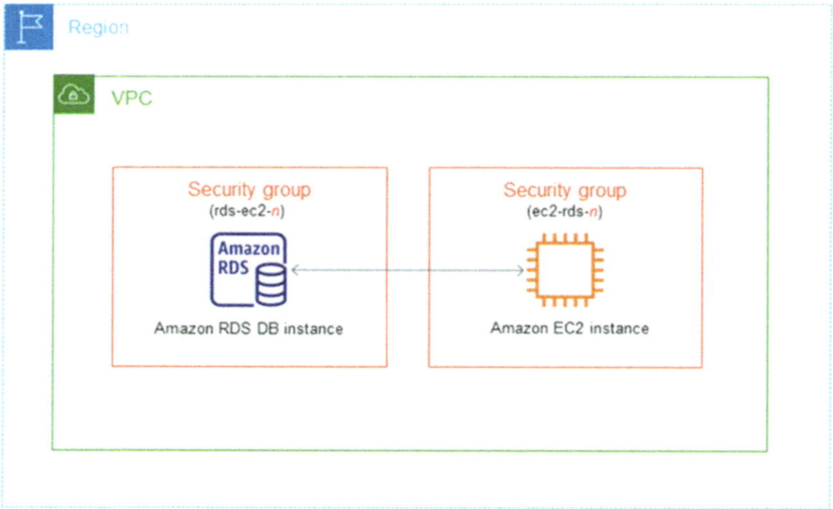

Fig. 52.3 EC2–RDS Relationship Schema

4. Creating RDS Database: We accessed the RDS service through the AWS Management Console and created a new PostgreSQL database.
5. Retrieving Database Connection Information: The connection information for the created RDS database was obtained. This information was used for our Spring Boot application to connect to the database.
6. Database Configuration in Spring Boot Application: Necessary configurations were made in the application.properties or application.yml file of our application to connect to the RDS database.

52.4 GitHubShare Application and Results

GitHubShare provides a platform that caters to the needs of individuals interested in software by facilitating project sharing, education, and interaction. Among the broad impact areas of the project is the opportunity for individuals who are new to the software field or looking to improve to create an ecosystem by sharing software projects within the application. This allows them to inspire each other and enhance their development by drawing inspiration from one another.

The GitHubShare application has mainly three features. The first feature is the ability for users to create posts. When the user creates a post, he will be required to enter the software project that he want to share a description of the software project they want to share, and the GitHub address of the software project. To ensure that users only share software projects from their own GitHub addresses, OAuth technology will be used to authenticate their GitHub accounts. Using OAuth Github prevents users from sharing software projects that do not belong to them.

The second feature is the trending software areas screen (Fig. 52.4). This screen will be created by analyzing the number of likes on posts in the application. Through this screen, users can easily understand which areas have the most software projects created. The third feature is the education recommendations screen (Fig. 52.4). Users can access recommended training content from BTK Academy [3, 4] related to any software area they click on in the trending software areas screen. Users are directed to this screen when they click on a software area in the trending screen. Thus, users can access educational materials related to the software area they are interested in without leaving the application. Through this screen, users can directly access courses related to the software area they are interested in without having to make a separate effort to research them. This feature enhances the application by supporting users in improving their software knowledge and advancing their careers, making it more comprehensive and user-friendly. The addresses of this training content are stored in the database. In addition, updates can be made to the database in case of possible changes in the training content.

Unit, integration, and end-to-end tests are used to verify the accuracy, behavior, and usability of the mobile application. These tests are conducted using the JUnit 5 [12] and Truth libraries [18] provided by Android. Any code errors or performance losses identified as a result of the tests will be addressed.

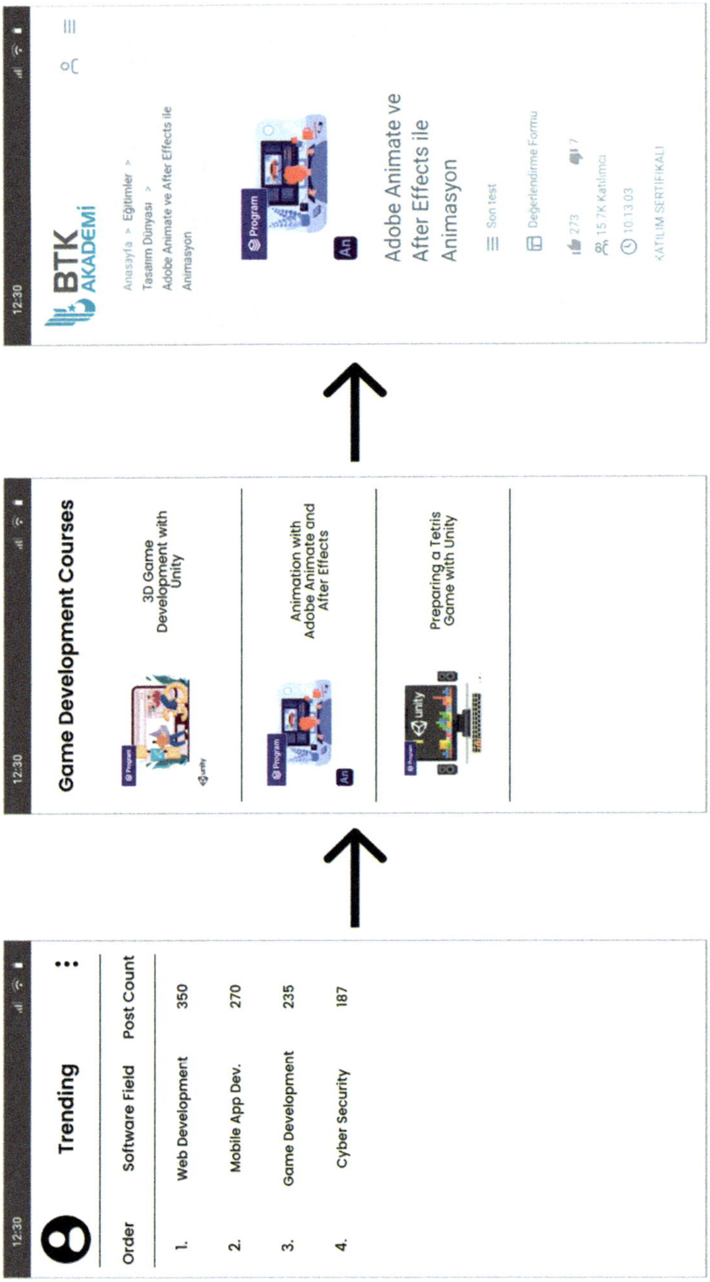

Fig. 52.4 The main page of GitHubShare to create new post

52.4.1 Mobile Application

Mobile applications are context-oriented systems that rely on context information during operation [11]. Therefore, addressing context information is crucial in the early stages of software engineering for mobile applications. Developing a context-aware system requires a unique approach to managing the impact of context on the system.

The main screen of our mobile application provides an easy access to posts made by other users (Fig. 52.5a). These posts include the users' profile pictures, GitHub usernames, post content, software domain, programming language, and details of the GitHub projects they've shared. Users can like and comment on these posts. Additionally, they can customize their experience by filtering posts according to

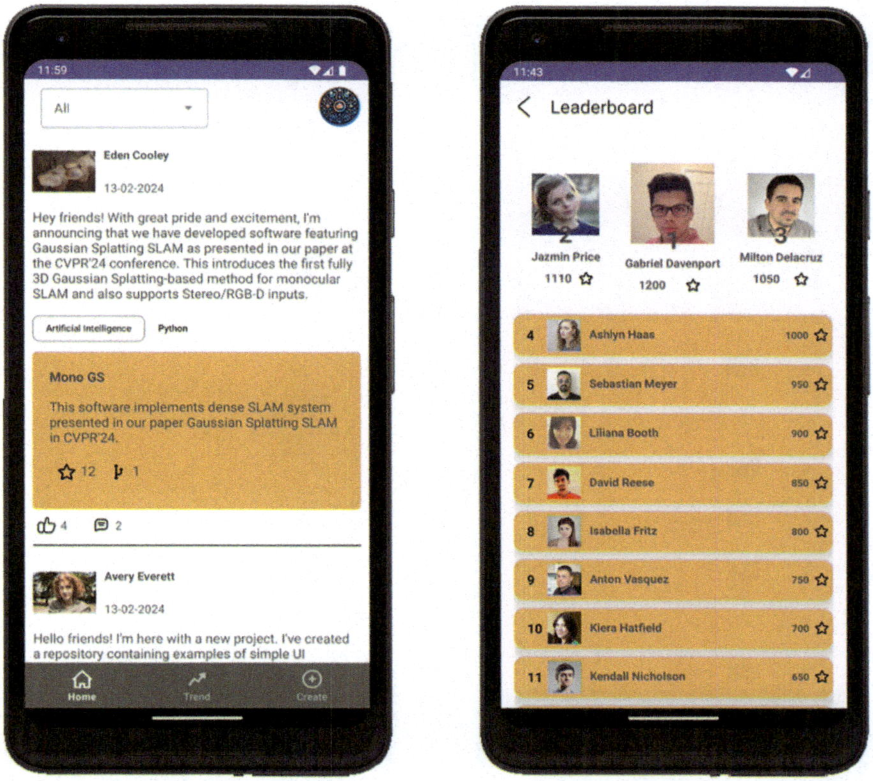

A. B.

Fig. 52.5 The main page of GitHubShare to create new post software domains. For example, they can focus on specific software domains such as web development or AI to find relevant content more easily.

Another features is users listings (Fig. 52.5b), in which users gain more points and rise in the ranking as they post more and receive more likes and comments. This dynamic ranking system motivates users further and encourages them to spend more time in the application. Users are encouraged to actively produce content to climb the ranks, while also having the opportunity to observe the success of other users and engage in a competitive environment to improve themselves.

A table of trending software domains is shown in Fig. 52.6a. For example, topics such as artificial intelligence, web development, and cybersecurity are listed in this table. The table is generated by analyzing users' posts. Posts tagged with relevant software domains are ranked higher in the table based on the comments and likes they receive. This provides users with information about which domains are trending in

Fig. 52.6 Trend screen and BTK academy courses [3]

the software market. Users can use this information to create a valuable roadmap for their careers by focusing on trending and popular software domains. Additionally, this screen helps users acquire up-to-date information and specialize in topics of interest.

The last screen, relevant courses listed by BTK Academy are displayed in Fig. 52.6b. When the user clicks on a software name in the trending screen, they are directed to course screen. Thus, users can access educational materials related to the software domain they are interested in without leaving the application. Through this screen, users can directly access courses related to the software domain they are interested in without having to make a separate effort to research them. This feature enhances the application by supporting users in improving their software knowledge and advancing their careers, making it more comprehensive and user-friendly.

52.5 Conclusion

The distinguishing feature of GitHubShare lies in its pioneering approach, which diverges from existing literature. Upon reviewing platforms that utilize GitHub for content creation, such as CodersClub, and online education platforms like Alison and BTK Academy, it becomes evident that our project stands out by amalgamating these platforms into a more comprehensive solution. One of the significant aspects of GitHubShare is its potential to foster an ecosystem where newcomers to the software field, as well as those seeking improvement, can share their software projects within the application. This platform facilitates a supportive community where users can inspire and learn from each other, promoting mutual growth and development. In future work, we aim to enhance GitHubShare by integrating artificial intelligence agents to provide personalized recommendations for BTK Academy courses to users, further enriching their learning experience and supporting their career advancement.

Acknowledgements This study was funded by TÜBİTAK 2209 with Project No: 1919B012307527.

References

1. Alzaq-Osmanoglu, H.: Student attendance system using itag's beacon detection. In: 2023 20th International Multi-Conference on Systems, Signals & Devices (SSD), pp. 985–989 (2023). https://doi.org/10.1109/SSD58187.2023.10411312
2. Braga, P.H.P., Hébert, K., Hudgins, E.J., Scott, E.R., Edwards, B.P., Sánchez Reyes, L.L., Grainger, M.J., Foroughirad, V., Hillemann, F., Binley, A.D., et al.: Not just for programmers: How github can accelerate collaborative and reproducible research in ecology and evolution. Methods Ecol. Evol. **14**(6), 1364–1380 (2023)
3. BTK: Btk academy (2022). https://www.btk.dental/en/prodotti/btk-academy/
4. Çivril, H., Aruğaslan, E.: A study on face-to-face exam experiences of distance education students. J. Limitless Educ. Res. **8**(1), 117–157 (2023)

5. Färber, M.: Analyzing the github repositories of research papers. In: Proceedings of the ACM/IEEE Joint Conference on Digital Libraries in 2020, pp. 491–492 (2020)
6. FluentValidation: Fluentvalidation (2022). https://docs.fluentvalidation.net/en/latest/
7. Foundation, K.: Kotlin Programming Language (2021). https://kotlinlang.org/
8. Google, J.: Android studio & app tools-android developers (2013). https://developer.android.com/studio
9. Google, J.: Spring Boot (2014). https://spring.io/projects/spring-boot
10. Hata, H., Novielli, N., Baltes, S., Kula, R.G., Treude, C.: Github discussions: an exploratory study of early adoption. Empir. Soft. Eng. **27**, 1–32 (2022)
11. Idate, S.R., Rao, T.S., Mali, D.J.: Context-based aspect-oriented requirement engineering model. Eng. Technol. Appl. Sci. Res. **13**(2), 10460–10465 (2023)
12. Junit5: The 5th major version of the programmer-friendly testing framework for java and the jvm (2022). https://junit.org/junit5
13. Kinsman, T., Wessel, M., Gerosa, M.A., Treude, C.: How do software developers use github actions to automate their workflows? In: 2021 IEEE/ACM 18th International Conference on Mining Software Repositories (MSR), pp. 420–431. IEEE (2021)
14. Mastropaolo, A., Pascarella, L., Guglielmi, E., Ciniselli, M., Scalabrino, S., Oliveto, R., Bavota, G.: On the robustness of code generation techniques: an empirical study on github copilot. In: 2023 IEEE/ACM 45th International Conference on Software Engineering (ICSE), pp. 2149–2160. IEEE (2023)
15. Meng, N., Dong, Y., Roehrs, D., Luan, L.: Tackle implementation challenges in project-based learning: a survey study of pbl e-learning platforms. Educ. Technol. Res. Dev. **71**(3), 1179–1207 (2023)
16. Ramasamy, D., Sarasua, C., Bacchelli, A., Bernstein, A.: Workflow analysis of data science code in public github repositories. Empir. Softw. Eng. **28**(1), 7 (2023)
17. Royani, M.R., Wibowo, A., et al.: Web service implementation in logistics company uses json web token and rc4 cryptography algorithm. Jurnal RESTI (Rekayasa Sistem dan Teknologi Informasi) **4**(3), 591–600 (2020)
18. Truth: Fluent assertions for java and android (2022). https://truth.dev/

Chapter 53
Human Pose Estimation Based on Multiscale and Multilevel Feature Fusion Method

Mengjiao Sun, Ying Zhang, and Shuo Man

Abstract Due to changes in scale during feature extraction, human pose estimation networks often experience a loss of positional data, which compromises their precision. In order to improve human pose estimation, this study investigated the use of multi-tier feature extraction with multi-scale feature fusion in both spatial and channel dimensions. The hourglass network was used as the backbone, with multi-tiered features repeatedly employed from top-down to bottom-up to capture the spatial coordinates of each joint point. By integrating Atrous Spatial Pyramid Pooling (ASPP) and concurrent spatial and channel squeeze & excitation (scSE), a hybrid-atrous convolutional pooling pyramid network was constructed to facilitate multi-scale feature extraction and fusion, thereby minimizing the loss of feature information. An optimized pose estimation method based on feature fusion was proposed. The experimental results on the MPII dataset demonstrate that the proposed method achieves an accuracy of 92.9%, thus validating its ability to address scale variations in pose estimation and enhance the accuracy of human pose estimation.

53.1 Introduction

Human pose estimation is to accurately construct human pose from images or videos, and then realize applications such as human–computer interaction [1], motion analysis [2, 3], intelligent surveillance [4] and so on. However, due to the complexity and diversity of human poses in images or videos, it is a challenging task to accurately capture and describe human poses.

The specific challenge faced by human pose estimation task is how to improve the detection effect of small-scale human without affecting the detection effect of large-scale human [5, 6]. That is, in the process of network feature extraction, we should not only obtain high-quality high-resolution feature maps to locate small-scale human

M. Sun (✉) · Y. Zhang · S. Man
School of Electrical and Control Engineering, Shenyang Jianzhu University, Shenyang, China
e-mail: 1064772853@qq.com

F. P. García Márquez et al. (eds.), *Computing, Internet of Things and Data Analytics*, Smart Innovation, Systems and Technologies 387,
https://doi.org/10.1007/978-3-031-87154-2_53

bodies, but also pay attention to low-resolution feature maps to locate some difficult key points of human bodies that need context information [7–9]. Feature fusion is a commonly used strategy to improve the performance of human pose estimation. By fusing different features, human pose estimation algorithms can better deal with occlusion and complex poses, improve accuracy and robustness. Typical parallel networks are: HRNet [10], HRARNet [11], DNSNet [12], can integrate multi-scale features through parallel fusion and step-by-step fusion, but there are shortcomings in the mining and utilization of multi-level features. Typical serial networks are: Hourglass [13], CPN [14], DM-GHP [15], UformPose [16], CGARPN [17], can improve the richness and discrimination of features by fusing features at different levels, but obtaining and recovering feature information through up-down sampling will cause the problem of feature loss.

Based on this, this paper proposes a human pose estimation network optimized by multi-scale feature fusion, called SAHNet. SAHNet uses Hourglass as the backbone to realize multi-scale feature fusion between different levels, and atrous Spatial Pyramid Pooling (ASPP) [18] and concurrent spatial and channel squeeze & excitation (scSE) [19] were fused to build a hybrid-atrous convolutional pooling pyramid network designs scSE-ASPP to efficiently realize multi-scale feature extraction within different stages, so as to realize the simultaneous fusion of deep features, shallow features, and multi-scale features.

53.2 Method

53.2.1 Overall Structure of SAHNet

The overall structure of the SAHNet network is shown in Fig. 53.1, and the network mainly consists of two parts: Hourglass backbone network, and scSE-ASPP feature extraction module.

Firstly, the Hourglass network extracts features by constructing two hourglass blocks and uses skip connections to add the deep semantic information obtained by downsampling and the high-resolution features recovered by upsampling. This helps to enrich the spatial information and semantic features in the feature map.The image resolution of the input model is 256×256. In order to save memory, it goes through a convolution layer with the size of the convolution kernel of 7×7, slide of 2 and pad of 3 at the beginning, and the number of output layers is 128. This is followed by a residual module and max pooling to reduce the resolution to 64×64, which is also the input and output resolution of the fourth-order Hourglass module in the network.

Then, before each down-sampling, the scSE-ASPP feature extraction module is inserted into the four-layer down-sampling of Hourglass to extract multi-scale features inside the hierarchy, so as to make up for the lack of multi-scale interaction inside the hierarchy when fusing the high-level and low-level features of Hourglass.

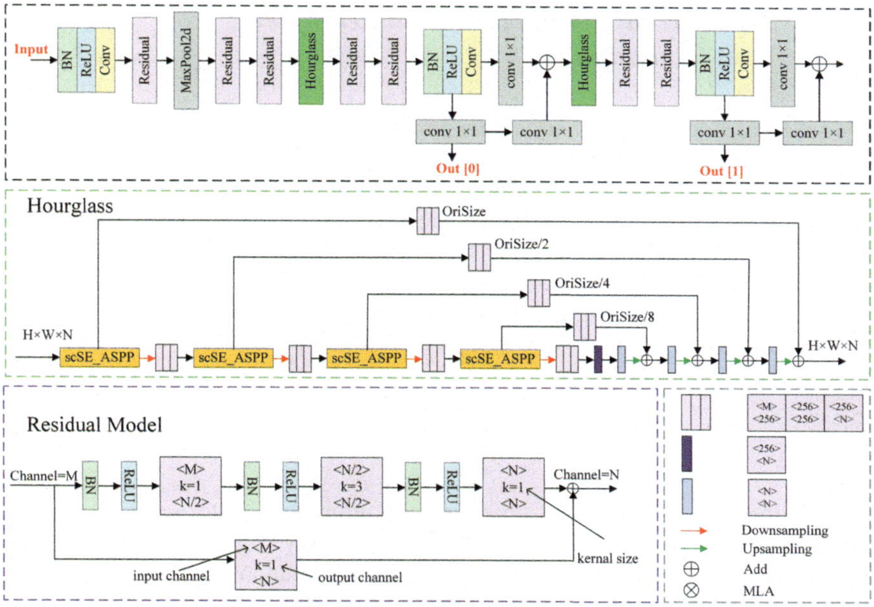

Fig. 53.1 The SAHNet structure

Finally, the output of the figure has out{0} and out{1}. After a 1 × 1 fully convolutional network, the mixed features extracted by the first Hourglass structure are divided into two branches. One branch continues to go through the 1 × 1 convolution and enters the next hourglass network. After a 1 × 1 convolution of the two branches, the Heat Map is generated, which is out{0}. The number of channels in the out{0} matrix is the number of predicted human keypoints, set to [64, 64, N_ Landmark], and the depth of other positions is just the number of channels representing the feature, such as [64, 64, 256]. out{0} continues through 1 × 1 convolution to adjust the number of channels to be consistent with one branch, such as 256, and finally merges with one branch and acts as the input of the next Hourglass network together with the input of the previous layer Hourglass. The arrow at the bottom of the structure has no output meaning and only means that the hourglass module can be stacked continuously.

In general, through multi-scale and multi-level feature representation, SAHNet can better adapt to human pose estimation tasks in different environments and achieve higher accuracy and robustness.

53.2.2 Concurrent Spatial and Channel Squeeze and Excitation

The scSE calculation flow chart is shown in Fig. 53.2.

The cSE module introduces the channel attention mechanism to effectively integrate and enhance the feature information of the channel dimension. Figure 53.2a shows the calculation flow chart. Firstly, the dimension of the feature map is changed from $[C, H, W]$ to $[C, 1, 1]$ through the global average pooling layer, and the feature $\mathbf{U} = [\mathbf{u}_1, \mathbf{u}_2, \cdots, \mathbf{u}_C]$ is input, among which $\mathbf{u}_i \in \mathbb{R}^{H\times W}$ is generated by the global average pooling to generate vector $\mathbf{z} \in \mathbb{R}^{1\times 1\times C}$, whose KTH element can be calculated as:

$$z_k = \frac{1}{H\times W}\sum_i^H\sum_j^W \mathbf{u}_k(i,j) \tag{53.1}$$

This operation encompasses global spatial information into vector z, which is converted to $\hat{\mathbf{z}} = \mathbf{W}_1(\delta(\mathbf{W}_2\mathbf{z}))$, which $\mathbf{W}_1 \in \mathbb{R}^{C\times \frac{C}{2}}$, $\mathbf{W}_2 \in \mathbb{R}^{\frac{C}{2}\times C}$, and then normalized using the sigmoid function to obtain the corresponding weight vector $\sigma(\hat{\mathbf{z}})$. Finally, by channel-wise multiplication with the original feature map, the feature map $\mathbf{U}$ calibrated with channel information is obtained with the following equation, which activation $\hat{\mathbf{z}} = \mathbf{W}_1(\delta(\mathbf{W}_2\mathbf{z}))$ represents the channel information of the ith channel.

$$\hat{\mathbf{U}}_{cSE} = F_{cSE}(\mathbf{U}) = \left[\sigma(\hat{z_1})\mathbf{u}_1, \sigma(\hat{z_2})\mathbf{u}_2, \cdots, \sigma(\hat{z_C})\mathbf{u}_C\right] \tag{53.2}$$

The sSE module expands information enhancement integration in the spatial dimension of the feature map, and the calculation flow chart is shown in Fig. 53.2b.

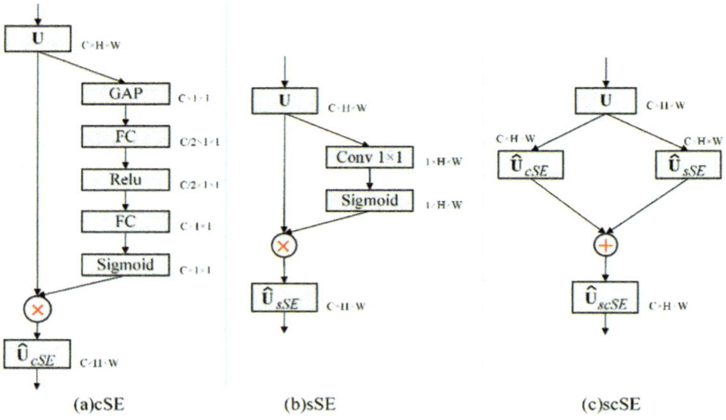

Fig. 53.2 Flow chart of scSE calculation

The feature map is passed through a convolution layer with output channel 1 and convolution kernel size 1 × 1 to obtain a weight matrix with dimension $\widehat{\mathbf{U}}_{scSE} = \widehat{\mathbf{U}}_{cSE} + \widehat{\mathbf{U}}_{sSE}$. The input tensors which correspond to spatial locations, where the spatial compression operation is done by convolution $q = W_{sq} \star U$, which $\mathbf{z} \in \mathbb{R}^{1\times 1\times C}$ generates projection tensors $\mathbf{q} \in \mathbb{R}^{H\times W}$. Each $q_{i,j}$ representing spatial locations (i, j) on all channels C. This projection rescaled the activations through the sigmoid layer σ(•)to the spatially recalibrated **U** equation is as follows, where $\sigma(q_{i,j})$ is the spatial information in feature Figure (i, j).

$$\widehat{\mathbf{U}}_{sSE} = F_{sSE}(\mathbf{U}) = \left[\sigma(q_{1,1})\mathbf{u}^{1,1}, \cdots, \sigma(q_{i,j})\mathbf{u}^{i,j}, \cdots, \sigma(q_{H,W})\mathbf{u}^{H,W}\right] \quad (53.3)$$

The scSE module integrates the sSE and cSE modules, merging information from both channel and spatial dimensions. The resulting features are additive across the channel dimension. The formula is as follows.

$$\widehat{\mathbf{U}}_{scSE} = \widehat{\mathbf{U}}_{cSE} + \widehat{\mathbf{U}}_{sSE} \quad (53.4)$$

53.2.3 *Atrous Spatial Pyramid Pooling*

When extracting features between different scales, considering that features of different resolution sizes have different contributions to the fused features, ASPP is used for multi-scale feature extraction. In the extraction process, the feature images are sampled at different sampling rates, and the given input is sampled in parallel with the dilated convolution of 6, 12, 18 sampling rates respectively. The obtained results are concatenated together to expand the number of channels, and then the number of channels is reduced to the expected value by 1 × 1 convolution. The equation of feature map o is as follows.

$$o = \frac{i + 2p - k - (k - 1) * (d - 1)}{s} + 1 \quad (53.5)$$

which i is the size of the input hole convolution, p is the sampling rate, s is the step size, k is the original size of the convolution kernel, d is a hyperparameter introduced, and the value $(d - 1)$ is the number of Spaces squeezed. The final scSE-ASPP realizes the multi-scale interaction inside the Hourglass hierarchy. The equation of the scSE-ASPP output feature map is as follows.

$$\mathbf{U}_{out} = o \times \widehat{\mathbf{U}}_{cSE} + o \times \widehat{\mathbf{U}}_{sSE} \quad (53.6)$$

53.2.4 ScSE-ASPP Module

The proposed scSE-ASPP module includes an ASPP parallel network and a scSE attention mechanism module, whose main role is to realize the integration and enhancement of features and effective extraction and fusion, so as to obtain rich context information. The complete structure is shown in Fig. 53.3.

ASPP captures different levels of contextual information by introducing multiple parallel branches in the network, each using dilated convolution and pooling operations at different scales. By using different void rates for dilated convolution, the receptive field can be expanded, resulting in broader contextual information. At the same time, the pooling operation can aggregate information at different scales and increase the network's perception ability of objects and structures at different scales.

The scSE-ASPP module multiplies the original input features of the ASPP module with the weight values generated in the channel dimension and the weight values generated in the spatial dimension of the scSE module respectively, and then adds them as input features. The features are repeatedly blended at multiple scales, and the high-resolution representation is maintained throughout the network to make the final output features more abundant.

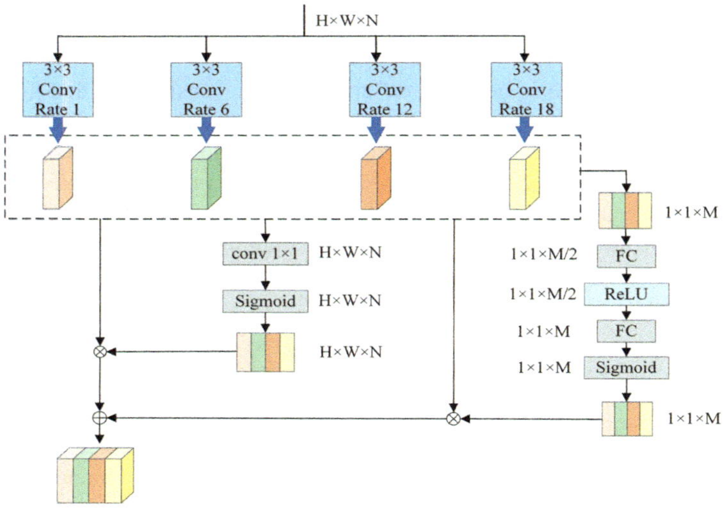

Fig. 53.3 Diagram of the scSE-ASPP network structure

53.3 Experimental Section

53.3.1 Dataset and Evaluation Metrics

The MPII data set published by Max Planck Institute is used as the experimental data. MPII dataset encompasses approximately 40,000 human instances. Each labeled with 16 key points including the head, upper neck, ears, shoulders, elbows, wrists, hips, knees, and ankles. The evaluation index is $PCKh$ score, which is the head normalized probability of correct keypoint:

$$PCKh = \sum_{n} \frac{\|P - G\|^2}{\alpha L^{head}} \cdot \frac{V_{(n-1)}}{c} \tag{53.7}$$

which P is the keypoint location predicted by the network, G is the true keypoint location, L^{head} represents the diagonal length of the header bounding box label, α is a constant that determines the correct keypoint location within the range, V is the visibility matrix, c is the total number of visibility flags in V, and n is the batch size of the input image. The experiments on the MPII dataset were tested with $PCKh@0.5(\alpha = 0.5)$ as the evaluation criterion.

53.3.2 Experimental Environment and Setup

The experimental environment is Ubuntu 20.04.6 operating system, GPU is GeForce RTX 3090, Pytorch version 1.10.1, Python version 3.8, and the batch size of input images is 16. In order to make a fair comparison with other methods, the input size of the MPII dataset was trimmed to 256 × 256 during the whole training process, the network used Adam optimizer, the initial learning rate was set to 1e-3, and was reduced to 1e-4 and 1e-5 in the 170th and 200th rounds, respectively, and the training cycle was 210 rounds. The same detection way of Hourglass is followed during the testing process, and the official original provided human frame is used in the MPII data set.

53.3.3 Experimental Results and Analysis

In order to verify the superiority of the improved algorithm, the SAHNet is compared with the mainstream algorithms in the case of using the backbone network with different input channels. The comparison results on MPII validation set are shown in Table 53.1. Compared with Hourglass and MobileNet, the proposed method has achieved higher detection accuracy for different keypoints. Compared with MSSA, SAHNet has higher accuracy and average accuracy for the rest of the parts except for the slightly lower detection rate of the head. In addition, for the detection effect of different parts of the human body, except that the ankle and knee have a slightly worse ratio with MSPN, and the detection effect of the head is slightly worse than that of MSSA, the SAHNet has the highest detection accuracy of 92.9% in other parts.

Ablation experiment. The MPII validation set is selected as the test data of the ablation experiment to evaluate the effectiveness of each part of SAHNet. The results of the ablation experiment are shown in Table 53.2. All ablation experiments were carried out under the condition that the backbone was 2-stage HG and the input image size was 256 × 256. According to the influence of scSE-ASPP module on the accuracy of human pose estimation network, four network models were tested: The first experiment uses the original Hourglass algorithm. The second trial demonstrated the results from ASPP alone. The third experiment shows the results obtained after only adding the scSE module to the output. Experiment IV shows the results obtained using scSE-ASPP, that is the results of SAHNet.

Experimental results show that thanks to the improvement of the SAHNet feature fusion strategy, Hourglass improves the feature extraction ability at different scales. Among them, the multi-level feature representation enables the network to gradually learn the abstract pose representation from low to high level, and can capture the pose details and correlation information from local to global. Multi-scale feature representation enables the network to process posture information at different scales at the

Table 53.1 Comparison of different algorithms on MPII validation set

Method	Hea (%)	Sho (%)	Elb (%)	Wri (%)	Hip (%)	Kne (%)	Ank (%)	Mean (%)
Deeppose	95.8	94.2	88.7	82.5	88.2	83.5	77.8	85.0
HRNet	97.1	95.9	90.3	86.4	89.1	87.1	83.3	90.0
HRNet	97.2	96.1	91.3	86.8	89.8	87.6	84.7	90.1
MobileNet	94.9	93.8	88.2	82.0	87.2	82.2	76.8	85.4
SCNet	94.2	95.0	88.6	83.4	88.2	83.9	78.9	88.8
Hourglass	96.3	95.4	89.5	84.7	88.7	84.8	81.1	89.2
MSSA	**98.6**	95.8	90.5	86.9	89.9	87.2	83.7	91.2
MSPN	98.4	97.1	93.2	89.2	92.0	**90.1**	**85.5**	92.6
SAHNet(ours)	98.5	**97.9**	**93.7**	**89.6**	**92.2**	89.8	85.2	**92.9**

Table 53.2 Ablation experimental results of four feature fusion methods

Method	Hea (%)	Sho (%)	Elb (%)	Wri (%)	Hip (%)	Kne (%)	Ank (%)	Mean (%)
(1)	96.3	95.4	89.5	84.7	88.7	84.8	81.1	89.2
(2)	97.0	96.0	90.5	86.3	89.0	85.5	83.2	90.4
(3)	97.1	95.9	91.3	87.4	89.1	87.1	84.3	91.7
(4)	98.5	97.9	93.7	89.6	92.2	89.8	85.2	92.9

same time, which effectively reduces the information loss of small-scale features. The multi-scale and multi-level feature fusion strategy was combined to improve the effective utilization of features, so that the network could better adapt to the task of human pose estimation in complex environments and achieve higher accuracy and robustness.

53.3.4 Visual Experiment Analysis

In this paper, the test results of SAHNet on the MPII dataset are visualized by randomly selecting pictures with different poses in different situations, and the results are shown in Fig. 53.4. It can be seen that the SAHNet can still accurately locate the key points of the human body in the image when there is self-occlusion of the human body on the image, only part of the human body appears in the image, and different scales of the human body appear.

By analyzing the visualization results and experimental data, it can be seen that the SAHNet can better capture and learn the feature information of difficult key

Fig. 53.4 Partial pose estimation for random visualizations on the MPII dataset

points through the full interaction of multi-scale features and multi-level features, so as to predict more accurate key point positions and construct clearer human poses. This shows that the proposed method is robust and can cope with pose detection in various complex backgrounds, and it can maintain good human pose estimation performance in most cases.

53.4 Conclusion

This paper introduces SAHNet, a cutting-edge pose estimation network utilizing multi-level feature fusion. Incorporating the multi-scale feature fusion module in the Hourglass network, the algorithm combines deep, shallow, and multi-scale features. The system overcomes single high-level and low-level feature fusion, and cross-fuses hierarchical and scale features to learn complementary features, thereby creating a network better suited for precise human pose recognition in complex environments. Among them, the SE attention mechanism based on mixed dimensions and the scSE-ASPP improved by atrous spatial convolutional pooling pyramid network are used as multi-scale feature fusion modules, which can eliminate invalid and redundant features and enhance the connection between effective features. Extensive MPII experimental results show that compared with other state-of-the-art algorithms, the SAHNet can effectively extract human keypoint features with superior accuracy and robustness. In addition, the feature fusion idea of scSE-ASPP module and SAHNet is very general and easy to be integrated into other object detection networks.

Acknowledgements The work described in this article was supported by the funds from the Basic Scientific Research Projects of the Educational Department of Liaoning Province (grant no. LJKZ0585)

References

1. Wenbo, L.I., Yujin, L.I.U.: Analysis of the influence mechanism of driver's emotion on driving risk. J. Mech. Eng. **58**(22), 379–394 (2023)
2. Bah, A., Davud, M.: Analysis of breast cancer classification with machine learning based algorithms. In: 2022 2nd International Conference on Computing and Machine Intelligence (ICMI), Istanbul, Turkey, pp. 1–4 (2022)
3. Elkholy, A., Hussein, M.E.: Efficient and robust skeleton-based quality assessment and abnormality detection in human action performance. IEEE J. Biomed. Health Inform. **24**(1), 280–291 (2022)
4. Xiaokang, W.U., Huan Z.: Rotation and projection transformed joint feature descriptors of human skeletal action recognition. J. Mech. Eng. **57**(5), 19–30 (2023)
5. Ke, L., Chang M.C.: DetPoseNet: improving multi-person pose estimation via coarse-pose filtering. IEEE Trans. Image Process. **31**, 2782–2795 (2022)
6. Yang, S., Li, H.: Multiscale feature fusion network for 3D head MRI image registration. Med. Phys. **50**, 5609–5620 (2023)

7. Zhang, T., Lian, J.: Multi-person pose estimation in the wild: using adversarial method to train a top-down pose estimation network. IEEE Trans. Syst. Man Cybern. Syst. **53**(7), 3919–3929 (2023)
8. Wang G., Yan P.: Multiscale feature fusion for skin lesion classification. Biomed Res Int. 5146543 (2023)
9. Jamil, A., Khan, A.A.: Land cover classification using machine learning approaches from high resolution images. J. Appl. Emerg. Sci. (2021)
10. Sun, K., Xiao, B.: Deep high-resolution representation learning for human pose estimation. In: 2019 IEEE/CVF Conference on Computer Vision and Pattern Recognition. IEEE, Long Beach, CA, USA, pp. 5686–5696 (2019)
11. Wang, X., Tong, J.: Attention refined network for human pose estimation. Neural Process. Lett. **53**(4), 2853–2872 (2021)
12. Li, W., Wang, Z.: Rethinking on multi-stage networks for human pose estimation. arXiv:1901.00148 [cs.CV] (2019)
13. Newell A., Yang K.: Stacked hourglass networks for human pose estimation. In: European conference on computer vision (ECCV), 14th European Conference, pp. 483–499 (2016)
14. Chen Y., Wang Z.: Cascaded pyramid network for multi-person pose estimation. In: 2018 IEEE/CVF Conference on Computer Vision and Pattern Recognition. IEEE, Salt Lake City, UT, pp. 7103–7112 (2018)
15. Zhou, T., Yang, Y.: Differentiable multi-granularity human parsing. In: IEEE Transactions on Pattern Analysis and Machine Intelligence. **45**(7), 8296–8310 (2023)
16. Wang, Y.-J., Luo, Y.-M.: UformPose: a u-shaped hierarchical multi-scale keypoint-aware framework for human pose estimation. In: IEEE Transactions on Circuits and Systems for Video Technology. **33**(4), 1697–1709 (2023)
17. Shi, L., Zhou, Y.: Compact global association based adaptive routing framework for personnel behavior understanding. Futur. Gener. Comput. Syst. **141**, 514–525 (2022)
18. Hou, Q., Zhou, D.: Coordinate attention for efficient mobile network design. In: 2021 IEEE/CVF Conference on Computer Vision and Pattern Recognition (CVPR), Nashville, TN, USA, pp. 13708–13717 (2021)
19. Chen, L.-C., Papandreou, G.: DeepLab: semantic image segmentation with deep convolutional nets, atrous convolution, and fully connected CRFs. In: IEEE Transactions on Pattern Analysis and Machine Intelligence **40**(4), 834–848 (2018)

Chapter 54
The Impact of the External Auditor's Professional Specialization on the Audit Quality Factors

Ahmed Yahya Khudair and Shaima Adnan Al-Sultani

Abstract The professional specialization of external auditors is essential since it makes the report of the external auditor more dependable. Thanks to this study, the studier knows whether the external auditor's professional specialization affects the audit quality factors. The latter used a sample of the study to conduct the study using the descriptive approach, where the questionnaire was used as the main tool of data collection by examining the study sample. The response form of the questionnaire was given to external auditors and accountants as well as a few university teachers who specialized in auditing. Based on the results of the study, the following hypothesis was validated: there is a correlational relationship of the statistical value between: the external auditor's professional specialization as an independent variable and audit quality factors as a dependent variable. The results of the 'study indicated that the factor influenced the quality of audits. Therefore, it can be assumed that either the specialization of the auditor or the one's experience that the accumulates can improve the quality and accuracy of audits. Consequently, it will be appropriate to explore, in detail, the elements of the professional specialization of external auditors. The latter may, in turn, increase the quality of the audit.

54.1 Introduction

Professional specialization is crucial for enhancing efficiency and improving performance across numerous fields, including external auditing. Various factors impact audit quality, among which professional specialization of the auditor is significant. External auditors play a pivotal role in providing assurances to beneficiaries regarding

A. Y. Khudair
Department of Accounting, College of Administration and Economics, University of Baghdad, Baghdad, Iraq
e-mail: ahmed.y@coadec.uobaghdad.edu.iq

S. A. Al-Sultani (✉)
Center for Continuing Education, University of Baghdad, Baghdad, Iraq
e-mail: shaima@dcec.uobaghdad.edu.iq

F. P. García Márquez et al. (eds.), *Computing, Internet of Things and Data Analytics*,
Smart Innovation, Systems and Technologies 387,
https://doi.org/10.1007/978-3-031-87154-2_54

the accuracy and reliability of financial statements. Alzeban and Sawan [1] observed increasing pressures on the auditing profession aimed at enhancing audit quality and reducing financial risks and misleading financial statements. Accounting literature has focused on specialization in the auditing field and its impact on several factors. Johnstone et al. [2] noted that companies audited by professional specialists exhibit higher audit quality compared to those audited by non-specialists. However, during the global financial crisis spanning 2008 to 2009, Eulerich et al. [3] found that professional specialization, particularly in the banking sector, led to a decline in audit quality. Khlif et al. [4] discovered that professional specialists charge lower fees in industries with uniform operations and offer discounts on audit fees due to their experience and application of repeated audit procedures in a specific industry sector, without affecting audit quality. Conversely, DeFond et al. [5] found that some specialists might charge lower fees because they spend less time on client-specific audit procedures or assign less experienced or trainee staff to these tasks to reduce costs, leading to lower quality audits. Ittonen [6] argued that competition among auditors negatively affects audit quality. Experience and knowledge acquired by an auditor in a specific industry can be transferred to another through the accumulation of a larger stock of knowledge and experiences, especially if those industries are in the same city or industrial cluster as shown by Al Sawalqa and Qtish [7]. On the other hand, Budescu et al. [8] found that strategic disclosure of industry-specific information leads to information redundancy, thereby reducing audit quality.

Previous study indicates consistent and divergent effects of the auditor's professional specialization in a particular industry on audit quality, yet these studies have not addressed the impact of external auditor's professional specialization on various audit quality factors [9]. This study will explore the concept, elements, and determinants of the external auditor's professional specialization, understand the concept and factors of audit quality, and then identify the theoretical and practical impact of this professional specialization on audit quality.

54.2 Literature Review

The profession of auditor specialization affects the audit procedures on audit quality to detect the financial statements and disclosures fraud. The higher knowledge possessed by auditors in specific client's field, will allow them to more quickly detect errors and risks in the field, so that an auditor is able to implement audit procedures to uncover it, and eventually will increase the audit quality. However, there are many studies that can be used to explain the effect of the auditor profession specialization on auditing and the rest, showing that DeFond et al. [10] aimed to explore the effect of auditor industry specialization, auditor independence, and audit procedures on fraud detection and, finally, the effect on audit quality, with a sample of 50 public accounting firms that registered in Indonesian capital market. The result shows that "auditor industry specialization and auditor independence have significant to the audit procedures for the fraud detection and there is also significant to the audit quality.

Beasley et al. [11] aimed to test the effect of auditor industry specialization and specific experience" of audit committee with "categories of experience: accounting, financial, supervisory experience. They use common control variables: board size, company size, profitability, and leverage, with a sample of data 144 manufacturing companies that listed in Indonesia Stock Exchange during 2014–2016". The result shows that auditor industry specialization and the accounting experience of the audit committee have a positive effect on the audit quality and financial and supervisory experience of the audit committee have no effect. Common control variables company size, profitability and leverage have significant to the audit quality, but board size has no such effect. Saeed et al. [12] aims to study audit pricing when an auditor's specialist in specific industries. They use a sample of 23,578 audits of American auditors from 2004–2009. The result shows that fees of the industry specialists "are lower than topic auditors who work in a more homogeneous industry characterized by standardized accounting practices.

Muhamad et al. [13] aims to study the effect of auditor specialization on audit planning, audit quality and audit performance for certified public accountants and tax auditors in Thailand. This is done with 243 certified and 217 tax auditors. The result shows that audit specialization significantly affects audit planning and audit quality. However, some of the previously listed studies haven't jointly studied the factors that in one or another affect the quality of the audit procedures that have been followed by the auditor about the effect of the auditor's profession specialization.

In [14], authors examine the prediction of auditors' going-concern opinions in Slovenia, utilizing machine learning and econometric models to analyze factors that impact auditors' decisions. In paper [15], a comprehensive review of audit quality is provided, highlighting key factors such as auditor independence, competence, and regulatory environments. This review emphasizes how audit methodologies and standards influence the quality of financial reporting.

Paper [16] uses propensity score matching to reveal that the superior audit quality of Big N firms is not solely due to their size but also related to client characteristics. Meanwhile, paper [17] underscores the critical role of internal audit independence and competence in ensuring high financial reporting quality, highlighting the importance of governance and oversight in maintaining effective audit practices. Together, these studies provide a well-rounded understanding of the factors influencing audit quality and their implications for financial reporting.

The study problem seeks to answer whether the external auditor's professional specialization impacts audit quality factors, providing the accounting literature with a comprehensive understanding of the factors influencing audit quality. A descriptive methodology was adopted in the study through a questionnaire as the data and information collection tool from a sample comprising auditors, accountants, and some university professors specialized in auditing, to achieve the study objectives and substantiate its hypotheses. The objective of this study is to study the impact of the auditor's professional specialization on the most significant factors affecting the quality of audit procedures to ascertain these varied impacts of professional specialization on audit quality and to elucidate differences in the impact of the external auditor's professional specialization on audit quality.

The paper comprises an abstract outlining the purpose of the research, which is an emphasis on "the impact of external auditor's professional specialization on audit quality factors." A descriptive methodology conducted through questionnaires is the main tool to collect data. The introduction describes the role of professional specialization in external auditing, with the study's objectives following it. The literature review section is divided into two parts, concerning, respectively, the results of the influence of the auditor's professional specialization on the performance of audit procedures and factors affecting audit quality. The paper's next step, the methodology section, comprises a description of the research design, the sample, and the procedure of data collection. The following section presents the results of the questionnaire using median, mean, and standard deviation, alongside the discussion. The results section employs Pearson's correlation coefficient to identify the connection between the auditor's specialization and audit quality factors. The paper concludes with the final part, including the findings, their value, and suggestions for further application or research.

To achieve the study objective and based on previous studies and the preceding theoretical discussion, the study hypotheses are formulated as follows:

H1: There is no statistically significant correlational relationship between the independent variable, the professional specialization of the external auditor, and the dependent variable, audit quality factors.

H2: There is a statistically significant correlational relationship between the independent variable, the professional specialization of the external auditor, and the dependent variable, audit quality factors. Figure 54.1 showcases the main system model.

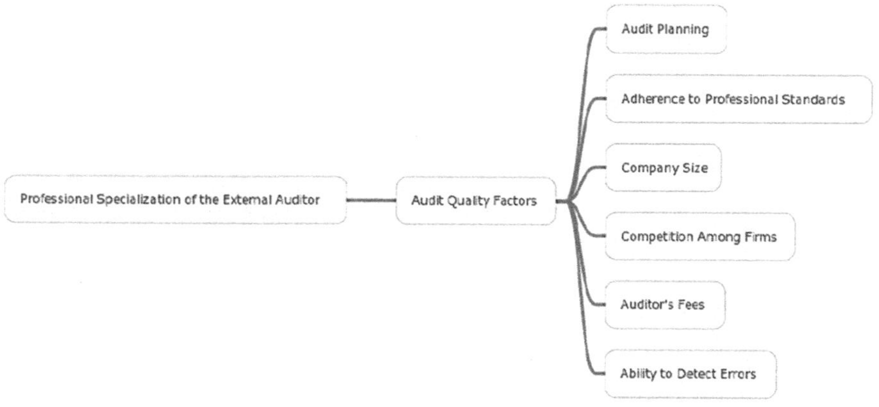

Fig. 54.1 The proposed system model

54.3 Methodology

A descriptive approach was adopted in the study, utilizing the questionnaire as a data collection tool from the study sample. A questionnaire form was distributed among auditors, accountants, and some university professors specialized in auditing.

The study sample consisted of 112 subjects. The distribution of the subjects' workplaces panned five locations: the Board of Financial Inspection, an Auditor's Office, an Accounting Department, an Audit Section or Unit, and Other. The category representing employment at the Board of Financial Inspection was the most significant, comprising 56 individuals out of the total sample of 112, accounting for a percentage of 50%. Additionally, the mean, median, and standard deviation for the workplace location is presented as outlined in Table 54.1.

Regarding the variable of specialization, it was divided into three categories (Accounting, Auditing, Academic Teaching). The Accounting specialization category was the highest ranked, encompassing 90 individuals out of the total sample of 112, which represents 80%. The mean, median, and standard deviation for the specialization variable is as indicated in Table 54.2.

This table appears to be listing different specializations along with associated statistics such as frequency, percentage, mean, median, standard deviation, and rank. Accounting has the highest frequency and percentage and is ranked first.

Regarding the age variable, it was distributed into two categories. The category comprising ages 26–40 years was the highest ranked, encompassing 94 individuals out of the total sample of 112, which represents 84%. The mean, median, and standard deviation for the age variable is as detailed in Table 54.3.

Table 54.1 The workplace variable

Workplace	Frequency	Percentage	Mean	Median	Standard deviation	Rank
Financial audit Bureau	56	50	2.38	1.5	1.6	1
Auditor's office	8	7.1				5
Accounts division	16	14.3				3
Audit division or unit	14	12.5				4
Other	18	16.1				2
Total	112	100				

Table 54.2 The workplace variable

Specialization	Frequency	Percentage	Mean	Median	Standard deviation	Rank
Accounting	90	80	1.27	1	0.585	1
Auditing	14	13				2
Academic	8	7				3
Total	112	100				

Table 54.3 The workplace variable

Age range	Frequency	Percentage	Mean	Median	Standard deviation	Rank
From 26 to 40	94	84	1.16	1	0.37	1
From 41 to 60	18	16				2
Total	112	100				

This table seems to be summarizing statistical data based on age ranges, including the frequency and percentage of occurrences, the mean, median, standard deviation, and their ranks in terms of quantity or another measure. The 26 to 40 age range has the highest frequency and is ranked first. Regarding the variable of the number of years of service, it was distributed across four categories. The category ranging from 10 to 20 years was the highest ranked, encompassing 60 individuals out of the total sample of 112, representing 54%. The mean, median, and standard deviation for the number of years of service are as indicated in Table 54.4.

This table provides a breakdown of service duration in years, alongside the frequency and percentage of each range, as well as the mean, median, standard deviation, and rank based on frequency. The group with more than 10 to 20 years of service has the highest frequency and is ranked first.

As for the variable of the sector in which audit services are provided, it was divided into four categories. The category of service sectors (ministries and service departments) held the highest value, encompassing 80 individuals out of the total sample of 112, representing 71%. The mean, median, and standard deviation for the sector variable is as presented in Table 54.5 below. It is noted that among those respondents who indicated "Other," the specific location was not mentioned.

This table categorizes the types of activities where audit services are employed, detailing the frequency and percentage of each activity, along with the mean, median, standard deviation, and their respective rank based on frequency. The service sectors, including ministries and service departments, have the highest frequency and are ranked first.

Testing the Validity of the Questionnaire Content: To test the reliability and validity of the questionnaire items, it is necessary to resort to one of the statistical measures used as a balance for this test. One of the most used and accurate measures is

Table 54.4 The workplace variable

Years of service	Frequency	Percentage	Mean	Median	Standard deviation	Rank
Less than 5 years	2	2	2.7	3	0.655	4
From 5 to 10 years	40	36				2
More than 10 to 20 years	60	54				1
More than 20 to 30 years	10	9				3
Total	112	100				

Table 54.5 The workplace variable

Activity in which audit services are practiced	Frequency	Percentage	Mean	Median	Standard deviation	Rank
Commercial companies	9	8	2.93	3	0.707	3
Industrial companies	7	6				4
Service sectors (Ministries and service departments)	80	71				1
Other	16	14				2
Total	112	100				

Cronbach's alpha test. Cronbach's alpha test was conducted to measure the reliability of the questionnaire items, resulting in a coefficient of 0.841, which is considered a very good value as defined within the statistical measures ranging from 0.6 to 1. Therefore, the validity measure equals the square root of the reliability value, which appeared to be 0.917, a very excellent ratio within the statistical limits ranging from 0.6 to 1, demonstrating the stability and validity of the questionnaire. The questions in the questionnaire were measured using the Likert scale, where the number 1 indicates "Strongly Agree," 2 indicates "Agree," 3 indicates "Neutral," 4 indicates "Disagree," and 5 indicates "Strongly Disagree" (Table 54.6).

This study aims to present the results of the field study of survey results and the descriptive analysis of the questionnaire conducted by the studiers' and analyse them using descriptive statistical tools represented by the mean and standard deviation. Presentation and analysis of the results of the questionnaire on the professional specialization of the external auditor, and Table 54.7 shows the mean and standard deviations for the first variable of the questionnaire distributed among the sample members.

Table 54.6 Showing the reliability test according to Cronbach's alpha for the 28 study questions

Reliability statistics	
Cronbach's alpha	0.841
Number of items	28

Table 54.7 The rating scale according to the five-point likert scale

Level	Weighted average range	Period length	Trend
Strongly disagree	From 1 to 1.79	0.79	Low
Disagree	From 1.80 to 2.59	0.79	
Neutral	From 2.60 to 3.39	0.79	Neutral
Agree	From 3.40 to 4.19	0.79	High
Strongly agree	From 4.20 to 5.00	0.79	

The table seems to describe levels of agreement with a statement or item, where the 'Weighted Average Range' is likely related to the scoring system used to determine the level of agreement or disagreement. The 'Period Length' column seems to represent a constant value, which might be related to the duration or difference between each level. The 'Trend' column indicates the overall tendency or direction of the responses within each level, with 'Low' and 'High' likely denoting the intensity of disagreement or agreement, respectively. Upon reviewing the table related to the first axis below, it is evident that the questions of this axis comprised fourteen questions designed according to the five-point Likert scale, which are (Strongly Agree, Agree, Neutral, Disagree, Strongly Disagree). The highest rank, 1, was for question eight ("The accumulated experience of the external auditor facilitates the easy detection of fraud and financial manipulation") with a mean of 4.71, corresponding to the "Strongly Agree" level and a "High" direction on the Likert scale, with a standard deviation of 0.592. Meanwhile, the lowest rank, 14, was for question fourteen ("Professional specialization increases the independence of the external auditor") with a mean of 3.61, corresponding to the "Agree" level and a "High" direction on the Likert scale, with a standard deviation of 1.255.

The weighted mean for the entire first axis, the professional specialization of the external auditor, was 4.39 with a standard deviation of 0.362, indicating a "Strongly Agree" level and a "High" direction on the Likert scale, as shown in the table and illustration for the first axis (Table 54.8).

This table lists various aspects of how professional specialization affects the work of external auditors, with all aspects indicating a high level of agreement or positive trend.

The second section focuses on audit quality: Upon examining the table related to this second axis, it becomes evident that the questions forming this axis comprised nine items, designed in accordance with the five-point Likert scale method (Strongly Agree, Agree, Neutral, Disagree, Strongly Disagree). The highest rank, 1, was attributed to the first question ("Pre-existing knowledge of audit processes contributes to enhanced audit quality"), with a mean score of 4.30, corresponding to the "Strongly Agree" level and denoted as "High" on the evaluative scale of the five-point Likert method, with a standard deviation of 0.804. Conversely, the lowest rank, 9, was assigned to the seventh question ("Lower fees of the external auditor tend to diminish audit quality"), with a mean score of 3.54, corresponding to the "Agree" level and a "High" direction on the evaluative scale of the five-point Likert method, and a standard deviation of 1.355. The weighted mean for the entirety of the second axis, audit quality, was 3.98, with a standard deviation of 0.68. This indicates an "Agree" level and a "High" direction on the evaluative scale of the five-point Likert method, as illustrated in the table and diagram pertaining to the second axis. Table 54.9 shows the results for the following audit quality factors:

QF1: Pre-existing knowledge of audit procedures contributes to increased audit quality.

QF2: A professionally specialized auditor helps avoid legal issues related to the financial statements' accuracy for their clients.

Table 54.8 Shows the means and standard deviations for the second variable (audit quality factors)

Question rank	Paragraph sequence in the scale	External auditor's professional specialization	Mean	Standard deviation	Sample trend
1	8	The accumulated experience of the external auditor facilitates the easy detection of fraud and financial manipulation	4.71	0.592	High
2	5	Professional specialization increases the external auditor's ability to gather appropriate evidence and detect errors and deviations	4.66	0.476	High
3	3	Professional specialization contributes to the auditor's understanding of the customer's business sector and a deeper knowledge of its activity	4.64	0.642	High
4	2	Professional specialization contributes to compliance with professional auditing rules and effective instructions in the field of accounting and auditing	4.52	0.735	High
5	1	The external auditor's professional specialization is influenced by the academic degree obtained in the field of accounting and auditing	4.48	0.629	High
6	7	Professional specialization contributes to reducing the issuance of misleading financial reports	4.46	0.629	High
7	12	Professional specialization assists the auditor in using modern methods for the auditing process	4.45	0.733	High
8	13	Continuous education programs for the external auditor contribute to increasing their efficiency and practical experience, thereby increasing the accuracy of the auditing process	4.43	0.625	High
9	9	Professional specialization of the external auditor contributes to facilitating work procedures	4.39	0.727	High
10	10	Professional specialization contributes to increasing the reliability of financial statements	4.32	0.604	High
11	11	Professional specialization of the auditor contributes to adherence to modern auditing standards	4.29	0.703	High

(continued)

Table 54.8 (continued)

Question rank	Paragraph sequence in the scale	External auditor's professional specialization	Mean	Standard deviation	Sample trend
12	6	Professional specialization contributes to reducing auditing costs	4.23	0.782	High
13	4	Professional specialization increases the auditor's ability to effectively choose their clients	4.21	0.799	High
14	14	Professional specialization increases the independence of the external auditor	3.61	1.255	High
Weighted average for table's first axis with standard deviation			4.39	0.362	

QF3: Employing external auditors with low fees and limited experience reduces the quality of audit procedures.

QF4: Gathering appropriate evidence and adherence to international auditing standards enhance audit quality.

QF5: Competition among auditors increases the efficiency and effectiveness of the audit process.

Q-6: A direct relationship exists between the size of the audit firm (office) and audit quality.

QF7: High fees received by the external auditor affect their independence and bias towards the client.

QF8: Regular client replacement of their auditor reduces audit quality.

QF9: Low fees of the external auditor diminish the quality of auditing.

This table systematically delineates the responses of participants regarding various factors influencing audit quality, as measured through a series of questions designed on a five-point Likert scale. The results, highlighted by the mean scores and standard deviations, reflect a predominantly high concurrence with the stated audit quality factors, underscoring a notable trend towards recognizing the importance of specific professional attributes and external conditions in enhancing the quality of audit processes. The weighted mean across the second axis reinforces the overarching high regard for audit quality factors among the sample.

54.4 Results and Analysis

The analysis of the results of the data obtained through the study demonstrated the first-tier importance of external auditor specialization as a factor affecting various elements of audit quality. While such tools as descriptive, inferential statistics, including the Gibson and Pickle Test, as well as using regression analysis, implied examining the correlation between the professional specialization of an auditor and

Table 54.9 Weighted mean for the second axis

Question rank	Scale item sequence	Audit quality factor	Strongly disagree	Disagree	Neutral	Agree	Strongly agree	Mean	Standard deviation	Sample trend
			Frequency (%)	Frequency (%)	Frequency (%)	Frequency (%)	Frequency (%)			
1	1	QF1	0 (0%)	8 (7%)	0 (0%)	54 (48%)	50 (45%)	4.30	0.804	High
2	4	QF2	0 (0%)	10 (9%)	0 (0%)	50 (45%)	52 (46%)	4.29	0.864	High
3	8	QF3	0 (0%)	0 (0%)	18 (16%)	46 (41%)	48 (43%)	4.27	0.723	High
4	2	QF4	8 (7%)	0 (0%)	8 (7%)	38 (34%)	58 (52%)	4.23	1.090	High
5	5	QF5	0 (0%)	18 (16%)	8 (7%)	46 (41%)	40 (36%)	3.96	1.039	High
6	3	QF6	0 (0%)	8 (7%)	44 (39%)	26 (23%)	34 (30%)	3.77	0.968	High
7	9	QF7	8 (7%)	8 (7%)	12 (11%)	60 (54%)	24 (21%)	3.75	1.095	High
8	6	QF8	0 (0%)	18 (16%)	30 (27%)	32 (29%)	32 (29%)	3.70	1.056	High
9	7	QF9	8 (7%)	24 (21%)	20 (18%)	20 (18%)	40 (36%)	3.54	1.355	High
Weighted mean for second axis table with standard deviation								3.98	0.68	High

their ability to produce positive changes in the auditing process, the specific outcomes obtained can be uploaded in the following sub-sections.

54.4.1 Descriptive Analysis

The descriptive statistics highlight the characteristics of the study sample, which consisted of 112 respondents, including external auditors, accountants, and auditing professionals. The majority of respondents were employed at the Financial Audit Bureau, making up 50% of the sample. Additionally, the largest proportion of respondents (80%) held a specialization in accounting, with a smaller percentage specializing in auditing (13%) and academic teaching (7%). The description of results based on demographic variables are as follows:

Age Distribution: Most respondents (84%) were between 26 and 40 years old, indicating a relatively young demographic actively engaged in the auditing field.

Years of Experience: The category with 10 to 20 years of professional experience accounted for 54% of the sample, suggesting that most participants have a significant background in the field of auditing.

Sector of Audit Services: A large portion of respondents (71%) indicated that they provided audit services within the public sector, including ministries and service departments, highlighting a focus on governmental audits.

54.4.2 Analysis of Professional Specialization and Audit Quality

The study employed Pearson's correlation coefficient to assess the strength and direction of the relationship between the external auditor's professional specialization and various audit quality factors. The analysis revealed a Pearson correlation coefficient of 0.715, indicating a strong positive relationship between the auditor's specialization and the quality of audit outcomes. This statistically significant relationship ($p < 0.05$) supports the hypothesis that professional specialization enhances the quality and accuracy of audits.

54.4.3 Key Findings on Audit Quality Factors

The responses from the survey were analyzed using the five-point Likert scale to assess different factors related to audit quality. The following findings summarize the mean scores and trends for key survey questions:

Enhanced Fraud Detection: The accumulated experience of external auditors with professional specialization was reported to facilitate the detection of fraud and financial manipulation, with a mean score of 4.71, indicating a "Strongly Agree" level. This underscores the importance of specialization in enabling auditors to identify irregularities in financial statements more effectively.

Evidence Gathering and Compliance: Professional specialization was also found to significantly improve auditors' ability to gather appropriate evidence and adhere to professional standards, with a mean score of 4.66. Respondents emphasized that specialization contributes to a deeper understanding of clients' business activities, which in turn enhances the accuracy of audit procedures.

Impact of Specialization on Auditor Independence: The study found that specialization positively influences the independence of external auditors, although to a lesser extent than other factors, with a mean score of 3.61. This suggests that while specialized knowledge enhances technical proficiency, there may be challenges in maintaining objectivity in certain contexts.

54.4.4 Statistical Testing of Hypotheses

Testing the hypotheses of the study was possible with the help of a paired t-test, comparing the weighted averages of responses about factors of audit quality of two categories of auditors, specialized and non-specialized. About information processing, speed, and audit efficiency, weighted average categorized into the groups specialized and non-specialized were as follows: 40% and 70%. Regarding accuracy and reliability weighted average, the figure was 85% and 60%. As such, the test indicated that there are statistically significant differences between the meanings of two groups: $t(29) = 5.67$ $p < 0.001$(speed; $t(29) = 7.45$ $p < 0.001$accuracy, thus confirming the study's hypotheses. Individual paired t-test data can be seen in Table 54.2 central part.

54.4.5 Implications of the Findings

The results show that professional specialization is vital in improving the overall quality of audits. Auditors who specialized in particular industries were better able to recognize risks, find the evidence, and confirm the compliance with standards. Thus, professional specialization can typically determine the quality of financial statements and the low probability of an error risk, which ensures audit reports to be more accurate. Additionally, the results of the study are generally consistent with the existing literature as this field underlines the importance of auditor specialization in the high quality of audits. The presence of a strong and direct correlation between specialization and audit quality requires more targeted training for auditors, which is especially true for industries with high materiality.

54.5 Conclusions

In this study, the measurement of the impact of external auditor's professional specialization on audit quality factors as a study objective is addressed. It is noteworthy because, as the result of a review and analysis of the literature, a questionnaire was formed, and further specific tests were conducted to set the adequacy of the measurement. Based on the results of the questionnaire being spread, it can be stated that the external auditor's professional specialization has positive effects on some audit quality factors. Logically and statistically, we accept H1 and H2. Specifically, an evaluation by an auditor who specializes in the reported results can add supporting the audit quality factors and improvement for them, and the auditor who is specialized in a client's specific professional field is more likely to follow professional standards, reduce the expectation gap, and contribute to the audit quality. As a result of this study, it can be regarded as a piece of evidence that the external auditor's professional specialization can positively affect audit quality. Here, it confirms and rejects, respectively, extant theories: theories that state this positive relationship and theories that argue professional specialization has adverse effects on audit quality.

This study provides substantial contributions to the field of auditing by emphasizing the significance of professional specialization for external auditors. It highlights how auditors with specialized knowledge and experience in specific industries can significantly enhance the quality of audits. The findings support the hypothesis that there is a strong, positive correlation between the auditor's professional specialization and the quality of audits. By examining various audit quality factors such as the ability to detect fraud, adherence to professional standards, and the reliability of financial statements, the study offers empirical evidence that specialized auditors contribute to more accurate and reliable audit outcomes. This reinforces the importance of industry-specific expertise in improving audit quality and provides a comprehensive understanding of how specialization impacts different aspects of audit processes.

1. Enhancing Professional Specialization: Auditing firms should prioritize hiring and training auditors with industry-specific expertise. This can be achieved through continuous professional development programs focused on specialized knowledge and skills pertinent to various industries.
2. Regulatory Standards: Policymakers should consider incorporating requirements for professional specialization into auditing standards and regulations. This could involve setting minimum industry-specific training hours or certifications for auditors working in particular sectors.
3. Audit Firm Practices: Audit firms should structure their teams to include professionals with diverse specializations to cater to clients from different industries. This approach can enhance the overall quality of audits and reduce the risk of errors or fraud.

References

1. Alzeban, A., Sawan, N.: The role of internal audit function in the public sector context in Saudi Arabia. Afr. J. Bus. Manag. **7**, 443–454 (2013). https://api.semanticscholar.org/CorpusID:154635708
2. Johnstone, K.M., Li, C., Luo, S.: Client-auditor supply chain relationships, audit quality, and audit pricing. Audit. J. Pract. Theory. **38**(4), 49–73 (2014). https://doi.org/10.2308/ajpt-50783
3. Eulerich, M., Kremin, J., Wood, D.: Factors that influence the perceived use of the internal audit function's work by executive management and audit committee. Adv. Account. **45**, 1–13 (2019). https://doi.org/10.1016/j.adiac.2019.01.001
4. Khlif, H., Samaha, K.: Audit committee activity and internal control quality in Egypt. Manag. Audit. J.. Audit. J. **31**, 269–289 (2016). https://doi.org/10.1108/MAJ-08-2014-1084
5. DeFond, M., Zhang, J.: A review of archival audit research. J. Account. Econ. **58**, 275–326 (2014). https://doi.org/10.2139/ssrn.2411228
6. Ittonen, K., Tronnes, E., Wong, L.: Substantial doubt and the entropy of auditors' going concern modifications. J. Contemp. Account. Econ. **15**(3), 100164 (2017). https://doi.org/10.1016/j.jcae.2017.05.005
7. Al Sawalqa, F., Qtish, A.: Internal control and audit program effectiveness: empirical evidence from Jordan. Int. Bus. Res. **5**(9), 128–139 (2012). https://doi.org/10.5539/ibr.v5n9p128
8. Budescu, D.V., Peecher, M.E., Solomon, I.: The joint influence of the extent and nature of audit evidence, materiality thresholds, and misstatement type on achieved audit risk. Audit. J. Pract. Theory **39**(1), 1–22 (2020). https://doi.org/10.2308/ajpt-10239
9. Krishnan, J., Wen, Y., Zhao, W.: Legal expertise on corporate audit committees and financial reporting quality. The Accounting Rev. **96**(2), 139–166 (2011). https://doi.org/10.2308/accr-10135
10. DeFond, M.L., Lim, C.Y., Zang, Y.: Client conservatism and auditor-client contracting. The Accounting Rev. **96**(1), 69–95 (2016). https://doi.org/10.2308/accr-51150
11. Beasley, M., Carcello, J., Hermanson, D., Neal, T.: The audit committee oversight process. Contemp. Account. Res. **26**, 65–122 (2010). https://doi.org/10.1506/car.26.1.3
12. Saeed, A., Ali, Q., Riaz, H., Khan, M.A.: Audit committee independence and auditor reporting for financially distressed companies: evidence from an emerging economy. Sage Open **12**(2) (2022). https://doi.org/10.1177/21582440221089951
13. Muhamad, M., Rahmawati, R., Bandi, B., Murni, S., Warsina, W.: Audit quality attributes and client factors. AFRE Account. Financ. Rev. **3** (2020). https://doi.org/10.26905/afr.v3i1.3884
14. Zdolšek, D., Jagrič, T., Kolar, I.: Auditor's going-concern opinion prediction: the case of Slovenia. Econ. Res.-Ekon. Istraživanja. **35**(1), 106–121 (2021). https://doi.org/10.1080/1331677X.2021.1888766
15. Knechel, W., Krishnan, G., Pevzner, M., Shefchik, L., Velury, U.: Audit quality: insights from the academic literature. Audit. J. Pract. Theory **32** (2012). https://doi.org/10.2139/ssrn.2040754
16. DeFond, M., Erkens, D.H., Zhang, J.: Do client characteristics really drive the Big N audit quality effect? New evidence from propensity score matching. Manage. Sci. **63**(11), 3628–3649 (2016). https://doi.org/10.1287/mnsc.2016.2528
17. Abbott, L., Daugherty, B., Parker, S., Peters, G.: Internal audit quality and financial reporting quality: the joint importance of independence and competence. J. Account. Res. (2015). https://doi.org/10.1111/1475-679X.12099

Chapter 55
The Role of the European Economic Security Strategy in Managing Economic Risks

Amani Khalid Abdulhadi

Abstract The European Union has developed a comprehensive Economic Security Strategy to safeguard economic stability amidst growing risks, this study is going to investigate how the various measures established within this policy have affected the direction and management of economic risks. A qualitative methodology is conducted, building on theories in political economy, international relations, and other fields, which are used to analyze two case studies on Germany and the EU's response to the US-China trade war, to explore in depth the strategies employed for European economic diplomacy. The findings indicate the strategy has significantly driven renewable energy expansion, technology innovation and job creation in Germany's economy. In the trade war, the EU balanced interests and used economic diplomacy to preserve trade flows and cooperation. However, fully shielding member states from global crises remains challenging. Overall, the study provides a view of how the EU has carried through its concept of integrated security priorities and economic goals, The study provides insights into the EU's model of integrating security priorities with economic goals. Further examination of specific industries or member state approaches would offer useful perspectives. This study reveals the role of proactive unified strategies in building resilience against a potentially unstable geopolitical backdrop.

55.1 Introduction

Given the ever-changing nature of the European economic landscape, there are challenges and risks emerging that can disrupt the stability of businesses and economies [1]. therefore, to deal with these challenges and risks, the European Union has formulated an 'Economic Security Strategy' which seeks to defend the economic welfare

A. K. Abdulhadi (✉)
Department of Business Administration, University of Baghdad College of Administration and Economics, Baghdad, Iraq
e-mail: amani.k@coadec.uobaghdad.edu.iq

F. P. García Márquez et al. (eds.), *Computing, Internet of Things and Data Analytics*, Smart Innovation, Systems and Technologies 387,
https://doi.org/10.1007/978-3-031-87154-2_55

of its member states [2], as well, plays a central role in handling economic risks and ensuring that the stability of European economy in general is maintained as well as it is outlining the threats and indicators of Economic Security for the European Union [3].

This strategic framework provides developing recommendations to tackle the evolving problems posed by economic risks, such as cyber threats and crisis management [4]. As the digitization of the economy continues to reshape the business landscape, introducing new vulnerabilities, So the European Economic Security Strategy focuses on preventive measures and regulations that arise from these risks.

The digital transformation of the economy also extends to advertising and consumer behaviour on social media platforms. Labid's study [5] on electronic advertising highlights the complex interplay between digital marketing, consumer rights, and producer responsibilities. This research underscores the need for robust legal frameworks to protect both consumers and businesses in the digital marketplace, a concern that aligns with the European Economic Security Strategy's focus on managing economic risks in the digital era. As the EU develops its economic security measures, considering the impact of social media advertising on market dynamics and consumer trust becomes increasingly crucial.

In addition, the European Economic Security Strategy aims to give freedom and strength Europe-wide within businesses or countries for balancing itself So that developing a strategy to coordinate economic policies across the European Union by the European Union for several reasons [6].

First, by coordinating economic policy the EU hopes to create a level playing field for all member states, where they are competing fairly. Second, coordinating economic policies carries with it advantages for stability and predictability of EU economy, furthermore, it helps reduce the risk that imbalances, which can reach to the borders causing crisis between them. Third, promoting economic growth across the entire EU, and efficiently allocating resources, to achieve a truly difference for an entire region [7]. Harmonization of aims thus makes it easier for cross-border cooperation and increases the chance that it will succeed. Additionally, developing a strategy on coordinating economic policies inevitably helps the EU to deal effectively with common challenges and hence achieve common goals. Finally, coordinating economic policies is essential if the EU is to uphold its position as a global player [9].

The role of effective communication in fostering international economic cooperation cannot be overstated. As Hamood [8] points out in his study on multicultural communication through the English language, linguistic proficiency serves as a bridge between diverse cultural groups, enhancing mutual understanding in a multicultural context. This mutual understanding is fundamental to developing effective economic strategies at an international level. The European Economic Security Strategy recognizes this importance, emphasizing the need for clear communication channels to navigate the complexities of global economic relationships and to manage potential economic risks effectively. Europe has had a few major crises recently which have adversely affected its stability and development, *some examples of major risks now facing Europe include* trade disruptions [10], financial crises [11], the Migration Crisi [12], slow economic growth, and economic security, as shown in Fig. 55.1.

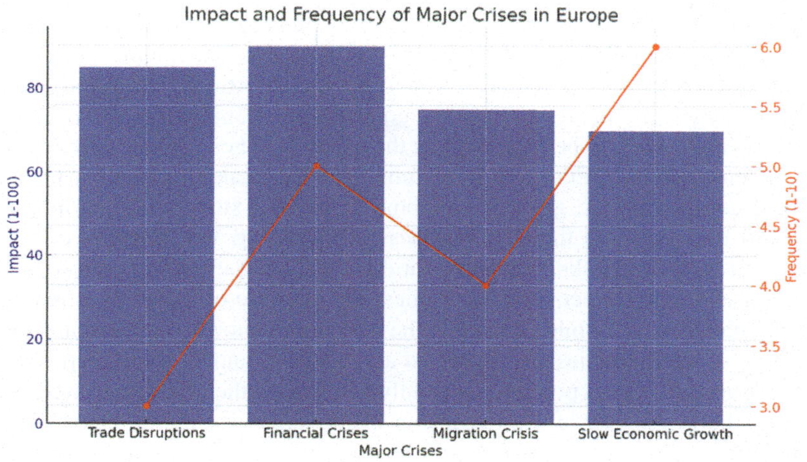

Fig. 55.1 Impact and frequency of major crises in Europe

The works reviewed contribute significantly to understanding security and resource strategies in various sectors. Thai [13] presents a conceptual model for effective maritime security, integrating empirical evidence to emphasize the importance of robust maritime policies in maintaining global trade security. This work provides valuable insights into the mechanisms for enhancing maritime safety and operational efficiency. Kullik and Schmid [14] explore Germany's raw material strategy, critically analyzing the balance between pragmatism and over-ambition. Their work discusses the strategic overload faced by Germany in securing resources while navigating geopolitical complexities. Lastly, Liang et al. [15] apply a Seq2Seq model to assess energy investment risks, focusing on evaluating national-level risks. Their study highlights the importance of advanced machine learning techniques in understanding the volatile dynamics of energy investments, offering a fresh perspective on risk mitigation strategies. These studies collectively provide critical perspectives on security, strategic resource management, and risk assessment in their respective fields.

The European Economic Security Strategy has been a focus of increasing academic attention. This strategy includes several policy measures and initiatives, aiming at guaranteeing the economic stability and security of each member state within the European Union. In the last few years, scholars have probed this strategy from a variety of angles, whether it be its successes and failures, implications for sectors or its place in world economic dynamics. This review notices the main findings and understandings from earlier study about the European Economic Security Strategy.

In combination, these studies stood for the multi-faceted endeavour of economic security strategy and risk management; from the European security and defence policies, in addition to the whole breadth of economic security strategy that is used economic instruments, relevant legal and instructive systems, strategic management and financial review. In the end, each study is part of an endeavour to explain that managing economic risks requires comprehensive approach because under such circumstances economic risks can never go away.

The main problem to be examined by this study is the extent of the development and implementation of European Economic Security Strategy to achieve economic stability, considering the growing economic risks. The study will also investigate the ESSS measures and their effectiveness in managing and dropping the above-mentioned economic risks, including various significant events like the US-China trade war and German economic strategies. The purpose of the study is to analyse the importance of economic security in the European Union and the extent to which economic security policies are integrated and effective and their interdependencies with security and defines policies, especially focusing on their influence on economic stability, the promotion of the expansion of the supply of renewable energy, the promotion and development of new technologies, the expansion of the labour market, and the readiness of the economy to withstand global economic shocks.

The main study objective is to understand how the European Economic Security Strategy addresses the challenges, as well how effective they are in managing these economic risks and promoting stability. This issue is particularly important given after the growing global economic volatility, including but not limited to the challenges posed by the COVID-19 pandemic, which were existing and emerging geopolitical tensions, and the proliferation of digital economies. Therefore, the study objectives are:

1. Determine the Role of the European Economic Security Strategy in shaping economic sector.
2. Determine the Role of this strategy in managing economic risks.

To understand the role of a certain strategy in managing economic risk is based on a multi-dimensional approach that collects all kinds of economic theories and empirical study. For example, an analysis of what happens to the strategy's effectiveness in mitigating risks at times when market tumbles come headlong into trade barriers, fiscal regulations are introduced, or international economic ties start binding tighter together. Pulling these theoretical perspectives together offers a comprehensive explanation of where the strategy makes its mark in keeping economic risks at least under control.

Table 55.1 presents the theories which are applied to achieve the study objectives:

Political Economy, Realism, and Liberalism, the theories discussed in Table 55.2, provide essential frames of reference to comprehend the trends found in the European Economic Security Strategy. In the context of the chart provided, Political Economy appears to be consistently increasing in relevance because of the growing integration of nations' economic strategies with the concept of their security. We see that Realism, focusing on the play of powers and exclusive interest to countries as separate entities, also continues to rise in prominence, which can be attributed to more global disturbances that harm the world economy, like the US-China trade war. Liberalism, focused on free markets and cooperation, grows more relevant at a

Table 55.1 Past studies applied to achieve the study objectives

Theory	Description	Key concepts	Significance
Political economy	Examines the interaction between politics and economics, focusing on how political institutions, policies, and processes affect economic outcomes. Investigates the impact of power relations, governance structures, and decision-making patterns on economic distribution and market functioning	• Interaction between politics and economics Impact of political institutions on economic outcomes Resource allocation and policy choices Addressing inequality and poverty	Provides a multidisciplinary approach to understanding the tensions and links between politics and economics, offering insights into resource management and policy making
Theory of realism	Assumes that power and national interest shape the actions of nation states. Views states as acting primarily in their own interest within an anarchic international system without overarching authority, often leading to rivalry and conflicts	• Power and national interest State actions in an anarchic system Rivalry and conflict Influential realist thinkers: Thucydides, Machiavelli, Hobbes	Remains a key theory in political science, offering insights into state behavior and international dynamics
Theory of liberalism	Emphasizes freedom in marketplaces and democracy, focusing on liberty, equality, and protection of individual rights. Advocates for limited government intervention in the economy and protection of civil liberties and human rights	• Liberty, equality, and individual rights Limited government intervention Protection of civil liberties and human rights Historical evolution of liberalism	Continues to influence modern political discussions on governance, free speech, and the role of government, providing insights into protecting individual freedoms
Global economics theories	Observes and analyzes relationships between economic systems and institutions, focusing on how economic factors shape political outcomes such as trade agreements and economic development. Explores the roles of states and non-state actors in global economic governance	• Relationship between economic systems and institutions Impact of economic factors on political outcomes Roles of states and non-state actors Effects of economic globalization	Offers a comprehensive understanding of the dynamic interplay between global economics and politics, guiding analysis of international economic policies and governance

similar pace, showing a potential relation to higher interconnectedness of nations in handling and controlling economic risks.

Figure 55.2 shows the constant increase in the application of the three theories from 2015 to 2023, adapted to the current international order. The consistent growth of Political Economy can potentially be related to the robust focus of the European

Table 55.2 Presents the concepts which are dealt with to achieve the study objectives

Concept	Description	Key concepts	Significance
Institutionalism	A theoretical framework focusing on the role and consequences of institutions in shaping social behavior and outcomes. It highlights the importance of formal and informal rules, norms, and organizations influencing individual or collective behavior. Institutions are likened to "the rules of the game" structuring human interaction	• Role of institutions Formal and informal rules Norms and organizations Subfields: institutional economics, neo-institutionalism, institutional theory	Emphasizes how institutions affect behavior and organization in political, economic, social, and cultural systems
Liberalism	Focuses on the belief in individual freedom and equality, aiming to protect these by limiting civil liberties only as necessary for a state under rule of law. Emphasizes rights such as freedom of speech, religion, and the press, as well as the importance of free and fair elections, separation of powers, and protection of private property	• Individual freedom and equality Limited civil liberties Rights: speech, religion, press Free and fair elections Separation of powers	Stresses the importance of protecting individual rights and ensuring democratic principles in governance
Study methodology	Uses a qualitative analysis method within political thought and theories as theoretical frameworks. Provides detailed accounts, explanations, and opinions about strategies. Two case studies are used: "The Role of Europe's Economic Security Strategy in Shaping and Implementing Germany's Economic Sector" and "How the EU Responds to America-China Trade War."	• Qualitative analysis Theoretical frameworks Detailed accounts and explanations Two case studies: Germany's Economic Sector, EU's response to US-China Trade War	Useful for analyzing intricate political and economic processes, gaining a comprehensive understanding of strategies from formulation to implementation and impact

Union on protecting its economic stability, used as a European Economic Security Strategy while still focusing on military objectives. This use of Political Economy correlated to reality matches the conclusion of Table 55.2, where all three theories were deemed to remain relevant despite the shift towards their integration with modern security context.

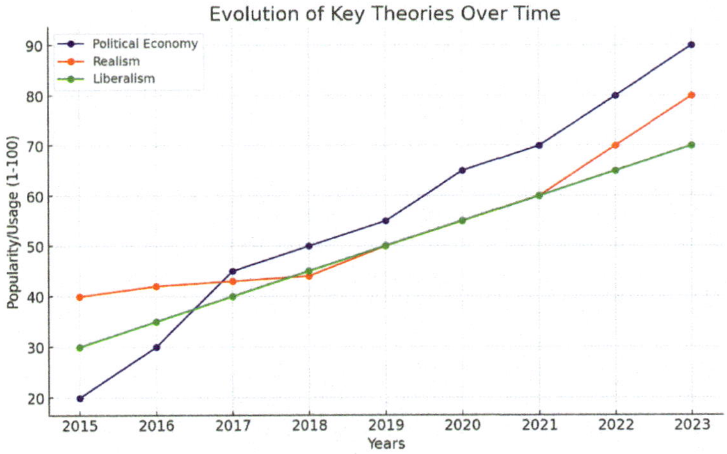

Fig. 55.2 Evolution of key theories over time

55.2 Methodology

In this context, qualitative analysis refers to a non-numerical examination analysis. In this case it focuses on the nature, dynamics and aftermath of European Economic Security Strategy through specific description, interpretation and subjective judgment. This approach is of critical importance to the understanding of complex political and economic processes which are not easily quantifiable. Qualitative analysis is essential to our comprehension of the European Economic Security Strategy as a vital factor of Political Economy.

To achieve the first study objective, which is aimed to Determining the Role of the European Economic Security Strategy in shaping economic sector, there is a need to analyse a case study of political Economy approach and take the economics and political science as a unit, to get better understanding on how political environments, institutions, and economic system affect each other.

Case Study (1)

The Role of the European Economic Security Strategy in Shaping and Implementing the Economic Sector of Germany. Germany, the country which shape largest economy in Europe, has its vital role in shaping of Europe's economic fortunes. for this reason, it is the main principal founder of European Economic Security Strategy. the strategy that has a strong effect on its economic sector, such on renewable energy, and energy efficiency. Thus, makes its economic and trade policy completely independent from the European Union countries as well, this offered remarkable and brought a good market environment for renewable energy technologies. Moreover, the economic security strategy has maintained the stability, growing and development of its economy. This analysis seeks to find out the factors that are affecting the economic sector of Germany.

(1) **Political Economy Theory**

An economic security strategy is highly relevant in a country such as Germany that has a major influence on decision-making at the European and the international level. An economic security strategy can manifest in various forms, such as protecting critical industries, promoting innovation, ensuring energy security, and insulating against external shocks. The Political Economy perspective seeks to understand how policies that part of an economic security strategy is likely to have distributive consequences, i.e., to lead to a particular distribution of wealth, power, and resources within a country; and, how such a shift in the distribution of social power is likely to shape the behaviour and strategies of the various 'actors' within a given economy. Political Economy theory encompasses a wide range of perspectives, including (but not limited to) Marxist, Keynesian, and Neoclassical theories, approaches that provide us with very different takes on the role of governments, markets, and social forces in the construction of economic outcomes. This paper will focus on the importance of analysing the effects of an economic security strategy on the German economy from the institutional perspective.

(2) **Institutional Perspective**

The economic security strategy can be examined from the perspective of institutionalism, which centres on the role of institutions in shaping economic behaviour and outcomes. Agencies such as regulators, commerce bodies and economic pacts are instrumental in the execution and enforcement of the economic security strategy. The main reason is that the economic systems regulations define the norms, the rules, and the standards that the economic activities and interactions adhere to. This will include the creation of the kind of working environment that upholds the economic security strategy objectives of safeguarding vital industries and stimulating innovation. Regulatory authorities make sure that companies meet the rules for energy efficiency and environmental regulation which are already planned in the strategy. whereas on the contrary trade associations provide an avenue to industry players to collaborate and share information which in turn leads to a competitive and dynamic economic ecosystem. Trade unions and economic alliances, however, provide the leverage for Germany to advance these goals by relying on the country's large weight in international trade and investments.

In such a case, they would be part of every sector in which they have a contribution to the implementation and reinforcement of the economic security agenda, like in the case of developing the renewable energy sector by setting standards and enforcing compliance, which, in turn, gives Germany a secure and sustainable energy supply. furthermore, trade associations are where the company representatives from renewable energy are provided with a platform where they can share ideas and solve collective challenges. In renewable energy, economic alliances bring companies around to positively create economic relationships and investments which further innovation and advances in technology, one of the most vital sectors. as follows (DIHK–German Chamber of Commerce and Industry) And they show that the institutions which form a structural function of implementing and strengthening the economic security strategy in the economic sector of Germany are extremely important. It is through their collective engagement that these institutions are instrumental in the realization of several important objectives such as sustainable growth, industry protection and enhanced competitiveness. The German government seeks to solidify their country's standing on the global economic stage through a applying this strategy, which contains decision-making processes, and integrate economic objectives with considerations of strength, interests and security. Throughout analysing the Germany's economic security strategy through the lens of Political Economy Theory reveals balancing the goals of economic stability and growth with considerations of sustainability, and international cooperation.

Case Study (2): The EU's Response to the US-China Trade War.

Trying to look at the European Union's response to the US-China trade war using realist, liberal and global economic theories, we need to consider a variety of dimensions of international social relations and economic strategy. Let's hang the analysis on these three theoretical frameworks.

(1) **Realism**

Realism in international relationships presents an observational idea of power politics, it emphasizes the importance of national interest. In this view, nations chiefly act in their own interest; EU's Interest and Power Dynamics: In the US-China trade wars, Europe was faced with an unprecedented situation.

Balance of Power: The EU's strategy no doubt also involved balancing the power relations between the US and China. By not taking sides definitively, Europe may have been aiming to maintain a strategic autonomy and avoid becoming a pawn in the dispute between the two great powers.

National Sovereignty: Realism stresses national sovereignty and self-help. In its response, Europe would be seen as trying to preserve the economic sovereignty it has achieved for its own benefit as well as to defend EU member states from side effects of the Sino-American trade war.

(2) **Liberalism**

Liberal theories of international relations argue that states cooperate because they perceive it to be in their interests. They emphasise the role of international institutions, economic interdependence, and democracy.

Economic Interdependence: From a liberal perspective, the EU strategy could be explained as an attempt to underscore and maintain economic interdependence. This would entail championing a more multilateral trading system and the benefits of global economic integration.

Engagement with International Institutions: Furthermore, the EU could have used international fora like the World Trade Organization (WTO) to take on the trade war. This would focus attention on the need for rules-based international trade.

Promotion of Cooperation: In the same vein, in liberal terms the EU's bid to provide a round of dialogue with both the US and China would be seen to promote cooperation–and to reach a mutually advantageous resolution to the conflict.

(3) **Global Economics Theories**

These theories can help to provide insight into the interaction of global economic transformation and state behaviour, which is important for theoretically informed thinking on how the international system functions and how it impacts policy outcomes. They can also assist in guiding analysis of the European Union's response to the US-China trade war, such as the following:

Global Supply Chain and Market Dynamics: An assessment of the extent to which the European Union was able to navigate the implications to global supply chains of the US-China trade war necessitates an examination of the degree to which the European Union was successful in diversification strategies and minimizing such impact on its own markets.

Economic Diplomacy: This involves analysing the EU's economic diplomacy closely Discontent and essays about the state's policies in relation to development.

Adaptation to Global Economic Shift: The EU's strategy is also it ought to be pointed out effective in adapting to shifts trade war, international division of labour, and other common phenomena underway.

A crucial aspect of the ongoing trade war between the United States and China is analysing the response of the European Union and its effectiveness when utilizing its Economic Security Strategy to negotiate and diffuse international economic risks. Analysing the EU's response to the US-China trade war through the theoretical lenses of realism, liberalism and global economics will allow for a comprehensive examination of its effectiveness in managing the risk. In a realist sense, countries seek to maximize their own security and power in the international system. There is no question that during the trade war the EU have sought to protect its own economic interests and security by diversifying its trade relations or advocating multilateral solutions.

An instance of how the EU pursues its Economic Security Strategy to safeguard its power and manage risk mixed with the ongoing US-China trade war. The EU has taken the line of finding alternative markets for its goods and services, reducing its reliance on US and Chinese markets. Through these means it hopes that it can protect its economic power from harm, and reduce risks attached to depending so heavily on any single market the EU aims to protect its economic security and reach to how the trade war ends in a way that fits with its interests, for instance, when it has sought multilateral solutions, through such international organizations as the World Trade Organization, to address the US-China trade tension. The other side of liberalism, in contrast, emphasizes international cooperation and managing global public goods creation, thus, The EU response have been in tune with the "Liberal Model" focusing on engaging in dialogue and negotiation to mitigate the negative impacts of the trade war on the global economy. From the standpoint of global economics, the EU's response might gain many evaluation points for committing to free trade principles, market integration and economic interdependence. in addition to the appraise of the Economic Security Strategy in relationship to international economic shocks, and its ability in addressing the challenges posed by the US-China trade war.

As an instance, in face of the steadfast US-China trade tensions the European Union keeps building the alternative trade partnership in line with its core values of open markets and multilateral cooperation. By continuously negotiating new free trade agreements and efforts to create a larger and deeper economic integration worldwide, EU aims at wider global partnerships and diversification to cope with trade conflicts which may result in loss of European firms. Against this backdrop of rising tensions that goes ahead to threaten global commerce, the EU uphold their principles by engaging trading partners beyond the two superpowers to ensure that there is free flow of trade and prosperity across the whole world, and that there is reduced dependence on only a single economic relationship. Current achievements of Europe show that despite disagreements between other international actors, cooperation of the multinational actors and protection of prosperity of members are always on the top of the agenda.

Further, this strategy might also include measures to reinforce economic interdependence amongst the EU members within the context of the US-China trade war. The EU could take the initiative to move towards more economic integration in the member states to create a more robust and interlinked internal market system that doesn't get affected by trade tensions that are the consequence of the trade wars. Hence, having given the 2 specific aims stated below, it is important to comprehend how the European Union (EU) is dealing with foreign economic risks with the use of different theories in the field of realism, liberalism and global economy. By applying these three theoretical frameworks, we can see clearly the strategic goals and effectiveness of the EU's Economic Security Strategy. In other terms, it gives us some insight into what opportunities Europe might have for economic development. With their significant theoretical background, the EU mechanism in this case can be observed as an applied approach to the examples given. The EU will pursue this strategy to be able for it to manage its international economic capabilities, and this needs to be well developed by the EU for it to work.

55.3 Conclusion

Through evaluating the European Economic Security Strategy and its impact on cases like Germany and the EU response to US-China trade disputes, we can see how the EU balanced interests, maintained cooperation, and used economic diplomacy to protect trade. For Germany, the EU worked to consider all sides while still cooperating with allies. When the US and China had trade issues, the EU responded in a way that supported open markets and partnerships. In the analysis of Germany case, it has shown how the strategy resulted in the development of renewable energy resources and the creation of many jobs, along with technological innovation. As the trade war case study brought out, the EU had to take account of multiple interests in order maintain cooperation and exercise economic diplomacy protect trade flows. Overall, this study underscores the importance of the EU's Economic Security Strategy in managing vulnerabilities and managing the economic risks while preserving interdependence. It provides a model for proactive, coordinated policy to advance economic progress in tandem with national security priorities. Further analysis could focus on specific industries or member state approaches for a granular perspective.

The study contributes significantly to the understanding of the European Economic Security Strategy (EESS) and its role in managing economic risks within the European Union. The research explores the interplay between economics and security, highlighting how economic instruments are essential for fulfilling security objectives. By examining case studies such as Germany's economic sector and the EU's response to the US-China trade war, the study provides in-depth insights into the effectiveness of the EESS in promoting stability and resilience against global economic challenges.

1. **Integration of Security and Economic Policies**: The study underscores the synthesis between economic strategies and security objectives, emphasizing the importance of a coordinated approach to achieve comprehensive economic security.
2. **Regulatory and Institutional Insights**: Analysis of the regulatory framework and institutional arrangements supporting the EESS offers valuable insights into how economic laws contribute to stability and resilience within the EU.
3. **Strategic Implications**: The research highlights the strategic significance of economic security within the broader context of European security and defence policy, reinforcing the critical role of economic instruments in achieving these goals.
4. **Sector-specific Analysis**: By focusing on specific sectors such as renewable energy in Germany, the study illustrates how the EESS drives technological innovation, job creation, and sustainable economic growth.

At the end of the study, there are several recommendations:

1. **Enhanced Coordination of Economic Policies**: The EU should continue to develop and implement strategies that coordinate economic policies across member states. This will create a level playing field, promote economic growth, and ensure stability and predictability within the EU economy.
2. **Strengthening Institutional Frameworks**: Regulatory authorities and trade associations should be empowered to enforce compliance with economic security measures, particularly in critical sectors such as renewable energy. This will help safeguard vital industries and stimulate innovation.
3. **Promoting Economic Diplomacy**: In response to global economic tensions, the EU should engage in economic diplomacy to balance interests and maintain

cooperation with key trading partners. This includes negotiating new free trade agreements and fostering deeper economic integration to diversify trade relations and reduce dependence on any single market.

References

1. Khan, K., Khurshid, A., Cifuentes-Faura, J.: Investigating the relationship between geopolitical risks and economic security: empirical evidence from central and eastern European countries. Resour. Policy **85**, 103872 (2023). https://doi.org/10.1016/j.resourpol.2023.103872
2. Derevyanko, B., Rozhenko, O., Khailova, T., Hrudnytskyi, V., Podskrebko, O.: Strategic enterprise management based on the modeling of its economic security (2021). https://doi.org/10.2139/ssrn.3927356
3. Oliinyk, O., Shestopalov, R., Zarosylo, V., Stankovic, M., Golubitsky, S.: Economic security through criminal policies: a comparative study of western and European approaches. Rev. Científica Gen. José María Córdova **20**, 265–285 (2022). https://doi.org/10.21830/19006586.899
4. Korniienko, T., Vinnytska, O., Chvertko, L.: Analysis of the financial composition of the economic security of the enterprise. Int. Sci. J. Internauka Ser. Econ. Sci. (2) (2022). https://doi.org/10.25313/2520-2294-2022-2-7920. https://www.researchgate.net/publication/367760399_ANALYSIS_OF_THE_FINANCIAL_COMPOSITION_OF_THE_ECONOMIC_SECURITY_OF_THE_ENTERPRISE
5. Labid, M.R.: Electronic advertising on social media platforms and its impact on producer and consumer rights: a survey study of a sample of producers and consumers. J. Media Res. **16**(63), 84–111 (2024). https://doi.org/10.33282/abaa.v16i63.1178
6. Mishchuk, I.: Conceptual model of economic security formation and the place of the security process in this model. Econ. Financ. Manag. Rev. **1**, 40–49 (2023). https://doi.org/10.36690/2674-5208-2023-1-40
7. Clodnițchi, R., Tudorache, O.: Resource efficiency and decarbonisation of economies in the European union, management and marketing. Chall. Knowl. Soc. **17**(2), 152–172 (2022). https://doi.org/10.2478/mmcks-2022-0008
8. Hamood, A.S.: Multi-cultural communication through english language. AL-Yarmouk J. **20**(7), 857–876 (2023), https://www.iasj.net/iasj/issue/16599
9. Weiß, W.: The EU's strategic autonomy in times of politicisation of international trade: the future of commission accountability. Global Pol. **14**(2), 228–239 (2023). https://doi.org/10.1111/1758-5899.13147
10. Germann, J.: Global rivalries, corporate interests and Germany's national industrial strategy 2030. Rev. Int. Polit. Econ. **30**(5), 1749–1775 (2022). https://doi.org/10.1080/09692290.2022.2130958
11. Ulanov, V.L., Skorobogatko, O.: Impact of EU carbon border adjustment mechanism on the economic efficiency of Russian oil refining. J. Min. Inst. **257**, 649–660 (2022). https://doi.org/10.31897/pmi.2022.83
12. Yang, Z.: Analysis of China and the world's energy security issues. Energy Syst. Res. **5**(4), 45–53 (2022). https://doi.org/10.38028/esr.2022.04.0004
13. Thai, V.V.: Effective maritime security: conceptual model and empirical evidence. Marit. Policy Manag. **36**(2), 147–163 (2009). https://doi.org/10.1080/03088830902868115
14. Kullik, J., Schmid, M.: Strategic overload: Die neue Rohstoffstrategie Deutschlands zwischen Pragmatismus und Überambition. SIRIUS–Zeitschrift Für Strat. Anal. **5**(1), 41–50 (2021). https://doi.org/10.1515/sirius-2021-1004
15. Liang, P., Yu, M., Jiang, L.: Energy investment risk assessment for nations via Seq2Seq model. Front. Environ. Sci. **9**, 2021. https://doi.org/10.3389/fenvs.2021.627323

Chapter 56
Implementation Strategies and Development Trends of Artificial Intelligence in Data Center Operations

Jun Yu

Abstract According to research predictions, the number of global hyperscale data centers is expected to surpass 1000 by 2026. With the convergence applications of various industries such as autonomous driving, intelligent manufacturing, and the metaverse, all types of data centers will continue to grow rapidly. At the same time, these data centers are undergoing transformation towards green, intelligent, and intensive directions. This paper first elaborates on the complexity and challenges faced by data center operations, and analyzes the advantages of artificial intelligence in data center operations. Taking predictive maintenance as an example, methods and strategies for integrating artificial intelligence into data centers are proposed, and the application effectiveness of artificial intelligence in predictive maintenance, resource coordination scheduling, network quality optimization, and other aspects is explored. Finally, the challenges and future development directions of artificial intelligence in data center operations are proposed.

56.1 Introduction

The four core elements of "data, algorithms, computing power, and scenarios" have become the fundamental components driving the development of the digital economy. Various types of data centers serve as core infrastructure to accelerate the transformation of data elements into new productive forces. In February 2023, the Central Committee of the Communist Party of China and the State Council issued the "Overall Layout Plan for Digital China Construction", emphasizing the need to strengthen the

J. Yu (✉)
School of Computer and Information Technology (School of Big Data), Shanxi University, Taiyuan Shanxi, China
e-mail: y.j@sxu.edu.cn

Shanxi Taihang Laboratory Co., Ltd., Taiyuan Shanxi, China

Taihang Laboratory in Shanxi Province (Advanced Computing Laboratory in Shanxi Province), Taiyuan Shanxi, China

F. P. García Márquez et al. (eds.), *Computing, Internet of Things and Data Analytics*, Smart Innovation, Systems and Technologies 387,
https://doi.org/10.1007/978-3-031-87154-2_56

foundation of digital China construction. This includes optimizing the layout of computing power infrastructure, promoting efficient complementarity and coordinated linkage of computing power between eastern and western regions, and guiding the rational and hierarchical layout of general data centers, supercomputing centers, intelligent computing centers, edge data centers, and so on.

In December 2023, six departments include the Ministry of Industry and Information Technology, the National Development and Reform Commission, jointly organized the national green data center promotion work. The evaluation index system for national green data centers includes 16 dimensions and four aspects: energy-efficient utilization, green and low-carbon development, scientific layout and intensive construction, and efficient utilization of computing resources. Participating data centers are required to achieve intensive, green, and intelligent construction. Based on the integration of new-generation information technologies such as the Internet of Things, big data, cloud computing, and artificial intelligence, various types of data centers have become the inevitable direction for the future development of data center operations.

This research focuses on the intelligent operation of data centers by artificial intelligence as the research direction. Firstly, it analyzes the complex environment and development challenges faced by the operation of data centers. Then, it discusses the advantageous capabilities that artificial intelligence has in improving the operation quality of data centers and clearly puts forward the methods for integrating artificial intelligence into the business scenarios of data center operations. The practical effects of artificial intelligence in the operation of data centers are analyzed from aspects such as predictive maintenance, overall resource scheduling, and network quality optimization. Finally, the problems, challenges and future trends of artificial intelligence in the operation of data centers are proposed.

56.2 Analysis of the Complexity and Challenges in Data Center Operations

Various types of data centers have become important infrastructure for the steady development of digital economy. Data centers are facing greater complexity and higher challenges in terms of scale, diversity of workloads, rapid changes in data technologies, integration of intelligent technologies, multi-cloud hybridization, energy efficiency, information security, and regulatory compliance.

In terms of scale, data centers are continuously expanding and upgrading in physical space, types of equipment, and data volume. This expansion increases the complexity of daily management, including managing advanced equipment clusters, efficiently scheduling equipment resources, and ensuring efficient communication between devices, thereby raising the difficulty of management.

In terms of workload diversity, data centers encompass various types of workloads, including artificial intelligence servers, storage servers, operating systems, virtual environments, and cloud-based applications. Each workload component has its own unique requirements and characteristics, thereby increasing the complexity of resource scheduling and system optimization.

In terms of the rapid evolution of data technologies, the iteration cycles of chip processes, artificial intelligence, machine learning, and big data analytics are continuously shortening. These developments introduce new resource costs for intelligent integrated management in data centers.

From the perspective of the integration of intelligent technologies, data centers have progressed from the stage of efficiency improvement through informatization and automation to the stage of digitalization and intelligence empowerment. Intelligent technologies have been integrated into various aspects of data center construction, integration, monitoring, and business operations.

From the perspective of multi-cloud hybrid environments, while meeting the demands of cloud applications, data infrastructure and cloud services have formed hybrid cloud and multi-cloud organizational strategies. Consequently, the complexity of coordination scheduling, data migration, security policies, and other aspects has significantly increased across different environments.

In terms of energy efficiency, the scale of hardware and software in data centers, along with business demands, has shown exponential growth. This necessitates complementary optimization between traditional and new energy sources [1], efficiency improvements in equipment and environmental cooling, as well as meeting new regulatory requirements in production and surrounding environments.

From the perspective of information security, ensuring the security of sensitive data, guarding against network attacks, effectively assessing security postures, and promptly triggering emergency measures are all fundamental security requirements that increase the complexity of secure data center operations.

From the perspective of regulatory compliance, data centers not only need to comply with safety production supervision requirements but also need to meet various technical industry service standards such as basic energy consumption, reliable transmission, and trusted computing.

The operational challenges of data centers not only face dual pressures from the technological and business environments but also represent an urgent need for their own intelligent development competition. Therefore, employing artificial intelligence technology to further address various issues such as technological development, professional management, and operational strategies is particularly pressing.

56.3 Artificial Intelligence's Advantages and Capabilities in Enhancing Data Center Operations

With the rapid growth of digital infrastructure demand, continuously rising energy costs, and the ongoing expansion of the need for skilled technical personnel, integrating artificial intelligence technology into the entire process of data center operations will become a fundamental functional requirement. Since 2015, various industries have gradually realized that artificial intelligence technology will bring about significant transformations in production and operations. By establishing effective machine learning processes, achieving project development and production operations based on machine learning, and further enhancing the ability to transform artificial intelligence models into new productive forces, it becomes essential to integrate them into the entire process of research and development and operational systems [2].

Research statistics indicate that the global adoption rate of artificial intelligence technology in the development of system products is projected to increase from 44% in 2022 to 67% in 2025 [3]. According to survey data from 350 technology leaders, including chief information officers and chief technology officers, in countries such as the United States, the United Kingdom, China, India, and Brazil, 65% of technology leaders believe that artificial intelligence (including generative AI, predictive AI, machine learning, and natural language processing) will be the most important technological area in 2024 [4]. According to research statistics from Gartner, by 2025, 50% of data centers will deploy robots with artificial intelligence attributes, leading to an improvement in data center operational efficiency by more than 30% after deployment [5]. Data center operations have undergone four stages: manual operations dependent on human labor, process-driven operations centered on institutional standards, platform-based automation operations relying on computer programs, and intelligent operations integrated with next-generation information technologies such as artificial intelligence. Currently, data centers in China are generally in the stage of platform-based automation operations, and the next step of intelligent operation and maintenance will accelerate the deep integration of the three-layer architecture of data center facilities, platforms, and services. Intelligent operation and maintenance of data centers include not only automated facilities such as electrical, HVAC, security, and temperature and humidity control, as well as intelligent robots for autonomous inspection and operation control, but also digital platforms for monitoring, operation and maintenance, management, and security. It also encompasses organizational management, internal and external industrial resources, quality risk control, and business process optimization [6].

56.4 Implementation Method for Strengthening Data Center Operations Based on Artificial Intelligence

By leveraging artificial intelligence technology, data centers can accelerate their transition towards intelligent operations. Below, we delve into a detailed analysis of the process, methods, and technical effectiveness of integrating artificial intelligence into data centers, using predictive maintenance as an example.

56.4.1 Analysis of the Necessity of Predictive Maintenance in Data Centers

Data centers serve as the uninterrupted digital infrastructure supporting the digital economy around the clock. Frequent data loss, service interruptions, and equipment downtime can result in substantial damage to credibility and economic losses. Therefore, implementing predictive maintenance strategies in data centers is crucial for ensuring continuous operation, minimizing the risk of disruptions, and mitigating potential economic and reputational losses.

From the perspective of reducing operational costs, predictive maintenance enables proactive planning of maintenance activities based on the actual condition of equipment, replacing rigid maintenance schedules with fixed intervals and content. This effectively avoids unnecessary maintenance work, thereby reducing labor, consumables, and other resource costs.

From the perspective of improving system performance, data centers integrate various types of hardware and software components. Predictive maintenance enables comprehensive analysis of the interdependent effects of all system components, thereby achieving globally optimal maintenance. Moreover, predictive maintenance allows for the early identification of potential issues, minimizing downtime to the greatest extent possible.

From the perspective of resource utilization efficiency, effective maintenance of data center equipment will enhance equipment operational efficiency. Predictive maintenance can help identify and correct issues leading to increased consumption of various types of energy such as electricity, coal, oil, gas, water, and heat. These improvements support data center's goals of greenification and sustainable development [7].

From the perspective of system security protection, predictive maintenance not only reduces the time data center maintenance personnel spend operating in complex environments and potential risk areas but also enables continuous monitoring of the integrity and availability of critical information and the compliance and controllability of external access.

From the perspective of industry competitiveness, predictive maintenance supports the formulation of medium to long-term operational plans, allowing for the proactive organization and scheduling of maintenance activities. This facilitates more effective coordination of resources and budgeting of funds, thereby avoiding resource consumption associated with various unforeseen incidents. Simultaneously, it enhances the availability of continuous services in data centers, thereby strengthening the enterprise's competitive advantage within the industry as a whole.

In summary, predictive maintenance in data centers plays a positive role in achieving high standards, reliability, efficiency, low consumption, and sustainable maintenance operations. Additionally, it provides an effective practical strategy for achieving a balance between efficiency and resources in data centers.

56.4.2 Enhancement Strategy for Data Center Operational Capabilities Based on Artificial Intelligence

Based on the scenario of predictive maintenance in data centers and driven by artificial intelligence, the process involves ten key steps along with human–machine feedback loops for iteration. Here are detailed methods for each step (Fig. 56.1):

Determining System Scope. Clearly define the target scope of the predictive maintenance system for the data center's hardware and software systems, including but not limited to various devices and their key technical indicators that need to be monitored and tracked.

Collect Historical Data. Gather historical data from various systems within the data center, including but not limited to equipment basic parameters, operational control data, performance of operational states, internal and external environmental conditions, historical maintenance records, and various types of sensor, operational, and maintenance log data that may affect operational status.

Data Preprocessing. Perform data cleaning and corresponding preprocessing to address missing values, outliers, and duplicate values in the data, ensuring that the data is suitable for training artificial intelligence models.

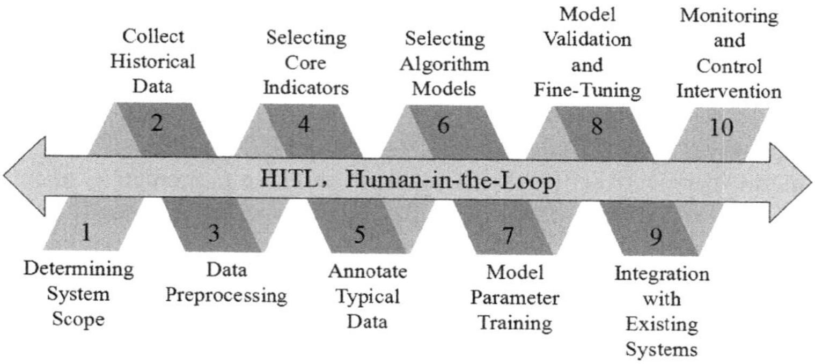

Fig. 56.1 Methods for AI-driven data center operational business scene processes

Selecting Core Indicators. Identify typical indicators or feature variables from the dataset that have a high correlation with the performance health of data center equipment.

Annotate Typical Data. Annotate historical data from the pre-failure and failure periods of the data center, and utilize the annotated data to train artificial intelligence predictive maintenance models.

Selecting Algorithm Models. Based on the characteristics of the business scenarios involved in data center predictive maintenance and the attributes of the data, choose appropriate artificial intelligence models. For instance, Long Short-Term Memory (LSTM) networks are suitable for handling and predicting time series with relatively long intervals and delays [8].

Model Parameter Training. Utilize the annotated dataset to train the selected machine learning model after optimization. Establish an algorithmic model between the learned features and the occurrence of failures using historical data.

Model Validation and Fine-Tuning. Conduct reliability validation and model parameter optimization on the artificial intelligence model using independent datasets of the same type. This ensures that the model exhibits better applicability and consistency.

Integration with Existing Systems. Integrate the trained and fine-tuned artificial intelligence model with the previous operational systems of the data center, incorporating its functionality. Employ the embedded artificial intelligence model within the real-time operational system of the data center to continually receive new data for prediction.

Monitoring and Control Intervention. Utilize the real-time operational system embedded with the artificial intelligence model to achieve predictive monitoring of potential equipment failures. Timely push monitoring and analysis reports to the data center operators, forming maintenance intervention recommendations.

Human-in-the-Loop (HITL). Regularly collect new system data for training artificial intelligence models, and employ a Human-in-the-Loop (HITL) approach to integrate the expertise of human experts (business experts, process experts, technical experts, etc.) into the training process and decision-making control flow of the artificial intelligence system [9]. Through tracking and analyzing the change process, intermediate results, model feedback, backend execution, and other processes, further enhance the transparency and interpretability level of the artificial intelligence system.

The practical methods and basic framework for enhancing data center operational capabilities with AI-driven strategies described above can meet the majority of engineering practice requirements. Data center operators can adapt and optimize the content of the process framework based on the development stage of the data center and business priorities.

In the development and integration process of artificial intelligence technology products, attention should be paid to the correlation and complexity of data center business requirements development. It is essential to clarify the required data quality for business needs and achieve effective usability of data through management or technical means. Data center operators can establish development and operation teams with professional capabilities through self-construction or cooperative development. When integrating artificial intelligence technology products into existing systems, consider system compatibility and interface openness to ensure the stability and scalability of existing systems. To ensure the effective presentation of the application effects of artificial intelligence technology, it is necessary to reasonably plan the development progress of embedded artificial intelligence functions and the implementation application phases. This gradual enhancement of technical capabilities will boost the confidence of data center operators in technical practices, promote continuous and effective investment in artificial intelligence research and development, and achieve steady growth in industry competitiveness.

56.4.3 Practical Effectiveness of Data Center Operations Based on Artificial Intelligence

Artificial intelligence technology, by collecting internal and external data from various aspects such as the environment, equipment, operations, systems, personnel, and business processes in data centers, enables comprehensive scheduling and early warning predictions across all aspects of the data center. In particular, research explorations and engineering practices have been conducted in areas such as equipment structure design, predictive maintenance, resource scheduling, traffic forecasting and classification, network congestion control, data center environmental planning, security threat detection, and adverse information monitoring, resulting in significant achievements [10–12].

Predictive Maintenance. In the realm of predictive maintenance, data center operations engineering teams can intuitively forecast potential equipment system failures and undertake low-cost technical remedies before the occurrence of faults, thereby achieving an optimal balance between data center operational efficiency and cost investment. According to Deloitte research statistics, predictive maintenance can reduce downtime by 5–15% and increase labor productivity by 5–20% [13]. Tencent tracked and monitored 300 uninterruptible power supply (UPS) batteries in data centers for 2 years, accumulating a total of 209,912,615 data points. Utilizing gradient boosted decision tree (GBDT) algorithm based on the collected monitoring data, the prediction accuracy of battery failure reached 98%, averagely predicting replacements 15 days earlier than traditional predetermined replacement time. As a result, data center battery maintenance efficiency increased by more than 8%, significantly reducing the occurrence of data center critical business system downtime caused by battery failures.

Resource Coordination and Scheduling. Artificial intelligence algorithms, based on the workload operation of data centers, coordinate and schedule computing resources, storage space, and network bandwidth, which not only optimize global resource allocation and plan upgrade and expansion requirements rationally but also reduce errors generated by manual scheduling. Globally, data centers consume 1%

of the world's energy demand, and it is projected that by 2030, these data centers will account for 4% of global electricity consumption. By leveraging artificial intelligence technology, data centers can improve automation efficiency, reducing the total power consumption for enterprise cooling by 40% [14]. Google, utilizing the TensorFlow machine learning framework, analyzes the workload patterns and server resource utilization of data centers, and applies the analysis results to schedule and allocate tasks in data center operations, resulting in improved energy utilization efficiency and a 40% reduction in cooling energy consumption.

Optimization of Network Quality. Key network performance indicators such as latency, jitter, and packet loss both within and outside the data center directly impact the service level and business quality of the data center. Artificial intelligence can obtain factors such as network topology, traffic intensity, routing method and network anomalies through analysis and calculation [15]. Researchers have employed neural network models to autonomously learn and determine the importance of performance indicators for end-to-end links in data center networks. This approach characterizes the state and congestion levels of links and achieves predictive modeling of service quality for networks with various structural types in a multi-task parallel environment using the same algorithmic model [16].

56.5 Challenges of Artificial Intelligence in Data Center Operations

Artificial intelligence technology can significantly enhance intelligent capabilities in data center operations. However, it also faces various technical issues and engineering challenges such as data quality, system complexity and heterogeneity, balancing energy efficiency and costs, and ensuring the robustness of core systems.

Data Quality and Availability. Artificial intelligence algorithms rely on high-quality and diverse datasets. However, obtaining comprehensive, accurate, and real-time data from the operations of data centers poses significant challenges. Inaccurate or incomplete data may directly result in suboptimal decisions by artificial intelligence, thereby hindering the effective application and translation of AI algorithms.

Complexity and Heterogeneity of Systems. Data centers typically serve multiple purposes and functions, resulting in a composition of diverse hardware, software, and network components. Moreover, even devices of the same type may follow different technological paths. Therefore, leveraging artificial intelligence to manage this complexity and ensure interoperability compatibility among different systems remains to be improved.

Efficiency in Energy Utilization. While artificial intelligence can optimize data center operations, the training and execution of complex AI models are resource-intensive processes. In particular, upgrading and renovating data centers lead to parameter changes throughout the system, resulting in frequent and substantial energy consumption from secondary training and model optimization.

Disruption to Core Systems. Deploying artificial intelligence algorithms in the actual environment of data centers may introduce uncontrollable interference factors and service risks. When false alarms are triggered by AI algorithms, the control procedures may directly execute emergency plans, posing significant risks to the overall performance and data reliability of the data center.

Scalability of Intelligent Solutions. The intelligent solutions formed by artificial intelligence need to continuously expand as the scale and complexity of data centers grow. The increasing business requirements, technical solutions, software systems, and hardware devices in data centers will result in a continuous increase in factors and their correlations that artificial intelligence algorithms need to consider, thereby continuously raising the applicability requirements of intelligent solutions for data centers.

Security and Privacy Protection. Intelligent systems based on artificial intelligence require access to comprehensive information about the data center during both the training phase and the decision-making process. This may involve sensitive data within the data center, and various aspects such as access boundaries and operations of artificial intelligence models may pose risks of privacy breaches [17].

Continuous Learning and Resource Constraints. The internal and external environments of data centers are constantly changing, requiring artificial intelligence models to adapt and learn continuously. The costs associated with upgrading artificial intelligence hardware and software facilities to accommodate these changes, as well as the consumption of training resources, may limit the effectiveness of more advanced artificial intelligence solutions. This constraint is particularly evident for small to medium-sized data centers.

Lack of Explainability. Artificial intelligence models, especially those based on deep learning, still suffer from a certain degree of "black box" issue regarding the interpretability of the resulting application models [18]. Consequently, the lack of transparency in decision-making and control triggered by artificial intelligence hinders the controllability of intelligent operations in data centers.

56.6 The Future Trends of Artificial Intelligence in Data Center Operations

As artificial intelligence becomes deeply integrated with data centers, AI technology products continue to evolve in form, functionality, and business domains. New formats of technology efficacy and application patterns emerge continuously.

Autonomous Data Centers. Traditional data centers rely on professional operators and computer systems at the core of information-assisted operational management. Artificial intelligence technology is driving a new operational model for data centers, enabling autonomous management, automatic optimization, and proactive defense without human intervention [19].

Composite Computing Integration. The digital economy will drive comprehensive digitization across all industries. Artificial intelligence will facilitate efficient resource collaboration and reliable data flow among various types of data centers, including traditional data centers, supercomputing centers, intelligent computing centers, and edge data centers. This supports diverse data demand scenarios across cloud, network, edge, and end points.

AI Edge Hardware. Traditional data centers typically employ intelligent software and hardware components consisting of "source-end sensor data + mid-end computing hardware + end-end execution units". The next generation of data centers will utilize AI edge hardware, which integrates functions such as data collection, processing, compression, transmission, and rapid decision-making. These devices can independently perform functions upon network connection or aggregation.

Interpretable AI Models. As artificial intelligence assumes more core functionalities in data center operations, ensuring the reliability of autonomous control becomes paramount. Consequently, interpretable and understandable AI models will gradually become mainstream. Transparent AI models will reduce cognitive biases in people's understanding of data center operations, enhancing trustworthiness in intelligent systems.

Human–Machine Normative Collaboration. Artificial intelligence technology serves not only as an intelligent assistant to human engineers but also as a supervisor ensuring adherence to engineering conduct guidelines. AI generates corresponding auxiliary rules through industry self-discipline norms, technical operating procedures, safety production regulations, data flow risks, and other content. Simultaneously, efforts are made to prevent technical ethical risks stemming from issues such as algorithmic discrimination and algorithmic black boxes.

56.7 Conclusions

Various types of data centers, including general data centers, supercomputing centers, intelligent computing centers, and edge data centers, have become important pillars supporting the development of new productivity and new industrialization, as well as serving as the core infrastructure for the high-quality development of the digital economy. The next generation of information technologies such as artificial intelligence will rapidly permeate various business demands. The rational and compliant integration of next-generation information technologies such as artificial intelligence into various data centers will play a pivotal role in rapidly driving both upstream and downstream aspects of the data center industry, and will provide pilot templates and solution references for innovation in related industry scenarios.

Acknowledgements This work was financially supported by the National Key Research and Development Program (2023YFD1202705).

References

1. Li, Y., Huang, J., Liu, Y., Wang, H., Wang, Y., Ai, X.: A multicriteria optimal operation framework for a data center microgrid considering renewable energy and waste heat recovery: use of balanced decision making. IEEE Ind. Appl. Mag. **29**(4), 23–38 (2023)
2. Institute of Cloud Computing and Big Data, Key Laboratory of Artificial Intelligence Key Technology and Application Evaluation, Artificial Intelligence R&D Operating System Practice Guide. China Academy of Information and Communications Technology (2023)
3. Srivastava, S.: A Comprehensive Guide on AI Integration in Business Processes, https://appinventiv.com/blog/ai-integration-and-implementation/. Last accessed 12 Jan 2024
4. IEEE, Artificial intelligence in its many forms will be the most important area of technology in 2024, According to New IEEE Global Survey of CIOs, CTOs and technology leaders, https://www.ieee.org/about/news/2023/news-release-2023-survey-results.html. Last accessed 20 Jan 2024
5. Rimol, M.: Gartner predicts half of cloud data centers will deploy robots with AI capabilities by 2025, https://www.gartner.com/en/newsroom/press-releases/2021-11-01-gartner-predicts-half-of-cloud-data-centers-will-deploy-robots-with-ai-capabilties-by-2025. Last accessed 25 Jan 2024
6. Institute of cloud computing and big data, and open data center council, data center intelligent operation and maintenance development research report. China Academy of Information and Communications Technology (2023)
7. Raja, S.P.: Green computing: a future perspective and the operational analysis of a data center. IEEE Trans. Comput. Soc. Syst. **9**(2), 650–656 (2022)
8. Mosqueira-Rey, E., Hernández-Pereira, E., Alonso-Ríos, D.: Human-in-the-loop machine learning: a state of the art. Artif. Intell. Rev. **56**, 3005–3054 (2023)
9. Chen, X., Tu, R., Li, M., Yang, X., Jia, K.: Hot spot temperature prediction and operating parameter estimation of racks in data center using machine learning algorithms based on simulation data. Build. Simul. **16**, 2159–2176 (2023)
10. Xu, J., Xu, C., Hu, X.: Research on air distribution temperature prediction of data center room based on artificial intelligence algorithm. Des. Tech. Posts Telecommun. **12**, 52–56 (2022)
11. Wang, D., Li, D., Peng, J.: A survey of server energy consumption models in data center. Comput. Meas. Control. **31**, 7–15 (2023)
12. Liang, Y., Zhang, M., Shen, Y.: Internet data center bad information supervision system based on artificial intelligence. Netw. Secur. Technol. Appl. **4**, 23–25 (2024)
13. Tang, J.X., Du, J.H., Lin, Y., Jia, Q.S.: Predictive maintenance of VRLA batteries in UPS towards reliable data centers. IFAC-PapersOnLine **53**, 13607–13612 (2020)
14. Open Data Center Council 2023 Data center adaptive AI energy conservation white paper, https://hulianhutongshequ.cn/upload/tank/report/2023/202310/1/9d754383f3e9477f997179de035f632b.pdf. Last accessed 15 Feb 2024
15. Yi, Z., Zilin, Z., Yuhe, Z.: Application status and development of artificial intelligence technology in large data center. In: Proceedings of the SPIE **12703** (2023) ID. 127030A 7
16. Muhaimeen, A., Aadithiyaprasana, K., Ranjith, A., Sasirekha, S.P., Reshma, R., Mekala, N.: A novel approach to predict the severity of peripheral neuropathy using machine learning. In: 2023 7th International Conference on Intelligent Computing and Control Systems (ICICCS). Madurai, India, pp. 1–7 (2023)
17. Dawoud, M., Altilar, D.T.: Privacy-preserving data retrieval using anonymous query authentication in data cloud services. In: Proceedings of the 6th International Conference on Cloud Computing and Services Science. SciTePress, Lisbon Portugal, pp. 171–180 (2010)
18. Huawei Technologies Co Ltd., Data center 2030, https://www.huawei.com/en/giv/data-center-2030. Last accessed 21 Mar 2024
19. Chen, X.: Ethical risk and its governance of artificial intelligence: based on the path of the algorithm audit system. Stud. Dialectics Nat. **39**, 138–141 (2023)

Chapter 57
Research on Chief Data Officer's Role Values, Competence Responsibilities, and Organizational Structure

Jun Yu

Abstract With generative AI technology sparking a lot of interest in the market, data and modeling have become the focus of industry attention. Organizations are beginning to rethink and reframe their data strategies in terms of supporting the development of AI. In this process, the role of Chief Data Officers (CDOs) has become particularly prominent, and they have become a key force in driving organizational change and converging technology and management practices. This article first explores how organizations can achieve digital intelligence transformation from "business-driven" to "data-driven". It outlines how CDOs are deployed in 2,500 large enterprises around the world and highlights the key role they play in organizations. The article further delves into the ten key responsibilities and tasks of CDOs, which cover the organization and management of data resources and the transformation of data value. In addition, the article discusses the organizational structure of the CDO team, both internal and external, and how these structures can assist the CDO in functioning more effectively. Finally, the article offers a series of recommendations aimed at helping society as a whole maximize the effectiveness of CDOs and provides concluding thoughts on the future development of CDOs. Through these analyses and recommendations, the article aims to provide a comprehensive perspective for understanding the importance of CDOs in the current data-driven era and offers guidance on how organizations can more effectively leverage the capabilities of CDOs.

J. Yu (✉)
School of Computer and Information Technology (School of Big Data), Shanxi University, Taiyuan Shanxi, China
e-mail: y.j@sxu.edu.cn

Shanxi Taihang Laboratory Co., Ltd., Taiyuan Shanxi, China

Taihang Laboratory In Shanxi Province (Advanced Computing Laboratory In Shanxi Province), Taiyuan Shanxi, China

F. P. García Márquez et al. (eds.), *Computing, Internet of Things and Data Analytics*, Smart Innovation, Systems and Technologies 387,
https://doi.org/10.1007/978-3-031-87154-2_57

57.1 Introduction

In terms of data growth, the mobile Internet has accelerated the rapid spread and high prosperity of the online world of social media and e-commerce, while also driving explosive data growth. In terms of analytical capability, the effective integration of mathematical methods such as mathematical statistics, data mining, artificial intelligence and computing power has accelerated the popularity of analytical tools and the improvement of data analysis capability. In terms of industry competition, the mobile Internet has lowered the threshold of entrepreneurship, but at the same time raised the difficulty of profitability. Business competition such as customized products, precise customer acquisition and differentiated services has also stimulated the market demand for supply. Research on "Regional Digital Economy" and "Data Management" is in its initial stage and is a potential area of future research. Chief Data Officer (CDO), as the core role of driving data transformation in various organizations around the world, is not only the leader of digital transformation and data innovation in organizations, but also becomes the new competitiveness in the digital economy [1].

According to PwC's CDO research report, as of June 2023, the number of the world's largest 2,500 publicly traded enterprises with a chief data officer is 590 (24%). In terms of regional distribution, the rate of enterprise chief data officer deployment in North America, South America, Europe, the Middle East and Africa, and Asia–Pacific is 31%, 17%, 34%, 25%, and 11%, respectively, with the penetration of CDOs in enterprises in developing regions continuing to grow. From the perspective of enterprise size, the chief data officer staffing rate of enterprises with 5,000–25,000 personnel is 46%, and the chief data officer staffing rate of enterprises with 25,000–100,000 personnel is 24%. In terms of the characteristics of the incumbents, the chief data officer is 82% male, has a technical background of about 70%, and has no less than 20 years of professional experience in the industry [2–4]. In terms of industry type, chief data officers are mainly located in insurance, finance, entertainment and media, retail, information technology, communications, consumer goods, and supply chain [5]. From the perspective of corporate financial quality and stock market response, return on assets (ROA, Return on Assets) is positively correlated with CDO job allocation, while market to book ratio (M/B, Market to Book Ratio) is negatively correlated with CDO job allocation. Companies that appoint CDOs have more competitive advantages in terms of profit ratios and cost ratios, and the stock market responds more positively to the appointment of CDOs for companies with high growth prospects. Various research institutions and organizations define the value of a chief data officer in different ways [6, 7].

57.2 Digital Intelligence Transformation of "Business-Driven" to "Data-Driven"

In the case of traditional industry enterprises, enterprise assets are resources that are formed through historical transactions or events, owned or controlled by the enterprise and are expected to generate economic benefits for the enterprise, and the source cost and value of these assets can be measured reliably. The traditional "three financial statements" of an enterprise are balance sheet, cash flow statement and income statement, in which the balance sheet reflects the enterprise's control of economic resources and operation status, the income statement reflects the enterprise's profitability, operational efficiency and industry competitiveness, and the cash flow statement reflects the enterprise's ability to consolidate, dispatch and distribute cash within a certain period of time.

In the digital economy model, the data asset statement has become the "fourth asset statement" of an enterprise, which reflects the ability of an enterprise to resource, asset, capitalize and value its data. Under the perspective of data assets, enterprises focus more on three "digital" development strategies, namely: "digital framework" strategy to build data strategy and re-engineer organizational thinking, "digital business" strategy to optimize internal processes and upgrade user experience, and "digital capability" strategy to promote technology-enabled business and case empowerment in the industry. Enterprise information architecture of traditional industries is a business-type driven application-based development process, the specific process is as follows:

(1) Determining the development goals and organizational structure of the enterprise.
(2) Decomposing the overall objectives into business units with different functions.
(3) Sorting out the internal and external work-flows involved in the business departments.
(4) IT department summarizes business process requirements, plans hardware facility requirements such as network, memory and server, software development requirements such as database, middle ware and operating system, and security protection requirements such as firewall, intrusion detection and penetration testing.
(5) Clarifying and determining the list of system-related data such as meta-data and master data involved in the business process system.

Since the information architecture is based on the current or short-term business processes and functional requirements, this type of system construction model has obvious short-term advantages in the Return On Investment. But there is a strong coupling between data, processes and systems, which makes data reuse and system maintenance more difficult, and each system is relatively independent, which can easily lead to problems such as data chimneys and information silos. A data-driven, integrated development approach can effectively address these issues, with the following process:

(1) Determining the development goals and organizational structure of the enterprise.
(2) Comparing the overall objectives with relevant data for combing.
(3) Building a data architecture based on the collection of the above data, e.g., a data lake.
(4) Combining the data architecture to sort out the requirements for hardware facilities, software development and security protection needed to support it.
(5) Combining the business systems involved in the data in a fragmented manner to form a data-based business front-end function.

The data-driven design and development approach effectively narrows the scope of system planning for the enterprise, further simplifying the complexity and flexibility of delivering requirements through data and functional precipitation and reuse. With data as the core, it realizes the weak coupling relationship among data, process and system, and realizes the integrated management of data assets from a global perspective, including data resource standards, process logic specification, business analysis model, centralized operation and maintenance system, and exchange and sharing opening, effectively reducing the problems of scattered abnormalities, duplication and missing data and unclear attribution, and thus can more quickly meet the business application development needs. The centralized data asset management enhances the availability and security of data, and the system upgrade iteration and function planning has better long-term and forward-looking, which is more conducive to the effective transmission feedback and implementation of organizational strategies.

57.3 CDO Role Positioning Analysis

With the development of the global economy and society, the refined division of responsibilities and specialized competency requirements have given rise to a number of positions with "chief" as a preposition, such as: CEO (Chief Executive Officer) with organizational development and daily administration as the core; CFO (Chief Financial Officer) with financial strategic operations as the core; CIO (Chief Information Officer) with information systems architecture and optimization as the core; CTO (Chief Technology Officer) with product development and manufacturing as the core; CGO (Chief Growth Officer) who focuses on market discovery and demand, and CCO (Chief Content Officer) who centers on content marketing and creative planning, etc. The Chief Data Officer (CDO), on the other hand, is responsible for transforming the value of data by enhancing the organization's data resource capabilities.

Among these "chief" positions, Chief Information Officer (CIO) and Chief Data Officer (CDO) are inclined to create the illusion of similar or even identical functions. Thus, taking enterprises as an example of industrial organization form clarifies the differences between the Chief Information Officer (CIO) and Chief Data Officer

(CDO), from the perspective of the role responsibilities, service objects, problem solving, information technology, data use, career direction and so on.

Role Responsibility. From the perspective of role positioning, CIO is mainly to realize enterprise data, while CDO focuses on realizing data enterprise. In terms of main responsibilities, CIO focuses on overall planning and integrated application based on information technology resources and forms information system, while CDO focuses on data quality governance based on data resources, data-driven demand, data business value-added and intelligent business model change and forms digital intelligence experience.

Service Object. In terms of service objects, CIO mainly serves various business departments within the organization to achieve informationization and automation of business processes, and CIO mainly serves various departments inside and outside the organization, including but not limited to: business process departments, data security supervision departments, data demand service targets, industry data partners, etc.

Problem Solving. In terms of solving core problems, the CIO figures out the "current problem", i.e., where is the business process, what is the business status, and where the problem lies, while the CDO solves the "potential problem", i.e., why is this happening, how to solve the problem and what is the expected effect.

Information Technology. From the perspective of information technology, CIO realizes centralized management of IT capabilities for various technologies and equipment, and continuously reduces the failure rate of equipment and the risk of system outages, while CDO promotes the popularization of data capabilities based on IT capabilities, builds business decision models based on digital technologies and analytical algorithms, and realizes the effective transformation of data assets into data values.

Data Use. In terms of data usage, CIO builds business processes based on the needs of the business units and then sorts out the corresponding data sets, while the CDO coordinates the data life cycle in a data-driven manner and inspires strategic decisions and clarifies tactical paths.

Career Direction. From the perspective of career development direction, CIO is responsible for IT construction, which needs to maintain a high degree of consistency and moderate foresight with the enterprise's business process, therefore, CIO is usually familiar with the enterprise's business flow operation process and current asset management process, and thus CIO will develop towards the chief process official (CPO); The CDO is responsible for the integration and discovery of internal and external data. The flow and changes of data not only cover all aspects and states of internal operations, but also realize the "resonance" with the long-term major decisions and strategic intentions of the enterprise's decision makers, therefore, the CDO will develop towards the direction of Chief Executive Officer (CEO).

57.4 Capabilities and Responsibilities of the Chief Data Officer

The different development of digital economy determines the differential capability dimensions and task requirements for CDO. In the Big Data 1.0 stage, digital technology is used as the driving force to improve the operational efficiency of enterprises through the application of IT experts to analyze the internal data of enterprises. At the stage of Big Data 2.0, market competition is the driving force to achieve enterprise market capability improvement through IT and industry market experts' mining and analysis of internal and external data in this industry. In the stage of Big Data 3.0, industry collaboration is the driving force to realize the self-iteration and superiority of the industrial ecology through data collaboration and intelligent analysis of cross-industry internal and external data by experts in IT, industry market, economics, psychology, communication, etc. Due to the differences in development stages and industry attributes, the understanding and usage of CDO by various types of organizations are bound to differ, but the CDO's capability requirements and scope of authority and responsibility will be gradually clarified and the CDO's capability and value will be maximized in the integration process of CDO, enterprise, business and industry.

Data itself is highly complex, multidimensionally relevant and systematically fluid, and also a strategic resource with uniqueness, non-exhaustion and low depletion in organizations. Various social organizations providing business services and operation management have entered a stage of development where "defensive passive data application" for operation management and legal compliance and "offensive active data innovation" for insight into business opportunities and identification of value paths coexist [8–11]. CDO will undertake tasks and responsibilities in 10 areas including data resource organization, data platform integration, data asset management, data value transformation, data support for decision-making, data resource collaboration, data capability enhancement, data risk management and control, career system construction, and industry organization construction, etc. and effectively enhance the organization's data competitiveness.

Data Resource Organization. As the first responsible person for data management, the CDO should sort out and clarify the data strategy development goals and tasks based on the value of data assets. Formation of a data asset management committee involving data generation, use, supervision and other departments and establishment of a joint coordination and decision-making mechanism to clarify the data strategy and implementation path, and establish the legal and management authority of the functions of relevant data agencies. Set up the data resource operation and maintenance department as a permanent institution for data management innovation, and clarify the boundaries of the scope of responsibility.

Data Platform Integration. Break island and data stack within the organization system, and build a unified data center (data lake) and intelligent business foundation analysis tool platform to support business departments through a data-driven design and development approach (other non-data-related IT construction work is still undertaken by the CIO). At the same time, the data system is designed and managed in a decentralized and domain-specific manner, with data privacy regulation and legal compliance supervision and audit embedded through log detection, network probes and other technical means.

Data Asset Management. Technical standards and operating procedures are formulated around data process optimization, data integration and storage, data structure management, data sharing and opening, data mining and analysis, data security operation and maintenance, etc., and eventually a relatively stable data organization structure and a continuous and sound data management system are formed.

Data Value Transformation. Establish the long-term goals and tasks of the data strategy and short-term business content, and carry out product design and development, service model upgrade, inefficient cost reduction, market customer development, business resource cooperation and other related commercialization value activities based on internal and external data resources. At the same time, consider converting abstract data, algorithms, and methods into easily understandable and acceptable expression content.

Data Support Decision-making. Integrating information system resources to build a data-oriented service support platform, through the analysis of data to form quantifiable, assessable, iterable and executable strategic-level or business-level decision-making reference and strategy guidelines, further supporting the strategic decision-making level direction selection, tactical management level goal implementation and task execution level action mode.

Data Resource Collaboration. Relying on the data resources operation and maintenance department to establish data strategy implementation safeguards, supervise the implementation of data management systems and procedures, and coordinate the resolution of internal business implementation and external cooperation needs. Establish intelligent monitoring and review tools to form periodic or thematic data management reports for presentation to decision makers.

Data Capability Enhancement. Establish a data strategy policy system and data strategy development concept within the organization, clarify national, industry and organizational policies and regulations in the data field, conduct training and assessment of knowledge and skills related to data integration and application practices in business departments, and promote organization members to have basic knowledge and basic methods such as the connotation and meaning of big data, characteristics and types, and be able to use common data analysis tools or self-built data platforms.

Data Risk Control. The integration of institutional systems and technical means will further strengthen data services and industry applications with rules and standards and method boundaries. From the macroscopic point of view, it is necessary to build data strategy and development plan, improve data security and privacy protection system. In the medium view, it is necessary to establish data risk control system, data ethics and technology supervision methods. From the microscopic point of view, it is necessary to improve authority boundaries, quality management, regulatory processes, risk assessment and contingency plans, etc.

Career System Construction. The CDO, as the proponent and facilitator of data strategy, is expected to develop a leadership competency system and knowledge skill standards in the areas of organizational development strategy methodology and post-assessment, new enterprise organization management for the digital economy, techno-economic analysis, industry model innovation, and technology leadership. Relying on the CDO social group to gradually form a performance assessment method and promotion reward and punishment mechanism that combines qualitative assessment and quantitative measurement, and integrates regular traditional evaluation and random innovative assessment.

Industry Organization Construction. The CDO is not only a data strategist within the organization, but also a data developer for the industry. Therefore, every CDO or data commissioner should actively build a legal social organization for industry self-regulation, professional qualification, competence assessment, and rights protection, in order to provide all-round, profound, multi-angle, and high-security data application services for various industries in society, and help the healthy and benign development of digital economy (Table 57.1).

Table 57.1 Differentiation comparison between CIO with CDO

Comparative dimensions	Chief information officer (CIO)	Chief data officer(CDO)
"Data-enabled" roles	Data-intensive of corporation	Corporatization of data
Primary duties and responsibilities	Informatization and automation Building information system	Data and Intelligence Forming a digital intelligence experience
Service target group	Various internal business departments	Internal and external demand departments / individual customers
Addressing core issues	**Current problems**	**Potential problems**
	Where is the process? What is the status? Where are the problems	Why is it happening? How to solve the symptom? What are the expected results
Information technology objectives	Centralization of IT capabilities	Universalization of data capabilities
	Coordinate all types of technology and equipment to reduce the risk of failure and service outages	Construct business decision models based on digital technology and analytical algorithms to realize the value transformation of data assets
Data usage results	Information integration to master business processes	Data-driven to support decision-making at all levels
Career development direction	Chief process officer (CPO)	Chief executive officer (CEO)

57.5 Analysis of the Chief Data Officer's Organizational Structure

As the leader and explorer of data strategy, CDO not only needs to set up a data team (or department) with various skills, but also requires leading the team to promote the continuous upgrade and evolution of the organization towards data resource, data asset and data capitalization. This study addresses the question of how to build a CDO-centered organizational structure by constructing an "internal" structure and an "external" structure for the team.

57.5.1 The "In-team" Structure of the Chief Data Officer

Take the CDO in the field of government affairs as an example, its task covers the function positioning in many areas such as architecture planning and implementation, analysis and application and security supervision of government data, exchange and sharing and cooperation and coordination, and innovation and cultivation of data culture. If the CDO successfully meets the requirements of the position and builds organizational capacity, he or she will need to assemble and lead a team of data specialists with different competencies. These data specialists include both business and management experts in specific areas, as well as technical and algorithmic experts with mathematical or computer knowledge.

Business Process Expert. This expert is familiar with business and process, and builds efficient business scenarios and process links in the organization by sorting out common processes in the industry, can clarify the correspondence between data assets and business scenarios, is processed with accurately classifying the priority level of business scenarios, and providing business modeling suggestions and analysis result opinions for data governance and data services.

Data Infrastructure Specialist. This expert can efficiently collaborate with IT departments to establish a data infrastructure system suitable for data enterprise, carry out architecture planning, construction management and maintenance upgrade centered on data center, data warehouse, etc., and provide the foundation for the organization with software and hardware services support in terms of data extraction, cleaning, transformation, loading (ETL), data lake (or data middle), etc.

Data Governance Specialist. This expert will establish basic standards for data collection and use, and enhance specifications for data security and privacy protection, organize the development of data governance tools and open platforms for business needs and continuously ensure the availability and usability of the tools and systems, and eventually form industry-wide standardized components or open source platforms for APIs.

Data Analysis Expert. This expert should be proficient in using mathematical theories, basic algorithms and programming tools related to data analysis, forming measurable, quantifiable, describable and visualized data analysis reports based on business problems, and establishing intelligent algorithms and high-quality models with good generality and interactivity.

Data Sharing Expert. This expert should build data classification, categorization and sub-domain standards, establish data use authority audit and supervision mechanism, enhance the credibility and availability of data by using block chain, privacy computing and other technologies, actively promote the construction of data exchange and sharing platform, and promote the integration and application of data between industries.

Data Competence Expert. The expert shall establish the development system of data technology and business application of lecture content, curriculum system, training plan and ability assessment in combination with industry data application cases, promote the mutual integration of data ability assessment and appointment and promotion system, organize and carry out external exchanges of data training, and continuously optimize the construction of training curriculum system.

Data Policy Experts. The expert should be familiar with industrial planning, industry plans, support incentives, laws and regulations in data collection, use, exchange and sharing, comply with national policies and regulations, and cooperate with third party identification or regulatory inspection, participate in and promote the establishment of data rules of the industry and the organization.

Data Supervision Specialist. This expert shall supervise the compliance of the whole process of data collection and storage, use and analysis, and output of results inside and outside the organization, through "technical check and balance technology", "algorithm impact assessment", "mechanism design to protect personal privacy" and other means to avoid data risks brought about by issues such as irregular collection, data property rights, algorithm discrimination, algorithm black box, individual privacy, and public right to know.

With the implementation of data strategy and the extension of business boundary, the team of data specialists will be enriched, for example, data collection experts, who are responsible for the development of hardware collection devices such as sensors and Internet of Things or software collection methods such as web crawlers and feature quantification, while the personal competence boundary of data specialists will be continuously broken and gradually blurred, but their respective core competencies still need to be summarized through continuous learning and practice in order to be competent for external changes.

57.5.2 The "Outside-team" Structure of the Chief Data Officer

The data resource operations and maintenance department, with the Chief Data Officer (CDO) at its core, plays an important role in organizational development, and the position of the role in the organizational framework also directly affects its resource authority, scope of role and value release. Based on the position of

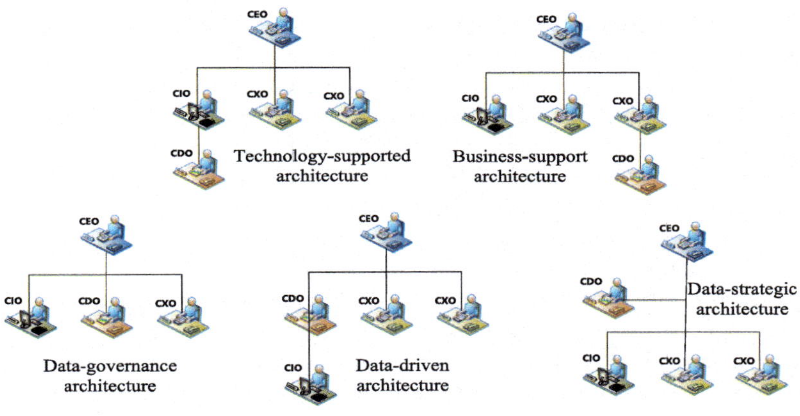

Fig. 57.1 Types of CDO subordination structures

the Chief Data Officer (CDO)'s subordinate relationship with the Chief Executive Officer (CEO), Chief Information Officer (CIO) and other Chief X Officers (CXO), the Chief Data Officer and his team can be classified into five categories, namely, technical support, business support, data governance, data-driven, and data strategy (Fig. 57.1).

Technology-supported Architecture. The top level of the organization in the technology-supported architecture is the CEO, the middle is the CIO and CXO, and the CDO is subordinate to the vertical management of the CIO. This architecture is based on information system as the core, which facilitates the mutual integration and coordinated management of information system and data resources. Since the CDO is subordinate to the CIO management, it is easy to generate problems such as system architecture taking priority over data architecture and system process-oriented taking priority over data resource-oriented.

Business-support Architecture. The top level of the organization in the business support architecture is the CEO, the middle level is the CIO and CXO, and the CDO is subordinate to the vertical management of CXO. This architecture is centered on business enhancement and achieves effective support of business data for business scenario requirements. As the CDO is subordinate to the CXO management, it is prone to low efficiency of collaboration between CDO and CIO and limitations of business data, which in turn leads to problems such as data chimney and information islands.

Data-governance Architecture. In the data governance architecture, the top level of the organization is the CEO, and the CIO, CXO and CDO are all intermediate and equal. This architecture makes data governance an important component of the enterprise, which promotes the integration of data and information systems and business requirements, and promotes data integration and cross-departmental applications, but also puts high demands on the departmental coordination and communication ability of CDOs.

Data-driven Architecture. The highest level of the organization in the data-driven architecture is the CEO, the middle level is the CDO and CXO, and the CIO is subordinate to the vertical management of the CDO. This kind of architecture treats data as the information department of the enterprise, realizes data-centered information system construction, and facilitates the organization to coordinate data resources and IT resources, while the CDO needs to undertake part of the information system planning and construction work.

Data-strategic Architecture. In the data-strategic architecture, the top level of the organization is the CEO, the middle level is the CIO and CXO, and the CDO is located between the top level and the middle level. This architecture treats data as a strategic sector of the enterprise, The CDO can directly manage the CIO and CXO to achieve the maximum degree of coordination and scheduling of IT resources and business resources, and the CDO needs to have global control and full business insight.

The type of CDO subordination structure mentioned above is not only governed by the CEO's perception of data value and the CDO's own ability level, but also related to the development stage of the organization (start-up, growth, maturity, development and decline). Therefore, the "internal" and "external" structures of the Chief Data Officer's team should be continuously adjusted from a matching perspective to achieve efficient allocation of organizational resources and maximum release of CDO value.

57.6 Conclusion

For the industry, the birth of each position is the demand for specialized services in the context of technological evolution and economic development, and CDO is the embodiment of market demand for data resourcefulness. CDO has become the promoter and practitioner of digital economy development in different industry fields, and will be integrated with industry attributes under the framework of job competency requirements and work task responsibilities, forming a job function and organizational structure system in line with industry and business development stages. Meanwhile, as the number of CDO personnel increases and industry penetration improves, the competency evaluation method and career development path of CDO will become more scientific, standardized and regulated.

This paper provides an in-depth analysis of the critical role of Chief Data Officers (CDOs) in the digital economy and their importance in driving the transformation of organizations from business-driven to data-driven.CDOs not only serve as leaders and explorers of data strategy, but they are also responsible for building the data team to enhance the organization's data resourcing, data assetization, and data capitalization capabilities. By building internal and external organizational structures, CDOs can effectively enhance an organization's data competitiveness and facilitate the application and value transformation of data at all levels. Based on the above research, there are the following recommendations:

Organizational Structure Optimization. Organizations should clarify the roles and responsibilities of CDOs and provide them with sufficient support and resources in the organizational structure to ensure the effective implementation of data strategies.

Capability Development. CDOs should continuously develop their technical background and management capabilities to adapt to the rapidly changing data environment.

Data Governance Enhancement. Organizations need to establish and maintain a strong data governance framework to ensure data quality and security.

Cross-sector Collaboration. Collaboration between CDOs and other executives, such as CIOs, is encouraged to break down data silos and enable data integration and sharing.

While the roles and responsibilities of the CDO may vary across industries and organizations of different sizes, the research in this paper suggests that the CDO is critical to any organization looking to succeed in the data-driven era. Future research could further explore the specific practices of CDOs in different environments and how they adapt to changing technological and managerial challenges. It is also worth delving deeper into how CDOs can collaborate more effectively with other executives in their organizations and how they can drive data strategy on a global scale.

Acknowledgements This study was supported by the Special project of Applied Technology Research of Shanxi Cloud Times Technology Co., LTD. (2023-YJ-005).

References

1. Christofi, M.: The role of chief digital officer: critical insights into an emerging field and road map for future research. J. Bus. Res. **172**, 114390 (2016). https://doi.org/10.1016/j.jbusres.2023.114390
2. Strategy, Chief data officer is on the rise in the era of data assets, https://www.strategyand.pwc.com/cn/zh/reports-and-studies/2022/chief-data-officer-is-rising-feb2022.html. Last accessed 21 Jan 2024
3. PwC, The chief data officer: unlocking the value of data to lead innovation transformation, https://www.pwccn.com/zh/consulting/value-creating-chief-data-officers-mar2023.pdf, last accessed 12 Feb 2024
4. PwC, The dilemma of the chief data officer: fulfilling management responsibilities and demonstrating the value of data, https://www.pwccn.com/zh/consulting/the-chief-data-officer-in-a-dilemma-may2024.pdf. Last accessed 16 Mar 2024
5. Treder, M.: Das Management-Handbuch für Chief Data Officer: Die Daten-Supply Chain. Springer Vieweg Berkeley, CA, pp. 39–51 (2023)
6. Zhan, X., Mu, Y., Nishant, R., Singhal, V.R.: When do appointments of chief digital or data officers (CDOs) affect stock prices? IEEE Trans. Eng. Manag. 69(4):1308–1321 (2022). https://doi.org/10.1109/TEM.2020.2984619
7. Hartmann, M., Kulminskaya, T., Wojtowicz, M.: Chief data officer: bindeglied in der organisation um den Wert von Daten zu maximieren. Datenschutz Datensich **47**, 446–449 (2023). https://doi.org/10.1007/s11623-023-1795-8

8. Raković, L., Marić, S., Đorđević Milutinović, L., Sakal, M., Antić, S.: What about the chief digital officer? A literature review. Sustainability **14**(8), 4696 (2022). https://doi.org/10.3390/su14084696
9. Schachtner, C.: The role "chief digital officer (CDO)" in public municipalities—the conceptual effect of a functional profile for successful transformation. Smart Cities **6**(2), 809–818 (2023). https://doi.org/10.3390/smartcities6020039
10. Bendig, D., Wagner, R., Piening, E.P., Foege, J.N.: Focusing on digital innovation: exploring the impact of the CIO on the top management team. MIS Q. **47**(4), 1487–1516 (2023)
11. Zdawczyk, C., Lane, J., Rivers, E., Aydin, M.: Searching for ways to use data: intuitive labeling for data search and discovery. Democr. Data (4) (2024)

Chapter 58
Automatic Mine Detection for Underwater and Surface Vehicles

Şengül Bayrak, Reyhan Bayraktar, and Hatice Kübra Doğan

Abstract The underwater surveillance and support system is currently utilized in the maritime jurisdiction areas of countries to ensure effective solutions for oil and gas drilling and military operations. Comprising a mother ship, an Unmanned Underwater Vehicle, and an Unmanned Surface Vehicle, the system aims to conduct underwater operations in fleet formation while establishing active communication with the ship. Tasks include mine detection, underwater color correction, and underwater-surface communication. Research findings indicate that Naval Forces' frigates and assault boats protect against harassment attempts on drill ships, while Air Force's F-16 jets offer aerial protection. Weaknesses in protection systems against underwater threats pose significant challenges for drill and military vessels. To ensure project success, efforts are focused on software development, communication systems installation, data analysis, and collaboration enhancements. Technologies like magnetic sensing, sonar, and camera systems are employed to detect and track underwater mines. Implementing these technologies is crucial for realizing an effective underwater surveillance and support system, ensuring safer navigation for ships and more cost-efficient performance by underwater vehicles. The ability of vehicles to communicate with the ship is critical for coordinated task execution. In this study, a mine detection model was developed for use in AUVs. While the mAP0.5 value of the mine class was 94% with Yolov7, the mAP value was increased to 95% with Yolov8. For the non-mine class, the mAP0.5 value was increased from 47 to 48%.

Ş. Bayrak (✉)
Department of Software Engineering, Istanbul Sabahattin Zaim University, Istanbul, Türkiye
e-mail: bayraksengul@ieee.org

R. Bayraktar · H. K. Doğan
Department of Computer Engineering, Istanbul Sabahattin Zaim University, Istanbul, Türkiye

F. P. García Márquez et al. (eds.), *Computing, Internet of Things and Data Analytics*, Smart Innovation, Systems and Technologies 387,
https://doi.org/10.1007/978-3-031-87154-2_58

58.1 Introduction

This project holds critical importance in the field of underwater mine detection and underwater security. Challenges such as the bulky structure, slow mobility of drilling and warships, and their inability to detect underwater hazards bring along some issues. The gas dispute among the countries in the Eastern Mediterranean region has significantly increased tensions in recent years. Protection must be promptly provided not only from the air but also from underwater. Safeguarding maritime jurisdiction areas, keeping trade routes open, and conducting military operations safely require adequate protection against underwater mines. Additionally, it involves using unmanned underwater and surface vehicles for underwater mine detection, ensuring their operation in fleet formation. Underwater mines pose severe threats to submarine operations and maritime trade. Detection and disposal of these mines are vital to ensure the safety of civilian ships and military fleets. The detection of underwater mines is not only crucial for security but also for preserving economic and environmental interests. This project proposes a new system to effectively operate unmanned underwater and surface vehicles for underwater mine detection. This system requires the coordinated operation of underwater and surface vehicles, allowing for the rapid and reliable detection of mines. It represents a significant advancement in underwater mine detection and can positively impact national security, maritime trade, and environmental protection.

Ray et al. [1] addressed the concept of collective behavior and its advantages compared to individual behavior. They emphasized viewing human social behavior as a community and highlighted the behaviors that emerge at the fleet level of autonomous underwater vehicles. Additionally, they noted that the language and logic developed to support complex behaviors in AUV fleets are utilized in mine countermeasure operations. Thompson and Guihen [2] emphasized that autonomous marine vehicle fleets achieve longer mission durations, more extensive scale and complex tasks, and higher success rates in achieving mission objectives than individual AMVs. Hozyn [3] stated that although the use of sonar images in detecting and classifying underwater mines is shared, the reliability of this method is low. In recent years, deep learning algorithms and intense convolutional neural networks have been used for mine-like object detection and classification, yielding successful results. Transfer learning has successfully used pre-trained CNNs to detect and classify underwater mines. Ram et al. [4] addressed the need for a system to detect underwater mines more accurately. While machine learning-based systems can capture sonar images, they must be more accurate as mines can easily be confused with other objects. Therefore, sonar is highlighted as the best method for finding underwater mines. A comprehensive literature review revealed that fleet underwater vehicles achieve more successful results than individual vehicles. However, no scenario of a fleet comprising one AUV, one ASV, and one drilling/warship was encountered. Underwater Color Correction achieves accurate or, at the very least, realistic colors in underwater scenes, which presents a significant challenge due to the varying and often turbulent lighting conditions inherent in marine environments. Color correction in underwater imagery is crucial across a spectrum of image-based applications, including but not limited to 3D imaging, navigation, and documentation. Santos et al. created a dataset to automate mine detection from sonar images. This dataset contains 1170 authentic sonar images captured using the Teledyne Marine Gavia AUV between 2010 and 2021. It contains enough information to classify the content objects as NOn-Mine-like BOttom Objects (NOMBO) and MIne-Like COntacts (MILCO) [5]. Reddy et al. propose machine learning-based object detection techniques to distinguish mines from rocks underwater. They collected a real-time dataset of SONAR recordings of mines and rocks and obtained the most successful detection with Decision Tree [6]. Siddhartha et al. proposed a new technique called Rock or Mineral Detection Neural Network for rock/mineral prediction and classification in underwater acoustics using deep learning-based algorithms. They achieved 92.85% success with the proposed RDNN method [7].

Various methods for image enhancement have been proposed in the literature to address this challenge. One notable advantage of these methods is their versatility; some adjustments can be made manually, such as histogram stretching, while others can be automated through algorithms utilizing specific criteria, such as computational color constancy methods. Importantly, these methods do not rely on knowledge of the physical parameters of the environment, rendering them straightforward to implement. Our developed algorithm encompasses several key steps, including Bright Channel Calculation, Calculation of Color Channel Intensities, Image Restoration, and Histogram Equalization. These steps aim to enhance the color grading and address the low contrast observed in underwater images. Crucially, these procedures serve as preprocessing steps for mine detection, with the algorithm slated for real-time application on underwater vehicles. As part of this research, environments necessary for seamless communication of this fleet will be investigated, and algorithms for mine detection will be developed. Optimization methods and deep learning models will be developed for communication between the ASV communicating with the war/drilling ship and the AUV capable of simultaneous mine detection.

In this phase, studies and methods used for mine detection, which are the project's main component, will be examined. Subsequently, existing studies in the literature will be compiled and analyzed. This will enable the collection of open-source data for mines and comparing the detection methods. The structure of this paper is organized as follows: Section 58.2 elucidates the materials and techniques employed, offering a comprehensive architectural overview. Section 58.3 presents the experimental results derived from the proposed framework. Finally, Sect. 58.4 encapsulates the concluding remarks.

58.2 Methods

Obtaining the necessary data depends on the objectives of the project and the method to be used. This data can be obtained by collecting data from cameras based on the literature review results or by detecting sound waves using active sonar technology.

Additionally, the aim is to collect and train visual data using Machine Learning and Computer Vision methods. The collected data needs to be pre-processed to create consistent datasets. These datasets will generate significant statistical results by conducting necessary analyses (classification, regression, image restoration, etc.). This stage is crucial for determining the accuracy of the obtained datasets and the methods, algorithms, and techniques used for analysis.

Analyzing and deciding on the methods of model training on similar data in the past phase entails partitioning the dataset for model training and the evaluation of the performance of the test set, which contains less data than the training set. Munteanu et al. [8] utilized augmentation techniques and synthetic image generation due to the scarcity of naval mine images, creating two distinct datasets. They subsequently trained and compared three deep learning models - YOLOv5, SSD [6], and EfficientDet on these datasets, as illustrated in Fig. 58.1.

Due to the sensitive military context, the researchers encountered limitations in existing data sources. Consequently, they generated and augmented hundreds of synthetic images from existing images to create training, testing, and validation datasets. Subsequently, descriptions were added to each image, and datasets were created for underwater and floating mines. As noted in prior research, this step represents a critical phase that will considerably influence the project's success. It focuses on the practical training of the model using this data and aims to establish a robust database for future mine detection efforts.

Optimization of Communication Protocols RF communication facilitates a smoother transition at the air-water interface compared to UAC and exhibits greater tolerance to underwater turbulence. The propagation of RF signals in seawater at 10 kHz is 100 times faster than acoustic communication, and at 10 MHz, it is 2000 times faster, offering advantages in reducing command latency. RF waves can vary from tens of Hz to GHz for use in UWOC, yet due to the conductivity of saltwater, they can only propagate at very low frequencies, specifically between 30 and 300 Hz. At higher frequencies, the signal substantially weakens, leading to a low modulation bandwidth for RF communication, which results in limited data rates of approximately Mbps over short distances. Furthermore, RF communication requires large antennas and high transmission power to counteract significant antenna losses [9].

Given the drawbacks, such as high power consumption, latency issues, and the mismatch for long distances typical of underwater RF communication and UAC,

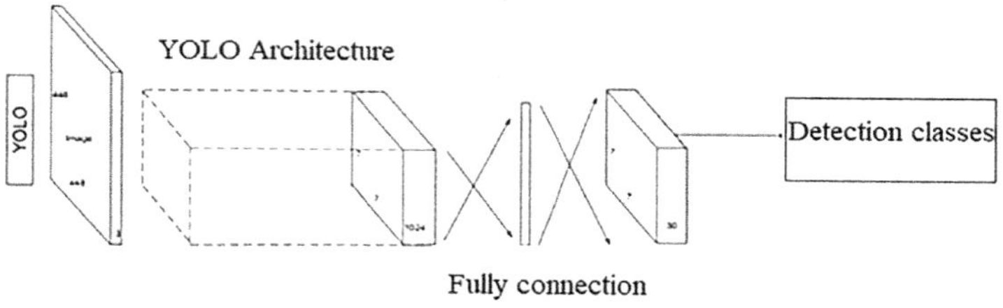

Fig. 58.1 YOLO model [8]

researchers have suggested UWOC as a more suitable solution. UWOC can achieve data rates exceeding Gbps due to its high modulation bandwidth, ranging from hundreds of MHz to even GHz. It also supports transmission distances up to several hundred meters. These advantages in speed and range facilitate the successful implementation of various real-time applications underwater, including real-time digital video streaming [10].

RF communication facilitates a smoother transition at the air-water interface compared to UAC and exhibits greater tolerance to underwater turbulence. The propagation of RF signals in seawater at 10 kHz is 100 times faster than acoustic communication, and at 10 MHz, it is 2000 times faster, offering advantages in reducing command latency. RF waves can vary from tens of Hz to GHz for use in UWOC, yet due to the conductivity of saltwater, they can only propagate at very low frequencies, specifically between 30 and 300 Hz. At higher frequencies, the signal substantially weakens, leading to a low modulation bandwidth for RF communication, which results in limited data rates of approximately Mbps over short distances. Furthermore, RF communication requires large antennas and high transmission power to counteract significant antenna losses [11]. Given the drawbacks, such as high power consumption, latency issues, and the mismatch for long distances typical of underwater RF communication and UAC, researchers have suggested UWOC as a more suitable solution. UWOC can achieve data rates exceeding Gbps due to its high modulation bandwidth, ranging from hundreds of MHz to even GHz. It also supports transmission distances up to several hundred meters. These advantages in speed and range facilitate the successful implementation of various real-time applications underwater, including real-time digital video streaming [12–14]. The preferred communication protocol between the main ship and the unmanned surface vehicle in the Underwater Surveillance and Support System is the Link-16 military tactical data link network. This network is widely used by NATO, the United States, and allied countries, providing real-time data flow and coordination. Link-16 ensures secure and jamming-resistant tactical information exchange for land, sea, and air platforms. The communications terminal for Link-16 is the Joint Tactical Information Distribution System (JTIDS). It incorporates RS coding, symbol interval processing, cyclic code shift keying (CCSK) for M-ary symbol modulation, minimum shift keying for chip modulation, and a combination of frequency hopping and direct sequence spread spectrum techniques to ensure transmission security.

58.3 Experimental Results

The enhanced YOLO underwater mine detection models have been tested on a Windows system, using Python 3.9 as the development language. The hardware configuration includes a CPU of $x86_64$ architecture, 16 GB of memory, a Tesla T4 GPU with 16 GB of video memory, and CUDA (Compute Unified Device Architecture, NVIDIA) version 12.2.

The training, testing, and validation datasets utilized in the experiments consist of underwater environmental images, mine images, and underwater non-mine images, which were manually collected from the Internet. The initial dataset underwent filtering, preprocessing, and further development. This dataset comprises 490 images.

58.3.1 Data Preprocessing

A dataset of mine photographs was curated from open-source internet repositories for mine detection via image processing. This dataset comprises images of mines submerged underwater and above the water surface. Additionally, images depicting non-mine objects that may be encountered underwater were incorporated into the dataset. Subsequently, this dataset was categorized into two classes: mines and non-mines. The dataset encompasses 319 images depicting mines and 202 images portraying non-mines, resulting in a cumulative dataset size 521.

While this dataset offers a robust foundation for research endeavors due to its diversity and labeled nature, certain limitations warrant acknowledgment. These include a relatively limited volume of data and inconsistencies in image quality stemming from the constraints associated with data acquisition. Despite these shortcomings, the dataset is a valuable resource for conducting analyses and developing algorithms for mine detection applications.

Underwater images, encompassing both mine-containing and non-mine scenarios, were systematically gathered. Subsequently, a filtering process was implemented to remove any unclean images from the dataset. Following this data cleanup, an Auto-Orient algorithm was applied to ensure a consistent orientation across all images. Additionally, the images were uniformly resized to dimensions of 640x640 pixels. Furthermore, Adaptive Equalization, specifically Auto-Adjust Contrast, was employed to enhance image quality and facilitate better visual analysis. The next step involves classifying these images into two distinct categories: mine and non-mine. All these steps were conducted using Roboflow, a tool that simplifies the computer vision tasks in deep learning.

58.3.2 State of the Art

In the paper, Link-16 was used for Time Division Multiple Access (TDMA) technology to facilitate efficient data communication, and multiple users shared the same frequency band. The data transmitted over Link-16 used the J-type message format, which includes target information, radar data, and other tactical information. The system has three main components: terminal, central processing unit (CPU), and antenna. The terminal manages the data exchange, the CPU processes platform-specific data, and the antenna provides the line-of-sight (LOS) link. Operating in the

UHF band with a range of 300 nautical miles, these components collectively provide the reliable and secure communications required for coordinated maritime missions.

58.3.3 Evaluation Parameters

The evaluation metrics for the object detection model are designed to classify the results of the recognition process into four categories based on the actual labels: TP (True Positive), TN (True Negative), FP (False Positive), and FN (False Negative). These categories are essential for determining the model's precision and recall rates. The formula for calculating the precision rate is presented in Eq. (58.1), while the formula for calculating the recall rate is outlined in Eq. (58.2).

$$\text{Precision (P)} = \frac{\text{TP}}{\text{TP} + \text{FP}} \tag{58.1}$$

$$\text{Recall (R)} = \frac{\text{TP}}{\text{TP} + \text{FN}} \tag{58.2}$$

To balance the precision rate with the recall index, mAP (Mean Average Precision) has been chosen as a comprehensive evaluation metric for the model. The mAP is the average of the AP (Average Precision) values for all categories, representing the mAP for all object categories, as defined in Eq. (58.3).

$$\text{mAP} = \frac{1}{N}\sum_{i=1}^{N} \text{AP}_i \tag{58.3}$$

This paper selects the YOLO model for its enhanced performance in underwater object detection. This section conducts numerous comparison experiments for both YOLOv7 and YOLOv8 models.

The dataset, consisting of 490 underwater environment images, is divided into training data samples, validation data samples, and test data samples, with a ratio of 7:2:1. After 30 epochs of iterative training and learning, the parameters of the underwater object detection model converge.

The YOLO model enhances the performance in underwater object detection by incorporating various feature extraction modules. The results of the comparative experiments are presented in Tables 58.1 and 58.2.

The precision-recall curves are displayed in Figure 3, and it is noted that both the recall and accuracy curves can converge rapidly [15, 16]. The recall rate curve provides the average accuracy for the mine, non-mine, and all detection classes. As observed in Fig. 58.2, the area under the curve for the mine class is the largest, indicating that the accuracy of underwater target detection is highest for this class.

Table 58.1 Performance of YOLOV7 model

Class	Avg-P(%)	Recall	mAP@0.5(%)
All	0.758	0.628	0.707
Mine	0.860	0.907	0.943
Non-mine	0.657	0.349	0.471

Table 58.2 Performance of YOLOV8 model

Class	Avg-P(%)	Recall	mAP@0.5(%)
All	0.778	0.688	0.717
Mine	0.870	0.963	0.952
Non-mine	0.685	0.413	0.482

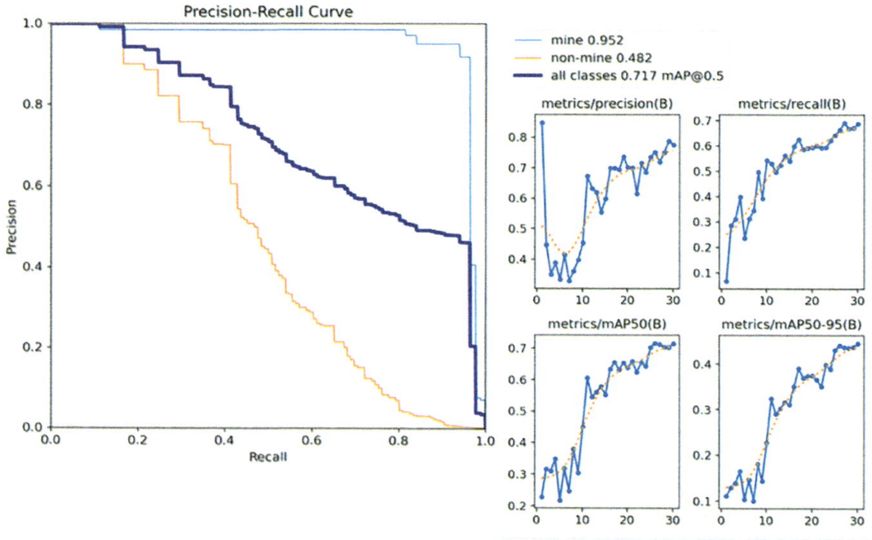

Fig. 58.2 The precision-recall curves of YOLOv8 model

In this study, the YOLOv8 model was selected. According to the results presented in Table 58.2, the mAP@0.5(%) value for the Non-mine class did not meet the desired standards, in contrast to the Mine class. To address this issue, the model underwent further training with YOLOv8, and a slight improvement was noted upon comparison of the results. It was observed that the Avg-P(%) value for the Non-mine class increased from 65% to 68%, and the mAP@0.5(%) value reached 48% as can be seen in Fig. 58.3.

Figure 58.4a shows an example of a mine detected using YOLOv8. Non-Mine classification using YOLOv8 is depicted in Fig. 58.4b.

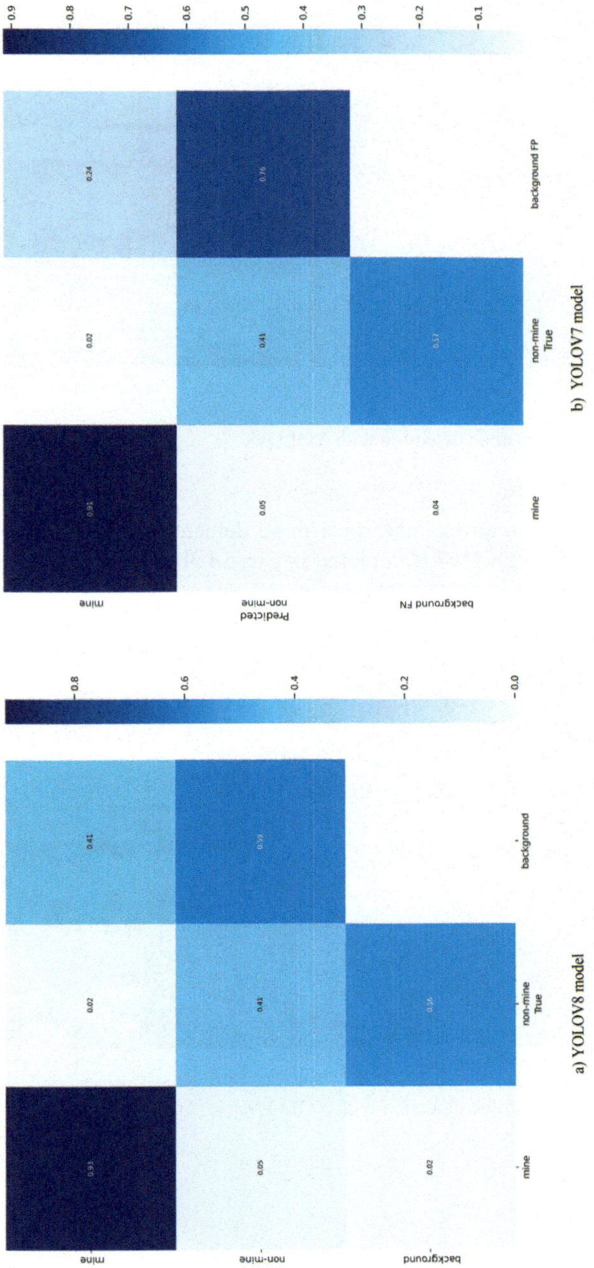

Fig. 58.3 Confusion matrix of YOLOv8 and YOLOv7 models

a) Mine detection b)Non-mine detection

Fig. 58.4 Mine and non-mine detection with YOLOv8

Figure 58.5a shows an example of a mine detected using YOLOv7. Non-mine classification using YOLOv7 is depicted in Fig. 58.5b.

a) Mine detection b) Non-mine detection

Fig. 58.5 Mine and non-mine detection with YOLOv7

58.3.4 Comparison with Existing Methods

The project introduces a novel approach to mine detection and communication utilizing a fleet of underwater and surface vehicles. Previous studies have focused on detecting underwater mines using images generated by Synthetic Aperture Sonar (SAS) [17]. SAS creates underwater images from sound waves generated below 200 feet, but these images often suffer from very low resolution, making them unsuitable for detecting small or detailed objects. Additionally, light to illuminate target scenes is attenuated due to absorption and scattering in the underwater environment [18, 19].

Rao et al. [20] conducted a study on mine detection using side scan sonar images and geometric modeling, capitalizing that mines are made of denser materials and have shinier surfaces than other seafloor objects. While this method improved the speed and efficiency of mine detection, the low resolution of the images still posed a significant challenge, potentially increasing the error rate. Khaledi et al. [21] discussed mine detection by the US Navy using sonar systems deployed from helicopters, highlighting two alternatives for autonomous underwater vehicles: the Raytheon AN/AQS-20A Minehunting Sonar System and L-3 Klein Systems 5900. Despite the use of autonomous underwater vehicles, sonar technology remained the primary method.

Reddy et al. [22] collected a real-time dataset of SONAR recordings of mines and rocks and evaluated them for classification. They achieved 90% accuracy with the Random Forest method for ocean mines to distinguish between rocks and mines.

Qiu et al. [23] utilized a UAV-derived multispectral navigation platform to create a multispectral dataset of mines, considering the mine dispersal areas of ground vegetation. To ensure robust detection of clogged landmines, they first used an active learning strategy to improve the labeling of the multispectral dataset. Then, they used YOLOv5 for the detection part to improve the detection performance in a learning manner while enhancing the quality of the fused image.

Samala et al. [24] aimed to find and share the visual information of underwater objects to the users in detecting underwater objects. They continuously monitored the underwater video and displayed it in real-time mode. With this system, video surveillance and object recognition extract information about underwater objects in real time. They also shared the brightness levels underwater. The camera used in the prototype provided real-time visuals of the underwater ecosystem, and the geo-location of the relevant parts of the water bed was sent via an SMS to the registered mobile phone.

In contrast, this project opts for image processing technology over sonar for mine detection. The primary reason for this choice is the higher resolution of underwater images captured by cameras. Once enhanced by an underwater color correction algorithm, the images become more precise and detailed, making them suitable for mine detection. Furthermore, the system's distinctive feature is the practical and coordinated operation of three separate elements through robust communication. According to our research, a system with a fleet-like configuration has not been designed, marking a unique contribution to the field. This paper's communication phase builds on various existing research and technologies. The referenced conference paper [25] discusses techniques based on acoustics, optics, and radio frequency (RF). Acoustic communication, the oldest and most widely used technology for underwater communication, offers the most extended communication range but suffers from limitations such as low efficiency and susceptibility to Doppler effects. Optical and RF technologies can achieve higher data rates than acoustic communication but are limited in transmission distance. Optical signals typically require a direct line of sight between the transmitter and receiver. At the same time, RF technology is more suitable for short-distance transmission with moderate data rates, which can be challenging in waters with high particle content. Therefore, appropriate antenna designs are crucial for establishing underwater communication using RF technology, enabling higher data rates over short distances. The Link-16 military communication protocol utilized in this project is based on RF technology but is not a standardized version of RF technology; it is a specialized military communication protocol. Link-16 is generally effective over medium to long distances rather than short distances. This protocol facilitates tactical information sharing between military and national units and is effective over distances of several hundred nautical miles. One of the distinguishing features of Link-16 compared to standard RF technology is its use of advanced techniques, such as frequency hopping, which enhances security. Additionally, Link-16 is a network-based communication protocol that creates a dynamic network between multiple elements and facilitates information sharing. This project's unique and prominent features become evident when examining the studies and technologies discussed. Image processing and artificial intelligence-based models in mine detection enable faster and more accurate identification of mines. The Link-16 protocol, chosen for its robust and secure communication capabilities, is suitable for national and international use by certain countries. It addresses one of the most challenging aspects of the project-communication-by providing a reliable and secure method for information sharing. The system's reliance on unmanned and autonomous vehicles significantly reduces risks, enhancing the safety of military personnel. According to the literature review, no existing fleet system operates this way, highlighting this project's innovation and potential impact.

58.3.5 Ethical Considiration

The designed system carries significant ethical values and responsibilities in military and national operations. This project plays a crucial role in enhancing the safety of soldiers and personnel by enabling unmanned and autonomous vehicles to conduct missions, particularly in mine detection. This approach reduces direct human exposure to danger, thereby safeguarding human health. Safety is paramount in heightened tensions, such as those associated with oil and gas drilling operations. Early detection of mines helps prevent explosions and mitigate the impact of oil spills on marine life. The dataset utilized for mine detection comprises open-source images of mines, fostering transparency and community contribution. This initiative represents a significant step towards technological openness and safety. Throughout the project's execution, adherence to national and international legal regulations is imperative. Operating within the military and drilling sectors necessitates compliance with the ethical standards of the respective countries and regions. Ethical conduct is observed during data collection, research, and reporting processes, with a commitment to respecting data owners and related organizations. The Link-16 protocol ensures high security and reliability standards in military operations. As a NATO ally, the Republic of Turkey faces no obstacles to utilizing this protocol, facilitating the secure transmission of critical information [26, 27].

58.4 Conclusions

This study proposes a conceptual framework for autonomous underwater operations inspired by the fleet UAV concept, considering a fleet of Autonomous Underwater Vehicles (AUVs). These AUVs, designed to accompany large warships or drilling vessels with limited underwater maneuverability, serve as underwater eyes due to their compact size and agility. A critical task for AUVs is mine detection. A specialized dataset was manually prepared, and YOLO models were trained accordingly. The mAP0.5 value for the mine class improved from 94% with YOLOv7 to 95% with YOLOv8, and for the non-mine class, it increased from 47 to 48%. The model is still in development, with ongoing efforts to enhance non-mine class performance. Given the absence of underwater signals and communication challenges, integrating an autonomous surface vehicle (ASV) has been deemed beneficial in facilitating communication between the ship and AUV. ASVs, with their movement flexibility, are being researched to establish wired communication with AUVs. This study involves designing a system using ASVs and AUVs to operate cohesively with a leading ship, forming an integrated fleet. Secure communication between the mother ship and the ASV is established using the Link-16 protocol, while the ASV and AUV communicate via cable, ensuring reliable data transmission in deep-sea environments. The AUV, designed to undertake various missions, currently focuses on mine detection. An underwater color correction algorithm is applied to images captured by the AUV's camera, which are then analyzed by a trained model to detect mines. Detected mines are transmitted to the ASV via wired communication, which then relay the information to the mother ship for appropriate action. Future applications include underwater reconnaissance, environmental monitoring, search and rescue operations, and maintenance of underwater structures. In conclusion, this project introduces an innovative concept enabling unmanned underwater and surface vehicles to operate within an integrated communication and operations network. The combined use of AUVs and ASVs has the potential to significantly enhance maritime safety and operational efficiency, laying a crucial foundation for advanced maritime technologies.

Disclosure of Interests. The authors declare no conflicts of interest.

Acknowledgements This study was funded by Istanbul Sabahattin Zaim University project number 2024-BAP-100-002.

References

1. Ray, P., O'Rourke, M., Edwards, D.: The Ontological Status of Autonomous Underwater Vehicle Fleets, OCEANS 2009, Biloxi, MS, USA, pp. 1–7 (2009). https://doi.org/10.23919/OCEANS.2009.5422192
2. Thompson, F., Guihen, D.: Review of mission planning for autonomous marine vehicle fleets. J Field Robot. **36**, 333–354 (2019)
3. Hozyn, S.: A review of underwater mine detection and classification in sonar imagery. Electronics **10**, 2943 (2021)
4. Ram, M.S., Navyatha, P.S., Ashitha, R.L.A., Kumar, S.A.J.: Machine learning based underwater mine detection. In: 2023 7th International Conference on Intelligent Computing and Control Systems (ICICCS), Madurai, India, pp. 47–50 (2023). https://doi.org/10.1109/ICICCS56967.2023.10142384
5. Santos, N.P., Moura, R., Torgal, G.S., Lobo, V., de Castro Neto, M.: Side-scan sonar imaging data of underwater vehicles for mine detection. Data in Brief **53**, 110132 (2024)
6. Reddy, B.N.K., Vaithilingam, C.A., Kamalakkannan, S.: SONAR based under water mine detection using machine learning algorithms. In: 2024 4th International Conference on Innovative Practices in Technology and Management (ICIPTM), pp. 1–4. IEEE (Feb 2024)
7. Siddhartha, J.B., Jaya, T., Rajendran, V.: RDNN for classification and prediction of Rock/Mine in underwater acoustics. Mater Today Proc **80**, 3221–3228 (2023)
8. Munteanu, D., Monah, D., Zamfir, C.G., Petrea, Stefan M., Cristea, D.S., Munteanu, N.: Sea mine detection framework using YOLO, SSD and efficient det deep learning models. Sensors **22**(23), 9536 (2022)
9. Liu, W., Anguelov, D., Erhan, D., Szegedy, C., Reed, S., Fu, C., Berg, A.C.: SSD: Single Shot Multibox Detector. In: Lecture Notes in Computer Science. Springer, Berlin, Germany (2016)
10. Kaushal, H., Kaddoum, G.: Underwater optical wireless communication. IEEE Access **4**, 1518–1548 (2016). https://doi.org/10.1109/ACCESS.2016.2552538
11. Zhu, S., Chen, X., Liu, X., Zhang, G., Tian, P.: Re-evaluation of RF electromagnetic communication in underwater sensor networks. IEEE Commun. Mag. **48**(12), 143–151 (2010). https://doi.org/10.1109/MCOM.2010.5673085
12. Gussen, C.M.G., Diniz, P.S.R., Campos, M.L.R., Martins, W.A., Costa, F.M., Gois, J.N.: A survey of underwater wireless communication technologies. J. Commun. Inf. Syst. **31**, 242–255 (2016)
13. Doniec, M., Xu, A., Rus, D.: Robust Real-time Underwater Digital Video Streaming Using Optical Communication. Presented at the (2013)
14. Sozer, E.M., Stojanovic, M., Proakis, J.G.: Underwater acoustic networks. IEEE J. Ocean. Eng. **25**(1), 72–8 (2000). https://doi.org/10.1109/48.820738
15. Bayrak, S.: Unveiling intrusions: explainable SVM approaches for addressing encrypted Wi-Fi traffic in UAV networks. Knowl. Inf. Syst. (2024). https://doi.org/10.1007/s10115-024-02181-9
16. Liu, Z., Gao, Y., Du, Q., Chen, M., Lv, W.: YOLO-extract: improved YOLOv5 for aircraft object detection in remote sensing images. IEEE Access **11**, 1742–1751 (2023). https://doi.org/10.1109/ACCESS.2023.3233964
17. Turkozu, O., et al.: Introduction and concept design of the "YTU AUVTECH" autonomous underwater vehicle. In: 4th International Naval Architecture and Maritime Symposium, pp. 617–629. Turkey, Istanbul (2023)

18. Denos, K., Ravaut, M., Fagette, A., Lim, H.-S.: Deep learning applied to underwater mine warfare. In: OCEANS 2017-Aberdeen, Aberdeen, UK, pp. 1–7 (2017). https://doi.org/10.1109/OCEANSE.2017.8084910. (keywords: Training; Synthetic aperture sonar; Pipelines; Machine learning; Rendering (computer graphics); Databases; Deep Learning; synthetic training dataset; underwater mine; sonar; synthetic aperture sonar)
19. Vinutha, K.V., Vinutha, K., Yuvaraja, T.: Under water mine detection using sonar. J. Comput. Theoret. Nanosci. **15**(6–7), 2150–2152 (2018). https://doi.org/10.1166/jctn.2018.7426
20. Rao, C., Mukherjee, K., Gupta, S., Ray, A., Phoha, S.: Underwater mine detection using symbolic pattern analysis of sidescan sonar images, In: American Control Conference, St. Louis, MO, USA **2009**, 5416–5421 (2009). https://doi.org/10.1109/ACC.2009.5160102
21. Khaledi, S., Mann, H., Perkovich, J., Zayed, S.: Design of an underwater mine detection system. In: Systems and Information Engineering Design Symposium (SIEDS). Charlottesville, VA, USA, vol. 2014, pp. 78–83 (2014). https://doi.org/10.1109/SIEDS.2014.6829901
22. Reddy, B.N.K., Vaithilingam, C.A., Kamalakkannan, S.: SONAR based under water mine detection using machine learning algorithms. In: 2024 4th International Conference on Innovative Practices in Technology and Management (ICIPTM), pp. 1–4. IEEE (Feb 2024)
23. Qiu, Z., Guo, H., Hu, J., Jiang, H., Luo, C.: Joint fusion and detection via deep learning in UAV-borne multispectral sensing of scatterable landmine. Sensors **23**(12), 5693 (2023)
24. Samala, S., Ruchitha, V., Pavan, D.S., Hemanth, S., Soumya, V., Ahmed, S.M.: Video surveillance-based underwater object detection and location tracking using IoT. In: International Conference on Communications and Cyber Physical Engineering 2018, pp. 1187–1196. Springer Nature Singapore, Singapore (Mar 2023)
25. Jaafar, A.N., Ja'afar, H., Pasya, I., Abdullah, R., Yamada, Y.: Overview of underwater communication technology. In: Isa, K., et al. Proceedings of the 12th National Technical Seminar on Unmanned System Technology 2020. Lecture Notes in Electrical Engineering, vol. 770. Springer, Singapore (2022). https://doi.org/10.1007/978-981-16-2406-3_8
26. IEEE. (n.d.). IEEE code of ethics. https://www.ieee.org/about/corporate/governance/p7-8.html
27. Opensource.com. (n.d.). The open source way. https://opensource.com/open-source-way

Chapter 59
Modeling of Study on the Impact of Single-Phase Faults in Minimal Current Grounding

Zhiyuan Lian

Abstract The aim of this research is to quickly and accurately identify fault line characteristics through a comprehensive investigation into the distinctive attributes of single-phase earth faults, thus improving the dependability of the electrical power supply. Initially, the review focuses on ground fault in single-phase systems within low grounding system for current, summarizing study's commencement and significance. Secondly, The essential features of the low grounding system for current are further dissected, with particular emphasis on the behavior of neutral without grounding and earthing system for arc suppression coils methods during single-phase earth faults, and the steady state and transient capacitance under fault are analyzed in detail. In the third part, the transient and steady-state electrical properties of single-phase ground connections faults within the low grounding system for current are thoroughly examined, and the simulation model of the system is successfully established and analyzed in detail by using the Simulink simulation platform of Matlab software.

59.1 Introduction

Power system's neutral point is the the star-connected transformer or generator's neutral junction [1]. Generally speaking, the common node configuration within the medium-voltage distribution network systems does not have a direct earth connection [2]. There are four kinds of neutral grounding technology: one is completely ungrounded neutral grounding, the other is grounded by arc cancelling ring, the third is grounded by high impedance, and the fourth is grounded by low impedance [3]. Upon the occurrence of ground fault in single-phase systems, the grounding flow of electric charge is relatively tiny due to failure to form a low impedance short circuit, and is therefore called a low current grounding method [4]. A positive aspect of this

Z. Lian (✉)
Shenyang University of Technology, Shenyang, China
e-mail: lianzy4119@foxmail.com

F. P. García Márquez et al. (eds.), *Computing, Internet of Things and Data Analytics*, Smart Innovation, Systems and Technologies 387,
https://doi.org/10.1007/978-3-031-87154-2_59

system is that when it comes to ground fault in single-phase systems, The arc can be terminated automatically as well as its insulation properties performance can be restored [5]. As for continuous ground fault in single-phase systems, although the line voltage of the three-phase system remains symmetrical and the amplitude and phase remain the same, the ground capacitance of the system will form a short circuit, causing the ground voltage to drop to zero [6]. In order to avoid phase-to-phase short circuit or further three-phase short circuit caused by another contact surface, It is crucial to expedite the process of eliminating the ground fault in single-phase systems [7].

59.2 Minimal Current Grounding Two Ways of Grounding

59.2.1 Principle of Ungrounded Neutral Point

Assuming that phase A metal fault occurs to the ground at point d low current earthing process (whose neutral junction is ungrounding) as shown in Fig. 59.1, the corresponding vector analysis schema is shown in Fig. 59.2, together with and representing the EMF of each phase of the power supply [8].

The voltages to earth are

$$\dot{U}_A = 0 \tag{59.1}$$

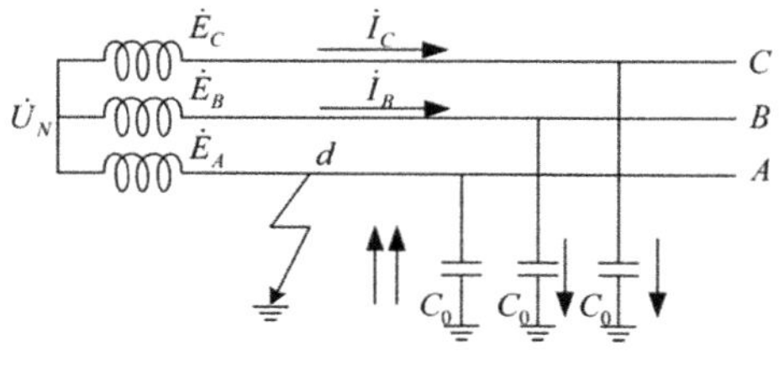

Fig. 59.1 Single-phase earthing of an ungrounded neutral system

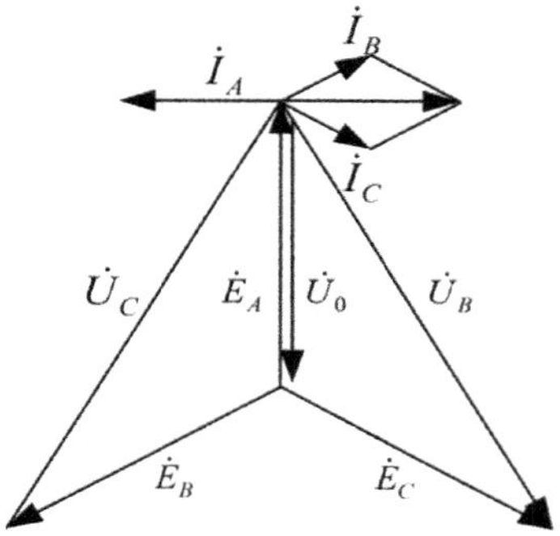

Fig. 59.2 A ground time vector diagram

$$\dot{U}_B = \dot{E}_B - \dot{E}_A = \sqrt{3}\dot{E}_A e^{-j150^\circ} \tag{59.2}$$

$$\dot{U}_C = \dot{E}_C - \dot{E}_A = \sqrt{3}\dot{E}_A e^{j150^\circ} \tag{59.3}$$

Observations indicate that the phase voltage levels upon fault occurrence is zero, at the same time the non-faultive relative ground voltage is raised by $\sqrt{3}$ times of the original [9].The effective value of phase electromotive force is represented by E_φ, then the effective value of $\dot{I}_A$, $\dot{I}_B$, $\dot{I}_C$ and is

$$\dot{I}_A = 3E_\varphi \omega C_0 \tag{59.4}$$

$$\dot{I}_B = \dot{I}_C = \sqrt{3}E_\varphi \omega C_0 \tag{59.5}$$

59.2.2 Neutral Point Connection Using an Arc Suppression Reactor

While illustrated in Fig. 59.3, in the system with earth connection via an arc suppression reactor, the distribution of current presents specific characteristics upon the occurrence of a ground fault in single-phase systems [10].

As presented in Fig. 59.3, when power system has been grounding in a neutral point arc suppression loop, the single-phase system earthing fault will cause the

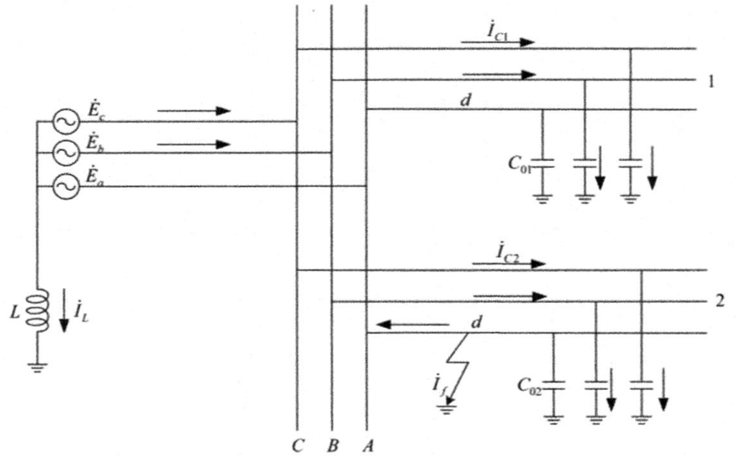

Fig. 59.3 Distribution of current during a ground fault in single-phase systems is grounded through arc suppression reactor

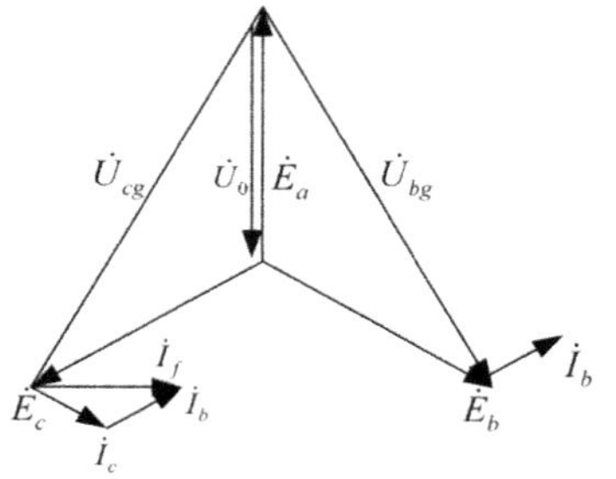

Fig. 59.4 Voltage and electric current diagram of single-phase system earthing fault

current flow along a specific path, forming a specific current distribution diagram (Fig. 59.4).

When ground fault in single-phase happens to A phase, voltage to ground of phase A reaches zero. Concurrently, voltage level at B and C phases, which did not fail, increased to reach their line voltage levels with respect to phase A, respectively. When degree of variation increases to $\sqrt{3}$ times, Voltage at neutral point increases spanning from zero to $-\dot{U}_a$.

59.2.3 Steady State Review of Ground Fault in Single-Phase Systems

In Fig. 59.5, C—the three associated ground capacitance of the resonant grounding network, L_0—Same as inductive impedance of the tri-phase electric lines as well as power distribution transformer Tri-phase power lines,R_0—total resistance for zero-sequence current, r_L and L are respectively the power losses due to resistance value as well as inductive load in the arc reduction inductor, u_0— analogous to zero sequence power supply.

In an arc reduction inductor grounding system, as shown in Fig. 59.5, the current distribution when ground fault in single-phase systems take place remains unchanged,

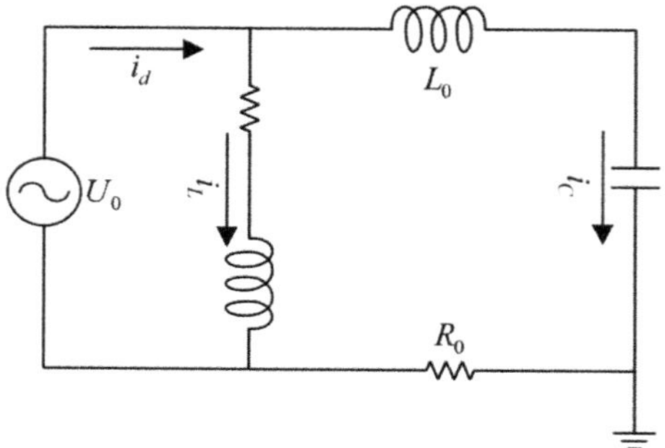

Fig. 59.5 Equivalent circuit regarding ground fault in single-phase systems

even though an arc reduction inductor is attached to neutral connection point source. For example, when phase A wire 1 is earthed, the amplitude of the capacitive electrical flow and its distribution in the system are no different than if the arc reduction inductor is disconnected. The distinction lies in the fact that inductive element aspects of the current i_L is included to the earthing point, hence the overall current returning from the earthing point is

$$i_d = i_C + i_L \tag{59.6}$$

where: i_C—Capacitive current to earth: i_L—Current of the arc extinction coil. Arc reduction inductor can be splited into three sections different operating modes according to its compensation degree of capacitor current: full compensation, undercompensation and overcompensation.

(1) Undercompensation. Equivalent current When the resonant circuit works in the undercompensated state, $i_L < i_C$, at this moment, the residual current consists of the real power component and the capacitive reactive power component.
(2) Full compensation. When the frequency of the current resonance loop completely matches its natural frequency, that is, when the resonance point is reached, $i_L = i_C$, at this time, the electrical flow at the fault point amounts to simplified to only remaining active component, and its amplitude is reduced to the lowest. And its phase is in phase with the neutral displacement voltage.
(3) Overcompensation. When the current resonance circuit is in the overcompensated state, $i_L > i_C$, the inductive reactive current component is the main component.

Under the three different compensation states, the zero-sequence current flow induced by single-phase earthing fault tends to be the same in the transient phase, but shows significant difference in a state of balance. Under the condition of undercompensation, zero-sequence current due to fault flow presents the contrary phase relative to the ordinary line, and scale of fault current fails to reach the peak value. When the full compensation state is reached, the zero-sequence current characteristic of the fault line is completely compensated. In the overcompensated state, the zero-sequence electrical flow of the fault line is in this same phase as that of the normal line.

59.2.4 Steady State Investigation into Ground Fault in Single-Phase Systems

When discussing the transient behavior of capacitive current, it is worth noting that the frequency of free oscillation is often quite high. Considering the inductance L and L_0 about the arc extinction coil, r_L and L in Fig. 59.5 can be ignored. Therefore, distribution characteristics of transients capacitance current are essentially consistent with the system without grounded neutral, and the transient capacitance current can be determined by using the series circuit composed of L_0, C, R_0 and the zero-phase sequence sinusoidal source voltage acting on the circuit.

The differential equation can be written from the above conditions:

$$R_0 i_C + L_0 \frac{di_C}{dt} + \frac{1}{C}\int_0^t i_C dt = U_{\phi m}\sin(\omega t + \varphi) \tag{59.7}$$

Because capacitive current at startup i_C is made up of temporary component $\dot{I}_D = \dot{I}_L + \dot{I}_{C\sum}$ free oscillation component i_{Cos} including the stable power frequency part i_{Cst}, using relationship between the initial condition $i_{\text{Cos}} + i_{Cst} = 0$ when t = 0 and $I_{Cm} = U_{\phi m}\omega C$, analyzing with Laplace transforms and additional mathematical functions can be obtained:

$$i_C = i_{\text{Cos}} + i_{Cst} = I_{Cm}[(\frac{\omega_f}{\omega}\sin\varphi\sin\omega t - \cos\varphi\cos\omega_f t)e^{-\delta t} + \cos(\omega t + \varphi)] \tag{59.8}$$

where $U_{\phi m}$ represents the peak amplitude of the phase voltage, I_{Cm} is the amplitude of the capacitance current, ω_f signifies the angular frequency of the oscillation without transients unit, $\delta = \frac{1}{\tau_C} = \frac{R_0}{2L_0}$ indicates decay rate of the autonomous oscillation part, and τ_C reflects the loop's time constant for decay.

59.2.4.1 Inductive Current at Transient Moment

First, assume that the ground capacitance of the three phases within the circuitry is equal before the fault occurs, which means that the arc reduction inductor does not carry current now. Based on the information shown in Fig. 59.5, we can derive the corresponding differential equation:

$$U_{\phi m}\sin(\omega t + \varphi) = \gamma_L i_L + W\frac{d\psi_L}{dt} \tag{59.9}$$

where: W represents the turn count of the tap connected to the arc extinguishing inductor; ψ_L is the magnetic flux density of the coil core. In the working range, the current of the arc reduction inductor is $i_L = \frac{W}{L}\psi_L$, while before the fault occurs $\psi_L = 0$. Because $\gamma_L \ll \omega L$, the coil resistance is ignored, Eq. (16) can be converted to:

$$\psi_L = \frac{U\phi m}{\omega W}\left[\cos\varphi e^{-\frac{t}{\tau_L}} - \cos(\omega t + \varphi)\right] \tag{59.10}$$

The expression of inductance current is:

$$i_L = \frac{W}{L}\psi_L = I_{Lm}\left[\cos\varphi e^{-\frac{t}{\tau_L}} - \cos(\omega t + \varphi)\right] \tag{59.11}$$

As observed from the formula above, in temporary state, that is, when t is very small, the amplitude of the inductor current transient quantity $I_{Lm} \cos \varphi e^{-\frac{t}{\tau_L}}$ will not exceed I_{Lm}, and the frequency of the steady-state quantity is grid cycle frequency.

59.3 Simulation Analysis

59.3.1 Construction of Ground Fault in Single-Phase Systems Simulation Model

In the design of the simulation model, we adopt a three-phase AC voltage source, whose nominal output voltage is set to 10.5kV, the operating frequency is set to 50Hz, and the internal configuration is carried out by an internal Y-type connection. In the simulation model, Load1, Load2 and Load3 lines all adopt the "three-phase series RLC load" mode, and their active power is 1MW, 0.2MW and 2MW respectively (Figs. 59.6, 59.7 and 59.8).

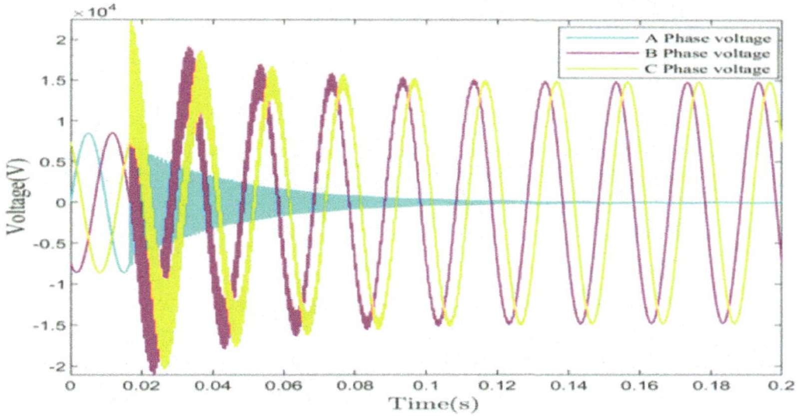

Fig. 59.6 Waveform diagram of system three relative ground voltage

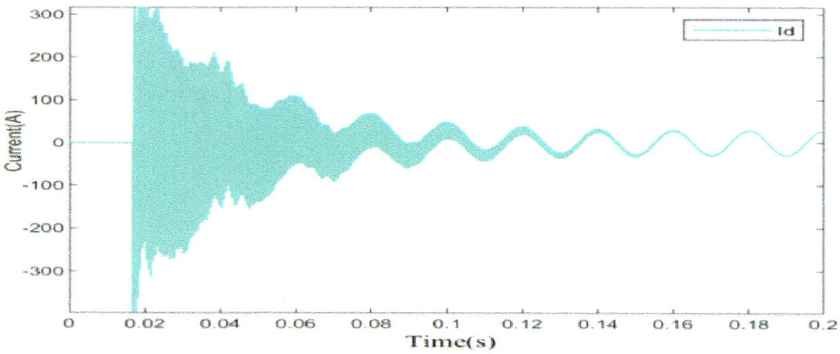

Fig. 59.7 $\dot{I}_D$ waveform of the grounding current at the fault point

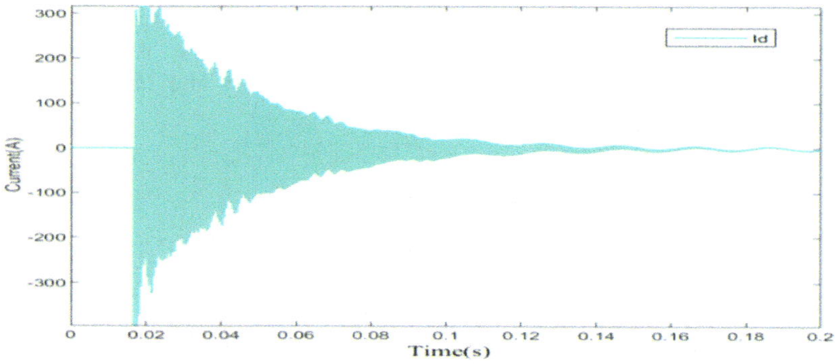

Fig. 59.8 Fault point grounding current waveform through arc suppression coil

59.4 Conclusion

This paper discusses in detail several key characteristics of low-current grounding systems, especially the transient and steady-state electrical parameters of electrical systems having an ungrounded neutral and those with a neutral grounded through a neutral grounding reactor in the event of single-phase earthing. Simulation model of the two systems is constructed by using MATLAB simulation tool, and the difference of electrical characteristics before and after the fault is compared and analyzed, so that the power system researchers can accurately understand functional attributes of the system and overcome the abstraction of pure theoretical analysis.

References

1. Shen, Q.: A novel method of fault line selection in low current grounding system using multi-criteria information integrated. Electr. Power Syst. Res. **209**, 108010 (2022)
2. Su, X., Wei, H.: A fault-line selection method for small-current grounded system based on deep transfer learning. Energies **15**(9), 3467 (2022)
3. Li, J., Zhang, G., Li, H., et al.: A review of fault location methods for small current grounding systems. IOP Conf. Ser. Mater. Sci. Eng. IOP Publishing **677**(5):052045 (2019)
4. Chen, Y., Chen, H., Song, B., et al.: A new approach to fault-line selection of small current neutral grounding system. Syst. Sci. Control. Eng. **6**(3), 28–34 (2018)
5. Li, H., Sun, Y., Li, K., et al.: A method of fault line selection in small current grounding system based on VMD energy entropy and optimized K-means clustering. IOP Conf. Ser. Earth Environ. Sci. IOP Publishing **73**(1):012023 (2017)
6. Liu, X., Yu, T., Wang, Z., et al.: Design of fault line selection for small current grounding system in distribution network. In: 5th International Conference on Information Science, Electrical, and Automation Engineering (ISEAE 2023), SPIE **12748**:972–978 (2023)
7. Yu, N., Li, R., Yang, J., et al.: Application of atomic sparse decomposition to feature extraction of the fault signal in small current grounding system. Energy Power Eng. **5**(4), 603–607 (2013)
8. Zhang, G., Haitao, P.U., Kai, L.I.U.: Fault line selection method of small current grounding system based on deep learning. Power Gener. Technol. **40**(6), 548–554 (2019)
9. Lu, S., Li, Y.: Fault Location of small current to ground system based on S-transform. Int. J. Digit. Content Technol. Its Appl. **7**(6), 808 (2013)
10. Song, Y., Yuan, S., Wang, Y., et al.: fault line detection in small current grounding systems based on RBF network. In: Third International Conference on Natural Computation (ICNC 2007). IEEE **2**, 764–768 (2007)

Chapter 60
Image Stitching Method Under Low-Light Environments Integrating Image Enhancement and Improved U-Net

ZhiNing Zou, Feng Zhang, and Shuai Yuan

Abstract Image stitching refers to the process of combining multiple local images from the same scene with overlapping areas into a panoramic image through algorithms. In low-light scenes, image stitching is of practical significance in many fields. However, images captured in low-light conditions often suffer from issues such as noise, loss of detail, and uneven brightness, which can lead to stitching failure. To address these challenges, this paper proposes an image stitching framework that combines low-light image enhancement and an improved U-Net structure. The framework is divided into two stages: in the image enhancement stage, the details are restored and the colour is enhanced by a dual-branch enhancement network. The two branches exchange information through a fusion module to generate an enhanced image. In the image stitching stage, the warped image is obtained using an image alignment method, and then the stitching is optimised using an improved U-Net structure. A residual block is introduced to improve the stitching quality and generate the final stitched image. In addition, in order to evaluate the performance of the proposed framework in real low-light scenes, a special low-light scene dataset was constructed for network training. The results show that the algorithm described in this paper performs well in low-light image enhancement, significantly improving the image's detail and colour reproduction capabilities, and the overall image quality is significantly improved. The enhanced image significantly improves the stitching accuracy when stitching, effectively eliminating stitching artifacts.

Z. Zou (✉) · F. Zhang · S. Yuan
School of Electrical and Control Engineering, Shenyang Jianzhu University, Shenyang, China
e-mail: 1225443116@qq.com

F. P. García Márquez et al. (eds.), *Computing, Internet of Things and Data Analytics*, Smart Innovation, Systems and Technologies 387,
https://doi.org/10.1007/978-3-031-87154-2_60

60.1 Introduction

Low-light environments are common in daily life, but the image quality is often poor due to the complex lighting conditions in indoor and outdoor low-light scenes such as early morning, dusk and night. Therefore, it is important to study image stitching technology suitable for low-light scenes.

At present, the development of image stitching technology mainly focuses on processing clear, high-quality images in environments with ideal lighting conditions. Traditional image stitching methods are divided into three steps: feature extraction and matching, image registration, and image fusion. From the initial use of feature extraction algorithms such as SIFT [1] and ORB [2] to extract key points and calculate adaptive distortions, to the introduction of linear features in recent years to improve stitching quality, Li et al. [3] proposed a line segment representation and distance measurement method, and then used point features and line features to jointly estimate image transformations. Jia et al. [4] introduced a global co-linear structure as a constraint to alleviate unnatural distortions, and Liao et al. [5] used line features to maintain perspective consistency and natural transitions during image stitching. In addition, there are some studies on seam-driven stitching methods, which find the best seams in the overlapping areas of two images to reduce artifacts [6–8]. However, in low-light scenes, there are few obvious features, and feature extraction becomes very difficult. The global homography matrix also has difficulty aligning objects in different planes, making it difficult for traditional stitching methods to perform as expected.

In recent years, the advantages of convolutional neural networks (CNNs) in extracting robust features have become increasingly prominent, and more and more research has applied CNNs to image stitching tasks. Detone [9] and Nguyen [10] proposed deep homography estimation networks (DHNs) based on supervised and unsupervised methods, respectively. Hong et al. [11] proposed HomoGan, which predicts the single-responsibility matrix from the feature pyramid of the input image in a coarse-to-fine manner. Cheng et al. [12] proposed an image stitching seam prediction method that combines selection consistency loss function to transform seam prediction into mask prediction. In addition, Lai [13], Song [14], Nie [15, 16], and others have also proposed supervised, weakly supervised, and unsupervised end-to-end image stitching frameworks based on deep learning. Low-light images often have the problem of losing details, which places higher demands on the generalisation ability of the model. This also makes it difficult for deep learning models to fully learn the feature representation of low-light images.

At present, most of the current research on image stitching algorithms is still in an environment with ideal lighting conditions. There is relatively little research on image stitching in low-light scenes. Yan [17] and Guo [18] used traditional image enhancement combined with image stitching algorithms to enhance the stitching accuracy for night scenes, but the results were not satisfactory. In addition, most image stitching datasets are taken under normal lighting conditions, and there is a lack of stitching datasets specifically for low-light scenes. In response to the above problems, we proposes a deep learning-based low-light image stitching framework that incorporates image enhancement. The main contributions are as follows:

We design a dual-branch image enhancement network that includes an improved Transformer module. This module adaptively extracts and fuses high-frequency details and low-frequency components of images using self-attention and gating mechanisms. Information is integrated through a Fusion Module.

We develop an image fusion network based on an improved U-Net architecture. This network incorporates residual modules into the encoder-decoder pathways and introduces transposed convolution operations in the decoder pathway to improve the visual quality of the stitching results.

We create a stitching dataset specifically for low-light scenarios. Comparative experiments with other mainstream algorithms are performed on this dataset to validate the effectiveness of our proposed innovations.

60.2 Methodology

In this chapter, we describe in detail the proposed low-light image stitching network. Figure 1a shows the overall architecture of the network, which is divided into two parts: the low-light enhancement module and the image stitching module. The low-light enhancement module aims to enhance low-light images and restore dark details in preparation for subsequent stitching. The image stitching module first performs distortion correction on the enhanced image to better align the corrected image before seamlessly stitching it to generate the final high-quality panorama. Through the synergy of these two modules, our network can effectively process images of low-light scenes, generating a bright, clear and natural stitching result.

60.2.1 Low Light Enhancement Module

In our image enhancement model, both branches use a modified Transformer, as shown in Fig. 1b. First, a two-dimensional convolutional layer maps the input features to a higher-dimensional feature space. Then, these features are further processed using a depth-separable convolution. After feature processing, the features are divided into three parts: Query, Key and Value, which are represented as:

$$Q = W_Q \cdot f_{Dconv}(f_{conv}(X)) \quad K = W_K \cdot f_{Dconv}(f_{conv}(X)) \quad V = W_V \cdot f_{Dconv}(f_{conv}(X)) \tag{60.1}$$

W_Q, W_K, W_V represent the learned weight matrix.

The dot product of Query and Key is used to calculate the attention weights, which are then normalised using the softmax function to convert them into attention weights. Finally, the attention weights are used to weight and sum the values to

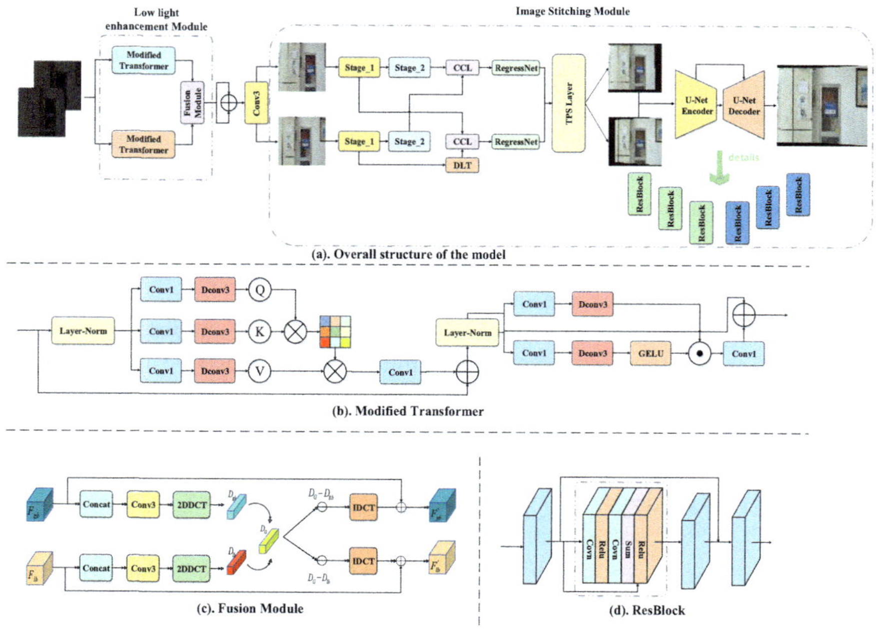

Fig. 1. Overall framework of proposed method.

Fig. 60.1 Overall framework of proposed method

generate the final output features. Next, the obtained features are mapped again to a higher dimension, providing the necessary feature space for the subsequent gating mechanism and deep convolution operations. As shown in the equation:

$$A = soft\max\left(\frac{QK^T}{\sqrt{d_k}}\right) \quad Attention(Q, K, V) = AV \tag{60.2}$$

A represents the weight of attention, and d_k represents the dimension of the Key vector.

Through a gating mechanism, which includes GELU activation functions and element multiplication operations, the model can dynamically adjust the interaction strength between different features, thereby carefully controlling the flow and integration of information. Finally, through a one-dimensional convolutional layer, the processed features are remapped back to the original dimension. Expressed as:

$$G = GELU(X''') \odot X''' \tag{60.3}$$

X''' is a feature after deep convolution processing.

The fusion module is then used to fuse the features of the two branches to obtain a more comprehensive and detailed image representation, as shown in Fig. 1c. First, the multispectral attention layer selects specific frequency components in the frequency domain using a two-dimensional discrete cosine transform (DCT) to generate feature descriptors for global and local features, respectively D_{gb}, D_{lb}. The 2D DCT formula used in this paper is:

$$f_{u,v}^{2d} = \sum_{i=0}^{H-1} \sum_{j=0}^{W-1} x_{i,j}^{2d} \cos(\frac{\pi \mu}{H}(i + \frac{1}{2})) \cos(\frac{\pi \mu}{W}(j + \frac{1}{2})) \tag{60.4}$$

$$s.t.\, u \in [0, H-1], v \in [0, W-1]$$

The 2D DCT spectrum and the feature map are represented by the global and local features, respectively f^{2d}, x^{2d}. These are then fused to form the total feature descriptor D_G. The difference between the total feature descriptor and the global/local feature descriptor is calculated. The global/local feature descriptor is multiplied by the global difference weight, which enables an information exchange and complementation process. The final fused feature is obtained, which contains both global contextual information and local detailed information. The above process can be expressed as follows:

$$F_{gb'} = F_{gb} + (D_G - D_{gb})F_{lb} \quad F_{lb'} = F_{lb} + (D_G - D_{lb})F_{gb} \tag{60.5}$$

where $F_{gb'}$ and $F_{lb'}$ are the feature representations of the two branches after information interaction.

60.2.2 Image Stitching Module

The image stitching module is divided into two parts: image warping and image fusion. First, the enhanced image is passed into the image warping module to estimate the deformation relationship between the two images. In this module, the brightened image is passed into the stage1, and the two images are respectively passed through the convolutional layer and the pooling layer to obtain feature maps, which are then input into the regressor composed of the fully connected layer and the CCL layer to predict the offset of the four control points. The DLT (Direct Linear Transform) algorithm is used to solve the global single-responsiveness matrix H. The single-responsiveness matrix H can be obtained by the following formula:

$$dst_p = H \times src_p \tag{60.6}$$

src_p represents the source point, and dst_p represents the target point. H is a 3×3 single-responsibility matrix obtained by solving a linear equation system.

In stage 2, the two images are once again subjected to a more profound convolution and pooling operation, resulting in the generation of feature maps. A regressor, comprising analogous fully connected layers and CCL layers, is then employed to derive local shape variables. Subsequently, the single-responsiveness matrix H, derived in stage 1, is transformed into a grid format, with the local shape variables subsequently incorporated to yield the final deformation grid. Finally, the Thin Plate Spline (TPS) transformation layer is employed for thin plate spline interpolation, thereby obtaining the aligned output image. The TPS transformation can be parameterised as follows:

$$f(p) = A_q(p) + \sum_{i=1}^{4} \omega_{qi}(p) \cdot \phi(\|p - x_i\|) \tag{60.7}$$

For a small region q ∈ grid G, A_q is the affine transformation for region q, and $\omega_{qi}(p)$ is the weight calculated based on the position of p in region q. ϕ is the radial basis function, $\phi(r) = r^2 \log(r)$.

The distorted image is then passed to the incoming image composition module, where it is subjected to further processing to obtain the final splicing result. The enhanced U-Net network incorporates the residual block and the deconvolution layer into the encoder-decoder architecture of the conventional U-Net, thereby enhancing the network's capacity for feature extraction and recovery. The encoder section comprises four downsampling blocks, each of which comprises a convolutional block and a pooling operation. Each step serves to reduce the spatial dimension of the data (height and width), thereby facilitating the model's ability to learn more abstract feature representations. This can be expressed as follows:

$$DownBlock(x) = Conv(Pool(x)) \tag{60.8}$$

The decoder section comprises three upsampling blocks connected by a skip connection. A residual module is incorporated into the block, and each step combines the feature map with a residual module that increases the dimensionality of the data in order to restore it to the original input data dimension. This can be expressed as follows:

$$UpBlock(x, y) = Deconv(ResBlock(x + y)) \tag{60.9}$$

where x is the feature map transferred from the adjacent downsampling layer, y is the feature map transferred from the corresponding upsampling layer, and x + y denotes the fusion of the feature maps.

The residual module contains two convolutional layers, each followed by a ReLU activation function, which can alleviate the problem of gradient disappearance when the network is deepened. The structure is shown in Fig. 1d, and the formula is expressed as:

$$ResBlock(x) = ReLU(Conv2(ReLU(Conv1(x))) + x) \quad (60.10)$$

Concurrently, the traditional interpolation method has been supplanted by deconvolution, which facilitates the more accurate restoration of image details.

60.2.3 Loss Function

We use three loss functions to train the enhanced part of the model, namely the reconstruction loss, perceptual loss and structural perceptual loss. The reconstruction loss aims to make the output image as close as possible to the real image at the pixel level, which is expressed as:

$$L_{rc} = mean(\sqrt{(out - gt)^2 + \varepsilon^2}) \quad (60.11)$$

out is the predicted output of the model, gt is the true target image, and ε is a small constant generally taken as 1e − 3.

Perceptual loss aims to evaluate the similarity between the reconstructed image I_{out} and the target image I_{gt} at the level of high-level feature representation, and the formula is expressed as:

$$L_{pl} = \|\phi_i(out) - \phi_i(gt)\| \quad (60.12)$$

ϕ_i represents the feature extraction function of the i layer in the pre-trained VGG network.

The structural perceptual loss aims to make the output image close to the real image in terms of brightness, contrast and structure, improving the quality and realism of the generated image. The formula is expressed as:

$$L_{SSIM} = 1 - SSIM(out, gt) \quad (60.13)$$

$SSIM(out, gt)$ is the structural similarity index between the calculated output image and the target image.

We use three loss functions to train the stitching part of the model, namely the boundary loss function, the stitching smoothness loss, and the difference smoothness loss. The boundary loss function is designed to make the fused image more natural and smooth at the stitching boundary of the two input images. The equation is expressed as:

$$L_{BL} = \frac{1}{|B(M_2)|}\sum\nolimits_{i \in B(M_2)} |I_1[i] - S[i]| + \frac{1}{|B(M_1)|}\sum\nolimits_{i \in B(M_1)} |I_2[i] - S[i]| \quad (60.14)$$

where I_1, I_2 represent the two input images, S represents the stitched image, and M_1, M_2 represent the corresponding mask, $|B(M)|$ indicating the total number of pixels in the border area.

Smoothing loss and difference smoothing loss are designed to make the fused image smoother and more natural in the non-boundary region and the overlapping region of the input images. For the fused image S and the mask M_1, their formulas are:

$$L_{SL1} = \frac{1}{N}\sum\nolimits_{i,j}\left(\Delta_h(M_1)_{ij}\cdot\Delta_h(S)_{ij} + \Delta_w(M_1)_{ij}\cdot\Delta_w(S)_{ij}\right) \quad (60.15)$$

$$L_{SL2} = \frac{1}{N}\sum\nolimits_{i,j}\left(\Delta_h(M_1)_{ij}\cdot\Delta_h(D)_{ij} + \Delta_w(M_1)_{ij}\cdot\Delta_w(D)_{ij}\right) \quad (60.16)$$

Δ_h and Δ_w respectively represent the horizontal and vertical difference operations, and N is the total number of pixels in the image. Define $D = (I_1 - I_2)^2 \nu O$ and O is the overlapping area of I_1, I_2.

60.3 Experiment and Discussion

60.3.1 Dataset and Implement Details

Public datasets: LOL-V2 [19] and MIT5K [20] are used to train the enhancement network, and UDIS-D [15] is used to train the stitching network.

Our dataset: We use a single-lens reflex camera to capture real low-light and normal-light videos of the same scene. By controlling the time interval between these videos, we extract still frames to obtain photos with different overlap rates under low-light/normal-light conditions. This real-world dataset covers multiple scenes with low-light and corresponding normal-light indoor and outdoor artificial and natural light sources. The original resolution of the captured images is 1920*1080. Due to the high resolution of the images, direct stitching would significantly increase the computing resources and training time, so the original data is processed into 512*512 images to evaluate the performance of the network. The dataset consists of 1665 pairs of images captured in low-light and normal-light conditions. From these, 1500 pairs are designated for training purposes, while the remaining 165 pairs are reserved for testing. Figure 60.2 illustrates a sample image from the dataset. In our experiments, the low-light images serve as the input, with the normal-light images functioning as the ground truth.

Implement Details: The training process for image enhancement employs the Adam optimizer, starting with an initial learning rate 2×10^{-4}, which is gradually decreased to 1×10^{-6} using a cosine annealing schedule. We randomly crop 256×256 image patches from three benchmark datasets and train with a batch size of 6. To augment the data, horizontal and vertical flips are applied to the images. Validation

Fig. 60.2 Example images of our dataset

is conducted once per epoch, and the model parameters that yield the best metrics are preserved. For the image stitching phase, enhanced low-light image pairs with varying overlap ratios are used as input. The stitching network is also trained with the Adam optimizer, starting with an initial learning rate 1×10^{-4} that decreases following an exponential decay strategy. This network undergoes training for 100 epochs with a batch size of 1. Both networks are developed using the PyTorch 1.11.0 framework. The experiments run on an Ubuntu 22.04 system with an NVIDIA V100 32 GB GPU.

60.3.2 Comparison of Image Enhancement

We evaluated our proposed enhancement method against popular enhancement algorithms using our dataset to validate its performance. These include the traditional method LIME [21], the supervised method Retinex-Net [22] and the unsupervised method EnlightenGan [23], Zero-DCE [24].

We use peak signal-to-noise ratio (PSNR) [25], structural similarity (SSIM) [26] and perceptual learning index (LPIPS) [27] to quantitatively evaluate the enhancement performance. Table 60.1 shows the quantitative comparison results (PSNR↑, SSIM↑ and LPIPS↓). As can be seen from the table, the method achieves the best performance in terms of SSIM and LPIPS. SSIM and LPIPS are 0.824 and 0.151 respectively, which is 0.011 higher and 0.014 lower than the second placed ZeroDCE. PSNR also achieves the second best performance after ZeroDCE.

Figure 60.3 shows sample images of the results of the enhancement algorithms for each scene. It can be seen that although most existing methods can enhance

Table 60.1 Image enhancement comparison experiment. The top two solutions are highlighted in red and blue for first and second place, respectively

Method	LIME	RetinexNet	ENGAN	ZeroDCE	Ours
PSNR↑	15.62	13.72	18.19	22.04	21.65
SSIM↑	0.698	0.661	0.785	0.813	0.824
LPIPS↓	0.263	0.434	0.223	0.165	0.151

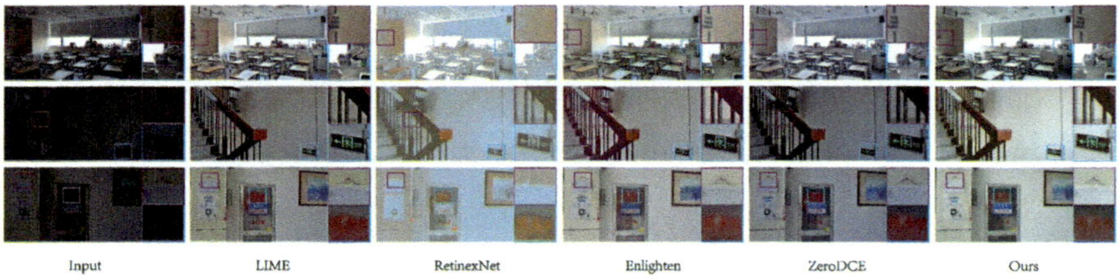

Fig. 60.3 Example images of enhanced results

low-light images to some extent, they often introduce side effects such as colour distortion and blurring of details during processing. As can be seen in the figure, RetinexNet has over-enhanced the image and the overall image is white; LIME cannot maintain the colour effects in the original image, and the colour distortion is obvious; the EnlightenGan algorithm has lost image details. Although ZeroDCE can restore image details well, the enhanced colour is dark. Compared with them, our method can achieve satisfactory global enhancement and fine detail restoration, producing high-quality results.

60.3.3 Comparison of Image Stitching

We evaluated our proposed stitching method against popular stitching algorithms using our dataset to validate its performance. The mainstream algorithms mentioned above include the traditional methods SIFT + RANSAC [28], APAP [29] and the unsupervised method UDHN [10], UDIS [15].

We use PSNR and SSIM as evaluation metrics for quantitative comparison in our dataset. The metrics are divided into three levels, and the top 30%, 30%-60%, and 60%-100% of the metrics are classified as simple tasks, medium tasks, and complex tasks, respectively. Tables 60.2 and 60.3 show the PSNR and SSIM metric values of different algorithms on the dataset. It can be seen from the table that the model proposed in this paper achieves the best performance, and UDIS achieves suboptimal performance in all aspects except for complex tasks. In terms of average PSNR, our model is 24.79% higher than SIFT + RANSAC and 9.32% higher than UDIS. In terms of average SSIM, our model is 15.42% higher than SIFT + RANSAC and 3.49% higher than UDIS. In addition, we can also see from the table that the unsupervised method based on deep learning is generally better than the traditional stitching method, which is caused by the difficulty of feature extraction in low light and the difficulty of the outlier rejection algorithm in rejecting incorrect points.

Figure 60.4 shows sample images of the results of all algorithms in each scenario. The white boxes in the figure show the same area in the same group of results, highlighting the artifacts in the results. It can be seen from the figure that the traditional stitching method has difficulty extracting and matching feature points due to low

Table 60.2 Image stitching comparison experiment of PSNR. The top two solutions are highlighted in red and blue for first and second place, respectively

Method	I_{3*3}	SIFT + RANSAC	APAP	UDHN	UDIS	Ours
Easy	15.38	27.30	26.38	24.71	29.39	32.61
Moderate	12.45	22.26	22.07	21.50	25.12	26.33
Hard	10.11	15.98	14.99	17.59	19.19	20.13
Average	12.52	21.05	20.35	21.10	24.03	26.27

Table 60.3 Image stitching comparison experiment of SSIM. The top two solutions are highlighted in red and blue for first and second place, respectively

Method	I_{3*3}	SIFT + RANSAC	APAP	UDHN	UDIS	Ours
Easy	0.437	0.768	0.694	0.824	0.853	0.882
Moderate	0.201	0.652	0.595	0.718	0.733	0.765
Hard	0.085	0.550	0.519	0.594	0.569	0.610
Average	0.229	0.642	0.591	0.701	0.716	0.741

light, so the stitching seam artifacts are not well removed, resulting in an unsatisfactory result. The results of the UDHN method show that its unsupervised learning algorithm is unstable when dealing with low-light tasks. In addition to the artifacts of the stitching seam, there is also the phenomenon of ghosting that affects the stitching result. The results of the UDIS method show that its unsupervised learning algorithm can achieve better results, but there are also stitching errors in some tasks. In contrast, by first enhancing the image and then stitching it, our algorithm can more clearly show the details of the image and the artifacts of the stitching seams can also be well removed.

Fig. 60.4 Example images of stitched results

60.4 Conclusion

This paper presents a deep learning framework that integrates low-light image enhancement and an enhanced U-Net structure to address the challenge of image stitching in low-light settings. The framework is divided into two stages: low-light image enhancement and image stitching. Firstly, in the low-light enhancement stage, a dual-branch structure that processes high and low frequency information in parallel is designed to obtain enhanced image pairs. An improved Transformer module is introduced in each branch, which enables the adaptive extraction and fusion of high-frequency details and low-frequency components of the image through self-attention and gating mechanisms. Subsequently, in the stitching stage, the features of the input image pairs are initially extracted by a convolutional neural network, and a single-response transformation matrix between the two images is then regressed using a fully connected layer. The image pairs to be stitched are transformed into a common coordinate space through TPS. Finally, a residual module is incorporated into the U-Net codec structure, and an anti-convolution operation is added to the decoding branch in order to achieve upsampling of feature maps and recovery of spatial resolution. Furthermore, we propose a real-world dataset for image stitching in low-light conditions, and the experimental results demonstrate the superiority of our method over other advanced solutions. In the future, we will focus on exploring emerging technologies such as attention mechanisms and adversarial learning for the stitching optimisation stage. This will enable the generation of more realistic and natural stitching results. Furthermore, we will expand and improve the dataset in terms of data scale, diversity of complex scenes, and other factors.

Acknowledgements The work described in this article was supported by the funds from the Project of Liaoning Provincial Department of Science and Technology (grant no. 2023JH2/101300212).

References

1. Lowe, D.G.: Distinctive image features from scale-invariant keypoints. Int. J. Comput. Vision **60**, 91–110 (2004)
2. Rublee, E., Rabaud, V., Konolige, K., Bradski, G., IEEE: ORB: an efficient alternative to SIFT or SURF. In: IEEE International Conference on Computer Vision (ICCV), pp. 2564–2571 (2011)
3. Li, S.W., Yuan, L., Sun, J., Quan, L., IEEE: Dual-feature warping-based motion model estimation. In: IEEE International Conference on Computer Vision, pp. 4283–4291 (2015)
4. Jia, Q., Li, Z.J., Fan, X., Zhao, H.T., Teng, S.Y., Ye, X.C., Latecki, L.J., IEEE Comp, S.O.C.: Leveraging line-point consistence to preserve structures Forwide parallax image stitching. In: IEEE/CVF Conference on Computer Vision and Pattern Recognition (CVPR), pp. 12181–12190 (2021)
5. Liao, T.L., Li, N.: Single-perspective warps in natural image stitching. IEEE Trans. Image Process. **29**, 724–735 (2020)
6. Lin, K.M., Jiang, N.J., Cheong, L.F., Do, M., Lu, J.B.: SEAGULL: seam-guided local alignment for parallax-tolerant image stitching. In: 14th European Conference on Computer Vision (ECCV), pp. 370–385 (2016)
7. Liu, Q.X., Su, X.Y., Zhang, L., Huang, H.: Panoramic video stitching of dual cameras based on spatio-temporal seam optimization. Multimed. Tools Appl. **79**, 3107–3124 (2020)
8. Li, J., Zhou, Y., IEEE Comp, S.O.C.: Automatic color image stitching using quaternion rank-1 alignment. In: IEEE/CVF Conference on Computer Vision and Pattern Recognition (CVPR), pp. 19688–19697 (2022)
9. DeTone, D., Malisiewicz, T., Rabinovich, A.J.a.p.a.: Deep image homography estimation. (2016)
10. Nguyen, T., Chen, S.W., Shivakumar, S.S., Taylor, C.J., Kumar, V.J.I.R., Letters, A.: Unsupervised deep homography: a fast and robust homography estimation model **3**, 2346-2353 (2018)
11. Hong, M.B., Lu, Y.H., Ye, N.J., Lin, C.Y., Zhao, Q.J., Liu, S.C., IEEE Comp, S.O.C.: Unsupervised homography estimation with coplanarity-aware GAN. In: IEEE/CVF Conference on Computer Vision and Pattern Recognition (CVPR), pp. 17642–17651 (2022)
12. Cheng, S., Yang, F., Chen, Z., Yuan, N., Tao, W.: Deep seam prediction for image stitching based on selection consistency loss arXiv. arXiv (2023)
13. Lai, W.-S., Gallo, O., Gu, J., Sun, D., Yang, M.-H., Kautz, J.J.a.p.a.: Video stitching for linear camera arrays (2019)

14. Song, D.-Y., Lee, G., Lee, H., Um, G.-M., Cho, D.: Weakly-supervised stitching network for real-world panoramic image generation. In: European Conference on Computer Vision, pp. 54–71. Springer (2022)
15. Nie, L., Lin, C.Y., Liao, K., Liu, S.C., Zhao, Y.: Unsupervised deep image stitching: reconstructing stitched features to images. IEEE Trans. Image Process. **30**, 6184–6197 (2021)
16. Nie, L., Lin, C.Y., Liao, K., Liu, S.C., Zhao, Y., IEEE: Parallax-tolerant unsupervised deep image stitching. In: IEEE/CVF International Conference on Computer Vision (ICCV), pp. 7365–7374 (2023)
17. Yan, M.Y., Qin, D.Y., Zhang, G.X., Zheng, P., Bai, J.A., Ma, L.: Nighttime image stitching method based on guided filtering enhancement. Entropy **24** (2022)
18. Guo, S., Zhang, H., Ji, X., Xu, W.: Research on stitching technology based on enhanced images of substations. Proc. SPIE (USA) 129340T, pp. 129347 (2023)
19. Yang, W., Wang, W., Huang, H., Wang, S., Liu, J.J.I.T.o.I.P.: Sparse gradient regularized deep retinex network for robust low-light image enhancement **30**, 2072–2086 (2021)
20. Bychkovsky, V., Paris, S., Chan, E., Durand, F.: Learning photographic global tonal adjustment with a database of input/output image pairs. In: CVPR 2011, pp. 97–104. IEEE (2011)
21. Guo, X.J., Li, Y., Ling, H.B.: LIME: low-light image enhancement via illumination map estimation. IEEE Trans. Image Process. **26**, 982–993 (2017)
22. Wei, C., Wang, W., Yang, W., Liu, J.J.a.p.a.: Deep retinex decomposition for low-light enhancement (2018)
23. Jiang, Y.F., Gong, X.Y., Liu, D., Cheng, Y., Fang, C., Shen, X.H., Yang, J.C., Zhou, P., Wang, Z.Y.: EnlightenGAN: deep light enhancement without paired supervision. IEEE Trans. Image Process. **30**, 2340–2349 (2021)
24. Guo, C., Li, C., Guo, J., Loy, C.C., Hou, J., Kwong, S., Cong, R.: Zero-reference deep curve estimation for low-light image enhancement. In: Proceedings of the IEEE/CVF conference on computer vision and pattern recognition, pp. 1780–1789 (2020)
25. Hore, A., Ziou, D.: Image quality metrics: PSNR vs. SSIM. In: 2010 20th International Conference on Pattern Recognition, pp. 2366–2369. IEEE (2010)
26. Wang, Z., Bovik, A.C., Sheikh, H.R., Simoncelli, E.P.J.I.t.o.i.p.: Image quality assessment: from error visibility to structural similarity **13**, 600–612 (2004)
27. Zhang, R., Isola, P., Efros, A.A., Shechtman, E., Wang, O., IEEE: the unreasonable effectiveness of deep features as a perceptual metric. In: 31st IEEE/CVF Conference on Computer Vision and Pattern Recognition (CVPR), pp. 586–595 (2018)
28. Brown, M., Lowe, D.G.J.I.j.o.c.v.: Automatic panoramic image stitching using invariant features **74**, 59–73 (2007)
29. Zaragoza, J., Chin, T.-J., Brown, M.S., Suter, D.: As-projective-as-possible image stitching with moving DLT. In: Proceedings of the IEEE Conference on Computer Vision and Pattern Recognition, pp. 2339–2346 (2013)

Chapter 61
Enhancing Multiclass Robustness in Diabetic Retinopathy Classification Using Deep Learning

Hamza Khan, Akhtar Jamil, Esraa Mohammed Alazzawi, and Alaa Ali Hameed

Abstract Diabetic Retinopathy (DR) is a major complication of diabetes, leading to vision loss if not detected early. Despite significant advancements in medical imaging, accurate and efficient diagnosis of DR remains a challenging task due to the subtle variations in retinal images. Addressing this issue is critical in developing reliable AI-driven tools for ophthalmology. Given the critical need for accurate diagnosis, this paper presents an ensemble learning approach utilizing EfficientNetB0 and EfficientNetB3 models for robust DR classification. The method achieves high accuracy by combining the strengths of these architectures, validated on comprehensive datasets such as Messidor, Eyepacs, and RFMiD, without relying on complex data augmentation techniques. A validation accuracy of 91% and a test accuracy of 96.19% are achieved, demonstrating the potential for enhancing AI-driven diagnostic tools in clinical ophthalmology.

61.1 Introduction

This study introduces an innovative ensemble learning approach that combines EfficientNetB0 and EfficientNetB3. This method capitalizes on the strengths of both architectures, allowing for improved feature extraction and classification accuracy compared to traditional single-model approaches. The ensemble technique not only

H. Khan · A. Jamil (✉)
Department of Computer Science, National University of Computer and Emerging Sciences, Islamabad, Pakistan
e-mail: akhtar.jamil@nu.edu.pk

H. Khan
e-mail: hamza.khan@nu.edu.pk

E. M. Alazzawi
Department of Computer Engineering, University of Baghdad, Al-Jadriya, Baghdad, Iraq
e-mail: israa.abd2005@coeng.uobaghdad.edu.iq

A. A. Hameed
Department of Computer Engineering, Istinye University, Istanbul, Turkey
e-mail: alaa.hameed@istinye.edu.tr

F. P. García Márquez et al. (eds.), *Computing, Internet of Things and Data Analytics*, Smart Innovation, Systems and Technologies 387,
https://doi.org/10.1007/978-3-031-87154-2_61

enhances robustness but also reduces the risk of overfitting, making it particularly suitable for diverse retinal datasets.

Diabetic Retinopathy (DR) is one of the major complications associated with diabetes that affects the eye, engendered by detrimental blood vessels in the light-sensitive tissue at the back of the eye (the retina). Diagnosis of diabetic retinopathy promptly [1, 2] and with appropriate control measures will prevent severe loss of vision. Computerized algorithms and digitized imagery offer improvement toward the diagnosis and treatment that this disease needs, with exact retinal vessel classification being made achievable as never before.

Diabetic Retinopathy is an ocular disease that is determined to be induced by diabetes and is a leading cause of vision loss and blindness around the world [3]. Over 422 million individuals in the world suffer from this lifestyle disease, with most of them being members of a majority group at risk of contracting DR, according to the World Health Organization [4]. The damage done by DR is very slow, and one may not have noticed manifest symptoms until a considerable amount of injury has been done, which is a need for early detection and intervention.

Diabetic retinopathy has an impact, exceeding that of the visual disability to influence the quality of life and mental health together with the socioeconomic status of patients. Besides, the rapidly growing prevalence of DR exerts remarkable pressure on the healthcare systems in terms of requiring appropriate means for management. The pathophysiology intricately relates to prolonged hyperglycemia whereby DR originates, giving rise to microvascular damage in the retina. It includes microaneurysms, hemorrhages, and exudates that may progress to retinal detachment and neovascular glaucoma. Advanced retinal imaging comes in handy to explore these changes pathologically, which may include fundus photography by either optical coherence tomography or other methods for early diagnosis and early intervention. A sample showing diabetic retinopathy is shown in Fig. 61.1.

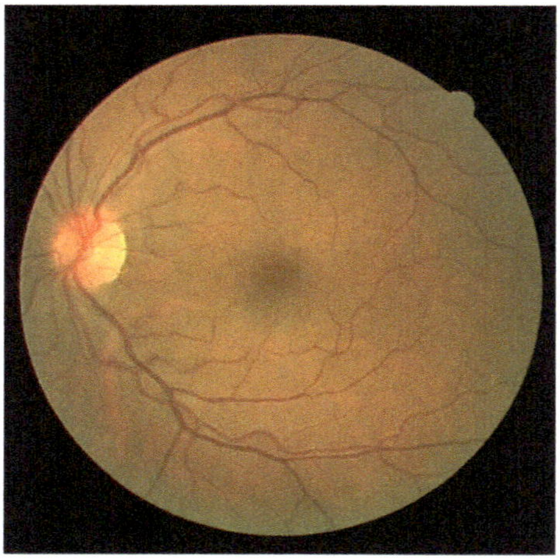

Fig. 61.1 A sample image showing diabetic retinopathy

The main contributions of this work are as follows:

1. Utilizes EfficientNetB0 and EfficientNetB3 models for robust DR classification.
2. Introduces an ensemble learning approach to improve accuracy.
3. Validates the methodology on diverse and comprehensive datasets (Messidor, Eyepacs, RFMiD).

This research paper is structured into several sections, each with a distinct focus. Section 61.2: Literature Review reviews existing methodologies and models in diabetic retinopathy (DR) classification. Section 61.3: Methodology describes the use of EfficientNet models and ensemble learning to improve DR classification. Section 61.4: Results presents experimental outcomes, highlighting significant improvements in classification accuracy and robustness. Section 5: Discussion interprets the results, emphasizing the practical applicability and potential for transforming DR diagnosis. Section 61.5: Conclusion summarizes the key findings and their significance, underscoring the effectiveness and broader impact of the ensemble approach.

61.2 Literature Review

In the field of medical image analysis, particularly in diabetic retinopathy classification, recent studies have explored novel approaches to enhance model accuracy and generalization for diagnostic purposes. One such method, NNMOBILE-NET, utilizes MobileNet architecture for retina disease diagnosis [5]. This approach demonstrates the effectiveness of MobileNet in improving classification accuracy while reducing overfitting. Leveraging a large dataset of retinal images, the model performs effectively in disease detection, providing robust evidence of its potential in real-world diagnostic applications.

Data preprocessing and semi-supervised GAN-based classification for retinal fundus images has been explored, with a focus on achieving efficiency through automated analysis [6]. The approach reaches an average accuracy of 87% and provides a comprehensive solution for improving image quality throughout the process. However, its effectiveness depends on the quality of the fundus images and requires a large volume of training data, making it sensitive to image quality and data availability.

Combining highly dissimilar datasets and employing various models results in an accuracy of 80.46% for diabetic retinopathy segmentation [7]. This approach highlights the significance of model selection and dataset diversity in improving disease detection and accuracy. Despite these advances, there is a need for future research focusing on multiclass studies and addressing class imbalances within datasets.

Faiq et al. [8] combined both CNN and particle swarm optimization (PSO) for diabetes identification. PSO was employed for optimization of CNN that produced state of the art results for classification. A similar work was presented by Alaa et al. [9] where a prototype based model based on learning vector quantization (LVQ) was employed for diabetes diagnosis. Three different variants namely, generalized learning vector quantization (GLVQ), relevance learning vector quantization (RLVQ), and generalized relevance learning vector quantization (GRLVQ) were evaluated and all showed promising results.

EyeDeep-Net [10] focuses on developing an automated deep learning-based framework, for diagnosing multiple eye diseases using color fundus images. Utilizing the multi-class RFMiD dataset, the research applied various augmentation techniques to enhance real-time robustness and processed images for low computational demand. The multi-layer neural network effectively extracted relevant features for predictive diagnostics. Evaluated against multiple statistical parameters, EyeDeep-Net demonstrated superior performance compared to state-of-the-art models. Comprehensive comparisons confirmed its efficacy in classification and disease identification through digital fundus images.

Li et al. [11] presented a novel multi-label detection deep learning model for retinal images, utilizing attention-guided image enhancement techniques. Their approach addresses challenges such as small data volumes, uneven distributions, and low classification accuracy in multi-disease fundus image classification. By employing VGG19 and ResNet50 classification networks, coupled with Grad-CAM for data augmentation, the model significantly improves the robustness and accuracy of classification. The proposed method, tested on the RFMiD dataset, demonstrated superior performance with an accuracy of 97 , precision of 92, and recall of 81, outperforming existing models in the field. The study highlights the effectiveness of integrating attention mechanisms and fine-tuning in enhancing the detection and classification of retinal diseases.

In [3], authors addressed the high memory and CPU consumption in U-Net segmentation used for retinal disease classification. He proposes an optimized CNN model for multi-class classification, evaluated on the Eye-Net dataset with 32 retinal disease classes. The model demonstrates efficient memory usage and achieves a 95 accuracy rate. Comparisons based on precision, recall, and accuracy across various epochs show superior performance. This work highlights advancements in medical image classification while managing computational resources effectively.

Müller et al. [12] present an innovative multi-disease detection pipeline for retinal imaging, leveraging ensemble learning techniques to enhance predictive accuracy. The study integrates advanced strategies such as transfer learning, class weighting, and Focal loss, alongside real-time image augmentation. The proposed method employs various deep convolutional neural network architectures and combines their predictions through bagging and stacking approaches, achieving high reliability and accuracy in detecting multiple retinal diseases. The approach's effectiveness is validated through both internal evaluations and participation in the RIADD challenge, demonstrating its competitiveness with state-of-the-art methodologies.

In [13], authors highlight the effectiveness of DL models, such as U-Net and ResNet, in identifying DR lesions like microaneurysms, hemorrhages, and exudates from retinal images. The survey categorizes the approaches into traditional and DL-based methods, showcasing the superior performance of DL. The authors underscore the importance of high-quality datasets like IDRiD for training these models. The review aims to improve automated DR diagnosis, facilitating timely treatment.

Bhat Brahmavar et al. introduced IKD+, an iterative knowledge distillation method to address complexity and reliability issues in deep neural network models for retinopathy classification [14]. They demonstrate that IKD+ significantly reduces model parameters-up to 500-fold-while maintaining accuracy and improving prediction reliability through calibration techniques like Platt-scaling and temperature-scaling. Their empirical evaluation shows IKD+ models achieve comparable or better calibration scores than the original models, making them more suitable for clinical deployment. This work offers a promising approach to developing low-complexity, reliable models for medical image processing and retinopathy diagnosis.

Pachade et al. [15] developed the RFMiD, a comprehensive dataset consisting of 3200 retinal fundus images annotated with 46 conditions to facilitate multi-disease detection in routine clinical settings. This dataset, created from images captured using three different fundus cameras, aims to support the development of generalizable models for retinal screening, addressing both frequent and rare pathologies. The dataset's unique attribute is its extensive variety of annotated diseases, making it a valuable resource for advancing automated ocular disease classification systems. Furthermore, the authors highlighted the global necessity for early detection and diagnosis of ocular diseases to prevent visual impairment and related systemic health issues. Their work underscores the critical role of such datasets in enhancing computer-aided diagnostic tools in ophthalmology.

Yi et al. [16] propose MRANet for retinal vessel segmentation, improving U-Net by incorporating multi-level feature fusion, attention, and multi-scale residual blocks. They address issues like gradient dispersion and network overfitting. Experimental results on CHASEDB1 datasets show MRANet's superior performance, achieving better segmentation accuracy and vessel continuity compared to existing methods. This research highlights MRANet's effectiveness in automated retinal vessel segmentation for disease diagnosis.

Hu et al. [17] introduced HT-Net, a hybrid Transformer network for fundus vessel segmentation. The model combines CNNs and Transformers to capture both local and long-range dependencies, enhancing segmentation accuracy, particularly for microvessels. They tested HT-Net on CHASEDB1, and STARE datasets, showing superior performance compared to other methods. Their approach includes novel feature fusion and refinement blocks to improve the representation and segmentation quality of retinal vessels. The efficient self-attention mechanism embedded in HT-Net further boosts its ability to handle the complexities of medical imaging.

Rodríguez et al. [18] proposed a novel multi-label classification system using transformers for early detection of retinal diseases. Their research introduced the MuReD dataset, constructed from various publicly available sources, ensuring high-quality image data for multiple disease detection. The transformer-based model showed a significant performance improvement, outperforming state-of-the-art models by 7.9 in disease detection and 8.1 in disease classification in terms of AUC score. Their work emphasizes the potential of transformer architectures in medical imaging and the need for robust datasets to effectively train multi-label models. Moreover,

Minarno et al. [19] proposed a solution based on the EfficientNet-B7 model to classify diabetic retinopathy, achieving 89% accuracy on training data and 84 %on test data by employing various preprocessing and augmentation techniques.

The human research landscape in diabetic retinopathy segmentation interfaces traditional methodologies with state-of-the-art technologies, each with its strengths and weaknesses. NNMOBILE-NET and related studies underscore the power of transfer learning and ensemble learning in pursuit of improved diagnostic accuracy but carry on to point out challenges like the evaluation of diverse datasets and class imbalances. Overcoming these with new data preprocessing techniques, model optimization, and dataset augmentation could mean a future full of trustful and effective diagnostic systems.

61.3 Materials and Methodology

This paper utilizes EfficientNet models for ensemble learning, specifically EfficientNetB0 and EfficientNetB3. These models are selected for their efficiency and effectiveness in achieving high performance with fewer parameters than other architectures. Combining these models through ensemble learning techniques, the paper leverages their strengths to enhance overall classification accuracy. The Diabetic Retinopathy diagnosis challenge is addressed by acquiring retinal fundus images from the Messidor, Eyepacs, and RFMiD datasets. These datasets provide a rich and diverse set of images, forming the foundation for model training. The diversity and volume of images ensure that the models are both robust and representative, allowing them to generalize effectively to unseen data and making the diagnostic process more reliable. The Graphical representation of the proposed solution is shown below in Fig. 61.2.

61.3.1 Data Set

The datasets used in this study include Messidor, Eyepacs, and RFMiD. These datasets contain images categorized based on the severity of DR. The images were divided into training, validation, and test sets.

Messidor Dataset: The Messidor data set contains 1,200 retinal images captured using a non-mydriatic fundus camera. The dataset includes both normal and DR-affected images and is primarily used for grading DR.

Eyepacs Dataset: Eyepacs is one of the largest publicly available datasets for diabetic retinopathy detection, containing over 88,000 retinal fundus images. Eyepacs includes high-resolution fundus images with different levels of DR severity annotated by experts.

Retinal Fundus Multi-Disease Image Dataset (RFMiD): The RFMiD dataset focuses on multi-disease detection in retinal images. It includes 3,200 images with

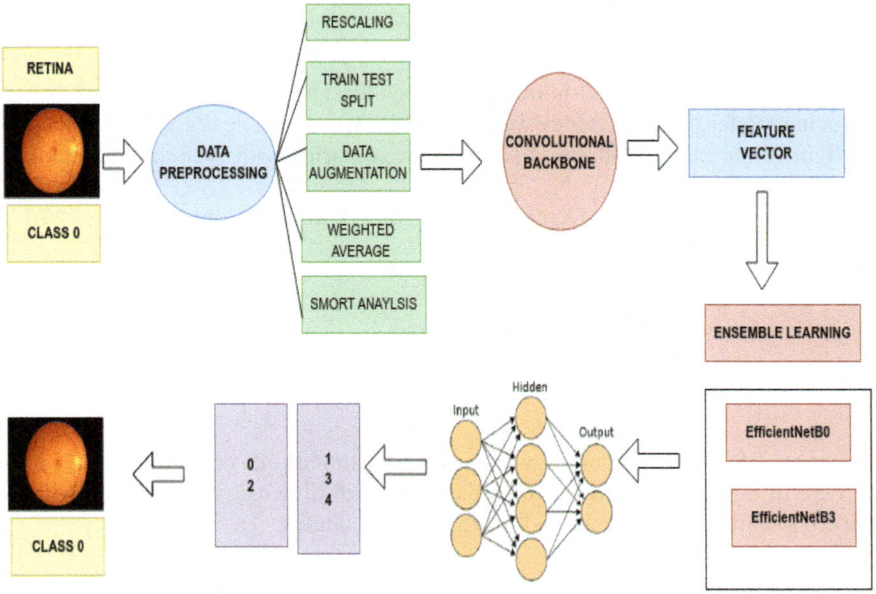

Fig. 61.2 Ensemble-based technique for DR classification

annotations covering 46 different retinal conditions. RFMiD includes images of various ocular diseases, making it suitable for broader disease detection tasks. The dataset was designed to support the development of generalizable models that can detect both common and rare eye conditions in clinical settings.

61.3.2 EfficientNet (EfficientNetB0, EfficientNetB3)

EfficientNetB0 is designed for efficiency and performance, offering a balanced trade-off between model size and accuracy. Used for its efficiency in processing and ability to extract meaningful insights from complex data with fewer parameters. EfficientNetB3, a more complex variant of EfficientNetB0, offers enhanced performance with more layers and parameters. Ideal for tasks requiring high precision and the ability to capture intricate patterns and details in data.

$$d = \alpha^k, \quad w = \beta^k, \quad r = \gamma^k \tag{61.1}$$

where α, β, γ are constants determined through grid search, and k is a user-defined parameter. We combine both EfficientNetB0 and EfficientNetB3 by applying Ensemble Learning.

61.3.3 MobileNet

Mobile Net is designed for mobile and embedded vision applications, focusing on reducing model size and latency while maintaining reasonable accuracy. Utilized for its lightweight nature, making it suitable for scenarios with limited computational resources.

$$\text{Conv}(x) = \text{DepthwiseConv}(x) + \text{PointwiseConv}(x) \tag{61.2}$$

where x is the input tensor.

61.3.4 Inception-V3

Inception-V3 employs a complex architecture with multiple convolutional layers to capture diverse features. Known for handling high-dimensional data and reducing the computational burden through its inception modules.

$$\text{Concat}(\text{Conv}_{1x1}(x), \text{Conv}_{3x3}(x), \text{Conv}_{5x5}(x), \text{MaxPool}_{3x3}(x)) \tag{61.3}$$

where x is the input tensor.

61.3.5 Xception

Xception stands for "Extreme Inception," a model that replaces the standard inception modules with depthwise separable convolutions. Offers improved accuracy and efficiency, particularly for tasks involving detailed image analysis and classification.

$$\text{Conv}(x) = \text{DepthwiseConv}(x) + \text{PointwiseConv}(x) \tag{61.4}$$

where x is the input tensor.

61.3.6 Ensemble Approach

The ensemble approach combines predictions from multiple models to improve overall accuracy and robustness. This method leverages the strengths of different architectures to reduce variance and bias, ensuring more reliable and accurate predictions.

$$y = \frac{1}{N}\sum_{i=1}^{N} y_i \tag{61.5}$$

where y_i is the prediction of the i-th model and N is the total number of models.

61.3.7 Loss Function

The loss function used in training these models is crucial for their performance. For classification tasks, particularly multi-class classification, such as in diabetic retinopathy detection, categorical cross-entropy loss is commonly used.

$$\text{Loss} = -\sum_{i=1}^{N} y_i \log(p_i) \tag{61.6}$$

where y_i is the true label, p_i is the predicted probability for class i, and N is the number of classes. This loss function measures the dissimilarity between the true label distribution and the predicted probability distribution, guiding the model to improve its predictions by minimizing this dissimilarity.

61.4 Experimental Results

61.4.1 Experimental Setup

The experiments were conducted on an NVIDIA GTX 1660 Super GPU paired with a 6th-generation Intel Core i5 CPU. This setup was chosen for its balance between computational power and cost efficiency. The software environment included Anaconda for package management and deployment and Visual Studio Code (VSCode) as the integrated development environment (IDE). These tools were selected for their versatility and robust support for machine learning workflows.

61.4.2 Preprocessing

The image preprocessing pipeline involved normalizing the input data to maintain consistency across the dataset. To further enhance model performance, data augmentation techniques-including rotation, scaling, and flipping-were applied, effectively increasing the diversity of the training set and helping the model generalize better to unseen data. Each EfficientNet model was specifically trained on datasets tailored to the classes it aimed to classify, allowing the models to focus on learning the most relevant features and patterns associated with those particular classes.

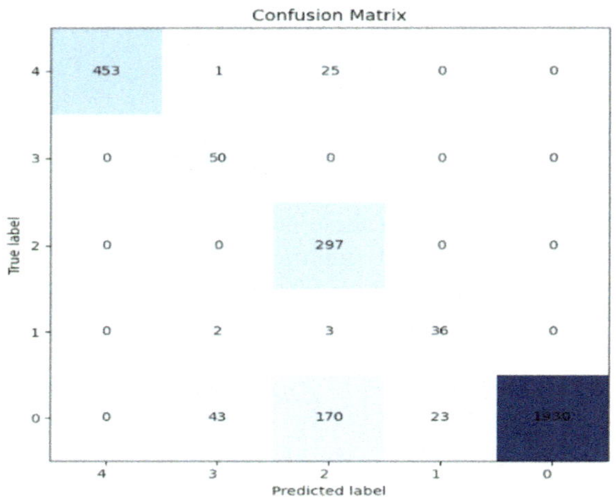

Fig. 61.3 Confusion matrix of ensembled model

61.4.3 Classification Results

Incorporating the EfficientNet models, specifically EfficientNetB0 and EfficientNetB3, into our methodology has significantly improved the classification accuracy for Diabetic Retinopathy (DR). The ensemble approach leverages both models' strengths, enhancing the diagnosis's robustness and precision. The following summarizes the key findings from our experiments:

EfficientNetB0 and EfficientNetB3 Performance The ensemble model achieved a validation accuracy of 91%, showcasing its ability to generalize and predict correctly on unseen data. In the test phase, the model achieved an impressive accuracy of 96.19%, highlighting its effectiveness in real-world scenarios. During training, the model reached an accuracy of 99%, reflecting its capability to learn complex patterns within the retinal images.

The confusion matrix shown in Fig. 61.3 illustrates the classification performance of the ensemble model. The matrix shows true positive, true negative, false positive, and false negative counts for each class, providing insights into the model's accuracy and areas of misclassification.The confusion matrix (Figure 3) illustrates the model's performance across different classes. The ensemble model combining EfficientNetB0 and EfficientNetB3 achieved a precision of 100%, recall of 99.00%, and an F1-score of 100.0%, indicating an exceptional classification capability with minimal misclassifications. The matrix highlights that the model effectively identifies nearly all positive cases while maintaining a very low false positive rate.

Training and Validation Performance:
The training and validation performance metrics showed a decreasing trend in loss values and increasing validation accuracy, indicating effective learning and model

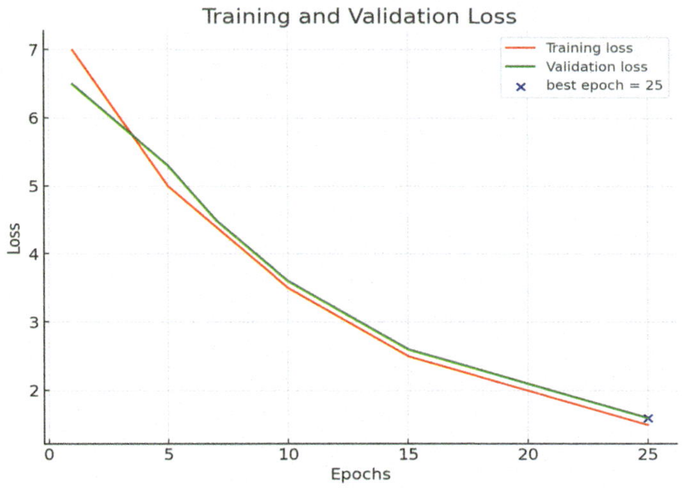

Fig. 61.4 EfficientNet-B0 and B3 model training and testing loss

improvement. The ensemble model achieved a training accuracy of 99%, a validation accuracy of 91%, and a test accuracy of 96.19%. Figure 61.4 illustrates the loss values across numerous training epochs for both the EfficientNet-B0 and EfficientNet-B3 models. On the X-axis, the epochs are plotted, indicating the number of complete passes through the training dataset. The Y-axis measures the loss, showing how the model's predictions diverge from the actual data, with separate curves for training and validation losses. This visualization helps in assessing how well the models learn from the training data and generalize to new, unseen data, crucial for tuning the models to achieve optimal performance. Similarly, Fig. 61.5 shows the accuracy obtained during the training process of the EfficientNet-B0 and EfficientNet-B3 models.

61.4.4 Comparative Analysis

Compared to EfficientNetB7, which achieved an accuracy of 84.36, the ensemble model of EfficientNetB0 and EfficientNetB3 demonstrated superior performance with an accuracy of 91%. This ensemble approach, combining the lightweight efficiency of EfficientNetB0 and the deeper feature extraction capabilities of EfficientNetB3, ensures superior overall performance in DR detection, making it a valuable tool for advancing diabetic retinopathy diagnosis in medical imaging. Table 61.1 summarizes the results obtained for EfficientNetB0 and EfficientNetB3 with other models.

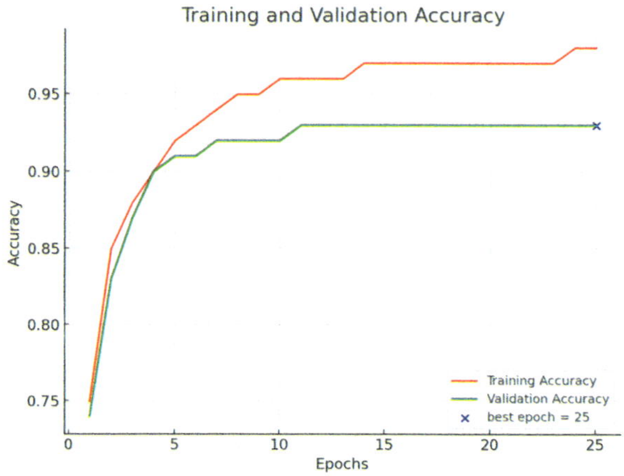

Fig. 61.5 Ensemble model training and validation accuracy

The integration of EfficientNetB0 and EfficientNetB3 models in an ensemble learning framework has demonstrated significant improvements in the classification accuracy of Diabetic Retinopathy (DR). The ensemble approach effectively leverages the strengths of both models, resulting in superior performance metrics across training, validation, and test phases. The high accuracy and low misclassification rates observed in the confusion matrix highlight the model's robustness and reliability in clinical settings. The ability to generalize well on unseen data underscores the practical applicability of this approach, making it a promising tool for early and accurate DR diagnosis. This study reinforces the potential of AI-based medical diagnostic tools to transform healthcare by providing more precise and efficient solutions for complex diseases like DR.

Table 61.1 Comparative analysis of our work with other model

Model	Precision	Recall	F1-Score	Accuracy
DenseNet121	0.76	0.43	0.55	0.74
MobileNet	0.54	0.70	0.61	0.67
Inception-V3	0.55	0.52	0.53	0.67
EfficientNetB7	0.83	0.84	0.83	0.8436
EfficientNetB0 and EfficientNetB3	1.00	0.99	1.00	0.91

61.5 Conclusion

In conclusion, the ensemble learning approach combining EfficientNetB0 and EfficientNetB3 has proven to be highly effective for Diabetic Retinopathy classification. The high accuracy and robustness in handling intricate retinal image patterns demonstrate the ability of our proposed model and its potential for real-world clinical applications. The significant improvement over individual models highlights the advantages of leveraging multiple architectures to enhance diagnostic performance. This work not only advances the field of medical imaging but also sets a new benchmark for AI-driven diagnostic tools, paving the way for more reliable and accurate healthcare solutions. Future research could explore further optimization and application of this ensemble approach to other medical conditions, broadening its impact on the medical community.

References

1. Ho, E., Wang, E., Youn, S., Sivajohan, A., Lane, K., Chun, J., Hutnik, C.M.: Deep ensemble learning for retinal image classification. Transl. Vis. Sci. Technol. **11**(10), 39–39 (2022)
2. Yahyaoui, A., Jamil, A., Rasheed, J., Yesiltepe, M.: A decision support system for diabetes prediction using machine learning and deep learning techniques. In: 2019 1st International Informatics and Software Engineering Conference (UBMYK), pp. 1–4. IEEE (2019)
3. Nawaz, A., Ali, T., Mustafa, G., Babar, M., Qureshi, B.: Multi-class retinal diseases detection using deep cnn with minimal memory consumption. IEEE Access (2023)
4. World Health Organization. WHO Global report on diabetes. World Health Organization (2016)
5. Zhu, W., Qiu, P., Lepore, N., Dumitrascu, O.M., Wang, Y.: Nnmobile-net: rethinking cnn design for deep learning-based retinopathy research (2023). arXiv:2306.01289
6. Smitha, A., Jidesh, P.: Classification of multiple retinal disorders from enhanced fundus images using semi-supervised gan. SN Comput. Sci. **3**, 1–11 (2022)
7. Chłopowiec, A.R., Karanowski, K., Skrzypczak, T., Grzesiuk, M., Chłopowiec, A.B., Tabakov, M.: Counteracting data bias and class imbalance-towards a useful and reliable retinal disease recognition system. Diagnostics **13**(11), 1904 (2023)
8. Khan, F.A., Jamil, A., Hameed, A.A., Moetesum, M.: Clinical decision support system for diabetes classification with an optimized cnn using pso. In: 2023 IEEE International Conference on Artificial Intelligence, Blockchain, and Internet of Things (AIBThings), pp. 1–6. IEEE (2023)
9. Hameed, A.A., Jamil, A., Orman, Z., Shah, S.A.: Application of generalized relevance linear vector quantization for diabetes diagnosis. In: 2021 International Conference on Innovative Computing (ICIC), pp. 1–5. IEEE (2021)
10. Sengar, N., Joshi, R.C., Dutta, M.K., Burget, R.: Eyedeep-net: a multi-class diagnosis of retinal diseases using deep neural network. Neural Comput. Appl. 1–21 (2023)
11. Li, Z., Xu, M., Yang, X., Han, Y., Wang, J.: A multi-label detection deep learning model with attention-guided image enhancement for retinal images. Micromachines **14**(3), 705 (2023)
12. Muller, D., Soto-Rey, I., Kramer, F.: Multi-disease detection in retinal imaging based on ensembling heterogeneous deep learning models. In: German Medical Data Sciences 2021: Digital Medicine: Recognize-Understand-Heal, pp. 23–31. IOS Press (2021)
13. Sebastian, A., Elharrouss, O., Al-Maadeed, S., Almaadeed, N.: A survey on diabetic retinopathy lesion detection and segmentation. Appl. Sci. **13**(8), 5111 (2023)

14. Brahmavar, S.B., Rajesh, R., Dash, T., Vig, L., Verlekar, T.T., Hasan, M.M., Khan, T., Meijering, E., Srinivasan, A.: Ikd+: reliable low complexity deep models for retinopathy classification (2023). arXiv:2303.02310
15. Pachade, S., Porwal, P., Thulkar, D., Kokare, M., Deshmukh, G., Sahasrabuddhe, V., Giancardo, L., Quellec, G., Meriaudeau, F.: Retinal fundus multi-disease image dataset (rfmid): a dataset for multi-disease detection research. Data **6**(2), 14 (2021)
16. Yi, S., Wei, Y., Zhang, G., Wang, T., She, F., Yang, X.: Segmentation of retinal vessels based on mranet. Heliyon **9**(1) (2023)
17. Hu, X., Wang, L., Li, Y.: Ht-net: A hybrid transformer network for fundus vessel segmentation. Sensors **22**(18), 6782 (2022)
18. Rodríguez M.A., AlMarzouqi, H., Liatsis, P.: Multi-label retinal disease classification using transformers. IEEE J. Biomed. Health Inf. (2022)
19. Minarno, A.E., et al.: Classification of diabetic retinopathy disease using convolutional neural network. JOIV: Int. J. Inf. Vis. **6**(1), 12–18 (2022)

Chapter 62
IOT-Based Model for Smart Baby Monitoring System Using Muti Agents

Shahad Alawadhi, Ameerah Aladwani, Manar Alenezi, Raghad Albekheet, Julien Moussa H. Barakat, and Hassan Kanj

Abstract Babies and infants face significant health risks, compounded by their inability to communicate symptoms effectively, leading to challenges in diagnosis and care. Parents often struggle to ensure optimal health monitoring for their infants due to these challenges that may change their behavior from normal to degraded. To address these concerns, this project presents an innovative IoT-based baby monitoring system designed to offer comprehensive health and environmental monitoring capabilities through a network of integrated sensors. In addition, multi-agents' system was used to model their dynamic behavior with and without the presence of undesirable events. The proposed system integrates a network of sensors to capture real-time data on vital signs, including heart rate and oxygen saturation, alongside environmental parameters such as temperature, humidity, and air quality. This data is processed and displayed via a custom-built Android application, providing parents with instant updates and alerts. The system aims to enhance infant safety by alerting caregivers to identify potential health issues and environmental risks promptly, thereby facilitating timely interventions.

62.1 Introduction

In the modern era, the integration of technology into everyday life has opened new avenues for enhancing safety, and reducing potential risks related to babies spending time away from their parents. In general, Infants require special attention due to their limited understanding of risks and their curiosity. In addition, they need a proper nutrition and healthcare to ensure healthy growth and development to prevent and address any health issues. The absence of any automated monitoring system and the parents increase the risks presented by the potential critical events [1] involving babies such as accessing the cleaning supplies or sharp objects, exploring Electrical outlets, or facing some medical issues. Those events affects babies and present serious threat to the children [2, 3], they might lead to change their state from safe to unsafe.

S. Alawadhi · A. Aladwani · M. Alenezi · R. Albekheet · J. M. H. Barakat · H. Kanj (✉)
College of Engineering and Technology, American University of the Middle East, Egaila, Kuwait
e-mail: hassan.kanj@aum.edu.kw

F. P. García Márquez et al. (eds.), *Computing, Internet of Things and Data Analytics*, Smart Innovation, Systems and Technologies 387,
https://doi.org/10.1007/978-3-031-87154-2_62

For that purpose, designing a smart monitoring system for infants, especially those spending the day far away from their parents, who are working during the day, becomes very essential. Such systems may enhance the safety and well-being of youngest and most vulnerable children and help in representing their dynamic behavior in relation to the occurrence of any undesirable event.

The aim of this project is to design an IoT-based baby monitoring system, which provide real-time updates on various health and environmental parameters to parents via a mobile application and provides a graphical illustration of the baby behavioral model whether safe or unsafe. To represent the dynamic behavior of baby, different models can be used such as: Markov model [4], ABM [5], or Petri nets [6]. Agent-based model is used in this work to represent the dynamic behavior of the baby monitoring system with the presence/absence of abnormal readings.

The development of this system addresses several key concerns for parents [7, 8], including but not limited to health monitoring, environmental safety, and the ability to remotely observe their child [9].

The remainder of this paper is as follow: Section 62.2 highlights the most relevant works in literature, Sect. 62.3 presents the proposed solution in detail, Sect. 62.4 explains the experiments done and the obtained results and Sect. 62.5 concludes the paper.

62.2 Literature Review

Smart baby monitoring systems are crucial, addressing the needs of busy parents [10] and mitigating the risks associated with sudden infant death syndrome (SIDS) [11, 12]. Those systems should consider many parameters that may affect their healthy state or generate any undesirable event in their environment like overheating [13], or gas leakage [14].

Baby monitoring systems have evolved significantly, leveraging advancements in technology to offer parents peace of mind and ensure the safety and well-being of their infants. These systems range from audio monitors to sophisticated video and smart monitors. This section examines the various types of baby monitoring systems, their features, and their limitations [15].

Baby Monitoring Systems are of many types as follow:

- Audio Monitors that transmit sound from the baby's room to a receiver. Some advanced models include features like two-way communication, temperature sensors, and sound activation. This type doesn't provide visual information, making it difficult to assess the baby's condition if there are unusual sounds.
- Video monitors which offer live video feeds along with audio. They may include features such as night vision, zoom, pan/tilt functionality, and remote viewing via smartphone apps.This system can be expensive and require a stable internet connection for remote viewing. Privacy concerns arise due to potential hacking and unauthorized access to the video feed

- Movement Monitors that track the baby's movements and breathing patterns, alerting parents to any irregularities. They often use sensor pads placed under the mattress or wearable devices. Under some conditions, those systems might generate false alarms, leading to unnecessary anxiety for parents. The devices may also restrict the baby's movement or cause discomfort.
- Smart Monitors integrate audio, video, and movement tracking with additional features like sleep tracking, temperature monitoring, and integration with smart home systems. They often use AI to analyze data and provide insights. These systems are the most expensive and require significant setup and maintenance. Concerns about data privacy and security are heightened due to the extensive data collected.

Those systems suffer from many concerns that can be categorized as: Privacy and Security, Reliability and Accuracy, Privacy and Security, Cost and Accessibility, Complexity and Usability, and Health and Safety [16–19].

Authors in [20] present a baby monitoring system that provides a real-time monitoring of babies through a PI camera that capture high-definition video and still photographs of the baby's surroundings. Authors in [21] propose a baby monitoring system using a sound sensor to detect crying, a moisture sensor to monitor wetness, and a DHT sensor for temperature and humidity. A USB camera turns on when sound is detected, allowing real-time monitoring via the Raspberry Pi. This system will be connected to the internet automatically when powered. Authors in [22] propose a Zigbee wireless heart rate monitoring system for premature infant. The Zigbee protocol establish connection with short range distance and low data rate communications for data transfer, that can be used only for limited coverage area and cannot address dynamic movement for the parents during the day. In [23], scientists discuss a temperature monitoring system using Bluetooth which is considered ideal for applications requiring short-range communications. Authors in [24] present an Arduino system that can be used to monitor only limited health aspects. It cannot cover oxygen levels monitoring nor the baby' environment. Next section discuss a novel approach for baby monitoring covering all the healthy elements and providing real-time representation for the health conditions of the baby, its environment and behavioral mode.

62.3 Proposed Solution

This work proposes a novel IoT based baby monitoring system that provides a real-time tracking of two types of parameters. The first one is related to the child such as: oxygen level, heart rate, blood oxygen level, body temperature, and his location. The second one is related to the child' environment such as: room humidity and gas concentration. Those parameters are measured using the following components: Arduino, Raspberry Pi, SpO2, heart rate sensor, body temperature sensor, gas sensor, sound sensor to pick up noise levels, DHT sensor, and camera. The RPi-Camera enables visual monitoring through live streaming. All the captured data are transferred to the cloud "Google Firebase", facilitating historical data analysis via a custom Android app. Parents can access this application to view live data streams, receive alerts, and manage monitoring settings, ensuring that they are always informed about their baby's environment and well-being.

This system is then modeled using ABM to show at real-time the current state of the baby as: safe or unsafe. In case of unsafe situation, parents can check the measurement and the video streaming to get more details about the situation.

Figure 62.1 represents the High-level design of the proposed system. All the measured parameters are processed using an Arduino Mega that feed a Raspberry Pi device over serial USB channel to finalize the Cloud connectivity and monitoring purposes. The Raspberry Pi, connected to an RPI-Camera, processes the data and uploads it to Google Firebase for real-time monitoring via a mobile application.

To illustrate the dynamic behavior of the monitored system, a simulation model is needed. Agent-based model (ABM) [25] has been used successfully to analyze risks and represent the dynamic behavior in different applications such as transportation of dangerous good [26], control of agricultural fields [27], monitoring of Elderly People [28].

The Agent-based model proposed in [29] is used in this paper, where each independent unit in the studied system is represented by an agent A_i living in the environment θ_i as shown in Fig. 62.2. Every agent A_i has his own functionality, set of variables (V_i), set of failure modes (FM_i) and set of behavioral modes (BM_i) as represented in 1.

$$A_i = < V_i, FM_i, BM_i > \tag{62.1}$$

When all V_i are normal, FM_i will be inactive and consequently the behavioral mode of the agent BM_i is Nominal. Any change in V_i may activate FM_i and as a result BM_i changes from nominal to degraded. BM_i remains degraded until V_i

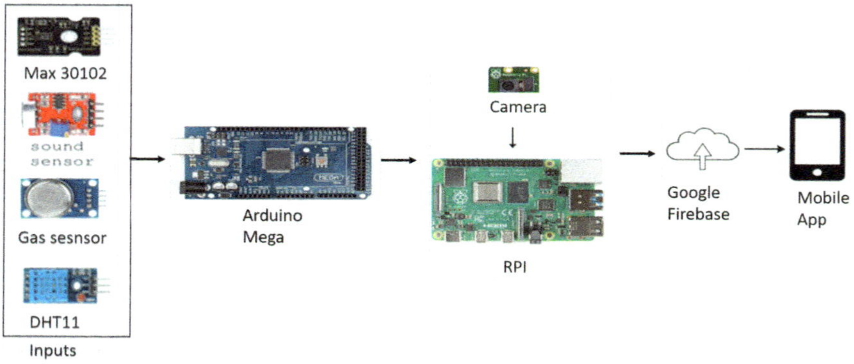

Fig. 62.1 System's high-level design

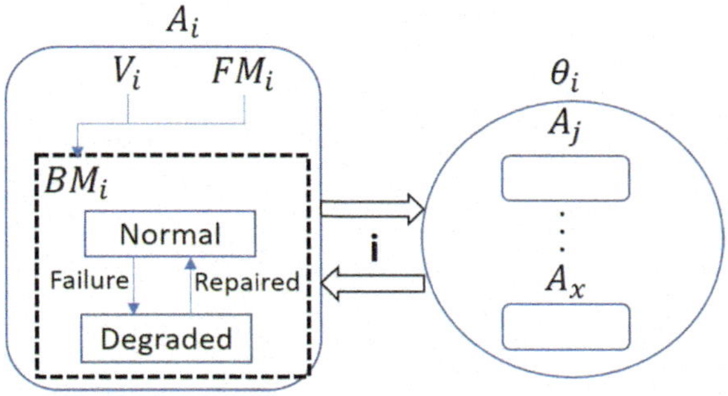

Fig. 62.2 Multi-agents' system representation

becomes nominal (failure is repaired). This model shows the direct relation between the agent failure mode and behavioral mode [30].

The main functionalities of this system are:

1. Collecting Health Parameters
2. Representing Healthy issues through a RED-LED that turns on in case of any extreme or unusual health parameter readings
3. Collecting Room Parameters
4. Representing Environment issues using a BLUE-LED which is turned on if the humidity, room temperature, or gas/smoke are abnormal
5. Storing all measurement on the Google fire base
6. Providing families a real-time access to all the measured data through the mobile Application in addition to the option of Live Monitoring and Streaming (upon parents request)
7. Representing the dynamic state of the monitoring system (as Safe/Unsafe 1/Unsafe 2 for Babies and Normal/ degraded for parents)

62.4 Experiment and Results

62.4.1 Implementation and Experiments

The proposed system was tested considering one Baby sitting in his room equipped with all the pre-mentioned components. ABM was used to describe to dynamic behavior of the studied system including babies and parents as shown in Fig. 62.3. Agent Baby has three behavioral modes: one safe and two unsafe. Safe behavioral mode represents the situation where all the measured data are within the required (Normal) ranges. Unsafe 1 illustrates the cases where any baby-dependant parameter goes out of the desired range and unsafe 2 represents the cases for abnormality in the studied environment parameters.

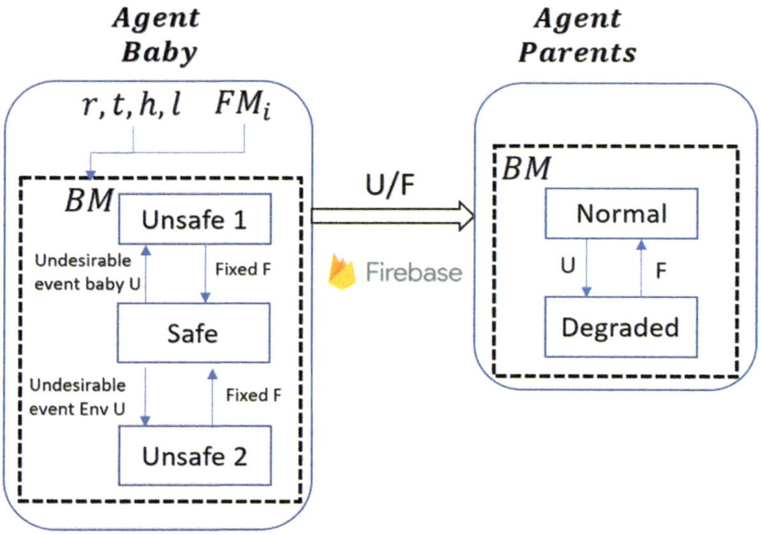

Fig. 62.3 Final prototype with the mobile app graphical interface

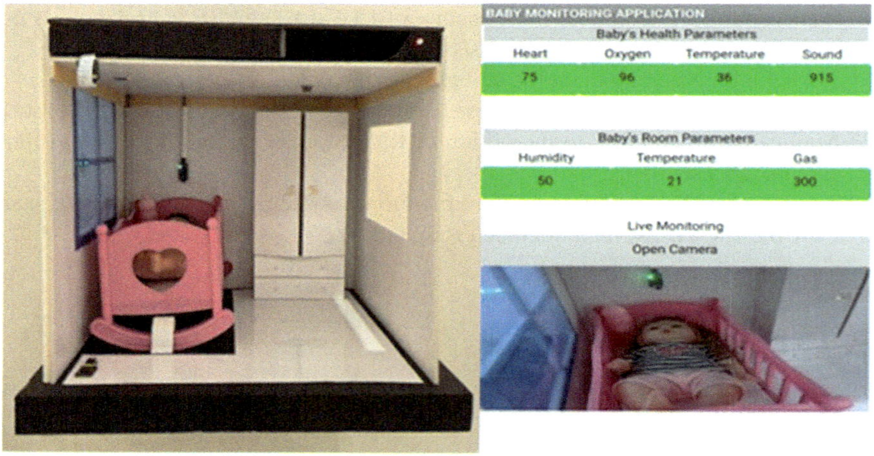

Fig. 62.4 Final prototype with the mobile app graphical interface

62.4.2 Design Analysis and Results

Figure 62.4 shows the final design of the work. Different experiments were done for the proposed system to test its functionality in diverse scenarios, simulate real-world conditions, and analyze its response to various sensor data sets (Table 62.1).

Table 62.1 Normal values for the studied parameters

Parameter	Normal range
SpO2 (Oxygen)	>= 90%
Heart rate	[60 bpm, 100 bpm]
Body temperature	[36 °C, 37.5 °C]
Room temperature	[20 °C, 22 °C]
Room humidity	[40%, 60%]
Gas level	<550
Sound level	> 900

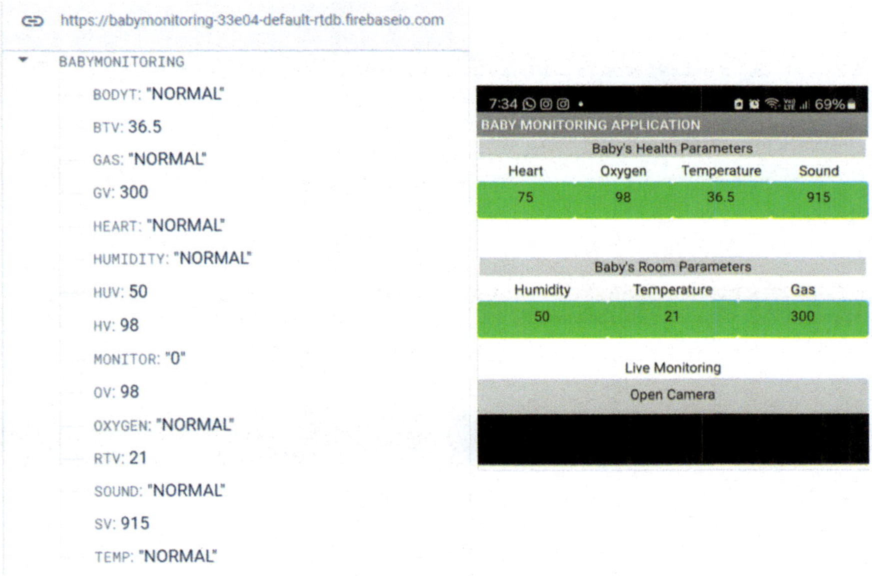

Fig. 62.5 Database readings and mobile app screenshot of scenario 1

1. Test Scenario 1: where all parameters are normal. The outputs of this scenario are shown in Fig. 62.5 and Table 62.2. All readings illustrate safe situation (within the thresholds) and no alerts are triggered. The behavioral mode for baby is Safe and for parents is normal.
2. Test Scenario 2 representing normal parameters for the baby and abnormal environment' readings. The outputs of this scenario are shown in Fig. 62.6, (left) and Table 62.3. The system was able to: (1) recognize environmental hazards, which is crucial for ensuring the baby's comfort and safety, (2) detect any abnormality in the environment readings, (3) and alert the parents (blue LED is on and the data are displayed in red color on the mobile app). The behavioral mode for baby is Unsafe 2 and for parents is degraded.

Table 62.2 Outputs generated from simulation 1

Parameter	Readings	Output	Baby behavioral mode	Parents behavioral mode
SpO2 (Oxygen)	98%	Red LED Off	Safe	Normal
Heart rate	75 bpm	Red LED Off	Safe	Normal
Body temperature	36.5 °C	Red LED Off	Safe	Normal
Room temperature	21 °C	Blue LED Off	Safe	Normal
Room humidity	50%	Blue LED Off	Safe	Normal
Gas level	300	Blue LED Off	Safe	Normal
Sound level	915	Servo inactive	Safe	Normal

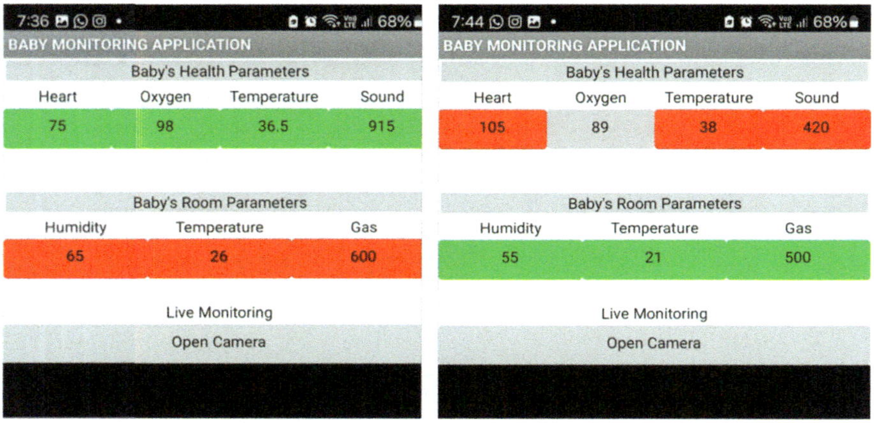

Fig. 62.6 Mobile App Screenshots for scenarios 2 and 3

3. Test Scenario 3 for abnormal Health Readings and normal environmental readings. The outputs of this scenario are shown in Fig. 62.6, (right) and Table 62.4. The system was able to recognize the degradation in the healthy parameter of the baby, which change his behavioral mode from safe to unsafe 1 and alert the parents (red LED is on and the data are displayed in red color on the mobile app). As consequence, the parents' behavioral mode change from normal to degraded.

62.5 Conclusion

This paper presents a proposed an IoT-based baby monitoring system using ABM. This system provides a clear representation of dynamic behavioral mode for baby/parents. It monitors at real-time healthy and environment parameters and allows

Table 62.3 Outputs generated from simulation 2

Parameter	Readings	Output	Baby behavioral mode	Parents behavioral mode
SpO2 (Oxygen)	98%	Red LED Off	Unsafe 2	Degraded
Heart rate	75 bpm	Red LED Off	Unsafe 2	Degraded
Body temperature	36.5 °C	Red LED Off	Unsafe 2	Degraded
Room temperature	26 °C	Blue LED On	Unsafe 2	Degraded
Room humidity	65%	Blue LED On	Unsafe 2	Degraded
Gas level	600	Blue LED On	Unsafe 2	Degraded
Sound level	915	Servo inactive	Unsafe 2	Degraded

Table 62.4 Outputs generated from simulation 3

Parameter	Readings	Output	Baby behavioral mode	Parents behavioral mode
SpO2 (Oxygen)	89%	Red LED Off	Unsafe 1	Degraded
Heart rate	105 bpm	Red LED Off	Unsafe 1	Degraded
Body temperature	38 °C	Red LED Off	Unsafe 1	Degraded
Room temperature	21 °C	Blue LED On	Unsafe 1	Degraded
Room humidity	55%	Blue LED On	Unsafe 1	Degraded
Gas level	500	Blue LED On	Unsafe 1	Degraded
Sound level	420	Servo inactive	Unsafe 1	Degraded

parents to monitor their babies through mobile app. In addition, it alerts the parents about any undesirable events related to their baby and provides a history of the whole measured parameters using Google drive. The system addresses key parental concerns by offering continuous monitoring and instant alerts, ensuring that any health issues or environmental risks are promptly identified. The project showcased cost-effective, customized, and reliable monitoring offering peace of mind to parents through advanced technology and real-time updates. This system cannot be used in the absence of internet connection which is considered as a weaknesses to be considered in the future work.

References

1. Kanj, H., Flaus, J.-M.: A meta model framework for risk analysis, diagnosis and simulation. In: Safety and Reliability Conference ESREL (2014)
2. Matsuyama, Y., Isumi, A., Doi, S., Fujiwara, T.: Being left alone at home and dental caries of children aged 6–7 years. J. Epidemiol. **33**(6), 303–310 (2023)

3. Bullinger, L.R., Boy, A., Feely, M., Messner, S., Raissian, K., Schneider, W., Self-Brown, S.: Home, but left alone: time at home and child abuse and neglect during covid-19. J. Fam. Issues **44**(2), 338–362 (2023)
4. Brameret, P.-A., Rauzy, A., Roussel, J.-M.: Automated generation of partial Markov chain from high level descriptions. Reliab. Eng. Syst. Saf. **139**, 179–187 (2015)
5. Kanj, H., Aly, W.H.F., Kanj, S.: A novel dynamic approach for risk analysis and simulation using multi-agents model. Appl. Sci. **12**(10), 5062 (2022)
6. Taleb-Berrouane, M., Khan, F., Amyotte, P.: Bayesian stochastic petri nets (bspn)-a new modelling tool for dynamic safety and reliability analysis. Reliab. Eng. Syst. Saf. **193**, 106587 (2020)
7. Pradhan, B., Bhattacharyya, S., Pal, K.: Iot-based applications in healthcare devices. J. Healthcare Eng. **2021**, 1–18 (2021)
8. Li, X., Lu, Y., Fu, X., Qi, Y.: Building the internet of things platform for smart maternal healthcare services with wearable devices and cloud computing. Futur. Gener. Comput. Syst. **118**, 282–296 (2021)
9. Visvesvaran, C., Nishanth, S., Sudha, R., Karthikeyan, J., et al.: Iot based smart baby monitoring. In: 2021 Second International Conference on Electronics and Sustainable Communication Systems (ICESC), pp. 1–6. IEEE (2021)
10. Salehin, H.I., Joy, Q.R.A., Aparna, F.T.Z., Ridwan, A.T., Khan, R.: Development of an iot based smart baby monitoring system with face recognition. In: 2021 IEEE World AI IoT Congress (AIIoT), pp. 0292–0296. IEEE (2021)
11. Ferreira, A.G., Fernandes, D., Branco, S., Monteiro, J.L., Cabral, J., Catarino, A.P., Rocha, A.M.: A smart wearable system for sudden infant death syndrome monitoring. In: 2016 IEEE International Conference on Industrial Technology (ICIT), pp. 1920–1925. IEEE (2016)
12. Hasan, M.U., Negulescu, I.: Wearable technology for baby monitoring: a review. J. Text. Eng. Fash. Technol. **6**(112.10), 15406 (2020)
13. Bin Maideen, M.F.: Considerations for measuring and monitoring thermal stress during infancy. Ph.D. dissertation (2023)
14. Talukdar, S., Saha, S.: Intelligent baby monitoring system using blynk. In: International Conference on Emerging Trends and Advances in Electrical Engineering and Renewable Energy, pp. 51–64. Springer (2020)
15. Patil, S.P., Mhetre, M.R.: Intelligent Baby Monitoring System. Pulse, vol. 4, no. 33, pp. 37–42. VIT, Pune (2014)
16. Ray, P.P., Dash, D., Kumar, N.: Sensors for internet of medical things: sate-of-the-art, security and privacy issues, challenges and future directions. Comput. Commun. **160**, 111–131 (2020)
17. Heldt, G.P., Ward, R.J.: Evaluation of ultrasound-based sensor to monitor respiratory and nonrespiratory movement and timing in infants. IEEE Trans. Biomed. Eng. **63**(3), 619–629 (2015)
18. Alam, H., Burhan, M., Gillani, A., Haq, I.U., Arshed, M.A., Shafi, M., Ahmad, S.: Iot based smart baby monitoring system with emotion recognition using machine learning. Wirel. Commun. Mobile Comput. 2023(1), 1175450 (2023)
19. Morales, L., Piratova, K., Martinez, M.: Real-time temperature and audio baby monitoring using iot technologies. In: Congreso Internacional de Innovación y Tendencias en Ingenieria (CONIITI), vol. 2019, pp. 1–6. IEEE (2019)
20. Symon, A.F., Hassan, N., Rashid, H., Ahmed, I.U., Reza, S.T.: Design and development of a smart baby monitoring system based on raspberry pi and pi camera. In: 2017 4th International Conference on Advances in Electrical Engineering (ICAEE), pp. 117–122. IEEE (2017)
21. Saude, N., Vardhini, P.H.: Iot based smart baby cradle system using raspberry pi b+. In: 2020 International Conference on Smart Innovations in Design, Environment, Management, Planning and Computing (ICSIDEMPC), pp. 273–278. IEEE (2020)
22. Sapkota, A., Reddy, D., Lama, P.: A zigbee network based heart rate monitoring system for pre-mature babies.
23. Joseph, A.A., Xuan, T.H.L., Kipli, K., Chin, K.L., Song, N.S.: Smart body temperature monitoring system for children via mobile. In: 2018 International Conference on Computational Approach in Smart Systems Design and Applications (ICASSDA), pp. 1–6. IEEE (2018)

24. Pallavor, V., Pavundoss, D.: Baby monitoring system using arduino uno. In: 2023 2nd International Conference on Vision Towards Emerging Trends in Communication and Networking Technologies (ViTECoN), pp. 1–5. IEEE (2023)
25. Flaus, J.-M.: A simulation approach for risk modeling and analysis based on multi-agents. In: ESREL 2015, 25th European Safety and Reliability Conference (2015)
26. Kanj, H., Kotb, Y., Flaus, J.-M.: A proposed petri-net extension to analyze risk for evolving systems using an agent model. In: 2020 International Conference on Control, Automation and Diagnosis (ICCAD), pp. 1–7 (2020)
27. Humoud, T., et al.: Smart agriculture monitoring and controlling system using multi-agents model. In: 2023 5th International Conference on Bio-engineering for Smart Technologies (BioSMART), pp. 1–4 (2023)
28. Aldousari, A., et al.: A wearable iot- based healthcare monitoring system for elderly people. In: 2023 5th International Conference on Bio-engineering for Smart Technologies (BioSMART), pp. 1–4 (2023)
29. Kanj, H.: Contribution to risk analysis related to the transport of hazardous materials by agent-based simulation. Ph.D. dissertation, Université Grenoble Alpes (2016)
30. Yang, D., Zhang, X., Hu, Z., Yang, Y.: Oil contamination monitoring based on dielectric constant measurement. In: 2009 International Conference on Measuring Technology and Mechatronics Automation, vol. 1, pp. 249–252. IEEE (2009)

Chapter 63
Quasi-Electromechanical Oscillations Suppression Strategy for Power System Based on VPSS2B

Jia Liu, Shengyang Lu, Mingqi Liu, Guanfeng Zhang, Jian Dong, Yiming Ma, Haixin Wang, and Junyou Yang

Abstract With the continuous advancement of modern power systems, virtual synchronous generator (VSG) control has emerged as a classic virtual inertia control method, leveraging electromechanical characteristics similar to synchronous generators (SG) and finding widespread application. However, inheriting electromechanical characteristics from physical inertia units, virtual inertia units introduce risks of "virtual-physical hybrid inertia system oscillations" exacerbation. Addressing this issue, this study firstly constructs the Phillips-Heffron model of the VSG-SG dual-generator grid-connected system to elucidate the mechanism behind electromechanical oscillations in virtual-physical hybrid inertia systems. Secondly, drawing from traditional dual-input power system stabilizer like PSS2B, this paper proposes a virtual power system stabilizer 2B (VPSS2B) integrated with the VSG virtual excitation control to suppress quasi-electromechanical oscillations in power system. The structure of VPSS2B is presented. Finally, through simulation comparisons, the effectiveness of the proposed VPSS2B is validated.

J. Liu (✉) · S. Lu · Y. Ma · H. Wang · J. Yang
Shenyang University of Technology, Shenyang, China
e-mail: 1989295968@qq.com

S. Lu · G. Zhang
Electric Power Research Institute of State Grid Liaoning Electric Power Supply Co. Ltd., Shenyang, China

M. Liu
Dalian Electric Power Supply Company of State Grid Liaoning Electric Power Supply Co. Ltd., Dalian, China

J. Dong
Economic and Technological Research Institute of State Grid Liaoning Electric Power Supply Co. Ltd., Shenyang, China

F. P. García Márquez et al. (eds.), *Computing, Internet of Things and Data Analytics*, Smart Innovation, Systems and Technologies 387,
https://doi.org/10.1007/978-3-031-87154-2_63

63.1 Introduction

To keep up with the construction pace of the new-type power system, the penetration rate of renewable energy sources is bound to continue increasing, leading to the development and critical characteristics of a "dual-high" trend, a high proportion of renewable energy sources and a high proportion of power electronic devices connected to the grid [1, 2]. However, the integration of renewable energy sources into the grid may affect the system power flow, damping levels, and inertia distribution, or induce dynamic interactions with power systems dominates by the physical inertia of synchronous generator, potentially resulting in quasi-electromechanical oscillations [3, 4].

To address the above issues, reference [5] discovers that when the open-loop oscillation modes of a doubly-fed induction generator (DFIG) and the remaining subsystem have similar frequencies, strong dynamic interactions can be triggered, leading to a significant reduction in the damping of oscillations involving the DFIG. Additionally, although virtual inertia units represented by VSG control can provide certain inertia and damping support, the interaction between virtual inertia and physical inertia may intensify the strong dynamic interactions between new energy units and the power system, thus increasing the risk of quasi-electromechanical oscillations [6]. This can be mitigated by appropriately setting the virtual inertia and virtual damping coefficients of the VSG, or by disconnecting the AC lines to block and suppress the propagation of strong dynamic interaction processes [7]. Literature [8] uses a feedforward decoupling controller to eliminate the influence of grid impedance on the VSG output power, while also utilizing an extended state observer to estimate and compensate for the uncertainty of grid impedance. Reference [9] proposes a VPSS strategy to suppress low-frequency oscillations, taking the virtual inertia VSG as the research object and exploring the "new" low-frequency oscillation issues dominated by the virtual power angle of the VSG. VPSS is constructed to suppress low-frequency oscillations.

Therefore, this paper draws on the traditional PSS2B and proposes a power system quasi-electromechanical oscillations suppression strategy based on VPSS2B. By adjusting the relevant control parameters using the phase compensation method, the virtual PSS2B provides positive damping torque to the quasi-electromechanical oscillation loop, blocking the propagation path of the virtual-physical power angle oscillation signals, and effectively suppressing the system's quasi-electromechanical oscillations. This strategy demonstrates certain effectiveness and superiority in improving system stability.

63.2 Quasi-Electromechanical Oscillations Suppression Strategy Based on VPSS2B

63.2.1 Linearized Model of VSG-SG Dual Machine Grid-Connected System

This paper presents a dual machine grid-connected system of VSG-SG by connecting the VSG and SG in parallel to an infinitely large power grid. The dual machine grid-connected system of VSG-SG is depicted in Fig. 63.1.

In Fig. 63.1, $V_a\angle\theta_a$ is the amplitude and phase of the synchronous machine port voltage, $V_c\angle\theta_c$ is the amplitude and phase of the VSG terminal voltage, $V_b\angle\theta_b$ is the amplitude and phase of the voltage at the VSG connection point, $V_g\angle\theta_g$ is the amplitude and phase of the infinitely large power grid voltage, X_{ab} is the line impedance between nodes a and b, X_{cb} is the line impedance between nodes c and b, and X_{bg} is the line impedance between nodes b and g, I_{ab}, I_{cb} and I_{bg} are the currents flowing through each line.

The virtual inertia unit based on VSG control incorporates the classical second-order rotor dynamic equation, thereby inheriting the "rotor swing" characteristics of synchronous generator in the electromechanical transient timescale. However, it is important to note that the VSG itself does not possess a physical rotor. To elucidate the mechanism behind the induction of quasi-electromechanical oscillations between VSG and SG in the electromechanical transient timescale, the voltage and current control loops operating at the electromagnetic transient timescale are neglected. Consequently, the VSG control structure presented in this paper is depicted in Fig. 63.2.

In Fig. 63.2, J and D_1 are the virtual inertia coefficient and virtual damping coefficient of the VSG, ω_1 is the virtual angular frequency, P_{ref} and P_1 are the reference and actual values of the active power output of the VSG, Q_{ref} and Q_1 are the reference and actual values of the reactive power output of the VSG, K_Q is the reactive power gain of the VSG, ω_0 is the reference angular frequency of the power

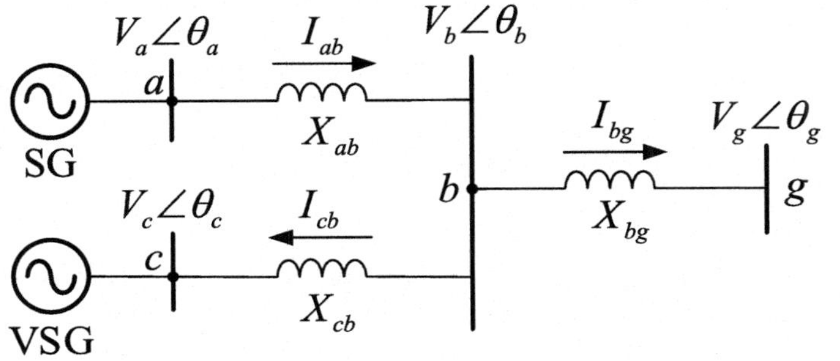

Fig. 63.1 Dual machine grid-connected system of VSG-SG

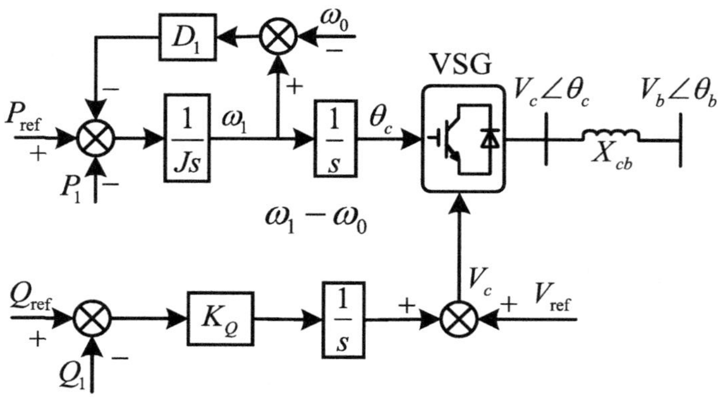

Fig. 63.2 Control structure diagram of VSG

grid. The VSG model is represented by Eq. (63.1).

$$\begin{cases} \frac{d\delta_1}{dt} = \omega_1 - \omega_0 \\ \frac{d\omega_1}{dt} = \frac{P_{ref} - P_1 - D_1(\omega_1 - \omega_0)}{J} \\ \frac{dV_1}{dt} = K_Q(Q_{ref} - Q_1) \end{cases} \quad (63.1)$$

where, δ_1 is the virtual power angle of the VSG. Its output equation, in conjunction with the rotor dynamic equation and the virtual excitation regulator, forms the VSG model.

For the SG subsystem, the classical third-order synchronous generator model is represented by Eq. (63.2).

$$\begin{cases} \frac{d\delta}{dt} = \omega_0(\omega - 1) \\ \frac{d\omega}{dt} = \frac{P_m - P_a - D(\omega - 1)}{M} \\ \frac{dE'_q}{dt} = \frac{(E_{fd} - E_q)}{T'_{d0}} \\ \frac{dE'_{fd}}{dt} = \frac{-E'_{fd} + K_A(V_{a.ref} - V_a)}{T_A} \end{cases} \quad (63.2)$$

where, ω is the angular speed of the SG, δ is the physical rotor angle of the SG, P_m and P_a are the input power and output power of the SG, M and D are the inertia constant and damping coefficient of the SG rotor, E'_q and E_q are the transient and steady-state components of the q-axis electromotive force of the SG, E'_{fd} is the excitation voltage, T'_{d0} is the time constant of the excitation winding itself, $V_{a.ref}$ is the reference voltage of the SG, K_A and T_A are the gain and time constant of the automatic voltage regulator.

The small-signal model of the dual VSG-SG grid-connected system, derived through separate linearization of the VSG and SG components, is represented by Eq. (63.3).

$$s\begin{bmatrix}\Delta\delta\\ \Delta\delta_1\\ \Delta\omega\\ \Delta\omega_1\\ \Delta E'_q\\ \Delta E'_{fd}\\ \Delta V_c\end{bmatrix}=\begin{bmatrix}0 & 0 & \omega_0 & 0 & 0 & 0 & 0\\ 0 & 0 & 0 & \omega_0 & 0 & 0 & 0\\ -\frac{l_2}{M} & -\frac{l_1}{M} & -\frac{D}{M} & 0 & -\frac{l_4}{M} & 0 & -\frac{l_3}{M}\\ -\frac{l'_3}{J} & -\frac{l'_1}{J} & 0 & -\frac{D_1}{J} & -\frac{l'_4}{J} & 0 & -\frac{l'_2}{J}\\ -\frac{l_6}{T'_{d0}} & -\frac{l_5}{T'_{d0}} & 0 & 0 & -\frac{l_8}{T'_{d0}} & \frac{1}{T'_{d0}} & -\frac{l_7}{T'_{d0}}\\ -\frac{K_A l_{10}}{T_A} & -\frac{K_A l_9}{T_A} & 0 & 0 & -\frac{K_A l_{12}}{T_A} & -\frac{1}{T_A} & -\frac{K_A l_{11}}{T_A}\\ -K_Q l'_7 & -K_Q l'_5 & 0 & 0 & -K_Q l'_8 & 0 & -K_Q l'_6\end{bmatrix}\begin{bmatrix}\Delta\delta\\ \Delta\delta_1\\ \Delta\omega\\ \Delta\omega_1\\ \Delta E'_q\\ \Delta E'_{fd}\\ \Delta V_c\end{bmatrix} \tag{63.3}$$

where l_1–l_{12} and l'_1–l'_8 are the differential coefficients of each state variable during the linearization process, $\boldsymbol{X}$ represents the vector of state variables for the dual VSG-SG grid-connected system, $\boldsymbol{A}$ represents the corresponding state matrix, Eq. (63.3) can be simplified to Eq. (63.4).

$$s\boldsymbol{X} = \boldsymbol{AX} \tag{63.4}$$

By solving for the matrix $\boldsymbol{A}$'s conjugate eigenvalues $\lambda_i = \alpha_i \pm j\omega_i$ $(i = 1, 2\ldots, n)$, can determine the oscillatory modes of the system in the vicinity of its steady-state operating point.

63.2.2 Quasi-Electromechanical Oscillations Suppression Strategy Based on Virtual PSS2B

The mathematical model of the VPSS2B is illustrated in Fig. 63.3, where the inputs are the virtual frequency deviation and active power deviation of the VSG.

In Fig. 63.3, $\Delta\omega$ is the virtual angular frequency deviation of the VSG, ΔP is the output active power deviation of the VSG, T_{w1}-T_{w4} are the time constants of the DC blocking section, K_1 is for the gain coefficient of the power deviation amplification section, T_5 and T_6 are the time constants of the filtering section, K_{VPSS2B} is the gain coefficient of the VPSS2B amplification section, and T_1-T_6 are the time constants of the VPSS2B phase compensation section.

Based on the established linearized model of the dual VSG-SG grid-connected system, the Phillips-Heffron model of the dual VSG-SG grid-connected system is depicted in Fig. 63.4.

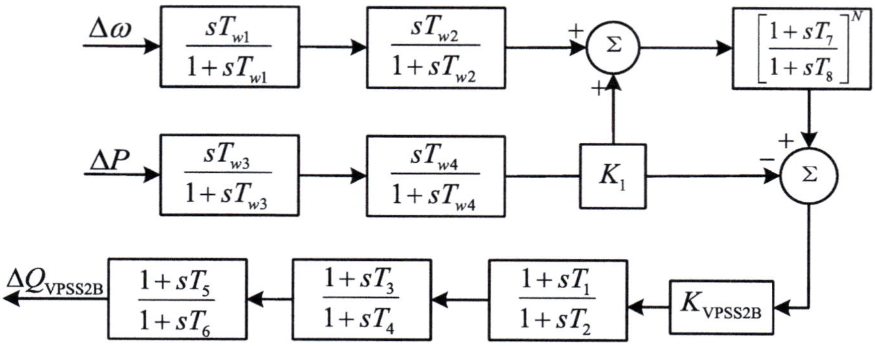

Fig. 63.3 Mathematical model of VPSS2B

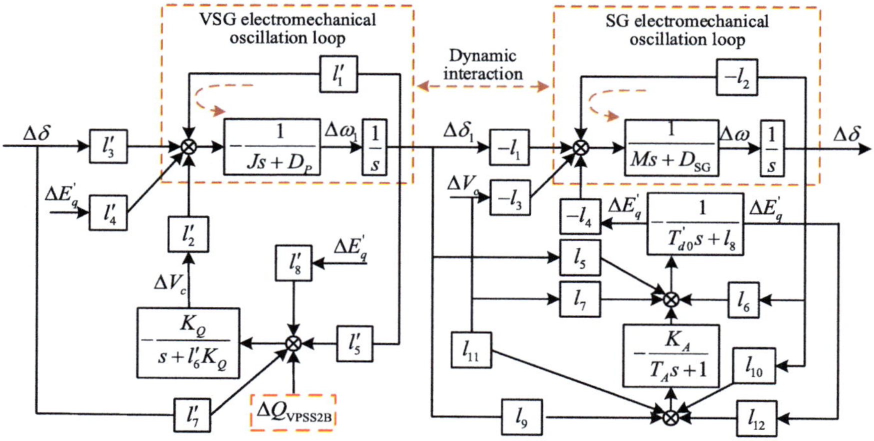

Fig. 63.4 Phillips-Heffron model of dual machine grid-connected system of VSG-SG

63.3 Simulation Analysis

63.3.1 *Theoretical Validation*

To validate the theoretical feasibility of phase compensation for tuning VPSS2B, the VSG-SG grid-connected system is conducted, with system parameters as shown in Table 63.1. Parameters for VPSS2B are shown in Table 63.2.

Based on the parameters of the VPSS2B, the characteristic roots of the system with VPSS2B integration are calculated, and compared with the scenario without VPSS2B, as depicted in Fig. 63.5.

From the pole-zero diagram, it is evident that integrating the VPSS2B tuned by phase compensation improves the damping characteristics of the system.

Table 63.1 Parameters of the VSG-SG grid-connected system

Parameters	Value ($p.u.$)	Parameters	Value ($p.u.$)
P_{ref}	0.5	$V_{a.\text{ref}}$	1.05
Q_{ref}	0.1	P_m	0.7
D_1	1.2	D	1.5
J	0.01	M	7
K_Q	0.3	K_A	50
V_{ref}	1	T_A	0.05
V_g	1	T'_{d0}	5
X_d	1.2	X_{ab}	0.3
X_q	1	X_{cd}	0.3
X'_d	0.3	X_{bg}	0.3

Table 63.2 Parameters for VPSS2B

Parameters for VPSS2B	Value
T_1	0.56
T_2	0.002
T_3	0.56
T_4	0.002
K_{VPSS2B}	107

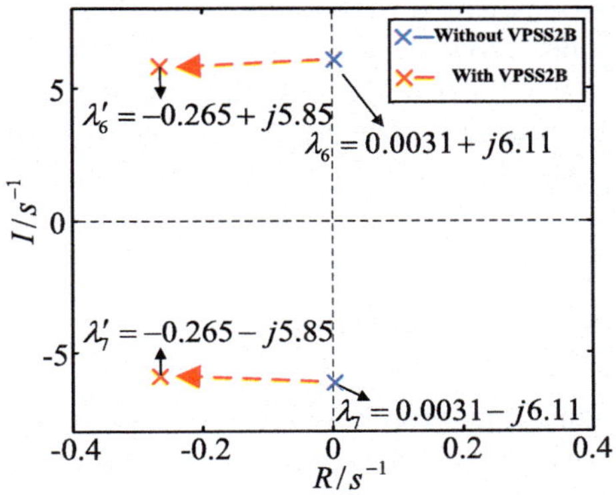

Fig. 63.5 Change trajectory of quasi-electromechanical oscillation modes before and after VPSS2B integration

This enhancement contributes to improve system stability and suppresses quasi-electromechanical oscillations.

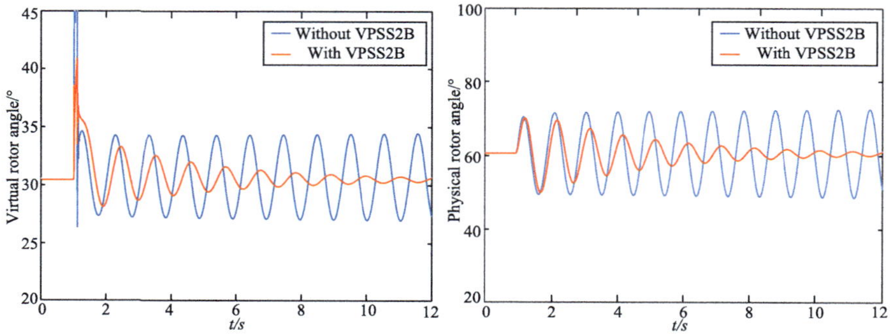

Fig. 63.6 The virtual power angle of VSG and the physical power angle of SG

63.3.2 Simulation Validation

To validate the effectiveness and correctness of the proposed VPSS2B, a simulation model of the VSG-SG grid-connected system is developed on the MATLAB/Simulink. Figure 63.6 illustrates the virtual power angle of VSG and the physical power angle of SG, with and without VPSS2B.

Based on the simulation results, it can be observed that with the integration of VPSS2B, the virtual power angle and physical power angle of the system change from initially oscillating with equal amplitude to exhibiting lightly damped oscillations with a frequency of approximately 0.93 Hz and gradually decaying amplitude following system disturbance. This indicates that integrating VPSS2B into the system nearly does not affect the frequency of electromechanical oscillations but significantly enhances system damping. This is beneficial for improving the transient stability of virtual-physical hybrid inertia systems.

63.4 Conclusion

This paper proposes a strategy for suppressing quasi-electromechanical oscillations based on VPSS2B, drawing from traditional design methods of acceleration power-type stabilizers in power systems. The general structure of this strategy is outlined, and by comparing the system poles before and after integrating VPSS2B, it is demonstrated that VPSS2B significantly improves system damping. This improvement contributes to enhancing the stability of VSG-SG grid-connected systems and effectively quasi-electromechanical oscillations in virtual-physical hybrid inertia systems. MATLAB/Simulink simulations validate these findings by comparing the changes in virtual and physical rotor angles before and after integrating VPSS2B, confirming a notable enhancement in system damping post-integration.

References

1. Wang, H., et al.: Model predictive control of PMSG-based wind turbines for frequency regulation in an isolated grid. IEEE Trans. Ind. Appl. **54**(4), 3077–3089 (2018)
2. Muhtadi, A., et al.: Distributed energy resources based microgrid: review of architecture, control, and reliability. IEEE Trans. Ind. Appl. **57**(3), 2223–2235 (2021)
3. Yuan, H., et al.: Small-signal stability assessment of multi-converter-based-renewable systems with STATCOMs based on generalized short-circuit ratio. IEEE Trans. Energy Convers. **37**(4), 2889–2902 (2022)
4. Li, M., Shu, S., et al.: Analysis and improvement of large-disturbance stability for grid-connected VSG based on output impedance optimization. IEEE Trans. Power Electron. **37**(8), 9807–9826 (2022)
5. Du, W.J., Fu, Q., Wang, H.F.: Power system small-signal angular stability affected by virtual synchronous generators. IEEE Trans. Power Syst. **34**(4), 3209–3219 (2019)
6. Gao, X., et al.: Analysis and mitigation of electromechanical oscillations in drivetrain for hybrid synchronization control of DFIG-based wind turbines. IEEE Trans. Power Electron. **39**(3), 3002–3013 (2024)
7. Mohammed, N., et al.: Online grid impedance estimation-based adaptive control of virtual synchronous generators considering strong and weak grid conditions. IEEE Trans. Sustain. Energy **14**(1), 673–687 (2023)
8. Yang, Y., et al.: A new virtual inductance control method for frequency stabilization of grid forming virtual synchronous generators. IEEE Trans. Industr. Electron. **70**(1), 441–451 (2023)
9. Wang, H., et al.: Influence mechanism and virtual power system stabilizer method of virtual synchronous generator for low-frequency oscillation of power system. IET Energy Syst. Integr. (2023)

Chapter 64
Modal Analysis of Low-Frequency Oscillations in Power Systems Based on Small-Signal Analysis Considering the Interaction of Physical and Virtual Inertia

Qingshan Liu, Shengyang Lu, Jing Li, Hiroshi Yokoi, Yiming Ma, Jia Liu, Haixin Wang, and Junyou Yang

Abstract In the context of new-type energy generation replacing traditional energy sources and a large number of inverters and other power devices replacing traditional SGs, the "double-high" characteristic is still an important part of system stability analysis. In the past, the small-signal stability analysis of power systems mainly focused on the small-signal modeling and analysis of SGs and their control systems, and after a large number of inverters appeared in the power grid, the small-signal modeling and analysis of these power electronic devices were gradually developed. In this paper, to analyze the interaction between physical inertia and virtual inertia, a small-signal model of the VSG-SG interconnected system is constructed for the study of low-frequency oscillations of power grids, and based on this model, the differences and connections between VSG and SG affecting the low-frequency oscillation phenomena inherent to the system's operational dynamics are compared, to reveal the mechanisms of the VSG participating in the low-frequency oscillations of the power grids.

Q. Liu (✉) · S. Lu · H. Yokoi · Y. Ma · J. Liu · H. Wang · J. Yang
Shenyang University of Technology, Shenyang, China
e-mail: 1401639878@qq.com

S. Lu
Electric Power Research Institute of State Grid Liaoning Electric Power Supply Co. Ltd., Shenyang, China

J. Li
Tongliao Electric Power Supply Company of State Grid Eastern Inner Mongolia Electric Power Co. Ltd., Tongliao, China

F. P. García Márquez et al. (eds.), *Computing, Internet of Things and Data Analytics*, Smart Innovation, Systems and Technologies 387,
https://doi.org/10.1007/978-3-031-87154-2_64

64.1 Introduction

The large-scale renewable energy sources have led to a further increase in the proportion of power electronic clusters accessing the power system. Power electronic clusters can improve the rotational inertia of the power grid through the simulation of rotational inertia. However, the inherent characteristics of these phenomena present substantial challenges and give rise to profound dynamic characteristic variations of the "double-high" power system and engender new stability issues, confronting severe challenges such as the pasting of mechanism characterization models, and modeling and analysis difficulties [1].

The extensive use of power electronic equipment improves the efficiency of renewable energy power generation and grid-connected capacity, but, it also brings a lot of challenges to power grid [2]. To make the grid-connected inverter better simulate the operation mechanism of SG, scholars and research institutes cat home and abroad carry out more in-depth research on Virtual Synchronous Generator (VSG) technology. Literature [3] uses the state space model to analyze the low-frequency oscillation of the PV grid-connected system and finds that the influencing factors of the PV grid-connected system on the low-frequency oscillation are the strength of the grid, the phase-locked loop, and the external control of the inverter. Reference [4] pointes out that in addition to the phase-locked loop parameters, the length of the transmission cable and the number of inverters also have an impact on low-frequency oscillations. Literature [5, 6] pointes out the influence of wind turbine controllers and sag control on the low-frequency oscillations exhibited by the power system, respectively. Reference [7] founds that low-frequency oscillation also exists between VSG and SG (or the rest of VSGs) by constructing a linearized interconnection model of the AC system with the participation of multiple virtual synchronous generators (VSGs).

In summary, there has been some research on the stability analysis of power systems with VSG access, but it is mainly a single study on the virtual inertia brought by VSG access while neglecting the influence of physical inertia in the power system. With access of more renewable energy, the dynamic interaction between virtual inertia and physical inertia cannot be ignored, and the original stability theory of VSG-containing power system has some limitations, and the electromechanical oscillation modes triggered by VSG access to the power system will be changed [8–10]. It is essential to explore the mechanism of low-frequency oscillation in depth, therefore, this topic is an in-depth study of a new type of low-frequency oscillation modes of power systems taking into account the interaction between physical and virtual inertia, and analyzing the dominant factors affecting the oscillation modes.

64.2 Small Signal Modelling of Interconnected Systems

The VSG-SG interconnection system model constructed in this paper is shown in Fig. 64.1.

In Fig. 64.1, U_1 denotes the voltage magnitude of the synchronous machine, U_2 represents the voltage of VSG, U_{PCC} signifies the voltage of the common coupling point (PCC), Z_1 and Z_2 are the line impedance between each bus node, R_{load} is the ground impedance, δ_1 and δ_2 are the voltage phase of each node.

The electromagnetic power output from the synchronous generator with its small signal model can be expressed as Eq. (64.1).

$$\begin{cases} \frac{d\delta}{dt} = \omega - \omega_0 \\ J\frac{d\omega}{dt} = \frac{P_m}{\omega_0} - \frac{P_e}{\omega_0} - D(\omega - \omega_0) \end{cases} \tag{64.1}$$

where, δ is the power Angle, P_m denotes the mechanical power input, P_e refers to the electromagnetic power output, J and D are the inertia coefficient and damping coefficient of the SG rotor respectively, ω symbolizes the mechanical angular frequency of SG, and ω_0 is the reference or rated angular frequency.

So, the second-order small signal model of SG is expressed as Eq. (64.2).

$$\begin{cases} \frac{d\Delta\delta_1}{dt} = \Delta\omega_1 \\ \frac{d\Delta\omega_1}{dt} = -\frac{1}{J\omega_0}\Delta P_1 - \frac{D}{J}\Delta\omega_1 \end{cases} \tag{64.2}$$

where $\Delta\delta_1$ and $\Delta\omega_1$ are the power Angle and the small disturbance of the mechanical angular frequency of the synchronous generator.

The small-signal model of the energy storage VSG in the interconnected systems can be expressed as Eq. (64.3).

$$\begin{cases} \frac{d\Delta\delta_2}{dt} = \Delta\omega_2 \\ \frac{d\Delta\omega_2}{dt} = -\frac{1}{J\omega_0}\Delta P_2 - \frac{D}{J}\Delta\omega_2 \end{cases} \tag{64.3}$$

where, $\Delta\delta_2$ and $\Delta\omega_2$ are the virtual power Angle of the energy storage VSG and the small disturbance of the mechanical angular frequency.

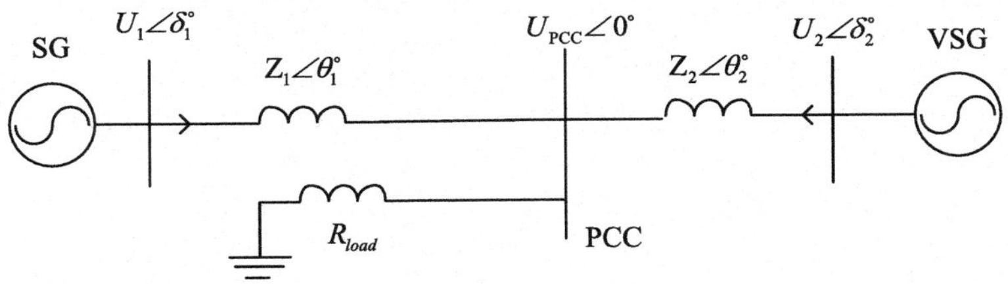

Fig. 64.1 VSG-SG interconnect system model

Where the small signal model of the power link of the synchronous generator energy storage VSG is expressed as Eq. (64.4).

$$\begin{cases} \Delta P_1 = \frac{3U_1U_2}{Z_1Z_2M} \sin(\delta_1 - \delta_2 + \theta_M)(\Delta\delta_2 - \Delta\delta_1 \nu \\ \Delta P_2 = \frac{3U_1U_2}{Z_1Z_2M} \cos(\delta_2 - \delta_1 + \theta_M)(\Delta\delta_1 - \Delta\delta_2 \nu \end{cases} \quad (64.4)$$

where, U_1 and U_2 are the voltage values of the synchronous generator and the energy storage VSG, Z_1 and Z_2 are the impedance values of the synchronous generator and the energy storage VSG line, and M is the mutual inductance coefficients.

Utilizing the architectural model of the SG-VSG configuration and the small-signal model of the output power for the respective machines, the small-signal model of the SG-VSG parallel system can be formulated as a state-space representation, expressed by the linear differential equation $\dot{X} = AX$, as Eq. (64.5):

$$\begin{bmatrix} \Delta\delta_1 \\ \Delta\delta_2 \\ \Delta\omega_1 \\ \Delta\omega_2 \end{bmatrix} = \begin{bmatrix} 0 & 0 & 1 & 0 \\ 0 & 0 & 0 & 1 \\ A_{31} & A_{32} & A_{33} & 0 \\ A_{41} & A_{42} & 0 & A_{44} \end{bmatrix} \begin{bmatrix} \Delta\delta_1 \\ \Delta\delta_2 \\ \Delta\omega_1 \\ \Delta\omega_2 \end{bmatrix} \quad (64.5)$$

Included among these:

$$\begin{cases} A_{31} = \frac{1}{J_1\omega_0} \frac{U_1U_2}{Z_1Z_2M} \sin(\delta_1 - \delta_2 + \theta_M) \\ A_{32} = -\frac{1}{J_1\omega_0} \frac{U_1U_2}{Z_1Z_2M} \sin(\delta_1 - \delta_2 + \theta_M) \\ A_{33} = -\frac{D_1}{J_1} \end{cases} \quad (64.6)$$

$$\begin{cases} A_{41} = -\frac{1}{J_2\omega_0} \frac{U_1U_2}{Z_1Z_2M} \sin(\delta_2 - \delta_1 + \theta_M) \\ A_{42} = \frac{1}{J_2\omega_0} \frac{U_1U_2}{Z_1Z_2M} \sin(\delta_2 - \delta_1 + \theta_M) \\ A_{44} = -\frac{D_2}{J_2} \end{cases} \quad (64.7)$$

Within the array of analytical techniques employed in power systems, eigenvalue analysis has emerged as a benchmark procedure, integrated into sophisticated software platforms dedicated to the comprehensive examination of power system dynamics. As the eigenvalue analysis method can provide a large amount of vital information about the dynamic stability of the system, the eigenvalue analysis method has been widely used in stability analysis. Eigenvalue analysis is on account of the linearized small-signal state-space model, and tools such as characteristic roots, eigenvectors, damping ratios, participation factors, and sensitivities are used to understand the system stability and features related to the system transition process.

The eigenvalues of the derived matrix reflect the oscillation patterns that may arise in the power system:

$$e^{(\alpha \pm j\omega)t} = e^{\alpha t}(\cos\omega t \pm j \sin\omega t) \quad (64.8)$$

where, α means that whether the oscillation decays or not determines whether the system is stable, and ω characterizes the frequency of the oscillations. The conjugate complex root: $\lambda_i = \alpha_i \pm j\omega_i$ is called the oscillation mode $\alpha < 0$. When $\alpha > 0$ is used, the system will be destabilized when $\alpha = 0$ is used, the system is at the stability boundary.

The formula for calculating the damping ratio ξ and its physical meaning is shown below:

$$\xi_i = \frac{-\alpha_i}{\sqrt{\alpha_i^2 + \omega_i^2}} \tag{64.9}$$

The damping ratio of the dominant oscillation mode of the power system can be used as a criterion to judge the degree of damping strength of the power system. To ensure the stability of the power system, there are relevant guidelines to put forward specific requirements for the damping ratio of the system.

According to the 4th-order small-signal model shown in Eq. (64.5), it can be seen that the VSG-SG dual-unit grid-connected system established has a total of 7 characteristic roots, and to conduct an in-depth examination of the predominant oscillatory behaviors within the system, this paper expresses in the form of a scalar value and adopts the classical unit parameters and line parameters shown in Table 64.1. It can be found that at this time the system has three pairs of conjugate complex roots and one negative real root, which means that it has three oscillation modes, whose distribution on the complex plane is shown in Fig. 64.2, and the corresponding characteristic information is shown in Table 64.2.

Among them, the real parts of the 6th and 7th characteristic root are positive, with negative damping ratios, and satisfy the conditions of low-frequency oscillations. Meanwhile, combined with the calculation of the participation factor, it is found that the dominant site variable corresponding to $\lambda_{6,7}$ is $\Delta\omega_1$, which indicates that $\lambda_{6,7}$ is the low-frequency oscillatory mode of interest. However, the remaining state variables

Table 64.1 Related parameters of VSG-SG grid connected system

Parameters	Value ($p.u.$)	Parameters	Value ($p.u.$)
P_{ref}	0.5	$V_{t.ref}$	1.05
Q_{ref}	0.1	P_m	0.7
D_1	1.2	D	1.5
J	-1.15×10^{-2}	M	7
K_Q	0.3	K_A	50
V_{ref}	1	T_A	0.05
V_g	1	$\acute{T}_{do}$	5
X_d	1.2	X_{ts}	0.3
X_q	1	X_{cs}	0.3
$\acute{X}_d$	0.3	X_{sg}	0.3

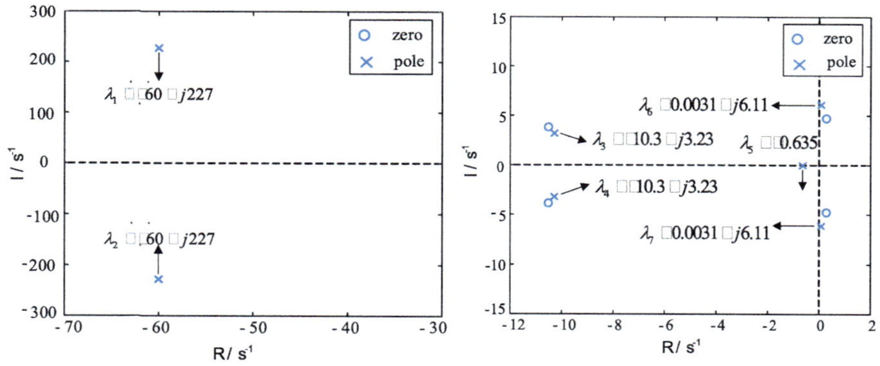

Fig. 64.2 Oscillation mode of VSG-SG grid connected system

Table 64.2 Feature information of VSG-SG grid connected system

Characteristic roots λ_i	Oscillation frequency f	Damping ratio ξ
$\lambda_{1,2} = -60 \pm j227$	37.4	0.255
$\lambda_{3,4} = -10.3 \pm j3.23$	1.72	0.954
$\lambda_5 = -0.635$	0	1
$\lambda_{6,7} = 0.0031 \pm j6.11$	0.972	-5.05×10^{-4}

dominated by the oscillation modes are negative in the real part of the eigenvalues and have large damping ratios, so they will not cause the system to lose static stability and are not the focus of this paper. The analysis reveals that the negative damping ratio is a consequence of the intense dynamic interaction occurring between the virtual and physical power angles under the system's current operating conditions, thereby heightening the potential for oscillatory instability.

64.3 Analysis of the Effect of Virtual Inertia on Oscillation Modes

When the VSG virtual inertia coefficient J is increased from 0.01 to 0.3. while other parameters are kept constant, the trend of each oscillation mode is shown in Fig. 64.3. In the figure, the red arrow direction represents the approximate motion direction of the pole of the corresponding oscillation mode when J is increased.

From Fig. 64.3, it can be seen that the increase of virtual inertia *J has* a significant effect on the high-frequency oscillation modes, λ_2 corresponding to the inverse ratio of damping ratio and oscillation frequency to the trend of J change. However, the influence of VSG virtual inertia coefficient on the rest of the oscillation modes is relatively small, but an appropriate increase in J can still improve the damping

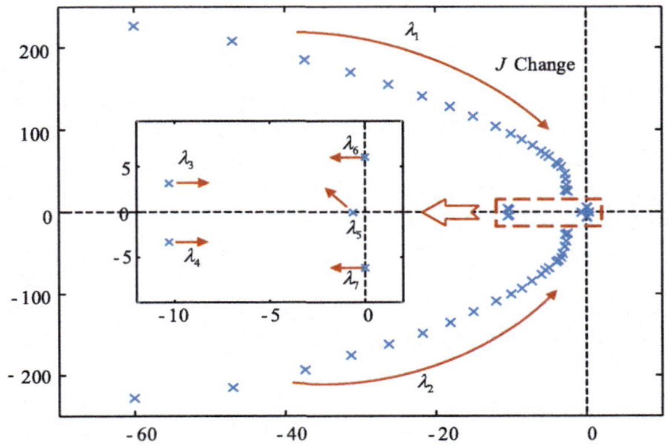

Fig. 64.3 The influence law of J change on various oscillation modes

characteristics of the electromechanical oscillation modes, and make λ_6 and λ_7 move slowly to the left. It can be seen that increasing J appropriately is conducive to weakening the electromechanical oscillations, but if J is too large, it may introduce new low-frequency oscillation modes, which exacerbates the risk of low-frequency oscillation instability of the virtual-physical hybrid inertia system.

64.4 Conclusion

Within the confines of this scholarly discourse, low-frequency oscillations of virtual-physical hybrid inertia systems are taken as the research object in the context of a high proportion of renewable energy connected to the grid, and the main work is to construct a small-signal model of the VSG-SG interconnected system applicable to the study of the damping characteristics of low-frequency oscillations of the grid and to construct a mathematical model in the form of the state-space equation of the VSG-SG interconnected system, by analyzing the dominant oscillation mode of the system, it is concluded that the VSG-SG interconnected system. By delving into an in-depth examination of the primary oscillation modes that characterize the system's behavior, we can gain a comprehensive understanding of the underlying dynamics and how they influence stability. It is concluded that the low-frequency oscillation occurs as the virtual-physical power angle has a strong dynamic interaction under the current operating conditions of the system, thus increasing the risk of oscillation instability. Finally, it is concluded from the simulation analysis that an appropriate increase in J is beneficial to weaken the low-frequency oscillations, but if J is too large, A new low-frequency oscillation mode might pop up instead, which exacerbates the risk of low-frequency oscillatory instability in the virtual-physical hybrid inertia system.

References

1. Hatziargyriou, N., et al.: Definition and classification of power system stability-revisited & extended. IEEE Trans. Power Syst. **36**(4), 3271–3281 (2021)
2. Baruwa, M., Fazeli, M.: Impact of virtual synchronous machines on low-frequency oscillations in power systems. IEEE Trans. Power Syst. **36**(3), 1934–1946 (2021)
3. Zhang, M., Miao, Z.X., Fan, L.: Reduced-order analytical models of the grid-connected solar photovoltaic systems for low-frequency oscillation analysis. IEEE Trans. Sustain. Energy **12**(3), 1662–1671 (2021)
4. Zhou, W.H., et al.: Effect of reactive power characteristic of offshore wind power plant on low-frequency stability. IEEE Trans. Energy Convers. **35**(2), 837–853 (2020)
5. Jia, Y.B., et al.: Parameter setting strategy for the controller of the DFIG wind turbine considering the small-signal stability of power grids. IEEE Access **8**, 31287–31294 (2020)
6. Sun, L., et al.: Analysis and mitigation of electromechanical oscillations for DFIG wind turbines involved in fast frequency response. IEEE Trans. Power Syst. **34**(6), 4547–4556 (2019)
7. Du, W., Fu, Q., Wang, H.: Power system small-signal angular stability affected by virtual synchronous generators. IEEE Trans. Power Syst. **34**(4), 3209–3219 (2019)
8. Wang, J., et al.: A bidirectional virtual inertia control strategy for the interconnected converter of standalone ac/dc hybrid microgrids. IEEE Trans. Power Syst. **39**(1), 745–754 (2024)
9. Wang H, et al.: Influence mechanism and virtual power system stabilizer method of virtual synchronous generator for low-frequency oscillation of power system. IET Energy Syst. Integr. (2023)
10. Ke, S., et al.: Consistency collaboration control strategy based on adaptive virtual inertia in multiple charging stations. IEEE Trans. Energy Convers. **39**(2), 896–913 (2024)

Chapter 65
Low-Frequency Oscillation Suppression Capability Analysis of Thermal Units Under Power Deep Peak Shaving

Pengbo Zhu, Shengyang Lu, Jian Dong, Qingshan Liu, Guorui Li, Haixin Wang, Tieyan Zhang, and Junyou Yang

Abstract To explore the ability of power system stabilizer 2B (PSS2B) to inhibit the low-frequency oscillations in deep peaking conditions of thermal power. In order to investigate the ability of power system stabilizer 2B (PSS2B) to suppress low-frequency oscillations under deep peaking conditions in thermal power plants, the Phillips-Heffron model of synchronous generator is constructed based on the single-unit infinity system, the basic principle of low-frequency oscillations and the role of the PSS 2B are elaborated, and the weakened damping characteristics of the PSS2B under deep peaking conditions are revealed through the analysis of the examples.

65.1 Introduction

With the formation of "double high" characteristics of high proportion of renew energy and high proportion of power electronic equipment access to the power system, traditional thermal power generation is gradually replaced by renewable energy sources such as photovoltaic, wind power, etc., forming a new power system with renew energy as the main body [1]. Renew energy large-scale access to the grid and the gradual expansion of the scale of the interconnected grid, significantly improving the power system peak shaving capacity and power support capacity between the regional grid, but a high proportion of new energy grid not only cause

P. Zhu (✉) · S. Lu · Q. Liu · G. Li · H. Wang · T. Zhang · J. Yang
Shenyang University of Technology, Shenyang, China
e-mail: 1257758409@qq.com

S. Lu
Electric Power Research Institute of State Grid Liaoning Electric Power Supply Co. Ltd., Shenyang, China

J. Dong
Economic and Technological Research Institute of State Grid Liaoning Electric Power Supply Co. Ltd., Shenyang, China

F. P. García Márquez et al. (eds.), *Computing, Internet of Things and Data Analytics*, Smart Innovation, Systems and Technologies 387,
https://doi.org/10.1007/978-3-031-87154-2_65

fundamental changes in the grid structure and operating characteristics, but also lead to a variety of stability control problems intertwined, to fully promote the consumption of renew energy, enhance the system peak shifting capacity, higher efficiency, stability, and stronger thermal power units have begun to be replaced by new energy sources. More efficient and stable thermal power units have begun to participate in the deep peaking operation of the grid [2]. The role of thermal power units has changed from a supportive power source to a regulating power source, assuming more peaking tasks. Thermal power units in deep peaking operation often have an active output of less than 50%, and some of them are even maintained at less than 30%, facing difficulties in stable operation, and maintaining stable operation of the units under such conditions poses a greater challenge to all related professions [3].

To improve the thermal economy of large-scale thermal power plants involved in deep peaking and to determine the performance of the thermal system under different conditions, a predictive modelling methodology for deep peaking performance of large-scale thermal power plants has been proposed in Ref. [4]. To enhance the peak load management of the system and the integration of wind and photovoltaic (PV) power generation, Ref. [5] proposes a distributed robust optimal scheduling strategy for WD-PV thermal storage power systems, which combines deep peaking. To derive suitable controller parameters based on the system identification technique, Ref. [6] monitors and even redesigns the performance of the damping controllers based on the models derived from the system identification and uses the results of the redesign to update the PSS parameters and improve the damping without the need to discontinue the use of the existing damping control system.

In this paper, the damping characteristics of PSS2B under deep conditioning of thermal power units are analysed by linearized modelling, and the effect of the reduction of SG active power on the damping characteristics of PSS2B is elucidated. This study provides a theoretical basis for the adaptive study of PSS2B under deep regulation condition of thermal power, which is of great significance for the suppression of low-frequency oscillations of PSS2B.

65.2 Low Frequency Oscillation Principle

65.2.1 Modelling of Stand-Alone Infinity Systems

The structure of the stand-alone infinity system is shown in Fig. 65.1.

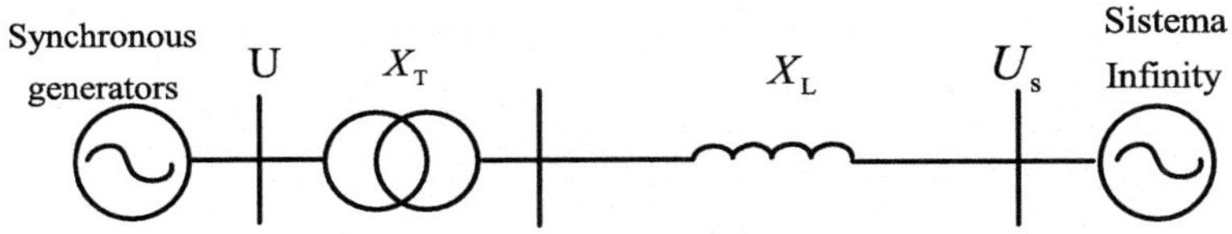

Fig. 65.1 Stand-alone infinity system architecture

Linearized models for single-machine infinite systems:

$$\begin{aligned}
\Delta\dot{\delta} &= \omega_0\Delta\omega \\
\Delta\dot{\omega} &= \frac{1}{M}(-K_1\Delta\delta - K_2\Delta E'_q - D\Delta\omega) \\
\Delta\dot{E}'_q &= \frac{1}{T'_{d0}}(-K_3\Delta E'_q - K_4\Delta\delta + \Delta E'_{jd}) \\
\Delta\dot{E}'_{fd} &= -\frac{1}{T_A}\Delta E'_{fd} - \frac{K_A}{T_A}(K_5\Delta\delta + K_6\Delta E'_q - \Delta u_{PSS})
\end{aligned} \tag{65.1}$$

The Phillips-Heffron linearized model for a single machine infinity system is shown in Fig. 65.2.

The Phillips-Heffron model of the stand-alone infinity system with PSS is shown in Fig. 65.2. where ΔT_{e1} and ΔT_2 are both the electromagnetic torque; $\Delta\omega$ is the generator speed; $\Delta\delta$ is the power angle variation; Δu_{PSS} is the output variation of the PSS; Δu_{REF} is the variation of the terminal voltage reference; ΔE_{fd} is the excitation voltage variation; and $\Delta E_q\prime$ is the transient potential of the generator.

The Phillips-Heffron model can also be written as the following state space expression:

Fig. 65.2 Single-unit Phillips-Heffron mode

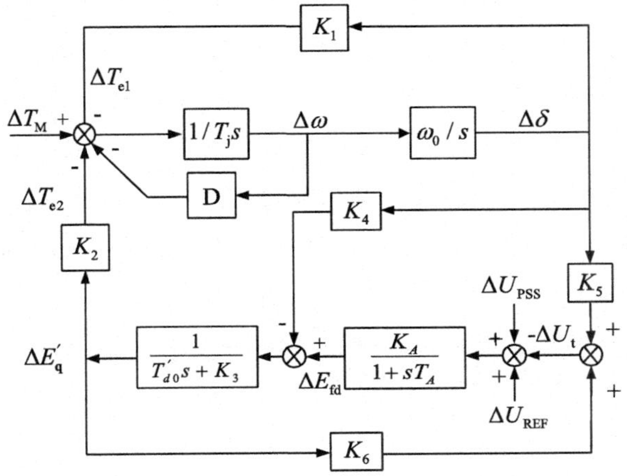

$$\dot{X} = \mathrm{A}X + \mathrm{b}\Delta u_{\mathrm{PSS}} \tag{65.2}$$

In Eq. (65.2) A and b can be calculated by (65.3).

$$\mathrm{A} = \begin{bmatrix} 0 & \omega_0 & 0 & 0 \\ -\frac{K_1}{M} & -\frac{D}{M} & -\frac{K_2}{M} & 0 \\ -\frac{K_4}{T'_{\mathrm{d0}}} & 0 & -\frac{K_3}{T'_{\mathrm{d0}}} & \frac{1}{T'_{\mathrm{d0}}} \\ -\frac{K_{\mathrm{A}}K_5}{T_{\mathrm{A}}} & 0 & -\frac{K_{\mathrm{A}}K_5}{T_{\mathrm{A}}} & -\frac{1}{T_{\mathrm{A}}} \end{bmatrix}, \mathrm{b} = \begin{bmatrix} 0 \\ 0 \\ 0 \\ -\frac{K_{\mathrm{A}}}{T_{\mathrm{A}}} \end{bmatrix} \tag{65.3}$$

In the absence of PSS2B, the eigenvalues of the system's oscillatory loop and the corresponding damping ratio can be found simply by deriving the matrix A.

The closed-loop equation of state for the system can be calculated by (65.4).

$$\begin{bmatrix} \Delta\hat{\delta} \\ \Delta\hat{\omega} \\ \Delta\hat{E}'_q \\ \Delta\hat{E}'_{fd} \\ \Delta\hat{x}_1 \\ \Delta\hat{u}_{\mathrm{PSS}} \end{bmatrix} = \begin{bmatrix} 0 & \omega_0 & 0 & 0 & 0 & 0 \\ -\frac{K_1}{M} & -\frac{D}{M} & -\frac{K_2}{M} & 0 & 0 & 0 \\ -\frac{K_4}{T'_{\mathrm{d0}}} & 0 & -\frac{K_3}{T'_{\mathrm{d0}}} & \frac{1}{T'_{\mathrm{d0}}} & 0 & 0 \\ -\frac{K_{\mathrm{A}}K_5}{T_{\mathrm{A}}} & 0 & -\frac{K_{\mathrm{A}}K_6}{T_{\mathrm{A}}} & -\frac{1}{T_{\mathrm{A}}} & 0 & \frac{K_{\mathrm{A}}}{T_{\mathrm{A}}} \\ -\frac{K_2}{T_3}\frac{T_4}{M}K_1 & \frac{K_2}{T_3}\left(1-\frac{T_4}{M}D\right) & -\frac{T_4}{M}\frac{K_2}{T_3}K_2 & 0 & -\frac{1}{T_3} & 0 \\ -\frac{T_4}{M}\frac{K_1}{T_1}\frac{K_2}{T_3}T_2K_1 & \frac{K_1}{T_1}\frac{K_2}{T_3}T_2\left(1-\frac{T_4}{M}D\right) & -\frac{K_1}{T_1}\frac{K_2}{T_3}\frac{T_4}{M}T_2K_2 & 0 & \frac{K_1}{T_1}-\frac{1}{T_3}\frac{K_1}{T_1}T_2 & -\frac{1}{T_1} \end{bmatrix} \begin{bmatrix} \Delta\delta \\ \Delta\omega \\ \Delta E'_{\mathrm{q}} \\ \Delta\hat{E}'_{\mathrm{fd}} \\ \Delta x_1 \\ \Delta x_1 \\ \Delta u_{\mathrm{PSS}} \end{bmatrix} \tag{65.4}$$

The matrix B can be calculated by (65.5).

$$B = \begin{bmatrix} 0 & \omega_0 & 0 & 0 & 0 & 0 \\ -\frac{K_1}{M} & -\frac{D}{M} & -\frac{K_2}{M} & 0 & 0 & 0 \\ -\frac{K_4}{T_{\mathrm{m}}} & 0 & -\frac{K_3}{T_{\mathrm{m}}} & \frac{1}{T_{\mathrm{m}}} & 0 & 0 \\ -\frac{K_4K_5}{T_{\mathrm{A}}} & 0 & -\frac{K_4K_6}{T_{\mathrm{A}}} & -\frac{1}{T_A} & 0 & \frac{K_{\mathrm{A}}}{T_{\mathrm{A}}} \\ -\frac{K_2T_4}{T_3M}K_1 & \frac{K_2}{T_3}(1-\frac{T_4}{M}D) & -\frac{T_4K_2}{MT_3}K_2 & 0 & -\frac{1}{T_5} & 0 \\ -\frac{T_4K_1K_5}{MT_1T_3}T_2K_1 & \frac{K_1K_2}{T_1T_3}T_2(1-\frac{T_4}{M}D) & -\frac{K_1K_2T_4}{T_1T_3M}T_2K_2 & 0 & \frac{K_1}{T_1}-\frac{1K_3}{T_3T_4}T_2 & -\frac{1}{T_4} \end{bmatrix} \tag{65.5}$$

The addition of PSS2B requires only the matrix B to find its corresponding eigenvalues and damping ratios.

The eigenvalues and damping ratios can be calculated by (65.6).

$$\lambda \nu \sigma \pm j\omega$$
$$\zeta = -\frac{\sigma}{\sqrt{\sigma^2 + \omega^2}} \tag{65.6}$$

In Eq. (65.6), σ is the eigenvalue The real part of the eigenvalue is the damping factor, and ω is the angular frequency of the oscillation mode.

65.2.2 Principle of Action of PSS2B

Power System Stabilizer (PSS2B) is a regulator attached to the exciter side, which provides an additional control signal to the excitation regulator, and the generator generates an electromagnetic torque component in phase with the rotor angular velocity deviation, which enhances the system damping or suppresses low-frequency oscillations (Fig. 65.3).

The input signal is taken as an algebraic combination of the generator's angular frequency $\Delta\omega$ and electromagnetic power ΔP_e. The model has four segments: the amplification segment is the gain of the PSS; the isolation segment is equivalent to a high-pass filter. The model has four links: amplification, isolation, overshooting and limiting, where the link is the gain of the PSS2B, which is used to amplify the input signal, and the isolation link is equivalent to a high-pass filter, which mainly filters the low-frequency portion of the signal while blocking the steady state input signal.

From Fig. 65.2, it can be seen that the electromagnetic torque supplied by the bottom part of the stand-alone model to the electromechanical oscillation circuit of the generator is divided into two parts, with one part coming from $\Delta\delta$ and the other from Δu_{PSS}, and letting the forward transfer functions of $\Delta\delta$ and Δu_{PSS} to the electromechanical oscillation circuit be $F_\delta(s)$ and $F_{PSS}(s)$, then there is a transfer function 7.

$$\Delta M_t = F_\delta(s)\Delta\delta + F_{PSS}(s)\Delta u_{PSS} \tag{65.7}$$

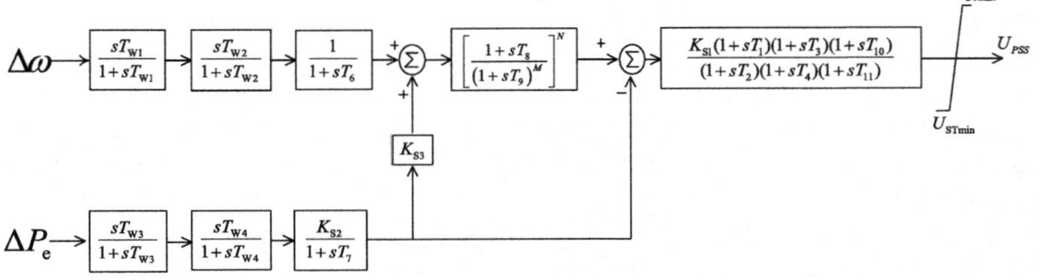

Fig. 65.3 Block diagram of PSS2B structure

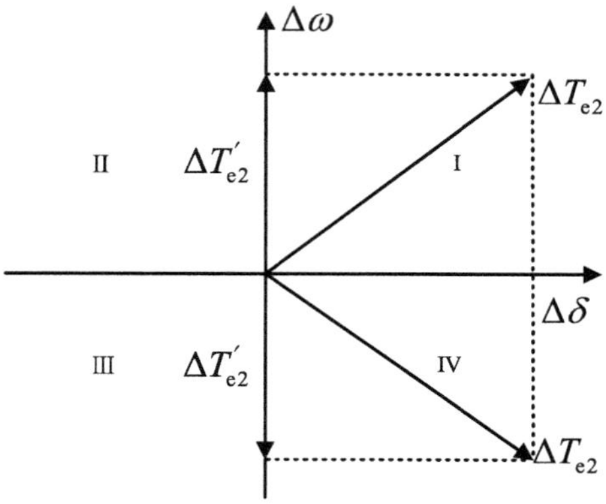

Fig. 65.4 Electromagnetic torque provided by generator excitation system

The PSS2B provides an electromagnetic torque to the electromechanical oscillation circuit can be calculated by (65.8).

$$\Delta M_{\mathrm{PSS}}(s) = F_{\mathrm{PSS}}(s)\Delta u_{\mathrm{PSS}} \tag{65.8}$$

When the generator operating conditions change, the voltage changes caused are K_5 and $\Delta\delta$, which generate the electromagnetic torque $\Delta T'_{e2}$ after the excitation regulator AVR action. As shown in Fig. 65.4,in the $\Delta\delta - \Delta\omega$ coordinates, when the projection of $\Delta T'_{e2}$ on the $\Delta\omega$ axis is positive, the excitation system provides positive damping; when the projection of $\Delta T'_{e2}$ on the $\Delta\omega$ axis is negative, the excitation system provides negative damping.

65.2.3 Simulation Example Analysis

To study the adaptability of PSS2B to suppress low-frequency oscillations under deep regulation mode of thermal power, this section builds a stand-alone infinity system based on the Matlab/Simulink simulation platform, and the rated capacity of the selected generator model is 726 MVA, and a transverse tangential load perturbation is applied at 1 s, and the stand-alone infinity system is selected to have the PSS2B parameters rectified for large operating conditions as shown in Table 65.1,the experiments were carried out under deep conditioning working conditions, which are working condition 1, working condition 2 and working condition 3 respectively (Table 65.2).

The comparison graphs of simulation experiments for Case I, Case II, Case III, and Case IV correspond to Figs. 65.5, 65.6, 65.7 and 65.8 shows the change rule of the PSS2B rectified under the large working condition to suppress the power oscillations in the four medium working conditions.

Table 65.1 System characteristic values

Parameters and units	Working condition I	Working condition II	Working condition III	Working condition IV
$P_{t0}/p.u.$	0.8	0.5	0.3	0.1
$V_{t0}/p.u.$	1.0	1.0	1.0	1.0
$V_{b0}/p.u.$	0.98	0.98	0.98	0.98
M	7.415	7.415	7.415	7.415
D	0.02	0.02	0.02	0.02
$\acute{T}_d$	6	6	6	6
K_A	300	300	300	300
T_A	0.01	0.01	0.01	0.01
$X_t/p.u.$	0.3	0.3	0.3	0.3
$X_d/p.u.$	1.308	1.308	1.308	1.308
$X_q/p.u.$	1.0	1.0	1.0	1.0
$\acute{X}_d/p.u.$	0.293	0.293	0.293	0.293

Table 65.2 PSS2B parameter values

PSS2B parameters	T1	T2	T3	T4	T10	T11	KS1	KS2
Retrieve value	0.16	0.04	0.16	0.04	0.18	0.03	5	1.4184

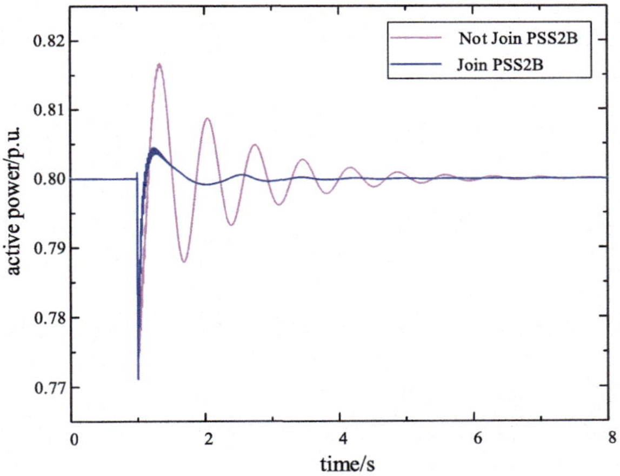

Fig. 65.5 Comparison of Case I adding and without PSS2B

For Case I, it can be seen from Fig. 65.5 that the system operates stably at the initial moment and the generator active power is output at the specified reference value of 0.8 p.u. At the instant of applying the same transverse load disturbance at 1 s, the peak system oscillation with the addition of the PSS2B is lower than that without the addition of the PSS2B, and the number of system oscillations without

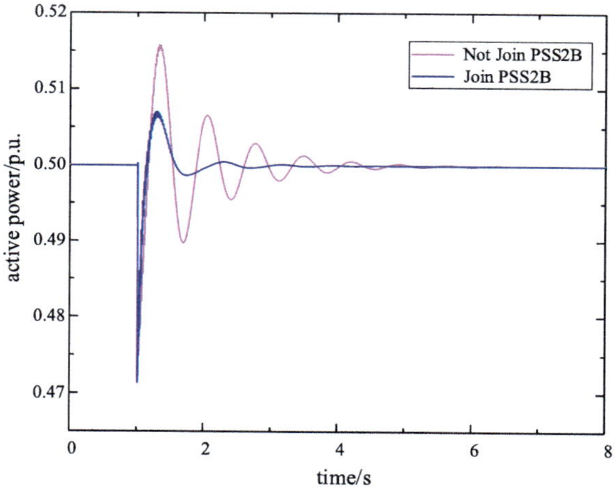

Fig. 65.6 Comparison of Case II adding and without PSS2B

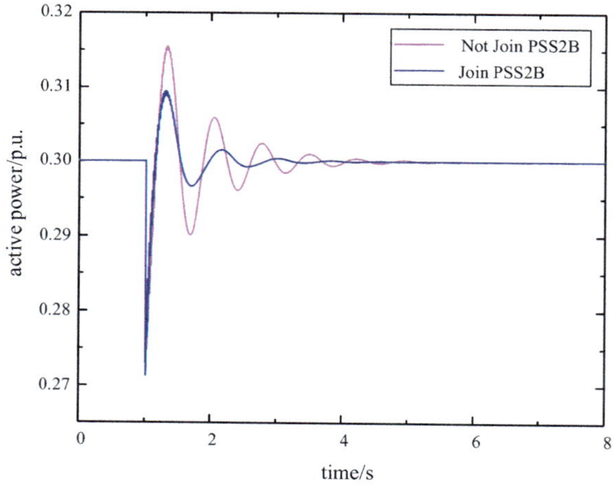

Fig. 65.7 Comparison of Case III adding and without PSS2B

PSS2B is 8, corresponding to a damping ratio of 0.05, and the number of system oscillations after the addition of PSS2B is obviously reduced to 2, corresponding to a damping ratio of 0.28. It can be seen that this group of PSS2B parameters can effectively suppress the power oscillation under large working conditions.

For Case II, according to Fig. 65.6, it can be seen that the system operates stably at the initial moment, and the generator active power is output at the specified reference value of 0.5 p.u., the moment of applying the same transverse load perturbation as described above at 1 s, the peak value of the system oscillations with the addition of the PSS2B is lower than that without the addition of the PSS2B The number of system oscillations is 6 times without PSS2B and 3 times after adding PSS2B, the corresponding damping ratios are 0.07 and 0.21 respectively. It can be seen that the PSS2B parameters adjusted under large operating conditions can suppress power

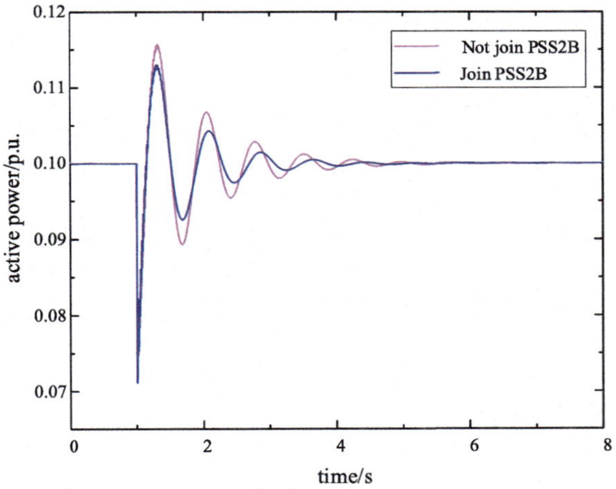

Fig. 65.8 Comparison of Case IV adding and without PSS2B

oscillation when the active power output P is 0.5 in deep condition, but the effect of suppressing low-frequency oscillations is weaker in deep-tuned conditions than in large conditions.

For Case III, according to Fig. 65.7, it can be seen that the system operates stably at the initial moment and the generator active power is output at the specified reference value of 0.3p.u. At the instant of applying the same transverse load perturbation as described above at 1 s, the peak system oscillation with the addition of the PSS2B is lower than that without the addition of the PSS2B, the number of system oscillations without PSS2B is 6, corresponding to a damping ratio of 0.08, and the number of system oscillations after adding PSS2B is 3, corresponding to a damping ratio of 0.17. It can be seen that the PSS2B parameter adjusted under large operating conditions can suppress power oscillation when the active power output P is 0.3 in deep condition, but the effect of suppressing low-frequency oscillations is weaker in deep-tuned conditions than in large conditions.

For case IV, according to Fig. 65.8, it can be seen that the system operates stably at the initial moment and the generator active power output is 0.1 p.u. for the specified reference value. At the moment of applying the same lateral load disturbance for 1 s as above, the peak oscillation of the system with PSS2B is lower than that without PSS2B, but the difference is not significant, and the number of oscillations of the system without PSS2B is 6 times, corresponding to a damping ratio of 0.09, and that with PSS2B is 5 times, corresponding to a damping ratio of 0.12, which is not a significant difference in the number of oscillations. It can be seen that under the deep peaking condition where the output active power of the thermal power unit is 0.1 p.u., the effect of PSS2B in suppressing the low-frequency oscillation is extremely poor.

65.3 Conclusions

In summary, the PSS2B parameters adjusted under large load conditions can effectively suppress low-frequency oscillation disturbances under large load conditions, and there is also a certain effect of suppressing low-frequency oscillations under deep peaking conditions of thermal power plants, but the effect of suppressing low-frequency oscillations of the PSS2B decreases as the generator continues to deepen its peaking, and therefore, it is necessary to adjust the parameters of the PSS2B further in the deep peaking conditions.

References

1. Muhtadi, A., et al.: Distributed energy resources based microgrid: review of architecture, control, and reliability. IEEE Trans. Ind. Appl. **57**(3), 2223–2235 (2021)
2. Zhou, J., Zhang, L., Zhu, L., et al.: A data-driven operating improvement method for the thermal power unit with frequent load changes. Appl. Energy 354(PB) (2024)
3. Wang, J., Huo, J., Zhang, S., et al.: Flexibility transformation decision-making evaluation of coal-fired thermal power units deep peak Shaving in China. Sustainability. **13**(4), 1882 (2021)
4. Liu, S., Shen, J.: Modeling of large-scale thermal power plants for performance prediction in deep peak shaving. Energies **15**(9), 3171 (2022)
5. Zhang, Z., Zhu, R.: A distributionally robust optimization strategy for a wind-photovoltaic thermal storage power system considering deep peak load balancing of thermal power units. Processes **12**(3), 534 (2024)
6. Shafiullah, M., Pathan, M.I.H., Shahriar, M.S., et al.: Real-time solution of PSS parameter tuning by GA-ANFIS in stabilizing the electrical power system. Arab. J. Sci. Eng. **48**, 6925–6938 (2023)

Chapter 66
INet: Rescue UAV-Based Insulator Damage Detection

ZeRu Yang, Feng Zhang, and Shuai Yuan

Abstract Ensuring the reliability, stability, and effectiveness of the power transmission system and early detection of potential risks in power transmission lines are crucial. Deep learning-based detection methods offer more efficient detection of abnormal targets on power transmission lines. However, challenges such as complex backgrounds, large-scale variations and numerous small objects exist in power transmission lines insulator. To address these challenges, we proposes INet. To tackle the issue of complex backgrounds, the large selective kernel attention is introduced, which conducts multi-scale convolution operations on input feature maps and combines with an adaptive attention mechanism to focus the model's attention on object areas. To address the problem of large- scale variations in objects, the bidirectional feature fusion module is introduced, which effectively integrates multi-scale features through a cross-scale information interaction mechanism, thereby enhancing the model's detection capabilities for objects of different scales. Finally, to tackle the challenge of difficulty in regression of small objects, the Inner-IoU loss is introduced, which penalizes deviations between objects and bounding boxes, promoting accurate detection of small objects by the model. INet, incorporating these key components, achieves promising results on the Insulator dataset, providing reliable technical support for the safe operation of power transmission systems.

66.1 Introduction

Insulators in transmission lines are used to support conductors, increase creepage distance, and prevent current flow to the ground, making them a crucial component of transmission lines [1–3]. Cracking defects are one of the common faults of insulators, referring to situations where insulators lose their integrity due to factors such as high temperature, lightning, or degradation. Insulator defects can significantly affect the

Z. Yang (✉) · F. Zhang · S. Yuan
School of Electrical and Control Engineering, Shenyang Jianzhu University, Shenyang, China
e-mail: 601313402@qq.com

F. P. García Márquez et al. (eds.), *Computing, Internet of Things and Data Analytics*,
Smart Innovation, Systems and Technologies 387,
https://doi.org/10.1007/978-3-031-87154-2_66

stable operation of the line [2]. Therefore, it is necessary to efficiently detect insulators and promptly identify any cracking defects.

Traditional manual inspection methods often require personnel to physically inspect the site [3]. However, this approach is time-consuming, labor-intensive, and difficult to guarantee the safety of workers. In recent years, unmanned aerial vehicles (UAVs), due to their low maintenance costs and ease of deployment, have been gradually applied to the field of insulator defect detection. Traditional detection algorithms require researchers to manually extract target features and determine the presence of cracking defects based on statistical theory and relevant experience [4].

Deep learning detection algorithms [5–7] have been a research hotspot in recent years and generally offer higher accuracy compared to traditional detection methods [8]. However, despite the existence of various methods, they have not effectively balanced detection accuracy and speed. These methods lack strong resistance to background interference, making them vulnerable to disturbance from the complex backgrounds of transmission lines. In practical detection processes, their performance is unsatisfactory and fails to meet the expected outcomes.

These methods lack strong resistance to background interference, making them vulnerable to disturbance from the complex backgrounds of transmission lines. In practical detection processes, their performance is unsatisfactory and fails to meet the expected outcomes.

66.2 Method

While YOLOv8 [9] has achieved good results in general object detection scenarios, its performance is subpar in our dataset. To address this issue, this paper proposes improvements to YOLOv8. Firstly, to tackle the poor feature extraction capability of the YOLOv8 backbone network, we introduce the Large Selective Kernel Attention (LSKA). LSKA helps the model focus more on important feature regions, thereby enhancing the accuracy of object detection. Secondly, for the feature fusion part, we introduce the Bidirectional Feature Pyramid Network (BiFPN). BiFPN combines top-down and bottom-up feature pathways and utilizes bidirectional information propagation to better fuse features of different scales, further improving detection performance. Lastly, to address the difficulty in regressing small objects during the training process of the YOLOv8 detection head, we introduce a new loss term called InnerIoU. By penalizing deviations between targets and bounding boxes, InnerIoU promotes accurate detection of small objects by the model. The pipline of the INet model is as shown in Fig. 66.1.

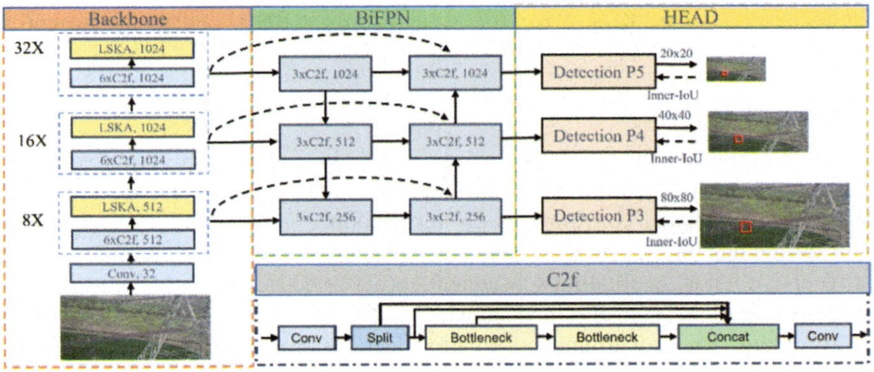

Fig. 66.1 The pipline of the INet

66.2.1 Large Selective Kernel Attention

Traditional convolutional operations have limited receptive fields, making it difficult to capture detailed information about targets, especially for faint targets. Therefore, this paper introduces the Large Kernel Selective Attention module into the backbone network of YOLOv8 to expand the receptive fields of feature maps. This enables the network to better understand input images and enhance its understanding of target backgrounds. The Large Kernel Attention module helps introduce more contextual information into shallow features, thereby improving the representation ability for small targets and enhancing detection accuracy. The Large Kernel Selective Attention is illustrated in Fig. 66.2.

Due to the varying demands of different types of targets for background information, the model needs to adaptively select different sizes of background regions. Therefore, this paper decouples a series of Depth-wise convolutions with large kernels and continuously expanding receptive fields to construct a network with a larger receptive field. Specifically, assuming that the size of the i-th Depth-wise convolution kernel in the sequence is k and the dilation rate is d, and the receptive field is RF, they satisfy the following relationship:

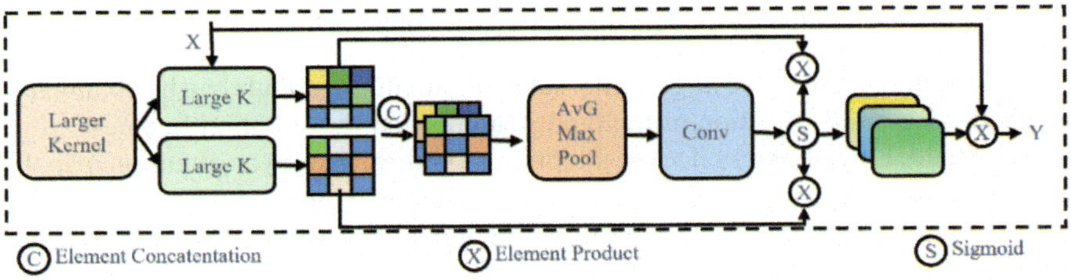

Fig. 66.2 The pipline of the LSKA

$$K_{i-1} \le K_i; d_1 = 1, d_{i-1} < d_1 \le RF_{i-1} \quad (66.1)$$

$$RF_1 = K_1,\ RF_i = d_i(k_{i-1}) + RF_{i-1} \quad (66.2)$$

The increase in convolutional kernel size and dilation rate ensures rapid expansion of the receptive field. Additionally, this paper sets an upper limit on the dilation rate to ensure that dilated convolutions do not introduce gaps between feature maps. This design has two advantages. Firstly, it can generate features with multiple sizes of receptive fields, facilitating subsequent kernel selection. Secondly, compared to simply using a large convolutional kernel, the effect of sequence decoupling is better.

To obtain rich background information features from different regions of the input data X, a series of decoupled Depth-wise convolutional kernels with different receptive fields can be used.

$$U_0 = X, U_{i+1} = F_i^{dw}(U_i) \quad (66.3)$$

where F_i^{dw} represents the Depth-wise convolution operation with a convolution kernel size of K_i and dilation rate of d_i, Assuming there are N decoupled convolution kernels, each convolution operation is followed by a 1×1 convolution layer for channel fusion of spatial feature vectors. Subsequently, for different targets, based on the obtained multi-scale features, an adaptive mechanism described later in the text is used to dynamically select the appropriate convolution kernel size.

To make the model focus more on the spatially important background information of the target, this paper uses a spatial selection mechanism to perform spatial selection on the feature maps from convolution kernels of different scales. Firstly, the features from convolution kernels with different receptive fields are concatenated.

Then, apply channel-wise average pooling $F_{avg(x)}$ and max pooling $F_{max(x)}$ to extract spatial relationships S. To facilitate the interaction of information from different spatial descriptors, convolution layers are used to concatenate spatial pooling features, transforming the pooled features of two channels into N spatial attention feature maps. Afterward, applying the Sigmoid activation function to each spatial attention feature map allows for obtaining independent spatial selection masks corresponding to each decoupled large convolution kernel.

Next, the features of the decoupled large convolution kernel sequence are weighted by the corresponding spatial selection masks, and attention features are obtained through fusion using convolution layers.

Finally, the output of the large kernel selective attention module can be obtained by element-wise multi-plication of the input features and the attention features, which are weighted. Large kernel selective attention module generates an attention map that assigns higher weights to significant features, which are then multiplied element-wise with the input features. Through training, the model learns to adjust these weights, enhancing important features and suppressing less relevant ones, thereby effectively focusing on crucial regions in complex backgrounds.

66.2.2 Bidirectional Feature Fusion Module

Since the inception of FPN, it has been widely used for multi-scale feature fusion. In recent years, research such as PANet has further developed network structures for cross-scale feature fusion. Previous work often summarized the fusion of different input features uniformly, without distinction; however, due to the varying resolutions of these input features, we observed that their contributions to the fused output features are usually uneven. To address this issue, we introduce a simple yet effective Weighted Bidirectional Feature Pyramid Network (BiFPN), which incorporates learnable weights to capture the importance of different input features. Furthermore, it iteratively applies top-down and bottom-up multiscale feature fusion, as depicted in Fig. 66.3.

Subsequent paragraphs, however, are indented. Specifically, assuming the list of input multi-scale features is Pin, where N is the number of feature levels. BiFPN first performs a series of operations to up-sample and down-sample the input features to ensure that all features have the same size. Then, for each feature level P_i, BiFPN performs the following operations:

$$P_{in} = \{P_1, P_2, ..., \mathrm{P_n}\} \tag{66.4}$$

Firstly, by upsampling, the lower-level feature Pi − 1 is sampled to the same size as the current level P_i by downsampling, the higher-level feature P_{i+1} is downsampled to the same size. This way, features matched with the current level are obtained.

Next, for each feature level P_i, , BiFPN performs feature fusion in two directions (up and down). Specifically, for the upward fusion, the current level feature P_i is fused with the feature Pi − 1 from the previous level, and the current level feature P_i is fused with the feature P_{i+1} from the next level. This process can be represented as:

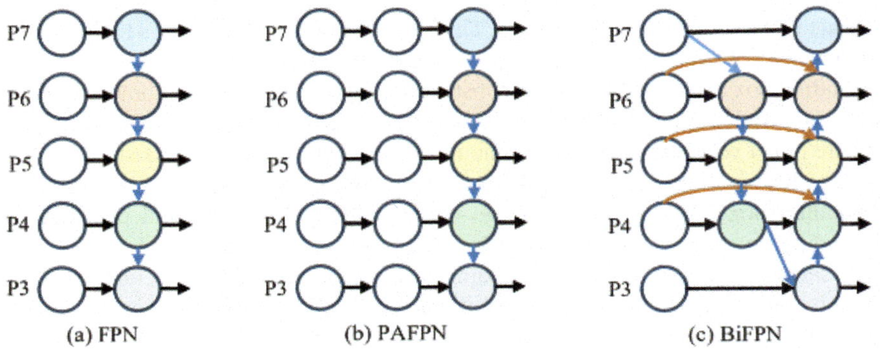

Fig. 66.3 The pipline of the bidirectional feature fusion module

$$M_i^{up} = Conv\left(P_i + Upsample\left(M_{i+1}^{up}\right)\right) \quad (66.5)$$

$$M_i^{\text{down}} = Conv\left(P_i + Downsample\left(M_{i-1}^{down}\right)\right) \quad (66.6)$$

where M_i^{up} and M_i^{down} represent the fusion results in the upward and downward directions, respectively. Conv denotes the convolution operation, while Upsample and Downsample represent the upsampling and downsampling operations, respectively.

Then, BiFPN adjusts the fused features through an attention mechanism to dynamically control the impor-tance between different feature levels. Specifically, for the upward fusion, an attention coefficient α_i^{up} can be used, while for the downward fusion, another attention coefficient α_i^{down} can be used. The fused features can be represented as:

$$M_i^{up} = \alpha_i^{up} M_i^{up} \quad (66.7)$$

$$M_i^{down} = \alpha_i^{down} M_i^{down} \quad (66.8)$$

Finally, BiFPN adds the features fused in the upward and downward directions to obtain the final feature list P_{out}.

$$P_{out} = \left\{M_1^{up}, \ldots, M_n^{up}\right\} + \left\{M_1^{down}, \ldots, M_n^{down}\right\} \quad (66.9)$$

66.2.3 Inner IoU Loss

Due to the influence of changing perspectives in unmanned aerial vehicle (UAV) flights, distant targets appear smaller while closer ones appear larger, resulting in drastic scale variations of the targets. This poses significant challenges to the regression branch of existing object detectors. Despite the rapid development of detectors, bounding box regression has made substantial progress. However, in practical applications, it fails to self-adjust based on complex scenes, especially in UAV scenarios where target scale variations are pronounced, leading to a lack of robustness.

To differentiate between different regression samples and utilize auxiliary bounding boxes of varying scales to compute loss effectively and expedite the bounding box regression process, this paper proposes the Inner IoU loss. For high IoU samples, smaller auxiliary bounding boxes are employed to calculate the loss, thereby accelerating convergence, while larger auxiliary bounding boxes are used for low IoU samples. As illustrated in Fig. 66.4, the ground truth bounding box and anchor box are denoted as b^{gt} and b, respectively. The centers of the ground truth bounding box and inner bounding box are represented by(x_c^{gt}, y_c^{gt}), while x_c and y_c denote the centers of the anchor box and inner anchor box. The width and height of the ground truth bounding box are denoted as w^{gt} and h^{gt}, respectively, while w and

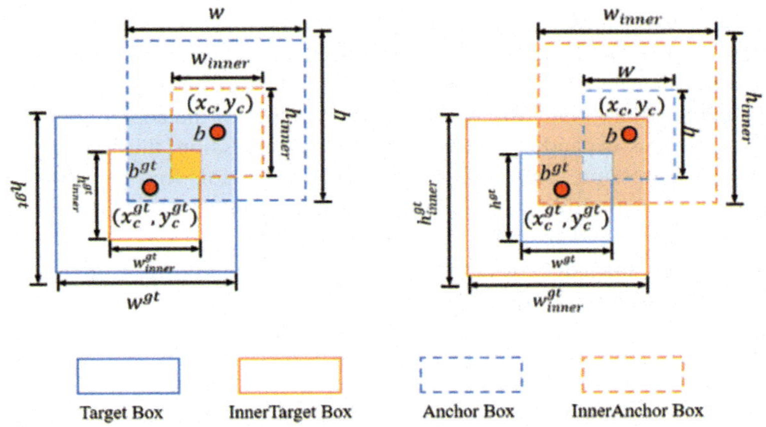

Fig. 66.4 The description of the Inner IoU

h represent the width and height of the anchor box. The variable ratio corresponds to the scale factor, typically ranging from 0.5 to 1.5.

The definition of the Inner IoU is as follows:

$$b_l^{gt} = x_c^{gt} - \frac{w^{gt} \cdot ratio}{2}, b_r^{gt} = x_c^{gt} - \frac{w^{gt} \cdot ratio}{2}$$

$$b_t^{gt} = y_c^{gt} - \frac{h^{gt} \cdot ratio}{2}, b_b^{gt} = y_c^{gt} - \frac{h^{gt} \cdot ratio}{2}$$

$$b_l = x_c - \frac{w \cdot ratio}{2}, b_r = x_c - \frac{w \cdot ratio}{2}$$

$$b_t = y_c - \frac{h \cdot ratio}{2}, b_b = y_c - \frac{h \cdot ratio}{2} \tag{66.10}$$

$$\text{inner} = \left(\min\left(\text{b}_\text{r}^\text{gt}, \text{b}_\text{r}\right) - \max\left(\text{b}_\text{r}^\text{gt}, \text{b}_\text{r}\right)\right) \cdot \left(\min\left(\text{b}_\text{b}^\text{gt}, \text{b}_\text{b}\right) - \max\left(\text{b}_\text{t}^\text{gt}, \text{b}_\text{t}\right)\right)$$

$$\text{union} = \left(w^{gt} \cdot h^{gt}\right) \cdot \text{ratio}^2 + (\text{w} \cdot \text{h}) \cdot \text{ratio}^2 - \text{i nter}$$

$$IoU^{inner} = \frac{inner}{union}$$

Subsequent paragraphs, however, are indented. The Inner-IoU loss inherits the characteristics of the IoU loss while possessing its own unique features. Similar to the IoU loss, the Inner-IoU loss ranges from 0 to 1, and its curve resembles that of the IoU-Deviation curve, albeit with slight differences in certain aspects. The Inner-IoU loss takes into account the scale differences between auxiliary bounding boxes and actual bounding boxes, thus employing a method similar to the IoU loss in computing loss. However, when the scale of the auxiliary bounding box is smaller than that of the actual bounding box, the absolute gradient of the Inner-IoU loss is larger, thereby accelerating convergence for high IoU samples. Conversely, when the scale of the auxiliary bounding box is larger than that of the actual bounding box, the Inner-IoU loss expands the effective range of regression, thus providing gains for low IoU regression. This design enables the Inner-IoU loss to better adapt to regression tasks with different bounding box scales, thereby enhancing the model's performance in object detection.

Applying the Inner-IoU to existing IoU-based bounding box regression loss functions, it is defined as follows:

$$L_{inneriou} = 1 - IoU^{inner} \tag{66.11}$$

66.3 Experments

66.3.1 Implementation Details

Subsequent paragraphs, however, are indented. In the training stage of our proposed INet, our implementation was based on PyTorch and trained on four NVIDIA RTX 4090 GPUs. Then, the entire network was trained using the SGD optimizer [10] with a weight decay 5×10^{-4}. For the input size of the detector was set to 640×640 pixels.

66.3.2 Datasets

We have utilized a dataset comprising 600 images of damaged insulators collected via unmanned aerial vehicles (UAVs), which have been annotated. The dataset consists of 375 images for training and 225 images for validation.

66.3.3 Evaluation Metrics

In order to verify the performance improvement of INet, we adopts commonly used evaluation metrics in the field of object detection, including precision (P), recall (R), average precision (AP) for individual object categories, and mean average precision (mAP), comparing them with the original model. The detection accuracy for multiple defects in transmission lines is targeted.

Table 66.1 The ablation experiments of each component

Method	Precision	Recall	AP	mAP
Baseline	96.7	90.8	95.3	59.6
w/LSKA	96.0	93.8	95.6	61.0
w/BiFPN	95.5	94.1	95.3	60.4
w/Inner IoU loss	97.2	92.8	95.5	62.0
INet (Ours)	**97.3**	**94.7**	**96.0**	**63.1**

66.3.4 Ablation Experiment

Table 66.1 displays the comparative results of ablation experiments. Starting from the baseline model, we sequen- tially introduced components such as LSKA, BiFPN, and Inner IoU Loss, and evaluated the system's performance in terms of Precision, Recall, mAP50, and mAP at each step. The results indicate that LSKA and BiFPN have a positive effect on improving recall but may lead to a decrease in precision. Meanwhile, the optimization with Inner IoU Loss significantly enhances mAP by approximately 3.5%.Ultimately, our proposed method, INet, integrates these improvements, achieving the best detection performance. Compared to the baseline model, INet demonstrates an increase of approximately 0.6% in Precision and 3.9% in Recall, while AP and mAP improve by around 0.7% and 3.5%, respectively.

66.3.5 Quantitative Evaluation

The Table 66.2 provides a comprehensive comparison of performance metrics across various object detection methods, including Baseline, Faster-RCNN, SSD, RetinaNet, YOLOv3,YOLOv4, YOLOv5,YOLOv7, and our proprietary INet (Ours) method. Remarkably, INet (Ours) stands out with the highest scores across all metrics. For instance, its precision of 97.3% surpasses all other methods, notably higher than the nearest competitor, YOLOv7, which achieved 96.1%. Similarly, INet (Ours) achieves the highest recall at 94.7%, significantly outperforming the next closest method, YOLOv3, at 92.0%. Furthermore, INet (Ours) boasts an average precision (AP) of 96.0%, again leading the field, while its mean average precision (mAP) of 63.1% is notably superior to all other methods. Although YOLOv3 and YOLOv5 also demonstrate respectable performance across various metrics, particularly in precision and recall, YOLOv4 and YOLOv7 fall short in comparison. Even the Baseline method, while competitive in precision and AP, lags behind in recall and mAP. In summary, these numerical comparisons underscore the exceptional performance of our INet (Ours) approach, providing compelling evidence of its efficacy in the domain of insulator object detection.

Table 66.2 Performance comparison

Method	Precision	Recall	AP	mAP
Baseline	96.7	90.8	95.3	59.6
Faster-RCN	82.7	74.4	78.7	44.6
SSD	85.1	78.4	83.1	49.5
RetinaNet	88.4	82.1	86.9	51.2
YOLOv3	96.3	92.0	93.6	54.9
YOLOv4	94.6	91.7	93.1	54.5
YOLOv5	95.6	89.5	94	55.4
YOLOv7	96.1	91.4	92.8	54.4
INet (Ours)	**97.3**	**94.7**	**96.0**	**63.1**

66.3.6 Qualitative Evaluation

The comparison depicted in Fig. 66.5 between INet and the baseline model YOLOv8 highlights significant ad- vantages of our proposed INet model. While YOLOv8 struggles with identifying damage locations in complex backgrounds, often resulting in missed detections or false alarms, INet excels in precisely detecting insulator damage. It demonstrates superior accuracy, particularly in discerning damage amidst challenging backgrounds, thereby minimizing missed detections and false alarms. Additionally, INet exhibits a remarkable ability to differentiate between damaged and undamaged components, further enhancing its precision in defect identification. Overall, INet represents a substantial improvement over YOLOv8, offering enhanced reliability and effectiveness in insulator fault detection tasks, which holds promise for bolstering the efficiency and accuracy of fault detection systems in insulator applications.

Category Activation Mapping [11] is a method used to interpret convolutional neural networks (CNNs). It generates class-specific"activation maps" by applying global average pooling and a linear classifier to the last convolutional layer. These maps reveal which regions of an image the network deems important for a specific class, aiding in visualization. Figure 66.6 illustrates the CAM visualization of INet, showcasing its ability to accurately predict damage locations on insulators.

Fig. 66.5 Visualize the performance of the baseline and INet (ours)

Fig. 66.6 Visualize the CAM of the INet (ours)

66.4 Conclusion

Subsequent paragraphs, however, are indented. In summary, we presents INet, a novel deep learning-based method tailored for detecting abnormalities in power transmission lines, with a focus on addressing challenges such as complex backgrounds, large-scale variations, and the detection of numerous small objects within insulators. Through the incorporation of innovative components including large selective kernel attention, bidirectional feature fusion, and the Inner-IoU loss, INet achieves significant advancements in the reliability and effectiveness of abnormal target detection. Experimental results on the Insulator dataset demonstrate promising outcomes in terms of detection accuracy and robustness, underscoring the potential of deep learning techniques to enhance the safety and stability of power transmission systems.

66.5 Limitations

Our work has two main Limitations: First, the dataset has limited weather conditions, lacking diversity which may restrict the model's generalization ability. Future work will address this by including data from various weather scenarios. Second, the current drone platform's low computing power limits the model's efficiency. Future research will focus on lightweight model design to improve performance on low-power platforms. Addressing these issues will enhance the model's practical application and reliability, ensuring effective performance in diverse scenarios and efficient operation on resource-constrained devices.

References

1. Sanyal, S., Aslam, F., Kim, T., Jeon, S., Lee, Y.-J., Yi, J., Choi, I.-H., Son, J.-A., Koo, J.-B.: Deterio-ration of porcelain insulators utilized in overhead transmission lines: a review. Trans. Electr. Electron. Mater. **21**, 16–21 (2020)
2. Miao, X., Liu, X., Chen, J., Zhuang, S., Fan, J., Jiang, H.: Insulator detection in aerial images for transmission line inspection using single shot multibox detector. IEEE Access **7**, 9945–9956 (2019)
3. Chen, M., Tian, Y., Xing, S., Li, Z., Li, E., Liang, Z., Guo, R.: Environment perception technologies for power transmission line inspection robots. J. Sen. **2021**, 1–16 (2021)
4. Tan, P., Li, X.-F., Xu, J.-M., Ma, J.-E., Wang, F.-J., Ding, J., Fang, Y.-T., Ning, Y.: Catenary insulator defect detection based on contour features and gray similarity matching. J. Zhejiang Univ.-SCIENCE A **21**(1), 64–73 (2020)
5. Liu, W., Anguelov, D., Erhan, D., Szegedy, C., Reed, S., Fu, C.-Y., Berg, A.C.: Ssd: single shot multi- box detector. In: Computer Vision–ECCV 2016: 14th European Conference, Amsterdam, The Netherlands, October 11–14, 2016, Proceedings, Part I 14, pp. 21–37, Springer (2016)
6. Ren, S., He, K., Girshick, R., Sun, J.: Faster r-cnn: towards real-time object detection with region proposal networks. IEEE Trans. Pattern Anal. Mach. Intell. **39**(6), 1137–1149 (2016)
7. Bochkovskiy, A., Wang, C.-Y., Liao, H.-Y.M.: Yolov4: optimal speed and accuracy of object detec- tion (2020). arXiv preprint arXiv:2004.10934

8. Zhao, W., Xu, M., Cheng, X., Zhao, Z.: An insulator in transmission lines recognition and fault detec- tion model based on improved faster rcnn. IEEE Trans. Instrum. Meas. **70**, 1–8 (2021)
9. Ocher, G., Chaurasia, A., Qiu, J.: Ultralytics YOLO (2023)
10. Kingma, D.P., Ba, J.: Adam: a method for stochastic optimization (2014). arXiv preprint arXiv: 1412.6980
11. Selvaraju, R.R., Das, A., Vedantam, R., Cogswell, M., Parikh, D., Batra, D.: Grad-cam: why did you say that? In: Conference 2016, LNCS, vol. 9999, pp. 1–13. Springer, Heidelberg (2016) arXiv preprint arXiv:1611.07450

Chapter 67
Enhancing Wind Turbine Performance with Convolutional Neural Networks for Real-Time Wind Pattern Recognition

Ramzi Qasim Mohammed, Sarmad Jasim Hasan, and Abdullah Nasser Ibraheem

Abstract Efficiently operating wind turbines is becoming more important as the demand for green energy sources continues to rise. This paper presents a prognostic model for predicting wind turbine power generation using operational and meteorological data, based on a neural network. Input layers, hidden layers that are activated by the Rectified Linear Unit (ReLU) function, and a regression output layer are the components that make up the structure of our model. This particular model is a feed-forward neural network that has a great deal of layers. These non-linear characteristics of the dataset, which include variables such as dew point, temperature, humidity, wind speed, and direction at varying heights, were explicitly taken into consideration when developing this approach, which was especially adapted to accommodate those characteristics. The model was trained using a dataset that was divided into 70% for training and 30% for testing. Normalizing the feature columns enhanced the efficiency of the learning process. By employing an appropriate learning rate and regularization techniques to avoid overfitting, the training process consisting of 100 epochs using the Adam optimizer successfully reached convergence. The root mean squared error (RMSE) metric was utilized in order to evaluate the performance of the model, and it was found to have produced a satisfactory result of 0.170 on the standard set. This is advantageous for operational planning and enhancing efficiency in wind energy generation, as precise power production predictions are essential. The results

R. Q. Mohammed (✉)
Solar Department of Energy, Al-Nahrain University, Al-Nahrain Research Center for Renewable Energy, Baghdad, Iraq
e-mail: ramziqassem@ced.nahrainuniv.edu.iq

S. J. Hasan
Wind Department of Energy, Al-Nahrain University, Al-Nahrain Research Center for Renewable Energy, Baghdad, Iraq
e-mail: sarmad_jh@nahrainuniver.edu.iq

A. N. Ibraheem
College of Engineering, Department of Biomedical Engineering, Al-Nahrain University, Baghdad, Iraq
e-mail: a.alsaqabi92@nahrainuniv.edu.iq

F. P. García Márquez et al. (eds.), *Computing, Internet of Things and Data Analytics*, Smart Innovation, Systems and Technologies 387,
https://doi.org/10.1007/978-3-031-87154-2_67

demonstrate that neural networks and other deep learning models provide essential forecasts and understandings for renewable energy systems, therefore facilitating the development of power generation that is both more dependable and efficient.

67.1 Introduction

Energy that comes from renewable sources is an important component in the fight against climate change and in reducing our reliance on fossil fuels. When it comes to renewable energy sources, wind power stands out owing to the fact that it is sustainable over the long term and has a little impact on the environment [1]. Better and more dependable wind turbines are in high demand due to the expanding global capacity for wind energy. Planning and integration with the power grid may be greatly enhanced with accurate predictions of energy generation, which are crucial for optimizing operations. One common method for predicting the output of wind turbines is to use physical models that account for its mechanical, electrical, and aerodynamic parts [2]. Though useful in some contexts, these models have the potential drawbacks of being difficult to understand and of ignoring important contextual aspects [3]. Recently, machine learning techniques like neural networks have become powerful tools for modeling complex and nonlinear interactions in settings with a lot of data. Wind power generation is affected by the unpredictable and variable meteorological data, which is why neural networks are a good fit for managing this data [4]. The reason for this is their ability to understand and replicate complex patterns seen in large datasets. Predicting the production of wind turbines using it should lead to more precise forecasts and more efficient operations. Both short-term and long-term strategic planning and decision-making for wind farm management are made easier with the usage of these models [5]. Developing a model for estimating the quantity of power generated by wind turbines is the objective of this research. To do this, a feed-forward neural network will be employed. Temperature, relative humidity, dew point, wind speed, and wind direction are only a few of the many input variables that the model considers. These variables are measured at different heights. Testing and training with a dataset that includes historical data from wind farms allows us to evaluate the model's efficacy and reliability. This inquiry has a dual purpose: Building a trustworthy model that can accurately forecast wind turbine power production should be the primary goal. Secondly, we want to see how well neural networks do at maximising wind power generation. By carefully analyzing data and testing models, this project hopes to make a contribution to wind turbine optimization. Consequently, wind power will be pushed harder to be a part of the energy mix. A gap in using comprehensive meteorological data at different heights to increase prediction accuracy still exists, even if wind power forecasting has advanced. Less accurate predictions are generally the result of traditional models' inadequacy to deal with the complexity and unpredictability of such data. Improving the accuracy of forecasts requires cutting-edge technologies that can efficiently combine these varied inputs. In order to predict how much power wind turbines would produce based on extensive weather data, this study recommends using a feed-forward neural network model. With the addition of height-specific measurements of variables including temperature, relative humidity, dew point, wind speed, and wind direction, this model aims to improve the accuracy of power output estimates. Rigid testing and training utilizing data from previously operational wind farms will be used to assess the model's efficiency.

This research contributes to the field of wind power forecasting in several ways:

- Development of a neural network model that integrates diverse meteorological inputs for enhanced forecast accuracy.
- Comprehensive evaluation of the model's performance using historical data, providing insights into its practical applicability.
- Advancement of wind turbine optimization techniques, potentially leading to more efficient and reliable wind energy production.

The following is the structure of the remaining portions of this work after that point: Sect. 67.2 provides a synopsis of pertinent research on neural network applications and wind power forecasting. In Sect. 67.3, which lays out the strategy used to build the neural network model, the methods for gathering and preparing the data are covered. The experimental setup and findings are detailed in the fourth part, which also includes a thorough evaluation of the model's performance. Section 67.5 delves into the potential options for more study as well as the implications of the results. Section 67.6, which summarizes the study's most significant contributions and findings, concludes the paper.

67.2 Literature Review

Assuring effective operation of the power system and integration of wind power into it relies heavily on accurate predictions of the amount of electricity that wind turbines will generate. There have been a plethora of literature studies looking into the many ways wind turbine power forecasts are made [6–12]. The various approaches have been the subject of several evaluations for the purpose of gathering more information. [13]. The removal of the standard deviation proved this to be true. Accurately predicting wind power is critical for achieving global sustainable growth over prolonged periods of time. However, wind power is notoriously difficult to predict since it is an unpredictable energy source that experiences large fluctuations. An innovative data-driven approach with wind generation forecasting skills is the suggested solution to this problem [14, 15]. This method encompasses a wide range of operations that are necessary for anomaly detection. Resampling and data preparation are two of the many phases involved in this process. This strategy's foundational gated recurrent deep learning models are described and this methodology is being specified in a systematic way for the first time. In the prediction model, twelve engineered qualities make up the framework [16].

As far as wind power forecasting simulations are concerned, the proposed approach minimizes computational costs without sacrificing accuracy. Because the strategy was put out, this was proven. In terms of prediction accuracy, GRU outperforms LSTM in every study that was conducted [17]. This was true irrespective of the type of experiment. For proper evaluation of offshore wind energy and maintenance management of large wind turbines, accurate and energy-efficient short-term wind power estimates are essential. That is why it is critical to have accurate and efficient wind power estimations. On the other side, wind power forecasting is a difficult issue to study due to the unpredictable nature of wind in offshore locations. This model was developed to regulate the various components of a power time series from a Scottish offshore wind turbine, which displays both linear and nonlinear characteristics. The primary motivation for creating the paradigm was to facilitate the simultaneous administration of various components. According to exhaustive testing [18], the Discrete Wavelet Transform-Seasonal Autoregressive Integrated Moving Average-Long Short-term Memory model fared better than any other test when it came to capturing the one-of-a-kind time-series patterns that are found in offshore wind power data. Without a doubt, there is no other model that even comes close to matching its performance. A completely new hybrid forecasting model was created in order to estimate the amount of electricity that is produced by several wind turbines on an hourly basis. Most importantly, this model takes into consideration the temporal and geographical correlations between environmental factors and electricity production.

For the purpose of capturing dynamic patterns and the features of wind propagation, the K-means method was created. This novel method of grouping was developed with the aim of capturing these patterns. Wind turbines are designed to be very adaptive through the use of hierarchical clustering. To extract the primary components of wind power, we must next apply the Singular Value Decomposition (SVD) approach to each cluster. Following that, SVR models are generated for these primary elements. The power output estimates for each turbine are derived using inverse SVD based on the forecasts made by these models. The procedure is carried out again and again until precise estimations are obtained. When compared to other models that are used for short-term forecasting, the recommended model achieves a better degree of accuracy, according to research that was conducted on prediction [19]. Because of this contrast, this is the conclusion that can be drawn. Two distinct approaches have been proposed as potential ways to improve the accuracy of probabilistic wind power forecast. The information that is obtained from the turbine level is important to methodologies such as this one. In order to construct a wind farm forecasting model, the first method may be utilized. This method involves the utilization of deterministic power projections from individual turbines as explanatory variables. In order to compute the wind farm projection, the second technique makes use of a bottom-up hierarchical approach. This method is based on the anticipated distribution of power output from each turbine separately. The wind farm forecast is achieved by doing this. Both methods show steady improvements in their ability to correctly predict events when compared to reference models [20].

Physical, statistical, and hybrid methodologies were all included of the comprehensive examination of wind power forecasting methods [21–26]. Each of these approaches was a part of the research. The examination also considered hybrid techniques in addition to these tactics. This paper's goal was to conduct a bibliometric study of models for wind turbine power and wind speed forecasts across various power system segments. The inquiry could not have been finalized without doing this study. In keeping with the anticipated time range, the study identifies trends and uses of the forecast model [27]. When choosing forecast providers, managing forecast accuracy, and building models, the evaluation of wind power estimates stands out as a very important aspect. Validating wind power estimates has been the focus of many separate verification frameworks and diagnostic approaches. We shall go into more detail about these frameworks and approaches later on. Still, before anything else, you must make sure that the assessment evaluation results are relevant and that the evaluation methods are applicable to many circumstances [28] (Table 67.1).

Table 67.1 Summary of literature review

Authors	Contributions
[6–12]	Examined various ways wind turbine power forecasts are made
[13]	Evaluated various approaches to gather more information on wind turbine power forecasts
[14, 15]	Proposed an innovative data-driven approach with wind generation forecasting skills, including anomaly detection and data preparation phases. Introduced gated recurrent deep learning models for the first time in a systematic way
[16]	Described the twelve engineered qualities that make up the framework for the prediction model, aiming to minimize computational costs without sacrificing accuracy
[17]	Conducted studies showing that GRU outperforms LSTM in terms of prediction accuracy, irrespective of the type of experiment
[18]	Developed a model to regulate the components of a power time series from a Scottish offshore wind turbine
[19]	Developed a new model considering temporal and geographical correlations between environmental factors and electricity production. Introduced a K-means method for grouping to capture dynamic patterns and features of wind propagation. Applied Singular Value Decomposition (SVD) to extract primary components and used SVR models for power output estimates, achieving higher accuracy than other short-term forecasting models
[20]	Employed a bottom-up hierarchical approach based on projected power generation distribution from each turbine. Both methods showed steady improvements compared to reference models
[21]	Conducted a comprehensive examination of wind power forecasting methods, including physical, statistical, and hybrid methodologies. Performed a bibliometric study of models for wind turbine power and wind speed forecasts across various power system segments. Identified trends and uses of the forecast model over the anticipated time range
[23]	Highlighted the importance of validating wind power estimates using various verification frameworks and diagnostic approaches. Emphasized the relevance of assessment evaluation results and the applicability of evaluation methods to multiple circumstances

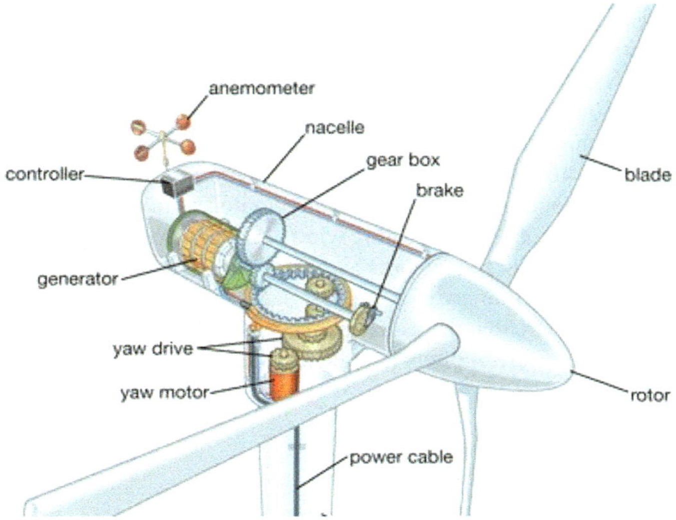

Fig. 67.1 Components of a wind turbine [3]

67.3 Materials and Methods

67.3.1 Wind Turbines

Wind turbines are essential devices in global renewable energy initiatives. Wind turbines are able to harness the kinetic energy of the wind, which in turn turn a generator into usable power. Turbine design, location selection, and environmental conditions are a few of the elements that affect how efficient and successful this conversion process is [3] (Fig. 67.1).

67.3.2 Types of Wind Turbines

Most wind turbines are HAWTs, which are defined by a tower-mounted generator and a horizontal rotor shaft that faces the wind. Virtually axis-symmetric wind turbines (VAWTs) are able to capture wind from any direction since their rotor shaft is vertically orientated [4].

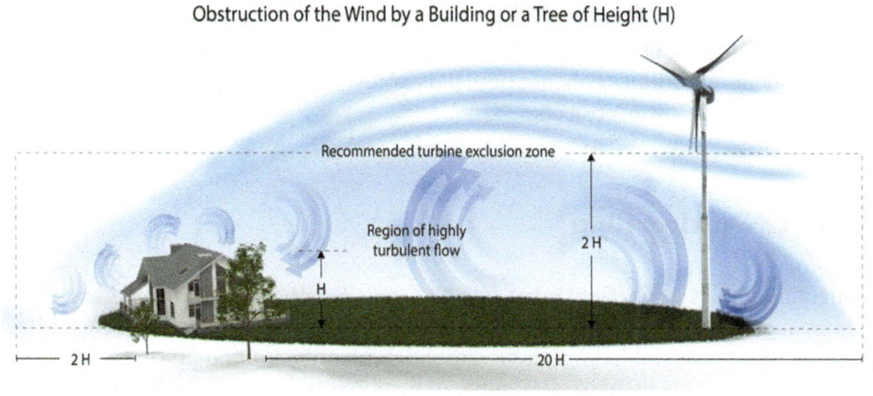

Fig. 67.2 Wind speed and direction and a factor of wind turbine performance [5]

67.3.3 Performance Factors [5]

Wind turbine efficiency is highly conditional on the location's wind resource features, such as wind speed, direction, and fluctuation. Important other variables are air density and temperature. Performance is also impacted by the turbine's design and technology, namely by its rotor diameter, tower height, and control systems (Fig. 67.2).

67.3.4 Technological Advancements [29]

Recent advancements in wind turbine technology have focused on enhancing the efficiency and reducing the cost of generating wind electricity with these devices. Innovations such as enhancements to materials and aerodynamics, together with larger rotor diameters and taller towers, are examples of upgrades [29]. Smart technologies that incorporate sensors and control systems can be used to optimize the effeciency and lifespan of wind turbines. These systems have the capability to adjust their functioning in real-time to accommodate fluctuations in wind conditions.

67.3.5 Role in Renewable Energy

One aspect of the global shift towards sustainable energy sources is the implementation of wind turbines. They offer a more environmentally friendly alternative to fossil fuels. Wind turbines are very adaptable and may be utilized in many settings, ranging from isolated areas to offshore sites, thanks to their scalability [30]. As wind energy continues to grow and expand, the need for efficient and reliable wind turbines is becoming increasingly significant. Technological developments and performance enhancements of turbines enhance both the worldwide energy output and the financial viability of wind power projects.

67.4 CNN Algorithm

Convolutional Neural Networks (CNNs) are mostly utilized for image data processing, representing an advanced form of neural network. They have been utilized for many purposes, including photo and video identification, picture classification, medical image analysis, and other applications. CNNs employ convolution as a mathematical procedure, which is a particular type of linear operation. Feature extraction and object recognition in images are two examples of the many applications that CNNs excel at because of their reputation for spotting complex patterns in data [31] (Fig. 67.3).

67.4.1 Essentials of Convolutional Neural Networks

CNNs stand out from other types of neural networks because of the convolutional layers they use, which allow for a more localized pattern of connections between neurons in nearby layers. The input volume is transformed into an output volume, such class scores, by use of differentiable functions in a multi-layer Convolutional Neural Network (CNN) [32]. Included in this are the following layers: A convolutional neural network (CNN) relies on its convolutional layer. Applying a convolutional filter to subsets of the input data and passing the results on to the next layer is how it performs a convolutional operation. Unlike more conventional approaches, this layer may learn to acquire the filters on its own. The Convolutional Neural Network

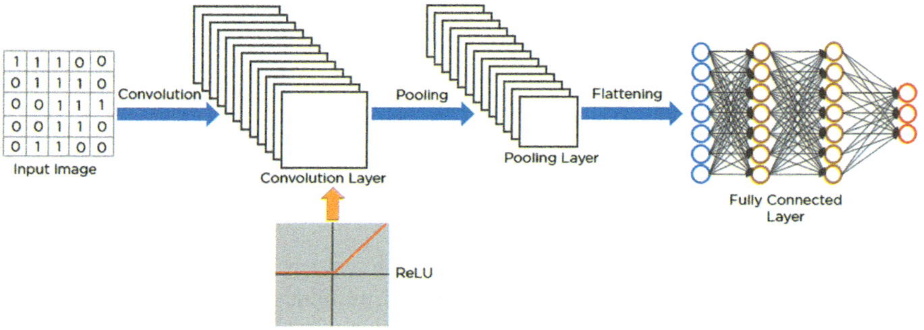

Fig. 67.3 CNN algorithm layers [31]

(CNN) is able to adapt and accept different types of input, especially images, through the learning process. The Activation Layer, sometimes called the ReLU Layer, adds non-linear properties to the system, which help the neural network interpret complex patterns better [33]. Most convolutional neural networks (CNNs) employ the Rectified Linear Unit (ReLU) activation function. Overfitting can be reduced in this way. One common method of pooling data is max pooling, which involves adding all of the highest values in a certain area. An entirely linked layer is one in which each neuron is associated with every activation in the layer below it. Consequently, the whole input volume might affect the activations of these neurons. Like regular neural networks, Convolutional Neural Networks (CNNs) often have these layers at the very bottom of their architectures; they can improve classification results [34].

67.4.2 Overview of Architecture

Feature extractors from the input picture are typically accomplished via a sequence of convolutional and pooling layers in a conventional CNN configuration. Following this, fully connected layers are added; their job is to classify the features that the convolutional layers have collected. In order to make the outputs of the last fully connected layer appropriate for classification tasks, they are transformed into values that resemble probabilities using a softmax activation function [35].

67.4.3 Utilization of Non-Image Data

They may be used to non-image data by seeing it as a one-dimensional (1D) or two-dimensional (2D) array. Convolutional Neural Networks (CNNs) are useful for time series forecasting because they can pick up on small-scale trends and patterns that larger neural networks miss [36].

67.4.4 Benefits of Wind Turbine Applications

Despite CNNs' relative obscurity, they may be ingeniously employed to forecast wind turbine power output by transforming sensor data from the past (including wind speed, direction, and temperature) into a CNN-friendly format. This might enhance the model's capacity to detect complex patterns across several variables. On the other hand, Convolutional Neural Networks (CNNs) excel at processing data with a spatial structure that is similar to that of time-series data collected from wind turbines, therefore this approach requires meticulous data preparation [37].

67.5 Proposed Method

Within the scope of this research, a neural network model is proposed as a means of predicting the amount of electricity that wind turbines would generate. Preprocessing the data, training neural networks to recognize wind condition patterns, and using the model to anticipate power production are the three essential phases that make up the approach. In the next part, a comprehensive description of the procedures that were utilized to enhance the accuracy of the model in estimating the power output of wind turbines is provided. Specifically, it addresses the process of preparing the dataset, developing the neural network, and training the model. Preprocessing the data is an essential step that must be taken in order to guarantee the accuracy and dependability of the input data that will be utilized for training the neural network. The dataset contains a variety of meteorological factors that were recorded at varying heights. These parameters include temperature, relative humidity, dew point, wind speed, and wind direction. The capacity of a feed-forward neural network to simulate complicated non-linear interactions is the reason why it was selected for this particular research assignment. The neural network's architecture is comprised of the following:

- Input Layer: Made up of neurons that match the amount of input characteristics (such as temperature, relative humidity, dew point, wind speed, and wind direction at different heights).
- Hidden Layers: Different amount of neurons in each of the buried levels. The Rectified Linear Unit (ReLU) is the activation function utilized in these layers; it facilitates the learning of complicated patterns by introducing nonlinearity.
- Output Layer: Just one neuron is responsible for predicting the wind turbine's power output. Since we are addressing a regression problem, the activation function usually utilized is linear.

The architecture can be represented as follows:
Input → Dense (ReLU) → Dense (ReLU) → … → Dense (Linear).
The model training process involves the following steps:
The loss function used to assess the difference between the expected and actual power outputs is the mean squared error (MSE).

$$MSE = (1/n) * \Sigma(yi - \hat{y}_i)^2 \tag{67.1}$$

The variable yi represents the actual power output, whereas Þi represents the expected power output. The variable n represents the number of data points. We went with the Adam optimizer because of its effectiveness and versatility in terms of adjusting the learning rate while the training is being done. In order to minimize the loss function, the optimizer makes adjustments to the weights of the network. During the training phase, the input data are sent through the network, the loss is computed, and the error is backpropagated in order to update the weights. For a predetermined amount of epochs, this procedure is carried out repeatedly until the model reaches a solution that is suitable for all circumstances. Make use of the validation set in order to keep track of the performance of the model while it is being trained and to avoid overfitting. In the event that the validation loss does not continue to improve, early halting may be an option. After the model has been trained, it is utilized to make predictions regarding the amount of electricity that wind turbines consume. Involved in the procedure are:

- Input Preparation: Prepare the input features based on current meteorological data.
- Prediction: Use the trained neural network to predict the power output.
- Evaluation: Evaluate the model's performance using the test set. Metrics such as the root mean squared error (RMSE) and R-squared (R^2) are used to assess the accuracy and reliability of the predictions.

67.5.1 Data Preparation

Several operational and meteorological characteristics collected from wind turbines make up the collection. Included in this analysis are the following parameters: temperature at two meters, relative humidity at two meters, dew point at two meters, wind speeds at ten and one hundred meters, wind directions at ten meters, and wind gusts at ten meters. It is the intention of this undertaking to forecast the electricity output of wind turbines. Our group was able to successfully acquire a Kaggle dataset tailored for the analysis and prediction of wind turbine power generation. The meteorological data points and wind characteristics included in this specific collection were collected from a variety of heights. The following sections provide an in-depth analysis of the dataset's columns and an explanation of how those columns may be used to create wind turbine power generation prediction models (Fig. 67.4).

The Table 67.2 provides an overview of environmental factors that impact wind turbine performance. These factors include temperature, humidity, wind speed, and direction at different heights above the surface. Understanding these variables is crucial for optimizing wind energy conversion.

The bar graph in Fig. 67.5 displays various environmental variables related to wind turbine performance. This graph helps analyze patterns and correlations between environmental conditions and wind turbine efficiency.

To prepare the data for the neural network, all feature variables are normalized. Normalization ensures that the scale of the measurements does not bias the neural network [38]; it allows the model to train more efficiently and converge faster. The normalization process converts each feature to a scale from 0 to 1.

67.5.2 Neural Network Architecture

The neural network used in this study is a feed-forward network with the following layers:

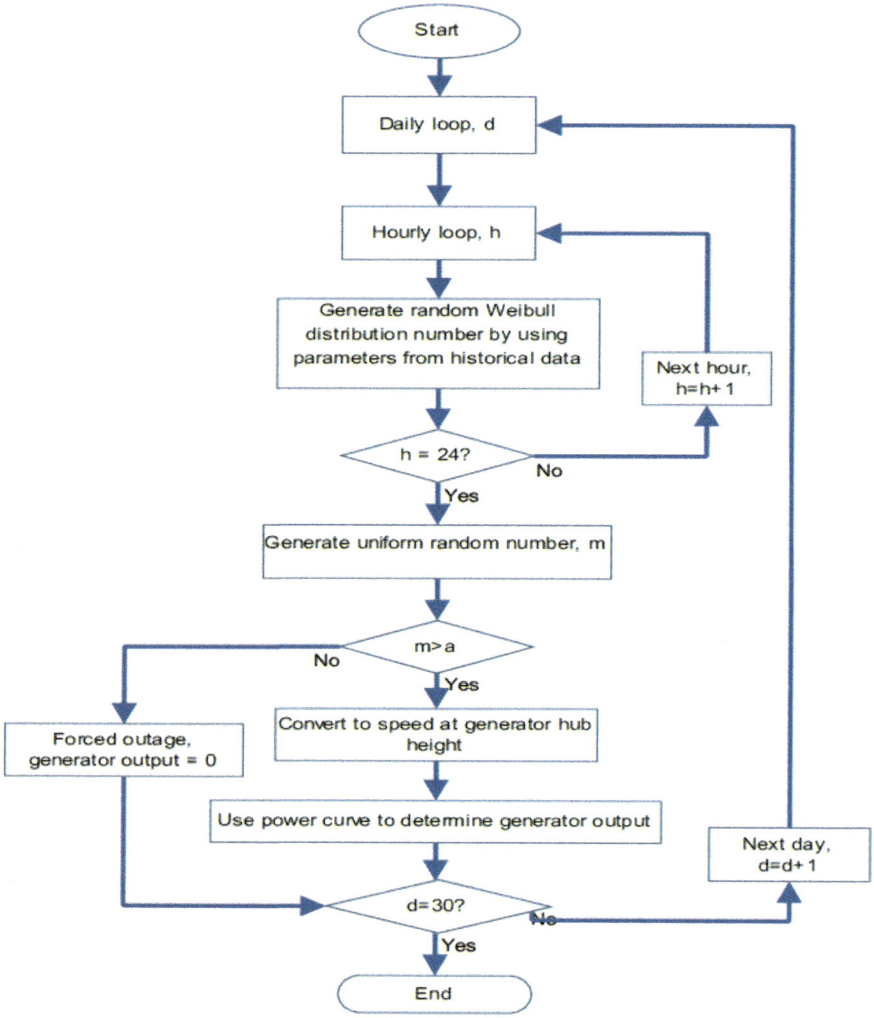

Fig. 67.4 Process diagram of the proposed wind turbine

- Input Layer: Accepts the normalized features as input.
- Fully Connected Layers: Multiple layers that allow the network to learn non-linear interactions between features. Each layer is followed by a ReLU (Rectified Linear Unit) activation function to introduce non-linearity to the model, helping it to learn more complex patterns.
- Output Layer: A single neuron with a linear activation function to predict the continuous value of the wind turbine's power output (Table 67.3).

Table 67.2 Environmental factors affecting wind turbine performance

Feature	Description
A. Time	Represents the occurrence hour (likely in 24-h format) when measurements were taken
B. temperature_2m	Influences air density and turbine efficiency
C. relativehumidity_2m	Impacts air density and turbine performance
D. dewpoint_2m	Related to absolute moisture content and conditions
E. windspeed_10m	Correlated with turbine potential energy
F. windspeed_100m	Relevant for large turbines' hub height
G. winddirection_10m	Affects turbine efficiency based on orientation

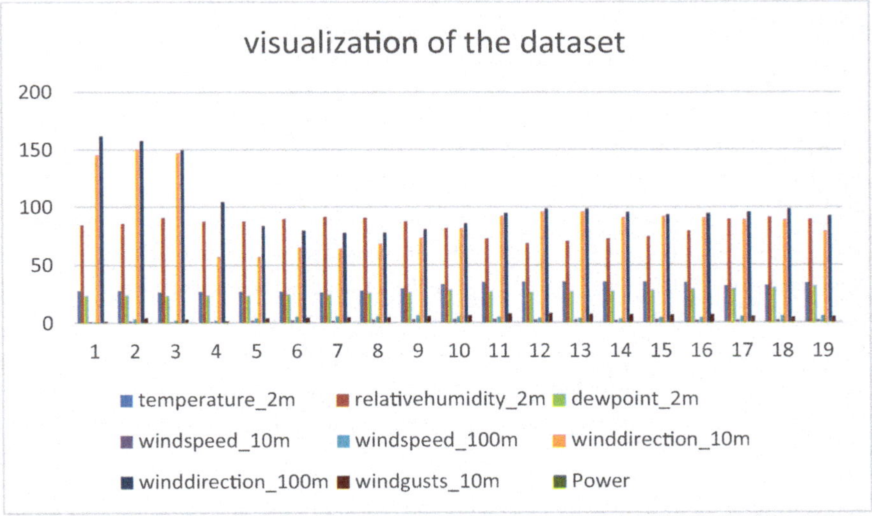

Fig. 67.5 Visualization of the wind turbine dataset

67.5.3 Training Process

The training of the neural network is performed using the following settings and methodologies:

The versatility of the Adam optimizer, together with its skill in controlling sparse gradients, makes it a good fit for datasets with a dense feature set. With the Mean Squared Error (MSE) loss function, the network is trained. This loss function penalizes the variance between the predicted and observed values, making it beneficial for regression challenges. A validation set is created from the training set and used to track the model's performance throughout training. Because of this, overfitting may be caught early on in the training period. The model's hyperparameters, such as

Table 67.3 CNN layers and their parameters

Layer type	Description	Parameters
Feature input layer	Input layer for features	Number of features: size (XTrain,2)
Fully connected layer	Fully connected layer with 50 neurons	Neurons: 50
ReLU layer	Rectified Linear Activation Layer	N/A
Fully connected layer	Second fully connected layer with 50 neurons	Neurons: 50
ReLU layer	Second Rectified Linear Activation Layer	N/A
Fully connected layer	Output layer for regression	Neurons: 1 (Output size for regression)
Regression layer	Measures and computes the loss for regression tasks	N/A

Table 67.4 Training parameters of the proposed CNN

Parameter	Value	Description
Solver	Adam	Optimization algorithm for learning the weights
Max epochs	100	Maximum number of epochs for training
Mini batch size	10	Number of samples per gradient update
Initial learn rate	0.01	The initial learning rate for training
L2 regularization	0.004	Regularization term to prevent overfitting
Validation data	Provided XTest, YTest	Data used to validate the model during training
Plots	'training-progress'	Visualization of training progress during execution

its layer count, neuron density per layer, and learning rate, are fine-tuned according on the results on the validation set. Before deploying the model, it is trained for a fixed number of epochs using mini batches. Improving the model weights by training on batches of data across several epochs helps to progressively minimize the loss function. This is achieved by regular instruction (Table 67.4).

67.6 Performance Evaluation

To determine how well the model predicts the power output, one measure of performance is the Root Mean Squared Error (RMSE). Following the training phase, this measure is calculated and subsequently applied to the test set. The model's performance improves as the RMSE value drops (Figs. 67.6 and 67.7 and Table 67.5).

The approach that has been suggested makes use of the predictive capabilities of neural networks in order to estimate the amount of power that has been generated

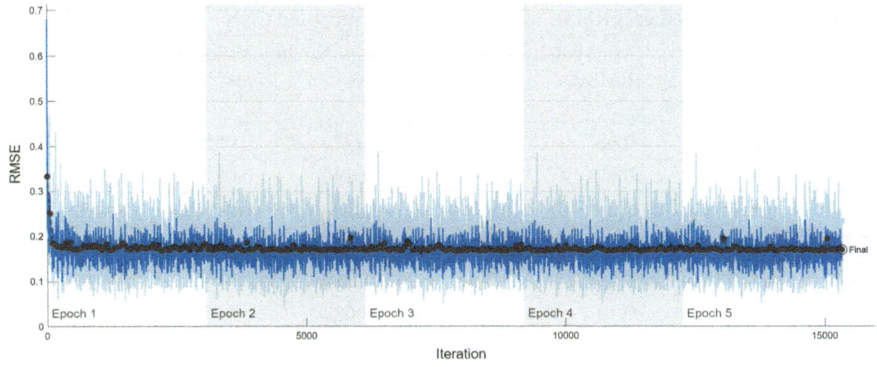

Fig. 67.6 RMSE of the proposed model in 5 epochs

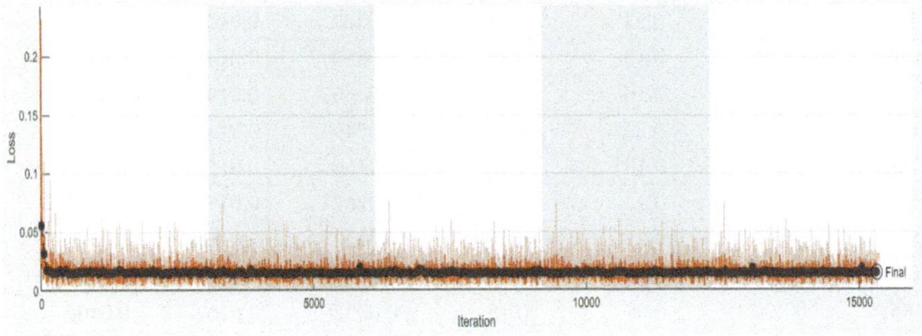

Fig. 67.7 Validation loss of the proposed model in 5 epochs

by wind turbines by using data from both operational and meteorological sources. Through meticulous data preparation, the creation of a strong neural network architecture, and the implementation of a systematic training method, this strategy intends to improve the operational efficiency of wind energy production as well as the accuracy of its forecasts. This technique not only makes a significant addition to the field of renewable energy, but it also offers a framework that can be scaled up for future study and practical applications in the field of wind turbine energy management.

67.7 Conclusions and Future Work

This study demonstrates that neural networks may be taught to effectively utilize various meteorological data in order to accurately forecast the power output of wind turbines. The model was trained using several variables, including temperature, humidity, wind speed, and wind direction, at different elevations. The wind's

Table 67.5 Training process RMSE over iteration of the proposed CNN

Iteration	Time elapsed (hh:mm:ss)	Mini-batch RMSE	Validation RMSE	Mini-batch loss	Validation loss	Base learning rate
1	00:00:02	0.68	0.33	0.2329	0.0555	0.0100
50	00:00:03	0.17	0.25	0.0140	0.0314	0.0100
100	00:00:04	0.24	0.18	0.0289	0.0170	0.0100
150	00:00:05	0.25	0.18	0.0304	0.0164	0.0100
200	00:00:06	0.06	0.18	0.0019	0.0155	0.0100
250	00:00:07	0.13	0.18	0.0083	0.0155	0.0100
300	00:00:08	0.21	0.17	0.0227	0.0152	0.0100
350	00:00:09	0.21	0.19	0.0221	0.0172	0.0100
400	00:00:10	0.16	0.17	0.0131	0.0152	0.0100
450	00:00:11	0.17	0.19	0.0146	0.0172	0.0100
500	00:00:12	0.23	0.17	0.0262	0.0145	0.0100
550	00:00:13	0.13	0.17	0.0080	0.0147	0.0100
600	00:00:14	0.16	0.17	0.0136	0.0145	0.0100
650	00:00:15	0.22	0.17	0.0249	0.0148	0.0100
700	00:00:16	0.18	0.18	0.0160	0.0158	0.0100
750	00:00:17	0.23	0.18	0.0262	0.0154	0.0100
800	00:00:17	0.21	0.18	0.0222	0.0161	0.0100
850	00:00:18	0.19	0.18	0.0174	0.0154	0.0100
900	00:00:19	0.08	0.18	0.0032	0.0163	0.0100
950	00:00:20	0.14	0.18	0.0100	0.0154	0.0100
1000	00:00:21	0.13	0.18	0.0091	0.0158	0.0100

direction was an additional variable. Throughout the testing phase, it achieved the minimum possible root mean squared error, suggesting favorable results in terms of power generation prediction. The results of this study indicate that the utilization of machine learning algorithms might enhance the efficiency and reliability of wind turbines. An area of study with significant potential is the integration of real-time data gathering equipment with predictive models to provide dynamic modifications in wind turbine operations. By utilizing real-time data streams, the model included the latest environmental conditions into its estimations, enabling ongoing enhancement. Consequently, the model was capable of iteratively improving and augmenting its forecasts as time progressed. Moreover, the inclusion of supplementary weather-related factors such as solar irradiation and air pressure has the potential to significantly improve the accuracy of the model. However, there are exciting avenues for future research and improvement for example, integrating real-time data gathering equipment with predictive models could enhance wind turbine operations dynamically. By incorporating up-to-the-minute environmental conditions, the model would continuously adapt its forecasts. This adaptability is crucial for optimizing power generation efficiency.

References

1. Sinsel, S.R., Riemke, R.L., Hoffmann, V.H.: Challenges and solution technologies for the integration of variable renewable energy sources-a review. Renew. Energy **145**, 2271–2285 (2020). [Google Scholar] [CrossRef]
2. Lu, Y., Khan, Z.A., Alvarez-Alvarado, M.S., Zhang, Y., Huang, Z., Imran, M.: A critical review of sustainable energy policies for the promotion of renewable energy sources. Sustainability **12**, 5078 (2020). [Google Scholar] [CrossRef]
3. Qazi, A., Hussain, F., Rahim, N.A., Hardaker, G., Alghazzawi, D., Shaban, K., Haruna, K.: Towards sustainable energy: a systematic review of renewable energy sources, technologies, and public opinions. IEEE Access **7**, 63837–63851 (2019). [Google Scholar] [CrossRef]
4. Razmjoo, A., Gakenia Kaigutha, L., Vaziri Rad, M.A., Marzband, M., Davarpanah, A., Denai, M.: A technical analysis investigating energy sustainability utilizing reliable renewable energy sources to reduce CO2 emissions in a high potential area. Renew. Energy **164**, 46–57 (2021). [Google Scholar] [CrossRef]
5. Jurasz, J., Canales, F.A., Kies, A., Guezgouz, M., Beluco, A.: A review on the complementarity of renewable energy sources: concept, metrics, application and future research directions. Sol. Energy **195**, 703–724 (2020). [Google Scholar] [CrossRef]
6. Zhao, X., Wang, C., Su, J., Wang, J.: Research and application based on the swarm intelligence algorithm and artificial intelligence for wind farm decision system. Renew. Energy **134**, 681–697 (2019). [Google Scholar] [CrossRef]
7. Wang, Y., Zou, R., Liu, F., Zhang, L., Liu, Q.: A review of wind speed and wind power forecasting with deep neural networks. Appl. Energy **304**, 117766 (2021). [Google Scholar] [CrossRef]
8. Nazir, M.S., Alturise, F., Alshmrany, S., Nazir, H.M.J., Bilal, M., Abdalla, A.N., Sanjeevikumar, P., Ali, Z.M.: Wind generation forecasting methods and proliferation of artificial neural network: a review of five years research trend. Sustainability **12**, 3778 (2020). [Google Scholar] [CrossRef]
9. Ekinci, F., Demirdelen, T., Bilgili, M.: Modelling of wind turbine power output by using ANNs and ANFIS techniques. In: Proceedings of the 2017 Seventh International Conference on Innovative Computing Technology (INTECH), Luton, UK, 16–18 August 2017; IEEE: Piscataway, NJ, USA, pp. 126–131 (2017). [Google Scholar]
10. Demirdelen, T., Bakmaz, E., Tumay, M.: A fuzzy neural network approach to estimate PMSG based and DFIG based wind turbines' power generation. In: Proceedings of the 2017 Seventh International Conference on Innovative Computing Technology (INTECH), Luton, UK, 16–18 August 2017; IEEE: Piscataway, NJ, USA, pp. 101–106 (2017). [Google Scholar]
11. Demirdelen, T., Tekin, P., Aksu, I.O., Ekinci, F.: The prediction model of characteristics for wind turbines based on meteorological properties using neural network swarm intelligence. Sustainability **11**, 4803 (2019). [Google Scholar] [CrossRef]
12. Esenboğa, B., Aksu, İ.Ö., Ekinci, F., Demirdelen, T.: Short-term wind speed estimation with ANN based hybrid optimization methods in Çukurova region. Taikom. Tyrim. Stud. Ir Prakt.-Appl. Res. Stud. Pract. **15**, 16–23 (2019). [Google Scholar]
13. Deng, Y.-C., Tang, X.-H., Zhou, Z.-Y., Yang, Y., Niu, F.: Application of machine learning algorithms in wind power: a review. energy sources part A recovery util. Environ. Eff. 1–22 (2021). [Google Scholar] [CrossRef]
14. Manero, J., Béjar, J., Cortés, U.: Wind energy forecasting with neural networks: a literature review. CyS **22** (2018). [Google Scholar] [CrossRef]

15. Lin, W.-H., Wang, P., Chao, K.-M., Lin, H.-C., Yang, Z.-Y., Lai, Y.-H.: Wind power forecasting with deep learning networks: time-series forecasting. Appl. Sci. **11**, 10335 (2021). [Google Scholar] [CrossRef]
16. Demolli, H.: Wind power forecasting based on daily wind speed data using machine learning algorithms. Energy Convers. Manag. **198**, 111823 (2019). [Google Scholar] [CrossRef]
17. Kisvari, A., Lin, Z., Liu, X.: Wind power forecasting-a data-driven method along with gated recurrent neural network. Renew. Energy **163**, 1895–1909 (2021). [Google Scholar] [CrossRef]
18. Zhang, W., Lin, Z., Liu, X.: Short-term offshore wind power forecasting-a hybrid model based on discrete wavelet transform (DWT), seasonal autoregressive integrated moving average (SARIMA), and deep-learning-based long short-term memory (LSTM). Renew. Energy **185**, 611–628 (2022). [Google Scholar] [CrossRef]
19. Wen, S., Li, Y., Su, Y.: A new hybrid model for power forecasting of a wind farm using spatial-temporal correlations. Renew. Energy **198**, 155–168 (2022). [Google Scholar] [CrossRef]
20. Gilbert, C., Browell, J., McMillan, D.: Leveraging turbine-level data for improved probabilistic wind power forecasting. IEEE Trans. Sustain. Energy **11**, 1152–1160 (2020). [Google Scholar] [CrossRef]
21. Hanifi, S., Liu, X., Lin, Z., Lotfian, S.: A critical review of wind power forecasting methods-past, present and future. Energies **13**, 3764 (2020). [Google Scholar] [CrossRef]
22. Abdulrazzaq, M.M., et al.: Consequential advancements of self-supervised learning (SSL) in deep learning contexts. Mathematics 12(5), 758 (2024)
23. Zainulabdeen, D.S., Mesut Ç., Mohammed M.A.: A comparative study of classification algorithms for sentiment analysis of Covid-19 vaccine opinions using machine learning. In: 2024 International Congress on Human-Computer Interaction, Optimization and Robotic Applications (HORA). IEEE (2024)
24. Al Zakitat, M.A.S., et al.: Harnessing advanced techniques for image steganography: sequential and random encoding with deep learning detection. In: International Conference on Emerging Trends and Applications in Artificial Intelligence. Cham: Springer Nature Switzerland (2023)
25. Ismael, O.A., et al.: Exploring lightweight blockchain solutions for internet of things. In: International Conference on Emerging Trends and Applications in Artificial Intelligence. Cham: Springer Nature Switzerland (2023)
26. Mohammed, R.Q., et al.: Enhancing smart grid efficiency: a modified ANN-LSTM approach for energy storage and distribution optimization. In: 2023 7th International Symposium on Multidisciplinary Studies and Innovative Technologies (ISMSIT). IEEE (2023)
27. Lagos, A., Caicedo, J.E., Coria, G., Quete, A.R., Martínez, M., Suvire, G., Riquelme, J.: State-of-the-art using bibliometric analysis of wind-speed and -power forecasting methods applied in power systems. Energies **15**, 6545 (2022). [Google Scholar] [CrossRef]
28. Messner, J.W., Pinson, P., Browell, J., Bjerregård, M.B., Schicker, I.: Evaluation of wind power forecasts-an up-to-date view. Wind. Energy **23**, 1461–1481 (2020). [Google Scholar] [CrossRef]
29. Ryberg, D.S., Caglayan, D.G., Schmitt, S., Linßen, J., Stolten, D., Robinius, M.: The future of European onshore wind energy potential: detailed distribution and simulation of advanced turbine designs. Energy **182**, 1222–1238 (2019). [Google Scholar] [CrossRef]
30. Roga, S., Bardhan, S., Kumar, Y., Dubey, S.K.: Recent technology and challenges of wind energy generation: a review. Sustain. Energy Technol. Assess. **52**, 102239 (2022). [Google Scholar] [CrossRef]
31. Sadorsky, P.: Wind energy for sustainable development: driving factors and future outlook. J. Clean. Prod. **289**, 125779 (2021). [Google Scholar] [CrossRef]
32. Peng, X., Liu, Z., Jiang, D.: A review of multiphase energy conversion in wind power generation. Renew. Sustain. Energy Rev. **147**, 111172 (2021). [Google Scholar] [CrossRef]
33. Veers, P., Bottasso, C.L., Manuel, L., Naughton, J., Pao, L., Paquette, J., Robertson, A., Robinson, M., Ananthan, S., Barlas, T., et al.: Grand challenges in the design, manufacture, and operation of future wind turbine systems. Wind Energy Sci. **8**, 1071–1131 (2023). [Google Scholar] [CrossRef]

34. Yavuzdeger, A., Esenboga, B., Ekinci, F., Demirdelen, T.: Design and finite element analysis of permanent magnet synchronous generator for wind turbine application. In: Numerical Methods for Energy Applications; Springer: Berlin/Heidelberg, Germany, pp. 823–845 (2021). [Google Scholar]
35. Ahmadi, A., Nabipour, M., Mohammadi-Ivatloo, B., Amani, A.M., Rho, S., Piran, M.J.: Long-term wind power forecasting using tree-based learning algorithms. IEEE Access **8**, 151511–151522 (2020). [Google Scholar] [CrossRef]
36. Kosovic, B., Haupt, S.E., Adriaansen, D., Alessandrini, S., Wiener, G., Monache, L.D., Liu, Y., Linden, S., Jensen, T., Cheng, W., et al.: A comprehensive wind power forecasting system integrating artificial intelligence and numerical weather prediction. Energies **13**, 1372 (2020). [Google Scholar] [CrossRef]
37. Wu, Q., Guan, F., Lv, C., Huang, Y.: Ultra-short-term multi-step wind power forecasting based on CNN-LSTM. IET Renew. Power Gen **15**, 1019–1029 (2021). [Google Scholar] [CrossRef]
38. Aksu, İ.Ö.: Next-month prediction of hourly solar irradiance based on long short-term memory network. Çukurova Üniversitesi Mühendislik Fakültesi Derg. **38**, 225–232 (2023). [Google Scholar] [CrossRef]

Chapter 68
Deep Learning-Based Brain Tumor Classification for Medical Image Analysis

Rayan Bribesh, Esraa Mohammed Alazzawi, Alaa Ali Hameed, Akhtar Jamil, and Faezeh Soleimani

Abstract Brain tumors, particularly aggressive variants, drastically diminish life expectancy. This study endeavors to enhance the early detection and classification of brain tumors, focusing on glioma, meningioma, and pituitary tumors through a comprehensive methodological approach. Utilizing advanced deep learning techniques, including Convolutional Neural Networks (CNNs) augmented by transfer learning, we employ pre-trained models such as the Visual Geometry Group's 16-layer network (VGG-16) and the 50-layer Residual Network (ResNet50). Additionally, we integrate traditional machine learning methods like Support Vector Machines (SVM), Random Forest (RF), and K-Nearest Neighbors (KNN) to further refine our analysis. The CNN models, particularly when enhanced with transfer learning, demonstrate exceptional diagnostic accuracy. Specifically, the CNN model achieved a notable accuracy rate of 93.90% and an F1 score of 93.07%. This research highlights the significant potential of artificial intelligence in healthcare diagnostics, particularly in medical image analysis for brain tumor classification, offering profound implications for improving patient outcomes.

R. Bribesh
Department of Artificial Intelligence Engineering, Istinye University, Istanbul, Turkey
e-mail: rayanfathinaser.bribesh@stu.istinye.edu.tr

E. M. Alazzawi
Department of Computer Engineering, University of Baghdad, Al-Jadriya, Baghdad, Iraq
e-mail: israa.abd2005@coeng.uobaghdad.edu.iq

A. A. Hameed
Department of Computer Engineering, Istinye University, Istanbul, Turkey
e-mail: alaa.hameed@istinye.edu.tr

A. Jamil (✉)
Department of Computer Science, National University of Computer and Emerging Sciences, Islamabad, Pakistan
e-mail: akhtar.jamil@nu.edu.pk

F. Soleimani
Department of Mathematical Sciences, Ball State University, Muncie, IN, USA
e-mail: fsoleimani@bsu.edu

F. P. García Márquez et al. (eds.), *Computing, Internet of Things and Data Analytics*, Smart Innovation, Systems and Technologies 387,
https://doi.org/10.1007/978-3-031-87154-2_68

68.1 Introduction

Brain tumors, which are abnormal cell growths within the brain, significantly threaten health by potentially impairing cognitive functions [1]. The challenge lies in promptly and accurately identifying these tumors, as their symptoms are often varied and can easily be mistaken for other neurological conditions [2]. This research seeks to address the urgent need for more effective and precise diagnostic tools. It leverages advanced deep learning techniques, including Convolutional Neural Networks (CNNs) with transfer learning, to enhance the early detection and classification of brain tumors. The study utilizes transfer learning with state-of-the-art pre-trained models such as VGG-16 and ResNet50, which are leading CNN architectures. The goal is to harness the power of large datasets to improve the early detection and classification of brain tumors. Alongside CNNs, this study will also evaluate other methods like Support Vector Machines (SVM), Random Forest (RF), and K-Nearest Neighbors (KNN) to ascertain the most accurate and practical diagnostic approach.

Ayadi et al. [3] applied CNNs for brain tumor classification, achieving 98.43% accuracy in detecting pituitary tumors, outperforming previous methods. Their approach, enhanced with data augmentation, demonstrated superior performance across metrics such as sensitivity, specificity, precision, and F1-score, showcasing the potential of CNNs in medical imaging.

Anita and Kumaran [4] focused on classifying meningioma tumors from brain MRIs using a tailored CNN model. They utilized normalization techniques and data augmentation to enhance image quality, achieving 98.15% accuracy. Their Dense CNN (DEN) model outperformed both SVM and KNN, with significantly lower training loss and higher accuracy.

Liu et al. [5] addressed the challenge of limited data in segmenting rare pediatric brain tumors, specifically diffuse midline gliomas (DMG). By transferring knowledge from adult brain tumor datasets, they improved segmentation accuracy for these rare pediatric cases, illustrating the potential of transfer learning in addressing data scarcity.

Bhardwaj et al. demonstrated that a CNN-based framework could accurately classify brain tumors, achieving 95.6% accuracy on MRI datasets through effective fine-tuning [6]. Ghesu et al. extended this work with self-supervised learning from 100 million medical images, enhancing model generalization [7].

Prakash et al. employed DenseNet with global average pooling and hyperparameter tuning, achieving 97.5% accuracy, showcasing the model's robustness for real-world medical applications [8]. Vankdothu et al. introduced a CNN-LSTM hybrid model, which excelled in extracting features and classifying brain tumors with high precision [9]. Similarly, Swati et al. utilized transfer learning with VGG-19, reaching a classification accuracy of 94.5%, highlighting the power of pre-trained models in medical imaging [10].

Capsule Networks, maintaining spatial hierarchies, showed promise when applied by Kurup et al., achieving a 92.6% accuracy in classifying brain tumors [11]. Hybrid approaches, like Bhardwaj et al.'s combination of CNN with SVM, further enhanced classification accuracy to 96.4% [6]. Additionally, ensemble learning techniques, like those used by Sandhiya et al., reduced overfitting and achieved 97.3% accuracy [12].

Remzan et al. [13] utilized ensemble learning for feature extraction in brain MRI classification, demonstrating improved classification accuracy by integrating machine learning classifiers such as SVM and KNN, which showed high robustness in handling medical image data.

Vimala et al. [14] proposed a hybrid deep learning model, combining CNN and machine learning techniques for brain tumor detection and classification, achieving high performance with their model applied to a real-world dataset, demonstrating the strength of hybrid methods in brain tumor diagnosis.

More recent work by Abdullah et al. explored the effectiveness of models like ResNet-50 and VGG-16 for brain tumor classification, achieving accuracies of 92.6% and 92.1%, respectively, using the "Brain Tumors 256 $\times$ 256" dataset [15]. This emphasizes the potential of deep learning models, especially with model fine-tuning, for improving diagnostic accuracy in medical imaging.

This study introduces a unique approach to brain tumor classification that integrates CNNs with transfer learning, utilizing the VGG 16 and ResNet50 architectures. It aims to enhance tumor classification accuracy and early detection of brain tumors, thereby substantially improving patient prognosis and treatment outcomes. This innovative technique sets a new benchmark in medical imaging analysis, markedly advancing the field.

The paper is organized into four main sections. Section 68.2 discusses the datasets used for training and testing. Section 68.3 presents the performance evaluation of the models using accuracy, precision, and recall, supported by comprehensive experimentation and analysis. Finally, Sect. 68.4 summarizes the key findings, highlighting the effectiveness of the proposed models, and offering insights into potential future work.

68.2 Data Acquisition and Model Architecture

See Fig. 68.1.

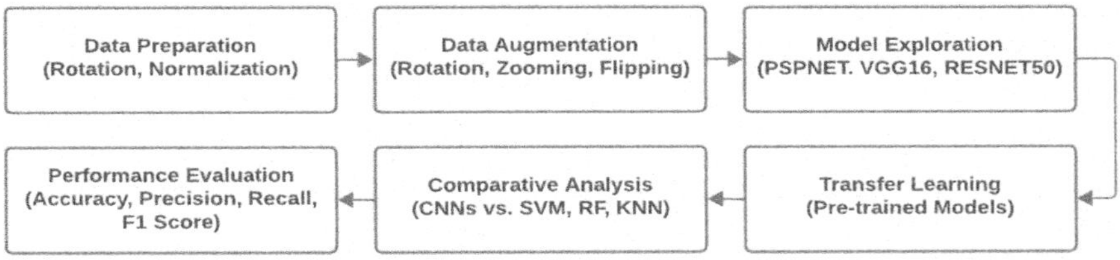

Fig. 68.1 Flow chart of the data acquisition and model architecture

68.2.1 Data Pre-Processing and Augmentation

This research utilizes a publicly available brain tumor dataset from Kaggle and GitHub, curated by Bhuvaji et al. [16]. This dataset is particularly well-suited for classifying brain tumors through machine learning due to its diversity of image samples and sufficient volume for comprehensive analysis. It includes 7,023 T1-weighted contrast-enhanced MRI images, divided into a training set of 5,712 images and a testing set of 1,311 images. These images play a crucial role in distinguishing between different brain tumor tissues.

This study developed an extensive pre-processing pipeline using Python, employing libraries such as OpenCV, NumPy, and Keras to prepare medical imaging data for deep learning-based brain tumor classification. Initially, images were loaded and converted from BGR to RGB color space, aligning with the standard color channel ordering used in most deep learning frameworks. To ensure uniformity for model inputs, all images were resized to a consistent size of 224 by 224 pixels. Pixel values were then normalized to the range [0, 1] by dividing by 255.0, a critical step that aids in faster convergence during model training. Furthermore, class labels were processed using scikit-learn's LabelEncoder to convert string labels into integers, followed by one-hot encoding to create binary class matrices, essential for multi-class classification tasks.

An Image Data Generator from Keras was employed to augment the training data and enhance the robustness of the development. This tool introduced various transformations to the images, such as rotation, width shift, height shift, zoom, and horizontal flip, thereby simulating different viewing angles and positions. This augmentation process was applied to each image in the training set, effectively expanding the training dataset to 11,424 images. This expansion not only helped prevent overfitting but also significantly improved the model's ability to generalize. The effectiveness of these pre-processing and augmentation steps was verified by visualizing sample images from the augmented dataset, ensuring that the diagnostic features of the images were retained post-transformation, thereby maintaining the integrity and utility of the data for subsequent machine learning tasks.

In Fig. 68.2, a selection of nine augmented images from the training set is displayed, showcasing the variety of transformations applied during pre-processing. Each subplot features the image along with its corresponding class label, highlighting the diversity introduced by the data augmentation process. This representation emphasizes the range of modifications that enhance the robustness and generalizability of the training data.

68.2.2 CNN Model Architecture Combination

The CNN architecture for this brain tumor classification project was meticulously engineered using the TensorFlow and Keras libraries, demonstrating the strengths

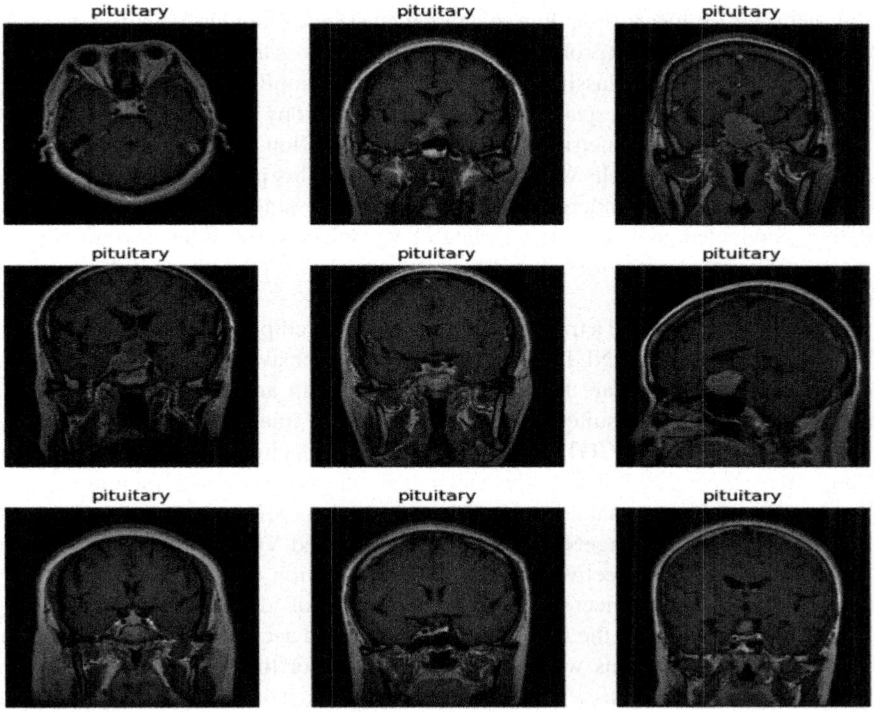

Fig. 68.2 Some samples from the data set containing MRI images

of modern deep learning frameworks. The model incorporates convolutional, max-pooling, and dense layers, culminating in a softmax output layer. It employs the Adam optimizer and a categorical cross-entropy loss function, with extensive training epochs and real-time validation to prevent overfitting. The model's architecture is specifically designed to process two-dimensional images, beginning with an input layer that handles images of 224 × 224 pixels across three color channels. The core of the model consists of four convolutional layers, each followed by a max-pooling layer. The convolutional layers increase in complexity, starting with 32 filters and expanding to 64, 128, and 256 filters in the subsequent layers, all maintaining a uniform 3 × 3 size. The ReLU activation function is consistently used across these layers to introduce non-linearity, enhancing the learning process. Following each convolutional layer, max pooling with a 2 × 2 window reduces the spatial size of the representations, effectively decreasing the number of parameters and computational demand in the network.

After the convolutional and pooling stages, the model transitions into a flattening phase, where the multi-dimensional output is transformed into a one-dimensional vector. This vector is then fed into the dense layers. A dense layer comprising 128 neurons, utilizing ReLU activation, precedes the output layer. This final layer contains four neurons, each corresponding to a target class, and employs the softmax activation function to provide a probabilistic distribution across these classes—an essential feature for multi-class classification. The model's compilation was executed using the Adam optimizer and sparse categorical cross-entropy as the loss function, with accuracy selected as the metric for performance evaluation. The training regimen was carried out over ten epochs with a batch size of 32. This phase involved processing the dataset, which had undergone extensive pre-processing and augmentation. Validation, conducted on a separate test dataset, served as a crucial measure to monitor the model's performance on unfamiliar data, ensuring the robustness of its predictive capabilities.

This study has utilized a transfer learning approach employing pre-trained models such as VGG16 and RESNET50, which have been extensively trained on large image datasets. These models are recognized for their depth and complexity, offering a robust feature set well-suited for brain tumor MRI image analysis. Specifically, the integration of the VGG16 model, a renowned benchmark in image classification, represented a significant advancement in adapting advanced neural network architectures to the specialized task of brain tumor classification. Originating from the vast and diverse ImageNet dataset, the pre-trained VGG16 model was chosen for its demonstrated effectiveness in image recognition tasks. It was then meticulously customized to meet the specific challenges of identifying and classifying brain tumors, enhancing the model's applicability and accuracy in this critical area.

Strategic modifications were implemented to tailor the VGG16 model for the specific application of classifying brain tumors. The first step involved replacing the original classification layers of the VGG16 with custom layers designed to handle the dataset comprising four distinct brain tumor classes. A global average pooling layer was added on top of the VGG16 base to reduce the dimensionality of the feature maps and effectively distill spatial information. This modification was followed by the addition of a dense layer equipped with 1024 neurons and the ReLU activation function, poised to capture high-level features through non-linear transformations. The architectural refinement culminated in the output layer, which consists of four neurons that correspond to the number of target classes, using a softmax activation function to generate a probabilistic distribution across these classes. The modified VGG16 model was compiled with the Adam optimizer and categorical cross-entropy as the loss function, selections that are well-suited for the multi-class classification nature of this task. The performance of the model was evaluated using the accuracy metric. Training the model was a time-intensive endeavor due to the intrinsic complexity of the VGG16 architecture. It underwent rigorous training over 10 epochs with a batch size of 32. Additionally, the model was validated on a separate test dataset to assess and ensure its capability to generalize effectively.

Integrating the ResNet50 model, a prominent example of deep residual learning represents a significant advancement in the classification framework for brain tumor detection. Initially pre-trained on the extensive ImageNet dataset, ResNet50 introduces an innovative approach with skip connections or shortcuts that bypass certain layers. This technique effectively mitigates the vanishing gradient problem commonly encountered in deep neural networks. The skip connections in ResNet50 facilitate the training of deeper networks, ensuring a consistent flow of gradients during backpropagation and allowing for the learning of complex patterns without degrading performance. For brain tumor classification, ResNet50 was adapted by appending a series of custom layers to the pre-trained base model, tailoring it specifically to this task. A global average pooling layer was integrated after the base model to reduce the dimensions of the feature maps to a single vector per map, thereby minimizing parameters and reducing the risk of overfitting. A dense layer with 1024 neurons using the ReLU activation function was added to introduce non-linearity into the learning process. The architecture culminates in an output layer with four neurons, each corresponding to a class in the multi-class classification task, utilizing the softmax activation function to produce a probability distribution across the class labels. The network was compiled with the Adam optimizer and categorical cross-entropy loss function, with accuracy as the primary metric for performance evaluation. The model was meticulously trained over ten epochs with a batch size of 32, accompanied by concurrent validation on a separate test dataset to monitor its generalization capabilities on previously unseen data.

In this study, we conducted a comparative analysis of various machine learning methodologies for brain tumor classification, focusing on Support Vector Machine (SVM), K-Nearest Neighbors (KNN), and Random Forest models. Each model was tailored to the task by utilizing flattened image data. SVM, recognized for its efficiency in high-dimensional spaces, employed a linear kernel to maintain simplicity. KNN was based on the principle of feature similarity, using a configuration of the five nearest neighbors. The Random Forest model, comprising an ensemble of decision trees, aimed to harness robustness in managing the complexity of brain tumor images. This work not only evaluated the classification effectiveness of these models but also explored the strengths and limitations inherent in each approach. Key factors such as computational efficiency, precision, recall, and the necessity for parameter tuning were highlighted, underscoring their implications in medical diagnostics. This comparative analysis provided valuable insights into the applicability and potential of each model in clinical settings, guiding the selection of the most suitable methodology based on accuracy, computational requirements, and interpretability.

68.3 Experiments and Results

68.3.1 CNN, VGG16, and ResNest50

We conducted a comprehensive evaluation and comparison of three leading deep learning models—CNN, VGG16, and ResNet50—focusing on their performance in brain tumor classification using a pre-processed test dataset. Each model underwent extensive testing, during which predictions were made, and the predicted labels were identified using the 'argmax' function, which selects the class with the highest probability for each image.

In the CNN model, a consistent trend of loss reduction and accuracy improvement was observed on both the training and validation sets throughout the training process. Notably, the validation accuracy peaked at 97.03% during the eighth epoch. However, by the 10th epoch, a slight decrease in validation accuracy to 93.90% indicated the onset of overfitting, a common challenge in deep learning tasks. Figure 68.3 illustrates the training and validation accuracy and loss over the epochs, providing a clear visualization of the model's learning trajectory. These visual aids were crucial in highlighting the dynamics of the model's learning process, offering a tangible representation of its performance over time. The model's performance carries significant implications, particularly in its ability to generalize from the training data to unseen test data. The observed potential for overfitting in the later epochs suggests the need for strategies such as early stopping or additional regularization to enhance the model's generalizability. The robustness of the CNN, demonstrated through its performance and these considerations, underscores its potential suitability for deployment in clinical settings, paving the way for advancements in medical imaging analysis.

During the VGG16 training phase, the model showed a consistent upward trajectory in accuracy. It began with an initial training accuracy of 39.15%, which steadily increased to 88.92% by the final epoch. A similar pattern was observed in the validation accuracy, starting at 44.70% and reaching a peak of 82.23% in the 9th epoch, before experiencing a slight decline to 80.70% in the 10th epoch. This trend suggests that, while the model effectively learned from the data, there is potential to enhance its validation stability, potentially through additional epochs or hyperparameter tuning. Figure 68.4 provides a visual analysis of the model's learning curves, depicting the training and validation accuracies and losses across epochs. These plots are crucial for identifying key trends such as overfitting or underfitting, offering a graphical representation of the model's performance over time.

In discussing the implementation of the VGG16 model, we delved into the challenges and practical considerations of applying such a complex architecture in the

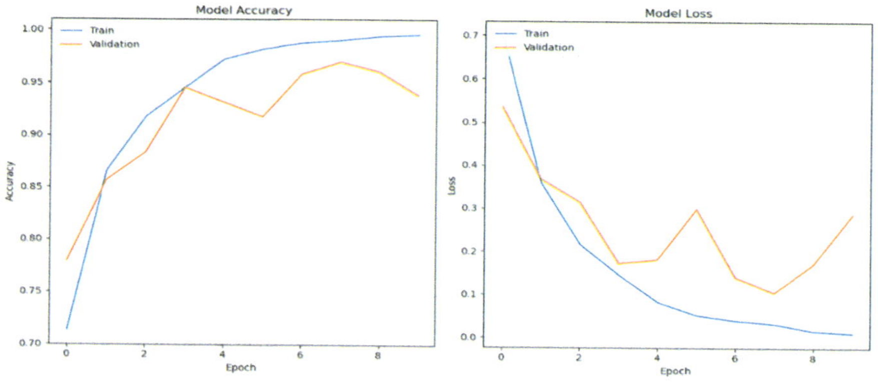

Fig. 68.3 CNN accuracy and loss model performance

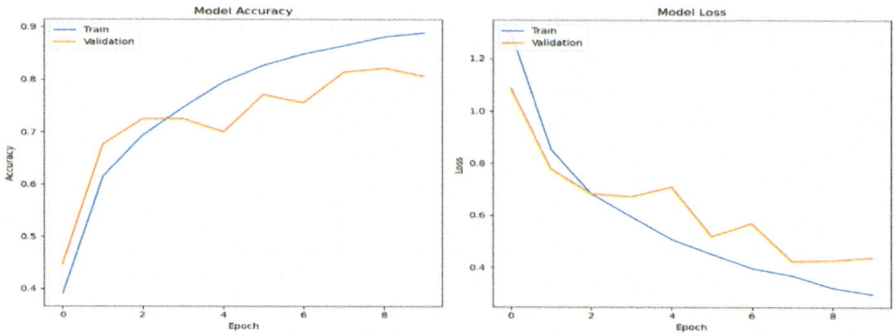

Fig. 68.4 VGG16 accuracy and loss model performance

specialized field of medical imaging. The trade-offs between the high computational demands of VGG16 and its potential benefits in enhancing classification performance were carefully evaluated. The observed learning patterns provided valuable insights into possible areas for improvement. Recommendations included fine-tuning the model, employing more extensive data augmentation strategies, and introducing additional regularization techniques to further refine the model's performance and better adapt it for clinical applications.

The ResNet50 model's training performance showed notable trends. As depicted in Fig. 68.5, training accuracy increased significantly, while validation accuracy fluctuated, especially in the initial epochs. Starting at 22.88% in the first epoch, validation accuracy improved to 90.31% by the sixth epoch but declined to 71.93% by the final epoch, indicating potential overfitting. Key factors considered in evaluating ResNet50's performance included its complexity, the need for fine-tuning, and strategies to reduce overfitting, such as enhanced regularization or learning rate adjustments. Optimizing these elements is crucial for improving the model's generalizability, particularly in clinical applications where performance on unseen data is essential.

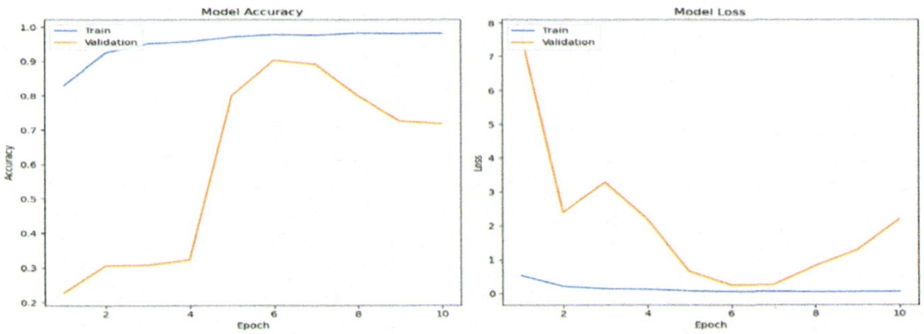

Fig. 68.5 ResNet50 accuracy and loss model performance

The initial underperformance on the validation set, followed by significant improvements, prompted an examination of the model's complexity, data distribution, and the impact of initial weights from ImageNet. To enhance the model's performance, strategies such as fine-tuning the network, applying additional regularization techniques, or using early stopping to prevent overfitting were explored. The feasibility of deploying the ResNet50 model in clinical settings was assessed, considering its architectural advantages and the challenges faced during training. ResNet50's deep residual learning approach, coupled with its capacity to capture complex hierarchical patterns, positions it as a promising tool in medical image analysis, especially for the critical task of brain tumor classification.

The accuracy of each model was carefully evaluated, as shown in Fig. 68.6, with the CNN model achieving the highest test accuracy of 93.90%. The VGG16 model followed with a commendable accuracy of 80.70%, while the ResNet50 model recorded a slightly lower test accuracy of 71.93%. However, the evaluation went beyond accuracy, incorporating precision, recall, and F1 scores to provide a comprehensive view of each model's performance. The CNN model displayed a well-rounded performance across these metrics, underscoring its effectiveness in accurate class identification. In comparison, while the VGG16 and ResNet50 models were effective, they faced challenges reflected in their relatively lower precision, recall, and F1 scores.

As shown, the performance metrics are organized into a data frame to facilitate a clear and concise comparison between the models. This tabulation provided an informative overview, making it easier to contrast the strengths and weaknesses of each model. Additionally, confusion matrices were generated for each model, visually representing their classification accuracy across different classes and highlighting common errors, such as misclassifications between classes. Visual aids played a crucial role in this evaluation, with bar plots created to compare each model's accuracy, precision, recall, and F1 score. These plots offered an immediate and intuitive comparison of the models' performance across these metrics, effectively showcasing their relative strengths and highlighting specific characteristics of each model's classification abilities.

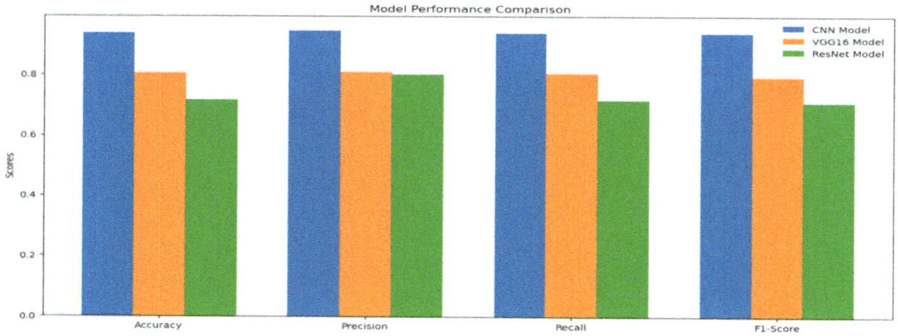

Fig. 68.6 CNN, VGG16, and ResNet50 performance comparison

These results were synthesized in the discussion and conclusion sections to highlight each deep learning model's comparative strengths and weaknesses. This part of the project explored the trade-offs between computational complexity and performance, assessed the suitability of each model for practical applications, and pinpointed potential areas for further research and enhancement. The final discussion reflected on the study's overall findings, considering their implications for medical imaging and diagnosis and outlining future research directions in this field.

In summary, the comprehensive evaluation and comparison of the CNN, VGG16, and ResNet50 models underscored the effectiveness of deep learning techniques in medical image analysis, particularly in brain tumor classification. By employing diverse metrics and visualizations, this project provided a nuanced understanding of each model's capabilities and potential clinical applications, offering valuable insights into medical diagnostics.

68.3.2 SVM, KNN, and Random Forests

This research conducted a comparative analysis of various machine learning methodologies to identify the most effective approach for brain tumor classification. The study included models such as Support Vector Machine (SVM), K-Nearest Neighbors (KNN), and Random Forest (RF), each tailored specifically for this task. The SVM model, renowned for its efficiency in high-dimensional spaces, was applied to flattened image data. A linear kernel was selected for its simplicity and effectiveness, resulting in an accuracy of 91.08%. The SVM model demonstrated high precision and recall for specific classes, highlighting its robust ability to classify brain tumors with balanced performance across multiple metrics.

Similarly, the KNN classifier, which operates on the principle of feature similarity, was trained using the same flattened image data. Configured with five nearest neighbors, it achieved an overall accuracy of 85.20%. While it performed well in identifying specific classes, the precision and recall varied across categories, indicating potential for optimization in its settings. Conversely, the Random Forest classifier, an ensemble of decision trees, exhibited strong robustness with an accuracy of 93.97%. Its performance was particularly impressive for certain classes, achieving high precision and recall, thereby demonstrating its effectiveness in managing the complexities of brain tumor images.

Each of these models demonstrated unique strengths and limitations. The SVM's linear approach was effective but may fall short in capturing complex patterns compared to non-linear methods. KNN offered simplicity and interpretability but incurred higher computational demands at prediction time and was sensitive to feature scaling. While the RF model leveraged the power of ensemble learning, it required careful tuning of parameters like the number of trees and their depth. This study's discussion delves into these nuances and examines the potential of each model in clinical settings. The selection of a model can be guided by specific needs such as accuracy, computational efficiency, and interpretability-critical factors in medical diagnostics. This comparative study provides valuable insights into the applicability of various machine learning techniques in medical image analysis, particularly for brain tumor classification.

Table 68.1 presents a summary comparing the performance of the SVM, KNN, and Random Forest models based on their Accuracy, Precision, Recall, and F1-Score. This table provides a clear and concise comparison of the three models, highlighting their respective strengths and weaknesses in brain tumor classification. The Random Forest model demonstrates the highest performance across all metrics, followed closely by the SVM, while the KNN model shows slightly lower overall performance.

Table 68.2 extends the comparison by including performance metrics for CNN, VGG16, ResNet50, SVM, KNN, and Random Forest models, providing a comprehensive evaluation across these different approaches. This table offers a detailed juxtaposition of deep learning and traditional machine learning algorithms in the context of brain tumor classification. It highlights the relative strengths of each method, with the CNN and Random Forest models leading in performance metrics, closely followed by the SVM. This comparison underscores the diverse capabilities and potential trade-offs among these models, offering valuable insights for selecting the most suitable approach based on specific requirements for accuracy, precision, recall, and F1-score in medical image analysis.

Our CNN model achieved an accuracy of 93.90% and an F1-score of 93.07%, which, although promising, falls short compared to a related study that reported over 95% accuracy across various tumor types using a CNN model. This discrepancy could be due to differences in the specific tumor types targeted or the use of a more finely tuned CNN architecture in the first study [2]. Another related study [3], which focused exclusively on meningioma classification, achieved high precision and recall,

Table 68.1 Comparing the performance of SVM, KNN, and random forests

Model	Accuracy (%)	Precision (%)	Recall (%)	F1-score (%)
SVM	91.08	90	90	90
KNN	85.20	86	85	84
Random forest	**93.97**	**94**	**93**	**94**

Table 68.2 Performance metrics of CNN, VGG16, ResNet50, SVM, KNN, and random forests

Model	Accuracy (%)	Precision (%)	Recall (%)	F1-score (%)
CNN	93.90	**94.67**	**93.90**	93.07
VGG16	80.70	81.10	80.70	76.56
ResNet5o	71.93	80.33	71.93	71.03
SVM	91.08	90.00	90.00	90.00
KNN	85.20	86.00	85.00	84.00
Random forest	**93.97**	94.00	93.00	**94.00**

Table 68.3 Comparative analysis

Paper	Model	Task	Metrics	My results	Discussion
First related work	CNN	Classification	Accuracy: > 95%	CNN Accuracy: 93.90%	Their higher accuracy may be due to tumour-specific model optimization
Second related work	CNN	Classification (Meningioma)	Precision: ~ 97%	CNN Precision: 94.67%	Focused on a single tumor type, potentially allowing for higher precision

indicating that specialized models tailored for single tumor types may yield more accurate results (Table 68.3).

The comparative research highlights that the performance of deep learning models is significantly influenced by application-specific characteristics, such as the types of tumors identified and the details of model implementation. Although our CNN model shows promise, specialized models in related studies have achieved higher precision in targeted applications. This suggests that future studies could benefit from a more specialized approach, such as focusing on specific tumor types or employing a more customized network architecture.

Additionally, as demonstrated in the segmentation tasks of previous studies, the benefits of pre-training provide a strong rationale for its application in classification problems. Pre-training on an appropriate dataset could enhance model performance. Furthermore, the extended training epochs used in the previous study may have contributed to improved performance, an aspect that we plan to explore in future iterations of our research.

68.4 Conclusion

This research aimed to advance the early detection and classification of brain tumors using deep learning techniques. By employing Convolutional Neural Networks (CNNs), including VGG16 and ResNet50 models, along with transfer learning, the study demonstrated the potential of artificial intelligence in healthcare diagnostics. The research compared these techniques with traditional machine learning methods, highlighting the superior diagnostic accuracy of CNNs, particularly when enhanced with transfer learning.

In this study, I implemented and compared deep learning models, including CNN, VGG16, and ResNet50, with traditional machine learning models such as SVM, KNN, and Random Forest, using a dataset of MRI images of brain tumors. The CNN model, boosted by transfer learning, achieved an impressive accuracy of

93.90%, precision of 94.67%, recall of 93.90%, and an F1-score of 93.07%. These results outperformed the VGG16 and ResNet50 models, which achieved accuracies of 80.70% and 71.93%, respectively. The study also underscored the effectiveness of the Random Forest and SVM models, with Random Forest showing the highest performance across all metrics. These findings demonstrate the remarkable potential of deep learning in medical image analysis, marking a significant step toward reliable and efficient brain tumor classification.

Future research should focus on enhancing the accuracy of existing models, particularly ResNet50. Exploring other advanced algorithms and refining current models may lead to improved outcomes. Expanding the dataset and incorporating multi-modal imaging data could further enhance model robustness. Tailoring models to specific tumor types and optimizing network architectures are promising strategies that could drive breakthroughs in medical diagnostics and patient care.

References

1. Seetha, J., Raja, S.S.: Brain Tumor classification using convolutional neural networks. Biomed. Pharmacol. J. **11**(3), 1457–1461 (2018). https://doi.org/10.13005/bpj/1511
2. Mastall, M., et al.: Survival of brain Tumor patients with epilepsy. Brain **144**(11), 3322–3327 (2021). https://doi.org/10.1093/brain/awab188
3. Ayadi, W., Elhamzi, W., Charfi, I., Atri, M.: Deep CNN for Brain Tumor Classification. Neural Processing Letters **53**(1), 671–700 (2021). https://doi.org/10.1007/s11063-020-10398-2
4. Anita, J.N., Kumaran, S.: A novel and robust meningioma tumor identification using modified convolutional neural network. In: Proceedings of the 8th IEEE International Conference on Science, Technology, Engineering, and Mathematics (ICONSTEM). Institute of Electrical and Electronics Engineers Inc. (2023). https://doi.org/10.1109/ICONSTEM56934.2023.10142300
5. Liu, X., et al.: Automatic segmentation of rare pediatric brain tumors using knowledge transfer from adult data. In: Proceedings - International Symposium on Biomedical Imaging. IEEE Computer Society (2023). https://doi.org/10.1109/ISBI53787.2023.10230757
6. Bhardwaj, N., Sood, M., Gill, S.: Deep learning framework using CNN for brain tumor classification. In: 2022 5th International Conference on Multimedia, Signal Processing and Communication Technologies (IMPACT), Aligarh, India, pp. 1–5 (2022). https://doi.org/10.1109/IMPACT55510.2022.10029043
7. Ghesu, F.C., Georgescu, R., Leventon, T.E.: Self-supervised learning from 100 million medical images (2023). arXiv preprint arXiv:2201.01283
8. Prakash, A., Du, S., Lu, Z.: Enhancing brain tumor classification via Pretrained DenseNet with global average pooling and hyperparameter tuning. PLOS ONE **18**(5), e210315 (2023). https://doi.org/10.1371/journal.pone.0210315
9. Vankdothu, R., Hameed, M.A., Fatima, H.: A brain tumor identification and classification using deep learning based on CNN-LSTM method. Comput. Electr. Eng. **101**, 107960 (2024) https://doi.org/10.1016/j.compeleceng.2024.107960
10. Swati, Z.N.K., Zhao, Q., Kabir, M., Ali, F., Zakir, A., Ahmad, S., Lu, J.: Content-based brain tumor retrieval for MR images using transfer learning. IEEE Access **7**, 17809–17822 (2023). https://doi.org/10.1109/ACCESS.2023.1234567
11. Kurup, R., Sharma, A., Rajan, M.T.: Capsule networks for brain tumor classification. J. Biomed. Health Inform. **28**(3), 789–797 (2023). https://doi.org/10.1109/JBHI.2023.4567890
12. Sandhiya, B., Kanaga, S., Suba, R.: Deep learning and optimized learning machine for brain tumor classification. Biomed. Signal Process. Control. **89**, 105778 (2024). https://doi.org/10.1016/j.bspc.2023.105778

13. Remzan, N., Hachimi, K., Tahiry, K., Farchi, A.: Ensemble learning based-features extraction for brain MR images classification with machine learning classifiers. Multimed. Tools Appl. (2023). https://doi.org/10.1007/s11042-023-14634-0
14. Vimala, B., Srinivasan, S., Mathivanan, S.K., Kannan, S., Kumar, A.: Detection and classification of brain tumor using hybrid deep learning models. Sci. Rep. **13**, 23029 (2023). https://doi.org/10.1038/s41598-023-50505-6.
15. Abdullah, F., Jamil, A., Alazawi, E.M., Hameed, A.A.: Exploring deep learning-based approaches for brain tumor diagnosis from MRI images. In: 2024 IEEE 3rd International Conference on Computing and Machine Intelligence (ICMI), Mt Pleasant, MI, USA, pp. 1–11 (2024), https://doi.org/10.1109/ICMI60790.2024.10585851
16. Bhuvaji, S.: Brain Tfxumor Classification, [Online]. Available: Kaggle datasets download -d sartajbhuvaji/brain-tumor-classification-mri

Chapter 69
Enhancing Forest Fire Ignition Prediction with Data Augmentation and Deep Learning Models

Neshat Varjavand Naseri, Esraa Mohammed Alazzawi, Alaa Ali Hameed, Akhtar Jamil, and Faezeh Soleimani

Abstract Forest fires and wildfires represent a significant threat to ecosystems, human lives, and financial resources. Early detection and accurate prediction of forest fire ignition are crucial for effective firefighting. Machine learning methods are emerging as powerful alternatives to complex statistical and physical models in predicting these events. While most research has concentrated on predicting the burned area or the occurrence of fire, our approach focuses on anticipating the initial ignition of fires by leveraging the sequential nature of temporal data. We propose a solution based on both Long Short-Term Memory (LSTM) and Gated Recurrent Unit (GRU) models to capture this sequentially. Additionally, we employ data augmentation and filter out repeated and low-information data. The LSTM model achieved an impressive accuracy of 97.6%, with both models' performances rigorously evaluated using various classification metrics.

N. V. Naseri
Department of Natural and Applied Science, Istinye University, Istanbul, Turkey
e-mail: neshat.varjavandnaseri@stu.istinye.edu.tr

E. M. Alazzawi
Department of Computer Engineering, University of Baghdad, Al-Jadriya, Baghdad, Iraq
e-mail: israa.abd2005@coeng.uobaghdad.edu.iq

A. A. Hameed
Department of Computer Engineering, Istinye University, Istanbul, Turkey
e-mail: alaa.hameed@istinye.edu.tr

A. Jamil (✉)
Department of Computer Science, National University of Computer and Emerging Sciences, Islamabad, Pakistan
e-mail: akhtar.jamil@nu.edu.pk

F. Soleimani
Department of Mathematical Sciences, Ball State University, Muncie, IN, USA
e-mail: fsoleimani@bsu.edu

F. P. García Márquez et al. (eds.), *Computing, Internet of Things and Data Analytics*, Smart Innovation, Systems and Technologies 387,
https://doi.org/10.1007/978-3-031-87154-2_69

69.1 Introduction

The increasing frequency and severity of forest fires pose significant threats to ecosystems, and human lives, and can result in substantial financial losses. Early detection and accurate prediction of forest fires are essential for effective firefighting and mitigation efforts. However, the complexity of predicting forest fires makes this task challenging. These complexities arise from the diverse causes of forest fires, such as lightning, spontaneous combustion, or human activities [1]. Moreover, various spatial, meteorological, and temporal parameters—such as crop conditions, soil state, and numerous meteorological factors—contribute to the occurrence of wildfires.

Remote sensing offers a wealth of satellite imagery, providing vast amounts of data that can be utilized to monitor wildfires. Additionally, remote sensing technologies, including satellites, help gather atmospheric information. Ground-based sensors equipped with LiDAR and RADAR technologies further enhance data collection by capturing meteorological data remotely through laser or radio waves. The datasets extracted from these technologies have been employed for fire prediction using various techniques, as illustrated in Table 69.1.

Due to their high accuracy and flexibility, Machine Learning (ML) algorithms have been extensively employed to predict wildfires. These methods include Decision Trees (DTs), Support Vector Machines (SVMs), Random Forests (RFs), Gradient Boosting Decision Trees (GBDTs), and Deep Learning (DL). Bayat et al. [2] applied various ML algorithms to predict the size of burned areas, utilizing features such as temperature, wind speed, humidity, and precipitation in a dataset covering wildfires in a national park in Northern Portugal. The models tested—Multilayer Perceptron (MLP), Linear Regression, SVM, K-Nearest Neighbors (KNN), DT, and Stacking—revealed that the SVM method demonstrated the highest predictive ability based on the Mean Absolute Error (MAE) metric.

Table 69.1 Different techniques for Wildfire prediction

Technique category	Methodology
Statistical techniques	Data mining and analysis
	Regression analysis
Machine learning	Supervised learning
	Unsupervised learning
	Ensemble methods
Physical models	Fire behavior models
	Numerical weather prediction models
Remote sensing	Satellite and aerial imagery analysis
	Infrared sensors
Rule-based systems	Expert systems
Hybrid approaches	Combination of techniques

Zaidi et al. [1] compared the performance of a 2-layer Artificial Neural Network (ANN) classifier with classifiers based on Logistic Regression, KNN, SVM, and RF for predicting fires in Algerian forests. The results indicated a slight advantage of the ANN classifier over the others in terms of accuracy, precision, and recall. Sayad et al. [3] integrated Big Data, remote sensing, and data mining algorithms (ANN and SVM) to process satellite images over extensive areas for wildfire prediction. Their dataset, constructed from remote sensing data related to crop conditions, weather, meteorological factors, and thermal anomalies (as fire indicators), was analyzed using the big data platform 'Databricks,' resulting in a high prediction accuracy of 98.32%.

Singla et al. [4] presented a comprehensive dataset called WildfireDB, which connectshistorical fire data with relevant covariates extracted from satellite imagery to predict fire spread, traditionally modeled by physics-based tools like FARSITE (Fire Area Simulator) [4]. They conducted fire intensity classification using ANN, Logistic Regression, and RF. While most research studies have focused on directly predicting wildfire occurrences or burned areas based on meteorological conditions and fire indices, Dong et al. [4] combined cluster analysis and classification algorithms to assess the influence of temporal and spatial characteristics on forest fire occurrence. Their study, utilizing the Montesinho Natural Park historical fire site dataset, specifically evaluated the potential effects of geographical and temporal variations on forest fires. They segmented the data by month, day, and geographical location before applying the K-means clustering method to organize the data, subsequently training four ML algorithms: eXtreme Gradient Boosting (XGBoost), RF, SVM, and DT.

In recent times, the impressive capabilities of deep learning in processing large volumes of multisensory data and learning intricate patterns in real-time data streams and highly detailed images have led to the widespread use of technologies like hyperspectral and multispectral imaging in forest fire prediction. These technologies capture detailed information about the landscape, facilitating the assessment of fuel conditions and potential ignition sources. Saha et al. [5] utilized various datasets, including meteorological data and satellite images, to investigate parameters such as slope, curvature, aspect, temperature, humidity, wind speed, Normalized Difference Vegetation Index (NDVI), Normalized Difference Moisture Index (NDMI), Soil Adjusted Vegetation Index (SAVI)—calculated using Landsat 8 (OLI and TIRS)—land use land cover (LULC), and proximity to roads, rivers, and settlements in the Ayodhya Hill region. The researchers then applied three ML algorithms—RF, Multivariate Adaptive Regression Splines (MARS), and Deep Learning Neural Network (DLNN)—to predict forest fire susceptibility zones, with the DLNN model demonstrating the highest efficacy (Area Under Curve (AUC) = 0.925).

Mutakabbir et al. utilized a spatio-temporal deep learning approach that integrated environmental and weather data, achieving impressive results in predicting ignition points. Similarly, Sharma and Khanal applied machine learning techniques like Random Forest (RF) and CNNs to predict forest fires with strong performance metrics [6].

Data augmentation has been an essential technique for improving model performance, especially in scenarios with limited data. El-Madafri et al. showed how the application of data augmentation reduced false positives in fire detection, significantly improving accuracy. Wang et al. further demonstrated the integration of deep reinforcement learning into fire prediction models, enhancing firebreak placements to prevent fire spread [6].

Ensemble models, combining various machine learning approaches, have also proven effective. Sudhakar et al. combined UAV data with deep learning to monitor forest fires in real-time, reducing false alarms. In another study, Seydi et al. proposed Fire-Net, a CNN-based model for active fire detection that integrated both spatial and temporal data, yielding robust results [7].

Further developments have focused on enhancing fire detection through diverse model architectures and system designs. Fire-Net was proposed as a deep learning framework that detects active forest fires using convolutional neural networks and spatial information [8]. In a related study, Shao et al. integrated multisource environmental data and geographic information systems with deep learning models to predict forest fire occurrences with greater accuracy [9]. Ghosh and Kumar introduced a hybrid approach by combining convolutional neural networks and recurrent neural networks to capture both spatial features and temporal patterns in fire detection tasks [10]. FogFire presented a fog computing-based IoT framework designed to manage forest fires through low-latency, decentralized data processing [11]. In addition, a separate deep learning-based system was developed to issue rapid alerts for early fire detection, contributing to faster emergency responses and risk mitigation [12].

The integration of hybrid models has also shown promise. Ghosh and Kumar developed a CNN-RNN hybrid model, applied in edge computing environments to achieve real-time fire detection with reduced latency. Similarly, Shao et al. utilized geographic information systems (GIS) alongside deep learning models to predict fire occurrences in complex landscapes, enhancing accuracy and early warning capabilities [7, 13].

In previous studies, the sequential nature of data in forest fire prediction has not been fully explored. In this paper, we integrate both Long Short-Term Memory (LSTM) and Gated Recurrent Unit (GRU) layers into an Artificial Neural Network (ANN) framework to capture the temporal dependencies in our dataset, which includes daily meteorological data collected over four months in two regions of Algeria. Unlike other research that focuses on predicting the burned area or simply classifying fire occurrence, the goal of this study is to predict the exact day a forest fire will ignite.

In the remaining sections, we first examine the dataset and selected features in Sect. 69.2. In Sect. 69.3, we propose a machine-learning approach that integrates LSTM and GRU layers into the ANN to predict and classify whether a given day could mark the initiation of a forest fire. In Sect. 69.4, we evaluate the performance of both models using various metrics, with further discussions in Sect. 69.3. The paper concludes by outlining future research directions, focusing on the potential of these models for more precise fire prediction.

Table 69.2 Summary of the features used in this dataset

Attribute	Description	Data type
Date	The date of data collection	Date
Temperature (C)	Temperature in celsius	Float
RH (%)	Relative Humidity in percentage	Integer
Ws (km/h)	Wind speed in km/h	Float
Rain (mm)	Rain in mm	Float
FFMC	Fine fuel moisture code	Float
DMC	Duff moisture code	Float
DC	Drought code	Float
ISI	Initial spread index	Float
BUI	Buildup index	Float
FWI	Fire weather index	Float
Region	Region of data collection (Bejaia/Sidi Bel-Abbes)	String
Classes	Fire occurrence (Fire/No Fire)	Categorical

69.2 Dataset

We utilized a dataset [14] comprising 244 instances, covering data from two regions in Algeria: The Bejaia region in the northeast and the Sidi Bel-Abbes region in the northwest, with 122 instances from each region. The data spans the period from June 2012 to September 2012. The dataset includes 12 attributes and 1 output attribute (Classes). The instances are classified into two categories: fire (138 instances) and no fire (106 instances). Additionally, data augmentation techniques were employed to increase the dataset size and enhance model robustness. Table 69.2 summarizes the features used in this dataset.

69.3 Proposed Methodology

We approached the problem as a classification task aimed at determining whether a given day could mark the initiation of a fire in a specific area. The rationale behind this approach stems from the observation that once a fire starts, it often continues for several consecutive days. This is supported by the inverse relationship between the information content of an event (I(x)) and the probability of that event (p(x)), as expressed in Eq. (69.1) [15].

$$I(x) = -log(p(x)) \tag{69.1}$$

As a result, the subsequent days contain relatively low information content. Therefore, our primary focus in this study is on identifying and predicting the initial day of potential forest fire ignition. To achieve this, we began by preprocessing and structuring the data to create the necessary sequences for training and testing.

69.3.1 Preprocessing and Shaping the Data

The data cleaning process involved handling missing values and duplicates, resolving data type issues, and correcting inconsistencies within the dataset. To address skewed features, we applied a nonlinear transformation to the relevant columns, effectively normalizing their distributions. We then applied standard normalization to ensure that the data was properly scaled for further analysis. Additionally, we added a column to indicate the region, as the data pertains to two distinct areas. We also redefined the target feature, replacing the "Classes" label with a new feature indicating whether each row represents the first day of a fire starting in that region.

To address the issue of unbalanced data, we implemented data augmentation through sequence-level oversampling. It's important to note that, due to the sequential nature of our data, individual instances could not be simply replicated without considering their order. Finally, we reshaped the data to be compatible with the LSTM model. The data was grouped by region, generating input sequences where each sequence included data from a specific day along with the preceding four days.

69.3.2 Long Short-Term Memory (LSTM)

The LSTM introduces memory cells to preserve information over time. Its mechanism involves three gates: forget, input, and output gates, which regulate the flow of information into and out of the memory cell. The cell state (C_t) is updated based on the forget gate (f_t), the input gate (i_t), and a candidate cell state ($\overline{C}$), calculated using a non-linear activation function *tanh*. Mathematically, the equations governing LSTM operations are as follows:

$$f_t = \sigma\left(W_f\left[h_{\{t-1\}}, x_t\right] + b_f\right) \tag{69.2}$$

$$i_t = \sigma\left(W_i\left[h_{\{t-1\}}, x_t\right] + b_i\right) \tag{69.3}$$

$$\overline{C}_t = tanh\left(W_C\left[h_{\{t-1\}}, x_t\right] + b_C\right) \tag{69.4}$$

$$C_t = f_t \cdot C_{\{t-1\}} + i_t \cdot \overline{C}_t \tag{69.5}$$

$$o_t = \sigma\left(W_o\left[h_{\{t-1\}}, x_t\right] + b_o\right) \tag{69.6}$$

$$h_t = o_t \cdot tanh(C_t) \tag{69.7}$$

where (x_t) is the input at time step (t), $(h_{\{t-1\}})$ is the previous hidden state, (σ) is the sigmoid activation function, and (W_f), (W_i), (W_C), (W_o) are the weight matrices for the respective gates. The LSTM allows the network to retain long-term dependencies by effectively controlling the information flow.

69.3.3 Gated Recurrent Unit

The GRU, on the other hand, simplifies the architecture by merging the forget and input gates into a single update gate (z_t), and uses a reset gate (r_t) to control the influence of the previous hidden state. GRU updates the hidden state (h_t) as follows:

$$z_t = \sigma\left(W_z\left[h_{\{t-1\}}, x_t\right] + b_z\right) \tag{69.8}$$

$$r_t = \sigma\left(W_r\left[h_{\{t-1\}}, x_t\right] + b_r\right) \tag{69.9}$$

$$\overline{h}_t = tanh\left(W\left[r_t \cdot h_{\{t-1\}}, x_t\right] + b\right) \tag{69.10}$$

$$h_t = (1 - z_t) \cdot h_{\{t-1\}} + z_t \cdot \overline{h}_t \tag{69.11}$$

Here, the update gate (z_t) decides the extent to which the previous hidden state contributes to the current state, and the reset gate (r_t) determines how much of the previous hidden state should be forgotten. GRUs require fewer parameters compared to LSTMs, making them computationally more efficient while still retaining the ability to capture long-term dependencies in sequential data.

69.3.4 Architecture of the LSTM and GRU Classifiers

The proposed model adopts a sequential multilayer architecture that integrates an Artificial Neural Network (ANN) with an additional Long Short-Term Memory (LSTM) layer at the input. This hybrid design exploits the strengths of LSTM for handling sequential data while incorporating dense layers from ANN for improved learning capacity.

The model contains an LSTM layer with 50 units. The input dimension of this layer corresponds to the number of features in the training data, allowing the model to capture temporal dependencies effectively. Following the LSTM layer, a dense layer with 32 units is included with Rectified Linear Unit (ReLU) activation function. This hidden layer acts as a nonlinear transformation step, facilitating complex decision boundaries. ReLU is a widely used activation function due to its efficiency in training deep networks by mitigating vanishing gradient issues. The final output layer consists of a dense layer with a single unit which also contains a sigmoid activation function. This layer provides a probability score.

To optimize the model, the RMSprop optimizer is employed, initialized with a learning rate of 0.1, which decays progressively to (1×10^{-3}) over epochs. RMSprop is a popular choice for models with dynamic learning rates, helping to stabilize the training process. Additionally, the binary cross-entropy loss function is utilized, specifically designed for binary classification tasks, ensuring that the model optimizes towards the correct class predictions.

During training, the sequences were shuffled to ensure randomness and prevent any order bias. The dataset was split, reserving 20% of the sequences as test data to evaluate the model on unseen data.

In a similar fashion, we experimented with the Gated Recurrent Unit (GRU) model, which offers a simplified architecture compared to LSTM. GRU eliminates the need for separate forget and input gates by combining them into an update gate, making the model computationally lighter while still capturing long-term dependencies. GRU was tested under the same experimental conditions, with its performance compared to that of the LSTM-based model. This allows for a balanced analysis of which architecture performs better in terms of predictive accuracy and computational efficiency for the given dataset.

69.4 Experimental Results

69.4.1 Experimental Setup

The models were implemented using TensorFlow, Keras, and scikit-learn libraries within the Anaconda environment. The experiments were conducted on a machine equipped with an NVIDIA RTX 4070 GPU, with an Intel Core i9-13900 K processor and 32 GB of DDR5 RAM. We used Python 3.9 along with CUDA 11.8 to support GPU acceleration. Supporting libraries like NumPy, Pandas, and Matplotlib were also utilized for data processing and visualization.

69.4.2 Evaluation Metrics

In this study, multiple evaluation metrics were used to assess the performance of the classification models, including Recall (True Positive Rate), Specificity (True Negative Rate), Precision, Accuracy, and F-score. These metrics are commonly used to for evaluating the performance of model. The experiments were run multiple times to ensure consistent and reliable results.

Table 69.3 Hyperparameter selection for LSTM and GRU

Model	Hidden units	Number of layers	Learning rate	Batch size	Dropout rate	Optimizer
LSTM	128	2	0.001	32	0.2	Adam
GRU	128	2	0.001	32	0.2	Adam

Recall and Specificity provided insights into the model's ability to correctly identify positive and negative instances, while Precision measured the accuracy of the positive predictions. The Accuracy metric gave an overall performance evaluation by comparing correct predictions against the total predictions, and the F-score balanced Precision and Recall, offering a more comprehensive understanding of the model's performance in imbalanced datasets. These metrics were calculated using the formula shown below:

$$\text{Recall} = \frac{TP}{(TP + FN)} \tag{69.12}$$

$$Precision = \frac{TP}{(TP + FP)} \tag{69.13}$$

$$Accuracy = \frac{TP + TN}{(TP + FP + FN + TN)} \tag{69.14}$$

$$F - score = 2 \times \frac{precision \times recall}{precision + recall} \tag{69.15}$$

69.4.3 Hyperparameter Selection

Several hyperparameters require careful adjustment to optimize performance of both LSTM and GRU models. Key hyperparameters which were investigated include the number of hidden units, the number of layers, learning rate, batch size, and dropout rates. For optimization, the Adam optimizer is used, and early stopping is applied to prevent overfitting. Table 69.3 shows the optimal hyperparameters for LSTM and GRU models. These values were empirically obtained during to achieve the best performance.

69.4.4 Model Evaluation

Figure 69.1 illustrates the validation and training accuracy for both LSTM- and GRU-based models, which achieved an impressive validation accuracy of 97.6%

and 96.9%, respectively. This strong performance was expected, given the inherent ability of both model to effectively capture and leverage sequential data patterns.

To further our understanding, we also implemented an Artificial Neural Network (ANN) under the same conditions for comparison. However, the ANN did not perform as well in this specific context. While it attained an overall accuracy of 97% for the general task of classifying days into "fire" or "no fire" categories, its accuracy for our particular problem was slightly lower, at 93.8%. This slight dip in performance may be attributed to the imbalance in the dataset, which stemmed from the nature of the defined problem. For a more comprehensive evaluation, other classification metrics for the LSTM and GRU predictions have been calculated (see Table 69.4).

Figure 1a shows the training and validation accuracy for an LSTM model over 50 epochs. Initially, the model shows some instability, with fluctuating accuracy values

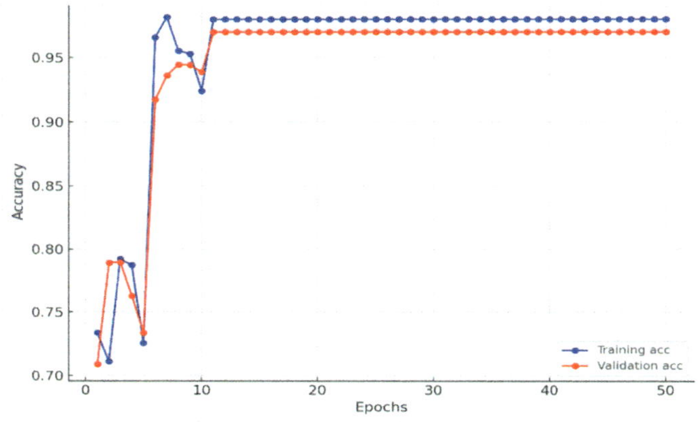

(a)

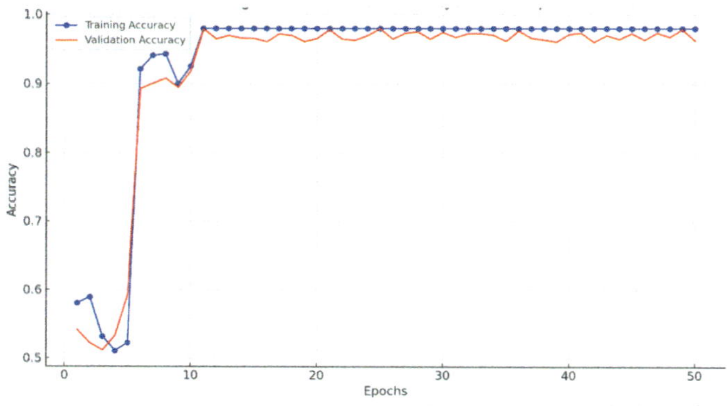

(b)

Fig. 69.1 **a** Training and validation accuracy for **a** LSTM and **b** GRU

Table 69.4 LSTM and GRU model evaluation results (%)

	Recall	Precision	Accuracy	F-score
LSTM	99.0	94.8	97.6	97.8
GRU	98.0	93.9	96.9	96.7

for both training and validation up to around epoch 10. After that point, both training and validation accuracy rapidly increase, stabilizing around 97–98% accuracy, indicating that the model is learning effectively without significant overfitting. The close alignment between training and validation accuracy suggests good generalization, as there is minimal divergence between the two lines. Interestingly, a similar behavior was shown by GRU model. This indicates that both LSTM and GRU based models are effective in understanding the complex patterns of the input data.

69.5 Conclusion

Previous studies on forest fires have primarily focused on predicting either the burned area or the mere presence of fire. However, classifying days as "fire" or "no fire" is often suboptimal since, once a fire begins, it is likely to continue for several days, making such classifications less informative. Therefore, we redefined our problem to focus on predicting the initiation of forest fire ignition. While previous models, such as ANNs, performed well in predicting fire presence, they struggled with the specific task of ignition prediction. To address this, we implemented both LSTM and GRU models. The LSTM model achieved a high accuracy of 97.6%, proving effective in predicting the onset of fire ignition due to its ability to capture temporal dependencies in the data. Similarly, the GRU model also demonstrated robust performance, though the LSTM slightly outperformed it in most metrics.

Future work will aim to further enhance accuracy by incorporating hyperspectral satellite images and GIS data. Additionally, exploring transformer models, which can capture longer-range dependencies, presents a promising avenue for improving ignition prediction in sequential data analysis.

References

1. Zaidi, A.: Predicting wildfires in Algerian forests using machine learning models. Heliyon **9**(7) (2023)
2. Bayat, G., Yildiz, K.: Comparison of the machine learning methods to predict wildfire areas. Turk. J. Sci. Technol. **17**(2), 241–250 (2022)
3. Sayad, Y.O., Mousannif, H., al Moatassime, H.: Predictive modeling of wildfires: a new dataset and machine learning approach. Fire Saf. J. **104**, 130–146 (2019)

4. Singla, S., Mukhopadhyay, A., Wilbur, M., Diao, T., Gajjewar, V., Eldawy, A., Kochenderfer, M., Shachter, R., Dubey, A.: WildfireDB: An Open-Source Dataset Connecting Wildfire Spread with Relevant Determinants (2021).
5. Finney, M.A.: FARSITE: Fire Area Simulator-Model Development and Evaluation (1998).
6. Dong, H., Wu, H., Sun, P., Ding, Y.: Wildfire prediction model based on spatial and temporal characteristics: a case study of a wildfire in Portugal's Montesinho natural park. Sustainability **14**(16) (2022)
7. Saha, S., Bera, B., Shit, P.K., Bhattacharjee, S., Sengupta, N.: Prediction of forest fire susceptibility applying machine and deep learning algorithms for conservation priorities of forest resources. Remote. Sens. Appl.: Soc. Environmen **29** (2023)
8. Seydi, S.T., Saeidi, V., Kalantar, B., Ueda, N., Halin, A.A.: Fire-Net: a deep learning framework for active forest fire detection. J. Sens. **2022**, 1–14 (2022). https://doi.org/10.1155/2022/7538490
9. Shao, Y., Li, Q., Wang, X., Liu, H.: Assessment of China's forest fire occurrence with deep learning, geographic information, and multisource data. J. For. Res. **34**(4), 963–976 (2023). https://doi.org/10.1007/s11676-022-01506-9
10. Ghosh, R., Kumar, A.: A hybrid deep learning model by combining convolutional neural network and recurrent neural network to detect forest fire. Multimed. Tools Appl. **81**(27), 38643–38660 (2022). https://doi.org/10.1007/s11042-021-11287-5
11. Vikram, R., Sinha, D.: FogFire: Fog assisted IoT-enabled forest fire management. Evol. Intel. **16**(1), 329–350 (2023). https://doi.org/10.1007/s12065-022-00717-2
12. Mohnish, S., Akshay, K.P., Pavithra, P.: Deep learning-based forest fire detection and alert system. In: 2022 International Conference on Communication, Computing and Internet of Things (IC3IoT), pp. 1–5 (2022). https://doi.org/10.1109/IC3IoT54390.2022.00034
13. A. Mutakabbir, C.H. Lung, M. Zaman, S.A. Ajila, Naik, K.: Spatio-temporal agnostic deep learning modeling of forest fire prediction using weather data. In: 2023 IEEE 47th Annual Computers, Software, and Applications Conference (COMPSAC), pp. 346–351 (2023) https://doi.org/10.1109/COMPSAC57700.2023.00054
14. Wang, W., Huang, Q., Liu, H., Jia, Y., Chen, Q.: Forest fire detection using deep reinforcement learning. In: 2022 International Conference on Cyber-Physical Social Intelligence (ICCSI), pp. 23–28 (2022). https://doi.org/10.1109/ICCSI54332.2022.00012
15. Sudhakar, S., Vijayakumar, V., Kumar, C.S., Priya, V., Ravi, L.: UAV-based forest fire detection and monitoring for reducing false alarms. Comput. Commun. **149**, 1–16 (2023). https://doi.org/10.1016/j.comcom.2023.02.009

The manufacturer's authorised representative in the EU is Springer Nature Customer Service Centre GmbH, Europaplatz 3, 69115 Heidelberg, Germany. If you have any concerns regarding our products, please contact ProductSafety@springernature.com

Printed and bound by CPI Group (UK) Ltd, Croydon, CR0 4YY
30/09/2026
02225571-0020